£52

J6

GW00686415

30130 117631001

Essex County Council

Many libraries in Essex have
facilities for exhibitions
and meetings —

enquire at your local library
for details

EMPIRE SHIPS

By the same authors

BRITISH STANDARD SHIP SERIES

Empire Ships of World War II (1965)
The Oceans, the Forts and the Parks
British Standard Ships of World War I

AMERICAN STANDARD SHIP SERIES

The Liberty Ships (1970)
  Revised Edition (1973)
  2nd Edition (1985)
Victory Ships and Tankers
From America to United States (in four parts)

MERCHANT SHIPS OF THE WORLD SERIES

Cruising Ships
Tankers

The Cunard Line—A post-war history
The Cape Run (1985)
  Revised Edition (1987)
Sailing Ship to Supertanker

The troopship *Empire Ken* in Southampton Water.

THE EMPIRE SHIPS

A Record of British-built and acquired Merchant Ships during the Second World War

W.H. Mitchell and L.A. Sawyer

SECOND EDITION

|L|L|P|

LONDON   NEW YORK   HAMBURG   HONG KONG
LLOYD'S OF LONDON PRESS LTD
1990

ESSEX COUNTY LIBRARY

Lloyd's of London Press Ltd.
Legal Publishing and Conferences Division
One Singer Street, London EC2A 4LQ

U.S.A. AND CANADA
Lloyd's of London Press Inc.
Suite 308, 611 Broadway
New York, NY 10012 USA

GERMANY
Lloyd's of London Press GmbH
59 Ehrenbergstrasse
2000 Hamburg 50, West Germany

SOUTH EAST ASIA
Lloyd's of London Press (Far East) Ltd.
Room 1101, Hollywood Centre
233 Hollywood Road
Hong Kong

First published 1965
Second edition 1990

©
W. H. Mitchell and L. A. Sawyer
1965, 1990

British Library Cataloguing in Publication Data
Mitchell, W. H. (William Harry) *1920–*
The empire ships: a record of British-built and acquired
merchant ships during the Second World War.—2nd. ed.
1. World War 2. Role of British merchant shipping
I. Title II. Sawyer, L. A. (Leonard Arthur) *1926–*
940.545941

ISBN 1–85044–275–4

All rights reserved. No part of this publication may be reproduced, stored
in a retrieval system, or transmitted, in any form or by any means,
electronic, mechanical, photocopying, recording or otherwise, without the
prior written permission of Lloyd's of London Press Ltd.

Text set 10 on 11½ pt Linotron 202 Bembo by
Wessex Typesetters, Frome, Somerset
Printed in Great Britain by
The Eastern Press Ltd., Reading

940
.545
941

CONTENTS

PREFACE

In 1939 a standard naming system was adopted by the Ministry of Shipping, in that all merchant ships ordered to be built in Britain to Government account, except very small ship types, would be given the prefix 'Empire' to their name. This also applied to ships acquired through purchase, requisition, or taken in prize, although in the event there were some exceptions.

In this record 'Empire' ships built are listed within general ship types and then sub-listed to each building yard. Then follows historical notes of each shipyard and ships built under private contract or licence during the 1939–1945 war years and the shoulder months of the war. The shipyard notes are in no way intended to be a full history of the company concerned.

Details of merchant ships include the yard number, gross tonnage (gt), which could subsequently change with any structural alteration to the vessel, the overall length (oa), followed by the length between perpendiculars and the breadth, in feet. Engines are shown as triple expansion (T3cyl.), compound (C2cyl.), turbine, or oil. Deadweight tonnage (tdw) is shown in some instances. Historical details include changes of name and/or ownership, from building to present disposition or final disposal. However, only casualties of a serious nature are shown.

Launching and completion dates, generally, are from Lloyd's Register Launching Forms or Shipbuilding Returns of the time. Yard numbers not shown are indications that the vessels were either warships built to Admiralty specification and not to Lloyd's Register class and, therefore, not on their Returns, or were minor craft or constructions of a non-marine nature, e.g., lock gates and the like.

The 'Empire' nomenclature also embraced the numerous ageing, but valuable, tramp ships acquired in 1941–1942 from the United States of America. There were also a number of modern C2 and C3-type ships on Lease/Lend arrangement to the United Kingdom during the late 1941–1942 period, for use in fast convoy work, and thirteen C1-type ships were converted to British Infantry Landing Ships in 1943–1944. All bore 'Empire' names.

During the course of the war many ships suffered serious damage, either through enemy action or as marine casualties. Of these, the bulk were, of course, repaired and sent on their ways, but others that were badly damaged, or even sunk, called for special effort. Where possible these ships were salved, even to the extent of fitting new foreparts, most then being requisitioned by the Ministry and allotted 'Empire' names.

At the outbreak of war a number of German ships were seized and several were captured on the high seas in subsequent years. A number of Italian ships were seized in Eritrea in 1941 and more taken when Italy surrendered in 1943. These, too, were generally renamed with an 'Empire' prefix.

In 1945 a large number of German ships were confiscated in North European and German ports and later given 'Empire' names. However, some were allocated to the U.S.S.R. by the Assembly of Inter-Allied Reparations Agencies and bore the 'Empire' nomenclature for only a short time, whilst a number of other ships, also re-allocated, did not bear an 'Empire' name at all.

In the Index of Ships, a number following a name, e.g. (II) is only shown if actually part of the name.

Other abbreviations used:

M.O.W.T. – Ministry of War Transport
M.O.T.   – Ministry of Transport
M.O.S.   – Ministry of Shipping
U.S.S.B. – United States Shipping Board
U.S.M.C. – United States Maritime Commission
C.T.L.   – Constructive Total Loss
LP   – Low Pressure
Cyl.   – Cylinder
DR   – Double Reduction

The authors wish to record their grateful thanks to those who have helped in the preparation of this book: Lloyd's Register of Shipping; the Corporation of Lloyd's and the Admiralty Library. Dennis Stonham, Bob Todd and David Hodge of the National Maritime Museum; Barbara Jones of Lloyd's Register of Shipping; Thomas Adams; John Freestone; Bob Childs; Ken Garrett; David Burrell; John Lingwood; Bill Lawes; Danny Lynch; James Barron (Clyde pilot); Bob MacDougall of New Zealand and George Schneider of the U.S.A.; and for photographic services, to Skyfotos Ltd; The National Maritime Museum; Tom Rayner; Paul Dalton; Roy Kittle; John Jedrlinic of the U.S.A. and Vic Young of New Zealand.

Southampton and London
July 1990

W. H. MITCHELL
L. A. SAWYER

INTRODUCTION

As the August of 1939 progressed, the blue skies of that fateful summer darkened with the quickening momentum of the long-gathering clouds of war. Each day the international situation grew more critical.

On the 19th August fourteen German U-boats, from a fleet of 57 operational submarines, quietly left their home ports of Kiel and Wilhelmshaven to await further instructions as they lay in the South Western Approaches and off the western shores of Britain. The pocket battleship *Admiral Graf Spee* left Wilhelmshaven on the 21st for South American waters and was followed three days later by the *Deutschland*, destined for the North Atlantic.

At dawn on 1st September the might of the German Wehrmacht smashed into Poland and the world stood aghast; on 3rd September Britain and France declared war on Germany.

At 7.30 p.m. that same day the Donaldson-Atlantic Line's *Athenia* (13,581 gt), outward bound from Glasgow and Liverpool for Montreal with 1,103 passengers and a crew of 315 was south of Rockall Bank when she was hit by a torpedo from the submarine *U.30*. She eventually sank at 10 a.m. on 4th September with a loss of 112 lives. She was Britain's first war loss. The titanic struggle had begun.

Fortunately, far-sighted planning in Britain enabled the convoy system to be activated quickly. Indeed, a special convoy sailed from Gibraltar for Cape Town on 2nd September and an eleven-ship convoy left the Clyde for Gibraltar on the 5th. The regular outward ocean convoys began on 7th September, assembling at Southend and then being joined by ships from the Channel ports; or from Bristol Channel ports, through St George's Channel and northabout to the Atlantic. The East coast convoys of the Firth of Forth–Thames shuttle run, with their colliers of latent power cargoes, began on the 6th. The first homeward-bound ocean convoy sailed from Freetown on the 14th; ships which had sailed independently prior to those dates had no choice but to run the enemy gauntlet.

For some time before the outbreak of war the Shipping Conference, comprised of shipowners, shipbuilders and shiprepairers, had worked on plans for putting their industries on a war footing, should the need arise, in particular to ensure that mistakes made in the Great War would not be repeated. Shipbuilders were asked as to the suitability of their yards for the construction of various ship types – cargo liners, tramps, tankers, colliers, coasters and naval vessels. From this basic information the overall capability was assessed.

The plans were very much advanced when war began and the Board of Trade quickly made Orders under the Defence Regulations for the control of shipbuilding and shiprepairing.

A Ministry of Shipping was formed in October 1939 with some departments from the Board of Trade, and set up within its structure was a Directorate of Merchant Shipbuilding and Repairs and an Advisory Committee on Merchant Shipbuilding Programme.

In January 1940 the decision was made that, effective from 1 February 1940, the Admiralty would be responsible for both naval and merchant ship building and repairs and the Merchant

Shipbuilding and Repairs Department was transferred from the Ministry of Shipping on that date. The aim of this centralisation was to assure the best use of all resources in materials and labour. A Controller of Merchant Shipbuilding and Repairs, being a member of the Admiralty Board, and through whom the industry was controlled, was appointed.

The Admiralty was responsible for ensuring the necessary production, not only for the Royal Navy, but for merchant shipping, to meet the requirements of the Ministry of Shipping and after consulting the owners.

Responsibility for construction was also with the Admiralty, although the ships would be Government-owned under the Ministry of Shipping, which would place them under shipping companies as agents for the Government.

Merchant ships could be built in two ways, either by direct orders of the Admiralty for new ships required for wartime strategy, or by issuing licences to firms to construct ships for private owners and built to specifications of wartime requirements.

On 1 May 1941 the Ministry of Shipping and Ministry of Transport were merged to become the Ministry of War Transport.

One of the tasks of the Advisory Committee was to consider and grant licences to build ships for private account, a condition being that the vessel be of the building yard's prototype plans and specifications and within the requirements of the overall Shipbuilding Programme. This arrangement continued until the end of 1944.

Prototypes of a yard's output were selected for group building, the standardisation of machinery being favoured rather than the construction of Government standard ships, as had been the requirement in the Great War. The yards could therefore build ships to which they were accustomed and of types that were their speciality, with their plans and patterns on hand.

By January 1940 the requisition of British ships was general, applying to deep sea ships after discharge of their first cargoes in a United Kingdom port from 1st February onwards.

Ships requisitioned were left under management of their owners under direction of the Ministry of Shipping; outward voyages were fixed through brokers on the commercial market, but home cargoes were on Government account and the question of market fixtures did not arise.

Twenty-five liners were Government-sanctioned for Admiralty acquisition on 24 August 1939 for conversion to armed merchant cruisers. This number was later increased to fifty-six. On 23 November 1939, the P & O SN Company's *Rawalpindi* was the first to be lost, sunk by the *Scharnhorst* whilst on patrol between Iceland and the Faroe Islands. Up to May 1941 another fourteen were lost and the remainder were gradually reconstructed to become troopships or naval auxiliaries.

Some tankers were requisitioned early in the war, but those that were not were requisitioned on the completion of discharge after 31 December 1940. If discharge had been completed prior to that date the vessel, if ready for service, was requisitioned on 1 January 1941; if under repair, then on the date available for employment.

Until then, tankers owned by the oil companies had been subject to direction at agreed rates of freight by a central committee, while the independent owners' tankers had been taken under requisition.

Apart from the general imports of grain, ores and oil, the strategies of war demanded, at times, not only alterations to the building programme, but modifications to the ships as well.

Some merchant ships building on the stocks were taken over for completion to escort carriers, or to various types of naval depot ships. In the early months of war there was a shortage of steel and at other times, of timber.

In late 1939–1940 there was the magnetic mine to contend with, counteracted by degaussing: an electric cable fitted around the hull of the ship and a current passed through, reversing the ship's magnetic field. In 1942 heavy lift derricks had to be fitted to ships of the Arctic convoys, enabling discharge at Murmansk; pre-fabrication was introduced for groups of tugs and coasters; a number of tramps were given insulated space of 250,000–300,000 cu ft, arranged in two or three holds and 'tween decks. And as war in Europe began to draw to a close there were coasting ships built for the Far East theatre of war.

Mid-war disposal of ships

In 1942 the M.O.W.T. and General Council of British Shipping met in discussions from which a scheme was introduced whereby British shipowners who had lost tonnage since the beginning of hostilities either by marine casualty, enemy action, or by Government acquisition were able to replace their losses. The ships, either built, or to be built during the war years, were made available for purchase at the cost of their construction, less depreciation. However, a condition was that they would still remain under M.O.W.T. control until hostilities ceased and the the new owner would manage the vessel on behalf of the Ministry. Owners of early losses were offered early war-built ships, the building costs being less than later buildings.

The most numerous losses were in the tramp section and replacements of steamers were offered with like propulsion or, if those were unavailable, diesel-driven ships were offered, and vice versa. Any deep sea liners (under 8,500 gt) lost would be under the same arrangement or, if needs be, substituted with a tramp vessel, but only a percentage of the tramps available was to be offered. Owners of fully-refrigerated ships had first option on similar ships. Tankers were treated as for tramps, although a larger tanker than the one lost could not be over 25% more in deadweight capacity.

If the acquired ship was subsequently lost, the arrangement became void. The acquired ship was to be kept by the same owner and under the British flag for three years from delivery, unless agreed otherwise by the M.O.W.T. The first batch of ships under this scheme were those built up to 30 September 1941; the second group were those built in the following year to 30 September 1942. Consideration was also to be given to the various Allied Governments for replacements to their war-torn fleets and an agreement was reached that vessels could be transferred to the various owners and flags of the Allies for the length of the war, but remaining available for the service of the M.O.W.T. This was in order that their new owners or managers could gain direct experience of the ships later to come under their control.

All tramps and colliers were easily sold, but the sale of smaller ships and coasters was slower, owing to the varied requirements of potential owners in these smaller ships. Those remaining unsold in the first allocation were offered to potential second owners.

Ships for the Allies

The German attack on western Europe began in May 1940 and such was the onslaught that within two months the coastline from the North Cape to the Pyrenees was under German domination. Many ports suffered bombing and with them much allied shipping was lost.

From 1941 and on through the years of war many 'Empire' ships were transferred to the Allies, to sail under the flags of the overrun countries, the governments or representatives of which were temporarily domiciled in London.

When Belgium was invaded on 10 May 1940, all 100 ships flying the Belgian flag were ordered to proceed to British ports, both ships and their cargoes being offered to the Allied cause. Unfortunately, thirteen vessels were detained in France and French Colonies, but the remainder of the Belgian fleet was in England by the following August. The ships were worked by their Belgian crews under charter arrangements with the Ministry of Transport but, by the end of 1942, the fleet had been decimated by forty-six ships, nearly half of the June 1940 figure.

In recognition of the services given by the Belgian fleet, the British Government decided to offer a number of ships to the exiled Belgian Government, then in London, and seven 'Empire' tramp ships were transferred to the Belgian flag, all then placed under the management of Cie. Maritime Belge (Lloyd Royal) S.A. A further four ships followed, including one of the 'Ocean'-type.

	Transferred	Renamed
Empire Lapwing	1941	*Belgian Fighter*
Empire Drayton	1942	*Belgian Sailor*
Empire Albatross	1942	*Belgian Fisherman*
Empire Masefield	1942	*Belgian Seaman*
Empire Selwyn	1942	*Belgian Soldier*
Empire Swan	1942	*Belgian Freighter*
Empire Ballantyne	1943	*Belgian Airman*
Empire Centaur	1943	*Belgian Captain*
Empire Claymore	1943	*Belgian Crew*
Empire Launcelot	1943	*Belgian Trader*

The American-built 'Ocean'-type tramp, *Ocean Veteran*, was transferred in 1943 and renamed *Belgian Veteran*. Later, a number of 'Liberty'-type ships were temporarily transferred from the United States' flag and placed under the management of Agency Maritime Internationale S.A. Subsequently, some were permanently acquired by the Belgian Government and placed in the fleet of Cie. Maritime Belge. They were given names of Belgian Merchant Marine war heroes under the 'Capitaine' nomenclature.

On 1 January 1940 the Dutch Mercantile Marine consisted of 915 ocean-going ships totalling 2,333,538 gt; on 1 September 1945 these figures had reduced to 637 ships totalling 1,185,185 gross tons.

To ease the losses, a number of 'Empire' tramp ships were transferred to the Government of the Netherlands in 1942–1943 and were all renamed after Dutch artists. Additional tonnage was also completed for Dutch account. Three American-built 'Ocean'-type tramps and a number of coasters were also put under the Dutch flag and in 1944 several American-flag ships were placed under bareboat charter arrangements.

	Transferred	Renamed
Empire Robin	1942	*Ferdinand Bol*
Empire Rennie	1942	*Frans Hals*
Empire Mavis	1942	*Jan van Goyen*
Empire Halley	1942	*Pieter de Hoogh*
Empire Penguin	1942	*Van de Velde*
Empire Raleigh	1942	*Vermeer*
Empire Hazlitt	1943	*Aelbert Cuyp*
Empire Galliard	1943	*Aort van der Neer*
Empire Iseult	1943	*Frans van Mieris*
Empire Spray	1943	*Gerard Dou*
Empire Courage	1943	*Philips Wouerman*
Empire Ruskin	1943	*Van der Capelle*

	Transferred	Renamed
Empire Sidney	1943	*Van der Helst*
Empire Fortune	1943	*Van Honthorst*
Empire Toiler	1943	*Van Ostade*
Empire Kamal	1944	*Van Ruisdael*
Empire Ribble	1945	*Oosterbeek*
Empire Trust	1942	*Rembrandt* (Fast cargo liner)
Empire Boy	1942	*Doorman* (Tanker)
Empire Fletcher	1944	*Backhuysen* (Tanker)
Empire Deep	1942	*Starkenburgh* (Dry cargo coaster)
Empire Sound	1943	*Zuiderhaven* (Dry cargo coaster)
Empire Reynard	1943	*Westerhaven* (Dry cargo coaster)
Empire Ford	1943	*Noorderhaven* (Dry cargo coaster)
Empire River	1943	*Oosterhaven* (Dry cargo coaster)
Empire Dyke	1943	*Prinses Margriet* (Dry cargo coaster)
Empire Lily	1946	*Pampus* (Dry cargo coaster)

The three 'Ocean'-type tramps, *Ocean Athlete*, *Ocean Merchant* and *Ocean Victory* were all transferred in 1943 and became *Govert Flinck*, *Jan Lievens* and *Jan Steen* respectively.

In 1939 France owned 2,950,000 gross tons of shipping which, by mid-1944 had been reduced to 850,000 gross tons with 228 ships. When France was liberated the French Government began rebuilding the fleet, purchasing from foreign countries, chartering and placing orders for new ships, so that by May 1945 the fleet tonnage was 970,000 gross tons. Thirteen 'Liberty'-type ships were bareboat chartered from the United States War Shipping Administration while a number of 'Empire'-type tramp ships were purchased from Britain and renamed after deceased seamen and personalities of the French Merchant Marine. All were transferred in 1945–1946.

	Renamed
Empire Call	*Ingenieur General Haarbleicher*
Empire Farmer	*Administrateur en chef Thomas*
Empire Stronghold	*Camille Porche*
Empire Crown	*Capitaine G. Lacoley*
Empire Falstaff	*Commandant Mantelet*
Empire Sedley	*Intendent J. Patrizi*
Empire Sceptre	*Jacques Bingen*
Empire Duke	*Lieutenant J. Le Meur*
Empire Welfare	*Matelot Becuwe*
Empire Friendship	*Matelots Pillien et Peyrat*
Empire Unicorn	*Pierre Corniou*
Empire Outpost	*Pilote Garnier*
Empire Symbol	*Professeur Emile Lagarde*
Empire Driver	*Radiotelegraphiste Biard*
Empire Jessica	*Joseph Blot*
Empire Dorrit	*Lieutenant Lancelot* (Dry cargo coaster)
Empire Gillian	*Brescou* (Dry cargo coaster)
Empire Mull	*Medea* (Coastal tanker)
Empire Rawlinson	*Monkay* (Fast cargo liner)
Empire Gala	*Bir Hakeim* (Fast cargo liner)
Empire Traveller	*Pechelbronn* (Tanker)
Empire Cadet	*Mascara* (Tanker)

Renamed

Empire Bute	*Miliana* (Tanker)
Empire Jupiter	*Saint Gaudens* (Tanker)

Ten 'Park'-type Canadian-built ships were acquired in 1946 and placed with the Gouvernement Générale de L'Indo-Chine, as were the *Empire Gala* and *Empire Jupiter* (above).

Most of the 'Empire'-named ships transferred to the Norwegian flag during the war years were given the name prefix of 'Nor' and some were named after members of the Norwegian Royal Family.

Renamed

Empire Pilgrim	*Astrid*
Empire Penn	*Kong Haakon VII*
Empire Grenfell	*Kong Sverre*
Empire Fairbairn	*Kronprinsen*
Empire Latimer	*Kronprinsessen*
Empire Field	*Prins Harald*
Empire Carey	*Ragnhild*
Empire Ptarmigan	*Norelg*
Empire Kittiwake	*Norfalk*
Empire Saxon	*Norfjell* (Tanker)
Empire Beaver	*Norhauk*
Empire Pearl	*Norheim* (Tanker)
Empire Druid	*Norholm* (Tanker)
Empire Eagle	*Norjerv*
Empire Pict	*Norland* (Tanker)
Empire Dunlin	*Norlom*
Empire Diamond	*Norsol* (Tanker)
Empire Onyx	*Nortind* (Tanker)
Empire Elk	*Norvarg*

Norway was invaded on 9 April 1940 and the ships, all transferred in 1941–1942, were operated by the Norwegian Shipping & Trading Mission, London, for the Norwegian Government.

The Polish merchant ship fleet lost fourteen ships during the war years, ten of which were sunk by enemy action. To offset these losses, the tramp *Baltyk* was completed in March 1942 by Swan, Hunter at Newcastle for Polish account and the following 'Empire' tramps were transferred to the Ministry of Industry, Commerce and Shipping, operating in London for the Polish Government:

	Transferred	Renamed
Empire Builder	1942	*Tobruk*
Empire Roamer	1942	*Narwik*
Empire Hunter	1943	*Boryslaw*

One U.S.-built 'Ocean'-type ship was also transferred, as were a number of U.S.-flag vessels.

The great assault

The invasion of Normandy came in June 1944, a culmination to the years of immense Allied war effort. Following the initial assault, some 250 merchant ships and 500 coasters, excluding the assault forces, began the great build-up of service personnel and military supplies. So many ships necessitated their loading in many British ports before they joined the cross-Channel convoys to discharge on the beaches or at the artificial Mulberry harbours at Arromanches in the British sector or St. Laurent, the American harbour which was destroyed by a vicious storm on 19th–22nd June. During the first three days there were thirty-eight convoys, totalling 753 major landing ships and supply ships, excluding assault forces, engaged in the build-up. Sixteen convoys and a similar number of landing groups were at sea at any time and by 16th June 500,000 personnel and 77,000 vehicles had been landed. On 6th July the millionth man had been landed and by the end of that month 1,600,000 personnel, 340,000 vehicles and 1,700,000 tons of stores had been put ashore.

Of the huge number of merchant ships employed in the 'Overlord' invasion, there were 612 British merchant vessels listed as being involved in the build-up period from D-Day to 14th June. This figure was exclusive of tugs and other small craft. There were 171 ships operating under the Ministry of War Transport, ninety-seven of which were 'Empire' ships, eleven were the American-built 'Ocean'-type, forty were 'Fort'-type Canadian-built tramps and there were twenty-three 'Sam'-named Liberty ships.

The 'Empire' C1-type Infantry Landing Ships (LSI) took part in the assault phase, code-named 'Neptune', landing troops by their assault landing craft (LCA), then continuing in the build-up, taking less than twenty-four hours from a South Coast roadstead to the beaches, disembarking their troops and returning to home anchorage.

There were many coasters employed, including 'Empire'-types, for it had been realised in planning the invasion that the burden of the initial build-up would fall on the small craft of about 3,000 tdw which would have to carry a variety of stores and equipment demanded from many sources.

Some coasters were beached so that vital supplies could be discharged direct to Army vehicles on the dry sand. Some coastal tankers did likewise, whilst many dry cargo coasters carried case petrol and oils.

After the initial build-up, the larger merchant ships anchored offshore, discharging overside to a myriad of small craft working to and from the beaches. By mid-June both Mulberry harbours were in use and on the 27th June Cherbourg was taken by U.S. forces. The first ship to arrive after clearing operations in the harbour was the *Empire Traveller*, with 10,000 tons of petrol for the U.S. Army.

The post-war scene

On 7 May 1945 there was unconditional surrender of all German fighting forces in Europe; on 14 August 1945 came the unconditional surrender of Japan and World War II ended.

In the shipping world there was much to do. Countless thousands of servicemen, prisoners of war and displaced persons had to be transported to their home countries. Long-established trade routes, closed down in 1939, had to be re-opened and new trades started. Facilities for drydocking, repairs, overhauls and conversions of ships were stretched to their utmost.

After six years of turmoil the world fleets had completely changed. Due to the vast shipbuilding programmes carried out in the United States during the war, their fleet numbered 5,521 merchant ships when hostilities ceased, totalling 56,800,000 tons deadweight, figures which excluded 604 ships lost by direct enemy action and 139 by marine casualty, but was a fourfold increase over the 1,401 ships of 12,100,000 tdw fleet of 1939.

All other Allied fleets, however, showed a reduction in carrying capacity; the British Empire (23,300,000 to 19,600,000 tdw), Norway (6,400,000 to 3,950,000 tdw), The Netherlands (3,300,000 to 2,090,000 tdw), France (2,900,000 to 1,300,000 tdw) Greece (2,700,000 to 1,700,000 tdw) and the U.S.S.R. (1,500,000 to 1,200,000 tdw).

At this time there were many ex-Axis ships sailing under the British flag and M.O.W.T. control, formerly of German, Italian and Finnish registry; indeed, up to the time of the Italian surrender on 3 September 1943, 129 vessels of some 450,000 gt had been seized. The majority of German ships had been confiscated in German ports and about half of those under the Italian flag which had been taken had been seized in British ports when war began, or in the ports of Eritrea. Some ships had been captured by the Royal Navy at sea.

Troopships

On 18 December 1945 it was announced by the Ministry of War Transport that the Government had decided that dry cargo ships on requisition would be released on termination of their voyages after 2 March 1946 when the charters expired. Tankers were released as they completed voyages after 31 December 1945. Passenger ships and other vessels employed on military and naval requirements were, however, to remain under requisition for the movement of troops and other special work to which they had been allotted, with huge numbers of people to be transported worldwide.

The pre-war policy for trooping was that all troopships would be privately owned and chartered by the Government when required. In 1939, nine were on charter, Bibby Line's *Dorsetshire* and *Somersetshire* of 1927, *Devonshire* of 1938 and the 1917-built *Lancashire*. British India SN Company owned the *Neuralia* of 1912, the *Nevasa* of 1913, *Dilwara* of 1935 and *Dunera* of 1937. In 1939 the *Ettrick* was completed for the P & O SN Company. Of these ships, two were lost in the war. War conditions, however, proved it necessary to use bigger and faster ships for hurrying troops to the battle fronts and many large passenger liners were requisitioned as troopships. When war ended these ships were again urgently required, this time by their owners, desirous of re-opening their services, and the Government found it necessary to convert a number of German passenger ships, condemned in prize, to troopships to supplement the trooping fleet. They were then given the troopship livery of white hull with blue line around the hull, and a buff funnel.

Largest of these were *Potsdam* (19,047 gt) of Norddeutscher Lloyd, which became *Empire Fowey*; *Pretoria* (17,362 gt) and *Ubena* (9,523 gt) of the Deutsche Ost-Afrika Linie which became *Empire Orwell* and *Empire Ken* respectively and the Hamburg Sud-Amerika Line ships *Antonio Delfino* (14,056 gt) and *Monte Rosa* (14,651 gt), renamed *Empire Halladale* and *Empire Windrush*. Another Hamburg Sud Amerika ship was *Cap Norte* which became *Empire Trooper* after capture by H.M.S. *Belfast*.

Other vessels taken over were British-flag casualties of war: Royal Mail Line's *Asturias* and their old *Atlantis*, Cunard White Star Line's *Georgic* and the Furness Withy ships *Monarch of Bermuda* and *Eastern Prince* (Prince Line). Of these, only the last was given an 'Empire' name.

There were also a number of smaller ships under Ministry control which were used for carrying troops. Four, *Empire Lifeguard*, *Empire Peacemaker*, *Empire Comfort* and *Empire Shelter* worked in the Mediterranean between British-held ports, having been turned over from their work as convoy rescue ships. Three others, *Empire Parkeston*, *Empire Wansbeck* and *Vienna* worked the Harwich/Hook of Holland run from 1948. The *Vienna* was requisitioned as a transport in 1940 and in 1944 was acquired by the M.O.W.T., but remained under Railway management, sometimes running the Tilbury/Ostend service. She was scrapped in 1960.

Emigrants to the Antipodes

Shortly after war ended there began a migration from war-torn Europe, particularly of British subjects, all seeking a new life in a fresh environment. They were greatly encouraged by the Australian and New Zealand Governments. Indeed, so great was the build-up of the movement that the numbers estimated by the British and involved governments were far beyond the capability of the ships employed in the passenger services at that time. From talks between government representatives and the Ministry of Transport, consideration was then given to the commissioning of ships which had worked as wartime transports, to carry the emigrants. Shipping companies that were involved as owners supported the plan and there began a build-up of a fleet of passenger ships, being so adapted for the carrying of emigrants. They sailed with full passenger lists and a further arrangement was that relatives and friends of British citizens, unable to obtain a passage on the regular liner services, could be carried on the return voyages. Some of these ships were Ministry-owned; others were chartered.

The first ship of the fleet was the *Ormonde*, chartered from the Orient SN Company, and after refitting by Cammell Laird & Company Ltd., Birkenhead, she left London on 10 October 1947 for Melbourne and served in this capacity until 1952. The *Ranchi* and *Chitral* of the P & O SN Company were also chartered and left London on 17 June 1948 and 30 December 1948 respectively, both bound for Sydney. They also worked in the service until 1952. Four Bibby Line ships were also taken up for the emigrant service, the troopships *Dorsetshire* and *Somersetshire* at the end of 1948; the 1912-built *Oxfordshire* from 1949 to 1950 and the *Cheshire*, working from Liverpool from 1949 to late 1952.

Largest of the emigrant ships to Australia was the motorship *Georgic* (27,759 gt) built for the White Star Line in 1932. Whilst at Port Tewfik on 14 July 1941 she was bombed by enemy aircraft from Crete and set on fire. After temporary repairs at Karachi and Bombay she was acquired in 1942 by the M.O.W.T. and sent to Belfast for refitting as a troopship. In 1948 another refit saw her as an emigrant ship, her first voyage from Liverpool to Sydney beginning on 11 January 1949. She worked with seasonal charters to the Cunard SS Company in the North Atlantic service.

Another large liner which also became a casualty of war was the Royal Mail Line's *Asturias*. She was acquired by the Ministry of Transport in 1946, rebuilt as a troopship, then worked as an emigrant ship from Southampton to Sydney between 1949 and 1953. The Anchor Line's *Cameronia*, built in 1920, was refitted from trooping to carry emigrants, making her first voyage on 1 November 1948. Bought by the M.O.T. in 1953, she returned to trooping as the *Empire Clyde*.

Emigration to New Zealand was on a much smaller scale. Three ships owned by the Ministry of Transport were put on the service, the first being the former Royal Mail Line's *Atlantis*, (15,135 gt) which left Southampton on 30 November 1948 for Wellington. Requisitioned when war broke out, she became *H.M. Hospital Ship No. 33*, being acquired by the M.O.W.T. in 1941. From 1948 she worked in a four-year charter agreement with the New Zealand Government until broken up at Faslane in 1952.

The *Captain Cook* (13,876 gt), originally the *Letitia*, sistership of the ill-fated *Athenia*, was built in 1925 for Anchor Donaldson Line, Glasgow. Acquired by the M.O.T. in 1946, she was renamed *Empire Brent*. In 1951 she was refitted as an emigrant ship and in 1951 was chartered by the New Zealand Government and renamed *Captain Cook*. She sailed from Glasgow in this service until 1960, when she was sold for breaking up. The *Captain Hobson* (9,300 gt) was built in 1920 as the *Amarapoora* for P. Henderson & Co. Ltd., Glasgow. During the war she, too, served as a hospital ship. In 1946 the M.O.T. bought her and had her fitted out as a migrant carrier and, under the name *Captain Hobson*, she worked under a New Zealand Government charter from Glasgow from 1952. But by mid-1953 there were no waiting lists of emigrants from Britain for New Zealand and the *Captain Hobson* became a troopship in August of the same year.

Over four years the ships sailed on many voyages with emigrants approved by Australian Government representatives, about half the number on Government-assisted passages. But by 1953 the numbers of emigrants that could be accepted had diminished and the number of assisted passages decreased. This caused a break-up of the Australian migrant fleet. The chartered *Ormonde* was scrapped in December 1952, followed by the *Ranchi* and the *Chitral* in 1953. The Bibby Line ships were returned to their owners. Both the *Asturias* and *Cameronia* were switched to trooping whilst the *Georgic* was chartered out to Cunard Line for a number of Atlantic crossings.

Only one ship continued the service, the *New Australia*, able to make three or four round trips each year with 1,500 or more emigrants each voyage. Of 22,424 gt she was built in 1931 as *Monarch of Bermuda* for Furness, Withy & Company and was requisitioned in 1939 as a troop transport. On 24 March 1947 she caught on fire whilst in drydock at Hebburn and was later moved to Granton Harbour where she was surveyed. She was then purchased by the Ministry of Transport for conversion to an emigrant carrier and was sent to Southampton, under tow, in June 1949 for conversion by J. I. Thornycroft & Company. Completed in 1950, she then had a capacity to carry 1,548 emigrants, was renamed *New Australia* (20,256 gt) and left Southampton on 15th August on her first voyage. In 1958 she was sold to Greece.

Disposal of the 'Empire' ships

In January 1946 the Government published the first of several lists of Government-owned 'Empire' ships offered for sale, or for three- or five-year charters. Tenders were restricted to United Kingdom or British Commonwealth shipowners who had lost ships.

Vessels of many types were listed, from the most numerous 10,000 tdw steam and motor tramps, tankers, coasters and dredging craft to the small prefabricated TID tug. At the end of 1946 came the list inviting tenders for the purchase or charter of the ex-German ships. Most of these were condemned in prize and there was a condition that a tender for the purchase of a ship not then condemned in prize would only be accepted subject to condemnation of the vessel in prize. A further condition was that the ship could not be transferred to any person, or cease to be registered in the United Kingdom for three years from the delivery date, except by sanction of the Ministry of Transport.

The British-built 'Empire' ships on offer had been ever-present in the great convoys which had rounded the Cape of Good Hope and worked their way northwards, through the Red Sea to the Middle East. They carried tanks, guns and vehicles in their thousands and countless quantities of other war impedimenta for the Allied armies in North Africa. These were the ships that had crossed the Atlantic westward to the United States in ballast convoys, to load with food, raw materials and the articles of war, then to assemble in convoys at the Nova Scotian ice-free port of Halifax or, later, at New York. Then they sailed eastward, defying the U-boat, the bomber and the elements, to reach the shores of Britain. They were in Britain's coastal convoys; in the Mediterranean convoys which struggled to replenish the vital defences of Malta under vicious onslaughts by bomber and submarine; and they had sailed in the numerous convoys to North Russia with the addition of the Arctic elements to contend with. They helped to back up the invasions of North Africa, Sicily and Italy, were present in the Mulberry harbours of Normandy, and followed the Allies northwards as, one after another, the ports of Western Europe were freed. One hundred and eighty-two 'Empire' ships were lost through enemy action. The first, the *Empire Commerce*, was lost on 9 June 1940; the last, the *Empire Gold*, on 18 April 1945.

Cause	1940	1941	1942	1943	1944	1945	Total
Mine	1	3	1	2	4	1	12
Submarine torpedo	13	21	65	21	10	2	132
Aircraft bomb	2	7	9	4			22
Aircraft torpedo				2			2
Raider		2	2				4
E-boat		1			1		2
Blockships at Normandy					8		8
	16	34	77	29	23	3	182

BUILDERS OF STANDARD TYPE MERCHANT SHIPS

Ailsa Shipbuilding Co. Ltd.	'Scandinavian'-type, 'Icemaid'-type colliers, 'C'-type dry cargo coasters.
Armstrong Whitworth & Co. Ltd.	Tramps (own prototype).
Ardrossan Dockyard Ltd.	'Tudor Queen'-type coaster.
S. P. Austin & Sons Ltd.	'C'-type dry cargo coasters.
Barclay, Curle & Co. Ltd.	Tramps (own prototype). Fast cargo liners.
Bartram & Sons Ltd.	PF (B), PF (C), PF (D), 'Bartram' design tramps, 'C'-type dry cargo coasters, 'Tes'-type coastal tankers.
Blyth Dry Docks & Shipbuilding Co. Ltd.	'B'-type dry cargo coasters, Far East coasters, 'Stella'-type tugs.
Blythswood Shipbuilding Co. Ltd.	'Ocean' tankers, 'Empire Cadet'-class coastal tankers. 'Empire Pym'-type coastal tanker.
G. Brown & Co. (Marine) Ltd.	'Chant'-type coastal tankers, 'Tudor Queen'-type coasters, 'Stella'-type tugs.
Browns Shipbuilding & Dry Dock Co. Ltd.	'Vic' Lighters.
Burntisland Shipbuilding Co. Ltd.	Tramps (own prototype). 'B'-type dry cargo coasters. 'Chant'-class coastal tankers.
Caledon Shipbuilding & Engineering Co. Ltd.	PF (B) Tramps, Fast cargo liners, 'Scandinavian'-type.
Cammell Laird & Co. Ltd.	'Y' tramp, 'Ocean' tankers.
Clelands (Successors) Ltd.	Far East coasters, 'Larch'-class tugs, Dry cargo coasters. 'Warrior'-type tugs.
Cochrane & Sons Ltd.	'C'-type dry cargo coasters, 'Stella'-type tugs. 'Warrior'-type tugs. River tugs.
C. Connell & Co. Ltd.	PF (B) tramps (own prototype), Fast cargo liners.
Cook, Welton & Gemmell Ltd.	'C'-type dry cargo coasters, 'Warrior'-type tugs.
J. Crown & Son Ltd.	'Icemaid'-type colliers, 'Warrior'-type tugs.
Wm. Denny & Bros. Ltd.	Tramps (own prototype).
Wm. Doxford & Sons Ltd.	Tramps (own prototype).
R. Dunston Ltd.	'Vic' lighters, 'Maple'-type tugs, TID tugs, 'Severn'-type colliers, River tugs.
Ferguson Bros. Ltd.	Dredgers, hoppers, 'Warrior'-type tugs. 'Stella'-type tugs.

Fleming & Ferguson Ltd.	Dredgers, hoppers, 'Stella'-type tugs.
Furness Shipbuilding Co. Ltd.	PF (B) Tramps, Fast cargo liners, 'Ocean'-tankers, 'Norwegian' tankers, Standard Fast-type tankers, 'Chant'-class coastal tankers.
Goole Shipbuilding & Repairing Co. Ltd.	'Shelt'-type dry cargo coasters, 'Vic' lighters, 'Empire F'-type dry cargo coasters, 'Chant'-type coastal tankers, 'Larch'-class tugs, 'Warrior'-type tugs.
Grangemouth Dockyard Co. Ltd.	'Scandinavian'-type, 'Ocean' tankers, 'Icemaid'-type colliers, 'Empire Pym'-type coastal tanker. 'Empire Cadet'-class coastal tankers, 'Ted'-type coastal tankers.
Wm. Gray & Co. Ltd.	PF (C), PF (D), tramps (own prototype), 'Empire Malta'-class, 'Scandinavian'-type, Colliers.
Greenock Dockyard Co. Ltd.	'X' tramp, 'Y' tramp, Refrigerated ships, 'Bel'-type heavy lift ships.
A. Hall & Co. Ltd.	'C'-type dry cargo coasters, 'Warrior'-type tugs.
Hall, Russell & Co. Ltd.	'Warrior'-type tugs.
Wm. Hamilton & Co. Ltd.	'Y' tramp, 'B'-type dry cargo coasters.
J. Harker Ltd.	'Severn'-type colliers, 'Vic' lighters, 'Isle'-class coastal tankers.
Harland & Wolff Ltd., Belfast	'X'-tramps, Tramps (own prototype), Refrigerated ships, 'Ocean'-tankers.
Harland & Wolff Ltd., Govan	'X' tramp, 'Y' tramp, 'Ocean'-tankers, Standard Fast type tanker, Dry cargo coasters, 'Tes'-type coastal tankers.
Hawthorn, Leslie & Co. Ltd.	'Ocean' tankers.
J. Hay & Sons Ltd.	'Vic' lighters.
C. Hill & Sons Ltd.	'C'-type dry cargo coasters.
Hong Kong & Whampoa Dock Company	Tramps
A. & J. Inglis Ltd.	'Empire Cadet' coastal tankers, 'Ted'-type coastal tankers.
Sir J. Laing & Sons Ltd.	Tramp (own prototype), Fast cargo liners, 'Scandinavian'-type, 'Ocean' tankers, 'Norwegian' tankers, Standard Fast type tankers. 'Intermediate'-type tankers. 'Ted'-type coastal tankers.
J. Lewis & Sons Ltd.	'Tudor Queen'-type dry cargo coasters.
Lithgows Ltd.	'X' Tramp, 'Y' Tramp, Fast cargo liners. 'Scandinavian'-type, Ore carriers.
Lobnitz & Co. Ltd.	Hoppers, dredgers.
Wm. Pickersgill & Sons Ltd.	Tramps (own prototype), TID tugs.
I. Pimblott & Sons Ltd.	Dry cargo coasters, 'Vic' lighters, 'Empire Lad'-class coastal tankers.
J. Pollock & Sons Ltd.	Dry cargo coasters, 'Vic' lighters.
J. Readhead & Sons Ltd.	PF (B), PF (C), PF (D) Tramps, 'Readhead' design tramps, 'Chant'-type coastal tankers.
Richards Ironworks Ltd.	Dry cargo coasters, 'Vic' lighters.
Rowhedge Ironworks Co. Ltd.	'Vic' lighters, 'Empire Lad'-class coastal tankers.
H. Scarr Ltd.	'Empire F'-type dry cargo coasters, 'C'-type dry

	cargo coasters, 'Warrior'-type tugs, 'Chant'-type coastal tankers. 'Shelt'-type dry cargo coasters.
Scott & Sons Ltd.	'C'-type dry cargo coasters, 'Warrior'-type tugs.
Shipbuilding Corporation Ltd. (Tyne)	Dry cargo coasters, 'Vic' lighters, PF (C), PF (D), Tramps (own prototype).
Shipbuilding Corporation Ltd. (Wear)	PF (C), PF (D), Tramps (own prototype).
Short Bros. Ltd.	PF (C) tramps, Tramps (own prototype), 'Ted'-type coastal tankers.
Wm. Simons & Co. Ltd.	Dredgers, hoppers, 'Stella'-type tugs.
Smith's Dock Co. Ltd.	'B'-type dry cargo coasters.
Swan, Hunter & Wigham Richardson Ltd.	Tramps (own prototype), 'Ocean' tankers, 'Tes'-type coastal tankers, Ferries.
Taikoo Dockyard & Engineering Co. Ltd.	Tramps.
J. L. Thompson & Sons Ltd.	Tramps (own prototype), Fast Cargo liners, 'Ocean' tankers. 'Intermediate'-type tankers.
Vickers–Armstrongs Ltd.	'Y' tramp, 'Bel'-type heavy lift ships. Dry cargo coasters.
J. S. Watson Ltd.	Dry cargo coasters, 'Vic' lighters, 'Warrior'-type tugs.
W. J. Yarwood & Sons Ltd.	Water carriers, Dry cargo coasters.

THE BUILT SHIPS

PART ONE

TRAMPS

When war began some builders were instructed to continue building to the design of their own prototypes. Of the standard designs, the X and Y types were the earliest, but in 1940 it was decided to produce ships of one standard design, applying, in part, the prefabrication method to their construction. From a survey of the several prototypes of ships within the 9,000–10,500 tdw capacity that were under construction it was decided that a ship of 425 ft length bp and a beam of 56 ft was the most suitable and plans were drawn up for a standard ship known as PF(A).

However, owing to the fall of France, some yards which were to have built the PF(A) were involved in a change of policy and committed in other ways and as the PF(A) design incorporated certain heavy units which only the larger yards could handle, plans for the PF(A) were never passed. Instead, the design was altered to break down the units for easier handling and type PF(B) emerged. This type had a split superstructure, there being some distance between funnel and bridge. The profile differences between the X/Y types and the B-type was that in the latter the funnel was slightly further aft and there was a space between funnel and kingpost. Derricks of 1×30-ton, 2×10-ton and 8×5-ton were fitted.

As the war progressed, military weapons and equipment became more bulky and heavier and in 1942 the design of the PF(B) was altered to provide bigger hatchways and greater facilities in the handling and stowage of heavy and awkward lifts and the PF(C) appeared with composite superstructure and equipped with 1×50-ton, 1×30-ton, 5×10-ton and 5×5-ton derricks.

The last type to be built, the PF(D) type was very similar to the PF(C). Both had V-shaped transom sterns. The PF(D) type, however, had a poop of full height whereas, in the PF(C) type, only a half-height poop was almost hidden by the bulwarks.

All PF types were generally of 10,000/10,500 tdw, had a speed of 10–11 knots and were 7,050 gross tons (approximately) for the B-type, 7,320 for C and 7,370 for the D-type. Some ships were partially equipped with refrigeration machinery and refrigerated space of 250,000 cubic feet.

At the end of the war, although 'Empire' names had been allocated to some newbuildings, the fact that the ships were acquired for private ownership whilst on the stocks caused them to be launched in their new owner's nomenclature, thus not bearing an 'Empire' prefix.

The number preceding the ship's name in all the following lists is the shipbuilder's yard number.

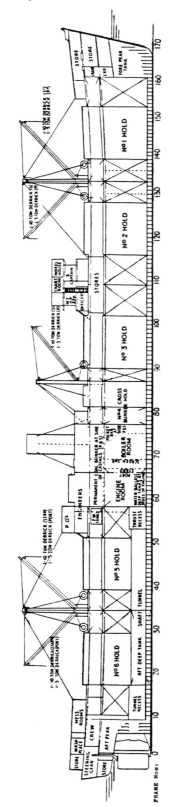

The standard partially fabricated 'B'-type cargo steamship.

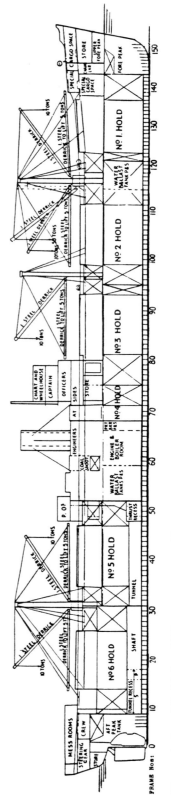

The standard partially fabricated 'C'-type cargo steamship.

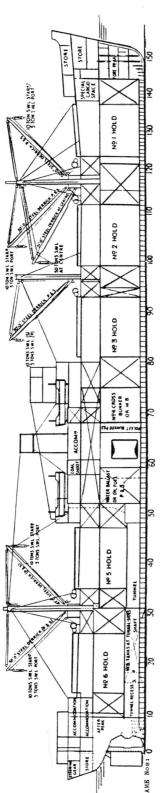

The standard partially fabricated 'D'-type cargo steamship.

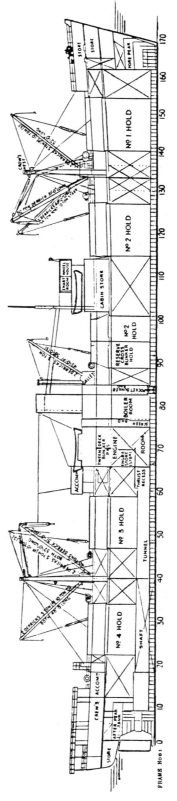

The 'Y'-type standard cargo steamship.

Built by Sir W. G. Armstrong, Whitworth & Co (Shipbuilders) Ltd., Walker Shipyard, Newcastle-on-Tyne

1   *Empire Standard* 7,050 gt, 'B' type.   446 ft (oa), 431 ft × 56 ft. Engines: T3cyl.
Launched: 29.6.1942.
Completed: 10.1942.
9.3.1943: Damaged by submarine (*U.596*) torpedo off Algiers (voyage: U.K./Algiers). Struck in No. 3 hold, the only one not stowed with explosives. Proceeded, and:
10.3.1943: Arrived Algiers. Discharged, moved to a repair berth.
26.3.1943: Struck by aerial torpedoes; broke back. Constructive total loss. Wreck towed to sea and scuttled.

2   *Empire Claymore* 7,050 gt. Details as Yard No. 1.
Launched: 19.11.1942.
Completed: 1.1943.
1943: *Belgian Crew* (Government of Belgium).
1946: *Capitaine Paret* (Cie. Maritime Belge).
1960: *Ardenode* (Mullion & Co., Hong Kong).
1966: *Tynlee* (Tynlee Navigation Co., Panama).
7.1969: Scrapped Kaohsiung.

3   *Empire Farmer* 7,050 gt. Details as Yard No. 1.
Launched: 8.3.1943.
Completed: 5.1943.
1945: *Administrateur en Chef Thomas* (Government of France).
1950: *Santagata* (A. Lauro, Italy).

24.11.1950: Aground on Goodwin Sands, 3 miles NE of South Goodwin Light Vessel. Abandoned: broke in two, then broke up further. Total loss (voyage: Casablanca/Leith – phosphate).

4   *Empire Flag* 7,050 gt. Details as Yard No. 1.
Launched: 2.6.1943.
Completed: 10.1943.
1946: *Carmia* (Donaldson Atlantic Line Ltd.).
1949: (Donaldson Line Ltd.).
1954: *Victoria Star* (Blue Star Line Ltd.).
1955: *Inchearn* (Williamson & Co. Ltd., Hong Kong).
8.1966: Scrapped Osaka.

5   *Empire Stronghold* 7,050 gt. Details as Yard No. 1.
Launched: 14.9.1943.
Completed: 12.1943.
1945: *Camille Porche* (Government of France).
1948: *Colonel Vieljeux* (Soc. Navale Delmas-Vieljeux, France).
1954: *Indian River* (International Nav. Corp., Liberia).
1960: *Atticos* (Vita Shipping Corp., Liberia).
1961: *Valor* (Supreme Shipping Co. Inc., Panama).
28.3.1963: Aground near Mukho, South Korea. Buckled amidships and settled. Salvage uneconomic; constructive total loss. Wreck reported sold (voyage: Korea/——, iron ore).

William George Armstrong, engineer and inventor of the modern gun in the mid-19th century, was the founder of the company. His venture into business was the Newcastle Craneage Company, its first hydraulic cranes being erected on Newcastle's Quayside in 1845. The company was later reformed to the Elswick Engine Company.

In the mid-1850s the company entered the ordnance field, with the manufacture of guns at Elswick, and in 1859 the Elswick Ordnance Company was set up from Government contracts. But in 1862 the contracts were cancelled and in the following year Armstrong took over the plant at Elswick. In 1864 Elswick Engine Works and Elswick Ordnance Company were combined under the title of Sir. W. G. Armstrong & Company for engineering and ordnance work, the latter including the production of many naval guns for ships building in Britain for foreign navies.

Armstrongs began shipbuilding in 1867 when they approached Charles Mitchell & Company, founders of the Low Walker Yard on the Tyne, to join them in building a gunboat in which the gun was to be a product of the Armstrong Elswick Ordnance Works. H.M.S. *Staunch* was duly built and equipped with one nine-inch gun, becoming a prototype ship for twenty-seven more gunboats known as the 'Ant'-class, these with a ten-inch gun and built between 1867 and 1881.

Armstrongs acquired the Low Walker Yard in 1882, the company name being re-styled to Sir W. G. Armstrong, Mitchell & Co. Ltd., and in 1884 a yard was opened at Elswick for the building of naval ships, the Low Walker Yard being retained for merchant ships. The company name was altered in 1896 to Sir W. G. Armstrong & Company, but within a few months merged with Sir

Joseph Whitworth & Company, long-standing rival engineers in the ordnance industry. Their Openshaw Works at Manchester then came under the control of yet another title, Sir W. G. Armstrong Whitworth & Co. Ltd.

In 1909 some land with a good river frontage was acquired at Walker for the fitting-out of ships, the previous yard above the Swing Bridge having proved inconvenient for the movement of ships. More land was leased in 1912 and the High Walker Yard was laid down. This was an excellent site, although some excavations of the surrounding high ground were necessary. When finished, the yard had nine building berths for ships of 500 ft to 1,000 ft and well superseded the Elswick Yard.

A number of large naval ships were turned out during the Great War. The battleship *Malaya*, a gift from the Federated Malay States, was laid down in October 1913, launched on 18 March 1915 and completed in 1916. The battle cruiser *Courageous* was completed in 1916; the *Furious* in 1917, both later converted to aircraft carriers, and the 'D'-class cruisers *Danae*, *Delhi* and *Dunedin* were also finished in 1918–1919.

When war ended the company, of necessity, turned to commercial work. The Cunard liner *Aquitania* arrived at the yard in November 1919 for overhaul and conversion from coal to oil-burning. Two more Cunarders, *Ausonia* and *Ascania*, both 14,000 gt, were completed in 1921 and 1925 respectively, the P & O liner *Mongolia*, 16,600 gt in 1923 and *Gripsholm*, 17,700 gt for the Svenska Amerika Linien in 1925.

In 1922 the world's largest floating dock was constructed for the Southern Railway Company at Southampton Docks. The huge structure was 960 ft in length, 175 ft overall width and 134 ft clear width at the entrance. The floor area was $3\frac{1}{4}$ acres; the displacement tonnage lift weight was 60,000 tons. But orders dwindled as the world moved into the biting post-war depression, shipbuilding slumped and steel and iron prices became influenced by foreign control. A scheme was begun for land development in Newfoundland, but faltered due to costs and the company faced financial difficulties.

So it came about that a merger of the two great companies, Vickers of Barrow and Armstrong Whitworth was put forward in early 1927 and on the last day of October it was agreed that a company be formed as Vickers-Armstrong Ltd., to cover all ordnance and naval shipbuilding.

In 1928 Armstrongs took over the Tyneside yards of W. Dobson & Co. Ltd., and the Tyne Iron Shipbuilding Co. Ltd., and with the Low Walker yard, limited in size of ships it could build, was reformed in 1930 as Sir W. G. Armstrong, Whitworth (Shipbuilders) Ltd. But the continuing depression and the yard's incapacity to accept orders for sizeable tankers that came their way caused the company to offer the three-berth Dobson yard at Walker and the three-berth Tyne Iron yard at Willington to National Shipbuilders Security Ltd., a company formed in 1930 for the elimination of redundant and surplus shipyards, and they were closed down in 1934. In this same year the Low Walker yard was also closed.

But when war came again, the Low Walker yard was opened in 1942 under the management of Sir W. G. Armstrong, Whitworth (Shipbuilders) Ltd., and five standard 'B'-type tramps (Yards 1–5) were built to Government orders.

In 1944 the yard became the Tyne Branch of the Shipbuilding Corporation Ltd., to construct more war tonnage, the yard numbers continuing from 6 to 28 when the yard closed in 1948.

Built by Barclay, Curle & Co. Ltd., Clydeholm Shipyard, Whiteinch, Glasgow

677   *Empire Light* 6,828 gt, 442.5 ft (oa),
428 ft × 57.5 ft. Engines: T3cyl.
Launched: 5.7.1940.
Completed: 11.1940.
25.4.1941: Sunk by German auxiliary cruiser *Pinguin*,
02.00S, 61.00E (approx.) off Seychelles Islands.

Note: The Hansa Line's *Kandelfels*, 7,766 gt, of 1936, was
taken over by the German Navy in 1940 and became the
Pinguin, (Raider F). After sinking or capturing twenty-eight
ships she was caught by the cruiser H.M.S. *Cornwall* on 8
May 1941 near the Seychelles and, after heavy bombardment,
blew up and sank.

678   *Empire Voice* 6,902 gt. Details as Yard No. 677,
but: Engines: T3cyl and LP turbine.
Launched: 3.9.1940.
Completed: 11.1940.
1946: *Bernard* (Booth SS Co. Ltd.).
1947: *Byron* (Lamport & Holt Line Ltd.).
1953: Renamed *Lalande*.
1961: *Uncle Batt* (Wm. Brandt Sons & Co.) for
delivery voyage, and:
8.9.1961: Arrived Moji for breaking up.

681   *Empire Faith* 7,061 gt. 432 ft (oa),
418 ft × 57.5 ft. Engines: Oil.
Launched: 4.3.1941.
Completed: 6.1941.
1946: *Jessmore* (Johnson Warren Lines Ltd.).
1958: *Antiope* (Maritime & Commercial Corp. Inc.,
Panama).
1964: *Global Venture* (Global Navigation Co. Inc.,
Panama (Wah Kwong & Co., Hong Kong)).
1965: (Glory Carriers Inc. (Wah Kwong & Co., Hong
Kong)).
8.1971: Arrived Kaohsiung for breaking up.

682   *Empire Glade* 7,006 gt. 425.7 ft (oa),
418 ft × 57.5 ft. Engines: Oil.
Launched: 12.6.1941.
Completed: 9.1941.
28.11.1942: Damaged by gunfire from submarine
U.67, north-east of Barbados, 17.16N, 48.44W.
Repaired.
1945: *Inishowen Head* (Ulster SS Co. Ltd.).
1962: *Maria N* (Platsani Ltda S.A. (L. Nomicos,
Greece).
10.7.1972: Arrived Istanbul, in tow, for breaking up.

685   (Laid down as) *Empire Penn* 5,326 gt, 446.4 ft
(oa), 431.3 ft × 56.4 ft. Engines: Oil.
Launched: 19.12.1941 as *Kong Haakon VII*.
Completed: 4.1942 for Government of Norway.
1946: (H. Staubo & Co., Norway).

1951: *Cavofrigelo* (Cia. Naviera Arica S.A., Panama).
1953: *Emporios* (Cia. de Nav. Golfo Azul S.A.,
Panama).
1967: *Aguinaldo* (7,068 gt) (Philippine President Lines
Inc).
1969: Renamed *Liberty Three*.
1972: Renamed *President Magsaysay*.
1972: Renamed *Liberty Three* (6,855 gt).
17.7.1972: Arrived Kaohsiung for breaking up.

The River Clyde pilot who was appointed to her launch
received the order 'Attend launch of *Empire Penn* 1200 19
December 1941, Barclay Curle's to Diesel', i.e., Builder's
Diesel Wharf, for engines and fitting out.
   On arrival at the Whiteinch Yard the pilot found the name
of the ship had been changed to *Kong Haakon VII* and King
Haakon himself was present, with many other Norwegian
and British dignitaries. Unfortunately, no sooner had the
Kong Haakon VII cleared the ways than she came in collision
with the Blue Funnel Line's *Myrmidon* (1930, 6.278 gt) which
was proceeding, fully laden, up river to Princes Dock. Both
ships were extensively damaged, the *Kong Haakon VII* with
stern damage and the *Myrmidon* with damage amidships.
   The maiden voyage of the *Kong Haakon VII* did not take
place until April 1942; the *Myrmidon* was sunk by submarine
U.506 torpedo off Freetown, 00.45N 06.27W on 5 September
1942.
   The *Kong Haakon VII* was the first merchant vessel to be
handed over to an Allied Government from a British shipyard
in replacement of ships lost in the Allied cause.
   At the time of her launch Norway had lost 173 ships of
750,000 gross tons.

686   (Laid down as) *Empire Fairbairn* 7,073 gt,
446.4 ft (oa), 431.3 ft × 56.3 ft. Engines: Oil.
Launched: 17.2.1942.
Completed: 4.1942 as *Kronprinsen* for Government
of Norway.
9.6.1942: Damaged by submarine (*U.432*) torpedoes
south of Cape Sable, NS., 42.53N 67.11W (voyage:
Baltimore/U.K.). Stern blown off, deck cargo on fire.
Towed in, beached Pubnico Fairway to discharge
cargo, including carbide. Temporary repairs made;
then 23.7.1942: Towed to Halifax, and 9.10.1942:
Towed to Boston, Mass. Repaired.
1945: (Olsen & Ugelstad, Norway).
1952: *Vori* (Cia. Nav. Porto Alegre S.A., Panama).
1967: *Lukia M* (Liminship Cia. Nav., Greece).
10.2.1969: Sprang leak in Yellow Sea, 50 miles SW
of Barren Island, 29.29N 124.16E (voyage:
Safaga/Korea). Abandoned. Later towed to Shanghai.
Reported subsequently seized by Government of
People's Republic of China. No further trace.

689   *Empire Courage* 7,089 gt. Details as Yard No.
681.

Launched: 21.12.1942.
Completed: 5.1943.
1943: *Philips Wouerman* (Government of the Netherlands).
1947: *Ceram* (NV Stoom. Maats. Nederland, Holland).
1953: *Amsteltoren* (Amsterdam NV., Rederi, Holland).
1953: Renamed *Amstelbrug*.
1959: *Armathia* (Cia. Nav. Alameda S.A., Greece).
1965: *Calliman* (Velamar Cia. Nav., Greece).
4.1968: Arrived Kaohsiung for breaking up.

690 *Empire Highway* 7,166 gt. Details as Yard No. 681.
Launched: 26.8.1942.

Completed: 10.1942.
27.7.1943: Bombed and damaged west of Gibraltar. Repaired.
1946: *Ionic Star* (Blue Star Line Ltd.).
1946: Renamed *Napier Star*.
1949: (F. Leyland & Co.).
1950: (Lamport & Holt Line Ltd.).
1953: (Booth SS Co. Ltd.).
20.7.1965: Aground in heavy seas off Bahia Potrero, 60 miles from Montevideo, Uruguay (voyage: Rio Gallegos/London – meat).
18.8.1965: Refloated; towed to Montevideo.
19.9.1965: Grounded whilst moving to drydock: refloated, returned to port.
23.9.1965: Drydocked: serious hull damage found.
Sold, and: 2.1966: Scrapped Montevideo.

This was one of the oldest of Clyde yards, dating back to 1818 when John Barclay leased ground at Stobcross Pool. In those days there were many shallows in the river and Barclay chose a site to erect his new patent slip for 200-ton ships where there was an adequate depth of water. But it was his son Robert who later joined with Robert Curle to begin the Barclay, Curle partnership. In 1855 the Whiteinch yard was acquired and in 1857 engine works were set up, four years later being enlarged on the site of the old Finnieston Cotton Spinning and Print Works.

Barclay, Curle launched the three-masted, square-rigged, iron steamer *Edina* (Yard No. 9) on 5 July 1854, a ship which was to last for eighty-four years. Just 171 ft long and of 322 gross tons, she arrived in Australia in 1863 at the time of the gold rush, there destined to become almost an institution until 1938 when her then owners, Australian Steamships (Propy) Ltd., sold her to become a lighter.

The company became limited in 1884 and when the century turned, built Union-Castle's *Dover Castle*, 8,000 gt in 1904, Allan Line's *Corsican* (11,400 gt) and Ellerman's *City of Paris* (9,000 gt) in 1907 and P & O's twin screw *Morea* of 11,000 gt in 1908. The Elderslie yard was purchased in 1912 and in 1913 the West Yard was opened. Then came the Great War and as well as completing twelve merchant ships, the company built thirty convoy escort sloops, five 'P'-class submarine hunters, four river gunboats and six tankers, a total of fifty-seven ships during hostilities.

One of the best-known yards at the turn of the century was the Jordanvale yard of John Reid & Co. Ltd., where many fine sailing ships and steamships had been built. The yard closed in 1909, but during the Great War, when Belgium was overrun, the British Government permitted the Belgian Government to build ships there and in 1916 Lloyd Royal Belge (GB) Ltd., at first under the management of Brys & Gylsen Ltd., re-opened the yard. The site covered 7½ acres, with a long frontage to South Street, Whiteinch, on the North side, and to the River Clyde on the South. There were two building berths for ships to 440 ft, one to 330 ft and two to 250 ft. The building list ran to twenty-five vessels before the yard was taken over by Barclay, Curle in 1924.

When war broke out again in 1939 five ships were fitting out and as well as continuing to build merchant ships under government licence, the company was awarded contracts for seven 'Empire' tramp ships, two fast sixteen-knot refrigerated cargo 'Empire' ships and for the Admiralty the 'Castle'-class corvette *Berkeley Castle* (Yard 699) which was launched on 19 August 1943 and the 'Loch'-class frigate *Loch Alvie* (Yard 700), 14 April 1944. Another frigate, *Loch Erisort* was cancelled.

Two transport ferries (LST(3)) were also constructed:
3014 Launched 11.11.1944.
3015 Launched 16.3.1945.
When war ended the yard had five berths for ships up to 700 feet. The Clydeholm shipyard closed in 1965.

MERCHANT SHIPS BUILT UNDER PRIVATE CONTRACT OR LICENCE

673   *Ozarda* 6,895 gt, 441.9 ft (oa), 428 ft × 57.2 ft.
Engines: Oil.
Launched: 14.11.1939.
Completed: 1.1940 for British India SN Co. Ltd.
1970: *Epidavros* (Troodos Shipping & Trading Ltd.).
23.9.1972: Arrived Kaohsiung for breaking up.

674   *Trevaylor* 5,257 gt, 447.8 ft (oa),
432.5 ft × 56.2 ft. Engines: Oil
Launched: 9.1.1940.
Completed: 3.1940 for Hain SS Co. Ltd.
1955: *Inchstaffa* (Williamson & Co. Ltd., Hong Kong).
1966: *Ardstaffa* (Mullion & Co. Ltd., Hong Kong).
1967: *Nankwang* (Southern Shipping & Enterprise
Co., Hong Kong).
30.11.1967: Aground and sank at Woosung
Anchorage, Shanghai, after moorings parted in heavy
weather (voyage: Whampoa/Shanghai – iron ore).

675   *Itria* 6,854 gt, 442.6 ft (oa), 428 ft × 57.6 ft.
Engines: T3cyl and LP turbine.
Launched: 12.3.1940.
Completed: 5.1940 for British India SN Co. Ltd.
1958: *Iqbalbaksh* (United Oriental SS Co., Karachi.)
6.1971: Scrapped Gadani Beach, Karachi.

676   *Burnside* 5,659 gt. Details as Yard No. 675.
Launched: 23.5.1940.
Completed: 10.1940 for Burns, Philp & Co. Ltd.,
Sydney, NSW.
1964: *Ever Sure* (Teck Hwa Shipping Co. Ltd.,
Singapore).
1966: Scrapped Singapore.

683   *Urlana* 6,852 gt. Details as Yard No. 675.
Launched: 8.8.1941.
Completed: 11.1941 for British India SN Co. Ltd.
5.9.1943: Ashore, west entrance to Loch Bracadale,
Scotland, 57.20N 6.39W (voyage: Buenos
Aires/Freetown/London – general).
Total loss.

684   *Umaria* 6,852 gt. Details as Yard No. 675.
Launched: 17.10.1941.
Completed: 1.1942 for British India SN Co. Ltd.
29.3.1943: Damaged by submarine (*U.662*) torpedo,
WSW of Ushant, in convoy SL 126
(voyage: Ceylon/Freetown/U.K.).
30.3.1943: Sank in position 46.44N 16.38W.

The *Umaria* left her builder's yard on trials on Boxing Day,
1941. Her life span was a brief 15 months.

Early in January 1943 she sailed from Ceylon with manganese ore and general cargo, bound for the United Kingdom.
She joined a convoy at Durban, reached Freetown safely and
then joined another convoy, consisting of 37 ships plus escort.

On 29 March the first ship was sunk by U-boat attack,
then the *Umaria* was struck by a torpedo. The ship did not

sink and ten minutes later was underway again, listing and
down by the head. She wallowed on, steaming well and
slowly catching the convoy, when another explosion shook
her. Her bows went deeper and her propeller came almost
clear of the water.

As dawn of 30 March broke, the vessel's foredeck was
completely under water and sea after sea was breaking over
her in quick succession. It was obvious that the ship could
not reach port and she was abandoned. The survivors were
later rescued by H.M.S. *Wear* and the almost-submerged
wreck of the ship sunk by gunfire.

(See also *Empire Bowman*, C. Connell & Co., Yard No.
437).

687   *Canara* 7,024 gt, 485.8 ft (oa),
465.7 ft × 62.9 ft. Engines: Oil, Twin screw.
Launched: 29.5.1942.
Completed: 8.1942 for British India SN Co. Ltd.
7.1968: Scrapped Kaohsiung.

688   *Chyebassa* 7,043 gt. Details as Yard No. 687.
Launched: 23.10.1942.
Completed: 12.1942 for British India SN Co. Ltd.
9.6.1969: Arrived Hong Kong for breaking up.

691   *Socotra* 7,754 gt. Details as Yard No. 687.
Launched: 18.3.1943.
Completed: 5.1943 for P & O SN Co. Ltd.
16.6.1965: Arrived Hong Kong for breaking up.

692   *Behar* 7,840 gt. Details as Yard No. 687.
Launched: 24.5.1943.
Completed: 8,1943 for Hain SS Co. Ltd.

Late in February 1944 a force of three Japanese cruisers –
Aoba, *Tone* and *Chikuma* – was despatched 'to disrupt Allied
communications in the Indian Ocean'.

The force operated under the control of the C. in C.,
South-west Area Fleet, and included in his orders was one
'That all members of merchant ship crews captured were to
be killed, with the exception of certain categories, such as
W/T operators, who were to be kept for interrogation'.

The operation was supported by the light cruisers *Kinu*
and *Oi* and three destroyers which formed a Security and
Supply Formation, to screen the raiders out of the Sunda
Strait and to give similar escort on their return. Reconnaissance aircraft from Java and Sumatra – ten bombers and four
large seaplanes – probed deeply in the direction of Ceylon
and four submarines of the 8th Flotilla kept watch on Allied
movements from Ceylon, the Maldives and the Chagos
Archipelago.

The three raiders sortied from the Sunda Strait on 1 March
and headed for the central Indian Ocean, on the main shipping
route between Aden and Fremantle. On 9 March, about
halfway between Fremantle and Colombo, they destroyed
their only victim.

On 29 February the *Behar* had sailed from Melbourne,
bound for Bombay and Colombo with a cargo of war stores
and zinc. At mid-morning on 9 March, in overcast weather
and frequent rain squalls, she was in position 20.32S 87.10E,

in the Indian Ocean, south-west of the Cocos Islands. Visibility improved as she ran clear of a lengthy squall, only to sight a cruiser four miles to starboard, on a converging course. As the Japanese vessel signalled with a lamp so the *Behar* turned sharply away, whereupon the cruiser *Tone* hoisted her Battle Ensign and opened fire, quickly scoring hits. Less than five minutes after the first sighting the *Behar* was abandoned: at this time the remaining two cruisers were in sight, though they took no part in the action. As a result of *Tone*'s shelling, the *Behar* rapidly settled by the stern, then capsized and sank.

When attacked, the British ship had managed to send a distress message: the Japanese considered it too risky to remain in the Indian Ocean and the operations of the cruisers were abandoned. Returning to port, the force anchored in Tanjong Priok Roads on 16 March.

The cruiser *Tone* was heavily damaged, set on fire and reduced to a wreck at Kure, Japan, on 24 and 28 July 1945 by aircraft of the United States 3rd Fleet.

Note: *Behar* is a P & O SN Company name. With the influence of the P & O over the Hain SS Co., which had come under P & O control in 1917, Hain were asked to manage a number of P & O cargo liners on the Eastern service. The first two, *Nimoda* and *Nohata*, were launched in 1927. These were followed by the *Bangalore*, *Burdwan*, *Behar* and *Bhutan*, all launched in 1928 and all permanently employed in P & O services although registered under the Hain title. All were war losses, but in May 1941 another *Behar* (as above) was ordered for Hain. Completed in August 1943, she lasted for less than eight months.

693 *Herefordshire* 8,398 gt, 492.6 ft (oa),
471.7 ft × 64.4 ft. Engines: Oil. Twin screw.
Launched: 1.10.1943.
Completed: 1.1944 for Bibby Bros. & Co.
1954: *Port Hardy* (Port Line Ltd., charter).
1961: *Herefordshire* (Bibby Bros. & Co.).
1969: *Merryland* (Merith Cia. Nav., Panama (Troodos Shipping & Trading Co. Ltd.)).
7.2.1973: Arrived Kaohsiung for breaking up.

694 *City of Chester* 8,520 gt. Details as Yard No. 693.
Launched: 30.12.1943.
Completed: 3.1944 for Ellerman's Hall Line Ltd.
1960: (Ellerman City Lines Ltd.).
1971: *Chester* (Embajada Cia. Nav., Greece).
10.1971: Scrapped Whampoa.

695 *Chanda* 6,957 gt, 484.9 ft (oa), 465 ft × 62.9 ft.
Engines: Oil.
Launched: 9.5.1944.
Completed: 7.1944 for British India SN Co. Ltd.
1969: *Precious Pearl* (Jebshun Shipping Co. Ltd., Hong Kong).
1971: (Development Navigation Co., S.A., Singapore).
15.10.1971: On fire in engine room when 150 miles east of Hong Kong, 22.00N 116.54E
(voyage: Kaohsiung/Saigon – cement and steel).
16.10.1971: Taken in tow by Dutch tug *Elbe*, but:

17.10.1971: Sank in position 22.16N 118.07E.

696 *Chupra* 9,657 gt. Details as Yard No. 695.
Launched: 16.9.1944.
Completed: 12.1944 for British India SN Co. Ltd.
17.1.1971: Arrived Hong Kong for breaking up.

697 *Perim* 9,550 gt, 499.6 ft (oa), 480.2 ft × 64.9 ft.
Engines: 3 Steam turbines.
Launched: 16.4.1945.
Completed: 11.1945 for P & O SN Co. Ltd.
1967: *Ann* (Astroguarda Ci. Nav. S.A.), for delivery to shipbreakers.
28.7.1967: Arrived Shanghai for breaking up.

698 *City of Khartoum* 9,955 gt, 497.6 ft (oa),
475.7 ft × 64.3 ft. Engines: Oil. Standard Fast type.
Launched: 11.1945.
Completed: 1.1946 for Ellerman Hall Line Ltd.
1968: *Benalligin* (Ben Line Steamers Ltd.).
10.9.1972: Arrived Kaohsiung for breaking up.

703 *City of Swansea* 9,959 gt. Details as Yard No. 698.
Launched: 21.12.1945.
Completed: 4.1946 for Ellerman Hall Line Ltd.
1968: *Benkitlan* (Ben Line Steamers Ltd.).
3.9.1972: Arrived Kaohsiung for breaking up.

704 *Eucadia* 7,142 gt. Details as Yard No. 698.
Launched: 4.1946.
Completed: 7.1946 for Anchor Line Ltd.
1963: *Ionian* (Transfruit Shipping Co. Ltd., Piraeus). Later renamed *Macedon*.
11.11.1964: Aground on rocks at Ras Beirut (voyage: Houston/Bombay – general). Flooded; listed and abandoned in heavy weather. Broke in three, and:
21.11.1964: Sank.

705 *Landaura* 7,289 gt, 447 ft (oa),
432.6 ft × 58.4 ft. Engines: Oil.
Launched: 6.1946.
Completed: 9.1946 for British India SN Co. Ltd.
1965: *Belle Etoile* (Mauritius SN Co. Ltd.).
1970: *Agios Stylianos* (Agios Stylianos Cia. Nav.).
1972: *Spyridon* (Spiritala Cia. Nav., S.A.).
4.5.1972: Arrived Shanghai for breaking up.

706 *Dumra* 4,867 gt, 398.8 ft (oa),
382.3 ft × 54.8 ft. Engines: Oil. Passenger/cargo.
Launched: 16.9.1946.
Completed: 12.1946 for British India SN Co. Ltd.

The *Dumra* was the first of four sisterships, all built by Barclay, Curle in the immediate post-war years for the Bombay to Arabian Gulf Ports service, with calls at Karachi, Basrah, Muscat, Bahrain and Kuwait and to other ports with sufficient inducement. The other three ships were *Dwarka*, completed in June 1947; *Dara* in June 1948 and *Daressa* in June 1950.

The quartet was broken when the *Dara* was lost by an

explosion on board on 8 April 1961 when the ship was some 100 miles west of the Straits of Hormuz, and she sank next day. Investigations concluded that her loss was due to sabotage – the placing of a bomb.

The *Daressa* was sold in 1965 to A. & D. Chandris and renamed *Favorita*; she became *Kim Hwa* of the Guan Guan Shipping Company of Singapore and was eventually scrapped at Hong Kong in 1974.

In 1973 *Dumra* joined the P & O fleet: in 1976 was sold to

Damodar Bulk Carriers Ltd., Goa, as the *Daman* and was broken up at Bombay in 1979.

In September 1980 the Iraq–Iran war began and with passenger figures falling and severe competition from airlines, the *Dwarka* made her last voyage in the spring of 1982 and arrived at Karachi on 19 May 1982 for breaking up. She was the last British ship on a regular scheduled deep-sea passenger route anywhere in the world.

Built by Bartram & Sons Ltd., South Dock, Sunderland

286   *Empire Surf* 6,640 gt. Bartram design: 432 ft (oa), 417 ft × 56 ft. Engines: T3cyl. 9,850 tdw.
Launched: 13.1.1941.
Completed: 4.1941.
5.7.1942: Sunk by submarine (*U.43*) torpedo southeast of Faeroe Islands, 58.42N 19.16W while in convoy ON 55 (voyage: U.K./North America).

287   *Empire Heath* 6,640 gt. Details as Yard No. 286.
Launched: 27.4.1941.
Completed: 7.1941.
11.5.1944: Sunk by submarine (*U.129*) torpedo north-east of Rio de Janeiro, (approx.) 19S 31W (voyage: Brazil/U.K. – ore).

288   *Empire Gilbert* 6,640 gt. Details as Yard No. 286.
Launched: 28.7.1941.
Completed: 10.1941.
2.11.1942: Sunk by submarine (*U.586*) torpedo, off east coast of Iceland, 70.15N 13.50E.

289   *Empire Byron* 6,640 gt. Details as Yard No. 286.
Launched: 6.10.1941.
Completed: 1.1942.
5.7.1942: Damaged by aerial torpedo from He 111 aircraft of German Bomber Group 26, then sunk by submarine (*U.703*) torpedo in Barents Sea, 76.18N 33.30E (Convoy PQ 17) (voyage: U.K./North Russia – war supplies).

290   *Empire Ballad* 6,640 gt. Details as Yard No. 286.
Launched: 17.12.1941.
Completed: 3.1942.
1946: *Bibury* (Alexander Shipping Co. Ltd (Houlder Bros. Ltd.)).
1951: *Stad Maassluis* (Halcyon Lijn NV., Holland).
1962: *Jaguar* (Cia. Nav. Jaguar (Palomba & Salvatori, Italy)).
1966: *Goldfield* (Olamar S.A. (Palomba & Salvatori, Italy)).
1968: *Poseidone* (Cia. de Nav. Sulemar (V. Coccoli, Italy)).

9.1969: Grounded on voyage Rouen/Egypt with grain. Put into Naples. Sold, and:
21.11.1969: Arrived Split, in tow, for breaking up.

292   *Empire Banner* 6,640 gt. Details as Yard No. 286.
Launched: 29.6.1942.
Completed: 9.1942.
7.2.1943: Sunk by submarine (*U.77*) torpedo in Mediterranean 36.48N 01.32E.

The *Empire Banner* (above) and *Empire Webster* (built by Short Bros. Ltd.) were both lost while in a supply convoy from the United Kingdom to North Africa (KMS 8), off Algiers. For escort the convoy had six British and eight Canadian corvettes. Enemy attacks began on 6 February when torpedo aircraft sank the Canadian 'Flower'-type corvette *Louisburg* (K. 143) off Oran. At daylight on the same day attacks by *U.596* had been repulsed but, at night, the submarine reported the sinking of *LCI 162*. After the escort was detached off Algiers, a fan of four torpedoes from *U.77* in the early hours of the 7th hit both 'Empire' ships, which were both sunk by gunfire an hour or so later.

The *U.77* was also responsible for sinking the steamship *Hadleigh* (1930, 5,222 gt) of the Atlantic Shipping & Trading Co., and damaging the motorship *Merchant Prince* (1939, 5,229 gt) owned by the Drake Shipping Co., in another supply convoy off Oran on 16 March before she, herself, was bombed and sunk by British aircraft on 28 March.

293   *Empire Kinsman* 6,640 gt. Details as Yard No. 286.
Launched: 29.8.1942.
Completed: 12.1942.
6.3.1943: Damaged by aircraft bombing at Murmansk. Repaired.
1948: *Umzinto* (Bullard King & Co.).
1956: *Vastric* (Cia. Ltda. Filia, Costa Rica).
30.8.1966: Arrived Onomichi for breaking up.

294   *Empire Prospero* 6,640 gt. Details as Yard No. 286.
Launched: 29.11.1942.
Completed: 3.1943.

1947: *Corinthic* (W. H. Cockerline & Co. Ltd., Hull).
1951: *Marine Flame* (Marine Enterprises Ltd. (Lyras Bros.)).
1951: *Shahreza* (Reliance SS Co. S.A., Panama).
1952: *Faustus* (Cia. Nav. Acapulco, Panama (S. G. Embiricos, London)).
6.11.1952: Ashore 150 yards off North breakwater, Hook of Holland, in a storm.
7.11.1952: Listed; driven through breakwater and rolled over, almost blocking the Nieuw Waterweg Channel. Sank 10 ft into sand. Suction dredgers and explosives used to excavate more sand and silt for the complete settling of the wreck (voyage: Hampton Roads/Rotterdam – coal).

295 *Empire Deed* 6,640 gt. Details as Yard No. 286.
Launched: 6.2.1943.
Completed: 5.1943.
24.5.1943: Damaged by aircraft bombs at Sunderland. Repaired.
1946: *Deed* (Sussex SS Co. Ltd. (S. G. Embiricos Ltd., London)).
1951: *Doro* (Cia. Nav. Doro, Panama).
1956: *Leonidas Cambanis* (Z. L. Cambanis & others, Greece).
1964: *Ever Fortune* (First SS Co. Ltd., Taiwan).
1964: Renamed *Ever Happiness*.
6.1967: Scrapped Kaohsiung.

296 *Empire Rock* 7,064 gt. 'B'-type. 446.3 ft (oa), 431 ft × 56.3 ft. Engines: T3cyl.
Launched: 22.4.1943.
Completed: 7.1943.
1946: *Admiral Codrington* (S. G. Embiricos Ltd., London).
1956: *Sandro Primo* (E. Szabados, Italy).
1959: *Amalie B* (D. Lijnzaad Transport-en-Handel, Rotterdam).
8.1960: Scrapped Hamburg.

297 *Empire Tourist* 7,064 gt. Details as Yard No. 296.
Launched: 17.7.1943.
Completed: 10.1943.
4.3.1944: Sunk by submarine (*U.703*) torpedo southeast of Bear Island, Barents Sea, 73.25N 22.11E while in convoy RA 57 (voyage: Kola Fjord/Loch Ewe).

298 *Empire Blessing* 7,064 gt. Details as Yard No. 296.
Launched: 1.10.1943.
Completed: 1.1944.
19.3.1945: Mined and sunk in approaches to River Schelde, Belgium, 51.24N 03.17E.

301 (Laid down as) *Empire Penang* 'C'-type. 447.8 ft (oa), 431 ft × 56.3 ft. Engines: T3cyl.
Launched: 10.7.1944 as *Mullion Cove* (F. 186) and completed as a Maintenance Ship for Hull Repairs.

1948: Converted to cargo ship, renamed *Margaret Clunies* (7,416 gt) (Clunies Shipping Co., Greenock).
1951: *Waynegate* (Turnbull, Scott & Co. Ltd.).
1961: *Katingo* (Pacifico Cia. Nav. S.A., Panama).
1964: *President Magsaysay* (Philippine President Lines, Manila).
1968: Renamed *Magsaysay*.
19.7.1968: On fire in engine room off Korea, 34.48N 125.51E (voyage: Philippines/Inchon – logs). Abandoned. Later reboarded; fire extinguished; towed to Pusan. Constructive total loss.
12.1968: Scrapped Pusan.

302 *Empire Mauritius* 7,320 gt. Details as Yard No. 301.
Launched: 30.10.1944.
Completed: 2.1945.
1947: *Markab* (Bury Hill Shipping Co. Ltd.).
1956: *Matador* (Motor Shipping Corpn. of Seven Seas, Panama).
1958: *San Jeronimo* (J. Manners & Co. Ltd., Hong Kong).
1958: Renamed *Yangtse Breeze*.
1959: *Hoping Wu Shi San* (Government of China.)
1979: (*circa*): Renamed *Ho Ping 53*.
1985: (*circa*): Renamed *Zhan Dou 53*.

303 *Empire Aden* 7,320 gt. Details as Yard No. 301.
Launched: 13.2.1945.
Completed: 5.1945.
1948: *Etivebank* (A. Weir & Co. Ltd.).
1955: *Alcyone Fortune* (A. Vergottis Ltd., London).
1958: *Northern Venture* (Pan Norse SS Co. (Wallem & Co.)).
9.6.1967: Aground off South Adaga Shima, Okinawa, 26.44N 128.21E (voyage: Tsukumi/Manila – cement). Broke in two; constructive total loss. Sold to local shipbreakers.

304 *Empire Tobago* 7,320 gt. Details as Yard No. 301.
Launched: 28.5.1945.
Completed: 10.1945.
1947: *Crowborough Hill* (Counties Ship Management Co. Ltd.).
1951: *Gryfevale* (A. Crawford & Co. Ltd., Glasgow).
1955: *Sterling Valour* (Sterling Shipping Co. Ltd., Nassau).
1958: *Madda Primo* (G. Bozzo, Italy). Renamed *Madda Bozzo*.
1963: *Kriss* (Seastar Shipping Corpn., Somali Republic).
21.2.1968: Arrived Kaohsiung for breaking up.

306 (Launched as) *Empire Southwold* 7,370 gt. 'D'-type. 449 ft (oa), 431 ft × 56.3 ft. Engines: T3cyl.
Launched: 16.1.1946.

Completed: 5.1946 as *Hesperia* for Houston Line Ltd.
1960: *Clan Murdoch* (Clan Line Steamers Ltd.).
1961: (King Line Ltd. (Dodd, Thomson & Co. Ltd.).

1962: *Mustafa* (Sadikzade Denizcilik Ltd., Turkey).
1974: *Denizhanlar* (Z. Sonmez, Turkey).
3.1979: Scrapped Aliaga, Turkey.

The last tramp ship from the above yard for Government account was the 'D'-type *Empire Southwold*, in 1946, although Government orders were received for four coasters for work in the Far East. During the war years a new berth was built in the yard, with realignment of an adjoining berth and when war ended the yard consisted of three berths.

In 1968 the company was acquired by Austin & Pickersgill and in March 1978 the South Yard closed after the launch of its last building, the motorship *Australind* (Yard No. 464) for the Australind SS Co. Ltd., on 23 March.

The first shipyard site of the company was set out at South Hylton, near Sunderland, in 1837, when George Bartram and John Lister joined in a partnership which was to last for nearly two decades, during this period launching an average of two sailing ships each year into the River Wear.

Robert Bartram, son of the founder, took over the business in 1871 and, with George Haswell as a partner, had a new yard laid down at Sunderland's South Dock. In 1890 the title changed again, from Bartram, Haswell & Company to Bartram & Sons and from then on the buildings were predominantly of tramp ships, these being launched directly into the North Sea between the piers of the dock system.

For most shipbuilding yards in Britain the later 1920s and early 1930s were very difficult years. Indeed, in 1932 and 1933 the whole shipbuilding industry's output was practically negligible.

During this depression Bartram & Sons laid down a 370 ft speculative hull, the only ship they completed between 1930 and 1936. She was to test their then latest ideas in cargo ship construction and a streamlined rudder and fins to Bartram design were incorporated. The hull lay on the stocks for some time before completion in October 1934 as *Eskdene* for Dene Shipmanagement Co. Ltd., London. Of 3,829 gt and a deadweight capacity of 6,640 tons, she had had triple expansion engines. But she was an early casualty of war for on 2 December 1939, while carrying a cargo of timber, she was struck by a torpedo from submarine *U.56* in position 56.30N 01.40W, fifty-four miles East of St. Abbs Head and reported as abandoned and sinking.

Two tugs, *Hendon* and *George V* put out from the Tyne and, battling with the elements, the almost unmanageable tow was brought into the Tyne. Helped by two more tugs, the *Eskdene* was beached on the Herd Sands and later unloaded, refloated and berthed in Albert Edward Dock for repairs.

At dawn on 8 April 1941 the *Eskdene* was again torpedoed in the Western Atlantic by *U.107* and sank in position 34.43N 24.21W, south of the Azores.

Between 1936 and 1939 eleven ships were constructed, due mainly to the 'Scrap and Build' programme introduced by the Government and in the first thirteen months of war, two were launched for J. & C. Harrison and two for Counties Ship Management Co. Ltd. (Rethymnis & Kulukundis Ltd., London).

Orders then came for ten ships, all to a Bartram 'standard' war design. Nine were for Government account and one (Yard No. 291) for Sir Wm Reardon Smith & Sons Ltd., which was named *Jersey City*. More Government orders for five standard Admiralty 'B'-type ships were received, the first three for Government account, one for Reardon Smith (Yard No. 299, *Indian City*) and *Stanrealm* (Yard No. 300) for Stanhope SS Co. Ltd. Four Admiralty 'C'-type were then built, one hull (Yard No. 301) being completed as a hull repair ship for naval service in the Far East.

MERCHANT SHIPS BUILT UNDER PRIVATE CONTRACT OR LICENCE

282 *Harpagus* 5,173 gt, 450.8 ft (oa),
437 ft × 58.5 ft. Engines: T3cyl.
Launched: 27.11.1939.
Completed: 4.1940 for J. & C. Harrison Ltd.

There were two ships of the same name lost in the war, both built for J. & C. Harrison Ltd. The first *Harpagus* (above) lasted just over a year. She was in convoy HX 126 (Halifax/United Kingdom) and was well south-east of Cape Farewell when she was torpedoed by *U.94* on 20 May 1941 and sank in position 56.47N 40.55W.

Another *Harpagus*, a cargo motorship, was completed by Doxford & Sons Ltd., Sunderland, in November 1942 and worked under requisition for the Ministry of War Transport. In May 1944 she was sold to Hain SS Company and was taken up as a stores ship for the Normandy landings. On 19 August 1944 she was 1½ miles north of the west breakwater at Arromanches when there was a violent explosion, presumed to have been caused by a mine, and she broke in two and sank. The afterpart was later refloated, towed across the English Channel to Southampton Water and then towed on to Wallsend. Here a 190 ft fore-end was built at the Shipbuilding Corporation's Walker yard and this was fitted to the aft part of the *Harpagus* in the Swan, Hunter & Wigham Richardson's drydock at Wallsend.

On 1 June 1960 she went aground on the Madira Reef in the Persian Gulf, was refloated on 7 June, sailed for Falmouth and was there declared a constructive total loss. On 21 September 1960 she arrived at Briton Ferry in tow of the tug *Tradesman* for breaking up.

283 *Harpalyce* 5,169 gt. Details as Yard No. 282.
Launched: 22.3.1940.
Completed: 6.1940 for J. & C. Harrison Ltd.
25.8.1940: Sunk by (*U.124*) torpedo,
58.52N 06.34W, north-west of Orkney Islands
(Convoy HX 65A) (voyage: Halifax/U.K.).

284 *Richmond Hill* 7,579 gt, 432.2 ft (oa),
421.2 ft × 60.5 ft. Engines: T3cyl.
Launched: 10.7.1940.
Completed: 11.1940 for Putney Hill SS Co. Ltd.
(Counties Ship Management Co. Ltd.).
1949: (London & Overseas Freighters Ltd.).
1950: renamed *London Craftsman*.
1951: *Italgloria* (S.A. Importazione Carbonie Nav. Italy).
1951: Renamed *Fiducia*.
1960: *Searaven* (Cia. de Nav. Almirante S.A.).
8.7.1968: Arrived Yokosuka for breaking up.

285 *Pentridge Hill* 7,579 gt. Details as Yard No. 284.
Launched: 4.10.1940.
Completed: 1.1941 for Dorset SS Co. (Counties Ship Management Co. Ltd.).
1949: (London & Overseas Freighters Ltd.).
1950: renamed *London Dealer*.

1951: *Centaurus* (Soc. Transoceanica Canopus S.A. (Liberia), (Rethymnis & Kulukundis, London)).
1961: *Najla* (Cia. Nav. Adriatica Ltda., Lebanon).
1965: Scrapped Tamise, Belgium.

291 *Jersey City* 6,686 gt. Details as Yard No. 286.
Launched: 16.4.1942.
Completed: 7.1942 for Reardon Smith Line Ltd.
1955: *Jacqueline* (E. Kekonius, Stockholm).
1959: *Kopalnia Szombierki* (Government of Poland).
1964: *MP PZZ-1* (grain storage hulk at Szczecin) (Rejonowe Zaklady Zbozowe PZZ).
1970 (*circa*): (Zaklady Obrutu Zbozami Importawanymi i Eksportowymi PZZ).
11.9.1978: Arrived Faslane, in tow, for scrapping.

299 *Indian City* 7,079 gt. Details as Yard No. 296.
Launched: 26.1.1944.
Completed: 3.1944 for Reardon Smith Line Ltd.
1957: *Gruz* (Atlanska Plovidba (Government of Yugoslavia)).
1969: *Diamando* (Aurora Borealis Shipping Co. Ltd., Cyprus).
2.4.1972: Arrived Istanbul for breaking up.

300 *Stanrealm* 7,062 gt. Details as Yard No. 296.
Launched: 25.4.1944.
Completed: 7.1944 for Stanhope SS Co. Ltd.
1960: *Fortune Lory* (Liberty Shipping Co. Ltd. (K. T. Wong, Hong Kong)).
27.6.1962: Arrived Hong Kong; laid up.
1.9.1962: Grounded Tolo Harbour, Hong Kong, in typhoon.
17.10.1962: Refloated with bottom damage. Repairs uneconomic. Sold, and: 6.1963: Scrapped Hong Kong.

305 *Pemba* 7,449 gt, 449 ft (oa), 431.2 ft × 56.3 ft.
Engines: T3cyl.
Launched: 24.8.1945.
Completed: 12.1945 for British India SN Co. Ltd.
1960: *Maqboolbaksh* (United Oriental SS Co. Ltd., Karachi).
12.1972: Scrapped Karachi.

309 *Margay* 4,972 gt, 437.5 ft (oa), 421.3 ft × 57 ft.
Engines: T3cyl.
Launched: 3.4.1946.
Completed: 7.1946 for Kaye Son & Co. Ltd., London.
1962: *Star Pink* (Wing Tak SS Co., Hong Kong).

P & O's *Socotra* heading for trials in 1943. (Barclay Curle & Co. Ltd., Yard No. 691.)   *Strathclyde Regional Archives*

The *Indian City*, built in 1944. (Bartram & Sons Ltd., Yard No. 299.)   *Skyfotos*

The *Empire Martaban* at Cape Town in 1948. (Burntisland Shipbuilding Co. Ltd., Yard No. 287.)

1966: renamed *Ocean Pink*.
1967: *Maria Ana* (Pac-Trade Nav. Co. (Madrigal Shipping Co. Inc., Manila)).
1969: *Velta* (Velta Cia. Ltda., Costa Rica (M. Y. McCormick, New York)).

13.2.1971: Sprang leak during gale, sank 200 miles south of Azores, 32.07N 23.26W
(voyage: Macapa/Bilbao – iron ore).

Built by Burntisland Shipbuilding Co. Ltd., Burntisland, Fifeshire

261   *Empire Rosalind* 7,290 gt, 436 ft (oa), 420 ft × 58 ft. Engines: T3cyl. 10,000 tdw.
Launched: 10.11.1942.
Completed: 1.1943.
1949: *Rosemoor* (W. Runciman & Co. Ltd.).
1952: *Helga* (W. H. Schlieker & Co., Germany).
1956: *Helga Bolten* (Aug. Bolten, Germany).
1960: *Sollingen* (Krupp Seeschiffahrt GmbH., Germany).
1960: *Mar Feliz* (Oversea Shipping Co. S.A. (Mariner Shipping Co. Ltd., Hong Kong)).
17.9.1960: Aground Straat Kidjang, Indonesia, and damaged bottom. Proceeded to Singapore, thence Hong Kong.
Sold, and: 1960: Scrapped Hong Kong.

266   *Empire Glory* 7,290 gt. Details as Yard No. 261.
Launched: 20.4.1943.
Completed: 6.1943.
1948: *Goalpara* (British India SN Co. Ltd.).
1953: *Bharatveer* (Bharat Line Ltd., India).
21.10.1963: Driven ashore five miles north of Madras after diverting from voyage during a cyclone (voyage: Calcutta/Cuddalore – coal). Abandoned.
23.10.1963: On fire; gutted. Constructive total loss.
1.1964: Sold to Bombay buyers for breaking up.

286   *Empire Fancy* 7,123 gt, 443 ft (oa), 427 ft × 57 ft. Engines: Oil.
Launched: 16.11.1944.
Completed: 1.1945.
1947: *Sheaf Mount* (W. A. Souter & Co. Ltd., Newcastle).
1957: *Valldemosa* (Harrisons (Clyde) Ltd.).
1961: *Ardfinnan* (Mullion & Co. Ltd., Hong Kong).
1968: *Court Harwell* (Mullion & Co. Ltd., Gibraltar).
9.6.1969: Arrived Hong Kong for breaking up.

287   *Empire Martaban* 7,542 gt, 437.8 ft (oa), 421.7 ft × 58 ft. Engines: T3cyl.
Launched: 15.9.1944.
Completed: 11.1944.
1951: *Avistone* (Aviation & Shipping Co. Ltd. (Purvis Shipping Co. Ltd.)).
1960: *Turkiye* (Faik Zeren, Turkey).
2.1972: Scrapped Istanbul.

288   *Empire Freetown* 7,131 gt. Details as Yard No. 286.
Launched: 29.1.1945.
Completed: 3.1945.
1946: *Inverness* (B. J. Sutherland & Co. Ltd.).
1953: *Redgate* (Turnbull Scott & Co. Ltd.).
1963: *Agia Elpis* (Cia. Marvalia Nav., S.A., Panama).
1967: (Southern Cross Shipping Co. Ltd., Cyprus).
7.1968: Scrapped Shanghai.

289   *Empire Calshot* 7,131 gt. Details as Yard No. 286.
Launched: 10.7.1945.
Completed: 11.1945.
1946: *Derrycunihy* (McCowan & Gross Ltd.).
1952: *Argobeam* (Argobeam Shipping Co. Ltd. (A. Lusi Ltd., London)).
19.8.1955: On fire in engine room during hurricane in Atlantic (voyage: Hampton Roads/Copenhagen – coal).
Fire extinguished; vessel flooded, 40 degrees list to port with bulwarks submerged. Abandoned.
21.8.1955: Taken in tow by tug *Salveda* in position 58.40N 15.14W.
25.8.1955: Arrived Stornaway, Isle of Lewis. Pumped out; towed to Copenhagen for discharge, then towed to Hamburg. Sold; repaired, and:
1955: *Parkgate* (Turnbull, Scott & Co. Ltd.).
1960: *Panagos* (Cia. Nav. Patlem S.A., (G. Lemos, Greece).
26.9.1968: Arrived Shanghai for breaking up.

The war shipbuilding programme of the Burntisland Shipbuilding Co. Ltd., extended from the collier *Foreland* (Yard No. 229), which was fitting out when war began, to Yard No. 300, another collier, *Oliver Bury*, for the London Power Company, launched at the end of 1945.

Construction was in two main categories, tramps and colliers, and in Government orders nine 'Empire' ships were built and four Channel Tankers ('Chants') in 1944, in time for the Normandy invasion.

Two of the 'Empire' ships were completed as Merchant Aircraft Carriers (MAC ships) and one was a coaster for Far East service. The yard also built three 'Loch'-class frigates: *Loch Killin* (Yard No. 283), launched on 29 November 1943; *Loch Fyne* (Yard No. 284) on 24 May 1944 and *Loch Glendhu* (Yard No. 285) on 18 October 1944.

In the tramp section ten ships were built for R. Chapman & Son, the old-established Newcastle company, shipowners since 1880. Early in 1940 Chapman's sought consent to place private orders and this was given, providing they used a standard design of ship. Short Brothers were approached but were unable to help and so negotiations were opened with the Burntisland Shipbuilding Company. All the vessels were 436 ft (oa) × 420 ft × 58 ft and driven by triple expansion engines.

Situated in Burntisland's West Dock, the company had four berths at the end of the war and a capacity for ships to 450 ft. The company went into liquidation in November 1968. The last ship built was the *Helen Miller*, 5,143 gt (Yard No. 442), launched on 3 April 1969 and delivered in July 1969 to the St. Vincent Shipping Co. Ltd. (Monroe Bros., Liverpool). In 1969 the shipbuilding assets of the Burntisland Shipbuilding Co. Ltd., established in 1918, were acquired by Robb Caledon Shipbuilders Ltd., Dundee.

MERCHANT SHIPS BUILT UNDER PRIVATE CONTRACT OR LICENCE

229 *Foreland* 1,870 gt, 276 ft (oa), 265 ft × 39.5 ft. Engines: T3cyl. A collier.
Launched: 3.7.1939.
Completed: 9.1939 for Shipping & Coal Co. Ltd.
3.1965: Scrapped Grays, Essex.

230 *Dalhousie* 7,072 gt, 431.5 ft (oa), 415 ft × 56.5 ft. Engines: Oil.
Launched: 6.8.1940.
Completed: 10.1940 for Dalhousie Steam & Motorship Co., London.
9.8.1942: Sunk by German raider *Stier* (raider No. 23) south-east of Abrolhos Islands, Brazil, 20.22S 24.40W.

The raider *Stier* was converted from the Atlas-Levante Linie A.G., Bremen, motorship *Cairo*, 4,778 gt, built in 1936 by Fr. Krupp, Kiel. She was equipped with 6 × 5.9-inch, 2 × 37mm and 4 × 20mm AA guns. She also had two torpedo tubes and carried two Arado seaplanes.

The *Stier* left Rotterdam on 12 May 1942 to cruise in the Central and South Atlantic. She blew up and sank in the South Atlantic on 27 September 1942 after severe damage caused by action with the United States' Liberty-type ship *Stephen Hopkins*, which was also lost.

The *Stier* was British-listed as raider 'J'.

231 *Cormarsh* 2,848 gt, 322 ft (oa), 312 ft × 44.5 ft. Engines: T3cyl. A collier.
Launched: 15.8.1939.
Completed: 10.1939 for Cory Colliers Ltd. (Wm. Cory & Sons, London).
8.4.1941: Damaged in air attack off Sheringham

Buoy, Norfolk coast. Repaired.
29.11.1941: Sunk by German E-boat in North Sea, north-west of Cromer, Norfolk.

232 *Cormead* 2,848 gt. Details as Yard No. 231.
Launched: 14.9.1939.
Completed: 12.1939 for Cory Colliers Ltd. (Wm. Cory & Sons, London).
17.3.1941: Damaged by aircraft torpedo east of Southwold, Suffolk. Repaired.
11.9.1941: Damaged by aircraft bombs south-east of Cromer.
25.12.1941: Mined off Lowestoft: taken in tow by H.M. tug, but
26.12.1941: Flooded, listed and sank (voyage: London/N.E. coast).

233 *Merton* 7,195 gt, 436 ft (oa), 420 ft × 58 ft. Engines: T3cyl.
Launched: 12.5.1941.
Completed: 7.1941 for R. Chapman & Son, Newcastle.
21.12.1941: Stranded off Pluckington Bank, entrance to Herculaneum Dock, Liverpool. Broke back (voyage: Baltimore/Liverpool). Refloated in two halves; repaired Birkenhead.
1960: *Union Pacific* (Union Nav. Corpn., Panama (T. L. Tsong, Hong Kong)).
3.12.1964: Aground on reef off Naha, Okinawa (voyage: Mormugao/Osaka – iron ore). Holed, flooded and abandoned. Constructive total loss.

13.2.1965: Salvage commenced, using four tugs and 300 workers to discharge cargo. No further trace.

234 *Ambrose Fleming* 1,555 gt, 256.8 ft (oa), 247 ft × 39.6 ft. Engines: T3cyl. A collier.
Launched: 15.2.1941.
Completed: 4.1941 for London Power Co. Ltd., London.
28.4.1941: Sunk by E-boat torpedo off Cromer, 53.13N 01.10E (voyage: London/Burntisland).

235 *Adams Beck* 2,816 gt, 330 ft (oa), 315 ft × 44.5 ft. Engines: T3cyl. A collier.
Launched: 24.4.1941.
Completed: 6.1941 for Gas, Light & Coke Co. Ltd., London.
29.7.1941: Bombed and damaged off 20c buoy, River Tyne.
30.7.1941: Sank; total loss (voyage: Tyne/Thames – coal).

236 *Uskbridge* 2,715 gt, 324 ft (oa), 314 ft × 45.2 ft. Engines: T3cyl.
Launched: 26.3.1940.
Completed: 6.1940 for Uskport SS Co. Ltd.
17.10.1940: Sunk by submarine (*U.93*) torpedo west of Faeroe Islands, 60.40N 15.50W while in convoy OB 228 (voyage: Liverpool/North America).

237 *Eastgate* 5,032 gt, 441 ft (oa), 424.2 ft × 57 ft. Engines: Oil.
Launched: 20.6.1940.
Completed: 9.1940 for Turnbull, Scott & Co. Ltd.
1952: *La Estancia* (Buries, Markes Ltd.).
1959: *Kapetan Kostis* (Cia. Nav. Palma S.A., Greece).
1.1966: Aground on Yugoslav coast, 45.12N 14.16E (voyage: Rijeka/Gibraltar – ballast). Towed back to Rijeka, damaged.
Sold, and: 7.3.1966: Arrived Split for breaking up.

238 *Charlbury* 4,836 gt, 430.3 ft (oa), 416 ft × 57 ft. Engines: T3cyl.
Launched: 27.12.1939.
Completed: 4.1940 for Alexander Shipping Co. Ltd. (Capper, Alexander & Co.).
28.5.1942: Sunk by Italian submarine (*Barbarigo*) torpedo and gunfire, north-east of Recife, Brazil, 06.22S 29.44W.

239 *Dan-Y-Bryn* 5,117 gt. Details as Yard No. 233.
Launched: 11.11.1939.
Completed: 1.1940 for Ambrose, Davies & Matthews Ltd., Swansea.
9.5.1941: Damaged by aircraft bombs at Hull. Repaired.
1946: (Cook Shipping Co., Jersey).
1949: (Jersey United Shipping Co. Ltd.).
1952: (United Transports Ltd., Jersey).
1960: *Ocean Gem* (Transoceanic Shipping Co. Ltd., Hong Kong).

1962: *Tosa Bay* (Gladiator Shipping Co. Ltd., Hong Kong).
2.1967: Scrapped Hong Kong.

240 *Suncrest* 5,117 gt. Details as Yard No. 233.
Launched: 30.10.1940.
Completed: 12.1940 for Crest Shipping Co., London (Overseas Navigation Trust Ltd.).
1949: (Ivanovic & Co. Ltd., London).
1952: *Atsmaut* (Zim Israel Navigation Co., Haifa).
1956: *Sunrise* (Cia. Sol de Nav., Panama (Anthony & Bainbridge, Newcastle)).
1959: *Silver Prince* (Silver Star Shipping Co., Liberia, (P. Vrangos, Greece)).
1963: *Aura* (Siderline Cia. de Nav. S.A., Panama (Palomba & d'Amato, Italy)).
1.1972: Scrapped Spezia.

241 *Elmdale* 4,872 gt, 441 ft (oa), 424.2 ft × 57 ft. Engines: T3cyl.
Launched: 14.12.1940.
Completed: 2.1941 for Morrison SS Co. (J. Morrison & Co., Newcastle).
6.4.1942: Damaged by Japanese submarine (*I. 3*) gunfire in Indian Ocean, 06.52N 78.50E (voyage: Karachi/Durban). Put into Colombo for temporary repair: permanent repairs made in U.S.A.
1.11.1942: Sunk by submarine (*U.174*) torpedo northeast of Brazil, 00.17N 34.55W (voyage: Baltimore/Alexandria – coal and military stores).

242 *Ger-Y-Bryn* 5,108 gt. Details as Yard No. 233.
Launched: 14.3.1940.
Completed: 5.1940 for Ambrose, Davies & Matthews Ltd., Swansea.
5.3.1943: Sunk by submarine (*U.130*) torpedo approx. 300 miles west of Cape Finisterre, Spain, 43.50N 14.45W (Convoy XK 2) (voyage: Lagos/Hull – general).

243 *Edencrag* 1,529 gt, 273.3 ft (oa), 264.3 ft × 40.3 ft. Engines: T3cyl.
Launched: 3.9.1940.
Completed: 12.1940 for Hartlepools SS Co. Ltd.
14.12.1942: Sunk by submarine (*U.443*) torpedo near Oran, 35.49N 01.25W (voyage: Gibraltar/North Africa – military stores).

244 *Seapool* 4,820 gt, 425 ft (oa), 415 ft × 57 ft. Engines: T3cyl.
Launched: 9.3.1940.
Completed: 5.1940 for Pool Shipping Co. Ltd. (Sir R. Ropner & Co. Ltd.).
1951: *Grunewald* (Hamburg America Line).
1953: *Esther Schulte* (Schulte & Bruns GmbH and A. C. Toepfer Schiffs, Hamburg).
22.1.1962: Arrived Hamburg for breaking up.

245 *Channel Queen* 567 gt, 176.5 ft (oa),

169.8 ft × 28.1 ft. Engines: Oil. 700 tdw.
Launched: 10.6.1940.
Completed: 9.1940 for British Channel Islands
Shipping Co. Ltd.
1947: Renamed *Channel Coast*.
1959: *Glenfield* (Zillah Shipping Co. Ltd., Liverpool).
1960: *Alderney Coast* (British Channel Islands
Shipping Co. Ltd.).
1966: *Astronaftis* (N. Grigoriou, Greece).
1975: Renamed *Sea Horse*.
1975: *Mastro Costas* (Namar Shipping Co., Greece).
21.2.1976: Engine breakdown on voyage Greece for
Lagos with pipes and tomato paste. Towed into
Monrovia by *Rethymnon* (1966, 1,127 gt). Abandoned.
10.3.1978: Towed out of harbour by Port Authority
and beached between Monrovia and the Lofa River.

246   *Coral Queen* 303 gt, 138 ft (oa), 132 ft × 24.6 ft.
Engines: Oil. 380 tdw.
Launched: 27.6.1940.
Completed: 1.1941 for British Channel Traders
Ltd., London.
1943: (Queenship Navigation Ltd.).
1948: *Coral Coast* (British Channel Islands Shipping
Co. Ltd.).
1949: *Fulladu* (Government of Gambia).
9.1.1965: Towed from Bathurst to Las Palmas for
breaking up.

247   *Tudor Queen* 1,029 gt, 212.3 ft (oa),
204.2 ft × 32.8 ft. Engines: T3cyl. 1,400 tdw.
Launched: 31.12.1940.
Completed: 2.1941 for British Channel Islands
Shipping Co. Ltd.
1946: (British Channel Traders Ltd.).
1947: (Queenship Navigation Ltd.).
1959: (Coast Lines Ltd.).
25.9.1959: Arrived Troon for breaking up.

248   *Norton* 7,195 gt. Details as Yard No. 233.
Launched: 8.7.1941.
Completed: 8.1941 for R. Chapman & Son,
Newcastle.
1956: *Mastro-Stelios* (Cia. de Vapores Realma S.A.,
Panama).
1960: *Hoping Ssu Shi Chi* (Government of China).
1974: *Ho Ping 47* (China Ocean Shipping Co.).
1979: *Zhan Dou 47* (People's Republic of China).

249   *Earlston* 7,195 gt. Details as Yard No. 233.
Launched: 23.8.1941.
Completed: 10.1941 for R. Chapman & Son,
Newcastle.

The *Earlston*, with a cargo of military equipment, fighter
planes and hundreds of tons of ammunition, was one of 35
ships in the ill-fated convoy PQ 17 to North Russia in June
1942.
  After four days of constant attack by enemy submarines
and bombers, the convoy was north-east of Bear Island,

Barents Sea, when, on 4 July, it was ordered to scatter and
most of its naval escort withdrawn to face the enemy when
it was thought to be in danger of attack by a German surface
fleet. So, as a convoy, it ceased to exist and its ships were on
their own, still under constant attack and with the enemy
able to pick them off, one by one.
  Many of the vessels headed for the shelter of the northern
ice, to gain protection on one side at least. Among them was
the *Earlston*, her crew witnessing at long range the sinking
of the *Empire Byron* on 5 July. A few hours later the *Earlston*
was herself under attack and for over three hours bombs and
aerial torpedoes straddled the ship as plane after plane came
in. For a time it seemed *Earlston* bore a charmed life. Then
her luck ran out: it was a near miss but enough to lift the
ship out of the water. Her main engine shifted off its bedplate,
every piece of machinery was smashed and the ship began
flooding. She was abandoned.
  Then four U-boats surfaced: three torpedoes were fired at
the helpless ship, two missed but one from *U.334* struck her.
Still she did not sink. The submarines submerged as the
planes resumed their attacks. Then a bomb hit No. 1 hold,
stowed with ammunition. There was an enormous explosion
and the fore-end of the ship disintegrated. Her stern rose
from the water, she turned over and slid beneath the waves.

250   *Allerton* 7,195 gt. Details as Yard No. 233.
Launched: 4.10.1941.
Completed: 11.1941 for R. Chapman & Son,
Newcastle.
1957: *North Lady* (Cia. Nav. Petunia S.A., Panama).
1961: *Ypapanti* (Anatoli SS Co., Greece).
1964: *Ever Fortune* (First National SS Co. Ltd.,
Taiwan).
1968: Scrapped Kaohsiung.

251   *Sir Leonard Pearce* 1,580 gt. Details as Yard No
234.
Launched: 5.8.1941.
Completed: 9.1941 for London Power Co. Ltd.
(Stephenson Clarke Ltd., London).
1948: (British Electricity Authority).
1955: (Central Electricity Authority).
1958: (Central Electricity Generating Board).
6.1960: Scrapped Sunderland.

252   *Fulham VI* 1,552 gt. Details as Yard No. 234.
Launched: 18.11.1941.
Completed: 12.1941 for Fulham Borough Council,
London.
1948: (British Electricity Authority).
1955: (Central Electricity Authority).
1958: (Central Electricity Generating Board).
29.5.1959: Arrived Rotterdam for breaking up.

253   *Fulham VII* 1,552 gt. Details as Yard No. 234.
Launched: 15.12.1941.
Completed: 1.1942 for Fulham Borough Council,
London.
14.2.1946: In collision with *Alfred Victory* (1945,
7,607 gt) nine miles from Beachy Head, Sussex. Sank
(voyage: Barry/London – coal).

254 *Derryheen* 7,217 gt. Details as Yard No. 233.
Launched: 3.12.1941.
Completed: 2.1942 for McCowan & Gross Ltd.,
London.
22.4.1942: Sunk by submarine (*U.201*) torpedo,
approx. 400 miles west of Bermuda, 31.20N 70.35W.

255 *Ingleton* 7,203 gt. Details as Yard No. 233.
Launched: 2.4.1942.
Completed: 5.1942 for R. Chapman & Son,
Newcastle.
1960: *Tarseus* (Santa Spyridon Maritime Co. Ltd.,
Lebanon).
1964: *Maria Renee* (Levant Shipping Co., S.A.L.,
Lebanon).
3.1967: Scrapped Sakai, Japan.

256 *Corfoss* 1,849 gt, 264.9 ft (oa), 257 ft × 39.5 ft.
Engines: T3cyl. A collier.
Launched: 31.12.1941.
Completed: 2.1942 for Wm. Cory & Son, London.
14.5.1966: Arrived Santander for breaking up.

257 *William Pearman* 1,552 gt. Details as Yard No.
234.
Launched: 3.2.1942.
Completed: 4.1942 for London Power Co. Ltd.
1948: (British Electricity Authority).
1955: (Central Electricity Authority).
1958: (Central Electricity Generating Board).
5.1961: Scrapped Zelzate, Belgium.

258 *Flamma* 2,825 gt, 325.8 ft (oa), 315 ft × 44.5 ft.
Engines: T3cyl. A collier.
Launched: 16.4.1942.
Completed: 5.1942 for Gas, Light & Coke Co. Ltd.
1949: (North Thames Gas Board).
1963: *San George* (Stassa Corpn., Panama (Kollakis
Bros, London)).
8.2.1967: Arrived Bremen for breaking up.

259 *Winsor* 2,825 gt. Details as Yard No. 258.
Launched: 14.5.1942.
Completed: 6.1942 for Gas, Light & Coke Co. Ltd.
1949: (North Thames Gas Board).
1964: *Ypapanti* (Seahorse Cia. Nav. Turistica (K & M
Shipbrokers, London)).
17.11.1966: Aground in heavy weather off Walton-
on-the-Naze, Essex. Broke in two. Total loss
(voyage: Tyne/Lisbon – coke).

260 *Lambrook* 7,038 gt. Details as Yard No. 237.
Launched: 13.6.1942.
Completed: 8.1942 for Austin Friars SS Co.
(Galbraith, Pembroke & Co.).
1951: *St. Merriel* (South American Saint Line Ltd.).
1963: *Proodos* (Cia. Nav. Agelef S.A., Panama).
1965: *Elpis* (Elpida Cia. Nav., Panama).
26.6.1966: On fire in engine room sixty miles off
Colombo, Ceylon. Abandoned (voyage:

Mormugao/Japan). Taken in tow by *Exemplar* (1940,
6,736 gt) but: 28.6.1966: Anchored, unable to
proceed due to monsoon swell.
30.6.1966: Fire extinguished – vessel burnt out. Vessel
not allowed into Colombo harbour
and: 10.7.1966: Towed to Trincomalee by Dutch tugs
Maas (1954, 295 gt) and *Orinoco* (1964, 670 gt).
27.4.1967: Arrived Piraeus, in tow. Constructive total
loss. Sold and 1.1968: Scrapped Split.

262 *Cormain* 2,883 gt. Details as Yard No. 259.
Launched: 28.8.1942.
Completed: 10.1942 for Wm. Cory & Son Ltd.
1946: *Coldridge* (Coastwise Colliers Ltd.).
1949: *Cormain* (Wm. Cory & Son Ltd.).
1969: (A/S Klaveness, Oslo) – a storage barge. Later
renamed *Bulkhandling 2* (bauxite discharging barge at
Burntisland) (A & N Vogel Ltd.).
29.9.1979: Arrived Faslane, in tow, for breaking up.

263 *Carlton* 7,210 gt. Details as Yard No. 233.
Launched: 15.7.1942.
Completed: 9.1942 for R. Chapman & Son,
Newcastle.
1963: *Ivy Fair* (Ivy Shipping Co. Ltd., London).
1964: *Cosmo Trader* (Southland Nav. & Commerce
Ltd., Hong Kong).
1964: (Eastland Nav. & Commerce Ltd., Hong
Kong).
5.9.1964: Aground on Kau Shau Island, Hong Kong,
in typhoon.
4.11.1964: Refloated, but constructive total loss. Sold
and scrapped locally.

264 *Highland Prince* 7,043 gt. Details as Yard No.
237.
Launched: 25.9.1942.
Completed: 12.1942 for Prince Line Ltd.
1955: *Inchstuart* (Williamson & Co. Ltd., Hong
Kong).
1966: (Douglas SS Co. (Mullion & Co., Hong
Kong)).
6.6.1969: Arrived Hong Kong for breaking up.

265 *Windsor Queen* 1,033 gt. Details as Yard No.
247.
Launched: 17.12.1942.
Completed: 2.1943 for British Channel Islands
Shipping Co. Ltd.
1946: (British Channel Traders Ltd.).
1947: (Queenship Navigation Ltd.).
3.10.1959: Arrived Boom, Belgium, for breaking up.

267 *Firelight* 2,841 gt. Details as Yard No. 258.
Launched: 20.1.1943.
Completed: 5.1943 for Gas, Light & Coke Co. Ltd.
4.11.1943: Torpedoed by E-boat near Cromer
(voyage: Thames/Tyne).
5.11.1943: Towed to Gt. Yarmouth, bows missing.

5.12.1943: Towed to Sunderland; repaired.
1949: (North Thames Gas Board).
1964: *Mari* (Panaghia Nav. S.A. (A. J. & D. J. Chandris, Greece).
1968: *Klabb* (A/S Klaveness, Oslo) – a storage barge. Later renamed *Bulkhandling 3* (bauxite discharging barge at Burntisland (A. & N. Vogel Ltd.)).
29.9.1979: Arrived Faslane, in tow, for breaking up.

269   *Cormarsh* 2,878 gt. Details as Yard No. 258.
Launched: 3.5.1943.
Completed: 7.1943 for Wm. Cory & Son Ltd.
4.1961: Arrived Willebroek for breaking up.

Note: Fitted as a heavy lift ship (60-ton derrick) during the war.

271   *Brighton* 7,345 gt. Details as Yard No. 233.
Launched: 17.6.1943.
Completed: 8.1943 for R. Chapman & Son, Newcastle.
1959: *Pelopidas* (Tharros Shipping Co. Ltd.).
1959: (Troodos Shipping & Trading Co. Ltd., London).
18.2.1965: Arrived Hong Kong for breaking up.

272   *Riverton* 7,307 gt. Details as Yard No. 233.
Launched: 2.8.1943.
Completed: 9.1943 for R. Chapman & Son, Newcastle).
23.4.1945: Damaged by submarine (*U.1023*) torpedo off north Cornwall coast. Towed to St. Ives Bay. Later repaired.
1960: *Eftychia* (D. P. Margaronis, Greece).
1965: *Boaz* (Cia. Nav. Pearl S.A., Panama (Teh-Hu SS Co., Hong Kong)).
3.1969: Scrapped Kaohsiung.

275   *Derrycunihy* 7,093 gt. Details as Yard No. 237.
Launched: 11.11.1943.
Completed: 2.1944 for McCowan & Gross Ltd., London.
24.6.1944: Mined off assault beaches, Normandy. Back broken, stern on bottom. Constructive total loss. Abandoned.

278   *Demeterton* 7,344 gt. Details as Yard No. 233.
Launched: 25.1.1944.
Completed: 3.1944 for R. Chapman & Son, Newcastle.
1964: *Jayshree* (Panamerica Pacific Corpn. (Hornbeam & Co., Hong Kong)).
1965: *Freedom Venture* (Interocean Nav. Corpn. (Wah Kwong & Co., Hong Kong)).
1969: (Freedom Carriers Inc. (Wah Kwong & Co., Hong Kong)).
1.1971: Scrapped Kaohsiung.

279   *Cormoat* 2,886 gt. Details as Yard No. 259.
Launched: 29.3.1945.

Completed: 5.1945 for Wm. Cory & Son Ltd., London.
1965: *Chrigal* (Chrigal Cia. Nav. S.A., Panama (G. Vlassis, Greece).
1972: *Marianik* (Sissini Nav. Co., Cyprus (N. J. Nomikos, Greece)).
10.1974: Scrapped Split.

280   *Scottish Prince* 7,138 gt, 443.1 ft (oa), 427 ft × 57 ft. Engines: Oil.
Launched: 24.4.1944.
Completed: 6.1944 for Prince Line Ltd.
1952: *Vitali* (Cia. Nav. Rio Bello S.A., Panama).
1952: *Hillcrest* (Crest Shipping Co. (Ivanovic & Co. Ltd., London)).
1959: *Sophia* (Fidelitas SS Co. (Rethymnis & Kulukundis Ltd., London)).
13.4.1966: Fire in engine room while repairing at Piraeus. Towed out, beached Ambeliki; fire extinguished.
25.4.1966: Refloated but constructive total loss. Sold to Halcoussis & Co., Greece. Repaired as *Yannis* (Janice Shipping Co., Cyprus).
6.11.1969: Arrived Shanghai for breaking up.

282   *Frumenton* 7,542 gt, 437.8 ft (oa), 421.7 ft × 58 ft. Engines: T3cyl.
Launched: 6.7.1944.
Completed: 9.1944 for R. Chapman & Son, Newcastle.
1962: *Garthdale* (Esk & Eskgarth Shipping Co. Ltd. (H. M. Lund)).
1964: *Jeb Lee* (Hong Kong United Investments Ltd., Newcastle (Jebshun Shipping Co. Ltd., Hong Kong)).
26.1.1970: Arrived Hong Kong for breaking up.

290   *Padana* 7,541 gt, 436.6 ft (oa), 421.7 ft × 58 ft. Engines: T3cyl.
Launched: 13.4.1945.
Completed: 7.1945 for British India SN Co. Ltd.
1961: *Apj Rita* (Surrendra Overseas Ltd., Bombay).
1967: Renamed *Samudra Apj Rita*.
7.1970: Scrapped Bombay (as *Apj Rita*).

295   *Chessington* 1,750 gt, 271 ft (oa), 260 ft × 39.5 ft. Engines: T3cyl. A collier.
Launched: 17.1.1946.
Completed: 4.1946 for Wandsworth & District Gas Company.
1966: (T. Johannisson, Sweden). Resold (Goteborgs Bogserings og Bargnings A/B, Gothenburg). Machinery removed, converted to a non-propelled barge/storage hulk.

296   *Cormist* 2,886 gt. Details as Yard No. 258.
Launched: 7.9.1945.
Completed: 1.1946 for Wm. Cory & Son Ltd.
1968: Machinery removed, converted to a storage hulk (Skrot & Aufullsprodukter, Gothenburg).

297 *Derryclare* 4,810 gt, 436 ft (oa), 420 ft × 57 ft.
Engines: Oil.
Launched: 5.11.1945.
Completed: 1.1946 for McCowan & Gross Ltd.,
London.
1951: *Cape Clear* (Lyle Shipping Co. Ltd., Glasgow).
1962: *Golden Sigma* (Dynasty Shipping Co. Ltd.,
Hong Kong).
1964: *Laurel* (Pluto Shipping Co. Ltd. (World Wide
Shipping Co., Hong Kong)).
1965: (Laurel Navigation Ltd., Hong Kong).
11.1967: Scrapped Hong Kong.

299 *Kittiwake* 2,016 gt, 308 ft (oa), 296 ft × 43.2 ft.
Engines: T3cyl.

Launched: 19.12.1945.
Completed: 4.1946 for British & Continental SS
Co. Ltd.
1955: *Germania* (Hellenic Lines Ltd., Greece).
1977: *Hanan* (W. Nseir, Syria).
1979: *Hanan Star* (Sea Transport Agency, Syria).

300 *Oliver Bury* 2,904 gt. Details as Yard No. 258.
Launched: 20.11.1945.
Completed: 3.1946 for London Power Co. Ltd.
1948: (British Electricity Authority).
1955: (Central Electricity Authority).
1958: (Central Electricity Generating Board).
1970: *Alycia* (Ayios Stylianos Shipping Ltd., Cyprus).
19.2.1973: Arrived Spezia for breaking up.

Built by Caledon Shipbuilding & Engineering Co. Ltd., Caledon Shipyard, Dundee

392 *Empire Rhodes* 7,050 gt. 'B'-type. 446 ft (oa),
431 ft × 56 ft. Engines: T3cyl.
Launched: 19.9.1941.
Completed: 12.1941.
18.12.1945: Cargo on fire at Gdynia after arriving
from Calcutta with jute. Towed alongside
breakwater, grounded and scuttled in attempt to
extinguish fire.
3.1.1946: Still afire forward; holds gutted, sides and
deck buckled. Extinguished.
23.2.1946: Towed to Kiel, then Falmouth.
11.4.1946: Towed to Glasgow: to be scuttled, but:
25.2.1947: Sold, to be repaired.
1947: *Culter* (South Georgia Co. (C. Salvesen & Co.,
Leith)).
1959: *Virginia Ipar* (M. Ipar, Istanbul).
27.4.1963: Laid up Istanbul, and:
9.1970: Scrapped Istanbul.

393 *Empire Heywood* 7,050 gt. Details as Yard No.
392.
Launched: 21.10.1941.
Completed: 3.1942.
1947: *Saint Gregory* (Saint Line Ltd. (Mitchell, Cotts
& Co. Ltd.).
1962: *Andros* (Stuart Nav. Co. (Bahamas) Ltd., Hong
Kong).
1963: *Abiko* (Escort Shipping Co. (World Wide
Shipping Co., Hong Kong)).
1963: (Pine SS Co. (Mariner Shipping Co., Hong
Kong)).
15.3.1967: Arrived Hong Kong for breaking up.

394 *Empire Prince* 7,050 gt. Details as Yard No. 392.
Launched: 31.3.1942.

Completed: 5.1942.
1945: *Clan Angus* (Clan Line Steamers Ltd.).
1956: *Umkuzi* (Bullard, King & Co. Ltd.).
1959: *Clan Angus* (Clan Line Steamers Ltd.).
4.1962: Scrapped Hirao.

396 *Empire Archer* 7,050 gt. Details as Yard No.
392.
Launched: 29.6.1942.
Completed: 8.1942.
13.9.1944: Stranded on Rathlin Island, N. Ireland,
foreholds flooded (voyage: Sunderland/U.S.A.).
Refloated, beached off Bangor for safety. Again
refloated, towed to Belfast then:
25.9.1944: Arrived Glasgow for repairs.
1946: *Baron Murray* (H. Hogarth & Sons).
1959: *Cathay* (Cathay Shipping Corpn. (P. S. Li,
Hong Kong)).
24.7.1963: Arrived Yokosuka for breaking up.

408 *Empire Canyon* 7,050 gt. Details as Yard No.
392.
Launched: 11.11.1943.
Completed: 12.1943.
1947: *Holmbury* (Alexander Shipping Co. Ltd.
(Houlder Bros. Ltd.)).
1960: *Ilyasbaksh* (United Oriental Shipping Co.,
Karachi).
12.8.1965: Arrived Bombay; placed under restraint
while undergoing rudder repairs during
Pakistan/India war, and:
11.1966: Impounded by Indian Government.
12.1970: Scrapped Bombay.

411   *Empire Favour* 7,050 gt. Details as Yard No. 392.
Launched: 22.8.1945.
Completed: 11.1945.
1947: *Epsom* (Britain SS Co. Ltd. (Watts, Watts & Co. Ltd.)).
1950: *Errington Court* (Haldin & Philipps Ltd.).
1956: *Penelope* (M. A. Embiricos, Greece).
1964: *Andromachi* (Franco Shipping Co., Greece).
25.6.1969: Damaged by Israeli shelling whilst lying at Suez during Arab/Israeli war. Set on fire and abandoned. Later sold for breaking up, and:
3.1976: Scrapped Adabiya, south of Suez.

412   *Empire Canning* 7,050 gt. Details as Yard No. 392, but: Engines: Oil.

Launched: 30.10.1944.
Completed: 12.1944.
1946: *Willesden* (Britain SS Co. Ltd. (Watts, Watts & Co. Ltd.)).
1958: *Golden Lambda* (World Wide Shipping Co. Ltd., Hong Kong)).
1960: *Marine Explorer* (Neptune Shipping Co., Hong Kong).
1962: *East Vim* (Viking Shipping Co., Hong Kong).
1963: *Wakasa Bay* (Marine Navigation Co. Ltd., London).
1966: *Golden Wind* (Leo Shipping Co. Ltd. (World Wide Shipping Co. Ltd., Hong Kong)).
16.11.1966: Arrived Wakayama, Japan, for breaking up, and:
12.1966: Scrapped Hiroshima.

The founder of the Caledon company was engineer W. B. Thompson, his first four ship buildings being steam launches, conveyed by cart from his inland foundry at Stobswell to the dock area of Dundee to take the water. Yard No. 5, the *Ilala*, was launched from his new shipyard at Dundee in 1874 and the next vessel constructed was a yacht, *Banshee*, for the Earl of Caledon and it was this peer who agreed to his name being adopted for the yard's title.

In 1882 activities were extended to the old Laurie Yard at Whiteinch, on the River Clyde, where a score of craft were built before a slump in trade closed the yard. At Dundee the famous four-masted barques *Juteopolis* and *Lawhill* were built in 1891–1892 and which, initially, worked in the Calcutta–Dundee jute trade.

In 1886, then as W. B. Thompson & Co. Ltd., the yard launched the Clyde Shipping Company's *Eddystone*; they were to build over thirty 'Lighthouse'-named ships. In 1896 the Caledon Shipbuilding & Engineering Co. Ltd., took over and new customers included the Wilson Line of Hull; Limerick SS Co.; Leyland Line, Liverpool; Blue Funnel and Yeoward Bros., and when war broke out in 1939 the yard building number had reached 370.

During hostilities Government orders included seven 'B'-type standard cargo ships, three 'Empire'-type refrigerated ships and a smaller 'Scandinavian'-type 'Empire' ship. For the Royal Navy some 1,200 repair and refit jobs were carried out in the maintenance of submarines and destroyers. Three 'Ranger'-class tankers were built in 1941, *Gold Ranger*, launched 12 March; *Grey Ranger* launched on 27 May and *Green Ranger* on 21 August, under Yard Nos. 389–391. All were single screw twelve-knot motor ships, of 3,300 gt and 3,800 tdw. Two were lost.

The *Grey Ranger* was torpedoed on 22 September 1942 by submarine *U.435* in position 71.23N 11.03W, whilst in convoy QP 14 (North Russia/Iceland). Damaged in the engine room, she was sunk by gunfire from Royal Navy ships, due to the presence of enemy submarines.

On 18 November 1962 the *Green Ranger* was driven ashore at Sennen Cove, near Hartland Point, in a gale and while in tow of the Alexandra Towing Co.'s tug *Caswell* (ex *Empire Sybil*) during a voyage to Cardiff from Plymouth for a refit. The *Green Ranger* broke in two and was a total loss.

The *Gold Ranger* was sold commercially, to Singapore owners, in 1973.

At the end of World War II the twenty-acre Caledon Yard had six berths with ship capacity to 560 feet.

In 1968 the Caledon Shipbuilding & Engineering Co. Ltd. was acquired by Henry Robb Ltd., Leith, and became Robb Caledon Shipbuilders Ltd.

Alfred Holt & Co's *Telemachus*, built under licence in 1943. (Caledon Shipbuilding & Engineering Co. Ltd., Yard No. 397.)
Dundee City Archives

MERCHANT SHIPS BUILT UNDER PRIVATE CONTRACT OR LICENCE

368   *Glenearn* 9,886 gt.
Launched: 29.6.1938.
Completed: 11.1938 for Glen Line Ltd.
10.1939: Requisitioned as a Fleet Supply Ship.
1941: Converted to a Landing Ship (Infantry) (Large).
LSI (L) Pennant: 4.250.
4.1941: Heavily damaged in military evacuation of Greece.
1946: (Glen Line), (9,784 gt).
11.12.1970: Arrived Kaohsiung for breaking up.

372   *Glengyle* 9,919 gt.
Launched: 18.7.1939.

1940: Requisitioned and completed as a Fleet Supply Ship.
1941: Converted to a Landing Ship (Infantry) (Large).
LSI (L) Pennant: 4.196.
1946: (Glen Line), (9,919 gt).
1970: *Deucalion* (Ocean SS Co. Ltd.).
9.6.1971: Arrived Kaohsiung for breaking up.

373   *Glenartney* 9,795 gt.
Launched: 27.12.1939.
Completed: 1940 for Glen Line Ltd.
4.1967: Scrapped Onomichi.

These three ships belonged to a class of eight vessels ordered in 1936 following acquisition of the Glen & Shire Lines by Alfred Holt & Co. Ltd. (Blue Funnel Line). Twin screw motorships designed for eighteen knots with a two knots extra maximum, all were 507 ft (oa) 483.1 ft and a breadth of 66.4 ft, had three decks, possible accommodation for twelve passengers and a deadweight capacity of 9,700 tons. Hopefully, all eight were to be in service by 1940.

But such ships had been earmarked for Admiralty use and within a month or so of war the *Glenearn* and *Glengyle* together with the Shire Line's *Breconshire*, another of the 'Glenearn'-class building at Hong Kong, were requisitioned and converted to Fleet Supply Ships. As such, the *Breconshire* was lost in the Mediterranean in 1942 (see Taikoo Dock & Engineering Co. Ltd.).

Both *Glenearn* and *Glengyle* took part in 'Operation Demon' in late April 1941 when some 50,000 servicemen were evacuated from Greece. The *Glengyle*, with four cruisers and three destroyers, also began the evacuation of Crete on 29 May 1941, lifting 7,000 men and continued working in the Mediterranean, later in the war joining the Pacific Fleet, as did the *Glenearn*.

The *Glenartney* worked in Malta convoys and she too, joined the Pacific Fleet later in the war.

Scotts of Greenock delivered the *Glenroy* (9,809 gt) in 1938 and in 1939 she, too, became a Fleet

Supply Ship. Damaged in an air attack on Liverpool on 12 September 1940, she was later made a Landing Ship Infantry (L) in 1941 and with the *Glenearn* and *Glengyle*, formed part of the 'Z' Force operating in the Mediterranean. On 23 November 1941 she was hit by an aerial torpedo and beached at Mersa Matruh. Repaired, she continued in the same role, taking part in the Normandy landings, Indonesia and the Far East. The *Glenroy* survived the war and was eventually scrapped at Onomichi, Japan, in November 1966.

The Taikoo Yard at Hong Kong also built another of the class in 1939, the *Glenorchy* (8,982 gt), which was lost in the Mediterranean on 13 August 1942.

Two of the eight ships were ordered from Continental yards. The *Denbighshire* came from NV Nederlandsche Scheep. Maats in 1938 and worked in the Malta convoys, and with the exception of a small fire whilst at Malta in 1942, came through the war unscathed. She then worked in the fast service to the Far East until early 1968 when she was transferred to the China Mutual SN Co. Ltd. (A. Holt & Co. Ltd.) and was renamed *Sarpedon*. On 11 August 1969 she arrived at Kaohsiung to be broken up.

The other order was placed with Burmeister & Wain, Copenhagen, for the *Glengarry*, but she was captured by German forces when Denmark was invaded in April 1940 and was planned to be completed as a raider for the German Navy. Instead, she became the training ship *Hansa* and in May 1945 was recaptured at Kiel and renamed *Empire Humber* (*q.v.*) and in September 1946 joined the Glen Line as *Glengarry*. Apart from the Glen & Shire ships, A. Holt & Co. ordered two of the same type for themselves from the Caledon Yard, *Priam* (Yard No. 387) and *Telemachus* (Yard No. 388).

383   *Morialta* 1,365 gt, 227.4 ft (oa), 217 ft × 41.1 ft. Engines: Oil.
Launched: 7.5.1940.
Completed: 10.1940 for Adelaide SS Co. Ltd.
1957: *Waiben* (John Burke Ltd., Brisbane).
1964: *Jacques del Mar* (Soc. Maritime Caledonienne, New Caledonia).
1968: *Longlife* (Seaview Nav. Corpn., Panama).
1972: Renamed *Royal Martin*.
1973: *Island Pearl* (Empire Navigation Co., Singapore).
23.12.1973: Cargo broke loose in heavy weather, capsized and sank seven miles from Vung Tau Lighthouse, 10.14N 106.59E (voyage: Phnom Penh/Singapore – rubber and cartridge scrap).

384   *Tottenham* 4,762 gt, 432 ft (oa), 417.6 ft × 56.8 ft. Engines: T3cyl. 9,200 tdw.
Launched: 21.3.1940.
Completed: 6.1940 for Britain SS Co. (Watts, Watts & Co. Ltd.).
19.3.1941: Mined on anchorage at Southend, Essex (voyage: London/Halifax NS – ballast). Repaired.
17.6.1941: Captured, then sunk by German raider *Atlantis* which was masquerading as the Norwegian-flag *Tamesis*, after two torpedoes, shelling and placing of a time bomb; position 07.38S 19.12W, in South Atlantic (voyage: Tyne/Middle East – military equipment and supplies).

385   *Twickenham* 4,826 gt. Details as Yard No. 384.
Launched: 17.9.1940.
Completed: 11.1940 for Britain SS Co. (Watts, Watts & Co. Ltd.).
15.7.1943: Torpedoed and forefoot blown away by

submarine *U.135* whilst in convoy OS 51 off Canary Islands, 28.36N 13.18W (voyage: Hull/Buenos Aires – coal). Ship remained afloat, and:
16.7.1943: Began voyage to Dakar (1,000 miles), at first under tow, then under own steam.
31.7.1943: Arrived Dakar; temporarily repaired and:
21.10.1944: Sailed to United Kingdom.
15.12.1944: Arrived Middle Docks, South Shields. Repaired.
1958: *Jag Mata* (Great Eastern Shipping Co. Ltd., Bombay).
1963: Scrapped Bombay.

386   *Teddington* 4,830 gt. Details as Yard No. 384.
Launched: 10.1.1941.
Completed: 3.1941 for Britain SS Co. (Watts, Watts & Co. Ltd.).
17.9.1941: Damaged by E-boat torpedo in 'E-boat Alley' off Norfolk coast, 53.04N 1.34E (voyage: London/Durban and Calcutta – war supplies). On fire, taken in tow, but drifted ashore three miles from Cromer Pier. Decks collapsed, shell plating buckled, holds and engine room flooded. Part of cargo salved, but ship broke her back.
23.9.1941: Completely submerged: Total loss.
7.1954: Wreckage dispersed by explosives.

387   *Priam* 9,321 gt, 512.9 ft (oa), 486.1 ft × 66.4 ft. Engines: Oil.
Launched: 25.6.1941.
Completed: 1941 for Blue Funnel Line (A. Holt & Co. Ltd.).
1948: *Glenorchy* (Glen Line Ltd.).
1970: *Phemius* (Ocean SS Co. Ltd. (A. Holt & Co. Ltd.)).
27.4.1971: Arrived Kaohsiung for breaking up.

388 *Telemachus* Details as Yard No. 387.
Laid down: 1.2.1940 for Ocean SS Co. Ltd. (A. Holt
& Co. Ltd.). Requisitioned by Ministry of War
Transport for possible conversion to an auxiliary
aircraft carrier; renamed *Empire Activity*.
Acquired by the Admiralty, and:
30.5.1942: Launched as *Activity*.
10.1942: Completed as an escort carrier (15 aircraft):
the flight deck was 492 ft × 66 ft.
Until October 1943 was used for training; then served
in Atlantic and with Arctic convoys and in 1945 was
with the East Indies Fleet as an aircraft ferry and,
later, as a stores ship.
5.1946: Purchased by Glen Line Ltd. (A. Holt & Co.
Ltd.) and converted at Palmers Hebburn Co. Ltd. to
a cargo motorship. Renamed *Breconshire* (9,061 gt).
26.4.1967: Arrive Mihara for breaking up.

397 *Telemachus* 8,265 gt, 489 ft (oa),
462.2 ft × 61.4 ft. Engines: Oil.

Launched: 18.5.1943.
Completed: 10.1943 for Ocean SS Co. Ltd. (A. Holt
& Co. Ltd.).
1957: *Monmouthshire* (Glen Line Ltd.).
1963: *Glaucus* (Ocean SS Co. Ltd. (A. Holt & Co.
Ltd.)).
1964: *Nanchang* (Ocean SS Co. Ltd.). (On charter to
China Navigation Co. Ltd.).
1.4.1968: Arrived Hong Kong for breaking up.

398 *Ascot* 7,005 gt, 434.5 ft (oa), 419.2 ft × 56.8 ft.
Engines: T3cyl.
Launched: 8.10.1942.
Completed: 12.1942 for Britain SS Co. Ltd. (Watts,
Watts & Co. Ltd.).
29.2.1944: Hit by torpedoes from Japanese submarine
(*I.37*) east of Seychelles, in position 05.00S 63.00E
and despite gunfire she wallowed, awash, for eight
hours and was finally despatched by time bombs set
by the submarine's crew (voyage:
Calcutta/Mauritius).

In 1939 the fleet of Watts, Watts & Co. Ltd. comprised nine ships, five of them Caledon-built. Eight
were operated by the Britain SS Co. Ltd. and one, *Willesden* (4,826 gt), originally the *Antinous* of
1925 and built by Workman, Clark, Belfast for the New Egypt & Levant Shipping Co. Ltd.,
London, by Watts Shipping Co. Ltd. She was to be caught by the raider *Thor* on 1 April 1942 and
sunk in position 16S 16W (approx.).

Of the eight pre-war ships, six were lost, the first sinking being the *Deptford* on 13 December
1939 when she was torpedoed by submarine *U.38* near Honningsvaag on a voyage Narvik/United
Kingdom with iron ore. On 8 June 1940 the German armies were nearing the port of Rouen where
the *Dulwich* was discharging coal. In an attempt to escape capture, she grounded on a bank in the
Seine and was scuttled. She was taken by the Germans and repaired and later sunk by the Allies.
The third of the 'D' trio, all built by Smiths Dock Co. Ltd., Stockton on Tees in 1930–1931, the
Dartford (4,023 gt) was hit by a torpedo on 12 June 1942 from submarine *U.124* while in convoy
ON S 100, in the North Atlantic. Of four ships built by Caledon during the war, three were lost
and in 1945 the fleet numbered seven vessels: *Beckenham* and *Beaconsfield* (4,790 gt) of 1937–1938,
Twickenham and *Willesden* (ex *Empire Canning*) all by Caledon; *Chertsey* and *Chiswick* by Pickersgill
in 1943 and the Doxford-built motorship *Greenwich* (7,292 gt) of the same year.

The Watts, Watts company has shipping traces back to 1715. In 1853 they sent the sailing ship
Brilliant with coal to the Continent and three years later were moving coal in sailing ships across the
North Sea under the name of Watts, Milburn & Co. In 1869 the company began building steamships,
opened its own collieries to fill their holds and changed its name to Watts, Ward & Co.

The Britain SS Co. Ltd. was formed in 1885 and in 1896 the Watts, Watts & Co. Ltd. title came.
In the wars in South Africa at the end of the century, shiploads of hay were moved from England
and South America for the horses of the British Forces there.

399 *Tarkwa* 4,716 gt, 460 ft (oa), 438 ft × 59.4 ft.
Engines: Oil.
Launched: 30.8.1943.
Completed: 4.1944 for Elder, Dempster Lines Ltd.
1967: *Golden Lion* (Guan Guan Shipping Ltd.,
Singapore).
5.1971: Arrived Shanghai for breaking up.

400 *Norman Monarch* 7,005 gt, 446.5 ft (oa),
434 ft × 56.7 ft. Engines: T3cyl.
Launched: 21.12.1942.
Completed: 2.1943 for Monarch SS Co. Ltd.
(Raeburn & Verel Ltd.).
1957: *Ragni Paulin* (Paulins Rederi A/B, Finland).
30.9.1969: Arrived Shanghai for breaking up.

401   *Scottish Monarch* 7,005 gt. Details as Yard No. 400.
Launched: 5.3.1943.
Completed: 4.1943 for Monarch SS Co. Ltd. (Raeburn & Verel Ltd.).
1957: *Demetrius D.S.* (Eastern Seafaring & Trading Co., Panama).
1958: *Wishford* (Hemisphere Shipping Co. Ltd., Hong Kong (Far East Enterprising Co. Inc., Hong Kong)).
1959: *Hoping Wu Shi Wu* (Government of China).
1979: Renamed *Ho Ping 55*.

402   *Lapland* 2,881 gt, 328 ft (oa), 315.5 ft × 46.7 ft. Engines: T3cyl.
Launched: 8.9.1942.
Completed: 11.1942 for Currie Line Ltd., Leith.
1959: *Pavlos* (Halcophil Cia. Nav. S.A., Beirut).
1967: Renamed *Liana*.
12.1973: Scrapped Piraeus.

403   *Iceland* 2,879 gt. Details as Yard No. 402.
Launched: 30.4.1943.
Completed: 6.1943 for Currie Line Ltd., Leith.
1956: *Moyle* (Shamrock Shipping Co. Ltd., Larne).

1960: *Wingrove* (Osprey (Bermuda) Ltd.).
1961: *Cannonbury* (Cannon Corporation of Panama).
1962: *Kyriakatsi* (La Naias Cia. Mar. S.A., Panama).
1968: Renamed *Efstathios*.
1979: Scrapped Eleusis, Greece.

409   *Rhexenor* 10,195 gt, 497.3 ft (oa), 475.8 ft × 64.4 ft. Engines: Oil.
Launched: 25.5.1945.
Completed: 12.1945 for China Mutual SN Co. Ltd. (A. Holt & Co. Ltd.).
1975: *Hexeno*. Renamed for delivery voyage only. Left Singapore 13.5.1975, and
18.5.1975: Arrived Kaohsiung for breaking up.

410   *Stentor* 10,195 gt. Details as Yard No. 409.
Launched: 4.12.1945.
Completed: 6.1946 for Ocean SS Co. Ltd. (A. Holt & Co. Ltd.).
1958: *Glenshiel* (Glen Line Ltd.).
1963: *Stentor* (Ocean SS Co. Ltd.).
1975: *Tento* Renamed for delivery voyage only. Left Singapore 1.4.1975, and
6.4.1975: Arrived Kaohsiung for breaking up.

In 1939, Alfred Holt's Blue Funnel Line totalled 69 ships, 22 of them in the China Mutual SN Company Ltd. and 47 under the Ocean SS Co. Ltd.

As with most liner companies, the fleet suffered severely during the war, no less than 41 ships being lost (321,940 gross tons of shipping) – some 55% of the fleet.

423   *Anchises* 7,642 gt, 487 ft (oa), 462.9 ft × 62.3 ft. Engines: Oil.
Launched: 25.9.1946.
Completed: 4.1947 for Ocean SS Co. (A. Holt & Co.).
1973: *Alcinous* (China Mutual SN Co. (Ocean Shipping & Trading Co., Liverpool)).
1975: (Glen Line Ltd.).
1975: (China Mutual SN Co. Ltd.).
5.9.1975: Arrived Kaohsiung for breaking up.

424   *Szechuen* 3,033 gt, 318.5 ft (oa), 307.2 ft × 46.3 ft. Engines: Oil.
Launched: 18.12.1945.
Completed: 7.1946 for China Navigation Co. Ltd.
1966: *Tong Hin* (Asia Selatan Enterprises Ltd. (Kie Hock Shipping Co. Ltd., Singapore)).
1966: *Gambaris* (Africa Shipping Co. S.A., Panama (Kie Hock Shipping Co. Ltd.)).

1968: Renamed *Karingo*.
1969: (Karingo Shipping Co. S.A., Panama (Kie Hock Shipping Co. Ltd.)).
1977: (Tay Chye Chuan, Malaysia).
10.1978: Scrapped Hong Kong.

425   Launched as *Shetland* 2,271 gt, 334 ft (oa), 322.2 ft × 46.2 ft. Engines: Oil.
Launched: 15.5.1946.
Completed: 10.1946 as *Scotland* for Currie Line Ltd.
1967: *Eleftheria* (L. Govdelas, Greece).
1971: (Dyros Cia. Nav. S.A., Greece).
1974: *Alexandra K* (Alandra Maritime S.A., Panama (Madina Maritime S.A., Greece)).
18.9.1976: On fire in Aegean Sea: taken in tow but abandoned in position 35.10N 30.20E. Presumed sank (voyage: Eleusis/Jeddah – timber).

Built by Cammell Laird & Co. Ltd., Birkenhead

1060   *Empire Flame* 7,069 gt. 'Y'-type 447.6 ft (oa), 432.3 ft × 56.2 ft. Engines: T3cyl.
Launched: 12.5.1941.
Completed: 6.1941.
1945: *Dunkery Beacon* (Crawford Shipping Co. Ltd., London).
1955: *Rissa* (R. Simberg, Finland).
1961: *Augusta Paulin* (Paulins Rederi A/B, Finland).
5.1969: Scrapped Shanghai.

1061   *Empire Clive* 7,069 gt. Details as Yard No. 1060.

Launched: 28.7.1941.
Completed: 8.1941.
1946: *Charlbury* (Alexander Shipping Co. Ltd. (Houlder Bros.)).
1958: *Isabel Erica* (Red Anchor Line Ltd., Hong Kong).
1964: (St Merryn Sg Co. Ltd. (C. Moller, Hong Kong)).
8.1969: Scrapped Hong Kong.

This large shipbuilding company was first established in 1824 by John Laird, later to become John Laird, Sons & Company, Laird Bros., then Laird Bros. Ltd., until 1903, when an amalgamation with Charles Cammell & Co. Ltd., steelmakers of Sheffield, was made and the company title became Cammell Laird & Co. Ltd.

Actually, the first ship had been constructed in 1829 and the yard had steadily progressed with the building of both merchant and naval craft. With the amalgamation, large capital outlay provided large development on the Merseyside site at Tranmere which, by World War II, covered 108 acres. There were ten building berths, seven graving docks of which Nos. 6 and 7 were 707 ft and 862 ft respectively and there was a wet basin of 14 acres.

A number of notable ships were constructed; three passenger ships were built for the Norwegian America Line, *Kristianiafjord*, 10,669 gt, and *Bergensfjord* 11,016 gt, both in 1913 and *Stavangerfjord*, 13,156 gt, in 1918; Cunard's *Samaria*, 19,597 gt, in 1921; P & O's *Moldavia*, 16,556 gt, in 1922, the CGT liner *De Grasse*, 18,435 gt, in 1924; and three of Blue Star Line's five 'A'-class 15,000 gt ships, *Almeda Star, Andalucia Star* and *Arandora Star* in 1926–1927. The Cunard White Star Line's *Mauretania* of 35,738 gt, which made her maiden voyage from Liverpool to New York on 17 June 1939, was also built by Cammell Laird.

Only four 'Empire'-named ships were constructed by Cammell Laird during the 1939–1945 war years, two 'Y'-type tramps, a merchant aircraft carrier and a tanker, although a number of merchant ships were built under private contract or licence.

For many years Cammell Laird were builders of naval ships, and building in the Great War included five light cruisers, six 'Admiralty'-type destroyer leaders and two escorts. In 1921 an order was received for a 48,000 displacement tons battle-cruiser, but this was reduced in size to 33,900 tons under the limits of the Washington Treaty of 1921. Named *Rodney*, the battleship with sixteen-inch guns was completed in August 1927.

On 3 May 1939 the yard launched another battleship, the 35,000 ton *Prince of Wales* which was fated to be bombed and sunk on 10 December 1941 by Japanese aircraft off the East coast of Malaya. Another major building was an aircraft carrier, laid down in May 1943 as *Irresistible*, then renamed *Ark Royal* in 1945, launched on 3 May 1950 and commissioned on 2 May 1955.

MERCHANT SHIPS BUILT UNDER PRIVATE CONTRACT OR LICENCE

1046   *City of Calcutta* 8,063 gt, 515.7 ft (oa), 496.7 ft × 62.4 ft. Engines: 6 Steam turbines. Twin screw. Passenger/cargo ship.
Launched: 24.4.1940.
Completed: 8.1940 for Ellerman Lines Ltd. (City Line Ltd.)).
1961: *Grosvenor Pilot* (Grosvenor Shipping Co. Ltd., London (Mollers Ltd., Hong Kong)).
1962: Scrapped Hong Kong.

1112   *John Holt* 4,964 gt, 390.7 ft (oa), 370.4 ft × 52.8 ft. Engines: T3cyl and LP turbine.
Launched: 9.12.1942.
Completed: 3.1943 for John Holt & Co. (Liverpool) Ltd.
5.3.1944: Sunk by submarine (*U.66*) torpedo, in position 03.56N 07.36E, south of Opobo River, Nigeria.

1113   *Jonathan Holt* 3,778 gt. Details as Yard No. 1112.
Launched: 20.7.1943.
Completed: 10.1943 for John Holt & Co. (Liverpool) Ltd.
1950: (John Holt Line Ltd.).
1950: (Guinea Gulf Line Ltd.).
1962: *Zermatt* (Andermatt Shipping Co., Liberia).
18.5.1968: Arrived Split for breaking up.

1133   *City of Durham* 10,025 gt, 497.4 ft (oa), 475.5 ft × 64.4 ft. Engines: 2 steam turbines. 'Standard fast' type.
Launched: 3.10.1944.
Completed: 3.1945 for Ellerman City Line Ltd.
1962: *Yon Lee* (Waywiser Nav. Corp. (W. H. Eddie Hsu, Taiwan)).
7.1969: Scrapped Kaohsiung.

1151   *Tamele* 7,172 gt, 451 ft (oa), 434.5 ft × 58.7 ft. Engines: Oil. Twin screw.
Launched: 3.10.1944.
Completed: 12.1944 for Elder, Dempster Lines Ltd.
1967: *Golden City* (Guan Guan Shipping (Pte.) Ltd., Singapore).
6.4.1973: Arrived Hong Kong for breaking up.

1156   *City of Carlisle* 9,913 gt. Details as Yard No. 1133.
Launched: 24.10.1945.
Completed: 2.1946 for Ellerman & Bucknall SS Co. Ltd.
1963: *Jeannie* (Far Eastern Nav. Corp. (W. H. Eddie Hsu, Taiwan).
5.1969: Scrapped Kaohsiung.

1159   *King Orry* 2,485 gt, 345 ft (o.a.), 329.7 ft × 47.2 ft. Engines: 4 steam turbines. Twin screws. A passenger ferry.
Launched: 22.11.1945.
Completed: 4.1946 for Isle of Man S.P. Co. Ltd.
1975: Sold for breaking up, then:
1978: resold and scrapped at Rochester, Kent.

1160   *Sacramento* 7,096 gt, 451 ft (oa), 434.5 ft × 58.7 ft. Engines: Oil. Twin screws.
Launched: 8.6.1945.
Completed: 8.1945 for Ellerman's Wilson Line Ltd.
1964: *City of Bristol* (Ellerman & Bucknall SS Co. Ltd.).
1969: *Felicie* (Anna Shipping Co. Ltd., Cyprus (Shipping & Produce Co. Ltd., London)).
1970: *30 de Noviembre* (Expresa Nav. Mambisa (Government of Cuba)).
27.7.1977: Arrived Faslane for breaking up.

1170   *Mona's Queen* 2,485 gt. Details as Yard No. 1159.
Launched: 5.2.1946.
Completed: 6.1946 for Isle of Man S. P. Co. Ltd.
1962: *Barrow Queen* (Marivic Nav. Inc. (A. J. & D. J. Chandris, Greece)).
1963: renamed *Carissima* for delivery voyage to Greece.
1963: refitted at Piraeus for cruising, renamed *Carina* (3,696 gt) (International Cruises S.A. (A. J. & D. J. Chandris).
1964: renamed *Fiesta*.
20.7.1974: (Laid up Piraeus).
9.1981: Scrapped Piraeus.

1171   *John Holt* 3,821 gt, 391.2 ft (oa), 370 ft × 52.8 ft. Engines: T3cyl and LP turbine.
Launched: 16.4.1946.
Completed: 9.1946 for John Holt & Co. (Liverpool) Ltd.
1950: (John Holt Line Ltd.).
1950: (Guinea Gulf Line Ltd.).
1963: *Kavo Matapas* (Alpha Cia. Nav. S.A., Liberia).
1966: *Tung Lee* (Tung Lee Nav. Co. S.A., Liberia (Deacon & Co. Ltd., Hong Kong)).
18.8.1968: Arrived Kaohsiung for breaking up.

1172   *Robert L. Holt* 3,821 gt. Details as Yard No. 1171.
Launched: 30.7.1946.
Completed: 11.1946 for John Holt & Co. (Liverpool) Ltd.
1950: (John Holt Line Ltd.).
1950: (Guinea Gulf Line Ltd.).
30.9.1962: Arrived Bruges for breaking up.

John Holt became a pioneer of the West African trade in the 1860s when he acquired a trading post and began business on the humid island of Fernando Po, in the Gulf of Guinea, working his trade to and from the mainland by transhipment from the calling Elder, Dempster ships, In 1868 he owned a small sailing ship, then gradually built up a fleet of small coastal ships with which to connect his growing chain of trading stations and then, in 1907, ventured into deep sea steamship owning with the purchase of the *Balmore*, a vessel of 1,272 gt, built in 1890 by T. & W. Smith, of South Shields. She was sold in 1922 to German buyers, being renamed *Johannes Tiemann*.

The *Balmore* was followed by two new buildings, *Jonathan Holt* and *Thomas Holt*, in 1910. So John Holt & Co. (Liverpool) Ltd. came about and by the mid-1920s five deep sea ships, most of them with 'Holt' names, and two coasters formed the fleet.

In 1939 the shipowning interests of John Holt & Co. (Liverpool) Ltd., as an ancillary to the West African trading business, comprised six ships and as war broke out they were placed on 'open berth' as common users for West African shippers. The six ships were *John Holt* and *Jonathan Holt*, both 3,800 gt (later 4,975 gt) of 1938, *Thomas Holt* and *Godfrey B. Holt*, 3,600 gt of 1929, *Robert L. Holt*, 2,918 gt of 1926 and a coastal feeder ship based at Lagos.

For such a small fleet, war losses were high. The first was on 24 February 1941 when the 1938-built *Jonathan Holt* was torpedoed by *U.97* whilst in the Liverpool–United States convoy OB 289. She sank west of the Shetlands, in position 61.10N 11.55W.

Next was the *Robert L. Holt* of 1926. In June 1940 she had helped in the evacuation of troops and equipment from France and transported a large number of survivors from the Cunard White Star liner *Lancastria*, which had been bombed and sunk off St. Nazaire on 17 June. Just a year later the *Robert L. Holt* was lost. She left the Mersey for Freetown and Warri on 20 June 1941 but, considerably overdue, was posted missing. It later transpired that she was actually sunk by torpedo from *U.69* on 4 July and sank in position 24.15N 20.00W.

Two months later the *John Holt* of 1938 was torpedoed by *U.107* about 300 miles south of the Azores. She sank on 24 September in position 31.12N 23.32W. She, too, had previously assisted with the survivors from the *Lancastria*: on 17 June 1940 she embarked over 1,000 who had been taken from the sea by the armed Grimsby trawler *Cambridgeshire* and landed them at Plymouth on the 18th.

To replace these losses, Cammell Laird & Co. completed the *John Holt* (Yard No. 1112) in March 1943, but she was to last only one year, being torpedoed by *U.66* on 5 March 1944 some sixty miles south of the Opobo River, Nigeria, in position 03.56N 07.36E. However, her sistership, *Jonathan Holt* (Yard No. 1113), survived the war, as did the two 1929-built ships.

As hostilities ceased, two more vessels were laid down at the Cammell Laird shipyard, another *John Holt*, another *Robert L. Holt*.

In the 1950s the shipping side of the Holt business became John Holt Line Ltd., and then, effective from 1954, the Guinea Gulf Line Ltd. The ships involved were *Jonathan Holt* (1943), the two 1946-built ships, and two 1953-built turbine-driven ships from Cammell Laird, the *Elizabeth Holt* and *Florence Holt*, the latter being the tenth ship built by Cammell Laird for the company.

One other ship, *Mary Holt*, 5,577 gt, was built in 1959 by William Gray & Co. Ltd., Hartlepool, but in 1965 the Guinea Gulf Line was sold to the Elder, Dempster Group and the *Mary Holt*, the last ship of the Holt era, was sold to the National Shipping Corporation of Pakistan.

Built by C. Connell & Co. Ltd., Scotstoun Yard, Scotstoun, Glasgow

431   *Empire Snow* 6,327 gt, 420 ft (oa),
407 ft × 55 ft. Engines: T3cyl.
Launched: 16.12.1940.
Completed: 2.1941.
1946: *Cairnavon* (Cairns, Noble & Co. Ltd.).
1961: *Vergolivada* (Cia. Nav. Sirikari, Panama
(Lebanese flag)).
19.9.1966: Rope round propeller, stranded
Doganarslan Bank, north Dardanelles
(voyage: Novorossisk/Persian Gulf – cement).
Jettison of cargo commenced, but stopped by the
Authorities due to build-up of a reef of artificial rocks
alongside.
29.9.1966: Remaining cargo transhipped,
and: 1.10.1966: Refloated, proceeded Piraeus.
11.1968: Arrived Shanghai for breaking up.

432   *Empire Zephyr* 6,327 gt. Details as Yard No.
431.
Launched: 2.3.1941.
Completed: 4.1941.
1946: *Valewood* (Kelston SS Co. Ltd. (J. I. Jacobs &
Co. Ltd.)).
1949: *Ampleforth* (Ampleforth SS Co. Ltd. (C. Cravos
& Co., Cardiff)).
12.8.1959: Arrived Port Glasgow for breaking up.

433   *Empire Glen* 6,327 gt. Details as Yard No. 431.
Launched: 24.5.1941.
Completed: 7.1941.
1945: *Aylesbury* (Alexander Shipping Co. (Capper,
Alexander & Co.)).
1948: *West Wales* (Gibbs & Co., Cardiff).
1961: *Persian Xerxes* (Iranian Lloyd Co. Ltd., Iran).
9.1964: Scrapped Hendrik Ido Ambacht.

434   *Empire Mallory* 6,327 gt. Details as Yard No.
431.
Launched: 9.7.1941.
Completed: 8.1941.

1946: *Ampleforth* (C. Cravos & Co., Cardiff).
23.1.1947: Dragged anchor, ashore off Tel Aviv
(voyage: Cardiff/Haifa/Alexandria – general).
3.3.1947: Refloated, and: 10.3.1947: Arrived
Alexandria. Constructive total loss. Sold; towed to
Genoa, then:
6.11.1947: Arrived Palermo, in tow. Repaired.
1948: *Bangor Bay* (Irish Bay Lines Ltd. (H. P.
Lenaghan & Sons Ltd., Belfast)).
1954: *Jag Shanti* (Great Eastern Shipping Co. Ltd.,
Bombay).
9.9.1961: Arrived Bombay for breaking up.

Note: The above four ships were of Connell design. They
had counter sterns.

435   *Empire Rennie* 6,626 gt, 444.7 ft (oa),
415.6 ft × 55 ft. Engines: Oil.
Launched: 7.10.1941.
Completed: 12.1941.
1942: *Frans Hals* (Government of the Netherlands).
1946: *Alchiba* (NV Van Nievelt, Goudriaan & Co.'s
Stoomvaart Mij., Rotterdam).
1956: *Rheinfels* (Hansa, Damp-Ges., Bremen).
1968: *Peramataris* (Peramataris Shipping Co. Ltd.,
Cyprus).
6.6.1975: Afire in engine room east of Malta,
36.45N 16.25E. Abandoned, but reboarded.
12.6.1975: Arrived Augusta, Sicily; laid up.
11.7.1976: Arrived Piraeus; laid up.
2.1979: Scrapped Piraeus.

436   (Launched as) *Empire Roamer* 7,030 gt. 'B'-type.
446 ft (oa), 431 ft × 56 ft. Engines: T3cyl.
Launched: 5.1.1942.
Completed: 3.1942 as *Narwik* for Government of
Poland.
1951: (Polskie Linie, Poland).
1967: (Polska Zegluga Morska, Poland).
7.3.1972: Arrived Bilbao for breaking up.

The highlight in the life of the *Narwik* was on 10 October 1942. That day the Orient SN Co.'s *Orcades*, 23,456 gt, built in 1937, was on the return leg of a troop voyage from the United Kingdom to Durban. After a call at Capetown, where she had embarked over 1,000 passengers in a miscellany of troops, seamen, civilian sick, wounded and other distressed subjects, she was 280 miles northwest of Capetown when two torpedoes fired from *U.172* struck her. She was down by the head and unmanageable, though on an even keel, but when a third hit was made, all passengers and most of the crew were sent off in boats; the position was 31.51S 14.40E.

At 12.30 pm a ship was sighted but was signalled to keep away and was lost to sight in a rainstorm. Just after 2 pm the *Orcades*, with holds flooding, was again hit and all 55 remaining crew took to the boats before the liner turned on her starboard side and sank.

Later, in darkness, the ship that had been faintly sighted now literally came in the picture. This was the *Narwik*, with a Polish crew and 10,000 tons of iron ore and which, without lights, had come across the fleet of lifeboats from the *Orcades*, one of which lighted a flare. Then alongside the *Narwik* they came, boat after boat, the survivors climbing the scrambling nets in the dimness of the night until eventually all had been taken on board. The *Narwik*, with her 1,000-plus extra passengers, then moved on at ten knots, taking two days to reach Capetown, on the second day being accompanied by two destroyers. It later transpired that the *Narwik* had seen the *Orcades* before the squall and presumed that she had foundered.

In 1942–1943 the submarine *U.172* torpedoed and sank twenty-six Allied ships. Her end came on 12 December 1943 when the escort carrier U.S.S. *Bogue*, with convoy GUS 23 (Gibraltar–USA) came upon her refuelling from *U.219* in the Central Atlantic. The supply submarine escaped, but *U.172* was sunk by aircraft and American destroyers.

437 *Empire Bowman* 7,030 gt. Details as Yard No. 436.
Launched: 4.4.1942.
Completed: 5.1942.
30.3.1943: Sunk by submarine (*U.404*) torpedo, 47.26N 15.53W whilst in convoy SL 126 (voyage: West Africa/United Kingdom – ore).

At the end of March 1943, convoy SL 126, comprising thirty-seven ships and six escorts homeward bound from Freetown, was spotted by the enemy some 700 miles SSW of Ushant. Five U-boats were deployed to the area and *U.404* made contact on the 28th and was joined next day by *U.662*.
In the late evening of the 29th, *U.404* began the torpedo attack, hitting the Royal Mail Line's *Nagara*, a twin screw refrigerated ship, 8,790 gt, packed with Argentine meat in her forty-one insulated chambers. She began to sink and was abandoned, the crew later being taken aboard an escort. Low in the water and listing, a tow was begun, but she sank seven days later.
The attack continued when some two hours later *U.662* fired a torpedo spread and three more ships were hit. The British standard 'Ocean'-type ship *Ocean Viceroy* was struck but did not sink, but the *Empire Whale* and *Umaria* both received mortal hits. The *Empire Whale* of 1919 was a purchase from the United States and *Umaria* a British India SN Company cargo ship launched by Barclay, Curle in October 1941.
In the early hours of the 30th the *U.404* again struck. Her target was the *Empire Bowman*. The six hours of U-boat action caused the loss of four ships totalling 29,000 tons, plus one badly damaged.

438 *Empire Mordred* 7,030 gt. Details as Yard No. 436.
Launched: 15.6.1942.
Completed: 8.1942.
7.2.1943: Damaged by mine 35.58N 05.59W, off Tangier. Broke in two; bow sank, stern part remained afloat. Tug despatched but stern section sank before tug's arrival.

439 *Empire Geraint* 7,030 gt. Details as Yard No. 436.
Launched: 1.9.1942.
Completed: 12.1942.
6.3.1945: Damaged by submarine (*U.775*) torpedo off Milford Haven (voyage: New York/Liverpool). Towed in, beached. Broke across deck.
30.4.1945: Refloated, towed to Newport, Mon., repaired.
1946: *Millais* (Lamport & Holt Line Ltd.).
1952: *Oregon Star* (Blue Star Line Ltd.).
1954: *Captayannis* (Iris Shipping & Trading Corp., Panama (Syros Shipping Co. Ltd., London)).
28.2.1962: Aground off Goeree Lightvessel, Dutch coast, 51.40N 3.25E. Refloated, towed to Rotterdam (voyage: Vassiliko Bay/Rotterdam – ore). Repairs uneconomic: sold and: 4.1962: Scrapped Hendrik Ido Ambacht.

440 *Empire Carpenter* 7,030 gt. Details as Yard No. 436.
Launched: 21.11.1942.
Completed: 1.1943.
1944: *Dickson* (U.S.S.R.).
1946: *Empire Carpenter* (M.O.W.T.).
1947: *Petfrano* (Petrinovic & Co. Ltd., London).
1955: *Amipa* (Cia. di Nav. Amipa S.A., Panama).
1958: *Apex* (Cia. Mar. Apex S.A., Panama).
1968: Renamed *Afros*.
1971: (Campos Shipping Co., Cyprus).
3.1971: Scrapped Shanghai.

441 *Empire Celia* 7,030 gt. Details as Yard No. 436.
Launched: 7.2.1943.
Completed: 4.1943.
1948: *Putney Hill* (Counties Ship Management Co. Ltd.).
1949: *Forest Hill* (London & Overseas Freighters Ltd.).
1950: Renamed *London Statesman*.
1951: *Morella* (Eastern & Panama Transport Corp., Panama).
1952: *Jednosc* (Polish Ocean Lines).
29.4.1963: Arrived Hong Kong for breaking up.

443 *Empire Symbol* 7,030 gt. Details as Yard No. 436.
Launched: 30.7.1943.

Completed: 10.1943.
1943: *Professeur Emile Lagarde* (Government of
France).
1957: *North Baroness* (Cia. Nav. Primula S.A. (A. G.
Pappadakis, Greece)).

1959: *Anadolu* (Faik Zeren, Turkey).
7.1967: Scrapped Istanbul.

The Connell family controlled the Scotstoun yard for over one hundred years, from 1861 until 1968. Yard No. 1, delivered in 1861, was the small steamer *Palermo* of 289 gross tons, and in the next years came the sailerman *City of Paris*, of almost 1,000 tons. In the following decade more than eighty vessels were constructed, some 25 per cent of them being sailing vessels. In fact, the yard's last sailing ships, *Dunhope, Forth* and *Mersey*, (Yard Nos. 211–213) were constructed in 1894.

Twenty years on, to the outbreak of World War I, the yard list reached to No. 360 and during that conflict four 'standard' ships were built for the Shipping Controller, seven sloops for the Admiralty and seventeen vessels for private account.

The recession of the 1920s caused a slight slump in output, although in that time another thirty vessels were built. But in 1930, following the construction of the 5,943 gt *Benlawers* (Yard No. 420) for the Ben Line, shipbuilding ceased for some eight years, resuming only in 1938 with the completion of the 4,648-ton sisterships *Mountpark* and *Wellpark* for J. & J. Denholm Ltd.

Charles Connell & Co. Ltd., with a yard of four berths and a building capability for ships to 570 feet, averaged an output of four vessels each year during World War II. The first four ships were to a Connell design and these were given counter sterns. There were a number of 'B'-type tramp ships constructed and a standard fast cargo liner, *Empire Wilson*, in 1944.

Private building under licence, and up to 1946, included eight ships for James Nourse Ltd., three for Ben Line, one for T. & J. Harrison and two for the Denholm Line. One other Government order for a Transport Ferry (LST 3), although launched as No. *3032* on 27 April 1945, was eventually completed at Rio de Janeiro in October 1950 as *Rio Mondego* for the River Plate to Trinidad service of E. G. Fontes & Cia., Rio de Janeiro.

In 1968, effective from 7 February, the Upper Clyde Shipbuilders Ltd. consortium came into being, of which Connell's yard was included in the Scotstoun Division. But in June 1971 Upper Clyde Shipbuilders went into liquidation and in the following year the Scotstoun yard of Connell, Stephen's old Linthouse Yard and the former Govan Yard were fused to become Govan Shipbuilders Ltd.

The last vessel built under the Connell name was Yard No. 512, the motorship *Benstac*, 12,011 gt, for the Ben Line Ltd., launched on 20 November 1967 and delivered in January 1968. In all, twenty-nine Ben Line ships were built under the Connell name.

MERCHANT SHIPS BUILT UNDER PRIVATE CONTRACT OR LICENCE

427   *Indus* 5,187 gt, 431.8 ft (oa), 415.6 ft × 55.2 ft.
Engines: Oil.
Launched: 28.11.1939.
Completed: 2.1940 for J. Nourse Ltd.
20.7.1942: Sunk by German raider *Thor*, south-east of Mauritius, 26.44S 82.50E (voyage: Colombo/Fremantle).

The raider *Thor* (German ship No. 10; Raider E under British designation) was a conversion of the *Santa Cruz*, a refrigerated fruit ship built for Oldenburg-Portugiesische Damp. Rhederei in 1938 at the Deutsche Werft yard, Hamburg, who also made the conversion. She left Kiel on 6 June 1940 on her first cruise to the South and Central Atlantic areas, and by the time she had returned to Hamburg on 30 April 1941, had sunk twelve ships. On her second cruise, leaving Kiel on 30 November 1941, she sank ten ships in the ensuing nine months.

The career of the *Thor* ended at Yokohama on 30 November 1942, when her supply tanker *Uckermark* blew up. The *Thor* caught fire and was completely burnt out.

428   *Sutlej* 5,187 gt. Details as Yard No. 427.
Launched: 8.2.1940.
Completed: 3.1940 for J. Nourse Ltd.
26.2.1944: Sunk by Japanese submarine (*I. 37*)

torpedo in Indian Ocean, 08.00S 70.00E
(voyage: Aden/Fremantle).

429 *Benalbanach* 7,153 gt, 436 ft (oa), 421 ft × 57 ft.
Engines: Quad. expansion.
Launched: 20.6.1940.
Completed: 10.1940 for Ben Line Steamers Ltd.
1941: Taken over by M.O.W.T. as a training ship
for Dock Operating Groups, Royal Engineers. Later
reverted to commercial status, and:
7.1.1943: Sunk by aerial torpedo 150 miles from
Algiers, 37.07N 04.38E (voyage: Clyde/Bona –
troops and supplies).

430 *Trader* 6,087 gt, 435 ft (oa), 421 ft × 55 ft.
Engines: T3cyl.
Launched: 18.10.1940.
Completed: 12.1940 for T. & J. Harrison.
1961: *Pempto* – renamed for delivery voyage to
shipbreakers (Margalante Cia. Nav. S.A., Panama
(Mavroleon Bros. Ltd.)).
20.9.1961: Arrived Hong Kong for breaking up.

442 *Hughli* 6,589 gt. Details as Yard No. 427.
Launched: 18.5.1943.
Completed: 7.1943 for J. Nourse Ltd.
1960: *Nancy Dee* (Red Anchor Line Ltd. (C. Moller,
Hong Kong)).
8.4.1971: Arrived Kaohsiung for breaking up.

444 *Benlawers* 7,804 gt, 475 ft (oa), 458 ft × 60 ft.
Engines: 2 steam turbines.
Launched: 27.3.1944.
Completed: 6.1944 for Ben Line Steamers Ltd.
20.2.1968: Arrived Kaohsiung for breaking up.

445 *Megna* 6,595 gt. Details as Yard No. 427.
Launched: 29.12.1943.
Completed: 3.1944 for J. Nourse Ltd.
1959: *Enrico M* (E. Mazzarella, Italy).
1964: *Orsa* (F. Grimaldi, Italy).
7.1969: Scrapped Genoa.

447 *Benvorlich* 9,767 gt, 497.4 ft (oa),
475.7 ft × 64.3 ft. Engines: 2 steam turbines.
'Standard Fast' type.
Launched: 23.10.1945.
Completed: 3.1946 for Ben Line Steamers Ltd.
1970: *Kavo Akritas* (Mardestino Cia. Nav. S.A.,
Greece).
27.9.1973: Arrived Shanghai for breaking up.

448 *Tapti* 6,618 gt. Details as Yard No. 427.
Launched: 8.6.1945.
Completed: 10.1945 for J. Nourse Ltd.
17.1.1951: Ashore on Soy Rocks, Eilean Soa, Coll
Island, Hebrides, 56.34N 6.37W
(voyage: Irwell/Tyne – ballast).
Flooded and abandoned.

22.1.1951: Slipped off rocks and sank in deep water.
Total loss.

449 *Kallada* 6,607 gt. Details as Yard No. 427.
Launched: 8.1.1946.
Completed: 3.1946 for J. Nourse Ltd.
1964: *Merryn Elizabeth* (Red Anchor Line Ltd. (C.
Moller, Hong Kong)).
18.4.1972: Arrived Hong Kong for breaking up.

450 *Mountpark* 6,722 gt, 431.8 ft (oa),
415.8 ft × 55.2 ft. Engines: T3cyl.
Launched: 3.1946.
Completed: 7.1946 for Denholm Line Steamers Ltd.
(J. & J. Denholm Ltd.).
1959: *Korcula* (Atlanska Plovidba (Government of
Yugoslavia)).
1966: *Grifone* (Palomba & Salvatori, Italy).
12.12.1967: Rudder and engine damage in heavy
weather, drifted aground on islet of Mavro, ten miles
east of Naxos Island, Greece, 36.00N 26.23E.
Abandoned, and:
15.12.1967: Sank.

451 *Wellpark* 6,722 gt. Details as Yard No. 450.
Launched: 5.1946.
Completed: 9.1946 for Denholm Line Steamers Ltd.
(J. & J. Denholm Ltd.).
1958: *Inver* (Shamrock Shipping Co. Ltd., Larne).
1962: *Dogan* (N. Dogan ve Ortaklari Kom. Sirketi,
Turkey).
4.1980: Scrapped Aliaga, Turkey.

452 *Marjata* 6,656 gt. Details as Yard No. 427.
Launched: 27.8.1946.
Completed: 10.1946 for J. Nourse Ltd.
1963: *Denny Rose* (Red Anchor Line Ltd. (C. Moller,
Hong Kong)).
31.8.1967: Sailed from Cebu, Philippines, for Chiba,
Japan, with iron ore.
13.9.1967: Last reported in position 25.15N 134.23E.
No further trace: presume foundered.

453 *Mutlah* 6,652 gt. Details as Yard No. 427.
Launched: 8.11.1946.
Completed: 1.1947 for J. Nourse Ltd.
1963: *Delwind* (Zephyr SS Co. (Deh Ling Wu, Hong
Kong)).
19.3.1965: Aground on Bombay Reef, 380 miles
south of Hong Kong, 16.30N 112.36E. Abandoned;
looted by pirates.
7.4.1965: Refloated by salvage tug, but unable to
control vessel in swell: grounded again. Salvage
attempts abandoned: constructive total loss. Wreck
offered for sale and reported later broken up
(voyage: Hong Kong/Thailand – ballast).

James Nourse, a ship's master at 23 years of age, gained much experience in command of sailing ships in the late 1850s, and kept his first ship, the iron barque *Adamant* until 1872, when she was sold to the Shaw, Savill & Albion Company. By then he had begun his company with orders for five iron sailing ships from T. R. Oswald, Sunderland. In fact two were built there and three at Woolston, Southampton, where Oswald had moved his business. These ships enabled Nourse to compete with Sandbach Tinne & Company, then already established in the coolie trade between India and the West Indies sugar plantations. The ships built were given Indian and Irish river names; those purchased retained their old names. Over thirty sailing ships were owned by him, twenty came from the Connell yard.

In 1894 the first steamship was acquired and the sailing ship fleet gradually declined. A private company was effective from 1903, a regular trade then existing from Calcutta and Rangoon to the West Indies and Cuba via the Cape of Good Hope. The ships were specially built for the tropics and in 1917 the company, with its eastern connections, was acquired by the Peninsular & Oriental SN Company Ltd, and slotted in with P & O/British India SN Company services. By 1926 seven steamers of 4,500/5,500 gt were owned; in 1939 there were six: *Saugur* (1928), *Jumna* (1929), *Ganges* (1930), *Jhelum* (1936), *Johilla* (1937) and *Bhima* (1939). Only *Johilla* survived the war.

Of the eight ships launched for J. Nourse from the Connell yard between November 1939 and November 1946 two, *Indus* and *Sutlej* were lost during the war.

Built by William Denny & Bros. Ltd., Leven Shipyard, Dumbarton

1356   (Laid down as) *Clan Buchanan* 9,909 gt, 487 ft (oa), 457 ft × 63 ft. Engines: T3cyl and LP turbines. Twin screw.
Launched: 26.5.1941.
Taken over by Admiralty for proposed conversion to an armed boarding vessel; allocated name *Empire Might*.
Then proposed to be an auxiliary seaplane carrier but eventually completed as an aircraft transport to ferry boxed or unboxed replacement planes to operational squadrons.
11.1941: Completed as *Engadine*.
5.1946: *Clan Buchanan* (Clan Line Steamers Ltd.).
14.11.1962: Arrived Cartagena for breaking up.

1358   *Empire Cameron* 7,015 gt. 'Y'-type: 448 ft (oa), 432 ft × 56 ft. Engines: T3cyl.
Launched: 19.11.1941.
Completed: 12.1941.

1946: *St Margaret* (Shakespear Shipping Co. Ltd. (South American Saint Line Ltd., Cardiff)).
1960: *Agna* (Agna Cia. Nav. S.A. Panama (Tharros Shipping Co. Ltd., London)).
16.7.1963: Arrived Yawata, Japan, for breaking up.

1367   *Empire Guinevere* 7,085 gt. 'Y3'-type. Details as Yard No. 1358.
Launched: 14.5.1942.
Completed: 6.1942.
1947: *Grelrosa* (Cardigan Shipping Co. Ltd. (W. T. Gould & Co. Ltd. Cardiff)).
1960: *Shun Tai* (Kam Kee Navigation Co. Ltd. (Jebshun & Co. Ltd., Hong Kong)).
1968: (Chan Moo Chu (Somali flag) (Jebshun Shipping Co. Ltd., Hong Kong)).
11.3.1969: In collision with *World Carrier* (1936, 6658 gt) approximately three miles south of Singapore; sank 1.12N 103.51E
(voyage: Canton/Colombo – rice).

The Denny story started in 1814 when Archibald M'Lauchlan and his yard manager William Denny began work at a small site on the River Leven, at Dumbarton, in the construction of a 68-ft-long paddle steamer, *Trusty*, acquired in 1815 by the Clyde Shipping Company, which was quickly followed with another paddle steamer, *Margery*, 63 ft in length and named after M'Lauchlan's daughter. After a few months of work on the Clyde, the *Margery* was acquired for work on the River Thames and was put on the Long Ferry, running between Wapping Old Stairs near London

Docks and Milton, near Gravesend, augmenting the *Richmond*, which was running the London–Richmond ferry service and was the first steamship on the Thames.

After four years, Denny took over the yard on his own account and William Denny & Son turned out small ships from building sites on both banks of the River Leven until 1833. Some of these small sites on the eastern bank of the river were later joined to become the Leven Yard.

In succession to him, Denny's three sons William, Alexander and Peter began a partnership in Glasgow as marine architects, but returned to shipbuilding in 1844 and in the primitive condition of a silting river and without gas, tap water and drainage, launched Yard No. 1, a 150 ft-long excursion steamer *Loch Lomond* at Dumbarton in 1845 for work on the Clyde.

The title of William Denny & Brothers lasted until 1918 when the firm became a limited company. The quality of their early buildings is, perhaps, exemplified by Yard No. 6, the paddle steamer *Premier*, which was completed in 1846 for Clyde River work. After moving to a Weymouth owner in 1852 she was purchased by Captain Joseph Cosens, also of Weymouth, in 1872. Later, she came under Cosens & Company, was lengthened to 133 ft in 1878 and re-engined. She worked as an excursion steamer until 1937 and an age of 91 years.

One of the best known clipper ships, the *Cutty Sark*, was linked with the Denny yard. Although laid down by Scott & Linton at the Woodyard, Dumbarton, the partners went bankrupt and the China-tea clipper, launched on 22 November 1869 was moved to Denny's yard for completion for John Willis & Son, London, although some final work was done in early 1870 when she was loading on the Thames. In December 1954 the *Cutty Sark* was placed in a drydock at Greenwich for permanent preservation.

In 1890 the Union Steamship Co.'s *Scot* was built for the Southampton–Cape Town service and quickly lowered the passage time. In 1901 the Clyde steamer *King Edward* was completed as the first turbine passenger steamer in the world. Thirty years later Denny Brothers delivered the *Lochfyne*, the first diesel-electric-propulsion ship in home waters.

Over the years many cross-Channel and Irish Sea ferries have come from the Denny yard. In particular many were built for the London & South Western Railway which, with the London, Brighton & South Coast and South Eastern & Chatham companies, became the Southern Railway in 1923. Indeed, many of these ships became very well-known; the *Canterbury* of 1901, the turbine-driven *Riviera* and *Engadine* of 1911, *Biarritz*, and the later *Canterbury*, built specially for the London/Dover-Calais/Paris 'Golden Arrow' service in 1929. From Southampton the ferries sailed to the Channel Islands, to Havre and to St. Malo. The Channel Islands were served by the three 'Isle'-class of 1929–1932 of which the *Isle of Sark* was built with a Maierform bow and in 1934 was fitted with the first Denny–Brown fin stabilisers. For many years the *St. Briac* and *Dinard* served on the St. Malo service and in 1947 the *Falaise* was also built for the St. Malo run. The *Normannia*, for the Havre service, came in 1952.

The Denny yard built a number of merchant ships during the 1939–1945 war and Government orders included two 'Empire' tramp ships, two hulls completed as MAC ships and a hull completed as an aircraft transport.

There was also a large warship-building programme which included ten destroyers, sloops, some minesweepers and experimental craft. When war ended the yard had nine berths, with a building capacity to 540 ft.

In 1962, in order to keep their work force employed, the Denny yard laid down a 15,000 tdw motor ship for their own account. However, in July 1963 it was announced that the company was to go into voluntary liquidation and the yard closed down. At the end of the year their own-account hull, Yard No. 1504, was purchased by J. A. Billmeir & Co. Ltd., on behalf of Duff, Herbert & Mitchell Ltd. Launching of the hull took place on 27 February 1964 and, as the *Melbrook*, was towed to Linthouse for completion by Alex. Stephen & Sons Ltd. She was delivered in the August.

Yard No. 1503, the *City of Gloucester* (4,961 gt), for Ellerman & Bucknall SS Co. Ltd., was the last ship to be completed by Denny, in March 1963.

The *Empire Guinevere* of the 'Y3'-type, as *Grelrosa*, in the English Channel. (Wm. Denny & Bros. Ltd., Yard No. 1367.)
Skyfotos

MERCHANT SHIPS BUILT UNDER PRIVATE CONTRACT OR LICENCE

1344   *Invicta* 4,178 gt, 347.5 ft (oa), 336.5 ft × 50 ft.
Engines: 4 steam turbines. Twin screws.
Launched: 14.12.1939.
Completed: 7.1940 for Southern Railway
Company.
1941: Requisitioned by Admiralty; converted to an
Assault Landing Ship, to carry six LCA's.
1945: (M.O.W.T.).
1946: (Southern Railway Company). Placed on
Dover/Calais 'Golden Arrow' service to Paris.
1948: (British Transport Commission).
22.9.1972: Arrived Nieuw Lekkerland, Holland, in
tow of tug *Michel Petersen* for breaking up, but resold,
and: 1.1973: Scrapped Bruge, Belgium.

1347   *Ardenvohr* 5,025 gt, 428.8 ft (oa),
414.8 ft × 56 ft. Engines: Oil.
Launched: 23.7.1940.
Completed: 10.1940 for Australind Steam Shipping
Co. Ltd. (Trinder, Anderson & Co. Ltd., London).
10.6.1942: Sunk by submarine (*U.68*) torpedo in
Caribbean, 12.45N 80.20W.

1348   *Kalewa* 4,389 gt, 421 ft (oa),
409.2 ft × 55.2 ft. Engines: T3cyl.
Launched: 2.2.1940.
Completed: 4.1940 for British & Burmese SN Co.
Ltd. (P. Henderson & Co. Ltd.).
1.8.1942: In collision with *Boringia* (1930, 5,821 gt)
300 miles off Cape Town. Sank in position
30.16S 13.38E (voyage: Glasgow/Table Bay/Port
Sudan/Aden).

1351   *Saturn* 400 gt, 223.8 ft (oa), 200 ft × 38 ft.
Engines: T3cyl. A stern-wheel passenger and cargo
river steamer.
Launched: 4.1941.
Completed: 5.1941 for India General Navigation &
Railway Co. Ltd., Calcutta.

1357   *Kanbe* 6,057 gt. Details as Yard No. 1348.
Launched: 11.8.1941.
Completed: 11.1941 for British & Burmese SN Co.
Ltd. (P. Henderson & Co. Ltd.).
Reported missing after 8 May 1943.
Probably sunk by torpedo from submarine (*U.123*)
off the coast of Liberia.

1368   *Pegu* 7,838 gt, 461 ft (oa), 446.4 ft × 61 ft.
Engines: 3 steam turbines.
Launched: 11.12.1942.
Completed: 6.1943 for British & Burmese SN
Co. Ltd. (P. Henderson & Co. Ltd.).
1950: *Benattow* (Ben Line Steamers Ltd.).
1963: *Newhill* (Trafalgar SS Co. Ltd. (Tsavliris
(Shipping) Ltd., London)).
16.3.1964: Aground at entrance to Santiago, Cuba
(voyage: St. Johns/Santiago – fertiliser).
23.3.1964: Refloated with severe bottom damage;
entered port. Constructive total loss. Sold.
19.6.1964: Towed Syra, Cuba. Repaired.
11.11.1967: Arrived Castellon for breaking up.

1371   *Australind* 7,214 gt. Details as Yard No. 1347.
Launched: 20.7.1944.
Completed: 9.1944 for Australind Steam Shipping
Co. Ltd. (Trinder, Anderson & Co. Ltd.).

1959: *Portalon* (Argus SS Co. Inc., Liberia (A. Zubizarrela, Spain)).
1959: (Argus SS Co. Inc. (E. de Aznar, Spain)).
13.3.1972: Arrived Santander for breaking up.

1377 *Cuillin* 24 gt, 44 ft × 17.5 ft. Engines: Oil. Motor car ferry.
Launched: 3.7.1942.
Completed: 7.1942 for London, Midland & Scottish Railway Company. For service on Isle of Skye/mainland service.

1388 *City of Lucknow* 9,961 gt, 497.3 ft (oa), 465 ft × 64 ft. Engines: 3 steam turbines. 'Standard Fast' type.
Launched: 21.11.1945.
Completed: 5.1946 for Ellerman's Hall Line Ltd.
1963: *Lisboa* (Alexandria Navigation Corp. Ltd., Panama (W. H. Eddie Hsu, Formosa)).
1969: (Outerocean Navigation Corp. Ltd., Formosa).
3.1971: Scrapped Kaohsiung.

1390 *Bhopal* 450 gt, 200 ft × 60 ft. Engines: T3cyl. A paddle steamer.
Completed: 1945 for India General Navigation & Railway Company, Calcutta.

1391 *Vigore* 450 gt. Details as Yard No. 1390.
Completed: 1945 for Rivers Steam Navigation Company, Chittagong.

1392 *Indore* 450 gt. Details as Yard No. 1390.
Completed: 1945 for Rivers Steam Navigation Company, Chittagong.

1393 *Mysore* 450 gt. Details as Yard No. 1390.
Completed: 1945 for Rivers Steam Navigation Company, Chittagong.

1394 *Ashburton* 5,032 gt, 430.2 ft (oa), 416.4 ft × 56 ft. Engines: Oil

Launched: 1945.
Completed: 9.1946 for Australind Steam Shipping Co. Ltd., (Trinder, Anderson & Co. Ltd., London).
1962: *Pacific Breeze* (South Breeze Navigation Co. Ltd. (J. Manners & Co. Ltd., Hong Kong)).
1965: *San Roberto* (San Fernando SS Co. S.A., Panama (J. Manners & Co. Ltd., Hong Kong)).
8.1.1967: In collision with *Emilia Rosello* (1965, 17,374 gt) off southern Japan, 33.25N 136.40E. Disabled with engine damage; partly flooded; drifted.
13.1.1967: Arrived Tokyo, in tow. Repairs uneconomic; sold and:
4.4.1967: Arrived Muroran, Japan, in tow, for breaking up.

1399 *Princess Victoria* 2,694 gt, 322.8 ft (oa), 309.8 ft × 48 ft. Engines: Oil. Twin screws.
Launched: 27.8.1946.
Completed: 3.1947 for London, Midland & Scottish Railway Company.
1948: (British Transport Commission).
31.1.1953: During a voyage from Stranraer to Larne with passengers, stormy seas were experienced; heavy following waves burst over the stern, flooded the aft car deck and the ship listed badly, rolled over and capsized five miles northeast of Mew Island Lighthouse, near Belfast Lough, N. Ireland.

1400 *Falaise* 3,710 gt, 314 ft (oa), 299.8. ft × 48.1 ft. Engines: 4 steam turbines. Twin screws.
Launched: 25.10.1946.
Completed: 1947 for Southern Railway Company for Southampton/St. Malo service.
1948: (British Transport Commission).
1964: Converted to a stern-loading car ferry at Palmers Hebburn yard for the Newhaven/Dieppe service.
31.12.1974: Arrived Bilbao in tow of tug *Fairplay XII* for breaking up.

The *Empire Drum* at New York, 20 April 1942. She was lost four days later. (Wm. Doxford & Sons Ltd., Yard No. 684.)
U.S.C.G.

Built by William Doxford & Sons Ltd., Pallion, Sunderland

With the exception of the first three buildings listed below, which were equipped with triple expansion engines, all vessels built were motorships.

679   *Empire Selwyn* 7,167 gt, 442.9 ft (oa), 428.8 ft × 56.5 ft.
Launched: 27.8.1941.
Completed: 10.1941.
1942: *Belgian Soldier* (Government of Belgium).
7.8.1942: Sunk by submarine (*U.552*) torpedo southeast of Newfoundland, 45.52N 47.13W whilst in convoy ON 115.

681   *Empire Cowper* 7,161 gt. Details as Yard No. 679.
Launched: 23.9.1941.
Completed: 12.1941.
11.4.1942: Bombed by JU 88 aircraft and sank in Barents Sea, 71.01N 36.00E whilst in convoy QP 10 (Murmansk/Iceland).

682   *Empire Dryden* 7,164 gt. Details as Yard No. 679.
Launched: 22.10.1941.
Completed: 2.1942.
20.4.1942: Sunk by submarine (*U.572*) torpedo, north of Bahamas, 34.21N 69.00W.

669   *Empire Mist* 7,241 gt, 442.9 ft (oa), 427 ft × 56.5 ft.
Launched: 29.10.1940.
Completed: 3.1941.
1945: *King David* (King Line Ltd.).
1963: *Hong Kong Venture* (Wallem & Co. Ltd. (T. Y. Chao) Hong Kong).
1966: (Unity Carriers Inc., Liberia (Wah Kwong & Co. Ltd., Hong Kong)).
19.4.1969: Arrived Hong Kong for breaking up.

670   *Empire Dawn* 7,241 gt. Details as Yard No. 669.
Launched: 14.12.1940.
Completed: 4.1941.
11.9.1942: Sunk by German raider *Michel* (Ship No. 28) south-west of Cape Town, approx. 34S 02.00E (voyage: Durban/Trinidad).

671   *Empire Spray* 7,308 gt, 443 ft (oa), 429 ft × 56.5 ft.
Launched: 11.2.1941.
Completed: 5.1941.
1943: *Gerard Dou* (Government of the Netherlands).
1947: *Marken* (NV Stoomvaart Maats., Rotterdam).
1955: *Inchmull* (Douglas SS Co. Ltd. (Williamson & Co. Ltd., Hong Kong)).
1966: (Douglas SS Co. Ltd. (Mullion & Co., Hong Kong)).
2.1969: Scrapped Kaohsiung.

673   *Empire Day* 7,242 gt. Details as Yard No. 671.
Launched: 27.3.1941.
Completed: 7.1941.
7.8.1944: Sunk by submarine (*U.198*) torpedo southeast of Zanzibar, 07.06S 42.00E (voyage: Lourenço Marques/Port Said – coal).

676   *Empire Lugard* 7,241 gt. Details as Yard No. 671.
Launched: 28.4.1941.
Completed: 9.1941.
13.9.1942: Sunk by submarine (*U.558*) torpedo north of Trinidad, 12.07N 63.32W while in convoy TAG 5 (voyage: Trinidad/Aruba/Guantanamo).

677   *Empire Raleigh* 7,240 gt. Details as Yard No. 671.
Launched: 12.6.1941.
Completed: 10.1941.
1942: *Vermeer* (Government of the Netherlands).
1946: *Zonnewijk* (NV Stoom. Maats. Wijklijn (Erhardt & Dekkers, Rotterdam)).
1961: *Antonakis* (Cia. Nav. del Egeo, Panama (Lemos & Pateras Ltd.)).
6.12.1961: Aground in fog two miles west of Cape Spartel, near Tangier, 35.43N 5.57W. Broke in two; total loss (voyage: Santiago/Shanghai – sugar).

678   *Empire Grenfell* 7,238 gt. Details as Yard No. 671.
Launched: 30.6.1941.
Completed: 11.1941.
1942: *Kong Sverre* (Government of Norway).
1946: *Martha Kleppe* (A/S P. Kleppe, Norway).
1959: *Reina* (A/S Rona (T. J. Skogland A/S, Norway)).
1960: *Miami* (Cia. Nav. Overseas Transport S.A. (J. W. Elwell & Co., U.S.A.)).
1965: *Impala* (Tenodian Shipping Co., Liberia).
1.5.1968: Arrived Kaohsiung for breaking up.

680   *Empire Latimer* 7,244 gt. Details as Yard No. 671.
Launched: 14.8.1941.
Completed: 12.1941.
1942: *Kronprinsessen* (Government of Norway).
1946: *Polytrader* (E. Rasmussen, Norway).
1962: *Flora M* (Marenviado Cia. Nav. (L. G. Matsas, Greece)).
27.12.1968: Arrived Mihara for breaking up.

683   *Empire Field* 7,244 gt. Details as Yard No. 671.
Launched: 23.9.1941.

The *Lapland*, fitted with heavy-lift derricks. (Caledon Shipbuilding & Engineering Co. Ltd., Yard No. 402.)

National Maritime Museum

The *Empire Lankester* at Cape Town in 1945. (Wm. Gray & Co. Ltd., Yard No. 1161.)

The *Clan Urquhart* in the Clyde, following trials. (Greenock Dockyard Co. Ltd., Yard No. 454.)   *Tom Rayner collection*

Completed: 1.1942.
1942: *Prins Harald* (Government of Norway).
20.11.1942: Sunk by submarine (*U.263*) torpedo 240 miles west of Gibraltar, 35.55N 10.14W (Convoy KRS 3).

684   *Empire Drum* 7,244 gt. Details as Yard No. 671.
Launched: 19.11.1941.
Completed: 3.1942.
24.4.1942: Sunk by submarine (*U.136*) torpedo (approx.) 300 miles south-east of New York, 37.00N 69.15W.

685   *Empire Knight* 7,244 gt. Details as Yard No. 671.
Launched: 15.1.1942.
Completed: 4.1942.
11.2.1944: Ashore in blizzard on Boon Island Ledge, twelve miles from York, Maine, 43.08N 70.24W.
12.2.1944: Abandoned; broke in two: afterpart foundered, and: 15.2.1944: Bow section slipped off reef and sank (voyage: St. John, NB/New York, Norfolk/Bombay and Calcutta).

702   *Empire Cheer* 7,297 gt. Details as Yard No. 671.
Launched: 9.3.1943.
Completed: 7.1943.
1946: *Cornish City* (Reardon Smith Line Ltd.).
8.12.1962: Fire in engine room whilst lying at Aden. Badly damaged (voyage: Baton Rouge/Calcutta). Temporarily repaired, then towed Bombay.
7.3.1963: Arrived Hong Kong in tow of tug *Pacific Star* (1944, 582 gt) for breaking up.

703   *Empire Beauty* 7,297 gt. Details as Yard No. 671.
Launched: 8.4.1943.
Completed: 7.1943.
27.7.1944: Damaged by E-boat torpedo in English Channel, 50.55N 01.02E. Repaired.
1946: *Polycrown* (E. Rasmussen, Norway).
1962: *Ioannis Aspiotis* (Lamda Shipping Enterprises Corp. S.A., Lebanon).
1968: *Laurel* (Laurel Shipping Co., Cyprus).
1.1969: Scrapped Kaohsiung.

708   *Empire City* 7,295 gt. Details as Yard No. 671.
Launched: 15.7.1943.
Completed: 11.1943.
6.8.1944: Sunk by submarine (*U.198*) torpedo in Mozambique Channel, 11.33S 41.25E (voyage: Lourenço Marques/Aden – coal).

Note: Six days later, on 12 August, a Catalina aircraft spotted *U.198* and called up the R.I.N. sloop *Godavari* and the R.N. frigates *Findhorn* and *Parret*, which sank the submarine.

709   *Empire Housman* 7,359 gt, 445 ft (oa), 431 ft × 56.5 ft.
Launched: 31.8.1943.
Completed: 12.1943.

31.12.1943: Damaged by submarine (*U.545*) torpedo 60.30N 24.35W (convoy ON 217) (U.K./North America).
3.1.1944: Again damaged, by submarine (*U.744*) torpedo, south of Iceland, 60.50N 22.07W.
Abandoned: taken in tow, but: 5.1.1944: Sank.

710   *Empire Sceptre* 7,359 gt. Details as Yard No. 709.
Launched: 16.9.1943.
Completed: 1.1944.
1945: *Jacques Bingen* (Government of France).
1954: *Sottern* (Rederi A/B Sigyn (Lundren & Borjesson, Sweden)).
1963: *Red Rose* (Zirda Cia. Nav. S.A. (F. Italo Groce, Italy)).
1967: (Garden City Shipping Co., Panama (F. Italo Groce, Italy)).
16.2.1970: Arrived Spezia for breaking up.

711   *Empire Lord* 7,359 gt. Details as Yard No. 709.
Launched: 11.10.1943.
Completed: 2.1944.
1946: *Aldington Court* (United British SS Co. Ltd. (Haldin & Co. Ltd.)).
1959: *Anacreon* (Cosmar Shipping Corp., Liberia).
1966: *White Daisy* (Garden City Shipping Co. Inc., Panama, (F. Italo Groce, Italy)).
1968: *Robertina* (Cia. Nav. Rivabella S.A., Panama (World Shipping S.A.)).
15.6.1970: Sprung leak off Cape Palmas. Later beached two miles west of Cape Garraway, Liberia. Flooded; abandoned. Constructive total loss (voyage: Takoradi/Leith – bauxite).

712   *Empire General* 7,359 gt. Details as Yard No. 709.
Launched: 11.11.1943.
Completed: 3.1944.
1947: *Hendonhall* (West Hartlepool SN Co. Ltd.).
1958: *Taxiarhis* (Lebanesa Ltda S.A., Panama (L. Nomikos, Greece)).
3.6.1958: On fire in engine room and No. 4 hold whilst at Bahrain. Beached (voyage: London/Persian Gulf.)
8.6.1958: Refloated; later returned to South Shields, in ballast, for repairs.
1971: Renamed *Tony C.*
4.1972: Scrapped Skaramanga, Greece.

713   *Empire Earl* 7,359 gt. Details as Yard No. 709.
Launched: 8.12.1943.
Completed: 5.1944.
1945: *Cressington Court* (United British SS Co. Ltd. (Haldin & Co. Ltd.)).
1958: *East Wales* (Gibbs & Co. Ltd., Newport, Mon.).
1966: *Universal Skipper* (Dalkeith Shipping Co. Ltd. (International SS Co. Ltd., Hong Kong)).
11.1970: Scrapped Whampoa.

722   *Empire Tavoy* 7,381 gt. Details as Yard No. 709.
Launched: 2.10.1944.
Completed: 2.1945.
1946: *Great City* (Leeds Shipping Co. (Reardon Smith Line Ltd.)).
1964: *Shipwind* (Taiship Co. Ltd., Hong Kong).
1968: *Wing Kwong* (Southern Shipping & Enterprises Co. Ltd., Hong Kong).
1970: (Poon Shun Po, Hong Kong (Somali flag)).
15.11.1973: Left Hong Kong for Pasuo, and:
6.1975: Scrapped Shanghai.

723   *Empire Singapore* 7,381 gt. Details as Yard No. 709.
Launched: 15.11.1944.
Completed: 3.1945.
1946: *Fresno City* (Reardon Smith Line Ltd.).
1964: *Sea Captain* (Vergocean SS Co. Ltd. (Vergottis Ltd., London)).
1970: Scrapped Shanghai.

732   *Empire Tilbury* 7,312 gt. Details as Yard No. 671.
Launched: 9.7.1945.

Completed: 12.1945.
1946: *Trevean* (Hain SS Co. Ltd.).
1957: (P & O SN Co. Ltd.).
1957: (Hain SS Co. Ltd.).
1963: *East Lion* (East Asia Navigation Co., Hong Kong).
1964: Renamed *Kawana*.
2.6.1966: Fire in holds while in Chittagong Roads; beached off Norman Point Light. Fire extinguished; broke in two; total loss (voyage: Chinwangtao/Chittagong – coal).

733   *Empire Northfleet* 7,311 gt. Details as Yard No. 671.
Launched: 16.7.1945.
Completed: 1.1946.
1946: *Chulmleigh* (Stephens, Sutton Ltd.).
1961: Renamed *Rugeley*.
1964: *Madura* (Union Fair Shipping Co., Liberia).
28.5.1964: Aground on rocks in typhoon at Hong Kong.
10.7.1964: Refloated, but constructive total loss. Sold, and:
8.1964: Scrapped Hong Kong.

William Doxford began his small shipbuilding yard in 1840 in the upper reaches of the River Wear, his wooden sailing ships soon gaining for him a reputation for design and workmanship. In 1857 Doxford, then joined by his two sons, moved his expanding business down river to a larger site at Pallion and in 1870 an even larger site was acquired there, for by that time wooden hulled ships had evolved to composite wood and iron vessels and then to iron hulls as steamships began to be built.

The Admiralty gave Doxfords an order for three composite gunboats and in the mid-1870s the 'Forester'-class gunboats *Contest, Cygnet* and *Express*, 450 tons displacement and 125 feet long, were built. In 1881 the steel corvette *Magician* was completed and a single-screw torpedo boat *El Rayo* was built for company account. At first she was steam driven by a coal-burning locomotive boiler which gave her twenty-one knots, but was converted to oil fuel. But the British Government showed no interest and she was sold to Venezuelan interests. Sail was gradually yielding to the steam engine and in 1878 steam engine and boiler shops were erected.

A number of torpedo-boat destroyers were built for the Royal Navy in the later years of the century. The 'A'-class turtle-backed ships *Hardy* and *Haughty* in 1896; the three-funnelled *Violet* in 1898 and *Sylvia* in 1899, both 400 tons full load displacement with engines of 6,300 ihp; the 'C'-type, thirty knot, *Lee*, laid down in 1898 for completion in 1901 and the three-funnelled *Success* completed in 1902. Also in the 1890s Wm. Doxford & Sons were designing and building their first turret steamers of which the first hundred standard type ships were built in eleven years. They had a patent Doxford-type turret, either one or two decks, 340 ft length hull, 45½ ft breadth and a deadweight capacity of 4,500 tons. Triple expansion steam engines had twenty-five and twenty-six inch HP cylinders and forty-two inch stroke. Altogether 178 of these ships were constructed totalling over one million gross tons.

In 1901 the Doxford business was converted to a public company; in September of that year the engine works were destroyed by fire but were quickly rebuilt in more modern and larger form and by 1902 the small West yard of 1870 had become a mere part of the then thirty-six acre site. In 1906 twenty-six ships were built and during the Great War the firm was quickly given orders for Government barges, nine 'A'-type and three 'B'-type standard tramps, submersible oil-tanks and in 1916 a group of nine 'M', four 'R', three 'S', two 'V' and two 'W'-class destroyers.

For many years prior to the Great War Doxfords were engaged in research work for production of an efficient oil engine for a motor-driven tramp. A test house was built and in 1909 an experimental ship was constructed. In 1912 there came a single-cylinder unit of 450 hp – the prototype of the Doxford opposed piston airless injection engine. Then a larger experimental shop was erected and there came a four-cylinder 3,000 hp, but rather heavy engine installed in the *Yngaren*, 5,247 gross tons completed by Doxford in March 1921 and followed by a sistership, *Eknaren* in September 1922, both for Rederi Transatlantic A/B, Gothenburg. These were the first Doxford motorships. Later came the much improved type of standard Doxford opposed piston oil engine giving an eleven-knot speed in a motorship of 9,000 tdw and a length of about 420 ft which featured so much in the 1930s.

In that decade Doxfords concentrated on their own standard cargo motorship, fitting their own diesel machinery and, in the development, changed over to all-welded construction of the bed plate and framework. So successful was the design and construction of the ships that the Admiralty permitted Doxfords to continue the type throughout the war, subject to modifications for war time requirements in deck arrangements, derricks and defence ability. Ships earmarked for Arctic convoys had extra ballast tanks fitted. The Pallion yard and its six berths was continuously improved during the war years, sheds, lofts and stores being added. A new canteen was the only building to be bombed. In the five years eighty-one merchant ships were completed of which twenty-six were for Government account and bore an 'Empire' prefix.

In March 1961 Wm. Doxford & Sons Ltd. merged with Sunderland Drydock & Shipbuilding Co. Ltd., the latter company also bringing in Sir James Laing & Sons Ltd., Joseph L. Thompson & Sons Ltd. and T. W. Greenwell & Co. Ltd., who were ship repairers at South Dock, Sunderland, under the title Doxford & Sunderland Shipbuilding & Engineering Co. Ltd., shortened in 1970 to Doxford & Sunderland Ltd., then to Sunderland Shipbuilders in 1973. At the end of 1972 Court Shipbuilders Ltd. was established as the holding company for Appledore Shipbuilders, North East Coast Shiprepairers and Doxford & Sunderland Ltd., but with the collapse of the Court Line Group in 1974 Sunderland Shipbuilders Ltd. was acquired by the Government.

MERCHANT SHIPS BUILT UNDER PRIVATE CONTRACT OR LICENCE

651   *Merchant Prince* 5,229 gt, 443 ft (oa), 427 ft × 56.5 ft. Engines: Oil.
Launched: 16.8.1939.
Completed: 9.1939 for Drake Shipping Co. Ltd. (Lykiardopulo & Co. Ltd., London).
16.3.1943:   Damaged by submarine (*U.77*) torpedo, east of Oran, Algeria, 36.10N 00.30W. Beached.
8.4.1943: Refloated; later docked and repaired.
6.1963: Scrapped Hong Kong.

652   *La Estancia* 5,185 gt, 445 ft (oa), 429.8 ft × 56.5 ft. Engines: Oil.
Launched: 14.9.1939.
Completed: 1.1940 for Buries, Markes Ltd.
20.10.1940: Sunk by submarine (*U.47*) torpedo, 57N 17W, northwest of Ireland (convoy HX 79) (voyage: Mackay/Methil – sugar.).

653   *Beignon* 5,218 gt. Details as Yard No. 651.

Launched: 29.9.1939.
Completed: 11.1939 for Nolisement SS Co. Ltd. (Morel Ltd.).
1.7.1940: Sunk by submarine (*U.30*) torpedo, 47.20N 10.30W., approx. 300 miles SW of Land's End.

654   *Rodsley* 5,000 gt, 439 ft (oa), 423.5 ft × 54 ft. Engines: Oil.
Launched: 12.10.1939.
Completed: 12.1939 for Thomasson Shipping Co. Ltd. (Stephens, Sutton Ltd.).
1952: *Reserv* (A. Johnson, Sweden).
1953: *Sirenes* (A. I. Langfeldt & Co., Norway).
1963: *Marcos G.F.* (J. Livanos & Sons Ltd. (Loutra Maritime Corpn., Greece)).
1965: *Sampaguita* (Benigno Ltda, Manila).
1966: *Philippine Sampaguita* (Laguna Nav. Inc., Manila).
1972: Scrapped Singapore.

655 *La Cordillera* 5,185 gt. Details as Yard No. 652.
Launched: 28.11.1939.
Completed: 3.1940 for Buries, Markes Ltd.
5.11.1942: Sunk by submarine (*U.163*) torpedo
south-east of Barbados, 12.02N 58.04W
(voyage: Suez/New York – ballast).

656 *Catrine* 5,218 gt. Details as Yard No. 651.
Launched: 24.1.1940.
Completed: 5.1940 for Pontypridd SS Co. (Morel
Ltd.).
1956: *Tove* (Transportes Maritimes Atlas (Panama)).
1963: *Tona* (Panamanian Oriental SS Corpn.,
Panama) (World-Wide Shipping Ltd. (Y. K. Pao)
Hong Kong)).
23.8.1966: Engine breakdown in typhoon 300 miles
off Nagasaki (voyage: Moji/Tamano).
27.8.1966: Towed to Moji.
15.9.1966: In tow Moji–Kobe but broke adrift and
went aground near Mihara; refloated; severe bottom
damage.
10.10.1966: Arrived Aioi, laid up.
9.3.1967: Arrived Hirao for breaking up.

657 *Derwenthall* 6,854 gt, 442 ft (oa), 426 ft × 54 ft.
Engines: Oil.
Launched: 9.1.1940.
Completed: 4.1940 for West Hartlepool SN Co. Ltd.
1952: *Kildale* (Rowland & Marwood's SS Co. Ltd.).
1961: *Glaisdale* (Headlam & Sons SS Co. Ltd.).
1968: *Rama Lesmana* (Rama Shipping Co. Ltd.,
Singapore).
2.6.1969: Arrived Hong Kong for breaking up.

658 *Sutherland* 5,170 gt. Details as Yard No. 651.
Launched 26.2.1940.
Completed: 5.1940 for B. J. Sutherland & Co. Ltd.,
Newcastle.
1953: *Grainton* (Chapman & Willan Ltd., Newcastle).
1957: *La Bahia* (Buries, Markes Ltd.).
1961: *San John* (Valerosa Cia. Nav., Panama
(Lebanese flag) (M. J. Lemos & Co. Ltd., London).
4.10.1961: Aground 20 miles (approx.) NW of
Churchill, Hudson Bay 59N 94.34W
(voyage: Tyne/Churchill).
5.10.1961: Refloated, constructive total loss.
Repaired.
1965: *Ledra* (Atlas Shipping & Trading Co. Ltd.,
Cyprus (M. J. Lemos & Co. Ltd.)).
11.11.1967: Aground on Alphee Shoal, Ceylon,
7.25N 81.51E (voyage: Madras/Poland – iron ore).
14.11.1967: Broke in two; constructive total loss.

659 *Putney Hill* 5,215 gt. Details as Yard No. 651.
Launched: 23.4.1940.
Completed: 7.1940 for Putney Hill SS Co. Ltd.,
London.
26.6.1942: Sunk by submarine (*U.203*) torpedo and

gunfire, 24.20N 63.16W., east of Bahamas (voyage:
Haifa/ New York – ballast).

660 *Tower Grange* 5,226 gt. Details as Yard No.
651.
Launched: 22.6.1940.
Completed: 7.1940 for Tower SS Co. Ltd., London.
18.11.1942: Sunk by submarine (*U.154*) torpedo, in
Indian Ocean 06.20N 49.10W (voyage:
Calcutta/U.K. – ore).

661 *Rawnsley* 4,998 gt. Details as Yard No. 654.
Launched: 21.3.1940.
Completed: 7.1940 for Red 'R' Shipping Co. Ltd.
(Stephens, Sutton Ltd.).
8.5.1941: Torpedoed by air attack south of Crete,
34.59N 25.46E.
9.5.1941: Taken in tow for Makryallo Bay, Crete, to
beach, but anchored in Hierapetra Bay due to bad
weather.
12.5.1941: Bombed and set on fire in air attack: Sank
(voyage: Haifa/Suda Bay – military stores).

662 *Atlantic City* 5,133 gt, 432.5 ft (oa),
415 ft × 55 ft. Engines: Oil.
Launched: 4.9.1940.
Completed: 5.1941 for Leeds Shipping Co. Ltd. (Sir
Wm. Reardon Smith & Sons Ltd.).
1962: *Achillet* (Achillet Cia. Nav. S.A. Lebanon)
(Halcoussis & Co., Greece).
17–18.2.1971: Sprang leaks in heavy weather and
25.2.1971: abandoned and awash about 300 miles NW
of Walvis Bay. Foundered off Rocky Point
19.00S 10.19E (voyage: Sfax/Madras – phosphate).

663 *Rookley* 4,998 gt. Details as Yard No. 654.
Launched: 18.5.1940.
Completed: 8.1940 for Thomasson Shipping Co.
Ltd. (Stephens, Sutton Ltd.).
1956: *Despoina* (D. P. Margaronis & Sons, Greece).
1966: *Jumbo* (Cristalinamar S.A. Panama (G. Della
Gatta, Italy)).
1969: Renamed *Ibis II*.
24.6.1971: Arrived Split for breaking up.

664 *Fultala* 5,051 gt. Details as Yard No. 657.
Launched: 6.8.1940.
Completed: 11.1940 for British India SN Co. Ltd.
8.4.1942: Sunk by Japanese submarine (*I.3*) torpedo,
06.52N 76.54E, 250 miles west of Colombo, Ceylon.

665 *Duke of Athens* 5,217 gt. Details as Yard
No. 651.
Launched: 18.7.1940.
Completed: 10.1940 for Trent Maritime Co. Ltd. (S.
Livanos & Co. Ltd., London).
1961: *Breeze* (Atlantic Freighters Ltd., Liberia).
1965: *San John P* (Cia. Nav. Prodromos S.A., Panama
(Liberian flag) (M. J. Lemos & Co. Ltd., London)).

1967: *Theokletos* (Mardinamico Cia. Nav., Panama
(Manlemos Shipping Agencies, Piraeus)).
21.9.1969: Arrived Karachi for breaking up.

666   *Reaveley* 4,998 gt. Details as Yard No. 654.
Launched: 24.8.1940.
Completed: 12.1940 for Stephens, Sutton Ltd.,
Newcastle.
1948: *Grenehurst* (Grenehurst Shipping Co. Ltd.).
1956: *La Barranca* (Buries, Markes Ltd.).
1959: *Westwind* (Eastwind Nav. Co. Ltd. (Deh Ling
Wu, Hong Kong)).
1965: *Universal Mariner* (Dalcape Shipping Co. Ltd.
(International Steamship Co. Ltd., Hong Kong)).
12.1969: Scrapped Whampoa.

667   *Eastern City* 5,185 gt. Details as Yard No. 662.
Launched: 15.10.1940.
Completed: 6.1941 for Leeds Shipping Co. Ltd.
(Sir Wm. Reardon Smith & Sons Ltd.).
1962: *Helmos* (Helmos, Cia. Nav. S.A. Lebanon).
1969: renamed *Nicopaul*. Sold to Taiwan shipbreakers;
resold to Japanese shipbreakers, but 8.4.1970:
delivered to shipbreakers at Whampoa.

668   *Antar* 5,222 gt. Details as Yard No. 651.
Launched: 1.11.1940.
Completed: 2.1941 for New Egypt & Levant
Shipping Co. Ltd. (T. Bowen Rees & Co. Ltd.,
Alexandria).
1948: *Garbeta* (British India SN Co. Ltd.).
4.1963: Scrapped Hong Kong.

672   *Daltonhall* 5,175 gt. Details as Yard No. 651.
Launched: 28.12.1940.
Completed: 6.1941 for West Hartlepool SN Co.
Ltd.
1957: *Altis* (Altis Shipping Co., Liberia, (Tharros
Shipping Co. Ltd., London)).
1965: (Salamis Maritime Co. Ltd., Cyprus (Pegasus
Ocean Services Ltd., London)).
11.5.1967: Arrived Whampoa for breaking up.

674   *Daghestan* 7,248 gt. Details as Yard No. 651.
Launched: 12.3.1941.
Completed: 8.1941 for Hindustan Steam Shipping
Co. Ltd. (Common Bros. Ltd.).
1956: *Annefield* (Asimarfield Shipping Corpn., Liberia
(GEARNAVI SpA, Italy)).
21.2.1969: Arrived Santander for breaking up.

The *Daghestan* was one of the first CAM ships (Catapult
Armed Merchantmen); her equipment was fitted by her
builders and she then proceeded to Glasgow to pick up her
aircraft and carry out launching trials in the Firth of Clyde.
   In 1943 the CAM-ship idea was developed further, the
Daghestan being fitted with a helicopter deck at Baltimore.
At Bridgeport, Connecticut, she took a Sikorsky helicopter
aboard and a few test flights/landings were made. The main
problem was not one of defence or the slowness of the
aircraft, but that of not being able to land on the ship in

anything except exceptionally calm weather. And so this
early wartime conception of carrying helicopters aboard ship
was abandoned. (See CAM-MAC ships, Part 3)

675   *Kafiristan* 7,250 gt. Details as Yard No. 651.
Launched: 30.4.1941.
Completed: 9.1941 for Hindustan Steam Shipping
Co. Ltd. (Common Bros. Ltd.).
1954: *Avisglen* (Aviation & Shipping Co. Ltd.,
London (Purvis Shipping Co. Ltd.)).
1961: *Noelle* (Cia. de Nav. Skiathos, Panama
(Lebanese flag).
1969: (Camelia Shipping Co. Ltd., Cyprus).
7.1972: Scrapped Shanghai.

686   *Tarantia* 7,268 gt. Details as Yard No. 652.
Launched: 17.12.1941.
Completed: 3.1942 for Anchor Line Ltd.
1959: *Cape Vamvakas* (Cia, de Nav. Scardana S.A.,
Panama (Greek flag).
1967: *Buonavia* (Lembus Shipping Co. Ltd., Cyprus
(A. Halcoussis & Co., Greece)).
8.1971: Scrapped Whampoa.

687   *Tahsinia* 7,250 gt, 442.8 ft (oa),
428.8 ft × 56.5 ft.
Launched: 30.1.1942.
Completed: 6.1942 for Anchor Line Ltd.
1.10.1943: Sunk by submarine (*U.532*) torpedo in
Indian Ocean, west of Ceylon, position
06.51N 74.38E.

688   *Fresno City* 7,261 gt. Details as Yard No. 687.
Launched: 18.3.1942.
Completed: 6.1942 for Reardon Smith Line Ltd.
(Sir Wm. Reardon Smith & Sons Ltd.).
12.4.1943: Damaged by submarine (*U.168*) torpedo,
54.15N 30.00W, south-east of Cape Farewell while
in convoy HX 232. Later sunk by *U.706*.

689   *Vancouver City* 7,261 gt. Details as Yard No.
687.
Launched: 31.3.1942.
Completed: 7.1942 for Reardon Smith Line Ltd.
(Sir Wm. Reardon Smith & Sons Ltd.).
1963: *Everbloom* (Prosperity Nav. Corpn., Liberia
(Wah Kwong & Co. Ltd.)).
10.9.1965: Dragged moorings in typhoon and went
aground at Wakanoura, Wakayama (Voyage:
Kure/Wakayama – ballast). Refloated: constructive
total loss.
11.1965: Scrapped Wakayama, Japan.

690   *Avristan* 7,266 gt. Details as Yard No. 687.
Launched: 29.4.1942.
Completed: 7.1942 for Strick Line (1923) Ltd. (F. C.
Strick & Co. Ltd.).
1963: *Paulia* (Monique Nav. Corp. Liberia (P. S. Li,
Hong Kong)).

1966: (Oriental Union Maritime Corpn (Y. C. Cheng, Hong Kong)).
1966: *Victoria Loyal* (Victoria Ocean Transport Ltd. (P. S. Li, Hong Kong)).
1967: *Grand Loyal* (Victoria Ocean Transport Ltd., Liberia (R. Y. T. Chen, Hong Kong)).
13.2.1970: Arrived Kaohsiung for breaking up.

691   *Houston City* 7,262 gt. Details as Yard No. 687.
Launched: 29.5.1942.
Completed: 8.1942 for Reardon Smith Line Ltd. (Sir Wm. Reardon Smith & Sons Ltd.).
1960: *Castle Peak* (Anglo-Chinese Shipping Co. Ltd. (Mollers Ltd., Hong Kong)).
1961: *Sandys River* (River Line Ltd. (Mollers Ltd., Hong Kong)).
1967: *Juliana* (Shun Yu Investment Co. Ltd., Hong Kong).
1968: *Prominent Star* (Holly Navigation Co., Panama).
1968: *Goodwin* (Clara Shipping Corpn., Panama (Q. Chuang, Hong Kong)).
15.10.1968: Arrived Hong Kong for breaking up.

692   *Hardingham* 7,250 gt. Details as Yard No. 687.
Launched: 1.6.1942.
Completed: 9.1942 for Willis SS Co. Ltd. (J. & C. Harrison Ltd., London).
1944: (Hain SS Co. Ltd.).
5.4.1945: Caught fire at Colombo when attempting to relight boiler-room burners. Fire spread rapidly – vessel soon ablaze from stem to stern; abandoned. Exploded and sank in outer anchorage (voyage: New York/Calcutta – general and explosives).

693   *Coombe Hill* 7,268 gt. Details as Yard No. 687.
Launched: 26.6.1942.
Completed: 10.1942 for Putney Hill SS Co. Ltd. (Counties Ship Management Co. Ltd.).
1949: (London & Overseas Freighters Ltd.).
1950: renamed *London Artisan*.
1953: *Jag Laadki* (Great Eastern Shipping Co. Ltd., Bombay).
1965: *Vyzas* (Centre Shipping Co., Liberia (Calafatis & Co. Ltd., Greece)).
11.1968: Scrapped Etajima, Japan.

694   *Harpalyce* 7,269 gt. Details as Yard No. 687.
Launched: 30.6.1942.
Completed: 10.1942 for National SS Co. Ltd. (J. & C. Harrison Ltd., London).
1944: (Hain SS Co. Ltd.).
1946: Renamed *Trewellard*.
1956: (P & O SN Co. Ltd.).
1958: (Hain SS Co. Ltd.).
1962: *Artemon* (Cia. Mar. Santa Marina S.A., Greece).
7.10.1965: Arrived Piraeus, engine trouble (voyage: Cebu/Rotterdam – copra) and:
1.11.1965: fire in cargo whilst at Piraeus.

6.11.1965: Beached in Ambelaki Bay.
8.11.1965: Fire extinguished, but severe damage. Constructive total loss.
8.10.1966: Arrived Valencia, in tow, for breaking up.

695   *Harpagus* 7,271 gt. Details as Yard No. 687.
Launched: 28.8.1942.
Completed: 11.1942 for National SS Co. Ltd. (J. & C. Harrison Ltd., London).
1944: (Hain SS Co. Ltd.).
19.8.1944: Struck mine, 1½ miles N of West Breakwater, Arromanches Harbour, Normandy. Broke in two, forepart sank (voyage: Southend/Arromanches – military stores). Stern half salved; towed to Southampton, thence to River Tyne.
5.1946: New forepart fitted; vessel renamed *Treworlas*.
1956: (P & O SN Co. Ltd.).
1958: (Hain SS Co. Ltd.).
1.6.1960: Aground, Madaira Reef, off Kuwait, Persian Gulf. Severe bottom damage.
7.6.1960: Refloated by tugs.
20.6.1960: Sailed for Falmouth under own power but declared constructive total loss.
21.9.1960: Arrived Briton Ferry, in tow of tug *Tradesman* for breaking up.

696   *Tower Hill* 7,268 gt. Details as Yard No. 687.
Launched: 25.8.1942.
Completed: 12.1942 for Tower SS Co. Ltd. (Counties Ship Management Co. Ltd.).
1949: (London & Overseas Freighters Ltd.).
1950: renamed *London Banker*.
1953: *Avisbank* (Aviation & Shipping Co. Ltd. (Purvis Shipping Co. Ltd.)).
1959: *Southern Venture* (Pan Norse SS Co. S.A. Panama).
31.10.1960: Broke moorings in cyclone, driven aground by tidal wave in Karnaphuli river, Chittagong. Holed & flooded; left high and dry. Patched and
15.11.1960: Refloated, proceeded to Kobe for repairs.
1966: (Bianca Carriers Inc., Panama (Wah Kwong & Co. (H.K.) Ltd.)).
8.7.1970: Arrived Kaohsiung for breaking up.

697   *Bardistan* 7,264 gt. Details as Yard No. 687.
Launched: 25.9.1942.
Completed: 12.1942 for Strick Line (1923) Ltd. (F. C. Strick & Co. Ltd.).
1963: *Pacific Mariner* (Mariner Ocean Transport Co. Ltd. (Wallem & Co. Ltd., Hong Kong)).
1966: *Eastern Enterprise* (Mariner Ocean Transport Co. Ltd. (Ping An SS Co., Hong Kong)).
20.5.1972: Arrived Kaohsiung for breaking up.

698   *Bradford City* 7,266 gt. Details as Yard No. 687.
Launched: 9.11.1942.

Completed: 2.1943 for Leeds Shipping Co. Ltd. (Sir Wm. Reardon Smith & Sons Ltd.).
1962: *Vercharmian* (Vergocean SS Co. Ltd. (Vergottis Ltd., London)).
1968: *Shun Wah* (Jebshun Shipping Co. Ltd., Hong Kong).
5.1972: Scrapped Tadotsu, Japan.

699   *Harlesden* 7,271 gt. Details as Yard No. 687.
Launched: 23.10.1942.
Completed: 3.1943 for J. & C. Harrison Ltd., London.
1944: *Trewidden* (Hain SS Co. Ltd.).
1959: *Ankobra River* (Black Star Line Ltd., Ghana).
1964: *Eland* (Tenes Shipping Co. S.A. Panama (C. G. Calafatis & Co. Ltd., Greece)).
29.10.1968: Arrived Kaohsiung for breaking up.

700   *English Prince* 7,275 gt. Details as Yard No. 687.
Launched: 22.12.1942.
Completed: 4.1943 for Prince Line Ltd. (Furness, Withy & Co. Ltd.).
1961: *Simos* (Amanda Shipping Co. Ltd. (G. C. Calafatis & Co. Ltd., Greece)).
22.7.1972: Aground in fog, ½ mile NE of Cape St. Vincent, Portugal (voyage: Ashod/France – phosphates).
22.8.1972: Refloated leaking and
24.8.1972: Arrived Setubal. Laid up.
31.8.1973: Arrived Bilbao in tow for breaking up.

701   *Jersey Hart* 7,275 gt. Details as Yard No. 687.
Launched: 20.12.1942.
Completed: 5.1943 for Nolisement SS Co. Ltd. (Morel Ltd.).
1945: *Stanpark* (Stanhope SS Co. Ltd. (J. A. Billmeir & Co. Ltd., London)).
1951: *Queen Eleanor* (Queen Line Ltd. (T. Dunlop & Sons, Glasgow)).
1956: *Inchdouglas* (Douglas SS Co. Ltd. (Williamson & Co. Ltd., Hong Kong)).
4.11.1970: Arrived Kaohsiung for breaking up.

704   *Trevelyan* 7,292 gt. Details as Yard No. 687.
Launched: 8.4.1943.
Completed: 7.1943 for Hain SS Co. Ltd.
1956: (P & O SN Co. Ltd.).
1958: (Hain SS Co. Ltd.).
5.11.1962: Arrived Hong Kong for breaking up.

705   *Trevince* 7,291 gt. Details as Yard No. 687.
Launched: 4.5.1943.
Completed: 8.1943 for Hain SS Co. Ltd.
1959: *Densu river* (Black Star Line Ltd., Accra).
1967: *Vicky* (Cia. de Nav. Victoria S.A., Panama (SOARMA, Italy)).
1974: (Holivian Shipping Co. S.A., Panama).
4.6.1974: Arrived in tow at Saigon, Vietnam, after engine breakdown during voyage from Penang.

Repairs uneconomic; towed to Hong Kong. Minor repairs made, and
24.7.1974: Sailed to Chinese shipbreakers, and
8.1974: Scrapped Whampoa.

706   *Avonmoor* 7,268 gt. Details as Yard No. 687.
Launched: 18.5.1943.
Completed: 9.1943 for Moor Line Ltd. (Runciman Shipping Co. Ltd.).
1959: *Yu Tung* (Yu Tung Navigation Corp., Formosa).
1966: *Union Success* (China Union Lines Ltd., Taipei).
1.2.1968: Arrived Kaohsiung for breaking up.

707   *Greenwich* 7,292 gt. Details as Yard No. 687.
Launched: 1.7.1943.
Completed: 10.1943 for Britain SS Co. Ltd. (Watts, Watts & Co. Ltd.).
1959: *Portador* (Argus SS Co. Inc., Liberia (E. de Aznar, Spain).
13.4.62: On fire, abandoned approx. 250 miles SW of Ireland, 51.15N 15.34W (voyage: Manchester/Comeau Bay – ballast). Presumed sunk.

714   *Arabistan* 7,369 gt, 444.8 ft (oa),
431 ft × 56.5 ft. Engines: Oil.
Launched: 24.1.1944.
Completed: 5.1944 for Strick Line (1923) Ltd. (F. C. Strick & Co. Ltd.).
1963: *Panagiotis Lemos* (Cia. Pacifica Financierea S.A. Panama (Liberian flag)).
1967: *Polyxeni* (Astromando Cia. Nav. Liberia (Somali flag) (Lemos & Pateras, London)).
29.9.1968: Struck submerged object, sprang leak (voyage: Sundsvall/Bombay – nitrate).
30.9.1968: Beached Fort Dauphin, Madagascar. Flooded; settled into sand, considered not salvable. Total loss.

715   *Trevethoe* 7,355 gt. Details as Yard No. 714.
Launched: 8.2.1944.
Completed: 6.1944 for Hain SS Co. Ltd.
1951: (P & O SN Co. Ltd.).
1958: (Hain SS Co. Ltd.).
1959: *Alcyonis* (Herculiania Maritime Co. Ltd., Greece).
13.8.1969: Arrived Kaohsiung for breaking up.

716   *Trevose* 7,354 gt. Details as Yard No. 714.
Launched: 25.4.1944.
Completed: 8.1944 for Hain SS Co. Ltd.
1951: (P & O SN Co. Ltd.).
1958: (Hain SS Co. Ltd.).
1962: *Ruthy Ann* (Red Anchor Line Ltd. (C. Moller Ltd., Hong Kong)).
9.9.1968: Collided with *Cuu Long* (1,157 gt) in typhoon at Haiphong, N. Vietnam; ran aground. Extensive damage to shell and bottom plating.
30.9.1968: Refloated, and

26.11.1968: Arrived Hong Kong. Repaired.
2.1971: Scrapped Whampoa.

717 *Welsh Prince* 7,354 gt. Details as Yard No. 714.
Launched: 12.4.1944.
Completed: 9.1944 for Rio Cape Line Ltd. (Furness, Withy & Co. Ltd.).
1961: *Vergmont* (Vergocean SS Co. Ltd.) (Vergottis Ltd., London).
23.2.1971: Arrived Whampoa for breaking up.

718 *Floristan* 7,368 gt. Details as Yard No. 714.
Launched: 12.6.1944.
Completed: 10.1944 for Strick Line (1923) Ltd. (F. C. Strick & Co. Ltd.).
1963: *Uje* (Cia. de Nav. Bayano S.A., Panama).
22.9.1973: On fire in engine room at Antwerp Docks. Gutted.
23.10.1973: Arrived Bilbao, in tow, for breaking up.

719 *Brockleymoor* 7,368 gt. Details as Yard No. 714.
Launched: 20.6.1944.
Completed: 11.1944 for Moor Line Ltd. (Runciman Shipping Co. Ltd.).
1960: *Restormel* (Cardigan Shipping Co. Ltd. (J. Cory & Sons Ltd., Newport)).
1964: *Newglade* (Waterloo Shipping Co. Ltd. (Tsavliris Ltd., London)).
7.11.1968: On fire in engine room while under repair at Kynosoura. Beached in Ambelaki Bay.
10.11.1968: Fire extinguished, vessel badly damaged.
19.11.1968: refloated, and
20.11.1968: re-moored at Kynosoura.
13.6.1969: Arrived Spezia in tow.
3.7.1969: Towed to Vado for breaking up.

720 *Registan* 7,373 gt. Details as Yard No. 714.
Launched: 9.8.1944.
Completed: 12.1944 for Strick Line (1923) Ltd. (F. C. Strick & Co. Ltd.).
1945: *Tresillian* (Hain SS Co. Ltd.).
1951: (P & O SN Co. Ltd.).
30.11.1954: Cargo shifted, capsized and sank in heavy seas, 51.14N 07.30W, twenty-five miles off Ballycotton, Ireland (voyage: Sorel PQ/Avonmouth and Glasgow – grain).

721 *Roybank* 7,368 gt. Details as Yard No. 714.
Launched: 31.8.1944.
Completed: 12.1944 for Bank Line Ltd. (A. Weir & Co. Ltd.).
1962: *Silver Lake* (Transportes Maritimos Mundiales S.A., Liberia (C. S. Koo, Hong Kong)).
1965: (Silver Lines Inc., Liberia (C. S. Koo, Hong Kong)).
16.4.1968: Arrived Kaohsiung for breaking up.

724 *Weybank* 7,368 gt. Details as Yard No. 714.
Launched: 30.11.1944.
Completed: 4.1945 for Bank Line Ltd. (A. Weir & Co. Ltd.).
1962: *Silver Moon* (Pacific Overseas Nav. Corp. S.A., Liberia).
8.4.1968: Arrived Kaohsiung for breaking up.

725 *Pundua* 7,295 gt. Details as Yard No. 689.
Launched: 27.2.1945.
Completed: 6.1945 for British India SN Co. Ltd.
1967: *Shun On* (Jebshun Shipping Co. Ltd., London).
9.12.1971: Laid up Singapore Roads; and
1972: Reported scrapped Singapore.

728 *Meadowbank* 7,307 gt. Details as Yard No. 689.
Launched: 10.2.1945.
Completed: 7.1945 for Bank Line Ltd. (A. Weir & Co. Ltd.).
1963: *Hsing Yung* (Van Yung Maritime Co. Ltd., China).
1968: Scrapped Kaohsiung.

729 *Moraybank* 7,307 gt. Details as Yard No. 689.
Launched: 26.4.1945.
Completed: 8.1945 for Bank Line Ltd. (A. Weir & Co. Ltd.).
1962: *Ardrowan* (Mullion & Co. Ltd., Hong Kong).
1968: *Tetrarch* (Tetrarch Shipping Co. Ltd., Gibraltar (Mullion & Co. Ltd., Hong Kong)).
3.12.1969: Arrived Hong Kong for breaking up.

730 *Ambassador* 7,312 gt, Details as Yard No. 689.
Launched: 29.3.1945.
Completed: 10.1945 for Hall Bros. SS Co. Ltd. (Hall Bros., Newcastle).
18.2.1964: Hatches stove in, in heavy seas after engine failure in Atlantic (voyage: Philadelphia/London – grain). Taken in tow by Dutch tug *Elbe* (1959, 797 gt), but tow parted and:
21.2.1964: Sank, 37.22N 48.51W.

731 *Hartington* 7,325 gt. Details as Yard No. 689.
Launched: 24.5.1945.
Completed: 11.1945 for National SS Co. Ltd. (J. & C. Harrison Ltd.).
1962: *Abaco* (Stuart Navigation Ltd. (World Wide Shipping Co. Ltd.)).
1963: *Funabashi* (Sycamore SS Co. Ltd. (World Wide Shipping Co. Ltd.)).
16.2.1966: In collision with *White Mountain* (1943, 7,167 gt, Liberian-flag) about nine miles from Singapore. Beached on Pulau Ramunia Island, 1.22N 104.15E.
22.2.1966: Refloated, towed to Singapore Roads.
12.1966: Scrapped Singapore.

Built by Furness Shipbuilding Co. Ltd., Haverton Hill-on-Tees

345   *Empire Beaumont* 7,044 gt, 'B'-type, 446 ft (oa), 431 ft × 56 ft. Engines: T3cyl.
Launched: 31.3.1942.
Completed: 6.1942.
13.9.1942: Attacked by aircraft of KG (Bomber Group) 26 and sank in position 76.10N 10.05E whilst in convoy PQ 18 (Iceland/North Russia).

Bombers and torpedo aircraft of KG 30 and KG 26 made many attacks on the convoy, which consisted of forty-three merchant ships and large naval escort and covering forces. The attacks lasted three days. Three ships, an American 'Liberty', a British tanker and a Russian cargo ship were sunk by U-boat torpedoes and ten more by air attack. Three U-boats were sunk and twenty aircraft destroyed.

346   *Empire Guidon* 7,041 gt. Details as Yard No. 345.
Launched: 30.5.1942.
Completed: 8.1942.
31.10.1942: Sunk by submarine (*U.504*) torpedo, 30.10S 33.50E, south of Mozambique Channel, approx. 150 miles east of Durban.

MERCHANT SHIPS BUILT UNDER PRIVATE CONTRACT OR LICENCE

307   *African Prince* 4,653 gt, 437.4 ft (oa), 421.8 ft × 56.7 ft. Engines: Oil.
Launched: 31.7.1939.
Completed: 9.1939 for Prince Line Ltd. (Furness, Withy & Co. Ltd.).
1961: *Ardmore* (Mullion & Co. Ltd., Hong Kong).
1965: *Kali Elpis* (Craft Shipping Co. Ltd. (Fraternidad Cia. de Nav. Ltd., London)).
28.3.1967: Arrived Bombay from Aden; laid up.
1969: Placed under restraint by creditors; to be sold by Order of the Court. Sold by Public Auction to Indian shipbreakers.
9.1969: Scrapped Bombay.

310   *Madras City* 5,092 gt, 437.4 ft (oa), 421.6 ft × 56.7 ft. Engines: Tcyl.
Launched: 8.2.1940.
Completed: 5.1940 for Reardon Smith Line Ltd. (Sir W. R. Reardon Smith & Sons Ltd.).
1958: *Chittagong City* (Chittagong SS Corpn. Ltd., Pakistan).
13.2.1971: Arrived Karachi for breaking up.

311   *Orient City* 5,095 gt. Details as Yard No. 310.
Launched: 7.3.1940.
Completed: 7.1940 for Leeds Shipping Co. Ltd. (Sir W. R. Reardon Smith & Sons Ltd.).

1958: *Feronia* (East & West SS Co. (Cowasjee & Sons, Karachi)).
9.1970: Scrapped Karachi.

351   *Kumasian* 7,221 gt, 439 ft (oa), 423 ft × 57.2 ft. Engines: T3cyl.
Launched: 22.1.1943.
Completed: 3.1943 for United Africa Co. Ltd.)).
1949: *Kumasi Palm* (Palm Line Ltd. (United Africa Co. Ltd.)).
1960: *Flower* (Cia. Nav. Zirda, Panama (F. I. Groce, Genoa)).
1967: (Garden City Shipping Co. Inc. Panama (F. I. Groce)).
5.4.1968: Arrived Spezia for breaking up.

352   *Lafian* 7,221 gt. Details as Yard No. 351.
Launched: 25.3.1943.
Completed: 5.1943 for United Africa Co. Ltd.
1949: *Oguta Palm* (Palm Line Ltd. (United Africa Co. Ltd.)).
1960: *Aristoteles* (Aristides SS Co., Panama. (Greek flag) (Rallis Shipping Co. Ltd., London)).
15.12.1962: Sprang leak in No. 2 hold approximately 260 miles west of Cape St. Vincent, Portugal (voyage: Detroit/Calcutta). Abandoned and
16.12.1962: sank in position 36.48N 14.40W.

Built by William Gray & Co. Ltd., West Hartlepool

1109   *Empire Sunbeam* 6,711 gt, 432 ft (oa), 419 ft × 57 ft. Engines: T3cyl.
Launched: 16.1.1941.

Completed: 3.1941.
1945: *Swainby* (Ropner Shipping Co. Ltd. (Sir R. Ropner & Co. Ltd.)).

1962: *Newgate* (Trafalgar SS Co. Ltd. (Tsavliris (Shipping) Ltd., London)).
1967: (Kantara Shipping Co. Ltd., Cyprus).
1968: (Newgate Shipping Co. Ltd., Cyprus).
2.10.1971: Arrived Istanbul for breaking up.

1110 *Empire Ocean* 6,765 gt. Details as Yard No. 1109.
Launched: 15.3.1941.
Completed: 5.1941.

The *Empire Ocean*, bound from Newport to Halifax with coal, was in convoy ON 115, close to the Canadian coast, when it was attacked by a U-boat pack. More than forty ships scattered, but on 4 August 1942 in an effort to escape, the *Empire Ocean* ran aground 1½ miles east of Shingle Head, Cape Race, Newfoundland. On a steep shore, with only her bows on the rocks, damage seemed only slight, but as a salvage tug arrived, the ship slid from the rocks and filled by the head.

Towed stern first, a course was set for the only safe coastal beaching place in the area and she reached Aquaforte Harbor, between two close headlands at night only to find all navigation lights removed.

With the ship's foredeck awash another course was set, for Ferryland Harbor, further north. As they neared the harbour next day, it became necessary to shorten the tow and as the ships slowed, the suction on the *Empire Ocean* eased and the full pressure of the sea was put on her bulkheads. Some collapsed; the ship slid under bows first, her stern stood upright, the remaining bulkheads carried away and the *Empire Ocean* plunged into deep water, in position 47.01N 52.50W.

1111 *Empire Darwin* 6,765 gt. Details as Yard No. 1109.
Launched: 13.5.1941.
Completed: 7.1941.
29.7.1943: Bombed and damaged by a near miss, 44.52N 16.00W, west of Cape Finisterre, Spain.
4.8.1943: Arrived Glasgow; repaired.
1946: *Culrain* (South Georgia Co. Ltd. (Chr. Salvesen & Co)).
1959: *Mersinidi* (North Europe & Persian Gulf Transports Corpn. (J. Livanos & Sons Ltd.)).
30.12.1966: Arrived Singapore for breaking up.

1118 *Empire Cabot* 6,722 gt. Details as Yard No. 1109.
Launched: 9.7.1941.
Completed: 9.1941.
1945: *Clearpool* (Pool Shipping Co. Ltd. (Sir R. Ropner & Co. Ltd.)).
1955: *Grelmarion* (Cardigan Shipping Co. Ltd. (T. Walter Gould & Co. Ltd., Cardiff)).
1959: (Bowring & Curry Ltd. (R. M. Sloman Jr. (Germany)); renamed *Rachel* for delivery to shipbreakers.
8.11.1959: Arrived Hong Kong for breaking up.

1121 *Empire Parsons* 6,742 gt. Details as Yard No. 1109.
Launched: 23.8.1941.

Completed: 10.1941.
12.1.1942: Ashore, east of Stroma Island, Pentland Firth, 58.41N 3.06W. Buckled, flooded and tidal. Abandoned. Broke in three. Total loss (voyage: Tyne/Baltimore – ballast).

1122 *Empire Marlowe* 6,768 gt. Details as Yard No. 1109.
Launched: 6.10.1941.
Completed: 12.1941.
1946: *Cape St David* (Sun Shipping Co. Ltd. (Mitchell, Cotts & Co. Ltd., London)).
1960: *Happy Seafarer* (Escort Shipping Co. Ltd. (Mariner Shipping Co. Ltd. (Hong Kong)).
7.1966: Scrapped Hirao.

1123 (Launched as) *Empire Builder* 7,048 gt, 446 ft (oa), 431 ft × 56 ft. Engines: T3cyl.
Launched: 19.11.1941.
Completed: 1.1942 as *Tobruk* for Government of Poland (Gdynia America Shipping Lines Ltd.).
1951: (Polskie-Linie Oceaniczne.)
6.1968: Scrapped Gdynia.

1124 *Empire Purcell* 7,049 gt. Details as Yard No. 1123.
Launched: 17.1.1942.
Completed: 3.1942.
27.5.1942: Bombed and sunk in Barents Sea, 74.00N 26.08E. (Convoy PQ16, Iceland/N. Russia).

1127 *Empire Arnold* 7,045 gt. Details as Yard No. 1123.
Launched: 6.3.1942.
Completed: 5.1942.
4.8.1942: Sunk by submarine (*U.155*), 10.45N 52.30W, Gulf of Aden (voyage: U.S.A./Middle East – military stores).

1128 *Empire Lionel* 7,012 gt. Details as Yard No. 1123.
Launched: 2.5.1942.
Completed: 6.1942.
1945: *Levenpool* (Pool Shipping Co. Ltd. (Sir R. Ropner & Co. Ltd.)).
1962: *Newlane* (Trafalgar SS Co. Ltd. (Tsavliris Shipping Ltd., London)).
1968: (Kantara Shipping Ltd., Cyprus (Tsavliris Shipping Ltd., London)).
1969: (Newlane Shipping Ltd., Cyprus (Tsavliris Shipping Ltd., London)).
23.10.1969: Arrived Chittagong for breaking up.

1133 *Empire Clarion* 7,031 gt. Details as Yard No. 1123.
Launched: 30.6.1942.
Completed: 9.1942.
1946: *Cedarpool* (Pool Shipping Co. Ltd. (Sir. R. Ropner & Co. Ltd.)).
20.7.1959: Arrived Hamburg for breaking up.

1134   *Empire Centaur* 7,041 gt. Details as Yard No.
1123.
Launched: 30.7.1942.
Completed: 10.1942.
12.12.1942: Damaged by Italian assault craft at
Algiers.
1943: *Belgian Captain* (Government of Belgium).
1946: *Capitaine Lambe* (Cie. Maritime Belge (Lloyd
Royal) S.A.).
1960: *Ardee* (Mullion & Co. Ltd., Hong Kong).
1964: *Alpha Trader* (Sigma Shipping Co. Ltd. (Trinity
Development Co. Ltd. (Hong Kong)).
11.1967: Arrived Shanghai for breaking up.

1137   *Empire Driver* 7,042 gt. Details as Yard No.
1123.
Launched: 24.9.1942.
Completed: 11.1942.
1945: *Radiotelegraphiste Biard* (French Government
(Chargeurs Reunis)).
1950: *Dea Mazzella* (P. Mazzella, Naples).
1956: *Maria Mazzella* (P. Mazzella, Naples).
1960: *Falzarego* (Pala and Franceschini, Genoa).
1964: *Grazia Prima* (Societa per Azioni Costanza,
Genoa).
1965: *Missouri* (Luzmar S.A., Liberia).
8.2.1969: Arrived Santander, in tow from Antwerp
for breaking up.

1138   *Empire Cato* 7,039 gt. Details as Yard No.
1123.
Launched: 10.11.1942.
Completed: 12.1942.
1948: *Clan Mackenzie* (Clan Line Steamers Ltd.).
14.10.1960: Arrived Hong Kong for breaking up.

1141   *Empire Mortimer* 7,051 gt. Details as Yard No.
1123.
Launched: 23.12.1942.
Completed: 3.1943.
1947: *Lord Gladstone* (Norwood SS Co. Ltd. (Ships
Finance & Management Co. Ltd., London).
1958: *Olga Minacoulis* (Cia. de Nav. San Antonio
Ltd., Costa Rica).
1964: *St Antonio* (San Antonio Shipping Co. Ltd.,
Malta).
1966: Sold Denmark for breaking up; resold Spanish
shipbreakers and
3.2.1966: Arrived Santander, in tow.

1142   *Empire Prowess* 7,058 gt. Details as Yard No.
1123.
Launched: 6.2.1943.
Completed: 4.1943.
1947: *Harperley* (J. & C. Harrison Ltd., London).
1955: *Elstead* (J. A. Billmeir & Co. Ltd.).
22.10.1959: Arrived Nagasaki for breaking up.

1147   *Empire Stalwart* 7,045 gt. Details as Yard No.
1123.

Launched: 23.3.1943.
Completed: 5.1943.
1946: *Eastbury* (Alexander Shipping Co. Ltd.
(Houlder Bros & Co. Ltd., London)).
1958: *Constitucion* (Transportes Maritimos Mexicanos
S.A.).
10.1968: Scrapped Veracruz, Mexico.

1148   *Empire Peak* 7,045 gt. Details as Yard No.
1123.
Launched: 4.5.1943.
Completed: 7.1943.
1947: *Charmouth Hill* (Dorset SS Co. Ltd. (Counties
Ship Management Co. Ltd.)).
1949: (London & Overseas Freighters Ltd.).
1950: renamed *London Mariner*.
1951: *Leone* (Ragruppamento Armatore Fratelli
Grimaldi).
1960: (Aldebaran, Cia. de Nav. S.A.).
1963: *Marianella* (Vinti Freighters Ltd., Cyprus
(E. M. Vintiadis, Genoa)).

The *Marianella* sailed from Houston, Texas, on 19 October
1967, bound for Calcutta with a bulk cargo of sulphate of
ammonia. After some eight months the ship had only
travelled as far as Cape Town.

On the first leg of the voyage she put into Kingston,
Jamaica, having developed leaks during heavy weather, with
cargo in Nos. 1 and 2 holds severely water damaged. While
at sea her fan engine had also broken down and efforts to
steam on natural draught choked the boiler tubes. The vessel
was powerless and adrift for some days before repairs were
completed. At Kingston her main pumps were found to be
in need of repair, due to continuous use in pumping, and
spares were air-freighted from Europe.

She sailed on 11 January 1968, bound for Dakar, but must
have suffered further troubles, for the next report is dated 10
May, when she sailed from Takoradi for Luanda. Leaving
this port on 15 June, she arrived at Cape Town on the 26th,
with boiler trouble, and was put to anchorage in Table Bay.
The voyage was abandoned when it was found that repairs
would exceed the value of the ship.

The *Marianella* stayed at anchor in the open roadstead for
another five months, a source of concern to the authorities
because of the corrosive action of seawater through hull leaks
to the cargo. The ship was not fit to proceed to sea, but
entered port once a fortnight to take fresh water for her
leaking boilers. With fertiliser manufactured locally there was
no local market for her cargo and it was finally transhipped
for onward delivery. Local offers for the ship itself were
considered derisory and she was sold to Italian shipbreakers.

On 9 December 1968 she left Cape Town for Genoa, in
tow of the tug *Smjeli* (ex *Empire Larch*) and on 6 March 1969
arrived at Vado for breaking up.

1151   *Empire Rival* 7,045 gt. Details as Yard No.
1123.
Launched: 19.6.1943.
Completed: 9.1943.
1948: *Amberton* (R. Chapman & Son, Newcastle).
1957: *Parmarina* (Cia. de Vapores Marina Ltda, Costa
Rica (N. & J. Vlassopulos Ltd., London)).

1963: (Oceanica Armadora S.A. (Lebanese flag) (Vlassopulos Ltd., London)).
10.1.1967: Wrecked off Keelung, Formosa, 25.10N 121.43E after anchor chain broke in heavy weather while waiting to berth (voyage: Keelung/Tokyo).

Within a year or so of the end of the war, displaced persons – mostly of the Jewish faith – were converging on Palestine to set up a new nation. However, the British Government, with a mandate of the territory, decided that such movement must not be allowed.

It became the task of the Royal Navy to stop the ancient and mostly unseaworthy vessels used for the traffic, culled from all corners of the world, whilst they were still at sea.

The vessels were then boarded by Army personnel, generally against strong opposition, and the refugees – sick and diseased people, many having suffered for years at the hands of the Nazis – were forced from their own ships into landing craft. They were then transhipped to merchant vessels, generally only converted by the addition of barbed-wire barriers, for transport to prison camps in Cyprus.

The refugee opposition, ashore and afloat, stiffened to war proportions, with frequent sabotage operations against the British ships involved.

On the night of 22 August 1946, in Haifa Bay, limpet mines were attached to the hull of the *Empire Rival*, one of the vessels used in taking illegal immigrants from their haven of Palestine to Famagusta. Explosions blew a large hole in the side of the ship and as she began to settle by the stern she was beached in shallow water. Raised and patched, she later proceeded to Alexandria for repairs. Four days before this casualty an attempt was made to sink the *Empire Heywood* soon after she left Haifa for Cyprus with 750 immigrants on board. But the explosion of gelignite concealed in electric torches caused more delay than damage and the vessel again proceeded with her human cargo.

The next year the *Empire Rival* was again involved, this following the detention, at sea, on 17 July 1947, of the much-publicised refugee ship known as *Exodus* (unregistered full name *Exodus From Europe 1947*) – an ex-Baltimore ferry boat, built in 1928 as *President Warfield*, and of 1,814 gt.

With more than 4,000 refugees on board, the *Exodus* was escorted to Haifa by a cruiser and five destroyers, where the immigrants were transferred to the *Empire Rival*, the *Ocean Vigour* (1942, 7,174 gt) and the *Runnymede Park* (1944, 7,139 gt). The passenger list was divided as:

Empire Rival: 629 men, 601 women, 291 children
Ocean Vigour: 654 men, 658 women, 259 children
Runnymede Park: 616 men, 443 women, 405 children.

The three ships returned their passengers to their embarkation port of Port de Bouc, France, but they refused to land and the vessels lay there from 29 July to 22 August, each fitted with an upper-deck wire cage to contain the refugees while on deck and each ship guarded by ninety men of the 6th Airborne Division. The vessels then sailed for Hamburg, escorted from Gibraltar by the cruiser *Phoebe*, the destroyer *Chevron* and the frigate *St. Bride's Bay*. At Hamburg the refugees were landed and sent to European camps.

Strangely, at the same time, July 1947, the *Empire Lifeguard* (*q.v.*) was sunk by limpet mines at Haifa after disembarking immigrants carried from the camps in Cyprus under a 1,500-persons-per-month quota.

1152 *Empire Nigel* 7,067 gt. Details as Yard No. 1123.
Launched: 20.7.1943.
Completed: 9.1943.
1944: *Archangel*, then changed to *Archangelsk* (U.S.S.R. (lease-lend-agreement)).
1946: *Empire Nigel* (M.O.T.).
1947: *Nandi* (W. & R. Carpenter & Co., Suva, Fiji).
1948: *Bristol City* (Bristol City Line of Steamships Ltd.).
1957: *Zelengora* (Splosna Plovba, Yugoslavia).
1971: *Taras* (Cia. de Nav. Portland S.A., Panama).
6.7.1972: Arrived Split for breaking up.

1154 *Empire Ploughman* 7,049 gt. Details as Yard No. 1123.
Launched: 14.9.1943.
Completed: 11.1943.
1946: *Baron Geddes* (H. Hogarth & Sons Ltd.).
1959: *Jytte Paulin* (Paulins Rederi A/B, Finland).
22.10.1968: Arrived Shanghai for breaking up.

1155 *Empire Unicorn* 7,067 gt. Details as Yard No. 1123.
Launched: 29.10.1943.
Completed: 12.1943.
1945: *Pierre Corniou* (Government of France).
1950: *Saint Andre* (Soc. Navale de l'Ouest).
1953: *Otello* (O. Wallenius, Stockholm).
1956: *Apollo* (L. Jeansson A/B, Stockholm).
1961: *Kopalnia Wujek* (Polska Zegluga Morska, Poland).
1971: Converted to a storage vessel (*MP–ZP–GDY* 7) for use at Gdynia.

1161 *Empire Lankester* 7,067 gt. Details as Yard No. 1123.
Launched: 24.2.1944.
Completed: 4.1944.
1948: *Clan Mackellar* (Clan Line Steamers Ltd.).
1961: *Ardgroom* (Mullion & Co. Ltd., Gibraltar).
1966: sold, to be renamed *Nearco* but:
20.2.1967: arrived Hong Kong for breaking up.

1162 *Empire Irving* 7,071 gt. Details as Yard No. 1123.
Launched: 25.4.1944.
Completed: 6.1944.
1946: *Bellerby* (Ropner Shipping Co. Ltd. (Sir R. Ropner & Co. Ltd.)).
1960: *Persian Cambyssis* (Iranian Lloyd Co. Ltd., Iran)
1964: *Iranian Trader* (Iranian Shipping Lines S.A. (Pan Shipping Ltd., Iran)).
1964: Renamed *Shiraz*.
7.5.1966: Arrived Dammam, and
15.5.1956: Placed under arrest for debt; to be sold by Order of the Court.
1969: Lying derelict, and
26.1.1970: Broke moorings, deliberately beached and

partly flooded to secure, as anchors missing. Refloated while still under arrest: sold.

9.1970: *Sayhet* (E. Matrood & Essa Zeers Bayrainis, Bahrein (Saudi Arabian flag).

18.9.1970: Arrived Sitra Roads, Bahrain, in tow, for provision of anchor, dumping of 3,000 tons of wheat (aboard since 1966) and for fumigation.

1972: Sold to Gulf Navigation Co., Saudi Arabia. Resold to Euroasia Carriers Ltd. for demolition, and

12.1972: Scrapped Gadani Beach, Pakistan.

1165   *Empire Malacca* 7,071 gt. Details as Yard No. 1123.

Launched: 10.6.1944.

Completed: 8.1944.

1946: *Mandasor* (T. & J. Brocklebank Ltd.).

1962: *Fotini Tsavliris* (Tsavliris Shipping Ltd., London).

1963: *Free Trader* (Pancristo Shipping Co. S.A. (Lebanese flag) (Tsavliris Shipping Ltd., London)).

1965: (Kantara Shipping Ltd., Cyprus (Tsavliris Shipping Ltd., London)).

1969: (Free Trader Shipping Ltd., Cyprus (Tsavliris Shipping Ltd., London)).

16.9.1970: Aground four miles off Terschelling Lighthouse, 53.25N 05.00E (voyage: Brunsbuttel/Antwerp – ballast).

18.9.1970: Refloated, towed to Amsterdam.

29.9.1970): Towed to Piraeus by tug *Nisos Zakynthos* (1944, 1,047 gt) and laid up.

1.5.1972: Arrived Derince, Turkey, for breaking up.

1166   (Laid down as) *Empire Labuan* 'C'-type. 448 ft (oa), 431 ft × 56 ft. Engines: T3cyl.

Launched: 5.9.1944.

Completed: 11.1944 for Admiralty as H.M.S. *Holm Sound*, a maintenance ship for aircraft components.

1949: Reconverted to a cargo ship, *Avisbay* (7,339 gt) (Aviation & Shipping Ltd. (Purvis Shipping Co. Ltd., London)).

1950: *Prah* (Elder, Dempster Lines Ltd., Liverpool).

1959: *Naprijed* (Atlanska Plovidba (Government of Yugoslavia)).

13.5.1969: Arrived Split for breaking up.

1171   (Laid down as) *Empire —— Details as Yard No. 1166.

Launched: 2.11.1944.

Completed: 1.1945 for Admiralty as H.M.S. *Cuillin Sound*, a maintenance ship for aircraft components.

1948: Reconverted to a cargo ship, *James Clunies* (7,850 gt) (Olsen, Johnston & Co. Ltd., Glasgow).

21.4.1949: Ashore in fog 1½ miles from Punta Mogotes, Argentina. Flooded and abandoned. Total loss (voyage: Bahia Blanca/Italy – grain).

1172   *Empire Takoradi* 7,318 gt. Details as Yard No. 1166.

Launched: 29.12.1944.

Completed: 3.1945.

1948: *Shielbank* (A. Weir & Co. Ltd.).

1956: *Asteropes* (Cia. de Nav. Andes, Panama (F. D'Amico, Italy)).

1962: (Cia. Baleniera Italiana SpA., Italy).

2.11.1964: Arrived Spezia for breaking up.

1176   *Empire Eddystone* 7,318 gt. 'D'-type. 448 ft (oa), 431 ft × 56 ft. Engines: T3cyl.

Launched: 11.5.1945.

Completed: 7.1945.

1947: *Winston Churchill* (Aegean Shipping Co. Ltd. (S. G. Embiricos Ltd., London)).

1952: *Marialaura* (Fratelli D'Amico, Italy).

5.1966: Scrapped Trieste.

1177   *Empire Dunnet* 7,373 gt. Details as Yard No. 1176.

Launched: 10.7.1945.

Completed: 9.1945.

1946: *Clan Mackinnon* (Clan Line Steamers Ltd.).

1961: *Ardross* (Mullion & Co. Ltd., Hong Kong).

1963: *Labuan Bay* (Kinabatangan Shipping S.A., Panama (United China Shipping Co. Ltd., Hong Kong)).

20.3.1967: Aground on Bancoran Island, North Borneo, 7.58N 118.04E (voyage: Philippines/Hamburg, Rotterdam).

24.3.1967: Refloated, fire damaged.

27.3.1967: Arrived Manila.

11–12.7.1967: Further fire damage to cargo. Extinguished.

13.7.1967: Left for Hong Kong, arrived 16.7.1967, then

11.1967: Scrapped Kaohsiung.

As with so many shipbuilding companies of north-east England, William Gray & Co.'s origins can be traced to the early years of the 19th century when, in 1836, one S. P. Denton began building sailing ships in a small yard at Hartlepool. This he continued to do until 1862 when William Gray (later to become Sir William) joined him in a partnership to become Denton, Gray & Company and within two years the new concern launched its first iron steamship, *Dessouk* (Yard No. 56), for the Pasha of Egypt. With expanding business the company then moved to the dockyard at West Hartlepool in 1869 which had been established by John Pile in 1853 and who built up Pile, Spence & Company with a high shipbuilding reputation. In 1872 the business was sold to William Gray and became Wm. Gray & Company, their first building, *Minerva* (Yard No. 142) being completed in

September 1874. The 1880s saw more expansion; in 1883 the Central Marine Engine Works was established; in 1887 the three-berth Central Shipyard was formed to build larger ships to 450 ft and two years later the firm became Wm. Gray & Co. Ltd. In 1900 two more berths were added, giving a capability for 500-ft-long hulls.

In 1914, just prior to the outbreak of war, land was purchased for the construction of a shipyard and drydock on the north bank of the River Tees, but this never came to fruition due to the outbreak of hostilities and it was 1924 before the first ship entered drydock there. But in 1917 a shipyard was laid out on the south bank of the Wear at Sunderland under another name. This yard was absorbed into the Gray company in 1919, the company title then being William Gray & Co. (1918) Ltd.

In January 1929 the company celebrated the delivery of its thousandth ship, the 7,958 gt *City of Dieppe* for Ellerman, the thirty-fifth ship built by Gray for that company, twenty of them since the end of the Great War. By the 1930s the company had seventeen ship berths; four at the Dockyard, five at the Central Yard and at the Wear Yard and Tees Yard there were four each.

William Gray & Company continued to build merchant ships throughout the 1939–1945 war, although two hulls were completed as Naval auxiliaries: Yard Nos. 1166 and 1171. Government orders were for three standard types, tramps, a general purpose ship of 4,700 tdw and colliers, the last of which was completed in March 1946. Grays then turned back to peacetime construction with orders for three vessels for the China Navigation Co. Ltd., two for the British India SN Co. Ltd. and six for Ellerman's Wilson Line.

On 22 October 1962 Wm. Gray & Co. Ltd., went into voluntary liquidation although shiprepair work continued for a short time under a newly-formed company, Gray (Tees) Ltd., but this was sold off to Smiths Dock Company in 1963. In the same year the lease of the thirty-five acre Central Shipyard reverted to the then named British Transport Docks Board

The last ship built by Wm. Gray & Company was the *Blanchland* (Yard No. 1303), a 12,800 tdw, 478 ft bulk carrier for Stephenson Clarke Ltd., completed in 1961.

MERCHANT SHIPS BUILT UNDER PRIVATE CONTRACT OR LICENCE

1094   *Atlantic* 5,414 gt, 425.3 ft (oa), 413.3 ft × 57 ft. Engines: T3cyl.
Launched: 18.7.1939.
Completed: 9.1939 for Sir W. H. Cockerline & Co., Hull.
1950: *Kingsford* (Kingsford Shipping Co. Ltd. (P. D. Hendry & Sons, Glasgow)).
1954: *Landspride* (Landsdowne & Co. Ltd. (Wheelock, Marden & Co. Ltd., Hong Kong)).
1959: *Ilexia* (Ilex Shipping Co. Ltd. (Wheelock, Marden & Co. Ltd., Hong Kong)).
3.9.1961: Arrived Nagasaki for breaking up.

1095   *Elmdene* 4,853 gt, 431.5 ft (oa), 416 ft × 56 ft. Engines: T3cyl.
Launched: 14.10.1939.
Completed: 12.1939 for Elmdene Shipping Co. Ltd. (Dene Management Co., London).
8.6.1941: Sunk by submarine (*U.103*) torpedo, south west of Freetown 08.16N 16.50W (voyage: Tyne/Alexandria – coal, stores & aircraft).

1096   *Vasco* 2,878 gt, 354.7 ft (oa), 342 ft × 48 ft. Engines: T3cyl.
Launched: 12.10.1939.
Completed: 12.1939 for Ellerman's Wilson Line Ltd., Hull.
1964: *Brookfield* (Union Enterprise Shipping Co. S.A., Panama (M. Scufalos, Greece)).
1969: *Evangelos Z* (Evasaze Shipping Co. Ltd., Cyprus (S. Zervos, Greece)).
6.1973: Scrapped Split.

1097   *Ruckinge* 2,869 gt, 338 ft (oa), 325 ft × 46.5 ft. Engines: T3cyl.
Launched: 11.11.1939.
Completed: 12.1939 for Constants Ltd., Cardiff.
19.12.1941: Damaged by submarine (*U.108*) torpedo approx 500 miles west of Portugal, 38.20N 17.15W (Convoy HG 76). Abandoned: sunk by gunfire from naval escort.

1098   *Ottinge* 2,870 gt. Details as Yard No. 1097.
Launched: 25.1.1940.
Completed: 3.1940 for Constants Ltd., Cardiff.
1955: *Sofia* (Socoa Shipping Co. Ltd., Liberia (R. de la Sota Jr., France)).
1965: *Dias* (Palamisto General Enterprises S.A., Liberia).
12.3.1967: On fire in engine room, off south coast of Portugal. Later extinguished, but leaking and abandoned. Exploded and sank 36.39N 8.3W, some sixty miles off Cape Vincent (voyage: Bremen/Civitavecchia – steel products).

1099   *Florian* 3,174 gt, 358.8 ft (oa), 345.7 ft × 50 ft.
Engines: T3cyl and LP turbine.
Launched: 26.1.1940.
Completed: 4.1940 for Ellerman & Papayanni Lines Ltd.
20.1.1941: Sunk by submarine (*U.94*) torpedo in North Atlantic, approx. 300 miles NW of Hebrides, 61.00N 12.00W (voyage: Oban/New York).

1100   *Industria* 4,861 gt, 431.5 ft (oa), 416 ft × 56 ft.
Engines: T3cyl.
Launched: 23.3.1940.
Completed: 5.1940 for Metcalfe Shipping Co. Ltd. (Metcalfe, Son & Co. Ltd.).
5.5.1941: Damaged by aircraft bombing at Liverpool. Repaired.
1957: *Teresa* (Socoa Shipping Co. Ltd. (R. de la Sota Jr., France)).
8.11.1968: Arrived Hirao for breaking up.

1101   *Cape Breton* 6,044 gt, 448.2 ft (oa), 432 ft × 57.1 ft. Engines: T3cyl.
Launched: 8.5.1940.
Completed: 7.1940 for Bowring SS Co. Ltd. (C. T. Bowring & Co. Ltd.).
5.5.1941: Bombed and damaged at Belfast; grounded. Refloated and repaired.
24.12.1962: Arrived Bo'ness for breaking up.

1102   *Itola* 6,793 gt, 442.8 ft (oa), 426.8 ft × 57.6 ft.
Engines: T3cyl and LP turbine.
Launched: 21.5.1940.
Completed: 7.1940 for British India SN Co. Ltd.
1958: *Pakistan Promoter* (Karachi SN Co. Ltd.).
3.1967: Scrapped Karachi.

1103   *Itaura* 6,793 gt. Details as Yard No. 1102.
Launched: 6.7.1940.
Completed: 10.1940 for British India SN Co. Ltd.
1959: *Jahangirabad* (Pakistan SN Co. Ltd., Chittagong).
1965: (East Bengal SS Co. Ltd., Karachi).
5.1968: Scrapped Karachi.

1104   *Duke of Sparta* 5,397 gt, 457.5 ft (oa), 441 ft × 57.8 ft. Engines: T3cyl.
Launched: 9.7.1940.

Completed: 10.1940 for Trent Maritime Co. Ltd. (S. Livanos & Co. Ltd., London).
1951: *Aquila* (Ragruppamento Armatori Fratelli Grimaldi, Italy).
28.4.1958: Bombed by Indonesian rebel aircraft while lying off Amboina Harbour, Moluccas, Eastern Indonesia, waiting to load copra for Copenhagen. Extensively damaged: Abandoned.
1.5.1958: Bombed again, and
27.5.1958: Sank, Total loss.

1105   *Ismaila* 6,793 gt. Details as Yard No. 1102.
Launched: 3.9.1940.
Completed: 12.1940 for British India SN Co. Ltd.
1958: *Safina-E-Jamhooriyat* (Pan-Islamic SS Co. Ltd., Karachi).
4.11.1966: Arrived Karachi for breaking up.

1106   *Ikauna* 6,793 gt. Details as Yard No. 1102.
Launched: 30.11.1940.
Completed: 3.1941 for British India SN Co. Ltd.
1958: *Fatehabad* (Pakistan SN Co. Ltd., Chittagong).
1965: (East Bengal SS Co. Ltd., Karachi).
5.1968: Scrapped Gadani Beach, Pakistan.

1139   *Nordeflinge* 2,873 gt, 327.9 ft (oa), 315.5 ft × 46.5 ft. Engines: T3cyl. 'Scandinavian'-type.
Launched: 25.8.1942.
Completed: 10.1942 for Constants Ltd., Cardiff.
30.5.1944: Bombed and sunk by German aircraft operating from Southern France, 37.02N 03.47E whilst in convoy UGS 42 (USA–Gibraltar).

1158   *Dallas City* 7,079 gt, 446.7 ft (oa), 431.5 ft × 56 ft. Engines: T3cyl.
Launched: 29.12.1943.
Completed: 2.1944 for Leeds Shipping Co. Ltd. (Sir Wm. Reardon Smith & Son Ltd.).
1956: *Hangklip* (South African Railways & Harbours Administration).
1966: *Jeannie K* (First Freighters (Pty.) Ltd., Johannesburg).
15.11.1967: Arrived Shodoshima for breaking up.

1175   *Pachumba* 7,283 gt, 447.8 ft (oa), 431.3 ft × 56.2 ft. Engines: T3cyl.
Launched: 15.3.1945.
Completed: 5.1945 for British India SN Co. Ltd.
1961: *Sun Pink* (Wing Tak SS Co. (Panama) S.A., (Great East Asia Shipping Co., Hong Kong)).
1966: *Crystal* (Crystal Maritime (Panama) S.A., Hong Kong).
28.4.1970: Arrived Hirao for breaking up.

1183   *Cattaro* 2,883 gt, 355.5 ft (oa), 342.2 ft × 48.1 ft. Engines: T3cyl.
Launched: 25.8.1945.
Completed: 11.1945 for Ellerman's Wilson Line Ltd.

1966: *Vrachos* (Manovas Shipping Co. S.A. (Panama) (Roussos Bros., Greece)).
10.1.1971: Fire in engine room while at Galatz, Romania, Beached in Sulina Canal. Later sold locally for scrapping to meet Romanian Government salvage claim.

1185 *Foochow* 3,279 gt, 328.5 ft (oa), 315 ft × 47 ft. Engines: T3cyl.
Launched: 24.8.1945.
Completed: 12.1945 for China Navigation Co. Ltd., London.
1965: *Eternity* (Prosperity SS Co. Panama).
12.3.1970: Listed in heavy weather, capsized and sank off Tan-Kan Island, south of Hong Kong, 22.2N 114.17E (Phnom Penh/Hong Kong – buffalo and rice).

1186 *Fengtien* 3,279 gt. Details as Yard No. 1185.
Launched: 20.11.1945.
Completed: 2.1946 for China Navigation Co. Ltd., London.
1965: *Chung Lien* (Chung Lien Nav. Co. (Great Pacific Navigation Co. Ltd., Taiwan)).
1968: Renamed *Tung Hong No. 1*.
9.1969: Scrapped Kaohsiung.

1187 *Fukien* 3,279 gt. Details as Yard No. 1185.
Launched: 23.10.1945.
Completed: 1.1946 for China Navigation Co. Ltd., London.
1965: *Felicity* (Prosperity SS Co., Taiwan (Panama flag)).
5.1975: Scrapped Whampoa.

1188 *Rinaldo* 2,957 gt, 355.5 ft (oa), 342 ft × 50 ft. Engines: T3cyl.
Launched: 6.1946.
Completed: 11.1946 for Ellerman's Wilson Line Ltd.
1967: *Emerald* (United Maritime Lines Corp. (M. Scufalos, Greece)).
1968: (4,119 gt).
1970: (C. A. Athanassiades, Greece).
1974: *Midas* (Dag Hope Shipping Co., Cyprus).
10.1974: Scrapped Split.

1189 *Ariosto* 2,208 gt, 306.7 ft (oa), 295.2 ft × 44.2 ft. Engines: T3cyl.
Launched: 5.3.1946.

Completed: 6.1946 for Ellerman's Wilson Line Ltd.
1967: Scrapped Tamise.

1190 *Albano* 2,239 gt, 308.5 ft (oa), 295 ft × 46.2 ft. Engines: T3cyl.
Launched: 30.7.1946.
Completed: 1.1947 for Ellerman's Wilson Line Ltd.
1962: *Magister* (Cayman Islands Shipping Co. Ltd. (J. Webster & Sons Ltd., Jamaica)).
1971: (Lewis Lines Ltd., Jamaica).
1973: *Peten* (Amagua Line Armadora Maritime, Guatemala).
6.11.1974: Arrived Karachi for breaking up.

1191 *Malmo* 1,779 gt, 297 ft (oa), 283.8 ft × 42.2 ft. Engines: T3cyl.
Launched: 31.5.1946.
Completed: 9.1946 for Ellerman's Wilson Line Ltd.
1965: *Akti* (Lisboa Cia. Nav., Panama (Greek flag)).
16.10.1965: On fire in hold, off Nieuwe Waterweg, Holland (voyage: Assab/Copenhagen – fish meal and maize cakes). Towed into Europoort and beached in the Elbehaven.
17.10.1965: Fire extinguished: later capsized.
6.10.1966: Righted; constructive total loss; sold and
7.11.1966: Arrived Rotterdam for breaking up.

1192 *Livorno* 2,957 gt. Details as Yard No. 1188.
Launched: 28.8.1946.
Completed: 12.1946 for Ellerman's Wilson Line Ltd.
1967: *Antonis* (Margerencia Cia. Nav. S.A., Panama) (J. A. Livanos, Greece).
4.1973: Scrapped Spezia.

1193 *Urlana* 6,835 gt. Details as Yard No. 1106.
Launched: 18.2.1946.
Completed: 5.1946 for British India SN Co. Ltd.
13.10.1962: Arrived Osaka for breaking up.

1194 *Umaria* 6,835 gt. Details as Yard No. 1106.
Launched: 3.4.1946.
Completed: 10.1946 for British India SN Co. Ltd.
1964: *Amonea* (Cia. Nav. Pearl S.A., Panama (Teh Hu SS Co., Hong Kong).
5.9.1964: Broke from moorings at Hong Kong during typhoon 'Ruby'; in collision with other vessels, grounded on Datum Rocks.
11.10.1964: Refloated, but 14.10.1964: Grounded again during typhoon 'Dot'. Stern submerged, flooded and wrecked. Total loss.

Built by Greenock Dockyard Co. Ltd., Greenock

445   *Empire Rainbow* 6,942 gt, 'X'-type. 447.2 ft (oa), 432 ft × 56.2 ft. Engines: Oil.
Launched: 27.12.1940.
Completed: 5.1941.
26.7.1942: Sunk by submarine (*U.607*) torpedo, 47.08N 42.57W, 300 miles (approx) East of Cape Race whilst in convoy ON 113 (U.K.—U.S.A.).

446   *Empire Ray* 6,919 gt. Details as Yard No. 445.
Launched: 25.3.1941.
Completed: 6.1941.
1945: *King Alfred* (King Line Ltd.).
16.3.1963: Arrived Hamburg for breaking up.

447   *Empire Stanley* 6,942 gt. Details as Yard No. 445.
Launched: 15.7.1941.
Completed: 9.1941.
17.8.1943: Sunk by submarine (*U.197*) torpedo,

27.08S 48.15E, South of Madagascar (voyage Durban/Aden).

448   *Empire Kingsley* 6,996 gt. 'Y'-type. 448 ft (oa), 432 ft × 56 ft. Engines: T3cyl.
Launched: 19.9.1941.
Completed: 12.1941.
22.3.1945: Sunk by submarine (*U.315*) torpedo, 50.08N 05.51W, off Coast of Cornwall (voyage: Ghent/Manchester – ballast).

449   *Empire Homer* 6,996 gt. Details as Yard No. 448.
Launched: 19.11.1941.
Completed: 12.1941.
15.1.1942: Blown ashore on Sandray Island, South of Barra, Outer Hebrides. Completely tidal; broke in two; abandoned. Total loss (voyage: Greenock/New York – ballast).

In 1918 the Clan Line, of Cayzer, Irvine & Co. Ltd. established in 1877, acquired control of Turnbull, Martin & Co.'s Scottish Shire Line, prominent in the frozen meat trade, thereby adding to the activities of the Clan Group in the Australian trade. In the same year they acquired the Houston Line of Steamers whose British & South American SN Co. Ltd., worked in the United States, South America and South African trades. The combined fleets then totalled some fifty ships and in order to exercise more control in the building of its own vessels, the Clan Line Board – Cayzer, Irvine & Co. Ltd. – purchased a large proportion of the shares of the Greenock Dockyard Co. Ltd. and practically all new shipbuilding orders were placed with them.

When war began in 1939 the Clan Line was claimed to be the world's biggest purely cargo concern. Some Clan ships were completed in the early war years and then the Greenock Dockyard Company received Government orders for a number of general cargo ships and three refrigerated vessels. Four heavy-lift 'Empire' ships were also built in the latter years of the war. Ten 'Clan' ships were also built during hostilities.

Three ships building at Greenock Dockyard were taken over before completion and converted for naval work. Yard No. 444, which became an aircraft transport; *Clan Davidson*, which was used as a mother ship for midget submarines, and *Clan Lamont*, which was completed as an Infantry Landing Ship.

At the end of the war there were four berths at the Cartsdyke Shipyard, Greenock, with a capability of building ships to 600 ft in length.

MERCHANT SHIPS BUILT UNDER PRIVATE CONTRACT OR LICENCE

436   *Clan MacDonald* 9,653 gt, 503.3 ft (oa), 481.9 ft × 64.7 ft. Engines: Oil. Twin screws.
Launched: 15.8.1939.
Completed: 12.1939 for Clan Line Steamers Ltd.
1960: (Houston Line Ltd.) (8,141 gt.).
6.8.1970: Arrived Shanghai for breaking up.

437   *Lanarkshire* 8,167 gt. Details as Yard No. 436 but Engines: six steam turbines.
Launched: 30.11.1939.
Completed: 4.1940 for Scottish Shire Line Ltd.
1959: *Umgazi* (Bullard, King & Co. Ltd.).
1960: *Grysbok* (Springbok Shipping Co. Ltd., South Africa).

1961: *South African Farmer* (Safmarine).
20.1.1963: Arrived Aioi for breaking up.

438 *Clan Lamont* 7,132 gt, 487.7 ft (oa),
463.7 ft × 63 ft. Engines: T6cyl and LP turbine. Twin screws.
Launched: 23.3.1939.
Completed: 5.1939 for Clan Line Steamers Ltd.
1942: Requisitioned by the Admiralty and converted to an Infantry Landing Ship to carry 800 personnel and twenty landing craft: Renamed *Lamont*.
1945: Renamed *Ardpatrick*.
1946: *Clan Lamont* (Clan Line Steamers Ltd.).
1961: (King Line Ltd.).
31.8.1961: Arrived Mihara for breaking up.

444 (Laid down as) *Clan Brodie* 7,473 gt. Details as Yard No. 438 but Engines: T6cyl.
Launched: 1.10.1940. Requisitioned by the Admiralty for conversion to an Aircraft Transport.
Completed: 10.1941 as *Athene* to carry forty aircraft.
1946: *Clan Brodie* (Clan Line Steamers Ltd.).
19.7.1963: Arrived Hong Kong for breaking up.

452 (Laid down as) *Clan Campbell*. Details as yard No. 438.
Acquired by Admiralty whilst still on stocks, and: Launched as *Bonaventure*: 27.10.1942
Completed as H.M.S. *Bonaventure*, a depot ship for midget submarines ('X' craft) 1.1943: Fitted with heavy derricks for hoisting submarines stowed on deck.
1948: *Clan Davidson* (8,047 gt) (Clan Line Steamers Ltd.).
1961: (King Line Ltd.).
25.12.1961: Arrived Hong Kong for breaking up.

453 *Clan Campbell* 7,804 gt. Details as Yard No. 438.
Launched: 23.2.1943.
Completed: 5.1943 for Clan Line Steamers Ltd.
27.9.1961: Arrived Hong Kong for breaking up.

454 *Clan Urquhart* 9,726 gt, 500.5 ft (oa),
477 ft × 65.8 ft. Engines: T6cyl and LP turbine. Twin screws.
Launched: 30.6.1943.
Completed: 1.1944 for Clan Line Steamers Ltd.
1960: (Houston Line Ltd.).
8.4.1966: Arrived Kaohsiung for breaking up.

455 *Clan MacDougall* 9,710 gt, 500.5 ft (oa),
482 ft × 64.7 ft. Engines: Oil. Twin screws.
Launched: 10.11.1943.
Completed: 5.1944 for Clan Line Steamers Ltd.
1963: (Houston Line Ltd.).
1971: *Vrysi* (Castle Shipping Co. Ltd., Cyprus).
12.1971: Scrapped Kaohsiung.

456 *Clan Chattan* 9,545 gt. Details as Yard No. 438.
Launched: 9.3.1944.
Completed: 6.1944 for Clan Line Steamers Ltd.
14.5.1962: Arrived Hong Kong for breaking up.

457 *Clan Chisholm* 9,581 gt. Details as Yard No. 438.
Launched: 23.6.1944.
Completed: 10.1944 for Clan Line Steamers Ltd.
7.5.1962: Fire in holds (voyage: Glasgow/Dar es Salaam, with general cargo, explosives and ammunition)
8.5.1962: Arrived Mombasa.
10.5.1962: Fire extinguished. Deck, coamings, beams and bulkheads buckled. Repairs uneconomic.
19.8.1962: Arrived Hong Kong for scrapping; moored in harbour.
25.8.1962: Leaking, listed and heeled over. Pumped out, righted and towed to breaking-up berth in Junk Bay, Hong Kong.

459 *Clan Cumming* 7,812 gt, 486.5 ft (oa),
463.8 ft × 63 ft. Engines: T6cyl and LP turbine. Twin screws.
Launched: 3.5.1946.
Completed: 8.1946 for Clan Line Steamers Ltd.
18.10.1962: Arrived Vigo for breaking up.

Built by William Hamilton & Co. Ltd., Port Glasgow

458 *Empire Trumpet* 7,059 gt. 'Y4'-type. 447.5 ft (oa), 432.7 ft × 56.2 ft. Engines: T3cyl.
Launched: 9.3.1943.
Completed: 4.1943.
1946: *Naturalist* (T. & J. Harrison).
1959: *Persian Cyrus* (Iranian Lloyd Co. Ltd., Iran).
1965: *Hamadan* (Iranian Shipping Lines, S.A.).
1966: *Koula F* (P. J. Frangoulis & A. I. Cliafas, Greece).

25.7.1966: Aground near Qais Island, Persian Gulf. Holed and abandoned. Total loss (voyage: Bandar Shapur/Greece).

459 *Empire Daring* 7,059 gt. Details as Yard No. 458.
Launched: 29.6.1943.
Completed: 8.1943.
1946: *Marietta* (Leith Hill Shipping Co. Ltd. (Counties

Ship Management Ltd., London)).
1948: (Leith Hill Shipping Co. Ltd. (Phocean Ship Agency Ltd., London)).
1958: (Bury Hill Shipping Co. (Phocean Ship Agency Ltd., London)).
1959: Scrapped Split.

462 *Empire Call* 7,067 gt. Details as Yard No. 458.
Launched: 10.2.1944.
Completed: 4.1944.
1945: *Ingenieur General Haarbleicher* (Government of France).
21.11.1945: Ashore on Stromboli Island, Sicily. Abandoned; broke in two. Total loss (voyage: Marseilles/Saigon – explosives).

463 *Empire Swordsman* 7,067 gt. Details as Yard No. 458.
Launched: 11.5.1944.
Completed: 7.1944.
1948: *Granrock* (Goulandris Bros. Ltd., London).
1950: *Benloyal* (Ben Line Steamers Ltd.).
1951: *Loch Ranza* (Glasgow United Shipping Co. Ltd. (Maclay & McIntyre Ltd.)).

1960: *Tertric* (Trico Corp., S.A., Lebanon (V. Tricoglu, London)).
26.4.1968: Arrived Kaohsiung for breaking up.

465 *Empire Kumasi* 7,021 gt. 'Y'-type. 447.8 ft (oa), 432.7 ft × 56.2 ft. Engines: T3cyl.
Launched: 30.10.1944.
Completed: 12.1944.
1947: *Ixia* (Stag Line Ltd. (J. Robinson & Sons)).
1951: *Empire Trader* (Century Shipping Corp., Liberia (Southern Star Shipping Co. Inc., New York)).
1954: *North River* (Cia. Atlantica Pacifica S.A. (Tidewater Commercial Co. Inc., Baltimore)).
31.1.1960: Arrived Savona for breaking up, but: later scrapped at Spezia.

466 *Empire Goodwin* 7,179 gt. Details as Yard No. 465.
Launched: 6.8.1945.
Completed: 12.1945.
1947: *Garvelpark* (Denholm Line Steamers Ltd. (J. & J. Denholm Ltd.)).
1958: *Ocean Ensign* (Trans Oceanic SS Co. Ltd., Pakistan).
1.1971: Scrapped Gadani Beach, Karachi.

The Hamilton story began in 1867 when William and John Hamilton were invited to complete two ships being built at the Bay Yard, Port Glasgow, owned by the Port Glasgow Harbour Trust.

In 1871 the Hamiltons then opened their own yard at Port Glasgow and two years later the old, derelict Newark Yard of John Reid was acquired, all the company's building activities being moved to the new site. In 1891 Reid's Glen Yard was sold to Hamiltons.

These early years of the company saw the building of a number of sailing ships, the names of which are prominent in maritime history. The *Grace Harwar*, 1,816 gt and 266 ft in length was built in 1889 and later joined Gustaf Erikson's grain fleet under the Finnish flag. The last of the single-rigged ships, she was broken up at Charlestown, Fife, in 1935. In 1904 two four-masted barques, *Kurt* and *Hans*, 3,100 gt were completed for German owners. The *Kurt* later became the *Moshulu* and joined Erikson's fleet in 1935. She survived the war and in 1974 arrived at Philadelphia to become a tourist attraction. The *Hans* became the *Mary Dollar*, of Robert Dollar & Co. Inc., San Francisco after the Great War, was relegated to a gambling ship named *Tango* in 1934, became a six-masted schooner in 1943 and two years later was registered at Lourenço Marques as the *Cidade do Porto*.

Construction during the Great War included merchant vessels for private account, standard-type tankers for the Shipping Controller – delivered in 1919 – more than a dozen warships, mostly sloops, and thirty-six 'X' lighters for the War Office, being landing craft known as 'Beetles'. (See shipyard notes, James Pollock & Sons.)

In 1919 William Hamilton finished working and the shareholding subsequently became almost halved between Lithgows and the old-established shipowners T. & J. Brocklebank Ltd. From then on the yard lists contained many Brocklebank ships and with the delivery of the *Mathura* in 1960 thirty-one cargo ships had been built by Hamilton for T. & J. Brocklebank Ltd.

Between the wars, despite the years of depression, the building list reached Yard No. 438, the *Martand*, for Brocklebanks, delivered in June 1939, although Yard No. 437, the *Saint Bernard*, for Mitchell, Cotts & Company, was not delivered until the early days of World War II.

In the war years, apart from Government orders for 'Y'-type 'Empire' ships, William Hamilton & Company built a number of general cargo ships for the private sector. Seven of them were for T.

& J. Brocklebank Ltd. In June 1941 a half-ship (Yard No. 453) was built, this being a new forepart for Furness Withy's tanker *Imperial Transport* (1931, 8,022 gt), the stern part of which had been brought home by her crew after the ship had been torpedoed and broke in two, in the Atlantic.

In the early 1960s agreement was reached for the Glen Yard of Wm. Hamilton & Co. Ltd. to be joined with the East yard of Lithgows Ltd., during the reconstruction and consolidation of the yards in the Lithgow Group which had a controlling interest in the Hamilton concern.

The last ship built by Hamilton was the *Treneglos* (Yard No. 527), a 9,976 gt motorship launched for the Hain SS Company, but completed in August 1963 for the New Zealand Shipping Co. Ltd. However, the last ship to be launched from the Glen Yard was the *Freetown*, on 19 September 1963, under the Lithgow Yard No. 1149. A motorship of 7,689 gt, she was completed for Elder, Dempster Lines in February 1964. After that the slipways were replaced by a new platers' shop for the larger yard, resulting from the merger of the former Hamilton Yard and the adjacent East Yard.

MERCHANT SHIPS BUILT UNDER PRIVATE CONTRACT OR LICENCE

437 *Saint Bernard* 5,183 gt, 447.3 ft (oa),
432.1 ft × 56.2 ft. Engines: T3cyl.
Launched: 3.8.1939.
Completed: 9.1939 for The Saint Line Ltd. (Mitchell, Cotts & Co. Ltd., London).
1956: *Jean Marie* (Soc. Commerciale Antoine Vloeberghs S.A., Antwerp).
1962: *Aristos* (Argo Cia. Maritima S.A., Panama (D. Lecanides, Greece)).
1962: (Argo Shipping Co., S.A. (G. Dracopoulos, Greece)).
28.8.1967: Collision in fog with *Linde* (1965, 13,882 gt). Sank sixteen miles from Beachy Head, Sussex, 50.30N 00.00 long. (voyage: Antwerp/Piraeus).

439 *Marietta E* 7,628 gt, 434.5 ft (oa),
420.8 ft × 60.4 ft. Engines: T3cyl.
Launched: 10.4.1940.
Completed: 6.1940 for Leith Hill Shipping Co. Ltd. (Counties Ship Management Co. Ltd.).
4.3.1943: Sunk by submarine (*U.160*) torpedo, south of Durban, 31.49S 31.11E in convoy DN21 (voyage Durban/Aden–Alexandria).

440 *Lulworth Hill* 7,628 gt. Details as Yard No. 439.
Launched: 24.6.1940.
Completed: 9.1940 for Dorset SS Co. Ltd. (Counties Ship Management Co. Ltd.).
19.3.1943: Sunk by Italian submarine (*Da Vinci*) torpedo in South Atlantic, 10.10S 01.00E (voyage Mauritius/Liverpool – sugar and rum).

441 *Kingston Hill* 7,628 gt. Details as Yard No. 439.
Launched: 17.10.1940.
Completed: 12.1940 for Putney Hill SS Co. Ltd. (Counties Ship Management Co. Ltd.).
22.2.1941: Damaged by air attack northwest of Hebrides. Flooded, abandoned. Taken in tow, and:

25.2.1941: Arrived Loch Ewe. Towed to Glasgow and repaired.
7.6.1941: Sunk by submarine (*U.38*) torpedo in Atlantic, southwest of Cape Verde Islands, 09.35N 29.40W (voyage Cardiff/Alexandria – coal and general).

446 *Michael E* 7,628 gt. Details as Yard No. 439.
Launched: 13.2.1941.
Completed: 5.1941 for Bury Hill Shipping Co. Ltd. (Counties Ship Management Co. Ltd.).
2.6.1941: Sunk by submarine (*U.108*) torpedo in North Atlantic, 48.50N 29.00W.

Note: The above vessel commenced her maiden voyage on 27 May 1941 – the first CAM-ship to put to sea. There was no necessity to launch her plane in the North Atlantic danger zone and she was sunk when only six days out.

447 *Manaar* 8,007 gt, 494.7 ft (oa),
475.7 ft × 62.7 ft. Engines: 3 steam turbines.
Launched: 6.1.1942.
Completed: 4.1942 for T. & J. Brocklebank Ltd.
18.4.1943: Sunk by Italian submarine (*Da Vinci*) torpedo south east of Durban, 30.59S 33.00E.

448 *Primrose Hill* 7,628 gt. Details as Yard No. 439.
Launched: 25.6.1941.
Completed: 9.1941 for Putney Hill SS Co. (Counties Ship Management Co. Ltd.).
29.10.1942: Sunk by submarine (*UD 5*) torpedo, north west of Cape Verde Islands, 18.58N 28.40W.

454 *Matheran* 8,051 gt. Details as Yard No. 447.
Launched: 28.5.1942.
Completed: 9.1942 for T. & J. Brocklebank Ltd.
20.5.1963: Arrived Osaka for breaking up.

455 *Malakand* 8,078 gt. Details as Yard No. 447.
Launched: 9.9.1942.

Completed: 12.1942 for T. & J. Brocklebank Ltd.
13.12.1966: Arrived Kaohsiung for breaking up.

457   *Mahanada* 8,489 gt, 505 ft (oa),
485.9 ft × 62.7 ft. Engines: three steam turbines.
Launched: 19.8.1943.
Completed: 12.1943 for T. & J. Brocklebank Ltd.
1967: *Corona* (Sincere Navigation Co. Inc., Panama
(Gibson Shipping Co. Inc.)).
1967: (Progessive Mariners S.A., Panama (W. H. C.
Tang, Hong Kong)).
3.1968: Scrapped Kaohsiung.

460   *Magdapur* 8,561 gt. Details as Yard No. 457,
but Engines: two steam turbines.
Launched: 3.8.1944.
Completed: 2.1945 for T. & J. Brocklebank Ltd.
1969: *Magda* (Cia. Nav. Embajada S.A.) for delivery
voyage to shipbreakers, and, 4.1970: Scrapped
Whampoa.

461   *Manipur* 8,569 gt. Details as Yard No. 460.
Launched: 6.1945.
Completed: 12.1945 for T. & J. Brocklebank Ltd.
6.1.1967: Arrived Whampoa for breaking up.

464   *Maidan* 8,566 gt. Details as Yard No. 460.
Launched: 21.3.1946.
Completed: 8.1946 for T. & J. Brocklebank Ltd.
1969: *Pretty* (Cia. Nav. Pretty S.A., Cyprus (Troodos
Shipping & Trading Ltd., London)).
1972: *Taighetos* (Cia. Nav. Witty S.A., Cyprus).
28.8.1972: Arrived Kaohsiung for breaking up.

468   *Mahronda* 8,537 gt. Details as Yard No. 460.
Launched: 10.10.1946.
Completed: 3.1947 for T. & J. Brocklebank Ltd.
1969: *Lucky* (Cia. Nav. Gloriath, Cyprus (Troodos
Shipping & Trading Ltd., London)).
14.5.1970: Cargo on fire whilst discharging at
Rotterdam, on voyage from Indonesia with copra.
Fire later extinguished, but ship badly damaged.
17.12.1970: Arrived Split for breaking up.

Built by Harland & Wolff Ltd., Queen's Island, Belfast

1118   *Empire Sidney* 6,904 gt. 'X'-type. 447 ft (oa),
433 ft × 56 ft. Engines: Oil.
Launched: 4.9.1941.
Completed: 5.1942.
1943: *Van der Helst* (Government of the Netherlands).
1946: *Tjimenteng* (Koninklijke Java-China-Japan Line,
Holland).
1963: *Diamandis* (Diamandis Eidiki Naftiliaki Eteria
(A. Halcoussis & Co., Greece).
20.1.1970: Arrived Carthagena for breaking up.

1119   *Empire Splendour* 7,335 gt. 'D'-type. 448.5 ft
(oa), 431.4 ft × 57.4 ft. Engines: Oil.
Launched: 18.12.1941.
Completed: 9.1942.
1946: *Medon* (Ocean SS Co. Ltd. (A. Holt & Co.
Ltd.)).
1963: *Tina* (Olistim Navigation Co. S.A., Greece).
1.1970: Scrapped Shanghai.

1120   *Empire Strength* 7,355 gt. Details as Yard No.
1119.
Launched: 28.5.1942.
Completed: 12.1942.
1946: *Saxon Star* (Blue Star Line Ltd.).
1961: *Redbrook* (D. L. Street Ltd., Cardiff).
1965: *E. Evangelia* (Hegif Cia. Nav. S.A. (H.
Embiricos, Greece)).
15.10.1968: Aground on rocks off Constantza,
43.58N 28.39E. Refloating attempts unsuccessful.

Constructive total loss (voyage: Rijeka/Constantza –
ballast).

1125   *Empire Castle* 7,356 gt. Details as Yard No.
1119.
Launched: 27.8.1942.
Completed: 1.1943.
1946: *Gothic Star* (Blue Star Line Ltd.).
1947: Renamed *Nelson Star*.
1958: Renamed *Patagonia Star*.
1961: *Eirini* (Gregory Maritime Ltd. (G. A.
Theodorou & Sons Ltd., London)).
1970: *Byzantum* (Angila Shipping Co. Ltd., Cyprus
(G. A. Theodorou & Sons Ltd., London)).
29.9.1970: Put into Gibraltar with machinery damage
(voyage: Algeria/China – phosphate). Not repaired:
laid up.
6.2.1971: Caught fire whilst laid up; accommodation
and bridge deck gutted. Sold, and
8.7.1971: Arrived Malaga for breaking up.

1165   *Empire Grange* 6,981 gt. Details as Yard No.
1118.
Launched: 23.9.1942.
Completed: 3.1943.
1946: *King Robert* (King Line Ltd. (Dodd, Thomson
& Co. Ltd.)).
1961: *Ardgem* (Mullion & Co. Ltd., Hong Kong).
1967: *Kelso* (Kelso Shipping Co. Ltd., Gibraltar
(Mullion & Co. Ltd., Hong Kong).
2.9.1969: Arrived Kaohsiung for breaking up.

1219 *Empire Outpost* 6,978 gt. Details as Yard No. 1118.
Launched: 31.5.1943.
Completed: 8.1943.
1945: *Pilote Garnier* (Government of France).
1960: *Kyra Hariklia* (Cia. Nav. Olisman Ltda (A. Frangistas & S. Manessis, Greece)).
1962: (Cia. Nav. Olisfan S.A., Panama (Franco Shipping Co. Ltd., Greece)).
7.2.1966: Grounded outside Malmo, Sweden (voyage: Cuba/Malmo – sugar).
11.2.1966: Refloated, towed in; discharged.
22.2.1966: Proceeded Hamburg: drydocked; entire bottom buckled and stern gear smashed. Repairs uneconomic. Sold, and
4.1966: Scrapped Hamburg.

1234 *Empire Rangoon* 7,028 gt. Details as Yard No. 1118.
Launched: 25.1.1944.

Completed: 5.1944.
1947: *Homer City* (Reardon Smith Line Ltd. (Sir Wm. Reardon Smith & Sons Ltd.)).
1960: *Grosvenor Mariner* (Grosvenor Shipping Co. Ltd., London (Mollers Ltd., Hong Kong)).
1966: *Red Sea* (Tat On Shipping & Enterprise Co. Ltd. (Yick Fung Shipping & Enterprise Co. Ltd., Hong Kong)).
17.8.1971: Driven aground on Lantau Island, Hong Kong by typhoon 'Rose'. Refloated, and
9.1971: Scrapped Hong Kong.

1276 *Empire Falkland* 6,987 gt. Details as Yard No. 1118.
Launched: 2.9.1944.
Completed: 2.1945.
1946: *Stirlingshire* (Scottish Shire Line Ltd. (Turnbull, Martin & Co. Ltd., Glasgow)).
1960: (Houston Line Ltd.).
2.9.1966: Arrived Bruges for breaking up.

Belfast, a city since 1888, stands on the River Lagan where it enters Belfast Lough. In its history it has records of shipbuilding on the Lagan's shores which date back to the late 17th century. It has seen the formation and growth of a company that was to become one of the world's largest shipbuilders.

The origins of Harland & Wolff began in the mid-19th century when Robert Hickson commenced shipbuilding in a small yard on Queen's Island, his first vessel, the *Silistria* being launched in 1854 for Edward Bates of Liverpool. Later that year, Hickson recruited a new manager and from England's north-east arrived Edward Harland. The next move was for Harland to appoint an assistant and in 1857 Gustav Wilhelm Wolff, an engineer, joined the staff.

But Hickson was destined to build only eight ships before he was overcome by financial difficulties and in 1858 offered the shipyard at Queen's Island to Harland. It duly changed hands and then, in 1861, came under the Harland and Wolff partnership.

At the end of that decade orders came for five ships for the newly-formed Oceanic Steam Navigation Company, to sail under the White Star Line flag, beginning a connection that was to last some sixty-three years; through the *Teutonic* and *Majestic* era of the 1890s; the planned great trio *Olympic*, *Titanic* and *Britannic* of the early 20th century, to the motorships *Britannic* and *Georgic* of the early 1930s. The first of the giants was the *Olympic*, whose keel was laid on 16 December 1908 and which was launched on 20 October 1910, by which time the *Titanic*, laid down on 31 March 1909, was half-built. She was launched on 31 May 1911, on which day the *Olympic* was completed. The ill-fated *Titanic* began her maiden voyage from Southampton on 10 April 1912, never to return. Third of the planned trio was the *Britannic*, launched on 26 February 1914 and lost by mine on 21 November 1916 in the Aegean Sea whilst serving as a hospital ship. She had never sailed commercially.

By the 1870s the Harland & Wolff establishment had six slipways for launching into the Abercorn Basin and the next decade saw another four slips at the north end of the yard. In 1885, for political expediency, the firm was sold to become a limited company, Queen's Island Shipbuilding & Engineering Co. Ltd., changing again to Harland & Wolff Ltd., when political tension eased three years later.

The company instituted their Govan Yard at Glasgow in 1912 with the acquisition of the London & Glasgow Engineering & Iron Co. Ltd., Govan, and in 1916 also took over the old-established yard of Caird & Company, Greenock. With the surge of war work some orders were subcontracted in 1916 to A. & J. Inglis at Pointhouse and to D. & W. Henderson at Meadowside, on the Clyde, both companies being taken over by Harland & Wolff in 1919.

During the Great War, at Government request, Harland & Wolff and Hendersons designed 'A' and 'B'-type standard ships, the first two being laid down in February 1917. Many tramp steamers of the 'A' and 'B' types and, later, the 'N'-type, were built for the Ministry of Shipping, which came into being on 19 December 1916.

The late 1920s saw the start of the world trade depression and in September 1928 the old Caird yard at Greenock was closed down, the last ship, *Behar*, of the Hain SS Company Ltd., launched in August, being towed to Govan and completed in November. The deepening depression at the end of the decade saw Harland & Wolff in serious financial difficulties. Freight rates were at rock bottom, many slipways were closed, Cairds Greenock yard was sold and the yards at Belfast relegated to care and maintenance only. In 1935 the adjacent shipbuilding business of Workman, Clark was acquired by the National Shipbuilders' Security Ltd., founded for the elimination of surplus shipyards but, with a slow upturn in trade having begun, Harland & Wolff purchased Workman Clark's Victoria Shipyard and Engine works. A restyling of the Harland & Wolff yards was undertaken and when war began in 1939 the North Yard had become Queens Shipyard and the South yard, Abercorn Shipyard; Workman Clark's South Yard was Victoria Shipyard and their old East Yard become Musgrave Shipyard.

The war effort of Harland & Wolff Ltd. at their many yards and works was enormous, not only in naval and commercial shipbuilding and shiprepairing, but in war production of armaments, tanks, AA guns, aeroplane parts, gun-mountings etc. The group constructed 139 naval ships, 132 merchant ships and the number of ships taken in hand for repairs etc. at all establishments including the Clyde, Liverpool, London and Southampton totalled 22,271. Under the emergency conditions the peacetime workforce of the Group almost doubled, from 26,000 to 51,000. Naval construction included corvettes, minesweepers, frigates, landing craft etc. and as the slipways were much too large for these smaller types, some berths were adapted to take up to six keels at the same time. Great damage was done by bombing to the establishments at Belfast, Liverpool, London and Southampton and quite extensive damage to those on the Clyde.

The 'D'-type *Empire Splendour*, as Blue Funnel Line's *Medon*, with a deck cargo of railway rolling stock and a tug. (Harland & Wolff Ltd., Belfast, Yard No. 1119.)   *Skyfotos*

MERCHANT SHIPS BUILT UNDER PRIVATE CONTRACT OR LICENCE

1005 *Andes* 25,689 gt, 669 ft (oa), 630 ft × 83.3 ft.
Engines: Turbine. Twin screws.
Launched: 7.3.1939.
Completed: 9.1939 for Royal Mail Lines Ltd.

The maiden voyage of Royal Mail Line's passenger/cargo flagship *Andes*, from Southampton to the River Plate, was fixed for 26 September 1939, the centenary day of the Royal Charter incorporating the Royal Mail Steam Packet Company in 1839, but war intervened and instead the *Andes* was sent to the Holy Loch, in Scotland.

21.11.1939: Requisitioned as a troopship; and
9.12.1939: First voyage, from Liverpool to Halifax, N.S.
7.3.1947: Arrived Southampton on last trooping voyage; reconverted by Harland & Wolff, Belfast, to passenger liner status.
22.1.1948: First commercial voyage from Southampton to River Plate.
1960: Converted to a cruising ship.
7.5.1971: Arrived Ghent for breaking up.

1019 *Waiotira* 12,823 gt, 535.9 ft (oa),
516.9 ft × 70.4 ft. Engines. Oil. Twin screws.
Launched: 1.8.1939.
Completed: 11.1939 for Shaw, Savill & Albion Co. Ltd.
26.12.1940: Sunk by submarine (*U.95*) torpedo in north Atlantic, NW of Rockall, 58.05N 17.10W (voyage: Sydney, N.S.W./U.K.).

1025 *Pardo* 5,400 gt, 450.3 ft (oa),
433.3 ft × 61.3 ft. Engines: Oil. Twin screws.
Completed: 8.1940 for Royal Mail Lines Ltd.
1965: *Aristarchos* (Cia. Nav. Fortune Gate S.A. (S. Triandafyllakis, Greece)).
1966: (Cia. Nav. Fortune Gate S.A. (M. Karageorgis, Greece)).
30.5.1967: Arrived Kaohsiung for breaking up.

1026 *Potaro* 5,410 gt. Details as Yard No. 1025.
Launched: 4.9.1940.
Completed: 11.1940 for Royal Mail Lines Ltd.
14.6.1942: Damaged by aircraft bombs 450 miles east of Malta.
Reached port; repaired.
1965: *Ariptipos* (Cia. Nav. Ioannitsa S.A. (S. Triandafyllakis, Greece)).
1966: (Cia. Nav. Ioannitsa S.A. (M. Karageorgis, Greece)).
3.1970: Arrived Shanghai for breaking up.

1027 *Pampas* 5,415 gt. Details as Yard No. 1025.
Launched: 2.11.1940.
Completed: 1.1941 for Royal Mail Lines Ltd.

20.3.1942: Left Alexandria in convoy MW 10, for Malta.
23.3.1942: Arrived Valletta.
24.3.1942/20.4.1942: Subjected to continual bombing while discharging in Grand Harbour; grounded, and
20.4.1942: destroyed and sunk after heavy bombing raid. All told there were recorded eighteen hits on the ship. Of her 6,000-ton cargo, 3,500 tons were discharged.

1028 (Laid down as) *Pelotas* 5,419 gt. Details as Yard No. 1025.
Launched: 14.1.1941.
Completed: 4.1941 as *Palma* for Royal Mail Lines Ltd.
20.7.1941: Damaged by submarine (*U.95*) gunfire in north Atlantic, south-west of Ireland,
50.14N 17.53W. Slightly damaged, and
22.7.1941: Arrived Liverpool; repaired.
29.2.1944: Sunk by submarine (*U.183*) torpedo, south of Ceylon, 05.51N 79.58E (voyage: Liverpool/Calcutta).

1029 *Debrett* 6,244 gt, 456 ft (oa), 438.8 ft × 62.3 ft.
Engines: Oil.
Launched: 23.3.1940.
Completed: 5.1940 for Lamport & Holt Line Ltd.
1955: *Washington Star* (Blue Star Line charter).
1956: *Debrett* (Lamport & Holt Line Ltd.).
1964: Sold to Embajada Cia. Nav., S.A. Panama, renamed *Ambasciata* for delivery to shipbreakers.
28.12.1964: Arrived Osaka for breaking up.

1030 *Defoe* 8,462 gt. Details as Yard No. 1029.
Launched: 20.6.1940.
Completed: 8.1940 for Lamport & Holt Line Ltd.
24.9.1942: Explosion, on fire 600 miles WSW of Land's End, 52.11N 19.32W (voyage: Manchester/Famagusta – liquid chlorine in drums and aeroplane varnish). Bow as far aft as foremast blown off: remainder remained afloat, but abandoned due to chlorine gas.
26.9.1942: Sighted in position 51N 18.10W, but no further trace. Presumed sunk.

1034 *Araybank* 7,258 gt, 450.4 ft (oa),
432.2 ft × 57.3 ft. Engines: Oil.
Launched: 6.6.1940.
Completed: 10.1940 for Bank Line Ltd. (A. Weir & Co. Ltd.).
16.5.1941: Bombed and sunk by German aircraft whilst discharging military stores at Suda Bay, Crete.
1947: Wreck sold to A. Lauro, Italy. Salved and towed to Genoa for repair. Fitted with new oil engine, and

1948: Renamed *Napoli* (8,082 gt).
3.4.1971: Arrived Spezia for breaking up.

1035   *Shirrabank* 7,274 gt. Details as Yard No. 1034.
Launched: 20.7.1940.
Completed: 12.1940 for Bank Line Ltd. (A. Weir & Co. Ltd.).
17.9.1963: Arrived Hong Kong for breaking up.

1036   *Fanad Head* 5,038 gt, 424.5 ft (oa),
407.3 ft × 58.9 ft. Engines: T3cyl and LP turbine.
Launched: 3.9.1940.
Completed: 12.1940 for Ulster SS Co. Ltd. (G. Heyn & Sons Ltd.).
1961: *Bogota* (Haven Crest (Hong Kong) Ltd. (Wallem & Co. Ltd., Hong Kong)).
20.1.1964: Grounded Fehmarn Island, Baltic Sea (voyage: Gdansk/Chittagong – cement).
22.1.1964: Refloated, extensively damaged. Proceeded to Kiel. Temporarily repaired for completion of voyage, then
13.6.1964: Laid up Hong Kong.
5.9.1964: Broke from moorings in harbour, driven ashore on Lantao Island by typhoon 'Ruby'.
13.10.1964: Further damaged by typhoon 'Dot'.
26.10.1964: Refloated. Sold, and
3.1965: Scrapped Hong Kong.

1082   *Deseado* 9,630 gt, 468.9 ft (oa),
453.3 ft × 65.3 ft. Engines: Oil. Twin screws.
Launched: 17.3.1942.
Completed: 11.1942 for Royal Mail Lines Ltd.
2.1968: Scrapped Hamburg.

1091   (Intended name not known) 540 ft (oa),
510 ft × 70 ft.
Laid down: 5.8.1941 for Shaw, Savill & Albion Co. Ltd., as a refrigerated meat carrier of the modified 'Waimarama'-type.

Whilst still on the stocks, the hull was taken over by the Admiralty for completion as an aircraft carrier and launched as *Campania* on 17 June 1943, named after a ship of the 1914–1918 war which was the first vessel to carry an aeroplane. Completion date was 7 March 1944 and H.M.S. *Campania* began serving as an escort carrier, particularly on the munitions convoys to North Russia, in which her aircraft were involved with enemy raiders from the Norwegian airfields.

In October, while in convoy RA 60, her Swordfish planes sank submarine *U.922.* From 29 October 1944 to 6 November 1944, with a cruiser and twelve destroyers, she escorted two troopships carrying 11,000 Russian ex-P.O.W.s from the United Kingdom to Murmansk. On 13 December 1944 her aircraft sank the submarine *U.365.*

Placed in reserve when war ended, the *Campania* was withdrawn in 1950 to be refitted by Cammell Laird & Co. Ltd. as a floating exhibition ship of British Industry, Arts and Achievements, for the Festival of Britain, marking the centenary of the Great Exhibition of 1851, much of the exhibition being in the 300 ft hangar deck and on the flight deck. She visited ten ports around Britain's coastline, then

went back into reserve only to be refitted, again at Birkenhead, for transporting scientific equipment to the atomic weapons test at the Montebello islands site, 136 miles north of Onslow, off the north-west coast of Australia, on 3 October 1952, returning to reserve in December 1953.

In late 1955 she was towed from Sheerness to Blyth, where she arrived on 11 November for breaking up.

A twin screw motorship, the *Campania* was of 12,450 displacement tons.

1148   *Darro* 9,733 gt. Details as Yard No. 1082.
Launched: 21.11.1942.
Completed: 6.1943 for Royal Mail Lines Ltd.
1967: (Embajada Cia. Nav., S.A. Panama (Rethymnis & Kulukundis Ltd.)), renamed *Surrey* for delivery to shipbreakers.
12.1967: Arrived Kaohsiung, in tow, for breaking up.

1149   *Pampas* 8,244 gt. Details as Yard No. 1025.
Launched: 25.9.1943 as *Parramatta* for Royal Mail Lines Ltd. Requisitioned by the Admiralty and completed as *Pampas* (HQ Infantry Landing Ship (LSI (H)). Carried 650 personnel and 18 Landing Craft. Displacement 12,680 tons. Used as a troop transport to the Normandy beaches.
7.9.1944: Refitted for Far East service, renamed H.M.S. *Persimmon*.
7.1946: *Pampas* (Royal Mail Lines Ltd.).
1964: *Aristodimos* (Amigos Cia. Nav. S.A., Panama (S. Triandafyllakis, Greece).
1966: (Amigos Cia. Nav. S.A., Panama (M. Karageorgis, Greece)).
28.4.1967: Arrived Kaohsiung for breaking up.

1150   *Rowallan Castle* 7,950 gt, 474.2 ft (oa),
457.4 ft × 63.3 ft. Engines: Oil.
Launched: 23.12.1942.
Completed: 4.1943 for Union-Castle Mail SS Co. Ltd.
2.9.1971: Arrived Kaohsiung for breaking up.

1152   *Paraguay* 5,560 gt. Details as Yard No. 1025.
Launched: 8.2.1944.
Completed: 9.1944 for Royal Mail Lines Ltd.
1965: *Elire* (Mount Pleasant Cia. Nav. S.A., Panama (M. A. Karageorgis, Greece)).
25.6.1969: Arrived Shanghai for breaking up.

1156   *Samanco* 8,336 gt, 466.4 ft (oa),
448.2 ft × 62.8 ft. Engines: Oil.
Launched: 23.3.1943.
Completed: 8.1943 for Pacific SN Co. Ltd.
18.1.1945: Dragged anchor, grounded Belfast Lough. Broke back; flooded and tidal.
19.2.1945: Refloated, beached Ballyholme Bay.
10.4.1945: Towed Belfast, and
29.11.1945: Towed to Glasgow. Repaired (voyage: Liverpool/Calcutta – general).

1956: *Reichenfels* (6,263 gt) (Deutsche Damps. Gesell. Hansa, Bremen).
20.4.1962: Arrived Bilbao for breaking up.

1157 *Sarmiento* 8,335 gt. Details as Yard No. 1156.
Launched: 17.8.1943.
Completed: 10.1943 for Pacific SN Co. Ltd.
1967: *Monomachos* (Eagle Ocean Shipping Co. Ltd., Cyprus (G. Lemos Bros. & Co. Ltd., London)).
1969: *Gladiator* (Eagle Ocean Shipping Co. Ltd., Cyprus (Efploia Shipping Co., S.A., Greece)).
4.1971: Arrived Shanghai for breaking up.

1161 *Waiwera* 12,029 gt, 540.5 ft (oa),
520.8 ft × 70.4 ft. Engines: Oil. Twin screws.
Launched: 30.9.1943.
Completed: 10.1944 for Shaw, Savill & Albion Co. Ltd.
1967: *Julia* (Embajada Cia. Nav. S.A., Panama (Rethymnis & Kulukundis Ltd.)), renamed for delivery voyage to shipbreakers.
31.8.1968: Arrived Kaohsiung for breaking up.

1176 *Drina* 9,785 gt. Details as Yard No. 1082.
Launched: 30.12.1943.
Completed: 7.1944 for Royal Mail Lines Ltd.
1966: *Romanic* (Shaw, Savill & Albion Co. Ltd.).
14.7.1968. Arrived Kaohsiung for breaking up.

1177 *Durango* 9,801 gt. Details as Yard No. 1082.
Launched: 5.9.1944.
Completed: 12.1944 for Royal Mail Lines Ltd.
1966: *Ruthenic* (Shaw, Savill & Albion Co. Ltd.).
1967: (Embajada Cia. Nav. S.A., Panama (Rethymnis & Kulukundis Ltd., London)), renamed *Sussex* for delivery voyage to shipbreakers.
26.12.1967: Arrived Kaohsiung for breaking up.

In 1912 the Royal Mail Steam Packet Company added five new Belfast-built refrigerated steamers of the 'D'-class (*Darro*, *Demerara*, *Deseado*, *Desna* and *Drina*) to its fleet. Of some 11,500 tons, with accommodation for nearly 1,000 passengers and among the largest meat carriers of their day, they were placed on a new Intermediate service between Liverpool and the River Plate, complementing the main service operated by their Southampton-based 'A'-class ships. The *Drina* was torpedoed in 1917, the others lasted until the slump period of the 1930s.

Towards the end of World War II another generation of 'D'-class ships was built, also in Belfast. These were the (above) Yard Nos. 1082 (*Deseado*), 1148 (*Darro*), 1176 (*Drina*) and the *Durango* – Yard No. 1177. These vessels, too, gave service in the River Plate trade, but in 1966 the *Drina* and *Durango* became Shaw, Savill's *Romanic* and *Ruthenic*, on the run to the Antipodes. However, they did not last long, all four ships being broken up in 1968.

1178 *Richmond Castle* 7,971 gt. Details as Yard No. 1150.
Launched: 23.2.1944.
Completed: 9.1944 for Union-Castle Mail SS Co. Ltd.

27.8.1971: Arrived Shanghai for breaking up.

1181 *Devis* 8,148 gt. Details as Yard No. 1029.
Launched: 12.4.1944.
Completed: 8.1944 for Lamport & Holt Line Ltd.
1955: *Oakland Star* (Blue Star Line charter).
1956: *Devis* (Lamport & Holt Line Ltd.).
4.7.1962: Arrived Spezia for breaking up.

1182 *Defoe* 8,454 gt. Details as Yard No. 1029.
Launched: 28.2.1945.
Completed: 5.1945 for Lamport & Holt Line Ltd.
1954: *Geelong Star* (Blue Star Line charter).
1958: *Defoe* (Lamport & Holt Line Ltd.).
1966: *Argolis Star* (Astrofeliz Cia. Nav. S.A. (Phoenix Shipping Co. Ltd., London)).
1967: (Argolis Shipping Co. S.A., Greece).
29.10.1969: Arrived Shanghai for breaking up.

1187 *Roxburgh Castle* 8,003 gt. Details as Yard No. 1150.
Launched: 31.10.1944.
Completed: 2.1945 for Union-Castle Mail SS Co. Ltd.
19.7.1971: Arrived Shanghai for breaking up.

1192 *Santander* 6,648 gt. Details as Yard No. 1156.
Launched: 17.1.1946.
Completed: 5.1946 for Pacific SN Co. Ltd.
1967: *Navmachos* (Navmachos Shipping Co. of Cyprus (G. Lemos Bros. & Co. Ltd.)).
9.12.1971: Arrived Valencia for breaking up.

1193 *Salaverry* 6,647 gt. Details as Yard No. 1156.
Launched: 2.4.1946.
Completed: 8.1946 for Pacific SN Co. Ltd.
1967: *Pelias* (Detebe Cia. Nav. (Stravelakis Bros., Greece)).
12.12.1972: Sprang leak in heavy weather about 250 miles south-east of Durban; sank 31.15S 35.40E (approx.) (voyage: Maceio/Saigon – sugar).

In 1943 the Pacific Steam Navigation Company obtained a licence to build two ships and these were named *Samanco* and *Sarmiento*, each 6,400 gt and the first of the 'S'-class.

Just after the war these two were joined by another four similar ships, although slightly larger, *Santander* and *Salaverry* (1946), *Salinas* (1947) and *Salamanca* (1948). Of 10,000 tdw and with accommodation for twelve passengers, these 15½-knot ships were employed in the United Kingdom and Continent service to the West Coast of South America via Caribbean ports and the Panama Canal. All were built by Harland & Wolff Ltd., Belfast.

1277 *Riebeeck Castle* 8,342 gt. Details as Yard No. 1150.
Launched: 23.10.1945.
Completed: 3.1946 for Union-Castle Mail SS Co. Ltd.
2.9.1971: Arrived Kaohsiung for breaking up.

1278　*Rustenburg Castle* 8,342 gt. Details as Yard No. 1150.
Launched: 5.3.1946.

Completed: 6.1946 for Union-Castle Mail SS Co. Ltd.
9.1971: Arrived Shanghai for breaking up.

Built by Harland & Wolff Ltd., Govan Shipyard, Glasgow

1093 (G)　*Empire Ballantyne* 6,959 gt. 'X'-type 447 ft (oa), 432.7 ft × 56 ft. Engines: Oil.
Launched: 21.10.1941.
Completed: 2.1942.
1943: *Belgian Airman* (Government of Belgium).
14.4.1945: Sunk by submarine (*U.879*) torpedo off Chesapeake Bay, Maryland 36.09N 74.05W.

1094 (G)　*Empire Bede* 6,959 gt. Details as Yard No. 1093.
Launched: 6.1.1942.
Completed: 3.1942.
18.8.1942: Damaged by submarine (*U.553*) torpedo, in N. Atlantic 19.35N 76.25W while in convoy TAW 13 (voyage Alexandria/USA – cotton). Later sunk in position 19.41N 76.50W, by gunfire from H.M.S. *Pimpernel* which picked up survivors from the *Empire Bede* and other sunken ships from the same convoy.

1168 (G)　*Empire Torrent* 7,076 gt. 'Y'-type 448 ft (oa), 432 ft × 56 ft. Engines: T3cyl.
Launched: 29.10.1942.
Completed: 12.1942.
1948: *Argos Hill* (Ernels Shipping Co. Ltd. (Counties Ship Management Co. Ltd., London)).

1951: *Queen Maud* (Queen Line Ltd. (T. Dunlop & Sons, Glasgow)).
1954: *Scotia* (Nueva Valencia Cia. Nav. S.A., Panama (N. J. Goulandris Ltd., London)).
1960: renamed *Skotia* (Greek flag).
7.1962: Scrapped Hong Kong.

1169 (G)　*Empire Nerissa* 7,076 gt. Details as Yard No. 1168.
Launched: 23.12.1942.
Completed: 2.1943.
1949: *Daydawn* (Claymore Shipping Co. Ltd., Cardiff).
1954: *Loch Don* (Maclay & McIntyre Ltd., Glasgow).
1959: *Kraljevica* (Kvarnerska Plovidba (Government of Yugoslavia).
1961: (Jugoslavenska Linijska Plovidba).
24.6.1966: Arrived Split for breaking up.

1283 (G)　*Empire Gambia* 7,074 gt. Details as Yard No. 1168.
Launched: 14.5.1944.
Completed: 7.1945.
1946: *King Edgar* (King Line Ltd. (Dodd, Thompson & Co. Ltd., London)).
4.5.1959: Arrived Kobe for breaking up.

Harland & Wolff's Govan Yard was founded in 1841 by Rober Napier, born in 1791. After working as a smith in Glasgow, Napier had turned to marine engineering, working with various shipbuilders, but mainly with John Wood of Port Glasgow. Cunard's first thirteen wooden-hulled ships for the Liverpool–Boston service, built between 1840–1853 by either Robert Duncan & Co., John Wood & Co., or Robert Steele & Son, had Napier engines, but Napier's ambition was to build both ships and engines and he acquired a small yard at Dumbarton.

In 1841 Napier moved to a larger six-acre site which had been acquired by MacArthur & Alexander and laid out for shipbuilding in 1840 as the Govan Shipbuilding Yard, but had not been used. Here, Napier began his building of iron ships, the site becoming known as the Old Yard. Expansion was made in 1850 when nine acres of nearby land was purchased. This was to be called the New Yard but, unfortunately, the land was not immediately adjacent, for in 1843 Smith & Rodger had begun their business next to the Old Yard and would not sell, so the new nine-acre Govan East Yard was next to that.

In 1864 Smith & Rodger formed the London & Glasgow Engineering & Iron Shipbuilding Company and eventually, in 1912, the yard was acquired by Harland & Wolff Ltd.

In 1876 Napier died and his business was taken over by William Beardmore & Company, although not known under that title until 1900. But in 1905 Beardmores moved to Dalmuir to enable larger warship production and for a time Napier's Govan East Yard lay unoccupied. In 1909, after four years of idleness, Govan East Yard was taken over by the London & Glasgow Company for fitting-out work and, in 1912, also came under Harland & Wolff ownership.

Meanwhile, the Old Yard had seen several owners, one of which, Dobie & Company, built over 100 sailing ships and steamers from 1866 until their liquidation in 1884. Dobie's business was then taken over by the newly-formed Govan Shipbuilding Company. This lasted but one year, closed down and lay dormant until 1888 when Mackie & Thomson took over the yard and began building.

In 1912 Harland & Wolff acquired the yard from Mackie & Thomson, who moved to Irvine, and with the two yards of the London & Glasgow Company, combined all three yards in the development of their Govan Yard.

One of the last ships completed by the London & Glasgow Company was the *Indraghiri* (5,723 gt), delivered in March 1912. She later became the *Eurylochus* of Alfred Holt's China Mutual SN Co. Ltd. The cruisers *Yarmouth* and *Sydney* and three 'K'-class destroyers were also completed under the L. & G. name. In December 1914 the keel of the first Royal Navy monitor was laid down and completed in June 1915 as H.M.S. *Raglan*. Several more followed in the same year whilst six 'R'-class destroyers were completed in 1916–1917, these by Harland & Wolff Ltd.

During World War II tanker construction dominated the building programme. Nine dry cargo ships were also built and five coasters, three of which were of the 'Tes'-type for Far East service.

On 22 October 1963 came the announcement that the Govan shipbuilding and repair yards were to be placed on a care and maintenance basis and two years later the property began to be sold, mainly to the Glasgow Corporation.

MERCHANT SHIPS BUILT UNDER PRIVATE CONTRACT OR LICENCE

1032 (G) *Lavington Court* 5,372 gt, 449.8 ft (oa), 433 ft × 57.8 ft. Engines: Oil.
Launched: 21.3.1940.
Completed: 6.1940 for Court Line Ltd. (Haldin & Philipps Ltd.).
19.7.1942: Damaged by submarine (*U.564*) torpedo, north of Azores, 42.38N 25.28W whilst in convoy OS 34 (U.K./Freetown). Bows blown off, engine useless. Abandoned. Tugs despatched, taken in tow but
1.8.1942: sank in position 49.40N 18.04W.

1033 (G) *Novelist* 6,133 gt, 438.3 ft (oa), 423.4 ft × 54.5 ft. Engines: T3cyl.
Launched: 4.6.1940.
Completed: 8.9.1940 for T. & J. Harrison.
11/12.3.1941: Damaged by aircraft bombs at Manchester. Repaired.
1.1.1943: Damaged by aircraft bombs at Bone Harbour, Algeria. Repaired.
1961: renamed *Phoenix* for delivery to shipbreakers

(Eastbound Tanker Co. (Lebanese flag) (Rethymnis & Kulukundis Ltd.).
25.8.1961: Arrived Hong Kong for breaking up.

1200 (G) *Parima* 7,543 gt, 450.4 ft (oa), 433.3 ft × 61.3 ft. Engines: Oil.
Launched: 25.1.1944.
Completed: 6.1944 for Royal Mail Lines Ltd.
1962: *Michalios X* (Mary Shipping Co., S.A., Panama).
1966: *Fortune Dragon* (Ionia Shipping Co., S.A. (South East Asia Shipping & Trading Co. Ltd., Hong Kong)).
1.5.1967: Arrived Hong Kong for breaking up.

1279 (G) *Pilcomayo* 7,540 gt. Details as Yard No. 1200 (G).
Launched: 21.8.1945.
Completed: 12.1945 for Royal Mail Lines Ltd.
1965: *Aristagelos* (Varkiza, Cia. Nav. S.A., Panama (M. A. Karageorgis, Greece)).
23.5.1967: Arrived Kaohsiung for breaking up.

In September 1939 there were thirty-four ships in the Royal Mail Lines fleet, of which ten were passenger ships. In the ensuing war twenty-one were to be lost, fourteen by torpedo, two by aircraft bombing, two from mines and three by torpedo/gunfire, one, the *Natia*, caught by the raider *Thor* on 8 October 1940 in mid-Atlantic. Largest of the ships sunk was the *Highland Patriot*, 14,172 gt, torpedoed by *U.38* 317 miles west of Valentia Island, Eire, on 1 October 1940.

The newly-built *Darro*, in 1943. (Harland & Wolff Ltd., Belfast, Yard No. 1148.)   *Tom Rayner collection*

The *Empire Bruce* at New York, June 1942. (Sir J. Laing & Sons Ltd., Yard No. 737.)   *U.S.C.G.*

The 'Y2'-type *Empire Spartan* in Ellerman Line colours, August 1947. She retained her 'Empire' name until 1951. (Lithgows Ltd., Yard No. 962.)

Tom Rayner collection

A major casualty was the *Asturias*, 22,048 gt, under requisition as an armed merchant cruiser. In a seemingly peculiar, but nevertheless, important task, the *Asturias* was detailed, with five anti-submarine vessels, to escort a floating dock from Bahia to Freetown. About 400 miles from that port on 25 July 1943 she was torpedoed by the Italian submarine *Cagni* and badly damaged. The Dutch tug *Zwarte Zee* managed to get her to Freetown and there she lay for eighteen months before being towed by the *Zwarte Zee* and another Dutch tug, *Thames*, some 2,000 miles, via Gibraltar where she spent three months, to Harland & Wolff, Belfast, arriving on 8 June 1945. Declared a constructive total loss, the Ministry of Transport had her repaired to become a troop transport and emigrant ship until she was scrapped at Faslane in September 1957.

Two other ships of the 1939 fleet were sold, the *Atlantis* in 1939 to become a hospital ship and the *Nela* just after war ended.

Twelve new ships from Harland & Wolff helped to soften the harsh war loss figures, although two of these were also lost. The new ships were four 'D'-class, each with an insulated capacity of 500,000 cu. ft., and accommodation for twelve passengers, and eight 'P'-class general cargo carriers of which the first two built, *Pampas* and *Palma*, were those lost. Helped with these new ships, the very old-established River Plate and West Indies trade routes were soon re-opened when hostilities ceased and were quickly supplemented with two more newbuildings plus acquisitions of war-built tonnage which included four 'Empire' and three 'Liberty'-type ships.

Built by Sir James Laing & Sons Ltd., Deptford Yard, Sunderland

737   *Empire Bruce* 7,459 gt. A James Laing prototype design: 436 ft (oa), 423.8 ft × 59.9 ft.
Engines: T3cyl.
Launched: 11.6.1941.
Completed: 8.1941.
18.4.1943: Sunk by submarine (*U.123*) torpedo approx. 100 miles off Freetown, W. Africa, 06.40N 13.17W (voyage: Buenos Aires/U.K. – linseed).

Note: Submarine *U.123* scuttled herself at Lorient on 19 August 1944.

The first Laing-built ship is recorded as the *Horta*, completed in 1794. When yard numbering began, the first twenty-eight ships were constructed on the Sands, Sunderland, but Yard No. 29 was built at Bridge Dock, Sunderland. By 1816, building was being done at Southwick yard, Yard 81, launched as *Cerberus*.

In 1844, James Laing took control of the Deptford Yard, his first ship, *Agincourt*, launched on 19 January of that year, but nearly twenty years were to pass before the yard built its first iron ship. This was the steamship *Amity*, with three masts and sails, launched on 20 September 1863. The Yard numbers had now reached 211. Within a decade ships were built for the P & O SN Company, in 1873 two ships building for the Ryde Line being acquired for P & O and completed as the cargo/passenger ships *Khiva* (Yard 359) and *Kashgar* (360), whilst Yard No. 363, *Durban*, was completed in 1887 for the Union SS Company Ltd. By the turn of the century Laings were turning out ships for Pacific SN Company; Bullard, King; British India SN Company; Hamburg-America and Union-Castle . . . etc.

During the 1914–1918 war, Laings built nine 'War' standard ships, mostly tankers, for the Shipping Controller and when the 1939–1945 war came, Government orders were also predominant in the building programme when thirty-one 'Empire' standard ships were built.

There were five berths in the Deptford Yard for ships to 550 feet when war ended. Then in the 1950s Laings joined with Jos. L. Thompson & Son Ltd. and the ship repairers T. W. Greenwell & Co. Ltd., to form Sunderland Shipbuilding, Dry Docks and Engineering Co. Ltd.

MERCHANT SHIPS BUILT UNDER PRIVATE CONTRACT OR LICENCE

726   *Bolton Castle* 5,203 gt, 454.3 ft (oa), 438.5 ft × 57.1 ft. Engines: T3cyl.
Launched: 1.9.1939.
Completed: 12.1939 for Lancashire Shipping Co. Ltd. (J. Chambers & Co., Liverpool).

After the dispersal of the thirty-one ships of the ill-fated PQ 17 convoy to North Russia in the Barents Sea on 4 July 1942, the *Bolton Castle* headed north towards the ice, the intention being to steam north of Novaya Zemlya and then turn south on the eastern side of the islands and down through the Kara Sea.

In mid-afternoon of 5 July, with the ship still in the Barents Sea, north-east of Bear Island, in position 76.40N 36.30E, a group of enemy planes swept in, a Ju 88 bomber obtaining direct hits. The upper part of the *Bolton Castle* virtually disintegrated as cordite in No. 2 hold ignited – not as an explosive force, but into a searing cloud of white-hot flame which melted steelwork. The vessel wallowed, then seemed to heave herself out of the water before sliding below the surface, stern first.

727   *Beechwood* 4,897 gt, 431.8 ft (oa), 415 ft × 58.2 ft. Engines: T3cyl.
Launched: 9.11.1939.
Completed: 1.1940 for J. I. Jacobs & Co. Ltd., London.
3.2.1940: Damaged by aircraft bombs and gunfire three miles east of Smith's Knoll Light Vessel, North Sea (voyage: Tyne/Gibraltar – coal). Kept afloat only by use of the ship's pumps, she was diverted to the Thames, discharged and later repaired.
26.8.1942: Sunk by submarine (*U.130*) torpedo, south-west of Monrovia, Liberia, 05.30N 14.04W (voyage: Haifa/Lourenço Marques/U.K. – general). A stowaway was found aboard the ship when she was abandoned after being torpedoed.

728   *Glenwood* 4,897 gt. Details as Yard No. 727.
Launched: 21.2.1940.
Completed: 4.1940 for J. I. Jacobs & Co. Ltd., London.
1948: *Durham Trader* (Trader Navigation Co. Ltd., London).
1957: *Jag Sevak* (Great Eastern Shipping Co. Ltd. (A. H. Bhandiwalla & Co., Bombay).
15.7.1965: Aground Visakhapatnam, when leaving port with cargo of cement and general; badly damaged, constructive total loss; broke in two. Wreck removed and scuttled.

729   *Wandby* 4,947 gt, 422.3 ft (oa), 418 ft × 58.8 ft. Engines: Oil.
Launched: 7.5.1940.

Completed: 7.1940 for Ropner Shipping Co. Ltd. (Sir R. Ropner & Co. Ltd.).
19.10.1940: Damaged by submarine (*U.47*) torpedo, 56.45N 17.07W, northwest of Rockall on homeward maiden voyage in convoy HX 79.
21.10.1940: Sank (voyage: Halifax/New York/United Kingdom).

730   *Tynemouth* 3,182 gt, 357 ft (oa), 343.3 ft × 48 ft. Engines: T3cyl.
Launched: 9.4.1940.
Completed: 7.1940 for Burnett SS Co. Ltd., Newcastle.
1952: *Sandhoe* (Sharp SS Co. Ltd., Newcastle).
1963: *Andreas Panou* (Aninomi Cia. Mar., Panama).
3.7.1966: In collision, in fog, with *Hoegh Aiglonne* (1953, 4,534 gt), five miles west of Cabo Villano, NW Spain; sank (voyage: Setubal/Sas van Ghent).

731   *Charlton Hall* 5,199 gt, 453.7 ft (oa), 440.5 ft × 57 ft. Engines: T3cyl.
Launched: 21.6.1940.
Completed: 8.1940 for C. G. Dunn Shipping Co. Ltd., Liverpool.
1944: (Shakespear Shipping Co. Ltd., Cardiff (South American Saint Line Ltd.)).
1946: renamed *St. Elwyn*.
1954: *Ocean Endurance* (Trans Oceanic SS Co. Ltd., Pakistan).
1966: renamed *Ocean Endeavour*.
2.1967: Scrapped Karachi.

732   *Fishpool* 4,950 gt. Details as Yard No. 729.
Launched: 19.8.1940.
Completed: 11.1940 for Pool Shipping Co. Ltd. (Sir R. Ropner & Co. Ltd.).
14.11.1940: Bombed, southwest of Rockall, 55.00N 17.04W (approx.) whilst on maiden voyage. Abandoned, towed to Clyde by tug *Assurance*.
9.5.1941: Bombed and damaged during air raid on Barrow. Repaired.
26.7.1943: Bombed, exploded and sank at Syracuse, after invasion of Sicily. Total loss.

769   *Asia* 8,723 gt, 508.8 ft (oa), 488.5 ft × 64 ft. Engines: two steam turbines.
Launched: 12.9.1946.
Completed: 4.1947 for Cunard White Star Ltd.
1963: *Shirley* (Waywiser Nav. Corp. (W. H. Eddie Hsu, Taiwan)).
1.1969: Arrived Kaohsiung for breaking up.

The 'Y4'-type *Empire Treasure* at completion of trials. (Lithgows Ltd., Yard No. 977.)   *Tom Rayner collection*

Built by Lithgows Ltd., Kingston Shipbuilding Yard, Port Glasgow

939   *Empire Frost* 7,005 gt. 'Y'-type. 447.7 ft (oa), 433 ft × 56.2 ft. Engines: T3cyl.
Launched: 2.9.1940.
Completed: 11.1940.
12.3.1941: Bombed and damaged in St. Georges Channel, 51.36N 05.40W.
13.3.1941: Taken in tow by Dutch tug *Seine* (1908, 308 gt), but bombed again and sunk.

940   *Empire Dew* 7,005 gt. Details as Yard No. 939.
Launched: 21.11.1940.
Completed: 1.1941.
12.6.1941: Sunk by submarine (*U.48*) torpedo in mid-Atlantic, 51.09N 30.16W (voyage: Tyne/St. Lawrence).

941   *Empire Comet* 6,978 gt, 'X'-type. 447.7 ft (oa), 433 ft × 56.2 ft. Engines: Oil.
Launched: 11.1940.
Completed: 1.1941.
19.2.1942: Sunk by submarine (*U.136*) torpedo west of the Hebrides, 58.15N 17.10W; a straggler from convoy HX 174.

943   *Empire Hail* 7,005 gt. Details as Yard No. 939.
Launched: 27.12.1940.
Completed: 2.1941.
23.2.1942: Sunk by submarine (*U.94*) torpedo in North Atlantic, east of St. John's, 44.48N 40.21W.

944   *Empire Spring* 6,946 gt. Details as Yard No. 941.
Launched: 8.3.1941.

Completed: 6.1941.
15.2.1942: Sunk by submarine (*U.576*) torpedo in North Atlantic, approx. 42N 55W.

945   *Empire Tide* 6,978 gt. Details as Yard No. 941.
Launched: 27.5.1941.
Completed: 10.1941.
1945: *Thirlby* (Ropner Shipping Co. Ltd.).
1956: *Guri* (Transportes Maritimos Atlas S.A., Panama).
1963: *Anto* (Panamanian Oriental SS Corp., Panama (World-Wide Shipping Ltd.)).
1965: (Eastern Giant Nav. Co. Ltd., Bahamas (World-Wide Shipping Ltd.)).
1966: (Apollo Shipping Co. S.A., Panama).
11.1966: Arrived Ikeda for breaking up.

947   *Empire Dell* 7,065 gt. Details as Yard No. 939.
Launched: 26.5.1941.
Completed: 8.1941.
11.5.1942: Sunk by submarine (*U.124*) torpedo in mid-Atlantic, 53.00N 29.57W whilst in convoy ONS 92 (voyage: U.K./U.S.A.).

953   *Empire Shackleton* 7,068 gt. Details as Yard No. 939.
Launched: 23.7.1941.
Completed: 10.1941.
28.12.1942: Sunk by submarine (*U.225*) torpedo in mid-Atlantic, 43.23N 27.14W.

954   *Empire Livingstone* 6,997 gt. Details as Yard No. 939.

Launched: 24.7.1941.
Completed: 10.1941.
31.12.1943: Dragged anchor in a gale, ran ashore near Bizerta (in ballast). Total loss. Scrapped *in situ*.

957   *Empire Ridley* 6,838 gt. 'Y1'-type. Details as Yard No. 939.
Launched: 21.8.1941.
Completed: 11.1941.
1943: Taken over by the Admiralty and converted to a cable-laying vessel for Operation 'Pluto' (Pipe Line Under The Ocean). Renamed H.M.S. *Latimer*.
7.1945: *Empire Ridley* (M.O.W.T.).
4.1947: Sold to Norway; sent to Italy for conversion. Resold.
1947: *Acheo* (Societa Ligure di Armamento, Italy).
1964: Scrapped Sakai, Japan.

958   *Empire Baffin* 6,978 gt. Details as Yard No. 957.
Launched: 28.8.1941.
Completed: 10.1941.
5.1942: Propeller, shaft and bearings damaged and stern gland leaking after near misses from aircraft bombs (Convoy PQ 16; U.K.–Murmansk – war supplies). Reached Kola Inlet, Barents Sea, after Chief Engineer spent three days and nights shut in the shaft tunnel, tending the bearings. Repaired.
1943: Taken over by the Admiralty and converted to a cable-laying vessel for Operation 'Pluto'. Renamed H.M.S. *Sancroft*.
1946: *Empire Baffin* (M.O.T.).
1946: *Clintonia* (Stag Line Ltd. (J. Robinson & Sons, N. Shields).
1960: *Aspis* (Alcestis Shipping Co. S.A. (Faros Shipping Co. Ltd., London)).
12.1963: Scrapped Yokosuka.

Forward planning of the invasion of Europe began soon after the debacle of Dunkirk. Included in the logistics of the immense undertaking was the problem of supplying fuel to the mechanised armies. A pipeline under the ocean (PLUTO) was first thought of in April 1942, using ordinary submarine electric power cable, but without its conductors and insulation, i.e., merely a hollow tube. Its code name was HAIS. Within a few weeks a satisfactory trial in the Thames, using a Post Office cable ship, resulted in orders being placed for many miles of cable of slightly larger three-inch diameter and in December 1942 the first experimental cable was laid by H.M.S. *Holdfast* across the Bristol Channel from Swansea to Ilfracombe.

H.M.S. *Holdfast* was the first HAIS cable ship, converted from the Dundee, Perth & London Shipping Co.'s coastal passenger ship *London*, 1,499 gross tons and built in 1921 by Hawthorns & Co. Ltd., Leith. Conversion began in July 1942 and was completed in October 1942. Modifications included replacing bow and stern sheaves with an assemblage of rollers so that cable was laid over the stern and recovered over the bow. She could carry thirty miles of HAIS cable in two cable tanks, each thirty feet in diameter (see *Empire Taw*).

The *Algerian* was similarly converted. She was a larger steamship, 2,315 gross tons, constructed by Barclay, Curle & Co. Ltd., Glasgow, in 1924 for Ellerman & Papayanni Lines Ltd. She became H.M.S. *Algerian*.

From this progression emerged the two largest cable ships in the world when two 10,000 tdw 'Empire' tramp ships, *Empire Ridley* and *Empire Baffin* were each altered to carry 100 miles of HAIS piping. The *Empire Ridley* was commissioned as H.M.S. *Latimer*; *Empire Baffin* as H.M.S. *Sancroft*. All these conversions were by Green & Silley Weir Ltd., London. For the laying of the shore ends the work had to be transferred to smaller self-propelled barges; *Britannic* (ex *Miner V*), *Oceanic* and *Runic*, all carrying 2½ miles of cable and from September 1943 the twin screw motor barges *Goldbell* and *Goldrift* were requisitioned as well as a number of smaller auxiliary craft.

There was also another pipe introduced, this made of steel and in diameters of two and three inches. Its code name was HAMEL. The two-inch cable was used experimentally in a steam dockyard hopper barge, *W.24*, 725 tons and built in 1904. She was converted at Portsmouth in April 1943 for laying the cable by having a great cable drum, forty-eight feet in diameter, fitted in the hold which rotated in trunnions on the ship's deck as the cable unwound. She was commissioned H.M.S. *Persephone*.

From experiments in June 1943 came the Conun, a floating drum (Conundrum), sixty feet in length and forty feet in diameter and capable of carrying sixty-five miles of pipeline. The prototype, *Conun 1*, was built in August 1943 and next month five more, in a simplified design of No. 1, were ordered for delivery between March and July 1944. They could carry up to ninety miles of cable in an emergency and the drum was thirty feet in diameter. The Conuns were prefabricated in a Scunthorpe factory, erected at Tilbury Docks and launched by slipway. The weight of *Conun 1* was 300 tons; the others 250 tons.

Towing was by tugs of the 'Bustler' class, 3,200 ihp and 'Brigand'-class of 3,000 ihp. Force PLUTO was then complete, the major part of conversion and building being achieved after the successful trials of *Holdfast*, *Persephone* and *Conun 1*.

By D-Day, 6 June 1944, a network of internal supply pipes and pumping stations had been built from tanker ports in the Mersey and Bristol Channel and included a spur under the Solent to connect to the Isle of Wight and Shanklin Pier. The headquarters of PLUTO was H.M.S. *Abatos*, a shore base at the old, damaged Supermarine Aircraft Works at Southampton, blitzed in 1940. Sandown Bay had been chosen as the terminal for pumping the petrol, with pumps at Shanklin and Sandown feeding two HAIS and two HAMEL pipelines.

The first laying operation was by H.M.S. *Latimer* from Shanklin to Nacquerville, west of Cherbourg; distance sixty-five miles; time ten hours. H.M.S. *Sancroft* began two days later. However, there were difficulties in the sea/shore connections and pumping did not begin in the four lines until 22 September 1944. As the armies advanced through northern France and Belgium eleven HAIS and six HAMEL lines were laid between Dungeness and Boulogne and one million gallons of fuel per day was pumped to the armies in France, 172 million gallons by VE day.

With war over, the valuable piping was recovered for salvage and recycling. Marine Contractors Ltd. was the recovery company, operating from Southampton, and the recovered piping was discharged to a bombed shed site at 102 berth Southampton Docks. Ships employed in the recovery were *Empire Ridley*, *Empire Taw* (ex H.M.S. *Holdfast*), an ex-German coastal tanker *Georg*, renamed *Empire Tigness*, a Mark III Tank Landing Craft named *Wrangler*, and *Redeemer*, a wooden-hulled 172 gt salvage ship built by Rowhedge Ironworks Co. Ltd. in 1940. The smaller ships were used mainly in the collection of eastern Channel piping. Some 770 miles of piping was collected and the operation ceased in 1949.

959 *Empire Howard* 6,985 gt. Details as Yard No. 939.
Launched: 22.10.1941.
Completed: 12.1941.
16.4.1942: Sunk by submarine (*U.403*) torpedo 73.48N 21.32E while in convoy PQ 14 (voyage: Iceland/Murmansk).

960 *Empire Ranger* 7,008 gt. Y2 type. Details as Yard No. 939.
Launched: 3.12.1941.
Completed: 2.1942.
28.3.1942: Bombed and sunk in Arctic Ocean, 72.10N 30.00E by JU 88s after being scattered from convoy PQ 13 in heavy storm (voyage: Glasgow/North Russia).

961 *Empire Zeal* 7,009 gt. Details as Yard No. 960.
Launched: 29.12.1941.
Completed: 3.1942.
2.11.1942: Sunk by Italian submarine (*Da Vinci*) torpedo and gunfire in South Atlantic, 00.30S 30.45W (voyage: Basrah/New York).

962 *Empire Spartan* 6,987 gt. Details as Yard No. 960.
Launched: 17.2.1942.

Completed: 4.1942.
1951: *City of Cardiff* (Ellerman & Bucknall SS Co. Ltd.).
1959: *Shun Wing* (Kam Kee Nav. Co. Ltd. (Jebshun Shipping Co. Ltd., Hong Kong)).
1971: (Chan Moo Chu, Somali flag) (Jebshun Shipping Co. Ltd., Hong Kong)).
1.1972: Arrived Hong Kong from Onahama, Japan, after detention following bankruptcy of owner. Laid up.
10.5.1972: Dragged anchor, ranged alongside and collided with ferry *Macau* (1931, 3,670 gt).
12.5.1972: Remoored. Sold, and:
23.9.1972: Arrived Kaohsiung for breaking up.

963 *Empire Conrad* 7,009 gt. Details as Yard No. 960.
Launched: 23.3.1942.
Completed: 5.1942.
1952: *Franta* (P. Atychides, Marseilles).
1954: *Nia* (Refast SS Co. (Marcou & Sons Ltd., London)).
1954: *Eugenia* (Ocean Tramp Tankers Corpn., Panama).
4.1967: Scrapped Niihama, Japan.

964   *Empire Prairie* 7,010 gt. Details as Yard
No. 960.
Launched: 2.12.1941.
Completed: 2.1942.
10.4.1942: Sunk by submarine (*U.654*) torpedo,
35N 60W (approx.) in north Atlantic, east of
Philadelphia.

965   *Empire Addison* 7,010 gt. Details as Yard
No. 960.
Launched: 30.12.1941.
Completed: 3.1942.
1945: *Philosopher* (T. & J. Harrison).
1959: *Aiolos* (Concordia Sg. Corpn., Liberia (T. L.
Boyazides, Greece)).
1963: Scrapped Hong Kong.

969   *Empire Austen* 7,057 gt. 'Y3'-type. Details as
Yard No. 939.
Launched: 24.3.1942.
Completed: 5.1942.
1949: *Frinton* (Frinton Shipping Co. Ltd.
(Counties Ship Management Co. Ltd.)).
1951: *Freecrest* (Crest Shipping Co. Ltd.
(Ivanovic & Co. Ltd., London)).
1955: *Fairwater* (International Nav. Corpn., Liberia
(Tidewater Commercial Co. Inc., Baltimore,
U.S.A.)).
1961: *Apj Usha* (Surrendra (Overseas) Private Ltd.,
Bombay).
6.1962: Scrapped Bombay.

970   *Empire Galahad* 7,046 gt. Details as Yard
No. 969.
Launched: 18.5.1942.
Completed: 7.1942.
1946: *Celtic Star* (Blue Star Line Ltd.).
1947: *Murillo* (Lamport & Holt Line Ltd.).
1952: *Bogliasco* (Industriale Maritima SpA, Genoa).
1963: *Ocean Peace* (Ocean Shipping & Enterprises
S.A., Panama).
13.9.1967: Arrived Kaohsiung for breaking up.

971   *Empire Lancer* 7,037 gt. 'Y4'-type. Details as
Yard No. 939.
Launched: 31.8.1942.
Completed: 11.1942.
16.8.1944: Sunk by submarine (*U.862*) torpedo,
15S 45E (approx.) in Mozambique Channel.

972   *Empire Pennant* 7,069 gt. Details as Yard
No. 971.
Launched: 30.9.1942.
Completed: 12.1942.
1946: *Langton Grange* (Houlder Bros. & Co. Ltd.).
5.10.1960: Arrived Hong Kong for breaking up.

977   *Empire Treasure* 7,022 gt. Details as Yard
No. 971.
Launched: 28.12.1942.

Completed: 3.1943.
1946: *Gracia* (Donaldson Line Ltd.).
1954: *Oregon Star* (Blue Star Line Ltd.).
1955: *Inchleana* (Williamson & Co. Ltd., Hong Kong).
1966: *Tetulia* (National Shipping Corpn., Pakistan).
9.1969: Scrapped Chittagong.

The *Empire Treasure* was in the Atlantic, in position
50.27N 33.56W, bound from Liverpool for Halifax and New
York when, in a violent storm on 15 January 1944, her stern
frame fractured, she lost a propeller blade and her rudder
became inoperative. She quickly dropped out of her convoy.
The weather worsened and she lost the rest of her blades.
Drifting, she wallowed and rolled alarmingly, with her crew
needing lifelines to move around the deck. For three days the
ship maintained radio silence, then short wave
communication was established.
    The tug *Bustler* was despatched by the Admiralty and the
Empire Treasure was taken in tow in storm conditions, with
waves up to forty-five feet from trough to crest. Nursed
gently along for more than 1,000 miles, tug and tow finally
reached a respectable seven knots in improving weather
before arriving in the Bristol Channel on the 29th of the
month.

978   *Empire Beatrice* 7,046 gt. Details as Yard
No. 971.
Launched: 23.2.1943.
Completed: 4.1943.
27.7.1944: Damaged by E-boat torpedo in Straits of
Dover.
1948: *Beatrice N* (Cheriton Shipping Co. Ltd. (P. B.
Pandelis Ltd., London)).
1952: *Mary K* (N. G. Kyriakides Shipping Co. Ltd.,
London).
1964: *Winchester Prowess* (Winchester Shipping Co.
Ltd. (G. O. Till, London)).
1966: *Grazia Bottiglieri* (B. Bottigliere di Giuseppe,
Naples).
3.1969: Scrapped Split.

In 1944 the *Empire Beatrice* was torpedoed by E-boats in
the Straits of Dover, in position 50.55N 01.02E. Severely
damaged, she was taken in tow and beached at Dungeness
with her stern shattered and No. 5 hold and engine room
flooded. Taken in hand by a salvage team, she was refloated
on 2 August and fifty feet of tangled metal was cut off her
stern. Rebeached, patching commenced and bulkheads were
shored up. No. 4 hold and 1,000 tons of sand ballast were
discharged and a cement box fitted over the shaft tunnel. The
engine room was pumped out, the vessel made buoyant and
moored stern-on to the beach with bow anchors.
    Refloated again, on 16 August, the ship left in tow of the
tugs *Empire Humphrey* and *Empire Betsy*, bound for the River
Thames, where she was beached on Blyth Sands six days
later. Here, her after bulkheads were rebuilt and the tunnel
resealed, but on 20 September, when the *Empire Beatrice* was
refloated, the cement box washed away. A stronger one was
refitted and the ship then towed to Tilbury, where she was
finally discharged and further temporary repairs carried out.
The vessel was then towed to Glasgow, for permanent
repairs.

979 *Empire Buckler* 7,046 gt. Details as Yard
No. 971.
Launched: 30.6.1942.
Completed: 9.1942.
1946: *Ovingdean Grange* (Houlder Bros. & Co. Ltd.).
1959: *Sabrina* (Devon Shipping Co. Ltd., Liberia
(Empresa Navegacion Proamar SRL,
Argentina)).
1961: *Noemi* (Cia. Nav. Marcasa S.A. (Lebanese flag),
(S. Catsell & Co. Ltd., London)).
27.12.1965: Aground one mile SW of Ras Abu ar
Rasas, south of Masirah, Oman. Abandoned.
Constructive total loss (voyage: Matanzas,
Cuba/Basra – sugar).

980 *Empire Pibroch* 7,046 gt. Details as Yard
No. 971.
Launched: 2.9.1942.
Completed: 11.1942.
1946: *Urmston Grange* (Houlder Bros. & Co. Ltd.).
1959: *Argo Grange* (Argonaut Shipping &
Trading Co. Ltd. (C. Y. Tung, Hong Kong)).
18.12.1959: Arrived Hong Kong for breaking up.

981 *Empire Falstaff* 7,067 gt. 'Y5'-type. Details as
Yard No. 939.
Launched: 8.4.1943.
Completed: 5.1943.
1945: *Commandant Mantelet* (Government of France).
1950: *Commandant le Biboul* (Soc. Navale
Delmas-Vieljeux, France).
1954: *Monrovia* (Eastern Shipping Corp., Liberia (J.
Livanos & Sons Ltd., London)).
25.6.1959: In collision, in fog, with Great Lakes vessel
Royalton (1924, 7,164 gt) in Lake Huron, Canada.
Abandoned, and: 26.6.1959: Sank, eleven miles off
Thunder Bay Island (voyage: Antwerp/
Duluth – general).

982 *Empire Service* 7,067 gt. Details as Yard
No. 981.
Launched: 20.5.1943.
Completed: 7.1943.
1945: *Selector* (T. & J. Harrison).

1960: *Margalante II* (Cia. Nav. Margalante, Panama).
9.5.1961: Arrived Hirao for breaking up.

983 *Empire Miranda* 7,054 gt. 'Y6'-type. Details as
Yard No. 939.
Launched: 18.3.1943.
Completed: 4.1943.
1947: *Merchant* (T. & J. Harrison).
1961: *Trito* (Cia. Nav. Margalante, Panama).
26.5.1961: Arrived Hong Kong for breaking up.

990 *Empire Florizel* 7,056 gt. 'Y5'-type. Details as
Yard No. 981.
Launched: 21.4.1943.
Completed: 6.1943.
21.7.1943: Bombed by aircraft and sunk at Augusta
during Allied invasion of Sicily.

997 *Empire Talisman* 7,201 gt. 'Y7'-type. Details as
Yard No. 939.
Launched: 20.4.1944.
Completed: 6.1944.
1949: *Tacoma Star* (Blue Star Line Ltd.).
1957: *Murillo* (Lamport & Holt Line Ltd.).
16.3.1961: Arrived Vigo for breaking up.

998 *Empire Balfour* 7,201 gt. Details as Yard
No. 997.
Launched: 27.6.1944.
Completed: 9.1944.
1949: *Barton Grange* (Houlder Bros. & Co. Ltd.).
1958: *Sunlight* (Western SS Co. Ltd. (Wang Kee &
Co. Ltd., Hong Kong)).
1962: (Pan-Norse SS Co., S.A., Panama (Wallem &
Co. Ltd., Hong Kong)).
30.3.1967: Arrived Hong Kong for breaking up.

1005 *Empire Cyprus* 7,189 gt. Details as Yard
No. 997.
Launched: 18.4.1945.
Completed: 6.1945.
1948: *North Britain* (North Shipping Co. Ltd. (H.
Roberts & Son, Newcastle)).
1962: *Jesselton Bay* (Kinabatangan Shipping Co. Ltd.
(United China Shipping Co. Ltd., Hong Kong)).
2.4.1968: Arrived Kaohsiung for breaking up.

Joseph Russell was one of the outstanding shipbuilders of the mid-1800s. In a partnership with
Anderson Rodger in 1874 he leased the small Bay Yard in the east end of Port Glasgow, but business
was so good that expansion was necessary and in 1879 the old yard of J. E. Scott in Main Street,
Greenock, was acquired. Within one year seven sailing ships and four steamer hulls were built. But
at this time the tramp steamer was being rapidly developed and Russell began the construction of
standardised sailing ships to reduce capital cost in construction and to maintain competitive prices.

In the year 1881 he purchased Henry Murray & Co.'s Kingston Yard at Port Glasgow. Here,
there were more facilities, but more so was the bonus of the yard's chief draughtsman, William
Lithgow, who showed such quality and drive in reorganising the shipyard that Russell and Rodger
took him in as a partner. Russell retired in 1891, the business then being shared between Anderson
Rodger who had the Bay Yard as A. Rodger & Company, whilst William Lithgow continued to

control the Greenock and Kingston yards, which remained under the Russell title. In succession the sons James and Henry Lithgow took over the business of William Lithgow, who died in 1908. Four years later the Bay Yard was taken over by Russell & Company when Anderson Rodger died. In 1918 the company was restyled in the name of Lithgows Ltd.

Russell built 'H' and 'Z'-type war standard ships during the 1914–1918 war and the last ship under the Russell name was the *War Ermine* (Yard 716), launched in 1918. The largest buildings between the wars were the turbine-driven *Doric Star* (10,098 gt) completed in October 1921; the twin-screw turbine ships *Rodney Star* (11,803 gt) completed in January 1927 and the similar *Napier Star* in March 1927, all for the Blue Star Line Ltd. Two twin-screw motorships, *Northern Prince* and *Southern Prince*, of 10,917 gt, were delivered in April and August 1929 and the 10,386 gt turbine-driven *Tjibesar* for the Java-China-Japan Lijn, Amsterdam, was handed over in October 1922.

The first launching in the 1939–1945 war was the *Broompark* (Yard 921) on 12 September 1939, for J. & J. Denholm Ltd. Lithgows built ninety-seven ships during this war period. Standard 'Empire' ships included three 'X'-type, thirty 'Y'-type, two fast cargo liners, two MAC-ships and three 'Scandinavian'-type vessels. Fifty-four merchant ships were built under licence and three Transport Ferries were constructed in the closing years of war.

In 1947 there were fifteen building berths, nine at the Kingston Shipbuilding yard, Port Glasgow, for ships to 550 ft and six at the East Shipbuilding yard, Port Glasgow, for vessels to 700 ft.

In late 1961 it was announced that the Glen Yard of Wm. Hamilton & Co. Ltd., was to be merged with Lithgow's adjoining East Yard, to become a 'super yard' at Port Glasgow, alongside Lithgow's then-recently-reconstructed Kingston Yard.

In 1967 Lithgows, with Scotts Shipbuilding & Engineering Company, jointly acquired the Firth of Clyde Dry Dock Co. Ltd., and Scott, Lithgow Drydocks Ltd. was formed to operate the acquired Inchgreen Drydock. The two companies then agreed to become one concern, styled Scott Lithgow Ltd., one of the Clyde's two groups of shipbuilders.

In 1970 Campbeltown Shipyard Ltd. was acquired, then, two years later, on 2 March 1972 the last ship, *Brimnes*, a 32,300 tdw bulk carrier, was launched by Lithgows for Tenax SS Co. Ltd. (Kristian Jebsen (U.K.) Ltd.), ending a history dating back to the *Comet* of 1812.

In July 1974 the Government announced that the Scott Lithgow Group was to be nationalised with many other shipbuilding companies into British Shipbuilders, with headquarters at Newcastle.

The *Barton Grange*, built as the 'Y7'-type *Empire Balfour*. (Lithgows Ltd., Yard No. 998.)

MERCHANT SHIPS BUILT UNDER PRIVATE CONTRACT OR LICENCE

921 *Broompark* 5,136 gt, 447.5 ft (oa),
431.9 ft × 56.3 ft. Engines: T3cyl.
Launched: 12.9.1939.
Completed: 10.1939 for Denholm Line Steamers Ltd.
(J. & J. Denholm Ltd.).
21.9.1940: Damaged by submarine (*U.48*) torpedo
approx. 350 miles west of Ireland, 55.08N 18.30W,
whilst in convoy HX 72
(voyage: Vancouver/Glasgow – lumber). Flooded
but stayed afloat; escorted to port.
23.9.1940: Bombed by enemy aircraft off Isle of Islay.
25.9.1940: Arrived Rothesay Bay, and
14.10.1940: Arrived Greenock; repaired.
25.7.1942: Damaged by submarine (*U.552*) torpedo
600 miles east of Newfoundland, whilst in convoy
ON 113. Taken in tow, but 1.8.1942: Sank in position
47.42N 51.55W (voyage: Tyne/New York – ballast).

922 *Glenpark* 5,136 gt. Details as Yard No. 921.
Launched: 28.9.1939.
Completed: 11.1939 for Denholm Line Steamers Ltd.
(J. & J. Denholm Ltd.).
1951: *Stad Arnhem* (Halcyon Lijn N.V., Rotterdam).
1961: *Elli* (Cia. Nav. Marfomento S.A. (Bray
Shipping Co. Ltd.).
1967: *Fecondo* (Maritime Coal Transport, Lebanon).
17.12.1970: Aground in storm near Bizerta, Tunisia
(voyage: Sicily/Algeria – pumice stone).
20.12.1970: Refloated; towed Bizerta. Constructive
total loss. Sold, and:
7.1971: Scrapped Spezia.

923 *Marsdale* 4,890 gt, 436.4 ft (oa),
420.3 ft × 56.9 ft. Engines: T3cyl.
Launched: 13.12.1939.
Completed: 4.1940 for 'K' SS Co. Ltd. (Kaye Son
& Co. Ltd.).
1957: *Volta River* (Black Star Line Ltd., Ghana).
1965: *Psara* (Psara Shipping Co. (G. C. Calafatis &
Co. Ltd., Greece)).
24.5.1967: Arrived Spezia for breaking up.

924 *Baron Scott* 4,575 gt, 431 ft (oa),
415.7 ft × 56.5 ft. Engines: T3cyl.
Launched: 15.11.1939.
Completed: 1.1940 for Kelvin Shipping Co. Ltd.
(H. Hogarth & Sons).
1961: *Cissoula* (Aristides SS Co. S.A. (Rallis Shipping
Co. Ltd., Panama).
1964: (F. A. Theodorides, Greece).
24.9.1969: Arrived Hsinkang for breaking up.

925 *Ribera* 5,559 gt, 447.2 ft (oa), 432.2 ft × 58 ft.
Engines: T3cyl.
Launched: 22.2.1940.

Completed: 4.1940 for Bolton Steam Shipping Co.
Ltd.
1955: *Okeanis* (Cia. Robion de Oro S.A., Panama
(Goulandris Bros. Ltd., London)).
1959: *Jolanda* (Cia. de Nav. Jolanda S.A., Liberia
(SOARMA, Italy)).
1964: (Cia. de Nav. Victoria S.A., Panama).
10.6.1971: Arrived Split for breaking up.

926 *Baron Herries* 4,574 gt. Details as Yard No. 924.
Launched: 26.12.1939.
Completed: 2.1940 for Kelvin Shipping Co. Ltd.
(H. Hogarth & Sons).
1960: *Athos II* (Avlis Shipping Co. S.A., Greece).
16.3.1962: Aground in fog on Hairsis Island, entrance
to Bosporus. Constructive total loss
(voyage: Constantza/Antwerp – grain). Sold, and:
6.1962: Scrapped Riva Deresi, Turkey.

927 *Dalesman* 6,343 gt, 459.6 ft (oa), 445 ft × 56 ft.
Engines: T3cyl.
Launched: 26.3.1940.
Completed: 5.1940 for T. & J. Harrison.
14.5.1941: Bombed by aircraft at Suda Bay, Crete;
salved by Germans and renamed *Pluto*; later sunk
again by bombing at Trieste. Salved by British, and:
1946: *Empire Wily* (*q.v.*)

928 *Trevilly* 5,296 gt, 448.5 ft (oa),
431.9 ft × 56.2 ft. Engines: Oil.
Launched: 29.4.1940.
Completed: 6.1940 for Hain SS Co. Ltd.
12.9.1942: Sunk by submarine (*U.68*) torpedo and
gunfire in South Atlantic, 04.30S 07.50W
(voyage: Middlesbrough/Beira – general and military
stores).

929 *Temple Arch* 5,138 gt. Details as Yard No. 921.
Launched: 27.11.1939.
Completed: 1.1940 for Temple SS Co. Ltd.
(Lambert Bros. Ltd.).
1959: *Marihora* (Marivic Nav. Inc., Liberia (A. & D.
Chandris, Greece)).
1964: (General Carriers S.A., Panama).
3.11.1966: Aground in cyclone, broke in two, two
miles south of Madras (voyage: Singapore/Madras –
ballast).

930 *Cape Hawke* 5,081 gt, 447.5 ft (oa),
431.9 ft × 56.2 ft. Engines: Oil.
Launched: 21.5.1940.
Completed: 3.1941 for Cape York Motorship Co.
Ltd. (Lyle Shipping Co. Ltd.).
1963: *Kalliopi* (Kalliopi Cia. Nav. S.A., Panama).
1963: *Roy* (Cia. Nav. Skaros S.A., Panama (Lemos
& Pateras Ltd.)).

31.3.1967: Towed into Honolulu with fractured crankshaft.
18.7.1967: Arrived Yokohama in tow. Repairs uneconomic; sold, and:
28.8.1967: Left, in tow, for Mihara and broken up.

931   *Temple Inn* 5,218 gt. Details as Yard No. 921.
Launched: 27.12.1939.
Completed: 2.1940 for Temple SS Co. Ltd. (Lambert Bros. Ltd.).
1959: *Mariviki* (Marivic Nav. Inc., Liberia (A. & D. Chandris, Greece)).
1964: (General Carriers S.A., Panama).
22.7.1965: Sprung leak, beached near Mormugao, 15.11N 73.55E.
23.7.1965: Broke in two. Total loss (voyage: Madras/Constantza – iron ore).

932   *Havildar* 5,407 gt, 425 ft (oa),
409.5 ft × 53.9 ft. Engines: T3cyl.
Launched: 21.5.1940.
Completed: 7.1940 for Asiatic SN Co. Ltd.
1960: *Amoy* (China Pacific Navigation Co. Ltd., Hong Kong).
1963: (Eastland Nav. & Commerce Ltd., Hong Kong).
1965: *Continental Trader* (Oriental Trader Nav. Co., Panama).
2.1966: Scrapped Kaohsiung.

933   *Risaldar* 5,407 gt. Details as Yard No. 932.
Launched: 26.6.1940.
Completed: 8.1940 for Asiatic SN Co. Ltd.
1958: *Al Ahmadi* (Muhammadi SS Co. Ltd., Karachi).
8.1966: Scrapped Karachi.

934   *Cape Wrath* 4,512 gt, 426.6 ft (oa),
411.8 ft × 54.2 ft. Engines: T3cyl.
Launched: 29.4.1940.
Completed: 6.1940 for Cape of Good Hope Motorship Co. Ltd. (Lyle Shipping Co. Ltd.).
1958: *Mansoor* (Gulf Steamships Ltd., Pakistan).
11.1966: Scrapped Karachi.

935   *Cape Rodney* 4,512 gt. Details as Yard No. 934.
Launched: 25.6.1940.
Completed: 9.1940 for Cape of Good Hope Motorship Co. Ltd. (Lyle Shipping Co. Ltd.).
5.8.1941: Torpedoed by submarine (*U.75*) west of Ushant while in convoy SL 81 (Sierra Leone/U.K.). Abandoned. Reboarded, drifting, but: 9.8.1941: Sank 52.44N 11.41W whilst salvage being attempted by R.N. vessel.

936   *Aircrest* 5,237 gt, 447.6 ft (oa),
432.2 ft × 56.2 ft. Engines: T3cyl.
Launched: 7.1940.
Completed: 10.1940 for Crest Shipping Co. Ltd. (Overseas Navigation Trust Ltd., London).

30.6.1942: Torpedoed and sunk by aircraft, north of Gaza, Palestine, 31.49N 34.04E.

937   *Rembrandt* 7,121 gt. Details as Yard No. 925.
Launched: 30.8.1940.
Completed: 1.1941 for Bolton Steam Shipping Co. Ltd.
1957: *Capetan Antonis* (Navigation Transport Co. Inc., Liberia).
1963: Renamed *Mastromitsos*.
1965: (Bluebird Maritime Co. Ltd., Liberia (N. D. Koulos, Greece)).
29.4.1967: Arrived Kaohsiung for breaking up.

938   *Coulbeg* 5,237 gt. Details as Yard No. 936.
Launched: 26.8.1940.
Completed: 11.1940 for Dornoch Shipping Co. Ltd. (Lambert Bros. Ltd.).
1951: *Jutland* (Nile SS Co. Ltd. (Glen & Co. Ltd., Glasgow)).
1953: *Marianthe* (Trafalgar SS Co. Ltd. (Tsavliris Shipping Ltd.)).
1955: *Berna* (S. Catsell & Co. Ltd., London).
1958: *Marianthe Tsavliris* (Maritime Co. Ltd., Greece).
1965: *Free Merchant* (Kantara Shipping Ltd. (Tsavliris Shipping Ltd., London)).
9.6.1967: Sprang leak in storm 700 miles from Colombo, Ceylon (voyage: Beirut/Yokohama – scrap). Abandoned: settled by stern, broke in two, and:
10.6.1967: Sank, 9.14N 68.11E.

942   *Cape Verde* 6,914 gt, 447.6 ft (oa),
432.7 ft × 56.2 ft. Engines: Oil.
Launched: 13.1.1941.
Completed: 3.1941 for Cape of Good Hope Motorship Co. Ltd. (Lyle Shipping Co. Ltd.).
4.4.1941: Bombed and damaged on maiden voyage, forty miles north of The Smalls 52.12N 05.42W (voyage: Clyde/South Wales). Repaired.
9.7.1942: Sunk by submarine (*U.203*) torpedo 11.32N 60.17W, east of Grenada, B.W.I.

946   *Mooncrest* 5,202 gt. Details as Yard No. 921.
Launched: 13.4.1941.
Completed: 5.1941 for Crest Shipping Co. Ltd. (Overseas Navigation Trust Ltd., London).
1956: *Kori* (Cia. Auxilar. Maritima Ltda. (A. Ramirez Escudero, Spain).
14.4.1970: Arrived Sakaide for breaking up.

952   *Helencrest* 5,233 gt. Details as Yard No. 921.
Launched: 23.6.1941.
Completed: 8.1941 for Crest Shipping Co. Ltd. (Overseas Navigation Trust Ltd., London).
1958: *Zonguldak* (D. B. Deniz Nakliyati T.A.S., Turkey).

1968: (Corra. Umumi Nakliyat, Vapurculuk Ticaret, Turkey).
14.6.1969: Arrived Istanbul for breaking up.

955   *Nurani* 5,414 gt. Details as Yard No. 932.
Launched: 21.10.1941.
Completed: 12.1941 for Asiatic SN Co. Ltd.
1960: *Hui An* (Hai An Shipping Co. Ltd., Hong Kong).
1965: *Jin An* (Jin An Shipping Co. Ltd. (Jinford & Co. Ltd., Hong Kong)).
9.1.1967: Arrived Hong Kong for breaking up.

956   *Nairung* 5,414 gt. Details as Yard No. 932.
Launched: 20.11.1941.
Completed: 1.1942 for Asiatic SN Co. Ltd.
18.8.1944: Sunk by submarine (*U.862*) torpedo, off coast of Madagascar, 15S 45E (approx.) (voyage: Durban/Bombay).

966   *Shahjehan* 5,454 gt. Details as Yard No. 932.
Launched: 30.4.1942.
Completed: 6.1942 for Asiatic SN Co. Ltd.
6.7.1943: Torpedoed by submarine (*U.453*) off Grennah, Libya.
Caught fire; taken in tow, but
7.7.1943: Sank, 32.51N 21.10E, 150 miles NE of Benghazi.

967   *Shahzada* 5,454 gt. Details as Yard No. 932.
Launched: 17.6.1942.
Completed: 9.1942 for Asiatic SN Co. Ltd.
9.7.1944: Sunk by submarine (*U.196*) torpedo 15.30N 65.30E, in Arabian Sea, 500 miles west of Goa.

968   *Junecrest* 6,945 gt. Details as Yard No. 936.
Launched: 26.6.1942.
Completed: 8.1942 for Crest Shipping Co. Ltd. (Overseas Navigation Trust Ltd., London).
1958: *Aydin* (D. B. Deniz Nakliyati T.A.S., Turkey).
11.1966: Scrapped Istanbul.

973   *Coulgorm* 6,997 gt. Details as Yard No. 936.
Launched: 28.10.1942.
Completed: 12.1942 for Dornoch Shipping Co. Ltd. (Lambert Bros. Ltd.).
1953: *Temple Mead* (Temple SS Co. Ltd. (Lambert Bros. Ltd., London)).
1955: *Theodore N. Vlassopulos* (Cia. Mar. Bee Ltda., Costa Rica) (Vlassopulo, Bros., London).
1963: *Ais Giannis* (Transmarina Armadora S.A., Panama (N. & J. Vlassopulos Ltd., London)).
12.11.1966: Arrived Kaohsiung for breaking up.

974   *Triona* 7,283 gt, 462.8 ft (oa),
447.8 ft × 56.3 ft. Engines: T3cyl.
Launched: 26.11.1942.
Completed: 2.1943 for British Phosphate Commissioners, Victoria, Australia.
2.5.1960: Arrived Hong Kong for breaking up.

976   *Cape Howe* 6,997 gt. Details as Yard No. 936.
Launched: 21.12.1942.
Completed: 2.1943 for Cape of Good Hope Motorship Co. Ltd. (Lyle Shipping Co. Ltd.).
1961: *World Pink* (Wing Tak SS Co. (Hong Kong) Ltd. (Great East Asia Shipping & Trading Corpn., Hong Kong)).
1962: (Wing Tak SS Co., Panama).
3.3.1967: Arrived Kaohsiung for breaking up.

984   *Mahadevi* 5,459 gt. Details as Yard No. 932.
Launched: 30.6.1943.
Completed: 8.1943 for Asiatic SN Co. Ltd.
1962: *Nalanda* (Shipping Corpn. of India Ltd., Bombay.)
8.1964: Scrapped Bombay.

985   *Trevanion* 7,375 gt, 447.2 ft (oa),
432.6 ft × 57.9 ft. Engines: Oil.
Launched: 11.11.1943.
Completed: 1.1944 for Hain SS Co. Ltd.
1955: *Avisbrook* (Aviation & Shipping Co. Ltd. (Purvis Shipping Co. Ltd.)).
1960: *Michalis* (Integritas Shipping Co. Ltd. (Rethymnis & Kulukundis Ltd., London)).
23.10.1967: Arrived Kaohsiung for breaking up.

986   *Trevider* 7,376 gt. Details as Yard No. 985.
Launched: 15.2.1944.
Completed: 5.1944 for Hain SS Co. Ltd.
1955: *Eastgate* (Turnbull, Scott & Co. Ltd., London).
1956: *Balkan* (Navigation Maritime Bulgare, Bulgaria).
16.1.1968: Aground on rocks at Lattakia, Syria; flooded (voyage: Bourgas/Lattakia – grain).
24.7.1968: Refloated; taken in tow for Bulgaria, but sold and:
4.8.1968: Arrived Split, in tow, for breaking up.

987   *Malika* 5,459 gt. Details as Yard No. 932.
Launched: 23.8.1943.
Completed: 10.1943 for Asiatic SN Co. Ltd.
1962: *Ajanta* (Shipping Corporation of India Ltd., Bombay).
17.3.1965: Arrived Bombay for breaking up.

988   *Prospector* 6,201 gt, 435 ft (oa),
420.3 ft × 54.6 ft. Engines: T3cyl.
Launched: 14.10.1943.
Completed: 1.1944 for Charente SS Co. Ltd. (T. & J. Harrison).
1961: *Ekton* (renamed for delivery voyage to shipbreakers); (Cia. Nav. Margalante S.A., Panama (Mavroleon Bros. Ltd.).
25.3.1962: Arrived Yokosuka for breaking up.

989   *Geologist* 6,202 gt. Details as Yard No. 988.
Launched: 9.10.1943.
Completed: 1.1944 for Charente SS Co. Ltd. (T. & J. Harrison).

13.7.1955: In collision off Corozal Point, Trinidad, with mv *Sunprincess* (1943, 5,221 gt); sank in position 10.49N 61.40W (voyage: Glasgow/Maracaibo – general).

991   *Lloydcrest* 7,020 gt. Details as Yard No. 936.
Launched: 14.2.1944.
Completed: 4.1944 for Crest Shipping Co. Ltd. (Overseas Navigation Trust Ltd., London)).
1958: *Sinop* (D. B. Deniz Makliyati T.A.O., Turkey).
1963: *Hakan* (Hakan Vapuru Donatma Istiraki, Turkey).
10.1979: Scrapped Aliaga, Turkey.

996   *Rivercrest* 6,998 gt. Details as Yard No. 936.
Launched: 6.4.1944.
Completed: 5.1944 for Crest Shipping Co. Ltd. (Overseas Navigation Trust Ltd., London).
1959: *Kolocep* (Maritenia Shipping Co. Ltd. (Government of Yugoslavia)).
1963: (Atlanska Plovidba (Government of Yugoslavia)).
31.12.1968: Arrived Split for breaking up.

999   *Egidia* 9,952 gt, 497.2 ft (oa), 476 ft × 64.3 ft.
Engines: Oil. 'Standard Fast' type.
Launched: 29.1.1945.
Completed: 5.1945 for Anchor Line Ltd.
1962: *Benhope* (Ben Line Steamers Ltd).
23.7.1972: Arrived Kaohsiung for breaking up.

1000   *Elysia* 9,979 gt. Details as Yard No. 999.
Launched: 30.5.1945.
Completed: 10.1945 for Anchor Line Ltd.
1963: *Athenian* (Efcarriers Co. Ltd., Liberia (Franco Shipping Co. Ltd., Greece)).
1965: *Ninghai* (China Navigation Co. Ltd., London).
1971: *Venus Ninghai* (Venus International Corp., Liberia).
1.9.1973: Arrived Kaohsiung for breaking up.

1001   *Beaverdell* 9,901 gt. Details as Yard No. 999, but: Engines: two steam turbines to electric motor.
Launched: 27.8.1945.
Completed: 2.1946 for Canadian Pacific Steamships Ltd. (Canadian Pacific Railway Company).
1952: Renamed *Mapledell*.
1956: Renamed *Beaverdell*.
1963: *Luisa Costa* (Giacomo Costa Fu Andrea, Italy).
29.3.1971: Arrived Spezia for breaking up.

1002   *Beaverglen* 9,824 gt. Details as Yard No. 1001.
Launched: 10.12.1945.
Completed: 5.1946 for Canadian Pacific Steamships Ltd. (Canadian Pacific Railway Company).
1963: *Bermuda Hibiscus* (Hibiscus Ltd., Bermuda).
1965: *Ping An* (Teh-Hu SS Co. Ltd., Hong Kong).
24.11.1965: Engine failed whilst on trials after engine repairs; anchor chains parted; ship aground in heavy weather at Terheidan, about five miles north of Hook of Holland. Sold, as lies, for breaking up.

Canadian Pacific Steamships Ltd., suffered great losses during hostilities, losing five of their great liner fleet during the first half of the war. The first blow was the loss of the giant 42,348 gt *Empress of Britain*. Bombed by a long-range Focke-Wulf 200 aircraft some seventy miles north-west of Donegal Bay on 26 October 1940 and on fire, the *Empress of Britain* was taken in tow by the naval tugs *Marauder* and *Thames*, but they slipped the tow when she was torpedoed by *U.32* in the early hours of 28 October. She sank in position 55.16N 09.50W. A few weeks later the merchant cruiser H.M.S. *Forfar* was torpedoed west of Ireland by *U.99* and sank on 2 December. She had been taken over by the Admiralty in September 1939, changing her name from *Montrose*, under which she had been completed by the Fairfield Company, Glasgow, in 1922.

Fifteen months were to pass before another liner was lost. On 5 February 1942 the *Empress of Asia*, 16,900 gt, built in 1913 and with 2,600 people on board, was attacked off Singapore by Japanese bombers and after five direct hits and well afire, ran aground on Sultan Shoal, west of Ayer Chawan Island, and sank. Many troops of the 18th Division were taken aboard the Australian corvette *Yarra* which, at great risk, went alongside the *Empress of Asia* as she heeled over. Others were rescued by Royal Navy patrol boats and the steam tug *Veruna*, 333 gt of 1906, belonging to the Singapore Harbour Board. On 15 February 1942 Singapore surrendered to the Japanese army.

The 1928-built *Duchess of Atholl*, 20,119 gt, was another U-boat victim when she was torpedoed by *U.178*, 200 miles east of Ascension, on 10 October 1942, homeward bound from Durban, and on 13 March 1943 the 21,560 gt *Empress of Canada*, also completed by Fairfields in 1922, was sunk by torpedo when the Italian submarine *Da Vinci* attacked her on the night of 13/14 March 1943 in the South Atlantic.

Another passenger ship, the 5,875 gt *Princess Marguerite* was lost in the Mediterranean on a voyage from Port Said to Cyprus on 17 August 1942. She belonged to the British Columbian fleet of Canadian Pacific Railway.

But these were not the only Canadian Pacific ships to be lost, for all five of the 'Beaver'-class ships built in 1927–1928 did not survive the war. They had provided a most important service between the United Kingdom and Canada prior to 1940. Both *Beaverburn* and *Beaverdale* were torpedoed; the *Beaverford* was sunk by the German battleship *Admiral Scheer* in the 'Jervis Bay' convoy in November 1940; the *Beaverbrae* was bombed and sunk in the North Atlantic in 1941 and the *Beaverhill* stranded on Hillyards Reef, Saint John N.B., on 24 November 1944.

In 1943 Government authority was obtained for the building of four 16-knot cargo ships to replace the earlier 'Beavers' of the London/Canada service, but Fairfield, with full yard lists of warship construction, could only accept one, completed as *Beavercove* in 1947, and the remainder were sub-contracted to Lithgows, to be launched as *Beaverdell, Beaverglen* and *Beaverlake*. These ships were a variation of the Standard Fast 15-knot type.

1003 *Beaverlake* 9,824 gt. Details as Yard No. 1001.
Launched: 20.5.1946.
Completed: 10.1946 for Canadian Pacific Steamships Ltd. (Canadian Pacific Railway Company).
1962: *Bice Costa* (Lloyd Tirrenico SpA (Giacomo Costa Fu Andrea, Italy)).
1968: (Costa Armatori SpA., Italy).
23.4.1971: Arrived Spezia for breaking up.

1004 *Nadir* 5,497 gt. Details as Yard No. 932.
Launched: 14.9.1944.
Completed: 11.1944 for Asiatic SN Co. Ltd.
1961: *Kulangsu* (China Pacific Navigation Co. Ltd., Hong Kong).
1963: Scrapped Hong Kong.

1006 *Palamcotta* 6,704 gt, 446.8 ft (oa),
432 ft × 56.2 ft. Engines: T3cyl.
Launched: 19.9.1945.
Completed: 11.1945 for British India SN Co. Ltd.
1961: *Doria* (Marine Industry Corp. Ltd. (P. S. Li, Hong Kong)).
1962: *New Hweisung* (Taiwan Ming Sung Industrial Co. Ltd.).
10.1968: Scrapped Kaohsiung.

1007 *Pentakota* 6,704 gt. Details as Yard No. 1006.
Launched: 20.11.1945.
Completed: 2.1946 for British India SN Co. Ltd.
1961: *M. Mehmet* (Cerrahogullari Umumi Nakliyat Vapurculuk ve Ticaret T.A.S., Turkey).
25.1.1969: Arrived Istanbul for breaking up.

1008 *Tahsinia* 5,680 gt. Details as Yard No. 985.
Launched: 7.3.1946.
Completed: 5.1946 for Anchor Line Ltd.
1959: *Caracas* (Atlantic Shipping Inc., Liberia (J. W. Elwell & Co. Inc., New York)).
1963: *Agios Therapon* (San Therapon Cia. Nav. S.A., Panama, (Lemos & Pateras Ltd., London)).
1969: *Paralos* (Marsiadora Cia. Nav. S.A. (P. A. Lemos & Associates)).
1.9.1969: In collision at Colombo, Ceylon, with

Priamos (1930, 4,184 gt). Later proceeded (voyage: Calcutta/Mormugao).
Sold, and:
3.11.1969: Arrived Shanghai for breaking up.

1012 *Shahjehan* 5,460 gt. Details as Yard No. 932.
Launched: 1946.
Completed: 10.1946 for Asiatic SN Co. Ltd.
1961: (Hai San Shipping Co. Ltd.).
1963: *Nan An* (Cia. Nav. Peace Ltda. (Hai An Shipping Co., Hong Kong)).
4.4.1965: Aground in fog in Mirs Bay, Hong Kong New Territories, 22.24N 114.24E
(voyage: Kaohsiung/Hong Kong – cement).
Abandoned. Looted and set on fire. Total loss; scrapped locally.

1013 *Shahzada* 5,469 gt. Details as Yard No. 932.
Launched: 27.9.1946.
Completed: 12.1946 for Asiatic SN Co. Ltd.
1963: *Sanchi* (Shipping Corporation of India Ltd.).
10.1964: Scrapped Osaka.

1014 *Cape Ortegal* 5,098 gt. Details as Yard No. 942.
Launched: 16.4.1946.
Completed: 8.1946 for Cape of Good Hope Motorship Co. Ltd., (Lyle Shipping Co. Ltd.).
1964: *Megara* (6,907 gt): (Acres Shipping Co., Greece (G. C. Calafatis & Co. Ltd., Greece)).
17.8.1966: Aground off Bancoran Island, Sulu Sea, north of Borneo, 7.58N 118.38E
(voyage: Philippines/Antwerp – copra).
9.9.1966: Refloated with hull and machinery damage; towed to Manila.
30.3.1967: Arrived Kaohsiung, in tow, for breaking up.

1022 *Cape Rodney* 6,939 gt. Details as Yard No. 942.
Launched: 9.1946.
Completed: 11.1946 for Cape of Good Hope Motorship Co. Ltd., (Lyle Shipping Co. Ltd.).

1955: (Lyle Shipping Co. Ltd.).
1963: *Blue Dolphin* (Blue Shark SS Co., S.A., Panama (Philippine Merchants SS Co. Inc.)).

1965: *Hariet* (H. Eidiki Anon. Naf. Etairia (A. Halcoussis, Greece)).
31.5.1971: Arrived Shanghai for breaking up.

Built by William Pickersgill & Sons Ltd., Southwick, Sunderland

244   *Empire Thunder* 5,965 gt, 415 ft (oa), 401 ft × 54 ft. Engines: T3cyl.
Launched: 6.8.1940.
Completed: 1.1941.
6.1.1941: Sunk (on maiden voyage) by submarine (*U.124*) torpedo north-west of Hebrides, 59.14N 12.43W (voyage: Oban/Panama).

246   *Empire Cloud* 5,969 gt. Details as Yard No. 244.
Launched: 27.12.1940.
Completed: 4.1941.

In May 1941 the *Empire Cloud* was on her maiden voyage, bound in ballast from the Tyne via Loch Ewe to the U.S.A. in convoy OB 318.

On 7 May the convoy was sighted by submarine *U.94* south of Iceland and during the next three days five U-boats sank or damaged ten ships. On 9 May, east of Cape Farewell, Greenland, the *Empire Cloud* was damaged by a torpedo from *U.201*. The ship remained afloat although the shell plating in the way of the engine and boiler rooms was missing, the engine was shattered and pushed to port and the holds were flooded. Taken in tow by the tug *Thames* (1938, 624 gt), it took nearly two weeks to tow her to the Clyde, where she was beached at Kames Bay, Isle of Bute. Refloated on 22 June, the *Empire Cloud* was drydocked and repaired.

It was February 1942 before she sailed again, carrying military stores to the Army in North Africa. Returning in ballast, via the Cape of Good Hope, the ship was some eighty miles out from Trinidad, in convoy TAW(S) when, on 19 August 1942, she was torpedoed by *U.564*. Again she remained afloat, though listing, and was taken in tow by the Dutch tug *Roode Zee* (1938, 468 gt). However, the vessel slowly flooded and sank two days later, in position 10.54N 62.10W.

247   *Empire Eve* 5,979 gt. Details as Yard No. 244.
Launched: 26.4.1941.
Completed: 6.1941.
18.5.1943: Sunk by submarine (*U.414*) torpedo west of Algiers, 36.37N 00.46E.

248   *Empire Marriott* 5,970 gt. Details as Yard No. 244.
Launched: 25.8.1941.
Completed: 10.1941.
1946: *Graigddu* (I. Williams & Co. Ltd., Cardiff).
1952: *Jayshoor* (New Dholera Steamships Ltd., India).
9.1969: Scrapped Bombay.

249   *Empire Cromwell* 5,970 gt. Details as Yard No. 244.
Launched: 8.7.1941.
Completed: 9.1941.
28.11.1942: Sunk by submarine (*U.508*) torpedo south-east of Trinidad, 09.00N 58.30W (voyage: Cape Town/New York).

252   *Empire Chaucer* 5,970 gt. Details as Yard No. 244.
Launched: 18.3.1942.
Completed: 5.1942.
17.10.1942: Sunk by submarine (*U.504*) torpedo, south of Cape Town, 40.20S 18.30E.

255   *Empire Hunter* 5,967 gt. Details as Yard No. 244.
Launched: 11.9.1942.
Completed: 11.1942.
1943: *Boryslaw* (Government of Poland).
1950: *Bytom* (Polskie Linie Oceanienze (Government of Poland)).
27.9.1963: Arrived Szczecin; converted to a floating grain warehouse for use in that port. Renamed *MP-PZZ-2* (Rejonowe Zaklady Zbozowe PZZ).
(*circa*) 1970: (Zaklady Obrutu Zbozami Importawanymi i Eksportowymi, P.Z.Z.). Presume vessel now scrapped.

260   *Empire Copperfield* 5,998 gt. Details as Yard No. 244.
Launched: 16.7.1943.
Completed: 9.1943.
1946: *Graigwen* (I. Williams & Co. Ltd., Cardiff).
1958: *Jag Devi* (Great Eastern Shipping Co. Ltd., Bombay).
19.7.1963: Arrived Bombay for breaking up; dismantled by owners, parts/sections/scrap sold individually, as required.

277   *Empire Flamborough* 4,191 gt, 401 ft (oa), 384 ft × 53.8 ft. Engines: T3cyl.
Launched: 19.11.1945.
Completed: 3.1946.
1946: *Vindeggen* (C. Ostberg, Norway).

1948: *Bulgaria* (Nav. Maritime Bulgare, Bulgaria).
9.1976: Scrapped Split.

278 (Laid down as) *Empire——* 4,251 gt. Details as Yard No. 277.

Launched: 5.2.1946.
Completed: 6.1946 as *Hubert* for Booth SS Co. Ltd.
1951: Renamed *Cuthbert*.
1953: *Mandanya* (Austasia Line, Singapore).
1965: *Loucia N* (Mouzakies Ltda. S.A., Panam., (L. Nomikos, Greece)).
26.11.1970: Arrived Shanghai for breaking up.

William Pickersgill began building ships at North Dock, Sunderland, in 1838 and there came a partnership of Pickersgill & Miller. After a few years this was dissolved and soon after that the firm of W. Pickersgill & Sons was established, building mainly tramp steamers over the years. Indeed, the company had just celebrated a century of ship building when war broke out, the first ship to be launched under war conditions being the *Daydawn*, on 9 December 1939.

Twenty cargo ships were built by the company during the war, the first three from pre-war orders. In August 1940 their first 'Empire' ship was launched, to Pickersgills' own prototype; seven more were built during the war and another nine ships were constructed under licence for private owners. Seven of these were for J. A. Billmeir's Stanhope SS Company and the pre-war order for a slightly smaller vessel made a total of eight ships built for Stanhope during the war.

In 1954 Pickersgills merged with S. P. Austin & Sons Ltd., and in January 1957 a consortium took over Austin & Pickersgill Ltd.; a half interest by London & Overseas Freighters Ltd., the remainder by Lambert Bros. Ltd. and Philip Hill, Higgins & Co. Ltd. In 1968 another Sunderland shipbuilding company, Bartram & Sons, joined the group. Austin & Pickersgill began building their first SD 14-class ship on 4 October 1967 at the Southwick shipyard.

MERCHANT SHIPS BUILT UNDER PRIVATE CONTRACT OR LICENCE

241 *Daydawn* 4,768 gt, 421 ft (oa), 406 ft × 54.8 ft.
Engines: T3cyl.
Launched: 9.12.1939.
Completed: 1.1940 for Claymore Shipping Co. Ltd., Cardiff.
21.11.1940: Sunk by submarine (*U.103*) torpedo WNW of Ireland, 56.30N 14.10W whilst in convoy OB 244 (voyage: Barry/Rio Santiago – coal.)

242 *Winkleigh* 5,468 gt, 447 ft (oa), 430 ft × 56 ft.
Engines: T3cyl.
Launched: 24.2.1940.
Completed: 5.1940 for W. J. Tatum Ltd., London.
1959: *St. Anthony* (St. Anthony Shipping Co., Liberia (S. Catsell & Co., London)).
1961: (Cia. Nav. Marcasa S.A., Panama (Lebanese flag)).
20.2.1966: Arrived Valencia, Spain, for breaking up.

243 *Stanmore* 4,975 gt, 442 ft (oa), 425.6 ft × 56.7 ft. Engines: T3cyl.
Launched: 22.5.1940.
Completed: 8.1940 for Stanhope SS Co. Ltd., London.
1.10.1943: Damaged by submarine (*U.223*) torpedo east of Oran, Algeria, 36.41N 01.10E. Towed in and

beached at Tenes; decks buckled and bulkheads carried away. Constructive total loss (voyage: Middlesbrough/Sicily – military stores).

245 *Stanford* 5,696 gt, 415 ft (oa), 401 ft × 54 ft.
Engines: T3cyl.
Launched: 3.10.1940.
Completed: 2.1941 for Stanhope SS Co. Ltd., London.
1952: *Jalamohan* (Scindia SN Co. Ltd.).
1961: *Nigean Star* (Nigean Shipping Co., S.A., Greece (Tsavliris (Shipping) Ltd., London)).
8.1962: Scrapped Perama.

250 *Stangarth* 5,966 gt. Details as Yard No. 245.
Launched: 21.10.1941.
Completed: 1.1942 for Stanhope SS Co. Ltd., London.
12.3.1942: Sunk by Italian submarine (*Morosini*) torpedo, approx. 400 miles west of Bahamas, 22.00N 65.00W (voyage: New York/St. Thomas/India).

251 *Stanbank* 5,966 gt. Details as Yard No. 245.
Launched: 18.12.1941.

Completed: 3.1942 for Stanhope SS Co. Ltd.,
London.
5.5.1942: Sunk by submarine (*U.103*) torpedo
approx. 750 miles SE of New York, 34.55N 61.47W
(voyage: New York/India).

253   *Stancleeve* 5,970 gt. Details as Yard No. 245.
Launched: 4.5.1942.
Completed: 7.1942 for Stanhope SS Co. Ltd.,
London.
1951: *Akera* (Skibs-A/S Preba (Prebenson & Blakstad,
Norway)),
9.10.1961: Arrived Hirao for breaking up.

254   *Stanhill* 5,969 gt. Details as Yard No. 245.
Launched: 30.6.1942.
Completed: 9.1942 for Stanhope SS Co. Ltd.,
London.
11.5.1947: Struck rocks off Cape Palmas, Liberia,
4.29N 7.13W; abandoned. Tidal: stripped and set on
fire by native looters (voyage: Lagos/Clyde –
general).

256   *Stanlodge* 5,976 gt. Details as Yard No. 245.
Launched: 9.11.1942.
Completed: 1.1943 for Stanhope SS Co. Ltd.,
London.

1951: *Bharatvijaya* (Bharat Line Ltd., India).
11.1963: Scrapped Bombay.

257   *Chertsey* 6,001 gt. Details as Yard No. 245.
Launched: 6.1.1943.
Completed: 3.1943 for Watts, Watts & Co. Ltd.,
London.
1947: *Kingsborough* (Kingsborough Shipping Co. Ltd.
(P. Hendry & Sons, Glasgow)).
1951: *Graiglwyd* (I. Williams & Co. Ltd., Cardiff).
1959: *Nordwind* (Wallem & Co., Hong Kong).
1959: *Nan Hai 145* (Government of China).
circa 1977: renamed *Hong Qi 145*. Still listed in ship
registers but existence doubtful.

258   *Stanridge* 5,975 gt. Details as Yard No. 245.
Launched: 22.3.1943.
Completed: 5.1943 for Stanhope SS Co. Ltd.,
London.
1952: *Jalajyoti*: (Scindia SN Co. Ltd., Bombay).
5.1965: Scrapped Bombay.

259   *Chiswick* 6,006 gt. Details as Yard No. 245.
Launched: 20.5.1943.
Completed: 7.1943 for Watts, Watts & Co. Ltd.,
London.
1952: *Olga* (W. H. Schlieker & Co., Germany).
26.5.1960: Arrived Boom, Belgium for breaking up.

Built by John Readhead & Sons Ltd., West Docks, South Shields

520   *Empire Rain* 7,290 gt. Readhead design: 449 ft
(oa), 432.4 ft × 56.7 ft. Engines: T3cyl.
Launched: 30.10.1940.
Completed: 1.1941.
1945: *Amersham* (Thompson Steam Shipping Co.
Ltd., London (Clan Line Ltd.)).
1952: *Janeta* (Malabar SS Co. Ltd., Bombay).
12.1961: Sold to Bombay shipbreakers, and
3.1963: Scrapped.

521   *Empire Storm* 7,290 gt. Details as Yard No. 520.
Launched: 27.1.1941.
Completed: 3.1941.
29.5.1941: Sunk by submarine (*U.557*) torpedo in
North Atlantic, 55N 39.50W in convoy HX 128S.

522   *Empire Franklin* 7,292 gt. Details as Yard
No. 520.
Launched: 28.4.1941.
Completed: 6.1941.
1945: *Hazelbank* (Bank Line Ltd. (A. Weir Shipping
& Trading Co. Ltd.)).
1957: *Irinicos* (Cia. Nav. Nuevo Mundo S.A., Panama
(Syros Shipping Co. Ltd., London)).

1962: (Paleocrassas Bros., Greece (Syros Shipping
Co. Ltd., London)).
1963: *Iris II* (Salinas Cia. Nav. S.A., Panama
(Paleocrassas Bros., Greece (Syros Shipping Co. Ltd.,
London))).
15.2.1967: Arrived Hong Kong for breaking up.

523   *Empire Scott* 6,150 gt. Readhead design: 421.3 ft
(oa), 405.8 ft × 53.5 ft. Engines: T3cyl.
Launched: 10.7.1941.
Completed: 8.1941.
1946: *Walter Scott* (Chine Shipping Co. Ltd. (Anglo-
Danubian Transport Co. Ltd., London)).
1960: *Zafiro* (Lanena Shipping Co. Ltd., Hong Kong
(T. Engan, Manila)).
1961: *Oriental* (Sigma Shipping Co. Ltd. (Trinity
Development Co. Ltd., Hong Kong)).
1963: Scrapped Hong Kong.

524   *Empire Stevenson* 6,209 gt. Details as Yard
No. 523.
Launched: 25.8.1941.
Completed: 10.1941.
13.9.1942: Blew up and sank after being struck by

aircraft torpedoes north of Bear Island, Barents Sea, 76.10N 10.05E (Convoy PQ 18) (voyage: Loch Ewe/Archangel – ammunition).

Note: The American freighter *Wacosta* (1920, 5032 gt) laden with war supplies and a deck cargo of tanks, was stationed immediately astern of the *Empire Stevenson* and took the full force of the blast when the 'Empire' ship exploded. Aboard the *Wacosta*, steam pipes, fuel lines, the electrical system, instruments and other mechanism were all smashed and the main engine displaced. As the vessel drifted to a standstill, a torpedo bomber released a missile from such close range that it landed on No. 2 hatch, penetrated it and exploded from inside the hold, blowing a large hole in the side of the ship. The *Wacosta* was abandoned and later sunk by the escort.

In fact, in just thirteen minutes and at a cost of only five aircraft, German torpedo bombers had sunk the eight ships which had formed columns 9 and 10 of the convoy. Official records suggest that column 10 failed to make its emergency turn with necessary promptness, while the *Empire Stevenson* and the rest of column 9 made no turn at all; thus all the ships failed to avoid the torpedoes aimed at them.

527 *Empire Clough* 6,147 gt. Details as Yard No. 523.
Launched: 2.4.1942.
Completed: 6.1942.
10.6.1942: Sunk by submarine (*U.94*) torpedo in mid-Atlantic 51.50N 35.00W (approx.) whilst in convoy ONS 100 and on maiden voyage.

531 *Empire Fortune* 6,140 gt. Details as Yard No. 523.
Launched: 9.11.1942.
Completed: 1.1943.
1943: *Van Honthorst* (Government of The Netherlands).
1946: *Stad Schiedam* (Halcyon Lijn N.V., Rotterdam).
2.12.1961: Arrived Rotterdam for breaking up.

535 *Empire Path* 6,140 gt. Details as Yard No. 523.
Launched: 5.7.1943.
Completed: 9.1943.
24.12.1944: Struck mine near Dunkirk, 51.22N 02.52E. Beached; broke back, abandoned; submerged. Total loss.

539 *Empire Grey* 6,140 gt. Details as Yard No. 523.
Launched: 9.3.1944.
Completed: 5.1944.
1947: *Burhill* (Zinal SS Co. Ltd. (J. Burness & Sons Ltd., London)).
1951: *London City* (Golden Cross Line Ltd., London).
1951: *Chepman* (Barberry's SS Co. Ltd. (Runciman (London) Ltd.)).
1957: *Jag Janani* (Great Eastern Shipping Co. Ltd., Bombay).
5.1961: Scrapped Bombay.

525 *Empire Squire* 7,044 gt. 'B'-type. 446.4 ft (oa), 430.9 ft × 56.2 ft. Engines: T3cyl.
Launched: 4.11.1941.

Completed: 1.1942.
1943: *Makedonia* (Royal Hellenic Government).
1947: (A. G. Pappadakis, Piraeus).
1962: *Anthas* (Cia. Nav. y de Comercio Adonis Ltd., Costa Rica (Aegis Shipping Co. Ltd., Greece)).
23.6.1967: Arrived Shanghai for breaking up.

526 *Empire Forest* 7,025 gt. Details as Yard No. 525.
Launched: 15.1.1942.
Completed: 3.1942.
1946: *Clan Allan* (Clan Line Steamers Ltd.).
1958: *Umtali* (Bullard, King & Co. Ltd.).
1959: *Clan Allan* (Clan Line Steamers Ltd.).
1961: *Ardsirod* (Mullion & Co., Hong Kong).
12.10.1966: Arrived Kaohsiung for breaking up.

528 *Empire Hazlitt* 7,036 gt. Details as Yard No. 525.
Launched: 14.5.1942.
Completed: 7.1942.
1943: *Aelbert Cuyp* (Government of The Netherlands).
1946: *Delfshaven* (Van Uden's Scheep & Agentuur Maats N.V., Rotterdam).
1960: *Edina* (Zenith Transportation Corp., Liberia (F. Delfino S.R.L., Italy)).
1961: *Confidence* (Consolidated Navigation Corpn., Liberia (Expedo & Co. (London) Ltd.)).
12.1966: Arrived Kaohsiung for breaking up.

529 *Empire Ruskin* 7,037 gt. Details as Yard No. 525.
Launched: 14.7.1942.
Completed: 9.1942.
1943: *Van der Capelle* (Government of The Netherlands).
1947: *Delfland* (Koninklijke Hollandsche Lloyd N.V., Amsterdam).
1959: *M. Esref* (Cerrahogullari Umumi Nakliyat T.A.S., Vapuculuk ve Ticaret, Istanbul).
13.10.1968: Arrived Istanbul for breaking up.

530 *Empire Lakeland* 7,015 gt. Details as Yard No. 525.
Launched: 14.9.1942.
Completed: 11.1942.
11.3.1943: Sunk by submarine (*U.190*) torpedo west of Hebrides 59N 15W (approx.) (Convoy SC 121) (voyage: New York/Glasgow).

532 *Empire Capulet* 7,044 gt. Details as Yard No. 525.
Launched: 20.1.1943.
Completed: 3.1943.
1946: *Hesione* (British & South American SN Co. Ltd. (Houston Line (London) Ltd.)).
5.10.1960: Arrived Hong Kong for breaking up.

533 *Empire Perdita* 7,028 gt. Details as Yard No. 525.

Launched: 10.3.1943.
Completed: 5.1943.
1948: *Navarino* (Ensign SS Co. Ltd. (S. G. Embiricos Ltd., London)).
1952: *Fortunato B* (Navigazione Dani SpA (Dani & Co., Genoa)).
12.1964: Arrived Vado for breaking up.

536 *Empire Pickwick* 7,068 gt. Details as Yard No. 525.
Launched: 31.8.1943.
Completed: 11.1943.
1948: *Clan Mackendrick* (Clan Line Steamers Ltd.).
1961: *Ardpatrick* (Mullion & Co. Ltd., Hong Kong).
1966: *Haringhata* (National Shipping Corpn., Karachi).
16.7.1968: Arrived Karachi for breaking up.

537 *Empire Crown* 7,070 gt. Details as Yard No. 525.
Launched: 16.10.1943.
Completed: 1.1944.
1945: *Capitaine G. Lacoley* (Government of France).
1961: *Mparmpa Petros* (Mparmpapetros Shipping Co. S.A. (Pateras Shipbrokers Ltd., London)).
22.5.1963: Aground at Porto de Pedras, 40 miles north of Maceio, Brazil. Flooded and abandoned. Constructive total loss (voyage: Buenos Aires/Naples – grain).

538 *Empire Curzon* 7,067 gt. Details as Yard No. 525.
Launched: 24.12.1943.
Completed: 2.1944.
2.9.1944: Driven ashore by heavy weather, Normandy coast. Refloated, drifted on to wreck of British steamer *Iddesleigh* (1927, 5,025 gt).
29.9.1944: towed to Southampton; found to require entire new bottom.
27.11.1944: towed to Falmouth; laid up.
12.1944: Moored in River Fal.
11.1945: Sold for breaking up, and
14.12.1945: Towed to Briton Ferry for scrapping.

540 *Empire Moulmein* 7,047 gt. Details as Yard No. 525, but: Engines: T3cyl and LP turbine.
Launched: 8.6.1944.
Completed: 8.1944.
1945: *Colonel Vieljeux* (Government of France).
1948: *Ville de Diego Suarez* (Nouvelle Compagnie Havraise Peninsulaire de Nav., Paris).
1961: *Vimy* (Soc. Anon. Monegasque d'Armement et de Nav., Monaco).
1962: *Demirhan* (Sadikoglu, Riza ve Aslan, ve Ortagi Adi Komandit Sirketi, Turkey).
1966: *Manizade* (Manizade Vapuru Donatma Istiraki (Z. Sonmez ve Ziya).
later restyled:
(Manioglu Gemi Isletmeciligi A.S., Turkey), (and

later as S. Manioglu, Denizcilik Isletmesi Donatma).
3.1976: Scrapped Aliaga, Turkey.

541 (Laid down as) *Empire Sarawak* 'C'-type.
447.8 ft (oa), 431.2 ft × 56.3 ft. Engines: T3cyl.
Launched: 24.8.1944.
Taken over by the Admiralty and:
Completed: 1945 as *Beauly Firth*, a hull repair and maintenance ship.
1948: *Stanfirth* (7,285 gt) (Stanhope SS Co. Ltd. (J. A. Billmeir & Co. Ltd.)).
1961: *Akamas* (Cia. Nav. y de Comercio Degedo Ltds., Costa Rica (Aegis Shipping Co. Ltd., Greece)).
1966: (Akamas Shipping Co. Ltd., Cyprus (Aegis Shipping Co. Ltd., Greece)).
1968: Renamed *Skepsis*.
23.8.1968: Arrived Shanghai for breaking up.

542 (Laid down as) *Empire Pitcairn* Details as Yard No. 541.
Launched: 10.7.1944.
Taken over by the Admiralty and renamed *Moray Firth*;
Completed as a repair and maintenance ship for aircraft components.
1947: *Linaria* (7,333 gt) (Stag Line Ltd. (J. Robinson & Sons Ltd.)). Converted to a dry cargo ship by Tyne Dock Engineering Co. Ltd.
1954: *Eskglen* (Chellew Navigation Co. Ltd., London).
1956: (Esk Shipping Co. Ltd. (H. M. Lund, London)).
1961: *Marine Fortune* (Fortune Shipping Co. Ltd., Hong Kong).
1961: (Herald Shipping Co. Ltd., Hong Kong).
8.1967: Arrived Yokosuka for breaking up.

543 *Empire Rabaul* 7,307 gt. Details as Yard No. 541.
Launched: 27.11.1944.
Completed: 2.1945.
1947: *Dumfries* (B. J. Sutherland & Co. Ltd., Newcastle).
1953: *Charles Dickens* (Chine Shipping Co. Ltd. (Anglo-Danubian Transport Co. Ltd., London)).
1956: *Pohorje* (Government of Yugoslavia).
21.4.1967: Arrived Trieste for breaking up.

545 *Empire Fawley* 7,392 gt. 'D'-type. 449 ft (oa), 431.2 ft × 56.3 ft. Engines: T3cyl.
Launched: 25.4.1945.
Completed: 5.1945.
1946: *Clan Mackinlay* (Clan Line Steamers Ltd.).
2.11.1962: Arrived Hong Kong for breaking up.

547 *Empire Gunfleet* 7,387 gt. Details as Yard No. 545.

The *Bulgaria*, formerly *Empire Flamborough*, in West India Docks, London, October 1964. (Wm. Pickersgill & Sons Ltd., Yard No. 277.)

The 'B'-type *Empire Curzon* at New York, March 1944. (J. Readhead & Sons Ltd., Yard No. 538.) U.S.C.G.

The *Lakoja Palm*, completed in 1947, was intended to be the *Empire Birdsay*. (Shipbuilding Corporation Ltd., Newcastle, Yard No. 21.)

Launched: 4.1945.
Completed: 6.1945.
1946: *Clan Mackay* (Clan Line Steamers Ltd.).

1962: *Babylon* (Cia. de Nav. Victoria Neptuno S.A.,
Panama (Teh Hu SS Co. Ltd., Taiwan)).
25.9.1966: Arrived Hong Kong for breaking up.

John Readhead started his working life as a colliery millwright. In 1850, aged thirty-two and now a shipwright, he moved to Thomas Marshall's shipyard where the first iron vessel built on the Tyne had been constructed. Readhead soon became manager and served Marshall for fifteen years.

Then branching out, John Readhead took a partner and Readhead & Softley began shipbuilding in March 1865 with a small iron collier brig, Yard No. 1, named *Unus* for Hodge & Williamson. The partnership was dissolved in 1872, but in the next sixteen years 152 ships were constructed, establishing for Readhead a reputation for quality. A paddle tug built in 1870 lasted eighty-two years, the screw steamer *Sagunto*, Yard No. 114, launched in 1875 was still in service as the *Enrique Maynes* over ninety years later and another tug, the *President* (Yard No. 124) built in 1876 was scrapped after giving eighty-three years of service.

In 1875 Edward Hain of St. Ives, Cornwall, began his family's long-standing connection with Readhead when he placed an order for a 1,200-ton screw steamship. Named *Trewidden* (Yard No. 146) she was launched in 1878 and a second order soon followed. The friendship established between the two families became outstanding in owner/builder associations in the building of 'Tre'-named ships for the Cornish owners.

In 1880 an adjacent wood-ship yard, known as the West Docks, was acquired for the construction and repair of iron and steel vessels and in 1892 a drydock was added to the shipyard facilities. The firm became a limited company in 1909, the first ship under the new title being the *Trelissick* (Yard No. 408) for Hains. These owners continued to dominate the yard's building list and when war broke out in 1914 sixty-five ships had been built by Readheads for them.

During the war years the shipyard completed twenty cargo vessels, including 'B'-type standard ships for the Shipping Controller, as well as a number of smaller craft. One ship, converted during construction, became the Royal Fleet Auxiliary vessel *Oletta*, the first and only deep-sea oil tanker built by the company.

By the mid-1920s the world depression took effect and shipbuilding orders dropped. Then another association commenced when Yard No. 482 was laid down as *Arabistan* for F. C. Strick & Company. This ship was acquired by Turnbull, Scott & Company and completed as *Southgate*, but in 1927 a vessel was delivered to Strick and further orders for a run of thirteen ships carried the shipyard, working at full capacity, into the early 1930s. Then the depression enveloped the West Docks again; grass did, indeed, grow on the slipways and only one vessel was completed in the next six years, but the company survived, solely on its ship repairing activities.

In the late 1930s shipbuilding recommenced and the riverside property which separated the shipbuilding yard from its repair facilities was purchased. The old docks were filled with spoil from a nearby ballast hill dating from the days of the sailing brigs and, for the first time, the yard became one inter-connected unit.

During World War II, Government orders were for twenty-five tramp steamers, nine to Readhead designs and the remainder being eleven 'B's, three 'C's and two of the 'D' type. Two 'C'-type hulls were taken over by the Admiralty as repair ships, H.M.S. *Moray Firth* and H.M.S. *Beauly Firth*. The latter was completed up-river, at the Palmer's yard, but *Moray Firth* became the only ship of her type to be wholly completed by one firm. Two small 'Chant'-type tankers were also completed and ten vessels were built to private contracts, including three for the Strick Line. When war ended the yard capacity was three berths for ships to 500 feet.

By 1965 Readhead's had completed forty-four vessels for the Strick Line and by the same year, when the Hain name became part of Hain-Nourse Ltd., under a P & O merger, the shipyard had delivered eighty-seven ships to Hain ownership.

The last order for the yard was a 27,000-ton bulk carrier, launched as *Zinnia* for the Stag Line on 26 July 1968. Meanwhile, in late 1967, Readhead's had merged to become a wholly-owned subsidiary of Swan, Hunters, this company, in turn, becoming Swan, Hunter & Tyne Shipbuilders Ltd., in 1968 and being restyled as Swan, Hunter Shipbuilders Ltd., in 1969.

MERCHANT SHIPS BUILT UNDER PRIVATE CONTRACT OR LICENCE

516 *Afghanistan* 6,992 gt, 472.5 ft (oa), 454 ft × 58.5 ft. Engines: T3cyl.
Launched: 11.12.1939.
Completed: 3.1940 for Strick Line (1923) Ltd. (F. C. Strick & Co. Ltd.).
1962: *Samareitis* (Cia. Nav. Marprisa S.A., Panama (N. & J. Vlassopulos Ltd.)).
1965: *Cyrenian* (Cia. Minotauros S.A., Liberia (N. & J. Vlassopulos Ltd.)).
14.3.1967: Arrived Kaohsiung for breaking up.

517 *Baluchistan* 6,750 gt. Details as Yard No. 516.
Launched: 22.3.1940.
Completed: 6.1940 for Strick Line (1923) Ltd. (F. C. Strick & Co. Ltd.).
8.3.1942· Sunk by submarine (*U.68*) torpedo south of Ivory Coast, 04.13N 08.32W.

518 *Thursobank* 5,575 gt, 451.8 ft (oa), 435.2 ft × 56.7 ft. Engines: T3cyl.
Launched: 18.6.1940.
Completed: 10.1940 for Bank Line Ltd. (A. Weir & Co. Ltd.).
22.3.1942: Sunk by submarine (*U.373*) torpedo (approx.) 350 miles south-east of New York, 38.05N 68.30W (voyage: New York/Cape Town/Alexandria).

519 *North Britain* 4,635 gt, 421.5 ft (oa), 405.6 ft × 53.6 ft. Engines: T3cyl.
Launched: 16.9.1940.
Completed: 11.1940 for North Shipping Co. Ltd. (H. Roberts & Son, Newcastle).
5.5.1943: Sunk by submarine (*U.125*) torpedo south of Cape Farewell, Greenland, 55.08N 42.43W, a straggler from convoy ONS 5 (voyage: Glasgow/Halifax – fireclay).

534 *Kelmscott* 7,039 gt, 446.5 ft (oa), 430.9 ft × 56.2 ft. Engines: T3cyl.
Launched: 7.5.1943.
Completed: 7.1943 for Pachesham SS Co. (Runciman (London) Ltd.).
9.2.1944: Damaged by submarine (*U.845*) torpedo off St. John's, NF. Towed in, flooded and listing (voyage: Canada/U.K. – paper).
17.8.1944: Sailed Baltimore for repairs; but
24.8.1944: In collision off Atlantic City, N.J., with American Liberty ship *William Leavitt* (1944,

7,176 gt). Holed and flooded; beached then towed to Delaware Breakwater thence Baltimore. Repaired.
1949: *Queen Anne* (Cadogan SS Co. (T. Dunlop & Sons, Glasgow)).
1954: *Marian Buczek* (Polish Ocean Lines, Gdynia).
30.3.1968: Arrived Whampoa for breaking up.

544 *Shahristan* 7,311 gt, 447.8 ft (oa), 431.2 ft × 56.3 ft. Engines: T3cyl.
Launched: 7.2.1945.
Completed: 4.1945 for Strick Line (1923) Ltd. (F. C. Strick & Co. Ltd.).
19.12.1962: Arrived Monfalcone for breaking up.

546 *Palikonda* 7,434 gt. Details as Yard No. 544.
Launched: 22.6.1945.
Completed: 9.1945 for British India SN Co. Ltd.
1959: *Sadikzade* (Sadikzade Nazim Og. Vapurculuk Konandit, Turkey).
1964: *Preveze* (Sadikzade Rusen Og. Denizilik, Turkey).
9.1.1969: On fire in engine room near Cape Verde Islands.
11.1.1969: Extinguished, but heavy damage (voyage: Ashdod/Santos – potash). Towed in to St. Vincent C.V., by Russian *Cherniakhovsk* (1961, 5,382 gt). Constructive total loss; towed Antwerp; discharged; then 23.6.1969: Arrived Istanbul, in tow, for breaking up.

548 *Obra* 5,695 gt, 446 ft (oa), 430 ft × 57.5 ft.
Engines: T3cyl and LP turbine.
Launched: 20.11.1945.
Completed: 3.1946 for British India SN Co. Ltd.
1962: *Dairen* (China Pacific Nav. Co. (Hornbeam & Co. Ltd.)).
1962: *Adri XIV* (a military auxiliary; Government of Indonesia).
25.9.1964: Capsized and sank in Kobe harbour in a typhoon. Later raised and laid up at Nadahama. No further trace.

549 *Okhla* 5,732 gt. Details as Yard No. 548.
Launched: 17.1.1946.
Completed: 5.1946 for British India SN Co. Ltd.
1961: *Ruthy Ann* (Red Anchor Line Ltd. (C. Moller & Co., Hong Kong)).
1962: *Adri XV* (a military auxiliary; Government of Indonesia).

1969: Transferred to Indonesian Navy.
4.2.1971: Engine breakdown 250 miles east of
Singapore (voyage: Indonesia/Taiwan). Taken in
tow, and: 21.2.1971: Arrived Singapore. Sold,
and: 27.2.1971: Arrived local shipbreakers for
scrapping.

550 *Baskerville* 5,571 gt, 452 ft (oa),
434.5 ft × 56.7 ft. Engines: T3cyl.
Launched: 31.5.1946.
Completed: 8.1946 for Barberry's SS Co. Ltd.
(Runciman (London) Ltd.).

1950: *Birmingham City* (Bristol City Line of
Steamships (C. Hill & Sons)).
1963: *Semporna Bay* (Kinabatangen Shipping Co.,
Hong Kong (United China Shipping Co. Ltd., Hong
Kong)).
1966: Renamed *Victoria Bay*.
20.6.1969: Aground leaving Chittagong on voyage
to Chalna.
6.7.1969: Refloated. Repairs uneconomic. Sold, and:
10.8.1969: Arrived Hong Kong for breaking up.

Built by Shipbuilding Corporation Ltd., Tyne Branch, Newcastle

The low Walker yard of Armstrong-Whitworth Ltd., closed in 1934 during the depression, was re-opened in 1942 under the management of Sir W. G. Armstrong Whitworth & Co. (Shipbuilders) Ltd. Yard Nos. 1–5 were completed by them and the yard then became the Tyne Branch of the Shipbuilding Corporation Ltd., before closing again in 1948. During the latter period Yard Nos. 6–14 and 21 were completed as tramps, with the remaining vessels (to Yard No. 28, the last) built as coasters or Military Oil Barges.

6 *Empire Abbey* 7,032 gt. 'B'type. 446.3 ft (oa),
430.9 ft × 56.2 ft. Engines: T3cyl.
Launched: 10.12.1943.
Completed: 3.1944.
1946: *Teviot* (Royal Mail Lines Ltd.).
1960: *Ardellis* (Mullion & Co. Ltd., Hong Kong).
1963: *Tung An* (Hai An Shipping Co. Ltd., Hong
Kong).
6.8.1966: Arrived Kaohsiung for breaking up.

7 *Empire Mandarin* 7,078 gt. Details as Yard No. 6.
Launched: 9.3.1944.
Completed: 5.1944.
1947: *Lulworth Hill* (Dorset SS Co. Ltd. (Counties
Ship Management Co. Ltd.)).
1949: Renamed *Castle Hill*.
1950: *London Builder* (London & Overseas Freighters
Ltd.).
1950: *Silver Wake* (Soc. Armadora Insular S.A.,
Panama).
1954: *Navarino* (Eastern Seas SS Co. Ltd., London).
1955: *Stanthorpe* (Stanhope SS Co. Ltd. (J. A. Billmeir
& Co. Ltd.)).
1961: *Ardbrae* (Mullion & Co. Ltd., Hong Kong).
1.3.1966: Arrived Onomichi for breaking up.

8 *Empire Lady* 7,046 gt. Details as Yard No. 6.
Launched: 20.6.1944.
Completed: 8.1944.

1946: *Tweed* (Royal Mail Lines Ltd.).
20.8.1959: Arrived Newport, Mon., for breaking up.

9 *Empire Asquith* 7,082 gt. Details as Yard No. 6.
Launched: 4.9.1944.
Completed: 11.1944.
1947: *Brockley Hill* (Brockley Hill SS Co. Ltd.
(Counties Ship Management Co. Ltd.)).
1950: (Vandar Shipping Co. Ltd. (Ivanovic & Co.
Ltd., London)).
1951: *Starcrest* (Crest Shipping Co. (Ivanovic & Co.
Ltd.)).
1957: *Argosy* (Codemar Cia. de Empresa
Maritimas, Panama).
1960: *Nezihi Ipar* (Ipar Transport Ltd., Turkey).
9.1970: Scrapped Istanbul.

10 *Empire Morley* 7,068 gt. Details as Yard No. 6.
Launched: 28.11.1944.
Completed: 2.1945.
1947: *Tower Grange* (Tower SS Co. Ltd. (Counties
Ship Management Co. Ltd.)).
1950: *London Trader* (London & Overseas Freighters
Ltd.).
1950: *Nico* (Cia. Mar. Azores, Liberia).
6.1969: Scrapped Etajima.

11 *Empire Prospect* 7,331 gt, 447.8 ft (oa),
431.2 ft × 56.3 ft. Engines: T3cyl.

Launched: 15.3.1945.
Completed: 6.1945.
1947: *Ronald M. Scobie* (Goulandris Bros. Ltd.,
London).
1954: *Plover* (Goulandris Bros., Ltd.).
1965: *Kowloon Venture* (Kowloon Carriers Inc. (Wah
Kwong & Co. (Hong Kong) Ltd.)).
27.4.1969: Arrived Kaohsiung for breaking up.

12   *Empire Antigua* 7,331 gt. Details as Yard No. 11.
Launched: 20.11.1945.
Completed: 2.1946.
1946: *Culross* (South Georgia Co. Ltd. (Chr. Salvesen
& Co.)).
1960: *Akastos* (Aegis Shipping Co. Ltd., Greece).
1966: (Agenor Shipping Co. Ltd., Cyprus).
1967: *Marina* (Blue X Transocean Co. Ltd. (I.
Chiotakis, Greece)).
4.8.1968: Arrived Hamburg for breaking up.

13   (Laid down as) *Empire Gantock* 7,331 gt. 'D'
type. Details as Yard No. 11.
Launched: 16.4.1946.
Completed: 8.1946 as *Martita* for 'K' Steamships
Ltd. (Kaye, Son & Co. Ltd.).
1960: *Maroudio* (Cia. Nav. Almadin, Greece).
1965: *Thalie* (Panafrica Atlantic Corp., Panama) (East
and West Africa Shipping Co.).
15.6.1968: Arrived Vado for breaking up.

14   (Intended name) *Empire Stroma* 5,123 gt. Details
as Yard No. 11.
Launched: 23.3.1947.
Completed: 7.1947 as *Ashantian* for United Africa
Co. Ltd.
1949: *Ashanti Palm* (Palm Line Ltd. (United Africa
Co. Ltd.)).
18.11.1962: Dragged anchors, aground on rocks, then
sank at entrance to Naples Harbour, Italy.
Constructive total loss (voyage: Genoa/Port
Harcourt – general).

21   (Intended name) *Empire Birdsay* 5,122 gt. Details
as Yard No. 11.
Launched: 16.8.1947.
Completed: 12.1947 as *Zarian* for United Africa Co.
Ltd.
1949: *Lokoja Palm* (Palm Line Ltd. (United Africa Co.
Ltd.)).
1966: *Despina L* (Cia. Nav. Kea S.A., Panama (Lemos
& Pateras Ltd.)).
1969: *Nova* (Nova Shipping Co. Ltd., Cyprus
(Pergamos Shipping Co. Ltd.)).
12.1971: Scrapped China.

In May 1946 the Tyne Branch of the Shipbuilding Corporation launched a half-ship, this being a new fore-end for the *Harpagus* (see Doxford, Yard No. 695), which had been towed to the River Tyne after breaking in two off the Normandy beaches in August 1944.

Early in 1947 the last two 'standard' ships (Yard Nos. 14 and 21) were still on the stocks, construction having been delayed by a shortage of materials. In the March they were sold to the United Africa Company, launched soon afterwards and completed in the second half of the year.

Built by Shipbuilding Corporation Ltd., Wear Branch, Sunderland

1   *Empire Trail* 7,083 gt. 'D'-type. 449 ft (oa),
429.8 ft × 56.3 ft. Engine: T3cyl.
Launched: 19.8.1943.
Completed: 12.1943.
1947: *Trail* (Steamship 'Mombassa' Co. Ltd. (Maclay
& McIntyre Ltd.)).
1951: *Loch Maddy* (Maclay & McIntyre Ltd.).
1960: *Ocean Glory* (Panamanian Oriental SS Corp.
(Wheelock, Marden & Co., Hong Kong)).
28.8.1962: Laid up with propeller damage at Hong
Kong.
2.9.1962: Broke from moorings, damaged in collision

with *Grosvenor Navigator* (ex *Empire Pendennis*) in
typhoon at Hong Kong.
1963: Sold to Japanese shipbreakers.

2   *Empire Tudor* 7,087 gt. Details as Yard No. 1.
Launched: 23.5.1944.
Completed: 7.1944.
1948: *Grandyke* (Goulandris Bros., London).
1949: *Benvannoch* (Ben Line Steamers Ltd.).
1956: *Medina Princess* (Helmville Ltd. (M.
Alachouzos, London)).
3.8.1962: Aground on reef near Djibouti. Moored.

1.9.1964: Broke moorings, grounded in damaged condition, with stern submerged.
1967: Reported sold to Greek buyers for breaking up.

3   *Empire Gladstone* 7,090 gt. Details as Yard No. 1.
Launched: 24.2.1944.
Completed: 5.1944.
5.9.1950: Ashore on Haystack Rock, eight miles north of Twofold Point, near Sydney, N.S.W., 36.56N 149.57E
(voyage: Whyalla/Adelaide/Sydney – iron ore and vehicle bodies).
Total loss.
21.9.1950: Wreck sold locally for salving of portable equipment.

4   *Empire Cowdray* 7,072 gt. 'C'-type. 447.8 ft (oa), 433 ft × 56.3 ft. Engines: T3cyl.
Launched: 19.8.1944.
Completed: 10.1944.
1948: *Granhill* (Goulandris Bros., London).
1951: *Baxtergate* (Turnbull, Scott & Co. Ltd.).
1.12.1960: Arrived Barrow for breaking up.

5   *Empire Mandalay* 7,086 gt. Details as Yard No. 1.
Launched: 29.10.1944.
Completed: 12.1944.
1946: *Tribesman* (T. & J. Harrison).
1961: *Delta* (Margalante Cia. Nav., Panama).
1961: (Sigma Shipping Co. Ltd.).
12.1961: Scrapped Hong Kong.

6   *Empire Prome* 7,086 gt. Details as Yard No. 1.
Launched: 1.3.1945.
Completed: 4.1945.
1947: *Martagon* (Kaye, Son & Co. Ltd., London).
1959: *Mehmet Ipar* (Ipar Transport Ltd., Turkey).
9.1970: Scrapped Istanbul.

7   *Empire Mombasa* 7,319 gt. Details as Yard No. 4.
Launched: 28.5.1945.
Completed: 2.1946.
1946: *Indian Enterprise* (India SS Co. Ltd., Calcutta).
19.6.1950: Explosion, sank 300 miles south of Suez, 25.31N 35.27E (voyage: Bremen, London/Calcutta – explosives and general).

8   (Laid down as) *Empire Kedah* 7,311 gt. Details as Yard No. 4.
Launched: 6.11.1945.
Completed: 4.1946 as *Marshall* for Kaye, Son & Co. Ltd., London.
1962: *M. Nurfan* (Cerra Umumi, Turkey).
25.9.1969: Arrived Istanbul for breaking up.

9   (Laid down as) *Empire Longstone* 7,301 gt. Details as Yard No. 1.
Launched: 2.5.1946.
Completed: 8.1946 as *Hesperides* for Houston Line Ltd.
1960: *Clan Murray* (Clan Line Steamers Ltd.).
9.1962: Scrapped Osaka.

10   (Laid down as) *Empire Stronsay* 7,318 gt. Details as Yard No. 1.
Launched: 26.9.1946 as *Louis E. Durand*.
Completed: 12.1946 as *Chef Mecanician Durand* (Government of France).
1949: *Rollon* (Cie. Maritime Normande (J. Chastellain et Cie., Rouen)).
1963: *Aeakos* (Aegis Shipping Co. Ltd., Greece).
9.9.1965: Aground on reef off Borneo, South China Sea, 5.07N 112.33E (voyage: Zamboanga/Europe – copra). Abandoned.
11.11.1965: Salvage vessel left from Singapore.
5.12.1965: Ship seized by 100 pirates: salvage vessel returned to base.

11   (Laid down as) *Empire Ronaldsay* 7,331 gt. Details as Yard No. 1.
Launched: 28.4.1947.
Completed: 7.1947 as *Lagosian* for United Africa Co. Ltd., London.
1949: *Lagos Palm* (Palm Line Ltd. (United Africa Co. Ltd.)).
1961: Renamed *Oguta Palm*.
1964: *Heraclitos* (Skaramanga Shipping Co. (M. Scufalos, Greece)).
1968: (Skaramanga Shipping Co. (G. Eleftheriou, Greece)).
1969: *Herodemos* (Helean Nav. Co. (G. Eleftheriou, Greece)).
4.4.1973: Arrived Split for breaking up.

The Wear Branch of the Shipbuilding Corporation was the old Robert Thompson yard. Robert Thompson began shipbuilding on the banks of the River Wear in 1819 with the construction of small sailing coasters. He took his three sons, Robert, John and Joseph, into the business and in the 1840s worked a small site at Washington Staithes, but was forced to close down owing to a slump in those 'Hungry Forties' years.

In 1846 he re-started in a small yard at North Sands and the first order was a 240-ton brig. Robert Thompson Jr. left the business in 1854 to open his own yard at Southwick; his brother John began his own business in 1861 at North Dock and Joseph carried on until his own sons were old enough to join him in what became the well-known firm of Joseph L. Thompson & Sons.

Robert Thompson Jr. built his first barque, *Graces*, 449 gt, in 1855, a vessel which spent much of her life carrying coal via the Cape of Good Hope to Aden to bunker P & O ships stationed east of Suez. He built many barques, but in 1870 turned out his first iron screw coastal collier, forerunner of many more. The hull of the Royal Mail Steam Packet Co.'s *Derwent*, 2,402 gt, was delivered in 1879. Robert Thompson Jr.'s yard became Robert Thompson & Sons when his two boys joined the business in 1881, purchasing the Bridge Dockyard on the Wear's north bank, and which included a 320 ft dry dock.

The Southwick yard was enlarged and modernised in 1901 with longer building berths and the Bridge yard was improved. The business became a limited company in 1906; cargo steamers continued to be turned out in a steady stream and in the 1914–1918 war many 'C'-type steamers of 5,100 tdw were built. In the late 1920s, with depression and an overstocked market, tramp ship building was discontinued, the last ships being *Harmonic* and *Harmattan* for J. & C. Harrison in 1930. Two motor trawlers for Portuguese owners were built, but the buyers defaulted on payment and in 1932 the business was offered for sale. The Southwick yard went to the National Shipbuilders Security, plant and machinery being sold by auction and in 1933 the Bridge yard closed down.

In 1942 the Southwick yard was resuscitated under the Shipbuilding Corporation title to build a number of 'Empire' tramp ships for the Government and a number of small craft were also turned out.

In February 1947 there was still one large 'Empire' ship on the stocks for Government account, this a reprieve of the yard's originally-intended closing date of January 1947, due to a shortage of materials to complete the ship. She was sold to the United Africa Company and launched three months later, but it was 1952 before the shipyard finally closed down.

Built by Short Brothers Ltd., Pallion, Sunderland

462 *Empire Lightning* 6,942 gt, 439.8 ft (oa), 427.5 ft × 57 ft. Engines: T3cyl.
Launched: 4.9.1940.
Completed: 1.1941.
7.10.1942: In collision with British steamer *Milcrest* (1919, 5,278 gt) sixty miles south-east of Halifax, NS, in which the *Milcrest* sank. The *Empire Lightning* put back to Halifax with bow damage: repaired.
1946: *Trident* (Hall Bros., Steamship Co. Ltd., Newcastle).
9.11.1959: Arrived Osaka for breaking up.

464 *Empire Summer* 6,949 gt. Details as Yard No. 462.
Launched: 27.12.1940.
Completed: 5.1941.
1946: *Stonegate* (Turnbull, Scott & Co. Ltd., London).
1955: *Hastedt* (C. Meentzen Schiffahrt und Handel GmbH, Bremen).
1959: *Hoping Wu Shi Err* (Government of China).
1973: (China Ocean Shipping Co.).
1979: Renamed *Ho Ping 52*.
circa 1985: Renamed *Zhan Dou 52*.
1987: Name removed from ship registers.

465 *Empire Sun* 6,952 gt. Details as Yard No. 462.
Launched: 10.4.1941.

Completed: 6.1941.
7.2.1942: Sunk by submarine (*U.751*) torpedo, south of Halifax NS, 43.55N 64.22W.

466 *Empire Burton* 6,966 gt. Details as Yard No. 462.
Launched: 29.5.1941.
Completed: 8.1941.
19.9.1941: Sunk by submarine (*U.74*) torpedo, 61.30N 35.11W, east of Cape Farewell, Greenland in convoy SC 44 (Sydney NS/United Kingdom).

467 *Empire Wyclif* 6,966 gt. Details as Yard No. 462.
Launched: 28.7.1941.
Completed: 9.1941.
1946: *North Anglia* (North Shipping Co. Ltd. (H. Roberts & Sons Ltd., Newcastle)).
1960: *Happy Mariner* (Mariner Shipping Co. Ltd., Hong Kong).
3.1967: Scrapped Hirohata, Japan.

468 *Empire Newton* 7,037 gt, 446.5 ft (oa), 431 ft × 56.3 ft. Engines: T3cyl.
Launched: 21.10.1941.
Completed: 1.1942.

1946: *Artisan* (Charente SS Co. Ltd. (T. & J. Harrison)).
21.8.1959: Arrived Grays, Essex for breaking up.

469   *Empire Story* 7,037 gt. Details as Yard No. 468.
Launched: 19.12.1941.
Completed: 3.1942.

On 3 May 1942 the *Empire Story* sailed from St. John, N.B., loaded with army tanks and trucks, to join a convoy forming up at Bedford Basin, Halifax NS, bound for Bombay via Table Bay.

The following day, due to thick fog and the strong set of the tides in the Bay of Fundy, she was well off course and ran ashore on the rocks of North West Ledge, near Briar Island, N.B.

Severely damaged, the *Empire Story* was abandoned as soon as an S.O.S. had been sent. The Canadian tug *Foundation Franklin* (1918, 653 gt) was despatched, only to be told by the Master of a fisheries vessel that the ship had refloated herself at high tide (the tidal range in this area being about thirty feet) and had drifted off, derelict, into the fog.

Located, half submerged, she was taken in tow for the nearby port of Digby but when only a few miles from that destination the ship's stern became submerged, her bows reared high out of the water and she slid into the murky depths, in position 44.35N 66.19W.

470   *Empire Keats* 7,035 gt. Details as Yard No. 468.
Launched: 19.3.1942.
Completed: 5.1942.
1943: *Ionion* (Government of Greece).
1947: *Ioannis Chandris* (E. & J. Chandris, Greece).
1955: *Ioannis Inglessis* (Navigation de Samos (D. Inglessi fils S.A., Greece)).
1965: *Thai Long* (Welfare Marine Corpn., Liberia (Tai Chong Nav. Co. Ltd., Taiwan)).
10.1966: Scrapped Keelung.

471   *Empire Southey* 7,041 gt. Details as Yard No. 468.
Launched: 15.5.1942.
Completed: 7.1942.
1946: *Hollybank* (Bank Line Ltd. (A. Weir & Co. Ltd.)).
1953: *Stad Rotterdam* (Halcyon-Lijn N.V., Netherlands).
1963: *Ocean Unity* (Ocean Shipping & Enterprises S.A., Panama (Great East Asia Shipping & Trading Corpn. Hong Kong)).
8.3.1967: Arrived Kaohsiung for breaking up.

472   *Empire Webster* 7,043 gt. Details as Yard No. 468.
Launched: 28.7.1942.
Completed: 10.1942.
7.2.1943: Sunk by submarine (*U.77*) torpedo, west of Algiers 36.47N 01.37E whilst in convoy KMS 8.

473   *Empire Envoy* 7,046 gt. Details as Yard No. 468.
Launched: 25.9.1942.

Completed: 12.1942.
1946: *Cheltenham* (Thompson Steam Shipping Co. Ltd., London).
1952: *La Orilla* (Buries, Markes Ltd., London).
1955: *Stallberg* (Skiold & Lundberg A/B, Stockholm).
1962: *Verna Paulin* (Paulins Rederier, Finland).
19.7.1969: Arrived Bruges for breaking up.

474   *Empire Bardolph* 7,017 gt. Details as Yard No. 468.
Launched: 8.12.1942.
Completed: 3.1943.
1946: *Memling* (Lamport & Holt Line Ltd.).
1953: *Vancouver Star* (Blue Star Line Ltd.).
1957: *Memling* (Blue Star Line Ltd.).
23.10.1959: Arrived Flushing for breaking up.

475   *Empire Friendship* 7,058 gt. Details as Yard No. 468.
Launched: 19.2.1943.
Completed: 5.1943.
1945: *Matelots Pilien et Peyrat* (Government of France).
1945: (Cie. Havraise de Nav. a Vapeur, Paris).
29.10.1962: Dragged anchors, broke moorings whilst laid up in Etang de Berre in vicinity of Port de Bouc, near Marseilles, and driven on breakwater of Canal de Marseilles au Rhône.
3.11.1962: refloated; constructive total loss.
11.1962: Scrapped La Seyne.

476   *Empire Manor* 7,036 gt. Details as Yard No. 468.
Launched: 8.4.1943.
Completed: 7.1943.

On 22 January 1944 a forty-ship escorted convoy sailed from New York, bound for the River Mersey laden with food and war supplies.

On 27 January the ships were some 200 miles south-east of Newfoundland, driving through heavy seas and blinding snow, with visibility almost nil. Among the merchantmen was the *Empire Manor*, with the vague grey outline of the American Liberty ship *Edward Kavanagh* (on her maiden voyage only seventeen days after being launched) in the next line, off to starboard. Suddenly, at 11.30 a.m. the American vessel veered sharply to port and as she loomed up, leaving the 'Empire' ship no time to take avoiding action, struck the British vessel amidships, cutting her almost in two. Within minutes the Liberty ship backed out of the huge hole but as she did so the seas poured in and the *Empire Manor* was soon flooded and awash. But she did not sink, and was taken in tow. In adverse weather the towline carried away time and time again, and then, on the 28th, the ship caught fire as chemicals in drums came in contact with water. No pumps were available and the vessel was abandoned.

The next morning, with the rescue tug *Tenacity*, from St. John's, standing by, there was the sound of tearing steel as the damaged ship broke in two, and the stern part sank. The bow section, still floating, was considered a danger to navigation and the convoy escort was ordered to sink it. Pounded by shells, the wreck of the *Empire Manor* was finally despatched by depth charges from the corvette H.M.C.S. *Kenogami*.

Then, from shore, came a coded signal to the ships involved: 'What happened to the bullion on board?' . . .

In 1953 the wreck of the *Empire Manor* was located by the salvage vessel *Twyford*, of the Risdon Beazley Marine Salvage Company, of Southampton, a firm which had already spent some years in pin-pointing sunken ships with valuable cargo still *in situ*.

Twenty years later, on 22 September 1973, an Admiralty 'Notice to Mariners' warned seafarers to keep clear of a salvage operation taking place off the Newfoundland coast, in position 43.53N 53.04W. An attempt was being made to salvage the bullion still aboard the wreck.

In appalling weather conditions, with winds of hurricane force on the surface, salvors from *Twyford*'s 1,300-ton sister ship *Droxford*, in two special diving bells so small that the only seat they could give the operator was a bicycle saddle, blasted their way through a mass of tangled wreckage 330-feet below, then removed hundreds of tons of machinery and cargo before finding their prize of dozens of gold bars, some still in the ship, others on the seabed, yet more buried in the mud.

Then, one morning in November 1973 the bullion was landed at Southampton's Town Quay and taken, under escort, to the Bank of England, in London.

477 *Empire Camp* 7,052 gt. Details as Yard No. 468.
Launched: 17.6.1943.
Completed: 10.1943.
1946: *Valacia* (Cunard White Star Ltd.).
1951: *New York City* (Bristol City Line of Steamships Ltd. (C. Hill & Sons, Bristol)).
1955: *Loch Morar* (Glasgow United Shipping Co. Ltd. (Mackay & McIntyre Ltd., Glasgow)).
1959: *Yelkenci* (Yelkenci Lufti Evlatlari Donmata Istiraki, Turkey).
20.2.1971: Arrived Istanbul for breaking up.

478 *Empire Duchess* 7,067 gt. Details as Yard No. 468.
Launched: 14.8.1943.
Completed: 12.1943.
1949: *Braemar Castle* (Union-Castle Mail SS Co. Ltd.).
1950: *King James* (King Line Ltd.).
1958: *Tyne Breeze* (Cambay Prince SS Co. Ltd. (J. Manners & Co. Ltd., Hong Kong)).
1963: *Cathay Trader* (Cathay Trader SS Co. (J. Manners & Co. Ltd., Hong Kong)).
1964: *Pearl Light* (Pacific Pearl Nav. Co. Ltd., Hong Kong).
1966: *Habib Marikar* (Marikar Navigation & Agencies Ltd., Hong Kong).
3.11.1967: Engines broke down in heavy weather 16.37N 113.2E (voyage: Dairen/Chittagong – bagged cement).
4.11.1967: Drifted ashore on Lincoln Island, near Paracel Islands, 350 miles SSW of Hong Kong, 16.38N 112.45E. Abandoned. Constructive total loss.

479 *Empire Stuart* 7,067 gt. Details as Yard No. 468.
Launched: 29.10.1943.
Completed: 2.1944.
1946: *Lord Lloyd George* (Norwood SS Co. Ltd. (Ships Finance & Management Co. Ltd., London)).
1955: *Atje-Ray-S* (N. V. Rotterdamsche Kolen Centrale, Holland).
1957: *Gianfranco* (Insulare Cia. Sicula di Armamento, Sicily (CITMAR, Genoa)).
12.1964: Scrapped Vado, Italy.

480 *Empire Cromer* 7,058 gt. Details as Yard No. 468.
Launched: 21.12.1943.
Completed: 4.1944.
1946: *Corrientes* (Donaldson Line Ltd., Glasgow).
1954: *Inchmay* (Williamson & Co. Ltd., Hong Kong).
1966: *Kaukhali* (National Shipping Corpn. of Pakistan).
2.4.1968: Arrived Karachi for breaking up.

481 *Empire Pendennis* 7,053 gt. Details as Yard No. 468.
Launched: 11.4.1944.
Completed: 6.1944.
1946: *Vasconia* (Cunard White Star Ltd.).
1950: *Fresno Star* (Blue Star Line Ltd.).
1957: Renamed *Millais*.
1960: *Grosvenor Navigator* (Grosvenor Shipping Co. Ltd., London (Mollers Ltd., Hong Kong)).
9.9.1966: Arrived Kaohsiung for breaking up.

482 (Laid down as) *Empire Perak* 7,058 gt. Details as Yard No. 468.
4.1944: Taken over by the Admiralty.
Launched: 4.9.1944 as *Dullisk Cove*; transferred to Smiths Dock Co. Ltd., Middlesbrough, for fitting out, and:
Completed: 6.1945 as a hull repair ship; laid up in Holy Loch, for disposal.
1947: *Kefalonia* (7,327 gt) (Kefalonian SS Co. Ltd. (Haddon SS Co. Ltd., London)).
1951: *Tyalla* (Commonwealth of Australia Shipping Board).
1957: (Australian National Line).
1957: *Wear Breeze* (Cambay Prince SS Co. Ltd. (J. Manners & Co. Ltd., Hong Kong)).
3.1962: Grounded at Jeddah (voyage: Hamburg/Colombo). Refloated by Danish salvage tug *Svitzer* (1921, 666 gt) and drydocked at Port Said: badly damaged in forward holds. Repairs uneconomic; sold, and:
7.1962: Scrapped Yokosuka.

483 (Laid down as) *Empire Lagos* 7,058 gt. Details as Yard No. 468.
Taken over by the Admiralty, and:
Launched: 31.10.1944 as *Solway Firth* (aircraft engine repair ship), but:

Completed in 1947 as a cargo ship by Amsterdam Drydock Co.; renamed *Kongsborg* (7,339 gt) (Skibs. Kongsborg., (A. G. Olsen, Norway)).
1955: *Olofsborg* (Rederi A/B Borgtramp (J. A. Zachariassen, Finland)).
1959: *Huta Florian* (Polish SS Co., Szczecin).
26.8.1971: Arrived Bilbao for breaking up.

484   *Empire Nairobi* 7,290 gt. Details as Yard No. 468.
Launched: 12.2.1945.
Completed: 4.1945.
1946: *Dover Hill* (Dover Hill SS Co. Ltd. (Counties Ship Management Co. Ltd.)).
1951: *Basil* (Cia. Nav. Castellana S.A., Panama).
1954: *Ravenshoe* (British SS Co. Ltd. (John Cory & Sons Ltd., Newport, Mon.)).
1960: *Plate Shipper* (Plate Shipping Co. S.A., Panama, (Greek flag) (P. B. Pandelis Ltd., London)).
1961: *Umran* (Sadikoglu, Riza ve Aslan, Turkey).

1966: *Tan 2* (L. Yelkenci Evatlari Donatina, Turkey).
7.9.1968: Arrived Istanbul for breaking up.

485   *Empire Dominica* 7,306 gt. Details as Yard No. 468.
Launched: 26.4.1945.
Completed: 8.1945.
1946: *Indian Endeavour* (India SS Co. Ltd., Calcutta).
22.9.1966: Arrived Hong Kong for breaking up.

486   *Empire Honduras* 7,320 gt. Details as Yard No. 468.
Launched: 27.6.1945.
Completed: 10.1945.
1948: *Lochybank* (Bank Line Ltd. (A. Weir & Co. Ltd.)).
1954: *Stad Haarlem* (Halcyon Lijn NV., Netherlands).
1963: *Union Fair* (Union Fair Shipping Co. Inc., Liberia, (P. S. Li, Hong Kong)).
4.1969: Scrapped Kaohsiung.

Short Brothers began in 1850 when the barque *Defiance* of 315 tons was built by George Short, a shipwright of Pallion, at Sunderland's Mowbray Quay. In line with the developing industry of the North-East, Shorts soon turned to the building of steamships and more and more general cargo ships were turned out, with a move made to the Pallion yard in 1870.

By the end of the Great War in 1918 a 10,000 tdw-capacity ship had almost been reached with two 9,900 tdw Prince Line ships, *Celtic Prince* (Yard No. 395) and *Gaelic Prince* (Yard No. 396), both 8,570 gross tons and a year or so later the *Sandown Castle* of 1921 and *Sandgate Castle* of 1922 aroused interest as the first turbine-driven ships for the Union-Castle Mail SS Co. Ltd.

Between the wars and during the years of depression, Shorts constructed sixty ships, in particular for Common Brothers, Chapman of Newcastle and for the Australian trade of Nitrate Producers SS Co. Ltd. (Lawther, Latta & Co. Ltd.).

Twenty-four 'Empire' tramp ships were ordered from Government sources during the 1939–1945 war, most of them constructed to Shorts' own prototype, but towards the end of 1944 partially prefabricated 'C'-type ships were delivered. Two small motor tankers were also delivered for Far East duties as the war drew to a close. The yard at that time had four berths and at the end of the 1940s they began building tankers, completing the Swedish-flag *Soya Christina* for O. Wallenius in April 1950.

In February 1964 the bulk carrier *Carlton* 16,303 gt (Yard No. 542) was handed over to Chapman & Willan Ltd., successors in 1950 to R. Chapman & Son of Newcastle. Of 642 ft in length and 24,710 tdw, she was to be Shorts' largest building, for on the 13th of that month it was announced that they were to cease shipbuilding and that the Pallion Yard, situated between the works of Doxford (Engineers) Ltd., and Steel & Co. Ltd., would be sold, after 114 years of shipbuilding.

MERCHANT SHIPS BUILT UNDER PRIVATE CONTRACT OR LICENCE

457   *Hermiston* 4,813 gt, 439 ft (oa), 427 ft × 54 ft.
Engines: T3cyl.
Launched: 30.8.1939.
Completed: 10.1939 for Carlton SS Co. Ltd. (R.

Chapman & Sons, Newcastle).
1960: *Nego Trader* (Wallem & Co., Hong Kong).
1966: *Kien An* (Kien An SS Co. Ltd., Hong Kong).
16.12.1967: Dragged anchors and went aground in

heavy weather east of Kakizaki, Naoetsu, Japan, 37.17N 138.34E. Broke in two. Total loss (voyage: Thailand/Naoetsu – manganese ore).

458 *Scorton* 4,813 gt. Details as Yard No. 457.
Launched: 30.10.1939.
Completed: 12.1939 for Carlton SS Co. Ltd. (R. Chapman & Sons, Newcastle).
13.7.1941: Bombed and damaged by German aircraft off Smiths Knoll Buoy, North Sea. Repaired.
1955: *Fro* (A/S D/S Ask (A. Kjerland & Co. A/S, Norway).
1965: *Winsome* (Winsen SS Co. S.A. (Winley Shipping Co., Hong Kong)).
10.6.1967: Caught fire in No. 4 hold in China Sea, south-east of Hainan Island. Abandoned, listing and sinking by stern, and:
11.6.1967: Sank 16.45N 116.45E
(voyage: Kaohsiung/Bangkok – general).

459 *Barnby* 4,813 gt. Details as Yard No. 457.
Launched: 25.1.1940.
Completed: 2.1940 for Rowland & Marwoods SS Co. Ltd. (Headlam & Son, London).
22.5.1941: Sunk by submarine (*U.111*) torpedo in North Atlantic, east of Cape Farewell, Greenland, 60.30N 34.12W.

460 *Hindustan* 5,245 gt, 450 ft (oa), 437 ft × 56.5 ft. Engines: Oil.
Launched: 23.4.1940.
Completed: 6.1940 for Hindustan Steam Shipping Co. Ltd. (Common Bros. Ltd., Newcastle).
1954: *Almen* (Rederi A/B Atos (Lundgren & Borjessons, Sweden)).
1963: *Sas* (G. Sigalas, Greece).
18.10.1976: Put into Las Palmas with engine trouble.
12.11.1976: Sailed, but put back next day.
29.12.1976: Sailed; developed leaks in heavy weather, and:
8.1.1977: Put into Rosas Bay.
19.1.1977: Arrived Sete in tow.

9.2.1977: Towed Piraeus: laid up; not repaired.
5.1979: Sold to German shipbreakers; resold, and:
23.7.1979: Arrived Santander, in tow, for breaking up.

461 *Hazelside* 5,297 gt, 441.5 ft (oa), 428.5 ft × 57 ft. Engines: T3cyl.
Launched: 24.6.1940.
Completed: 9.1940 for Charlton Steam Shipping Co. (Charlton, McAllum & Co. Ltd., Newcastle).
28.10.1941: Sunk by submarine (*U.68*) torpedo in South Atlantic, west of Walvis Bay, South Africa, 23.10S 01.36E.

463 *Newbrough* 5,255 gt. Details as Yard No. 460.
Launched: 31.10.1940.
Completed: 2.1941 for Northumbrian Shipping Co. Ltd. (Common Bros. Ltd., Newcastle).
1955: *Avisbay* (Aviation & Shipping Co. Ltd. (Purvis Shipping Co. Ltd., London)).
1962: *Giannis* (Aegean Nav. Co. Inc. (L. Nomikos, Greece)).
9.1969: Arrived Hong Kong with engine trouble. Sold, and:
10.1969: Scrapped Hong Kong.

488 *Taksang* 3,318 gt, 328 ft (oa), 315 ft × 47 ft. Engines: T3cyl.
Launched: 6.9.1945.
Completed: 1.1946 for Indo-China SN Co. Ltd., Hong Kong.
1962: *Rochford* (Peninsular Shipping Co. Ltd., (K. T. Wong, Hong Kong)).
9.1971: Scrapped Whampoa.

489 *Loksang* 3,318 gt. Details as Yard No. 488.
Launched: 17.11.1945.
Completed: 3.1946 for Indo-China SN Co. Ltd., Hong Kong.
1961: *Frankford* (Ocean Tramping Co. Ltd. (K. T. Wong, Hong Kong)).
14.10.1971: Arrived Kwangchow for breaking up.

Built by Swan, Hunter & Wigham Richardson Ltd., Wallsend Shipyard, Wallsend (W) and Neptune Works, Newcastle on Tyne (N)

1639(W) *Empire Masefield* 7,023 gt. 'Y'-type. 447.4 ft (oa), 433 ft × 56 ft. Engines: T3cyl.
Launched: 26.8.1941.
Completed: 10.1941.
1942: *Belgian Seaman* (Government of Belgium).

13.1.1942: Damaged by aircraft bombs off coast of Yorkshire, 54.22N 00.19W. Repaired.
1946: *Anvers* (Armement Deppe S.A., Belgium).
1952: *Clervaux* (Cie. Belge d'Expansion Maritimes, Belgium).

1960: *Mihalis Angelos* (M. Angelos Ltd., London).
1963: (Maradelanto Cia. Nav. S.A. (Angelos Ltd., London)).
1965: *Gloria* (Celestial Shipping Corp. S.A., Panama (Gloria Shipping Ltd., Hong Kong)).
6.12.1967: Arrived Kaohsiung for breaking up.

When the *Empire Masefield* was attacked by aircraft in January 1942, she was hit by bombs which exploded in the 'tween decks and tore a hole in the ship's port side, causing her to flood. Returning to the River Tees for refuge, with only thirty inches of freeboard, she stranded on the North Gare Sands.

On the morning of 14 January the tugs *Euston Cross* (1924, 226 gt), *Lingdale* (1882, 174 gt) and *Acklam Cross* (1933, 150 gt) attempted to salve the ship, but without success. Later, two more tugs joined the force and the following day the combined efforts of the five tugs was successful. The vessel was towed to Middlesbrough, docked and repaired.

When the tugs *Euston Cross* and *Acklam Cross* cast off from the casualty on 14 January, after their first refloating attempts, both stranded on the North Gare Sands: both were safely refloated.

1641(W) *Empire Drayton* 7.023 gt. Details as Yard No. 1639(W).
Launched: 23.10.1941.
Completed: 2.1942.
1942: *Belgian Sailor* (Government of Belgium).
1946: *Capitaine Biebuyck* (Cie. Maritime Belge S.A., Belgium).
1958: *Kastav* (Kvarnerska Plovidba (Government of Yugoslavia)).
1965: *Ivory Tellus* (Ivory Shipping Co. Ltd. (Aries Shipping Co. Ltd., Hong Kong)).
22.4.1970: Arrived Hirao for breaking up.

1694(N) *Empire Foam* 7,047 gt. Details as Yard No. 1639(W).
Launched: 13.3.1941.
Completed: 5.1941.
1946: *Graigaur* (Graig Shipping Co. Ltd. (I. Williams & Co. Ltd., Cardiff)).
1957: *Maltezana* (Marinos & Frangos Ltd., London).
1958: *Johore Bahru* (Great Southern SS Co. Ltd., Hong Kong).
24.7.1963: Arrived Kure for breaking up.

1714(N) *Empire Portia* 7,058 gt. Details as Yard No. 1639(W).
Launched: 9.11.1942.
Completed: 1.1943.
26.2.1943: Damaged by bombs from JU 88s, 69.17N 33.20E, off Murmansk, in convoy JW 53 (voyage: Loch Ewe/North Russia). Repaired.

On 30 June 1944 the *Empire Portia* was mined off Selsey Bill, the engine room was flooded and the ship taken in tow by *LST 416*. Just off Ryde Pier (Isle of Wight) the towline parted, this causing the LST to fall out of control and collide with several other craft, while the *Empire Portia* went aground just north of the pier, her portside badly holed and the engine room, stokehold and cross bunker tidal.

1.7.1944: Beached; all holds were tight, the ship drawing thirty-one ft aft and sixteen ft forward. A salvage vessel stood by.
3.7.1944: The *Empire Portia* was moved further up the beach to a safer position.
4.7.1944: The ship's back broke right across; engines and boilers were smashed. The vessel then considered irrepairable, but floatable. Guns, equipment and all gear removed.
25.9.1944: Last load of equipment shipped to Southampton; aft section of vessel salved, and:
3.10.1944: Vessel handed to shipbreakers, and:
30.4.1945: Arrived Briton Ferry for breaking up.

.   .   .

In Channel activities between Selsey Bill and Seine Bay at the end of June 1944 the 'Flower'-class sloop *Pink* was severely damaged by submarine *U.988* on 27 June. On 28 June the Southern Railway steamer *Maid of Orleans* (2,388 gt) was also sunk whilst on a trooping voyage to Normandy and two days later the *Empire Portia* was damaged.

At first all three casualties were attributed to submarine *U.988*; however, on the 29th an attack was made by the 3rd Support Group (U.S.-flag 'Captain'-class frigates *Duckworth, Essington, Domett* and *Cooke*) on a submarine and as the *U.988* never returned from her patrol it later transpired that the 'Empire' ship must have been the victim of a mine.

This huge company, one of Britain's largest shipbuilding concerns, was established in June 1903, a fusion of C. S. Swan & Hunter and Wigham Richardson & Company, Wallsend Ship & Pontoon Company and the Wallsend Slipway Company.

The Swan, Hunter story began in 1874 when C. S. Swan acquired a small yard at Wallsend, established by Coulson, Cook & Company in the 1840s, and he at once began constructing coastal colliers, building up a sound business as larger steamers were constructed.

Unfortunately, C. S. Swan was drowned in 1879 and G. B. Hunter, of S. P. Austin & Hunter, was offered the job of continuing the Swan yard. In 1880 the company was named C. S. Swan & Hunter and began business in a seven-acre yard with 270 feet water frontage and a work force of 600 men. Hunter was sole partner until C. S. Swan (junior) joined the Board. By 1900 many well-known steamship owners were ordering ships, including Canadian Pacific, Harrison and Cunard.

The *Empire Honduras*, at Cape Town in November 1946, was completed after war had ended. (Short Bros. Ltd., Yard No. 486.)

The *Aronda*, one of three British India Company sisterships. (Swan, Hunter & Wigham Richardson Ltd., Newcastle, Yard No. 1640(N).)

The *Baltyk*, built for Polish account in 1942. (Swan, Hunter & Wigham Richardson Ltd., Newcastle, Yard No. 1704(N).)
Skyfotos

Wigham, Richardson & Company began in 1860 when John Wigham Richardson purchased the old yard at Walker, which J. H. Coutts had started in 1842. It became the Neptune Works, a three-berth, four-acre site with 320 feet river frontage, and steam colliers were soon being built. Expansion came in 1879, with engine and boiler works added.

From the amalgamation in 1903, Swan, Hunter & Wigham Richardson began adding to an impressive yard list and in 1907 delivered Yard No. 735, the Cunard liner *Mauretania* (30,696 gt), until 1911 the largest and, for twenty years, the fastest liner in the world. They also built Cunard's *Aurania* (13,936 gt) in 1916 and *Laconia* (19,680 gt) in 1921; Cie. Generale Atlantique's 11,337 gt *Cuba* in 1923; *Giulio Cesare* (21,848 gt) for the Navigazione Generale Italiana, completed in 1922 and in the mid-1930s the train ferries *Hampton Ferry*, *Shepperton Ferry* and *Twickenham Ferry*, whilst many tankers for United Molasses and British Petroleum and passenger/cargo ships for Ellerman Lines were evident. In 1912, a four-berth yard was opened at Southwick, Sunderland, to build cargo ships, floating docks and other port equipment. One of the last ships built was Stephenson Clarke's collier *Flathouse*, in 1931, before the yard closed down in the depression year of 1933.

When war began in 1939 the company's building list was extensive with private orders; indeed, during the war years from 1939 to early 1946 fifty-five ships were completed under Government licence for private companies, prominent among them being Port Line with six ships, the Ellerman Group with nine vessels, tankers for the British Petroleum Company and Anglo-Saxon Petroleum Company, and a number of cable ships. Four 'Empire' tramp ships were ordered by the Government, of which two went to the Belgian flag; four 'Ocean'-type tankers were built and two MAC-ships, converted from commercial hulls. Three ferries took 'Empire' names and two 'Empire Tes'-type coastal tankers were completed as war ended. A number of ferries were also built for the Turkish Government.

Warship construction was enormous, major buildings being the battleship *Anson*, three aircraft carriers, four cruisers, thirty destroyers and escort destroyers and numerous smaller craft.

At the end of hostilities the Tyneside works covered eighty acres, with a river frontage of 4,000 ft. There were seventeen berths for ships to nearly 1,000 feet in length and three Graving Docks for vessels to 490 ft, 560 ft and 570 ft in length.

MERCHANT SHIPS BUILT UNDER PRIVATE CONTRACT OR LICENCE

1567(N)   *Hav* 5,062 gt, 432.4 ft (oa),
420.8 ft × 57.2 ft. Engines: Oil.
Launched: 15.7.1939.
Completed: 9.1939 for Helmer Staubo & Co., Norway.
14.5.1942: Struck mine off Port Said; beached. Holed, flooded and tidal.
23.6.1942: Abandoned.
25.6.1942: Fire broke out whilst fittings and equipment being removed. Left to burn out. Total loss.

Note: This vessel was a victim of mine barrages laid by German U-boats off several Eastern Mediterranean ports in April 1942.

1569(N)   (Launched as) *Port Napier* 9,847 gt, 523.9 ft (oa), 503.3 ft × 68.2 ft. Engines: Oil, Twin screw.
Launched: 23.4.1940 for Port Line Ltd.
1940: Requisitioned by the Admiralty and completed

as a minelayer, H.M.S. *Port Napier*, to carry 500 mines for mine barrages.
On trials: 16.6.1940. Laid 6,331 mines in several operations.

Was to have sailed in Operation SN 11, minelaying in the Denmark Strait, between Greenland and Iceland, but was left behind when her port propeller was fouled by the collier *Balmaha* during a gale on the night of 22 November 1940. 27.11.1940: Caught fire when at Lochalsh and abandoned after forty un-primed mines were jettisoned overside. Following several explosions of mines remaining on board, the *Port Napier* settled, only her forepart above water. The wreck was later partly cut up where she lay, and: (*circa*) 1980: Remains were finally dispersed after mines still on board had been removed and made safe.

1607(W)   *Pandorian* 3,146 gt, 359.5 ft (oa), 345.7 ft × 50 ft. Engines: T3cyl and LP turbine.
Launched: 12.12.1940.

Completed: 3.1941 for Ellerman & Papayanni Lines Ltd.
1963: *Kyrakali* (Kalimana Shipping Co., Liberia (T. N. Epiphaniades Co. Ltd., Greece)).
1964: *Bluesky* (Bluesky Corp. (Victoria SS Co., London)).
1969: (Bluesky Corp., (Middle East Maritime Co., Greece)).
1969: *Varosi* (Nereus Maritime Co. (Etab. Atilmar, Greece)).
28.3.1970: Arrived Shanghai for breaking up.

1608(N) *Hoperidge* 5,222 gt, 425 ft (oa),
418.9 ft × 57.4 ft. Engines: Oil.
Launched: 7.7.1939.
Completed: 9.1939 for Hopemount Shipping Co. Ltd. (Stott, Mann & Fleming Ltd., Newcastle).
1963: *Bethlehem* (Cia. Nav. Pearl S.A., Panama (Teh Hu SS Co. Ltd., Taiwan)).
2.8.1969: In collision with motor tanker *Showa Maru*, (1957, 13,183 gt) 30 miles from Singapore. Flooded, broke in three parts and sank, 1.16N 104.08E (voyage: Tokyo/Aden – cement).

1609(W) *Port Phillip* 9,947 gt. Details as Yard No. 1569(N).
Launched: 7.10.1941.
Completed: 3.1942 for Port Line Ltd.
2.1971: Scrapped Shanghai.

1626(N) *Ariel* 1,479 gt, 250.5 ft (oa),
237.5 ft × 35.2 ft. Engines: T6cyl. Twin screws. A cable ship.
Launched: 1.9.1939.
Completed: 12.1939 for H.M. Postmaster General, London.
1969: *C. S. Ariel* (The Post Office, London).
12.1976: Scrapped River Medway, Kent.

1638(W) *Hopetarn* 5,231 gt. Details as Yard No. 1608(N).
Launched: 9.11.1939.
Completed: 1.1940 for Clive Shipping Co. Ltd. (Stott, Mann & Fleming Ltd., Newcastle).
29.5.1943: Sunk by submarine (*U.198*) torpedo east of Durban, 30.50S 39.32E (voyage: Calcutta/U.K. – general).

1640(N) *Aronda* 8,396 gt, 464 ft (oa),
444.6 ft × 61 ft. Engines: six steam turbines. Twin screws.
Launched: 5.8.1940.
Completed: 3.1941 for British India SN Co. Ltd.
8.5.1963: Arrived Hong Kong for breaking up, but resold to Kaohsiung shipbreakers, and:
21.7.1963: Left adrift by tug *Cabrilla* with engine trouble in typhoon (voyage to Kaohsiung for breaking up).
Grounded on Chinese coast near Macao. Refloated by Chinese authorities, who insisted on 'repairing' the vessel before its return. 'Repaired', then returned to owner at Hong Kong; sold to local shipbreakers, and:
3.1964: Scrapped Hong Kong.

The *Aronda* was the last of a group of three passenger/cargo ships, the first of which, *Amra*, was completed in November 1938 for the Calcutta/Rangoon mail service. In November 1940 she was taken over to become a hospital ship and served in the East and Mediterranean areas. After war ended she was put on the Bombay/East Africa service.

The *Amra* arrived at Keelung in early December 1965 for breaking up. When built her boilers were designed to burn Calcutta coal and she was one of the relatively few ships to be fitted with mechanical stokers; she was converted to oil burning in 1951.

The second ship, *Aska*, 8,323 gt, completed in August 1939, was not so fortunate. She left Freetown for Liverpool in September 1940 with 350 French troops and on the night of the 16th was zig-zagging between Rathlin Island and Maidens Rock, off the north coast of Ireland, when she was struck by three heavy bombs. She was abandoned and sank in position 55.15N 05.55W, survivors being picked up by H.M.S. *Jason* and some trawlers.

1646(N) *Ariosto* 2,176 gt, 306.2 ft (oa),
295.2 ft × 44.2 ft. Engines: T3cyl and LP turbine.
Launched: 24.1.1940.
Completed: 3.1940 for Ellermans Wilson Line Ltd.
24.10.1941: Sunk by submarine (*U.564*) torpedo, 36.20N 10.50W, south-west of Cape St. Vincent, whilst in convoy HG 75.

1648(N) *Angelo* 2,199 gt. Details as Yard No. 1646(N).
Launched: 22.2.1940.
Completed: 4.1940 for Ellermans Wilson Line Ltd.
1963: *Nevada II* (Demetra Maritime Corp., Liberia (J. Livanos & Sons Ltd., London)).
1964: *Spyros L* (S. Lalis & Co. Ltd., Greece).
1970: (Biala Nav. Co. Ltd., Cyprus (S. Lalis & Co. Ltd., Greece)).
1971: *Manos I* (Itea Shipping Co., Panama).
3.1973: Scrapped Piraeus.

1650(N) *Iris* 1,480 gt. Details as Yard No. 1626(N).
Launched: 26.3.1940.
Completed: 6.1940 for H.M. Postmaster General, London.
1969: *C. S. Iris* (The Post Office, London).
6.1976: Scrapped Viane, Zeeland, Holland.

1659(N) *Port Victor* 12,411 gt. Details as Yard No. 1569(N).
Launched: 27.6.1941.
Completed: 10.1942 for Port Line Ltd.

A refrigerated ship, with accommodation for twenty-four saloon and ninety-eight second class passengers, the *Port Victor* left Buenos Aires for the United Kingdom on 14 April 1943 with a full cargo and sixty-five passengers. The ship was travelling independently when, at 8.30pm on 30 April she was hit in the engine room by a torpedo from the submarine *U.107* some 600 miles south-west of Ireland. Lights failed, two lifeboats were smashed and another damaged when another torpedo hit her amidships. A fourth torpedo finally struck and the *Port Victor* sank at 01.00 hours on 1 May. When daylight came a Liberator plane spotted a line of five lifeboats and three rafts connected by ropes and guided the sloop H.M.S. *Wren* to the spot. The *Port Victor* sank in position 47.49N 22.02W.

1661(W)   *City of Bristol* 8,424 gt, 493 ft (oa), 471.6 ft × 64.3 ft. Engines: six steam turbines. Twin screws.
Launched: 28.7.1942.
Completed: 1.1943 for Ellerman's City Line Ltd.
1960: (Hall Line Ltd.).
1961: *Tung Lee* (Far Eastern Navigation Corp (W. H. Eddie Hsu, Formosa)).
11.9.1963: Arrived Kaohsiung for breaking up.

1685(W)   *Port MacQuarie* 9,072 gt, 487.9 ft (oa), 470.9 ft × 62.2 ft. Engines: Oil.
Launched: 19.8.1943.
Completed: 2.1944 for Port Line Ltd.
13.9.1968: Arrived Kaohsiung for breaking up.

1697(W)   *City of Madras* 8,582 gt. Details as Yard No. 1661(W).
Launched: 19.9.1944.
Completed: 2.1945 for Ellerman's Hall Line Ltd.
1961: *Wei Lee* (Far Eastern Navigation Corp (W. H. Eddie Hsu, Formosa)).
12.1963: Scrapped Kaohsiung.

1704(N)   *Baltyk* 7,001 gt, 447.5 ft (oa), 431.6 ft × 56.2 ft. Engines: T3cyl.
Launched: 15.1.1942.
Completed: 3.1942 for Government of Poland (Gdynia America Shipping Lines Ltd.).
1951: (Polish Ocean Lines).
1964: (Polish Steamship Co.).
13.7.1973: Arrived Lubeck; sold to German shipbreakers; then resold to Spanish shipbreakers; renamed *Atty* and:
11.9.1973: Arrived Santander for breaking up.

1707(W)   *Port Lincoln* 7,246 gt. Details as Yard No. 1685(W).
Launched: 23.8.1945.
Completed: 1.1946 for Port Line Ltd.
27.10.1971: Arrived Castellon for breaking up.

1719(W)   *City of London* 8,434 gt, 500 ft (oa), 478.9 ft × 64.3 ft. Engines: six steam turbines. Twin screws.
Launched: 28.8.1946.
Completed: 5.1947 for Ellerman & Bucknall SS Co. Ltd.
1967: *Sandra N* (Cia. Maritime Somia S.A. (M. Scufalos, Greece)).
30.12.1968: Arrived Kaohsiung for breaking up.

1740(N)   *Umtata* 7,288 gt, 470 ft (oa), 452.8 ft × 59.2 ft. Engines: T6cyl and LP turbines. Twin screws.
Launched: 1.9.1943.
Completed: 1.1944 for Bullard, King & Co. Ltd.
1960: *Klipbok* (Springbok Shipping Co. Ltd., South Africa).
9.1961: Scrapped Yokosuka.

1741(W)   *Port Pirie* 10,561 gt, 529 ft (oa), 508.5 ft × 68.4 ft. Engines: Oil. Twin screws.
Launched: 29.5.1946.
Completed: 1.1947 for Port Line Ltd.
2.7.1972: Arrived Castellon for breaking up.

1749(W)   *Port Napier* 11,384 gt, 559.5 ft (oa), 536.9 ft × 70.3 ft. Engines: Oil. Twin screws.
Launched: 12.11.1946.
Completed: 9.1947 for Port Line Ltd.
10.2.1970: Arrived Kaohsiung for breaking up.

1768(N)   *Monarch* 8,056 gt, 483.6 ft (oa), 458.8 ft × 55.7 ft. Engines: T6cyl. Twin screws. A cable ship.
Launched: 10.1945.
Completed: 2.1946 for H.M. Postmaster General, London.
1969: Renamed *CS Monarch*.
1970: *Sentinel* (Cable & Wireless Ltd., London).
25.10.1977: Arrived Blyth for breaking up.

1770(N)   *City of Poona* 9,962 gt, 497.5 ft (oa), 475.7 ft × 64.2 ft. Engines: Oil. 'Standard Fast' type.
Launched: 18.1.1946.
Completed: 7.1946 for Ellerman Lines Ltd. (Hall Line Ltd.).
1968: *Benarkle* (Ben Line Steamers Ltd.).
16.6.1974: Arrived Kaohsiung for breaking up.

In 1941–1942 the Admiralty requested that some merchant hulls be acquired through the Ministry of War Transport for completion as escort carriers. One ship in this category was a Port Line order in October 1941 to Swan, Hunters, with the allocated name of *Port Sydney*, whose hull was laid down on 21 July 1942.

On 20 October 1942 the hull was acquired by the Ministry of War Transport for conversion to an auxiliary aircraft carrier and the intended name altered.

1783(W) (Laid down as) *Port Sydney* Details as Yard No. 1569(N).
Launched: 4.5.1943 as H.M.S. *Vindex*.
Completed: 3.12.1943; Commissioned as an escort carrier with eighteen aircraft; flight deck 495 ft.
1947: Laid up in Firth of Forth; Re-acquired by Port Line and:

8.1948: Towed to Wallsend for reconversion by her builders.
6.1949: Completed as *Port Vindex* (10,489 gt) – a refrigerated cargo motorship for the United Kingdom/Australia service.
22.6.1949: Maiden voyage from London.
23.8.1971: Arrived Kaohsiung for breaking up.

Formerly the Commonwealth & Dominion Line, the name Port Line was adopted in 1936 and in November 1937 became the registered title. Coinciding with this move was the introduction of a new design of ship to the fleet, the first vessel, *Port Jackson*, in 1937. She differed greatly from other Port Line ships but, owing to economic conditions, was not immediately followed by a sistership, although a number subsequently built can be closely identified with her, *Port Napier* (Yard 1569) launched in 1940, *Port Victor* of 1942 (Yard 1659) and *Port Phillip* (Yard 1609) in 1941, all by Swan, Hunter.

At the beginning of war the Port Line had fifteen motorships and thirteen steamships working in their United Kingdom–Australia/New Zealand and United States services. The *Port Napier* and *Port Victor* were both lost, as were another eleven Port Line ships.

Another two, *Port Vindex* (Yard 1783) (allocated name *Port Sydney*) building by Swan, Hunter, and Hull No. 557, building at John Brown's yard at Clydebank, were taken over by the Admiralty and completed as escort carriers.

At the end of 1945 the fleet consisted of seventeen pre-war ships and two war-built, *Port Phillip* and *Port Macquarie*; a total of nineteen plus three more under construction, *Port Lincoln*, *Port Wellington* and *Port Hobart*.

The old Commonwealth & Dominion Line was an original amalgamation of four family businesses; Tyser & Company, J. P. Corry & Co.'s Star Line, a part of T. B. Royden & Co.'s Indra Line and the Anglo-Australasian SN Company, founded by Wm. Milburn & Company. The 'Port' nomenclature tradition began with the last-named company.

1822(N)   *Tasso* 1,648 gt, 295.2 ft (oa), 283.9 ft × 40.2 ft. Engines: T3cyl and LP turbine.
Launched: 11.5.1945.
Completed: 9.1945 for Ellerman's Wilson Line Ltd.
1963: *Sophia* (C. M. Sarlis & Co., Greece).
14.8.1972: Arrived Perama for breaking up.

1828(N)   *Dwarka* 4,851 gt, 398.6 ft (oa), 382.3 ft × 54.8 ft. Engines: Oil.
Launched: 25.10.1946.
Completed: 6.1947 for British India SN Co. Ltd.
22.5.1982: Arrived Gadani Beach, Karachi, for breaking up.

The *Dwarka* was one of four similar ships built for the India/Persian Gulf trade, a trade which began in 1862, and she carried both passengers and cargo. Her accommodation was for twenty first class, thirty second and 1,500 deck passengers. The original mail service was from Bombay; the last was from Karachi to the Gulf ports in 1982, by then an eighteen-days round trip.

The *Dwarka* represented the P & O ship *Arabia* (1898) in the film 'Ghandhi'.
(See also Yard No. 706, *Dumra*, built by Barclay, Curle & Co. Ltd., Glasgow).

1830(N)   *Volo* 1,797 gt, 296.8 ft (oa), 283.8 ft × 42.2 ft. Engines: T3cyl and LP turbine.
Launched: 15.7.1946.
Completed: 12.1946 for Ellerman's Wilson Line Ltd.
1969: *Avolos* (Maltese National Lines Ltd., Malta).
1974: *Mdina* (Sea Malta Co. Ltd., Malta).
1979: Scrapped Catania, Sicily.

1836(N)   *Bassano* 4,986 gt, 419.6 ft (oa), 401.5 ft × 55.8 ft. Engines: T3cyl and LP turbine.
Launched: 1946.
Completed: 6.1946 for Ellerman's Wilson Line Ltd.
1967: *Athanasia* (Greek Sea Shipping Co., Panama (S. A. Daifos, Greece)).
22.10.1969: Arrived Shanghai for breaking up.

Built by J. L. Thompson & Sons Ltd., North Sands Shipyard, Sunderland

601   *Empire Wind* 7,459 gt, 444 ft (oa),
426 ft × 60 ft. Engines: T3cyl.
Launched: 9.7.1940.
Completed: 9.1940.
13.11.1941: Bombed by aircraft; sank in Atlantic 250
miles west of Ireland, 53.48N 15.52W.

602   *Empire Meteor* 7,457 gt. Details as Yard
No. 601.
Launched: 3.9.1940.
Completed: 12.1940.
29.6.1941: Damaged by aircraft bombs in North Sea,
53.05N 01.30E. Towed to River Humber; patched
and proceeded to Hull. Repaired.
1946: *Dorington Court* (United British SS Co. Ltd.
(Haldin & Co. Ltd.)).
1956: *Giada* (Insa Soc. di Nav., Genoa).
1960: *Sheikh* (P. Kyprianou & Partners (P. J.
Angouras, Greece)).
2.10.1961: Ashore in typhoon at Kita Daito Jima,
Japan. Broke in two; total loss
(voyage: Osaka/Philippines – ballast). Sold locally for
scrapping.

603   *Empire Breeze* 7,457 gt, 439 ft (oa),
424 ft × 60 ft. Engines: T3cyl.
Launched: 3.10.1940.
Completed: 1.1941.

In early February 1941 the *Empire Breeze* left the Tyne with
a cargo of coke, turned northwards and then, on the 5th,
went ashore on Bondicar Rocks, Amble. Her decks and sides
cracked at No. 3 hold, boiler and engines were set up and
holds Nos. 1, 4 and 5 became tidal. There was water in her
engine room and some buckling and fracturing amidships.
On 13 March 1941 she was refloated and with an attendant
salvage tug, *Bullger* (1907, 270 gt) owned by the Leith Salvage
& Towage Co., sailed south. However, the tug struck a mine
in Druridge Bay on the 16th, only a few miles south, and
sank some sixteen miles north of the Tyne. The *Empire Breeze*
anchored off Cresswell and was later taken to Sunderland for
repairs.

25.8.1942: Sunk by submarine (*U.438*) torpedo in
mid-Atlantic, 49.22N 35.52W, whilst in convoy
ON 122 (voyage: U.K./U.S.A.).

604   *Empire Sunrise* 7,459 gt. Details as Yard
No. 603.
Launched: 13.11.1940.
Completed: 2.1941.
2.11.1942: Damaged by submarine (*U.402*) torpedo
550 miles NE of Newfoundland, 51.50N 46.25W.
Later sunk by *U.84*. (Convoy SC 107) (voyage: Three
Rivers/Belfast).

605   *Empire Moon* 7,472 gt. Details as Yard No. 601.
Launched: 15.12.1940.
Completed: 5.1941.
22.7.1943: Damaged by submarine (*U.81*) torpedo
off Sicily, 36.43N 15.20E. Towed to
Syracuse, beached.
6.1945: Refloated; berthed, and:
22.7.1945: Towed to Palermo: repaired.
1949: *Ionian Moon* (Mediterranean SS Co. Ltd.,
London).
1953: *Sterling Victory* (Sterling Shipping Co. Ltd.,
Bahamas, (A. Vergottis Ltd., London)).
1957: *Alma* (Cia. Nav. Campos, Panama (Liberian
flag)).
1968: *Campos* (Cia. Nav. Campos, Panama
(Michalinos Maritime & Commercial Co. Ltd.,
Greece)).
3.1970: Scrapped Shanghai.

606   *Empire Sky* 7,455 gt. Details as Yard No. 603.
Launched: 10.2.1941.
Completed: 6.1941.
14.11.1942: Sunk by submarine (*U.625*) torpedo
south of Spitzbergen, Barents Sea, 76.20N 17.30E
(voyage: U.K./Archangel – war supplies).

Note: The above vessel was not in convoy, but on an
independent sailing.

607   *Empire Wave* 7,463 gt. Details as Yard No. 603.
Launched: 28.3.1941.
Completed: 7.1941.
2.10.1941: Sunk by submarine (*U.562*) torpedo ESE
of Cape Farewell, Greenland, 59.08N 32.26W, while
in convoy ON 19 (voyage: U.K./U.S.A.).

608   *Empire Hudson* 7,465 gt. Details as Yard
No. 603.
Launched: 9.5.1941.
Completed: 8.1941.
10.9.1941: Sunk by submarine (*U.82*) torpedo in
Greenland Sea, 61.28N 40.51W, whilst in convoy
SC 42 (voyage: Sydney, N.S./U.K.).

609   *Empire Lawrence* 7,457 gt. Details as Yard
No. 603.
Launched: 10.6.1941.
Completed: 9.1941.
27.5.1942: Bombed and sunk by aircraft east of Bear
Island, Barents Sea, (approx.) 74.00N 25.10E (convoy
PQ 16) (voyage: Iceland/North Russia – war
supplies).

610   *Empire Cranmer* 7,460 gt. Details as Yard
No. 603.

Launched: 8.7.1941.
Completed: 10.1941.
1942: *Thraki* (Government of Greece).
1947: *Arietta* (Livanos Maritime Co. Ltd., Greece).
17.3.1961: Aground near Novorossisk
(voyage: Novorossisk/Liverpool – grain). Fractured amidships: severe damage to engine room.
1.4.1961: Refloated; towed Novorossisk, but constructive total loss.

611 *Empire Liberty* 7,157 gt, 441 ft (oa),
423.8 ft × 57 ft. Engines: T3cyl.
Launched: 23.8.1941.
Completed: 11.1941.
1943: *Kyklades* (Government of Greece).
1947: *Mentor* (H. C. Dracoulis, Greece).
10.1960: Scrapped Osaka.

612 *Empire Halley* 7,168 gt. Details as Yard
No. 611.
Launched: 26.9.1941.
Completed: 12.1941.
1942: *Pieter de Hoogh* (Government of the Netherlands).
1947: *Britsum* (Stoom. Maats. Oostzee (Vinke & Zonen, Amsterdam)).
24.8.1959: Arrived Osaka for breaking up.

613 *Empire Johnson* 7,168 gt. Details as Yard
No. 611.
Launched: 20.10.1941.
Completed: 1.1942.
1942: *Paulus Potter* (Government of the Netherlands).
5.7.1942: Damaged by aircraft bombs west of Novaya Zemlya, Barents Sea, after scattering of convoy PQ 17 to North Russia. Abandoned, drifting, and:
13.7.1942: Sunk by submarine (*U.255*) torpedo in Barents Sea, approx. 70N 52E.

614 *Empire Nomad* 7,167 gt. Details as Yard
No. 611.
Launched: 16.12.1941.
Completed: 2.1942.
13.10.1942: Sunk by submarine (*U.159*) torpedo south-west of Cape Town, 37.50S 18.16E.

615 *Empire Barrie* 7,168 gt. Details as Yard No. 611.
Launched: 17.1.1942.
Completed: 4.1942.
1945: *Clan Alpine* (Clan Line Steamers Ltd.).
1957: *Umvoti* (Bullard, King & Co. Ltd.).
1959: *Clan Alpine* (Clan Line Steamers Ltd.).
1959: Sold to Japanese shipbreakers for delivery in 11.1960.
31.10.1960: Broke moorings in cyclone at Chittagong; driven ashore; left high and dry in paddy fields, eleven miles from entrance to Chittagong River. Constructive total loss (voyage: Glasgow/Chittagong – general).
2.1961: Sold locally and scrapped *in situ*.

617 *Empire Tristram* 7,167 gt. Details as Yard
No. 611.
Launched: 6.4.1942.
Completed: 7.1942.
23.6.1944: Damaged by flying bomb, Surrey Commercial Docks, London.
12.7.1944: Again damaged by bombs, Surrey Commercial Docks, London. Towed to Blyth for repairs.
1946: *Hollypark* (Denholm Line Steamers Ltd. (J. & J. Denholm Ltd.).
1955: *Gogovale* (Buchanan Shipping Co. Ltd. (A. Crawford & Co. Ltd., Glasgow)).
1957: *Avisvale* (Aviation & Shipping Co. Ltd. (Purvis Shipping Co. Ltd., London)).
1961: *St. Nicolas* (Cia. Nav. Marcasa S.A. (S. Catsell & Co. Ltd., London)).
28.1.1967: Arrived Split for breaking up.

618 *Empire Iseult* 7,170 gt. Details as Yard No. 611.
Launched: 14.5.1942.
Completed: 7.1942.
1943: *Frans van Mieris* (Government of the Netherlands).
1946: *Farmsum* (Stoom. Maats. 'Oostzee' (Vinke & Co., Holland)).
1959: *Kin Ming* (E-Hsiang SS Co. Ltd., Hong Kong).
1965: *Kai Quen* (Kai Tai Marine Lines Ltd., Formosa (China Union Lines Ltd.)).
9.1969: Scrapped Kaohsiung.

619 *Empire Galliard* 7,170 gt. Details as Yard
No. 611.
Launched: 27.6.1942.
Completed: 9.1942.
1943: *Aert van der Neer* (Government of the Netherlands).
1946: *Maasland* (Koninklijke Hollandsche Lloyd, Holland).
1959: *M. Bingul* (Cerrahogullari Umumi Nakliyat, Vapurculuk ve Ticaret T.A.S., Turkey).
10.1966: Scrapped Istanbul.

624 *Empire Brutus* 7,233 gt. Details as Yard
No. 611.
Launched: 18.12.1942.
Completed: 3.1943.
26.7.1943: Damaged by aircraft bombs,
39.50N 13.38W.
8.7.1944: Damaged by mine off Normandy.
1948: *Vergmor* (Haddon SS Co. Ltd., London).
1950: *Southgate* (Turnbull, Scott Shipping Co. Ltd., London).
1955: *Fatih* (Sadikzade Rusen Ogullari KS, Turkey).
2.1968: Scrapped Istanbul.

On 26 July 1943 the *Empire Brutus* was in convoy in the Atlantic, bound for the Mediterranean, when German bombers attacked. The ship was carrying a highly dangerous cargo of ammunition, incendiary bombs and military trucks. Bombs showered among the ships but only one, the *Empire Brutus*, was hit. A gaping hole was torn in her side and the engine room, stokehold, cross bunker and No. 3 hold flooded. Abandoned, the ship remained afloat and was reboarded. The tug, *Empire Samson*, arrived and took the wallowing, waterlogged vessel in tow. Next morning the tug was running short of fuel and the crew of the damaged ship climbed down into her flooded bunkers, filled buckets with coal and passed it aloft to be dumped aboard the tug, which was alongside. The two vessels continued in this way for five days and eventually, after travelling 230 miles at an average of two knots, reached the safety of the River Tagus. The *Empire Brutus* later returned home from Lisbon and was repaired.

Less than a year later, off Normandy in July 1944, the ship suffered further damage when she struck a mine off Juno Beach Light Vessel and was beached. Again, her engine and boiler room and bunker space were flooded but she was refloated and towed to Middlesbrough for repairs, where she arrived on 17 July.

628 *Empire Duke* 7,240 gt. Details as Yard No. 611.
Launched: 20.7.1943.
Completed: 11.1943.
1945: *Lieutenant J. Le Meur* (Government of France).
1949: *Zelidja* (Cie. Franco-Cherifienne de Nav., Morocco).
1955: *Propontis* (Cia. de Nav. Hellespont S.A., Liberia).
1957: (Cia. de Nav. Propontis Liberia (A. M. Embiricos, Monaco)).
24.5.1966: Arrived Kaohsiung for breaking up.

630 *Empire Welfare* 7,083 gt, 450 ft (oa), 429.8 ft × 56.3 ft. Engines: T3cyl.

Launched: 11.11.1943.
Completed: 1.1944.
1945: *Matelot Becuwe* (Government of France).
1949: *Marcel Schiaffino* (Soc. Algerienne de Nav. (Charles Schiaffino et Cie., Algiers)).
1965: *Desmin* ('Bulet' State Economic Enterprise, Bulgaria).
1968: *Stefan Karadja* (Navigation Maritime Bulgare, Bulgaria).
1973: Scrapped Yugoslavia.

632 *Empire Pitt* 7,086 gt. Details as Yard No. 630.
Launched: 28.1.1944.
Completed: 5.1944.
11.11.1946: Aground off Berville-sur-Mer, Seine Estuary, France. Abandoned; back broken. Constructive total loss (voyage: Rouen/Havre/West Indies – liqueurs, champagne and phosphates).

634 *Empire Haldane* 7,087 gt. Details as Yard No. 630.
Launched: 20.6.1944.
Completed: 9.1944.
1947: *Granford* (Goulandris Bros. Ltd., London).
1957: *Fulmar* (San Pedro Cia. Armadora S.A., Panama, (Goulandris Bros. Ltd.)).
1965: *Bianca Venture* (Bianca Carriers Inc., Liberia (Wah Kwong & Co. (Hong Kong) Ltd.)).
8.11.1965: Aground forty miles north of Mukho, South Korea, 38.09N 128.36E. Flooded and abandoned.
11.11.1965: Broke in two. Total loss (voyage: Daepori/Japan – iron ore).

The harsh reality of the war at sea came after nine months of hostilities when the tally of Atlantic losses was counted at 150 ships. The U-boats were sinking ships at a faster rate than British yards could build them.

Britain alone was then facing the enemy. Many merchant ships were needed to maintain the war effort and in September 1940 a British Shipbuilding Mission, led by a representative from the J. L. Thompson & Sons shipyard, left for the U.S.A. with a brief to order merchant ships for Britain.

The plans taken were similar to those of the *Dorington Court*, a Thompson-built general cargo ship of 1938, but with less beam. The ships to be ordered would be of 10,000 tdw and of eleven knots.

Sixty ships evolved from the contracts signed on 20 December 1940 by the Mission to the United States, to be built in two yards which, themselves, had to be laid down, one near Richmond, California, and the other at Portland, Maine, on the East coast. Each ship bore an 'Ocean' prefix and became an 'Ocean'-type ship. All were delivered in 1942 and eventually added 633,000 dwt capacity to the British merchant ship fleet.

From this came a change of policy in the United States when it was decided in January 1941 that a general cargo ship of 10,400 tdw and of eleven knots would be constructed under emergency conditions and based on the British design. The initial 200-ship programme was to expand to over 2,700 Liberty ships by the end of the war.

In Sunderland, Thompson's built twenty-three 'Empire' tramps to their own prototype, nine following the same dimensions of the *Empire Liberty*. Four standard 'Intermediate' tankers and four cargo liners were also built and a number of ships were constructed under licence for private owners.

MERCHANT SHIPS BUILT UNDER PRIVATE CONTRACT OR LICENCE

593 *Port Quebec* 5,800 gt, 468 ft (oa),
451 ft × 59.7 ft. Engines: Oil.
Launched: 17.8.1939.
Completed: 11.1939 for Port Line Ltd.
1940: Requisitioned by the Admiralty and converted to a minelayer. Capable of carrying 500 mines for laying in barrage. Served in same minelaying squadron as *Port Napier* (see Swan, Hunter & Wigham Richardson, Yard No. 1569).
1943: Minelaying squadron disbanded. Refitted as aircraft repair ship, renamed H.M.S. *Deer Sound*.
1947: *Port Quebec* (Port Line Ltd.).
23.3.1968: Arrived Keelung for breaking up.

594 *Argyll* 4,897 gt, 431.8 ft (oa), 415.1 ft × 58.2 ft.
Engines: T3cyl.
Launched: 14.9.1939.
Completed: 12.1939 for B. J. Sutherland & Co. Ltd., Newcastle.
1941: Seized at Dakar by Vichy French forces; renamed *Saint Henri*.
1943: Recaptured by Allies; reverted to original name and owners.
1954: (Savolex Shipping Co. Ltd., London (Jonason, Bray & Co.)).
1954: *Inkeri Nurminen* (J. Nurminen O/Y, Finland).
1967: *Someri* (I. Tuuli, Finland).
26.12.1971: Arrived Split for breaking up.

595 *Inverness* 4,897 gt. Details as Yard No. 594.
Launched: 10.11.1939.
Completed: 1.1940 for B. J. Sutherland & Co. Ltd., Newcastle.
9.7.1941: Sunk by submarine (*U.98*) torpedo, 42.46N 32.45W, north-west of Azores.

596 *Royal Emblem* 4,900 gt. Details as Yard No. 594.
Launched: 27.11.1939.
Completed: 2.1940 for Hall Bros. SS Co. Ltd., Newcastle.
7.1961: Scrapped Hong Kong.

597 *Confield* 4,956 gt. Details as Yard No. 594.
Launched: 9.1.1940.
Completed: 4.1940 for Confield SS Co. Ltd. (E. J. Sutton & Co. Ltd., Newcastle).
8.10.1940: Damaged by submarine (*U.58*) torpedoes north-west of Ireland, 56.48N 10.17W.
9.10.1940: Torpedoed again; sank.

598 *Graiglas* 4,312 gt, 407.7 ft (oa), 389.3 ft × 54.7 ft. Engines: T3cyl.
Launched: 23.2.1940.
Completed: 5.1940 for Graig Shipping Co. Ltd. (I. Williams & Co. Ltd.).

1952: *Lantao* (Lantao SS Co. Ltd. (Wallem & Co. Ltd., Hong Kong)).
1966: *Shia* (General SS Co. Ltd. S.A. of Hong Kong).
3.1967: Scrapped Hong Kong.

599 *Thistlegorm* 4,898 gt. Details as Yard No. 594.
Launched: 9.4.1940.
Completed: 6.1940 for The Albyn Line Ltd. (Allan, Black & Co. Ltd.).
6.10.1941: Bombed and sunk by aircraft in Strait of Jubel, Gulf of Suez (voyage: Glasgow/Suez – military stores and transport).

600 *St. Essylt* 5,634 gt, 459.6 ft (oa), 442.5 ft × 58.1 ft. Engines: Oil.
Launched: 23.5.1940.
Completed: 7.1940 for South American Saint Line Ltd., Cardiff.
4.7.1943: Damaged by submarine (*U.375*) torpedo, 36.44N 01.31E, fifteen miles from Sicily. Caught fire, and:
5.7.1943: Blew up and sank (Convoy KMS 18B) (voyage: Clyde/Sicily – military stores).

616 *Elmwood* 7,167 gt, 441.5 ft (oa), 423.8 ft × 57.2 ft. Engines: T3cyl.
Launched: 3.3.1942.
Completed: 6.1942 for John I. Jacobs & Co. Ltd., London.
27.7.1942: Sunk by submarine (*U.130*) torpedo in Atlantic, west of Sierra Leone, 04.48N 22.00W (voyage: New York/Kuwait).

620 *Thistledale* 7,227 gt. Details as Yard No. 616.
Launched: 30.7.1942.
Completed: 10.1942 for The Albyn Line Ltd. (Allan, Black & Co. Ltd.).
1959: *Nedi* (Cia. Nav. Altis S.A., Panama (Tharros Shipping Co. Ltd., London)).
1961: (Troodos Shipping & Trading Co. Ltd., London).
29.11.1966: Grounded in gale on Fehmarn Island shortly after leaving Lubeck for Taiwan with a cargo of scrap.
2.12.1966: Refloated: towed to Kiel; drydocked. Temporary repairs made; vessel sold for scrapping.
15.4.1967: Arrived Keelung for breaking up.

621 *Middlesex Trader* 7,241 gt. Details as Yard No. 620.
Launched: 28.8.1942.
Completed: 11.1942 for Trader Navigation Co. Ltd., London.
1955: *Strovili* (Strovili Cia. Nav., Costa Rica (K. Lusi Ltd., London)).
1956: *Anker* (Anker Kolen Maats. N.V., Holland).

1958: *Carnia* (Mariscula SpA, Sicily (Pala &
Franceschini, Genoa)).
4.1965: Scrapped Spezia.

622   *Thistlemuir* 7,227 gt. Details as Yard No. 620.
Launched: 29.9.1942.
Completed: 12.1942 for The Albyn Line Ltd. (Allan,
Black & Co. Ltd.).
1961: *Nunez de Balboa* (Cia. Auxiliar Mar. Ltda (A.
Ramirez Escudero, Spain)).
5.1968: Arrived Osaka for breaking up.

623   *Essex Trader* 7,237 gt. Details as Yard No. 620.
Launched: 9.11.1942.
Completed: 1.1943 for Trader Navigation Co. Ltd.,
London.
1957: (Esk Shipping Co. Ltd. (H. M. Lund,
London)).
1958: Renamed *Eskcliffe*.
1960: *Sandra* (Empresa Naviera La Libertad, Panama
(Valles SS Co., Hong Kong)).
1961: (Empresa Naviera La Libertad, Panama (C. S.
Koo, Hong Kong)).
26.3.1967: Arrived Kaohsiung for breaking up.

625   *Chinese Prince* 9,485 gt, 490.3 ft (oa),
469.8 ft × 63.5 ft. Engines: Oil.
Launched: 23.3.1943.
Completed: 10.1943 for Prince Line Ltd. (Furness
Withy & Co. Ltd.).
1950: *Nordic* (Shaw, Savill & Albion Co. charter).
1.11.1964: Arrived Hirao for breaking up.

626   *Denewood* 7,241 gt. Details as Yard No. 620.
Launched: 20.4.1943.
Completed: 12.1943 for John I. Jacobs & Co. Ltd.,
London.

1945: *Indore* (Maritime Shipping & Trading Ltd.
(Michalinos & Co. Ltd.)).
1961: *Polegate* (United Merchants Shipping Co. Ltd.
(Michalinos & Co. Ltd.)).
10.11.1967: Arrived Hamburg, in tow, for breaking
up.

627   *Caxton* 7,271 gt. Details as Yard No. 620.
Launched: 2.6.1943.
Completed: 10.1943 for Barberrys SS Co. Ltd.
(Runciman (London) Ltd.)).
1957: *La Costa* (Buries, Markes Ltd., London).
1958: *Hong Kong Breeze* (North Breeze Nav. Co. Ltd.
(J. Manners & Co. Ltd., Hong Kong)).
1965: *Panam Trader* (San Fernando SS Co. S.A.,
Panama (China Pacific Nav. Co. Ltd., Hong Kong)).
7.1967: Scrapped Keelung.

629   *Silveroak* 6,597 gt. Details as Yard No. 625.
Launched: 14.10.1943.
Completed: 6.1944 for Silver Line Ltd. (S. & J.
Thompson Ltd., London).
1955: *Port Stephens* (Port Line Ltd. charter).
1956: *Benvannoch* (Ben Line Steamers Ltd.).
15.1.1969: Arrived Kaohsiung for breaking up.

644   *Bencruachan* 8,047 gt, 482.6 ft (oa),
461 ft × 60 ft. Engines: two steam turbines.
Launched: 19.10.1945.
Completed: 6.1946 for Ben Line Steamers Ltd.
1966: *Annunciation Day* (Twenty Five March Shipping
Co. S.A., (M. Scufalos, Greece)).
1969: (Golden Star Shipping Co. Ltd., Cyprus).
1974: (Twenty Five March Shipping Co. S.A. (G.
Eleftheriou, Greece)).
1974: *Demis* (Demis Navigation Co. S.A., Greece).
19.3.1979: Arrived Split, in tow, for breaking up.

Built by Vickers-Armstrongs Ltd., Naval Construction Works, Barrow in Furness

768   *Empire Gale* 7,122 gt, 'Y' type, 448 ft (oa),
433 ft × 56 ft. Engines: T3cyl.
Launched: 29.4.1941.
Completed: 6.1941.
1946: *Langleegale* (Medomsley Steam Shipping Co.
Ltd.).
1953: *Entopan* (Cia. Nav. Logos S.A., Greece).
12.7.1968: Arrived Whampoa for breaking up.

769   *Empire Morn* 7,117 gt. Details as Yard No. 768.
Launched: 1.7.1941.
Completed: 9.1941.

26.4.1943: Damaged by mine off Rabat,
32.52N 07.50W. Stern blown off but vessel remained
afloat. Towed in: beached. Constructive total loss.
Refloated, and:
1.9.1943: Arrived Gibraltar in tow: used as a store
ship. Later sold, and:
1947: *San Antonio* (F. M. Pereda, Spain).
12.3.1947: Towed to Cadiz. Renamed *Rio Pas*;
Repaired (new afterpart: Length: 454 ft (oa), 7,117 gt).
1962: (Maritima Colonial y de Comercio S.A.,
Spain).
1.973: Scrapped Santander.

787 *Empire Baxter* 7,079 gt. Details as Yard
No. 768.
Launched: 8.10.1941.
Completed: 12.1941.
1946: *Paris City* (Reardon Smith Line Ltd.).
1954: *Westford* (Duff, Herbert & Mitchell Ltd.,
Liverpool).
1958: *Severn River* (Cia. Atlantica-Pacifica S.A.,
Panama).
1959: *Huseyin Kaptan* (R. & E. Sadikoglu Ortaktari,
Turkey).
1963: Scrapped Istanbul.

788 *Empire March* 7,090 gt. Details as Yard
No. 768.
Launched: 20.2.1942.
Completed: 4.1942.
1.1.1943: Sunk by gunfire and torpedoes of raider
Michel in South Atlantic, 40.00S 05W (approx.)
(voyage: Calcutta/Durban/Trinidad/U.K. – general).

The raider *Michel* (German ship No. 28) was completed in
April 1939 by Danziger Werft as *Bielsko* for the Gdynia
America Line. A motorship of 4,740 gt, she was seized by the
Germans, renamed *Bonn* and placed under the Norddeutscher
Lloyd as an accommodation ship, until converted to an ocean
raider, carrying torpedo tubes and two seaplanes as well as
six 5.9-inch guns and lighter weaponry.
  Her first cruise began from Kiel on 9 March 1942 and
ended in the Japanese-controlled port of Tanjong Priok, Java,
338 days later, having sunk fourteen ships – the first the
Patella (1927, 7,468 gt) on 19 April 1942 and the last, *Empire*

March (as above) on New Year's Day, 1943. She then left for
a Japanese home port, arriving at the Mitsubishi repair yard
in Kobe, for a refit, on 2 March.
  The *Michel* sailed again on the last day of April, on a cruise
that lasted 173 days. She sank only three more vessels.
  The raider *Michel* was herself torpedoed by the submarine
U.S.S. *Tarpon* off Yokohama on the night of 17–18 October
1943. Struck by three torpedoes, one of them opened up the
cavernous Nos. 3 and 4 holds, where the ship's seaplanes and
torpedo boat were housed. She was soon listing and settled
by the stern, her main deck awash. A fourth torpedo spelled
Michel's end. Her bow rose high in the air and she slid under
by the stern, with the screech of tearing steel.

827 *Empire Noble* 7,125 gt. Details as Yard No. 768.
Launched: 13.11.1943.
Completed: 1.1944.
1946: *Amicus* (W. H. Seager & Co. Ltd., Cardiff).
1963: *Leela* (Southland Navigation & Commerce
Ltd., Hong Kong).
1964: *Pacific Fir* (Fir Line Ltd. (Ta Hing Co. (Hong
Kong) Ltd.)).
5.2.1968: Sprang leak in heavy weather, approx.
seventy miles east of Tai Tung, Taiwan,
22.37N 121.42E (voyage: Mormugao/Osaka – iron
ore).
6.2.1968: Holds and engine room flooded.
Abandoned. Later found adrift off coast; towed in
and beached on Koto Soh, twenty-five miles off
southern Taiwan. Broke in two and forepart sank.
Total loss.

This great company dates back to the 1820s, to Edward Vickers, a steel miller of Sheffield, who
built up his business in worldwide exports.
  In 1867, then under the control of his son, Tom, the company became limited under the title of
Vickers, Sons & Company and began forming connections in the field of armaments. Within two
decades they had moved firmly into the industry. The next step, after turning out huge naval guns,
was to build the actual ships for which the guns had been made and for this Vickers turned to the
Naval Construction & Armaments Company of Barrow, taking over that concern in 1897.
  The origins of the Naval Construction & Armaments Company were in the Barrow Shipbuilding
Company, whose yard for iron ships had been set in 1871 at the northern end of Barrow Island.
The yard was soon under way, turning out the steamers *Duke of Devonshire* and *Duke of Buccleuch*
for Ducal Line's service from Calcutta, while three iron steamships were built for the directors of
the yard under the name of the Barrow Ocean Steamship Company, but the *Anchoria*, *Devonia* and
Circassia soon moved to the Anchor Line. The yard's first ship of steel, the 8,400 gt *City of Rome*
was built in 1882 for the Inman Line. In 1886 came the first steel warship, the small torpedo-cruiser
Fearless. Two years later the company was transformed into the Naval Construction & Armaments
Co. Ltd., the aim being to build warships with full armament and equipment. The first four-
funnelled cruiser, *Powerful*, was delivered in 1895.
  In 1897 came the great amalgamation, Vickers first of all acquiring the fifty-seven acre yard of
the Naval Construction & Armaments Company and then in the same year the gunmakers Maxim
Nordenfelt, becoming Vickers, Son & Maxim Ltd. It could now construct the complete warship,
but in 1911 was renamed Vickers Ltd.
  Apart from huge orders for guns and munitions in the 1914–1918 war, the yard was fed with
orders for naval ships of all types, including sixty-four submarines.

After four years of naval construction, Vickers turned to merchant ships. In 1920 the Anglo-American tanker *Narragansett* was delivered, Cunard's 19,800 gt *Scythia* was also launched in March of that year and the same owner's *Antonia*, 13,800 gt was completed in 1922. Three of five 13,800 gt 'Bay'-class ships, *Moreton Bay, Hobsons Bay* and *Jervis Bay* were constructed for the Australian Commonwealth Shipping Board and four oil carriers for Tankers Ltd., all in 1921–1922. Another 20,000 gt liner, *Carinthia*, was handed over to Cunard in 1925 and orders for three 20,000 gt Orient liners, *Orama* (1924), *Otranto* (1925) and *Orford* (1928) were interspersed with two 7,000 gt ships *Newfoundland* and *Nova Scotia* for the Warren Line. But, by 1926, the world trade was in deepening depression and the shipbuilding industry suddenly slumped.

In 1927 came the merger of the Armstrong, Whitworth Company and Vickers, two giant enterprises working almost in parallel form, the new concern becoming Vickers-Armstrongs Ltd. And with the merger, the Walker Yard on the Tyne and the Elswick Works became additions to the Barrow facilities.

But the depression remained and in April 1928, with no work, the Naval Yard on the Tyne closed down. Then, in March 1930, it was re-opened for the Furness Withy turbo-electric liner *Monarch of Bermuda* to be laid down as Yard No. 1 of the Vickers-Armstrongs building list. Launched on 17 March 1931, the 22,000 gt liner sailed from the Tyne on 4 November 1931 and the yard closed again, not being re-opened until May 1934, when the cruiser *Newcastle* was laid down in a worrying international situation.

As in the 1914–1918 war, the now-merged two great shipbuilding companies of Vickers-Armstrongs were turned mainly to naval construction when war broke out again in 1939. However, there were a number of merchant ships constructed. Four 'Y'-type tramps were built at Barrow in the early war years and one in 1944; a coaster was turned out in 1941 and the company was also given orders to build a number of heavy-lift ships of which four were built at Barrow and two on the Tyne.

Naval construction was enormous. At Barrow the aircraft carriers *Illustrious* and *Indomitable* and the smaller *Majestic* and *Pioneer* were built, the last-named as a maintenance ship. Two cruisers were launched in the early war years. From the Tyne naval yard, Vickers-Armstrongs launched the battleship *King George V* and the 15-inch gun monitor *Abercrombie*. Other major naval buildings included four aircraft carriers and three cruisers.

In April 1965 the name of the company became Vickers Ltd.

The Hong Kong Shipyards

The only yards outside of Britain to construct 'Empire' ships to the order of the Ministry of War Transport during the war years were the two yards at Hong Kong. Steel supplies were obtained from Australia and the United States with some difficulty and some materials had to be shipped out from Britain, but five ships were completed before Hong Kong was occupied by Japanese forces.

Built by Hong Kong & Whampoa Dock Co. Ltd., Kowloon Docks, Hong Kong

841 *Empire Moonrise* 6,854 gt, 450 ft (oa), 429.7 ft × 56.7 ft. 9,800 tdw. Engines: T3cyl. Launched: 14.6.1941.

Completed: 8.1941.
9.4.1942: Damaged by aircraft bomb at Colombo, Ceylon. Repaired.

The *Empire Starlight*, rebuilt as the Soviet ship *Murmansk*, at Yokohama in 1979. (Hong Kong & Whampoa Dock Co. Ltd.,
Yard No. 842.)   *Vic Young*

The *Empire Haven*, built in Hong Kong in 1941. (Taikoo Dockyard & Engineering Co. Ltd., Yard No. 296.)
                                                                                                         Tom Rayner collection

The *Viti*, built for the Government of Fiji, at Wellington in July 1943. (Taikoo Dockyard & Engineering Co. Ltd., Yard
No. 285.)

1945: *Hartland Point* (Gowan SS Co. Ltd. (D. J. McLaren & Co., London)).
1947: *Burmount* (James Burness & Sons Ltd., London).
1954: *Marilena* (Maritima Mensabe S.A. (J. P. Hadoulis Ltd., London)).
1957: *Athamas* (Cia. y de Comercio Athamas Ltda, Costa Rica).
1966: (Agenor Shipping Co. Ltd., Cyprus).
27.9.1966: Arrived Whampoa for breaking up.

842   *Empire Starlight* 6,854 gt. Details as Yard No. 841.
Launched: 4.4.1941.
Completed: 7.1941.
3.4.1942–1.6.1942: Bombed repeatedly at Murmansk (voyage: Loch Ewe/North Russia – war supplies) (Convoy PQ 13). Sank. Abandoned. Total loss.
1945: Salved by U.S.S.R., renamed *Murmansk* (7,153 gt, Length: 448.9 ft oa).
12.10.1979: Left Nagoya for Nakhodka; reported converted for use as a storage barge.

On 20 March 1942 convoy PQ 13 left Reykjavik, Iceland, on its way to North Russia with a covering force of the cruiser *Trinidad*, destroyers *Eclipse* and *Fury*, two anti-submarine trawlers and three minesweeping whalers. After a day or so the weather deteriorated and in heavy storms the convoy's nineteen ships became scattered between the 24th and 27th.

On the 27th they were spotted by a German plane and next day, still in heavy seas, six ships made contact with one another but were then subjected to submarine and destroyer torpedo attacks as well as incessant air attacks from JU 88s, at the same time experiencing navigational difficulties due to ice, in which five of the ships became stuck fast. The *Empire Starlight* managed to stay free, cutting the ice around the other ships and freeing them so that they managed to reach open water. Eventually, however, the *Empire Starlight* lost contact with the other ships as they proceeded independently and she reached Murmansk on her own. In all, fourteen ships arrived at Murmansk, two having been sunk by bombs, two by U-boats and one by the German destroyer *Z 26*.

On 3 April the German bombers then switched their air attacks to the port, sometimes as many as four attacks in one day. The *Empire Starlight* was hit twice whilst discharging and on 1 June, after repeated attacks, was struck by a stick of bombs on her port side and settled on the bottom, her decks awash. She was abandoned as a war loss, but after the war was salved and rebuilt by the Russians, being renamed *Murmansk*.

843   *Empire Moonbeam* 6,849 gt. Details as Yard No. 841.
Launched: 31.3.1941.
Completed: 6.1941.
12.9.1942: Damaged by submarine (*U.211*) torpedo; finally sunk by submarine *U.608*, in the Atlantic in position 48.55N 33.38W, while in convoy ON 127.

847   *Empire Dragon* Details intended to be as Yard No. 841.
Launched: 6.12.1941.
Completed by the Japanese; reported to be named *Gyoko Maru*, but believed to have been *Gyokuyo Maru*, and:
14.11.1944: Sunk by submarine U.S.S. *Spadefish* in East China Sea, 31.04N 123.56E.

848   *Empire Pagoda* Details intended to be as Yard No. 841.
Laid down: 6.12.1941 (on berth vacated by Yard No. 847 (above)).
Completed by the Japanese as *Gyoten Maru*.
17.2.1944: Sunk by submarine U.S.S. *Tang* west of Truk, Pacific, in position 8.04N 149.28E.

850   *Empire Lantern* Details intended to be as Yard No. 841.
Laid down: 26.5.1941.
Launched: 8.12.1942 by Japanese and completed as *Gyoku Maru*.
18.9.1944: Sunk by submarine U.S.S. *Thresher* in Yellow Sea, South of Korea, in position 35.05N 124.24E.

851   *Empire Wall* Details intended to be as Yard No. 841.
Laid down: 24.6.1941.
1945: Still on stocks as had been left, 80 per cent plated-up, decks incomplete. All material needed for completion available. Slight bomb damage in No. 2 hold. Engine and boiler parts ready, but not assembled. British Government (M.O.W.T.) asked if work was to be resumed, but:
5.1950: Dismantled for scrap.

855	Not named:	Admiralty Merchant Ship No. A/MS 275	
856	Not named:	Admiralty Merchant Ship No. A/MS 304	
857	Not named:	Admiralty Merchant Ship No. A/MS 305	Vessels ordered but not built.
859	Not named:	Admiralty Merchant Ship No. A/MS 338	
860	Not named:	Admiralty Merchant Ship No. A/MS 339	

MERCHANT SHIPS BUILT UNDER PRIVATE CONTRACT

818 *Hermelin* 1,683 gt, 291.2 ft (oa), 277 ft × 43 ft.
Engines: Oil.
Launched: 1939.
Completed: 1940 for Bruusgaard Kiosterud & Co.,
Norway.
1972: *Treasure Country* (Kwok Wah Shipping Co.,
Panama (Kim Wah Maritime Co., Hong Kong)).
8.1977: Scrapped Hong Kong.

819 *Karuah* 1,353 gt, 241.6 ft (oa),
232.2 ft × 39.1 ft. Engines: T3cyl.
Launched: 1939.
Completed: 3.1940 for Newcastle & Hunter River
Steamship Company, N.S.W.
1962: *Milo's Del Mar* (Soc. Mar. Caledonienne, New
Caledonia).
1965: (General Marine Corporation, Panama, (Power
Navigation Co., Hong Kong)).
3.1970: Scrapped Singapore.

827 *Heinrich Jessen* 3,300 gt, 319.5 ft (oa),
305 ft × 46.6 ft. Engines: T3cyl.
Launched: 22.2.1940.
Completed: 9.1940 for Rhederi M. Jebsen A/S,
Denmark.
1940: Requisitioned: British flag; Served as a destroyer
depot ship in Indian waters.

1946: Returned to builders for refit, then
1947: (Government of Denmark).
1948: (Returned to owners).
1964: *Aru Mariner* (United Marine S.A., Liberia
(United China Shipping Co., Hong Kong)).
12.1970: Scrapped Hong Kong.

837 *Ranger* 512 gt, 142.5 ft (oa), 130.2 ft × 32.1 ft.
Engines: Oil. Twin screw. A tug.
Launched: 15.8.1940.
Completed: 9.1940 for Luzon Stevedoring Co.,
Manila.
12.1941: Sunk by Japanese at Manila, Philippines.

842 *Hinsang* 4,644 gt, 372 ft (oa), 357.1 ft × 53.2 ft.
Engines: Oil.
Launched: 12.1940.
Completed: 6.1941 for Indo-China SN Co. Ltd.,
London.
22.11.1941: Arrived Hong Kong from Sandakan for
repairs.
25.12.1941: Scuttled at Hong Kong.
28.2.1942: Salved by Japanese: renamed *Kensei Maru*.
12.1.1945: Bombed and sunk by U.S. aircraft south-
east of Cam-Ranh Bay, South Vietnam,
11.10N 108.55E.

Before Hong Kong became a British Crown colony in 1841 there were Chinese-owned mud docks at Whampoa. The Peninsular & Oriental SN Company had contracted to use these docks, but concluded that they could not entrust the docking and repair of their coastal steamers entirely to Chinese without European supervision and so it was that one of their master carpenters, John Couper, was sent to Whampoa as their representative, charged with looking after the company's interests when their ships were docked.

He quickly realised the requirements of the shipping trade as a whole, as well as the needs of his employers, and also saw the possibilities and potential of expanding this business, both for his own account and for that of the near-landlocked harbour. The ship-docking business was a lucrative one and his first step was to lease the Whampoa Mud Docks from their Chinese owners. Out of his large profits he built the Couper Dock at Whampoa and was running an extremely prosperous business when an incident occurred which led to war. This was when some of the crew of the British lorcha (similar to a junk, but built on European lines) *Arrow* were imprisoned as pirates. Demands for their release were not met and the incident developed into hostilities between Britain and China in 1856, drifting on to 1860, which put the Whampoa Docks into a period of decline.

The Chinese set about the destruction of the granite-built Couper Dock. Its side walls were ripped out and hurled to the bottom and the machinery and working plant were destroyed by Chinese troops. Couper was himself kidnapped, and his fate never known. Both peace and indemnities followed, Couper's son being awarded compensation. The dock was pumped out and the same Chinese who had been so eager to destroy it were employed to replace the wall blocks and rebuild its facilities. In less than three months the dock was again in working order.

On 1 July 1863 the Hongkong & Whampoa Dock Company was founded. The company took over the Couper Dock and the more-recent Lockson Dock at Whampoa and two years later concluded negotiations for the purchase of property in the local district of Aberdeen, comprising the Lamont Dock, in working order, and the Hope Dock, under construction, together with workshops and all equipment. On 11 October 1866 the Hongkong & Whampoa Dock Co. Ltd. was registered under the Companies Ordinance, to take over the affairs of the original company. The Hope Dock was opened in June 1867 and in subsequent years was mainly used for docking H.M. ships and large vessels. Then, in March 1870, an amalgamation was made with the Union Dock Company, which owned property at Kowloon.

By January 1877 the properties at Whampoa were no longer remunerative and were sold to the Chinese Government on the condition that no vessel, other than of Chinese nationality, should be docked there. The Company was now based at Kowloon, and in August 1877 two patent slips were purchased and moved to enhance the Kowloon dock facilities. In December 1880 the Cosmopolitan Dock Company was acquired, the assets including a number of steam launches. In the same year a series of low tides caused great difficulty in placing H.M.S. *Audacious* in the Hope Dock. The British Admiralty, which was contemplating the necessity of sending larger vessels to the China Station, instructed its Commander-in-Chief to see what could be done to provide increased facilities for docking the largest vessels in the fleet. The result was that construction of No. 1 dock at Kowloon was begun in 1882, and completed six years later. A grant from the British Government ensured the Royal Navy priority of entrance to the dock for twenty years. In 1910 the dock was extensively rebuilt, being widened, lengthened and deepened.

In common with many other places in the British Empire, Hong Kong was given its greatest task during the years of the Great War. To speed the efforts of shipbuilding, engineering and repairs, land was purchased from the Government and a new yard, with three building berths, was constructed to the east of the old yard. Construction included five 'standard' 'B'-type merchant vessels, each of over 8,000 tons deadweight and one 'C'-type ship of 5,050 tdw, these orders forming part of the British Shipping Controller's wartime shipbuilding programme. The ships, however, were not completed until after war ended, three in 1919, two in 1920 and the 'C'-class ship in 1919, all after sale to private buyers.

In the immediate post-war years shipyard expansion continued. By 1924 No. 1 dock, 700 ft long and 86 ft wide, was already proving too small and plans were drawn up for the construction of a new dock, 1,200 ft in length and 120 ft wide. However, Hong Kong was also affected by the world-wide depression which followed the war and the Company was forced to curtail many of its ambitious schemes, including the contemplated new dry dock.

The Hongkong & Whampoa Dock Co. Ltd. survived during these years of depression and by the later 1930s the rumblings of another global war brought renewed activity to the yard.

Hong Kong was invaded by the Japanese in December 1941 and surrendered to them on Christmas Day. By this time the Company had built and delivered three World War II 'standard' 'Empire'-type ships, each of 10,000 tons deadweight, and had others in various stages of construction as well as a variety of smaller craft, including minesweepers and tugs, to the order of the Admiralty. By this time many improvements had been made to the yard facilities, including new machine shops, erection of tower cranes, a lengthening of No. 2 drydock and extensions to the building berths and workshops.

But there was a great deal of war destruction. Some buildings, irreparable, had to be rebuilt subject to availability of materials; new machinery and drydock pumping plant was needed; new cranes had to be installed . . .

The first post-war vessel was built and delivered in 1948 – a waterboat for the Government of Hong Kong.

Built by Taikoo Dockyard & Engineering Company of Hong Kong Ltd., Quarry Bay, Hong Kong

296 *Empire Haven* 6,603 gt, 9,975 tdw, 450 ft (oa), 429.7 ft × 56.8 ft. Engines: T3cyl.
Launched: 28.4.1941.
Completed: 6.1941.
13.8.1943: Torpedoed by aircraft north of Oran, 36.15N 02.23W. Towed to Gibraltar by H.M. ship. Temporarily repaired, then towed to U.K. for permanent repairs.
1947: *Clearton* (R. Chapman & Sons, Newcastle).
1956: *Amaconte* (Cia. Mar. Amaconte, Liberia (J. Ponte Naya, Spain).
1.1970: Arrived Aviles for breaking up.

297 *Empire Almond* 6,840 gt. Details as Yard No. 296.
Launched: 23.7.1941.
Completed: 9.1941.
1946: *Marquita* ('K' SS Co. Ltd. (Kaye Son & Co. Ltd.)).

1951: *Marsland* (Coolham SS Co. Ltd. (Kaye Son & Co. Ltd.)).
1959: *Huta Zgoda* (Polish SS Co., Poland).
(circa) 1967: Converted to a grain storage vessel for use at Gdansk (Rejonowe Zaklady Zbozowe PZZ).
(circa) 1969: Renamed *MP-ZOZIE-12* (Zaklady Obrutu Zbozami Importawanymi i Eksportowymi PZZ).
10.7.1978: Arrived Faslane in tow for scrapping.

303 *Empire Blossom* Details as Yard No. 296.
Laid down: 5.1941.
12.1941: Ready for launching, but taken by Japanese and reported completed.

Note: The engine and boilers for *Empire Blossom*, together with machinery for other ships building and such machinery as Hong Kong & Whampoa Dock Co. had ready were shipped out of Hong Kong per Blue Funnel Line's (A. Holt & Co.) *Ulysses* (1913, 14,647 gt) on 1 December 1941 and discharged at Singapore.

OTHER ORDERS

	Admiralty merchant ship No.:	
307	A/MS 214	Hull materials, machinery and boilers ready, but ship not built.
308	A/MS 237	
310	A/MS 276	Not laid down, although the steel for all four vessels was assembled in the yard.
311	A/MS 306	
316	A/MS 340	

MERCHANT SHIPS BUILT UNDER PRIVATE CONTRACT

276 *Breconshire* 9,776 gt, 507 ft (oa), 475 ft × 66.5 ft. Engines: Oil. Twin Screw.
Launched: 2.2.1939.
Completed: 1939 for Glen Line Ltd.
1939: Requisitioned by the Admiralty as a Fleet Supply Ship (Pennant Y1.3).

The *Breconshire* was employed in the Mediterranean, working mainly from Alexandria in heavily-supported naval convoys with supplies for Malta. On 20 March 1942 she was one of four ships in supply convoy MW 10, which left Alexandria for Malta, escorted by the anti-aircraft cruiser *Cairo* and six destroyers. A covering force was made up of three cruisers, four destroyers and six flanking submarines in danger areas. There was activity from both German and Italian submarines in storm force seas on 22 March.

Early on 23 March the convoy was nearing Malta and was very soon under attack by German bombers. Some eight miles off Valletta, the *Breconshire* was hit in the engine room by a single bomb and badly damaged. Disabled, she struggled on in tow of H.M.S. *Penelope*, taking eleven hours to travel four miles to Marsa Xlok Bay, in south Malta, on 25 March. The *Breconshire* was again bombed on 29 March, but sank while salvage attempts were being made. As she lay on the bottom, her side was above water, which enabled a hole to be cut, allowing oil to be pumped out for use by the Malta garrison.

Three other ships of the convoy were also lost: *Clan Campbell* about twenty miles south of Malta; the Norwegian-flag *Talabot* of Wilh. Wilhelmsen of Oslo, bombed and set on fire in Valletta Harbour on 26 March and which had to be sunk by the Army to prevent further damage, and the

Royal Mail Line's *Pampas*, continually bombed in port and finally sunk on 20 April.

In April 1950 work began to lift the *Breconshire* for disposal at sea, but it was found to be a more practicable proposition to refloat her if she were to be raised bottom up. Work for this began on 7 August 1950, with naval salvage ships *Dispenser, Retriever* and *Sea Salvor*. The raising was successful and during it the ship was purchased by a Maltese firm for scrapping. However, on 31 August 1950, delivery was made to her new owners and she left, in tow, bottom up, for Messina and was there beached. In 1952 she was towed to Taranto, where she was righted and broken up.

277   *Glenorchy* 8,982 gt, 501 ft (oa), 483 ft × 66.4 ft.
Engines: Oil. Twin screw.
Launched: 1939.
Completed: 1939 for Glen Line Ltd.
13.8.1942: Sunk by Italian torpedo boats, NW of Kelibia Light, Tunisia, during 'Operation Pedestal' supply convoy to Malta (see details below).

'OPERATION PEDESTAL'

This Operation was planned to take urgent supplies to the tiny, beleaguered island of Malta, a British possession since 1814, so strategically important in its position in the Mediterranean, but in those dark days of 1942 almost surrounded by Axis-dominated territory.

The convoy had to be fast and fourteen ships capable of sustaining fifteen to sixteen knots over lengthy periods were chosen. Three ships, including a tanker, flew the United States' flag; the remainder were British, including the *Empire Hope*, only completed seven months previously. After loading at Liverpool, Belfast and Glasgow the ships gathered to leave the Clyde in the evening of 2 August 1942 to form convoy WS 21S. Three cruisers, an anti-aircraft ship and twelve destroyers formed the close naval escort.

There was a powerful covering force; *Nelson* and *Rodney* in battleship power; the aircraft carriers *Eagle, Victorious* and *Indomitable* mustering seventy-two fighter aircraft, three cruisers and twelve destroyers. Also attached was the carrier *Furious*, with thirty-eight fighter planes to be flown off to Malta and eight destroyers as escorts. An ocean tug was attached and eight British submarines had been strategically placed in Mediterranean waters.

The huge force moved through the Straits of Gibraltar in thick fog on the 10th August, from where Force 'R', the oilers *Dingledale* and *Brown Ranger*, four corvettes and a tug, joined in support.

Next morning, the 11th, enemy spotter planes hovered overhead, forewarning of action to come. South of the Balearic Islands the fighter planes on the *Furious* were flown off to Malta, the carrier then returning to Gibraltar. But at 1 pm the first blow to the convoy came when a four-torpedo salvo from *U.73* struck the carrier *Eagle* and she sank within eight minutes, her fighter planes tumbling overside as the flight deck angled. Bombers arrived in the evening and from then on there was little respite; enemy submarines were ever present, seven German and thirteen Italian boats already positioned, whilst E-boat and Italian torpedo-boat attacks were expected in the Sicilian Channel.

The morning of the 12th began with bombing by JU 88s and attacks continued all day. The *Deucalion* of Alfred Holt's Blue Funnel Line suffered bomb damage and was disabled and in the early evening JU 87s caused heavy damage to the *Indomitable*, whilst an Italian aerial torpedo damaged the destroyer *Foresight* so badly that she was sunk by H.M.S. *Tartar*.

Later the same evening Italian submarines struck, a torpedo from the *Dessie* damaging the stern of the *Brisbane Star*, but she managed to continue. At this time the disabled *Deucalion* was hit by an aerial torpedo and sank five miles west of Cani Rocks, off Tunisia. The cruiser *Nigeria* turned to Gibraltar with escorts after being torpedoed by the *Axum* when nearing the Skerki Channel, the same submarine also sinking the anti-aircraft ship *Cairo* and damaging the tanker *Ohio*. An attack by JU 88s hit the *Empire Hope* and the *Glenorchy*. Already disabled with engine damage from previous attacks, the *Empire Hope* was later torpedoed by the *Bronzo* and had to be sunk off Galeta Island by an R.N. escort. At dusk the submarine *Alagi* entered the attack, damaging the cruiser *Kenya* and sinking the *Clan Ferguson* twenty miles north of Zembra Island.

The covering naval force had made its planned return to Gibraltar that day and the remaining merchant ships and close escort of two cruisers and nine destroyers rounded Cape Bon at midnight. Valletta, in Malta, was 225 miles away; inshore the E-boats and torpedo boats were waiting to pounce.

The first casualty on the 13th was the cruiser *Manchester*, which suffered so badly from torpedo boat attacks that she was abandoned and scuttled. She was soon followed by the damaged *Glenorchy*, sunk by MS 31.★ More sinkings were made by 'MAS'-class★ and 'S'-class★ boats (★See notes below); two American ships, the Grace Line's C2-type *Santa Elisa* and Lykes Line's C3-type *Almeria Lykes* were followed by the Shaw, Savill & Albion Co.'s *Wairangi*, whilst the Union-Castle Line's refrigerated motorship *Rochester Castle* was damaged.

There was no rest from air attacks. As the ships moved nearer to Malta JU 88 and JU 87-type planes, Heinkel 111s and Savioa S79 planes continuously attacked. Another Shaw, Savill ship, *Waimarama*, carrying high octane spirit, was hit, violently exploded in a sheet of flame and sank in four minutes. The Federal Steam Navigation Co.'s *Dorset* was hit in the engine room and flooded badly; she began to settle and was abandoned. At 6 pm another bomb, another fire, and she sank two hours later. More hits were registered on the *Rochester Castle* and on the now seriously damaged tanker *Ohio*, with her precious cargo of oil.

In the afternoon of the 13th the Malta-based minesweepers met the first of the battered ships, the *Rochester Castle*, followed by the *Melbourne Star* and *Port Chalmers*, with thousands of cheering Maltese and island-based servicemen lining the harbour as the ships arrived.

At noon next day the *Brisbane Star*, which had remained at Sousse for a time with torpedo damage, entered the harbour. Then came the tanker *Ohio*, the fifth and last of the fourteen-ship convoy. Hit time and time again, with only a three feet and lessening freeboard and almost unmanageable, she limped in at 09.30 hours on the 15th and moved into Grand Harbour with crowds cheering. Her back was broken and water lapped over the deck amidships: she was gently moved with the destroyers *Penn* and *Ledbury* closed on each side and the *Rye* towing – a wreck but in her tanks was 14,000 tons of petrol for the survival of Malta. With her precious cargo discharged the tanker settled on the bottom. Later raised, she was used as a storage hulk until 19 September 1946, when she was towed out and sunk by gunfire in the blue waters in which she had sailed so bravely.

These were the five ships of the fourteen-ship convoy, carrying the supplies and food which enabled the fortress of Malta to continue its resistance. The price was high. Nine merchant ships were lost; the aircraft carrier *Eagle*, two cruisers and a destroyer were sunk. An estimated 400 bombers, torpedo planes and long-range fighters had attacked the ships through Tunisian waters.

Note: (★) Ms – Motosiluranti (Italian), two 21-inch torpedo tubes. Thirty-two knots.

MAS – Motoscafi Anti-Sommergibili (Italian), two 18-inch torpedo tubes. Forty-seven knots.

S – Schnellboote (German), two 19.7-inch torpedo tubes. Thirty-one knots.

285 *Viti* 676 gt, 167.6 ft (oa), 159 ft × 31.6 ft.
Engines: Oil. Twin screws.
Launched: 1939.
Completed: 7.1940 for Government of Fiji.
1948: (Tasman SS Co. Ltd., Auckland).
1961: (Seafoods Ltd., Auckland).
1967: *Audrey B* (M. J. Batty (Panama) Ltd.).
1986: Name deleted from ship registers: existence of vessel in doubt.

The *Viti* was built for inter-island communications in the region of the S.W. Pacific administered by the Western Pacific High Commission, in Suva.

Early in the war she was fitted as a minor combatant ship but still used for administrative duties. In January 1941 she was used to train Fiji's naval volunteer force and in the April

became H.M. Fijian Ship. At the end of the year *Viti* was accepted into the Royal Navy and although based at Fiji she refitted annually in New Zealand.

Into late 1945 the vessel carried stores, passengers and troops around the South Pacific and was then returned to her owners. She made several more similar voyages, but was put up for sale at the end of 1946.

289 *Hanyang* 2,865 gt, 308 ft (oa),
299.7 ft × 44.2 ft. Engines: T3cyl.
Launched: 3.1940.
Completed: 1940 for China Navigation Co. Ltd.
11.4.1943: Bombed by Japanese aircraft; disabled (voyage: Milne Bay/Oro Bay, Papua New Guinea). Later proceeded to Townsville, thence to Sydney, N.S.W., for repairs.

1964: *Bidford* (Hemisphere Shipping Co. Ltd., Hong Kong (Ocean Tramping Co., Hong Kong)).
6.1969: Scrapped Whampoa.

291 *Pakhoi* 2,865 gt. Details as Yard No. 289.
Launched: 12.1940.
Completed: 1941 for China Navigation Co. Ltd.
1963: *Longford* (Peninsular Shipping Co. Ltd., Hong Kong (Ocean Tramping Co., Hong Kong)).
4.1969: Scrapped Whampoa.

295 *Poyang* 2,873 gt. Details as Yard No. 289.
Launched: 10.6.1941.
Completed: 1941 for China Navigation Co. Ltd.
5.1942–11.1945: (Used by R.A.N. as Arms Supply Vessel).
1946: Reverted to owner.
1963: *Bali Steer* (Steering Line (Hong Kong) Ltd., Panama).
1965: *Rosalina* (Cia. Nav. Viento del Sur., S.A., Panama (Lam Soon Shipping Co. Ltd., Hong Kong)).
7.1970: Scrapped Singapore.

Built by Blythswood Shipbuilding Co. Ltd., Glasgow

CARGO SHIPS BUILT UNDER PRIVATE CONTRACT OR LICENCE

58 *Manchester Merchant* 7,264 gt, 446.5 ft (oa), 432 ft × 57 ft. Engines: three steam turbines.
Launched: 10.2.1940.
Completed: 4.1940 for Manchester Liners Ltd.
25.2.1943: Sunk by submarine (*U.628*) torpedo in mid-Atlantic, 45.10N 43.23W whilst in convoy ON 166 (voyage: United Kingdom/U.S.A.).

59 *Manchester Trader* 7,363 gt. Details as Yard No. 58.
Launched: 15.2.1941.
Completed: 5.1941 for Manchester Liners Ltd.
5.1963: Broken up Split.

60 *Welsh Prince* 5,148 gt, 432.5 ft (oa), 418 ft × 56 ft. Engines: T3cyl.
Launched: 23.4.1940.
Completed: 6.1940 for Prince Line Ltd. (Furness, Withy & Co. Ltd.).
26.9.1940: Bombed and damaged, northeast of

Aberdeen (voyage: London/New York). Put into port; repaired.
7.12.1941: Mined in vicinity of Spurn Head, River Humber; abandoned 53.24N 0.59E; grounded; broke in two; sank; total loss.

71 *Manchester Shipper* 7,881 gt, 461.4 ft (oa), 443.3 ft × 58.1 ft. Engines: three steam turbines.
Launched: 30.6.1943.
Completed: 10.1943 for Manchester Liners Ltd.
10.7.1969: Arrived Trieste for breaking up.

75 *Javanese Prince* 8,875 gt, 482.3 ft (oa), 464 ft × 62.1 ft. Engines: Oil.
Launched: 7.8.1944.
Completed: 11.1944 for Rio Cape Line Ltd. (Furness, Withy & Co. Ltd.).
1954: (Prince Line Ltd. (Furness, Withy & Co. Ltd.)).
1961: *Benlarig* (Ben Line Steamers Ltd.).
6.9.1969: Arrived Hong Kong for breaking up.

Built by R. & W. Hawthorn, Leslie & Co. Ltd., Newcastle-upon-Tyne

CARGO SHIPS BUILT UNDER PRIVATE CONTRACT OR LICENCE

653 *Rippingham Grange* 10,365 gt, 464.5 ft (oa), 447.5 ft × 65.5 ft. Engines: Oil. Twin screw refrigerated cargo ship.
Launched: 6.3.1943.
Completed: 9.1943 for Houlder Line Ltd. (Furness, Withy & Co. Ltd., London).

1961: *Abbey Wood* (Far East Marine Enterprises Ltd., Hong Kong).
23.4.1962: Arrived Hakodate for breaking up.

655 *Condesa* 10,367 gt. Details as Yard No. 653.
Launched: 17.8.1943.

Completed: 4.1944 for Furness–Houlder Argentine Lines Ltd. (Furness, Withy & Co. Ltd., London). 31.10.1960: Chartered by French Government and used as a storeship for frozen meat at Boulogne. 6.1962: Arrived Spezia for breaking up.

683 *Hornby Grange* 10,785 gt, 470 ft (oa), 463 ft × 65.8 ft. Engines: Oil. Twin screw refrigerated cargo ship.

Launched: 31.5.1946. Completed: 12.1946 for Houlder Line Ltd. (Furness, Withy & Co. Ltd., London)). 1969: *Douro* (Royal Mail Lines Ltd., London). 1970: (Prince Line Ltd. (Shaw, Savill & Albion Co. Ltd.)). 6.6.1972: Arrived Aviles, Spain, for breaking up.

The *Manchester Shipper* in war guise. (Blythswood Shipbuilding Co. Ltd., Yard No. 71.)

The *Rippingham Grange*, built under licence in 1943. (R. & W. Hawthorn, Leslie & Co. Ltd., Yard No. 653.)   *Skyfotos*

PART TWO

DEEP SEA TANKERS

Oil was the life blood of Britain's war machine; the Royal Navy, Royal Air Force and the mechanised armies depended on it, as did the many factories engaged in war production. Practically all refined oil products had to be brought to Britain and the tanker was special to that single purpose. Up to the outbreak of war tankers could be generally classified to two types, those that worked in routes for the major oil companies and the 'tramp' tankers operated by private companies, available for chartering out to the major companies through the workings of the London Baltic Exchange.

Tankers were quite obviously going to be victims in the war at sea, precious ships with their precious cargoes singled out by the ever-seeking U-boat, and Government orders for the oil carrier were soon forthcoming. Conforming to the war policy the orders were given to those yards which had been producing tankers in the pre-war period, so that the builders had prototypes on which to build.

Three types of ocean-going tanker dominated the tanker building programme. First was the 'Ocean' type, based on a 'Shell' design which was sometimes known as the 'Three Twelves'-type, the vessels being of 12,000 tons deadweight and having a speed of twelve knots on a fuel consumption of twelve tons per day. They were capable of carrying many types of fuel including the high-octane fuel required for aircraft; they could also be used for fuelling at sea. The plans were for diesel drive, some forgings to be brought from the Continent, but this was frustrated by the speed of the German invasion of the Low Countries. Some 'Ocean'-type tankers were therefore fitted with triple expansion steam engines. In addition a group of 'Ocean'-type tankers was acquired by the Admiralty under the 'Dale' nomenclature.

Next came the slightly larger 'Norwegian'-type. The prototypes of this class were the sisterships *Sandanger* and *Eidanger*, built by Sir James Laing & Sons Ltd., Sunderland, in 1938 for the Norwegian owners, Westfal-Larsen & Co. A/S, of Bergen. Again, machinery was the main problem and the ships were built with any set that could be produced from the various engine works. At the start a 3,800 ihp triple expansion set was installed, then some 3,300 bhp diesel engines became available and finally the 4,000 bhp engine was fitted. The 'Norwegian'-type twelve-knot ships were constructed by two builders, Furness Shipbuilding Co. Ltd., and Sir James Laing & Sons.

In 1943 the machinery supply had much improved and a new design for a 12,000 tdw tanker was introduced. These ships, however, were eventually to have turbine machinery and water tube boilers, their speed of fifteen knots enabling them to sail free of convoy. Six sets of tanks and a pumproom simplified the hull and the deck was parallel to the keel from the aft engine casing to the foremast. They were actually designed with oil engines but when yard space became available the urgency for them had lessened and they were given two steam turbines to a single shaft.

The first of the type, *Empire Bounty*, was completed in 1944. However, in planning for the Far East war the Admiralty required fast tankers and the whole class of twenty ships was acquired, all 'Empire' names being changed to the 'Wave' prefix. Four, *Wave Emperor*, *Wave Governor*, *Wave*

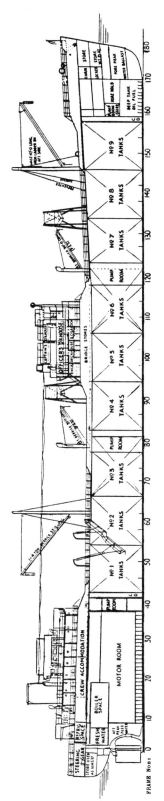

The 'Ocean'-type tanker.

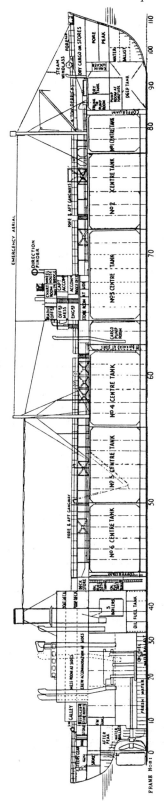

The 'Norwegian'-type tanker.

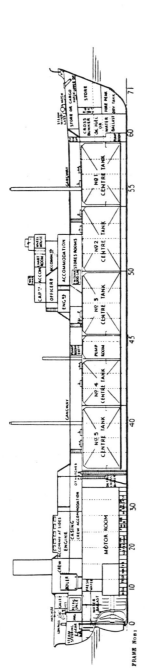

The standard 'Intermediate'-type tanker.

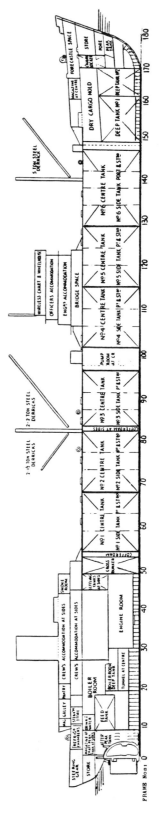

The standard fast tanker.

King and *Wave Monarch* ended the war in the British Pacific Fleet. The remainder, at first, worked commercially, then became Fleet Auxiliaries. Eight were altered to become Fleet Replenishment Ships: *Wave Baron*, *Wave Chief*, *Wave Knight*, *Wave Master*, *Wave Prince*, *Wave Ruler*, *Wave Sovereign* and *Wave Victor*. Two of these, *Wave Ruler* and *Wave Victor*, spent some years as aviation fuel hulks at Gan, in the Maldive Islands, which was classed as a 'staging post in the Indian Ocean'.

The first of the class to be broken up was *Wave Liberator*, which had suffered serious engine defects all her short life of $12\frac{1}{2}$ years.

There was one other ship built to this design, *Beechwood*, completed by Laing in 1945 for Oil & Molasses Tankers Ltd., and which worked in the commercial sector.

'Ocean'-type

Built by Blythswood Shipbuilding Co. Ltd., Glasgow

63 *Empire Jet* 8,134 gt, 479.3 ft (oa),
463.2 ft × 61.2 ft. Engines: Oil.
Launched: 27.5.1941.
Completed: 8.1941.
1946: *Regent Jaguar* (Bowring SS Co. Ltd. (C. T. Bowring & Co. Ltd.)).
2.6.1958: Arrived Briton Ferry for breaking up.

64 *Empire Pict* 8,134 gt. Details as Yard No. 63.
Launched: 11.9.1941.
Completed: 11.1941.
1942: *Norland* (Government of Norway).
20.5.1942: Sunk by submarine (*U.108*) torpedo, 31.29N 55.37W, east of Bermuda whilst in convoy ON 93 (voyage: Clyde/Corpus Christi – ballast).

80 *Empire Trinidad* 8,130 gt, 484 ft (oa),
466 ft × 59.2 ft. Engines: Oil.
Launched: 10.7.1945.
Completed: 11.1945.
1946: *Regent Lion* (Bear Creek Oil & Shipping Co. Ltd. (C. T. Bowring & Co. Ltd.)).
1950: (Bowring SS Co. Ltd. (C. T. Bowring & Co. Ltd.)).
1955: renamed *Camillo*.
7.1.1960: Arrived Faslane for breaking up.

The Blythswood Shipbuilding Co. Ltd., was registered on 6 October 1919, its yard of five berths situated on the north bank of the River Clyde, at Scotstoun, Glasgow.

It was to specialise in oil carriers and cargo/passenger ships, and even before the yard was actually completed contracts for five tankers had been received, Yard No. 1, *British Architect*, 7,388 gt, being delivered to the British Tanker Co. Ltd., in December 1922.

There then followed a succession of tanker orders, interspersed with newbuildings for Manchester Liners, Furness, Withy, Prince Line . . . etc.

Blythswood also completed the tanker *San Demetrio* in December 1938 for the Eagle Oil & Shipping Co. Ltd., whose encounter with the German raider *Admiral Scheer* on 5 November 1940 is recorded as an epic in maritime history.

During World War II the company yard list was dominated by tanker building, twenty-one being delivered including eight for Anglo-Saxon, four for the British Tanker Co., one for Eagle Oil and eight for Government account.

By mid-1961 work was so short that the yard was turned to the construction of caravans to keep carpenters employed. On 22 December 1964 it was announced that the yard would close from January 1965 and it was taken over by the adjacent Yarrow & Co. Ltd., who were the original owners of much of the Blythswood site; in the following May Yarrow announced integration of the yard.

The last ship constructed was the lighthouse tender *Fingal* (Yard No. 140), 1,342 gt, launched on 8 August 1963 and completed in January 1964 for the Commissioners of Northern Lights, Leith.

Built by Cammell Laird & Co. Ltd., Birkenhead

1053   *Empire Steel* 8,138 gt, 484 ft (oa), 466 ft × 59.2 ft. Engines: Oil.
Launched: 4.12.1940.
Completed: 3.1941.

24.3.1942: Sunk by submarine (*U.123*) torpedo and gunfire north-east of Bermuda, in position 37.45N 63.17W.

Built by Furness Shipbuilding Co. Ltd., Haverton Hill-on-Tees

326   *Empire Granite* 8,028 gt, 479 ft (oa), 463.5 ft × 61.2 ft. Engines: T3cyl.
Launched: 12.12.1940.
Completed: 3.1941.
1946: *Kennerleya* (Anglo-Saxon Petroleum Co. Ltd.).
4.2.1960: Arrived Spezia for breaking up.

327   *Empire Oil* 8,029 gt. Details as Yard No. 326.
Launched: 11.2.1941.
Completed: 5.1941.
10.9.1942: Crippled by submarine (*U.659*) torpedoes, at bow and stern and eventually sunk by submarine (*U.584*) in mid-Atlantic 51.23N 28.13W. (Convoy ON 127) (voyage: U.K./North America).

328   *Empire Mica* 8,032 gt. Details as Yard No. 326.
Launched: 10.4.1941.
Completed: 7.1941.
29.6.1942: Sunk by submarine (*U.67*) torpedo in Gulf of Mexico 29.25N 85.17W.

329   *Empire Sapphire* 8,031 gt. Details as Yard No. 326.
Launched: 27.5.1941.
Completed: 7.1941.
1946: *Esso Saranac* (Anglo-American Oil Co. Ltd.).
25.1.1959: Arrived Antwerp for breaking up.

330   *Empire Amethyst* 8,032 gt. Details as Yard No. 326.
Launched: 8.7.1941.
Completed: 9.1941.
13.4.1942: Sunk by submarine (*U.154*) torpedo near Jamaica 17.40N 74.50W (voyage: New Orleans/Freetown).

334   *Empire Emerald* 8,032 gt. Details as Yard No. 326.
Launched: 26.8.1941.
Completed: 10.1941.
1946: *El Gallo* (Lobitos Oilfields Ltd.). (C. T. Bowring & Co. Ltd.).
5.2.1959: Arrived Briton Ferry for breaking up.

335   *Empire Celt* 8,032 gt. Details as Yard No. 326.
Launched: 7.10.1941.
Completed: 1.1942.
24.2.1942: Damaged by submarine (*U.158*) torpedo, south-east of Newfoundland, 43.50N 43.38W. Broke in two, both parts remained afloat, but with forepart slowly sinking. Attempts to take afterpart in tow failed; adrift but considered salvable with adequate towing assistance.
9.3.1942: Canadian tug *Foundation Franklin* left port to assist, but search for vessel unsuccessful, and
17.3.1942: Search abandoned. Vessel presumed to have sunk, date and position uncertain.

Built by Harland & Wolff Ltd., Belfast

1053 *Empire Diamond* 8,236 gt, 483 ft (oa),
465.6 ft × 59.5 ft. Engines: Oil.
Launched: 10.7.1941.
Completed: 11.1941.
1942: *Norsol* (Government of Norway).
1946: *Kollbjorg* (A/S Kollbjorg (O. Berg, Oslo)).
1956: *Storo* (Rederi Norland (Odmark & Andersson,
Sweden)).
20.11.1959: Arrived Hong Kong for breaking up.

1079 *Empire Spenser* 8,194 gt. Details as Yard No.
1053.
Launched: 17.2.1942.
Completed: 7.1942.
8.12.1942: Sunk by submarine (*U.524*) torpedo in
mid-Atlantic, 57.04N 36.01W (voyage:
Curaçao/New York/Stanlow – oil).

1080 *Empire Chapman* 8,194 gt. Details as Yard No.
1053.
Launched: 17.1.1942.
Completed: 6.1942.
1946: *British Commando* (British Tanker Co. Ltd.).
3.3.1959: Arrived Bruges for breaking up.

1081 *Empire Fletcher* 8,191 gt. Details as Yard No.
1053.
Launched: 4.4.1942.
Completed: 7.1942.
1944: *Backhuysen* (Government of The Netherlands).
1947: *Chama* (N.V. Petroleum Maats. "La Corona",
Holland).
1955: *Anastasia* (Derna Cia. Nav. S.A., Panama (J.
Livanos & Sons Ltd., London)).
9.9.1959: Arrived Savona for breaking up.

1158 (Launched as) *Empire Fusilier* 8,202 gt. Details
as Yard No. 1053.
Launched: 8.8.1942.
Completed: 2.1943 as *Empire Bombardier*.
1946: *British Bombardier* (British Tanker Co. Ltd.).
13.3.1959: Arrived Tamise, Belgium, for breaking
up.

1159 *Empire Industry* 8,203 gt. Details as Yard No.
1053.
Launched: 4.5.1943.
Completed: 9.1943.
1946: *Flammulina* (Anglo-Saxon Petroleum Co. Ltd.).
22.8.1960: Arrived Hong Kong for breaking up.

1164 *Empire Benefit* 8.202 gt. Details as Yard No.
1053.
Launched: 24.11.1942.
Completed: 4.1943.
1945: *Athelqueen* (Athel Line Ltd.).
1955: *Mariverda* (Mariblanca Nav. S.A. (Chandris
(England) Ltd.)).
6.9.1961: Arrived Kure for breaking up.

1189 *Empire Traveller* 8,201 gt. Details as Yard No.
1053.
Launched: 29.6.1943.
Completed: 10.1943.
1946: *Pechelbronn* (Government of France).
1956: *Eagle* (African Carriers Corpn. (J. A. Galani,
Paris)).
1959: *Jajce* (Maritenia Shipping Co. Ltd.
(Government of Yugoslavia)).
1963: (Jugoslavenska Tankerska Plovidba
(Government of Yugoslavia)).
1.1969: Scrapped Valencia.

1242 *Empire Saturn* 8,224 gt. Details as Yard No.
1053.
Launched: 6.5.1944.
Completed: 9.1944.
1946: *Nayadis* (Anglo-Saxon Petroleum Co. Ltd.).
10.1961: Scrapped Hirao.

Built by Harland & Wolff Ltd., Govan

1045 (G)   *Empire Gem* 8,139 gt, 479.4 ft (oa),
463.2 ft × 61.2 ft. Engines: Oil.
Launched: 29.5.1941.
Completed: 9.1941.
24.1.1942: Torpedoed by submarine (*U.66*) off the
Virginia Capes, U.S.A., 35.06N 74.58W. Broke in
two; afterpart sank; bow section remained afloat, but
later sank in position 35.02N 75.33W.

1083 (G)   *Empire Onyx* 8,221 gt, 483 ft (oa),
465.6 ft × 59.5 ft. Engines: Oil.
Launched: 21.8.1941.
Completed: 12.1941.
1942: *Nortind* (Government of Norway).
20.6.1942: Damaged by submarine (*U.67*) torpedo in
Gulf of Mexico, 28.41N 89.34W. Put back to New
Orleans, then proceeded Mobile for repairs.
26.1.1943: Sunk by submarine (*U.358*) torpedo
58.40N 33.10W, east of Cape Farewell, Greenland,
whilst straggling in convoy HX 223s (voyage:
Curaçao/New York/River Mersey – oil).

1116 (G)   (Launched as) *Empire Vigilance* 8,093 gt.
Details as Yard No. 1045 (G).
Launched: 18.2.1942.
Completed: 5.1942 as *British Vigilance* for British
Tanker Co. Ltd.
3.1.1943: Damaged by submarine (*U.514*) torpedo,
20.58N 44.40W, in mid-Atlantic. Abandoned, drifted
and
24.1.1943: Sunk by submarine (*U.105*) torpedo
(voyage: Curaçao/Gibraltar).

1160 (G)   *Empire Metal* 8,201 gt. Details as Yard No.
1083 (G).

Launched: 30.6.1942.
Completed: 9.1942.
2.1.1943: Bombed and sunk at Bone Harbour,
Algeria.
8.1949: Raised, broke in two.
5.1950: Stern section removed and beached at
Grenouilliere for demolition *in situ*.
29.8.1950: Forepart arrived Savona for breaking up.
Machinery removed and shipped to Canada for
installation in the Great Lakes vessel *Captain C. D.
Secord* (1900, 6,943 gt) in 1954.

1197 (G)   (Launched as) *Empire Grenada* 8,231 gt.
Details as Yard No. 1083 (G).
Launched: 20.12.1945.
Completed: 4.1946 as *British Piper* (British Tanker
Co. Ltd.).
10.11.1961: Arrived Newport, Mon., for breaking
up.

1243 (G)   *Empire Jupiter* 8,217 gt. Details as Yard
No. 1083 (G).
Launched: 21.9.1944.
Completed: 12.1944.
1946: *Saint Gaudens* (Government of France).
1948: *Sevane* (Les Petroles d'Outre-Mer, France).
1958: *Progres* (Jugoslavenska Tankerska Plovidba,
Jugoslavia).
9.11.1970: Arrived Split for breaking up.

Built by R. & W. Hawthorn, Leslie & Co. Ltd., Newcastle-upon-Tyne

627   *Empire Bronze* 8,149 gt, 483.3 ft (oa),
465.3 ft × 59.3 ft. Engines: Oil.
Launched: 19.8.1940.
Completed: 11.1940.
1946: *Esso Cadillac* (Anglo-American Oil Co. Ltd.).
1956: *Maribella II* (Mariblanca Nav. S.A. (Chandris
(England) Ltd.)).
14.8.1959: Arrived Osaka for breaking up.

666   *Empire Neptune* 8,285 gt. Details as Yard
No. 627.
Launched: 13.4.1945.
Completed: 8.1945.
1946: *San Virgilio* (Eagle Oil & Shipping Co. Ltd.).
3.12.1958: Arrived Hong Kong for breaking up.

The beginning of this company was in 1817, when engineer Robert Hawthorn started a steam
engine works at Forth Banks, Newcastle, he and his brother turning to the building of marine
engines in 1820 with 7 hp machinery for the *Indefatigable*, a small packet boat for work on the River
Tyne. Another event recorded in history was the building of the first locomotive for the Stockton
& Darlington Railway in 1831. An engine set for the gunboat H.M.S. *Shearwater* came in 1862

which heralded Admiralty and overseas orders for engine sets for all types of warships over the ensuing years.

The shipbuilding side of the company was begun by Andrew Leslie in 1853, the first ship, *Clarendon*, being completed at Hebburn in 1854. Eleven of the first seventeen ships were for Russia and the yard also constructed most of the Russian Volunteer Fleet, formed by a combine of Russian merchants.

In 1885 R. & W. Hawthorn amalgamated with A. Leslie & Company and received their first Admiralty order for a small stores carrier in the following year. In 1890 the 1,830 ton H.M.S. *Bellona*, a nineteen-knot 'protected' cruiser was completed.

The amazing performance of the turbine-driven *Turbinia* at the Fleet Review of 1897 when she reached 34½ knots was followed by an Admiralty order to Hawthorn, Leslie for a turbine-driven destroyer, and H.M.S. *Viper*, with quadruple shafts for eight screws to give thirty-four knots, was completed in 1899. From then on Hawthorn, Leslie's yard list contained many naval vessels. Twenty-seven warships were constructed in the Great War and one, H.M.S. *Verdun*, a destroyer of 1917, was chosen to bring home the body of the Unknown Warrior. The *Verdun* was broken up in 1946 at Granton.

The yard also constructed many merchant ships, including tankers, refrigerated vessels and passenger ships. In 1922 the *Andania* (Yard No. 500) (13,950 gt) was completed for Cunard Line and in 1925 the P & O liners *Ranpura* (Yard No. 532) and *Ranchi* (Yard No. 534), each of 16,500 gt, entered the London–Bombay route. During the 1939–1945 war twelve tankers and three large refrigerated meat carriers were constructed, although the main output was of naval ships. The yard consisted of nine building berths to 700 ft long ships and a drydock 502 ft × 66 ft, when war ended.

Operative from January 1968, the company merged with John Readhead & Sons Ltd., the Swan, Hunter Group Ltd., and Vickers Ltd., under the title of Swan Hunter & Tyne Shipbuilders Ltd.

Built by Swan, Hunter & Wigham Richardson Ltd., Wallsend

1601 *Empire Flint* 8,129 gt, 483.1 ft (oa), 468.4 ft × 59.4 ft. Engines: T3cyl.
Launched: 29.3.1941.
Completed: 8.1941.
1945: *Athelstane* (Athel Line Ltd. (United Molasses Co. Ltd.)).
1952: *Oakley* (Skibs A/S Vaholm (Holmen & Vaboen)).
1959: (H. A. Moller A/S (T. Klaveness, Oslo)).
2.1962: Scrapped Hamburg.

1706 *Empire Saxon* 8,129 gt, 483.1 ft (oa), 465.9 ft × 59.4 ft. Engines: T3cyl.
Launched: 2.12.1941.
Completed: 2.1942.
1942: *Norfjell* (Government of Norway).
1946: *Nordfonn* (Skibs A/S Ringfonn (S. Bergesen, Oslo)).
1947: New (oil) engine.
1957: *Norsk Jarl* (Mil Tankrederi A/S (Norsk Braendselolje A/S, Oslo)).
27.6.1960: Arrived Bo'ness for breaking up.

1710 *Empire Garrick* 8,128 gt. Details as Yard No. 1706.
Launched: 14.5.1942.
Completed: 7.1942.
1945: *British Guardsman* (British Tanker Co. Ltd.).
1951: *Alan Evelyn* (British Oil Shipping Co. Ltd. (Stevinson, Hardy & Co. Ltd., London)).
1955: *Westbrook* (Duff, Herbert & Mitchell Ltd.).
28.7.1959: Severely damaged amidships by fire while laid up at Barry, Glam. Sold, and
15.3.1960: Arrived Newport, Mon. in tow: grounded in river entrance; refloated same day.
16.3.1960: Berthed at Cashmore's yard for breaking up.

1712 *Empire Reynolds* 8,128 gt. Details as Yard No. 1706.
Launched: 16.7.1942.
Completed: 9.1942.
1946: *Luminous* (Aral SS Co. Ltd. (H. E. Moss & Co., London)).
1956: *Potere* (Cia. Sicula di Armamento SpA, COSARMA, Sicily).
1956: renamed *Miriella*.
10.1960: Scrapped Trieste.

The 'Ocean'-type tanker *Empire Chapman*, June 1943. A dummy funnel amidships conceals her tanker status and her aft funnel is replaced by twin 'kingpost'-type uptakes. (Harland & Wolff Ltd., Belfast, Yard No. 1080.) *National Maritime Museum*

The 'Dale'-class tanker *Dewdale* as a Gantry Landing Ship, in 1946. (Cammell Laird & Co. Ltd., Yard No. 1054.)
Wright & Logan

The *Empire Metal* as the Admiralty 'Dale'-class tanker *Eaglesdale*, in 1958. (Furness Shipbuilding Co. Ltd., Yard No. 339.)
Wright & Logan

'Ocean'-type (The Admiralty 'Dale'-class)

The origins of the 'Dale'-class of naval tankers date back to pre-war times, when it was decided that the Admiralty needed its own fleet of tankers. The first group of six vessels (*Abbeydale, Aldersdale, Arndale, Bishopdale, Boardale* and *Broomdale*) were purchased on the stocks and entered service in 1937.

Two vessels (*Cairndale* and *Cedardale*) formed the second group, these being purchased from the Anglo-Saxon Petroleum Company while still building. They entered service in 1939, being used to evaluate future needs when compared with the earlier six vessels.

On the outbreak of World War II it was realised that the Admiralty would need to increase its tanker fleet and a third group, of ten war-built vessels, was acquired from the merchant shipbuilding programme, a number of them originally intended for operation by the Eagle Oil Company on behalf of the M.O.W.T. In the event, three of the ten ships were converted to LSG's (Gantry Landing Ships) (see *Dewdale*, etc.).

Built by Blythswood Shipbuilding Co. Ltd., Glasgow

61 *Empire Oil* 8,145 gt, 483 ft (oa), 460 ft × 59 ft.
Engines: Oil.
Launched: 15.11.1940.
Completed: 2.1941 as *Darkdale* (R.F.A.).
22.10.1941: Sunk by submarine (*U.68*) torpedo whilst anchored off St. Helena Island, South Atlantic.

62 *Empire Silver* 8,145 gt, 479.3 ft (oa),
463.2 ft × 61.2 ft. Engines: Oil.
Launched: 19.10.1940.

Completed: 1.1941 as *Denbydale* (R.F.A.).
19.9.1941: Damaged by human chariot limpet charge from Italian submarine *Scire* whilst lying at the Detached Mole, Gibraltar. Back broken; remained at Gibraltar as a fuelling hulk. Engines removed and sent to United Kingdom; some parts lost en-route when the carrying vessel was sunk; remainder later fitted in *Derwentdale*.
27.7.1957: Arrived Blyth, in tow, for breaking up.

Built by Cammell Laird & Co. Ltd., Birkenhead

1054 *Dewdale* 8,265 gt, 483.3 ft (oa),
465.3 ft × 59.3 ft. Engines: Oil.
Launched: 17.2.1941.
Completed: 6.1941 as a Gantry Landing Ship (LSG).
20.11.1942: Bombed and damaged at Bougie, Algeria, during the Allied landings in North Africa.
29.11.1942: Further damaged (by mine) at Algiers.
4.1943: Arrived Liverpool for repairs.
6.1946: Refitted as a tanker at Portsmouth.
23.12.1959: Arrived Antwerp for breaking up.

As a Gantry Landing Ship the above vessel was equipped with four gantry crane extensions which travelled the main deck on rails and lowered the fifteen landing craft carried, over the side in a thirty-minute period. These landing craft were 50 ft in length and 26 tons deadweight.

The *Dewdale* was the first R.F.A. ship to enter Singapore after its capture from Japanese occupation.

Two other tankers were requisitioned for conversion to Gantry Landing Ships, *Derwentdale*, built by Harland & Wolff Ltd., Govan, and *Ennerdale*, built by Swan, Hunter & Wigham Richardson Ltd., Newcastle.

Built by Furness Shipbuilding Co. Ltd., Haverton Hill-on-Tees

325   *Empire Gold* 8,028 gt, 479 ft (oa),
463.5 ft × 61.2 ft. Engines: T3cyl.
Launched: 4.10.1940.
Completed: 2.1941.
Allocated name *Eppingdale*, but vessel not taken over by the Admiralty.
18.4.1945: Damaged by submarine (*U.1107*) torpedo west of Bay of Biscay, 47.47N 06.26W, while in convoy HX 348. Caught fire; broke in two: both parts later sank (voyage: Philadelphia/Antwerp).

339   *Empire Metal* 8,032 gt. Details as Yard No. 325.
Launched: 18.11.1941.
Completed: 1.1942 as *Eaglesdale* (R.F.A.).
29.11.1959: Arrived Hamburg for breaking up (see *Easedale*, Yard No. 340, below).

Note: As *Eaglesdale* the ship was used for trials of refuelling equipment following the capture of a German supply ship. This included the fitting of rubber hoses and deck rollers.

340   *Easedale* 8,032 gt. Details as Yard No. 325.
Launched: 18.12.1941.
Completed: 2.1942 (R.F.A.).
23.11.1959: Sold (Soc. Misr de Nav. Mar. SAE., Egypt); reported renamed *N. Tisir*, but deal not completed, and
18.2.1960: Sold to Belgian buyers for breaking up.

Note: Some sources show the above sale (to Egypt) as applying to the *Eaglesdale* (Yard No. 339, above) but this is not borne out by R.F.A. records. However, the dates of sales, which are confirmed, indicate that such transaction did concern the *Easedale*.

Built by Harland & Wolff Ltd., Belfast

1052   *Derwentdale* 8,393 gt, 483 ft (oa),
465.6 ft × 59.5 ft. Engines: Oil.
Launched: 12.4.1941.
Completed: 8.1941 as a Gantry Landing Ship (LSG).
9.9.1943: Severely damaged by bombing during Operation 'Avalanche' (Allied landings at Salerno, Italy); engine room hit, vessel towed to Malta by tug *Hengist*.
1944: Towed to United Kingdom. Engines replaced with parts salvaged from the *Denbydale* (ex *Empire Silver*, *q.v.*).
1946: Returned to service as a tanker.

1.1960: *Irvingdale I* (Atlantic Traders Ltd. (K. C. Irving, St. John, N.B.)).
23.7.1966: Arrived Ferrol for breaking up.

1078   *Empire Norseman* 8,214 gt. Details as Yard No. 1052.
Launched: 21.10.1941.
Completed: 4.1942 as *Dinsdale* (R.F.A.).
31.5.1942: (on maiden voyage) Sunk by Italian submarine (*Cappellini*) torpedo north-east of Pernambuco, Brazil, 00.45S 29.50W (voyage: Trinidad/Port Elizabeth – petrol).

Built by Harland & Wolff Ltd., Govan

1044 (G)   *Dingledale* 8,145 gt, 479.4 ft (oa),
463.2 ft × 61.2 ft. Engines: Oil.
Launched: 27.3.1941.
Completed: 9.1941 (R.F.A.).
1959: *Royaumont* (Cie. d'Armement Maritime S.A., Djibouti).

1966: Sold to German buyers; resold, and
23.1.1967: Arrived Santander, in tow, for breaking up.

Built by R. & W. Hawthorn, Leslie & Co. Ltd., Newcastle-on-Tyne

628 (Laid down as) *Empire Granite* 8,150 gt, 483.3 ft (oa), 465.3 ft × 59.3 ft. Engines: Oil. Launched: 29.11.1940.

Completed: 3.1941 as *Echodale* (R.F.A.).
20.9.1961: Arrived Spezia for breaking up.

Built by Swan, Hunter & Wigham Richardson Ltd., Newcastle

1656 *Ennerdale* 8,219 gt, 483.1 ft (oa), 468.4 ft × 59.4 ft. Engines: T3cyl.
Launched: 27.1.1941.
Completed: 7.1941 as a Gantry Landing Ship (LSG).
10.7.1943: Bombed and damaged at Sicily during Allied landings; Repaired.
4.12.1945: Struck mine at entrance to Perak River, Port Swettenham, Malacca Strait, on voyage from Penang. Seriously damaged, bottom plating blown away, vessel afloat on main deck. Later reached Singapore, then returned to United Kingdom, and 5.1946: Repaired at Devonport and refitted as a tanker.
14.4.1959: Arrived Faslane for breaking up.

'Norwegian'-type

Built by Furness Shipbuilding Co. Ltd., Haverton Hill-on-Tees

341 *Empire Dickens* 9,819 gt, 503.8 ft (oa), 483.6 ft × 68.3 ft. Engines: T3cyl.
Launched: 14.2.1942.
Completed: 4.1942.
1946: *Esso Appalachee* (Anglo-American Oil Co. Ltd.).
1947: (Esso Petroleum Co. Ltd.).
2.8.1960: Arrived Faslane for breaking up.

342 *Empire Norseman* 9,811 gt. Details as Yard No. 341.
Launched: 20.4.1942.
Completed: 6.1942.
23.2.1943: Damaged by submarine (*U.202*) torpedo; later sunk by submarine (*U.558*) torpedo, south of the Azores, 31.18N 27.20W (voyage: Clyde/U.S.A.).

343 *Empire Lytton* 9,807 gt. Details as Yard No. 341.
Launched: 16.6.1942.
Completed: 8.1942.
9.1.1943: Sunk by submarine (*U.442*) after three attacks by torpedo, 28.08N 28.20W south west of Canary Islands (convoy TM 1s) (voyage: Trinidad/Gibraltar).

344 *Empire Grenadier* 9,811 gt. Details as Yard No. 341.
Launched: 25.8.1942.
Completed: 10.1942.
1946: *Ficus* (Shell Company of Gibraltar Ltd.).
1951: Oil hulk at Gibraltar.
6.8.1960: Arrived Clyde Anchorage in tow of tug *Gele Zee* for breaking up at Port Glasgow.

349 *Empire Nugget* 9,807 gt. Details as Yard No. 341.
Launched: 28.9.1942.
Completed: 11.1942.
1946: *Adellen* (Adellen Shipping Co. Ltd. (B. L. Shipping Co. Inc., London)).
10.1961: Scrapped Sakai City, Japan.

350 *Empire Cobbett* 9,811 gt. Details as Yard No. 341.
Launched: 19.11.1942.
Completed: 12.1942.
1945: *San Wilfrido* (Eagle Oil & Shipping Co. Ltd.).
10.11.1959: Arrived Hong Kong for breaking up.

Many commercial enterprises had been formed in the 1870s by Christopher Furness, but when he obtained an interest in a Hartlepool shipbuilding company in 1883, his name rose to the fore and there so remained.

Yet it was not until five years after his death that the yard at Haverton Hill was built by his son, Viscount Furness. Sanction for the eight-berth yard was given at the end of 1917, and by March 1918 plans were made to transform a ninety-acre grassland site on the River Tees, opposite Middlesbrough, to a prefabricating shipyard. Some of the site land was actually below river level at high water and a million tons of slag, sand, etc., had to be used to raise the level by twelve or fifteen feet, this done with the help of several hundred women, for with Europe then in the turmoil of war, manpower was in short supply.

Eight N1-type prefabricated ships were ordered by the Government and the first ship of the order, *War Energy* (Yard No. 9) was completed in October 1919 as *Danier*. In fact, all eight of the order were completed before Yard Nos. 1–8 were constructed. Yard No. 1, *Benares* (5,762 gt) for the Swedish East Asiatic Company, was not delivered until September 1920, whilst Yard No. 8, *La Crescenta*, was not delivered until June 1923. Many tramps and tankers were built and in 1928 two passenger liners, the 7,800 gt *Santa Barbara* and *Santa Maria*, the largest liners built on the Tees, were delivered to Grace Line Inc., New York.

During World War II a total of twenty-nine deep-sea tankers were constructed, as well as sixteen of the coastal 'Chant'-type. Two 'B'-type standard cargo ships and two of the 'Standard Fast'-type were also built.

When war ended the Furness yard had twelve berths for ships to 750 feet and in the early 1960s work was done to provide facilities for the building of larger ships. However, in March 1968, it was announced that after severe losses over the previous five years the Haverton Hill shipbuilding yard would be phased out and later in that year it was placed on a care and maintenance basis. Yard numbers finally reached beyond the 500-mark, but almost half were allocated to land works of various kinds, rather than to ship construction.

Built by Sir J. Laing & Sons Ltd., Sunderland

733   *Empire Silver* 8,602 gt, 12,523 tdw, 493.8 ft (oa), 474.6 ft × 62.1 ft. Engines: T3cyl.
Launched: 28.11.1940.
Completed: 3.1941.
1946: *Sylvafield* (Northern Petroleum Tankship Co. Ltd. (Hunting & Son Ltd.)).
1952: *Radiant* (Castro Bello Cia. Armadora S.A., Panama).
1957: Renamed *Andros Sun*.
1958: *Capetan Theo* (Star Line Shipping Co. Inc., Panama).
14.11.1960: Arrived Split for breaking up.

734   *Empire Coral* 8,602 gt. Details as Yard No. 733.
Launched: 11.2.1941.
Completed: 4.1941.
1946: *Derwent River* (British Empire SN Co. Ltd. (Furness Withy & Co. Ltd.)).

1947: *Derwentfield* (Northern Petroleum Tankship Co. Ltd. (Hunting & Son Ltd.)).
1.9.1952: Explosions, on fire at Balik Papan, Borneo, during tank cleaning operations. Extensively damaged forward of bridge; deck ripped open, large hole in hull; midship deckhouse gutted. Grounded, with bows submerged.
16.9.1952: Abandoned: constructive total loss.
1953: Refloated; sold (Cia. Globo de Nav. S.A., Panama).
15.5.1953: Arrived Osaka for repairs; then repairs considered uneconomic and vessel beached in Kitzu River, Osaka, for breaking up.
21.8.1953: Scrapping commenced.

735   *Empire Opal* 9,811 gt, 501.3 ft (oa), 484 ft × 68.3 ft. Engines: T3cyl.
Launched: 28.4.1941.
Completed: 7.1941.

1945: *Southern Opal* (The South Georgia Co. Ltd. (Chr. Salvesen & Co.)). Converted to a whaling tanker (12,874 gt, 14,560 tdw).
15.5.1961: Laid up Tonsberg.
8.1964: Scrapped Hamburg.

736 *Empire Pearl* 9,881 gt. Details as Yard No. 735.
Launched: 29.7.1941.
Completed: 10.1941.
1942: *Norheim* (Government of Norway).
1945: *Kollgrim* (O. Berg, Oslo).
1950: converted to motorship.
1955: *Walton* (Dingwall Shipping Co. Ltd., Halifax N.S. (Nordstrom & Thulin A/B, Sweden).
Converted to an ore carrier (10,080 gt, 14,350 tdw).
1963: *James Hamel* (United Shipping and Trading Co. Ltd.).
1963: *Paget Trader* (Paget Traders Inc., Liberia (Ship Services Ltd., Bermuda)).
1968: (Pecos SS Co. Inc., Liberia (Elkan Ltd., Bermuda)).
1.1969: Scrapped Vinaroz, Spain.

Note: The first attempt to launch the *Empire Pearl* was made on 10 July 1941, but the vessel stuck when halfway down the ways. Tugs and yard equipment failed to move her and she was reblocked aft and made safe. The ship then settled firmly on both end ways and there was insufficient time to remove, regrease and replace the cradles in time for another launch attempt the following day. Thus, the launching had to be postponed for over fourteen days, to await the next suitable tide.

738 *Empire Druid* 9,829 gt, 503.2 ft (oa), 484 ft × 68.3 ft. Engines: T3cyl.
Launched: 10.9.1941.
Completed: 12.1941.
1942: *Norholm* (Government of Norway).
1946: *Haukefjell* (Olsen & Ugelstad, Oslo).
1949: converted to a motorship.
1952: *Bluewater* (Cia. Atalantica Pacifica S.A., Panama (Tidewater Commercial Co. Inc., Baltimore, U.S.A.)).
27.7.1959: Arrived Osaka for breaking up.

739 *Empire Airman* 9,813 gt, 503.8 ft (oa), 484 ft × 68.3 ft. Engines: T3cyl.
Launched: 18.11.1941.
Completed: 1.1942.
1946: *San Wenceslao* (Eagle Oil & Transport Co. Ltd.).
20.7.1959: Arrived Hong Kong for breaking up.

740 *Empire Marvell* 9,821 gt. Details as Yard No. 739.
Launched: 17.1.1942.
Completed: 4.1942.

1946: *Bloomfield* (Northern Petroleum Tank SS Co. Ltd. (Hunting & Son Ltd.)).
1955: *Letizia Montanari* (D. B. & E. A. Montanari, Italy).
1955: Converted to a bulk carrier.
1959: *Panaghia T* (Pacific Ruler Corpn., Liberia (Tsakalatos Navigation Corpn., New York)).
8.8.1960: Aground, six miles south of Tamandare, Brazil, after fire had broken out in engine room (voyage: Hampton Roads/Rio de Janeiro).
5.9.1960: Refloated, towed to Recife.
31.8.1961: Towed from Recife to Ymuiden, arriving 7.10.1961.
19.12.1961: Arrived Vigo, for breaking up.

741 *Empire Coleridge* 9,798 gt. Details as Yard No. 739.
Launched: 17.3.1942.
Completed: 5.1942.
1946: *Esso Cheyenne* (Anglo-American Oil Co. Ltd.).
1947: (Esso Petroleum Co. Ltd.).
15.4.1961: Arrived Boom, Belgium, for breaking up.

742 *Empire Wordsworth* 9,891 gt, 503.8 ft (oa), 482.7 ft × 68.3 ft. Engines: Oil.
Launched: 29.5.1942.
Completed: 9.1942.
1945: *British Lancer* (British Tanker Co. Ltd.).
10.9.1960: Arrived Briton Ferry for breaking up.

743 *Empire Cavalier* 9,891 gt. Details as Yard No. 742.
Launched: 27.8.1942.
Completed: 11.1942.
1945: *British Cavalier* (British Tanker Co. Ltd.).
13.11.1957: Laid up Swansea.
23.5.1959: Arrived Briton Ferry for breaking up.

745 *Empire Collins* 9,796 gt. Details as Yard No. 739.
Launched: 26.9.1942.
Completed: 12.1942.
1945: *Southern Collins* (The South Georgia Co. Ltd. (Chr. Salvesen & Co.)).
1956: *Cassian Sailor* (San Felicia Cia. Nav. S.A., Panama).
1960: *Mushtari* (Gulf Steamships Ltd., Karachi).
2.1964: Scrapped Karachi.

747 *Empire Alliance* 9,909 gt. Details as Yard No. 742.
Launched: 8.3.1943.
Completed: 6.1943.
1945: *British Dragoon* (British Tanker Co. Ltd.).
12.12.1962: Arrived Blyth for breaking up.

749   *Empire Inventor* 9,912 gt. Details as Yard No. 742.
Launched: 22.4.1943.
Completed: 1.1944.
1946: *Vivian Louise* (British Oil Shipping Co. Ltd. (Stevinson, Hardy & Co. Ltd.)).
1955: *Stanloch* (Stanhope SS Co. Ltd. (J. A. Billmeir)).
20.3.1959: Arrived Savona for breaking up.

753   *Empire Beresford* 9,804 gt. Details as Yard No. 739.
Launched: 15.9.1943.
Completed: 12.1943.
1945: *Stanbell* (Stanhope SS Co. Ltd. (J. A. Billmeir)).
1955: Converted to ore carrier (14,810 tdw).
1960: *Kelantan* (Malaya Shipping Co., Hong Kong (United Shipping & Investment Co. Ltd., Hong Kong)).

1960: (Malaya Shipping Co. Ltd., Hong Kong (Gibson Shipping Co. Inc., Macao)).
1964: (Phoenix Shipping Co. Inc., Liberia (Gibson Shipping Co. Inc., Macao)).
3.1965: Scrapped, Hirao.

756   *Empire Chancellor* 9,917 gt. Details as Yard No. 742.
Launched: 4.9.1944.
Completed: 7.1945.
1946: *Stanglen* (Stanhope SS Co. Ltd. (J. A. Billmeir)).
1952: *Newminster* (Minster SS Co. Ltd. (Mitchell, Cotts & Co. Ltd.)).
1954: *Stanpark* (Trafalgar SS Co. Ltd., London).
2.1960: Scrapped Piraeus.

'Intermediate'-type

A class of ten tankers somewhat smaller than the 'Ocean' and 'Norwegian' types was commenced in 1943 and completed in 1945. They were of 5,000 tdw on measurements of 358 ft (oa), 344 ft (bp) and a breadth of 48 ft. Oil engines developing some 2,500 bhp gave twelve to thirteen knots.

The hull was divided into five sets of port, centre and starboard tanks; the pumproom was amidships.

The absence of an overall sheer and a simplified camber were features of this wartime design. The upper deck had no sheer from the fore-end of the bridge structure to the stern and, to ease construction, the deck between the longitudinal bulkheads was flat transversely, a camber being provided by making a 'knuckle' in the region of the longitudinal bulkheads and from which point the deck plating over the wing tanks ran down in a flat slope to the gunwale.

The vessels were intended for lightening the cargoes of larger ships and for working in the smaller harbours of the war zones. Most of these ships were purchased by the Anglo-Saxon Petroleum Co. Ltd., when war ended and were based at Singapore.

Two more of this type were constructed without 'Empire' names for the Anglo-Saxon Petroleum Co. Ltd. Both came from the Laing shipyard, *Bela* (Yard No. 762), launched on 28.12.1943 and the *Borus* (Yard No. 763), launched on 29.3.1945.

Built by Sir J. Laing & Sons Ltd., Sunderland

748   *Empire Commerce* 3,750 gt.
Launched: 23.12.1942.
Completed: 3.1943.
1.10.1943: Damaged by submarine (*U.410*) torpedo north-west of Philippeville, Algeria, 37.19N 06.40E. Broke in two, afterpart sank; forepart taken in tow and beached Algiers, but gutted by fire (voyage: Bona/Algiers).

752   *Empire Gain* 3,750 gt.
Launched: 17.6.1943.
Completed: 9.1943.
1946: *Barbatia* (Anglo-Saxon Petroleum Co. Ltd.).
1955: (Shell Tankers Ltd. (Shell Petroleum Co. Ltd.)).
11.1956: Seized by Egypt during Anglo/French action after nationalisation of the Suez Canal.
1957: (Egyptian General Petroleum Organisation (Government of Egypt)). Renamed *Magd*.
1961: (United Arab Maritime Co. (Government of Egypt)).
8.6.1967: Attacked by Israeli planes at south end of Suez Canal and sank, during Israeli/Arab 'Six-day war'.
1975: Wreck cleared for re-opening of canal.

757   *Empire Russell* 3,750 gt.
Launched: 28.10.1943.
Completed: 2.1944.
1946: *Batissa* (Anglo-Saxon Petroleum Co. Ltd.).
1956: (Shell Tankers Ltd. (Shell Petroleum Co. Ltd.)).
1960: (Estrella Maritima S.A., Argentina).

On the night of 7 June 1970 the *Batissa* and the Italian motor tanker *Italmotor* (1953, 17,173 gt) were in collision in the River Paraná, Argentina, seven miles above San Pedro, when the *Batissa*, inwards from Buenos Aires and proceeding upstream to load oil at San Lorenzo, and the *Italmotor*, having loaded a part cargo of grain at Rosario, was heading down river to complete loading at Bahia Blanca, before sailing for Italy.
   The *Batissa* was badly holed amidships, there were explosions and fire broke out. She grounded and was abandoned. Later refloated, she was laid up in damaged condition at Buenos Aires, with her previously-arranged sale to new owners (Toba, S.A.M.C.I.F., Argentina) and name-change to *Toba Pegaso*, not proceeded with.
   By 1975 the position of the vessel was unchanged, with a claim against the owner of *Italmotor* still unresolved. Two years later *Batissa* was sold and broken up at Buenos Aires.

760   *Empire Crest* 3,750 gt.
Launched: 7.7.1944.
Completed: 9.1944.
1946: *Bursa* (Anglo-Saxon Petroleum Co. Ltd.).
1955: (Shell Tankers Ltd. (Shell Petroleum Co. Ltd.)).
7.1961: Scrapped Sungei Perampuan, Singapore.

765   *Empire Cross* 3,750 gt.
Launched: 28.6.1945.
Completed: 11.1945.
1946: (Anglo-Saxon Petroleum Co. Ltd.). To be renamed *Balea* but
2.8.1946: On fire, explosions, capsized and sank in Haifa Roads whilst discharging high octane aviation fuel. Total loss.
1952: Raised, broken up by Mediterranean Salvage Company.

Note: The Royal Navy destroyers *Virago* and *Venus*, anchored nearby, led the rescue work, but the Admiralty discounted the theory that the rupture of a fuel line, which led to the fire on the tanker, was caused by the detonation of a depth charge dropped from a destroyer as a security measure against terrorist swimmers with limpet mines.

766   *Empire Maldon* 3,750 gt.
Launched: 19.11.1945.
Completed: 4.1946.
1946: *Imperial Halifax* (Imperial Oil Co. Ltd., Canada).
1970: *Congar* (Johnston Shipping Ltd., Canada).
11.1977: Scrapped Hamilton, Ontario.

Built by J. L. Thompson & Sons Ltd., Sunderland

636   *Empire Ganges* 3,750 gt.
Launched: 18.9.1944.
Completed: 1.1945.
1946: *Bolma* (Anglo-Saxon Petroleum Co. Ltd.).
1955: (Shell Tankers Ltd. (Shell Petroleum Co. Ltd.)).

1955: *Astrality* (F. T. Everard & Sons Ltd.).
1965: *Monte Berico* (Marittima Fluviale Meridionale (V. Bellerino, Italy)).
1967: (Venezia Tankers S.A.S., Italy).
1973: (Misano di Nav. SpA, Palermo).

The 'Norwegian'-type tanker *Empire Beresford* as *Stanbell*, in 1950. (Sir J. Laing & Sons Ltd., Yard No. 753.) *Skyfotos*

The 'Intermediate'-type tanker *Empire Maldon* on trials in 1946. (Sir J. Laing & Sons Ltd., Yard No. 766.)

The 'Standard Fast'-type tanker *Empire Law*, following completion. (Furness Shipbuilding Co. Ltd., Yard No. 357.)

National Maritime Museum

The *Empire Flodden*, as *Wave Baron*, of the Admiralty 'Wave'-class. (Furness Shipbuilding Co. Ltd., Yard No. 378.)

The *Empire Herald*, of the Admiralty 'Wave'-class, was completed in 1946. (Sir J. Laing & Sons Ltd., Yard No. 761.)

The *Airsprite*, in the English Channel in 1953. (Blythswood Shipbuilding Co. Ltd., Yard No. 72.) *Skyfotos*

1976: (F. S. Salonia, Rome).
1977: (Maralba SpA, Palermo).
11.1978: Scrapped Spezia.

637   *Empire Ensign* 3,750 gt.
Launched: 16.12.1944.
Completed: 3.1945.
1946: *British Drummer* (British Tanker Co. Ltd.).
1957: *Anella* (A. Blystad, Norway).
1958: *Norse Commander* (Bucha, Godager & Co., Norway).
6.9.1966: Arrived Singapore, in tow, with severe boiler damage. Repairs uneconomic, sold.
11.1966: Scrapped Singapore.

641   *Empire Arrow* 3,750 gt.
Launched: 27.4.1945.
Completed: 8.1945.
1947: *British Bugler* (British Tanker Co. Ltd.).

1957: *Montmajour* (Cie. d'Armement Maritime, France).
1963: *Mantinia* (Greek Tanker Shipping Co. Ltd. (C. Diamantis, Greece)).
1.1.1978: Laid up Piraeus District, Greece.
6.1981: Scrapped Kynosoura, Greece.

642   *Empire Senlac* 3,750 gt.
Launched: 27.6.1945.
Completed: 10.1945.
1946: *Bullina* (Anglo-Saxon Petroleum Co. Ltd.
1955: *Bulmar* (Bulmar SpA Siciliania di Armamento, Italy).
1967: *Volina* (Cia. Arm. Sicula Adriatica SpA, Italy).
1969: (Maritime Aragua S.A., Venezuela).
3.1977: Scrapped Cartagena.

'Standard fast'-type (The Admiralty 'Wave'-class)

Built by Furness Shipbuilding Co. Ltd., Haverton Hill-on-Tees

356   *Empire Bounty* 8,128 gt, 492.4 ft (oa), 473.8 ft × 64.3 ft. Engines: two steam turbines.
Launched: 30.9.1943.
Completed: 2.1944.
10.1946: *Wave Victor* (R.F.A.).
1.1954: On fire in engine room in Bristol Channel. Abandoned; later towed to Swansea.
4.1954: Towed to North Shields, repaired.
8.1960: Air Ministry charter; placed as fuelling hulk for military aircraft at Gan, Maldive Islands, when air transport superseded troopships.
4.1971: Towed to Singapore for breaking up but
3.1975: reported to be lying hulked in Manila Bay, Philippines.

357   *Empire Law* 8,127 gt. Details as Yard No. 356.
Launched: 27.11.1943.
Completed: 3.1944.
1946: *Wave Conqueror* (R.F.A.).
1958: (H. G. Pounds, Portsmouth) Oil hulk at Le Havre.
6.4.1960: Left Le Havre, in tow, and
23.4.1960: Arrived Spezia for breaking up.

358   *Empire Milner* 8,135 gt. Details as Yard No. 356.
Launched: 9.2.1944.
Completed: 6.1944.
12.1946: *Wave Liberator* (R.F.A.).
4.5.1959: Arrived Hong Kong in tow of tug *Golden Cape* (1942, 552 gt) for breaking up.

359   *Empire Paladin* 8,141 gt. Details as Yard No. 356.
Launched: 21.4.1944.
Completed: 8.1944.
12.1946: *Wave Commander* (R.F.A.).
9.5.1959: Arrived Inverkeithing for breaking up.

360   *Empire Protector* 8,158 gt. Details as Yard No. 356.
Launched: 20.7.1944.
Completed: 10.1944.
11.1946: *Wave Protector* (R.F.A.).
3.1958: Storage hulk and jetty at Ras Hanzir in Grand Harbour, Malta. (Replaced *War Hindoo*, scrapped 5.1958 at Blyth.)
8.1963: Scrapped Le Grazie, Italy.

361   *Wave Emperor* 8,196 gt. Details as Yard No. 356.
Launched: 16.10.1944.
Completed: 12.1944 (R.F.A.).
19.6.1960: Arrived Barrow for breaking up.

362   *Wave Governor* 8,190 gt. Details as Yard No. 356.
Launched: 30.11.1944.
Completed: 3.1945 (R.F.A.).
9.8.1960: Arrived Rosyth for breaking up.

363   *Wave Regent* 8,184 gt, 491 ft (oa), 473.6 ft × 64.3 ft. Engines: two steam turbines.
Launched: 29.3.1945.
Completed: 6.1945 (R.F.A.).
29.6.1960: Arrived Faslane for breaking up.

364   *Wave Sovereign* 8,182 gt. Details as Yard No. 363.
Launched: 20.11.1945.
Completed: 2.1946 (R.F.A.).
6.1967: Scrapped Singapore.

373   *Empire Evesham* 8,138 gt. Details as Yard No. 363.

Launched: 17.1.1946.
Completed: 4.1946.
2.1947: *Wave Ruler* (R.F.A.).
10.1970: Placed as a fuelling hulk for military aircraft at Gan, Maldive Islands (replacing the tanker *Wave Victor*, which was broken up in 1971).
1.1976: Sold 'as lies' for demolition (Straits Engineers Contracting Pte. Ltd., Singapore) and towed to Singapore.
11.1976: Vessel lying off Johore (Singapore Straits), Malaysia.
1977: Sold and towed away to Taiwan shipbreakers.

378   (Launched as) *Empire Flodden* 8,182 gt. Details as Yard No. 363.
Launched: 19.2.1946.
Completed: 6.1946 as *Wave Baron* (R.F.A.).
12.1969: Laid up Devonport.
3.1972: Sold to Dutch shipbreakers; resold, and
23.4.1972: Arrived Bilbao for breaking up.

389   (Launched as) *Empire Marston* 8,175 gt. Details as Yard No. 363.
Launched: 27.6.1946.
Completed: 12.1946 as *Wave Premier* (R.F.A.).
11.6.1960: Arrived Inverkeithing for breaking up.

Built by Harland & Wolff Ltd., Govan

1222 (G)   (Laid down as) *Empire Sheba* 8,189 gt, 492.4 ft (oa), 473.8 ft × 64.3 ft. Engines: two steam turbines.
28.1.1944: Taken over by the Admiralty; name cancelled.
Launched: 6.4.1944.
Completed: 7.1944 as *Wave King* (R.F.A.).
9.8.1956: Struck rock north of São Luis de Maranhao, Brazil, 1.04S 44.32W. Refloated but badly damaged (voyage: Rio de Janeiro/Belem). Returned to United Kingdom; docked South Shields. Later sold, and
3.1960: (H. G. Pounds, Portsmouth) for demolition, but resold, and
16.4.1960: Arrived Barrow for breaking up, in tow of tug *Merchantman* (ex *Empire Bess*).

1223 (G)   (Laid down as) *Empire Venus* 8,159 gt. Details as Yard No. 1222 (G).
28.1.1944: Taken over by the Admiralty; name cancelled.
Launched: 6.7.1944.
Completed: 11.1944 as *Wave Monarch* (R.F.A.).
3.1960: (H. G. Pounds, Portsmouth). Became an oil hulk at Le Havre, replacing *Wave Conqueror* which was scrapped 4.1960.
1960: *Noema* (Soc. Miroline) – oil storage hulk.
8.4.1964: Arrived Bilbao for breaking up.

1306 (G)   (Launched as) *Empire Edgehill* 8,097 gt. Details as Yard No. 1222 (G).
Launched: 4.4.1946.
Completed: 8.1946 as *Wave Chief* (R.F.A.).
13.11.1974: Arrived Inverkeithing for breaking up.

Built by Sir J. Laing & Sons Ltd., Sunderland

754　*Empire Salisbury* 8,199 gt, 493.8 ft (oa), 473 ft × 64.1 ft. Engines: two steam turbines.
Launched: 20.5.1944.
Completed: 12.1944.
12.1946: *Wave Master* (R.F.A.).
4.1963: Arrived Jurong, Singapore, in tow, for breaking up.

755　*Empire Mars* 8,199 gt. Details as Yard No. 754.
Launched: 16.11.1944.
Completed: 4.1945.
1946: *Wave Duke* (R.F.A.).
25.12.1969: Arrived Bilbao, in tow, for breaking up.

761　*Empire Herald* 8,204 gt. Details as Yard No. 754.
Launched: 27.7.1945.
Completed: 3.1946.

12.1947: *Wave Prince* (R.F.A.).
16.12.1971: Arrived Burriana, Spain, for breaking up.

764　*Empire Naseby* 8,187 gt. Details as Yard No. 754.
Launched: 22.10.1945.
Completed: 5.1946.
1.1947: *Wave Knight* (R.F.A.).
12.1964: Scrapped Willebroek, Belgium.

767　(Launched as) *Empire Dunbar* 8,187 gt. Details as Yard No. 754.
Launched: 3.4.1946.
Completed: 9.1946 as *Wave Laird* (R.F.A.).
3.1970: Scrapped Gandia, Spain.

'Empire Pym'-type

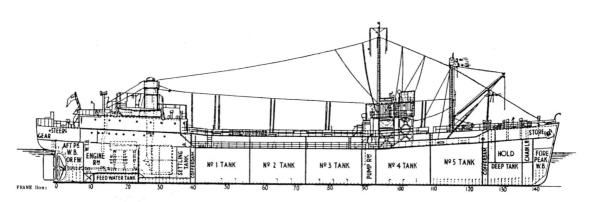

The 'Empire Pym'-type tanker.

Some smaller tankers were constructed for special purposes and four 3,200 tdw ships, with steam machinery aft, were built in 1944–1945. The draught was eighteen feet and they were built for access to ports that were quickly taken and cleared during the Allied assault on Normandy.

Built by Grangemouth Dockyard Co. Ltd.

448 *Empire Pym* 2,370 gt, 301.8 ft (oa),
290.7 ft × 44.1 ft. Engines: T3cyl.
Launched: 27.11.1943.
Completed: 3.1944.
1946: *Refast* (Refast SS Co. (Stevinson Hardy Ltd.,
London)).
1948: (Counties Ship Management Ltd.).
1952: (Marcou & Sons Ltd., London).
1952: *Cassian* (Nolido Cia. de Nav. S.A., Costa Rica).
1954: *Mobilsud* (Soc. Mazout Transports, France).
1964: *Janson* (Soc. Anon. Monegasque d'Armement
et Nav., Monaco).
1966: *Capo Mannu* (Sarda Bunkers SpA (A. Garolla
& Co., Italy)).
1976: Laid up Naples.
1980: Scrapped Italy.

458 *Empire Jumna* 2,370 gt. Details as Yard No. 448.
Launched: 31.10.1944.
Completed: 1.1945.
1946: *Fossularca* (Anglo-Saxon Petroleum Co. Ltd.).
1960: (Shell Tankers Ltd.).
5.1964: Scrapped Singapore.

462 *Empire Jewel* 2,370 gt. Details as Yard No. 448.
Launched: 12.6.1945.
Completed: 9.1945.
1946: *Fossarus* (Anglo-Saxon Petroleum Co. Ltd.).
1960: (Shell Tankers Ltd.).
10.1960: Scrapped Singapore.

Built by Blythswood Shipbuilding Co. Ltd., Glasgow

77 *Empire Rosebery* 2,370 gt, 301.8 ft (oa),
290.7 ft × 44.1 ft. Engines: T3cyl.
Launched: 22.5.1944.

Completed: 7.1944.
24.8.1944: Struck mine off Normandy coast; sank.
Total loss.

Built by Barclay, Curle & Co. Ltd., Clydeholm Shipyard, Whiteinch, Glasgow

DEEP SEA TANKER BUILT UNDER PRIVATE CONTRACT

672 *Polarsol* 10,022 gt, 519.2 ft (oa),
501.7 ft × 66.9 ft. Engines: Oil.
Launched: 14.9.1939.

Completed: 12.1939 for Melsom & Melsom,
Norway.
1959: *Dale* (H. Kuhnle, Norway).
7.1961: Scrapped Split.

Built by Blythswood Shipbuilding Co. Ltd., Glasgow

DEEP SEA TANKERS BUILT UNDER PRIVATE CONTRACT OR LICENCE

57 *Donacilla* 8,113 gt, 482.8 ft (oa),
464.9 ft × 59.3 ft. Engines: Oil.
Launched: 30.8.1939.
Completed: 10.1939 for Anglo-Saxon Petroleum Co.
Ltd.
1955: (Shell Petroleum Co. Ltd. (Shell Tankers Ltd.)).
5.1961: Scrapped Hong Kong.

65 *Nasprite* 965 gt, 214 ft (oa), 204.5 ft × 33.2 ft.
Engines: T3cyl. A petrol carrier.
Launched: 28.11.1940.
Completed: 2.1941 for the Admiralty (R.F.A.).
1963: (Lamico Shipping Co., Sussex).
2.1964: Scrapped Willebroek, Belgium.

66 *San Victorio* 8,136 gt, 480 ft (oa),
463.3 ft × 61 ft. Engines: Oil.

Launched: 20.1.1942.
Completed: 4.1942 for Eagle Oil & Shipping Co.
Ltd.
17.5.1942: Sunk by submarine (*U.155*) torpedo west
of Grenada, West Indies, 11.40N 62.33W, on maiden
voyage (voyage: Aruba/U.K. – oil).

68   *Nassa* 8,134 gt. Details as Yard No. 57.
Launched: 1.6.1942.
Completed: 10.1942 for Anglo-Saxon Petroleum Co.
Ltd.
1955: (Shell Petroleum Co. Ltd. (Shell Tankers Ltd.)).
18.9.1963: Arrived Pulau Bukom, Singapore, for use
as a bunkering vessel.
9.1964: Scrapped Hong Kong.

69   *Naranio* 8,134 gt. Details as Yard No. 57.
Launched: 13.10.1942.
Completed: 1.1943 for Anglo-Saxon Petroleum
Co. Ltd.
1955; (Shell Petroleum Co. Ltd. (Shell Tankers Ltd.))
3.3.1961: Arrived Bruges for breaking up.

70   *Ninella* 8,134 gt. Details as Yard No. 57.
Launched: 9.3.1943.
Completed: 5.1943 for Anglo-Saxon Petroleum Co.
Ltd.
1955. (Shell Petroleum Co. Ltd. (Shell Tankers Ltd.)).
Later used as an oil storage vessel at Saigon.
4.1966: Scrapped Kaohsiung.

72   *Airsprite* 970 gt. Details as Yard No. 65.
Launched: 22.12.1942.
Completed: 2.1943 for the Admiralty (R.F.A.).
14.3.1965: Arrived Antwerp for breaking up.

74   *Neocardia* 8,211 gt. Details as Yard No. 57.
Launched: 18.10.1943.
Completed: 12.1943 for Anglo-Saxon Petroleum
Co. Ltd.
1955: (Shell Petroleum Co. Ltd. (Shell Tankers Ltd.)).
30.8.1960: Arrived Hong Kong for breaking up.

76   *Northia* 8,210 gt. Details as Yard No. 57.
Launched: 10.2.1944.

Completed: 4.1944 for Anglo-Saxon Petroleum Co.
Ltd.
1955: (Shell Petroleum Co. Ltd. (Shell Tankers Ltd.)).
8.7.1960: Arrived Hong Kong for breaking up.

78   *British Wisdom* 8,295 gt, 482 ft (oa),
466.6 ft × 61.2 ft. Engines: Oil.
Launched: 12.4.1945.
Completed: 7.1945 for British Tanker Co. Ltd.
10.2.1958: Laid up Falmouth.
5.1962: Scrapped Briton Ferry.

79   *Nuttallia* 8,210 gt. Details as Yard No. 57.
Launched: 28.12.1944.
Completed: 4.1945 for Anglo-Saxon Petroleum
Co. Ltd.
1954: (Shell Company of Gibraltar Ltd. (Shell
Tankers Ltd.)); stationed at Gibraltar as a depot ship.
10.1960: Scrapped Faslane.

81   *British Success* 8,200 gt, 484 ft (oa),
466 ft × 59.3 ft. Engines: Oil.
Launched: 7.11.1945.
Completed: 2.1946 for British Tanker Co. Ltd.
29.8.1961: Arrived Troon for breaking up.

82   *Neothauma* 8,229 gt. Details as Yard No. 57.
Launched: 21.3.1946.
Completed: 6.1946 for Anglo-Saxon Petroleum Co.
Ltd. Sold, and
21.6.1955: Arrived Kiel, in tow, for repairs.
1956: *Jaspis* (Spermacet Whaling & Shipping Co.,
Panama (A. Jahre & Co. A/S, Norway)). Converted
to a whale factory supply ship (8,503 gt).
3.1961: Scrapped Osaka.

83   *Neritopsis* 8,231 gt. Details as Yard No. 57.
Launched: 1.7.1946.
Completed: 10.1946 for Anglo-Saxon Petroleum Co.
Ltd.
1955: (Shell Petroleum Co. Ltd. (Shell Tankers Ltd.)).
16.11.1956: Struck submerged reef off Palawan
Island, near Borneo, 8.32N 116.40E. Flooded
and abandoned (voyage: Miri/Shimotsu – crude oil).
17.11.1956: Sank; total loss.

Built by Caledon Shipbuilding & Engineering Co. Ltd., Caledon Shipyard, Dundee

DEEP SEA TANKER BUILT UNDER PRIVATE CONTRACT

382   (Launched as) *Silenus* 8,108 gt, 483.2 ft (oa),
466.3 ft × 59.4 ft. Engines: Oil.
Launched: 19.7.1940 for Axel Johnson, Stockholm.
Completed: 3.1941 as *Athelvictor* for Tankers Ltd.
(Athel Line Ltd.).

1952: *California* (S. Chiarella Soc. di Nav., Italy).
1961: (Comp. Sicula di Nav. SpA (COSINA), Italy)).
9.2.1962: Arrived Spezia for breaking up.

Built by Cammell Laird & Co. Ltd., Birkenhead

DEEP SEA TANKERS BUILT UNDER PRIVATE CONTRACT OR LICENCE

1067 *British Tradition* 8,443 gt, 482 ft (oa),
466 ft × 62 ft. Engines: Oil.
Launched: 5.3.1942.
Completed: 8.1942 for British Tanker Co. Ltd.
2.9.1958: Laid up Portland; then
29.10.1960: at Cardiff.
20.1.1961: Arrived Briton Ferry for breaking up.

1068 *British Promise* 8,443 gt. Details as Yard
No. 1067.
Launched: 30.7.1942.
Completed: 11.1942 for British Tanker Co. Ltd.
20.11.1942: Damaged by submarine (*U.518*) torpedo,
in position 43.53N 55.02W, approximately 200 miles
south of Newfoundland.
22.11.1942: Arrived Halifax N.S., with severe
damage; repaired.

3.1.1958: Laid up Methil, then
24.2.1959: Arrived Rosyth for breaking up.

1105 *British Restraint* 8,443 gt. Details as Yard No.
1067.
Launched: 8.4.1943.
Completed: 7.1943 for British Tanker Co. Ltd.
31.12.1957: Laid up Falmouth.
29.5.1959: Arrived Spezia (after removal of
machinery by purchasers) in tow of tug *Turmoil*
(1945, 1,136 gt) for breaking up.

Built by Furness Shipbuilding Co. Ltd., Haverton Hill-on-Tees

DEEP SEA TANKERS BUILT UNDER PRIVATE CONTRACT OR LICENCE

347 *British Vigour* 5,844 gt, 420.9 ft (oa),
406.2 ft × 56.3 ft. Engines: Oil.
Launched: 21.12.1942.
Completed: 2.1943 for British Tanker Co. Ltd.
1959: *Thoronet* (Cie. d'Armement Maritime,
Djibouti).
28.6.1964: Arrived Aviles for breaking up.

348 *British Purpose* 5,845 gt. Details as Yard
No. 347.
Launched: 22.2.1943.
Completed: 4.1943 for British Tanker Co. Ltd.
1959: *Anella* (A. Blystad, Norway).
22.12.1961: Arrived Bremerhaven for breaking up.

387 *Southern Venturer* 14,066 gt, 555.4 ft (oa),
539.7 ft × 74.4 ft. Engines: T6cyl: Twin screws. A
whaling factory ship.
Launched: 11.6.1945.
Completed: 10.1945 for Sevilla Whaling Co. Ltd.
(Chr. Salvesen & Co.).
1962: *Southern Venturer Maru* (Nippon Suisan KK.,
Tokyo).
6.1964: Scrapped Mihara, Japan.

388 *Norhval* 13,830 gt. Details as Yard No. 387.
Launched: 26.7.1945.
Completed: 11.1945 for Hvalfangersisk Polaris A/S
& Globus A/S (Melsom & Melsom, Larvik).
9.1962: Laid up Sandefjord.
16.2.1966: Arrived Bilbao in tow of Dutch tug *Utrecht*
(1956, 638 gt) for breaking up.

392 *Southern Harvester* 15,088 gt. Details as Yard
No. 387.
Launched: 2.5.1946.
Completed: 10.1946 for South Georgia Co. (Chr.
Salvesen & Co.).
1963: (Nippon Suisan KK., Tokyo).
1966: (South Georgia Co.).
1968: Sold to Norwegian shipbuilders Akers Mek.
Verkstad A/S., Oslo, for conversion to a floating
workshop.

Built by Harland & Wolff Ltd., Belfast

DEEP SEA TANKERS BUILT UNDER PRIVATE CONTRACT OR LICENCE

1090   *San Veronico* 8,189 gt, 483 ft (oa),
465.7 ft × 59.6 ft. Engines: Oil.
Launched: 30.5.1942.
Completed: 12.1942 for Eagle Oil & Shipping Co. Ltd.
22.2.1964: Arrived Hamburg for breaking up.

1173   *Narica* 8,213 gt. Details as Yard No. 1090.
Launched: 7.2.1943.
Completed: 5.1943 for Anglo-Saxon Petroleum Co. Ltd.
1955: (Shell Petroleum Co. Ltd.).
9.1960: Scrapped Hong Kong.

1194   *Norrisia* 8,246 gt. Details as Yard No. 1090.
Launched: 14.10.1943.
Completed: 3.1944 for Anglo-Saxon Petroleum Co. Ltd.
1955: (Shell Petroleum Co. Ltd.).
1958: (Shell Company of Gibraltar Ltd.). Stationed at Gibraltar as a floating oil depot.
5.2.1960: Arrived Spezia in tow of tug *Praia de Adraga* (1952, 517 gt), for breaking up.

1195   (Laid down as) *Novaculina* 8,246 gt. Details as Yard No. 1090.
Launched: 14.12.1943 as *Nassarius*.
Completed: 3.1944 for Anglo-Saxon Petroleum

Co. Ltd.
1955: (Shell Petroleum Co. Ltd.).
2.8.1959: Arrived Hong Kong for breaking up.

1198   *Niso* 8,273 gt. Details as Yard No. 1090.
Launched: 3.8.1944.
Completed: 12.1944 for Anglo-Saxon Petroleum Co. Ltd.
1955: (Shell Petroleum Co. Ltd.).
29.6.1959: Arrived River Blackwater for lay up.
11.1961: Scrapped Dalmuir.

1199   *Newcombia* 8,272 gt. Details as Yard No. 1090.
Launched: 17.11.1944.
Completed: 3.1945 for Anglo-Saxon Petroleum Co. Ltd.
1955: (Shell Petroleum Co. Ltd.).
26.9.1959: Arrived Antwerp, in tow of tug *Clyde* (1957, 820 gt) for breaking up.

1284   *British Supremacy* 8,242 gt. Details as Yard No. 1090.
Launched: 26.7.1945.
Completed: 12.1945 for British Tanker Co. Ltd.
26.9.1961: Arrived Troon for breaking up.

Forty-four ocean tankers owned by Anglo-Iranian Oil Company (British Tanker Co. Ltd.) were lost during the war as a result of enemy action, while others suffered damage and were repaired and re-commissioned. As opportunity offered, the company had built and acquired other ships and at the end of hostilities the fleet numbered sixty-nine vessels of 758,000 tdw compared with ninety-three of 980,000 tdw at the beginning of war.

1285   *Neothyris* 8,243 gt. Details as Yard No. 1090.
Launched: 24.10.1945.
Completed: 1.1946 for Anglo-Saxon Petroleum

Co. Ltd.
1955: (Shell Petroleum Co. Ltd.).
5.1960: Scrapped Hong Kong.

The whaling factory ship *Southern Harvester*, April 1954. (Furness Shipbuilding Co. Ltd., Yard No. 392.)

Built by Harland & Wolff Ltd., Govan

DEEP SEA TANKERS BUILT UNDER PRIVATE CONTRACT OR LICENCE

1117 (G) *British Merit* 8,093 gt, 479.4 ft (oa),
463.2 ft × 61.2 ft. Engines: Oil.
Launched: 16.4.1942.
Completed: 7.1942 for British Tanker Co. Ltd.
25.7.1942: Damaged by submarine (*U.552*) torpedo,
approx. 600 miles east of Newfoundland,
49.03N 40.36W, in convoy ON 113 (U.K./U.S.A.).
Taken in tow, and
2.8.1942: Arrived St. John's;
24.8.1942: Towed to New York: repaired.
17.3.1961: Arrived Briton Ferry for breaking up.

1163 (G) *San Vulfrano* 8,167 gt. Details as Yard
No. 1117 (G).
Launched: 23.9.1942.
Completed: 12.1942 for Eagle Oil & Shipping Co.
Ltd.
14.1.1960: Arrived Inverkeithing for breaking up.

1166 (G) *British Patience* 8,097 gt. Details as Yard
No. 1117 (G).
Launched: 23.3.1943.

Completed: 6.1943 for British Tanker Co. Ltd.
8.6.1961: Arrived Troon for breaking up.

1174 (G) *Neritina* 8,222 gt, 483.5 ft (oa),
465.6 ft × 59.5 ft. Engines: Oil.
Launched: 31.8.1943.
Completed: 12.1943 for Anglo-Saxon Petroleum Co.
Ltd.
1953: (Shell Tankers Ltd., London).
7.1961: Scrapped Hirao.

1183 (G) *San Vito* 8,163 gt. Details as Yard
No. 1117 (G).
Launched: 2.11.1943.
Completed: 12.1943 for Eagle Oil & Shipping Co.
Ltd.
7.5.1962: Arrived Antwerp for breaking up.

1196 (G) *British Might* 8,245 gt. Details as Yard No.
1174 (G).
Launched: 29.3.1945.
Completed: 5.1945 for British Tanker Co. Ltd.
9.5.1961: Arrived Troon for breaking up.

Built by R. & W. Hawthorn, Leslie & Co. Ltd., Newcastle-on-Tyne

DEEP SEA TANKERS BUILT UNDER PRIVATE CONTRACT OR LICENCE

622 *Dolabella* 8,142 gt, 483.3 ft (oa),
465.3 ft × 59.3 ft. Engines: Oil.
Launched: 15.8.1939.
Completed: 11.1939 for Anglo-Saxon Petroleum Co.
Ltd.
1955: (Shell Petroleum Co. Ltd. (Shell Tankers Ltd.,
London)).
6.1958: Scrapped Hong Kong.

631 *Donovania* 8,149 gt. Details as Yard No. 622.
Launched: 13.3.1941.
Completed: 6.1941 for Anglo-Saxon Petroleum Co.
Ltd.
21.7.1942: Sunk by submarine (*U.160*) torpedo, off
Trinidad in position 10.56N 61.10W.

632 *Diplodon* 8,149 gt. Details as Yard No. 622.

Launched: 28.6.1941.
Completed: 10.1941 for Anglo-Saxon Petroleum Co.
Ltd.
1955: (Shell Petroleum Co. Ltd. (Shell Tankers Ltd.,
London)).
26.8.1960: Arrived Hong Kong for breaking up.

636 *San Venancio* 8,152 gt. Details as Yard No. 622.
Launched: 8.10.1941.
Completed: 1.1942 for Eagle Oil & Shipping Co.
Ltd.
25.9.1958: Arrived Hong Kong for breaking up.

648 *Nicania* 8,179 gt. Details as Yard No. 622.
Launched: 2.2.1942.
Completed: 5.1942 for Anglo-Saxon Petroleum Co.
Ltd.

1955: (Shell Petroleum Co. Ltd. (Shell Tankers Ltd., London)).
23.6.1960: Arrived Hong Kong for breaking up.

649   *Nuculana* 8,179 gt. Details as Yard No. 622.
Launched: 2.6.1942.
Completed: 9.1942 for Anglo-Saxon Petroleum Co. Ltd.
1955: (Shell Petroleum Co. Ltd. (Shell Tankers Ltd., London)).
1958: *Ave*; converted to bulk carrier (North Bulk Carriers Ltd., Liberia (M. Yllera, Spain)).
29.3.1968: Arrived Kaohsiung for breaking up.

652   *Naticina* 8,179 gt. Details as Yard No. 622.
Launched: 25.9.1942.
Completed: 1.1943 for Anglo-Saxon Petroleum Co. Ltd.
1955: (Shell Petroleum Co. Ltd. (Shell Tankers Ltd., London)).
23.8.1962: Arrived Yokosuka for breaking up.

661   *San Velino* 8,210 gt. Details as Yard No. 622.
Launched: 10.11.1943.
Completed: 6.1944 for Eagle Oil & Shipping Co. Ltd.
24.4.1962: Arrived Grimstad, Norway, for breaking up.

663   *Navicella* 8,255 gt. Details as Yard No. 622.
Launched: 4.8.1944.
Completed: 12.1944 for Anglo-Saxon Petroleum Co. Ltd.
1955: (Shell Petroleum Co. Ltd. (Shell Tankers Ltd.)).
1960: (Shell Tankers N.V. (Shell-Royal Dutch Group, Holland)).

25.2.1963: Arrived Bruges, Belgium, for breaking up.

670   *Neaera* 8,254 gt. Details as Yard No. 622.
Launched: 9.11.1945.
Completed: 3.1946 for Anglo-Saxon Petroleum Co. Ltd.
1955: (Shell Petroleum Co. Ltd. (Shell Tankers Ltd.)).
3.8.1960: Arrived Hong Kong, in tow, for breaking up.

671   *Auricula* 8,257 gt. Details as Yard No. 622.
Launched: 17.4.1946.
Completed: 8.1946 for Anglo-Saxon Petroleum Co. Ltd.
1955: *Don Demetrio* (Nueva Vista Cia. Nav. S.A., Panama).
1956: Converted to dry cargo.
1957: (Lerida Cia. Nav. S.A., Panama).
1959: *Seaway Discoverer* (Falaise SS Co. Ltd., Bermuda (Mavroleon Bros. Ltd., London)).
1961: *Captain Minas* (Valmonte Cia. Nav. S.A. (Helikon Shipping Enterprises Ltd., London)).
23.3.1969: Arrived Kaohsiung for breaking up.

684   *Latia* 6,442 gt, 446.2 ft (oa), 430 ft × 54.5 ft.
Engines: Oil.
Launched: 15.2.1946.
Completed: 5.1946 for Anglo-Saxon Petroleum Co. Ltd.
1955: (Shell Petroleum Co. Ltd. (Shell Tankers Ltd.)).
18.1.1961: Laid up River Blackwater.
9.1962: Scrapped Inverkeithing.

Built by Sir James Laing & Sons Ltd., Sunderland

DEEP SEA TANKERS BUILT UNDER PRIVATE CONTRACT OR LICENCE

725   *Athelcrest* 6,825 gt, 426.3 ft × 59.3 ft.
Engines: Oil.
Launched: 9.1.1940.
Completed: 4.1940 for Athel Line Ltd.
25.8.1940: Sunk by submarine (*U.48*) torpedo, 58.24N 11.25W, whilst in convoy HX 65A (voyage: Halifax/New York/U.K.).

The *Athelcrest* was commissioned on 5 April 1940, shortly afterwards sailing on her maiden voyage to the Gulf of Mexico, there loading oil for France. But *en route*, in May, France fell and she was diverted, moving to several anchorages before being ordered to Aruba, in the Dutch West Indies, where she exchanged her cargo, taking on one for the United Kingdom. But she never arrived, for on 25 August she was torpedoed in the early hours west of the Hebrides, and sank.

From a fleet of thirty-two tankers, United Molasses Co. Ltd., lost twenty-two ships by enemy action from their two operating companies, seventeen from Athel Line Ltd., five from Tankers Ltd. One other Athel Line ship was a marine loss in 1943.

746 *Wearfield* 9,795 gt, 503.8 ft (oa), 484 ft × 68.3 ft. Engines: T3cyl.
Launched: 23.11.1942.
Completed: 3.1943 for Northern Petroleum Tank SS Co. Ltd. (Hunting & Son Ltd.).
1953: (Hunting SS Co. Ltd.).
1955: *Transmars* (Transatlantic Navigation Corpn., Liberia (Caldel Petroleum Corpn., New York).
1.8.1960: Arrived Onomichi for breaking up.

750 *Thamesfield* 9,801 gt. Details as Yard No. 746.
Launched: 16.7.1943.
Completed: 11.1943 for Northern Petroleum Tank SS Co. Ltd. (Hunting & Son Ltd.).
1954: (Stanhope SS Co. Ltd.).
2.1955: Converted to an ore carrier, renamed *Stanfield*.
1961: *August Moon* (East Sun Shipping Co. Ltd., Hong Kong).
15.9.1966: Aground on Pratas Reef, South China Sea (voyage: Calcutta/Yokohama – iron ore). Broke in two. Total loss.

759 *Beechwood* 8,197 gt, 494 ft (oa), 473 ft × 64 ft.
Engines: two steam turbines. 'Standard Fast' type.
Launched: 14.3.1945.
Completed: 8.1945 for Oil & Molasses Tankers Ltd. (J. I. Jacobs & Co. Ltd.).
1955: (Galbraith, Pembroke & Co. Ltd.).
1955: Converted to dry cargo ship (8,966 gt), renamed *City of Athens* (Soc. de Nav. Magliveras, Panama) – vessel on charter to Ellerman Lines.
1957: Renamed *Marianne*.
10.1962: Oil engine installed.

1964: *Constellation* (8,492 gt) (Patt, Manfield & Co. Ltd., Hong Kong (Panama flag)).
1969: *Golden Moon* (Golden Moon Shipping Corpn. (C. T. Chu, Hong Kong (Panama flag))).
17.2.1972: Arrived Kaohsiung; laid up, and
11.1973: Scrapped Kaohsiung.

762 *Bela* 3,735 gt, 357.6 ft (oa), 343.5 ft × 48.3 ft.
Engines: Oil. 'Intermediate'-type.
Launched: 28.12.1944.
Completed: 4.1945 for Anglo-Saxon Petroleum Co. Ltd.
1955: (Shell Petroleum Co. Ltd.).
7.1961: Scrapped Singapore.

763 *Borus* 3,735 gt. Details as Yard No. 762.
Launched: 29.3.1945.
Completed: 9.1945 for Anglo-Saxon Petroleum Co. Ltd.
1955: (Shell Petroleum Co. Ltd.).
13.10.1964: (At Hong Kong awaiting breaking up): Sank at moorings in typhoon 'Dot'. Later refloated and scrapped locally.

768 *British Princess* 8,582 gt, 490 ft (oa), 469.6 ft × 62 ft. Engines: Oil.
Launched: 30.4.1946.
Completed: 8.1946 for British Tanker Co. Ltd.
8.2.1962: Arrived Briton Ferry for breaking up.

770 *British Holly* 8,583 gt. Details as Yard No. 768.
Launched: 26.8.1946.
Completed: 12.1946 for British Tanker Co. Ltd.
23.3.1964: Arrived Faslane for breaking up.

Built by Lithgows Ltd., Port Glasgow

DEEP SEA TANKERS BUILT UNDER PRIVATE CONTRACT OR LICENCE

919 *Delphinula* 8,120 gt, 483 ft (oa), 465 ft × 59.2 ft. Engines: Oil.
Launched: 18.9.1939.
Completed: 12.1939 for Anglo-Saxon Petroleum Co. Ltd.
9.5.1943: Ashore, near Great Pass Beacon, Alexandria, Egypt (voyage: Haifa/Alexandria – benzine).

18.5.1943: Explosion, on fire, due to petrol vapour igniting; two assisting tugs also caught fire. All vessels abandoned.
20.6.1943: Fire extinguished; vessel holed, twisted and distorted.
21.7.1943: Broke in two. Constructive total loss.

920 *Desmoulea* 8,120 gt. Details as Yard No. 919.
Launched: 26.10.1939.
Completed: 12.1939 for Anglo-Saxon Petroleum
Co. Ltd.
31.1.1941: Torpedoed by destroyer or E-boat in
Mediterranean, 35.31N 02.34E. Abandoned;
reboarded and towed to Crete.

4.1941: Towed to Port Said, thence Suez.
5.8.1941: Damaged by air torpedo off West Beacon,
Suez. Taken over by Ministry of War Transport,
renamed *Empire Thane* (*q.v.*).

Built by Smith's Dock Co. Ltd., North Shields

DEEP SEA TANKERS BUILT UNDER PRIVATE CONTRACT OR LICENCE

1158 *Geomitra* 5,040 gt, 400 ft (oa),
383.7 ft × 62.8 ft. Engines: T6cyl. Twin screw.
Launched: 16.4.1946.
Completed: 7.1946 for N.V. Curaçaosche Scheepv.
Maats. N.V., Curaçao. (Anglo-Saxon Petroleum Co.
Ltd.).
1952: (Cia. Shell de Venezuela Ltd.).
1960: (Shell Tankers Ltd., London).
7.3.1965: Arrived Hong Kong for breaking up.

1159 *Gouldia* 5,040 gt. Details as Yard No. 1158.
Launched: 29.7.1946.
Completed: 11.1946 for N.V. Curaçaosche Scheepv.
Maats. N.V., Curaçao. (Anglo-Saxon Petroleum Co.
Ltd.).
1953: (Cia. Shell de Venezuela Ltd.).
1960: (Shell Tankers Ltd., London).
1965: (Serena Shipping Ltd., Liberia (Keystone
Shipping Co., U.S.A.)).

5.1965: Scrapped Hong Kong.

1160 *Cyrena* 4,373 gt, 379.8 ft (oa),
365.6 ft × 49.8 ft. Engines: Oil.
Launched: 10.11.1946.
Completed: 2.1947 for Anglo-Saxon Petroleum
Co. Ltd.
1954: *Hamilton Harbour* (converted to dry cargo)
(Harbour Line Ltd. (Mollers Ltd., Hong Kong)).
1957: *Tong Wee* (Kie Hock Shipping Co. Ltd.,
Singapore).
25.7.1970: On fire in engine room whilst undergoing
survey at Singapore; fire extinguished. Constructive
total loss. Sold, repaired and
1971: (Kie Hock (1971) (Pte.) Ltd., Singapore).
1977: (Cia. Nav. Thompson S.A. (Kie Hock (1971)
(Pte.) Ltd.)).
1978: (Gammewah Enterprise Ltd., Panama).
4.1979: Scrapped Kaohsiung.

Built by Swan, Hunter & Wigham Richardson Ltd., Wallsend (W) or Newcastle (N)

DEEP SEA TANKERS BUILT UNDER PRIVATE CONTRACT OR LICENCE

1563 (N) *Thiara* 10,364 gt, 525.3 ft (oa),
505.8 ft × 64.6 ft. Engines: Oil.
Launched: 1.8.1939.
Completed: 10.1939 for Anglo-Saxon Petroleum Co.
Ltd.
27.7.1940: Sunk by submarine (*U.34*) torpedo 400
miles WNW of Ireland in position 56.37N 17.56W.

1673 (W) *British Gratitude* 8,463 gt, 486.3 ft (oa),
470.1 ft × 61.9 ft. Engines: Oil.
Launched: 26.9.1942.
Completed: 12.1942 for British Tanker Co. Ltd.

12.5.1959: Arrived Tamise, Belgium, for breaking
up.

1675 (W) *Nacella* 8,196 gt, 483.6 ft (oa),
465.3 ft × 59.3 ft. Engines: Oil.
Launched: 21.3.1943.
Completed: 6.1943 for Anglo-Saxon Petroleum Co.
Ltd.
1955: (Shell Petroleum Co. Ltd.).
3.2.1958: Laid up Blackwater River and
7.3.1960: Arrived Bo'ness in tow of tug *Englishman*
(1945, 716 gt) for breaking up.

1687 (W)   *Neverita* 8,265 gt, 485.4 ft (oa),
467.4 ft × 59.2 ft. Engines: Oil.
Launched: 26.2.1944.
Completed: 7.1944 for Anglo-Saxon Petroleum Co.
Ltd.
1955: (Shell Petroleum Co. Ltd.).
18.2.1963: Arrived Bruges for breaking up.

1689 (W)   *Hyalina* 12,667 gt, 583 ft (oa),
561.8 ft × 70 ft. Engines: Steam turbines to electric
motor.
Launched: 28.12.1944.
Completed: 1945.
Building for Anglo-Saxon Petroleum Co. Ltd., but
acquired by the Admiralty before completion and
converted to a Fleet Oiler; renamed *Olna*.
1946: (Royal Fleet Auxiliary, Pennant A.216).
3.1967: Scrapped Castellon.

1696 (N)   *British Harmony* 8,465 gt, 481.6 ft (oa),
466.3 ft × 61.9 ft. Engines: Oil.
Launched: 9.6.1941.
Completed: 9.1941 for British Tanker Co. Ltd.
23.9.1957: Laid up Falmouth.
16.10.1960: Arrived Troon for breaking up.

1698 (N)   *British Character* 8,461 gt. Details as Yard
No. 1696 (N).
Launched: 25.8.1941.
Completed: 12.1941 for British Tanker Co. Ltd.
19.3.1959: Arrived Bo'ness for breaking up.

1701 (W)   *Regent Hawk* 8,169 gt, 485.2 ft (oa),
465.9 ft × 59.4 ft. Engines: T3cyl.
Launched: 27.3.1945.
Completed: 7.1945 for Trinidad Leaseholds Ltd.,
London.
1956: (Regent Petroleum Tankship Co. Ltd.,
London).
9.5.1960: Arrived Briton Ferry for breaking up.

1708 (N)   *Congonian* 6,082 gt, 430.2 ft (oa),
415.6 ft × 56.7 ft. Engines: T3cyl.
Launched: 2.3.1942.
Completed: 5.1942 for United Africa Co. Ltd.,
Liverpool.
1949: *Opobo Palm* (Palm Line Ltd. (United Africa Co.
Ltd.)).
1961: *Winwar* (Windward Shipping Co. Ltd. (Pioneer
Shipowners Ltd., Hong Kong)).
22.6.1963: Arrived Hong Kong for breaking up.

1711 (W)   *Helicina* 12,167 gt. Details as Yard
No. 1689 (W).
Launched: 4.4.1946.

Completed: 10.1946 for Anglo-Saxon Petroleum Co.
Ltd. Acquired prior to completion by the Admiralty
for conversion to a Fleet Oiler; allocated name
Oleander, but not completed when hostilities ceased
so returned to her owners.
1955: (Shell Petroleum Co. Ltd.).
1960: Sold for scrapping and
20.4.1962: Arrived Blyth for breaking up.

1724 (N)   *British Respect* 8,479 gt, 486.3 ft (oa),
469.8 ft × 61.9 ft. Engines: Oil.
Launched: 4.2.1943.
Completed: 4.1943 for British Tanker Co. Ltd.
13.6.1959: Arrived Barrow in tow of tug *Cruiser*
(1953, 304 gt), for breaking up.

1743 (W)   *Regent Tiger* 9,960 gt, 525 ft (oa),
505 ft × 67.5 ft. Engines: Oil.
Launched: 1.7.1946.
Completed: 10.1946 for Bowring SS Co. Ltd. (C. T.
Bowring & Co. Ltd., London).
1954: Renamed *Capulet*.
31.5.1966: Arrived Santander for breaking up.

1762 (N)   *British Virtue* 8,553 gt, 486.3 ft (oa),
469.1 ft × 61.9 ft. Engines: Oil.
Launched: 12.3.1945.
Completed: 6.1945 for British Tanker Co. Ltd.
4.5.1962: Arrived Troon for breaking up.

1764 (N)   *British Caution* 8,522 gt. Details as Yard
No. 1762 (N).
Launched: 21.9.1945.
Completed: 2.1946 for British Tanker Co. Ltd.
16.8.1959: Laid up Barry.
10.12.1961: Arrived Newport, Mon., for breaking
up.

1772 (N)   *British Earl* 8,573 gt, 490 ft (oa),
469.6 ft × 61.9 ft. Engines: Oil.
Launched: 28.6.1946.
Completed: 10.1946 for British Tanker Co. Ltd.
18.1.1947: Struck mine in Great Belt, Denmark;
beached off Langeland Island with severe damage
(voyage: Abadan/Stockholm – oil).
25.1.1947: Refloated, taken in tow for Nyborg, but
grounded south of Sprogo. Again refloated and towed
to Nyborg. Temporarily repaired, then towed to
United Kingdom. Repaired.
15.7.1957: Laid up Falmouth.
18.7.1961: Left Falmouth in tow of tug *Englishman*
(1945, 716 gt) and
9.1961: Scrapped Inverkeithing.

Built by J. L. Thompson & Sons Ltd., North Sands, Sunderland

DEEP SEA TANKERS BUILT UNDER PRIVATE CONTRACT OR LICENCE

643 *Galeomma* 5,042 gt, 400 ft (oa),
383.8 ft × 62.7 ft. Engines: T6cyl. Twin screws.
Launched: 16.1.1946.
Completed: 5.1946 for N.V. Curaçaosche Scheepv.
Maats. N.V. (Anglo-Saxon Petroleum Co. Ltd.,
London).
1953: (Cia. Shell de Venezuela Ltda., Maracaibo,
Venezuela).
1960: (Shell Tankers Ltd., London).
11.5.1962: Arrived Blyth for breaking up.

645 *Gansella* 5,042 gt. Details as Yard No. 643.
Launched: 7.2.1946.

Completed: 8.1946 for N.V. Curaçaosche Scheepv.
Maats. N.V. (Anglo-Saxon Petroleum Co. Ltd.,
London).
1953: (Cia. Shell de Venezuela Ltda., Maracaibo,
Venezuela).
1960: (Shell Tankers Ltd.).
1964: (Serena Shipping Ltd., Liberia).
7.3.1966: Arrived Hong Kong for breaking up.

646 *British Rose* 6,101 gt, 422.8 ft (oa),
406 ft × 56.3 ft. Engines: Oil.
Launched: 29.5.1946.
Completed: 10.1946 for British Tanker Co. Ltd.
16.6.1961: Arrived Bruges for breaking up.

The tanker *British Patience* in wartime guise and rigged with anti-torpedo nets and booms. (Harland & Wolff Ltd., Govan, Yard No. 1166(G).)
National Maritime Museum

The *Congonian*, leaving for trials, 11 May 1942. (Swan, Hunter & Wigham Richardson Ltd., Newcastle, Yard No. 1708.)

PART THREE

CAM-MAC SHIPS

From the debacle of Dunkirk in May/June 1940 over half a million Allied troops were evacuated to Britain, France collapsed and the whole coastline of Western Europe, from the North Cape to the Franco/Spanish border, became occupied by German forces.

The French naval bases of Brest, Lorient, Bordeaux and St. Nazaire on the Bay of Biscay coast quickly became operational bases for the German U-boats, and Allied shipping, moving on the transatlantic route to the south of Ireland, became wide-open to attack.

On 1 August 1940 Kampfgeschwader 40, a German bomber group of Focke-Wulf FW 200 Kondor planes took up station at Merignac, near Bordeaux. Britain's south coast ports had closed to ocean ships, the ports on the East coast were suffering continual bombing and the chief ports were now in the Bristol Channel area, the Clyde and at Liverpool, where the control centre for convoys, under the Commander-in-Chief, Western Approaches, was established. Shipping was re-routed around the north of Ireland, in the North West Approaches, but apart from the U-boats, which quickly followed their quarry to the new hunting grounds, the Kondors flew in an arc west of the Irish coastline, ever searching for targets and capable of circumnavigating Britain by refuelling at Stavanger or Trondheim, in Norway, on their return leg to Bordeaux. British ports were still turning round some two million tons of shipping each month and many ships were lost. The Kondor planes usually carried four 250 kg (551 lb) bombs, attacking at masthead height with a salvo of their full bomb-load. In November 1940 eighteen Allied ships were bombed and sunk, fourteen of which flew the Red Ensign.

Added to this was the appearance, in late 1940, of the German battleships *Scharnhorst* and *Gneisenau*, additions to the cruiser *Admiral Hipper* and the pocket battleship *Admiral Scheer*, in marauding the convoys.

In February 1941 seventy-four British ships were lost; during the six months ending in February the Kondors alone sank eighty-five Allied ships and in March 1941 all British efforts were turned to the announced 'Battle of the Atlantic'.

It became obvious that effective protection of shipping could only come from ship-borne fighter planes, but at that time the Royal Navy could offer little assistance, its resources stretched almost to breaking point. However, it was increasing in strength, with additional corvettes and anti-submarine vessels being turned out for convoy escort work.

In October 1940 the prototype of the Hawker Hurricane (Mark II) land-based fighter, modified for launching from a marine catapult, had been ordered and three months later sets of catapult equipment for fifty merchant ships were also ordered. Ten merchant ships were then taken up for conversion to catapult ships, followed by a further twenty-five, the work being done at Bristol, Cardiff, Clydeside and Liverpool. Each ship, however, would carry its normal cargo and sail as part of the convoy.

Meanwhile, in December 1940, the old *Ark Royal* of 1914 (renamed *Pegasus* in 1934) had embarked three Fulmar fighter planes and taken up duties as an escort ship. Four more merchant ships, already under Royal Navy requisition, were turned to convoy work, being fitted with a catapult and carrying one Fulmar plane. Two of the four, *Ariguani*, (1927, 6,746 gt) and *Patia*, (1922, 5,355 gt) were banana carriers of the Elders & Fyffes fleet, both having been taken up as Ocean Boarding Vessels in October 1940. Another banana carrier, owned by Morant SS Co. (Standard Fruit Corporation) was the *Erin* (1932, 5,824 gt), taken over on 30 September 1940 also as an Ocean Boarding Vessel and renamed *Maplin*. The fourth was Andrew Weir & Co.'s *Springbank* (1926, 5,155 gt), taken up in November 1940 as an anti-aircraft Ship. The five became known as Fighter Catapult Ships. All were ready for their new tasks in April 1941, but the *Patia* was bombed and sunk off the Tyne on 27 April without even embarking her fighter plane. Two of the remaining four were placed on the Gibraltar run, and two with the North Atlantic convoys.

On 27 September 1941 the *Springbank* was hit by a torpedo from *U.201*; abandoned, she became a menace to shipping and was sunk by the 'Flower'-class corvette H.M.S. *Jasmine* in the Atlantic, in position 49.10N 20.05W.

The thirty-five vessels, classified as CAM-ships (Catapult-Armed Merchantmen), began to appear in May 1941, the first to put to sea being the *Michael E*, of 7,628 gross tons, built in 1941 for the Counties Ship Management Ltd. But no use could be made of her aircraft before she was torpedoed by submarine *U.108* on 2 June 1941 in mid-Atlantic, in position 48.50N 29.00W. Another eleven CAM-ships were to be lost before they were superseded by the MAC-ships in 1943.

On the CAM-ship, the embarked Sea Hurricane fighter plane was launched from an 85-ft steel catapult runway, propelled some three-quarters of the running length by cordite rockets, to give a 75–80 mph lift-off. But there was no facility for a return to the ship and should a landing site ashore not be close enough, the R.A.F. pilot had no alternative other than to ditch the plane and hopefully await pick-up. The fact that each plane could make only one sortie seemed expensive and wasteful, both in planes and pilots.

However, the CAM-ships proved their worth in providing some form of air cover and defence for 170 West African, Russian and North Atlantic convoys, particularly through the 500-mile gap of undefended air space in the mid-Atlantic.

In June 1943, with escort carriers coming into convoy service, the Merchant Ship Fighter Unit and the Fighter Catapult Ships had become redundant. And so a message from the Admiralty which showed appreciation of the valuable service rendered to the convoys, also recommended that the association of the R.A.F. with the Merchant Navy should be brought to an end. The order to disband the Merchant Ship Fighter Unit went out on 8 June; at the time there were five CAM-ships left in service and the last two were expected back in the United Kingdom in early July.

In fact, the convoy with the last two CAM-ships – *Empire Tide* and *Empire Darwin* – was delayed and did not leave Gibraltar until 23 July 1943. German Intelligence had monitored the disbandment of the Fighter Unit and on 28 July, when the convoy was out of range of air cover from both Gibraltar and the U.K., enemy long-range planes commenced attacking the convoy – which was thought to have no air support. Both Hurricane fighters were launched from the CAM-ships and two German FW Kondors were shot down.

So ended the CAM-ship phase.

CAM-ships

Eight ships were taken up from private owners, the remainder were Government-owned 'Empire' tramp ships.

Daghestan	*Empire Burton*★	*Empire Franklin*	*Empire Rainbow*★
Daltonhall	*Empire Clive*	*Empire Gale*	*Empire Ray*
Eastern City	*Empire Darwin*	*Empire Heath*	*Empire Rowan*★
Helencrest	*Empire Day*	*Empire Hudson*★	*Empire Shackleton*★
Kafiristan	*Empire Dell*★	*Empire Lawrence*★	*Empire Spray*
Michael E★	*Empire Eve*★	*Empire Moon*	*Empire Spring*★
Novelist	*Empire Faith*	*Empire Morn*	*Empire Stanley*
Primrose Hill★	*Empire Flame*	*Empire Ocean*	*Empire Sun*
	Empire Foam		*Empire Tide*
		★ = lost	*Empire Wave*★

The CAM-ship *Empire Faith*, fitted with her aircraft catapult. (Barclay, Curle & Co. Ltd., Yard No. 681.)

National Martime Museum

MAC-ships

The CAM-Ships were superseded by the Merchant Ship Aircraft Carriers – MAC-ships – which flew the Red Ensign, with merchant navy crews and masters, and naval personnel for air crew and maintenance.

Development of the MAC-ships began in early 1942. Six American escort carriers had been transferred to Britain under Lend-Lease arrangements between October 1941 and March 1942, but the Admiralty saw fit to send them to shipyards for some modification, including a revision of the petrol system.

At that time there was much concern about the Battle of the Atlantic and the menace of the U-boat. Action was still urgently needed for convoy protection and there came a suggestion for the conversion of merchant ships to escort carriers – ships with a flight deck from which aircraft could fly off in convoy protection, yet continue to carry cargo. The planes would primarily be for defensive duties, rather than offensive – a role quite contrary to that of their fighting Royal Navy sisters and, unlike the earlier CAM-ships, would have the advantage of not losing their aircraft after they became airborne.

The conversion of merchant ships into aircraft carriers did not begin with the MAC-ships: the Admiralty had already converted some passenger liners and had acquired and converted, while still on the stocks, some cargo liner-type vessels. One which stimulated naval interest in the 'tramp'-type of ship was the conversion of the captured German merchantman *Hannover* to the escort carrier H.M.S. *Audacity* (see *Empire Audacity*). She served for only a short time, but a tribute was paid to the part she played in anti-submarine warfare by naming a MAC-ship after her commander, viz: *Empire MacKendrick*.

Once the need for merchant ship aircraft carriers became both apparent and urgent their development proceeded rapidly and the decision was made for the construction of two grain-carrying vessels, to be ready for service by the spring of 1943. The Burntisland Shipbuilding Company was given an outline plan and requested to draw up detailed plans, the Admiralty, at first, recommending a minimum flight deck length of 490 feet and a speed of fifteen knots, but these figures were later reduced to 390 feet and eleven knots to enable standard 'Empire' hulls to be used.

The new requirements were intended to cover both cargo ships and oil tankers, but with different problems in each type their application followed different courses. Nevertheless, it was no easy matter to add a complete superstructure some fifteen feet above the normal strength deck of the hull.

Grain ship merchant aircraft carriers

Subsequent amendments to the detailed plans submitted by the shipbuilder were agreed by the Admiralty Merchant Shipbuilding Department at three conferences held in May/June 1942 and from then on the design remained virtually unaltered. In October 1942 the programme was increased to a total of six grain ships to be given the additional role of MAC-ships—two vessels being ordered from each of three shipyards—Burntisland, Denny and Lithgows.

The hull form for all six vessels, being repeats of hulls already tank-tested, needed no further change, but it was necessary to seek guidance in relation to the aircraft carrier features. The length of flight deck for the two Burntisland ships was 413 ft 9 in, for the Denny-built vessels 423 ft 1 in, and 424 ft 4 in for the Lithgow buildings. In all cases the flight decks were longitudinally stiffened, without expansion joints and had a breadth of sixty-two feet, with the ends of each made similar in case planes needed to land over the bows, whilst the width at the ends was determined by the amount of overhang which could be supported by the simple bracing below.

Solid plating in the sides between sheerstrake top and underside of the flight deck was impracticable: nevertheless the openings in the side plating for lifeboats and rafts were limited in size and number. To offset any unbalancing effect caused by a broadside wind and to lessen the angle of helm required to maintain a steady course, the rudder area was increased by 15 per cent over normal requirements. Further stability problems, due to increased top weight, were overcome to ensure a moderate angle of heel when turning, but not to be considered as quick rolling.

It was accepted that only diesel engines could be considered for the ships' propelling machinery, having regard to the problems which would otherwise arise in getting rid of boiler smoke. So, with the oil engines, the main exhaust outlet was trunked under the flight deck and extended to both sides of the ship, a flap within each branch permitting diversion of gases to the lee side, in order not to affect flying operations.

The wartime 'standard tramp' machinery with an output of 2,500 bhp gave a speed of some eleven knots, but to have repeated this in these ships would have given no margin of power to

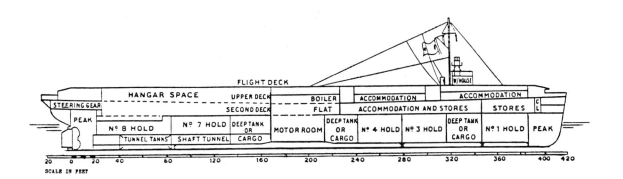

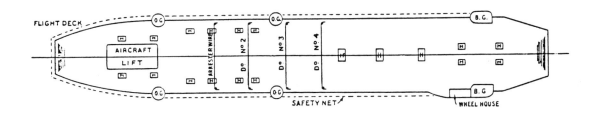

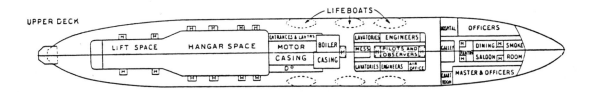

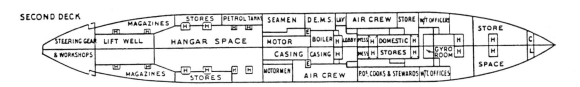

Merchant Aircraft Carrier, grain carrier-type.

enable them to get out of convoy station quickly for flying patrols or to overhaul the convoy if, in manoeuvring to a suitable take-off position, they had fallen astern. All the MAC-ships of this class were, therefore, given machinery of 3,300 bhp, the additional rating deemed sufficient to give any spurt required.

These grain ship aircraft carriers, the smallest of any produced during the war, were fitted with four arrester wires stretched across the flight deck at 30 ft intervals. Four Fairey Swordfish aircraft with folded wings could be accommodated in a hangar 142 ft × 38 ft × 24 ft height, this served by a platform lift 42 ft × 20 ft, electrically operated and able to lift a plane to flight deck level in fifty seconds. Special ventilation, heating, lighting and a fire-prevention sprinkler system were provided throughout the hangar space. The aircraft lifts – and the arrester gear for both the grain ship and tanker types – were, in fact, made available from equipment ordered for the escort carrier programme.

Whereas with normal naval practice spaces for magazines, explosive stores and petrol compartments were away from the ship's side and below the waterline, with these ships it was necessary to locate such spaces aft, with space available only at the side of the hangar, between the second and upper deck.

Cargo spaces were restricted to holds below the second deck and extra bulkheads were fitted to provide more subdivision, together with three deep tanks for use during westward ballast voyages. Loading and discharge of grain was by flexible pipe or spout and no above-deck cargo-handling gear impeded this.

The first MAC-ship, *Empire MacAlpine*, built by the Burntisland Shipbuilding Company, was ordered in June 1942 and the keel laid on 11 August 1942. The ship was launched on 23 December 1942, delivered on 21 April 1943 and took up duty a month later. The second MAC-ship, *Empire MacAndrew*, entered service in the July. All three shipbuilders shared in the development and detailed planning, with the fullest effort concentrated on production of the first vessel, so that problems could be solved before construction of the subsequent vessels had proceeded too far.

In man-hours and cost, construction of the ships required 25 per cent more than for a 'standard' ship; increased steel-weight amounted to some 20 per cent and the reduction in deadweight was 28 per cent.

The first homeward cargo, loaded in three days, saw the ship twenty-four hours at the grain elevator at a north-west port, with the complete 7,500 tons discharged by suction in sixteen hours.

After the October 1942 increase of grain-carrying MAC-ships to six, mercantile shipping losses in the following month were drastic, with over 700,000 tons of Allied shipping sunk; in fact, from August to November there was an appalling loss of some two million tons and in the following March total disruption of communications between the New and Old worlds came perilously close when ninety-seven Allied ships were destroyed in the first twenty days.

The German Kondor planes, which had left France for the Russian front in 1941, returned to the Biscay area in early 1943. Their work, however, was now changed to that of U-boat co-ordination, the previous patrol work being carried on by their successors, the Junkers 290s.

Built by Burntisland Shipbuilding Co. Ltd., Burntisland, Fife

268 *Empire MacAlpine* 7,954 gt, 435 ft (oa), 417.1 ft × 57 ft. Engines: Oil. A grain carrier.
Launched: 23.12.1942
Completed: 4.1943 as a MAC-ship.
1947: *Derrynane* (McCowan & Gross Ltd., London).
1951: *Huntsbrook* (Power SS Co. Ltd. (O. Gross & Sons Ltd., London)).
1959: *Suva Breeze* (South Breeze Navigation Co. Ltd. (J. Manners & Co. Ltd., Hong Kong)).
1965: *Djatingaleh* (San Fernando SS Co., Hong Kong (J. Manners & Co. Ltd., Hong Kong)).
1966: Renamed *San Ernesto*.

1968: *Pacific Endeavour* (San Fernando SS Co. Ltd.,
Panama (Jaguar Shipping Corp. Ltd., Hong Kong)).
1969: (Cia. Nueva del Oriente S.A., Panama (Jaguar
Shipping Corp. Ltd., Hong Kong)).
21.2.1970: Arrived Hong Kong for breaking up. (See
also *Empire Ibex*.)

277 *Empire MacKendrick* 7,933 gt. Details as Yard
No. 268.
Launched: 29.9.1943.
Completed: 12.1943 as a MAC-ship.
1947: *Granpond* (Mediterranean & Atlantic Lines Ltd.
(Goulandris Bros. Ltd., London)).

1951: *Condor* (Cia. Maritima del Este S.A., Panama
(Goulandris Bros. Ltd., Greece)).
1955: *Saltersgate* (Turnbull, Scott Shipping Co. Ltd.,
London).
1957: *Vassil Levsky* (Navigation Bulgare Maritime
(Government of Bulgaria)).
6.6.1967: Anchored in Bitter Lakes, Suez Canal and
detained during Arab/Israeli war, until Suez Canal
re-opened to shipping on 5 June 1975.
22.7.1975: Arrived Split, in tow, for breaking up.

Built by Wm. Denny & Bros. Ltd., Leven Shipyard, Dumbarton

1370 *Empire MacAndrew* 7,952 gt, 448.5 ft (oa),
429.8 ft × 56.3 ft. Engines: Oil. A grain carrier.
Launched: 3.5.1943.
Completed: 7.1943 as a MAC-ship.
1947: *Derryheen* (McCowan & Gross Ltd., London).
1951: *Cape Grafton* (Cape of Good Hope Motor Ship
Co. Ltd. (Lyle Shipping Co. Ltd., Glasgow)).
1963: *Patricia* (Patricia Cia. Nav. S.A., Liberia).
1968: (Pomos Shipping Co. Ltd., Cyprus (Chios
Nav. Co. Ltd., London)).
10.1970: Scrapped Hsinkiang, China.

1378 *Empire MacDermott* 7,952 gt. Details as Yard
No. 1370.
Launched: 24.1.1944.
Completed: 3.1944 as a MAC-ship.
1948: *La Cumbre* (Buries, Markes Ltd., London).
1959: *Parnon* (Canero Cia. Nav. S.A., Panama (Lyras
Bros. Ltd., London)).
1969: *Starlight* (Southern Shipping & Enterprises Co.
Ltd. (Yick Fung Shipping & Enterprises, Hong
Kong)).
1976: (Government of People's Republic of China).

Built by Lithgows Ltd., Port Glasgow

992 *Empire Macrae* 8,252 gt, 444.6 ft (oa),
429.5 ft × 57.9 ft. Engines: Oil. A grain carrier.
Launched: 21.6.1943.
Completed: 9.1943 as a MAC-ship.
1947: *Alpha Zambesi* (Alpha South African SS Co.
(Mollers Ltd., London)).
1949: (Motor Lines Ltd. (Olsen, Johnston & Co. Ltd.,
Glasgow)).
1954: *Tobon* (V. Torkildsen, Norway).
1960: (W. Kubon, Norway).
1967: *Despina P* (Aghia Paraskevi Corpn., Greece
(Pontikos Shipping Agencies Ltd., London)).
4.1971: Scrapped Kaohsiung.

993 *Empire MacCallum* 8,252 gt. Details as Yard
No. 992.
Launched: 12.10.1943.
Completed: 12.1943 as a MAC-ship.
1947: *Doris Clunies* (Doris SS Co. Ltd. (Olsen,
Johnston & Co. Ltd., Glasgow)).
1951: Renamed *Sunrover*.
1953: (Doris SS Co. Ltd. (Dracoulis Ltd., London)).
1957: Renamed *Eudoxia*.
1959: *Phorkyss* (Phorkyss Shipping Corpn., Panama
(H. C. Dracoulis, Greece)).
11.1960: Scrapped Osaka.

Oil tanker merchant aircraft carriers

Outline plans for the conversion work on tankers had been prepared along with the grain ship proposals, but the suggestion that tankers, which loaded in similar fashion to the grain ships, should also become MAC-ships met early opposition as to the fire hazard in such valuable vessels and their precious cargoes. But such argument was dismissed on the theory that a tanker with cargo was already a hazard and, thus, conversion would not make it more so and in October 1942, concurrent with the grain ship increase to six, came orders for the completion as MAC-ships of four tankers in the new construction programme and the conversion of nine tankers already in service with the Anglo-Saxon Petroleum Company. At the same time it was agreed that while in service as merchant aircraft carriers the tankers would only carry heavy-grade oil cargoes.

The plans for the four new vessels were prepared from an Admiralty outline by each individual shipbuilder, Harland & Wolff, Cammell Laird and Swan Hunter. Conversion plans for their nine existing vessels, all of similar dimensions and to be known as the 'Rapana'-class, were drawn up by marine technicians of the Anglo-Saxon company, in association with Palmers (Hebburn) Co. Ltd., and Smiths Dock Co. Ltd., North Shields.

The ships were larger than the grain carriers, with a 461 ft flight deck, although its breadth was the same. In appearance they were better balanced than the grain ships, this largely due to their extra length, more open superstructure and a two-deck bridge.

The primary difference between the two types of MAC-ships was the absence of a hangar in the tanker type. To have provided such space would have required a complete re-design, which was not the intention. Instead, the larger flight deck allowed a 100-ft length aft to be used as permanent deck parking for three Swordfish reconnaissance planes, an aim of which was the spotting of U-boats and/or torpedoes. The aircraft arrester gear was a repeat of that used on the grain ships. The flight deck itself was not a strength member, but arranged in sections with an expansion joint between each. This enabled the deck and its supports to be prefabricated and, in the nine existing tanker conversions, out of a total of 957 tons of additional steel, 51 per cent was fabricated by the structural industry and supplied to the conversion yards for assembly.

The small hold and 'tween decks forward were the only spaces available for use as magazines and inflammable stores, and they were fitted with a separate water-extinguishing system. With some 10 per cent of the deadweight lost as a result of the additional structure, it was possible to use one of the main centre cargo tanks for the storage of aviation fuel.

The lifeboats, normally aft in tankers, were relocated to the well spaces, four being placed aft and two forward, these fitted with special gravity davits that could stow the boats well inboard. Due to the elimination of the normal tanker funnel, a system similar to that used on the grain-carrier MAC-ships was adopted for the ejection of engine gases. At the same time accommodation was doubled for a combined crew of 122 men, and additional galley facilities were also necessary.

The inclusion of nine existing tankers in the programme precluded any increase in the propelling power of the new vessels. All thirteen vessels could develop the required 3,300 bhp and reach eleven knots, although they had but little reserve of power above the normal service speed.

The average time for conversion work on the Anglo-Saxon tankers was six months, while the extra time taken to complete the new tankers as MAC-ships was just under three months.

Subsequently, it was found that the flight decks kept remarkably dry in rough seas, much of the dryness attributed to the waves being free to pass over the tank decks, due to the maximum open spaces provided below the flight deck in order to free any gas vapour rising from the cargo. It was, in fact, one of the prime concerns in this conversion design that the tank decks be kept clear of any enclosing structure and that all tank hatches remained in the open.

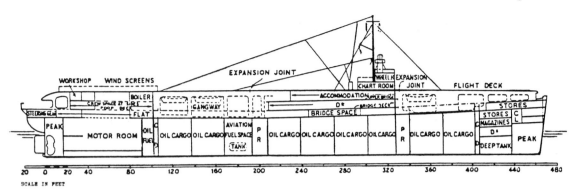

Flight deck and other arrangements
generally similar to *Rapana*-class
tankers

Merchant Aircraft Carrier, tanker-type.

The grain-carrying MAC-ship *Empire MacAlpine*, on trials. (Burntisland Shipbuilding Co. Ltd., Yard No. 268.)

The *La Cumbre*, formerly the grain-carrying MAC-ship *Empire MacDermott*. (Wm. Denny & Bros. Ltd., Yard No. 1378.)
Skyfotos

The tanker *British Pilot*, formerly the tanker MAC-ship *Empire MacColl*. (Cammell Laird & Co. Ltd., Yard No. 1106.)
Skyfotos

The tanker MAC-ship *Empire MacCabe*. Without an aircraft hangar, her 'Swordfish' planes are parked on the flight deck.
(Swan, Hunter & Wigham Richardson Ltd., Newcastle, Yard No. 1726(N).)
National Maritime Museum

Conclusion

In all, there were nineteen MAC-ships, the last, *Macoma*, entering service in May 1944. Thirteen more conversions had been planned, but were not required; two allocated names, *Empire MacSorley* and *Empire Mackenzie*, were cancelled.

Indeed, such was the situation then, that it was possible to place two, and sometimes even three MAC-ships with a convoy, the larger naval escort carriers being deployed elsewhere.

Some MAC-ships of the tanker type actually made eleven special voyages from the United States to the United Kingdom, bringing over 200 aircraft in the build-up for the forthcoming invasion of Normandy.

The short era of the MAC-ship ended with the arrival of the *Empire MacKay* in the U.K. on 28 June 1945. In the month previous, on 21 May, 836 Squadron, the largest in the Fleet Air Arm and the last to fly Swordfish planes, was disbanded. As each MAC-ship neared its completion for escort work a new flight for the squadron was formed in alphabetical sequence. It ended at 'S' and a total of sixty-three air crews.

Built by Cammell Laird & Co. Ltd., Birkenhead

1106 *Empire MacColl* 9,133 gt, 481.7 ft (oa), 466.3 ft × 61.9 ft. Engines: Oil. A tanker; 11,508 tdw.
Launched: 21.7.1943.

Completed: 11.1943 as a MAC-ship.
1946: *British Pilot* (British Tanker Co. Ltd.).
21.8.1962: Arrived Faslane for breaking up.

Built by Harland & Wolff Ltd., Govan

1167 (G) (Laid down as) *British Wisdom* 8,908 gt, 479.6 ft (oa), 463.2 ft × 61.2 ft. Engines: Oil. A tanker; 11,246 tdw.
Launched: 17.6.1943 as *Empire MacKay*.

Completed: 10.1943 as a MAC-ship.
1946: *British Swordfish* (British Tanker Co. Ltd.).
21.5.1959: Arrived Rotterdam for breaking up.

Built by Swan, Hunter & Wigham Richardson Ltd., Wallsend (W) or Newcastle (N)

1726 (N) *Empire MacCabe* 9,249 gt, 485.9 ft (oa), 469.8 ft × 61.9 ft. Engines: Oil. A tanker; 11,450 tdw.
Launched: 18.5.1943.

Completed: 11.1943 as a MAC-ship.
1946: *British Escort* (British Tanker Co. Ltd.).
1960: *Easthill Escort* (River Line Ltd., Bermuda (Mollers Ltd., Hong Kong)).
1962: Scrapped Hong Kong.

There were ninety-three ocean-going tankers in the British Tanker Company fleet in September 1939, with a carrying capacity of nearly one million tons. During the war years forty-four ships were lost. The British Tanker Co. Ltd., was formed in 1915 to carry the products of the Anglo-Persian Oil Company, established in 1909. It was restyled Anglo-Iranian Oil Company in 1913 and then, in 1954, British Petroleum Co. Ltd. From June 1956 the British Tanker Co. Ltd. became BP Tanker Co. Ltd., whose parent company is British Petroleum Co. Ltd.

1677 (W)   *Empire MacMahon* 8,856 gt, 483 ft (oa), 465.3 ft × 59.3 ft. Engines: Oil. A tanker; 11,000 tdw.
Launched: 2.7.1943.

Completed: 12.1943 as a MAC-ship.
1946: *Naninia* (Anglo-Saxon Petroleum Co. Ltd.).
17.3.1960: Arrived Hong Kong for breaking up.

'Rapana' class

ex Anglo-Saxon Petroleum Co. Ltd.

All ships: 481 ft (oa), 463 ft × 59.3 ft. Engines: Oil, twelve knots. Tankers, 11,009 tdw (as MAC-ships). Dutch-built ships:

Rapana 7,986 gt.
Completed: 4.1935 by N.V. Wilton Fijenoord, Schiedam, for N.V. Petroleum Maats. 'La Corona', The Hague.
1940: Transferred to Anglo-Saxon Petroleum Co. Ltd., London.
7.1943: Completed conversion to MAC-ship by Smiths Dock Co. Ltd., North Shields.
1945: Reverted to owners.
1950: *Rotula* (N.V. Petroleum Maats. 'La Corona', The Hague.
1.1958: Scrapped Hong Kong.

Miralda 8,003 gt.
Completed: 7.1936 by N.V. Nederlandsche Scheeps, Maats., Amsterdam, for N.V. Petroleum Maats. 'La Corona', The Hague.
1940: Transferred to Anglo-Saxon Petrolum Co. Ltd., London.
2.1944: Completed conversion to MAC-ship by Palmers (Hebburn) Co. Ltd.
1946: Reverted to owners.
1950: *Marisa* (N.V. Petroleum Maats. 'La Corona', The Hague.
21.7.1960: Arrived Hong Kong for breaking up.

Dutch-flag ships:

Gadila 7,999 gt.
Launched: 1.12.1934.
Completed: 4.1935 by Howaldtswerke A.G.,Kiel, for N.V. Petroleum Maats. 'La Corona', The Hague.
1940: Re-registered at Willemstad, N.W.I.; continued sailing under Dutch flag.
3.1944: Completed conversion to MAC-ship by Smith Dock Co. Ltd., North Shields.
1946: Reverted to owners.
6.6.1958: Arrived Hong Kong for breaking up.

Macoma 8,011 gt.
Launched: 3.12.1935.
Completed: 5.1936 by N.V. Nederlandsche Scheeps. Maats., Amsterdam, for N.V. Petroleum Maats. 'La Corona', The Hague.
1940: Re-registered at Willemstad, N.W.I.; continued sailing under Dutch flag.
5.1944: Completed conversion to MAC-ship by Palmers (Hebburn) Co. Ltd.
1946: Reverted to owners.
14.12.1959: Arrived Hong Kong for breaking up.

Note: The *Gadila* and *Macoma* were the first aircraft carriers to operate under the Dutch flag.

All ships: 483.2 ft (oa), 465 ft × 59.4 ft. Engines: Oil – twelve knots. Tankers, 11,009 tdw (as MAC-ships).

British-built ships:

Acavus 8,010 gt.
Launched: 24.11.1934.
Completed: 1.1935 by Workman, Clark Ltd., Belfast.
10.1943: Completed conversion to MAC-ship by Silley, Cox & Co. Ltd., Falmouth.
1946: Reverted to owners.
1952: *Iacra* (Soc. Maritime Shell, Paris).
18.4.1963: Arrived La Seyne for breaking up.

Ancylus 8,017 gt.
Launched: 9.10.1934.
Completed: 1.1935 by Swan, Hunter & Wigham Richardson Ltd., Newcastle.
10.1943: Completed conversion to MAC-ship by Palmers (Hebburn) Co. Ltd.
1946: Reverted to owners.
1952: *Imbricaria* (Soc. Maritime Shell, Paris).
4.12.1954: Arrived Spezia in tow of tug *Ursus* (1919, 515 gt) for breaking up.

German-built ship:

Alexia 8,016 gt.
Launched: 20.12.1934.
Completed: 4.1935 by Bremer Vulkan, Vegesack.
12.1943: Completed conversion to MAC-ship by T. W. Greenwell & Co. Ltd., Sunderland.

Amastra 8,031 gt.
Launched: 8.12.1934.
Completed: 3.1935 by Lithgows Ltd., Port Glasgow.
9.1943: Completed conversion to MAC-ship by Smith Dock Co. Ltd., North Shields.
1946: Reverted to owners.
1951: *Idas* (Soc. Maritime Shell, Paris).
27.6.1955: Arrived Spezia, in tow, for breaking up.

Adula 8,040 gt.
Launched: 28.1.1937.
Completed: 3.1937 by Blythswood Shipbuilding Co. Ltd., Glasgow.
1.1944: Completed conversion to MAC-ship by Silley, Cox & Co. Ltd., Falmouth.
1946: Reverted to owners.
15.5.1953: Arrived Briton Ferry for breaking up.

1946: Reverted to owners.
1951: *Ianthina* (Soc. Maritime Shell, Paris).
17.8.1954: Arrived Blyth for breaking up.

The roots of the Anglo-Saxon Petroleum Co. Ltd., are traceable to 1892, the year when M. Samuel & Company was formed to operate three small steamships, at first to carry shells and then to transport Middle East petroleum through the Suez Canal. In 1897 the Shell Transport & Trading Co. Ltd. was formed.

From 1 January 1907 the agreement between M. Samuel & Company for the management of its affairs was cancelled. Instead, the Shell Transport & Trading Company joined with N. V. Koninklijke Nederlandsche Petroleum Maatschappij (Royal Dutch Petroleum Company) which was founded in 1890, as parent holding companies of the Royal Dutch/Shell Group on a 60%/40% basis.

Income for the two holding companies mostly came from three operating companies, the N. V. Bataafsche Petroleum Maatschappij and Anglo-Saxon Petroleum Co. Ltd., both founded in 1907 and the Shell Petroleum Co. Ltd., founded in 1903. The Royal Dutch/Shell Group was to grow to a vast international empire of several hundred companies devoted to the oil industry.

Many national flags flew from the ships of the Anglo-Saxon Petroleum Co. Ltd., which became London Agent during the 1939–1945 war for the many carrying companies, the largest fleets being under the British and Dutch flags.

In the 1930s the motor tanker *Acavus* and seven sisterships were delivered, which began a design that was to last for some two decades. The design included raked bow, a rather long midships bridge structure, short poop and a capped, stumpy funnel. The design did not alter, although dimensions and tonnages varied. During the war some had exhausts leading to twin uptakes, disguised as derrick posts, with a dummy funnel abaft the bridge. This arrangement, it was hoped, would simulate a cargo ship and be less attractive to the U-boat. Up to the 1950s over 120 tankers were constructed in European yards for the Group. Of 12,000 tons deadweight, they had a speed of twelve knots.

In 1939 the Anglo-Saxon Petrolum Company owned 178 ships with a total deadweight capacity of 1,524,000 tons, of which seventy-two ships were lost during the war. In 1953 Shell Tankers Ltd. was formed to manage and operate the Shell fleet, although ownership was still with the Anglo-Saxon Company. At that time, Shell Group's owned and chartered tanker tonnage totalling $6\frac{3}{4}$ million tons in worldwide trading was about one-fifth of the world's tanker tonnage.

Shell tankers bear on their funnel the 'Shell' emblem in scarlet and practically all ships flying the Netherlands flag or the Red Ensign are named after some species of marine crustacean. A specimen of the shell after which the ship is named can be found in the dining saloon of each tanker.

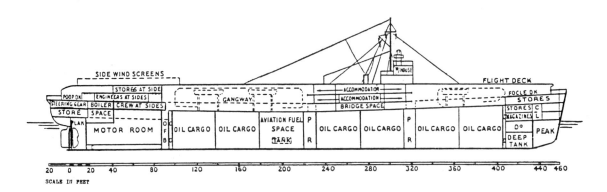

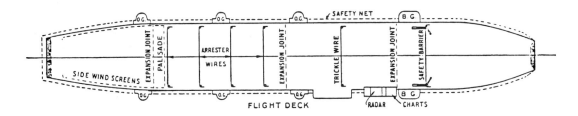

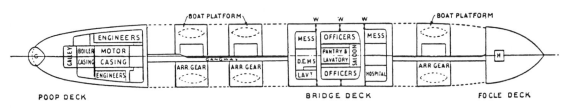

Merchant Aircraft Carrier, 'Rapana'-class.

PART FOUR

FAST CARGO LINERS

In the early years of the war the forecasting of shipping requirements was difficult in the changing patterns of strategy. The debacle of Dunkirk had given shipyards a great amount of repair work; conversions of passenger liners to armed merchant cruisers were urgent; warship construction was a priority; cargo ship hulls were requisitioned to become naval auxiliaries, whilst yards were receiving large orders for shipping, particularly for tramps and tankers.

To produce fast cargo ships depended on the availability of slipways and with the yards at full capacity, output was slow. Naval priority also demanded hulls being taken over in all stages of construction. Most were for completion as aircraft carriers: *Activity* (ex *Telemachus*), *Vindex*, *Nairana*, *Campania*, and the aircraft transports *Athene* (ex *Clan Brodie*) and *Engadine* (ex *Clan Buchanan*).

In 1941 some criticism was made against the Government through the Select Committee on National Expenditure that the ships building for Government account were slow and that the whole question of design and speed of merchant ships should be investigated.

At that time there was a high class fast cargo liner building for Government account by the Greenock Dockyard Company Ltd. She had twin screws driven by triple expansion steam engines and was designed for a variety of cargo requirements to a deadweight capacity of 11,170 tons.

Built by Greenock Dockyard Co. Ltd.

443 *Empire Song* 9,228 gt, 487.6 ft (oa), 463.8 ft × 63 ft. Engines: T3cyl and LP turbines. Twin screws. Sixteen knots.

Launched: 18.6.1940.
Completed: 10.1940.

In April 1941 a build-up of enemy tanks in North Africa caused concern and it became urgently necessary to build up the armoured equipment of British forces there. A large convoy (WS 8) of nine troop transports and supply ships for North Africa was already assembling when it was decided to detach five fast fifteen-knot ships, carrying tanks and aircraft, at Gibraltar and send them through the Mediterranean to Alexandria. The diversion was coded 'Operation Tiger' and the *Clan Campbell*, *Clan Chattan*, *Clan Lamont*, *New Zealand Star* and *Empire Song* passed Gibraltar on 5th/6th May with Force H and a large covering force.

On 9th May, when approaching the Narrows, the *Empire Song* and *New Zealand Star* struck mines. The *New Zealand Star*, although damaged, managed to continue, but the *Empire Song*, on

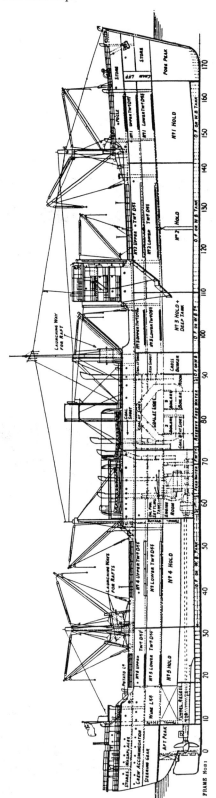

Fast cargo liner *Empire Song*.

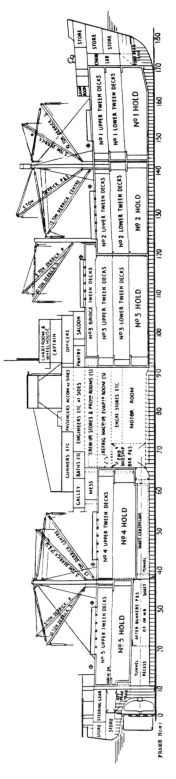

Refrigerated cargo liner prototype.

The *Empire Might*, as *Clan Macrae*. (Greenock Dockyard Co. Ltd., Yard. No. 450.) *Skyfotos*

The *Empire Wisdom*, in wartime guise. (Greenock Dockyard Co. Ltd., Yard No. 451.) *Tom Rayner collection*

The *Empire Life*, as *Good Hope Castle*, outward-bound from London. (Caledon Shipbuilding & Engineering Co. Ltd., Yard No. 407.) *Skyfotos*

fire, exploded and sank off Malta with her cargo of fifty-seven tanks. The remaining four ships were met by the Mediterranean Fleet and escorted to Alexandria carrying 238 tanks and forty-three Hurricane aircraft.

.   .   .

Convoys under the WS coding were arranged for the major strategies of war in the movement of large bodies of troops or in the movement of urgently needed tanks, guns and other vehicles of war. With the downfall of France in 1940 it was thought politic to reduce British shipping movements in the Mediterranean and with the entry of Italy into the war in June 1940, troop movements through the Mediterranean ceased. There then began the long haul of great convoys via the Cape of Good Hope to the Middle East, with some ships diverting off Mombasa for India and Singapore.

Convoy WS 5A, comprising twenty-four ships, left the United Kingdom in late December 1940; Convoy WS 5B, twenty-one ships carrying 40,000 personnel and their equipment, left in January 1941 and WS 6A, of twenty-nine ships, left one month later, merging with a six-ship convoy (WS 6B) from the Clyde, at Freetown.

In September 1941 it was decided to reinforce the Middle East with some 40,000 troops, but at that time British shipping was fully extended and Britain turned to the United States for the loan of some transports and fast cargo ships for a period of some five months. This was agreed, the transports with U.S. Navy crews sailing under the American Neutrality Act which allowed U.S. ships to go to any port and the fast cargo ships to be placed on the U.S.–U.K. Atlantic run in order that British ships could be withdrawn for the Middle East voyage.

Under code WS 12X the American ships, with over 20,000 British troops, which had assembled at Halifax N.S., left there on 10 November 1941, reaching Cape Town on 9 December where they were diverted to Bombay, and one ship, *Mount Vernon*, to Singapore. In this group were four ex United States Line's ships, *Wakefield*, 24,289 gt (ex *Manhattan*), *Mount Vernon*, 23,179 gt (ex *Washington*), *West Point*, 26,454 gt (ex *America*) and *Joseph T. Dickman*, 13,869 gt (ex *President Roosevelt*). Others were the *Leonard Wood*, 13,712 gt, formerly the Munson liner *Western World*, and the 6,937 gt *Orizaba*. The escort comprised the aircraft carrier *Ranger*, two cruisers and eight destroyers; also the fast tanker *Cimarron*.

Meanwhile, the British element WS 12Z comprising fifteen transports left the Clyde and Mersey on 12 November for Freetown, Durban and the Middle East.

Convoy WS 15 sailed on 11 January 1942, twenty-two ships carrying 38,000 personnel. Convoy WS 17 on 23 March had thirty ships carrying 59,200 men. On 19 May Cunard White Star Line's *Queen Mary*, sailing alone because of her speed, carried 9,500 in convoy coding WS 19W and one month later, on 17 June, the *Queen Elizabeth* left with 10,000 troops in a single-ship convoy WS 19Y.

These were some of the early troop convoys of the war; there were many more. On 10 July 1943 Allied troops landed in Sicily; on 3 September they invaded the Italian mainland; on 8 September an Armistice between Great Britain, the United States, Russia and Italy was announced and the Mediterranean was open again.

Winston Churchill only learned after war had ended that the initials which he had so often used were an Admiralty coding for 'Winston's Specials'.

.   .   .

The Greenock Dockyard Company also turned out two fast refrigerated ships in 1942 at a time when efforts were being made to avoid a reduction in the nation's meat ration. Three-deck ships, they were similar to the previous class of ten ships which began with *Clan Cameron* in 1937 and ended with the *Clan Lamont* in 1939, these being shelter-deckers with tonnages of 7,250 gross and 10,100 tons deadweight.

450   *Empire Might* 9,208 gt, 487.6 ft (oa), 463.8 ft × 63 ft. Engines: T6cyl and LP turbines. Twin screws. 16 knots. Refrigerated space: 306,400 cu. ft.
Launched: 17.4.1942.
Completed: 8.1942.
1946: *Clan Macrae* (Clan Line Steamers Ltd.).
1959: *Umgeni* (Bullard, King & Co. Ltd.).
1960: *Gemsbok* (Springbok Shipping Co. Ltd.).
1961: *South African Financier* (South African Marine Corpn. Ltd.).

1962: *Santa Maria de Ordaz* (N.V. Redwijs, Baarn, Holland).
3.1962: Scrapped Valencia, Spain.

451   *Empire Wisdom* 9,208 gt. Details as Yard No. 450, but: Refrigerated space: 305,200 cu. ft.
Launched: 29.7.1942.
Completed: 11.1942.
1946: *Royal Star* (Blue Star Line Ltd.).
10.1961: Converted to a motorship by Bremer Vulkan, Vegesack. Renamed *Caledonia Star*.
1.12.1971: Arrived Kaohsiung for breaking up.

Built by Harland & Wolff Ltd., Belfast

Six fast refrigerated cargo liners were built by this yard during the war, two in the early years and four as the war neared its close. Two of the later four were single screw ships; all were motorships of a Shaw, Savill design.

1050   *Empire Hope* 12,688 gt, 540.1 ft (oa), 521.4 ft × 70.4 ft. Engines: Oil. Twin screws. 16 knots.
Launched: 27.3.1941.
Completed: 10.1941.
With a refrigerated capacity of 495,000 cu. ft., the *Empire Hope* was placed under Shaw, Savill & Albion Company management, made two voyages to Australia and New Zealand and was then chosen, because of her speed, for a convoy to Malta. This was to be Operation 'Pedestal', coded WS 21, fourteen fast merchant ships with essential supplies for the beleaguered fortress and centrepoint of Mediterranean strategy.

The convoy passed Gibraltar on 10 August 1942. On the next day high-level bombing began; then continuous attacks by Junkers 88s and Heinkel 111s in the evening, and the following morning by Italian planes and Ju 88s, with fighter protection.

Later that day the *Empire Hope* suffered eighteen near misses in some thirty minutes. But these explosions shook and damaged her engines and she became a sitting target. Gun crews were blown out of their positions, some managing to clamber back to their guns to continue fighting. But two direct hits aft set the ship on fire; one set kerosene alight;

another started a fire in a hold containing explosives and nearby was a quantity of bagged coal. The explosion threw this upwards, with the fine dust piercing mens' skins. Boats at their davits were half-filled with coal dust, but were launched safely and the ship's crew were picked up later by the destroyer H.M.S. *Penn*. Then, just before midnight on the 12th, the *Empire Hope* was hit by a torpedo from the Italian submarine *Bronzo*. The wreck became a hazard to shipping and was later despatched by an escort destroyer, H.M.S. *Bramham*, off Galeta Island.

1051   *Empire Grace* 13,478 gt. Details as Yard No. 1050.
Launched: 25.8.1941.
Completed: 4.1942.
1946: *Wairangi* (Shaw, Savill & Albion Co. Ltd.).
14.8.1963: Aground at Kannholmsfjarden, near Sandhamn, Stockholm Archipelago (voyage: Rio Grande/Stockholm – coffee and oranges).
26.8.1963: Refloated. Constructive total loss.
25.10.1963: Arrived Faslane in tow of Dutch tug *Utrecht* (1943, 524 gt) for breaking up.

The shipyards and plant which were available in these early war years curtailed the construction of an adequate number of refrigerated ships and the difficulty was overcome by equipping some of the 10,000 tdw tramps with partial refrigeration of about 250,000 cu. ft. in 2 and 3 holds and 'tween decks. Four larger ships were completed by Harland & Wolff Ltd., Belfast, towards the end of the war.

1188   (Laid down as) *Empire Wessex* 11,138 gt.
Details as Yard No. 1050.
Launched: 5.12.1945.
Completed: 8.1946 as *Port Hobart* for Port Line Ltd.
9.1970 Arrived Shanghai for breaking up.

1230   *Empire Abercorn* 8,563 gt, 474.2 ft (oa),
457.3 ft × 63.3 ft. Engines: Oil. Single screw. 16
knots. Refrigerated capacity: 368,000 cu. ft.
Launched: 30.12.1944.
Completed: 6.1945.
1946: *Rakaia* (New Zealand Shipping Co. Ltd.).
1966: (Federal Steam Navigation Co. Ltd.).
22.8.1971: Arrived Hong Kong for breaking up.

1231   *Empire Clarendon* 8,577 gt. Details as Yard No.
1230, but: Refrigerated capacity: 421,000 cu. ft.
Launched: 14.5.1945.

Completed: 10.1945.
1947: *Tuscan Star* (Blue Star Line Ltd.).
1948: Renamed *Timaru Star*.
1950: (Lamport & Holt Line Ltd.).
1959: *California Star* (Lamport & Holt Line Ltd.).
1967: Reported sold to Far East buyers for conversion
to a fish factory ship, but sale not completed, and:
21.4.1969: Arrived Kaohsiung for breaking up.

1303   (Laid down as) *Empire Mercia* 11,085 gt.
Details as Yard No. 1050, but: Refrigerated capacity:
492,000 cu. ft.
Launched: 4.3.1946.
Completed: 12.1946 as *Empire Star* for Blue Star Line
Ltd.
1950: (Lamport & Holt Line Ltd.).
16.10.1971: Arrived Kaohsiung for breaking up.

Built by Barclay, Curle & Co. Ltd., Glasgow

679   *Empire Trust* 8,143 gt, 492.5 ft (oa),
471.7 ft × 64.3 ft. Engines: Oil. Twin screws. 15
knots. 10,910 tdw.
Launched: 15.11.1940.
Completed: 2.1941.
1942: *Rembrandt* (Government of Netherlands).
1947: *Amerskerk* (Vereenigde Nederlandsche Sheepsv.
Maats., The Hague).
1947: Renamed: *Rijnkerk*.
21.9.1963: Arrived Hong Kong for breaking up.

680   *Empire Pride* 9,248 gt, 495 ft (oa),
473.4 ft × 64.3 ft. Engines: Oil. Twin screws. 15
knots.
Laid down as a cargo liner, but converted on stocks.

Launched: 14.5.1941.
Completed: 9.1941 as a troopship for the Ministry
of War Transport. Accommodation for 1,600 troops.
Used in Madagascar, North Africa, Sicily and
Southern France landings. Postwar trooping to Far
East and Mediterranean areas.
1954: Withdrawn from service; sold, refitted at
Lubeck as a cargo liner (10,250 tdw), renamed
Charlton Pride (Charlton SS Co. Ltd. (Chandris
(England) Ltd.)).
1956: *Calgaria* (Donaldson Line Ltd. (Donaldson
Bros. & Black Ltd., Glasgow)).
1963: *Embassy* (Cia. Nav. Fortaleza, Panama).
27.6.1963: Arrived Hong Kong for breaking up.

Built by J. L. Thompson & Sons Ltd., Sunderland

640   (Laid down as) *Empire Gala* 9,074 gt, 483.3 ft
(oa), 460 ft × 62.7 ft. Engines: two steam turbines.
15 knots.
Launched: 27.8.1945.
Completed: 4.1946 as *Bir Hakeim* for Gouvernement
Generale de l'Indo-Chine, Indo-China (Government
of France).
1958: *Marionga Maris* (Ardena S.A., Panama
(Morland Navigation (London) Ltd.)).

13.9.1964: Aground on Etna Bank, forty-five miles
(approx.) north of Djakarta (voyage:
Manila/Canada – plywood).
13.10.1964: Refloated with bottom damage.
Proceeded Djakarta, thence Singapore then continued
voyage. Sold.
1965: *Everlucky* (Everlucky Nav. Co. Ltd., Monrovia
(Orient Star Nav. Corpn., Taiwan)).
1969: *Maritime Express* (Maritime Express Nav. Co.
Ltd. (Orient Star Nav. Corpn., Taiwan)).
1.1970: Scrapped Kaohsiung.

The 'Standard Fast' type

In 1942, with a slight ease in naval work, yard and engineering facilities became available for the introduction of a fast 15-knot, single screw cargo ship and by May 1942 Furness Shipbuilding Co. Ltd., from Ministerial instructions and an outline design prepared in 1941, had completed drawings, and exhaustive tank tests with a model had been finalised. The drawings were then forwarded to several yards and at the same time licences were granted to private owners for building.

Although fast cargo liners had been built in the early war years for both Government and private account similar to the *Empire Song* design, the new type to be introduced was quite different. The ship was to be a closed shelter-deck type, with three decks, a raked stem and cruiser stern and with a hull shape designed for speed. With post-war trade also in mind there was the usual cargo liner accommodation for twelve passengers (twenty-four in wartime) and a deadweight capacity of 12,000 tons, but 300 tons less in the heavier-engined motor ships. The hull structure was, for the most part, riveted, though welding was adopted for the assembly of bulkheads and other internal items and for the construction of deckhouses in substantial pre-fabricated sections. The design was distinctive in appearance in that the midship erections were condensed to a small proportion of the full length, the necessary accommodation having been secured by superimposing other deckhouses on the promenade and boat decks, so leaving the main deck roomy and free for working and also for deck cargo. In wartime, tanks and differing kinds of military transport, planes, locomotives, motor torpedo boats, tugs, landing craft, workboats and other items of military equipment were frequently in the cargo manifests and for this the upper deck was designed to cater for substantial loads without special reinforcement. For working the cargo there were electric cargo winches and four derrick-post masts fitted with twelve 5-ton and six 10-ton derricks, with facilities for a 50-ton lift on the foremast, an 80-ton lift at the mainmast and a 30-ton lift on the jigger mast, certain to be useful for postwar Eastern trades.

Propulsion for the first vessels in the series was by double reduction geared turbines, with the boilers disposed transversely, one at each side of the ship and with the boilers and turbines accommodated in a single compartment. Some later vessels were given oil engines, these vessels being fitted with a shorter, wider funnel.

The first 'Standard Fast' ship completed was the *Empire Chieftain* in October 1943, followed by the *Empire Regent* in the November. Altogether, twelve 'Empire'-named ships were completed for the Ministry of War Transport; one was transferred to the Dutch flag on completion in 1944, some others were built under licence, while other hulls still under construction at the end of the war were sold and altered on the stocks for their new owners' trade; included was Anchor Line Ltd., which added *Egidia*, *Elysia* and *Eucadia* to its fleet, and Canadian Pacific, which had four with diesel-electric propulsion built, three by Lithgows and one by the Fairfield yard.

Built by Caledon Shipbuilding & Engineering Co. Ltd., Dundee

404 *Empire Captain* 9,875 gt, 497.5 ft (oa), 475.8 ft × 64 ft. Engines: two steam turbines. Single screw.
Launched: 25.2.1944.
Completed: 7.1.1944.
1946: *Beaverburn* (Canadian Pacific SS Ltd.).

1960: *Bennachie* (Ben Line Steamers Ltd.).
1964: *Silvana* (Atlantic Navigation Corpn. Ltd. (W. H. Eddie Hsu, Formosa)).
6.4.1971: Arrived Kaohsiung for breaking up.

405 (Laid down as) *Empire Albion* 9,864 gt. Details as Yard No. 404.

Launched: 23.5.1944.
Completed: 9.1944 as *Terborch* for the Royal
Netherlands Government.
1946: *Eemdijk* (Nederlandsche Amerikaansche
Stoom. Maats., Rotterdam).
1960: *Orient Merchant* (Orient Mid-East Line).
27.4.1965: Aground, near Port Colborne, Lake Erie
(voyage: Chicago/Far East).
8.5.1965: Refloated, extensive bottom damage.
Constructive total loss. Sold.
1965: *Zambezi* (Cia. Nav. Labrador S.A., Panama).
19.11.1967: Arrived Kaohsiung for breaking up.

406   *Empire Kitchener* 9,881 gt. Details as Yard No.
404.
Launched: 18.8.1944.
Completed: 12.1944.
1946: *Beaverford* (Canadian Pacific SS Ltd.).
1963: *Hulda* (Alliance Marine Corpn., Panama (P.S.
Li, Hong Kong)).
1966: (International Marine Development Corpn.,
Liberia (Y. C. Cheng, New York)).
18.8.1969: Broke moorings during hurricane at
Gulfport; aground at Camille, Mississippi;
constructive total loss; sold for dismantling and broken
up 'as lies'.

407   *Empire Life* 9,879 gt. Details as Yard No. 404.
Launched: 12.1.1945.
Completed: 5.1945.
1946: *Good Hope Castle* (Union-Castle Mail SS Co.
Ltd.).
14.7.1959: Arrived Hong Kong for breaking up.

422   (Laid down as) *Empire —— 10,116 gt, 497.6 ft
(oa), 472.3 ft × 64.2 ft. Engines: Oil.
Launched: 30.6.1946.
Completed: 12.1946.
Laid down as a fast cargo motorship for the
M.O.W.T., but acquired by the Royal Netherlands
Government and completed as *Modjokerto* for
Rotterdamsche Lloyd for service between Holland
and the Dutch East Indies.
1963: *Dona Rita* (Socrates Nav. Co. Ltd. S.A.,
Panama (A. J. & D. J. Chandris, Greece)).
1968: *Atlas Promoter* (Hyundai International Inc.,
S. Korea).
23.9.1972: Arrived Kaohsiung for breaking up.

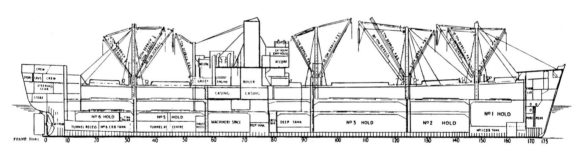

The standard fast cargo liner.

Built by C. Connell & Co. Ltd., Scotstoun, Glasgow

446 *Empire Wilson* 9,916 gt, 497.5 ft (oa), 475.7 ft × 64.3 ft. Engines: Oil.
Launched: 18.8.1944.
Completed: 12.1944.

1946: *Kenilworth Castle* (Union-Castle Mail SS Co. Ltd.).
4.6.1967: Arrived Hong Kong for breaking up.

Built by Furness Shipbuilding Co. Ltd., Haverton Hill-on-Tees

354 *Empire Chieftain* 9,904 gt, 497.6 ft (oa), 475.5 ft × 64.4 ft. Engines: two steam turbines.
Launched: 20.5.1943.
Completed: 10.1943.
1946: *Loch Ryan* (Royal Mail Lines Ltd.).
1960: *Fair Ryan* (Argonaut Shipping & Trading Co. Ltd., London).
2.7.1960: Arrived Nagasaki for breaking up.

355 *Empire Regent* 9,904 gt. Details as Yard No. 354.

Launched: 17.7.1943.
Completed: 11.1943.
1946: *Black Prince* (Rio Cape Line Ltd. (Furness, Withy & Co. Ltd.)).
1949: *Zealandic* (Shaw, Savill & Albion Co. Ltd. (charter)).
1952: *Beaverlodge* (Canadian Pacific Steamships Ltd.).
1960: *Benhiant* (Ben Line Steamers Ltd.).
1970: *Venus* (Witty Cia. Nav. S.A., Cyprus (Troodos Shipping & Trading Ltd., London)).
16.7.1971: Arrived Kaohsiung for breaking up.

Built by Sir J. Laing & Sons Ltd., Sunderland

751 *Empire Paragon* 9,892 gt, 500.3 ft (oa), 475.4 ft × 64.1 ft. Engines: three steam turbines.
Launched: 25.2.1944.
Completed: 8.1944.

1946: *Pinjarra* (Peninsular & Oriental SN Co. Ltd.).
1962: *Hongkong Importer* (International Export Lines Ltd. (C. Y. Tung, Hong Kong)).
26.12.1969: Arrived Kaohsiung for breaking up.

Built by Lithgows Ltd., Port Glasgow

994 *Empire Rawlinson* 9,912 gt, 497.4 ft (oa), 476 ft × 64.3 ft. Engines: Oil.
Launched: 22.6.1944.
Completed: 11.1944.
1946: *Monkay* (Government of France).
1950: (Cie. des Messageries Maritimes, France).
1959: *Dimitros* (Cia. Mar. Marmara S.A., Panama).
1969: *Tropero* (S.A. Widsom Ltda., Panama (A. Bottacchi S.A., Argentina)).
1.2.1972: Arrived Campana, Argentina for breaking up.

995 *Empire Haig* 9,923 gt. Details as Yard No. 994.
Launched: 6.10.1944.
Completed: 12.1944.
1946: *Dryden* (Lamport & Holt Ltd.).
1952: *Fremantle Star* (Blue Star Line Ltd.).
1957: renamed *Catalina Star*.
1963: *Devis* (Lamport & Holt Ltd. (bareboat charter)).
1969: *Mondia* (Bry Overseas Navigation Inc. (Panama)).
23.12.1969: Arrived Kaohsiung for breaking up.

Built by J. L. Thompson & Sons Ltd., Sunderland

631   *Empire Dynasty* 9,905 gt, 500.3 ft (oa), 475.4 ft × 64.1 ft. Engines: two steam turbines.
Launched: 22.5.1944.
Completed: 11.1944.
1946: *Eastern* (Eastern & Australian SS Co. Ltd., London).
1965: *Dori* (Eddie SS Co. Ltd. (W. H. Eddie Hsu, Taiwan)).
4.7.1969: Sold for breaking up whilst lying at Kaohsiung.

633   *Empire Allenby* 9,904 gt. Details as Yard No. 631.
Launched: 18.10.1944.
Completed: 6.1945.
1946: *Drakensburg Castle* (Union-Castle Mail SS Co. Ltd.).

5.8.1959: Arrived Hong Kong for breaking up.

635   *Empire Joy* 9,895 gt. Details as Yard No. 631.
Launched: 13.3.1945.
Completed: 12.1945.
1946: *Nellore* (Eastern & Australian SS Co. Ltd., London).
1966: *Oriana* (Austin Navigation Corpn. Ltd., Panama).
31.12.1966: Caught fire whilst moored in Kaohsiung harbour when removing partitions from hold. Burnt out; flooded by water used for fire-fighting; grounded.
1.1.1967: Fire extinguished, and:
4.1.1967: Refloated, but constructive total loss. Sold, and
12.1967: Scrapped Kaohsiung.

The 'Standard Fast'-type cargo liner *Empire Paragon*. (Sir J. Laing & Sons Ltd., Yard No. 751.)   *National Maritime Museum*

PART FIVE

HEAVY LIFT SHIPS

The heavy-lift ships were constructed on the basic design of the *Belpareil*, one of a fleet of ships which was built up between the wars by Christen Smith & Company, Oslo, for the movement of locomotives, tugs, lightships, lighters and other similar heavy and bulky cargo. The ships were of Norwegian registry with names prefixed 'Bel', under Belships Co. Ltd., and when war broke out there were five in the fleet, the largest being the twin screw *Belpareil*, 7,203 gross tons, of 1926. One ship, *Belmoira*, 3,214 gt of 1928 was torpedoed by submarine *U.102* and sank in position 48.15N 10.30W, but some ships later joined the Allied Merchant Navy, proving such assets with their heavy lift capacity and large unobstructed holds, that Vickers-Armstrongs Ltd. were asked by the Director of Merchant Shipbuilding to build similar ships.

The first was the *Empire Elaine*, with lifting equipment to 120 tons in each of three derricks, a 20 tons more lifting capacity that those of the *Belpareil*. Another difference was that the *Empire Elaine* was of single screw propulsion. Forward of the machinery were three large cargo holds, the two forward being separated by a cross bunker. Six main transverse water/oil-tight bulkheads extending to the upper deck were fitted.

Most important in the design was the cargo-handling equipment. Three derrick post masts, one forward and two abaft the amidship deckhouse were capable of supporting heavy loads on the derricks under all working conditions.

After completion of the *Empire Elaine*, a faster type for similar service was ordered from Vickers-Armstrongs and for more speed and power the ships were given steam turbines for propulsion, which needed more fuel storage for long-range working. The features were generally the same as the first pair, with large hatches, unobstructed holds and 120-ton derricks, as well as six 10-ton and six 5-ton. However, the new type was lengthened to obtain the same capacity, with an increase in speed from twelve to fifteen knots.

The final group of four were built by the Greenock Dockyard Co. Ltd., but as production of turbine sets had become strained, the ships were fitted with a turbine connected to an electric motor to drive a single screw.

Built by Vickers-Armstrongs Ltd., Barrow

856 *Empire Elaine* 7,513 gt, 10,300 tdw, 433.4 ft (oa), 416 ft × 66.7 ft. Engines: Oil. Launched: 30.7.1942.

Completed: 11.1942.
1947: *John Lyras* (Marine Enterprises Ltd. (Lyras & Lemos Bros. Ltd., London).

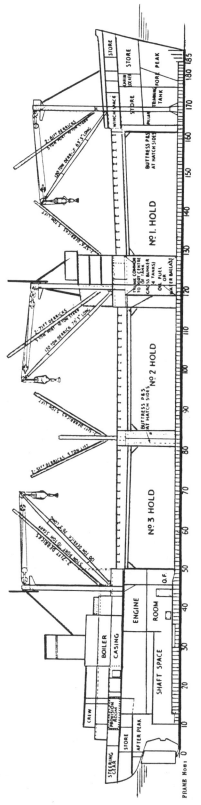

The 11-knot 'Bel'-type crane-ship.

The standard fast 'Bel'-type crane-ship.

The *Empire Athelstan* as Ben Line's *Benalbanach*, September 1953. (Vickers–Armstrongs Ltd., Newcastle, Yard No. 94.)

Launched as *Empire Ethelbert*, this ship was completed as the Norwegian *Beljeanne* in 1947. (Vickers–Armstrongs Ltd., Newcastle, Yard No. 95.)   *Skyfotos*

The *Empire Admiral*, June 1947. (Vickers–Armstrongs Ltd., Barrow, Yard No. 859.)   *Tom Rayner collection*

1959: (Viking Shipping Corp., Panama (Lyras Bros. Ltd., London)).
1970: *Boundary* (New Frontier Shipping Co. Inc., Panama (Grinrod, Gersigny & Co. (Pty.) Ltd., Durban)).
9.1972: Arrived Kaohsiung for breaking up.

857   *Empire Charmian* 7,513 gt, Details as Yard No. 856.
Launched: 25.11.1942.
Completed: 3.1943.
1951: *Vercharmian* (Vergottis Ltd., London).
31.5.1961: Struck rocks and grounded when entering Mormugao, India (voyage: Antwerp/Colombo). Refloated and:
7.7.1961: Sailed from port, leaking; put back to Mormugao Bay; beached.
5.10.1961: Refloated, towed to Karachi, and:
21.3.1962: Arrived Chittagong, in tow, for breaking up.

858   *Empire Viceroy* 7,803 gt, 10,360 tdw, 469.8 ft (oa), 451 ft × 66.7 ft. Engines: three steam turbines.

Launched: 8.4.1943.
Completed: 8.1943.
1954: *Harry Lundeberg* (Gypsum Carriers Inc. (Kaiser Gypsum Company, U.S.A.)).
1957: Renamed *Ocean Carrier*.
13.11.1971: Laid up Los Angeles.
11.7.1973: Arrived Kaohsiung in tow of tug *Viking* (1953, 497 gt) for breaking up.

859   *Empire Admiral* 7,884 gt. Details as Yard No. 858, but: Engines: two steam turbines.
Launched: 26.3.1945.
Completed: 8.1945.
1947: *Peter Dal* (Dalhousie Steam & Motor Shipping Co. Ltd., London).
1951: *Benledi* (Ben Line Steamers Ltd.).
1963: *Andros Tommeno* (Andros Navigation Co. Ltd., Nassau).
1964: (Frank Shipping Co. Ltd., Liberia).
1966: *Unique Carrier* (Unique Marine Corp., Liberia (P. S. Li, Hong Kong)).
27.2.1969: Arrived Kaohsiung for breaking up.

Built by Vickers-Armstrongs Ltd., Newcastle

94   *Empire Athelstan* 7,795 gt, 10,360 tdw, 469.8 ft (oa), 451 ft × 66.7 ft. Engines: two steam turbines.
Launched: 15.1.1946.
Completed: 6.1946.
1947: *Benalbanach* (Ben Line Steamers Ltd.).
1965: *Camelot* (Ministry of Transport (British India SN Co. Ltd.)).
1969: (Board of Trade Sea Transport Branch).
1969: *Dragon Castle* (Mercur Shipping Enterprise S.A., Panama).
1975: (Cuatebol Shipping S.A., Panama (Soc. Italia Gestioni, Italy)).
5.12.1975: Arrived Split for breaking up.

95   (Laid down as) *Empire Ethelbert* 7,843 gt. Details as Yard No. 94.
Launched: 14.8.1946.
Completed: 1.1947 as *Beljeanne* for Belships Co. Ltd. (C. Smith & Co., Norway).
1964: *Southern Cross* (Bacong Shipping Co. S.A., Panama (Southern Industrial Projects Inc., Philippines)).
1968: Renamed *Southern Hope*.
1968: *Virginia Second* (Peoples Bank & Trust Co. (M. M. Shipping Lines Inc., Philippines)).
1.1969: Arrived Aioi for breaking up.

Built by Greenock Dockyard Co. Ltd.

458   *Empire Byng* 7,832 gt, 10,000 tdw, 469.7 ft (oa), 451.3 ft × 66.9 ft. Engines: Steam turbine to electric motor. 14 knots.
Launched: 16.11.1944.
Completed: 5.1945.
1951: *Peter Dal II* (Dalhousie Steam & Motorshipping Co. Ltd. (Nomikos (London) Ltd.)).

1954: (Novacastria Shipping Co. Ltd. (Nomikos (London) Ltd.)).
1955: *Benwyvis* (Ben Line Steamers Ltd.).
1963: *Southern Comet* (Bacong Shipping Co. S.A., Panama (Southern Industrial Projects Inc., Manila)).
1968: *Marites* (Peoples Bank & Trust Co., Panama (M. M. Shipping Lines Inc., Manila)).

19.11.1970: Grounded off breakwater, Manila Bay, Philippines, in typhoon 'Patsy'.
29.11.1970: Refloated with bottom damage; anchored in South Harbour. Sold and
8.2.1972: Arrived Hong Kong for breaking up.

460   *Empire Marshal* 7,836 gt. Details as Yard No. 458.
Launched: 14.5.1945.
Completed: 11.1945.
1947: (Pandelis Shipping Co. Ltd., London).
14.7.1952:   Explosion in engine room whilst at Pusan, Korea.
8.1952: Towed to Nagasaki; laid up. Constructive total loss.
1954: Sold, and 20.12.1954: Left in tow, bound for Hong Kong for repair. Refitted by Taikoo Dockyard & Eng. Co., with oil engines (fitted 1946) taken from tanker *Elax* (1927, 7,403 gt), which was bought for the purpose. The hull of the tanker was scrapped.
1955: *Bermuda Trader* (Trader Line Ltd., Bermuda (Mollers Ltd., Hong Kong)).
9.3.1965: Aground in heavy weather near Sakata, Japan, 38.57N 139.49E (voyage: Timaru/ Sakata – timber).
14.3.1965: Broke in two. Constructive total loss.
10.1965 and 9.1966: Both parts refloated and towed to Japanese shipbreakers.

An example of the versatile capacity of these ships can be shown by just two vessels: when the *Empire Byng* sailed on her maiden voyage in May 1945, bound for Bombay, she had five TID-type tugs (Nos. 125/126 and 131/133) and landing craft stowed on deck. The maiden voyage of the *Empire Marshal* was made in November 1945, when she loaded nineteen small craft, including a number of TID tugs and lighters. But with this ship nine TID tugs (Nos. 127/128, 144/149 and 151) were stowed below deck, with the remaining ten craft on the upper deck, overhanging the bulwark rail. Also stowed on deck, athwartships, was an oil separator 100 feet in length. Loading of the small ships was done at Birkenhead, but with an overhang of sixteen feet each side for the separator, the *Empire Marshal* had to load it in the Gladstone Dock, Liverpool, where the locks were wide enough to allow the ship access to the river.

At the time this was regarded as one of the most cumbersome of loads ever carried on one ship's deck. The *Empire Marshal* sailed from Liverpool on 19 November 1945 and from the Clyde on the 24th, bound for Hong Kong.

461   *Empire Wallace* 7,800 gt. Details as Yard No. 458.
Launched: 4.9.1945.
Completed: 2.1946.
1956: *Benarty* (Ben Line Steamers Ltd.).
1962: Arrived Hong Kong. Sold. Engines removed for new installation.
1.9.1962: Grounded North Point, Hong Kong, in typhoon 'Wanda', then ashore at east end of Kowloon docks.
14.9.1962: Refloated; repaired, fitted with oil engine, and
1963: *Elys Harbour* (Harbour Line Ltd., Bermuda (Mollers Ltd., Hong Kong)).
1967: *Unique Developer* (Unique Development Co. Inc., Liberia (R. Y. Chen, Hong Kong)).
1969: *Fermenco* (Taboga Enterprises Inc., Panama).
1973: (Cia. Agropecuaria y Maritima Santa Rosa Ltd., Colombia).
1973: (Taboga Enterprises Inc., Panama).
1974: *Avalon* (Wayne Inc., Panama (A. Ochoa y Cia. Ltd., Colombia)).
1981: *Bahia Colombia* (Pizano S.A. (Abello Cia. Ltda., Barranquilla)).

462   *Empire Canute* 7,908 gt. Details as Yard No. 458.
Launched: 24.12.1945.
Completed: 6.1947 as *Belocean* for Belships Co. Ltd. (C. Smith & Co., Oslo).
10.1954: (Oil engines installed).
1964: *Southern Star* (Bacong Shipping Co. S.A., Panama (Southern Industrial Products Inc., Manila)).
1968: *Marie Ann* (Manila Interocean Lines Inc., Manila).
29.7.1976: Arrived Gadani Beach, Karachi, for breaking up.

Pioneer of the heavy-lift ship was shipowner Captain Christen Smith, with experience in the Norwegian Navy, who founded Christen Smith & Company, Oslo, in 1920.

At that time Armstrong, Whitworth & Company were constructing large numbers of steam locomotives for overseas railways, one large contract for 200 locomotives and their tenders being for the war-torn Belgian State Railways. It was then that Captain Smith saw his opportunity of putting his ideas into reality and secured the work of carrying the new locomotives, the loading and discharging to be done by his methods of lifting gear and slings, with some assistance from quayside cranes. The locomotives, able to be shipped complete, were then ready for self movement within a day of discharge.

Two steamships were acquired and converted to his plans and in 1921 twenty-four locomotives were moved from Elswick to Antwerp in the 2,100 gt *Belgot* and *Belfri*, the remaining 176 being moved in 1922.

But there was little enthusiasm for the idea until Christen Smith was entrusted with a big shipment of locomotives and their tenders for the Bombay, Baroda and Central India Railway and he was soon in Bombay to study port discharge facilities. In 1924 shipments were carried for the Argentine Railways and at Buenos Aires complete discharge was made of seventeen locomotives without quay crane assistance.

Adding to several one-ship companies, two larger 7,200 gt engine-aft motorships, *Beljeanne* and *Belpareil* were built by Armstrong Whitworth in 1926 and it was from this design that the first British wartime pair were based.

In 1935 the one-ship companies were amalgamated to form Belships Company Ltd., Skibs-A/S.

The *Empire Viceroy*, with a deck cargo of barges, TID-type tugs and a VIC-lighter. (Vickers-Armstrongs Ltd., Barrow, Yard No. 858.)   *Vickers Ltd.*

PART SIX

SCANDINAVIAN TYPE SHIPS

The 'three-island' ship of 4,700 tdw was based on the so-called 'Scandinavian' design of general cargo carrier in which Wm. Gray & Company played the leading part, constructing twenty-five ships between 1941 and 1944.

A single-deck ship, with high bulwarks in the wells, enabled deck cargoes, especially timber, to be carried without obstruction. All lifting and handling gear was placed on the three islands, the poop length 33 ft, bridge 82 ft and forecastle 34 ft. The hull length was 327.9 ft (oa), 315.5 ft (bp) and breadth 46.5 ft; propulsion was by triple expansion engines which gave 10 knots.

Although convoys to North Russia had been introduced in the summer of 1941, the entry of the United States into the war against the three Axis powers in the following December promoted huge programmes of armament production for 1942, in both America and Great Britain. But when heavy shipments of military aid to Russia began in 1942, problems arose in discharge at the North Russian ports. Although the newer British ships were equipped with heavy lift derricks, the ships were insufficient in number and rather than send more to the hard-pressed shipyards for fitting heavier lifting equipment, some 'Scandinavian'-type ships were adapted as crane ships and equipped with derricks of a length capable of lifting from the centre of a 10,000 tdw ship when placed alongside, and landing on the opposite side, the reach overside being thirty feet.

A number of ships were so adapted, with two 50-ton, two 15-ton and four 5-ton derricks, at the same time the ships being fitted out for Arctic service. They were quite successful in speeding up the turn-round of convoys in the North Russian ports, for in the summer of 1942 the demand for shipping was acute and not only was there the hazard of bombing of ports, but the cargoes of armour were urgently needed for the great tank battles of that time.

Some ships were later equipped with one 80-ton and one 50-ton derrick instead of two of 50-ton capacity. One ship, *Nordeflinge* was completed by Wm. Gray & Co. Ltd., under licence for Constants Ltd., Cardiff, in 1942.

Built by William Gray & Co. Ltd., West Hartlepool

1119 *Empire Wolfe* 2,888 gt.
Launched: 26.7.1941.
Completed: 9.1941.
1946: *Wicklow Head* (Ulster SS Co. Ltd. (G. Heyn & Sons Ltd.)).

2.5.1947: Ashore in fog at Joli Point, Port Mouton Island, Nova Scotia. Pounded by heavy seas; flooded. Salvage proposed, but:
8–12.6.1947: Further damaged in heavy weather. Abandoned. Constructive total loss (voyage: Ardrossan/St. John, N.B. – ballast).

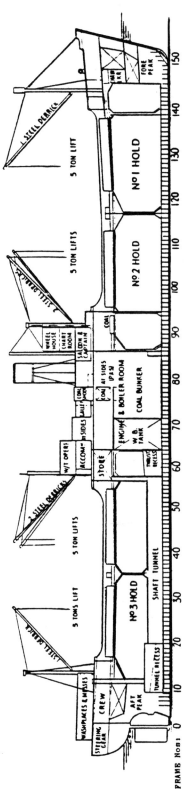

The 'Scandinavian'-type tramp.

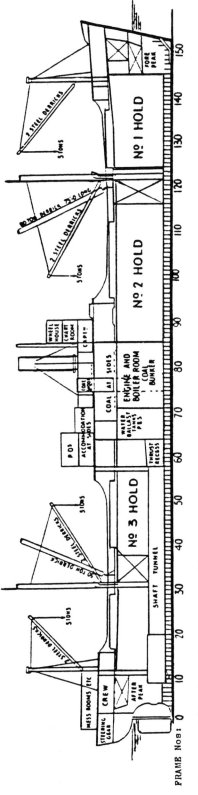

The converted 'Scandinavian'-type as a crane-ship.

1120 *Empire Newcomen* 2,840 gt.
Launched: 6.9.1941.
Completed: 11.1941.
30.11.1941: Sunk by E-boat torpedo, five miles south of Dudgeon Light, off Cromer, Norfolk (voyage: London/Sunderland).

1125 *Empire Carey* 2,833 gt.
Launched: 20.10.1941.
Completed: 12.1941.
1942: *Ragnhild* (Government of Norway).
1946: *Penelope* (John Wilson's Rederi, Norway).
1950: (Rederi A/B Pandia, Finland).
1955: (Lundqvist–Rederierna, Finland).
11.1972: Sold (Wackatz & Co., Gothenburg): rebuilt as a grain store/floating warehouse (engines removed).

1126 *Empire Pilgrim* 2,828 gt.
Launched: 20.11.1941.
Completed: 1.1942.
25.1.1942: Ashore in blizzard fourteen miles north of Aberdeen. Holed and flooded; abandoned.
5.2.1942: Salvage commenced, and:
16.2.1942: Refloated; towed to Aberdeen.
21.3.1942: Towed to Blyth by tug *Empire Larch*; repaired.
1942: *Astrid* (Government of Norway).
1945: *Tindefjell* (A/S Granli (R. Ugelstad, Norway)).
1948: *Ringhorn* (A. Schjelderup, Norway).
1951: (Jansens Rederi A/S (I. Jansen, Norway)).
1958: *Indonor* (Pan-Norse SS Co. (Wallem & Co., Hong Kong)).
3.2.1960: Aground on reef at Benkoan Island, Indonesia.
7.2.1960: Slipped off reef; sank. Total loss (voyage: Palembang/Surabaya).

1129 *Empire Tennyson* 2,880 gt.
Launched: 19.1.1942.
Completed: 3.1942.
1.10.1942: Sunk by submarine (*U.175*) torpedo, south-east of Trinidad, 09.27N 60.05W.

1130 *Empire Elgar* 2,847 gt.
Launched: 17.2.1942.
Completed: 4.1942.
1947: *Sea Minstrel* (Dover Navigation Co. Ltd., London).
1951: *Marandellas* (Drayton SS Co. Ltd., Newcastle).
1956: *Edward Jansen* (I. Jansen, Norway).
1960: *Slitan* (Skibs A/S Katlander, Norway).
1961: *Pirin* (Navigation Maritime Bulgare (Government of Bulgaria)).
1.10.1965: Arrived Split for breaking up.

1131 *Empire Caxton* 2,873 gt.
Launched: 31.3.1942.
Completed: 5.1942.
1945: *Letchworth* (Watergate SS Co. Ltd. (R. S. Dalgliesh Ltd., Newcastle)).
1956: *Peterland* (Sagland Ltd. (Buries, Markes Ltd.)).
1959: *Pamit* (Padre Cia. Nav. S.A. (A. Halcoussis & Co., Greece)).
1962: *Christos* (Solmare Cia. Mar. S.A. (T. Samourkas, Greece)).
31.3.1967: Aground on Kandeliusa Island, south of Kos, Greece (voyage: Constanza/Hodeidah – sugar). Floated off, but sprang leaks in Aegean Sea, and:
1.4.1967: Sank north of Crete, 36.32N 26.57E.

1132 *Empire Gareth* 2,873 gt.
Launched: 1.5.1942.
Completed: 6.1942.
1947: *Athenic* (W. H. Cockerline & Co. Ltd., Hull).
1954: *Astarte* (Soc. Anon. Maritime et Commerciale, Switzerland).
1960: *Yanix* (A. Halcoussis & Co., Greece).
1961: *Nicos* (Nicos Cia. Nav. S.A. (A. Halcoussis & Co., Greece)).
7.1.1968: Arrived Palermo, in tow, with machinery damage due to heavy weather (voyage: Augusta/Sfax). Laid up.
6.5.1968: Arrived Spezia, in tow, for breaking up.

1135 *Empire Boswell* 2,898 gt.
Launched: 2.6.1942.
Completed: 8.1942.
1947: *Aviswell* (Aviation & Shipping Co. Ltd. (Purvis Shipping Co. Ltd., London)).
1949: *Seniority* (F. T. Everard & Son Ltd.).
7.11.1950: Ashore at Leinish Point, Inner Hebrides, 56.57N 7.25W in heavy weather. Refloated; settled again, and:
8.11.1950: Sank off Bo Vich Chuan Rock (voyage: Ellesmere Port/Risor – ballast).

1136 *Empire Patriot* 2,893 gt.
Launched: 29.6.1942.
Completed: 8.1942.
1946: *Struan* (The South Georgia Co. Ltd. (Chr. Salvesen & Co.)).
1960: *Zannis* (Marconato Cia. Nav. S.A., Panama).
1967: *Orontes* (V. Roussos, Greece).
1970: (Marconato Cia. Nav. S.A., Panama (G. D. Patrikios Ltd., Greece)).
2.1974: Scrapped Istanbul.

1140 *Empire Lorenzo* 2,865 gt.
Launched: 25.9.1942.
Completed 12.1942.

1946: *Baron Elcho* (Hogarth Shipping Co. Ltd.
(H. Hogarth & Sons)).
1955: *Kismet II* (Cia. Mar. Ircar S.A., Liberia).
25.11.1955: Steering gear disabled; aground in
snowstorm on reef at Cape Breton Island,
47.5N 60.3W (voyage: Philadelphia/Summerside,
Prince Edward Island – ballast). Abandoned; total
loss.

1143   *Empire Record* 2,902 gt.
Launched: 24.10.1942.
Completed: 12.1942.
1948: *Stanway* (Stanhope SS Co. Ltd.).
1951: *Yorkbrook* (Williamson Shipping Co. Ltd.
(Comben, Longstaff & Co. Ltd.)).
1954: *Elisabeth Jansen* (I. Jansen, Norway).
1959: *Celia B* (Marine Venture Corp., New York).
1963: *Saint Mary* (Prymo Meltemi Cia. Nav. S.A.,
Panama).
1964: *Sea Maid* (Angelmar Shipping Co., Panama).
7.1.1965: Lost propeller, engine damaged, north-east
of Bonaire, N. Antilles
(voyage: Houston/Demerara – ballast).
11.1.1965: Towed to Willemstad; abandoned.
Constructive total loss; sold for scrapping at Curaçao,
but resold. Towed to Rotterdam, thence Spain and:
3.1969: Scrapped Bilbao.

1144   *Empire Candida* 2,908 gt.
Launched: 8.12.1942.
Completed: 2.1943.
1947: *Burdale* (Zinal Shipping Co. (Burness Shipping
Co. Ltd.)).
1948: *Peldale* ('Z' Shipping Co. (Burness Shipping
Co. Ltd.)).
1954: *Statius Jansen* (Jansens Rederi A/S, Norway).
1959: *Sunny* (New China SS Co. (Wallem & Co.,
Hong Kong)).
1961: *Indarung* (P. T. Maskapai Pelayaran Sumatera,
Djakarta).
5.4.1969: Leaking, north of Philippines
20.10N 120.25E (voyage: Indonesia to shipbreakers).
Towage not possible due to lack of ropes or wires on
board. Escorted, and:
8.4.1969: Arrived Kaohsiung for breaking up.

1145   *Empire Harmony* 2,906 gt.
Launched: 8.1.1943.
Completed: 3.1943.
1947: *Avisbrook* (Aviation & Shipping Co. Ltd.
(Purvis Shipping Co. Ltd., London)).
1950: *Menastone* (T. Stone (Shipping) Ltd. (Stone &
Rolfe Ltd., Swansea)).
1961: *Capetan Panaos* (Ypapanti A.S., Panama (K. &
M. Shipbrokers Ltd., London)).
1966: (Astrocierto Cia. Nav., Panama (N. J.
Nomikos, Greece)).

6/7.5.1969: Aground at Kilyos, near Black Sea
entrance to Bosporus (voyage: Galatz/
Alexandria – timber).
22.5.1969: Refloated, towed in; beached near
Buyukdere.
9.8.1969: Refloated again; cargo discharged, and:
2.11.1969: Arrived Piraeus, in tow, for breaking up.

1146   *Empire Valour* 2,906 gt.
Launched: 22.2.1943.
Completed: 5.1943.
1948: *Eskgarth* (Eskgarth Shipping Co. Ltd. (H. M.
Lund, London)).
1951: *Uskmouth* (Uskside SS Co. Ltd. (R. W. Jones
& Co., Newport)).
1963: *Alexandra K* (Cia. Marabello San Nicolas,
Panama).
1968: *Aristiois II* (Pateras Bros. Ltd., Greece).
1969: (Reinato Marino Nav., S.A. Panama).
6.1971: Scrapped Piraeus.

1149   *Empire Mountain* 2,906 gt.
Launched: 3.4.1943.
Completed: 6.1943.
1951: *Hannah Moller* (Moller Line Ltd. (Mollers Ltd.,
Hong Kong)).
1951: *Mount Parker* (Mount Line Ltd. (Mollers Ltd.,
Hong Kong)).
1952: *Carcoola* (Australian Shipping Board).
1956: *Tees Breeze* (Cambay Prince SS Co. Ltd.
(J. Manners & Co. Ltd., Hong Kong)).
1964: *Timur* (San Roberto SS Co. S.A., Panama
(J. Manners & Co. Ltd., Hong Kong)).
1966: *Victoria Trader* (Oriental Trader Nav. Co. S.A.,
Panama (China Pacific Navigation Co. Ltd., Hong
Kong)).
7.1967: Scrapped Kaohsiung.

1150   *Empire Buttress* 2,905 gt.
Launched: 6.5.1943.
Completed: 7.1943.
1946: *Wallsend* (Burnett SS Co. Ltd., Newcastle).
1959: *Bordagain* (Bordagain Shipping Co. Ltd.,
Liberia, (R. de la Sota Jr., France)).
1967: *Daring* (Cia. de Nav. Pinares S.A., Panama).
5.1976: Scrapped Split.

1153   *Empire Gulliver* 2,905 gt.
Launched: 8.6.1943.
Completed: 9.1943.
1946: *Bharatkhand* (J. & C. Harrison Ltd., London).
1954: (Bharat Line Ltd., India).
9.1962: Scrapped Bombay.

1156   *Empire Seaman* 2,905 gt.
Launched: 17.7.1943.

Completed: 10.1943.
1946: *Burnhope* (Burnett SS Co. Ltd., Newcastle).
1961: *Antonios Michalos* (N. Michalos & Sons
Maritime Co. Ltd., Greece).
6.3.1968: Struck submerged object; grounded
approaching berth at Braila, Romania. Refloated,
with extensive damage to stern gear.
17.4.1968: Arrived Monfalcone, in tow; discharged.
Constructive total loss. Sold.
27.4.1968: Arrived Trieste, in tow, for breaking up,
and:
5.1969: Scrapped Trieste.

1157   *Empire Ransom* 2,905 gt.
Launched: 31.8.1943.
Completed: 11.1943.
1946: *Baron Elibank* (Kelvin Shipping Co. Ltd.
(H. Hogarth & Sons Ltd.)).
1959: *Armenistis* (Empros Shipping Co. Ltd., Greece).
1966: (Empros Shipping Co., Special S.A., Greece).
6.7.1971: Arrived Tamise, Belgium, for breaking up.

1159   *Empire Beaconsfield* 2,905 gt.
Launched: 2.10.1943.
Completed: 12.1943.
1946: *Hawkinge* (Constants (South Wales) Ltd.,
Cardiff).
1951: *Angusbrae* (Dundee, Perth & London Shipping
Co. Ltd., Dundee).
1956: *Hispania* (Wm. Muller & Co. N.V.,
Rotterdam).
1960: *Dia* (West End Corp., Panama (P. E. Panas,
Greece)).
14.10.1964: Sank after springing a leak south of
Savona, 44.12N 8.38W (voyage: Antwerp/
Bourgas – superphosphate).

1160   *Empire Harcourt* 2,905 gt.

Launched: 30.10.1943.
Completed: 1.1944.
1946: *Baron Ailsa* (Kelvin Shipping Co. Ltd.
(H. Hogarth & Sons Ltd.)).
1955: *Iberia* (W. H. Muller & Co. N.V., Rotterdam).
1962: *Cycladiki Doxa* (Tankers Finance Corp., Greece
(S. Restis, Greece)).
1964: *Mount Sinai* (Cia. Mar. Sarita S.A., Greece
(N. Sotirakis & Co., Greece)).
4.1972: Scrapped Perama.

1163   *Empire Sedley* 2,905 gt.
Launched: 11.12.1943.
Completed: 2.1944.
1945: *Intendant J. Patrizi* (Government of France).
1949: *Menhir Braz* (Les Cargoes Algeriennes, S.A.).
1957: *Athina* (Pamel Shipping Co. (Michaelides et
Cie. S.A.R.L., Marseilles).
14.3.1962: Fire in cargo at St. Louis du Rhône, near
Port de Bouc, France.
16.3.1962: Fire extinguished; but constructive total
loss.
8.1962: Scrapped La Seyne.

1164   *Empire Osborne* 2,906 gt.
Launched: 28.1.1944.
Completed: 3.1944.
20.12.1944: Damaged by mine in River Seine.
Repaired.
1946: *Uskport* (Uskport SS Co. Ltd. (R. W. Jones &
Co., Newport)).
1957: *Rio Damuji* (Empresa Nav. Mambisa
(Government of Cuba)).
3.2.1970: Aground near Punta Maya, Varadero
Peninsula, north coast of Cuba, 23.06N 81.24W
(voyage: Neuritas/Havana – general). Equipment
removed; ship then abandoned after heavy weather
tore shell plating from side of ship.

Built by Ailsa Shipbuilding Co. Ltd., Troon, Ayrshire

441   *Empire Toiler* 2,932 gt.
Launched: 15.4.1942.
Completed: 6.1942.
1943: *Van Ostade* (Government of the Netherlands).
1947: (K.N.S.M., Holland).
1950: *Etal Manor* (Tanfield SS Co. Ltd., Newcastle).
1955: *Moto* (Pelton SS Co. Ltd., Newcastle).
1960: *Tirso* (Teulada SpA di Nav. (O. Rosini, Italy)).
1962: *Hamal* (Cia. Nav. General S.A. (N. Patella,
Italy)).
5.1969: Scrapped Trieste.

442   *Empire Launcelot* 2,890 gt.
Launched: 13.8.1942.
Completed: 10.1942.
1943: *Belgian Trader* (Government of Belgium).
1946: *Ostende* (Armement Deppe S.A., Belgium).
1954: *Kettwig* (H. Stinnes, Germany).
1963: (Monsun Schiffs. MBH & Co. A.G.,
Germany).
1965: *Honda* (Cia. de Nav. Saborga S.A. (N. Patella,
Italy)).
1974: Scrapped Split.

444   *Empire Jessica* 2,847 gt.
Launched: 24.3.1943.
Completed: 5.1943.
1945: *Joseph Blot* (Government of France).
1954: *Leon Mazzella* (Armement Leon Mazzella et
Cie., Algeria).
1960: *Loris* (Loris Cia. Nav. S.A., Panama).
1966: *Agia Varvara* (Cia. Mar. Santa Barbara S.A.
(N. & J. Vlassopulos Ltd., London)).
1.1975: Scrapped Izmir, Turkey.

447   *Empire Dirk* 2,942 gt.
Launched: 31.8.1943.
Completed: 12.1943.
1951: *Nancy Moller* (Moller Line Ltd., Hong Kong).
1951: *Mount Austin* (Mount Line Ltd. (Mollers Ltd.,
Hong Kong)).
1952: *Coolabah* (Government of Australia).
1956: *Troon Breeze* (Cambay Prince SS Co. Ltd.
(J. Manners & Co. Ltd., Hong Kong)).
1964: *Cachupin* (San Fernando SS Co. Ltd., Panama
(J. Manners & Co. Ltd., Hong Kong)).
1966: *Kowloon No 1* (Shui Cheung Shipping &
Trading Ltd., Hong Kong).
16.9.1967: Aground at Hachinohe, Japan,
40.32N 141.33E. Abandoned.
7.10.1967: Refloated, towed to Yokosuka;
constructive total loss. Sold, and:

6.1968: Scrapped Opama, Japan.

448   *Empire Crusoe* 2,958 gt.
Launched: 11.4.1945.
Completed: 10.1945.
1946: *Greenland* (Currie Line Ltd., Leith).
1955: *Heminge* (Constants Ltd., Cardiff).
1956: *Maria Luisa* (Socoa Shipping Co. Ltd. (R. de la
Sota, France)).
1963: *Santa Kyriaki* (Nereide Cia. Mar. S.A.,
Panama).
24.11.1965: Engine failure in heavy weather; dragged
anchors, aground one mile south of Ymuiden,
Holland (voyage: Cork/Ymuiden – ballast).
8.3.1966: Refloated; towed to Ymuiden. Constructive
total loss. Sold, and:
14.7.1966: Arrived Aviles, in tow, for breaking up.

449   (Launched as) *Empire Warner* 2,961 gt.
Launched: 21.3.1946.
Completed: 6.1946 as *Uskside* for Uskside SS Co.
Ltd. (R. W. Jones & Co., Newport).
1965: *Gero Michalos* (N. Michalos & Sons Maritime
Co. Ltd., Greece).
10.5.1968: Broke moorings in cyclone; aground at
Akyab, Burma, whilst loading rice.
12.5.1968: Partially submerged; breaking up. Total
loss.

Built by Caledon Shipbuilding & Engineering Co. Ltd., Dundee

396   *Empire Bard* 3,114 gt.
Launched: 30.12.1941.
Completed: 3.1942.
1946: *Angusburn* (Dundee, Perth & London Shipping

Co. Ltd., Dundee).
1955: *Brettenham* (Rederi A/B Hildegaard
(F. Lundqvist, Finland)).
24.4.1971: Arrived Carthagena for breaking up.

Built by Grangemouth Dockyard Co. Ltd.

437   *Empire Dunstan* 2,887 gt.
Launched: 19.11.1941.
Completed: 1.1942.
18.11.1943: Sunk by submarine (*U.81*) torpedo in
Ionian Sea, 39.24N 17.40E (voyage: Bona/
Brindisi – mines).

442   *Empire Melody* 2,883 gt.
Launched: 27.8.1942.
Completed: 11.1942.

1946: *Lucy Borchard* (Fairplay Towage & Shipping
Co. Ltd., Avonmouth).
1950: *Nordeflinge* (Constants (South Wales) Ltd.,
Cardiff)).
1955: *Ines* (Socoa Shipping Co. Ltd. (R. de la Sota,
France)).
1962: *Popi K* (Zanlouk Cia. Mar. S.A., Panama).
1968: *Gold Sky* (Astrovlanis Cia. Nav., Panama
(G. Vlanis Shipping Ltd., Greece)).

The Scandinavian-type ship *Empire Toiler*, on completion in 1942. (Ailsa Shipbuilding Co. Ltd., Yard No. 441.)
National Maritime Museum

The *Empire Bard*, fitted with heavy-lift masting. (Caledon Shipbuilding & Engineering Co. Ltd., Yard No. 396.)
Dundee City Archives

The *Empire Southwark*, of the 'Empire Malta'-class, as *Tempo*. (Wm. Gray & Co. Ltd., Yard No. 1181.)
Skyfotos

19.12.1968: Sprang leak, about twenty miles off Gibraltar, 35.57N 4.53W; sank (voyage: Split/ Gizan – cement).

This, however, was not the end of the story, for the loss of the *Gold Sky* led to a long trial in the British Courts of Law, lasting some sixty days, in 1972. The main issue was that of alleged scuttling and the burden of proof, with the ship's owners (the plaintiff) claiming the total loss of their vessel by perils of the sea, whilst the marine insurance underwriter (the defendant) sought that the plaintiff prove this and, furthermore, he alleged scuttling.

Outlining events on the day the ship sank, the court told of the motor boat of the German vessel *Otto Leonhardt* (1967, 23,414 gt) – the vessel which rescued the survivors – transferring them to the salvage tug *Herkules*, whose master then went alongside the *Gold Sky*. He was told that the engines of the ship were submerged and that there was water in Nos. 1, 3 and 4 holds, but he was refused permission to board or to commence salvage by three men still aboard the ship and who were seen frequently to look down an aft inspection hatch, as though watching the water level therein.

From time to time the master of the *Herkules* invited the three to leave the sinking ship, but was always told 'to wait a bit longer'. Eventually, as their vessel began to settle by the stern, they boarded a rubber raft and were towed to the *Herkules*. However, if the *Herkules* had been permitted to get its pumps aboard, the ship could have been saved, and it seemed that the ship's master deliberately kept the salvors off the ship so that it might sink.

The court concluded that no proof had been established of an alleged crack in the ship's side permitting the ingress of water – a witness, the ship's second engineer, failing to notice it on two visits to the engine room; that the plaintiffs stood to gain financially by the loss of the *Gold Sky* due to her high insured value; that the ship sank as soon as payment for carriage of the cargo had been made but whilst she was in calm weather and near the safety of Gibraltar and that the main sea suction valve, repaired at Alexandria in November 1968, had been seen by another witness being tampered with, its fixing bolts being loosened.

In judgment, it was said that the plaintiffs "had not proved, on the balance of probabilities, that the loss of the *Gold Sky* was fortuitous. Indeed, the weight of evidence was to the contrary effect, that the vessel was scuttled with the connivance of her owners."

Built by Sir J. Laing & Sons Ltd., Sunderland

744   *Empire Thackeray* 2,865 gt.
Launched: 1.7.1942.
Completed: 8.1942.
1945: *Thackeray* (Rodney SS Co. Ltd. (Anglo-Danubian Transport Co. Ltd., London)).
27.12.1946: Ashore half-mile west of Outer Cat Island, Cape Froels, near Argentia, N.F. (voyage: Hampton Roads/Botwood – ballast).
24.5.1947: Refloated, taken to St. Johns, N.F. Sold and repaired.

1948: *Theokeetor* (M. S. Polemis (Goulandris Bros. Ltd., Greece)).
1953: *Mozart* (Cia. Commercial Transatlantica S.A., Panama (S. Polemis & Sons Ltd., New York)).
1954: *Micaela* (Cia. Nav. Micaela S.A. (Soc. Arm. Marittimo (SOARMA), Italy)).
1960: *Onorato Secondo* (SOARMA, Italy).
1962: *Jelcz* (Polska Zegluga Morska, Poland)).
5.1968: Scrapped Ystad, Sweden.

The 'Empire Malta' class

Ten more 'Scandinavian'-type ships of a special series and known as the 'Empire Malta' class were completed by Wm. Gray & Co. Ltd., at West Hartlepool in 1944–1945. These were multi-purpose ships and, according to requirements, capable of working with crane lifts to 80 tons, as colliers, as cased-oil carriers, as general purpose cargo vessels or for the transporting of heavy vehicles.

The general measurements of the hull were the same as those of the standard 'Scandinavian' type, but the triple expansion machinery – which gave a service speed of $11\frac{1}{4}$ knots – was placed aft instead of amidships in order to reduce the fire risk when cased oil was carried.

They were well-deck type ships with a poop of 82 ft, raised quarter deck of 197 ft and forecastle of 29 ft. Tonnages were 3,539 gross, 4,310 deadweight and the total grain capacity was 250,700 cu. ft.

There were four holds served by large hatchways, one (No. 3) being 40.5 ft × 26 ft. The transverse bulkheads at either end of No. 3 hold were fitted with portable sections 14 ft wide by 20 ft high. When these were removed the openings gave clear access to Nos. 2 and 4 holds and enabled the vessels to carry in three holds large vehicles, tanks or locomotives which, owing to their size, could only be loaded through one hatchway.

In addition to the total water ballast capacity of 1,327 tons, a hundred tons of permanent ballast was arranged amidships, to assist in limiting the angle of heel during heavy lifts.

The cargo-handling gear was grouped around the masts: the 50-ton and four 3-ton derricks at the forward mast, the mainmast with the 80-ton and a further four 3-ton derricks.

Built by Wm. Gray & Co. Ltd., West Hartlepool

1167 *Empire Malta* 3,539 gt.
Launched: 24.3.1944.
Completed: 5.1944.
1946: (Williamson & Co., Hong Kong). Resold, and:
1946: *Hangsang* (Indo-China SN Co. Ltd., London).
1960: *Slight Wind* (Continental Navigation & Enterprises Ltd., Hong Kong).
1964: *Sunbeam* (Sunbeam Nav. Co. S.A., Panama (Patt, Manfield & Co. Ltd., Hong Kong)).
23.7.1969: Engine breakdown in South China Sea; towed to Kaohsiung. Sold, and
11.1970: Scrapped Kaohsiung.

1168 *Empire Perlis* 3,539 gt.
Launched: 22.5.1944.
Completed: 7.1944.
1946: *Hinsang* (Indo-China SN Co. Ltd., London).
1965: *Kowloon* (Kinabatangan Shipping Co. Ltd., Hong Kong (United China Shipping Co. Ltd., Hong Kong)).
1969: *Horis* (Concordia Kinabatangan Shipping Co., Panama).
25.12.1969: Heavy weather damages to No. 1 hold repaired at Surabaya, Indonesia. Sailed, but
28.12.1969: Water discovered in engine room and Nos. 3 and 4 holds; initially controlled by pumps, but
29.12.1969: Holds and engine room flooded. Abandoned; capsized and sank in Celebes Sea, 200 miles from Tawau, Sabah, 03.53N 119.23E (voyage: Surabaya/Hong Kong).

1169 *Empire Newfoundland* 3,539 gt.
Launched: 6.7.1944.
Completed: 9.1944.
1949: *Ethel Everard* (F. T. Everard & Sons Ltd.).
1954: *Hop Sang* (Indo-China SN Co. Ltd., London).
1962: Renamed *Hang Sang*.
1968: *Hoi Soon* (Fui Nam Co. Ltd., Hong Kong).

1969: (Chan Cheung Manufacturing Co., Somaliland).
3.1970: Scrapped Hong Kong.

1170 *Empire Labrador* 3,539 gt.
Launched: 19.8.1944.
Completed: 10.1944.
1949: *Incharran* (Williamson & Co. Ltd., Hong Kong).
1.5.1950: Seized by Chinese Nationalist warship while on voyage Hong Kong to Macao, with rice. Taken to Lafsami harbour. Released with assistance of H.M.S. *Mounts Bay*; proceeded to Hong Kong.
12.2.1953: Fired on by Chinese Nationalist warships in Formosa Strait when on voyage to Shanghai, following a Chinese Nationalist decree to intercept any vessel trying to enter Chinese mainland ports. Evaded capture; proceeded to Hong Kong.
1955: *Hosang* (Indo-China SN Co. Ltd., London).
1968: *Golden River* (Golden River Shipping Corp. (C. T. Chu, Hong Kong)).
7.4.1970: Arrived Sakaide for breaking up.

1173 *Empire Bermuda* 3,539 gt.
Launched: 30.9.1944.
Completed: 11.1944.
1949: *Hewsang* (Indo-China SN Co. Ltd., London).
1963: *Sunshine* (Sunshine Nav. Co. Ltd. (Patt, Manfield & Co. Ltd., Hong Kong)).
3.1970: Scrapped Kaohsiung.

1174 *Empire Jamaica* 3,538 gt.
Launched: 16.11.1944.
Completed: 1.1945.
1951: *Westway* (Western SS Co. Ltd. (Wang Kee & Co., Hong Kong)).
1958: *Djajapratama* (Djakarta Lloyd, Indonesia).
1967: (Trikora Lloyd, Indonesia).
23.12.1970: Arrived Hong Kong for breaking up.

1178   *Empire Barbados* 3,538 gt.
Launched: 28.12.1944.
Completed: 3.1945.
1948: *Tennyson* (Rodney SS Co. Ltd. (Anglo-Danubian Transport Co. Ltd., London)).
1950: *Berylstone* (T. Stone (Shipping) Ltd. (Stone & Rolfe Ltd., Swansea)).
1960: *Manticos* (Cia. Nav. Zannis (A. Halcoussis & Co., Greece)).
8.10.1963: Leaking, aground 210 miles south of Dakar.
16.10.1963: Tug alongside, pumping, but
22.10.1963: Leak increased, afterpart suddenly submerged. Total loss
(voyage: Libreville/Mediterranean – logs).

1179   *Empire Caicos* 3,538 gt.
Launched: 28.2.1945.
Completed: 3.1945.
1950: *Sugar Transporter* (Silvertown Services Ltd. (R. S. Dalgliesh Ltd.)).
1957: *Pattawilya* (J. Paterson & Co. (Pty.) Ltd., Australia).
1962: *Clovelly* (Cronulla Shipping Co. Ltd. (J. Manners & Co. Ltd., Hong Kong)).
6.1.1967: Heavy weather damage on voyage Yokohama to Surabaya.
9.1.1967: Put back to Sasebo, in tow.

13.5.1967: Arrived Uchiumi, Shodo Island, for breaking up.

1180   *Empire Aldgate* 3,485 gt.
Launched: 10.5.1945.
Completed: 7.1945.
1948: *Thackeray* (Rodney SS Co. Ltd. (Anglo-Danubian Transport Co. Ltd., London)).
1951: *Sugar Refiner* (Silvertown Services Ltd. (R. S. Dalgliesh Ltd.)).
1958: *San Patricio* (Valck & Monckton, Valparaiso).
1962: (Worldwide Maritime Co. Ltd., Liberia).
1965: *San Miguel* (Altair Maritime Corp., Liberia).
12.9.1965: Put into Las Palmas with boiler trouble (voyage: Jacksonville/Tarragona).
10.1965: Towed to Tarragona; abandoned by owners. Sold.
8.1967: Towed to Cartagena, and
9.1967: Broken up.

1181   *Empire Southwark* 3,486 gt.
Launched: 11.6.1945.
Completed: 9.1945.
1946: *Tempo* (Pelton SS Co. Ltd., Newcastle).
1961: *Nagusena* (Anemi Cia. Nav., Panama).
17.10.1967: Sank in heavy weather four miles off Esbjerg, Denmark, 55.23N 8.60E (voyage: Szczecin/Esbjerg – coal).

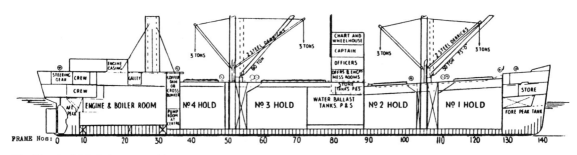

The 'Empire Malta'-class crane-ship.

PART SEVEN

COLLIERS

Every wartime convoy was of great importance and none was more vital than the east coast convoys from the Firth of Forth to the Thames, with their lines of colliers carrying coal from the coalfields of the north-east to London, capital of the British Empire and, in the early years of war, pulsating heart of the free world.

The east coast route had been worked for several hundred years, 'Geordie' brigs recorded as far back as 1730 when the two Clarke brothers began moving coal down the east coast, unknowingly founding what was to become Stephenson Clarke Ltd., in 1928, one of Britain's largest collier fleets.

The collier brigs, each carrying about 350 tons of domestic coal, became very numerous as time passed. In those days the voyage down the east coast was hazardous; bad weather, bad charts and bad lighting spelled danger; there were also pirates. According to the elements the brigs would frequently arrive in the Thames in large groups, all seeking their points of discharge. Over one hundred would arrive weekly and with a myriad of barges, lighters and other small craft working the coal from ship to shore, there was great confusion to the shipping of the Thames, a factor that was to weigh heavily towards the building of London's enclosed docks.

In 1784 there came the steam engine, followed by great expansion in the production of coal. More and more industrial machinery was developed, coal was moved in greater quantities, both for factory and domestic uses and with a merchant marine already the world's carrier, Britain enjoyed near monopoly of the industrial revolution. In its second stage there came the rapid development of steam transport on land and on sea. Competition from a growing network of railways began in the early 1800s and quickly increased and in 1852 the first iron-built steam collier, *John Bowes*, introduced a two-day run down the east coast. Within three years there were thirty-six on the route and within two decades steam colliers had ousted sail and were carrying four million tons of coal each year to Thameside's ever-growing gas undertakings.

Towards the end of the century, as well as the collier owners Stephenson Clarke and Wm. Cory & Son, who introduced floating derricks on the Thames in 1861 for the discharge of colliers, the gas companies began to operate their own ships, whilst the advent of the electricity generating stations forewarned of great competition from those companies producing electrical power and light. As the century turned, more and more coal was required for the highly industrialised south and at this time the floating derricks were superseded by wharves and discharge of the collier by crane.

In the Great War of 1914–1918, with such exposure to attack on the east coast route, German U-boats were very active against the collier and this pattern was resumed in the 1939–1945 conflict with the additional menace of E-boat and bomber.

The first east coast convoy between Methil, on the Firth of Forth, and the Thames began on 6 September 1939, under coding FS, the return FN. The ships left Methil, sailed past Blyth, the Tyne, Middlesbrough, Flamborough Head, the Humber estuary, through 'E-boat alley' and hazardous sandbanks off Cromer, and along the Norfolk coast to the Thames. Vital convoys of fifty-plus ships

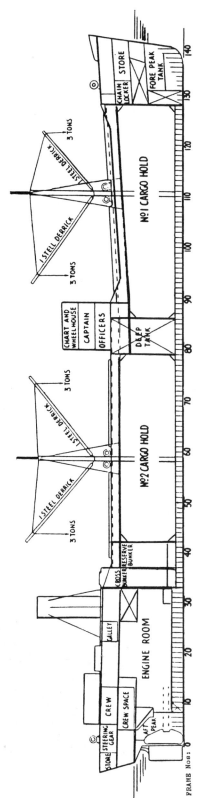

The 321 ft, 4,100 tdw-type collier.

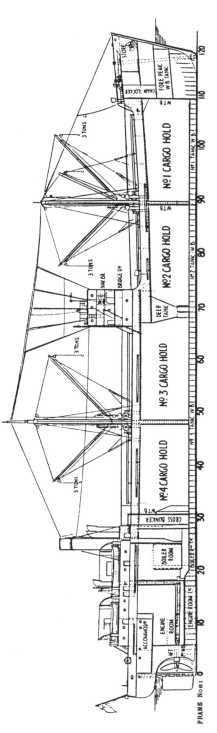

The 'Icemaid'-type collier *Empire Lagoon*.

were open to the attack of submarine or E-boat, or to the mine and when the German forces occupied the entire North Sea coastline of mainland Europe in 1940, suffered attacks by short-range dive bombers.

Almost daily the small ships faced attack as they fed the great Thameside gas and electricity power plants, absolutely essential to the very existence of London, for failure of supply would have seen industries reduced to near standstill. Some colliers continued on to the south coast ports and when France fell, although those ports were closed to ocean-going ships, it was necessary to continue supplies to them and some 40,000 tons was moved weekly in convoys from the Bristol Channel to the Thames under convoy codings CW and CE, the colliers running the gauntlet of air attack by day and the E-boat at night.

There were great losses of colliers in the coastal convoys. Of the power undertakings the Gas, Light & Coke Company lost ten ships by enemy action and one by marine casualty; the South Metropolitan Gas Company lost four from its 1939 fleet of seven and the London Power Company three from its ten-ship fleet, one of these through collision. Fulham Borough Council also lost one in collision and one from E-boat attack. The fleet of Stephenson Clarke was decimated by the loss of twelve colliers, three of these by marine casualty. One other was mined and sunk in 1947. Twelve colliers were also lost from the fleet of Wm. Cory & Son Ltd.

The importance of the collier was recognised and the gas and electricity undertakings were allowed to replace losses of up-river colliers, known as 'Flat-irons'. Three types of collier were also ordered for the Ministry of War Transport; the 4,100 tdw, a number of about 2,900 tdw and 350 tdw carriers.

Largest of the wartime M.O.W.T. colliers were nine built by Wm. Gray & Company of West Hartlepool, constructed with raised bridge deck with forecastle and poop. A deep ballast tank was arranged amidships. They had flat raked transom sterns.

The prototype of the second largest collier type was the *Icemaid*, completed in 1936. She was designed for discharging at Beckton or Regents Canal Dock, London. The *Icemaid* was damaged by mine on 11 October 1941 near Shipwash L.V., off Harwich, but did not sink. She later became *Papeira M* and was scrapped at Split in 1965.

Six small colliers of 350 tons deadweight capacity were built by two yards. Known as the 'Severn Collier'-type, they were built for transporting coal from South Wales ports to the power station at Gloucester.

The *Empire Lagoon*, an 'Icemaid'-type collier. (Grangemouth Dockyard Co. Ltd., Yard No. 433.)

Colliers

'Icemaid'-type – 2,825 tdw, 281.5 ft (oa), 272 ft × 40 ft. Engines: T3cyl. (aft) – 9½ knots

Built by Grangemouth Dockyard Co. Ltd.

433 *Empire Lagoon* 2,013 gt.
Launched: 15.3.1941.
Completed: 6.1941.
1946: *Hudson Bay* (Hudson SS Co. Ltd., London).
1964: Scrapped Blyth.

434 *Empire Ghyll* 2,011 gt.
Launched: 9.6.1941.
Completed: 9.1941.
18.10.1941: Struck mine, sank, in Barrow Deep,
Thames Estuary. Total loss (voyage:
Sunderland/London – coal).

438 *Empire Hearth* 2,020 gt.
Launched: 16.2.1942.
Completed: 5.1942.
1945: *Kentwood* (Wm. France, Fenwick & Co. Ltd.).
1956: *Mayfleet* (Ouse SS Co. Ltd. (E. P. Atkinson &
Sons, Goole)).
5.1961: Scrapped Dublin.

444 *Empire Clansman* 2,065 gt.
Launched: 10.10.1942.
Completed: 12.1942.
18.1.1945: Ashore on rocks off South Carr, North
Berwick. Flooded and abandoned. Broke in three
parts (voyage: Methil/Belfast – coal).
14.2.1945: Refloated; anchored Granton, then towed
to Leith; put aground.
14.3.1945: Drydocked; then
22.3.1945: Towed to Tyne; repaired.
1948: *Sheaf Field* (Sheaf SS Co. Ltd. (W. A. Souter
& Co. Ltd., Newcastle)).
1951: *Corfield* (Wm. Cory & Son Ltd.).
1964: *Spyros Armenakis* (M. Scufalos, Greece).
13.2.1965: Aground on Nolle Sandbank, off
Flushing, Holland. Abandoned, and
14.2.1965: Broke in three; sank (voyage:
Immingham/Terneuzen – coal).

449 *Empire Citizen* 2,066 gt.
Launched: 21.4.1943.

Completed: 6.1943.
1945: *Queenworth* (Watergate SS Co. (R. S. Dalgliesh
Ltd., Newcastle)).
1960: Scrapped Dunston-on-Tyne.

450 *Empire Islander* 2,066 gt.
Launched: 22.6.1943.
Completed: 8.1943.
1949: *Rattray Head* (Henry & McGregor Ltd., Leith).
1960: *Brick Quarto* (Gino Gardella, Italy).
10.1973: Scrapped Savona.

451 *Empire Villager* 2,066 gt.
Launched: 31.8.1943.
Completed: 11.1943.
1946: *Grit* (F. T. Everard & Sons Ltd.).
1957: *Bankstone* (Bankstone Shipping Co. Ltd. (Stone
& Rolfe Ltd., Swansea)).
1959: *Saver* (Virtu Steamship Co. Ltd., Malta).
1965: *Christoyannis* (Marespuma Cia. Nav., Panama
(A. P. Venetsanos, Greece)).
1967: (Ann Poulos, Greece).
11.1967: Sold for breaking up at Perama.

452 *Empire Daughter* 2,026 gt.
Launched: 27.12.1943.
Completed: 4.1944.
1946: *Glanrhyd* (Harries Bros. & Co. Ltd., Swansea).
1948: *Noeldale* (Tavistock Shipping Co., London).
1949: *Kinnaird Head* (Henry & McGregor Ltd., Leith).
1961: *Brick Quinto* (Gino Gardella, Italy).
13.7.1976: Arrived Savona for breaking up.

454 *Empire Peggotty* 2,066 gt.
Launched: 25.4.1944.
Completed: 7.1944.
1946: *Glanowen* (Harries Bros. & Co. Ltd., Swansea).
1965: *Balmoral* (Balmoral Shipping Corpn., Liberia
(Transocean Maritima S. M. Bull S.A., Spain)).
12.3.1967: Aground in River Weser Estuary in heavy
weather. Flooded; stern sank into sand.

5.4.1967: Pumped dry but failed to refloat. Constructive total loss. Broke in two. Forepart salved, and
12.10.1967: Arrived in tow at Bruges for breaking up (voyage: Ghent/Bremen – ballast).

457 *Empire Shepherd* 2,066 gt.
Launched: 10.7.1944.
Completed: 10.1944.
1948: *Sheaf Arrow* (Sheaf SS Co. Ltd. (W. A. Souter & Co. Ltd., Newcastle)).
1956: *Eva* (A. Kjerland & Co., A/S, Norway).
1969: (Poul Christensen, Denmark).
12.1969: Scrapped Antwerp.

459 *Empire Vauxhall* 2,025 gt.
Launched: 30.11.1944.
Completed: 3.1945.
1946: *Braywood* (Wm. France, Fenwick & Co. Ltd.).
1960: *Abdullah* (Faruk & Ozmelek, Turkey).
1976: *Taylan Kalkavan* (Kalkavan Ziya Koll. Sirketi, Turkey).
4.1982: Scrapped Aliaga.

461 *Empire Wapping* 2,025 gt.
Launched: 15.3.1945.
Completed: 5.1945.
1947: *Maystone* (Thomas Stone Shipping Ltd. (Stone & Rolfe Ltd., Swansea)).
18.10.1949: In collision in a gale with aircraft carrier H.M.S. *Albion*; sank four miles from Longstone Light, off Northumberland coast (voyage: Methil/London – coal).

At the time of this casualty H.M.S. *Albion* was in tow of three Tyne-based tugs (*Beamish* ex *Empire Paul*), *Hendon* (1924, 241 gt) and *George V* (1915, 224 gt), bound from Jarrow to Rosyth for drydocking. In the collision the aircraft carrier sustained a 15-ft-square hole torn in her stern, started to take water, and her tugs attempted to tow her to shallow water near St. Abbs Head. In this manoeuvre the tug *Hendon* was disabled with a wire rope round her propeller shaft and the *Albion* was finally hove-to as the two remaining tugs failed to make headway towards the coast in the continuing gale.

Another tug, H.M.S. *Restive* (1940, 700 tons) was despatched from Rosyth and the destroyer H.M.S. *St. James* arrived on the scene and took the disabled tug in tow before her crew finally managed to clear the wire from their ship's stern gear.

The *Albion* was finally berthed at Rosyth, where salvage pumps cleared her flooded compartments, including five feet of water from her engine room. After repair and drydocking the *Albion* was towed back to the Tyne.

Note: The *Albion* (18,300 displacement tons) was laid down at the Swan, Hunter yard in March 1944, launched in May 1947 and immediately laid up. She was scheduled for completion at the end of 1951, but was finally completed in May 1954. In August 1962 the vessel was commissioned as a Commando Carrier.

464 (Laid down as) *Empire Deptford* 2,040 gt.
Launched: 1946.
Completed: 9.1946 as *SNCF No 1* for Societe Nationale D'Affrétements, France.
1947: *Perrigny* (Societe Nationale Des Chemins de Fer Français, France).
1958: (Societe Navale Caennaise S.A., France).
1962: *Otto Pruss* (Hanseatische Keiswerke GmbH, Germany).
1962: (Converted to a gravel suction dredger; fitted with new (oil) engine).
1966: *Hanseat III* (Gesellschaft für Kiesgewinnung und Kiesvertrieb MbH. (O. A. Muller, Germany)).
1974: (Bredo Baltic Gravels S.A., Panama (O. A. Muller, Germany)).
8.1975: Scrapped Hamburg.

The construction of ships by the Grangemouth Dockyard Co. Ltd., during the 1939–1945 war was, chiefly, of two types, the 'Icemaid'-type collier and the 'Empire Cadet'-class coastal tanker.

The prototype of the colliers was the 'Icemaid', completed by S. P. Austin & Sons Ltd., Sunderland, in 1936 for the Gas, Light & Coke Company, London, the vessel's details being 279.7 ft length (oa), a breadth of 40 ft and 1,964 gross tons. Twenty-six of these colliers were constructed for the M.O.W.T. by five builders during the war, thirteen by the Grangemouth Dockyard Co. Ltd. The ships had four hatches arranged for easy trimming and four winches were set two at each mast, with a warping winch aft. Officers were housed amidships, the crew aft. The length of the war-built colliers was slightly more than the prototype, as was the gross tonnage.

The Grangemouth Dockyard Company Ltd. was a former constituent of the Greenock & Grangemouth Dockyard Co. Ltd., a title which had become effective in 1908 from the reversal of the Grangemouth & Greenock Dockyard company name. The Grangemouth Dockyard Company began in 1900 when the lease on Joseph Russell's old Kingston Yard was transferred by William Lithgow, a partner of Russell who had been running the yard for some years, to the Grangemouth Dockyard Company until it was restyled in 1908.

Construction was mostly for the coaster and short sea trade. In 1947 the yard had four berths for ships to 330 ft and three dry docks; 350 ft, 340 ft and 275 ft.

SHIPS BUILT UNDER PRIVATE CONTRACT OR LICENCE

425 *Robert Dundas* 1,120 gt, 222.5 ft (oa), 213 ft × 35 ft. Engines: Oil (aft).
Launched: 28.7.1939.
Completed: 1939 as a stores carrier (pennant A.204) for the Royal Fleet Auxiliary.
1972: Scrapped Grays, Essex.

Note: A sistership, *Robert Middleton*, was launched on 29 June 1938 (Yard No. 424), pennant A.241. In 1978 she became *Myrina* (Georgantis & Co. (Agem Maritime Enterprises, Greece)).

428 *Quentin* 500 gt, 173.8 ft (oa), 167.2 ft × 28.1 ft.
Engines: Oil (aft).
Launched: 9.5.1940.
Completed: 6.1940 for G. Gibson & Co. Ltd., Leith.
1965: (Converted to liquefied gas carrier (574 gt)).
1973: (Anchor Gas Tankers Ltd.).
1976: (Anchor Line Ltd.).
4.1976: Scrapped Milton Regis, Kent.

432 *Durward* 419 gt, 181 ft (oa), 174 ft × 30.2 ft.
Engines: Oil (aft).
Launched: 16.9.1940.
Completed: 12.1940 for G. Gibson & Co. Ltd., Leith.
1960: *Cupids* (H. B. Dawe Ltd., St. John's, N.F.).
1974: (Seatrade & Finance Corpn., St. John's, N.F.).
1975: (Domino Run SS Co., St. John's, N.F.).

1975: (Course Seatrade Ltd., St. John's, N.F.).
5.1.1977: Foundered in St. Pierre Harbour, Newfoundland.

443 *Bucklaw* 424 gt. Details as Yard No. 432.
Launched: 23.11.1942.
Completed: 5.1943 for G. Gibson & Co. Ltd., Leith.
1967: *Christina* (M. & D. Gigilinis & Partner, Greece).
1969: *Pelasgos* (Greek owners).
1969: *Thunder* (Nicos Cia. Nav. S.A., Panama).
22.3.1973: Listed in heavy weather, foundered north of Crete, 36.44N 26.11E (voyage: Eleusis/Cyprus – trucks and machinery).

445 *Fireguard* 2,015 gt, 282 ft (oa), 272 ft × 40 ft.
Engines: T3cyl (aft).
Launched: 9.12.1942.
Completed: 2.1943 for Gas, Light & Coke Company (Stephenson, Clarke Ltd.).
1949: (North Thames Gas Board).
1958: *Pothoula II* (Cia. Maritime Santa Madonna, Panama).
1962: *Thoula* (Nav. Intermar S.A., Panama (P. Belacchi, Italy)).
5.1968: Scrapped Split.

The contract for the following first three vessels was signed by the Singapore Straits SS Co. Ltd., in December 1944. Although a private contract, the vessels conformed to the standard 'B' type of dry cargo coaster specially built for service in the Far East. It may be noted here that the Singapore Straits SS Co. Ltd. later assumed the title of Straits SS Co. Ltd., and, subsequently, that of Straits Steamship Co. Ltd.

465 *Bruas* 957 gt, 224.5 ft (oa), 215 ft × 36.8 ft.
Engines: Oil (aft).
Launched: 10.7.1945.
Completed: 11.1945 for Sarawak SS Co. (Singapore Straits SS Co. Ltd.).
1972: (Hua Seng Sawmill Co. Bhd., Malaysia).

466 *Bidor* 980 gt. Details as Yard No. 465.
Launched: 5.9.1945.
Completed: 2.1946 for Singapore Straits SS Co. Ltd.
1954: (1,383 gt).
1967: (Sharikat Perk. Sendirian, Malaysia (Mansfield & Co.)).
1971: *Orchid Venture* (Orchid Line (Pvt.) Ltd., Singapore).
1975: (Seven Sea Maritime Co. (Pvt.) Ltd., Singapore).
1982: *Hock Siong* (Hock Chip Seong Shipping & Trading Co., Panama).

21.3.1984: Arrived Jurong, Singapore, for breaking up.

467 *Bentong* 980 gt. Details as Yard No. 465.
Launched: 23.10.1945.
Completed: 4.1946 for Singapore Straits SS Co. Ltd.
1955: (1,383 gt).
1966: *Breeze* (Madrigal Shipping Co., Philippines).
1978: (2,128 gt).

468 *Crichtoun* 870 gt, 210.5 ft (oa), 202.7 ft × 33 ft.
Engines: Oil (aft).
Launched: 18.3.1946.
Completed: 6.1946 for G. Gibson & Co. Ltd., Leith.
1965: *Vauquelin* (V. Bouchard, Quebec).
1966: *C. Omer Marie* (Euclide Bouchard Ltd., Quebec).
1967: Renamed *C. Omer*.
1972: *Marine Transport* (fitted with new oil engine) (Puddister Trading Co., St. John's, N.F.).

Built by Ailsa Shipbuilding Co. Ltd., Troon

443 *Empire Pioneer* 2,076 gt.
Launched: 10.11.1942.
Completed: 12.1942.
1946: *Hudson Bank* (Hudson Steamship Co. Ltd., London).
1959: *Gertrud C. Ertel* (Rebuilt; fitted with oil engine) (Ertel, Bieber & Co., GmbH., Germany).
1964: *Saga* (Deutsche-Nordische Schiffs. (Graue & Co., Germany)).

24.12.1965: Aground at Falsterbo, Sweden. Abandoned; broke in two. Constructive total loss (voyage: Klaipeda/France – coal).
7.1968: Refloated; and
29.7.1968: Arrived Oskarshamn in tow. Cargo discharged; wreck sold to Oskarshamn's Varv. Shipyard, and
8.1968: Scrapped Oskarshamn.

Colliers – 2,900 tdw, 284 ft (oa), 273 ft × 41 ft. Engines: T3cyl (aft) – 9½ knots

Built by J. Crown & Sons Ltd., Sunderland

214 *Empire Highlander* 2,135 gt.
Launched: 26.6.1945.
Completed: 10.1945.
1946: *Arnewood* (Wm. France, Fenwick & Co. Ltd.).
1960: *Elias K* (G. Kouremenos, Greece).
17.1.1967: Aground at Farasan, 16.23N 41.48E, in heavy seas (voyage: Varna/Gizan – cement).
24.1.1967: Refloated, and
28.1.1967: Arrived Aden Roads in tow. Later proceeded to Port Said.
1.4.1967: Sailed for Piraeus; drydocked. Extensive bottom damage found; repairs uneconomic; laid up. Sold, and
12.1967: Scrapped Split.

216 (Laid down as) *Empire Lowlander* 2,160 gt.
Launched: 4.3.1946.
Completed: 6.1946 as *Corflow* for Wm. Cory & Son Ltd.
1959: *Rosa Vlassi* (G. Vlassis & Co., Greece).
25.12.1959: Capsized and sank between Laurium and Makronisi, off east coast of Attica, Greece, 37.37N 24.02E, after cargo shifted in a storm. Total loss (voyage: Stratoni/Piraeus – iron pyrites).

217 (Laid down as) *Empire Lambeth* 2,250 gt.
Launched: 15.7.1946.
Completed: 9.1946 as *Dashwood* for Wm. France, Fenwick & Co. Ltd.
6.1961: Scrapped Hendrik Ido Ambacht, Holland.

Apart from nine 'Empire' tugs, three colliers were built by J. Crown & Sons Ltd., for the Ministry of War Transport. The company also built a number of small naval vessels.

John Crown was the originator of the business which became The Strand Slipway Company, returning to the John Crown title in 1900 and then becoming John Crown & Sons Ltd., a year or so later.

At the end of World War II there were two berths, a Graving Dock of 400 feet and a 225 feet-long slipway at the Strand Shipyard at Sunderland.

The company was taken over by J. L. Thompson & Sons Ltd. in 1946 and was later merged into the Doxford & Sunderland Shipbuilding & Engineering Co. Ltd. (a holding firm) with Thompson's, Sir James Laing & Sons Ltd., William Doxford & Sons Ltd., and T. W. Greenwell & Co. Ltd. (repairers).

The *Bruas*, built under licence to the 'B'-type Far East Coaster design, at Singapore. (Grangemouth Dockyard Co. Ltd., Yard No. 465.)

The *Empire Islander*, as *Rattray Head*, berthing at Gravesend. (Grangemouth Dockyard Co. Ltd., Yard No. 450.)

The collier *Empire Gower*, as *Rogate*, June 1963. (Wm. Gray & Co. Ltd., Yard No. 1184.)

The company ceased shipbuilding in 1960, the last vessel, Yard No. 247, *Silver Isle*, being completed for the Silver Isles Navigation Co. (Bermuda) Ltd., in February of that year.

SHIP BUILT FOR PRIVATE ACCOUNT

194 *Corfen* 1,848 gt, 257.2 ft × 39.5 ft.
Engines: T3cyl. A collier.
Launched: 11.11.1939.
Completed: 1940 for Wm. Cory & Son Ltd.
3.1.1942: Struck mine in Barrow Deep Channel,

Thames Estuary approaches. Taken in tow but capsized and sank. Total loss.

Note: This was the first vessel in the Cory fleet to be fitted with steel hatch covers.

Colliers – 4,100 tdw, 321 ft (oa), 310 ft × 44 ft. Engines: T3cyl (aft) – 9½ knots

Built by Wm. Gray & Co. Ltd., West Hartlepool

1107 *Empire Bay* 2,824 gt.
Launched: 20.8.1940.
Completed: 11.1940.
15.1.1942: Bombed, broke in two and sank in Tees Bay, off Middlesbrough. Total loss (voyage: Hartlepool/London – coal).

1108 *Empire Lough* 2,824 gt.
Launched: 1.10.1940.
Completed: 12.1940.
24.6.1944: Intercepted by German E-boats when taking her third cargo of explosives to the Normandy beach-heads; shelled, caught fire, and
25.6.1944: Beached near Folkestone, Kent. Became tidal; masts, superstructure and decks collapsed. Total loss (voyage: London/
Normandy – ammunition and petrol in cans).

1112 *Empire Strait* 2,841 gt.
Launched: 31.10.1940.
Completed: 12.1940.
28.4.1941: Damaged by bombs off Great Yarmouth, Norfolk (voyage: Ipswich/West Hartlepool). Repaired.
1945: *Granta* (Granta SS Co. Ltd. (Witherington & Everett, Newcastle)).
12.1960: Scrapped Harlingen, Holland.

1113 *Empire Knoll* 2,824 gt.
Launched: 16.12.1940.
Completed: 2.1941.
17.2.1941: Ashore in a gale on foundations of the old North Pier, Tynemouth. Badly damaged; fractured

amidships and stern frame carried away. Became tidal: broke in two. Total loss (voyage: Hartlepool/Lisbon – coal).

1114 *Empire Lake* 2,852 gt.
Launched: 30.1.1941.
Completed: 3.1941.
15.7.1943: Sunk by submarine (*U.181*) torpedo in Indian Ocean, southwest of Mauritius, 21.27S 51.47E (voyage: Durban/Aden).

1115 *Empire Brook* 2,852 gt.
Launched: 10.4.1941.
Completed: 5.1941.
1946: *Stancliffe* (Stanhope SS Co. Ltd. (J. A. Billmeir & Co. Ltd., London)).
3.4.1947: Grounded near entrance to Sharpness Docks, River Severn, Gloucester. Refloated but regrounded off North Pier (voyage:
Emden/Sharpness – timber). Abandoned; broke back, plating corrugated and masts buckled. Cargo later salvaged.
15.6.1947: Refloated; beached on foreshore. Constructive total loss. Sold, repaired, and
1948: *Gripfast* (Newbigin SS Co. Ltd. (E. R. Newbigin Ltd., Newcastle)).
1960: *Capetan Costis P* (Saints Anargyroi Cia. Ltda., Panama, (Ezkos Maritime Technical Co., Greece)).
1966: *Karine M* (Cia. de Nav. Patricio, Liberia (Mooringwell Steamship Co., Cardiff)).
1966: *Pitsa* (Siconen Shipping S.A., Panama (Kalamotusis Shipbroking Ltd., London)).

10.10.1967: Put into Djibouti with boiler damage
(voyage: Aqaba/Colombo). Found to be leaking,
with bottom damage.
1.12.1967: Left Colombo in tow of tug *Nisos Kerkyra*
for discharge and repairs, but
4.12.1967: Developed further leaks and:
6.12.1967: Sank off Socotra Island, west of Colombo,
Sri Lanka, 13.32N 55.00E.

1116   *Empire Hurst* 2,852 gt.
Launched: 10.5.1941.
Completed: 6.1941.
11.8.1941: Bombed and sunk south of Cape St.
Vincent, Portugal, 36.48N 9.50W (voyage:
Aquilas/Barrow – iron ore).

1117   *Empire Sedge* 2,852 gt.
Launched: 11.6.1941.
Completed: 7.1941.
1945: *Holmside* (Burnett Steamship Co. Ltd.,
Newcastle).

1956: *Gransha* (Shamrock Shipping Co., N.
Ireland).
1960: *Daniela T* (Paolo Tomei, Italy).
1962: (Capo Mannu Soc. di Nav. (Paolo Tomei,
Italy)).
1972: *Vulca* (Mediterranea Marittima Sarda SpA,
Sardinia).
6.1974: Scrapped Spezia.

1184   *Empire Gower* 2,849 gt.
Launched: 18.1.1946.
Completed: 3.1946.
1946: *Rogate* (Stephenson Clarke Ltd.).
1964: *Santa Barbara* (Aghia Barbara Cia. Mar.,
Panama (K. & M. Shipbrokers Ltd., London)).
1969: (Naveprimo Cia. Mar., Panama (P. Vlastos,
Greece)).
8.1972: Scrapped Perama, Greece.

'Severn collier'-type – 350 tdw, 148.9 ft (oa), 141.7 ft × 22 ft. Engines: Oil (aft) – 8 knots

Built by Richard Dunston Ltd., Thorne, near Doncaster

393   *Empire Laird* 313 gt.
Launched: 29.12.1942.
Completed: 7.1943.
1947: *Monkton Combe* (A. L. Duggan & Co. Ltd.,
Bristol).
1950: *Halronell* (J. Tyrrell, Bristol).
1954: (J. Tyrrell, Eire).
22.10.1961: Stranded in heavy weather on Black
Rock, outside Rosslare Harbour, Wexford, Eire.
23.10.1961: Broke in two; wreck driven across rocks
in storm; sank. Total loss (voyage: Newport,
Mon./Haulbowline, Cork – steel sheets).

394   *Empire Townsman* 313 gt.
Launched: 26.5.1943.
Completed: 8.1943.
1947: *Roselyne* (W. D. Tamlyn & Co. Ltd.).
1953: *Lantyan* (Fowey Harbour Commissioners).
1964: *Pen Arun* (Converted to a suction dredger/sand
carrier) (Seaborne Aggregate Co. Ltd.,
Southampton).
1970: (Amey Marine Ltd., Southampton).
1974: *Sir Cedric* (Dale Sand & Gravel Co. Ltd.,
Guernsey).
1976: (Roselyon Shipping Co., Guernsey).
1978: (Soc. Pte. Derrien-Bichue, France).

395   *Empire Skipper* 313 gt.
Launched: 23.8.1943.
Completed: 10.1943.
1947: *Sand Skipper* (Converted to a sandsucker)
(South Coast Sand & Gravel Co. Ltd.).
1950: (Zinal SS Co. Ltd. (J. Burness & Sons Ltd.,
London)).
1954: (South Coast Shipping Co. Ltd. (Burness
Shipping Co. Ltd., London)).
1956: (South Coast Shipping Co. Ltd. (Wm. Cory &
Son Ltd.)).
7.1970: Scrapped Southampton.

396   *Empire Runner* 313 gt.
Launched: 17.9.1943.
Completed: 11.1943.
1947: *Sand Runner* (Converted to a sandsucker) (South
Coast Sand & Ballast Co. Ltd.).
1950: (Zinal SS Co. Ltd. (J. Burness & Sons Ltd.,
London)).
1954: South Coast Shipping Co. Ltd. (Burness
Shipping Co. Ltd., London)).
1956: (South Coast Shipping Co. Ltd. (Wm. Cory &
Son Ltd.)).
1.8.1967: Arrived Northam, Southampton, for
breaking up.

Built by J. Harker Ltd., Knottingley, Yorkshire

146 *Empire Reaper* 332 gt.
Launched: 17.10.1942.
Completed: 4.1943.
1947: *Browning* (Anglo-Danubian Transport Co. Ltd., London).
1949: *Moreton Corbet* (Kerton Shipping Co. Ltd., Hull).
1953: *Lerryn* (Fowey Harbour Commissioners).
1964: *Pen Adur* (Converted to a sand carrier) (Seaborne Aggregate Co. Ltd., Southampton).
1969: *Sand Wren* (South Coast Shipping Co. Ltd., Southampton).
1973: *Margaret Smith* (Bowen & Caine, Southampton).
28.6.1978: Capsized after developing leaks when entering Cowes Harbour, I.O.W., with gravel after working in Solent. Drifted, towed to buoys off Yarmouth, I.O.W., but sank in position 52.42N 1.28W.

147 *Empire Rancher* 332 gt.
Launched: 2.1.1943.
Completed: 7.1943.
1947: *Shelley* (Anglo-Danubian Transport Co. Ltd., London).
1948: *Normanby Hall* (Coppack Bros. & Co., Hull).
6.6.1965: Stranded in fog near Tara, two miles from Strangford Bar Buoy, Strangford Lough, N. Ireland. Refloated, taken in tow for Belfast, but pumps unable to cope with influx of water, and
8.6.1965: Sank in Belfast Lough, N. Ireland. Total loss (voyage: Birkenhead/Belfast – flour and animal feed).

The origins of J. Harker Ltd. date from 1877, when the Aire Tar Works was established at Knottingley, on the Selby section of the Aire & Calder Canal, by M. Stainsby and J. G. Lyon. Crude tar was brought in barges to the Works from Leeds and York and the refined tar carried away to Goole and Hull for export. In 1893 this lighterage work was contracted to John Harker, works manager at the Tar Works, who acquired two open wooden barges and shipped the tar in barrels. He died in 1911 and seven years later, in his memory, Stainsby and Lyon formed John Harker Ltd., with a fleet of seven barges, towed by tugs.

In 1925 their first motor barge, *Michael H*, was delivered, this starting the company practice of naming its craft with the suffix 'H' added to the names. In the following year several Yorkshire gas companies and tar distilleries amalgamated and, in exchange for shares in the new concern, Stainsby and Lyon concentrated on its carrying business, retaining the Harker title.

The company grew steadily and in the mid-1920s, in addition to its normal cargoes of coal, tar and pitch, started to carry petroleum products for the major national oil companies. In 1929 the firm acquired a shipyard at Knottingley and, thereafter, built and repaired its craft at its own yard. The first launch, in August 1929, was the tank barge *William Kipping*, of 150 tdw. – a diversion from the new-style nomenclature, the vessel being named after the son-in-law of John Harker.

In 1937 a new naming-style was adopted, the craft being named after Yorkshire dales, but still with the suffix 'H', and in the same year the first 'Dale' motor barge, the tanker *Darleydale H*, 280 tons, was commissioned for River Severn service. Some twenty years later, on 20 December 1958, the vessel was involved in an accident when coming downstream from Worcester. She collided with the cast-iron Haw Bridge, just above Gloucester, and completely destroyed the structure. Severely damaged, the tanker was later sold to Denmark.

Two slightly smaller vessels followed in 1938 and in 1939 Harker's formed Gloucester Shipyard Ltd., situated in Gloucester docks, to provide maintenance to its 'western' fleet of craft.

The Harker shipyards built only one vessel for their own account during the war, the motor barge *Barnsdale H* (250 tons), in 1942. In addition to the two 'Severn'-type colliers (above) they also constructed four 'Isles'-class coastal tankers and three 'VIC' lighters for the M.O.W.T., whilst two Military Oil Barges (*MOB 1* and *2*) were launched at the end of 1945.

When war ended, the yard at Knottingley had six berths with a ship length capacity to 135 feet.

PART EIGHT

DRY CARGO COASTERS

Coasters were in constant demand throughout the war and some nine million tons of cargo and twenty-one million tons of coal were moved annually between British coastal ports, helping greatly to relieve the overburdened wartime railway and road transport systems.

The demand was further increased by military requirements for such vessels, to be used as back-up craft to military operations, and many different types of coastal ships – dry cargo, tankers and lighters – to a variety of measurements were provided for both military and Ministerial use. Orders given by the M.O.W.T. totalled well over 300 ships, whilst many dry cargo coasters and a few coastal tankers were constructed to private account, as well as specialised colliers for the coastal and River Thames coal trade.

In the dry cargo section the largest coasters were those of the 'Tudor Queen'-class, ten vessels constructed in Scotland during 1944–1946. The most numerous vessels were those of the 'Empire F' type, of straight-line, prefabricated construction and numbering twenty-five ships. They derived from hulls of the original 'Chant' (Channel Tanker) programme, its numbers reduced and so allowing completion of surplus hulls as dry cargo coasters.

The *Empire Atoll* was an unusual construction: ordered by private owners she was given 'Empire' nomenclature and had the distinction of being the only war-built coaster fitted for the carriage of refrigerated cargoes.

Of the smaller types of coaster, those of the 'Isles'-class, though few in number, were most useful in the carriage of lengthy cargo, their significant feature being one hold, over 40 ft in length and with a correspondingly long cargo hatchway. There was also an 'Isles'-class of coastal tanker.

The smallest type of coaster built during the war was the 'Clyde Puffer' type, coastal lighters known as Victualling Inshore Craft, of which sixty-three were constructed, fifty-four steam and nine diesel-driven and with measurements of some 67 ft × 18 ft and of 96 gross tons. They were followed by an 'Improved' version, mostly steam-driven and with dimensions of 80 ft × 20 ft. Both types were named 'VIC No. . . . .' and were built by several shipyards – Dunston, Harker, Pimblott, Pollock, Richards, Rowhedge, etc., whilst the last two completed, *VIC 105* and *VIC 106*, were 83.5 ft in length, diesel-engined and constructed by the Shipbuilding Corporation (Tyne Branch), Newcastle. Many of the craft found their way to ports throughout the world, where most carried out naval work as storeships, ammunition carriers, water boats and on other harbour duties. After the war many of them were transferred to permanent Admiralty ownership, although they were later disposed of as needs declined.

In 1944, with the end of the war in Europe in sight, attention was turned to the Far East and a build-up of the South East Asia Command (S.E.A.C.) began for the final effort in that theatre of war.

Had the atomic bomb – which brought about the end of the war – not been developed in time, a sea-borne invasion of Japanese-occupied territory would have been mounted, the date of March

216

The 'Severn Collier'-type *Empire Runner*, as *Sand Runner*, entering Portsmouth Harbour. (R. Dunston Ltd., Yard No. 396.)

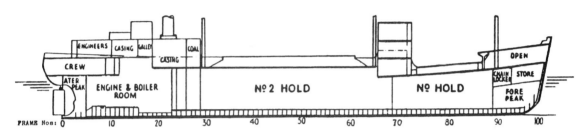

The 'Tudor Queen'-type coaster.

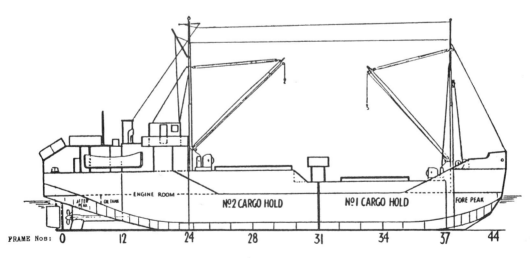

The standard fabricated 'F'-type coaster.

COASTERS FOR FAR EAST SERVICE

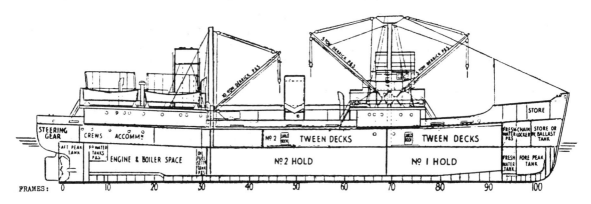

The 'B'-type coaster.

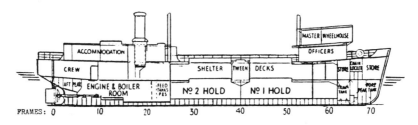

The 'C'-type coaster.

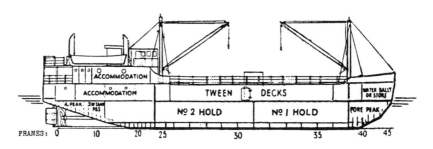

The 'Shelt'-type standard fabricated coaster.

1946 being set for Operation 'Olympic' – the American assault on Japan itself. No British participation in the initial assault fleet was planned, but a reserve fleet of some hundreds of British assault craft was due to assemble in the Pacific early in 1946, following landings in Malaysia, which were scheduled for September 1945. As well as the military and naval craft involved, there was an obvious need for follow-up vessels – small cargo carriers to service the forces and, ultimately, to open up trade – of the types which customarily operated in South East Asia and, in particular, in the area of the Malaysian peninsula.

To meet these needs three types of special coaster were ordered; the largest was the 'B' type, three-island, shelter-deck steamers of some 970 gross tons, 1,200 tdw., with machinery aft. The smaller 'C' type, of some 350 gross tons, were open shelter-deck vessels with their bridge placed forward, up to the foc's'le, and were not unlike many of the vessels engaged in the area's pre-war rubber trade.

Also included in the programme of coasters for the Far East was the prefabricated straight-line-built 'Shclt' (Shelter deck) type, somewhat similar in construction and appearance to the 'Chant' coastal tankers and the dry cargo 'Empire F' coasters, but with gangway doors serving the 'tween decks and the vessels capable of carrying a small number of troops.

Coasters

'Tudor Queen'-class

The largest of the dry cargo coasters were the ships of the 'Tudor Queen'-class, built from a prototype of that name which came from the Burntisland Shipbuilding Company in 1941 for Queenship Navigation Ltd., London.

There were ten 'Empire'-named ships in the class, of which five were built by J. Lewis & Sons Ltd., Aberdeen, four from George Brown & Company, Greenock, and one from Ardrossan Dockyard Ltd.

All were measured at 212 ft (oa), 205 ft × 32.7 ft and had T3cyl engines aft, to give 9½ knots. Deadweight capacity was 1,360 tons.

Their design was an adaptation of the easy-trimming collier, with No. 1 hold short in length and No. 2 hold almost 40 per cent of the length of the ship, with a hatchway 55 ft in length and over 20 ft in breadth. There were three masts, each with a steam winch for a single derrick. A feature of the design was that the crew was berthed aft, thus avoiding the need for accommodation in the foc's'le.

Built by John Lewis & Sons Ltd., Aberdeen

182 *Empire Cheyne* 1,051 gt.
Launched: 17.10.1944.
Completed: 12.1944.
1946: *Saltfleet* (Ouse SS Co. Ltd. (E. P. Atkinson & Sons, Goole).

3.10.1951: Ashore in fog at Reedness, near Goole, River Ouse, Yorks.
4.10.1951: Rolled over; submerged (voyage: Goole/Poole – coal).
12.1951: Salvage commenced.

10.1952: Salvage operations suspended.
4.1953: Salvage work recommenced, by which time the vessel had broken her back.
3.1954: Submerged wreck cut in two.
28.5.1954: Forepart lifted, beached on river bank; dismantled.
9.1954: Afterpart refloated, moved up-river, and
10.1954: Broken up.

184   *Empire Chelsea* 1,051 gt.
Launched: 18.12.1944.
Completed: 2.1945.
1947: *Humbergate* (Hull Gates Shipping Co. Ltd. (Craggs & Jenkins Ltd.)).
1955: *Springwear* (Efford Shipping Co. Ltd. (Springwell Shipping Co. Ltd., London)).
1959: *Lynnwear* (Lynn Shipping Co. Ltd. (Springwell Shipping Co. Ltd., London)).
1962: *Dumbo* (South Star Corporation, Panama (V. & J. A. Ensenat, Spain)).
10.1968: Under arrest: auctioned by Court Order. Sold (subject to ratification), but
24.11.1968: Driven ashore on Alcalavaneras beach, Las Palmas, during a storm. Left high and dry. Offer for purchase (by Naviera del Odiel, S.A.) withdrawn. Constructive total loss. Vessel taken over by local port authority.
5.1969: Refloated, towed to shallow water, beached.
10.12.1969: Sold at auction, for intended conversion to a floating nightclub, but resold (to Don Martin Juanatey Malvarez). Later broken up.

185   *Empire Kew* 1,052 gt.
Launched: 29.3.1945.
Completed: 5.1945.
1947: *Beltinge* (Constants (South Wales) Ltd.).
1950: *Monkton Combe* (Ald Shipping Co. Ltd. (A. L. Duggan & Co., Bristol)).
1958: *Astarte* (Ligure Fiorentina di Nav. (Danio Navigazione SRL, Italy)).
1959: (New oil engine).
1964: *Maria Dormio* (1,783 gt) (Ditta Giuseppi Dormio, Italy).
1975: (Ant. Scotto di Santolo, Italy).
3.2.1978: Sprang leak in heavy weather. Abandoned, sank fifty-six miles southwest of Cape Miseno, Tyrrhenian Sea (voyage: Baia/Porto Empedocle).

186   *Empire Richmond* 1,047 gt.
Launched: 11.6.1945.
Completed: 8.1945.
1946: *Pulborough* (Stephenson Clarke Ltd.).
1959: Renamed *Pulborough II*.
1959: *Nilgiri* (Ashok Line, India).
1969: Under arrest at Calcutta: sold by Court Order.
4.1970: Scrapped Calcutta.

187   *Empire Fenchurch* 1,047 gt.
Launched: 6.11.1945.
Completed: 2.1946.
1946: *Yewforest* (J. Stewart & Co. (Shipping) Ltd.).
1954: *Perelle* (O. Dorey & Sons Ltd., Guernsey).
1961: Towed to Gothenburg for breaking up, then leased out for one year as a floating store in Denmark.
8.1962: Reported dismantled in Sweden, but
1965: in service as a barge, named *Tor*.

John Lewis & Sons Ltd., of Albert Quay, Aberdeen, were builders of coasters and trawlers, the latter in particular for Acadia Fisheries Ltd., Newfoundland; R. Irvin & Sons and Iago Steam Trawlers Ltd. During the war, however, construction was turned to naval craft for the Admiralty, apart from the 'Tudor Queen'-class ships and some trawlers which were completed in the shoulder months.

At Aberdeen, the company had four berths to 300 ft capacity and the Torry slip, to lift to 750 tons. They also controlled several trawling companies, including the 'Dodds' Steam Fishing Co. Ltd., and North Eastern Fisheries Ltd., in which a number of trawlers were employed.

In the summer of 1972 John Lewis & Sons Ltd. were taken over by the John Wood Group.

SHIPS BUILT UNDER PRIVATE CONTRACT OR LICENCE

145   *Worthtown* 868 gt, 205 ft (oa), 197.7 ft × 30.7 ft. Engines: T3cyl. (aft).
Launched: 30.9.1939.
Completed: 11.1939 for Williamstown Shipping Co. Ltd. (Comben, Longstaff & Co. Ltd., London).

27.5.1940: Bombed by German aircraft at Dunkirk. Sank.
11.1940: Salvaged by Germans and taken in prize.
10.1943: *Ilse Schulte* (Schulte & Bruns, Emden).
1945: *Empire Worthtown* (q.v.).

149 *Mount Battock* 396 gt, 147 ft (oa),
141 ft × 25.6 ft. Engines: T3cyl. Trawler.
Launched: 14.11.1939.
Completed: 12.1939 for The 'Dodds' Steam Fishing
Co. Ltd.
1955: (North Eastern Fisheries Ltd.).
8.1968: Scrapped Montrose.

188 *Eminence* 555 gt, 174 ft (oa), 167.6 ft × 28 ft.
Engines: Oil.
Launched: 11.7.1945.
Completed: 10.1945 for London & Rochester
Trading Co. Ltd.
1967: *Elizabeth* (North Atlantic Bulk Cargoes Ltd.,
Newfoundland).

189 *Marinda* 342 gt, 148 ft (oa), 136 ft × 24.6 ft.
Engines: T3cyl. Trawler.
Launched: 6.10.1945.
Completed: 1.1946 for J. Marr & Sons Ltd.,
Fleetwood.
1947: (Seddon Fishing Co. (B. A. Parkes)).
1950: (National Trawling & Fishing Co. Ltd. (Irvin
& Johnson Ltd., South Africa)).
12.1968: Towed to sea (as useless) and sunk by gunfire
off South Africa.

190 *Braconvale* 341 gt. Details as Yard No. 189.
Launched: 4.12.1945.
Completed: 2.1946 for Don Fishing Co. Ltd.,
Aberdeen (B. A. Parkes).
1947: *Orion* (P. P. D. Dalmor (Government of
Poland)).
8.1973: Scrapped Boom, Belgium.

191 *Dunkinty* 307 gt, 144.8 ft (oa),
131.3 ft × 24.2 ft. Engines: T3cyl. Trawler.
Launched: 4.2.1946.
Completed: 4.1946 for Looker Fishing Co. Ltd.,
Aberdeen.
9.1964: Scrapped Inverkeithing.

192 *Avondow* 308 gt. Details as Yard No. 191.
Launched: 6.4.1946.
Completed: 4.1946 for North Star Fishing Co. Ltd.,
Aberdeen.
9.1967: Scrapped Bo'ness.

193 *Moray Firth* 567 gt. Details as Yard No. 188.
Launched: 16.2.1946.
Completed: 5.1946 for Firth Shipping Co. Ltd. (G.
T. Gillie & Blair Ltd., Newcastle).
1959: *Ferryhill* (Aberdeen Coal & Shipping Co. Ltd.).
3.1972: Scrapped Dunston-on-Tyne.

Built by Ardrossan Dockyard Ltd.

398 *Empire Drover* 1,047 gt.
Launched: 30.10.1944.
Completed: 12.1944.

1946: *Roman Queen* (Queenship Navigation Ltd.
(Coast Lines Ltd.)).
1961: Scrapped Hendrik Ido Ambacht.

Built by G. Brown & Co. (Marine) Ltd., Greenock

232 *Empire Balham* 1,063 gt.
Launched: 18.12.1944.
Completed: 5.1945.
1946: *Nordic Queen* (Queenship Navigation Ltd.
(Coast Lines Ltd.).
1958: *Maldive Star* (Maldivian National Trading
Corp. (Ceylon) Ltd.).
12.1972: Scrapped Gadani Beach, Karachi.

233 *Empire Bromley* 1,059 gt.
Launched: 26.5.1945.
Completed: 6.1945.
1946: *Levenwood* (Constantine Shipping Co. (J.
Constantine Steamship Line Ltd.)).
1961: *Basildon* (Panax (Overseas) Ltd., London).
1962: (Don Shipping Co. Ltd. (C. M. Willie & Co.
(Shipping) Ltd.)).

1963: (R. S. Braggs & Co. (Shipping) Ltd.).
10.1967: Scrapped Burcht, Belgium.

234 *Empire Lewisham* 1,059 gt.
Launched: 27.11.1945.
Completed: 2.1946.
1946: *The Monarch* (J. Hay & Sons Ltd., Glasgow).
1962: *Silver Cloud* (P. Vrangos, Greece (Lebanese
flag)).
9.1968: Scrapped Eleusis, Greece (as *Chrysanthi*).

235 (Launched as) *Empire Kingsway* 1,058 gt.
Launched: 27.7.1946.
Completed: 1946 as *The Emperor* for J. Hay &
Sons Ltd., Glasgow.
1963: Scrapped Boom, Belgium.

Prefabricated, 'Empire F' class

The 'Empire F' coasters were a dry cargo version of the 'Chant'-type coastal tankers. Some sixty-eight of the latter type had been ordered, but changing wartime plans, including those of the Normandy landings, showed that demands could be met with a smaller number. And so the 'surplus' hulls were re-designed to general cargo carriers.

As with the Chants, their straight-line, all-welded construction was from twenty-eight prefabricated units, supplied by inland factories and delivered to the shipyards for completion. Due to such fabrication the dry cargo version – totalling twenty-five vessels – were renamed with a 'Fabric' prefix and a figure (number) suffix, but this was soon amended to the standard 'Empire' nomenclature, the suffix commencing with the letter 'F'.

All the vessels originated from the River Humber area, thirteen being constructed by the Goole Shipbuilding & Engineering Co. Ltd., and the remaining twelve by H. Scarr Ltd., at Hessle.

Actual construction methods of the two types – the Chants and the Empire Fs – were similar and they also remained similar in appearance, the main structural difference of the dry cargo version being the greater length of the raised trunkdeck – reaching to midships – and allowing for No. 2 hold's 26-ft-long hatchway to be fitted at the poop deck level. The hatchway for No. 1 hold was 4 ft lower than this, whilst the open-railed welldeck was some 8 ft lower than the fo'c'sle and poop decks. Only two holds were arranged, as distinct from the four oil cargo tanks of the Chants, the two holds being served by two 30-cwt derricks. Cargo capacity was 19,200 cu. ft.

Dimensions at 148.2 ft (oa), 142.2 ft × 27 ft equated with the Chant tankers, but the gross tonnage was slightly more, at 410–411, with the corresponding deadweight around 460 tons. As with the Chant tankers they were driven by oil engines, generally of 300 bhp, and giving a speed of some 8 knots.

After the war many well-known British coaster owners supplemented their fleets with vessels of the 'Empire F' class; in particular F. T. Everard & Sons Ltd. purchasing nine of them, to become their own 'F' class. These owners, and others, too, often retained the vessels for fifteen or more years, until imminent and stringent 20-year Special Surveys sealed the vessels' fate. By the early 1950s a number of the Empire Fs were in Canadian ownership, operating in the St. Lawrence region, and generally replacing ageing, family-owned, wooden schooners which were no longer able to handle the quantity and size of machines and machinery needed by new industry. But even this trade was shortlived, the operators not able to compete with the growth of large vehicles and rail-car ferries which eliminated the need for cargo trans-shipment.

The last of the 'Empire F' type under British ownership was the *Farringay* (ex *Empire Farringay*), which lasted until 1979 although much modified and converted over the years. In that year she went to Panamanian-flag Spanish owners for further service, but lasted only another two years before being broken up. However, a few other vessels, under overseas ownership, were still listed in shipping registers into the late 1980s.

Built by Henry Scarr Ltd., Haven Shipyard, Hessle, nr. Hull

447   *Empire Fabric* Laid down as *Chant 14*, later renamed *Fabric 14*.
Launched: 6.1944 as *Empire Fabric*.
Completed: 7.1944.
1951: *Fenstock* (Harbour Specialists Ltd., Hull (P. Bauer, London).

1952: *Torridge Lass* (Torridge Coasters Ltd., Bideford).
1961: Sold to Canada, but deal not completed.
1963: *Ste. Marguerite* (E. Desgagne, Quebec).
1965: (A. Cote, Quebec).
1966: (Bouchard Navigation Ltd., Quebec).

The 'Tudor Queen'-class coaster *Empire Richmond*, as *Pulborough*, in the River Thames. (J. Lewis & Sons Ltd., Yard No. 186.)

The 'Empire F'-class coaster *Empire Factor*, as *Gansey*. (Goole Shipbuilding & Repairing Co. Ltd., Yard No. 417.)

The *Hullgate*, formerly the *Empire Facet*, in 1952. (Goole Shipbuilding & Repairing Co. Ltd., Yard No. 431.)   *Skyfotos*

1970: *Prince Loys* (F. Lussier, Quebec).
10.1972: Laid up with machinery damage. Later sold,
and
1977: Scrapped Ile-aux-Coudres, Canada.

448   *Empire Fabian* Laid down as *Chant 15*, later
renamed *Fabric 15*.
Launched: 9.7.1944 as *Empire Fabian*.
Completed: 7.1944.
1947: *Karani* (Booker Bros, McConnell & Co. Ltd.).
1950: (Booker Shipping (Demerara) Ltd.).
1969: *Gibmac* (L. Gibbs & M. McIntosh, Georgetown,
Guyana).

449   *Empire Fable* Laid down as *Chant 16*, later
renamed *Fabric 16*.
Launched: 23.7.1944 as *Empire Fable*.
Completed: 8.1944.
1946: (Cyprian Coastal Line Ltd. (P. Mantovani,
Cyprus).
1948: Renamed *Cyprus C*.
1950: *Yvonne Olivier* (De Malglaive Shipping Ltd.,
Windsor).
1954: *Antonios* (Hellenic Levant Lines Ltd., Greece).
1957: (S. Daifas & Co., Greece).
1958: *Copetrole I* (Soc. Co-operative des Petroles,
Egypt).

450   *Empire Farringdon* Laid down as *Chant 18*, later
renamed *Fabric 18*.
Launched: 8.1944 as *Empire Farringdon*.
Completed: 9.1944.
1946: *Susie Olivier* (De Malglaive Shipping Ltd.,
Windsor).
1948: (Booker Line Ltd. (Booker Bros., McConnell
& Co. Ltd.)).
1952: *Mabiri* (Booker Line Ltd.).
1960: (New oil engine).
1972: (Island Shipping Co. Ltd., Trinidad).
19.2.1974: Sprang leak ninety-four miles southeast of
Tobago, listed. Taken in tow but capsized and sank
in Gulf of Paria, 10.37N 61.34W.

451   *Empire Fanfare* Laid down as *Chant 19*, later
renamed *Fabric 19*.
Launched: 8.1944 as *Empire Fanfare*.
Completed: 10.1944.
1946: *Festivity* (F. T. Everard & Sons Ltd.).
8.1961: Scrapped Nieuw Lekkerland, Holland.

452   *Empire Faversham* Laid down as *Chant 17*, later
renamed *Fabric 17*.
Launched: 6.1944 as *Empire Faversham*.
Completed: 9.1944.
1947: *Fawdon* (Whitehaven Shipping Co. Ltd.
(Anthony & Bainbridge Ltd.).
1952: *Maduni* (Booker Line Ltd. (Booker Bros.,
McConnell & Co. Ltd.)).
1959: (New oil engine).

1970: *Herma A* (Pedonomou Lines Ltd., Trinidad).
19.7.1975: Foundered in a storm while moored at
Port of Spain, Trinidad.

453   *Empire Facility* Laid down as *Chant 20*, later
renamed *Fabric 20*.
Launched: 10.1944 as *Empire Facility*.
Completed: 10.1944.
1946: *Flexity* (F. T. Everard & Sons Ltd.).
1.1962: Scrapped Krimpen a/d Yssel, Holland.

454   *Empire Faraway* Laid down as *Chant 21*, later
renamed *Fabric 21*.
Launched: 10.1944 as *Empire Faraway*.
Completed: 11.1944.
1946: *Seabrook* (Seaway Coasters Ltd. (Howard &
Sons, London)).
1954: *Fortunity* (F. T. Everard & Sons Ltd.).
2.1962: Scrapped Nieuw Lekkerland, Holland.

455   *Empire Fanal* Laid down as *Chant 46*, later
renamed *Fabric 46*.
Launched: 10.1944 as *Empire Fanal*.
Completed: 11.1944.
1946: *Futurity* (F. T. Everard & Sons Ltd.).
1960: Vessel party dismantled by owners at
Greenhithe, Kent, then
18.5.1960: Hull arrived at Grays, Essex, for breaking
up.

456   *Empire Fastness* Laid down as *Chant 47*, later
renamed *Fabric 47*.
Launched: 11.1944 as *Empire Fastness*.
Completed: 12.1944.
1946: *Firmity* (F. T. Everard & Sons Ltd.).
1964: Sold to U.K. buyers for breaking up; resold,
and
12.1964: Scrapped Krimpen a/d Yssel, Holland.

457   *Empire Farrier* Laid down as *Chant 48*, later
renamed *Fabric 48*.
Launched: 11.1944 as *Empire Farrier*.
Completed: 12.1944.
1947: *River Ouse* (R. H. Hunt & Sons, Hull).
1952: *Braywick* (Braywick Shipping Co. Ltd. (J. P.
Hadoulis Ltd., London)).
1953: *Sand Diver* (converted to a sand suction dredger
at Appledore, 379 gt; 403 tdw) (South Coast Shipping
Co. Ltd. (Burness Shipping Co. Ltd., London)).
1956: (South Coast Shipping Co. Ltd. (Wm. Cory &
Sons Ltd.)).
1966: Scrapped Grays, Essex.

458   *Empire Fathom* Laid down as *Chant 49*, later
renamed *Fabric 49*.
Launched: 12.1944 as *Empire Fathom*.
Completed: 1.1945.

1946: *Fosdyke Trader* (B. W. Steamship, Tug & Lighter Co., Craggs & Jenkin Ltd., Hull).
1961: *Fort Carillon* (J. P. Desgagnes, Quebec).
1972: *Janolyne* (L. Tremblay, Quebec).
1975. *Fermont* (J. P. Benoit & G. Tremblay (Transport Maritime Harvey, Ltee., Quebec)).
1978: Laid up; beached at La Petite Riviere St. François.
1987: Reported sold for conversion to a floating restaurant.

In 1940 the shipyard of Henry Scarr Ltd., produced a number of Dockyard craft before turning to dry cargo coasters and tugs, completing a total of thirteen 'near Warrior'-type tugs between 1941 and 1945.

The twelve dry cargo coasters of the 'Empire F'-class were built in 1944 and these were followed in 1945 by twelve shelter-deck dry cargo coasters specially designed for the war with Japan, which it was thought would continue. All had names prefixed 'Empire Sea . . . .'. Two 'C'-type coasters, also for the Far East campaign, were constructed in 1945.

In the coastal tanker range the shipyard also built twelve vessels of the 'Chant'-class (Channel tankers).

When war ended the Haven shipyard had eight berths, with a ship capacity to 150 feet, and a 250 ft slipway.

SHIPS BUILT UNDER PRIVATE CONTRACT OR LICENCE

434 *Mallard* 377 gt, 149.8 ft (oa), 143.5 ft × 26.1 ft.
Engines: Oil.
Launched: 6.7.1944.
Completed: 8.1944 for General Steam Navigation Co. Ltd., London.
1948: *Norwich Trader* (Great Yarmouth Shipping Co. Ltd.).
1965: *Nikolaos* (G. & E. Zervas, Greece).
1972: (E. Kallikas & Efstathiou, Greece).
1978: (G. & E. Zervas, Greece).

462 *Mavis* 381 gt. Details as yard No. 434.
Launched: 22.11.1945.
Completed: 5.1946 for General Steam Navigation Co. Ltd., London.
1966: *Athanasios A* (B. Andrias & Partners, Greece).
1970: *Limnos* (G. Georgandis & others, Greece).
1983: (C. Markakis, Greece).

Built by Goole Shipbuilding & Repairing Co. Ltd.

417 *Empire Factor* Laid down as *Chant 29*, later renamed *Fabric 29*.
Launched: 5.1944 as *Empire Factor*.
Completed: 7.1944.
1946: *Coe Jean* (Coe Line Ltd., London).
1950: *Barrule* (Southern Shipping Co. Ltd., I.O.M.).
1954: *Gansey* (C. M. & D. M. Watterson, I.O.M.).
26.12.1964: Arrived Dalmuir for breaking up.

418 *Empire Fairhaven* Laid down as *Chant 30*, later renamed *Fabric 30*.
Launched: 22.6.1944 as *Empire Fairhaven*.
Completed: 7.1944.
1946: *Fixity* (F. T. Everard & Sons Ltd.).
3.3.1961: Arrived Grays, Essex, for breaking up.

419 *Empire Favourite* Laid down as *Chant 31*, later renamed *Fabric 31*.
Launched: 10.7.1944 as *Empire Favourite*.
Completed: 7.1944.
1946: *Formality* (F. T. Everard & Sons Ltd.).
9.1962: Scrapped Krimpen a/d Yssel, Holland.

420 *Empire Fashion* Laid down as *Chant 32*, later renamed *Fabric 32*.
Launched: 22.7.1944 as *Empire Fashion*.
Completed: 8.1944.
1946: *Frivolity* (F. T. Everard & Sons Ltd.).
8.1961: Scrapped Grays, Essex.

421   *Empire Fane* Laid down as *Chant 33*, later renamed *Fabric 33*.
Launched: 4.8.1944 as *Empire Fane*.
Completed: 9.1944.
1946: *Fluidity* (F. T. Everard & Sons Ltd.).
1956: (New oil engine).
1960: *Apar* (converted to a tug mooring and storage hulk for service at Limehouse Reach, River Thames (Gaselee & Son Ltd., London)).
(*circa*) 1974: Scrapped Dartford, Kent.

422   *Empire Farnham* Laid down as *Chant 34*, later renamed *Fabric 34*.
Launched: 2.9.1944 as *Empire Farnham*.
Completed: 9.1944.
1946: *Jim M* (Metcalf Motor Coasters Ltd.).
1959: (New oil engine).
12.1964: Engine removed by owners, and
1.1965: Scrapped Grays, Essex.

423   *Empire Farouche* Laid down as *Chant 35*, later renamed *Fabric 35*.
Launched: 19.9.1944 as *Empire Farouche*.
Completed: 10.1944.
1946: *Lizzonia* (J. Wharton (Shipping) Ltd.).
1956: (New oil engine).
16.3.1961: Damaged in collision, in fog, with mv *Arctic Ocean* (1948, 4,029 gt) three miles WNW of Varne Light Vessel, English Channel. Abandoned; sank (voyage: Antwerp/Plymouth).

424   *Empire Farringay* Laid down as *Chant 36*, later renamed *Fabric 36*.
Launched: 2.10.1944 as *Empire Farringay*.
Completed: 11.1944.
1946: *Farringay* (J. H. K. Griffin, Swansea).
(*circa*) 1972: Rebuilt; flush deck added to level of old trunk deck (461 gt, 533 tdw).
1965–1972: Re-engined at different times (oil engines), fitted with triple screws.
1979: *Claire* (Cia. de Nav. Panajosyane S.A., Panama).
3.1981: Scrapped La Corunna, Spain.

430   *Empire Farjeon* Laid down as *Chant 37*, later renamed *Fabric 37*.
Launched: 18.10.1944 as *Empire Farjeon*.
Completed: 11.1944.
1946: *Drakedene* (Drakelow Steamship Co., Cardiff).
1966: *Vivian* (K. Perrakis, Greece).
(*circa*) 1968: Converted to a tanker; fitted with new oil engine.
1970: (D. & P. Theodossiou & others, Greece).

(*circa*) 1987: Employed supplying fresh water to Spetsia Island, Greece, from the mainland.

431   *Empire Facet* Laid down as *Chant 38*, later renamed *Fabric 38*.
Launched: 4.11.1944 as *Empire Facet*.
Completed: 11.1944.
1946: *Hullgate* (Hull Gates Shipping Co. (Craggs & Jenkin Ltd.)).
1962: *Agios Nektarios* (Dendrinos & Varouchas, Greece).
1962: (T. D. Athanassiades, Greece).
18.3.1963: Caught fire in Ionian Sea, abandoned. Taken in tow by Yugoslav steamer *Lastovo* (1922, 1,039 gt) but sank near Patras, Greece (voyage: Piraeus/Trieste – cotton).

432   *Empire Fang* Laid down as *Chant 39*, later renamed *Fabric 39*.
Launched: 13.11.1944 as *Empire Fang*.
Completed: 1.1945.
1946: *Marion* (Wm. Robertson & Son, Glasgow).
1952: *Longboat* (N. Long & Co. Ltd., Glasgow).
1954: (G. Harvey, Quebec; later Transport Maritime Harvey Ltee.).
1956: (New oil engine).
1972: *De Lavoye* (E. Lavoie & Sons, Quebec; later Lavoie & Fils).
1978: (Vapores Orinoco, Panama (Honduras flag)).

433   *Empire Fairplay* Laid down as *Chant 40*, later renamed *Fabric 40*.
Launched: 16.12.1944 as *Empire Fairplay*.
Completed: 1.1945.
1949: *Helen Fairplay* (Overseas Fish Import Co., (Great Yarmouth Shipping Co. Ltd.)).
1951: *Lynn Trader* (Great Yarmouth Shipping Co. Ltd.).
1953: (New oil engine).
1960: *Hamza I* (Fouad Hassan Hamza, Port Said, Egypt).

434   *Empire Fairway* Laid down as *Chant 41*, later renamed *Fabric 41*.
Launched: 16.1.1945 as *Empire Fairway*.
Completed: 2.1945.
1949: *Helen Fairway* (Overseas Fish Import Co. (Great Yarmouth Shipping Co. Ltd.)).
1951: *Selborne* (J. Carter (Poole) Ltd.).
1956: *Tynehaven* (Whitehaven Shipping Co. Ltd. (Anthony & Bainbridge Ltd.)).
1959: *Champlain* (R. & D. Desgagnes, Quebec).
1959: (New oil engine fitted – made in 1936).
1970: *Gilani* (Desgagne & Perron Inc., Quebec) (rebuilt to one hold for carriage of bulk woodpulp).

22.4.1972: Capsized and sank at Vercheres wharf, Montreal, while loading steel on deck. Refloated and repaired.

1978: Reported sold (Honduras flag) and later reported lost, but loss unconfirmed: vessel still listed in ship registers.

Coaster – refrigerated

Built by Ardrossan Dockyard Ltd.

385   *Empire Atoll* 692 gt, 990 tdw, 210 ft (oa), 201 ft × 33 ft. Engines: Oil (aft) – 10½ knots.
Launched: 12.7.1941.
Completed: 1942.
1946: *Hadrian Coast* (Coast Lines Ltd.).
1967: *Elda* (E. Daviou & others, Greece).
10.1.1970: Dragged anchors and grounded on a beach near Mehidia, Morocco, after sustaining leakage and engine trouble in heavy weather (voyage: Ravenna/Kenitra – fertiliser). Total loss.

The *Empire Atoll*, although carrying the M.O.W.T. prefix to her name, was built to the order of Coast Lines Ltd., whose activities included a great number of services, with many specialised types of ship to operate them. The ship had the distinction of being the only all-refrigerated coaster built under the wartime building programme and with her introduction Coast Lines became the first company in Great Britain to operate a full 'reefer' coaster.

Of the machinery-aft, single screw type and intended primarily for meat carrying, the *Empire Atoll* had two holds and 'tween decks, all of which were insulated. The total hold capacity of 50,604 cu. ft. was also about 10 per cent of that of a large 'Empire' food-carrying ship, representing the amount of trans-shipment cargo which would normally be available for local carriage when a larger vessel, due to operating conditions, would not be expected to make short sea trips with a minimum of cargo.

The construction of Ardrossan Harbour was begun in 1806 and completed in 1833. From fishing, exports of coal and chemicals the port gradually expanded to include coastal passenger services, and private shipbuilders established small yards in the area. The Ardrossan Shipbuilding Company came into being in the 1870s and at the turn of the century was restyled under new ownership as the Ardrossan Drydock & Shipbuilding Company. From expansion of shipbuilding facilities in the Great War, when two yards, North and South, were worked, the company became Ardrossan Dockyard Ltd. in 1925, but from deteriorating trade conditions came the shipbuilding industry's plan for the elimination of surplus shipyards and the five-berth South Yard – the largest berth 450 ft – of the Ardrossan company was acquired by National Shipbuilders' Security Ltd., and closed.

During the 1939–1945 conflict the company not only constructed coasters for Government and private account, but also built a number of trawlers and boom defence vessels for the Admiralty. In 1947 there were four berths with a hull capacity of 275 ft and a drydock 340 ft × 46 ft.

In 1962 the yard was put up for sale as a going concern by its shareholders, J. G. Kincaid & Co. Ltd. and Coast Lines Ltd., and was acquired by Blake, Barclay Ltd., ship repairers and engineers.

The last ship constructed was the Coast Lines (Link Line) motor coaster *Buffalo* (Yard No. 430), of 2,163 gt with engines aft, completed in January 1962.

SHIPS BUILT UNDER PRIVATE CONTRACT OR LICENCE

378   *Stuart Queen* 1,224 gt, 247.9 ft (oa),
238.5 ft × 34.2 ft. Engines: T3cyl.
Launched: 14.11.1940.
Completed: 3.1941 for British Channel Islands
Shipping Co. Ltd. (Coast Lines Ltd., London).
1947: (Queenship Navigation Ltd. (Coast Lines
Ltd.)).
1952: *Hampshire Coast* (Tyne-Tees SS Co. Ltd. (Coast
Lines Ltd.)).
3.1959: Scrapped Hendrik Ido Ambacht.

379   *Moray Coast* 687 gt, 209.6 ft (oa),
201.8 ft × 33.2 ft. Engines: Oil.
Launched: 6.7.1940.
Completed: 11.1940 for Coast Lines Ltd., London.
1954: *Jersey Coast* (British Channel Islands Shipping
Co. Ltd. (Coast Lines Ltd.)).
1967: *Star of Ibrahim* (Orri Navigation Lines, Jeddah).
1973: *Bluesky* (H. M. Fayez & Sons, Jeddah).
5.7.1980: Reported to have machinery damage due
to engine breakdown.
9.2.1982: Towed to sea and scuttled outside port
limits of Jeddah, Saudi Arabia.

380   *Ulster Duke* 507 gt, 201.8 ft (oa),
194.2 ft × 30.3 ft. Engines: Oil.
Launched: 19.4.1942.
Completed: 7.1942 for Belfast SS Co. Ltd. (Coast
Lines Ltd.).
1947: *Guernsey Coast* (British Channel Islands
Shipping Co. Ltd. (Coast Lines Ltd.)).
1955: *Ulster Spinner* (Belfast SS Co. Ltd. (Coast Lines
Ltd.)).
1968: *Al-Amin* (M. A. Araktingi, Beirut).
1972: *Hamid* (Wafik Begdache, Lebanon).
1980: *Elvina* (Ayat Bakhirat Co. Ltd., Cyprus).

391   *Southern Coast* 883 gt, 243 ft (oa),
230 ft × 35.2 ft. Engines: Oil.
Launched: 25.1.1943.
Completed: 6.1943 for Coast Lines Ltd., London.
1955: *Colebrooke* (Belfast, Mersey & Manchester SS
Co., Belfast (Coast Lines Ltd.)).
1959: *Forth* (Wm. Sloan & Co. Ltd., Glasgow (Coast
Lines Ltd.)).
1962: *Southern Coast* (British Channel Islands
Shipping Co. Ltd. (Coast Lines Ltd.)).
1967: *Eleistria* (D. Varverakis & C. Hadjigeorgiou,
Greece).

1979: *Al Rubayia* (Al Rubayia Transport Co.,
Kuwait).
1980: (Naviglory Shipping Corp., Panama).
17.11.1983: Placed under arrest at Bombay.
18.2.1985: Sold to shipbreakers by auction under
Court Order.
27.6.1985: Sprang leak in monsoon, sank in Bombay
harbour. Raised and scrapped locally.

393   *Lairds Loch* 1,530 gt, 275 ft (oa),
256.5 ft × 41.2 ft. Engines: Oil, twin screw.
Launched: 9.3.1944.
Completed: 8.1944 for Burns & Laird Lines Ltd.
(Coast Lines Ltd.).
1969: *Hey Daroma* (Sefinot Ltd., Israel).
3.9.1970: Aground, ten km from Sharm el Shaikh,
Gulf of Aqaba, 28.05N 34.27E (voyage: Eilat/Sharm
el Shaikh). No salvage attempts made. Constructive
total loss.

397   *Norman Queen* 1,048 gt, 212.5 ft (oa),
204.5 ft × 32.7 ft. Engines: T3cyl.
Launched: 25.5.1944.
Completed: 10.1944 for British Channel Islands
Shipping Co. Ltd. (Coast Lines Ltd.).
1947: (Queenship Navigation Ltd. (Coast Lines
Ltd.)).
6.1961: Scrapped Hendrik Ido Ambacht.

399   *Highland Queen* 1,043 gt. Details as Yard No.
397.
Launched: 24.5.1945.
Completed: 9.1945 for British Channel Islands
Shipping Co. Ltd. (Coast Lines Ltd.).
1947: (Queenship Navigation Ltd. (Coast Lines
Ltd.)).
18.6.1959: Arrived Hendrik Ido Ambacht for
breaking up.

400   *Balmoral Queen* 1,043 gt. Details as Yard No.
397.
Launched: 22.10.1945.
Completed: 12.1945 for British Channel Islands
Shipping Co. Ltd. (Coast Lines Ltd.).
1947: (Queenship Navigation Ltd. (Coast Lines
Ltd.)).
15.6.1959: Arrived Hendrik Ido Ambacht for
breaking up.

The *Empire Atoll* as *Hadrian Coast*, in the River Thames, August 1953. This was the only war-built coaster fitted to carry refrigerated cargoes. (Ardrossan Dockyard Ltd., Yard No. 385.)

The coaster *Race Fisher*, formerly *Empire Jill*. (S. P. Austin & Sons Ltd., Yard No. 361.)

The *Empire Head*, as the coaster *Brendonia*. (Clelands (Successors) Ltd., Yard No. 57.)   *Skyfotos*

Coasters – 1,015 tdw, 193 ft (oa), 185 ft × 30 ft. Engines: Oil (aft) – 10 knots

Built by Vickers Armstrongs Ltd., Barrow

829   *Empire Jack* 734 gt.
Launched: 4.10.1941 as *River Fisher*.
Completed: 12.1941 as *Empire Jack*.
1946: *River Fisher* (J. Fisher & Sons Ltd., Barrow).
1967: *Owenduv* (Greenore Ferry Services, Dublin).

1971: (Cia. Mtma. Fogana S.A., Panama).
13.1.1972: Capsized and sank ten miles off Leixoes after cargo shifted in heavy weather (voyage: Villagarcia/Morocco – wood platex).

Built by S. P. Austin & Sons Ltd., Sunderland

361   *Empire Jill* 739 gt.
Launched: 15.1.1942.
Completed: 4.1942.
1946: *Race Fisher* (J. Fisher & Sons Ltd., Barrow).
1967: *Fardad* (M. J. Motraghi, Iran).

370   *Empire Judy* 738 gt.
Launched: 5.4.1943.

Completed: 6.1943.
1946: *Stream Fisher* (J. Fisher & Sons Ltd., Barrow).
1965: (Converted at Workington for carrying irradiated atomic fuel from Anzio, Italy, to Barrow-in-Furness).
1969: *Ramaida* (Grandport Shipping, Panama (J. H. Ramagge)).
9.1977: Scrapped Lisbon.

Coasters – 625 tdw, 170 ft (oa), 165 ft × 26 ft. Engines: Oil (aft) – 9 knots

Built by Clelands (Successors) Ltd., Wallsend

56   *Empire Dyke* 489 gt.
Launched: 15.1.1942.
Completed: 4.1942.
1943: *Prinses Margriet* (Government of Netherlands).
1954: *Sand Star* (South Coast Shipping Co. Ltd. (Burness Shipping Co. Ltd.)).
1955: (Converted to a sand dredger).
1956: (South Coast Shipping Co. Ltd. (Wm. Cory & Sons Ltd.)).
9.1966: Scrapped Grays, Essex

57   *Empire Head* 489 gt.
Launched: 13.5.1941.
Completed: 10.1941.
15.2.1942: Damaged by aircraft bombs eleven miles east of Hartlepool. Proceeded, arrived Middlesbrough. Repaired.
1945: *Brendonia* (J. Wharton (Shipping) Ltd., Goole).
1964: *Ifigenia* (N. Dimitriadis & Co., Greece).
1976: *Hamzi* (S. Mohamet, Syria).
19.1.1983: Found lying aground and abandoned at Golovasi, Yumurtalik Bay, Turkey. Refloated: taken over by local port authority for disposal.

Coasters – 1,125 tdw, 203 ft (oa), 198 ft × 30 ft. Engines: Oil (aft) – 9½ knots

Built by Goole Shipbuilding & Repairing Co. Ltd.

357 *Empire Cliff* 873 gt.
Launched: 16.10.1940.
Completed: 12.1940.
1945: *Marna* (South Georgia Co. Ltd. (Chr. Salvesen & Co., Leith)).
1960: *Harcliff* (Hargreaves Coal & Shipping Co. Ltd., London).
1963: *Ricardo Manuel* (Comp. Cia. Portuguesa de Nav., Panama).
4.9.1971: Sank off entrance to port of Casablanca after collision in fog with, and being cut in two by, mv *Zagora* (1956, 1,437 gt). Total loss (voyage: Lisbon/Casablanca).

358 *Empire Foreland* 873 gt.
Launched: 2.12.1940.
Completed: 3.1941.
1945: *Norfolkbrook* (Williamstown Shipping Co. Ltd. (Comben Longstaff & Co. Ltd.)).
1950: *Agate* (Gem Line Ltd. (Wm. Robertson, Glasgow)).
1961: *Silvana Tomei* (Di Guido Pio Tomei, Italy).
1972: *Sabbiatore Primo* (Naval Protector, Italy).
1984: Name deleted from shipping registers – vessel converted to a non-propelled barge.

Coasters – 430 tdw, 136 ft (oa), 130 ft × 25.2 ft. Engines: Oil (aft) – 8 knots

Built by J. Pollock & Sons Ltd., Faversham

1776 *Empire Creek* 332 gt.
Launched: 15.1.1941.
Completed: 4.1941.
13.6.1941: Disabled by aircraft bombs off Peterhead, Scotland. Towed to Aberdeen; repaired.
1946: *Springcreek* (Springwell Shipping Co. Ltd., London).
1948: *Goldcreek* (E. J. & W. Goldsmith Ltd., London).
1951: *Milborne* (J. Carter (Poole) Ltd.).
1964: *Georgios* (S. Skordalakis, Greece).
1978: *Ulysses* (Zoegeorge S.A., Panama).
20.12.1979: Driven aground near Naples in heavy weather. Wrecked and abandoned. Total loss.

1777 *Empire Crag* 332 gt.
Launched: 15.3.1941.
Completed: 6.1941.
1946 *Springcrag* (Springwell Shipping Co. Ltd., London).
1954: *Walcrag* (Walford Lines Ltd., London).
1962: *Colne Trader* (J. J. Prior (Transport) Ltd., London).
1976: *Spithead Trader* (G. C. Yell, London).

Note: Both *Empire Creek* and *Empire Crag* were replicas of the *Camroux I* and *Camroux II*, built by the yard in 1934–1935 for the Newcastle Coal & Shipping Co. Ltd., and themselves based on the yard's own standard 'Landina' design.

The origins of James Pollock & Sons Ltd., date back well over a century. James Pollock was born in 1838 and, as a young engineer, sailed in 1859 for Vladivostok in the barque *Orus*, which also carried the paddle steamer *General Kharsakov*, its hull in plates and angles, its engine in sections. James Pollock was there to supervise its building and, with himself as Chief Engineer, it was the first steamer to navigate the great River Amur. This was one of the earliest of prefabricated constructions.

In 1863 the blockade runner *Ruahine* was taken in hand for the American Civil War. Of 280 ft, her boilers worked at 25 pounds per square inch.

From 1875 James Pollock worked in London as a naval architect and then, in 1900, with his son, formed the firm of J. Pollock, Son & Company and over the next twenty years supervised the building of a variety of vessels: ferries for the Thames; a shallow-draught paddle steamer for the rivers of Iraq; a floating dock for Australia; and a group totalling forty special types of ships for the River Amazon. This group included a stern-wheeler named *Antonio Lemos*, with solid instead of feathering floats, which crossed the Atlantic under her own power. In fact, much of the business was for South American and African account.

After James Pollock died, in 1910, the company continued under the guidance of his son, Walter. Late in 1914 the Admiralty requested that a shipyard, to be known as Admiralty Shipyard Extension No. 15, be built at Faversham, Kent, to construct small craft for war purposes. In 1915 the Admiralty required a large number of shallow-draught landing craft, for putting an army ashore behind German lines in the Baltic. Pollock suggested that flat-bottomed barges be built, with the forefoot cut away, a hinged brow over the bows and an oil engine aft, enabling the barge to be driven directly on to the beach. Orders were placed for 250 of this design, Pollocks (as agents to the Swedish engine firm of Bolinder) supplying the engines and supervising the construction of these 'X'-class lighters, to become known as 'Beetles', although none were built at Faversham. But the original military plan was cancelled and some were shipped out for use in the Dardanelles/Gallipoli campaign, including the evacuation of Suvla Bay. Many of the remainder became naval dockyard craft in the 1920s.

Two experimental ferro-concrete coasters, *Molliette* and *Violette*, about 300 gt, were delivered by the yard in 1919 and in the ensuing years of peace Pollocks built tugs, especially for Thames work, coasters 'on spec' to their own design, small tankers, lighters and barges, many for overseas buyers.

Output during the 1939–1945 war included two small 'Empire' ships, two 'VIC'-class steam lighters, a tender for Turkish account and many military craft and cargo barges. The largest ships ordered at the yard were four aircraft transports, each of 1,000 tons displacement, for servicing Fleet Air Arm vessels. Two were completed, the *Ripon* (Yard No. 1838), launched 15 March 1945 and completed in the August, and the *Seafox* (Yard No. 1839) launched on 16 May 1946. But the end of the war had made both vessels surplus to requirements and they were sold. The former, as *Ripon M*, carried cargo around the West Indies far into the 1980s, whilst the *Seafox*, as *Roubahe Darya*, flew the flag of Iran into the same decade. The other two ships were cancelled, the partly-completed hulls purchased commercially to become the *Goldhind* and *Goldlynx* of E. J. & W. Goldsmith Ltd., London.

The yard continued with the construction of tugs, salvage plant and small craft in the postwar years, but announced its liquidation in February 1970, by which time the 'yard' numbers exceeded 2,000. But they were not all actual constructions, for prior to 1916 the company was associated with the design or procurement of 891 vessels, these given 'yard' numbers rather than 'job' numbers, but in the period 1916–1938 some 826 craft were constructed in their shipyard.

SHIPS BUILT UNDER PRIVATE CONTRACT OR LICENCE

1726 *Dominence* 261 gt, 118.6 ft (oa), 114 ft × 24.8 ft. Engines: Oil (aft).
Launched: 11.1.1940.
Completed: 1940 for London & Rochester Trading Co. Ltd.
1945: (New oil engine).
11.1969: Stripped by owners of usable equipment at Rochester, Kent; hull scrapped.

1781 *Imta Layteri* 207 gt, 110 ft (oa), 106 ft × 24 ft. Engines: Oil (aft).
Launched: 18.4.1942.
Completed: 1942 as a submarine tender for the Turkish Navy. Later renamed *Isin* (390 displ. tons).
(*circa*) 1960: In use as a diving tender.

The tender *Imta Layteri* was built to a pre-war contract, based on the shipyard's own standard coaster design. The main difference was that her hold was divided: the after part fitted with battery-charging equipment for submarines and the forepart fitted with a hatch of sufficient length to permit the stowage of torpedoes without their having to be slewed in the loading process.

1844 (Laid down as) *Sea Gladiator* 567 gt, 180 ft (oa), 165 ft × 30.1 ft. Engines: Oil (aft).
Laid down as an aircraft transport for the Fleet Air Arm, but contract cancelled: vessel sold commercially.

Launched: 18.12.1948.
Completed: 4.1949 as *Goldhind* for E. J. & W. Goldsmith Ltd., London.
1952: *Purple Emperor* (Coastal Tankers Ltd. (Springwell Shipping Co. Ltd.)).
1955: *Towai* (Anchor Shipping & Foundry Co., New Zealand).
1969: *Akana* (Akana (Pty.) Ltd., New Guinea).
1977: *Minaa Maaree* (A. Ahamed, Maldive Islands).
1979: *Masahi* (M. Yanagiya, Maldive Islands).

1845 (Laid down as) *Sea Hurricane* 552 gt. Details as Yard No. 1844.
Laid down as an aircraft transport for the Fleet Air Arm, but contract cancelled: vessel sold commercially.
Launched: 24.9.1949.
Completed: 2.1950 as *Goldlynx* for E. J. & W. Goldsmith Ltd., London.
1952: *Springwood* (Springwell Shipping Co. Ltd.).
1953: *Leafoam* (Leadenhall Shipping Co. (Springwell Shipping Co. Ltd.)).
1953: *Ballyedward* (J. Kelly Ltd., Belfast).
1970: *Lady Hyacinth* (Zodiac Shipping Ltd., N. Ireland).
1973: *Golden Trader* (Commercial Ferries Ltd., Eire).
1974: Scrapped Gijon, Spain.

Coasters – 320 tdw, 137 ft (oa), 132.5 ft × 24.6 ft. Engines: Oil (aft) – 8 knots

Built by I. Pimblott & Sons Ltd., Northwich

635 *Empire Kyle* 325 gt.
Launched: 1941.
Completed: 6.1941.
1945. (New oil engine).
1946: *Turgail* (Erskine Shipping Co. Ltd., Liverpool).
1956: *Ordinence* (London & Rochester Trading Co. Ltd.).
7.1972: Scrapped Queenborough, Kent.

636 *Empire Grove* 325 gt.
Launched: 5.6.1941.
Completed: 10.1941.
18.10.1941: Ashore at Long Peak, two miles south of Hartland Point, Devon. Driven across rocks and against cliffs. Holed, buckled, then fractured.

Constructive total loss (voyage: Hayle/Cardiff – ballast).

642 *Empire Lily* 325 gt.
Launched: 29.1.1942.
Completed: 6.1942.
1946: *Pampus* (Government of Netherlands).
1946: *Petit Frere* (L. Tercy, France).
1953: (New oil engine).
1962: *Dedalos* (A. Veroutis & Co., Greece).
1964: *Nikiforos* (S. D. Voudouris & Syriggas, Greece).
1973: *Gagnant* (Beekman Line S.A., Greece).
1988: (Still listed in shipping registers, but owners not specified) (existence of vessel in doubt).

Built by Richards Ironworks Ltd., Lowestoft

280   *Empire Firth* 325 gt.
Launched: 3.1941.
Completed: 8.1941.
1947: *Annick* (J. Campbell, Irvine).
1954: *Lones* (A/S Lo-nes Rederi (T. Horvi & Sandvik, Norway)).
1958: *Edenside* (Ross Line Ltd., Sunderland).
1968: *North Trader* (North East by East Shipping Co. Ltd.).
1969: (N. Jadavji & Hirji, Kenya).
1969: *Tanzania* (United Youth Shipping Co., Tanzania).

281   *Empire Sound* 325 gt.
Launched: 8.8.1941.
Completed: 12.1941.
1943: *Zuiderhaven* (Government of Netherlands).
1946: *Tamise II* (Entreprise Generale de Transport Maritimes S.A., France).
1950: *Cimcour II* (S.A. de Ciments de Dannes, France).
1953: *Sjaholm* (A/S Sjaholm, Norway).
1958: (New oil engine).
1965: *Pokal* (A. Remoy Partrederi, Norway).
1968: *Bjerkosund* (I/S Peddership-Pedersen & Sonner, Norway).
1972: *Eidsvag* (Nesset R/A., Norway).
1983: (G. Mallion, London).
1985: (Nick Ocean International, Honduras).

296   *Empire Punch* 325 gt.
Launched: 31.1.1942.
Completed: 5.1942.
1947: (Lovering & Sons, Cardiff).
1955: *Oakdene* (T. G. Irving Ltd., Sunderland).
1967: (G. & E. Sealy, Sunderland).
8.1966: Sailed from London for service in Barbados.

301   *Empire Reynard* 325 gt.
Launched: 11.7.1942.
Completed: 10.1942.
1943: *Westerhaven* (Government of Netherlands).
1946: *Orsuro* (S.A. Jean Negri, France).
1949: *Chassiron* (Cia. Charentaise de Transports Maritimes, Paris).

1951: *Kilbride* (R. T. V. Hall, Dublin).
1972: (T. Rive, Dublin).
1973: *Joyce* (Mrs. Joyce Hercock, Hull).
4.1974: Scrapped Hull.

310   *Empire Sportsman* 325 gt.
Launched: 6.5.1943.
Completed: 9.1943.
1946: *Norrix* (R. Rix & Sons, Hull).
1961: (New oil engine).
1963: *Ionion* (Odysseas & Charalabous, Greece).
1963: (N. T. Giannoutsos, Greece).
5.1985: Scrapped Perama, Greece.

311   (Intended to be) *Empire Chuzzlewit* 322 gt.
Launched: 14.10.1943.
Completed: 1943 as naval auxiliary coaster *Chattenden* (R.F.A. ammunition carrier).
1951–1967: Laid up Portchester Creek, Portsmouth.
1967: (H. G. Pounds, Portsmouth).
1969: *Mark Bowen* (T. Bowen & P. Caines) (converted to aggregates suction dredger).
(*circa*) 1978: Laid up River Itchen, Southampton. Later broken up.

333   *Empire Gillian* 306 gt.
Launched: 24.5.1944.
Completed: 8.1944.
1945: *Brescou* (Government of France).
1947: (Cie. Meridionele de Nav., France).
8.1970: Scrapped La Seyne, France.

337   *Empire Albany* 306 gt.
Launched: 3.10.1944.
Completed: 12.1944.
1946: *Albany* (Mrs. P. Dowds, Eire).
20.11.1946: Sailed from Port Talbot, South Wales, for Rosslare, Co. Wexford, Eire, with a cargo of coal during a gale.
22.11.1946: Two damaged ship's boats and name board of the vessel washed ashore near St. David's Head, Pembrokeshire. No further trace; presume to have foundered.

In 1876 and at the age of 24, Samuel Richards left his home town of Penzance and in the following year founded a shipyard, S. Richards & Company, at Kirkley Ham, a narrow creek off Lowestoft's inner harbour.

   The first vessel was the 56-ft sailing drifter *Nil Desperandum* and the yard went on to specialise in the construction of wooden-hulled fishing craft, later diverting to small ship production of many types.

At the start of World War I the company turned to repair work and naval contracts; trawlers were converted to minesweepers and numerous wooden minesweepers and patrol vessels were built. Postwar construction again added vessels to Britain's fishing fleet and in 1926 the first British diesel-powered drifter, the 86-ft *Veracity*, was delivered. Sold in 1934, she was rigged with square sails and her hull metal-sheathed before her owner took her to the Cocos Islands in an abortive search for pirate treasure, alleged to have been buried in 1823.

In the early 1930s the firm was restyled Richards Ironwords Ltd., in this period completing the last coal-burner for the Lowestoft fishing fleet, the 94-ft *Merbreeze*, for P. W. Watson & Sons. She was still in service more than forty years later.

Apart from the eight 'Empire' coasters built during World War II, Richards Ironworks built a number of smaller craft, including six VIC-type coasters, wooden minesweepers, a torpedo recovery vessel, *TRV 3* (Yard No. 300, launched 23.1.1943) and twenty-four motor fishing vessels (MFVs). There were over 700 of these small MFVs built in the United Kingdom during the war years, spread to four classes, all from Admiralty orders, while over a hundred were constructed in colonial yards. Construction contracts were shared by many companies. The four classes of MFV ranged from 49.7 ft (loa) to 64.5 ft., 75.5 ft., and 97.7 ft. Not all were diesel-driven, some being fitted with petrol engines due to wartime expediency; the speed ranged from $7\frac{1}{2}$–9 knots.

Intended shipment as deck cargo was denied these craft due to lack of shipping space and they made their voyages in flotillas on their own keels; in 1943 many sailed to the Mediterranean area, some 2,000 miles to Gibraltar in wartime diversions. These fishing vessels had numerous uses apart from their standard work. They were used as harbour runabouts; some were taken up as pilot boats; many worked on the Malta–Sicily shuttle service of the Sicilian landings in 1943 and, later, at the Normandy beaches, whilst large numbers ended up in India and the Far East. Those built by Richards were of the largest type, with classified numbers in the *MFV 1501–1607* range.

When war ended the company's yard at Lowestoft had seven berths to 150 ft. In 1957 the firm was acquired by United Molasses Co. Ltd., and expanded to build ships to 300 ft. It was renamed Richards (Shipbuilders) Ltd.

Built by J. S. Watson Ltd., Gainsborough

1520   *Empire Ford* 325 gt.
Launched: 28.5.1941.
Completed: 9.1941.
10.1.1943: Grounded, with engine room flooded, off Seahouses, North Sunderland.
11.1.1943: Abandoned in sinking condition.
Refloated and put to anchor, but broke adrift in heavy weather; drifted, unmanned, and grounded off Farne Islands, near Bamborough, Northumberland. Submerged (cargo of cement).
27.2.1943: Refloated, towed to Warkworth harbour.
6.3.1943: Arrived Tyne in tow: Repaired.
1943: *Noorderhaven* (Government of Netherlands).
1947: *Saint Honorat* (Soc. Nav. d'Import et d'Export, Dakar).
1951: (New oil engine).
1965: *Korali* (D. Vassilatos, Greece).

1966: *Maria S* (K. Savva Bros, Greece).
1967: *Sofia Gogi* (P. & M. Gogis, Greece).
1975: *Konstantinos Gaviotis* (owned in Greece).
1976: *Agios Georgios* (G. Atsalis & Co., Greece).

1521   *Empire River* 325 gt.
Launched: 8.9.1941.
Completed: 12.1941.
1943: *Oosterhaven* (Government of Netherlands).
1946: *Jean-Marc* (M. R. Couton, France).
1947: *Jean-Marc Richard* (Andre Richard, France).
1950: *Marshlea* (Hindlea Shipping Co. Ltd., Cardiff).
1952: *Peter Leigh* (F. A. Ashmead & Son Ltd., Bristol).
1956: (New oil engine).
1965: *Carbo-Centre* (converted to a sand carrier) (Carbo Centre S.A., France).

As well as the two dry cargo coasters, the J. S. Watson shipyard completed five 'Empire' tugs and a number of VIC-type coasters. The remainder of the ships built were mostly for dockyard work; five Torpedo Recovery Vessels (TRV) were also constructed.

Coasters – 1,160 tdw, 211 ft (oa), 203 ft × 33 ft. Engines: Oil (aft) – 10 knots

Built by Harland & Wolff Ltd., Govan

1092G   *Empire Shoal* 878 gt.
Launched: 13.2.1941.
Completed: 6.1941.
1946: *Angularity* (F. T. Everard & Sons Ltd.).
1967: *Elpis* (G. Tzortzis & others, Greece).
22.1.1968: Sprang leak in engine room, sank between Ameland and Schiermonnikoog, Holland, 53.35N 5.51E (voyage: London/Hamburg/Malta – cement).

1115G   *Empire Deep* 878 gt.
Launched: 9.9.1941.
Completed: 11.1941.

1942: *Starkenburgh* (Government of Netherlands).
1947: *Spaarnestroom* (Hollandsche Stoomboot Maats., Holland).
1961: *Erato Sartes* (Sartes Corporation Ltd., Greece).
1963: *Antonios P* (Antonios I. Petras, Greece).
16.2.1969: Stranded in fog outside Ravenna harbour, Italy, 44.35N 12.18E.
11.3.1969: Refloated, with stern gear damage; towed to *Ravenna* (voyage: Lattakia/Ravenna – barley).
7.1969: Scrapped Piraeus.

Built by A. & J. Inglis Ltd., Glasgow

1088P   *Empire Gat* 871 gt.
Launched: 13.11.1940.
Completed: 4.1941.
1947: *Borthwick* (G. Gibson & Co. Ltd.).
1960: *Agostino* (Ubaldo Gennari fu Torqueto & C., Italy).
1971: (Sinavi, Italy).
1972: *Ivy* (Ivy Shipping Co. S.A., Panama).
1986: Name deleted from ship registers – existence of vessel in doubt.

1089P   *Empire Spinney* 872 gt.
Launched: 26.6.1941.
Completed: 9.1941.
1946: *Peregrine* (General Steam Navigation Co. Ltd.).
1965: *Libya* (D. Vassilatos & others, Greece).
1965: (Elias Condos & others, Greece).
1971: *Rozmary* (S. Kondopoulos & Co., Greece).

Built by Scott & Sons, Bowling.

358 *Empire Beacon* 872 gt.
Launched: 24.9.1941.
Completed: 11.1941.
5.4.1942: Struck British mine and sank six miles from St. Ann's Head, North Devon, 51.41N 5.10W (voyage: Cardiff/Belfast).

359 *Empire Cape* 872 gt.
Launched: 27.3.1941.
Completed: 7.1941.

1945: *Gowrie* (Dundee, Perth & London Shipping Co. Ltd.).
1948: Renamed *Lochee*.
1966: *Aghios Spyridon* (D. & S. Zoulis & others, Greece).
1969: (S. C. Vazeos, Greece).
1970: *Anwar* (Abdel Razzak Sattout, Lebanon).
1979: (General United Trading & Shipping Co., S.A.R.L., Lebanon).

Coasters – 1,100 tdw, 205 ft (oa), 198 ft × 34 ft. Engines: T3cyl (aft) – 9½ knots

Built by Scott & Sons, Bowling

369 *Empire Rider* 965 gt.
Launched: 15.9.1943.
Completed: 10.1943.
1946: *Rocquaine* (O. Dorey & Sons Ltd., Guernsey).
1961: Scrapped Terneuzen, Holland.

370 *Empire Marksman* 965 gt.
Launched: 26.1.1944.
Completed: 3.1944.
1948: *Afon Morlais* (Afon Lliedi SS Co. (Wm. Coombs & Sons, Llanelli)).
1956: *Cliffville* (John S. Monks Ltd., Liverpool).
12.5.1958: Developed leak in engine room. Listed, heeled over and sank at Meadowside Granary Wharf, Glasgow (voyage: Liverpool/Glasgow – grain). Cargo discharged, and:
14.7.1958: Refloated, drydocked, but constructive total loss. Sold and scrapped Dublin.

372 *Empire Dorrit* 965 gt.
Launched: 4.10.1944.
Completed: 12.1944.
1945: *Lieutenant Lancelot* (Cia. Navale Caennaise, France).
1954: *Holdernith* (Holderness SS Co. (T. Kittlewell & Son Ltd., Hull)).
17.1.1957: Grounded on Whitton Sand, River Humber; engine room and No. 2 hold flooded. Abandoned, sank (voyage: Goole/London – wool).
19.1.1957: Refloated and patched, towed to Hull. Discharged, drydocked and repaired.
1963: Scrapped Grays, Essex.

The shipyard at Bowling was started by the Scott family, of Greenock, in 1851 and was to last for 128 years. Ship construction was in the smaller ship types, coasters, yachts and, in particular, tugs.

In 1935 they built the tug *Warrior* for Steel & Bennie Ltd., Glasgow, and from this design came the wartime 'Warrior'-class of 'Empire' tugs, of which Scott's built thirteen. Five 'Empire' coasters were also built.

When war ended the company was operating four berths for ships to 230 ft and two slips of 800 and 450 tons lift.

In 1965 the company was acquired by Scotts Shipbuilding & Engineering Co. Ltd., of Greenock and, in turn, they merged with Lithgows Ltd. in 1967 to become Scott Lithgow Ltd. On 29 October

1974 it was announced in the Queen's Speech to Parliament that the shipbuilding and shipping industries were to be nationalised and Scott Lithgow duly came under the British Shipbuilders banner.

Eventually, in 1979, the yard was closed on a care and maintenance basis. Two of the last buildings were the Voith tractor tugs *Carron* (Yard No. 458), launched on 30 April 1979 and the *Laggan* (Yard No. 459) launched on 25 June 1979, both for Forth Tugs Ltd.

SHIPS BUILT UNDER PRIVATE CONTRACT OR LICENCE

354 *Staley Bridge* 297 gt, 138 ft (oa), 131.4 ft × 24.6 ft. Engines: Oil (aft).
Launched: 27.3.1940.
Completed: 1940 for J. Summers & Sons Ltd., Shotton, Flintshire.
1967: (W. Wharton, Chester).
1970: (W. T. Bateman, London).
1972: Converted to a salvage ship (Salvage & Cable (Folkestone) Ltd.).
1977: (J. P. Rowland, London).

355 *Hawarden Bridge* 297 gt. Details as Yard No. 354.
Launched: 25.1.1940.
Completed: 1940 for J. Summers & Sons Ltd., Shotton, Flintshire.
1967: (I. W. Marshall, Chester).
3.11.1978: Towed out of Miami and sunk as an artificial fish reef.

Note: Both (above) Yard Nos. 354 and 355 (when owned by J. Summers & Sons) were employed working from Hawarden Bridge Steelworks, via the River Dee to Liverpool, and for general coasting.

356 *Saint Rule* 524 gt, 172.2 ft (oa), 166.2 ft × 27.1 ft. Engines: Oil (aft).
Launched: 3.9.1940.
Completed: 2.1941 for J. & A. Gardner & Co. Ltd.
1968: (Marine Enterprises (Malta) Ltd. (Maltese National Lines Ltd.)).
1972: *Maltese Trader* (Marsa Industries Ltd. (Maltese National Lines Ltd.)).
1973: *Mariam* (Wafik Begdache, Lebanon).
1980: *Fourat Star* (Wafik Begdache, Syria).
17.1.1981: Damaged by stranding in heavy weather at Limassol, Cyprus. Sold and scrapped *in situ*.

357 (Launched as) *Foremost 97* 181 gt, 95.3 ft (oa), 88.8 ft × 24.2 ft. Engines: T3cyl. A tug.
Launched: 23.5.1940.
Completed: 8.1940 as *Cardiff* for Great Western Railway Co.
1948: (British Transport Commission).
1963: (R. & J. H. Rea Ltd., Cardiff).
1964: Scrapped Newport, Mon.

Coasters – 'Empire Isle'-class – 480 tdw, 150 ft (oa), 144 ft × 26 ft. Engines: Oil (aft) – 9 knots

Built by Henry Scarr Ltd., Hessle

416 *Empire Isle* 402 gt.
Launched: 18.2.1941.
Completed: 7.1941.
1945: *Suffolkbrook* (Comben, Longstaff & Co. Ltd.).
1948: *Fennel* (Lovering & Sons, Cardiff).
1952: *Hindlea* (Hindlea Shipping Co. Ltd. (J. L. Hindmarsh, Cardiff)).
1954: (Lengthened to 170.9 ft; 506 gt, 725 tdw).
27.10.1959: Driven shorewards in Moelfre Bay, Anglesey, while sheltering from storm. Anchored and abandoned; dragged anchors and blown ashore. Pounded on rocks, broke in two. Some wreckage washed ashore, remainder of vessel looted by local inhabitants. Total loss (voyage: Weston Point/Newport, Mon. – ballast).

417 *Empire Bank* 402 gt.
Launched: 12.4.1941.
Completed: 8.1941.
1946: *Rose-Julie M* (Metcalf Motor Coasters Ltd., London).
1956: (MAC Shipping Co. Ltd., Glasgow (T. J. Metcalf, London).
1.1966: Scrapped Queenborough, Kent.

Coaster – 480 tdw, 149 ft (oa), 143.5 ft × 26.1 ft. Engines: Oil (aft) – 9 knots

Built by Shipbuilding Corporation, Tyne Branch, Newcastle

18 *Empire Sloane* 419 gt.
Launched: 17.1.1946.
Completed: 1946.
1948: (Broadway Holdings Ltd., London).
1948: *John Williams VI* (London Missionary Society).
1963: *Manutai* (Burns, Philp & Co. Ltd., London).
1975: (Rabi Holdings Ltd., London).

In 1948 J. S. Doig Ltd., Humber Bank, Grimsby, converted the *Empire Sloane* to a Children's Goodwill Ship, to assist in educational, social and Christian work among the islands of the South-West Pacific. Cargo space was turned into accommodation for missionaries, native passengers and children and the deck space at bridge level was extended. Before her maiden voyage as such, in October 1948, she called at seventeen British ports for public inspection. The vessel was named after *John Williams*, a martyr-missionary, who was murdered on Erromanga, in the New Hebrides, in 1839.

Coasters – 380 tdw, 133 ft (oa), 127 ft × 25 ft. Engines: T3cyl (aft) – 7½ knots

Built by W. J. Yarwood & Sons Ltd., Northwich

666   *Empire Bridge* 348 gt.
Launched: 26.2.1941.
Completed: 6.1941.

On 1 February 1946 the British steamer *Fort Massac* (1943, 7,150 gt), owned by the M.O.T. and operated for them by John Cory & Sons, bound from Middlesbrough to Table Bay with general cargo, and the *Thornaby* (1935, 1,174 gt) owned by the Tyne-Tees SS Co. (Coast Lines Ltd.) were in collision off the Sunk Light Vessel, some ten miles ESE of Harwich, Essex, in position 51.53N 1.32E. Struck on the starboard side, the *Fort Massac* was quickly down by the head and then abandoned, with her bows submerged and resting on the bottom, Nos. 1, 2 and 3 holds, stokehold and engine room flooded and her stern above water.

The *Thornaby* arrived at Harwich later the same day, with extensive bow damage. She proceeded to the Thames for repairs, and was later renamed *Northumbrian Coast*.

Salvage attempts on *Fort Massac* commenced on 7 February, but due to a succession of gales the situation deteriorated, the vessel flooding throughout and settling on the bottom, with 8 ft of water over the main deck. Again salvage operations started, this time for recovery of the ship's cargo.

On 9 April the coaster *Empire Bridge*, managed for the M.O.T. by the Springwell Shipping Co., was alongside the *Fort Massac*, loading salved cargo – mostly drums of oil – when she surged and struck the corner of the wreck's boat deck. With No. 2 hold and her boiler room holed, she quickly heeled over and was abandoned. A few minutes later the *Empire Bridge* sank alongside the *Fort Massac*. Salvage operations now commenced on the *Empire Bridge* and by July 1946 the Admiralty had placed lifting wires in position. On 23 August an attempt was made to raise the vessel, but only succeeded in turning the ship on to her port side. Further salvage attempts were abandoned and the vessel declared a constructive total loss.

Note: The sale of the *Empire Bridge* to her managers had been agreed by the M.O.T. just prior to her loss, her prospective purchasers intending to rename the vessel *Springbridge*.

Coasters – 400 tdw, 148.2 ft (oa), 142.2 ft × 27 ft. Engines: Oil (aft) – 7½ knots

These vessels were similar to the 'Empire F'-type, with identical hull form but completed as flush, single deckers and without the double hull.

Built by Clelands (Successors) Ltd., Wallsend

75   *Empire Seablue* 518 gt.
Launched: 28.7.1945.
Completed: 8.1945.
1950: *Seablue* (Instone Lines Ltd.).
13.2.1954: Struck wreck of steamer *Empire Blessing* (1945, 7,062 gt) in fog off Knocke, entrance to River Schelde, Belgium. Proceeded, but made water rapidly in both holds. Attempted to beach but listed; abandoned and sank five miles WSW of Flushing (voyage: London/Antwerp – general cargo and automobiles). Total loss.

76   *Empire Seagreen* 518 gt.
Launched: 6.9.1945.
Completed: 10.1945.

1950: *Seagreen* (Instone Lines Ltd.).
1959: *St. Pierre* ('tween deck removed: 386 gt), (H. Harvey, Quebec).
1962: (Transport Maritime Harvey Ltee., Quebec).
1969: (New oil engine, made in 1951).

9.5.1974: Holed after touching breakwater outside Lachine Canal, Montreal. Entered Canal, but capsized and sank. Raised, and:
6.1974: Broken up at entrance to Canal.

Built by Shipbuilding Corporation, Tyne Branch, Newcastle

15 *Empire Seaforth* 518 gt.
Launched: 2.1945.
Completed: 3.1945.
1947: *Seaforth* (Seaway Coasters Ltd. (C. Howard & Sons, London)).
1951: *Halfaya* (Seaway Coasters Ltd. (J. Fisher & Sons, Barrow)).
1955: *Beihan* (A. R. Mohamed Saleh Al Haddad, Dubai).

1964: *Napoleon* (Transportes Mar. de San Blas S.A., Panama (Guan Guan Shipping Ltd., Singapore)).
(*circa*) 1973: *Aquatic 2* (Thailand).
1975: *Red Eagle* (Thailand flag).
17.3.1975: Sank in Telok Ayer Basin, Singapore. Raised and sold, and
3.1976: Scrapped Jurong, Singapore.

16 *Empire Seabrook* 518 gt.
Launched: 28.3.1945.
Completed: 5.1945.
1947: *Legbourne* (Coastal Carriers Ltd., Grimsby (Gillie & Blair Ltd.)).
1951: *Maston* (Soon Bee SS Co. (Heap Eng Moh SS Co., Singapore)).
1951: Renamed *Bee Tong*.
1959: *Singa Mas* (Guan Guan Ltd. (Chek Guan & Co., Singapore)).

17 *Empire Seasilver* 518 gt.
Launched: 7.6.1945.
Completed: 8.1945.
1947: *Seasilver* (Seaway Coasters Ltd. (C. Howard & Sons, London)).
1951: *Sidi Barrani* (Seaway Coasters Ltd. (J. Fisher & Sons, Barrow)).
1955: *Seiyun* (Savon & Ries (Ethiopian Shipping) Co., Massawa, Ethiopia).

Coasters specifically designed for service in the Far East

At the end of 1944 the South East Asia Command (S.E.A.C.) was able to assess its future shipping requirements for the successful prosecution and completion of the war in its area of the Far East. It concluded that three broad categories of merchant ships would be needed to support its operational duties.

The outcome of this was that contracts were placed for the necessary ships and the M.O.W.T. appointed three shipping companies experienced in the area to manage the planned ships for them, although at the time many of the vessels were still to be completed. Jardine, Matheson & Co. were chosen to operate the bigger ships, the Anglo-Saxon Petroleum Co. (later Shell) the tankers and the Singapore Straits SS Co. (later Straits SS Co.) the coasters.

The coasters totalled eighty-six new ships; they were from a number of small British shipyards, including ones at Hessle, Goole, Sunderland, Bristol and Blyth and also from Canadian shipyards at

Prince Rupert, Hamilton and Vancouver. All these coasters conformed to the 'B', 'C' and 'Shelt' types, of which fifty-one were to be built in the United Kingdom and thirty-five in Canada.

The 'B' type was the largest of the three coaster types, carrying about 1,200 tdw, of shelter-deck type with a forecastle, bridge amidships and machinery aft. A cargo door was fitted in each side, in Nos. 1 and 2 'tween decks.

The British-built 'C' type coaster, of the open shelter-deck type, was not unlike many of the small ships trading around Singapore and in Malayan waters before the war, with the bridge and officers' accommodation at the fore end, up to the fo'c'sle. No tonnage well was provided in the way of the hatch, the required freeboard not needing the maximum allowance for the 'tween deck superstructure. The Canadian-built 'C' type coaster had its bridge situated aft, on the superstructure.

Also included in the programme of Far East coasters was the Shelter-deck type, a dry cargo coaster of some 400 deadweight tons. Known as 'Shelts', they were built on the same prefabricated straight-line form as were the 'Empire F'-type coasters and the 'Chant' tankers, the three types being similar in appearance and similar in length and breadth and with oil engines fitted aft. A gangway door serving the 'tween decks, was fitted to each side of the 'Shelt'-type ships.

For the British newbuildings the route to the Far East was to be from the U.K. to the Bay of Bengal, thence to Malaysian waters. The delivery convoys would be groups of the smaller types ('C' type and 'Shelts') escorted by the larger 'B'-type ships, which were fitted with wireless telegraphy. At the end of July 1945 the first convoy, consisting of one 'B' type, three 'C' types and nine 'Shelts', was ready to leave from Falmouth and a few days after it sailed, on 8 August, Japan surrendered. This enabled the remaining coasters to be despatched overseas in safety, without military personnel or armament.

Due to the sudden cessation of hostilities none of the ships took part in the operations for which they had been planned, whilst in Canada the contracts for many of the vessels specifically intended for service in South East Asia were cancelled.

'B'-type Coasters – 1,200 tdw, 224 ft (oa), 215 ft × 37 ft. Engines: T3cyl (aft) – 9½ knots

Built by Blyth Dry Docks & Shipbuilding Co. Ltd.

312 *Empire Pavilion* 974 gt.
Launched: 9.8.1945.
Completed: 11.1945.
1946: *Sapele* (Elder, Dempster Lines Ltd.).
1963: (Bergens Mek. Verkstad, Norway).
1963: *Mahia* (converted to a shrimp factory) (Ocean Industries Ltd., Pakistan).
1969: *Safina-E-Armer* (a shell-fish factory) (Pan Islamic SS Co., Pakistan).
10.1973: Scrapped Karachi.

313 *Empire Passmore* 974 gt.
Launched: 6.10.1945.
Completed: 2.1946.
15.4.1947: Struck mine near Horsburgh Light, off Singapore, 1.24N 104.34E (voyage: Kuching/Singapore – general); Main engines severely damaged.
16.4.1947: Towed to Singapore by steamer *Anhui* (1925, 3,494 gt). Discharged and repaired.
1949: *Beluru* (Straits SS Co. Ltd.).
1954: *Jalabala* (Scindia SN Co. Ltd., India.).
6.1964: Scrapped Bombay.

314 *Empire Park* 974 gt.
Launched: 20.11.1945.
Completed: 4.1946.
1952: *Benveg* (Ben Line Steamers Ltd.).
1962: *Grandhing* (Ta Hing Co. (Hong Kong) Ltd.).
1963: (China Pacific Navigation Co., Panama).
1964: *Sumbawa* (Cia. de Nav. Abeto, Panama).

1968: *Amarina* (Asia Maritime Co., Liberia).
Later chartered to Fushing Navigation Co., Hong Kong, and:
4.1970: Captured and confiscated by South Vietnam authorities when sailing off South Vietnam.
1975: (Vietnam Ocean Shipping Co. (Government of the Socialist Republic of Vietnam)).

Three 'B'-type dry cargo coasters were built by Blyth Dry Docks & Shipbuilding Co. Ltd., but none were launched before war ended. In fact, the Company was almost completely committed for naval work.

There were actually two Blyth Shipbuilding companies. The first was incorporated in 1883, lasting until May 1925, when a receiver and manager was appointed.

In November 1926 it was acquired by R. S. Dalgliesh who, at the same time, acquired ten acres of adjoining land, previously owned by Ritson's Shipbuilding Company, which had ceased operations. For some time the new organisation suffered badly from the great depression of that time, but there began an upturn in trade in the mid–1930s, followed by the large naval programme of the war years.

In 1947 the company had five drydocks, the largest 480 ft × 60 ft, and four berths to a capacity of 500–feet–length ships.

On 24 November 1966 the yard launched its last building, the *Rogate* (Yard No. 395), 4,997 gt, for Stephenson Clarke & Co. Ltd.

One of the most interesting of ships built by the company was the *Ark Royal*, laid down as a collier, but acquired by the Admiralty for completion as an aircraft carrier. She was launched on 5 September 1914 and completed to carry eight seaplanes, with cranes to lift them from holds to sea and back on board. Renamed *Pegasus* in 1934, she became a catapult fighter ship in 1941, for convoy protection.

Strangely, the shipyard was again involved with an aircraft carrier, during World War II, when, in 1941, it converted the ex-German ship *Hannover* – taken as a prize in 1940 and renamed *Empire Audacity* (*q.v.*) – to Britain's first escort carrier, H.M.S. *Audacity*.

Built by Burntisland Shipbuilding Co. Ltd.

298 *Empire Pacific* 984 gt.
Launched: 15.5.1945.
Completed: 8.1945.
1949: *Buloh* (Straits SS Co. Ltd.).
1957: *Tainamshan* (Tai Ping SS Nav. Co., Hong Kong).

23.11.1962: Aground outside Swatow, China. Listed and abandoned.
26.11.1962: Flooded and capsized; sank. Constructive total loss (voyage: Hong Kong/Foochow).

Built by Wm. Hamilton & Co. Ltd., Glasgow

469 *Empire Palace* 977 gt.
Launched: 6.1945.
Completed: 9.1945.
1949: *Belaga* (Sarawak SS Co., Kuching).

1958: *Kishni* (Devidas Gulab, Hong Kong).
1964: *Ocean King* (Avon Shipping & Trading Co., Hong Kong).
10.1971: Scrapped Kaohsiung.

Built by Smiths Dock Co. Ltd., Middlesbrough

1153   *Empire Pattern* 974 gt.
Launched: 27.4.1945.
Completed: 8.1945.
1948: *Forcados* (Elder, Dempster Lines Ltd.).
1962: *Barbalias* (S. L. Anghelatos, Greece).
1966: *Agia Varvara* (G. Tzortzis & C. Sykias, Greece).
12.12.1966: Caught fire in engine room and
accommodation in Jeddah Roads, Saudi Arabia.
Gutted, capsized and sank. Total loss (voyage:
Jeddah/Suez – ballast).

1154   *Empire Pampas* 974 gt.
Launched: 11.6.1945.
Completed: 10.1945.
1946: *Warri* (Elder, Dempster Lines Ltd.).
12.6.1956: Grounded in heavy surf at Iwerekun,
twenty miles east of Lagos. Hatches, bulwarks and
accommodation stove in; engine room and holds tidal.
Abandoned. Total loss (voyage: Sapele/Lagos – palm
kernels).

'C'-type Coasters – 300 tdw, 151 ft (oa), 144 ft × 27.1 ft. Engines: T3cyl (aft) – 9 knots

Built by Ailsa Shipbuilding Co. Ltd., Troon

458   *Empire Maytime* 394 gt.
Launched: 25.4.1945.
Completed: 7.1945.
1947: *Membau* (Straits SS Co. Ltd.).
1953: *Adelina* (Shun Cheong SN Co. (K. S. Pang,
Hong Kong)).
1955: *Nam Sanh* (Hong Phat Hang, Vietnam).
30.10.1971: Stranded and wrecked in Chulai harbour,
South Vietnam, during a typhoon (cargo: rice, sugar
and general).

459   *Empire Maytree* 394 gt.
Launched: 31.5.1945.
Completed: 8.1945.
1947: *Mantin* (Straits SS Co. Ltd.).
1953: *Lorinda* (554 gt) Shun Cheong SN Co. (K. S.
Pang, Hong Kong)).
1954: (G. Grimble & Co. Ltd., Hong Kong).
1955: (Soc. Franco-Chinoise de Transport Maritime
& Fluviaux, France).
1957: *Luen Hwa* (Government of Indonesia).

The Ailsa Shipbuilding Company was restyled from the Troon Shipbuilding Company in 1885, adopting the family name of its purchaser, the Marquis of Ailsa, who was well experienced in local boatbuilding.

The company built up a good reputation in the construction of coasters and short-sea ships and their yard list also contained several paddle steamers which became well-known to thousands of holidaymakers. P. & A. Campbell's *Glen Avon*, *Glen Usk* and *Glen Gower* appeared in 1912, 1914 and 1922 respectively; the *Bournemouth Queen* in 1908 and in 1924 the *Medway Queen* for the New Medway Steam Packet Co. Ltd. One of the largest ships built was the 4,441 gt passenger/cargo steamer *Jose Menendes*, for Argentina in 1922. They also built one of the last of the steel barques, *Killoran*, 1,817 gt for J. Hardie of Glasgow in 1900. She, later, joined Gustaf Erikson's fleet and was eventually sunk by the German raider *Widder* on 10 August 1940 in mid-Atlantic whilst on a voyage from the east coast of South America to Las Palmas with maize and sugar.

In 1902 the Ailsa Company acquired McKnights Yard at Ayr whose list of buildings included the paddlers *Balmoral* in 1900 and the *Britannia* (1896), *Ravenswood* (1891) and *Westward Ho* (1894) for P. & A. Campbell Ltd. A fair volume of shipbuilding and repair work was built up here, especially during the Great War, the launched hulls being towed to Troon, some six miles north, for their machinery.

But in the postwar years there was a big decline in coal exports and Ayr, on the estuary of the River Ayr and being the principal outlet for the South Ayrshire coalfields, was seriously affected, and the yard there was closed down in 1929, the last steamer built being the *Cobargo*, 869 gt, a twin screw coaster for the Illawarra & South Coast SN Company Ltd., Sydney. The yard then lay dormant until 1940 when it was requisitioned by the Admiralty for ship repair work, being returned to Ailsa control after three years.

On 1 July 1947 the Ayr Engineering & Construction Co. Ltd., acquired the yard, some work being in the repair of railway wagons. In 1947 facilities at Troon included four berths for ships to 350 ft and two drydocks, 289 ft and 400 ft in length.

SHIPS BUILT UNDER PRIVATE CONTRACT OR LICENCE

429   *Magician* 1,000 tons displ. 206 ft × 37.5 ft.
Launched: 27.9.1939.
Completed: 1939 to replace the ferries *Harlequin* and *Nimble* at Chatham, but taken over by the Army as a hospital ship.
1945: (Royal Navy).
1946: *Magician II*.
1952: Scrapped Faslane.

430   *Empress Queen* 1,781 gt, 281.9 ft (oa), 269.5 ft × 37.7 ft. Engines: four steam turbines. Twin screws.
Launched: 29.2.1940 for P. & A. Campbell Ltd. Requisitioned by the Admiralty, and:
Completed: 7.1940 as a troopship.
12.1940: *Queen Eagle* (after conversion to an anti-aircraft ship).
11.1943: Trooping in Irish Sea (M.O.W.T.).
1946: *Empress Queen* (P. & A. Campbell Ltd.).
1955: *Philippos* (Kavounides Bros., Greece).
1959: (New (oil) engines).
23.2.1972: On fire, explosion, whilst under repair at Keratsini, Piraeus. Towed out, beached; fire extinguished.

6.3.1972: Refloated, but constructive total loss. Sold and broken up.

445   *Zealand* 1,924 gt, 265 ft (oa), 254.3 ft × 40.3 ft.
Engines: T3cyl.
Launched: 24.5.1943.
Completed: 7.1943 for Currie Line Ltd., Leith.
1954: Renamed *Shetland*.
1959: *Curitiba* (Tibagi Transportes Maritimos Ltda., Brazil).
1970: ('Marina' Maritima Nactional Ltda., Brazil).
1974: Name erased from some ship registers; existence of vessel in doubt.

446   *Rutland* 1,907 gt. Details as Yard No. 445.
Launched: 8.11.1945.
Completed: 2.1946 for Currie Line Ltd., Leith.
1960: *Mahaganga* (South East Asia Shipping Co. Ltd. (J. P. Bragg, Bombay)).
12.1973: Scrapped Bombay.

The coastal pleasure steamer *Empress Queen*. (Ailsa Shipbuilding Co. Ltd., Yard No. 430.)

Built by S. P. Austin & Sons Ltd., Sunderland

380   *Empire Maya* 394 gt.
Launched: 27.3.1945.
Completed: 7.1945.
1947: *Merlimau* (Straits SS Co. Ltd.).
1957: *Margaret Rose* (A. Gill & Co. (Pvt.) Ltd., India).
9.6.1959: Encountered tidal wave off Port Okha, about 300 miles northwest of Bombay; capsized and sank off Dwarka. Total loss (voyage: Bombay/Port Okha – tin plate).

381   *Empire Maymount* 394 gt.
Launched: 12.4.1945.
Completed: 8.1945.
1947: *Meluan* (Straits SS Co. Ltd.).
1955: *Vir Pandian* (A. Gill & Co. (Pvt.) Ltd., India).
28.7.1955: Aground at Gopinath, fifty miles from Bhavnagar, India. Abandoned. Constructive total loss. Sold and broken up.

One of the earliest of the North-east shipbuilding establishments was the Austin yard, its founder, Peter Austin, starting the business at North Sands, Sunderland, in 1826, with the construction of ships for the coastal trade.

Twenty years later the company, then S. P. Austin & Son, moved upriver from their site at the mouth of the River Wear, to the proximity of the Wear bridge, and there they were to remain, becoming one of the sixty Wear shipyards of the mid-19th century years, building coasters, general cargo carriers and colliers.

One the largest ships built by Austins was the 3,431 gross tons Cory collier *Buffs*, built in 1917 and working in Government service until war ended. The King of Denmark, Honorary Colonel of the Buffs regiment, presented the ship with his portrait just before the ship was given Cory nomenclature, *Corland*, in 1920. She was bombed by aircraft off Spurn Head on 5 February 1942, and sunk.

'Empire' ships built during 1939–1945 included coasters and tugs, but construction was mainly of colliers and when war ended the Wear Dock Yard of S. P. Austin & Son Ltd. included three berths for ships to 360 ft, a 300-ft Graving Dock and a Pontoon Dock for ships to 390 ft along its $\frac{1}{4}$-mile river frontage.

In 1955 the company amalgamated with Wm. Pickersgill & Sons Ltd., Southwick, the combined companies of Austin & Pickersgill Ltd. building many of the SD 14-type ships in the 1960s at the Southwick Yard.

As shipbuilding decreased in the 1960s, Austin's old Wear Ship Yard was temporarily closed from time to time, eventually closing down permanently on 28 August 1964.

SHIPS BUILT UNDER PRIVATE CONTRACT OR LICENCE

351   *Lea Grange* 2,969 gt, 328 ft (oa),
316.8 ft × 45.2 ft. Engines: T3cyl.
Launched: 12.10.1939.
Completed: 12.1939 for Tanfield SS Co. Ltd., Newcastle.
1953: (Stephenson Clarke Ltd.).
1959: *Costicos* (Cia. Nav. Costicos S.A., Lebanon).
9.6.1973: Arrived Istanbul, in tow, for breaking up, but:
10.1973: Scrapped Halic, Turkey.

352   *Moorwood* 2,056 gt, 283.6 ft (oa),
273.3 ft × 41 ft. Engines: T3cyl.
Launched: 24.1.1940.
Completed: 3.1940 for Wm. France, Fenwick & Co. Ltd.
11.6.1941: Sunk by aircraft torpedo at 20C Buoy, off Hartlepool, Co. Durham (voyage: London/Blyth – ballast).

The collier *Sound Fisher*, as *Portwood*, April 1953. (S. P. Austin & Sons Ltd., Yard No. 360.)

The collier *Birdwood* in April 1961, after rebuilding and conversion to a motorship. (S. P. Austin & Sons Ltd., Yard No. 374.)

The tug *Danube VII*, in the River Thames. (Cochrane & Sons Ltd., Yard No. 1312.)

353   *Sea Fisher* 2,950 gt, 325.5 ft (oa),
311.4 ft × 46.7 ft. Engines: T3cyl.
Launched: 23.4.1940.
Completed: 5.1940 for Fenwick, Fisher SS Co. Ltd.
1945: (J. Fisher & Sons Ltd., Barrow).
1956: *Malcom* (Shamrock Shipping Co. Ltd., N.
Ireland).
1959: *New Country* (Great Ocean SS Co. (An Kuo SS
Co. Ltd., Taiwan)).
1966: (China Merchants SN Co. Ltd., Taiwan).
12.1967: Scrapped Keelung.

354   *Cornwood* 2,777 gt, 321.9 ft (oa),
311.4 ft × 44.5 ft. Engines: T3cyl.
Launched: 3.8.1940.
Completed: 9.1940 for Wm. France, Fenwick & Co.
Ltd.
1959: *Aris* (Ithaca Marine Transportation Inc.,
Liberia).
1961: *Gabriele* (E. di Pietro Canale, Italy).
1971: *Firmino* (Euronavi SpA (Soc. di Nav.
Carbonavi, Italy)).
1977: Reported scrapped in Italy in 1972.

355   *Capitol* 1,558 gt, 257 ft (oa), 247 ft × 39.7 ft.
Engines: T3cyl.
Launched: 25.4.1941.
Completed: 6.1941 for Gas, Light & Coke
Company.
1949: (North Thames Gas Board).
7.1963: Scrapped Willebroek, Belgium.

356   *Goodwood* 2,780 gt. Details as Yard No. 354.
Launched: 30.10.1940.
Completed: 1.1941 for Wm. France, Fenwick &
Co. Ltd.
22.2.1945: Sunk by E-boat torpedo off Lowestoft,
52.53N 02.12E (approx.) (voyage: Blyth/London –
coal).

357   *Murdoch* 2,717 gt. Details as Yard No. 354.
Launched: 25.1.1941.
Completed: 4.1941 for Gas, Light & Coke
Company.
26.4.1941: Struck submerged wreck; grounded on
Scroby Sands, off Norfolk coast. Submerged in heavy
weather; broke in two. Total loss (voyage:
Sunderland/London – coal).

358   *Betty Hindley* 1,738 gt, 266.8 ft (oa),
258 ft × 38.3 ft. Engines: T3cyl.
Launched: 7.6.1941.
Completed: 8.1941 for Stephenson, Clarke Ltd.
6.8.1941: Aground on Haisbro' Sands, off Cromer,
Norfolk, 52.54N 1.43E (voyage: Blyth/London –
coal).

The *Betty Hindley* was one of seven ships from a south-bound
East Coast convoy led on to Haisbro' Sands by the naval
escort. Other ships in the convoy, with Masters long-
experienced in the coastal trade, 'stood off' from danger by
disregarding the naval orders to maintain their position, but
the seven vessels were all lost, breaking their backs in heavy
seas and becoming submerged.
   The other losses were:

Aberhill	built 1915,	1,516 gt
Afon Towy	built 1919,	684 gt
Deerwood	built 1919,	1,875 gt
Gallois	built 1917,	2,684 gt
Oxshott	built 1915,	1,241 gt
Taara	built 1907,	1,401 gt

and the naval trawler:

Agate	built 1934,	627 gt

359   *Lambtonian* 2,781 gt. Details as Yard No. 354.
Launched: 4.11.1941.
Completed: 1.1942 for Tanfield SS Co. Ltd.,
Newcastle.
1953: (Stephenson Clarke Ltd.).
19.3.1960: Arrived Dunston-on-Tyne for breaking
up.

360   *Sound Fisher* 2,931 gt. Details as Yard No. 353.
Launched: 21.8.1941.
Completed: 10.1941 for Fenwick, Fisher SS Co. Ltd.
1946: *Colnbrook* (Coastwise Colliers Ltd., London).
1949: *Portwood* (Wm. France, Fenwick & Co. Ltd.).
1962: *Chrysanthi K* (George Corpn., Panama
(Kollakis Bros. Ltd., London)).
6.12.1966: Arrived Kiel, in tow, after fire in
machinery space. Sold.
24.11.1967: Arrived Nakskov, in tow, for breaking
up.

362   *Fireside* 2,757 gt. Details as Yard No. 354.
Launched: 16.3.1942.
Completed: 5.1942 for Gas, Light & Coke
Company.
1949: (North Thames Gas Board).
1962: *Dynamikos* (Grigorouse, Cia. Nav., S.A.,
Panama (Kronos Shipping Co. Ltd., London)).
1965: *Nikos V* (San Mitrofanes S.A., Panama (Globe
Shipping Co., Greece)).
29.12.1967: Aground two miles from Driana
Lighthouse, sixteen miles from Benghazi, Libya.
Abandoned; flooded and broke up. Total loss (voyage:
Varna/Benghazi – cement).

363   *Cormull* 2,865 gt, 328.5 ft (oa),
317.3 ft × 44.5 ft. Engines: T3cyl.
Launched: 28.5.1942.
Completed: 7.1942 for Wm. Cory & Son Ltd.
15.5.1943: Struck mine $\frac{1}{4}$ cable west of No. 7 Buoy,

fourteen miles north east of Yarmouth; badly
damaged (voyage: Blyth/London – coal). Repaired.
1946: *Coldharbour* (Coastwise Colliers Ltd., London).
1949: *Cormull* (Wm. Cory & Son Ltd.).
1960: *Christakis* (Dos Hermanos Corp. (G. Vlassis &
Co., Greece)).
30.10.1965: In collision in fog with Greek vessel
Mairoula (1918, 984 gt) off Nara Burnu; beached five
miles south of Canakkale, Dardanelles. Cargo
discharged, and:
15.11.1965: Refloated; anchored Canakkale Roads.
1.12.1965: Arrived Piraeus; beached Ambeliki.
Constructive total loss (voyage: Galatz/Alexandria –
superphosphates).

364 *Firedog* 1,557 gt. Details as Yard No. 355.
Launched: 14.7.1942.
Completed: 9.1942 for Gas, Light & Coke
Company.
1949: (North Thames Gas Board).
23.4.1959: Arrived Rotterdam for scrapping.
Breaking up commenced, but hull resold to Dutch
buyers, and
6.1959: named *Noordzee* (used for storage of sand).

365 *Bushwood* 2,842 gt. Details as Yard No. 363.
Launched: 24.9.1942.
Completed: 11.1942 for Wm. France, Fenwick & Co.
Ltd.
1958: *Evaggelistra* (Maristrella Nav. S.A. (A. J. & D.
J. Chandris, Greece)).
1960: (Panagia Nav. S. A., Panama (A. J. & D. J.
Chandris)).
1968: *Babb* (T. Klaveness, Norway).
1969: *Bulkhandling 4* (A/S Bulkhandling, Norway).
Used as a bauxite discharging barge at Burntisland,
Fife.
10.11.1978: Arrived Inverkeithing for breaking up.

366 *Betty Hindley* 1,771 gt. Details as Yard No. 358.
Launched: 23.11.1942.
Completed: 1.1943 for Stephenson, Clarke Ltd.
7.10.1947: Struck drifting mine three miles east of
Scarborough, Yorks. Taken in tow, with back
broken, by fishing vessels, for shallow water; beached
in South Bay by tugs, but sank with only tops of
masts, funnel and bridge showing. Total loss (voyage:
London/Tyne – ballast).

367 *Bowcombe* 2,760 gt. Details as Yard No. 354.
Launched: 20.2.1943.
Completed: 4.1943 for Stephenson, Clarke Ltd.
1946: *Colwyn* (Coastwise Colliers Ltd., London).
1949: *Bowcombe* (Stephenson, Clarke Ltd.).
1966: (T. Johannisson, Sweden).
1967: Converted in Sweden to a lighter.

368 *Wrenwood* 2,847 gt. Details as Yard No. 363.
Launched: 2.6.1943.
Completed: 10.1943 for Wm. France, Fenwick & Co.
Ltd.
1946: *Collingbourne* (Coastwise Colliers Ltd.,
London).
1949: *Wrenwood* (Wm. France, Fenwick & Co. Ltd.).
1959: *Ethel C* (Transportes Maritmos Catalia S.A.,
Panama (D. Caravias, London)).
16.4.1960: Cargo shifted while vessel en-route to
Newport News, Va., to refuel; hole punched in ship's
side. Flooded and abandoned; explosion in engine
room, stern blown off. Sank off Virginia coast,
37.21N 75.15W (voyage: New York/Rotterdam –
scrap iron).

369 *Cormead* 2,867 gt. Details as Yard No. 363.
Launched: 31.8.1943.
Completed: 12.1943 for Wm. Cory & Sons Ltd.
1964: *Panormitis* (Nafs, Cia. Nav. S.A., Panama (K.
& M. Shipbrokers Ltd., London)).
3.1971: Scrapped Antwerp.

371 *Fireglow* 1,549 gt. Details as Yard No. 355.
Launched: 20.7.1944.
Completed: 10.1944 for Gas, Light & Coke
Company.
1949: (North Thames Gas Board).
5.1965: Sold to Rotterdam shipbreakers. Breaking up
commenced, but hull sold to Boele & Oosterwijk
N.V., Holland, for use as a barge.

372 *Hawkwood* 2,850 gt. Details as Yard No. 363.
Launched: 25.1.1944.
Completed: 4.1944 for Wm. France, Fenwick & Co.
Ltd.
1965: *Ioannis P* (Sterpi Nav. S.A., Panama (S. L.
Pissis, Greece)).
14.7.1969: Arrived Hamburg for breaking up.

373 *Rogate* 2,871 gt. Details as Yard No. 363.
Launched: 22.5.1944.
Completed: 7.1944 for Stephenson, Clarke Ltd.
19.3.1945: Sunk by German E-boat (of 6th Flotilla)
off Lowestoft while in convoy FS 1759 (voyage:
Sunderland/London – coal).

374 *Birdwood* 2,862 gt. Details as Yard No. 363.
Launched: 10.1945.
Completed: 10.1945 for Wm. France, Fenwick &
Co. Ltd.
1959: Rebuilt; fitted with oil engine.
1968: *San Javier* (Transportactiones Combinadas
C.A., Venezuela).
1970: *Amacuro* (Cia. Anon. Naviera Orinoco,
Venezuela).
1972: *Tacamar I* (Tacarigua Marina C.A., Venezuela).

1976: (Tacamar Panamena S.A.).
5.1979: Scrapped Cartagena, Colombia.

375   *Cormount* 2,871 gt. Details as Yard No. 363.
Launched: 2.10.1944.
Completed: 12.1944 for Wm. Cory & Son Ltd.
1966: *Chriluck* (Chriluck Shipping Co. Ltd., Liberia
(G. & A. Vlassis, Greece)).
1972: *Marianik* (Sissini Nav. Co. Ltd., Cyprus (N. J.
Nomikos, Greece)).
10.1974: Scrapped Split.

376   *Pinewood* 2,853 gt. Details as Yard No. 363.
Launched: 12.1.1945.
Completed: 3.1945 for Wm. France, Fenwick & Co.
Ltd.
1946: *Coldstream* (Coastwise Colliers Ltd., London).
1949: *Pinewood* (Wm. France, Fenwick & Co. Ltd.).
4.1967: (T. Johannisson, Sweden). Later converted at
Gothenburg to a lighter.

379   *Moorwood* 2.034 gt. Details as Yard No. 352.
Launched: 24.5.1945.
Completed: 9.1945 for France, Fenwick & Co. Ltd.
28.10.1945: Struck wreck in Barrow Deep, Thames
Estuary. Holed, beached on Maplin Sands. Refloated,
proceeded London, repaired (voyage: Blyth/London –
coal).
1960: *Horsted* (Stephenson, Clarke Ltd.).
11.1966: Sold; engines removed, converted to canal
sand barge for Boele & Oosterwijk N.V., Holland.

382   *Keynes* 1,563 gt, 270 ft (oa), 261.2 ft × 36.5 ft.
Engines: T3cyl.
Launched: 19.12.1945.
Completed: 3.1946 for Stephenson, Clarke Ltd.
1966: *Granita IV* (T. Johannisson, Sweden).
3.7.1969: Arrived Gothenburg for breaking up.

383   *Effra* 2,701 gt, 319.3 ft (oa), 308.5 ft × 44.2 ft.
Engines: T3cyl.
Launched: 5.11.1945.
Completed: 2.1946 for South Metropolitan Gas
Company.
1949: (South Eastern Gas Board).
1967: (H. G. Pounds, Portsmouth). Resold, and:
1967: *Yannakis Fanis* (Cia. de Nav. Eli Gounaris S.A.,
Panama).
1969: *Giulia* (L. Decius Shipping Co., Panama).
23.3.1974: Developed leaks off La Nouvelle; towed
to Marseilles. Repairs uneconomic, and:
22.4.1974: Arrived Split for breaking up.

384   *Sir Alexander Kennedy* 1,714 gt, 270.5 ft (oa),
260 ft × 39.5 ft. Engines: T3cyl.
Launched: 4.4.1946.
Completed: 5.1946 for London Power Co. Ltd.
1948: (British Electricity Authority).
1954: (Central Electricity Authority).
1958: (Central Electricity Generating Board).
5.1968: Scrapped Willebroek, Belgium.

385   *Brixton* 1,635 gt, 257.5 ft (oa),
247.3 ft × 39.5 ft. Engines: T3cyl.
Launched: 15.5.1946.
Completed: 7.1946 for South Metropolitan Gas
Company.
1949: (South Eastern Gas Board).
1962: *Brunetto* (E. Canale, Italy).
1977: (Cia. Siciliana Trasporti Mare SpA (E. Canale,
Italy)).
1978: *Iginia Zeta* (San Gavino SpA di Nav., Italy).
1978: Renamed *Piero M.*
7.1981: Scrapped Spezia.

Built by Bartram & Sons Ltd., Sunderland

307   *Empire Mayrose* 394 gt.
Launched: 16.5.1945.
Completed: 8.1945.
1947: *Mawai* (Straits SS Co. Ltd.).
1954: *Meklong* (Pacific Shipowners Ltd. (W. R.
Carpenter & Co. Ltd., Australia)).
1957: (Lanena Shipping Co Ltd., Hong Kong (T.
Engan, Philippines)).
1960: *Karang Djawa* (Tonglik Shipping Co. Ltd. (P.
T. Garina Line, Indonesia)).

308   *Empire Mayflower* 394 gt.
Launched: 16.5.1945.
Completed: 9.1945.
1946: (Straits SS Co. Ltd.).
1947: Renamed *Malim*.
1956: (Eastern Starlines Ltd., Ceylon).
1957: Renamed *Starline Merchant*.
1.1962: Scrapped Bombay.

Built by Cochrane & Sons Ltd., Selby

1305   *Empire Mayring* 394 gt.
Launched: 8.1945.
Completed: 1.1946.
1947: *Sing Hing* (565 gt) (Ta Hing Co. (H. K.) Ltd.
(Mollers Ltd., Hong Kong)).
1949: (Wallem & Co., Hong Kong).
1951: *Islamabad* (Pakistan SN Co. Ltd. (A. K. Khan & Co., Chittagong)).
1972: (Bangladesh SN Co. Ltd. (A. K. Khan & Co., Chittagong)).

1306   *Empire Mayrover* 394 gt.
Launched: 8.9.1945.
Completed: 5.1946.
1947: *Wa Hing* (558 gt) (Ta Hing Co. (H. K.) Ltd.
(Mollers Ltd., Hong Kong)).
1949: *Mumtaz* (India General Navigation & Railway Co. Ltd., Calcutta).
1961: (Pakistan River Steamers Ltd., Pakistan).
1972: (Bangladesh River Steamers Ltd.).
1973: *C5-203* (Government of Bangladesh).

Cochrane & Sons, Selby, was founded by Andrew Cochrane in the early 1880s, the first ship built being a steam lighter, *Albion*, in 1884. Wooden sailing trawlers soon gave way to steel vessels and in 1914 the order list for trawlers, many for Icelandic fishing grounds, was long, with many of them passing to the Admiralty to serve as naval minesweepers.

The yard turned to the building of small craft of all kinds, particularly tugs, during the inter-war years and in 1939 received orders to build twenty-one rescue tugs of the 'Assurance' class. Thirty 'Empire'-type tugs were also constructed.

Trawlers of the 'Dance', 'Shakespeare' and 'Isles' classes were built and in February 1944 production went ahead on the first of six 'Envoy'-class tugs.

SHIPS BUILT UNDER PRIVATE CONTRACT OR LICENCE

1211   *Le Royal* 316 gt, 156 ft (oa), 142.6 ft × 24.6 ft.
Engines: Oil. A trawler.
Launched: 1941.
Completed: 11.1941 for Milford Steam Trawling Co. Ltd.
1946: Renamed *Milford Marquis*.
1951: *Postboy* (N. V. Viss. Onderneming De Vem., Holland).
1964: *St. Kitts* (Claridge Trawlers Ltd.).
4.10.1974: Towed into Lowestoft with engine trouble. Laid up.
11.1976: Sold for breaking up on River Humber.

1213   *Triton* 680 gt, 173.2 ft (oa), 170 ft × 29 ft.
Engines: T3cyl.
Ordered as a trawler for Boston Deep Sea Fishing Company; allocated name *Queen of the Waves*, but: acquired by The Corporation of Trinity House, and: Launched: 27.2.1940.
Completed: 6.1940 as a Lighthouse Tender.
24.7.1963: Left Harwich in tow of tug *Martine Letzer* for Bruges, where broken up.

1309   *St. Bartholomew* 550 gt, 193.5 ft (oa),
177.7 ft × 30.1 ft. Engines: T3cyl. A trawler.
Launched: 8.10.1945.

Completed: 3.1946 for St. Andrews Steam Fishing Co. Ltd., Hull.
1946: *Stella Arcturus* (Charleson-Smith Trawlers Ltd., Hull).
1950: (Trawlers Grimsby Ltd.).
1964: (Ross Trawlers Ltd.).
1965: Renamed *Ross Arcturus*.
1967: *Arctic Outlaw* (Boyd Line Ltd., Hull).
10.1968: Scrapped Bo'ness.

1310   *St. Mark* 550 gt. Details as Yard No. 1309.
Launched: 7.11.1945.
Completed: 3.1946 for St. Andrews Steam Fishing Co. Ltd., Hull.
1947: *Cape Trafalgar* (Hudson Bros. (Trawlers) Ltd., Hull).
1955: *Auburn Wyke* (West Dock Steam Fishing Co. Ltd., Hull).
1959: *Arctic Hunter* (Boyd Line Ltd., Hull).
10.1968: Scrapped Antwerp.

1311   *Northella* 550 gt. Details as Yard No. 1309.
Launched: 16.12.1945.
Completed: 4.1946 for J. Marr & Son Ltd., Hull.
1948: *Stella Canopus* (East Riding Trawlers Ltd.).
1950: (Trawlers Grimsby Ltd.).
1964: (Ross Trawlers Ltd.).

1965: Renamed *Ross Canopus*.
7.1967: Scrapped Antwerp.

1312   *Danube VII* 237 gt, 118.3 ft (oa),
110.6 ft × 27.6 ft. Engines: T3cyl. A tug.
Launched: 5.1.1946.
Completed: 5.1946 for Tilbury Contracting &
Dredging Co. Ltd., London.
1965: (Westminster Dredging Co. Ltd., London).

1969: *Giove Sailem* (Soc. Anon. Italiana Lavori
Marittimi, Italy).
1987: (Acc. Ferriere Palermo SpA, Italy).

1313   *Danube VIII* 237 gt. Details as Yard No. 1312.
Launched: 1.1.1946.
Completed: 5.1946 for Tilbury Contracting &
Dredging Co. Ltd., London.
1965: (Westminster Dredging Co. Ltd., London).
9.1968: Scrapped Antwerp.

Built by Cook, Welton & Gemmell Ltd., Beverley

749   *Empire Mayport* 394 gt.
Launched: 5.1945.
Completed: 9.1945.
1946: (Straits SS Co. Ltd.).
1947: Renamed *Mentakab*.
1953: *Debora* (Shun Cheong SN Co. (K. S. Pang,
Hong Kong)).
1954: (G. Grimble & Co. Ltd., Hong Kong).
1954: (554 gt) (Soc. Franco-Chinoise de Transports
Maritime et Fluviaux, France).
1960: (Malayan Navigation Co. Ltd., Malaya).
1965: *Bright Star* (Progress Shipping Co., Panama).
20.1.1966: Ashore and wrecked on a reef in South
China Sea, fifty miles southeast of Da-Nang,
Vietnam, 15.32N 109.09E.

750   *Empire Maybury* 394 gt.
Launched: 10.7.1945.
Completed: 10.1945.
1948: *Hong Ann* (Ho Hong SS Co. (1932) Ltd.,
Singapore).
1954: *Ai Sokula* (Pacific Shipowners Ltd. (W. R.
Carpenter & Co. Ltd., Australia)).
1963: *Nei Raete II* (Milne Bros., Marshall Islands –
U.S. Trust Territory of the Pacific).

The company of Cook, Welton & Gemmell Ltd. owed its foundations to a Scotsman, William Gemmell, and two colleagues from Earles Shipbuilding & Engineering Company, Hull, who began shipbuilding at a site formerly occupied by the Hull Garrison, in 1882. Their first building was, appropriately, named *Precursor*, a steam smack and the company went on to build up a reputation for the design, development and building of ships for the fishing industry, especially for the nearby fleets of Hull and Grimsby.

In 1902, their Yard building list then some 350 ships, they moved to Beverley, some eight miles northwest of Hull, on the river of that name, where they continued to specialise in trawlers and in the construction of lightships, estuarial craft and coasters. Shipbuilding on the Humber site finished in 1904. In the Great War, after building replacements of trawlers and whalers requisitioned by the Admiralty, the company turned to minesweepers and anti-submarine vessels.

A research steamship, *William Scoresby*, 300 gt, was built in 1926 for the Crown Agents for the Colonies, and its South Polar work included the marking of whales to learn of their ocean movements.

In World War II the same building pattern was applied as for the Great War, with construction of corvettes, landing craft, minelayers and anti-submarine ships; some 100 vessels were built and when war had ended the yard had six berths for ships to 200 ft.

In 1963 the company faced liquidation and closure of the yard was set for 31 March. At that time the Yard list had reached No. 984. However, the yard was acquired by C. D. Holmes & Co. Ltd., marine engineers of Hull, who had engined so many of the company's buildings over the years. Takeover of the Grovehill Shipyard, Beverley, was effective from 1 April 1963.

SHIPS BUILT UNDER PRIVATE CONTRACT OR LICENCE

650 *Lady Lilian* 581 gt, 193.7 ft (oa), 178 ft × 30 ft.
Engines: T3cyl. A trawler.
Launched: 2.9.1939.
Completed: 11.1939 for Jutland Amalgamated
Trawlers Ltd., Hull.
1.1940: Requisitioned as an anti-submarine
trawler.
16.3.1941: Sunk by aircraft attack, West of
Ireland.

651 *Lady Madeleine* 581 gt. Details as Yard No. 650.
Launched: 14.9.1939.
Completed: 11.1939 for Jutland Amalgamated
Trawlers Ltd., Hull.
2.1940: Requisitioned as an anti-submarine
trawler.
1946: *Kingston Diamond* (Kingston Steam Trawling
Co. Ltd., Hull).
1963: (Wyre Trawlers Ltd., Fleetwood).
4.1965: Scrapped Port Glasgow.

654 *St. Apollo* 580 gt. Details as Yard No. 650.
Launched: 14.12.1939.
Completed: 1940 for T. Hamling & Co. Ltd.,
Hull.
2.1940: Requisitioned as an anti-submarine
trawler.
22.11.1941: In collision with destroyer H.M.S.
Sardonyx off Hebrides, Scotland. Sank.

655 *St. Zeno* 580 gt. Details as Yard No. 650.
Launched: 12.2.1940.
Completed: 1940 for T. Hamling & Co. Ltd.,
Hull.
3.1940: Requisitioned by the Admiralty.
2.1942: (U.S. Navy).
10.1942: (Royal Navy).
1946: (Firth Steam Trawling Co. Ltd. (T. Hamling
& Co. Ltd., Hull)).
1952: *Banyers* (Henriksen & Co. Ltd.).
12.1966: Scrapped Antwerp.

656 *Vizalma* 580 gt. Details as Yard No. 650.
Launched: 11.4.1940.

Completed: 8.1940 for Atlas Steam Fishing Co.
Ltd., Grimsby.
12.1964: Scrapped Dunston-on-Tyne.

755 *Aby* 361 gt, 148 ft (oa), 136 ft × 25 ft. Engines:
T3cyl. A trawler.
Launched: 22.9.1945.
Completed: 12.1945 for Boston Deep Sea Fishing &
Ice Co. Ltd., Fleetwood.
1946: (Seddon Fishing Co. Ltd.).
1949: *Chaffcombe* (Neale & West Ltd., Cardiff).
1956: *Boston Gannet* (Don Fishing Co. Ltd.,
Fleetwood).
1963: (Boston Deep Sea Fisheries Ltd., Cardiff).
10.1963: Scrapped Troon.

756 *Bulby* 361 gt. Details as Yard No. 755.
Launched: 8.10.1945.
Completed: 1.1946 for Boston Deep Sea Fishing &
Ice Co. Ltd., Fleetwood.
1946: (Seddon Fishing Co. Ltd.).
1954: (National Trawling & Fishing Co. Ltd., South
Africa).
12.1968: Towed to sea and scuttled (as useless) off
South Africa.

757 *Navena* 360 gt. Details as Yard No. 755.
Launched: 25.10.1945.
Completed: 1.1946 for J. Marr & Son Ltd.,
Fleetwood.
1946: *Iolite* (Kingston Steam Trawling Co. Ltd.,
Hull).
1951: (National Trawling & Fishing Co. Ltd., South
Africa).
21.3.1969: Towed to sea and scuttled (as useless) off
South Africa.

758 *St. Botolph* 361 gt. Details as Yard No. 755.
Launched: 21.11.1945.
Completed: 2.1946 for St. Andrew's Steam Fishing
Co. Ltd., Hull.
1946: (Neale & West Ltd., Cardiff).
1956: (St. Christopher Steam Fishing Co.,
Fleetwood).
11.1963: Scrapped Glasson Dock, Lancs.

Built by A. Hall & Co. Ltd., Aberdeen

710   (Launched as) *Empire Maydream* 413 gt.
Launched: 4.4.1946.
Completed: 1946 as *Maydream* for Ta Hing (H.K.)
Ltd. (Mollers Ltd., Hong Kong).
1947: Renamed *Wing Hing* (563 gt).

1948: (Wallem & Co., Hong Kong).
12.2.1950: Ashore, on fire off Chilang Point, ninety
miles northeast of Hong Kong. Total loss (voyage:
Amoy/Hong Kong – ballast).
9.6.1950: Wreck reported sold to Chinese interests.

The company of A. Hall & Co. Ltd., took its name from Alexander Hall, who, born in 1760, arrived in Aberdeen in 1783 to join with James Cochar, a shipbuilder, then, after seven years, becoming a partner in the restyled Gibbon, Cochar & Hall. Later, the firm became Cochar & Hall.

Hall's son, William, continued the business and in 1818 launched Aberdeen's then largest-ever ship, the 119-ft long *Asia*. In 1839 came the schooner *Scottish Maid*, regarded as the precursor of the clipper ship era, which lasted some three decades until ousted by the steamship and the opening of the Suez Canal in 1869, just three years after the great tea race of 1866. The new waterway saw the end of the clippers on the China trade and they were turned to the Australian wool cargoes.

The company turned out a number of big sailing ships in the period. In 1855 they completed the 2,284-ton *Schomberg* for Baines & Co.'s Black Ball Line of Liverpool, the largest wooden ship built in Britain to that date. She was lost on her outward maiden voyage in December 1855, near Peterborough, on the Victoria coast, Australia. The *Sobraon*, 2,130 tons, 272 ft × 40 ft, was, at first, a steamship, but was converted to the largest composite sailing ship. Teak-hulled, iron-framed and beamed, she used her two acres of sail in the Australian trade, but later became a training ship for Devitt & Moore at Sydney and, later, H.M.S. *Tingira*; she was still afloat in 1940. In September 1869 the 914-ton *The Caliph* sailed on her maiden voyage to Australia; in 1871, on a voyage to Shanghai, she was last heard of off Angier Point, Java.

The yard also constructed the *Port Jackson*, 2,212 tons, a four-masted, 286-ft barque, considered by many to be the most beautiful sailing vessel ever built. Sold by J. Duthie, Sons & Company to Devitt & Moore as a cadet ship, she was torpedoed in 1917.

In 1906 Alexander Hall & Company, specialising in trawlers and drifters, became a limited company and in the Great War was parent company for all Admiralty-ordered steel drifters. During the following twenty years of peace, coasters and drifters continued in output and a number of dredgers and hoppers were also built for James Dredging, Towage & Transport Co.'s reclamation work in the building of Southampton's Western Docks extension.

In 1939 war again brought orders for trawlers, tugs, corvettes and salvage craft, the latter being specially designed for clearing invasion ports. One corvette, *Nettle*, was a gift from the Nizam of Hyderabad and was given the name *Hyderabad*. When war ended the yard had ten berths.

Built by C. Hill & Sons Ltd., Bristol

335   *Empire Mayland* 394 gt.
Launched: 8.1945.
Completed: 2.1946.
1948: *Hong Soon* (Ho Hong Steamship Co. (1932)
Ltd., Singapore).
1952: *D. Aleixo* (Government of Portuguese Timor).
1965: (Tat Pin Shipping & Trading Co.,
Singapore).

1966: (Name removed from ship registers).

336   *Empire Maymorn* 394 gt.
Launched: 31.12.1945.
Completed: 2.1946.
1947: *Mazaruni* (Government of British Guiana).
1966: (Government of Guyana).

James Martin Hilhouse, a shipowner, turned his attention to the building of ships in the 1770s at Hotwells, near Bristol. In the early 1800s a Charles Hill joined the firm, became manager of the dockyard in 1822 and a partner three years later. In 1840 the company was restyled Hilhouse & Hill and five years later Charles Hill took over the whole business, which became Charles Hill & Sons.

Expansion was made in 1857 when drydocks were constructed at Cardiff, but only one wooden schooner and four ships of iron were built there.

Over the years the company built many small ships of all types, coasters, tugs, canal barges, pontoons and also many ships for the Bristol City Line of Steamships Ltd. in the 2,000–3,000 gross tons range, owned by the same company.

In the Great War two 'D'-type standard ships were completed for the Shipping Controller a month or so before Armistice, but six 'H'-type were not finished until after hostilities ceased.

In World War II the first Admiralty order was quickly received for 'Flower'-class corvettes and the company went on to build frigates of the 'River' and 'Loch' classes. When war ended the yard facilities included four berths, each 325 ft in length, and a dry dock, 540 ft in length.

On 9 July 1976 the last ship was launched by Hills at their Albion Dockyard – Yard No. 477 *Miranda Guinness*, 1,541 gt, a tanker for Arthur Guinness Son & Co. (Dublin) Ltd.

SHIPS BUILT UNDER PRIVATE CONTRACT OR LICENCE

276   *St. Vincent* 484 gt, 161.9 ft (oa),
155 ft × 27.1 ft. Engines: Oil (aft).
Launched: 2.1.1940.
Completed: 4.1940 for Osborn & Wallis Ltd.,
Bristol.
1969: *Giankaros II* (M. Gigilinis & D. Kalkassinas,
Greece).
1970: (E. I. Koritsidis & others, Greece).
1987: Name removed from ship registers – existence
of vessel in doubt.

277   *Peter Joliffe* 80 gt, 78.8 ft (oa), 74 ft × 19 ft.
Engines: T3cyl. A tug.
Launched: 18.1.1940.
Completed: 5.1940 for Poole Harbour
Commissioners.
1960: Sold (H. G. Pounds, Portsmouth) to be broken
up, but used occasionally in confines of Portsmouth
Harbour in connection with purchaser's shipbreaking
business.

304	*Sabrina 1*	⎫ 100 gt, 89.5 ft × 18.6 ft.
305	*Sabrina 2*	⎪ 'Bird'-class dumb barges,
306	*Sabrina 3*	⎬ completed in 1944 for Ministry
307	*Sabrina 4*	⎪ of War Transport (Severn
308	*Sabrina 5*	⎪ Carrying Co. Ltd., Bristol).
309	*Sabrina 6*	⎭

334   *Bristol Queen* 961 gt, 258.5 ft (oa),
244.7 ft × 31.2 ft. Engines: T3cyl. A paddle steamer.
Launched: 30.6.1946.
Completed: 1946 for P. & A. Campbell Ltd.,
Bristol.
14.1.1968: Sustained considerable damage when
struck, whilst laid up at Cardiff, by the Liberian
tanker *Geodor* (1953, 12,235 gt) whose towline parted
in high winds while berthing.
3.1968: Scrapped Willebroek, Belgium.

Built by H. Scarr Ltd., Hessle

476   *Empire Maymead* 394 gt.
Launched: 5.1945.
Completed: 11.1945.
1948: *Hong Tat* (Ho Hong SS Co. (1932) Ltd.,
Singapore).
1955: (Chinese flag).
1957: *Hua Mui* (Hua Siang SS Co. (Chan Cheng
Kum, Singapore)).

1962: *Hong Tat* (Malayan Navigation Co. Ltd.,
Singapore).
1965: (Madam Poonsri Sutharom, Thailand).

477   *Empire Maytown* 394 gt.
Launched: 8.1945.
Completed: 2.1946.
1947: *Lady Berbice* (cargo ship and ferry) (Government
of British Guiana).
1966: (Government of Guyana).

Built by Scott & Sons, Bowling

376　(Launched as) *Empire Maysong* 394 gt.
Launched: 20.12.1945.
Completed:　12.1948　as *Lochbroom* (325 gt; oil engine) for David MacBrayne Ltd., Glasgow.

1972: *Focomar* (Focomar Shipping Co. Ltd., Cyprus (S. C. Vazeos, Greece)).
19.9.1974: Aground off northwest coast of Andros Island, Greece. Slipped off, sank in deep water. Total loss (voyage: Piraeus/Constantza – ballast).

'Shelt'-type coasters – Prefabricated shelter-deck vessels, 148 ft (oa), 143 ft × 27 ft. 400 tdw. Engines: Oil (aft) – 7½ knots

Built by Goole Shipbuilding & Repairing Co. Ltd.

437　*Empire Seascape* 522 gt.
Launched: 27.2.1945.
Completed:　4.1945.
1946: *Serdang* (Straits SS Co. Ltd.).
1947: (Sharikat Perk. Sendirian, Malaya).
3.1972: Scrapped Singapore.

438　*Empire Seashore* 522 gt.
Launched: 17.3.1945.
Completed:　5.1945.
1946: *Scudai* (Straits SS Co. Ltd.).
1967: (Sharikat Perk. Sendirian, Malaya).
1974: *Tropic Trader* (Borneo Maritime Transport (Pvt.) Ltd., Singapore).
1978: *Scudai* (Borneo Maritime Transport (Sabah) Sendirian, Labuan).
1986: Scrapped Singapore.

439　*Empire Seaward* 522 gt.
Launched: 12.4.1945.
Completed:　6.1945.
1946: *Senggarang* (Straits SS Co. Ltd.).
1960: *Anho* (Teck Hwa Shipping Co. Ltd., Singapore).
1965: (Kie Hock Shipping Co. Ltd., Singapore).
1977: *Sabah* (Borneo Maritime Transport (Sabah) Sendirian, Labuan).

440　*Empire Seaway* 522 gt.
Launched:　4.1945.
Completed:　7.1945.
1946: *Sedili* (Straits SS Co. Ltd.).
9.1966: Scrapped Singapore.

443　*Empire Seafarer* 522 gt.
Launched: 11.6.1945.
Completed:　7.1945.
1946: *Sumpitan* (Straits SS Co. Ltd.).
6.1965: Scrapped Singapore.

444　*Empire Seagrass* 522 gt.
Launched:　9.1945.
Completed:　9.1945.
1946: *Salong* (Straits SS Co. Ltd.).
1962: *Pulau Tekong* (Kee Lee Shipping Co. Ltd., Singapore).
1965: (Madam Dolly Seah, Singapore).
1968: (Ting Chu Ling, Sarawak).

445　*Empire Seaworthy* 522 gt.
Launched: 27.8.1945.
Completed: 10.1945.
1946: *Sidibarrani* (Middle East Coastal Services Ltd., Cyprus).
1951: *Semenyih* (Straits SS Co. Ltd.).
1967: (Sharikat Perk. Sendirian, Malaya).
12.1971: Scrapped Singapore.

446　*Empire Seaflower* 522 gt.
Launched: 21.9.1945.
Completed: 11.1945.
1946: *Mersamatruh* (Middle East Coastal Services Ltd., Cyprus).
1950: *Isle of Mahe* (Middle East & Caribbean Shipping Co., Bahamas).
1953: Renamed *Mersa Matruh*.
1956: *Shibam* (Savon & Ries (Aden Shipping) Ltd.).

1966: (Shipping Travel & Lighterage Co. of Aden Ltd.).
10.11.1966: Aground in cyclone while discharging off Risut jetty, Salalah, Oman. Holed and flooded; cargo of oil in drums jettisoned. Abandoned.
24.11.1966: Refloated; towed to Aden. Repaired. Sold, and:
1967: *Al Fateh* (Mohsin E. Aldarazy & Bros, Bahrain).

447 *Empire Seabright* 522 gt.
Launched: 8.10.1945.
Completed: 12.1945.
1949: *Helen Seabright* (Overseas Fish Import Co. Ltd. (Great Yarmouth Shipping Co. Ltd.)).
1951: *Ortolan* (General Steam Navigation Co. Ltd.).
1958: *Georgios K* (Panama flag).
1962: *Laut Mas* (Cathey Shipping Corp., Panama (Guan Guan Shipping Co., Singapore)).
1964: *Pasteur* (Transportes Mar. de San Blas S.A., Panama).
14.1.1971: Sank near Alida Shoal, 180 miles east of Singapore, 00.56N 107.53E (voyage: Sibu/Singapore – rubber, pepper and general).

Note: At the time of her loss the vessel was well off the normal route to Singapore.

448 *Empire Seabank* 522 gt.
Launched: 23.11.1945.
Completed: 1.1946.
1946: *Halfaya* (Middle East Coastal Services Ltd., Cyprus).
1950: *Semantan* (Straits SS Co. Ltd.).
1967: (Sharikat Perk., Sendirian, Malaya).
1970: *Tropic Seas* (Keenan Shipping (Pte.) Ltd., Singapore).
1973: *Moon River* (Panama flag).
1977: *Success Star* (River Navigation Co., Panama).
1.1977: Grounded off Jubakar, Tumpat, Malaya. Abandoned.
12.1979: Wreck offered for sale for scrapping.

449 *Empire Seafoam* 522 gt.
Launched: 4.2.1946.
Completed: 7.1946.
1946: *Mareth* (Middle East Coastal Services Ltd., Cyprus).
1949: *Teesta* (British India SN Co. Ltd.).
1950: (Rivers SN Co., London).
1961: (Pakistan River Steamers Ltd.).
1975: *C5-213* (Bangladesh Inland Water Transport Corpn.).

450 (Intended to be) *Empire Seaspray* – Construction cancelled.

The Goole Shipbuilding & Repairing Co. Ltd., had its origins in the early 1880s, when T. Scott & Company began building small craft at their Victoria Yard, beside the Dutch River, so named when it was cut as a drainage canal by Netherlands contractors many years before. Early in the new century the twin-screw *Sudan* (Yard No. 34) was launched, which proved to be Scott's last vessel before the Craggs family took over the site, founding the Goole Shipbuilding & Repairing Company in 1901.

Continuation of the yard numbers covered more small craft until 1902, when Yard No. 47, the 839-ton, 200-ft steel screw steamer *Bia*, for Swedish owners, proved to be their first sizeable vessel. In the next few years the constructions were mainly of trawlers. Over forty were for the Kelsall Brothers' 'Bird' fleet, among them the *Crane* (Yard No. 55), which was lost off the Dogger Bank on the night of 15 October 1904, sunk by gunfire from jittery Russian Baltic Fleet cruisers which had mistaken a small group of trawlers in the North Sea for the Japanese Fleet, at the time of the Russo-Japanese war. Other trawlers were also damaged in the incident.

By 1914 the larger vessels being built were proving difficult to launch into the confines of the narrow waterway and in that year a new ten-acre site, allowing launching directly into the River Ouse, was leased from the Aire & Calder Navigation Company. Wartime restrictions slowed its completion, but when the move was finally made in 1917 the new yard had seven building berths for vessels up to 350 ft in length. At this time the company was building paddle minesweepers and trawlers for the Admiralty and in the early postwar years built many vessels, including the notable four-ship 'Gitano'-class of 1921–1924 for Ellerman, Wilson Line. Orders continued during the lean years of the 1920s, but the recession reached the shipyard, with the order book empty, by 1931.

Work resumed in the mid-1930s with coasters, a grab dredger for Ramsgate Harbour in 1936 and a trawler-type vessel for the Missions to Fishermen, its fish hold fitted out as a chapel. But war clouds were forming and by 1937 the yard was in full production, Admiralty orders including the 700-ton Boom Defence ships *Barcombe* and *Barcroft* (Yard Nos. 332 and 333), delivered in 1938.

Apart from naval construction during the war, the merchant ship building programme was impressive with eleven tugs, two coasters and three coastal tankers under 'Empire' nomenclature. Prefabricated vessels built included nine 'Chant' tankers, thirteen dry cargo variations known as the 'Empire F'-type and eleven similar vessels of the 'Shelt' type for Far Eastern service. Four standard 'Vic' lighters were also built and there were a number of ships built under private contract, including coasters for F. T. Everard & Sons Ltd., and two sisterships for the Bristol Steam Navigation Company.

On 21 November 1967 the share capital of Goole Shipbuilding & Repairing Co. Ltd. was acquired by the Swan, Hunter Group, becoming part of their Small Ship Division, but in 1978 the shipyard was nationalised and its name changed again, to Goole Shipbuilders.

By 1980 orders had virtually ceased, the last, *Fort Good Hope* (Yard No. 604), an offshore supply ship for Townsend Holdings Ltd., being launched on 7 October 1983. In January 1984 British Shipbuilders (the nationalised shipyards) confirmed that shipbuilding at Goole had finished and the yard closed on 27 April 1984, after eighty-three years.

Five months later the yard was purchased by Cochrane Shipbuilders Ltd., of Selby (part of the North British Group). In four months eight ships were repaired and in 1985 building work at the yard restarted, in the form of an offshore platform supply vessel for Stirling Shipping, of Glasgow.

The *Scudai*, formerly the 'Shelt'-type coaster *Empire Seashore*, in Far East waters. (Goole Shipbuilding & Repairing Co. Ltd., Yard No. 438.)

SHIPS BUILT UNDER PRIVATE CONTRACT OR LICENCE

346　*Spirality*　554 gt, 176.3 ft (oa), 168.7 ft × 27.7 ft.
Engines: Oil (aft).
Launched: 15.8.1939.
Completed: 11.1939 for F. T. Everard & Sons Ltd.
16.1.1941: In collision with mv *Bonnington Court* (1929, 4,909 gt) off Cliff Quay, Ipswich; capsized and sank.
25.1.1941: Wreck run into by H.M. ship, and:
30.1.1941: by steamer *Sanfry* (1930, 946 gt).
27.2.1941: Vessel uprighted, and:
16.3.1941: Refloated, but settled again.
27.3.1941: Refloated again; beached. Repaired.
3.1969 Scrapped Antwerp.

347　*Alacrity*　554 gt. Details as Yard No. 346.
Launched: 14.12.1939.
Completed:　2.1940 for F. T. Everard & Sons Ltd.
21.8.1940: Damaged by aircraft bombs at Falmouth. Repaired.
5.3.1942: Damaged by aircraft bombs seven miles north-west of Bishop Rock; reached port (voyage: Drogheda/Newport, Mon. – ballast). Repaired.
13.9.1963: Aground during fog in Portheras Cove, north of Pendeen Lighthouse, Cornwall.
Constructive total loss (voyage: Swansea/Brussels – anthracite). Wreck later dispersed by explosives.

350 *Fiddown* 319 gt, 139.3 ft (oa), 133.8 ft × 24.7 ft. Engines: Oil (aft).
Launched: 9.5.1940.
Completed: 7.1940 for S. Morris Ltd., Goole.
29.11.1940: Run down and sunk by H.M.S. *Campbeltown* when entering River Mersey.
7.7.1942: Beached at Tranmere.
10.7.1942: Refloated; repaired, and:
1943: *Empire Estuary* (M.O.W.T.) (*q.v.*).

392 *Supremity* 2,074 gt, 270.2 ft (oa), 265 ft × 40.5 ft. Engines: Oil (aft).
Launched: 26.2.1944.
Completed: 10.1944 for F. T. Everard & Sons Ltd.
1964: *Kapa* (Kapa Shipping Enterprises (J. Capralos, Greece)).
1966: *Irene K* (Karmiros Bros, Greece).
12.1973: Scrapped Skaramanga, Greece.

394 *Ability* 881 gt, 202.8 ft (oa), 192.6 ft × 30.1 ft. Engines: Oil (aft).
Launched: 2.6.1943.
Completed: 9.1943 for F. T. Everard & Sons Ltd.
1975: *Eleni V* (Elmar Ltd., Greece) (Panama flag).
1977: *Nagla Star* (Tripolis Shipping Co. (Elmar Ltd., Cyprus flag)).
10.8.1981: Arrived Sami, Cephalonia, in tow after machinery damage on voyage Porto Nogaro/Beirut.
1982: Sold by auction to L. Kladias, and
10.11.1982: Left Sami in tow and subsequently broken up at Eleusis, Greece.

395 *Amenity* 881 gt. Details as Yard No. 394.
Launched: 14.9.1943.
Completed: 1.1944 for F. T. Everard & Sons Ltd.
5.1968: Scrapped Inverkeithing.

396 *Cerium* 532 gt, 181.2 ft (oa), 174.5 ft × 27.2 ft. Engines: Oil (aft).
Launched: 16.10.1943.
Completed: 12.1943 for I.C.I. (Alkali) Ltd.
1967: *G. R. Velie* (Continental Explosives Ltd., Vancouver (I.C.I. Ltd.)).
1974: (Westof Marine Ltd., Vancouver).
1976: (Centennial Towing Ltd., Vancouver).
1976: *G. B. Church* (Commander Leasing Ltd., Vancouver).

403 *Lapwing* 940 gt, 209.2 ft (oa), 202.6 ft × 31.4 ft. Engines: Oil (aft).
Launched: 4.10.1944.
Completed: 12.1944 for General Steam Navigation Co. Ltd.
22.3.1967: In collision in St. Clements Reach, River Thames, with *Carpathia* (1957, 2,040 gt). Holed and

flooded; berthed (voyage: Felixstowe/Deptford). Constructive total loss. Sold, and:
4.1967: Arrived Grays, Essex, for breaking up.

407 *Petrel* 921 gt. Details as Yard No. 403.
Launched: 15.2.1945.
Completed: 5.1945 for General Steam Navigation Co. Ltd.
1961: *Petrell* (T. Jensen, Norway).
1964: (Moeship A/S Pedersen's Rederi, Norway).
1965: *Costakis S* (I. K. Mimides, Greece).
1966: *Anna* (Varvakis & Co., Greece).
1974: (V. Andreou & Co., Greece).
1983: Tepeleni Shipping Co., Honduras).

425 *Adaptity* 945 gt, 209.4 ft (oa), 202.6 ft × 31.5 ft. Engines: Oil (aft).
Launched: 12.5.1945.
Completed: 7.1945 for F. T. Everard & Sons Ltd.
1.1970: Scrapped Inverkeithing.

426 *Actuality* 945 gt. Details as Yard No. 425.
Launched: 9.1945.
Completed: 11.1945 for F. T. Everard & Sons Ltd.
27.10.1963: In collision, in fog, four miles off Hastings, Sussex, with Dutch mv *Betty Anne-S* (1953, 499 gt). Capsized and sank. Total loss (voyage: Amble/Yelland – coal).

427 *Friargate* 945 gt. Details as Yard No. 425.
Launched: 22.12.1945.
Completed: 3.1946 for Hull Gates Shipping Co. Ltd. (Craggs & Jenkin Ltd.).
1950: *Yarmouth Trader* (Great Yarmouth Shipping Co. Ltd.).
1959: *Protoporos* (Seafarers Co. Inc., Liberia (C. Stergiopoulos, Greece)).
1960: *Yewcroft* (J. Stewart & Co. (Shipping) Ltd., Glasgow).
1965: *Georgios Kontos* (Kontos Bros. & Psarelis, Greece).
1971: Renamed *Panaghia*.
18.10.1971: Developed leaks four miles south of Cape Gata, near Limassol, Cyprus. Taken in tow by *Pelias* (1955, 781 gt) but abandoned, and:
19.10.1971: Sank off Cyprus, 34.27N 33.10E (voyage: Marina di Carrara/Beirut – marble).

428 *Ino* 945 gt. Details as Yard No. 425.
Launched: 5.2.1946.
Completed: 4.1946 for Bristol Steam Navigation Co. Ltd.
1954: *Maltara* (Adelaide SS Co. Ltd.).
1959: (Acco Transport Ltd. (Adelaide SS Co. Ltd.)).
1967: *Sandy* (Islander Nav. Corpn., S.A. (Asia–Africa Shipping Co., Hong Kong)).

1973: (Cia. de Nav. Amin S.A., Panama (Unique Shipping & Trading Co., Singapore)).
1974: *Bagas* (Bahari Bahtera P.T. Perusahan Pelayaran Nusantara, Indonesia).
1976: (Gesuri Lloyd P.T., Indonesia).
1979: (Nagah Berlian P.T., Indonesia).

442   *Cato* 945 gt. Details as Yard No. 425.
Launched: 14.4.1946.

Completed: 6.1946 for Bristol Steam Navigation Co. Ltd.
24.4.1963: Cut in two whilst moored in Avonmouth Docks, when a tug's stern line on mv *City of Brooklyn* (locking in) carried away and the ship sliced through the *Cato* at after end of No. 2 hatch. Sank.
26.5.1963: Raised, but constructive total loss. Sold, and:
13.6.1963: Arrived at Newport, Mon., for breaking up.

Built by Henry Scarr Ltd., Hessle

464   *Empire Seasheltie* 522 gt.
Launched: 2.1945.
Completed: 3.1945.
1947: *Selangor* (Straits SS Co. Ltd.).
1967: (Sharikat Perk. Sendirian, Malaya).
12.1967: Scrapped Singapore.

465   *Empire Seabeach* 522 gt.
Launched: 2.1945.
Completed: 4.1945.
1946: *Sedenak* (Straits SS Co. Ltd.).
1967: (Sharikat Perk. Sendirian, Malaya).
1969: *Selamat* (Tan Yong Sing Shipping Co., Singapore).
15.7.1971: Stranded in heavy weather on Kalampunian Island, north of Kudat, Borneo, 07.03N 116.44E. Abandoned. Total loss (voyage: Sandakan/Kuching – ballast).

466   *Empire Seahawk* 522 gt.
Launched: 3.1945.
Completed: 5.1945.
1946: *Seramban* (Straits SS Co. Ltd.).
12.1965: Scrapped Singapore.

467   *Empire Seafront* 522 gt.
Launched: 3.1945.
Completed: 5.1945.
1946: *Sadao* (Straits SS Co. Ltd.).
6.1965: Scrapped Singapore.

468   *Empire Seaboy* 522 gt.
Launched: 4.1945.
Completed: 6.1945.
1946: *Sirusa* (Straits SS Co. Ltd.).
1967: (Sharikat Perk. Sendirian, Malaya).
1971: *Darpo Lima* (Samudera P.T. Perusahan Pelayaran Nusantara, Indonesia).

469   *Empire Seabreeze* 522 gt.
Launched: 4.1945.
Completed: 6.1945.
1947: *Senai* (Straits SS Co. Ltd.).
1962: *Changi* (Tiong Lam Hang Shipping Co. Ltd., Hong Kong).
1962: *Mene* (Cosmos Shipping Co., S.A., Panama).
1983: *Mercury* (Naviera Voluntad Soc. de R.L., Honduras).
23.12.1984: Foundered off Tumpat, Malaya, 5.50N 102.36E, after taking water in engine room (voyage: Songkhla/Singapore).

470   *Empire Seacoast* 522 gt.
Launched: 6.1945.
Completed: 10.1945.
1946: *Birhakim* (Middle East Coastal Services Ltd., Cyprus).
1949: *Tanda* (Indian General Nav. & Railway Co., Calcutta).
1961: (Pakistan River Steamers Ltd.).
1975: *C5-212* (Bangladesh Inland Water Transport Corpn.).

471   *Empire Seagull* 522 gt.
Launched: 5.1945.
Completed: 7.1945.
1947: *Serampang* (Straits SS Co. Ltd.).
1967: (Sharikat Perk. Sendirian, Malaya).
1970: *Darpo Empat* (Samudera P.T. Perusahan Pelayaran Nusantara, Indonesia).

472   *Empire Seabird* 522 gt.
Launched: 26.6.1945.
Completed: 9.1945.
1947: *Stia* (Straits SS Co. Ltd.).
1960: *Anli* (Teck Hwa Shipping Co. Ltd., Singapore).
1965: (Kie Hock Shipping Co. Ltd., Singapore).
1972: *Global Trader* (Singapore owners).

1974: *Ever Faithful* (Lam Kok Shipping Co. Ltd., Singapore).
1981: *Blue Eagle* (Sunrise Asia Shipping Co., Panama).

473   *Empire Sealion* 522 gt.
Launched: 7.1945.
Completed: 9.1945.
1947: *Serudom* (Straits SS Co. Ltd.).
1962: *Jurong* (Tiong Lam Hang Shipping Co., S.A., Panama).

1967: *Soon Hong* (Cosmos Shipping Co., S.A., Panama).
(*circa*) 1975: Reported renamed *Soon Lee*, and:
3.1976: Scrapped Singapore.

474   *Empire Seaview* 522 gt.
Launched: 8.1945.
Completed: 10.1945.
1947: *Segamat* (Straits SS Co. Ltd.).
12.1966: Scrapped Singapore.

At the end of World War II, after the Malaysian Peninsula was freed from Japanese control, the Singapore Straits Steamship Co. Ltd. resumed trading in its customary areas of operations and the surviving ships, of those which had been requisitioned, were returned to company ownership.

Previously, in December 1944, a few months before war ended, the company was licensed to place private contracts with the Grangemouth Dockyard Company for the construction and purchase of three coasters of the 'B'-type, vessels similar to the seven standard 'Empire'-named vessels of the type which were already on order elsewhere in the United Kingdom. The three new vessels, each of 950 gt, were delivered during 1945–1946 and given the names *Bentong*, *Bidor* and *Bruas* (see Grangemouth Dockyard Company, ships built under licence). At the same time many of the three types of 'standard' coasters specially built for service in the Far East became surplus to Government requirements and were made available for purchase.

In 1946 the company name of Singapore Straits Steamship Co. Ltd., was restyled as Straits Steamship Co. Ltd., and in July of the same year it purchased sixteen vessels of the 'Shelt' type, which it had been managing and operating on behalf of the M.O.W.T.

A further three vessels of the 'B' type, Government-owned and with 'Empire' nomenclature – *Empire Pacific*, *Empire Palace* and *Empire Passmore* – which the Straits SS Company had also been operating, since their completion for the M.O.W.T., were, firstly, chartered by the company and then, in 1948, purchased outright under an 'option-to-purchase' agreement.

Also, a number of the 'C'-type, 'May'-class coasters were acquired. They were, in fact, part of a settlement by the M.O.W.T. in respect of the company's requisitioned vessels *Circe* (1912, 778 gt) and *Medusa* (1913, 793 gt), for which the reconditioning liability on these two old ships amounted to a large sum, and the company 'offered to accept, in lieu', eight of the coasters. Instead, the Ministry offered only five: these were accepted and the vessels were handed over during 1947, by which time the Straits SS Company had sold the *Circe* and the *Medusa* for breaking up. Soon after, the remaining three of the eight 'C'-type coasters which had been available, were purchased by the company.

During 1950–1951 two more vessels of the 'Shelt'-type were purchased, this time from a Cyprus-based firm, Middle East Coastal Services Ltd., and thus the Straits SS Co. Ltd. owned eighteen 'Shelts' from the total of twenty-three which had been built.

475   *Empire Seaport* 522 gt.
Launched: 8.1945.
Completed: 11.1945.
1946: *Eladem* (Middle East Coastal Services Ltd., Cyprus).

1949: *Torilla* (Pakistan River Steamers Ltd.).
1950: (Rivers Steam Navigation Co. Ltd., London).
1975: *C5-216* (Bangladesh Inland Water Transport Corpn.).

'Clyde Puffer' type coasters – The 'VIC' lighters

Early in the war years it was found that a large fleet of self-propelled cargo lighters would be needed and plans were prepared for a series of *Victualling Inshore Craft*, which became known as 'VIC' lighters.

The Admiralty Merchant Shipbuilding Department selected the 'Clyde Puffer' as the prototype, using the designs of the *Anzac* and *Lascar*, the last of the type built before the outbreak of war. These two vessels, launched by Scott & Son of Bowling, on the River Clyde, in August 1939 for coaster and 'Puffer' owners J. Hay & Sons Ltd., measured 66.7 ft in length by 18.5 ft in breadth and were of 97 gross tons.

The Clyde 'Puffer' had evolved in the previous century from the early Forth and Clyde Canal flat-bottomed barges (known as scows) and the similar coastal seagoing craft. With coal-fired boilers, their simple single- or twin-cylinder steam engines were without condensers and exhausted directly into the atmosphere, giving a peculiar puffing sound – similar to a steam railway engine – and from which the name derived. Later, improved versions developed and compound engines were fitted with condensers, but the nickname of the type remained. Gradually the 'Puffer' evolved into a standard form, with a large hold forward capable of holding more than a hundred tons of cargo and the wheelhouse placed abaft the funnel. Size of the craft was dictated by the size of the locks of the Forth and Clyde Canal (a maximum of 68 ft 6 ins), with shallow-draught vessels for canal work and deeper-draught craft for coastal and Scottish islands trade. Except for some variation in propulsion, the design remained virtually unaltered for many years.

Between 1941 and 1943 sixty-four 'VICs' conforming to the limitations of the Forth and Clyde Canal, and the smallest type of coaster produced during the war, were ordered. Their dimensions were 66.8 ft × 18.4 ft and tonnages were 96 gross, 140 deadweight. Most of them were steamers, twenty-seven of them – including the lead ship – from Richard Dunston Ltd., of Thorne, Yorkshire. Others were built at Goole, Hull, Gainsborough, Northwich, Faversham and one in Scotland. Dunston's also completed the nine diesel-engined craft from this group, the vessels destined for overseas service and described as cased petrol carriers, in 1944.

The only Scottish-built 'VIC' lighter (*VIC 18*) from J. Hay & Sons, was, in fact, part of a two-ship contract, but the second craft was not taken up as a 'VIC', being completed in 1944 as *Kaffir* for the builder's own 'Puffer' fleet, but still conforming to the standard 'VIC' dimensions.

There are no official records listing the construction of *VIC 13* and, indeed, it is said that she was not built. However, some sources suggest that the vessel served with the Royal Army Service Corps; nevertheless she is also listed as having been struck off the shipping register at Bathurst, West Africa, on 1 November 1945.

Later, following the initial order for sixty-four 'VIC' lighters, a series of larger 'Improved Puffer' craft was ordered, with the Canal limitations ignored. These craft had welded, not riveted, hulls, were without sheer or camber and, in order to save scarce wartime steel, as much plate work as possible was eliminated. They also had the wheelhouse placed forward of the funnel. Most of the vessels were completed to dimensions of 80 ft × 20 ft, with tonnages of 147 gross and 165 deadweight. Again, steam machinery was predominant, although five diesel-driven craft were of slightly smaller tonnage. Eight craft conforming to these measurements were cancelled. The final pair of 'VIC' lighters constructed were also diesel-powered, but were 83.5 ft in length.

Further details of the basic, original 'VIC' lighter show a straight stem and deep counter stern, a steam compound engine with vertical coal-fired boiler developing some 120 hp on a single shaft and giving 7½ knots. The eleven tons bunker capacity gave a range of some 700 miles. The single hold was 30 ft in length, served by a single 18-cwt safe-working-load derrick on the foremast. The

'Improved Puffer'-type coaster had a foc's'le and a raised quarterdeck, with sunk poop aft. The hold was almost 40 ft in length, with one cargo hatchway.

The war service of the 'VICs' was mostly naval, not only in home waters but also in many overseas locations, ranging from West Africa to Hong Kong. In February 1946 authority was granted to the Admiralty to 'take over, permanently, all the VIC lighters allocated to them for naval work and such others from the building programme as may be available'. Many 'VICs' were taken over, mostly in 1947. However, as the need for them later declined, many were sold into private ownership. Some went to the traditional 'Puffer' routes of their forebears, many others were converted to seagoing coasters and specialised craft. A number of them survive to the present time.

It has not proved possible to trace the full histories of a number of the VIC lighters, particularly when in Admiralty service or in any subsequent commercial service, and this fact is indicated.

'VIC' type lighters – 96 gt, 140 tdw, 66.8 ft × 18.4 ft. Engines: Compound 2 cyl (aft) – 7½ knots

Built by R. Dunston Ltd., Thorne

369   *VIC 1*
Launched: 2.10.1941
Completed: 11.1941.
1941–1946: (Naval work).
1946: (M.O.W.T.).
1947: (War Department – Army).
1948: (Port of London Authority). Fitted with new boiler and rebuilt as a mooring craft and buoy tender. Equipped with lifting horns over the bow, renamed *Glengall*.
1966: (M. Fielding, Dublin).
Later reported scrapped.

370   *VIC 2*
Launched: 23.10.1941.
Completed: 1.1942.
2.1942–9.1943: (Naval work).
10.1943: Shipped to Malta on Liberty ship *John Langdon* (1942, 7,176 gt), for War Department – Army.
5.1946: (Admiralty, Malta).
11.1950: Sold locally.
No further trace.

371   *VIC 3*
Launched: 26.12.1941.
Completed: 2.1942.
2.1942–5.1943: (Naval work).
5.1943: Shipped to Freetown, West Africa.
7.1943–10.1944: (M.O.W.T.).
11.1944–12.1945: (Naval work).

25.12.1945: Capsized and sank at Freetown, W. Africa. Total loss.
1949: Wreck sold 'as lies' to local salvors.

372   *VIC 4*
Launched: 10.2.1942.
Completed: 2.1942.
2.1942–3.1943: (War Department – Army).
3.1943: Shipped to Gibraltar.
10.1944: (Naval work).
1946: (Converted to a water carrier at Gibraltar).
3.1947: Transferred to Admiralty (Gibraltar).
(*circa*) 1966: *Lady Isle* (Irvine Shipping & Trading Co.).
1974: Sold to East Coast buyers, and:
1981: Lying at St. Davids on Forth, for breaking up.

378   *VIC 7*
Launched: 2.4.1942.
Completed: 4.1942.
4.1942–5.1943: (Naval work).
5.1943–8.1945: (Port duties, West Africa Command).
1945: (M.O.W.T.).
1948: (Sold to W. G. Garside).
1949: *Lady Isle* (J. L. McCorquodale, Oban).
11.8.1956: Stranded at Scarnish, Tiree Island, west coast of Scotland. Holed and abandoned.
25.9.1956: Vessel righted but further heavy damage revealed.
28.9.1956: Salvage work stopped due to gales, which caused vessel to split on starboard side from deck to keel. Salvage work abandoned. Total loss.

379   *VIC 8*
Launched: 13.5.1942.
Completed: 6.1942.
6.1942: (War Department – Army).
1946: (Naval work, Malta).
1949: Transferred to Admiralty.
1966: *Seahorse V* (Alfred Tanti, Malta).
1972: (Sold to buyers at Augusta, Sicily).
No further trace.

380   *VIC 9*
Launched: 4.6.1942.
Completed: 7.1942.
7.1942–4.1947: (Naval work).
1947: Transferred to Admiralty (Portsmouth),
renamed *C.667*, used as a waterboat.
1949: For disposal, but held in Reserve at Portland.
No further trace.

381   *VIC 10*
Launched: 20.7.1942.
Completed: 9.1942.
10.1942: (Naval work, West Africa Command).
1947: Transferred to Admiralty.
1948: (H. G. Pounds, Portsmouth).
1949: *Emmanuel* (converted to oil engine), (W. A.
Smit, Rotterdam).
1950: (M. Hovland, Norway).
No trace after 1976.

387   *VIC 21*
Launched: 29.7.1942.
Completed: 9.1942.
9.1942: (Naval work).
1950: Transferred to Admiralty.
No further trace.

388   *VIC 22*
Launched: 2.9.1942.
Completed: 10.1942.
10.1942: Allocated for naval work in West Africa,
but:
12.1942: Based at Greenock (pending shipment to
Freetown), then moved to Milford Haven and
Portsmouth.
3.1947: (Naval work – Ceylon).
5.1947: Transferred to Admiralty, Colombo.
8.1947: (Laid up).
11.1948: *Mazda* (Ruttanji Nussurwanji Nazir,
Bombay).
No further trace.

389   *VIC 23*
Launched: 4.10.1942.
Completed: 11.1942.

11.1942–1947: (Naval work).
1948: *Limelight* (Light Shipping Co. Ltd., Glasgow).
19..: *Cloch Lass* (M. Brown & Co., Greenock).
1966: Reported scrapped Dalmuir.

390   *VIC 24*
Launched: 5.11.1942.
Completed: 12.1942.
12.1942–5.1943: (Ministry of Supply).
5.1943–1947: (Naval work).
1947: Transferred to Admiralty – Harwich).
1957: (H. G. Pounds, Portsmouth).
1964: (W. J. Havens, London).
1967: *Advance* (Husbands Shipyard Ltd.,
Southampton). Restored and overhauled at shipyard.
1985: Reported sold Falmouth buyers for further
trade.

391   *VIC 25*
Launched: 4.1.1943.
Completed: 2.1943.
2.1943: (Naval work).
1949: Transferred to Admiralty.
No further trace.

392   *VIC 26*
Launched: 23.4.1943.
Completed: 5.1943.
5.1943–6.1946: (Naval work).
8.1946: *Polarlight* (Light Shipping Co. Ltd.,
Glasgow).
No further trace.

411   *VIC 32*
Launched: 3.7.1943.
Completed: 8.1943.
8.1943–7.1946: (Naval work).

For her war service the vessel was based at Fort William, carrying ammunition, aviation fuel and cement. Due to the volatile nature of some cargo she was fitted with fire hydrants and sprinklers. In 1947 *VIC 32* transferred to the Admiralty and in 1949 was renamed *C.702*, being based at Devonport and, later, at Rosyth. In December 1963 she was sold to Turner & Hickman Ltd., Glasgow, and three months later sold again, for scrapping, to J. A. White & Company, St. Davids on Forth.

But she was not broken up, pending a resale, and in 1970 the vessel was purchased by a steam enthusiast and moved to Whitby. In October 1975 she was sold yet again, and steamed to London in the following May, spending the next three years under conversion for 12-passenger 'Puffer' cruising. The hold was fitted with six 2-berth cabins and she was given a raised galley, dining and saloon areas, this accommodation being up to the level of the old hatch coamings. The vessel, which steamed north in 1978, still retains her original compound coal-fired steam engine and boiler. Her owners (N. & R. Walker) now offer 'Highland Steamboat Holidays' on the lochs and canals of Scotland.

412   *VIC 36*
Launched: 17.12.1943.
Completed: 1.1944.
3.1944–5.1946: (Naval work, as a waterboat).
1947: Transferred to Admiralty – Harwich.
1964: (A. E. Pierce & Sons, Essex).
Later reported scrapped.

413   *VIC 37*
Launched: 15.2.1944.
Completed: 3.1944.
3.1944: (Converted to a waterboat for naval work).
1947: Transferred to Admiralty – Rosyth.
1966: *Lady Morven* (Irvine Shipping & Trading Co.).
1988: At Maryport, Cumbria, Maritime Museum.

511   *VIC 83*
Launched: 15.6.1944.
Completed: 7.1944.
8.1944: Allocated for service in Ceylon.
10.1944: Shipped out per *Empire Viceroy* (1943, 7,803 gt).
1947: Transferred to Admiralty – Colombo.
1950: *Rutna* (Bombay Port Trust). Later converted and renamed *Salvage Lighter*.
1966: Name removed from ship lists.

512   *VIC 84*
Launched: 16.6.1944.
Completed: 10.1944.
1947: Transferred to Admiralty, renamed *C.704* (used as a collier).
No further trace.

513   *VIC 85*
Launched: 14.9.1944.
Completed: 11.1944.
11.1944: (Naval work).
1947: Transferred to Admiralty – Fort William.
1963: Sold.
No further trace.

514   *VIC 86*
Launched: 22.9.1944.
Completed: 11.1944.
1.1945: (Naval service, Antwerp, in conjunction with defence of River Schelde).
5.1945: (War Department – Army).
1947: Transferred to Admiralty – Singapore.
1948: Sold locally (Chain Utility Stores). Probably broken up.

515   *VIC 87*
Launched: 7.10.1944.
Completed: 12.1944.
1944: (M.O.W.T.).
1945: (Naval work).
1947: Transferred to Admiralty – Deptford, London.
1948: *King Hal* (Overseas Towage & Salvage Co. Ltd.).
1949: *Dane* (J. Hay & Sons Ltd.).
No trace after 1956.

516   *VIC 88*
Launched: 17.10.1944.
Completed: 2.1945.
3.1945: (Naval work – Greenock).
1947: Transferred to Admiralty – Singapore.
1948: Reported sold locally.
No further trace.

517   *VIC 89*
Launched: 8.12.1944.
Completed: 2.1945.
1945: (M.O.W.T.).
1947: (War Department – Army).
1947: *Glenaray* (Hamilton & McPhail, Glasgow).
1964: Scrapped.

518   *VIC 90*
Launched: 21.12.1944.
Completed: 2.1945.
4.1945: (Naval work – Portsmouth).
1947: Transferred to Admiralty – Gosport.
4.1961: Reported sold (Dundas Fose, Emsworth, Hants.).
No further trace.

519   *VIC 91*
Launched: 17.1.1945.
Completed: 3.1945.
1947: Transferred to Admiralty.
No further trace.

520   *VIC 92*
Launched: 19.1.1945.
Completed: 4.1945.
5.1945: Allocated for naval service in Ceylon.
3.1946: Shipped out per *Empire Admiral* (1945, 7,842 gt).
1947: Transferred to Admiralty – Trincomalee.
1948: *Buxor* (Ruttonji Nussurwanji Nazir, Bombay).
No further trace.

Built by Goole Shipbuilding & Repairing Co. Ltd.

377   *VIC 5*
Launched: 5.11.1941.
Completed: 12.1941.
2.1942–5.1943: (Naval work).
5.1943: (West Africa Command).
1948: (H. G. Pounds, Portsmouth).
No trace after 1955.

378   *VIC 6*
Launched: 18.3.1942.
Completed: 4.1942.
5.1942–10.1943: (War Department – Army).
10.1943: (Naval work).
1947: Transferred to Admiralty.
No further trace.

381   *VIC 11*
Launched: 1.5.1942.
Completed: 6.1942.
6.1942–5.1947: (Naval work).
1947: Transferred to Admiralty.
1948: *Zulu* (J. Hay & Sons, Glasgow).

29.12.1951: Sailed from Carnlough, N. Ireland,
bound for Paisley, Glasgow, with a cargo of
limestone.
30.12.1951: Storm of hurricane force in area. Vessel
overdue.
4.1.1952: Wreckage of vessel washed ashore at
Stranraer.

382   *VIC 12*
Launched: 6.5.1942.
Completed: 6.1942.
6.1942–3.1947: (Naval work).
1947: Transferred to Admiralty, renamed *C.713*.
1963: *Toward Lass* (W. Burke Ltd., Greenock). Later:
(M. Brown & Co., Greenock).
2.1980: Scrapped Dalmuir.

Note: The above vessel's naval work included that of carrying
torpedoes to submarines based in the Holy Loch and her
service in commercial use included that of a rubbish tender
to the U.S. submarine base in the same area.

Built by I. Pimblott & Sons Ltd., Northwich

646   *VIC 14*
Launched: 8.1942.
Completed: 9.1942.
9.1942–3.1947: (Naval work – fitted as a mobile
workshop).
3.1947: Transferred to Admiralty – Greenock.
1961: *Storford* (lengthened, fitted with oil engine); (J.
T. Palmer & Sons, Gravesend).
(*circa*) 1984: Sold, put into River Thames sand trade.
Resold (M. Murray, Sittingbourne). Engine
removed, and:
1988: Hull dismantled at Queenborough, Kent.

647   *VIC 15*
Launched: 10.1942.
Completed: 12.1942.
12.1942–10.1943: (War Department – Army).
10.1943: (War Department – Mediterranean).
5.1946: (Naval work – Malta).
1947: Transferred to Admiralty – Malta.
1951: Renamed *Y.C.390* (Yard Craft); converted to
electric power plant lighter at Malta.
No further trace.

648   *VIC 16*
Launched: 1.1943.
Completed: 3.1943.
4.1943–3.1944: (Converted to a waterboat; naval
work at Portsmouth, Chatham and Harwich).
1947: Transferred to Admiralty – Chatham.
1964: Sold (A. E. Pierce & Sons, Essex), later reported
scrapped.

649   *VIC 17*
Launched: 1.7.1943.
Completed: 7.1943.
7.1943–10.1943: (War Department – Army).
10.1943: (War Department – Mediterranean).
1946: (Naval work – Malta).
1947: Transferred to Admiralty – Malta.
1949: (At Gibraltar).
1967: Sold at Gibraltar.
No further trace.

644   *VIC 19*
Launched: 21.2.1942.
Completed: 4.1942.
4.1942–4.1943: (Naval work).

4.1943: (Naval work – Gibraltar).
1947: Transferred to Admiralty – Gibraltar.
1959: Sold (J. O. Viale, Gibraltar).
No further trace.

645   *VIC 20*
Launched: 16.4.1942.
Completed: 6.1942.
7.1942–5.1943: (M.O.W.T.).
5.1943: Port duties, (West Africa Command).
1946: Transferred to Government of Gambia.
1.1951: Ran short of fuel on voyage Bathurst for
Bissao, in ballast. Entered Casamance River in order
to anchor at Zighinkor, but carried by current and
grounded on river bank, smashing her propeller.
25.1.1951: Refloated by local port services, towed to
Zighinkor.
1951: Registry of vessel closed.

650   *VIC 27*
Launched: 17.7.1943.
Completed: 8.1943.
8.1943–4.1944: (Naval work).
4.1944: (Converted to a waterboat).
1.1945: (Naval work – Antwerp).
1947: Transferred to Admiralty – Devonport and
Harwich.
1966: (M. Kelly, Ardrossan Dockyard Co. Ltd.).
Resold (Glenburn Shipping Company, Glasgow).
1968: (Sir James Miller, Edinburgh). Vessel taken to
Granton, refitted and converted for parties of up to
twenty persons, and:
1969: Renamed *Auld Reekie* (Old Smokey).

Based at Oban, Scotland, in summer, the vessel is chartered
to youth organisations at nominal cost and used as a floating
base for activities such as sailing, swimming and local
exploration.
   The conversion of *Auld Reekie* included the addition of a
hatchway to the saloon/dining area built into the hold, this
fitted with a solid-fuel stove which also fired central heating.
Situated off the main saloon were two- and four-berth cabins,
washing facilities and a galley. With a crew of only two, the
young persons on board share all the chores, including that
of coal-fired stoking of the boiler.

(*circa*) 1988: Renamed *Vital Spark*.

651   *VIC 29*
Launched: 1944.
Completed: 3.1944.
4.1944–5.1945: (Naval work – a waterboat).
5.1945: (War Department – Army).
1947: Transferred to Admiralty.
1948: *Glen Rosa* (G. & G. Hamilton Ltd., Glasgow).

16.1.1958: Grounded on rocks on south coast of Isle
of Mull, Scotland. Holed and abandoned.
Submerged. Total loss (voyage: Troon/Mull – coal).

652   *VIC 28*
Launched: 1943.
Completed: 10.1943.
11.1943–8.1945: (Naval work).
1947: Transferred to Admiralty – Plymouth.
4.1961: (Sold).
No further trace.

653   *VIC 30*
Launched: 1944.
Completed: 3.1944.
4.1944: (For naval work; converted to a waterboat at
Bristol).
1947: Transferred to Admiralty – Gosport.
No trace after 1948.

654   *VIC 31*
Launched: 15.4.1944.
Completed: 5.1944.
5.1944–12.1946: (Naval work – Colombo).
21.12.1946: Ashore on Foul Point, Ceylon, while in
tow from Colombo to Trincomalee. Sunk.
Constructive total loss. Later sold, and:
1949: Salved, repaired and renamed *Rahumani* (T. P.
Abdul Rahuman & Co., Colombo).
No further trace.

656   *VIC 33*
Launched: 2.11.1944.
Completed: 1944.
1945: (M.O.W.T.).
1947: Transferred to War Department – Army.
1951: *Smeaton* (Mersey Docks & Harbour Board).
1961: (H. G. Pounds, Portsmouth).
No trace after 1965.

657   *VIC 34*
Launched: 14.3.1946.
Completed: 1946.
11.1946: (Naval work – a waterboat at Rosyth).
1947: Transferred to Admiralty – Greenock.
No further trace.

658   *VIC 35*
Launched: 27.9.1945.
Completed: 1945.
1945: (M.O.W.T.).
4.1946: (Naval work).
1947: Transferred to Admiralty – Greenock.
1970: (P. Herbert, Bude, Cornwall).
1976: (Cornish Wrecking Co., Penzance). Fitted with
an oil engine. Later refitted to a salvage craft at
Penzance; renamed *Crazy Diamond*.

Built by J. Hay & Sons Ltd., Kirkintilloch

60   *VIC 18*
Launched: 1942.
Completed: 3.1942.
4.1942–7.1946: (Naval work).
7.1946: (Laid up).

In August 1946 *VIC 18* was made over to J. Hay & Sons as a replacement for their 'Puffer' *Spartan*, which had been lost while on Government service when she blew up and sank off Lismore, Western Scotland, on 31 May 1946. The new addition to the fleet was also given the name *Spartan* and spent the rest of her career in the normal 'Puffer' trades – the carriage of coal, bricks, timber and a variety of general cargo around the west coast and western islands of Scotland.

In 1961 the *Spartan* was rebuilt and fitted with an oil engine. In 1980 she was withdrawn from service. Due to her historic importance – the last vessel afloat built on the Forth and Clyde Canal – her owners, Glenlight Shipping Co. (successors to J. Hay & Sons), presented her to the West of Scotland Boat Museum Association. The vessel was handed over on 22 April 1982 and later she sailed to Troon for survey, minor repairs and a refit. *Spartan* was to become the centrepiece of a display at the Scottish Maritime Museum at Irvine, Ayrshire.

61   *VIC ——*
Launched: 1944. Not taken up as a VIC lighter.
Completed: 1944 as *Kaffir* for builder's own 'Puffer' fleet.
1961: New (oil) engine.
1968: (Glenlight Shipping Co.).
23.9.1974: Stolen from Ayr (Scotland) harbour at night and taken to sea with a pilot cutter in pursuit. While attempting to return to harbour missed the entrance and ran aground on Newton Beach, north of harbour entrance. Severely damaged and flooded, but authorities prevented cargo of 118 tons of coal being jettisoned. Abandoned, constructive total loss; wreck still remaining visible at low water.

In 1847 William Hay started a canal transport business at Kirkintilloch, a town situated some halfway along the Forth and Clyde Canal, and gradually built up a fleet of scows to serve the iron, coal, timber and grain trades. Ten years later some of his craft were converted to screw propulsion and in the same year the first steam screw lighter to be built from the keel up was launched by David Swan, at Kelvin Dock, also on the canal. Named *Glasgow*, this craft came to be regarded as the beginning of the subsequent, numerous 'Clyde Puffer' type. But for a decade there was no local yard at Kirkintilloch which could service small vessels, although some had sprung up at the ends of the canal – at Glasgow to the west and Falkirk to the east.

Then, in 1867, William Hay's sons, James and John, already respected as shipping agents in the town, took over an unsuccessful, shortlived boatbuilding co-operative and used it for the maintenance of the family fleet of steam lighters, horse-drawn barges and scows.

Twelve years later the brothers started a line of coasting steamers, with James as its manager, whilst John concentrated his attention to the operations of the repair and maintenance yard. He quickly turned to shipbuilding, the yard launching its first vessel, the 64-ft, 50-ton iron screw lighter, *Helena*, in the same year.

In the decade of the 1880s the yard's output was eleven craft, ten for their own account and one, *Aniline*, for Falkirk owners. She was built as a tanker and fitted for the carriage of tar in bulk.

In 1888 John Hay took control of the coasting business and formed J. Hay & Sons. He also extended the shipbuilding and repair yard with a new dock and slipway and then retitled it as J. & J. Hay Ltd.

Progress into the twentieth century was still dominated by the company's own requirements and up to the start of World War I fourteen more craft were built. In 1917 the yard fitted a number of barges with tanks to carry Admiralty oil from Grangemouth to Bowling, on the Clyde, then, when the conversions were finished, the Admiralty decided to lay a pipeline instead.

In 1921 the two Hay-owned firms were combined, to become J. Hay & Sons Ltd., whilst in the twenty years between the wars and as general trade declined due to economic conditions, Hay's became the main users of the canal.

Only three ships were built at the yard during World War II, two VIC-type craft and the 'Puffer' *Boer* in 1941. The *Boer* lasted until 1965, when she was broken up at Troon.

After the war only one more vessel was built. This was Yard No. 62, the *Chindit* of 74 tons, launched on 23 September 1945 – the sixty-second and last coaster from Hay's shipyard. The old yard was demolished in 1954 and the last repair job at the slipway yard was in 1961.

Built by Brown's Shipbuilding & Drydock Co. Ltd., Hull

10   *VIC 38*
Launched: 1943.
Completed: 1943.
7.1943: (Naval work – Malta).
1947: Transferred to Admiralty – Malta.
1966: (Sold).
No further trace.

11   *VIC 39*
Launched: 12.1943.
Completed: 2.1944.
4.1944: (Naval work – a waterboat at Plymouth).
1947: Transferred to Admiralty – Plymouth.
1949: Reported for disposal.
1965: Offered for sale at Devonport.
No further trace.

13   *VIC 52*
Launched: 1.1944.
Completed: 2.1944.
2.1944: (Naval work – allocated for conversion to waterboat).
1947: Transferred to Admiralty – Harwich.
1967: For disposal.
No further trace.

14   *VIC 53*
Launched: 2.1944.
Completed: 4.1944.
5.1944: (Naval work).
6.1945: (Naval work – Ceylon).
1947: Transferred to Admiralty – Singapore.
1948: Sold to local buyers (Chain Utility Stores).
Reported broken up.

15   *VIC 72*
Launched: 1944.
Completed: 9.1944.

10.1944: (Naval work).
1947: Transferred to Admiralty – Devonport.
1964: (W. J. Havens, London).
19. .: *Eldesa*.
1983: (C. Nicholson, Argyll).
1984: *Eilean Eisdeal* (Easdale Island Shipping Line, Oban).

16   *VIC 73*
Launched: 1944.
Completed: 11.1944.
12.1944: (Naval work).
1.1945: (Naval work at Antwerp, for serving craft in connection with defence of River Schelde).
9.1945: (Naval work – Rosyth).
1948: *Lowlight* (Purdy Coal Co. Ltd., North Shields).
No further trace.

17   *VIC 74*
Launched: 1.1945.
Completed: 4.1945.
5.1945: (Naval work).
8.1945: Shipped to Ceylon per *Empire Admiral*, (1945, 7,842 gt).
1947: Transferred to Admiralty – Trincomalee.
1948: *Wisia* (Ruttonji Nussurwanji Nazir, Bombay).
1951: Transferred to Government of India; for coasting service in Andaman Islands.
No further trace.

18   *VIC 75*
Launched: 25.10.1945.
Completed: 12.1945.
1.1946: (Naval work).
1947: Transferred to Admiralty – Harwich.
1957: (H. G. Pounds, Portsmouth). Reported sold to Dublin shipbreakers, but:
22.4.1959: Arrived New Waterway, Holland, for scrapping.

'VIC' type lighters – 96 gt, 140 tdw, 66.8 ft × 18.4 ft. Engines: Oil (aft) – 8 knots. Cased petrol carriers

Built by R. Dunston Ltd., Thorne

452   *VIC 40*
Launched: 9.1.1944.
Completed: 5.1944.
5.1944: (Naval work – Hong Kong).
1947: *Hip Sang* (Hong Kong owners).
1953: *Southern State* (Converted to trawler; fitted with new oil engine) (Great South Fishing Industries Ltd., Hong Kong).
1965: *Yau Wing No. 103* (Yau Wing Co., Hong Kong).
No further trace.

453   *VIC 41*
Launched: 26.1.1944.
Completed: 5.1944.
4.1944: (M.O.W.T.).
1947: Transferred to Admiralty – Hong Kong.
9.1947: Transferred to Hong Kong Government.
No further trace.

454   *VIC 42*
Launched: 17.3.1944.
Completed: 4.1944.
30.4.1944: Broke adrift from tug *Empire Charles* off Corton Sands, grounded four miles from Great Yarmouth. Refloated, taken into port. Later continued voyage in tow.
5.1944: (Naval work).
1949: *Yarvic* (N. G. Parkinson, London).
1951: (B. W. Steamships, Tug & Lighter Co. Ltd., Hull). (Later East Anglia Shipping Co. Ltd.).
1967: (Zodiac Shipping Ltd.).
1968: *Taillefer* (Les Vedettes Vertes, France).
No further trace.

455   *VIC 43*
Launched: 7.4.1944.
Completed: 7.1944.
1944: (Naval work – Hong Kong).
1947: Transferred to Admiralty – Hong Kong.
1952: *Madonna Star* (Burns, Philp & Co., New Guinea). Reported trading later as *Rui*.
1961: Scrapped.

456   *VIC 44*
Launched: 17.6.1944.
Completed: 8.1944.
1944: (M.O.W.T.).
1947: Transferred to Admiralty.
No further trace.

457   *VIC 45*
Launched: 18.7.1944.
Completed: 9.1944.
4.1945: (Allocated for naval work at Sydney, N.S.W.) but
5.1945: Shipped to Hong Kong for naval work.
1947: Transferred to Admiralty – Hong Kong.
1948: For disposal.
No further trace.

458   *VIC 46*
Launched: 29.7.1944.
Completed: 10.1944.
11.1944: (R.A.S.C.).
1947: Transferred to Admiralty.
No further trace.

459   *VIC 47*
Launched: 5.11.1944.
Completed: 12.1944.
8.1945: Shipped to Ceylon per *Empire Admiral* (1945, 7,842 gt).
1947: Transferred to Admiralty – Trincomalee.
1953: Disposed of, locally.
No further trace.

460   *VIC 48*
Launched: 25.11.1944.
Completed: 1.1945.
8.1945: Shipped to Singapore per *Empire Admiral* (1945, 7,842 gt).
1947: Transferred to Admiralty – Calcutta.
1949: (Naval work – Singapore).
10.1961: Approval given for vessel to be sunk as a target ship.

Improved 'VIC' type lighters – 147 gt, 165 tdw, 80.5 ft × 20 ft. Engines: Compound 2cyl (aft) – 7½ knots

Built by I. Pimblott & Sons Ltd., Northwich

659 *VIC 49*
Launched: 27.4.1944.
Completed: 6.1944.
6.1944: (Naval work).
1947: Transferred to Admiralty, Portsmouth.
1952: (H. G. Pounds, Portsmouth).
1953: *Sund 2* (Norway).
1955: *Sundvag* (P/R Sundvag, Norway). Vessel rebuilt to a motor coaster.
1963: (New oil engine and C.P. propeller).
1964: Lengthened to 111.5 ft (183 gt).

660 *VIC 50*
Launched: 17.6.1944.
Completed: 7.1944.
8.1944: (Naval work).
1947: Transferred to Admiralty.
3.1948: (Sold).
No further trace.

661 *VIC 51*
Launched: 26.8.1944.
Completed: 9.1944.
12.1944: (Naval work).
1945: Barrage balloon service at Antwerp, in connection with defence of River Schelde.
1947: Transferred to Admiralty – Deptford, London.
1972: (P. M. Herbert, Bude, Cornwall).
1974: *Tsavo Lady* (F. W. Walters, Penryn).
1974: (M. A. Smith, Newport, I.O.W.).
No further trace.

664 *VIC 60*
Launched: 18.11.1944.
Completed: 3.1945.
4.1945: (Naval work).
1947: Transferred to Admiralty.
1964: (V. van der Bossche & Co., Belgium).
Later reported broken up.

665 *VIC 61*
Launched: 6.3.1945.
Completed: 4.1945.
6.1945: (Naval work).
1947: Transferred to Admiralty.

1964: (V. van der Bossche & Co., Belgium).
Later reported broken up.

666 *VIC 62*
Launched: 15.5.1945.
Completed: 6.1945.
6.1945: (Naval work – Plymouth and Milford Haven).
1947: Transferred to Admiralty – Devonport.

In the early 1970s this vessel was sold for scrapping, but was acquired by the Department of Industry (National Maritime Institute) to become the National Physical Laboratory's research craft, for their ship division had accumulated such a list of projects calling for practical work at sea that they decided the quickest way to get results was to go into the shipowning business themselves.

After confirming that her fixed ballast of forty-four rounds of 15-inch ammunition for battleships long-since scrapped were, in fact, solid practice shells, these were retained but her boiler was scrapped and her compound steam engine – said to be second-hand when installed and dating from the 1920s – was given to the Science Museum, London, as a relic of a bygone era.

Externally, *VIC 62* changed little, only her 'NPL' funnel marking hinting of her new owners. Internally, her engine room housed a new diesel engine, electric generator and gearbox whilst in the hold, on top of the shells, a 20-ft container housed a mass of electronic recording equipment for use in sea-going research. Thus, this mobile sea-going laboratory could be maintained and serviced at the NPL's shore base at Hythe, Hants.

For several years *VIC 62* served in Southampton Water, her first jobs aimed at studying the behaviour of rudders. Her original 'barn door' rudder was replaced by a new one embodying a rotating cylinder on the leading edge, enabling the rudder to be put over to an angle of 90 degrees yet still retain its 'bite' on the water. The ship was able to turn in her own length with 'full ahead' power – a manoeuvre beyond the powers of any ordinary merchant ship.

Other studies undertaken included the measurement of 'squat' – the sinkage due to under-bottom suction in shallow water, and the influence of shallow water upon steering behaviour.

When the test programmes finished in June 1979, *VIC 62* was sold to Calcified Seaweed Company, of Cornwall, and at Truro was fitted with a tank in her hold, becoming a sand dredger and seaweed carrier. In August 1986 the vessel left the River Fal, bound for Millom, Cumbria, for breaking up.

667   *VIC 63*
Launched: 1.9.1945.
Completed: 2.1946.
1946: (Naval work).
1947: Transferred to Admiralty.
1956: *Colonsay* (A. McNeill Ltd., Greenock).
9.11.1960: Sailed in ballast from island of Barra,
Outer Hebrides, Scotland, after discharging a cargo
of slates. Returned to Castlebay to shelter from a gale;
anchored in bay. Dragged anchor and grounded.
Abandoned; slid off rocks and sank in deep water.
Total loss.

668   *VIC 64*
Launched: 3.11.1945.
Completed: 12.1945.
1946: (M.O.W.T.).
1947: (War Department – Army).
1948: *Fishersvic* (J. Fisher & Sons Ltd., Barrow).
1954: *Celt* (J. Hay & Sons Ltd., Glasgow).
31.3.1960: Grounded at entrance to Annalong
Harbour, Co. Down, N. Ireland, in a gale. Severely
damaged, holed and flooded. Abandoned.
9.5.1960: Refloated; towed in. Sold.
8.1960: (Marine Transport Services, Cobh, Eire).
Refitted and converted to oil engine.
1985: Reported scrapped Bude, Cornwall.

669   *VIC 65*
Launched: 28.3.1946.
Completed: 1946.
1946: (M.O.W.T.).
1947: Transferred to Admiralty – Devonport;
converted to a waterboat.
1979: Sold for scrapping at Inverkeithing, but:
1980: Resold to a group of steam enthusiasts hoping
to form a Charitable Trust for the vessel's
preservation. The Trust was not formed.
Later reported sold again, for scrapping.

Note: The above vessel was the last 'VIC'-type lighter to be
owned by, and in the service of, the military forces (Ministry
of Defence).

670   *VIC 66*
Launched: 18.4.1946.
Completed: 1946.
1946: (M.O.W.T.).
1947: Transferred to Admiralty – Rosyth; converted
to a waterboat.
1970: Offered for sale at Rosyth.

671   *VIC 67*
Launched: 11.9.1946.
Completed: 1947.
1947: (M.O.W.T.).
1948: *Ann W* (Greenwood Shipping Co. Ltd.,
Liverpool).
1953: (Zanzibar Transport Co. Ltd.).

9.1955: Capsized and sank when entering Mombasa
Old Port. Salved and repaired: sold to R. J. Gadhavi,
Zanzibar.
1962: Reported scrapped.

672   *VIC 68* Contract cancelled. Assembled material
completed privately:
Launched: 18.9.1946.
Completed: 1.1947 as *Moealang* (121 gt, 85 ft ×
20 ft) a motor lighter for N.V. Dortsche Petroleum
Maats., Holland.
1955: (Republik Indonesia Perusahan Pelayaran,
Kalimantan, Indonesia).
1961: (New oil engine).
1962: *Kota Silat X* (Pelayaran Persatuan Nasional,
Indonesia).
4.7.1977: Foundered in Sunda Strait, Indonesia,
during heavy weather.

673   *VIC 69* Contract cancelled. Assembled material
completed privately:
Launched: —
Completed: 1.1948 as *Moebai* (122 gt, 85 ft × 20 ft),
a motor lighter for N.V. Dortsche Petroleum Maats.,
Holland.
1955: (Republik Indonesia Perusahan Pelayaran,
Kalimantan, Indonesia).
1957: (New oil engine).
1974: *Kota Silat II* (Pelayaran Persatuan Nasional,
Indonesia).
1985: (P. T. Pelayaran Lokel Gonotiro, Indonesia).

674   *VIC 70* Contract cancelled. Assembled material
completed privately:
Launched: —
Completed: 3.1948 as *Moeara* (147 gt, 85 ft × 20 ft),
a motor lighter for N.V. Dortsche Petroleum Maats.,
Holland.
1955: (Republik Indonesia Perusahan Pelayaran,
Kalimantan, Indonesia).
1957: (New oil engine).
1973: *Kota Silat VIII* (Pelayaran Persatuan Nasional,
Indonesia).
1985: (P. T. Pelayaran Lokel Gonotiro, Indonesia).

675   *VIC 71* Contract cancelled. Assembled material
completed privately:
Launched: —
Completed: 9.1948 as *Moeda* (123 gt, 85 ft × 20 ft),
a motor lighter for N.V. Dortsche Petroleum Maats.,
Holland.
1957: *Sang Muda* (Indonesian owners).
1961: (New oil engine).
1963: *Kota Silat XI* (Pelayaran Persatuan Nasional,
Indonesia).
1976: (P. T. Pelayaran Lokel Gonotiro, Indonesia).

Built by J. S. Watson (Gainsborough) Ltd., Gainsborough

1552 *VIC 54*
Launched: 3.10.1944.
Completed: 12.1944.
1944: (M.O.W.T.).
1947: Transferred to Admiralty.
No further trace.

1553 *VIC 55*
Launched: 16.12.1944.
Completed: 1945.
8.1945: (Naval work).
1947: Transferred to Admiralty – Gosport.
1948: Converted to a waterboat at Devonport.
1968: Offered for sale (lying at Portsmouth Dockyard).
No further trace.

1554 *VIC 97*
Launched: 8.1945.
Completed: 1946.
1947: Transferred to Admiralty.
No further trace.

1555 *VIC 98*
Launched: 5.11.1945.
Completed: 1.1946.
1946: (Naval work – Grangemouth/Rosyth).
1947: Transferred to Admiralty.
1964: (Mrs. A. Fielding, Dublin).
19. .: (M. Townsend, Leeds).
1972: Reported scrapped.

Built by J. Pollock & Sons Ltd., Faversham

1840 *VIC 56*
Launched: 22.11.1945.
Completed: 12.1945.
1946: (Naval work).
1947: Transferred to Admiralty – Rosyth.

While serving the Admiralty, the above vessel was used as a stores and ammunition carrier at Rosyth, Crombie, Port Edgar, in the Firth of Forth and in the Hebrides. In 1962 she sailed to the Isle of Rona (near Skye) via Inverness and the Caledonian Canal, with materials for a Government Research Station.

In 1974 the ship was laid up at Rosyth and in 1978 was sold to M. Cleary of Wealdstone, Middlesex, the ship sailing to London.

Included in a subsequent refit was the conversion of the boiler firebox to burn both coal and wood, the vessel then being partly sponsored by the National Coal Board, which supplied some of the fuel needed in return for a Coal Board slogan-banner carried on the ship's side.

In 1984 *VIC 56* had repair work carried out at Rochester, Kent, and in July of the following year was successfully showing her prowess at a Power Boat and Steam Rally in the London docks.

Note: The sale of this vessel, in 1978, then left only one VIC-type lighter (*VIC 65*, *q.v.*) owned by the military forces (Ministry of Defence).

1841 *VIC 57*
Launched: 8.3.1946.
Completed: 6.1946.

1946: (M.O.W.T.).
1948: *Arran Monarch* (Arran Sea Transport & Supply Co. Ltd.).
(*Circa*) 1953: (Wansborough Paper Co. Ltd., Watchet, Somerset).
1960: (P. Herbert, Bude, Cornwall). Vessel continued to carry coal to Watchet, Somerset, for the local paper mills.
1964: *Coedmor* (Converted to a sand dredger, fitted with oil engine, lengthened to 107.7 ft, 181 gt) (Hollacombe Aggregates Ltd., Wadebridge, Cornwall).
1985: (D. & C. Williams, Llanelli, S. Wales).

1842? *VIC 58* Contract cancelled. Hull completed privately.
Launched: –
Completed: 1948 as *Nervo* (109 gt) for London & Rochester Trading Co. Ltd.
7.1967: Sold (H. R. Horlock & Co., Essex) for use as a ballast lighter.

1843? *VIC 59* Contract cancelled. Hull completed privately.
Launched: –
Completed: 1949 as *Knox* (109 gt) for London & Rochester Trading Co. Ltd.
10.1967: Sold – reported scrapped.

Built by Rowhedge Ironworks Co. Ltd., Rowhedge, near Colchester, Essex

655   *VIC 76*
Launched: 31.1.1945.
Completed: 4.1945.
5.1945: (Naval work – Rosyth and Scapa Flow).
1947: Transferred to Admiralty – Crombie.
4.1966: Reported sold.
No further trace.

656   *VIC 77*
Launched: 1.3.1945.
Completed: 1945.

The VIC 77 served the Admiralty for many early years, much of the time at Portsmouth, being renamed *C.675* and later acquiring the name *Victual*. In 1970 she was sold to shipbreaker H. G. Pounds, of Portsmouth. Two years later she was purchased by Mr. R. Simon and in January 1973 was towed back to Rowhedge, Essex. After four months' work a 100-ft berth had been dug for her in the mud of the river bank and she was berthed just a few yards from the slipway of her construction.

Victual was found to be still in good basic order and after several more years of hard work was restored to steaming condition, many of her missing boiler fittings being replaced by those from sistership *VIC 78*, which was traced and found being taken 'out of steam'. Again in service, *Victual* made many trips and joined many rallies in and around the south-east of Britain.

In 1981 the *Victual* was sold to Dutch buyers and towed to Dordrecht, Holland, for use as a floating restaurant. But no such conversion was made and at the end of 1985 she was sold again, to J. Lehmann, of Lorrach, W. Germany. However, two years later the vessel was still berthed in Holland.

657   *VIC 78*
Launched: 27.8.1945.
Completed: 1945.
8.1946: (Naval work).
1947: Transferred to Admiralty – Plymouth, converted to a waterboat.
1972: Sold, and:
1976: Vessel taken out of steam and many boiler fittings transferred to the refitting of *VIC 77* (above).
No further trace.

Built by J. Harker Ltd., Knottingley

182   *VIC 81*
Launched: 19.8.1944.
Completed: 11.1944.
1945: (Naval work – Rosyth).
1947: Transferred to Admiralty, and:
1949: Renamed *C.711*.
1969: Sold (M. Townsend, Leeds). Taken to Hull, fitted with oil engine; intended to be used for salvage work.
28.10.1970: Drifted ashore after anchor cable broke in gale while waiting to cross Bideford Bar, Devon, after sailing from Goole for Appledore to collect pig-iron ballast from *VIC 98* (same owner). Grounded on beach at Westward Ho!; refloated three days later and returned to Hull. Proposed use as a salvage vessel not proceeded with.
1976: Offered for sale under name *Julia T*. Sold to Wexford, Eire, buyers: intended for use as a mussel dredger, but found her draught prevented her crossing Wexford Harbour Bar.
1977: Sold (M. Mylotte, Co. Galway, Eire).
1980: In use carrying live fish and crabs to Europe.

183   *VIC 82*
Launched: 16.12.1944.
Completed: 3.1945.
3.1945: (Naval Work).
1947: Transferred to War Department – Army.
1948: *Sir James* (A. E. Chapman).
1955: (J. Hay & Sons Ltd., Glasgow).
1961: (I. A. Dutch, Perth) To be used for sand dredging.

184   *VIC 99*
Launched: 28.3.1945.
Completed: 7.1945.
8.1945: (Naval work – Rosyth).
1947: Transferred to Admiralty – Crombie.
1968: Sold for breaking up; Resold and converted to a floating restaurant: in use at Stourport-on-Severn, Worcs.
22.11.1977: Set alight (arson) during a firemen's strike. Interior of vessel and superstructure badly burned.

1980: Sold (J. Bedworth, Bewdley) who intended to rebuild ship to original plans.
1.1984: Offered for sale (lying at Stourport) in 'as is' condition by Admiralty Marshal due to Court Order. Condition of vessel shown as: 'Engine and boiler removed. Tailshaft and propeller remain. After the fire certain interior rebuilding work undertaken, with wood internal accommodation and top deck fitted. Hardwood staircase and balustrade fitted, from maindeck down to lower accommodation, which is five cabins'.

185   *VIC 100* Contract cancelled.

Built by R. Dunston Ltd., Thorne

575   *VIC 93*
Launched: 6.3.1945.
Completed: 4.1945.
5.1945: (Naval work).
1947: Transferred to Admiralty – Deptford, London.
1961: *Sandor* (H. Sandoy, Norway).
1962: *Justi* (Norwegian owners).
1964: (Lengthened to 106 ft, 184 gt).
1967: *Engesund* (H. Stokka P/R., Norway).
1982: (New oil engine and C.P. propeller).
1985: (F. Steinsland, Norway).

576   *VIC 94*
Launched: 19.3.1945.
Completed: 5.1945.
6.1945: (Naval work – Portsmouth).
1947: Transferred to Admiralty – Gosport.
1977: Sold (Teeside Shipbreakers Ltd., Derby). Resold, and:
1980: Reported laid up at Plymouth without power and used as a storage vessel for local salvage industry.

577   *VIC 95*
Launched: 20.4.1945.
Completed: 5.1945.
7.1945: (Naval work – Rosyth).
1947: Transferred to Admiralty – Fort William.
1950: *Corpach* (Metal Industries (Salvage) Ltd., Faslane).
1952: Reported sold (D. Fitzpatrick, Cobh) and, later Marine Transport Services, Eire.
4.1978: Scrapped Passage West, Cork.

578   *VIC 96*
Launched: 24.4.1945.
Completed: 7.1945.
1947: Transferred to Admiralty, renamed *C.668*.
19. .: Reported sold (M. Fielding, Dublin). Later resold to U.K. buyers; subsequently laid up in various parts of London's docks for several years. Remained structurally and mechanically sound, but vandalised.
1981: Sold; steamed to Newcastle. Later taken to the steamship museum at Maryport, Cumbria, to become an exhibit.

Improved 'VIC' type lighters – 132 gt, 80.4 ft × 20.1 ft. Engines: Oil (aft) – 8 knots

Built by Richards Ironworks Ltd., Lowestoft

342   *VIC 79*
Launched: 16.11.1944.
Completed: 1.1945.
2.1945: (Naval work).
1947: Transferred to Admiralty – Sheerness.
1961: (H. G. Pounds, Portsmouth). Believed resold and renamed *Aner* (D. & R. Taylor (Contractors) Ltd., Perth) and:
16.6.1965: Arrived Inverkeithing for breaking up.

343   *VIC 80*
Launched: 27.1.1945.
Completed: 3.1945.
4.1945: (Naval work).
1947: Transferred to Admiralty – Plymouth; converted to a waterboat at Devonport.
1965: Offered for sale at Pembroke Dock. No further trace.

356   *VIC 101*
Launched: 10.4.1945.
Completed: 6.1945.
6.1945: (Naval work – Crombie and Rosyth).
1947: Transferred to Admiralty – Plymouth;
converted to a waterboat at Devonport.
1973: (P. Herbert, Bude, Cornwall).
No further trace.

357   *VIC 102*
Launched: 9.6.1945.
Completed: 10.1945.
10.1945: (Naval work – Rosyth).
1947: Transferred to Admiralty – Sheerness, and
1949: Renamed *C.716.*

1961: *Sandale* (H. Sandoy, Norway).
1962: (Lengthened to 109 ft, 171 gt).
1963: *Sandal* (F. S. Hansen, Norway).
1970: (New oil engine).
1986: (F. Sandfrakt, Norway).

358   *VIC 103*
Launched: 22.9.1945.
Completed: 1946.
1947: Transferred to Admiralty, renamed *C.676* (used
as a storeship and collier).
No further trace.

—   *VIC 104* Contract cancelled.

Improved 'VIC' type lighters – 154 gt, 83.5 ft × 20 ft. Engines: Oil (aft) – 8 knots

Built by Shipbuilding Corporation, Newcastle

27   *VIC 105*
Launched: 3.1946.
Completed: 6.1946.
7.1946: (Naval work – Gosport).
1947: Transferred to Admiralty – Portsmouth.
1948: (Fraser & White Ltd.).
1949: *Banjul* (H. Madi, Liverpool) (Vessel for West
Africa service).
1965: Reported scuttled.

28   *VIC 106*
Launched: 3.1946.
Completed: 1946.
9.1946: (Naval work – Gosport).
1947: Transferred to Admiralty – Portsmouth.
1970: (Sold).
No further trace.

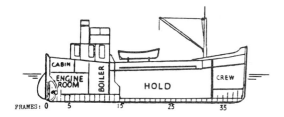

The 'Clyde Puffer'-type coaster.

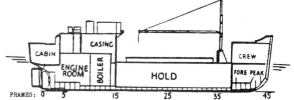

The Improved 'Puffer'-type coaster.

The *VIC 55* in June 1962. (J. S. Watson (Gainsborough) Ltd., Yard No. 1553.)

Wright & Logan

The *VIC 106* of the 'Improved'-type, at Devonport, June 1957. (Shipbuilding Corporation, Newcastle, Yard No. 28).

G. A. Osbon

PART NINE

COASTAL TANKERS

The 'Empire Cadet'-class of twenty-three vessels were the largest – by length – (202 ft) of the coastal tankers built during the war. Of some 850 deadweight tons, the prototype was Bulk Oil SS Company's *Pass of Balmaha*, built in 1933.

The class was fitted with triple expansion steam engines giving $9\frac{1}{2}$ knots, this type of machinery being the most readily available at the time of construction. There were three oil holds, one forward and two aft of the pump room. In addition there was a forward dry cargo hold and a deep tank. The vessels had counter sterns and a trunk deck and, initially, the foremast was fitted to the port side of the trunking. The bridge structure and accommodation was grouped around the machinery space, which was situated aft.

A number of coastal tankers were specially built for service in the Far East: these were the 'TED'-type (*T*anker, *E*astern, *D*iesel) and the 'TES'-type (*T*anker, *E*astern, *S*team), both types with a somewhat greater tonnage than those of the 'Empire Cadet'-class, but on a slightly shorter length of ship.

Also built for the Far East was a group of steam-driven coastal tank lighters, with dimensions of 104 ft (oa) × 100 ft × 19.8 ft, and with tonnages of 148 gross, 170 tdw. However, these vessels were constructed to military requirements and were known as Military Oil Barges (M.O.B.).

The most numerous class of coastal tankers was the 'Chant'-class, forty-three prefabricated vessels of straight-line construction and which were used extensively in the Normandy invasion and build-up of forces. They were an exception to the 'Empire' nomenclature of Ministry ships, their 'Chant' (Channel Tanker) names carrying a serial number suffix. A number of the originally-planned sixty-nine vessels were regarded as surplus to requirements and they were redesigned and completed as 'Empire F'-type dry cargo coasters, although both types remained similar in tonnage and measurements. Due to the redesigning of some 'Chant' vessels the serial numbers of the 'Chant' tankers themselves were not completely consecutive, being completed as Nos. 1–12; 22–28; 42–45 and 50–69.

There were also a number of other coastal tanker types built, including small vessels of an 'Isles'-class – a class name which was also applied to some small dry cargo coasters.

'Empire Cadet' class

850 tdw, 202 ft (oa), 193 ft × 31 ft. Engines: T3cyl (aft) – 9½ knots

Built by Blythswood Shipbuilding Co. Ltd., Glasgow

67 *Empire Bairn* 813 gt.
Launched: 23.10.1941.
Completed: 12.1941.

1948: *Chilka* (Indian Navy) (Harbour tanker).
1976: Name removed from Navy List.

Built by Grangemouth Dockyard Co. Ltd.

435 *Empire Lass* 813 gt.
Launched: 31.7.1941.
Completed: 1.1942.
1946: *Esso Juniata* (Anglo-American Oil Co. Ltd.).
1956: *Argosity* (F. T. Everard & Sons Ltd.).
1957: (Lengthened to 230.5 ft, 877 gt).
3.5.1969: Arrived Bruges, Belgium, for breaking up.

436 *Empire Cadet* 813 gt.
Launched: 22.9.1941.
Completed: 1.1942.
1946: *Mascara* (Government of France).
1948: (Soflumar Transport de Vins, France).
1951: *Aureity* (F. T. Everard & Sons Ltd.).
6.1968: Scrapped Barrow.

439 *Empire Arthur* 780 gt.
Launched: 5.3.1942.
Completed: 6.1942.
22.11.1943: Listed when nearing completion of loading with fresh water; seawater entered through deck openings, capsized and sank alongside Kissy jetty, Freetown, W. Africa.
20.1.1944: Removed from proximity of jetty; beached. Later refloated and secured, bottom up, alongside wreck of Liberty ship *Flora MacDonald* (1943, 7,177 gt). Constructive total loss.
1947: Wreck sold (Italian) and raised. Temporarily repaired, and
8.5.1948: Left Freetown for Genoa in tow of tug *Witte Zee* (1946, 328 gt). Repaired.
1949: *Merula* (Ape Azionaria Petroliere, Italy).

1951: *Adherity* (F. T. Everard & Sons Ltd.).
9.1962: Scrapped New Lekkerkerk, Holland.

440 *Empire Gawain* 784 gt.
Launched: 16.4.1942.
Completed: 6.1942.
1946: *Esso Dakotah* (Anglo-American Oil Co. Ltd.).
1951: (Esso Petroleum Co. Ltd.).
1962: Scrapped Boom, Belgium.

441 *Empire Damsel* 784 gt.
Launched: 29.6.1942.
Completed: 10.1942.
1947: *Pass of Balmaha* (Bulk Oil SS Co. Ltd., London).
3.1967: Scrapped Dalmuir.

446 *Empire Harbour* 797 gt.
Launched: 6.2.1943.
Completed: 5.1943.
1946: *Esso Genesee* (Anglo-American Oil Co. Ltd.).
1951: (Esso Petroleum Co. Ltd.).
1961: Scrapped Tamise, Belgium.

447 *Empire Wrestler* 797 gt.
Launched: 22.5.1943.
Completed: 7.1943.
1946: *Esso Tioga* (Anglo-American Oil Co. Ltd.).
1951: (Esso Petroleum Co. Ltd.).
23.9.1963: Arrived St. Davids on Forth for breaking up.

453   *Empire Settler*   797 gt.
Launched: 11.10.1943.
Completed: 11.1943.
1947: *Iran* (British Tanker Co. Ltd.).
1958: *Widad* (B.P. Tanker Co. Ltd.).
1962: *Motol VII* (N. E. Vernicos Shipping Co. Ltd., Greece).
4.1968: Scrapped Piraeus.

455   *Empire Trotwood*   797 gt.
Launched: 29.2.1944.
Completed: 5.1944.
1947: *Amir* (Kuwait Oil Co. Ltd. (Anglo-Iranian Oil Co. Ltd.)).
1952: *B.P. Distributor* (Shell Mex & B.P. Ltd.).
5.1965: Scrapped Willebroek, Belgium.

456   *Empire Mull*   797 gt.
Launched: 22.5.1944.
Completed: 8.1944.
1946: *Medea* (Government of France).
1950: (Cie. Franco-Africaine de Nav., France).
1951: (Societe Navale de L'Ouest, France).
1951: *Christine* (G. S. Stein K.G., Germany).
1956: *Pass of Kintail* (Bulk Oil SS Co. Ltd.).
1963: *Passamare* (Navalpetroli Soc. di Nav., Italy).
1965: *Kali Limenes* (Seka S.A., (N. Vardinoyannis, Greece)).

1987: Name removed from ship registers; existence of vessel in doubt.

460   *Empire Drury*   797 gt.
Launched: 7.10.1944.
Completed: 12.1944.
1947: *Shelbrit 6* (Shell Mex & B.P. Ltd.).
1952: Renamed *B.P. Refiner*.
1964: *Cosina* (Comp. Siciliana Navi Cisterna SpA, Italy).
6.1973: Scrapped Palermo.

463   *Empire Tavistock*   798 gt.
Launched: 29.1.1945.
Completed: 4.1945.
1946: *Sobat* (Van Castricum & Co. Ltd., London).
1951: *Allegrity* (F. T. Everard & Sons Ltd.).
13.12.1961: Grounded in a gale on Greeb Point, near St. Anthony Head, Cornwall (voyage: Le Havre/Stanlow – oil). Refloated by tide, drifted off, holed and awash. Grounded again on rocks at Veryan Beach, near Dodman Point. Flooded. Salvage attempts unsuccessful; vessel buckled and bottom set up for entire length.
22.12.1961: Capsized in a gale. Total loss.

Built by A. & J. Inglis Ltd., Glasgow

1151P   *Empire Maiden*   813 gt.
Launched: 20.12.1941.
Completed: 3.1942.
14.6.1943: Sunk by aircraft bombs at Pantellaria Island, Mediterranean, after island occupied by Allied forces.
1947: Wreck sold to Italian buyers. Raised, and:
5.7.1948: Towed to Messina, Sicily. Repaired and re-engined (C2cyl). Resold (G. Dagnino, Italy).
1953: *Asteria* (Astrolea Soc. Anon., Italy).
1958: *Sanjacopo* (Lugari & Filippi, Italy).
1962: (New oil engine).
1968: (Soc. Toscana di Arm. Navigazione, Italy).
1972: (Lidia Melodia Ved. Lugari, Italy).
7.1974: Scrapped Spezia.

1175P   *Empire Gypsy*   813 gt.
Launched: 31.8.1942.
Completed: 11.1942.
1948: *Sambhar* (Indian Navy) (Harbour tanker).
1976: Name removed from Navy List.

1184P   *Empire Fay*   814 gt.

Launched: 26.12.1942.
Completed: 3.1943.
1946: *Kleinella* (Shell Co. of East Africa Ltd. (Anglo-Saxon Petroleum Co. Ltd.)).
1948: *Shelbrit 7* (Shell Mex & B.P. Ltd.).
1952: Renamed *B.P. Marketer*.
1964: *Sarroch* (Sarda Bunkers SpA, Italy).
9.1983: Scrapped Naples.

1190P   *Empire Coppice*   814 gt.
Launched: 27.3.1943.
Completed: 6.1943.
1948: *Amin* (Kuwait Oil Co. Ltd. (Anglo-Iranian Oil Co. Ltd.)).
1952: *Shell Fitter* (Shell Mex & B.P. Ltd.).
1964: *Aliki* (D. I. Philippopoulos, Greece).
1966: (Naftiki Adrotiki, Greece).
1968: (Marine Water Supply Co. Ltd., Greece).
9.1969: Scrapped Perama, Greece.

1225P   *Empire Harvest*   814 gt.
Launched: 10.11.1943.
Completed: 12.1943.
1946: *Shelbrit 5* (Shell Mex & B.P. Ltd.).

The 'Empire Cadet'-class coastal tanker *Empire Trotwood* as *B. P. Distributor*. (Grangemouth Dockyard Co. Ltd., Yard No. 455.)   *Skyfotos*

The tanker *Allegrity*, formerly *Empire Tavistock*. (Grangemouth Dockyard Co. Ltd., Yard No. 463.)

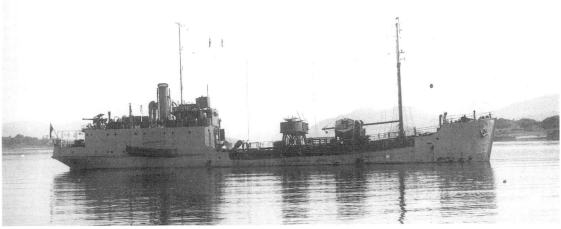

The *Empire Coppice*, in wartime livery. (A & J Inglis Ltd., Yard No. 1190P.)   *National Maritime Museum*

1952: Renamed *B.P. Engineer.*
6.1965: Scrapped Antwerp.

1227P   *Empire Dombey* 813 gt.
Launched: 15.5.1944.
Completed: 7.1944.
1947: *Allurity* (F. T. Everard & Sons Ltd.).
10.1964: Sold for scrapping in Holland, but resold, and:
4.1965: Scrapped Bruges, Belgium.

1282P   *Empire Jura* 813 gt.
Launched: 28.8.1944.
Completed: 10.1944.
1946: *Samshoo* (Van Castricum & Co. Ltd., London).
1951: *Pass of Glenogle* (Bulk Oil SS Co. Ltd.).
1961: *Marcello Garolla* (A. Garolla & Cie., Italy).
1969: *Marcello G* (Sarda Bunkers SpA, Italy).
19.2.1972: Developed list in heavy weather while undergoing annual repairs at Naples; heeled over and sank.
2.8.1972: Raised, but constructive total loss. Repaired and re-entered owners' service.
3.1979: Scrapped Naples.

1286P   *Empire Bute* 813 gt.

Launched: 19.10.1944.
Completed: 12.1944.
1946: *Miliana* (Government of France).
1948: *Rivoli* (A. Scotto Pugliese Fils & Cie., Algeria).
1952: *Pass of Drumochter* (Bulk Oil SS Co. Ltd.).
1962: *Santa Giulia* (Lugari & Filippi, Italy).
1970: (Chemigas SpA, Italy).
1971: (Ciana Anopo Comp., di Nav. & Bunkeraggi SpA, Italy).
1971: Scrapped Spezia.

1287P   *Empire Orkney* 813 gt.
Launched: 30.11.1944.
Completed: 3.1945.
1950: *Alchymist* (F. T. Everard & Sons Ltd.).
3.5.1969: Arrived Bruges, Belgium, for breaking up.

1288P   *Empire Shetland* 813 gt.
Launched: 19.1.1945.
Completed: 4.1945.
1948: *Adib* (Kuwait Oil Co. Ltd. (Anglo-Iranian Oil Co. Ltd.)).
1952: *B.P. Transporter* (Shell Mex & B.P. Ltd.).
6.1965: Scrapped Antwerp.

The name of Inglis, as engineers, began in 1847 when John Inglis joined brother Anthony in opening a small business at Finnieston, Glasgow. They built their first marine engine in 1850 and there followed an expansion in the production of engines, some orders including the ship hull. The time was now right for further expansion and in 1861 they acquired a yard site at Pointhouse, a peninsula at the point where the River Kelvin joins the River Clyde and where ships of iron were launched.

A. & J. Inglis launched their first steamer, the 150 ft *Blanche*, in 1862. Outstanding features of the yard came with the building of slips, angled for launching ships into the Kelvin, and a patent slipway and cradle so that ships could be built and drawn broadside on to the cradle for launching.

Through the era of sail the Inglis yard constructed several fine clipper ships whose names are recorded in the history of sail; the *Norman Court* was one, completed in 1869 and wrecked in Cymran Bay, Anglesey, on 28 March 1883 when homeward bound from Java with sugar. Another was the *Loch Etive*, an iron, full-rigged ship of 1,288 gt for the General Shipping Company (Aitken, Hilburn & Company, Glasgow). Completed in 1877, she was cut down to a barque in the early 1900s, sold to France in 1911, hulked and then scrapped at Genoa.

Throughout its years of shipbuilding the company constructed many ships for the railways, in particular for the London & North Eastern Railway Company. As early as 1865 two iron steamers were built for the Manchester, Sheffield & Lincolnshire Railway Company and in the same year came the steamers *Kinloch*, 334 gt, and the *Waverley*, 592 gt, both paddlers for the North British Railway Company. Better known was the *Dandie Dinmont*, a steel paddle steamer built in 1895 for the North British Company and transferred to the L. & N.E.R. in 1923. She worked the Humber ferry (New Holland/Hull) service from 1928 until broken up in 1936 at Ghent. A successor was the *Lincoln Castle*, launched in 1940.

When the 1914–1918 war ended the Pointhouse Yard suffered greatly in the severe shipbuilding crisis of the immediate post-war years, as did many other small yards, and in 1919 it was acquired by Harland & Wolff Ltd. Yard numbers for new buildings were allocated by Harland & Wolff with the suffix 'P' (Pointhouse).

After weathering the years of depression and the closure of the engine works in 1927 the yard completed the paddler *Talisman* in 1935 for the L. & N.E.R., the first direct-acting, diesel-electric paddle vessel in the world. Four diesel engines were set to drive electric generators, current being supplied to a double-armature motor on the paddle shaft. After thirty-two years the ship arrived at Dalmuir in October 1967 for breaking up.

During the 1939–1945 war many trawlers and corvettes were built for the Royal Navy, whilst coasters were turned out for the Ministry of War Transport. These were mostly coastal tankers and included four of the 'TED'-type diesel-powered ships specially designed for service in the Far East.

When hostilities ceased the yard had five berths, with a ship capacity to 425 ft in length; the cradle was 270 feet long, its lifting power was to 2,000 tons.

One of the first post-war ships was the paddle steamer *Waverley*, 693 gt (Yard No. 1330P), for the Caledonian Steam Packet Co. Ltd., and for a time thereafter the order book was full. But in 1962 the plant was considered as being out of date and the yard should be closed down. In 1965 the Pointhouse Yard was acquired by the Glasgow Corporation for redevelopment.

SHIPS BUILT UNDER PRIVATE CONTRACT OR LICENCE

1021P   *T. H. Watermeyer* 620 gt, 155.6 ft (oa), 146.7 ft × 33 ft. Engines: T6cyl. Twin screw salvage and firefighting tug.
Launched: 6.7.1939.
Completed: 10.1939 for Union of South Africa (Railways & Harbours Administration), Cape Town.
1941: (South African Railways Administration).
4.1982: Scrapped Cape Town.

1024P   *Lincoln Castle* 598 gt, 208.9 ft (oa), 199.7 ft × 56.6 ft. Engines: T3cyl.
Launched: 27.4.1940.
Completed: 7.1940 for London & North Eastern Railway Co. as a paddle ferry: the last coal-fired paddle steamer to service the Humber Ferry (Hull,

Yorks. – New Holland, Lincs.).
1948: (British Transport Commission; later British Railways Board).
1978: Boilers failed; laid up in Hull docks.
1979: (Sealink (U.K.) Ltd.).
1979: Sold (F. Daly).
1980: Moved to a non-tidal anchorage at Hessle, Yorks., for use as a Club/Restaurant.

1043P   *Vipya* 280 gt. (Measurements unknown.)
Launched: 7.1942.
Completed: 10.1942 for Lake service of the Nyasaland Railways. (A passenger/car ferry shipped in sections and re-erected; named after Vipya Mountains.)

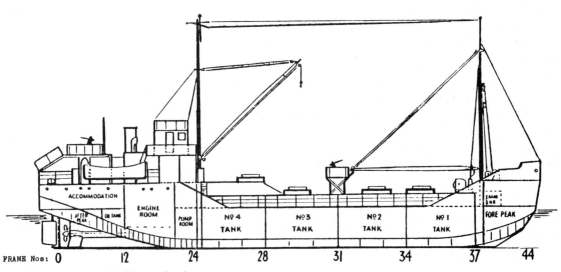

The 'Chant'-type standard fabricated tanker.

'Isles' class

300 tdw, 142 ft (oa), 136 ft × 21 ft. Engines: Oil – 10 knots

Built by J. Harker Ltd., Knottingley

166 *Empire Alderney* 288 gt.
Launched: 11.12.1943.
Completed: 6.1944.
1946: *Mil 50* (Norsk Tankanlaeg A/S., Norway).
1955: *Max S* (Partenrederei Max S, (M. Sotje, Germany)).
1958: (Marina Mercante Nicaraguense (Mamenic Lines, Nicaragua)).
1959: (Cia. Maritima Mundial, Nicaragua).
1980: (Trafford Holdings Ltd., Cayman Islands).

167 *Empire Lundy* 288 gt.
Launched: 11.4.1944.
Completed: 8.1944.
1946: *Scot* (Skibs A/S Scot (L. Lauritsen, Norway)).
1947: *Skeljungur* (Shell h/f., Iceland).
1956: *Bannister* (227 gt) (Bowker & King Ltd., London).
No trace after 1966.

168 *Empire Guernsey* 288 gt.
Launched: 21.10.1944.
Completed: 3.1945.
1947: *Beacon* (British Controlled Oilfields Ltd., Ecuador).
1957: *Billie* (Transpetroleo Compania Anonima, Ecuador).
1980: (Transnacoop, Ecuador).
1981: Reported disposed of by scuttling.

169 *Empire Anglesey* 288 gt.
Launched: 16.6.1945.
Completed: 10.1945.
1946: *Abadan* (A/S Tanks Rederi, Denmark).
1961: *Renee J* (Celtic Coasters Ltd., Ireland).
3.1969: Scrapped Cork, Eire.

'Empire Lad' class

300 tdw, 135 ft (oa), 128 ft × 24 ft. Engines: Oil – 9 knots

Built by Rowhedge Ironworks Ltd., Rowhedge, near Colchester, Essex

601 (Launched as) *Empire Garnet* 298 gt.
Launched: 10.7.1941.
Completed: 11.1941 as *Empire Lad*.
1946: *Esso Suwanee* (Anglo-American Oil Co. Ltd.).
1951: (Esso Petroleum Co. Ltd.).
1960: (P. L. Den Breejen, Holland).
1963: Renamed *U.S.A.* (Cia. Comercio Nav. Alpes, Panama), and converted to dry cargo (331 gt).
1966: *Pejerey* (Autco S.A., Panama).
1966: Renamed *Esterel*.
1968: *Westerend* (Colombo Shipping Co., Panama).

1970: *Sunrise* (Albina S.A., Panama).
1970: Renamed *Grace*.
1971: *Captain Stelios* (D. P. Gousetis, Greece).
1975: *San Liberal* (C. Dagadakis, Greece).
1977: *Kleopatra* (E. & G. Kottis, Greece).

607 *Empire Homestead* 296 gt.
Launched: 10.11.1942.
Completed: 2.1943.
1947: *Havskjell* (A/S Norske Shell, Norway (Anglo-Saxon Petroleum Co. Ltd.)).

1953: (Shell Tankers Ltd.).
1960: (A/S Shellbatane, Norway (Shell Tankers Ltd.).
1963: (Lengthened to 156.5 ft, 372 gt, 430 tdw).
1972: *Nigeria Shell 2* (Shell Nigeria Ltd.).

1976: *National Eagle 2* (National Oil Marketing Co., Lagos).
1984: Reported broken up.

Built by I. Pimblott & Sons Ltd., Northwich

643   *Empire Coast* 299 gt.
Launched: 9.1.1943.
Completed: 5.1943.
1946: *Esso Ottawa* (Anglo-American Oil Co. Ltd.).
4.1967: Scrapped Bruges, Belgium.

655   *Empire Cricketer* 299 gt.
Launched: 18.9.1943.
Completed: 2.1944.
1946: *Havstraum* (M/S Straum (Λ. Utkilen, Norway)).
1967: *Anne Berith* (A. A. Rasmussen, Norway).
1970: *Akstank* (Per Hagen, Norway).
1971: (New oil engine).
1977: *High Heat* (Bulk Product Shipping Trading (Pte.) Ltd., Singapore).

662   *Empire Tapley* 305 gt.
Launched: 12.8.1944.
Completed: 1.1945.

1946: *Haifa* (A/S Tankskibsrederiet (K. V. Tersling, Denmark)).
1957: *Nord* (Rederi A/B Castor, Sweden). Lengthened to 164.5 ft, 366 gt, 536 tdw.
1960: *Soren Rask* (S. P. Christensen, Denmark).
1964: (New oil engine).
1973: *Doriforos* (Argonaftis Argo Maritime, Greece).
1980: *Cyprus Star* (Cyprus Star Shipping Co., Cyprus).
1981: Renamed *Newluck*.
12.1984: Scrapped Barry, South Wales.

663   *Empire Nickleby* 306 gt.
Launched: 17.7.1945.
Completed: 12.1945.
1946: *Nickleby* (Cia. de Nav. Anne S.A., Panama (Tankers Transit & Shipping Co., London)).
1950: *Nirmala* (Bombay Port Trust) (a water tanker).

Wartime construction by Pimblotts at their Weaver Yard, Northwich, Cheshire, also included three dry cargo 'Empire' coasters (*q.v.*) and thirteen VIC-type coasters. When war ended the yard had twelve berths with a ship capacity to 150 ft.

Prefabricated – the 'CHANT' type

After a number of the prefabricated 'TID' tugs had been completed there arose, through the future anticipated demands of war – namely the planned D-day invasion of France – a need for a number of small coastal tankers. In the light of the experience gained during the construction of the tugs, it was decided that the building of these tankers should follow a similar procedure to that adopted for the tugs during the early stages of their development. A vessel, of shipshape form, on dimensions of 148 ft × 27 ft, was selected as a prototype and from this a straight-line design was developed into a type described as a *Chan*nel *Tanker* – to become commonly known as a CHANT.

Following tank tests of a model, modifications included the introduction of a second chine forward, at the sweep of the bow, making an 'easy' flow for water instead of the single 'abrupt' chine which had produced adverse resistance. A fin, or skeg, of aerofoil shape – of similar construction to that used in the prefabricated tugs – was added aft at the deadwood housing of the stern tube. Except for this skeg, there was not a curved or twisted plate in the whole vessel, every plate being flat or rolled in one direction only, with frame bending completely eliminated. The all-welded hull was devoid of sheer, giving a somewhat square, lumpy appearance.

The improved operating results obtained with the added skeg allowed the use of some lesser-powered oil engines, but, overall, the service speed of the class was somewhat lower than for similar-sized contemporary vessels. The engines installed in the CHANTs were of 220/270 hp, giving some $7\frac{1}{2}$ knots, but with the ships primarily intended for the short cross-channel route between southern England and the Continental beaches, this speed was considered sufficient.

The CHANT vessels, with a tonnage of 401 gross, were prefabricated by inland factories in twenty-eight separate units, the transverse ones some ten feet long and the midbody units twenty feet long. Methods of construction of these units were similar to those used for the 'TID' tugs, with flexibility in the plates attained by leaving seams unwelded for ten inches on each side of where a joint would come. The maximum weight of any unit was thirteen tons and, as with the 'TID' tugs, delivery to the assembling shipyards was by road transport. The CHANT tankers were assembled in five shipyards between February and July 1944, their assembly berths more conventional than those used for the tugs, with cranes being generally available to cover the berths and storage areas.

The CHANTs were originally intended for carrying petroleum spirit, either in bulk or in cans, and to be capable of grounding upon beaches. To minimise the chance of leakage they were given a double hull, the cargo holds forming four sub-divided tanks several feet less than the breadth of the hull, with void spaces flanking the lower parts of the holds as protection for the cargoes carried. The tanks themselves formed a trunk deck above the main deck, with the aftermost (No. 4 tank) trunking raised even more, to quarterdeck level. Each tank had a small, circular oil hatch fitted on top of a large, rectangular one, which could be removed for the stowage of cased oil and for which two derricks and winches were fitted.

However, the success of the D-day operation (Operation 'Overlord') and the subsequent laying of PLUTO (Pipe Line Under The Ocean) (see *Empire Ridley* and *Empire Baffin*) altered the demand for small, cross-channel tankers and a number of the CHANTs were redesigned, to become dry cargo carriers (see 'Empire F' type). In all, forty-three CHANTs were completed, twelve by Henry Scarr Ltd., nine by the Goole Shipbuilding Company, sixteen by the Furness Shipbuilding Company, two by Readheads and four by the Burntisland Shipbuilding Company. Serial number 13 was not used, whilst the redesigned hulls were firstly renamed as 'Fabrics' before final completion as vessels of the 'Empire F' type.

At the end of the war most of the CHANT tankers were sold to overseas buyers, British owners not showing much interest in them, although by the 1950s a few were to be found under the British flag. Into the late 1970s a number of CHANTs were still in service, whilst one, working out of Le Havre into the 1980s, still carried its original name.

'CHANT'-class – 450 tdw, 148.2 ft (oa), 142.2 ft × 27 ft. Engines: Oil – 7½ knots

Built by H. Scarr Ltd., Hessle

435   *CHANT 1*
Launched: 2.1944.
Completed: 3.1944.
1946: *Mil 52* (Norsk Tankanlag A/S, Norway (British Tanker Co. Ltd.)).
1955: Renamed *B.P. 52.*
1959: *Cenisio* (O. Novella, Italy).
1979: (Ciane-Anapo Comp. di Navigazione & Bunkeraggi, Italy).
1.1985: Scrapped Brindisi.

436   *CHANT 2*
Launched: 2.1944.
Completed: 3.1944.
15.9.1944: Shelled and damaged by German coastal batteries, Straits of Dover. Repaired.
1946: *Rosina* (Cia. de Nav. Rosina S.A., Panama).
1948: *Tiznit* (Cia. Cherifienne d'Arm. Transportes S.A., Morocco).
1954: *Petroblanc* (Societe Petromer, France).
1962: *N.S. Delle Grazie* (Petrolmar SpA Transporti Mar., Italy).

437   *CHANT 3*
Launched: 2.1944.
Completed: 3.1944.
1946: *Tresko* (Skibs. A/S Tripp, Norway).
1950: *Constantinos C* (G. C. Calafatis, Greece).
1955: *Tassia Politi* (N. Politis, Greece).
1965: (Greek Tanker Shipping Co. Ltd., Greece).
1974: Scrapped Greece.

438   *CHANT 4*
Launched: 2.1944.
Completed: 3.1944.
15.9.1944: Shelled and damaged by German coastal batteries, Straits of Dover. Repaired.
6.10.1944: Damaged in collision with trawler in Thames Estuary. Repaired.
14.11.1944: Damaged in collision with tug *Sun VIII* (1919, 196 gt) in Thames Estuary. Repaired.
1946: *Fia* (Per Bjorn Hansen, Norway).
1947: *Monty* (R. Bjornholdt & Co., Norway).
7.1.1951: In distress, listing and leaking in heavy seas four miles from Torungen Lighthouse, near Arendal, Norway. Capsized and sank
(voyage: Hervoya/Trondheim – fertiliser). Total loss.
8.1.1951: Wreckage washed ashore.

439   *CHANT 5*
Launched: 22.3.1944.
Completed: 4.1944.
1946: *B.T.V.* (A/B Bensintransport, Sweden (G. Reuter, Sweden)).
1960: *Union* (Bil & Verkstads A/B Union, Sweden).
1964: *Arita* (O/Y Finntank A/B, Finland).
11.1975: Scrapped Aminnefores, Finland.

440   *CHANT 6*
Launched: 3.1944.
Completed: 4.1944.
1946: *African Shell* (Shell Co. of East Africa Ltd. (Anglo-Saxon Petroleum Co. Ltd.)).
1955: *Motol II* (N. E. Vernicos Shipping Co., Greece).
1958: *Despina Politi* (N. Politis, Greece).
1976: (G. Kokaris & Co., Greece).
1986: Scrapped Greece.

441   *CHANT 7*
Launched: 4.1944.
Completed: 5.1944.
19.6.1944: Driven ashore in a gale, capsized on Normandy coast. Constructive total loss
(voyage: Thameshaven/Normandy – petrol).

Note: The above vessel was one of a number to be lost or damaged in the storm which struck shipping and the 'Mulberry' harbours of the Normandy beach-heads less than two weeks after the first invasion forces went ashore on 6 June 1944.

442   *CHANT 8*
Launched: 4.1944.
Completed: 5.1944.
1946: *Pollux* (Cia. Estrellia de Nav. S.A., Panama).
1947: *Elias A* (M. Arcoulis, Greece).
1963: *Sofoklis II* (E. & G. Revythis, Greece).
1971: (Megalonissis Co. Sea Transports & Exploitations, Greece).
1982: Reported broken up in Greece in 1977.

443   *CHANT 9*
Launched: 4.1944.
Completed: 5.1944.
1946: *B.T. VIII* (Rederi A/B Turego, Sweden (G. Reuter, Sweden)).
1952: (New oil engine).
1963: *Giraffa* (F. Visentini, Italy).
1968: *Lisert* (M. Amadi, Italy).
1978: (Arm. Soc. Lugari & Filippi, Italy).

444   *CHANT 10*
Launched: 4.1944.
Completed: 5.1944.
1946: *B.T. VII* (A/B Bensintransport, Sweden
(G. Reuter, Sweden)).
1952: (New oil engine).
1960: *Chresten Rask* (S. P. Christensen, Denmark).
22.3.1961: Struck submerged object; leaking, south
of Gronsund, Denmark. Sank near Stubbekobing
(voyage: Nyborg/Copenhagen – petrol).
16.5.1961: Refloated; taken to Copenhagen, but
constructive total loss. Sold and scrapped Lubeck.

445   *CHANT 11*
Launched: 5.1944.
Completed: 7.1944.
1946: *Pinard* (Van Castricum & Co., Panama).
1951: *Leadsman* (C. Rowbotham & Sons Ltd.).
1962: (H. G. Pounds, Portsmouth).
1964: (S. Bezzina, Malta).
1968: *Uaddan* (S. Bezzina & Sons, Malta).
1979: Reported scrapped in Spain in 1974.

446   *CHANT 12*
Launched: 6.1944.
Completed: 7.1944.
1946: (Government of France).
1957: *S.M.D. 1* (Soc. Maritime Degazage, France).
1971: *Success III* (a tank cleaning vessel; no longer

seagoing), (B.V. Vacuum Cleaning, Holland).
1983: Name deleted from ship registers.

447   *CHANT 14* See *Empire Fabric*.

448   *CHANT 15* See *Empire Fabian*.

449   *CHANT 16* See *Empire Fable*.

450   *CHANT 18* See *Empire Farringdon*.

451   *CHANT 19* See *Empire Fanfare*.

452   *CHANT 17* See *Empire Faversham*.

453   *CHANT 20* See *Empire Facility*.

454   *CHANT 21* See *Empire Faraway*.

455   *CHANT 46* See *Empire Fanal*.

456   *CHANT 47* See *Empire Fastness*.

457   *CHANT 48* See *Empire Farrier*.

458   *CHANT 49* See *Empire Fathom*.

The *CHANT 60*, built in 1944. (J. Readhead & Sons Ltd., Yard No. T.1.)   *National Maritime Museum*

Built by Goole Shipbuilding & Repairing Co. Ltd.

410 *CHANT 22*
Launched: 1.1944.
Completed: 2.1944.
1946: *Trond* (Jorgen Jahre, Norway).
1949: *Wodnik* (Government of Poland).
1960: Name removed from ship registers (used as a barge in inland waters).

411 *CHANT 23*
Launched: 10.2.1944.
Completed: 2.1944.
1946: *Sanny* (A. Johansson, Finland).
1954: (Laid up at Mariehamn, Finland), sold to Turkish buyers, renamed *Necati Pehlivan II* (C. M. Pehlivanlar & others), but:
26.9.1954: Aground outside Mariehamn, west of Lagskar, shortly after leaving on delivery voyage to new owners. Abandoned, sank. Total loss (voyage: Mariehamn/Istanbul – ballast).

412 *CHANT 24*
Launched: 28.2.1944.
Completed: 3.1944.
1946: *Ringa* (O. Novella SpA, Italy).
1983: Scrapped Spezia.

413 *CHANT 25*
Launched: 13.3.1944.
Completed: 4.1944.
1946: *Rakke* (A/S Troja Skibsrederi, Norway).
1951: *Porjus* (L. B. Kritensson & others, Sweden).
1957: (New oil engine).
1963: *Cedrino* (Teulada Soc. Azioni di Nav., Italy).
1965: *Comandante Ugo C* (Chiavari di Armamento, Italy).
1965: (Lengthened to 181 ft, 490 gt, 730 tdw).
1967: *Nonno Gigi* (Comp. Armatoriale Siculo-Adriatica, Italy).
1967: (New oil engine).
27.11.1969 and 3.12.1969: Severely damaged in heavy weather; put back to Genoa. Constructive total loss. Sold, and
6.1971: Scrapped Spezia.

414 *CHANT 26*
Launched: 28.3.1944.
Completed: 4.1944.
1946: *T.1* (Finska Angfartygs A/B., Finland).
1951: *B.T.IX* (Reuters Handels A/B., Sweden (H. Reuter, Sweden)).
1958: Renamed *Svartskar*. (Fitted with new oil engine).

1959: *B.T.IX* (A/B Bensintransport, Sweden (G. Reuter, Sweden)).
1963: *Foca* (F. Visentini, Italy).
1967: (Angelo Hopps, Italy).
1969: (Foca-Miriam SrL, Italy).
10.1974: Scrapped Spezia.

415 *CHANT 27*
Launched: 26.4.1944.
Completed: 5.1944.
1947: *Comagre* (Soc. de Nav. Comagre S.A., Panama).
1947: *Frans* (N.V. Terbedrijf Uithoorn, Holland).
1955: *Auspicity* (F. T. Everard & Sons Ltd.).
1969: (New oil engine).
1972: *Thekli* (P. Vourdahas & others, Greece).
1972: Scrapped Piraeus.

416 *CHANT 28*
Launched: 4.1944.
Completed: 5.1944.
1946: (Government of France – Port Authority, Le Havre).
1981: (Still in service at Le Havre).

417 *CHANT 29* See *Empire Factor*.

418 *CHANT 30* See *Empire Fairhaven*.

419 *CHANT 31* See *Empire Favourite*.

420 *CHANT 32* See *Empire Fashion*.

421 *CHANT 33* See *Empire Fane*.

422 *CHANT 34* See *Empire Farnham*.

423 *CHANT 35* See *Empire Farouche*.

424 *CHANT 36* See *Empire Farringay*.

430 *CHANT 37* See *Empire Farjeon*.

431 *CHANT 38* See *Empire Facet*.

432 *CHANT 39* See *Empire Fang*.

433 *CHANT 40* See *Empire Fairplay*.

434 *CHANT 41* See *Empire Fairway*.

435   *CHANT 50*
Launched: 10.5.1944.
Completed: 5.1944.
1947:   *Tank I* (Lysaker Kemiske Fabrik A/S.,
Norway).
1956:   *Tankholm* (Rederi A/B Bjornsund, Sweden).
1964:   (B. Gustafson Partrederi, Sweden).
1971:   *Vingo* (R/A Bjornsund, Sweden).
1974:   Scrapped Ystad, Sweden.

436   *CHANT 51*
Launched: 5.1944.

Completed: 6.1944.
1946:   *Dollie* (Tore Ulff A/B, Sweden).
1950:   *Gemma* (N.V. Terbedrijf Uithoorn, Holland).
28.12.1951:   Adrift in heavy weather with engine
trouble three miles north of Cape Machichaco, near
Bilbao, Spain. Taken in tow, but tow rope parted ten
miles from San Sebastian; capsized and drifted ashore.
Total loss (voyage: Bilbao/London – oleum).
Scrapped *in situ*.

Built by Furness Shipbuilding Co. Ltd., Haverton Hill

365   *CHANT 52*
Launched: 29.12.1943.
Completed: 2.1944.
1946:   *Lucia II* (Cominpek SrL, Italy).
1949:   (Cofra SrL, Italy).
1954:   (G. Colotronis di Giovanni, Italy).
1958:   Name deleted from ship registers.

366   *CHANT 53*
Launched: 10.1.1944.
Completed: 2.1944.
1946:   *Theodora* (N.V. Rederij Theodora, Holland).
1953:   *Averity* (F. T. Everard & Sons Ltd.).
1964:   (New oil engine).
6.1972:   Scrapped Troon.

367   *CHANT 54*
Launched: 24.1.1944.
Completed: 3.1944.
1946:   *Steinsfjell* (F. N. Nordbo, Norway).
1946:   *General Mitchell Baker* (Union SS Co. of South
Africa Ltd.).
1947:   Renamed *Klaver* (converted to dry cargo).
1949:   *Bechuana* (Thesens Steamship Co., South
Africa).
11.12.1950:   Aground near Port Nolloth, South
Africa. Holed and flooded; abandoned. Total loss
(voyage: Port Nolloth/Cape Town – crayfish).

368   *CHANT 55*
Launched: 31.1.1944.
Completed: 3.1944.
1947:   *Abdul Kader* (M. H. Kodsi, Syria).
1948:   *Tony* (Toufic Battache, Lebanon).
1956:   *Maria* (S. Kontos, D. Gioldassis & Co.,
Greece).
3.9.1966:   Sprang leak off south coast of Cyprus;
abandoned and sank in position 34.21N 34.50E
(voyage: Haifa/Famagusta – cement).

369   *CHANT 56*
Launched: 10.2.1944.
Completed: 3.1944.
1947:   *Milo* (N.V. Nederlands-Indonesische
Tankvaart Maats., Holland).
1958:   Sold to Indonesian Government for scrapping
at Palembang, but:
1960:   Reported transferred to Indonesian military
authorities. No further trace.

370   *CHANT 57*
Launched: 11.2.1944.
Completed: 4.1944.
1946:   *Grande* (Rederi A/B Staffen, Sweden (Svea
Line)).
1946:   Renamed *Gran*.
1953:   (New oil engine).
1966:   (Stockholms Rederi A/B Svea, Sweden).
1966:   *Kamran* (Maritime Co. Ltd., Iran).
18.1.1989:   Foundered in heavy weather off Abu
Musa, U.A.E., 25.50N 55.22E (voyage: Dubai/Iran).

371   *CHANT 58*
Launched: 23.2.1944.
Completed: 4.1944.
1946:   *Kamuni* (Booker Line Ltd. (Booker Bros.,
McConnell & Co. Ltd.)).
1946:   (Converted to dry cargo).
1950:   (Booker Shipping (Demerara) Ltd.).
1958:   (New oil engine).

372   *CHANT 59*
Launched: 29.2.1944.
Completed: 4.1944.
1946:   *Helny* (Rederi A/B Havnia (A. Johansson,
Finland).
1954:   *Maria Rosa* (Naval Agency Corp. S.A., Costa
Rica).

1958: (Marine Tankers S.L., Panama).
10.1965: Scrapped Barcelona.

374 *CHANT 62*
Launched: 10.3.1944.
Completed: 5.1944.
1946: *Pando* (Rethymnis & Kulukundis, Panama).
1946: *Pan* (Malmo Rederi A/B, Sweden).
1952: (New oil engine).
1956: *Tempo* (Rederi A/B Bjorno, Sweden).
1965: *Kaiwan* (Maritime Co. Ltd., Iran).

375 *CHANT 63*
Launched: 13.3.1944.
Completed: 5.1944.
5.6.1944: Capsized and sank off Flamborough Head, Yorkshire (voyage: Middlesbrough/ Portsmouth – fresh water).

376 *CHANT 64*
Launched: 28.3.1944.
Completed: 5.1944.
1946: *Castor* (Rethymnis & Kulukundis, Panama).
1954: (New oil engine).
1961: *Herman Rask* (S. P. Christensen Partrederi, Denmark).
1966: *Bellan* (Hans E. Bergmann, Denmark).
1969: (A/S H. J. Hansen, Denmark).
8.1972: Scrapped Odense, Denmark.

377 *CHANT 65*
Launched: 12.4.1944.
Completed: 5.1944.
1948: *Seladang* (Shell Company of Singapore Ltd.).
1959: (Tiong Lam Hang Shipping Co., Panama).
1986: Name deleted from ship registers – existence of vessel in doubt.

383 *CHANT 42*
Launched: 9.5.1944.
Completed: 6.1944.
1946: *Ramsfjell* (F. N. Nordbo, Norway).
1947: *Mercurius* (Amsterdamsche Scheep. Bedriff, Holland).

1956: (N.V. Amsterdamse Red. Tot. Exploitatie van Het. Mercurius, Holland).
1961: (Converted to a live fish carrier (Visgroothandel Fa. Joh., Kuyten, Holland)).
1972: (Schiffahrts & Handelsges. Hujo A.G., Holland).
5.1974: Scrapped New Lekkerland, Holland.

384 *CHANT 43*
Launched: 10.5.1944.
Completed: 6.1944.
1947: *Rusa* (Shell Company of Singapore Ltd.).
1959: (Tiong Lam Hang Shipping Co., Panama).
1986: Name deleted from ship registers – existence of vessel in doubt.

385 *CHANT 44*
Launched: 24.5.1944.
Completed: 6.1944.
1946: *Androniki* (converted to dry cargo); (C. E. Vlassopoulos, Greece).
1947: *Okiep* (Union SS Co. of South Africa Ltd.).
1949: *Mashona* (Coast Lines (Africa) Ltd.).
1951: (New oil engine).
1953: *Mashona Coast* (Thesens Steamship Co., South Africa).
1964: Engines removed; sold for use as a storage ship; and:
3.1965: (Converted to a barge); (Marine Diamond Corporation, South Africa).

386 *CHANT 45*
Launched: 25.5.1944.
Completed: 6.1944.
1947: *Maro* (C. Machairas, Panama (Union Maritime & Shipping Co.)).
1948: *Seid* (Les Cargos Fruitiers Cherifiens S.A., Morocco).
1951: *Sainte Francoise II* (Soc. Mar. de Transport Oceano-Mediterraneens, Morocco).
1958: (New oil engine).
1962: *Napoleone Primo* (Leone Bianchi & Figlio, Italy).
1974: Name deleted from ship registers; vessel reported converted to a non-propelled barge.

Built by J. Readhead & Sons Ltd., South Shields

T.1 *CHANT 60*
Launched: 11.4.1944.
Completed: 4.1944.
1946: *Arzella* (Shell Company (Malta) Ltd.).
1962: *Caravella Bunker* (Ciane-Anapo Cia. de Nav. Bunkeraggi SpA, Italy).
9.1986: Scrapped Savona, Italy.

T.2 *CHANT 61*
Launched: 11.4.1944.
Completed: 4.1944.
8.6.1944: Capsized and sank off Normandy beach-head, France (voyage: Thameshaven/Normandy – petrol).

Built by Burntisland Shipbuilding Co. Ltd., Fife

291   *CHANT 66*
Launched: 21.2.1944.
Completed: 5.1944.
5.1.1945: Capsized in Old Dock, Grangemouth,
while undergoing repairs to deck plating. Filled and
sank.
19.1.1945: Uprighted, and:
23.1.1945: Refloated, but repairs uneconomic.
4.1945: Scrapped Grangemouth.

292   *CHANT 67*
Launched: 23.2.1944.
Completed: 5.1944.
1946: *Norbensin* (Sporveienes Bensindepot Nor. A/S,
Norway).
1952: *Redo* (K. J. Rebensdorff & others, Sweden).
1956: *Redon* (Knut Hermansson, Sweden).

1961: (New oil engine).
1971: *Kambiz* (Maritime Co. Ltd., Iran).

293   *CHANT 68*
Launched: 29.2.1944.
Completed: 4.1944.
1946: *Leman* (N. E. Vernicos SS Co., Greece).
1961: Renamed *Motol VI*.
11.1969: Scrapped Piraeus.

294   *CHANT 69*
Launched: 10.3.1944.
Completed: 4.1944.
16.6.1944: Capsized off Normandy, France. Sunk by
gunfire from H.M. ship. Wreckage later dispersed.

Coastal tankers – 890 tdw, 196 ft (oa), 189 ft × 31 ft. Engines: T3cyl. (aft) – 9½ knots

Built by Goole Shipbuilding & Repairing Co. Ltd.

361   *Empire Boy* 859 gt.
Launched: 28.8.1941.
Completed: 12.1941.
1942: *Doorman* (Government of the Netherlands).
1947: *Flandria* (Verenigde Tankkustvaart N.V.,
Holland).
1951: *Alice* (Ulric Thomas (S. Stein K.G.,
Germany)).
1952: *Hammonia* (Bauermann & Metzendorff GmbH,
Germany).
1952: (Lengthened to 223 ft, 963 gt).
1954: *Petra* (R. Bauermann (Olea Tankschiff GmbH,
Germany)).
1962: *Anny* (Vittorio Rossetti, Italy).
1965: (New oil engine).
1972: Renamed *Tosco*.
1975: (Tosco Sardi di Nav. SpA, Italy).
6.1975: Scrapped Spezia.

371   *Empire Harp* 861 gt.
Launched: 22.11.1941.
Completed: 1.1942.
1948: *Anis* (Kuwait Oil Co. Ltd. (Anglo-Iranian Oil
Co. Ltd.)).
1954: *Authenticity* (F. T. Everard & Sons Ltd.).
1966: *Petrola I* (John S. Latsis, Greece).
1984: Scrapped Aspropyrgos, Greece.

389   *Empire Faun* 846 gt.
Launched: 12.10.1942.
Completed: 2.1943.
1951–1958: On loan to Greek Navy from Great
Britain; temporarily sailing under the name
Poseidon.
1959: Renamed *Sirios* (pennant A.345) when previous
name given to the submarine *Lapon* acquired from
the U.S.A. in 1958.
1962: Purchased outright by Royal Hellenic Navy
(classed as a harbour tanker).

Coastal tankers – 800 tdw, 184 ft (oa), 177 ft × 31 ft. Engines: Oil (aft) – 9 knots

Built by G. Brown & Co. (Marine) Ltd., Greenock

217 *Empire Ruby* 667 gt.
Launched: 26.6.1941.
Completed: 10.1941.
1946: *Athelruby* (Athel Line Ltd. (United Molasses Co. Ltd., London)).
1950: *Akinity* (F. T. Everard & Sons Ltd.).
4.1965: Scrapped Bruges, Belgium.

221 *Empire Dweller* 667 gt.
Launched: 19.2.1942.
Completed: 6.1942.
1945: *Asperity* (F. T. Everard & Sons Ltd.).
4.1967: Sold (A. E. Pearce Ltd., Essex) for breaking up.

5.1967: Resold and reported scrapped Belgium.

225 *Empire Audrey* 657 gt.
Launched: 23.2.1943.
Completed: 6.1943.
1946: *Audacity* (F. T. Everard & Sons Ltd.).
11.1.1967: Grounded near Terschelling Bank Light Vessel, Holland, 53.21N 5.06E (voyage: Kings Lynn/Hamburg – ballast). Bottom damaged; flooded.
21.1.1967: Refloated, towed to Harlingen. Temporarily repaired, and
25.1.1967: Towed to owner's repair yard at Greenhithe, Kent. Later sold for breaking up, and:
8.1969: Scrapped Boom, Belgium.

As well as the three coastal tankers (above), the Garvel Yard of G. Brown & Company also built five other 'Empire' ships, being four 'Tudor Queen'-type dry cargo coasters and one tug, *Empire Lola*.

The yard commenced building in the late years of the 19th century, then, as the century changed, was taken over as the family business of George Brown & Company. The first building under the new name was the *Princess Beara*, Yard No. 5, a steel, screw, cutter 115 feet long and of 212 gt, driven by a two-cylinder compound engine and completed in July 1901. Her owners were the Bantry Bay SS Co., Cork.

Over the years the company built up a reputation in the construction of tugs and coasters, particularly for the Everard fleet. In 1937 the company was restyled as George Brown & Co. (Marine) Ltd.

During the 1939–1945 war years, apart from merchant ship construction, orders were received for a number of ships for the Admiralty. In 1947 the yard comprised five berths for vessels to 370 feet.

In 1963, with the decline of the shipbuilding industry, the company announced that shipbuilding would cease in May 1963 and the yard put up for sale. The last ship built was the *Vasabha*, Yard No. 277, a twin screw motor tug of 111 ft, 275 gt, for the Colombo Port Commission, completed in the June of 1963.

SHIPS BUILT UNDER PRIVATE CONTRACT OR LICENCE

211 *Supremity* 554 gt, 176 ft (oa), 168.6 ft × 27.7 ft.
Engines: Oil (aft).
Launched: 27.9.1939.
Completed: 11.1939 for F. T. Everard & Sons Ltd.
6.12.1940: Mined, sank near East Oaze Light Vessel, Thames Estuary (voyage: Blyth/London – coal).

213 *Serenity* 557 gt. Details as Yard No. 211.

Launched: 8.8.1940.
Completed: 5.1941 for F. T. Everard & Sons Ltd.
1.10.1941: Bombed and gunned by aircraft ten miles off St. Govans Light Vessel, Pembroke. Repaired.
1967: *Agia Marina* (M. Gigilinas & D. Kalkassinas, Greece).
1979: Scrapped Spain.

The *Empire Harp*, as *Authenticity*. (Goole Shipbuilding & Repairing Co. Ltd., Yard No. 371.)

Coastal tankers – 400 tdw, 152 ft (oa), 147 ft × 24 ft. Engines: Oil (aft) – 10 knots

Built by Rowhedge Ironworks Ltd., Near Colchester, Essex

629   *Empire Boxer* 340 gt.
Launched: 14.10.1943.
Completed: 2.1944.
1946: *Chartsman* (C. Rowbotham & Sons Ltd.).
1967: *Baymead* (converted to a suction dredger for tin dredging in St. Ives Bay (Coastal Prospecting Ltd.)).
7.1974: Scrapped Northam, Southampton.

639   *Empire Barkis* 340 gt.
Launched: 8.6.1944.
Completed: 8.1944.
1946: *Sodok* (Van Castricum & Co. Ltd., London).
1947: *Guntur* (Shell Company of Singapore Ltd.).
1962: (Madam Dolly Seah, Singapore).
1972: (P. T. Perusahaan Pelayaran Palka Utama, Indonesia).

The Rowhedge Ironworks was involved mainly in the construction of coasters. Four 'Empire' coasters were built and three VIC-type coasters late in the war. Two small coastal tankers were built for private account:

585   *Ben Hann* 298 gt, 127.7 ft × 24.3 ft.
Engines: Oil (aft).
Launched: 25.1.1940.
Completed: 2.1940 for National Benzole Co. Ltd.
11.11.1941: Last reported off Mull of Kintyre, Scotland. Subsequently listed as an overdue vessel; no further trace (voyage: Inverness/ Glasgow – ballast).

640   *Trapp* 358 gt, 152 ft (oa), 146.8 ft × 23.7 ft.
Engines: Oil (aft).

Launched: 1.6.1946.
Completed: 8.1946 for Anglo-Saxon Petroleum Co. Ltd.
1947: *Shell Onze* (Companhia Shell, Portugal).
1958: (New oil engine).
1968: *Sonaptanque* (Sonap Maritima Ltda., Lourenço Marques).
1983: *Macuse* (Navique Empresa Moçambicana de Nav., Mozambique).

The Rowhedge Ironworks also built two Torpedo Recovery Vessels, *TRV 2* (launched 1.4.1942) and *TRV 4* (launched 20.2.1943) for the Admiralty.

In 1947 the shipyard facilities included fifteen berths with a ship capacity to 160 ft and three slips to a 180 ft maximum.

The yard closed down at the end of April 1964.

Coastal tankers – 900 tdw, 201 ft (oa), 193 ft × 32 ft. Engines: Oil (aft)

These tankers were similar to the 'TED' type tankers built for service in the Far East.

Built by A. & J. Inglis Ltd., Glasgow

1299P   *Empire Belgrave* 890 gt.
Launched: 16.3.1945.
Completed: 6.1945.
1947: *Aqueity* (F. T. Everard & Sons Ltd.).
11.11.1947: Struck mine near Terschelling, Holland.
Abandoned, flooded and awash; broke up in heavy
seas. Sank (voyage: Bremen/Bromborough – ballast).

1300P   *Empire Campden* 890 gt.
Launched: 30.4.1945.
Completed: 8.1945.
1947: *Anonity* (F. T. Everard & Sons Ltd.).
1966: *Petrola II* (John S. Latsis, Greece).
1969: *Kalymnos* (P. C. Chrissochoides & others,
Greece).
12.4.1970: Grounded on rocks off Rhodes. Refloated,
but constructive total loss. Towed to Piraeus, and:
5.1970: Scrapped Salmina, Greece.

1301P   *Empire Fitzroy* 890 gt.
Launched: 12.6.1945.
Completed: 10.1945.
1952: *Alignity* (F. T. Everard & Sons Ltd.).
11.1971: Scrapped Blyth.

1302P   *Empire Grosvenor* 890 gt.
Launched: 10.1945.
Completed: 11.1945.
1947: *Frenulina* (Anglo-Saxon Petroleum Co. Ltd.).
1954: (Lengthened to 230 ft, 1,041 gt).
1962: Laid up at Singapore, to be scrapped, but:
1962: Resold, renamed *Anlok* (Teck Hwa Shipping
Co., Panama).
1962: *Permina VI* (National Oil Co. Ltd. (Permina),
Indonesia).
1974: *Bimoli 01* (P. T. Bimoli, Indonesia).

Coastal tankers specially designed for service in the Far East

'TED' type (Tankers, Eastern, Diesel), 900 tdw, 201 ft (oa), 193 ft × 34 ft. Engines: Oil (aft) – 10 knots

Built by Grangemouth Dockyard Co. Ltd.

474   *Empire Tedson* 950 gt.
Launched: 17.1.1946.
Completed: 7.1946 as *Arduity* for F. T. Everard &
Sons Ltd.
1956: (Lengthened to 233.9 ft, 1,159 gt).

1969: *Bela* (Felisberto Valente de Almeida, Portugal).
1970: *Ariex* (for river service only).
1979: Name removed from ship registers.

Built by Sir J. Laing & Sons Ltd., Sunderland

772   *Empire Tedassa* 950 gt.
Launched: 8.9.1945.
Completed: 12.1945.
1947: *Fossarina* (Anglo-Saxon Petroleum Co. Ltd.).
1950: *Amity* (F. T. Everard & Sons Ltd.).
1965: Scrapped Great Yarmouth.

773   *Empire Tedilla* 950 gt.
Launched: 25.9.1945.
Completed: 2.1946.
1947: *Forskalia* (Anglo-Saxon Petroleum Co. Ltd.).
1949: *Danesdale H* (J. Harker (Coasters) Ltd.).
1952: *Shell Driller* (Shell Mex & B.P. Ltd.).
1966: Scrapped Faslane.

Built by Short Bros. Ltd., Sunderland

490   *Empire Tedlora* 950 gt.
Launched: 18.1.1946.
Completed: 6.1946.
1947: *Forreria* (Anglo-Saxon Petroleum Co. Ltd.).
1951: *Austility* (F. T. Everard & Sons Ltd.).
1969: *Piraeus IV* (Ionian Tank Shipping S.A.
(G. Kalogeratos & Co., Greece)).
1971: *Aspropyrgos* (G. Lyberis, Greece).
1985: (Converted to a non-propelled barge at
Perama).

491   (Launched as) *Empire Tedburgh* 950 gt.

Launched: 4.2.1946.
Completed: 6.1946 as *Dovedale H* for J. Harker
(Coasters) Ltd.
1953: *B.P. Supervisor* (Shell Mex & B.P. Ltd.).
1966: *Rainbow* (Antonia Shipping Co. Ltd.
(J. Livanos & Sons, Greece).
1967: *Piraeus II* (Ionian Tank Shipping S.A.
(G. Kalogeratos & Co., Greece)).
6.11.1977: Caught fire and sank in Eleusis Bay,
Greece, with a cargo of molasses. Total loss. Sold,
raised, and:
9.1978: Scrapped Piraeus.

Built by A. & J. Inglis Ltd., Glasgow

1311P   *Empire Tedship* 890 gt.
Launched: 20.10.1945.
Completed: 2.1946.
1947: *Fischeria* (Anglo-Saxon Petroleum Co. Ltd.).
1951: *Acuity* (F. T. Everard & Sons Ltd.).
1967: *Vittoriosa* (Betamar Carriers Ltd., Somali
Republic).
1968: (Converted to a water tanker).
1969: *Neptunia Terza* (Compania di Davide Russo &
Co., Italy).
1975: Scrapped Italy.

1312P   *Empire Tedport* 890 gt.
Launched: 30.11.1945.
Completed: 3.1946.
1947: *Felipes* (Anglo-Saxon Petroleum Co. Ltd.).
1948: *Shelbrit 10* (Shell Mex & B.P. Ltd.).
1952: Renamed *Shell Director*.
9.1966: Scrapped Bo'ness.

1313P   *Empire Tedmuir* 890 gt.
Launched: 5.2.1946.
Completed: 5.1946.
1947: *Fusinus* (Anglo-Saxon Petroleum Co. Ltd.).
1949: *Aqueity* (F. T. Everard & Sons Ltd.).
1.1965: Arrived Bruges for breaking up.

1314P   *Empire Tedrita* 890 gt.
Launched: 4.1946.
Completed: 9.1946.
1947: *Fusus* (Anglo-Saxon Petroleum Co. Ltd.).
1956: *Tong Lie* (Kie Hock Shipping Co.,
Singapore).
1957: (Converted to dry cargo; bridge resited aft).
1962: (Palembang Shipping Co., Panama (Kie Hock
Shipping Co., Singapore)).
1964: *Monaco* (Cia. de Nav. Gatun, Panama (Kie
Hock Shipping Co., Singapore)).

1965: *Hanna* (Cia. Nav. Thompson S.A., Panama
(Kie Hock Shipping Co., Singapore)).
1965: Renamed *Fataki*.
7.1976: Scrapped Hong Kong.

1319P   *Empire Tedmont* Cancelled.

1320P   *Empire Tedlake* Cancelled.

1321P   *Empire Tedellen* Cancelled.

1322P   *Empire Tedrose* Cancelled.

–   *Empire Tedfay* Allocated name, Cancelled.

–   *Empire Tedflora* Allocated name, Cancelled.

'TES' type (Tankers, Eastern, Steam), 900 tdw, 201 ft (oa), 193 ft × 34 ft. Engines: T3cyl. (aft) - 10 knots

Built by Bartram & Sons Ltd., Sunderland

310   *Empire Tesbury* 975 gt.
Launched: 21.11.1945.
Completed: 3.1946.
1951: *Rippledyke* (Owned by Admiralty, but
chartered to commercial service).
1958: Oil hulk at Gibraltar (Royal Fleet Auxiliary).
1960: (S. Lucchese & L. Esposito, Italy).
1961: (Converted to a suction dredger: 1,000 gt).
1965: *Ada* (Motia Comp. di Nav. SpA, Italy).
5.11.1966: Sank near northern breakwater at entrance
to Lido, port of Venice, after collision with Yugoslav
ship *Bocna* (1957, 5,215 gt).
4.2.1967: Refloated. Repaired and fitted with new
(oil) engine.
1978: (Reclassed as a barge).
11.1981: Sold for breaking up at Porto Nogaro, near
Venice.

Note: On 16 November 1966 the Italian wooden motor
vessel *Marina Di Sapri* sank after striking the wreck of the
Ada (above).

311   *Empire Tesville* 975 gt.
Launched: 21.11.1945.
Completed: 3.1946.
1952: *Fusinus* (Anglo-Saxon Petroleum Co. Ltd.).
1960: (Shell Tankers Ltd.).
1964: Scrapped Singapore.

312   (Allocated name) *Empire Tesgate* Contract
cancelled, not built.

313   (Allocated name) *Empire Tesrock* Contract
cancelled, not built.

Built by Harland & Wolff Ltd., Govan

1315G   *Empire Tesland* 975 gt.
Launched: 31.7.1945.
Completed: 9.1945.
1946: *Fulgar* (Anglo-Saxon Petroleum Co. Ltd.).
1948: *Shelbrit 9* (Shell Mex & B.P. Ltd.).
1952: Renamed *B.P. Manager*.
6.1967: Scrapped Antwerp.

1317G   *Empire Tescombe* 975 gt.
Launched: 4.10.1945.
Completed: 12.1945.
1952: *Fossarina* (Anglo-Saxon Petroleum Co. Ltd.).

1965: Scrapped Hong Kong.

1318G   *Empire Tesella* 975 gt.
Launched: 31.10.1945.
Completed: 2.1946.
1951: *British Pluck* (British Tanker Co. Ltd.).
4.1954: Scrapped Bombay.

1323G   *Empire Tesdown* Cancelled.

1324G   *Empire Tesgrove* Cancelled.

Built by Swan, Hunter & Wigham Richardson Ltd., Newcastle

1842   *Empire Teslin* 975 gt.
Launched: 5.10.1945.
Completed: 4.1946.
1946: *Fragum* (Anglo-Saxon Petroleum Co. Ltd.).
1948: *Shelbrit 8* (Shell Mex & B.P. Ltd.).
1952: Renamed *Shell Supplier*.
1954: (Lengthened to 240.6 ft, 1,157 gt).
1967: *Sofia* (Marine Water Supply Co. (N. E. Vernicos Shipping Co. Ltd., Greece)).
5.1971: Scrapped Perama, Greece.

1844   *Empire Tesdale* 975 gt.
Launched: 22.10.1945.
Completed: 5.1946.
1946: *Beme* (Burmah Oil Co. (Tankers) Ltd., Rangoon, (Burmah Oil Co. Ltd., London)).
1948: (Burmah Oil Co. (Burma Trading) Ltd.).
1963: (The People's Oil Industry, Burma).
1964: *Yenan* (Government of Burma – Rangoon Port Corporation).
1980: Broken up in Burma.

The 'Ted'-type diesel tanker *Empire Tedrita* as *Fataki*, after conversion to dry cargo. (A. & J. Inglis Ltd., Yard No. 1314P.)

The 'Tes'-type steam tanker *Empire Tesland* as *B. P. Manager*. (Harland & Wolff Ltd., Govan, Yard No. 1315G.)

PART TEN

TUGS

When war began it quickly became apparent that many tugs would be required to meet the demands of both the Royal Navy and the Merchant Marine. In fact, during the whole period of hostilities, the demand for tugs never ceased. All types were required, but a matter of immediate concern was the provision of rescue and salvage tugs to aid ships suffering from enemy action by aircraft or submarine or, perhaps, by marine peril.

Ocean-going naval tugs, working as target-towing ships in the days of peace, were quickly turned to rescue work and sent out to assist valuable war-damaged merchant ships struggling to reach a haven where precious cargo could be discharged and where the vessel itself might be repaired to rejoin the fray.

Requisitioning telegrams were quickly sent to British owners for tugs for rescue work and for harbour duties and by the end of 1942, when requisitioning had all but ceased, some fifty tugs for rescue work and thirty for harbour work had come under Government control. Among these the London owners, William Watkins, supplied four for harbour and two for rescue duties; three 'Danubes' were taken over from the Tilbury Contracting & Dredging Company and seven 'Sun' harbour tugs were supplied from W. H. J. Alexander's fleet. The Hull-based company, United Towing, supplied three – *Englishman, Seaman* and *Superman* – as rescue tugs plus two smaller vessels, whilst Dover Harbour Board handed over their twin-screw salvage steamer, *Lady Brassey*, for the duration of war.

And in June 1940, when the victorious German armies swept to the continental Channel ports, many tugs towing dredgers, hoppers, yachts and a miscellany of small craft, crossed the English Channel to join the Allies and continue the struggle. Included in the collection were several 'Abeilles' tugs from Le Havre, one, indeed, being the old Royal Navy 'Saint'-class tug *St. Minver*, dating from 1919. Three tug/tenders broke Cherbourg connections; two new French Navy tugs *Attentif* and *Champion* (672 tons displacement) and only completed at Bordeaux in 1939 arrived; and from Holland came Wijsmuller's *Amsterdam* and Smit's *Schelde* and *Thames*.

In the year of war Britain had few powerful tugs. In an attempt to restore the British flag in the work of marine salvage, the Overseas Towage & Salvage Co. Ltd. had built in 1938 the *Marinia*, 600 gt., with triple expansion engines. But she was not to last for long, being torpedoed and then sunk by gunfire from *U.29* on 13 September 1939 in the South Western Approaches, in position 49.20N 14.40W. Built by Cochranes of Selby, this company was to complete the slightly smaller 579 gt *Salvonia* for the same owners in January 1939. She was taken over by the Royal Navy when war began and was eventually released in October 1945.

Discussions had taken place in 1938 between Henry Robb Ltd., of Leith, and the Overseas Towage & Salvage Company regarding designs for a 3,000/4,000 hp tug. The builders favoured diesel machinery for propulsion, pointing out the very low standby charges and the advantages of full power within a few minutes of getting away. However, the tug company were in mind of single-screw propulsion as essential for maximum efficiency in towing over long distances. The builders then proposed geared diesel machinery, as in Smit & Co.'s Dutch-flag *Zwarte Zee*, 793 gt., completed in 1933 and the most powerful of pre-war tugs. From this came the preparation of design and specification to meet the owner's requirements and the contract was about to be signed when war broke out.

Then, through the collaboration between the Admiralty and the Overseas Towage & Salvage Company in the requisition of their salvage tugs, it became known that Henry Robb Ltd. had full designs of a tug for immediate use, and they were invited by the Admiralty to submit a proposal to build such vessels. Admiralty adjustments for wartime requirements were added to the plans and the Robb yard was ordered to proceed with the building of a class of very powerful rescue tugs of 1,100 gt, with two 8-cyl. engines – the first fleet tugs with diesel machinery – developing 4,000 bhp and giving 16 knots. They were known as the 'Bustler'-class and eight were built, in pairs:

	Yard No.	Launched:		Yard No.	Launched:
Bustler	321	4.12.1941	*Mediator*	335	21. 6.1944
Samsonia	322	1. 4.1942	*Reward*	336	31.10.1944
Growler	328	10. 9.1942	*Turmoil*	337	11. 5.1945
Hesper	329	10.11.1942	*Warden*	338	28. 6.1945

Note: The *Hesper* (later *Hesperia*) grounded on the Libyan coast on 9 February 1945 and was lost; *Growler* was later renamed *Cyclone*.

But, as with rescue tugs, there was a shortage of escort ships in the early war years and it was not possible to provide much defence. Some early convoys were allocated no more than four escort ships for part of the voyage across the Atlantic and none at all for the remainder of the way. In 1939 merchant ships had no anti-aircraft armament except, perhaps, a single Lewis gun; even destroyers were not able to elevate their guns enough to bear on some of the enemy bombers.

Henry Robb Ltd. was therefore given instructions to build the rescue tugs along with corvettes and frigates, all ships urgently required for the Battle of the Atlantic. The first tug, *Bustler*, was completed in June 1942; the eighth and last, *Warden*, in December 1945 and between these two the Robb yard turned out six 'Flower'-class and three 'Castle'-class corvettes, six 'River' and six 'Bay'-class frigates and two minelayers.

The Admiralty also had the 'Assurance'-class tugs completed by Cochranes, the name ship launched in May 1940. The twenty-first and last tug of the class – *Sesame* – was launched in October 1943. Smaller than the 'Bustlers', but sturdy rescue tugs, they each carried 275 tons of fuel oil, enough for a steaming range of three weeks duration. Triple expansion engines to 1,350 ihp gave a speed of 13 knots.

Six 'Envoy'-class tugs, slightly more powerful and larger than the 'Assurance'-class, were completed in 1944. Four 'Nimble'-class, twin screw tugs with triple expansion engines were also completed, the name-ship in 1941 and the *Capable, Careful* and *Expert* in 1945.

Twenty-four rescue tugs were lend/leased from the United States between 1942 and mid-1944. They had diesel-electric drive to twin screws and were of 1,875 bhp. Four more, of wooden-hull build, were launched early in 1944 and also joined the Royal Navy. These, however, had triple expansion engines to a single shaft.

During the war years the rescue service was operated by the Admiralty via the local naval officer-in-charge at ports and bases. In theory there was no reason why requisitioned tugs in this service could not continue to work under the Red Ensign and management of their owners, but the Admiralty wished to have the crews of the tugs they controlled under naval discipline. So an informal agreement was reached: ship tugs, including those built under the Ministry of War Transport's building programme for operation in the U.K. and the coastal towing service should be operated by their Sea Transport Division under the Red Ensign and commercial management, but the rescue service should be under the White Ensign and Admiralty management. There were, however, some exceptions to this arrangement, as changing wartime conditions demanded.

Tugs for the merchant sector were broadly classified to four types, all single screw. The largest was the tug for deep sea work; then the tug for coastal waters; the river and estuarial type, and the dock tug. The need for all types was urgent and it was decided that in order to enable yards to begin work, prototypes of proven buildings could be used for similar construction.

For the deep sea tug the prototype chosen was the *Englishman*, 487 gt, completed by Cochrane & Sons Ltd., Selby, in October 1937 for the United Towing Co. Ltd. of Hull. Her measurements were 143 ft (oa), 135 ft (bp) × 30 ft breadth and a moulded depth of 16 ft. Triple expansion engines developed 1,100 ihp. The *Englishman* was taken up by the Royal Navy in February 1940 as a rescue tug and was sunk on 21 January 1941 in an air attack by German FW200s of the I/KG (Bomber Group) 40, about forty miles west of Tory Island, Donegal, Ireland.

Of the first group of eight built to prototype measurements, the first two – *Empire Larch* and *Empire Oak* – launched in early 1941, were built to peace-time standards; wartime stringency and scarcity of materials were to be felt in the tugs that followed.

Details of the first tug, *Empire Larch*, included a curved stem, elliptical stern and monkey forecastle. She had three watertight and five oiltight bulkheads. Fore and aft peak tanks were fitted for water ballast and the aft port and starboard fuel tanks could, if necessary, also be used for a similar purpose. Oil fuel bunkers were two port and two starboard tanks and a wing tank either side of the boiler. Bunker capacity was 340 tons. The main machinery consisted of a set of vertical triple expansion steam engines, which developed some 1,200 ihp.

Accommodation for officers was forward, captain's berth on the main deck; chartroom and radio room on the bridge deck. The saloon, with its mahogany plywood panelling and furnished with upholstered settees, was below the main deck. There was also a large refrigerated room and a bathroom.

But the tugs were increasingly required to make longer deep-sea voyages; more armament was deemed necessary and additional crew required. The bigger crew necessitated more boats and rafts and, in turn, stability and trim were affected, so, in order to ensure stability, a variation in design increased the beam to 33 ft and became effective in the Cleland-built tugs, Yard Nos. 70–74. All tugs of this type were fitted with salvage pumps, fire-fighting monitors and fire hoses.

Larch Class

Built by Goole Shipbuilding & Repairing Co. Ltd.

353   *Empire Larch*
Launched: 30.1.1941.
Completed: 6.1941.
30.6.1941: Damaged by aircraft bombs off Great Yarmouth; repaired.
Naval work to:

1946: *Masterman* (United Towing Co. Ltd.).
1962: *Smjeli* (Brodospas, Yugoslavia).
1972: Scrapped Split.

Note: Another British war-built tug, *Bustler* (1942, 946 gt.), was acquired by Brodospas in 1973. Firstly named *Mocni*, she then perpetuated the name *Smjeli* in 1975.

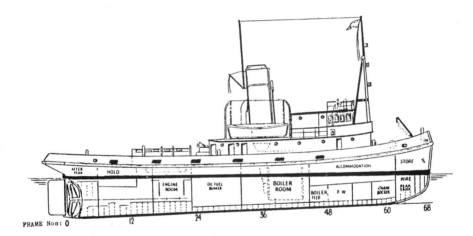

The 'Warrior'-type tug.

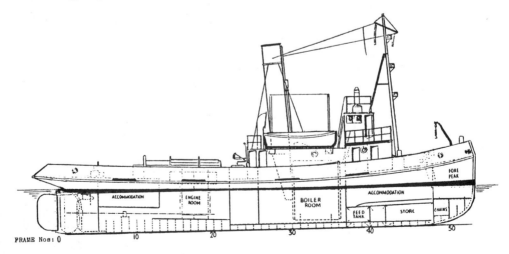

The 'Stella'-type tug.

The Modified 'Maple'-type tug.

The 'Warrior'-type tug *Empire Fir* as *Rampside*. (Scott & Sons Ltd., Yard No. 361.)   *Fotoship*

The 'Improved Larch'-class tug *Empire Susan*, as *Rumania*, in 1952. (Clelands (Successors) Ltd., Yard No. 71.)   *Skyfotos*

354   *Empire Oak*
Launched: 15.3.1941.
Completed: 7.1941.
22.8.1941: Sunk by submarine (*U.564*) torpedo in the
Atlantic, 40.43N 11.39W (in convoy OG 71,
U.K./Gibraltar).

Note: Between 19–23 August, four U-boats sank nine ships
of convoy OG 71, plus the Norwegian destroyer *Bath* and
the British corvette *Zinnia*.

387   *Empire Harry*
Launched: 12.10.1942.
Completed: 3.1943.
Naval work to:

6.6.1945: Ashore on rocks, in fog, at Beacon Point,
½ mile west of Bolt Tail, Bigbury Bay, Devon. Broke
up. Total loss (voyage: Falmouth/Antwerp – towing
U.S. Army barges).

388   *Empire Rupert*
Launched: 10.11.1942.
Completed: 5.1943.
24.1.1945: In collision with the steamer *Twickenham
Ferry* (1934, 2,839 gt) ten miles off Dover, Kent. Sank
in position 51.3N 1.32E. Total loss.

Built by Clelands (Successors) Ltd., Willington Quay-on-Tyne

66   *Empire Sandy*
Launched: 22.12.1942.
Completed: 7.1943.
1948: *Ashford* (Risdon Beazley Ltd.).
1952: *Chris M* (Great Lakes Paper Co. Ltd., Canada).
1979: *Empire Sandy* (J. E. Rogers, Canada).
1982: Converted to a ferry (Empire Sandy Inc.,
Canada).
1985: Converted to a three-masted schooner.

67   *Empire John*
Launched: 21.4.1943.
Completed: 10.1943.
Naval work to:
21.8.1947: Passed over a mine which exploded astern,
near Kiel (voyage: Harwich/Copenhagen, towing a
corvette). Damaged, but reached Kiel; docked and
repaired.

1951: (Dominion Coal Co. Ltd., Canada).
12.1965: Scrapped Bilbao.

68   *Empire Winnie*
Launched: 2.9.1943.
Completed: 1.1944.
1946: *Zealandia* (Wm. Watkins Ltd.).
1952: *Yuna* (Adelaide SS Industries Ltd., Australia).
1971: (C. R. Rotendella, Australia).
1973: Reported converted to a barge.
4.1974: Scrapped Bunbury Harbour, W. Australia.

69   *Empire Aid*
Launched: 27.11.1943.
Completed: 4.1944.
1952: *Marinia* (Overseas Towage & Salvage Co. Ltd.).
1954: *Huda* (Kuwait Oil Co. Ltd.).
1965: Sold (H. H. Deeb, Kuwait).
1967: Dismantled at Basrah, Iraq.

The following five tugs had a breadth of 33 ft and a gross tonnage of 593. They were known as the
IMPROVED 'LARCH'-CLASS.

70   *Empire Julia*
Launched: 22.4.1944.
Completed: 7.1944.
1946: *Tradesman* (United Towing Co. Ltd.).
1963: *Vernicos Kitty* (N. E. Vernicos Shipping Co.
Ltd., Greece).
12.1974: Scrapped Kartal, Turkey.

71   *Empire Susan*
Launched: 19.7.1944.
Completed: 10.1944.
1946: *Rumania* (Wm. Watkins Ltd.).
10.2.1956: Aground during heavy weather on Long
Sand Bank, Thames Estuary, while assisting Lloyd
Brasileiro's steamer *Loide-Honduras* (1948, 5,408 gt)
also aground on the same bank. The crew of the
Rumania were rescued by helicopter before she
submerged and became a total loss, 51.43N 1.37E.
The Brazilian ship was refloated on 12 February,

In 1946 Wm. Watkins Ltd. were contracted to make one of their longest tows, the work involving the delivery of two ex-Royal Navy sloops to Shanghai and which had been sold for commercial use. They were the 'Kingfisher'-class ships *Kittiwake* and *Sheldrake*, Thornycroft-built, which had become surplus to requirements. They were to be renamed *Tuch Sing* and *Tuch Loon*, respectively.

In January 1947 the *Rumania* left Southampton with the *Kittiwake* in tow; the *Zealandia* (ex *Empire Winnie*) with the *Sheldrake*. At Algiers the *Rumania* took over the *Sheldrake* and continued via Suez, Aden, Colombo and Singapore, arriving at Shanghai in May 1947.

From there she sailed for Sydney, N.S.W., and from there towed the Howard Smith ex-Interstate liner *Canberra* (7,170 gt) to Singapore, taking forty-seven days with one bunkering, ex-tow. Altogether, the *Rumania* was absent from Britain for sixteen months, during which time she had steamed 48,000 miles.

72 (Launched as) *Empire Jean*
Launched: 17.10.1944.
Completed: 1.1945 as *Empire Mary*.
1946: *Marinia* (Overseas Towage & Salvage Co. Ltd.).
1950: *W. Ponty* (Union des Remorq., de Dakar).
1954: Renamed *Ponty*.
1961: *Ocean Bull* (Soc. Belge Remorq. Oceanique, Ostend).
1965: *Nettuno S* (S.A. Italiene Lavori e Maritimi, Italy).
1984: Renamed *Nettuno Sailem*.
5.1985: Scrapped Palermo.

The Overseas Towage & Salvage Co. Ltd. was formed in Britain in 1937, being set up with French capital by the Le Havre-based 'Les Abeilles' tug firm after they had several import licences for British-built tugs refused. At the same time the move helped restore the Red Ensign to its old place in the salvage business. The intention was that, after sailing the new tugs under the British flag for a while, they would be imported, second-hand, into France.

In 1938 the tug/salvage vessel *Neptunia* (798 gt) was completed for the company by Cochranes, of Selby, and sent on station at Queenstown (Cobh), Eire. The second pre-war tug was *Salvonia*, 571 gt, completed in January 1939, also by Cochranes, and she was based at Falmouth. Two months later the same builders delivered the 327 gt *Nereidia*, but with import licence granted, she was almost immediately transferred to Le Havre to join the fleet of 'Les Abeilles' as *Abeille No. 4* and, as such, survived the war.

When war broke out both *Neptunia* and *Salvonia* were taken over by the Admiralty as rescue tugs. The *Neptunia* lasted only another few days, for on 13 September 1939 she was sunk by submarine *U.29* about 300 miles south-west of Cork when on her first wartime rescue task. The *Salvonia* sailed under Admiralty pennant number W. 43.

The company managed numerous 'Empire' tugs of the Ministry of War Transport during hostilities and at the end of the war were controlling twenty-six 'Empire' tugs and five ex-French-flag tugs as well as the *Turmoil* for the Admiralty, which was to be featured in the *Flying Enterprise* saga in the Atlantic and Western Approaches to the English Channel in late 1951. The tug *Nancy Moran*, 452 gt, built for the Moran Towing Company in 1912, had been acquired from the U.S. flag in 1943, but she was lost in collision on 30 May 1946 off the South Goodwin Light Vessel; but by 1950 the company had acquired the Admiralty tug *Dexterous* (1942, 600 gt) and, two years later, the *Marinia* (ex *Empire Aid*).

In January 1955 another seagoing tug, again named *Marinia* (392 gt) was delivered, and four years later, when the shares of Overseas Towage & Salvage and its associated Milford Haven Tug Services Ltd. were acquired by the Dutch tug and salvage firm L. Smit & Co., she was the only deep-sea tug in the fleet.

73 (Laid down as) *Empire Rosa*
Launched: 30.12.1944.
Completed: 4.1945 as *Empire Jean*.
1946: *Metinda III* (Metal Industries Ltd.).
1961: *R.A.3.* (Spanish Navy).

74 *Empire Bess*
Launched: 26.4.1945.
Completed: 7.1945.
1946: *Merchantman* (United Towing Co. Ltd.).
1962: *Tarentum* (Soc. Rim. Napoletani, Italy).
1982: Scrapped Naples.

Clelands (Successors) Ltd. stemmed from the Cleland Graving Dock & Slipway Company of Willington Quay-on-Tyne, which dated back to the 1890s. One outstanding building of this primary repair company was the tug *Majestic*, Yard No. 3, completed in August 1898. A small vessel, 107 ft × 22 ft and of 157 gt., she spent many years with the Dublin Port & Docks Board before moving to the Britannia Towing Company, Swansea. Her last job was in 1956 when, at fifty-eight years of age, she towed the 'Hunt'-class escort destroyer *Pytchley* to Llanelli for breaking up. After handing over her tow, the *Majestic* was also handed over for scrapping at the same yard.

Clelands (Successors) Ltd., built a number of tugs during World War II, four of which were for deep sea work and seven for coastal waters. Four coastal ships were also constructed and when war ended the yard consisted of two berths for ships to 250 ft and two slipways of 310 ft and 250 ft.

In October 1961 the company delivered the 1,595 gt *Cornishbrook* (Yard No. 250) under the Clelands (Successors) name; subsequent buildings were under the restyled Clelands Shipbuilding Co. Ltd.

One of the largest ships built was the *Wheelsman* (Yard No. 293), a 4,575 tdw (2,876 gt) tanker delivered to C. Rowbotham & Sons Ltd. in 1967. Later, the shipbuilding company became part of the Swan, Hunter Group Ltd. – Small Shipbuilding Division.

'Warrior' type

The most numerous type of tug was the coastwise type and these were most in demand. The prototype chosen for construction was the *Warrior*, built in 1935 for Steel & Bennie Ltd. of Glasgow. Details of this vessel were 114 ft (oa) × 107 ft × 26 ft breadth and a draught of 13 ft 6 ins. Her gross tonnage was 250 and coal-fired triple expansion engines developed 1,000 ihp. She was built by Scott & Sons, Bowling (Yard No. 332) and working drawings were given to several shipyards. However, some builders had constructed tugs of similar design to that of the *Warrior* and they were given orders, when possible, to build to their own 'near-Warrior' prototype. These vessels are listed as 'near-Warrior' type under their individual builders.

Built by Scott & Sons Ltd., Bowling

360   *Empire Pine*
Launched: 10.6.1941.
Completed: 9.1941.
1946: *Vanguard* (Steel & Bennie Ltd.).
1961: Renamed *Battleaxe*.
1961: *Dunfalcon* (Newport Screw Towing Co. Ltd.).
12.1968: Scrapped Newport, Mon.

361   *Empire Fir*
Launched: 9.10.1941.
Completed: 12.1941.

1946: *Central No. 3* (London & North Eastern Railway).
1949: (British Transport Commission, Grimsby).
1961: *Rampside* (British Transport Docks Board, Barrow).
1973: *Poseidon* (Maritime Commercial Enterprises, Greece).
1976: *Vernicos Fani II* (N. E. Vernicos, Greece).
1986: Scrapped Greece.

362   *Empire Palm*
Launched: 20.1.1942.
Completed: 4.1942.
1946: *Seaway* (Ardrossan Harbour Co.).
7.1969: Scrapped Dalmuir.

363   *Empire Farm*
Launched: 30.4.1942.
Completed: 6.1942.
Naval work to:
1947: *Lady Rosemary* (Wilson Sons & Co., Brazil).
1966: *Marte* (Wilson Sons S.A. Comercio Industria, Brazil).

364   *Empire Cupid*
Launched: 2.6.1942.

Completed: 7.1942.
Naval work to:
1947: *Integrity* (Admiralty).
21.12.1965: Arrived Inverkeithing for breaking up.

365   *Empire Sinew*
Launched: 14.7.1942.
Completed: 11.1942.
1948: *Faidherbe* (Union des Remoq. de L'Ocean, Dakar).
1954: (Adelaide SS Co.).
6.8.1954: Left Dakar on delivery voyage.
24.10.1954: Left Cape Town for Mauritius and Fremantle.
26.10.1954:   Last reported in distress off Cape Agulhas; foundered with loss of all hands.

'Near-Warrior' type

Built by A. Hall & Co. Ltd., Aberdeen

From the prototype *Foremost*, completed in July 1926 for Huddart, Parker Ltd., Melbourne. 235 gt, 113 ft (oa), 105 ft × 27 ft. Engines: T3cyl (750–900 ihp).

680   *Empire Minotaur*
Launched: 16.4.1942.
Completed: 7.1942.
Naval work (Ceylon) to:
1949: *Lalor* (Townsville Harbour Board, Australia).
1969: Stripped, then scuttled off Townsville, Queensland.

681   *Empire Gnome*
Launched: 30.4.1942.
Completed: 7.1942.
Naval work (Ceylon) to:
1949: *Jacobs* (Ned-Indonesia Steenkolen Handel Maats.).
1959: (Government of Indonesia).
1961: *Laut Jamdena* (P. T. Pelayaran Adhiguna, Indonesia).
1972: (Bahadjas Raya, Indonesia).

682   *Empire Ned*
Launched: 27.8.1942.
Completed: 11.1942.
Naval work to 1947, but:
1945: Renamed *Empire Edward*.
1947: (Admiralty).
1956: Renamed *Energetic*.
1965: *Nisos Lefkos* (Tsavliris Salvage & Towage Ltd., Greece).
1975: *Kronos* (Maritime Commercial Enterprises Ltd., Greece).
23.3.1978: Severely damaged when struck by passing cruise vessel *Romanza* (1939, 7,938 gt) whilst berthed at Piraeus. Constructive total loss. Sold, and:
3.1979: Scrapped Perama.

683   *Empire Fred*
Launched: 11.9.1942.
Completed: 11.1942.
1943: (Admiralty).
1970: (Accommodation vessel, Chatham Dockyard).

4.1974: Towed to Hendrik-Ido-Ambacht for breaking up.

689   *Empire Ann*
Launched: 9.1.1943.
Completed: 3.1943.
Naval work (Malta) to:
1948: *Solway* (United Steel Companies Ltd., Sheffield; operated by Workington Harbour & Dock Board).
21.4.1977: Arrived Fleetwood for breaking up.

690   *Empire Spitfire*
Launched: 23.1.1943.
Completed: 4.1943.
Naval work (Malta) to:
1947: *Warden* (Admiralty).
1951: Renamed *Prompt*.
1975: *Torque* (Thames Services Ltd., London).
1979: (Shoreham Salvage & Marine Ltd.).
1982: (Maryport Maritime Museum, Cumbria).
1986: Scrapped Millom, Cumbria.

693   *Empire Harlequin*
Launched: 2.8.1943.
Completed: 10.1943.
Naval work (Alexandria) to:
1947: *El Gadir* (Sudan Government Railways).
1965: Reported scrapped.

694   *Empire Pierrot*
Launched: 13.8.1943.
Completed: 10.1943.
Naval work (Mombasa/Singapore) to:
1948: *St. Patrick* (Government of Trinidad).
1966: *Empire Pierrot* (Trinidad Port Authority).
1978: (Name and nationality of owners deleted from ship registers).

697   *Empire Jonathan*
Launched: 27.1.1944.
Completed: 3.1944.
Naval work (India/Singapore) to:
1947: *Fidget* (Admiralty).
1971: (Government of Singapore).
1973: (Rebuilt, fitted with oil engine; Straits Engineers Ltd., Singapore).
1975: (World Dredging Ltd., Panama).
1983: (Strel Ltd., Panama).

698   *Empire Roger*
Launched: 10.4.1944.
Completed: 5.1944.
Naval work to:
1949: *Fisherstown* (J. Fisher & Sons, Barrow).
6.1968: Scrapped Barrow.

699   *Empire Jane*
Launched: 25.4.1944.
Completed: 6.1944.
Naval work (India/Singapore) to:
1947: *Taioma* (Union SS Co. of New Zealand).
1978: Preserved 'high and dry' as part of a maritime engineering display at Tauranga, New Zealand.

700   *Empire Polly*
Launched: 19.9.1944.
Completed: 11.1944.
1947: *Central No. 4* (London & North Eastern Railway).
1949: (British Transport Commission).
1961: *Roa* (British Transport Docks Board).
1973: *Apollo* (Maritime Commercial Enterprises Ltd., Greece).
1986: Scrapped Greece.

706   *Empire Shirley*
Launched: 27.6.1945.
Completed: 8.1945.
Naval work (India/Singapore) to:
1947: *Tapuhi* (Union SS Co. of New Zealand).
1973: *Tui Tawate* (Fiji owners).
1974: *Tui Tuate* (R. Discomb, Fiji).
1986: (C. Griffiths, Wellington, New Zealand).

Early in 1986 the *Tui Tuate*, laid up at Port Vila, Vanuatu, was given by her then owner to the businessman C. Griffiths. It was his intention to return the vessel to Wellington for conversion to a floating restaurant, but its condition was too bad to permit the tow. Instead, he purchased the Auckland Harbour Board's tug *Aucklander* (1958, 454 gt), which had been laid up for some eighteen months, and she arrived at Wellington under her own steam on 12 October 1986. Her machinery, shafts and propellers were removed and the afterdeck enclosed to become a restaurant area. The vessel was to be repainted in 'Union Steamship' colours and renamed *Tapuhi II*.

707   *Empire Connie*
Launched: 10.7.1945.
Completed: 9.1945.
Naval work (India/Singapore) to:
1946: *Mies* (Royal Netherlands Navy).
1947: (Government of the Netherlands East Indies).
1953: (Indonesian Navy).
1958: (Government of Indonesia).
1974: *Teluk Ambon* (Tanjung Priok Port Authority, Indonesia).

708   *Empire Roderick*
Launched: 21.12.1945.
Completed: 2.1946.
Naval work to:
1947: *Security* (Admiralty).
4.1966: Scrapped Burght, Belgium.

The 'Near Warrior'-type tug *Empire Jane* as *Taioma*, at Wellington, New Zealand. (A. Hall & Co. Ltd., Yard No. 699.)

Vic Young

The tug *Empire Ace* in Scottish waters. (Cochrane & Sons Ltd., Yard No. 1255.)

The *Empire Linden*, as *Linden*, at Dar es Salaam, in 1956. (Henry Scarr Ltd., Yard No. 419.)

709   *Empire Raymond*
Launched: 21.1.1946.
Completed: 5.1946.
1947: *Cervia* (Wm. Watkins Ltd.).
26.10.1954: Foundered at Tilbury while assisting the
P & O SN Co.'s *Arcadia* (1953, 29,734 gt).
28.10.1954: Raised: beached; repaired at Ramsgate.
Re-entered owners' service.
1972: (Medway Maritime Museum).
1973: (International Towing Ltd., Sittingbourne).
1984: (East Kent Maritime Museum, Ramsgate:
vessel to be preserved as an exhibit, in Wm. Watkin's
livery).

712   (Launched as) *Empire Leonard*
Launched: 5.5.1946.

Completed: 9.1946 as *Sun XVI* for W. H. J.
Alexander Ltd.
1962: *S. Cataldo* (Soc. Rim. Napoletani, Italy).
1983: Scrapped Naples.

713   (Laid down as) *Empire Margaret*
Launched: 14.6.1946 as *Sun XVII*.
Completed: 11.1946 for W. H. J. Alexander Ltd.
1968: *Rania G* (Soc. Rim. Napoletani, Italy).
6.1983: Scrapped Palermo.

714   *Empire George*
Contract cancelled when vessel two-thirds completed:
scrapped on stocks.

715   *Empire Keith*
Contract cancelled: vessel scrapped on stocks.

Built by Cochrane & Sons Ltd., Selby

From the prototype *Hoedic*, built in 1931 for Cie. Nazairienne de Remorquage et de Sauvetage, St.
Nazaire. 275 gt, 112 ft (oa), 105 ft × 27 ft. Engines: T3cyl (850 ihp).

1243   *Empire Fairy*
Launched: 5.1.1942.
Completed: 5.1942.
Naval work (East Africa) to:
1944: (Admiralty).
1948: *Nathamee* (Rangoon Port Commissioners).

1244   *Empire Goblin*
Launched: 19.1.1942.
Completed: 6.1942.
1948: *Bio Bio* (Angel, Gardella Ltd., Argentina).
1985: Name deleted from ship registers: existence of
vessel in doubt.

1249   *Empire Pat*
Launched: 30.5.1942.
Completed: 8.1942.
Naval work to:
1946: (Chartered to British Tanker Co. Ltd., Bandar
Mashur).
1949: *Himma* (Kuwait Oil Co. Ltd.).
1951: (J. Fenwick & Co. Ltd., Sydney, N.S.W.).
1972: (Pimco Shipping Co., Papua, N.G.).
1974: (W. J. Byers, Papua, N.G.).
1977: Scuttled off coast of New South Wales as an
artificial fish reef.

1250   *Empire Sam*
Launched: 1.6.1942.
Completed: 9.1942.
Naval work (Colombo) to:

1945: (Government of Hong Kong).
1965: *Yau Wing No. 23* (Yau Wing Co., Hong Kong).
1966: *Fedredge Sam* (Cheung Chau Shipping &
Trading Co., (Mollers Ltd., Hong Kong)).
9.1967: Scrapped Hong Kong.

1255   *Empire Ace*
Launched: 12.9.1942.
Completed: 12.1942.
Naval work to 1947, but:
15.3.1944: Sunk during an air attack on Malta.
10.5.1944: Salved and repaired.
1947: *Diligent* (Admiralty).
1961: *Empire Ace* (Secretary of State for Defence,
London).
3.1961: Loaned to U.S.N. in Scotland.
12.1964: Returned to Ministry of Defence, London.
11.11.1968: Aground in heavy seas near
Campbeltown, Mull of Kintyre, Scotland.
Abandoned.
6.1969: Refloated, but constructive total loss. Sold
for breaking up, and:
1971: Scrapped Campbeltown.

1256   *Empire Denis*
Launched: 26.9.1942.
Completed: 1.1943.
Naval work (Mediterranean) to:
1948: *Flying Meteor* (Clyde Shipping Co. Ltd.).
1962: *Royal Rose* (I. C. Guy Ltd., Cardiff).

1963: *Yewgarth* (R. & J. H. Rea Ltd.).
14.9.1965: Crushed against lock wall while assisting ore carrier *Aldersgate* (1960, 12,718 gt) into Cardiff docks. Holed, sinking, beached outside dock entrance. Submerged. Constructive total loss.
20.9.1965: Refloated; towed to shipbreaker's yard, and:
11.1965: Scrapped Newport, Mon.

1267   *Empire Sara*
Launched: 6.5.1943.
Completed: 8.1943.
1946: *Presto* (Ellerman Wilson Line Ltd.).
1968: (United Towing Co. Ltd.). Resold, and:
15.6.1968: Arrived Blyth for breaking up.

1268   *Empire Sybil*
Launched: 7.5.1943.
Completed: 8.1943.
1947: *Assistant* (Mersey Docks & Harbour Board).
1962: *Caswell* (Alexandra Towing Co. Ltd.).
25.3.1969: Arrived Passage West, Cork, for breaking up.

1273   *Empire Humphrey*
Launched: 2.9.1943.
Completed: 1.1944.
Naval work (India/Far East) to:
1947: *Suus* (Ned-Indonesia Steenkolen Handel Maats.).
1959: (Government of Indonesia).
1961: Renamed *Laut Sawu*.
1964: (Surabaya Port Authority).

1274   *Empire Vincent*
Launched: 3.9.1943.
Completed: 1.1944.
Naval work (India) to:
12.1945: Transferred to Government of Thailand.
Later renamed *Samaesan* (Royal Thai Navy; pennant YTB 7).
1982: Laid up in Chao Phraya river, Bangkok.
1983: Reported dismantled.

1279   *Empire Silas*
Launched: 13.12.1943.
Completed: 4.1944.
1946: *Fairplay Two* (Fairplay Towing & Shipping Co. Ltd., London).
22.6.1947: Capsized and sank in Flushing Roads, Holland, after sudden tightening of towing hawser when tug broadside to tide
(voyage: Cardiff/Antwerp – towing steamer *Kuurtanes* (1906, 3,088 gt)).
13.8.1947: Refloated, towed to Antwerp.
Constructive total loss; sold and repaired, and:

1948: *Ifrane* (Soc. Cherif de Rem. et Sauv., Casablanca).
1978: Scrapped Casablanca.

1280   *Empire Betsy*
Launched: 14.12.1943.
Completed: 5.1944.
1947: *Soegio* (Bataansche Petroleum Maats., Holland).
12.2.1948: Struck a mine, sank in Macassar Strait, Borneo, in position 2.36S 116.33E.

1285   *Empire Christopher*
Launched: 9.5.1944.
Completed: 8.1944.
Naval work (Burma/Singapore) to:
21.4.1946: Sunk by mine off Maungmagan Bay, Gulf of Martaban, Burma, 14.09N 98.03E
(voyage: Rangoon/Singapore).

1286   *Empire Josephine*
Launched: 10.5.1944.
Completed: 9.1944.
Naval work (Sydney/Hong Kong) to:
1945: (Admiralty).
1946: (Government of Hong Kong).
1965: *Yau Wing No. 25* (Yau Wing Co., Hong Kong).
1966: *Fedredge Josephine* (Cheung Chau Shipping & Trading Co. (Mollers Ltd., Hong Kong)).
9.1967: Scrapped Hong Kong.

1291   *Empire Jenny*
Launched: 4.10.1944.
Completed: 1.1945.
Naval work (Ceylon) to:
1947: *Aid* (Admiralty).
1960: (H. G. Pounds, Portsmouth).
1961: *Irving Teak* (J. D. Irving Ltd., Canada).
6.1977: Scrapped Canada.

1292   *Empire Barbara*
Launched: 5.10.1944.
Completed: 2.1945.
Naval work (Ceylon) to:
1947: *Adept* (Admiralty).
1957: *Aliya* (Government of Ceylon; allocated to Ceylon Navy).
1964: For disposal, but instead refitted for further naval service.
1978: Sold to Steel Corporation of Sri Lanka for breaking up.

1307   *Empire Helen*
Launched: 11.7.1945.
Completed: 6.1946.
1946: *Nereidia* (Overseas Towage & Salvage Co. Ltd.).

1951: *Abeille No. 7* ('Les Abeilles' Rem. et Sauv., Le Havre).
1965: *Sergio* (Rim. Sardi, Italy).
1984: Scrapped Porto Torres, Italy.

1308   (Launched as) *Empire Simon*
Launched: 11.7.1945.
Completed: 7.1946 as *Simonia* for Overseas Towage

& Salvage Co. Ltd.
1951: *Abeille No. 8* ('Les Abeilles' Rem. et Sauv., Le Havre).
1966: *Antonio D'Alesio* (G. D'Alesio, Italy).
1975: *Grecale* (Rim. Calabresi SpA., Italy).

When the war broke out in 1939 Cochranes were fitting out the twin screw salvage tug *Revue* (245 gt) for Beira Works Ltd., London; the motor tug *Silvertown* (83 gt) for Silvertown Services Ltd., and two trawlers. Another tug was completing for the Swedish flag from a pre-war order: her details were: 112 ft (oa), 105 ft bp × 26 ft breadth, with T3cyl engines. She became:

1206   *Empire Henchman*
Launched: 31.8.1939 as *Karl* for Goteborgs Bogserings & Bargnings Akt., Gothenburg.
Requisitioned by M.O.W.T.
Completed: 2.1940 as *Empire Henchman* (managed

by United Towing Co. Ltd., on behalf of the M.O.W.T.).
1946: (Reverted to original name and owners).
1963: *Capo Faro* (Soc. di Nav. Capieci, Italy).

United Towing Co. Ltd.

By the latter years of the 19th century tug owning had become a keen and competitive business. In the River Humber area there were numerous small companies and individual owners vieing for towage work, their tugs awaiting Hull-bound ships in the approaches and offering tows to homeward-bound sailing ships in windless waters.

An association of Hull tugowners began operating from 1 January 1914 and this was a step towards the formation of the United Towing Co. Ltd. in 1921, a grouping of several companies contributing thirty-nine tugs. They were City Steam Towing Company; T. Gray & Co. Ltd.; Humber Towing Co. Ltd.; Premier Tug Co. Ltd., T. C. Spink (tugowner) and the Troy Steam Tug Co. Ltd. The largest of the constituents was the sixteen-tug fleet of T. Gray & Co. Ltd., and United decided to adopt this company's nomenclature in naming all their tugs with the suffix 'man'.

By 1926 the United fleet consisted of twenty-four tugs, largest of which were the Cochrane-built *Seaman*, 369 gt, of 1924 and the *Nobleman* and *Prizeman*, each of 226 gt, by the same builders in 1925.

By the time war came, in September 1939, the company had built up considerable experience in long-distance towing work and within the fleet of twenty-two ships, possessed three of Britain's five ocean-going tugs, *Seaman* (above), *Superman* (1933, 359 gt) and the new *Englishman*, 487 gt of 1937. All were quickly requisitioned and served as naval rescue tugs. The *Englishman* was bombed and sunk on 21 January 1941. Three 1938-built, 230 gt, tugs – *Brahman*, *Krooman* and *Norman* – were also requisitioned, as was the 1905-built *Guardsman*, 102 gt, which fell foul of a mine off the North Foreland, Kent, and sank on 5 November 1940.

Many 'Empire' tugs were managed for the Ministry of War Transport during hostilities and there were two losses, *Empire Rupert* and *Empire Harry*. In 1946 there were still four under United Towing Company management. Eight 'Empire' tugs were acquired and took United Towing nomenclature. Also acquired were three 'TID'-type tugs in the early 1950s and in 1958 the company took over management of the Admiralty tug *Growler*, which was renamed *Welshman*.

From 1961 United Towing Co. Ltd. came under the control of B. A. Parkes, the Boston group operating over ninety trawlers under twenty-eight companies. By 1967 only four 'Empire' tugs remained in the fleet and these were gone within a year or so.

The largest tug ever built in British yards, *Englishman*, 5,000 hp, joined the fleet in 1965; then the New York-based Moran group's *Alice L. Moran* of 1966, 1,167 gt and of 12,000 hp was acquired in 1973 and renamed *Statesman*. But the largest was to be the *Lloydsman*, 2,040 gt, 16,000 hp, completed by Robb Caledon at Leith in September 1971. She served the company for only eight years or so, being disposed of in 1979 and becoming the Singapore-flag *Salviscount*.

In 1973 the company became fully independent as United Towing Ltd., with three management companies, United Towing (Ocean Tugs) Ltd., for sea-going vessels; Humber Tugs Ltd. (harbour and river movements) and, for salvage work, United Towing (Marine Services).

In 1977 United Towing Ltd., acquired the Kondyke Shipping Co. Ltd., and formed the North British Maritime Group as the controlling body. The largest-ever salvage tug came when the 20,000 hp *Salvageman* was accepted from the Chung Wah Shipyard, Hong Kong, in April 1980. The Klondyke Shipping Company was disposed of in 1985, being renamed North British Shipping Ltd. In 1987 the North British Maritime Group was taken over by the Australian company Howard Smith Ltd.

Built by Goole Shipbuilding & Repairing Co. Ltd.

263 gt, 115 ft (oa), 108 ft × 26 ft. Engines: T3cyl.

372   *Empire Bracken*
Launched: 24.9.1941.
Completed: 4.1942.
1946: *Flying Spitfire* (Clyde Shipping Co. Ltd.).
1963: *Tortoli* (Soc. Salvataggi Siciliana, Italy).
1968: Renamed *Lindoi*.
12.1983: Scrapped Cagliari.

373   *Empire Ivy*
Launched: 22.10.1941.
Completed: 7.1942.
Naval work to:

1946: *Flying Tempest* (Clyde Shipping Co. Ltd.).
1962: *Poetto* (Soc. Salvataggi Siciliana, Italy).
1968: Renamed *Montelungo*.
1982: Reported scrapped.

376   *Empire Pixie*
Launched: 27.8.1942.
Completed: 11.1942.
1946: *Flying Swordfish* (Clyde Shipping Co. Ltd.).
1957: *Fulgor* (D. Tripcovich & Co., Italy).
1978: Scrapped Italy.

Built by Clelands (Successors) Ltd., Willington Quay-on-Tyne

263 gt, 115 ft (oa), 108 ft × 26 ft. Engines: T3cyl.

64   *Empire Thistle*
Launched: 21.10.1941.
Completed: 2.1942.
1946: *Flying Hurricane* (Clyde Shipping Co. Ltd.).
1956: *Brynforth* (Britannia Steam Towing Co.).
1962: (Alexandra Towing Co. Ltd.).
8.1965: Scrapped Silloth.

65   *Empire Piper*
Launched: 28.5.1942.
Completed: 8.1942.
Naval work to:
1947: *Piper* (J. Cooper, Belfast).
1969: (R. & J. H. Rea Ltd.).
1970: (Cory Ship Towage Ltd.).
1971: *Sotirios* (A. P. Papayannis, Greece).
1984: Sold to shipbreakers at Rafina, but deal not completed; vessel remained in owner's fleet.
1985: Renamed *Lalrion*.
1986: Reported broken up.

Built by Hall, Russell & Co. Ltd., Aberdeen

263 gt, 114 ft (oa), 108 ft × 26 ft. Engines: T3cyl.

767   *Empire Cherub*
Launched: 16.3.1942.
Completed: 5.1942.

1946: *Tynesider* (Lawson-Batey Tugs Ltd.).
3.1970: Scrapped Blyth.

Hall, Russell & Co. Ltd.

In the mid–1860s the two sons of Alexander Hall, James and William, joined with Glasgow engineer, Thomas Russell, in acquiring the buildings and site of the Aberdeen Ironworks. So began the marine engineering works of Hall, Russell & Company. Although Alexander Hall's yard was still turning out their famous clipper ships, the new company looked towards the time which, sooner or later, would see the demise of the sailing ship and after three years of operating as marine engine builders, constructed their first ship, the 913-ton *Kwang Tung*, a Chinese river steamer, the precursor of twenty similar orders.

In 1869 the company turned out the iron barque *Umvoti* for John T. Rennie & Co.'s African trade and when that company introduced its steam services to Natal, built the 1,538-ton *Dabulamanzi* in 1882, going on to build fourteen other steamers for Rennie, the last, *Intaba*, in 1910.

Trawlers, tugs and coasters were added to the builder's yard list and they constructed some specialised craft in the early 1900s. In 1904, the 280 gt *Freya*, a steel steam trawler, was built for the Fishing Board of Scotland and in July 1911 the steel steam ketch *Watchful*, 378 gt, was completed for the Ministry of Finance and Customs of the Newfoundland Government. On 29 August 1913, the 415-ton, 110 ft dockyard tanker, *Zealous*, was launched. When war ended in 1918 she was renamed *Zest*, became *Zeal* in 1944 and eventually arrived at Rosyth for breaking up on 7 February 1949.

Between the wars trawlers continued to be built, some for Spanish owners in Atlantic fishing. In 1933 the *Acklam Cross* (150 gt) was completed for Robinson & Crosthwaite (Tees Towing Co. Ltd.), Middlesborough, the first diesel-electric-propelled ship-handling tug in Europe. Her diesels were connected to an electric motor, which drove the screw and which also enabled the tug master to operate the engines by remote control.

Constructions during World War II – Yard Nos. 750 to 789 – by Hall, Russell & Company, included only one 'Empire' tug and eight vessels to private account, the main output being in smaller-type naval ships. In 1942 the share capital of the company was acquired by the Burntisland Shipbuilding Co. Ltd. When war ended the company had four berths, with a 400-ft capacity and a slipway for a 160-ft vessel.

SHIPS BUILT UNDER PRIVATE CONTRACT OR LICENCE

750   *Auchmacoy* 255 gt, 132.3 ft (oa),
114.6 ft × 23 ft. Engines: Oil (aft).
Launched: 12.10.1939.
Completed: 11.1939 for Mitchell & Rae Ltd., Newburgh.
1941: (West African Lighterage & Transport Co. Ltd. (Elder, Dempster & Co. Ltd.)).
26.10.1950: Towed to sea and sunk (as useless) off Lagos.

751   *Bois Rose* 1,374 gt, 232.6 ft (oa),
218.3 ft × 35.6 ft. Engines: C4cyl. A steam trawler.
Launched: 12.12.1939.
Completed: 3.1940 for Soc. Anon. 'Les Pecheries de Fecamp', France.
3.1943: Reported lost.

773   *Edenwood* 1,874 gt, 267.8 ft (oa),
256.3 ft × 39.1 ft. Engines: Oil.
Launched: 15.7.1943.
Completed: 10.1943 for Joseph Constantine SS Line Ltd.
1947: (Whimster & Co. Ltd.).
1949: (Constantine Line Ltd.).
1953: Shortened to 258.9 ft (oa) (1,589 gt).
1960: *Paralos* (Piraeus Shipping Co. Ltd., Greece).
1961: (G. & N. Angelakis & others, Greece).
1965: *Ergina Ventouri* (C. G. Ventouris, Greece).
1972: *Apostolos B* (Kimolos Shipping Co., Cyprus).
1974: (Ventouris Shipping Co., Cyprus).
1975: *Mersini* (Mastrogeorgis Shipping Co., Cyprus).
28.8.1980: Arrived Perama for breaking up.

776   *Avonwood* 1,874 gt. Details as Yard No. 773.
Launched: 22.2.1944.
Completed: 5.1944 for Joseph Constantine SS Line Ltd.
1947: (Whimster & Co. Ltd.).

1949: (Constantine Line Ltd.).
1953: Shortened to 258.9 ft (oa) (1,596 gt).
1960: *Yewpark* (J. Stewart & Co. Shipping Ltd., Glasgow).
1966: *Filia* (Friendship Corp. S.A. (Eptanisiaki Shipping Co., Greece)).
1973: Renamed *Eleni M* (Cyprus flag).
23.8.1973: Aground off Libyan coast, 32.00N 24.40E. Flooded and abandoned. Total loss (voyage: Algiers/Alexandria – scrap iron).

781   *Corfen* 1,867 gt, 264.9 ft (oa), 257 ft × 39.5 ft. Engines: T3cyl.
Launched: 1.9.1944.
Completed: 11.1944 for Cory Colliers Ltd. (Wm. Cory & Sons Ltd.).
1949: (Wm. Cory & Sons Ltd.).
1965: (Cory Maritime Ltd.).
5.1965: Scrapped Antwerp.

785   *Firebeam* 1,554 gt, 256.6 ft (oa), 247 ft × 39.6 ft. Engines: T3cyl.
Launched: 16.3.1945.
Completed: 5.1945 for Gas, Light & Coke Co. Ltd.
1949: (North Thames Gas Board).
11.1962: (Metaalhandel en Sloopswerken NV., Rotterdam).
1962: Resold (Stenstore A/B, Gothenburg).
2.1963: (Portland Cement A/S, Oslo). Vessel converted to a cement storage barge.

788   *Sir Joseph Swan* 1,554 gt. Details as Yard No. 785.
Launched: 6.9.1945.
Completed: 11.1945 for London Power Co. Ltd.
1948: (British Electricity Authority).
1954: (Central Electricity Generating Board).
4.1967: Scrapped Bremen.

789   *Lestris* 2,025 gt, 308 ft (oa), 296 ft × 43.2 ft.
Engines: T3cyl.
Launched: 5.2.1946.
Completed: 5.1946 for British & Continental SS Co.
Ltd.
1955: *Belgion* (Hellenic Lines Ltd. (P. G.
Callimanopulos, Greece)).

9.4.1968: Aground off Tripoli, Libya, when leaving
harbour (voyage: Antwerp/Lattakia – general).
10.4.1968: Refloated: extensive bottom damage.
Constructive total loss. Sold, and:
7.9.1968: Arrived Split, in tow, for breaking up.

Built by J. Crown & Sons Ltd., Sunderland

268 gt, 115 ft (oa), 108 ft × 26 ft. Engines: T3cyl.

201   *Empire Ash*
Launched: 13.8.1941.
Completed: 10.1941.
1946: *Flying Fulmar* (Clyde Shipping Co. Ltd.).
1956: *Sea Alarm* (C. J. King & Sons Ltd., Bristol).
1973: Sold for scrapping at Briton Ferry. Resold to
the Welsh Industrial and Maritime Museum, Cardiff.
Restored, and:
1978: An exhibit at the Museum.

203   *Empire Wold*
Launched: 24.3.1942.
Completed: 6.1942.
10.11.1944: Sailed from Reykjavik, Iceland, to assist
the Baltic Trading Co.'s *Shirvan* (1925, 6,017 gt) in
U.K.–Reykjavik convoy UR 142.
13.11.1944: The *Empire Wold*, *Shirvan* (above) and the
Iceland SS Co.'s *Godafoss* (1921, 1,542 gt) all sunk by
torpedoes from the submarine *U. 300* in close
proximity to each other, in position 64.08N 22.38W.

Note: Official records list the *Empire Wold* as sunk by
submarine, but the tug is not claimed by German records as
a U-boat success and it is now believed that the tug was lost
when overwhelmed by the heavy weather prevailing at the
time.

206   *Empire Frank*
Launched: 2.9.1942.
Completed: 11.1942.
1946: *Brigadier* (Steel & Bennie Ltd.).
21.2.1960: Aground on rocks at Horse Island, off
Ardrossan. Holed and flooded. Salvage attempts
abandoned. Total loss.

207   *Empire Demon*
Launched: 31.12.1942.
Completed: 3.1943.
Naval work to:
1943: (Admiralty).
1945: (Ministry of Transport).
1949: (Admiralty).
1962: (Chartered to U.S. Navy; River Clyde area).
1964: Transferred to H.M.S. *Sea Eagle*, a training
school at Londonderry, N. Ireland. Later chartered
to local Harbour Commissioners.
26.3.1965: Damaged in collision with mv *Norse Lion*
(1953, 12,305 gt) in tow. Constructive total loss.
1.1966: Sold to Haulbowline Industries, Passage
West, Cork, for scrapping.
15.2.1966: While on voyage to shipbreakers, lost tow
(*Dredger No. 2* (1930, 213 gt) also bound for the
'breakers) in heavy weather off Wexford, Eire. Tug
put in to Dublin for stores and water: crew deserted.
Vessel resold to Dublin shipbreakers, and:
3.1966: Scrapped Dublin.

Built by Henry Scarr Ltd., Hessle

244 gt, 113 ft (oa), 107 ft × 27 ft. Engines: T3cyl (1,000 ihp).

418 *Empire Birch*
Launched: 9.8.1941.
Completed: 12.1941.
10.8.1942: Damaged by mine 150 miles north of
Lourenço Marques, 24.45S 34.47E. Beached and
abandoned. Slid off and sank in deep water. Total loss
(voyage: Clyde/Beira).

419 *Empire Linden*
Launched: 24.9.1941.
Completed: 2.1942.
Naval work (East Africa) to:
1944: Loaned to Kenya & Uganda Railways &
Harbours Admin., Mombasa.
1945: Chartered to British Petroleum Co. Ltd.,
Bandar Mashur.
1948: (Tanganyika Railways & Harbours Admin.,
Dar es Salaam).
1956: *Linden* (East African Railways & Harbours
Admin., Dar es Salaam).
1974: (Marino Engineering Works, Kenya).
9.1983: Sold for scrapping at Mombasa.

420 *Empire Teak*
Launched: 21.12.1941.
Completed: 4.1942.
Naval work to:
1950: *Brambles* (Alexandra Towing Co. Ltd.).
1969: (Northern Slipway Ltd., Dublin).
10.1971: Scrapped Briton Ferry.

421 *Empire Race*
Launched: 21.11.1941.
Completed: 6.1942.
Naval work to:
1962: *Capo d'Orlando* (Soc. di Nav. Capieci, Italy).

422 *Empire Sprite*
Launched: 17.2.1942.
Completed: 6.1942.
1946: *Inflexible* (Government of France).
1951: *Abeille No. 23* ('Les Abeilles' Rem. et Sauv., Le
Havre).
1961: *Capo Milazzo* (Soc. di Nav. Capieci, Italy).
1979: Reported scrapped at Augusta.

423 *Empire Titan*
Launched: 29.6.1942.
Completed: 10.1942.
1947: *Titan* (Gold Coast Government Railway).

1957: *Lenadee* (H. P. Lenaghan & Sons Ltd., Belfast).
1959: *Pioniere* (C. Picciotto, Italy).
30.11.1966: Capsized and sank at Messina while
assisting the liner *Guglielmo Marconi* (1963, 27,905 gt)
to leave berth.
22.1.1967: Refloated; repaired and re-entered owner's
service.

424 *Empire Oberon*
Launched: 24.11.1942.
Completed: 1.1943.
Naval work (Hong Kong) to:
1945: (Rangoon Port Authority).
1947: (Calcutta Port Authority).
7.9.1959: Sank near Akra, nine miles from Calcutta,
when barge lashed alongside filled and sank. Total
loss. Wreck partially blocked channel, and 10.1959:
Dispersed by explosives.

430 *Empire Mascot*
Launched: 8.3.1943.
Completed: 5.1943.
Naval work to:
1947: *Metinda IV* (Metal Industries Ltd.).
1948: *Flying Kestrel* (Alexandra Towing Co. Ltd.).
3.1969: Scrapped Passage West, Cork.

431 *Empire Maisie*
Launched: 23.5.1943.
Completed: 7.1943.
1947: *Flying Typhoon* (Clyde Shipping Co. Ltd.).
1961: *Dunhawk* (Newport Screw Towing Co. Ltd.).
1969: Scrapped Newport, Mon.

432 *Empire Charles*
Launched: 1.11.1943.
Completed: 1.1944.
Naval work to:
1947: *Fortitude* (Admiralty).
1962: (D. Arnold, Ashford, Middlesex).
4.1964: Towed by tug *Acklam Cross* (1933, 150 gt)
from London to Ravenna, Italy, for scrapping;
Resold, and:
1965: *Fortitudo* (Soc. Esercizio Rem. Salvataggi,
Italy).
1987: Name deleted from ship registers; existence of
vessel in doubt.

Note: Subsequent to this voyage to the Mediterranean the
towing tug was herself delivered to new owners – the
Mediterranean Towing & Salvage Co., of Malta.

433   *Empire Walter*
Launched: 30.12.1943.
Completed: 3.1944.
1946: *Sea Queen* (C. J. King & Sons Ltd., Bristol).
6.1974: Scrapped Gijon.

461   *Empire Elinor*
Launched: 4.10.1944.
Completed: 11.1944.
1946: *Vigoureaux* (Government of France).
1951: *Abeille No. 24* ('Les Abeilles' Cie. de Rem. et Sauv., Le Havre).
1964: *Labor* (Rim. Laziali SpA., Italy).
10.1985: Scrapped Naples.

463   *Empire Becky*
Launched: 2.12.1944.
Completed: 2.1945.
1947: *Forager* (Steel & Bennie Ltd.).
23.5.1962:   Capsized and sank in River Clyde while towing *Hororata* (1942, 12,090 gt) to Plantation Quay, Glasgow.
5.6.1962: Refloated: docked for inspection; Sold.
1962: *Mastino* (Soc. Rim. Napoletani, Italy).
3.1984: Scrapped Naples.

Built by Ferguson Bros. Ltd., Port Glasgow

254 gt, 116 ft (oa), 107 ft × 27 ft. Engines: T3cyl.

359   *Empire Lawn*
Launched: 1.4.1942.
Completed: 5.1942.
Naval work to:
1947: *Masterful* (Admiralty).
1958: *Sanantonio Primo* (Marittime Augustea SpA., Italy).
1968: (Soc. Rim. Napoletani, Italy).
3.1981: Scrapped Naples.

360   *Empire Mead*
Launched: 6.4.1942.

Completed: 6.1942.
Naval work (Singapore) to:
1948: *Bodeker* (Ned-Indonesia Steenkolen Handel Maats.).
1959: (Government of Indonesia).
1961: *Laut Belawan* (Tanjung Priok Port Authority, Indonesia).

361   *Empire Warlock*
Launched: 23.7.1942.
Completed: 9.1942.
1947: *Sakr* (Government of Egypt – Port & Lighthouse Administration).

Built by J. S. Watson Ltd., Gainsborough

242 gt, 113 ft (oa), 107 ft × 27 ft. Engines: T3cyl (1,000 ihp).

1528   *Empire Meadow*
Launched: 4.6.1942.
Completed: 8.1942.
1946: *Meadow* (J. Cooper, Belfast).
1963: (New (oil) engine).
1969: (R. & J. H. Rea Ltd.).
1970: (Cory Ship Towage Ltd.).
1973: *Hector* (Maritime Commercial Enterprises, Greece).
1978: (H. N. Spiliopoulos, Greece).
12.1978: Scrapped Perama, Greece.

1533   *Empire Ben*
Launched: 22.12.1942.
Completed: 3.1943.
Naval work to:
1948: *E. Nicholson* (Leith Salvage & Towage Co. Ltd.).
1951: *Victor* (Melbourne Harbour Trust Commissioners).
1957: (Geelong Harbour Trust Commissioners).
1968: (R. J. Phersson, Melbourne).
1970: (J. H. Nicholls, Melbourne).

1978: (Australian Oil Burners Pty. Ltd.).
1979: (A. Sullivan, Warragul).
1985: Laid up: under preservation at Geelong.

1534 *Empire Mustang*
Launched: 2.6.1943.
Completed: 8.1943.
1947: *Dundas Cross* (Tees Towing Co. Ltd.).
1958: *Duneagle* (Newport Screw Towing Co. Ltd.).
1965: *Nisos Syros* (Tsavliris Ltd., Greece).
1975: (Maritime Commercial Enterprises, Greece).
1976: Reported scrapped Greece.

1545 *Empire Paul*
Launched: 7.7.1944.
Completed: 9.1944.
1946: *Queensgarth* (R. & J. H. Rea Ltd.).
1949: *Beamish* (France, Fenwick Tyne & Wear Co. Ltd.).
1964: (New (oil) engine).
6.1970: *Rex Mellenger* (R. Mellenger, St. John, N.B.).
11.1970: *Beamish* (Industrial Insulators Ltd., Canada).

1973: *Thunder Cape* (Western Engineering Service Ltd., Canada).
1986: (Great Lakes Marine Contracting Co., Canada).

Note: The above vessel (as *Beamish*) was chosen to represent all the British tug fleets at the Coronation Review at Spithead, in 1953.

1546 *Empire Alfred*
Launched: 5.9.1944.
Completed: 10.1944.
1946: *Muscle* (Government of France).
1951: *Abeille No. 22* ('Les Abeilles' Cie. de Rem. Sauv., Le Havre).
6.1969: Scrapped Le Havre.

1556 *Empire Lucy*
Launched: 6.3.1946.
Completed: 6.1946.
Naval work to 1958.
1962: *Ognina* (Impresa Marittima Augustea, Italy).
1972: Reported transferred to Italian Navy.

'Modified-Warrior' type

As the war progressed more tugs were required for West African and North African ports of the Mediterranean. Although the 'Warrior'-type possessed a large coal bunker capacity, oil was undoubtedly the logical fuel to be used in those areas for ease of supply, yet in such quantity would cause instability on deep-sea voyages. Moreover, extra space for additional crew would be required. So it was that another design was chosen, the prototype being a Scott-built tug, *Roach* (Yard No. 330), completed at Bowling in August 1935 for the Government of Palestine. The class was termed 'Modified-Warrior'-type and measurements were 112.7 ft (oa), 105.7 ft × 30 ft breadth and 258 gross tons. Triple expansion engines developed 1,075 ihp to give 12 knots. Scott's began building this type in 1942 and construction of the tugs continued to the end of the war, when two more, already laid down, were cancelled and completed for private buyers.

Built by Scott & Sons, Bowling

366 *Empire Minnow*
Launched: 24.9.1942.
Completed: 4.1943.
Naval work (Mediterranean) to:
1948: *Thika* (British India SN Co. Ltd.).
1951: *Clyneforth* (Britannia Steam Towing Co. Ltd.).
1962: (Alexandra Towing Co. Ltd.).
1966: *Ena* (J. S. Latsis, Greece).
9.1969: Scrapped Piraeus.

367 *Empire Titania*
Launched: 21.12.1942.
Completed: 7.1943.
Naval work to:
1947: *Vagrant* (Admiralty).
1968: *Zancle* (C. Picciotto fu Gillseppe, Italy).
12.1987: Reported scrapped Spezia.

368   *Empire Griffin*
Launched: 22.4.1943.
Completed: 6.1943.
Naval work to:
1947: *Fortunate* (Condor Ltd., Glasgow).
1961: (Cory Hermanos S.A., Tenerife).
1974: Reported scrapped.

371   *Empire Doris*
Launched: 14.3.1944.
Completed: 4.1944.
Naval work (Persian Gulf) to:
1945: (Chartered to British Tanker Co. Ltd.).
1948: *Bahramand* (Petroleum SS Co. Ltd., London).
1958: (B.P. Tanker Co. Ltd.).
1968: *Tahamtan* (A. Shafei, Iran).

373   *Empire Madge*
Launched: 30.4.1945.
Completed: 6.1945.
Naval work (India/Singapore) to:
1947: *Weasel* (Admiralty).
11.1968: Scrapped Singapore.

374   *Empire Ruth*
Launched: 18.12.1944.
Completed: 2.1945.
Naval work (Ceylon) to:
1948: *Hadhir* (Government of Iraq).
1966: *Al Zab* (Iraqui Ports Administration).

375   *Empire Nan*
Launched: 26.9.1945.
Completed: 12.1945.
Offered for sale after completion, and:
1946: *Metinda II* (Metal Industries Ltd.).
1950: *Banbury Cross* (Tees Towing Co. Ltd.).
1955: *Wilga* (Adelaide SS Co., Fremantle).
1973: (Prioper Shipping Co., Fremantle).
1975: (Straits Engineers Ltd., Singapore).
1975: (Rebuilt and fitted with oil engine).
1976: (World Dredging Ltd., Panama).

377   (Laid down as) *Empire Doreen*
Launched: 1.5.1946 as *Nirumand* (307 gt).
Completed: 8.1946 for Petroleum SS Co. Ltd.,
London.
1955: *B.P. Defender* (British Tanker Co. Ltd.).
1956: Renamed *Nirumand*.
1958: (B.P. Tanker Co. Ltd.).
1971: *Niru* (Gulf Shipping Co. S.A., Iran).
Later reported lying sunk one mile north of Abadan.

378   (Laid down as) *Empire Terence*
Launched: 16.9.1946 as *Tanumand* (307 gt).
Completed: 11.1946 for Petroleum SS Co. Ltd.,
London
1958: (B.P. Tanker Co. Ltd.).
1971: (M. R. Samadpour, Iran).
1973: *Famshek* (Marine Service Co., Iran).

The *Wilga*, formerly *Empire Nan* of the 'Modified Warrior'-type, at Singapore in March 1981, after conversion to a motor tug, with funnel removed and lifeboats replaced. (Scott & Sons., Yard No. 375.)

Built by Goole Shipbuilding & Repairing Co. Ltd.

261 gt, 114 ft (oa), 106 ft × 30 ft. Engines: T3cyl.

397 *Empire Samson*
Launched: 8.4.1943.
Completed: 6.1943.
Naval work (Ceylon/India) to:
1948: *Sakti* (Government of India: Madras Port Authority).

398 *Empire Jester*
Launched: 6.5.1943.
Completed: 7.1943.
1946: *Napia* (Wm. Watkins Ltd.).
1971: *Tolmiros* (J. G. Efthinou, Greece).
1973: (L. G. Matsas, Greece).
2.1986: Scrapped Perama.

401 *Empire Sophy*
Launched: 13.12.1943.
Completed: 6.1944.
Naval work (Ceylon) to:
1947: *Behest* (Admiralty).
1957: (Colombo Port Authority).
Later reported lying sunk in Colombo Harbour.

402 *Empire Katy*
Launched: 18.12.1944.
Completed: 6.1945.
Naval work (India/Aden) to:
1948: *Sir Bernard Reilly* (Aden Port Trust).
1963: *Mar Siculo* (Soc. di Nav. Rim. Capiechi, Italy).
1979: Reported scrapped Milazzo.

Ship Towage (London) Ltd.

In January 1950 three of London's oldest tug firms combined their interests to form Ship Towage (London) Ltd., to manage the combined fleets of William Watkins Ltd. and Elliott Steam Tug Co. Ltd., also acquiring the newly-formed Gamecock Tugs Ltd. from the Ocean Salvage & Towage Co. Ltd.

Oldest of the group was William Watkins Ltd., indeed, the oldest private tug owner in the world, the business of towing being started in 1833 when John Roger Watkins acquired the wooden paddler *Monarch*, 64 ft 10 in long, 13 ft 10 in in breadth and driven by a 20 hp steam engine. William Turner sketched her as helping the old wooden-wall battleship *Temeraire* to Beatson's yard at Rotherhithe for breaking up and there followed his famous painting of 1839, 'The Fighting Temeraire'.

The Watkins business developed with two wooden paddle tugs of 150 gt in 1853–1854, *Victoria* and *Britannia*, whose work lay in seeking out the towing of sailermen to and from the Nore, especially those inward bound in the urgency of London's markets.

Another paddle tug, *Anglia*, was built in 1866 which, because of one funnel forward and two abreast further aft, was known as 'Three Finger Jack'. She was 140 ft in length, 22 ft breadth and at 275 gt was the largest of London's tugs.

The company steadily grew and by 1939 owned seventeen steam tugs. Three were lost during hostilities, the first, *Napia*, sunk by mine off Ramsgate on 20 December 1939 whilst on Naval examination service. She had only been hired two weeks previously. The *Muria* was also lost by mine on 8 November 1940 off the North Foreland. She was also on naval service. The third was the *Persia*, which caught fire when assisting H. E. Moss & Co.'s tanker *Lunula*, 6,363 gt, which touched off a mine at Thames Haven on 9 April 1941.

When war ended in 1945 Watkins owned thirteen tugs and another seven 'Empire' Ministry of War Transport tugs were under their management. Four 'Empire' tugs were acquired to rebuild the Watkins fleet and at the time the companies combined they owned thirteen, including the iron-built *Hibernia*, constructed in Holland in 1884 and the *Java* of 1905 which saw service in two world wars. The *Java* is reputed to have been the first tug from Britain in the Dunkirk evacuation and carried a 'Dunkirk' plaque which was lodged at the St. Andrews Waterside parish church, Gravesend, when the tug was broken up in 1965.

Another constituent was the Elliott Steam Tug Company Ltd., started in the 1860s by T. W. Elliott. Dick & Page Tugs took over in 1881 and the Elliott Company came about in 1897. In the 1920s there were eight tugs in the fleet; in 1946 three, *Challenge* and *Contest*, 212 gt sisterships built by A. Hall & Company, Aberdeen, in the early 1930s and the much older *Security*, built by J. P. Rennoldson & Sons, South Shields, in 1904 as *Kingfisher*. Purchased by the Admiralty in 1906 and renamed *Security* in 1914, she became an Elliott tug in 1927. Unfortunately, she capsized and sank about eight miles off Anvil Point Light on 8 December 1946 after breaking a tow in heavy weather on a voyage from Falmouth to the Tyne. This left the two sistertugs which joined with Watkins in Ship Towage (London) Ltd.

The third company in the combine was purchased. Formation of the Gamecock Towing Company was made in 1880 by a number of River pilots and, after becoming a limited company in 1927, was later acquired by L.H.G. Walford, of London. As war ended, the company owned five tugs. After disposal of the *New Stormcock* of 1921, there remained *Atlantic Cock* and *Ocean Cock* of 1932, *Crested Cock* of 1935 and *Watercock* of 1923, whose blue funnels had so long been a feature of the Thames. In 1947 these tugs were placed under the Ocean Salvage & Towage Co. Ltd. (L.H.G. Walford) and in 1950 became Gamecock Tugs Ltd.

In 1969 Gaselee & Son, which began operations nearly a century before, also joined Ship Towage Ltd. Also in 1969, W.H.J. Alexander Ltd., founder of Sun Tugs in 1883, came into the picture, merging with Ship Towage and forming London Tugs Ltd., only itself to be acquired in January 1975 by the Alexandra Towing Co. Ltd., which made the Liverpool company the largest tug operator in the United Kingdom.

Built by Cook, Welton & Gemmell Ltd., Beverley

259 gt, 114 ft (oa), 106 ft × 30 ft. Engines: T3cyl.

753 *Empire Peggy*
Launched: 5.1945.
Completed: 7.1945.
Naval work (India/Singapore) to:
1946: (French Navy: Indo-China area).
1949: *Coringa* (Williams & Co. Pty. Ltd., Brisbane).
1974: *Empire Peggy* (Northern Salvage Ltd., Australia).
6.1977: Scrapped Cairns.

754 *Empire Pam*
Launched: 24.8.1945.
Completed: 11.1945.
1946: *El Hank* (Soc. Rem. et D'Assistance, Casablanca).
1947: *El Baraka* (Soc. Cher. de Rem. D'Assistance, Casablanca).

760 *Empire Dorothy*
Launched: 1.8.1945.
Completed: 10.1945.
Naval work (Singapore/Japan) to:
1949: (Malaya Railways).
1958: *Dorothy* (Government of Malaya: Port Swettenham Port Authority).

1970: (Straits Engineers Ltd., Singapore).
1973: (New (oil) engine and rebuilt).
1975: *Straits Winner* (World Dredging Ltd., Panama).

1981: Sold to shipbreakers, and:
2.1983: Scrapped Jurong, Singapore.

Built by J. Crown & Sons Ltd., Sunderland

257 gt, 114 ft (oa), 106 ft × 30 ft. Engines: T3cyl.

210   *Empire Dolly*
Launched: 5.7.1943.
Completed: 9.1943.
1953: *Thunderer* (Steel & Bennie Ltd., Glasgow).
1958: *Ocean Osprey* (Saint John Tug Boat Co. Ltd., Bermuda).

211   *Empire Belle*
Launched: 31.10.1943.
Completed: 2.1944.
Naval work (India/Singapore) to:
1947: *Elf* (Admiralty).
1960: *Mare Jonio* (Imprese Maritíme Augustea, Italy).
1972: Reported transferred to Italian Navy.

215   *Empire Nicholas*
Launched: 8.5.1944.
Completed: 6.1944.
Naval work (Japan/East Indies) to:
1947: *Asta* (Ned-Indonesie Steenkolen Handel Maats.).
1957: (Government of Indonesia).
1961: *Laut Arafura* (Tanjung Priok Port Authority, Indonesia).

218   *Empire Phyllis*
Launched: 2.12.1944.
Completed: 1.1945.
Naval work (Ceylon/India) to:
1947: *Hayat* (Kuwait Oil Co. Ltd.).
1961: *Brucoli* (Imprese Maritíme Augustea, Italy).
1982: Transferred to Italian Navy, at Messina: not put into service and later dismantled.

219   *Empire Sally*
Launched: 18.9.1945.
Completed: 11.1945.
1947: *Daneshmand* (Petroleum SS Co. Ltd., London).
1958: (B.P. Tanker Co. Ltd.).
1972: *Danesh* (Gulf Shipping Co., Iran).
20.1.1975: Sank in Khor Musa Channel, Khorramshahr, after collision between *Arya Tab* (1971, 12,015 gt) and the barge *Gulf 107* (in tow of *Danesh*). Constructive total loss. Wreck later removed.

'Stella' type

This group consisted of eight tugs of a special design to accommodate eight engine sets from North America which had been found in excess of requirements. The tugs were 123 ft (oa), 116 ft × 28 ft breadth, giving a tonnage of 292 gross and were for long-haul work, the design including a bunkering capacity for 125 tons of fuel oil. The triple expansion machinery sets had cylinders of 12, 20 and 33 ins., with a 24 in. stroke, and developed 500 ihp to give 10 knots. They were from the Franklin Machine & Foundry Co., Providence, Rhode Island, U.S.A. The engines, however, did give some mechanical problems and a number of the tugs were soon re-engined.

Built by Cochrane & Sons Ltd., Selby

1297   *Empire Flora*
Launched: 16.3.1945.
Completed: 8.1945.
1948: *Topmast 14* (Risdon Beazley Ltd.).
1949: *Taurus* (Panfido Rim., Italy).
8.1984: Scrapped Porto Nogaro.

1298   *Empire Stella*
Launched: 16.3.1945.
Completed: 8.1945.
1.1.1946: Boiler explosion; laid up: later sold; and:
1946: *Serviceman* (new T3cyl engine ex *Empire Keith*),
(United Towing Co. Ltd.).
1961: (New (oil) engine).
1969: *Poetto* (Rim. Sardi, Italy).

1299   *Empire Sheila*
Launched: 30.3.1945.
Completed: 9.1945.
1949: *Sheilia* (Overseas Towage & Salvage Ltd.).
1950: *Sidi Belyout* (Soc. Cher. de Rem. d'Assistance, Casablanca).
1956: (New (oil) engine).
1963: *Tirso* (Rim. Sardi, Italy).
1978: (New (oil) engine).

1300   *Empire Clara*
Launched: 28.4.1945.
Completed: 10.1945.
1947: *Airman* (United Towing Co. Ltd.).
1949: (New T3cyl. engine).
11.1967: Scrapped Blyth.

1301   *Empire Martha*
Launched: 28.4.1945.
Completed: 10.1945.
1947: *Foremost 106* (James Contracting & Shipping Co. Ltd.).
1949: *Georges Letzer* (Union de Rem. et Sauv., Antwerp).
1964: (New (oil) engine, and rebuilt).

1302   *Empire Vera*
Launched: 14.5.1945.
Completed: 12.1945.
1947: *Rifleman* (United Towing Co. Ltd.).
1949: (New T3cyl. engine).
11.1967: Scrapped Blyth.

1303   *Empire Greta*
Launched: 12.6.1945.
Completed: 2.1946.
1947: *Foremost 105* (James Contracting & Shipping Co. Ltd.).
1949: *Francis Hallinan* (Cork Harbour Commissioners).

In November 1968 the *Francis Hallinan* was sold to a private owner and in the December left Cork for Penzance. She became disabled when water entered her boiler room and she was towed to her destination by the Wijsmuller tug *Groningen* (1963, 598 gt), of Ymuiden. The salved vessel then moved to Falmouth and there was arrested by the Admiralty Marshal on behalf of the owners of the salvage tug.

During a gale in February 1969 the *Francis Hallinan* broke loose from her buoy in Falmouth's Inner Harbour and drifted until remoored in a more sheltered spot. Later, in 1971, the vessel was acquired by the Sapsin Property Company, in Devon. Sold, she was towed from Falmouth and arrived at Bilbao on 12 March 1973 for breaking up.

1304   *Empire Nina*
Launched: 12.6.1945.
Completed: 2.1946.
1947: *Guardsman* (United Towing Co. Ltd.).
1947: (New T3cyl engine, ex *Empire George*).
11.1967: Scrapped Blyth.

'Modified-Stella' type

Orders for a second group of 'Stella'-type tugs were placed with various shipbuilders just prior to the end of hostilities. They were ordered for work in the Far East but in the event did not reach the area and, in fact, some contracts were cancelled and the vessels sold to commercial buyers. The

T3cyl. machinery for the tugs built was produced by local engineers situated near to the shipbuilders, but the machinery cylinders were 15 in, 25 in and 42 in, with a 27 in stroke, which gave 800 ihp, and some modifications had to be made to the engines, boiler and auxiliary seatings to suit the altered machinery. Hull measurements of the tugs were the same as the 'Stella'-type.

Built by Blyth Dry Docks & Shipbuilding Co. Ltd.

315   *Empire Rosa*
Launched: 6.12.1945.
Completed: 4.1946.
Naval work to:
1949: (Admiralty).
Later used as target tug for R.A.F. practice bombing runs, but:

3.12.1977: Broke from moorings, drifted ashore inLuce Bay, Drummore, Galloway, in a storm. Salved, but constructive total loss. Scrapped at Troon.

316   *Empire Hilda*
Launched: 19.12.1945.
Completed: 5.1946.
1949: *Fishershill* (J. Fisher & Sons Ltd., Barrow).
6.1968: Scrapped Barrow.

Built by George Brown & Co. (Marine) Ltd., Greenock

236   *Empire Lola*
Launched: 5.3.1946.
Completed: 4.1946.
Naval work (Bermuda) to:

1947: *Justice* (Admiralty).
1951: (Government of Bermuda).
21.7.1967: Sunk as a gunnery target off Bermuda, by H.M.S. *Leander*.

Built by Cochrane & Sons Ltd., Selby

1314   (Laid down as) *Empire Doreen*
Launched: 4.2.1946 as *Empire Hedda*.
Completed: 9.1946 as *Atlas* (327 gt) for Bergnings och Dykari A/B Neptun, Sweden.
1965: *Maroso* (Rim. Sardi, Italy).
1986: Scrapped Italy.

1315   *Empire Juna*
Launched: 8.2.1946.
Completed: 8.1946.
1947: *Balbus* (Government of Nigeria; Ports Authority).
1967: *Nisos Poros* (Tsavliris Salvage & Towage Ltd., Greece).
12.1970: Scrapped Greece.

Built by Ferguson Bros. Ltd., Port Glasgow

377   *Empire Frieda*
Launched: 22.10.1945.
Completed: 1.1946.
Naval work to:
1947: *Oriana* (Admiralty).

19.1.1948: Struck mine, sank off Clacton, Essex, while towing motor minesweeper *D. 366* from Chatham to Brightlingsea. Total loss.

Note: The minesweeper was picked up by the tug *Empire Lucy* and delivered to destination.

378   *Empire Rita*
Launched: 15.12.1945.
Completed: 5.1946.
Naval work to:

1946: (Admiralty).
1959: Renamed *Frisky*.
1970: *Creo* (S. O. Mar., Malta).
3.1979: Scrapped Naples.

Built by Fleming & Ferguson Ltd., Paisley

729   *Empire Netta*
Launched: 21.9.1945.
Completed: 12.1945.
Naval work to:
1949: (Admiralty).
11.1967: Scrapped Burght, Belgium.

730   *Empire Zona*
Launched: 26.10.1945.
Completed: 2.1946.
1949: (Admiralty).
1958: Renamed *Resolve*.
1974: *Georgios L. Matsas* (L. Matsas, Greece).

Built by Wm. Simons & Co. Ltd., Renfrew

778   *Empire Tessa*
Launched: 3.6.1946.
Completed: 6.1946.
Naval work (Bermuda) to:
1947: *Eminent* (Admiralty).
18.1.1951: Severely damaged by fire at Bermuda.
Towed to U.K. for repairs.
1975: *Goliath* (International Towing Ltd.,
Sittingbourne).
1982: (Maryport Maritime Museum, Cumbria; to
become an exhibit).

26.2.1986: Arrived Millom, in tow, for breaking up
(see also TID 164).

779   *Empire Nora*
Launched: 15.8.1945.
Completed: 9.1946.
1946: *Barman* (Government of Nigeria; Ports
Authority).
1967: *Nisos Aegina* (Tsavliris Salvage & Towage Ltd.,
Greece).
4.1970: Scrapped Piraeus.

River and estuarial tugs: 'Maple' type

Ten tugs were built by R. Dunston Ltd., Thorne, near Doncaster, the first being launched in May 1941. The measurements were 97.5 ft (oa), 92.5 ft × 20.5 ft beam, the beam restricted to this by the width of a lock from the shipyard for eventual access to the sea.

   Orders for the last eight had been placed before the first of the ten was completed and the added defence features gave some stability difficulties to overcome with such a narrow beam, exemplified by the capsizing of the *Empire Imp* when only a few days old, the ¾-inch mild steel wheelhouse, twin Lewis guns, larger and heavier lifeboats and their davits not only causing top-heaviness and restricting vision to a dangerous degree, but also causing compass problems. Topside modifications included reverting to a light steel wheelhouse, the heavier steel being used only to protect the small radio room, but the compass problems were not overcome until only timber was used within a 6 ft radius of the binnacle.

Below decks, the natural draught boiler, which could not produce the desired power on the breadth available, was modified to forced draught.

With four later tugs from the yard (Yard Nos. 383–386) the design was altered to take advantage of the (remeasured) lock width, resulting in vessels with a beam of 21.3 ft the extra nine inches giving more stability and, by dispensing with the side bunkers while retaining the same capacity, enabled the boilers to be fitted with sufficient heating surface to develop the full 500 ihp on natural draught.

All the tugs were coal-burners, for which a bunker capacity of 35 tons was provided. Engines were triple expansion. The first six tugs were fitted with open propellers and the remaining eight with Kort nozzles. The first ten tugs had a gross tonnage of 129, but this was increased to 138 for the last four.

In all the classes of tug building, lack of suitable wood was always a drawback, not only with deck sheathing but for fenders and the capping of towing rails and beams. With all the 'Maple'-class tugs, and with the 'Englishman' and 'Birch' classes, too, wood fenders and capping were dispensed with and iron ones fitted, but these presented harsh surfaces which quickly caused severe wear and tear to tow ropes.

Built by R. Dunston Ltd., Thorne

358   *Empire Maple*
Launched: 20.5.1941.
Completed: 9.1941.
1947: *Tarpan* (Government of Poland).
1962: Name deleted from ship registers; vessel classed for port service only (some sources suggest the vessel was scrapped).

359   *Empire Willow*
Launched: 29.5.1941.
Completed: 10.1941.
Naval work to:
1947: *Los* (Government of Poland).
1962: Name deleted from ship registers; vessel reported scrapped.

360   *Empire Cedar*
Launched: 26.9.1941.
Completed: 11.1941.
Naval work to:
1947: *Handyman* (United Towing Co. Ltd.).
4.1966: Scrapped Bo'ness.

361   *Empire Plane*
Launched: 9.11.1941.
Completed: 12.1941.
Naval work to:
1943: (Admiralty).
1958: *River Eskimo* (Shipping & Freighting Ltd., Southampton).

1964: Scrapped Southampton.

364   *Empire Spruce*
Launched: 13.1.1942.
Completed: 3.1942.
Naval work; and 9.1.1943: In collision with H.M. ship at entrance to Gareloch, Firth of Clyde: almost cut in two, sank.
24.2.1943: Refloated; towed to Glasgow: repaired.
1947: *Emulous* (Admiralty).
1958: (H. G. Pounds, Portsmouth).
1961: *Irving Oak* (new oil engine) (J. D. Irving Ltd., Canada).

365   *Empire Folk*
Launched: 18.3.1942.
Completed: 5.1942.
1947: (Government of France).
1950: *Jehan de Bethancourt* (Chamber of Commerce, Dieppe).
4.1970: Scrapped Fécamp, France.

373   *Empire Ariel*
Launched: 20.9.1942.
Completed: 11.1942.
Naval work to:
1947: *Ariel* (Cie. Rem. 'Les Tuyaux Bleus', Bordeaux).
1951: *Jolasry 5* (J. Lasry & Sons, Oran).
1956: *Velox* (D. Tripcovich & Co., Italy).

1976: Cut down to a barge, renamed *Manuella F* (Marittima Farsoura, Italy).

374   *Empire Seraph*
Launched: 25.10.1942.
Completed: 12.1942.
Naval work to:
1947: *Bizon* (Government of Poland).
1961: Name deleted from ship registers: vessel classed for port services only (some sources suggest the vessel was scrapped).

375   *Empire Imp*
Launched: 22.5.1942.
Completed: 7.1942.
1.8.1942: Capsized and sank alongside jetty at Pembroke Dock.

The following four tugs had a breadth of 21.3 ft:

383   *Empire Lewis*
Launched: 29.5.1943.
Completed: 8.1943.
1947: *Desdemona* (Government of Cyprus; Dept. of Ports).
1987: *Kaptan Dursun* (Turkey).

384   *Empire Percy*
Launched: 20.6.1943.
Completed: 9.1943.
1948: *Thorney* (Port of London Authority).
2.1968: Scrapped Bruges.

19.8.1942: Righted and refloated; towed to Milford Haven: repaired. Naval work to:
1960: (H. G. Pounds, Portsmouth).
1961: *Irving Walnut* (J. D. Irving Ltd., Canada).
3.1969: Dismantled and scuttled off east coast of Canada.

376   *Empire Toby*
Launched: 8.7.1942.
Completed: 8.1942.
1947: *Croisic I* (Union de Rem. d'Ocean, St. Nazaire).
1965: (Soc. Mir. Deros, St. Nazaire).
1969: (Soc. Algero-Provençale de Rem., France).
12.1973: Scrapped Spezia.

385   *Empire Lilliput*
Launched: 10.11.1943.
Completed: 1.1944.
1947: *Lembu* (Shell Company of Singapore Ltd.).
9.1958: Scrapped Singapore.

386   *Empire Andrew*
Launched: 27.11.1943.
Completed: 2.1944.
1948: *Dzik* (Government of Poland).
1961: Name deleted from ship registers; vessel for port work only, but later reported broken up.

Also in 1943 two tugs of somewhat similar dimensions to the above were delivered by Cochrane & Sons, but due to such dimensions they do not fit into any of the named classes or types. They were:

Built by Cochrane & Sons Ltd., Selby

203 gt, 104 ft (oa), 95 ft × 25 ft. Engines: T3cyl.

1261   *Empire Darby*
Launched: 8.1.1943.
Completed: 4.1943.
Naval work to:
1947: *Egerton* (Admiralty).
1958: (H. G. Pounds, Portsmouth).
1961: *Irving Beech* (J. D. Irving Ltd., Canada).

1962: (New (oil) engine).
1.12.1967: Ashore with tows (tanker *Lubrolake*, 1937, 1,622 gt, and a barge) after engine breakdown off New Waterford, near Sydney Harbour, Nova Scotia. Abandoned. Total loss.

Note: The two vessels in tow were also abandoned as total losses.

1262 *Empire Joan*
Launched: 8.1.1943.
Completed: 5.1943.
Naval work to:
1947: *Emphatic* (Admiralty).

1958: (E. Handcock (1929) Ltd., Cardiff).
1960: (Bristol Channel Towage Co. Ltd.).
1963: *Hallgarth* (R. & J. H. Rea Ltd.).
5.1966: Scrapped Newport, Mon.

'TID' type tugs

When urgent demands were made for small tugs for harbour and dock work, the terse statement made to satisfy the needs was simple: it stated 'design, organise and start work immediately toward achieving, in the shortest possible time, the delivery of one tug per week, using in the process, little or no shipyard labour'.

A survey showed that constructional engineering yards were already hard-pressed by the industry and could not accept orders for tugs, generally launched from conventional slipways. However, there was more capacity in manufacturing establishments for welded work rather than riveted work. It was evident that the planning must allow for the work to be placed with a number of different firms, and the basic design for an all-welded tug emerged.

Pre-fabricated construction in shipbuilding had risen to huge proportions in the United States but there was little, if any, in Britain. Now, however, its possibilities were investigated, with a tank-tested model requiring only minor modifications before acceptance. The result was a complete departure from normal British shipbuilding practice, in shape, in design detail and in the construction of pre-fabricated parts for the assembly of a vessel. It was an advance in technical and industrial development.

So came the 'TID' tug – the Admiralty abbreviation of *Tug, Inshore* and *Dock*. It was to be mass-produced and of straight-line form, all design lines of the same strake of plate being parallel, giving frames in straight lengths. There were to be no bent frames and curvature in the shell would apply in one direction only, i.e., with no twist in the plates.

Initially, contracts for parts were awarded to four contractors, but quickly increased to thirteen. The design was subdivided to eight units, cut right across the vessel, with all joints of units arranged to come midway between two frames. There were independent drawings for each unit, with the unit sizes restricted to maximums of 10 ft length, 17 ft width, 13 ft depth and a weight of six tons for transport by road, sometimes up to distances of 200 miles.

Some contractors were able to produce more than one unit, and with each the longitudinal seams of plates were left unwelded for a length of ten inches at either side of a joint, in order that the plates might be 'sprung' together if any slight deviation from the correct dimension occurred. Each separate unit was completed with many of its fittings in position: a special feature of the after-most unit being that it was completed with the rudder, propeller and tailshaft in place. At fitting-out stage – after completion and launch of the hull – the engine bedplate chocks were machined to dimensions taken from the engine after it had been packed and wedged up in alignment with the tailshaft.

However, with some fittings – namely engine room valves, pipework and auxiliaries – it was deemed unwise to have these fitted to the units by the sub-contractors, due to possible movement by vibration during transit. Therefore, such items were fitted at the shipyard, prior to the transverse all-round welding which turned eight separate units into a complete tug.

Hull measurements of the tug were 65 ft length (bp), 74 ft (oa), 17 ft breadth and 8 ft depth, giving 54 gross tons. The draught was 7.3 ft with bunkers and water tank full. Full displacement was 124 tons, bollard pull two tons and full bunker capacity eight tons (coal) or nine tons (oil). Assembly of the hull was done by Richard Dunston Ltd., at their Thorne and Hessle shipyards in Yorkshire and late in the programme, to keep up with demand, by William Pickersgill & Sons Ltd., at Southwick, Sunderland.

A hull was put together every five days – the record was four – and the vertical boiler, two-cylinder compound engine which developed 220 ihp, and superstructure were fitted after the launching. For this purpose, units Nos. 4, 5 and 6 had their upper casings merely tack-welded into position by the contractors. These were removed by cutting the tacks and were easily replaced afterwards.

With Dunston's constructions the first TID was towed to Hessle from Thorne, had her engine and boiler fitted, ran trials back to Thorne and as she left for delivery towed the next completed hull downstream for its machinery installation. This went on week after week, each completed TID towing the next one.

During the four years of TID building, their appearance changed little, only minor changes to the deckhouse, boiler room and accommodation being made, most of these on the Sunderland-built craft.

The initial order from the Ministry of War Transport for twelve TID tugs quickly became twenty-five; then, as production began, was altered to fifty, and as work quickly progressed the figure was doubled to 100. All were ordered as coal burners, to give 7–8 knots and with the liberation of Europe in mind, the main intention was for their use in smaller ports and anchorages.

Then came the likelihood of the use of TID tugs in the Mediterranean and the Far East and another fifty were ordered. But it was necessary to modify the design to make them burn oil, this due to the lack of coal – or its generally poor quality – at prospective bases and to give increased range to the vessels. Such conversion, including lowering funnels, required only slight structural modifications to two of each set of eight prefabricated units. At the same time it was decided to convert similarly the second batch of fifty tugs ordered, but with these already in production it was found possible to change only ten of them to oil.

Finally, a group of thirty-two oil-burners for tropical service was built, with generators to operate ventilator fans and fitted with electric light.

The tugs were numbered 1 to 12 and 14 to 183. Many were allocated to naval work and a number of them were shipped to Eastern waters as deck cargo aboard heavy-lift vessels. Such voyages can be exemplified by the departure from Liverpool on 22 May 1945 of the *Empire Byng*, with *TID*s Nos. *125, 126, 131, 132* and *133* as deck cargo. She arrived at Bombay on 19 June. Similarly, *TID*s Nos. *122, 123, 124, 129* and *130* were shipped to the Pacific and, in June 1945, joined the British Pacific Fleet at Manus, in the Admiralty Islands. The islands had been established as a forward base in the January, enabling the Royal Navy and its associated Fleet Train of supply vessels to operate successfully thousands of miles north of its main bases in Australia. A total of more than 800 ships – naval and merchant – were assigned to these operations, but the sudden end to hostilities in August 1945 caused many of the vessels to be diverted or dispersed.

By October 1945 a number of the TIDs had reached Hong Kong aboard the *Empire Charmian*, whilst others (*TID*s Nos. *127, 128, 144–149* and *151*) were despatched there from the U.K., as under-deck cargo on the *Empire Marshal*, on her maiden voyage in November 1945.

Earlier, in the July, a further batch of TID tugs, still in the U.K., were to be refitted and tropicalised for Eastern service, although in the event these plans were not carried out.

When the war ended some of the TID tugs engaged on naval work were given a permanent transfer to the Admiralty, for continued service at navy bases throughout the world. Most of those which had served with the Army reverted to Ministry of Transport jurisdiction before post-war disposal, with a number allocated to various dock and harbour authorities and others to towage and lighterage companies. In addition, a considerable number were sold to Continental buyers in France, Belgium, Holland, Finland, Norway and Sweden – and even one as far away as Uruguay. However, it has not proved possible to trace the entire subsequent history of a number of them.

The fourteen TID tugs sold to Finland made the passage to that country in three 'convoys', eight of them (see *TID 1*) sailing in October 1946, three (see *TID 69*) sailing from Great Yarmouth on 25 April 1947 and three (see *TID 19*) sailing from Dover two days later.

A batch of eleven went to the French Government in December 1945, then passed to the civilian administrators of various Channel ports. In 1948 one of them (*TID 20*), was shipped to French Indo-China and three years later five more followed, still retaining their TID prefix but renumbered *TIDs I* to *V*. And by 1947–1948 another ten or so had also passed into French ownership.

TID tug orders summarised:

50 coal burners
50 coal burners (10 changed to oil)
50 oil burners
32 oil burners (for tropical service)
182

Built by R. Dunston Ltd., Thorne

T. 399 *TID 1*
Launched: 26.2.1943.
Completed: 3.1943.
Naval work to:
1945: (M.O.W.T.).
10.1946: Sold to Government of Finland.

This vessel was delivered to Finland as part of a convoy of eight *TID* tugs. The sailing schedule was as follows:
9.10.1946: Sailed from River Mersey to Swansea.
29.10.1946: Arrived Dartmouth from Swansea, in convoy with *TID* Nos. *7, 25, 30, 35, 40, 41* and *74*.
31.10.1946: Sailed from Southampton.
6.11.1946: Arrived Rotterdam, via Dover.
19.11.1946: Sailed Delfzyl.
20.11.1946: Sailed Emden.
22.11.1946: Passed through Kiel Canal, bound for Helsinki.
No further trace.

T. 400 *TID 2*
Launched: 6.3.1943.
Completed: 4.1943.
4.1943–12.1945: (War Dept. – Army).
12.1945: (Admiralty).
4.1946: Renamed *C. 677*.
1958: (E. Mellenger, Canada).
1961: *Irving Fir* (J. D. Irving Ltd., Canada) (vessel converted to oil engine).
No further trace.

T. 401 *TID 3*
Launched: 16.3.1943.
Completed: 4.1943.
Naval work to:
1945: (Reported to have carried the name *Beacon* (Admiralty)).
1973: (Controlled Thermic Lancing Ltd., Barking, Essex), and:
1973: Cut up during thermic lance experiments.

T. 402 *TID 4*
Launched: 25.3.1943.
Completed: 4.1943.
Naval work to:
1948: (Admiralty).
9.1958: (H. G. Pounds, Portsmouth).
1958: *Irving Pine* (J. D. Irving Ltd., Canada) (vessel converted to oil engine).
No further trace.

T. 403 *TID 5*
Launched: 1.4.1943.
Completed: 5.1943.
5.1943: (M.O.W.T.).
4.1944: (War Dept. – Army).

1948: (F. T. Everard & Sons Ltd.).
1949: Renamed *E. A. Everard* (converted to oil engine).
1965: Withdrawn from service; engine removed.
1971: Hull sold to L. Todd and scrapped Greenhithe, Kent.

T. 404   *TID 6*
Launched: 10.4.1943.
Completed: 5.1943.
5.1943: (War Dept. – Army).
7.1945: (M.O.W.T.).
12.1945: Sold (Government of France, Civil Port Admin., Le Havre).
No further trace.

T. 405   *TID 7*
Launched: 16.4.1943.
Completed: 5.1943.
6.1943: (Naval work).
10.1946: Sold to Government of Finland, (see *TID 1*).

T. 406   *TID 8*
Launched: 23.4.1943.
Completed: 5.1943.
Naval work to:
9.1943: (Naval work – Mediterranean).
8.1946: Transferred to Government of Italy (Sea Transport Service, Sicily). Later renamed *Gabbiano*.
1951: *Gurjan*.
1955: *Capreno* (O. Novella, Genoa).
No trace after 1963.

T. 407   *TID 9*
Launched: 4.5.1943.
Completed: 6.1943.
Naval work (Mediterranean) to:
7.1946: Transferred to Government of Italy (Sea Transport Service, Sicily).
1948: *Riccardi 2* (Italy).
1953: *Fiume* (Italy).
No further trace.

T. 408   *TID 10*
Launched: 10.5.1943.
Completed: 6.1943.
Naval work (Mediterranean) to:
6.1947: Renamed *W. 91* (Civil Engineers, Malta).
1960: (Bailey Shipyard, Malta).
No further trace.

T. 409   *TID 11*
Launched: 17.5.1943.
Completed: 7.1943.
7.1943: (War Dept. – Army).

9.1943: Naval work (Gibraltar) to:
6.1963: *Sabo* (S. Bezzini & Son, Malta) (towed to Malta by *TID 56*) (converted to oil engine).
1974: Scrapped.

T. 410   *TID 12*
Launched: 28.5.1943.
Completed: 7.1943.

On 9 August 1943 the tugs *TID 12* and *TID 14* went aground at Tarlair Point, Macduff, Banffshire, after breaking adrift in heavy weather from the tugs *Empire Larch* and *Onward* when the towing bridle broke, on delivery voyage from Hull to the Clyde, via Inverness. Attempts to reconnect the tow failed and both drifting tugs stranded. Held between rocks, they were pounded by the weather, but then flooded by salvors to hold them in position. *TID 12* lost her stern gear, *TID 14* fractured her sternpost.

Refloated three days later, they were towed to Macduff and were then 'in reserve' until December 1943 while under repair. In the same month they were transferred to the War Dept. – Army and twelve months later *TID 14* was in naval service for port duties and by April 1945 was being managed by the Dutch Government. During 1948 the vessel was reported as sold to them, and at the same time *TID 12* was reported sold to Belgian buyers.

T. 414   *TID 14*
Launched: 2.6.1943.
Completed: 7.1943.
(For details, see *TID 12*, above.)

T. 415   *TID 15*
Launched: 10.6.1943.
Completed: 8.1943.
Naval work to:
9.1944: (U.S. Army).
3.1945: (M.O.W.T.).
10.1945: (Chartered to Milford Haven Docks Co.).
2.1946: Naval work to:
1949: *BP 2* (B. Perry & Sons, Bristol).
1958: Renamed *Salisbury*.
1964: (Converted to oil engine).
1980: (Laxey Towing Co., Isle of Man).

T. 416   *TID 16*
Launched: 19.6.1943.
Completed: 8.1943.
Naval work to:
1946: *Bonita* (Liverpool Lighterage Co.).
3.1957: (Offered for sale), and:
1963: Scrapped Liverpool.

T. 417   *TID 17*
Launched: 26.6.1943.
Completed: 8.1943.
12.1943: Naval work (West Africa) to:
8.1946: Sold (Sierra Leone Coaling Co., Freetown).
No further trace.

T. 418 *TID 18*
Launched: 20.7.1943.
Completed: 9.1943.
9.1943: (War Dept. – Army).
1948: Reported sold to Belgium.
No further trace.

T. 419 *TID 19*
Launched: 31.7.1943.
Completed: 9.1943.
9.1943: (War Dept. – Army).
7.1945: (Laid up).
1.1946: (Chartered to Westminster Dredging Co.
Ltd.).
6.1946: (Laid up).
4.1947: Sold to Finland.

This vessel was delivered to Finland as part of a three-ship
TID-tug convoy, as follows:
27.4.1947: Sailed from Dover for Helsinki via Rotterdam, in
company with *TID 34* and *TID 49*:
7.5.1947: Sailed Delfzyl:
8.5.1947: Passed Kiel Canal.
No further trace.

T. 420 *TID 20*
Launched: 19.7.1943.
Completed: 9.1943.
9.1943: (M.O.W.T.).
2.1944: (U.S. Army).
12.1944: Naval work to:
3.1945: (M.O.W.T.).
12.1945: Sold to Government of France.
1948: Transferred to French Indo-China.
No further trace.

T. 421 *TID 21*
Launched: 24.7.1943.
Completed: 9.1943.
9.1943: (M.O.W.T.).
2.1944: (U.S. Army).
12.1944: Naval work to:
1946: (M.O.W.T.).
1.1948: (Naval work – Malta; shipped out per ss
Pacific Liberty).
3.1959: (Bailey Shipyard, Malta).
No further trace.

T. 422 *TID 22*
Launched: 4.8.1943.
Completed: 10.1943.
10.1943: (M.O.W.T.).
2.1944: (U.S. Army).
7.1944: (War Dept. – Army).
No further trace.

T. 423 *TID 23*
Launched: 14.8.1943.
Completed: 10.1943.
10.1943: (War Dept. – Army).
9.1944: Naval work to:
11.1945: *Ashford 23* (Chartered to Lloyds Albert Yard
& Motorboat Packet Co. (Risdon Beazley Ltd.)).
1947: *Tidspur* (P. Foster & Co., Hull).
1956: (United Towing Co. Ltd., Hull).
4.1963: Scrapped Hendrik Ido Ambacht, Holland.

T. 424 *TID 24*
Launched: 19.8.1943.
Completed: 10.1943.
Naval work to:
12.1945: (Laid up).
1952: *Ashford 24* (Chartered to Lloyds Albert Yard &
Motorboat Packet Co. (Risdon Beazley Ltd.)).
1953: *Bowman* (United Towing Co. Ltd., Hull).
4.1963: Scrapped Hendrik Ido Ambacht, Holland.

T. 425 *TID 25*
Launched: 25.8.1943.
Completed: 10.1943.
Naval work to:
1945: (U.S. Army).
1945: (M.O.W.T.).
9.1946: *B3* (Government of Finland).
1947: *Motti* (Finland).
1959: Scrapped.
(See also *TID 1*.)

T. 426 *TID 26*
Launched: 3.9.1943.
Completed: 11.1943.
11.1943: (War Dept. – Army).
12.1944: Naval work to:
3.1945: (M.O.W.T.).
12.1945: Sold to Government of France.
(See note under *TID 91*.)

T. 427 *TID 27*
Launched: 9.9.1943.
Completed: 11.1943.
Naval work to:
0.1910: (Transferred to Admiralty).
1949: (Chartered to British Transport Docks, Hull).
1952: (Dashwood & Partners, London).
No further trace.

T. 428 *TID 28*
Launched: 17.9.1943.
Completed: 11.1943.
Naval work to:
1949: *Triune* (Hull Steam Trawlers Mutual Insurance
& Protection Association, Hull).
1966: Scrapped Newhaven.

T. 429   *TID 29*
Launched: 22.9.1943.
Completed: 11.1943.
11.1943: (War Dept. – Army).
1947: *Gedu* (United Africa Co. Ltd.).
No trace after 1955.

T. 430   *TID 30*
Launched: 21.5.1943.
Completed: 6.1943.
6.1943: (M.O.W.T.).
9.1944: (U.S. Army).
12.1944: Naval work (Portsmouth) to:
4.1945: (M.O.W.T.).
1946: *B4* (Government of Finland).
1948: *Oulu 12* (Oulu O/Y, Finland).
1970: Scrapped.
(See also *TID 1*.)

T. 431   *TID 31*
Launched: 2.6.1943.
Completed: 8.1943.
Naval work to:
11.1944: (War Dept. – Army).
12.1944: Naval work to:
5.1945: (M.O.W.T., Port duties – operated by
Government of Netherlands).
1947: (Sold to France).
1955: *Thaurion* (E. L. Chagnaud, Marseilles).
No further trace.

T. 432   *TID 32*
Launched: 17.6.1943.
Completed: 8.1943.
8.1943: (War Dept. – Army).
9.1944: (Admiralty).
1949: Renamed *C. 702*.
1967: (H. G. Pounds, Portsmouth).
1975: Reported scrapped Portsmouth.

T. 433   *TID 33*
Launched: 23.6.1943.
Completed: 9.1943.
9.1943: (M.O.W.T.).
12.1943: (War Dept. – Army).
19.6.1944: Sank in heavy weather, Arromanches,
Normandy beach-head, France.

T. 434   *TID 34*
Launched: 2.7.1943.
Completed: 9.1943.
9.1943: (M.O.W.T.).
12.1943: (War Dept. – Army).
7.1945: (Laid up).
1.1946: (Chartered to Westminster Dredging Co.
Ltd.).

1947: Sold to Finland.
(See *TID 19*.)

T. 435   *TID 35*
Launched: 7.7.1943.
Completed: 9.1943.
9.1943: (M.O.W.T.).
12.1943: (U.S. Army).
1.1945: Naval work to:
4.1945: (M.O.W.T.).
1946: *B5* (Government of Finland).
1947: *Tommi* (Finland).
1984: (Jonko & Aila, Finland).
(See also *TID 1*.)

T. 436   *TID 36*
Launched: 15.7.1943.
Completed: 9.1943.
9.1943: (M.O.W.T.).
2.1944: (U.S. Army).
10.1944: (War Dept. – Army).
1946: *Respite* (Cory Lighterage Co. Ltd.).
1957: (New (oil) engine).
No trace after 1957.

T. 437   *TID 37*
Launched: 4.8.1943.
Completed: 9.1943.
9.1943: (M.O.W.T.).
2.1944: (U.S. Army).
12.1945: (War Dept. – Army).
1948: Sold to Belgian buyers.
No further trace.

T. 438   *TID 38*
Launched: 16.8.1943.
Completed: 10.1943.
10.1943: (M.O.W.T.).
2.1944: (U.S. Army).
7.1944: (War Dept. – Army).
1948: Sold to Belgian buyers.
No further trace.

T. 439   *TID 39*
Launched: 20.8.1943.
Completed: 10.1943.
10.1943: (War Dept. – Army).
1949: Sold to Belgian buyers.
No further trace.

T. 440   *TID 40*
Launched: 30.8.1943.
Completed: 10.1943.
10.1943: (M.O.W.T.).
14.4.1945: Hull, engine and boiler damaged when
lock gates of Cambrian Dry Dock, Swansea, carried

away during a high tide. Repaired. (See also *TID 41*.)
1946: Sold to Government of Finland. No further
trace.
(See also *TID 1*.)

T. 441   *TID 41*
Launched: 3.9.1943.
Completed: 10.1943.
10.1943: (M.O.W.T.).
14.4.1945: Hull, engine and boiler damaged when
lock gates of Cambrian Dry Dock, Swansea, carried
away during a high tide. Repaired. (See also *TID 40*.)
1946: Sold to Government of Finland. No further
trace.
(See also *TID 1*.)

T. 442   *TID 42*
Launched: 14.9.1943.
Completed: 10.1943.
10.1943: (M.O.W.T.).
9.1944: Naval work to:
12.1945: Sold to Government of France, for service
at Boulogne.
(See note under *TID 91*.)

T. 443   *TID 43*
Launched: 17.9.1943.
Completed: 11.1943.
Naval work to:
1949: *Tideall* (James Contracting & Dredging Co.
Ltd.).
1953: (New (oil) engine) (Foremost Contracting &
Dredging Co. Ltd., Southampton).
1975: (Westminster Dredging Co. Ltd.). Later sold,
and:
1986: Vessel under arrest, sold by Admiralty Marshal,
Troon, to Kingsleydale Ltd., Liverpool. Renamed
Seaport Alpha.
1987: (Reported based at Penrhyn, N. Wales and
operating in Anglesey area).

T. 444   *TID 44*
Launched: 29.9.1943.
Completed: 11.1943.
Naval work to:
3.12.1944: Sank in Portsmouth Harbour while
assisting an LST.
16.3.1945: Refloated; repaired.
1949: *Kiero* (Hull Steam Trawlers Mutual Insurance
& Protection Association, Hull).
1964: Scrapped Newhaven.

T. 445   *TID 45*
Launched: 30.9.1943.
Completed: 11.1943.
Naval work to:

1952: (War Dept. – Army).
No further trace.

T. 446   *TID 46*
Launched: 30.10.1943.
Completed: 12.1943.
Naval work to:
1945: (Corporation of Trinity House).
1947: (Admiralty).
1959: (H. G. Pounds, Portsmouth).
Later reported scrapped.

T. 447   *TID 47*
Launched: 29.9.1943.
Completed: 12.1943.
Naval work to:
1944: (Admiralty).
1947: *Ashford 47* (Lloyds Albert Yard & Motorboat
Packet Co. (Risdon Beazley Ltd., Southampton)).
1953: *Fenman* (United Towing Co. Ltd.).
10.3.1954: Capsized and sank outside Alexandra
Dock, Hull, in fog and when taking towrope from
Swedish Steamer *Rudolf* during docking operations.
3.4.1954: Salved and docked; repaired.
1963: Scrapped Hendrik Ido Ambacht.

T. 448   *TID 48*
Launched: 6.10.1943.
Completed: 12.1943.
12.1943: (War Dept. – Army).
1947: Sold to Holland.
No further trace.

T. 449   *TID 49*
Launched: 12.10.1943.
Completed: 12.1943.
12.1943: (War Dept. – Army).
1947: Sold to Finland. No further trace.
(See *TID 19*.)

T. 450   *TID 50*
Launched: 18.10.1943.
Completed: 12.1943.
Naval work to:
1958: (Reported for disposal).
1968: (H. G. Pounds, Portsmouth).
Later scrapped.

T. 451   *TID 51*
Launched: 25.10.1943.
Completed: 1.1944.
29.2.1944: Capsized and sank in North Sea while in
tow (voyage: Harwich/Hull).

T. 461   *TID 52*
Launched: 9.11.1943.
Completed: 1.1944.
Naval work to:
1948: (Admiralty).
19. .: *MNS 52* (M. N. S. Fishing Ltd., Newhaven).
1963: (Lacmots Ltd., Sheerness, Kent).
1965: (New (oil) engine).
No further trace.

T. 462   *TID 53*
Launched: 16.11.1943.
Completed: 1.1944.
1.1944: (War Dept. – Army).
1946: *W. D. Teal* (converted to oil engine)
(Westminster Dredging Co. Ltd.).
14.8.1950: Stranded on sandbank in River Dee;
submerged. (See also *TID 84*.)
11.9.1950: Refloated, towed to Mostyn, then
Bromborough Dock. Repaired, renamed *Teal*.
1965 (*circa*): Shipped to New Zealand for use in
Gisborne Harbour building project. Later reported
sold to Far East buyers.

T. 463   *TID 54*
Launched: 23.11.1943.
Completed: 1.1944.
Naval work to:
1945: (Chartered to Westminster Dredging Co. Ltd.).
1948: *Biddick* (River Wear Commissioners,
Sunderland).
1973: Sold for preservation (M. Stephens,
Sittingbourne).
(*circa*) 1976: Resold; laid up in River Thames, and by
1987: Lying off Greenwich, London, derelict and
tidal.

T. 464   *TID 55*
Launched: 27.11.1943.
Completed: 1.1944.
1.1944: (War Dept. – Army).
1948: Sold to Belgian buyers; no further trace.

T. 465   *TID 56*
Launched: 6.12.1943.
Completed: 3.1944.
3.1944: (U.S. Army).
11.1944: (Admiralty).
12.1945: Renamed *C. 688* (Admiralty – Gibraltar).
6.1947: Reverted to name *TID 56*.
1963: *Sabe* (converted to oil engine) (Bezzina & Sons,
Malta).
No further trace.

T. 466   *TID 57*
Launched: 10.12.1943.
Completed: 2.1944.
2.1944: (U.S. Army).
12.1944: (Admiralty).
9.1958: Scrapped Bo'ness.

T. 467   *TID 58*
Launched: 17.12.1943.
Completed: 1.1944.
1948: Sold to Government of France. Later renamed
Var (based at Port du Bouc).
No trace after 1955.

T. 468   *TID 59*
Launched: 23.12.1943.
Completed: 2.1944.
2.1944: (War Dept. – Army).
10.1945: Naval work to:
1947: *Sunnyside* (P. Carney & Sons, Sunderland)
(vessel converted to oil engine).
1960: (Fenchurch Shipping Co., London.)
1962: (Metal Recoveries Ltd., Newhaven).
1965: *Trover* (Britannia Steam Towing Co. Ltd.,
Swansea).
Later resold, renamed *Lady of Menai* (private owner).
No further trace.

T. 469   *TID 60*
Launched: 2.1.1944.
Completed: 2.1944.
2.1944: (War Dept. – Army).
12.1945: (Government of France).
1947: (Civil Port Administration, Boulogne).
Later renamed *Boanamary* (based at Majunga,
Madagascar).
No trace after 1955.

T. 470   *TID 61*
Launched: 8.1.1944.
Completed: 3.1944.
3.1944: (U.S. Army).
1945: (Admiralty).
1958: (H. G. Pounds, Portsmouth).
1961: *Irving Elm* (converted to oil engine) (J. D.
Irving Ltd., Canada).
No further trace.

T. 471   *TID 62*
Launched: 14.1.1944.
Completed: 5.1944.
Naval work to:
1945: (Admiralty).
20.9.1946: Broke adrift from H.M.S. *Tenacity* in a
gale twelve miles off Beachy Head, Sussex. Taken in
tow by H.M.S. *Zephyr*, but hove-to, due to weather
conditions: *TID 62* suddenly capsized and sank five

miles south-east of Folkestone Pier after taking high seas aboard (voyage: Portsmouth/Sheerness).

T. 472   *TID 63*
Launched: 18.1.1944.
Completed: 4.1944.
4.1944: (War Dept. – Army).
12.1945: (Government of France: reported in service with French Navy).
1947: (Civil Port Administration, Boulogne).
(See note under *TID 91*.)

T. 473   *TID 64*
Launched: 25.1.1944.
Completed: 2.1944.
Naval work to:
12.1945: *Claude* (French owners).
1955: *P. B. Everard* (F. T. Everard & Sons Ltd.).
1969: Scrapped Harwich.

T. 474   *TID 65*
Launched: 8.2.1944.
Completed: 3.1944.
1944: (M.O.W.T.).
1946: *Sea Gem* (C. J. King & Son, Bristol).
3.1967: Scrapped Portishead.

T. 475   *TID 66*
Launched: 8.2.1944.
Completed: 2.1944.
Naval work to:
1946: (Anglo-Saxon Petroleum Co. Ltd., London).
1949: (National Coal Board, Hull).
19..: (Warkworth Harbour Board).
11.1.1963: Towed into Berwick, Scotland, after drifting in North Sea with engine trouble (voyage to River Clyde to be refitted for service at Benghazi). Repaired and proceeded, but:
16.1.1963: Broke down with engine trouble in a gale ENE of St. Abb's Head. Towed into Leith. Later broken up.

T. 476   *TID 67*
Launched: 11.2.1944.
Completed: 3.1944.
3.1944: (War Dept. Army).
12.1945: (Government of France).
(See note under *TID 91*.)

T. 477   *TID 68*
Launched: 16.2.1944.
Completed: 3.1944.
3.1944: (U.S. Army).
1945: (Admiralty).
1967: (Milford Haven Marine Services).
1968: (H. G. Pounds, Portsmouth).
Later broken up.

T. 478   *TID 69*
Launched: 21.2.1944.
Completed: 3.1944.
Naval work to:
1945: (Admiralty).
1947: (Luke, Thomas & Co. Ltd., Aden).
Later reported broken up.

T. 479   *TID 70*
Launched: 26.2.1944.
Completed: 3.1944.
3.1944: (U.S. Army).
23.12.1944: Struck mine in English Channel; sank while in tow of U.S. tug *LT 533*, south of Selsey Bill, 50.12N 0.52W.

T. 480   *TID 71*
Launched: 1.3.1944.
Completed: 3.1944.
3.1944: (U.S. Army).
12.1944: (Admiralty).
1962: (H. G. Pounds, Portsmouth).
1964: *Assurance* (converted to oil engine) (Husbands Shipyard, Marchwood, Southampton).

T. 481   *TID 72*
Launched: 6.3.1944.
Completed: 4.1944.
4.1944: (U.S. Army).
1944: (M.O.W.T.).
1945: (War Dept. – Army).
1947: Intended to be renamed *Evelyn* (River Wear Commissioners, Sunderland), but 1948: Renamed *Pallion*.

In 1947 the River Wear Commissioners (later Port of Sunderland Authority) bought two coal-fired TID tugs, Nos. *54* and *72*, from the Admiralty and in the following year renamed them *Biddick* and *Pallion*, respectively. For many years they were mainly employed on the towage and manoeuvring of dredgers and barges in the narrow confines of the River Wear. By the end of the 1960s only one TID tug was necessary to serve the dredging fleet, although both were retained due to the unreliability of their steam machinery.

In 1970 the National Ports Council was asked to suggest further ways of improving the river's dredging operations. Subsequently, one recommendation was that the efficiency of one of the TIDs be improved so that the other could be disposed of. Accepting this, the Wear Commissioners decided that the duties of their tugs should be extended to include buoy maintenance, the laying of anchors and moorings and light salvage work. Previously these duties had been carried out by a non-propelled, heavy-lift barge with steam deck machinery, which required a crew of seven men and the services of a tug, and it was reasoned that if a tug was equipped with a two-ton crane, it could perform all but major maintenance work.

The TID tug *Pallion* was selected for the new duties and her re-engining and modernising commenced at Gateshead in July 1972. She emerged from the refit three months later, with wheelhouse-control diesel machinery developing 440 bhp, new oil fuel bunker tanks, a modern funnel, extensively refitted accommodation and a hydraulic winch on the foredeck operating a buoy-handling boom with an outreach beyond the bow.

T. 482   *TID 73*
Launched: 9.3.1944.
Completed: 4.1944.
4.1944: (U.S. Army).
1945: (Dashwood & Partners Ltd.).
1949: Renamed *Dashound*.
1954:(New (oil) engine).
1955: Name reverted to *TID 73* (Admiralty).
1970: (H. G. Pounds, Portsmouth).
No further trace.

T. 483   *TID 74*
Launched: 14.3.1944.
Completed: 4.1944.
4.1944: (M.O.W.T.).
1.1945: Assisted American Liberty ship *George Hawley*, which had been torpedoed off the Lizard, Cornwall. Towed the disabled vessel some thirty miles before handing over to a salvage tug.
8.1946: (Sold to Government of Finland). No further trace.
(See also *TID 1*.)

T. 484   *TID 75*
Launched: 18.3.1944.
Completed: 4.1944.
Naval work to:
1948: (Admiralty).
1960: (H. G. Pounds, Portsmouth).
1965: *Adherance* (converted to oil engine) (Husband's Shipyard, Marchwood, Southampton).

T. 485   *TID 76*
Launched: 22.3.1944.
Completed: 4.1944.
5.1944: (U.S. Army).
12.1944: (M.O.W.T.).
1948: (Admiralty).
1960: (H. G. Pounds, Portsmouth).
Later broken up.

T. 486   *TID 77*
Launched: 28.3.1944.
Completed: 5.1944.
Naval work to:
1948: (Admiralty).
1950: *Ardol* (Olympic Oil & Cake Mills, Hull; later: British Oil & Cake Mills (Unilever Ltd.)).
Later reported broken up.

T. 487   *TID 78*
Launched: 31.3.1944.
Completed: 5.1944.
7.1944: (War Dept. – Army).
12.1945: *President Breward* (France).
1966: *Ower* (converted to oil engine) (Alexandra Towing Co.).
9.1978: Scrapped Southampton.

T. 488   *TID 79*
Launched: 6.4.1944.
Completed: 5.1944.
4.1944: (War Dept. – Army).
1946: *Hillman* (J. H. Piggott & Son, Grimsby).
30.10.1954: Capsized and sank while towing trawler *Kirknes* into Fish Dock, Grimsby.
8.11.1954: Refloated; sold and repaired, and:
1955: *Dagger* (converted to oil engine) (Hull Steam Trawlers Mutual Insurance & Protection Association, Hull).
19..: (M. N. S. Fishing Ltd., Newhaven).
No further trace.

T. 489   *TID 80*
Launched: 13.4.1944.
Completed: 5.1944.
Naval work to:
1948: (Admiralty).
1962: (Anglo Diesel Co., London).
1965: Broken up.

T. 490   *TID 81*
Launched: 18.4.1944.
Completed: 5.1944.
Naval work to:
1.1947: (Laid up).
1950: *Sea Prince* (C. J. King & Sons, Bristol).
16.10.1957: Run down off Avonmouth while towing *Cato*, (1946, 939 gt), the ship's bow running over the tug's stern and causing it to capsize. Sank. Total loss.

T. 491   *TID 82*
Launched: 21.4.1944.
Completed: 6.1944.
7.1944: (War Dept. – Army).
1948: Sold to Belgian buyers.
No further trace.

T. 492   *TID 83*
Launched: 26.4.1944.
Completed: 6.1944.
6.1944: (U.S. Army).
1945: (Admiralty).

1961: *Michael Hamilton* (conversion to oil engine commenced) (M. Williams, Orpington, Kent).
1966: Sold (incomplete) to Electro Marine Ltd., London, and:
1967: Scrapped Erith, Kent.

T. 493 *TID 84*
Launched: 29.4.1944.
Completed: 7.1944.
7.1944: (M.O.W.T.).
1946: *W. D. Duck* (Westminster Dredging Co. Ltd.).
14.8.1950: Stranded on a sandbank in River Dee.
23.8.1950: Refloated, and:
26.8.1950: Arrived in tow at Bromborough Dock.
Reported later sold to foreign buyers.
(See also *TID 53*.)

T. 494 *TID 85*
Launched: 2.5.1944.
Completed: 6.1944.
7.1944: (M.O.W.T.).
1948: Sold to Belgian buyers.
No further trace.

T. 495 *TID 86*
Launched: 6.5.1944.
Completed: 7.1944.
1944: (M.O.W.T.).
1946: *Bernie* (Hull Steam Trawlers Mutual Insurance & Protection Association, Hull).
No trace after 1955.

T. 496 *TID 87*
Launched: 10.5.1944.
Completed: 6.1944.
1944: (M.O.W.T.).

1946: *Gilder* (Hull Steam Trawlers Mutual Insurance & Protection Association, Hull).
No trace after 1955.

T. 497 *TID 88*
Launched: 15.5.1944.
Completed: 6.1944.
1944: (M.O.W.T.).
1948: Sold to Belgian buyers.
No further trace.

T. 498 *TID 89*
Launched: 17.5.1944.
Completed: 6.1944.
Naval work to:
12.1945: (Government of France).
(See note under *TID 91*.)

T. 499 *TID 90*
Launched: 13.6.1944.
Completed: 7.1944.
Naval work to:
12.1945: (Laid up).
1948: (Admiralty).
1952: *Ashford 90* (Lloyds Albert Yard & Motorboat Packet Co. (Risdon Beazley Ltd.)).
1953: *Yeoman* (United Towing Co. Ltd.).
4.1963: Scrapped Hendrik Ido Ambacht.

T. 500 *TID 91*
Launched: 16.6.1944.
Completed: 7.1944.
Naval work to:
1945: (M.O.W.T.).
12.1945: (Government of France – Civil Port Administration, Le Havre).

In 1945 seven TID-type tugs were transferred to the Government of France and put to work in various Channel ports. Later, in 1951, it was reported that five TIDs had been sent to Indo-China, this following the despatch of *TID 20* in 1948. The five TIDs retained the prefix of their names but were given new numbers, becoming *TIDs I* to *V*. Of these, one was transferred to Vietnam in March 1953 and renamed *H.Q.9502*, while the remaining four were either also given to Vietnam or discarded in 1956.

However, from six 'probable' TID tugs (Nos. *26, 42, 63, 67, 89* and *91*) it has not proved possible to ascertain which five went to the Far East. Additionally, no further history details have been traced and it is likely that six, not five, tugs were actually shipped.

T. 501 *TID 92*
Launched: 22.5.1944.
Completed: 8.1944.
Naval work to:
1944: (Admiralty).
1948: *Teshi* (United Africa Co. Ltd., Liverpool).
Presume subsequently scrapped.

T. 502 *TID 93*
Launched: 28.5.1944.
Completed: 8.1944.
Naval work to:
1950: *Nubia* (Elder, Dempster Lines Ltd.).
10.1959: Broken up.

The tug *TID 4*, built in 1943. (R. Dunston Ltd., Yard No T. 402.)

TID tugs in the River Humber, following trials.   *R. Dunston Ltd.*

The heavy-lift ship *Empire Byng* in Bromborough Dock, May 1945, with *TID* tugs Nos. *125, 126, 131, 132,* and *133* as deck cargo. Their folding funnels have been lowered, the wheelhouses are unprotected. (See story in TID tug Introduction.)

T. 503 *TID 94*
Launched: 1.6.1944.
Completed: 8.1944.
Naval work to:
1948: Sold to Belgian buyers.
No further trace.

T. 504 *TID 95*
Launched: 5.6.1944.
Completed: 8.1944.
1944: (M.O.W.T.).
1946: *Ernest Brown* (T. R. Brown & Sons, Bristol).
1966: (New (oil) engine).
19..: (Evans Marine Ltd., Maidenhead).
1986: (Reported sold to a London buyer; vessel sent
to work on civil engineering project near Paris, on
River Seine).

T. 505 *TID 96*
Launched: 9.6.1944.
Completed: 9.1944.
1944. (M.O.W.T.).
1947: (Admiralty).
No further trace.

T. 506 *TID 97*
Launched: 22.6.1944.
Completed: 9.1944.
Naval work to:
1945: (Admiralty).
29.12.1962: Capsized and sank at Chatham Dockyard
while assisting the R.F.A. *Hebe* to berth.
4.1.1963: Refloated; and
10.1963: Sold (R. F. Horlock, Mistley, Essex).
No further trace.

T. 507 *TID 98*
Launched: 29.6.1944.
Completed: 9.1944.
Naval work to:
1945: (Admiralty).
8.1947: (Government of Burma).
11.1947. (Inland Water Transport Board, Rangoon).
No further trace.

T. 508 *TID 99*
Launched: 5.7.1944.
Completed: 9.1944.
Naval work to:
1948: (Admiralty).
1963: Reported sold.
1973: (H. G. Pounds, Portsmouth).
Later reported scrapped.

T. 509 *TID 100*
Launched: 9.7.1944.
Completed: 9.1944.
9.1944: (War Dept. – Army).
1958: *Richard Abel* (R. Abel & Sons Ltd., Liverpool).
1966: Scrapped Barrow.

T. 510 *TID 101*
Launched: 12.7.1944.
Completed: 9.1944.
Naval work to:
1948: (Admiralty – Malta).
4.1964: *San Marco* (E. Cassar, Malta).
1968: (Sold Italy).
No further trace.

T. 523 *TID 102*
Launched: 17.7.1944.
Completed: 10.1944.
Naval work to:
2.1945: (War Dept. – Army).
1948: *Nuttall* (E. Nuttall & Sons, London).
1954: (African Lighterage & Transport Co., Lagos
(Elder, Dempster & Co. Ltd.)).
12.1960: Scrapped locally.

T. 524 *TID 103*
Launched: 20.7.1944.
Completed: 10.1944.
11.1944: (Naval work).
No further trace.

T. 525 *TID 104*
Launched: 25.7.1944.
Completed: 10.1944.
Naval work.
Later sold, and:
9.1947: Towed from Liverpool to Tunis (with *TID
105*) by tug *Empire Aid*.
No further trace.

T. 526 *TID 105*
Launched: 1.8.1944.
Completed: 10.1944.
Naval work.
Later sold, and:
9.1947: Towed from Liverpool to Tunis (with *TID
104*) by tug *Empire Aid*.
No further trace.

T. 527 *TID 106*
Launched: 14.8.1944.
Completed: 11.1944.
Naval work to:
1945: (Admiralty).
1949: *Tidtug* (Dashwood & Partners, London).
1953: *Nupe* (Elder, Dempster & Co. Ltd., Liverpool).

1956: (Government of Sierre Leone).
No further trace.

T. 528   *TID 107*
Launched: 12.8.1944.
Completed: 11.1944.
11.1944: (War Dept. – Army).
1948: (Admiralty – Harwich and Chatham).
1968: Sold for breaking up (T. W. Ward Ltd., Grays, Essex),
but 1970: *Chrianie* (Christiani & Nielsen Ltd.).
1973: (B. Pearce, Maldon, Essex). (Parts of the vessel used to refit this owner's tug *TID 172*), then:
12.1975: Scrapped Sittingbourne, Kent.

T. 529   *TID 108*
Launched: 26.8.1944.
Completed: 11.1944.
1944: (M.O.W.T.).
1947: *Zed* (C. R. Fry, Brixham).
1948: *Richard Wallace* (Cork Harbour Commissioners).
1980: Offered for sale;
No further trace.

T. 530   *TID 109*
Launched: 31.8.1944.
Completed: 1.1945.
1.1945: (Admiralty).
8.1947: (Government of Burma).
11.1947: (Inland Water Transport Board, Rangoon).
No further trace.

T. 531   *TID 110*
Launched: 6.9.1944.
Completed: 11.1944.
1945: (M.O.W.T.).
1949: *Taywood Tid* (Taylor Woodrow (West Africa) Ltd.).
17.1.1950: Arrived Takoradi from Dakar in tow of ss *Mendi Palm* (1936, 5,419 gt). Later surveyed in respect of damage received during passage.
No trace after 1955.

T. 532   *TID 111*
Launched: 11.9.1944.
Completed: 12.1944.
Naval work to:
1948: Sold to Belgian buyers.
No further trace.

T. 533   *TID 112*
Launched: 15.9.1944.
Completed: 3.1945.
Naval work to:
6.1945: (Shipped to Calcutta for Admiralty).

1946: (Calcutta Port Commissioners).
No further trace.

T. 534   *TID 113*
Launched: 15.9.1944.
Completed: 11.1944.
1945: (M.O.W.T.).
1948: Sold to Belgian buyers.
No further trace.

T. 535   *TID 114*
Launched: 25.9.1944.
Completed: 3.1945.
Naval work to:
1.1948: (War Dept. – Army).
No further trace.

T. 536   *TID 115*
Launched: 25.9.1944.
Completed: 12.1944.
Naval work to:
1947: *Dollar Bay* (Port of London Authority).
1969: Scrapped River Medway, Kent.

T. 537   *TID 116*
Launched: 4.10.1944.
Completed: 12.1944.
Naval work to:
1947: *Tidworth* (James Contracting & Dredging Co.).
1947: (British Transport Commission, Newhaven).
1966: *Castor* (Liverpool Grain Storage & Transit Co.) (vessel converted to oil engine).
No trace after 1975.

T. 538   *TID 117*
Launched: 9.10.1944.
Completed: 12.1944.
Naval work to:
7.1945: Scheduled for refit and tropicalisation for service in the Far East, but plan cancelled.
1947: Reported sold to Uruguay.
No further trace.

T. 539   *TID 118*
Launched: 13.10.1944.
Completed: 12.1944.
Naval work to:
7.1945: Scheduled for refit and tropicalisation for service in the Far East, but plan cancelled.
1947: *Oco* (Olympic Oil & Cake Mills, Hull. Later British Oil & Cake Mills Ltd. (Unilever Ltd.)).
18.1.1961: In collision with mv *Henfield* (1949, 1,098 gt) in Swinefleet Reach, near Goole, River Ouse. Capsized and sank (voyage: Hull/Selby – towing barges).

1.2.1961: Raised and beached.
14.2.1961: Refloated, berthed at Goole, then towed to Hull. Repaired. Reported to have taken the name *Selby Olympia*; but no further trace.

T. 540   *TID 119*
Launched: 19.10.1944.
Completed: 1.1945.
2.1945: Naval work (Flushing, Holland) to:
1945: Renamed *W. 60* (Admiralty).
19. .: *W. 93* (Ministry of Public Building & Works, London).
19. .: *TID 119* (Admiralty).
2.1964: (Van den Bosche, Antwerp.) Reported broken up.

T. 541   *TID 120*
Launched: 26.10.1944.
Completed: 1.1945.
Naval work to:
6.1945: Scheduled for refit and tropicalisation for service in Far East, but plan cancelled.
1947: *Tideway* (James Contracting & Dredging Co. Ltd.).
1953: (Foremost Dredging Co., Southampton).
19. .: (Converted to oil engine) (Westminster Dredging Co.).
1973: *Tiderip* (D. Miller, Newhaven). (Used for towing, tendering and diving services: small crane fitted on engine casing.)

T. 542   *TID 121*
Launched: 29.10.1944.
Completed: 1.1945.
Naval work to:
8.1945: (M.O.W.T.).
1947: *Takare* (United Africa Co. Ltd.).
Later broken up.

T. 543   *TID 122*
Launched: 5.11.1944.
Completed: 1.1945.
Naval work to:
4.1945: (Shipped to Singapore for Admiralty).
10.1945: (Shipped to Hong Kong for Admiralty, per *Empire Charmian*).
11.1958: *Yau Tuen* (Yau Wing & Co., Hong Kong).
No further trace.

T. 544   *TID 123*
Launched: 9.11.1944.
Completed: 2.1945.
2.1945: (Shipped to Manus, Admiralty Islands, Pacific).
10.1945: (Shipped to Hong Kong for Admiralty, per *Empire Charmian*).

1949: Renamed *C. 742* (Admiralty).
12.1959: Sold (Tai Chiong, Hong Kong).
Reported scrapped.

T. 545   *TID 124*
Launched: 14.11.1944.
Completed: 2.1945.
2.1945: (Shipped to Manus, Admiralty Islands, Pacific).
10.1945: (Shipped to Hong Kong for Admiralty, per *Empire Charmian*).
11.1959: Sold (Tai Chiong, Hong Kong).
Reported scrapped.

T. 546   *TID 125*
Launched: 20.11.1944.
Completed: 2.1945.
11.4.1945: Arrived Liverpool from Hull via Milford Haven.
22.5.1945: Shipped as deck cargo from Bromborough Dock per *Empire Byng*.
19.6.1945: Arrived Bombay, (for Admiralty). Later shipped to Hong Kong.
1947: Sold (Wang Kee & Co., Hong Kong).
1947: Resold (Leung Yew, Hong Kong).
1950: *Hailey* (Peters & Co., Hong Kong).
1954: *Red Leaf* (China Union Trading Co., China).
Later reported stranded in South China Sea.
Constructive total loss.

T. 547   *TID 128*
Launched: 25.11.1944.
Completed: 2.1945.
11.4.1945: Arrived Liverpool from Hull, via Milford Haven – a voyage of 873 miles at 7½ knots and seven days in convoy.
22.5.1945: Shipped as deck cargo from Bromborough Dock, per *Empire Byng*.
19.6.1945: Arrived Bombay, for Admiralty.
No further trace.

T. 548   *TID 127*
Launched: 1.12.1944.
Completed: 5.1945.
11.1945: Shipped to Hong Kong per *Empire Marshal*, for Admiralty.
2.1946: (Hong Kong Harbour Board).
1948: (Hong Kong & Whampoa Dock Co.).
No further trace.

T. 549   *TID 128*
Launched: 7.12.1944.
Completed: 6.1945.
11.1945: Shipped to Hong Kong per *Empire Marshal*.
2.1946: (Hong Kong Harbour Board).
1947: *Hai Ming* (Shell Company of China Ltd.).

1948: (Asiatic Petroleum Co. Ltd., Hong Kong).
1952: *Shih Tou Shan* (Shell Company of Singapore Ltd.).
1957: (Kon. Nederlandse Maats. Voor Haven Werken, N.V., Holland).
No further trace.

T. 550   *TID 129*
Launched: 13.12.1944.
Completed: 2.1945.
3.1945: Shipped to Manus, Admiralty Islands, Pacific.
10.1945: Shipped to Hong Kong, for Admiralty, per *Empire Charmian*.
1958: (Wah Hing Metals Co., Hong Kong). Broken up.

T. 551   *TID 130*
Launched: 18.12.1944.
Completed: 2.1945.
3.1945: Shipped to Manus, Admiralty Islands, Pacific.
10.1945: Shipped to Hong Kong, for Admiralty, per *Empire Charmian*.
11.1959: Sold (Tai Chiong & Co., Hong Kong).
Later reported scrapped.

T. 552   *TID 131*
Launched: 28.12.1944.
Completed: 3.1945.
19.4.1945: Arrived Liverpool from Hull, via Falmouth.
22.5.1945: Shipped as deck cargo from Bromborough Dock, per *Empire Byng*.
19.6.1945: Arrived Bombay. Later shipped to Hong Kong for Admiralty.
1947: Sold (Wang Kee & Co., Hong Kong).
1947: Resold (Leung Yew, Hong Kong).
1951: *Shunley* (Peters & Co., Hong Kong).
1953: Reported sold to French buyers.
No further trace.

T. 553   *TID 132*
Launched: 3.1.1945.
Completed: 3.1945.
22.5.1945: Shipped as deck cargo from Bromborough Dock, per *Empire Byng*.
19.6.1945: Arrived Bombay, for Admiralty.
1946: *Tentu* (Singapore Harbour Board).
1964: Reported sold to Malaysian buyers.
No further trace.

T. 554   *TID 133*
Launched: 13.1.1945.
Completed: 3.1945.
22.5.1945: Shipped as deck cargo from Bromborough Dock, per *Empire Byng*.

19.6.1945: Arrived Bombay, for Admiralty. Later shipped to Calcutta (Calcutta Harbour Commissioners).
1946: Sold locally.
No further trace.

T. 555   *TID 134*
Launched: 19.1.1945.
Completed: 3.1945.
3.1945: (M.O.W.T.).
1948: (War Dept. – Army).
No further trace.

T. 556   *TID 135*
Launched: 29.1.1945.
Completed: 4.1945.
1945: Shipped from Liverpool to Rangoon (Government of Burma).
11.1947: (Inland Water Transport Board, Rangoon).
No further trace.

T. 557   *TID 136*
Launched: 7.2.1945.
Completed: 4.1945.
1945: Shipped to Colombo, Ceylon.
9.1946: At Rangoon, but transfer to Government of Burma cancelled.
1.1948: Shipped to Mombasa (for Admiralty Reserve) per mv *Belray* (1926, 2,904 gt).
1948: *Bunduki* (Mombasa owners).
1960: (East Africa Marketing Co. Ltd., Nairobi).
Later reported scrapped.

T. 558   *TID 137*
Launched: 14.2.1945.
Completed: 4.1945.
1945: Shipped to Colombo, Ceylon.
9.1946: At Rangoon, but transfer to Government of Burma cancelled.
2.1948: *Plover* (Tanganyika Railways) (for special service in connection with the Ground Nuts Scheme).
1951: *Toroka* (East African Railways & Harbour Administration).
No further trace.

T. 559   *TID 138*
Launched: 20.2.1945.
Completed: 4.1945.
6.1945: Shipped from Liverpool.
22.9.1945: Arrived Rangoon, but transfer to Government of Burma cancelled.
1948: *Lapwing* (Tanganyika Railways) (for special service in connection with the Ground Nuts Scheme).
1951: *Taveta* (East African Railways & Harbour Admin.).
No further trace.

T. 560   *TID 139*
Launched: 26.2.1945.
Completed: 4.1945.
1945: Shipped from Liverpool to Rangoon
(Government of Burma).
1947: (Inland Water Transport Board, Rangoon).
No further trace.

T. 561   *TID 140*
Launched: 2.3.1945,
Completed: 5.1945.
6.1945: Shipped from Liverpool.
22.9.1945: Arrived Rangoon, but transfer to
Government of Burma cancelled.
1948: Shipped to Ceylon (for Admiralty Reserve) per
mv *Belray* (1926, 2,904 gt).
11.1948: *Tiddler* (East African Railways & Harbour
Admin.).
No trace after 1953.

T. 562   *TID 141*
Launched: 7.3.1945.
Completed: 4.1945.
4.1945: (M.O.W.T.).
1948: (War Dept. – Army).
No further trace.

T. 563   *TID 142*
Launched: 10.4.1945.
Completed: 5.1945.
6.1945: Shipped from Liverpool.
12.1945: (At Gibraltar – Admiralty).
2.1946: (At Singapore – Admiralty).
1969: (Siong Huat Hardware Co. Ltd., Singapore).
1970: *Jaram* (converted to oil engine) (Straits
Engineers & Contracting Co., Singapore).
1982: Sank in Bamu River, Papua, New Guinea.

T. 564   *TID 143*
Launched: 16.4.1945.
Completed: 5.1945.
6.1946: (Chittagong Port Commissioners).
No further trace.

T. 565   *TID 144*
Launched: 21.4.1945.
Completed: 5.1945.
11.1945: Shipped to Singapore, for Admiralty, per
Empire Marshal (voyage: Liverpool–Port Said–
Singapore and Hong Kong).
1971: (Government of Singapore).
1972: *Mutiara II* (converted to oil engine) (Straits
Engineers & Contracting Co., Singapore).
1975: Sank in collision off Singapore.

T. 566   *TID 145*
Launched: 2.4.1945.
Completed: 5.1945.
11.1945: Shipped to Singapore, for Admiralty, per
Empire Marshal.
1971: (Government of Singapore).
1972: *Straits Endurance* (converted to oil engine)
(Straits Engineers & Contracting Co., Singapore).
1978: (Seng Leong Seng & Co., Singapore). Later
reported scrapped.

T. 567   *TID 146*
Launched: 4.5.1945.
Completed: 6.1945.
11.1945: Shipped to Hong Kong, for Hong Kong
Harbour Board, per *Empire Marshal*.
1948: *Taikoo Fu* (Taikoo Dockyard & Engineering
Co. Ltd., Hong Kong).
1968: Scrapped locally.

T. 568   *TID 147*
Launched: 18.5.1945.
Completed: 6.1945.
16.7.1945: Sailed from Hull for Liverpool, and:
11.1945: Shipped to Singapore (for M.O.W.T.) per
Empire Marshal.
3.1948: (J. Manners & Co., Hong Kong).
29.7.1948: Lost in Hainan Strait, South China Sea,
during a typhoon (delivery voyage to Hong Kong).

T. 569   *TID 148*
Launched: 5.1945.
Completed: 7.1945.
11.1945: Shipped to Hong Kong, for Hong Kong
Harbour Board, per *Empire Marshal*.
1948: *Tsing Shan* (Asiatic Petroleum Co. Ltd., Hong
Kong).
1951: (Lu Bros., Hong Kong).
1959: (Shell Oil Co. Ltd., Hong Kong).
No further trace.

T. 570   *TID 149*
Launched: 5.1945.
Completed: 7.1945.
11.1945: Shipped to Singapore, for Admiralty, per
Empire Marshal.
1971: (Government of Singapore).
1972: *Straits Progress* (converted to oil engine) (Straits
Engineers & Contracting Co., Singapore).
(Currently operating in Papua, New Guinea area.)

T. 571   *TID 150*
Launched: 4.5.1945.
Completed: 7.1945.
7.1945: (M.O.W.T.).
1947: *Cragdale* (Harris Barges Ltd., Liverpool).

1949: *Neston* (Elder, Dempster Lines Ltd.) shipped to Lagos per mv *Mary Kingsley* (1930, 4,083 gt).
10.1959: Scrapped.

T. 572   *TID 151*
Launched: 5.1945.
Completed: 7.1945.
18.8.1945: Sailed from Hull for Liverpool.
11.1945: Shipped to Hong Kong, for Hong Kong Harbour Board, per *Empire Marshal*.
1947: *Penguin* (Hong Kong & Whampoa Wharf & Godown Co.).
No trace after 1955.

T. 629   *TID 168*
Launched: 1946.
Completed: 6.1946.
1946: (Chartered to Anglo-Iranian Oil Co. Ltd.).

1947: *Lea* (Port of London Authority).
1969: Scrapped River Medway, Kent.

T. 630   *TID 169*
Launched: 1946.
Completed: 7.1946.
1946: (Chartered to Anglo-Iranian Oil Co. Ltd.).
1947: (Chartered to Port of London Authority).
1947: Sold to Finland.

The above vessel was delivered to Finland as part of a three-ship TID-tug convoy, in company with *TID 175* and *TID 176*, as follows:
25.4.1947: Sailed from Great Yarmouth.
26.4.1947: Arrived Rotterdam.
7.5.1947: Sailed Delfzyl.
8.5.1947: Passed Kiel Canal, bound for Helsinki.

In 1858 the Dunston family moved northwards some forty miles from the village of Torksey, in Nottinghamshire, to Thorne, north-east of Doncaster, Yorkshire, and there, beside the river Don, established a small shipbuilding business.

During the following decades the company, which subsequently became known as Richard Dunston Ltd., prospered and specialised in small craft construction.

In 1918 the shipyard obtained its first Admiralty contract – for three wooden drifters – and this association between the parties, formed more than seventy years ago, still continues into the present time.

The company survived the years of depression in the 1920s and in 1932 took over the shipbuilding firm of Henry Scarr Ltd., based at Hessle, near Hull, on the river Humber. Both continued to trade under their own names until 1961, when the Henry Scarr title was changed to Richard Dunston (Hessle) Ltd.

Reduced output between the wars was enhanced by spasmodic building to Admiralty and War Department (Army) requirements, but from January 1941 much of the company's capacity was taken up by Ministry of Transport/M.O.W.T. contracts. In the ensuing four years the two firms (Thorne and Hessle yards combined) delivered approximately 350 vessels, a miscellany of small craft such as barges, launches, lighters, coasters, target vessels, steam and diesel puffers (VIC-type lighters) and some 150 prefabricated steam TID-type tugs.

During the second half of 1945 eighteen shallow-draught tugs (Yard Nos. 580–597) intended for Irrawaddy river service were built at Thorne and in the following year the company constructed further small craft, including small waterboats for Burma, lighters and swim-type barges for use on the River Thames.

During 1974 the Dunston family sold their interests in the Richard Dunston Ltd. Group to the Ingram Corporation of New Orleans, U.S.A., but by the early 1980s the demand for small steel vessels was rapidly decreasing and in 1985 it was considered necessary to cease trading at the Thorne shipyard, where the smaller craft were constructed. At the same time the Ingram Corporation wished to realise their assets in the U.K. and consequently the Group was put up for sale. In 1986 a Management buy-out was successful in obtaining the assets of the Dunston companies.

Shortly after, the company was further strengthened by the interests of the Dutch shipbuilding group Damen Shipyards, who are now the sole owners of Richard Dunston through their parent company, HODAMA.

Dunston company records indicate that between them the Thorne and Hessle shipyards have built some 2,400 vessels, of which 470 have been naval/military orders – almost twenty per cent. of the entire output.

MERCHANT SHIPS BUILT UNDER PRIVATE CONTRACT OR LICENCE

349 *Vista* 71 gt, 69 ft × 18 ft. Engines: Oil. A tug.
Launched: 1940.
Completed: 6.1940 for Vokins & Co., London.
19..: *General IX* (Hastings Bros., Brentford).

352 *Meads* 74 gt, 68 ft × 19.5 ft. Engines: C2cyl. A tug.

Launched: 1940.
Completed: 4.1940 for River Lighterage Co. Ltd., London. No further trace.

377 *Pinklake* 88 gt, 71.3 ft × 20.5 ft. Engines: C2cyl. A tug.
Launched: 1942.
Completed: 3.1943 for River Lighterage Co. Ltd., London.
1961: *R. A. Everard* (F. T. Everard & Sons Ltd.).
1962: (New oil engine).

Built by Wm. Pickersgill & Sons Ltd., Sunderland

279 *TID 152*
Launched: 8.1945.
Completed: 1945.
1947: *Sir Milne* (Belfast Harbour Commissioners).
1984: Reported lying derelict in a bankrupt shipbreakers' yard at Malahide, near Dublin, Eire.

280 *TID 153*
Launched: 9.8.1945.
Completed: 1945.
1947: *Aigle* (S. A. Ossude, Le Havre).
No trace after 1969.

281 *TID 154*
Launched: 8.1945.
Completed: 1945.
1947: (Wilkins & Devereux Ltd.).
1947: (Solea Barge Co., Cyprus).
No trace after 1953.

282 *TID 155*
Launched: 28.8.1945.
Completed: 11.1945.
Naval work to:
1946: *Danae* (A. Holt & Co. Ltd., Liverpool) (for harbour duties at Hong Kong).
1959: (Wang Kee & Co., Singapore).

1961: *Hailey* (Sarawak Co., Kuching).
No further trace.

283 *TID 156*
Launched: 8.9.1945.
Completed: 1945.
1946: *Somerton* (Belfast Harbour Commissioners).
1984: Reported lying derelict in a bankrupt shipbreakers' yard at Malahide, near Dublin, Eire.

284 *TID 157*
Launched: 1945.
Completed: 1945.
1947: *Shell Dezoito* (Cia. Shell Oil Portuguesa, Lisbon).
1971: Name deleted from ship registers: no further trace.

285 *TID 158*
Launched: 1945.
Completed: 1945.
(Laid up after completion.)
1948: (Chartered to Port of London Authority).
1949: *Kerbau* (Anglo Saxon Petroleum Co. Ltd.).
1949: (Shell Company of Singapore Ltd.).
No trace after 1958.

286   *TID 159*
Launched: 1945.
Completed: 1945.
1947: (Port of London Authority).
1948: Renamed *Brent*.
1969: Sold for scrapping (Stour Salvage Co., Mistley, Essex).
1971: Resold; refitted for private use (R. & J. Hall, Maldon, Essex).

Note: This was the last steam tug to be employed in London's enclosed docks system.

287   *TID 160*
Launched: 1945.
Completed: 10.1945.
1945: (Government of France).
1947: *Vautour* (S. A. Ossude, Le Havre).
1957: (Soc. Dumez, Le Havre).
No trace after 1966.

288   *TID 161*
Launched: 9.8.1945.
Completed: 10.1945.
1945: (Government of France).
1947: *Corbeau* (S. A. Ossude, Le Havre).
1957: (Soc. Dumez, Le Havre).
No trace after 1966.

289   *TID 162*
Launched: 28.8.1945.
Completed: 10.1945.
1945: (Government of France).
1947: *Cygne* (S. A. Ossude, Le Havre).
1957: (Soc. Dumez, Le Havre).
No trace after 1966.

290   *TID 163*
Launched: 8.9.1945.
Completed: 10.1945.
Naval work to:
1946: *Hecuba* (Ocean SS Co. Ltd., Liverpool).
1949: *Provence* (Worms & Co., France).
No further trace.

291   *TID 164*
Launched: 8.1945.
Completed: 11.1945.
Naval work to:
1947: (Chartered to Port of London Authority).
1948: (Admiralty).
1974: (Medway Maritime Museum, Chatham, Kent).
1975: *Hercules* (International Towing Ltd. – operated on behalf of the Maritime Museum).
1978: (Reverted to original name and number) (M. Stevens, Sittingbourne, Kent).

The International Towing Ltd, formed in 1974, built up a towing fleet at reasonable cost and as a check on their operating costs used their facilities on the River Medway.

The company took the tug *Hero* (ex *John H. Amos* (1931, 202 gt)) from the River Tees and gave it its former name, intending the vessel for preservation and/or 'tourist' trips on the river, but not for commercial work. They also took the ex-Watkins' Gravesend-based tug *Cervia* (ex *Empire Raymond*, q.v.), the ex-Navy tug *Goliath* (ex *Empire Tessa*, q.v.) and the *TID 164*, which was renamed *Hercules*. Under her original name, *TID 164*, now in private ownership, is still 'in steam' on the River Medway; the *John H. Amos* now lies semi-derelict at Chatham, only minor preservation work having been carried out.

292   *TID 165*
Launched: 9.1945.
Completed: 12.1945.
Naval work to:
1948: (Admiralty).
12.1969: Scrapped Inverkeithing.

293   *TID 166*
Launched: 9.1945.
Completed: 12.1945.
1946: *Christine* (Ned. Maats. Havenwerken N.V., Amsterdam).
1965: Name removed from ship registers.
No further trace.

294   *TID 167*
Launched: 1945.
Completed: 1.1946.
1946: *Deanbrook* (Port of London Authority).
1969: Scrapped River Medway, Kent.

296   *TID 177*
Launched: 1945.
Completed: 5.1946.
1946: *Marlis* (Ned. Maats. Havenwerken N.V., Amsterdam).
1965: Name removed from ship registers.
No further trace.

297   *TID 178*
Launched: 17.1.1946.
Completed: 8.1946.
1946: *Bogen* (Sand & Singel A/S, Norway).

1953: (New oil engine).
1979: Name deleted from ship registers.
No further trace.

298   *TID 179*
Launched: 17.1.1946.
Completed: 8.1946.
1946: *Tocia* (Ned. Maats. Havenwerken N.V.,
Amsterdam) (vessel registered at Curaçao and used
in Netherlands West Indies).
1965: Name removed from ship registers.
No further trace.

299   *TID 180*
Launched: 1946.
Completed: 11.1946.
1946: *Cement 7* (A/S Christiana Cementfabrik,
Norway).
1958: *Kranfjord* (Risor Traemasse-fabrik, Norway).
1964: (Kaarbos M/V A/S, Norway).
No trace after 1968.

300   *TID 181*
Launched: 1946.
Completed: 8.1946.
1946: (Goteborgs Bogserings & Bargnings, Sweden).
No further trace.

301   *TID 182*
Launched: 1946.
Completed: 11.1946.
1947: *Lackenby* (Tees Conservancy Commissioners).
No trace after 1965.

302   *TID 183*
Launched: 1946.
Completed: 11.1946.
1947: *Snorre Sel* (L. Lorentzen, Norway).
1950: (A. Collett, Norway).
19. .: (Bodo Skibsverft, Norway).
1.1967: Scrapped Norway.

Built by Henry Scarr Ltd., Hessle, near Hull

S.478   *TID 170*
Launched: 1945.
Completed: 11.1945.
1946: (Chartered to Port of London Authority).
1947: (British registry closed): no further trace;
reported sold to overseas buyers.

S.479   *TID 171*
Launched: 20.11.1945.
Completed: 2.1946.
1946: (Chartered to Port of London Authority).
1947: (British registry closed): no further trace;
reported sold to overseas buyers.

S.480   *TID 172*
Launched: 11.1945.
Completed: 2.1946.
2.1946: *Martello* (Admiralty).
7.1946: *TID 172* (Admiralty).
10.1946: *W.92* (Ministry of Public Building & Works,
London).
10.1959: *TID 172* (Admiralty) (the last TID tug in
service in Chatham Dockyard).
7.1973: sold to shipbreakers at Grays, Essex.
8.1973: Resold for preservation (B. Pearce, Maldon,
Essex). Refitted with parts from *TID 107*, which had
been vandalised while lying at the shipbreaker's yard.
1978: Sold (A. Groom, Ipswich).

23.4.1983: Explosion on board while moored at Old
Custom House, Ipswich. Bulkhead ripped open,
fittings and equipment destroyed. Laid up.
1987: Sold after some renovation work carried out at
Ipswich (Steam Tid Ltd., Ipswich) – sponsored by
Norfolk, Essex and Suffolk Training Services Ltd. –
to provide training and experience for engineering
trainees and apprentices in the area.

S.481   *TID 173*
Launched: 21.1.1946.
Completed: 3.1946.
1946: (Chartered to Port of London Authority).
7.1946: (Government of France).
1948: *Abeille No. 1* ('Les Abeilles' Rem. et Sauv.,
France).
1959: Renamed *Abeille No. 29*.
1961: *Diu* (Enterprise René Levaux, Le Havre).
1964: Name removed from ship registers.
No further trace.

S.482   *TID 174*
Launched: 10.1945.
Completed: 2.1946.
1946: (Government of France).
1948: *Abeille No. 13* ('Les Abeilles' Rem. et Sauv.,
France).
1958: (New (oil) engine).
1963: *Baie Comeau* (Sirespa Building Co. Ltd.).

1966: *Bonchurch* (Red Funnel Tugs Ltd.,
Southampton).
1983: (H. G. Pounds, Portsmouth).
Later reported sold to a private buyer at Torquay: to
be used in a search for a sunken treasure ship off the
Devon coast.

S.483   *TID 175*
Launched: 11.1945.
Completed: 2.1946.
1946: (Chartered to Port of London Authority).

1947: Sold to Finland.
No further trace.
(See *TID 169*.)

S.484   *TID 176*
Launched: 11.1945.
Completed: 2.1946.
1947: Sold to Finland.
No further trace.
(See *TID 169*.)

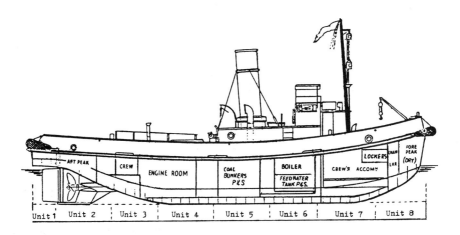

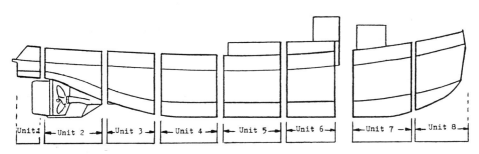

The 'TID'-type fabricated tug.

PART ELEVEN

MISCELLANEOUS

Section 1 Dredgers and hoppers

Built by Wm. Simons & Co. Ltd., Renfrew

767 *Empire Forager* 2,588 gt, 295.2 ft (oa),
287 ft × 52.6 ft. Engines: T6cyl – 10½ knots. A twin
screw suction hopper dredger.
Launched: 19.3.1946.
Completed: 4.1946.
1947: *M.O.P.229-C* (Government of Argentina).
1949: Renamed *La Descanisada*.
1958: Renamed *M.O.P.223-C*.
1986: Reported scrapped in Argentina in 1976.

768 *Empire Dockland* 683 gt, 167 ft (oa),
162 ft × 33 ft. Engines: T6cyl. Twin screw hopper
with bottom doors.
Launched: 24.6.1944.
Completed: 1944.
1944: *W.101* (Admiralty).
1947: Renamed *W.31*.
1963: (Ministry of Public Buildings & Works,
London).
1970: Offered for sale at Rosyth, by Board of Trade.
No further trace.

769 *Empire Portland* 683 gt. Details as Yard No. 768.
Launched: 7.9.1944.
Completed: 1944.
1948: *Morib* (Government of Federation of Malaya).
1953: (Queensland Cement & Lime Co.,
Australia).
1967: (Macquarie Plant Pool Pty. Ltd., Australia).
Name removed from ship registers – vessel non-
seagoing.

770 *Empire Upland* 683 gt. Details as Yard No. 768.
Launched: 26.12.1944.
Completed: 2.1945.
1945: (Superintendent Civil Engineer, Bombay).
1949: *Nirmal* (Indian Navy).

771 *Empire Sandboy* 512 gt, 160 ft (oa),
154 ft × 36 ft. Engines: C2cyl (aft). A bucket
dredger.
Launched: 15.12.1944.
Completed: 2.1945.
1945: (Superintendent Civil Engineer, Bombay).
1948: *M.O.P. 28-C.* (Government of Argentina).
1949: Renamed *Stella Maris, 28-C*.
1958: Renamed *M.O.P. 28-C, Stella Maris*.
1985: Name removed from ship registers – existence
of vessel in doubt.

774 *Empire Champion* 512 gt. Details as Yard No.
771.
Launched: 8.10.1945.
Completed: 12.1945.
1946: *W.94* (Admiralty).
1947: Renamed *St. Abbs* (W.3).
1963: (Ministry of Public Buildings & Works,
London). No further trace.

775   *Empire Moorland* 683 gt. Details as Yard No. 768.
Launched: 21.12.1945.
Completed: 1946.
1946: *W.98* (Admiralty).
1948: Renamed *W.29.*
1963: (Ministry of Public Buildings & Works, London).
1972: Offered for sale at Portsmouth, by Board of Trade. No further trace.

776   *Empire Marshland* 683 gt. Details as Yard No. 768.
Launched: 21.2.1946.

Completed: 1946.
1946: *W.30* (Admiralty).
1963: (Ministry of Public Buildings & Works, London).
1973: Offered for sale at Rosyth, by Board of Trade. No further trace.

777   *Empire Woodland* 683 gt. Details as Yard No. 768.
Launched: 17.4.1946.
Completed: 1946.
1946: *W.103* (Admiralty).
1948: Renamed *W.32.*
1963: (Ministry of Public Buildings & Works, London). No further trace.

The story of William Simons & Company began at Cartside, Greenock, in 1810. Two years later, in 1812, war broke out between Great Britain and the United States of America and with an urgent need for ships, Simons moved their yard to Canada, to be nearer the actual war, taking a site on Isle aux Noix, near Montreal, and where, for six years, until war ended, they built ships to 800 tons burthen. The company returned to Greenock in 1818.

This move lasted only a few years before another was made, to Whiteinch. One of the craft built here was the yacht *Tiara*. She was to have taken part in the America's Cup race against the schooner *America* in 1851, but in very rough seas from the Clyde to Cowes she was so delayed that she did not arrive in time.

Once again another move was made, this time to Renfrew in 1860 and within a few years the firm began building bucket dredgers and hopper barges and, in 1872, a hopper dredger. A Simons-built bucket hopper dredger, *Corozal*, was built for the Isthmian Canal Commission and did much work in moving the clay and rocks from the Pacific entrance to the Panama Canal and the spoil from the great landslides at the Culebra Cut.

Simons built some fifty smaller-type naval ships, sloops, minesweepers, tugs etc., in the 1914–1918 war and repeated this construction pattern in the 1939–1945 conflict.

In December 1930 the *Rietbok* was completed for the South African Railways & Harbours Administration. A twin-screw suction hopper dredger, she measured 374 ft in length, breadth was 57.7 ft and her gross tonnage 4,538 tons.

The last ship completed before World War II naval building began was the 2,790 gt, twin-screw suction hopper dredger *Baghdad* for the Government of Iraq, launched on 12 December 1939 and completed in February 1940. She was Yard No. 726. A private contract towards the end of hostilities was the *Lady Bourdillon* (Yard No. 766), another twin-screw suction hopper dredger, 345 ft × 53 ft and of 3,944 gross tons, launched 19 September 1944 and completed in the November for the Government of Nigeria.

When war ended the yard at Renfrew had seven berths for a ship capacity to 400 ft. In 1957 the company was acquired by G. & J. Weir; in 1959 the Weir Group also acquired Lobnitz & Co. Ltd., and Simons-Lobnitz Ltd. was formed. In 1964 the yard closed down.

Built by Lobnitz & Co. Ltd., Renfrew

966 *Empire Clydesdale* 1,747 gt, 290.6 ft (oa), 256.7 ft × 42 ft. Engines: T6cyl (aft). A suction hopper dredger.
Laid down as *Mazatlan* for Mexican Government; Requisitioned by M.O.W.T., and:

Launched: 30.10.1944 as *Empire Clydesdale*.
Completed: 12.1944.
1946: *Tuxpam* (Secretaria di Marina (Mexican Government)).
1977: Reported scrapped in Mexico in 1970.

The origins of Lobnitz & Company began in 1847 at the West Yard, Renfrew, but not in that name. The first occupier was James Henderson, who completed his first ship, the *Vesper*, 140 tons, 156 ft long, in 1848. Nine years later a Dane, Henry Lobnitz, joined the company. There was much expansion in the years that followed and in 1895 Lobnitz & Company was formed, by then specialists in the construction of dredgers – grab, bucket, suction, dipper and the related hoppers, barges and tugs.

Over one hundred craft were ordered for cutting the Suez Canal and more orders came from the original Panama Canal Company. The peculiar rockbreaker *Derocheuse* was built in 1887, a bucket dredger with ten rockcutters, each weighing three tons and there was much anxiety regarding its trim for its voyage through the Mediterranean.

Lobnitz built thirty-nine naval ships during the Great War and in September 1939 the company became an Admiralty-Controlled Undertaking. Boom Defence vessels were the first priority. The boom was a network arrangement which stretched across harbour entrances, acting as a submarine block, with the Boom Defence ships opening, closing, repairing and mooring the boom. Then in the yard's building list came minesweepers, landing craft, dredgers and store ships and much work on the construction of pierheads for the Mulberry Harbour installations. A dredger, laid down for the Mexican Government, was requisitioned and completed with 'Empire' nomenclature.

In 1957 Lobnitz & Company joined William Simons & Company to become Simons-Lobnitz Ltd., and in 1962 G. & J. Weir (Holdings) Ltd. acquired the company.

The last ship was *Hopper Barge No. 3*, 1,200 gt., for the Calcutta Port Commissioners and launched on 27 December 1963. She left the Clyde on 22 April 1964 and the yard closed.

. . .

As the Allied invasion fleet set out from Spithead on the eve of D-day, in June 1944, Admiral Sir Bertram Ramsay, in his Flagship, hoisted a signal to all the forces in the great assembly of ships in Spithead, 'Good Luck, Drive On'. The Senior Officer of the leading minesweeping flotilla was quick to reply, again in flags at the yard-arm, 'Aye, Aye, sir, Nelson in the van'. And it was Nelson, Commander George Nelson R.N., minesweeper flotilla leader on the Lobnitz-built H.M.S. *Pelorus*, leading the invasion fleet. The signal was repeated by all ships of the flotilla and attached craft and kept flying as they left. H.M.S. *Pelorus* was the first to arrive at the far shore.

SHIP BUILT UNDER PRIVATE CONTRACT

1016 *Prittlewell* 160 gt, 100.8 ft (oa), 96.7 ft × 25.1 ft. Engines: (two) diesel-electric, (aft). A grab hopper dredger.
Launched: 1.9.1939.

Completed: 6.1940 for the Borough of Southend-on-Sea, Essex.
1971: *Essex Lady* (Tartan Arrow Marine Ltd., London).
1977 (Bridlington Harbour Commissioners).

Launch of the dredger *Empire Sorcerer*. (Ferguson Bros. Ltd., Yard No. 375.)

Built by Ferguson Bros. Ltd., Port Glasgow

375   *Empire Sorcerer* 2,594 gt, 295 ft (oa),
285 ft × 52.5 ft. Engines: T6cyl (aft) – 10½ knots. A
twin-screw suction hopper dredger.
Launched: 21.2.1946.
Completed: 4.1946.
1947: *M.O.P.230-C* (Government of Argentina).
1949: Renamed *Miguel Miranda*.
1958: Renamed *M.O.P.224-C*.

The *Empire Sorcerer* was a twin-screw bow well, combined
trailing and suction cutting dredger, one of the largest and
most powerful of her type when built to Admiralty order.
She was designed to load 2,000 tons per hour into her own
hopper, or to deliver the spoil ashore by floating pipeline.
The hopper doors were hydraulically operated. Dredging
operations were controlled from a special control room on
the upper deck; the vessel was fitted out for working in the
tropics and a searchlight was fitted for night working.

When launched, the vessel was practically complete, with all
machinery fitted aboard.

376   *Empire Hartland* 683 gt, 167 ft (oa),
162 ft × 33 ft. Engines: T6cyl (aft). A twin-screw
hopper.
Launched: 16.5.1946.
Completed: 1946.
1946: *Mersey No. 3* (Mersey Docks & Harbour
Board).
1965: *WD Alpha* (Westminster Dredging Co. Ltd.,
London).
1968: *WK Alpha* (Hok Kiang Heng Co (PN Waskita
Karya, Indonesia)).
1972: *WD Alpha* (Qon Char Koon, Singapore).

The four Ferguson brothers began the Newark Shipyard in 1903, specialising over the years in
dredging equipment, tugs, ferries and estuarial craft. During the 1939–1945 period the yard built
trawlers, corvettes and Boom Defence vessels. Also completed were a number of ferries for the
Government of Turkey.

In July 1963 it was announced that the entire capital of Ferguson Brothers (Port Glasgow) Ltd.
had been acquired by Lithgows Ltd. The yard had four berths to a maximum of 350 feet.

SHIPS BUILT UNDER PRIVATE CONTRACT OR LICENCE

346   *St. George* 208 gt, 111.5 ft (oa), 105 ft × 26 ft.
Engines: T6cyl. A twin-screw tug.
Launched: 20.12.1941.

Completed: 5.1942 for Government of Trinidad.
6.3.1977: Foundered at Port of Spain, Trinidad.

Ferries built for the government of Turkey – see Ferries.

Built by Fleming & Ferguson Ltd., Paisley

699 *Empire Conjuror* 512 gt, 160 ft (oa),
154 ft × 37 ft. Engines: C2cyl (aft). A bucket dredger.
Launched: 5.10.1944.
Completed: 12.1944.
1945: (Superintendent Civil Engineer, Bombay).
1946: (Mitchell Engineering Group, London).
1948: *Seyhan* (Ministry of Public Works, Turkey).
1985: (Bayindirlik Bakanligi Makina Ve Ikmel, Turkey).

700 *Empire Downland* 683 gt, 167 ft (oa),
162 ft × 33 ft. Engines: T6cyl (aft). A twin-screw hopper with bottom doors.
Launched: 19.12.1944.
Completed: 4.1945.
1945: (Superintendent Civil Engineer, Bombay).
1947: *Chas. A. Phayer* (Melbourne Harbour Trust Commissioners).
1966: *Leven* (Devonport Marine Board, Tasmania). Sold, and:
6.1988: Scrapped Devonport, Tasmania.

701 *Empire Heathland* 683 gt. Details as Yard No. 700.
Launched: 2.4.1945.
Completed: 5.1945.
1945: (Superintendent Civil Engineer, Bombay).
1947: *Mersey No. 4* (Mersey Docks & Harbour Board).
1964: *WD Beta* (Westminster Dredging Co. Ltd., London).
1968: *WK Beta* (Hok Kiang Heng Co (PN Waskita Karya, Indonesia)).
1972: *WD Beta* (Qon Char Koon, Singapore).

702 *Empire Grassland* 683 gt. Details as Yard No. 700.
Launched: 16.5.1945.
Completed: 6.1945.
1945: (Superintendent Civil Engineer, Bombay).
1946: Acquired by Melbourne Harbour Trust Commissioners, and:
20.1.1947: Broke adrift after hopper doors broke off in heavy seas seventy miles NNW of Carnarvon, W. Australia, while being towed by sistership *Empire Downland* (Yard No. 700, above) from Singapore to Melbourne. No further trace; presumed to have foundered. Total loss.

708 *Empire Mammoth* 938 gt, 241.5 ft (oa),
195 ft × 40.1 ft. Engines: T3cyl (aft). A bucket dredger.
Launched: 6.7.1945.
Completed: 11.1945.
1946: *St. Ives* (Admiralty).
1963: *Bucket Dredger W.2* (Ministry of Public Buildings & Works, London).
1964: (Ministry of Defence, London).
(*circa*) 1970: (H. G. Pounds, Portsmouth).
1972: Sold (as *St. Ives*) to Italy, and:
27.12.1972: Capsized in heavy weather NW of Ferrol, Spain, while in tow of tug *Smit Pioneer* (1972, 495 gt) on voyage Portsmouth/Palermo. Sank in position 44.21N 08.57W.

The Phoenix Shipyard at Paisley dated from 1877, although at that time it was under the control of H. MacIntyre & Company. The company moved on to Alloa and in 1885 the two-families company, Fleming & Ferguson, acquired the yard and began building dredgers and other types of estuarial and coastal craft. The firm became a limited company in 1898 and continued to build up a reputation in the development of the reciprocating engine and continued building it after World War II had ended.

In January 1965 it was announced that Fleming & Ferguson Ltd. was to go into liquidation, but the yard was then acquired by the American Marine & Machinery Company and continued to build dredgers and the like. The last ship to be built was *Hopper Barge No. 4* (Yard No. 812), of 859 gross tons, completed in March 1968 for the Calcutta Port Trust. The yard finally closed down on 27 September 1968.

SHIPS BUILT UNDER PRIVATE CONTRACT OR LICENCE

557   *Baccalieu* 1,421 gt, 242.2 ft (oa),
233.5 ft × 37 ft. Engines: T3cyl. A ferry.
Launched: 28.11.1939.
Completed: 4.1940 for the Government of
Newfoundland (Railway SS Dept.).
1949: (Canadian National Railways).
12.1969: Scrapped St. John's, N.F.

558   *Burgeo* 1,421 gt. Details as Yard No. 557.
Launched: 7.2.1940.
Completed: 6.1940 for the Government of
Newfoundland (Railway SS Dept.).
1949: (Canadian National Railways).
9.1969: Scrapped St. John's, N.F.

732   *Cargo Fleet No. 3* 920 gt, 207.2 ft (oa),
201.1. ft × 31.1 ft. Engines: T3cyl (aft). A hopper
barge with bottom doors.
Launched: 22.11.1945.
Completed: 1.1946 for Cargo Fleet Iron Co. Ltd.,
Middlesbrough.
1953: (South Durham Steel & Iron Co. Ltd.).
1967: (Stephenson Clarke Shipping Ltd., London).
1972: Renamed *Megstone*.
1975: (Belcon Shipping & Trading Co.).
1981: Reported broken up in the U.K. in 1975.

733   *Larubi* 100 gt, 74 ft × 23 ft. A non-propelled
dredger fitted with pump-ashore equipment.
Launched: 27.9.1945.
Completed: 12.1945 for Anglo-Iranian Oil Co. Ltd.
(for port reclamation service in Middle East). No
further trace.

734   *Taff* 607 gt, 192.5 ft (oa), 172 ft × 54.2 ft. A
hopper dredger.
Launched: 5.3.1946.
Completed: 9.1946 for Great Western Railway
Company.
1948: (British Transport Commission).
1955: Deleted from ship registers as non-seagoing,
but:
(*circa*) 1969: Reported sold for tank cleaning services
on River Thames.

736   *Mandovi* 530 gt, 195.7 ft (oa),
176.9 ft × 32.2 ft. Engines: T6cyl (aft). A twin-screw
suction hopper dredger.
Launched: 1946.
Completed: 11.1946 for Portuguese Government
(Governo Geral do Estado da India (Later:
Exploradora do Porto Mormugao)).
1962: (Taken over by Government of India
(Mormugao Port Trust)).
1964: Deleted from ship registers as non-seagoing.
1978: Sold for breaking up.

Section 2   Landing Ships, Tank; Ferries

Landing ships

A Tank Landing Ship (LST (Mark 3)) type was ordered by the Admiralty in 1944 when agreement could not be reached with the United States over the allocation of the LST (2) type ships to the two Allies. The new ships were intended for invasions in the Far East theatre of war.

Over 100 ships of the new type were planned. In the event forty-five came from shipyards in Britain, with allocated pennant numbers from 3001–3045 and others came from Canadian yards,

The *Empire Gannet*, formerly *LST 3006*, with a deck cargo of vehicles. (Harland & Wolff Ltd., Belfast, Yard No. 1289.)

The Convoy Rescue Ship *Empire Shelter*, in the Clyde. (G. Brown & Co. (Marine) Ltd., Yard No. 230.)

Strathclyde Regional Archives

A ferry built for Turkish account and ready for her delivery voyage.

Davie Shipbuilding & Repairing Company, Lauzon; Canadian Vickers Ltd., Montreal, and Yarrows Ltd., Esquimalt, to be numbered 3501–up.

Propulsion of the ships was by T8cyl engines of 2,750 hp, driving twin screws to give 11 knots, diesel engines being unavailable for such a big programme. The engines were placed aft, as was the bridge. Tanks were loaded over a bow ramp into the interior and from another ramp leading from the tank deck heavy vehicles could be stowed on the open upper deck. Loaded displacement was 4,820 tons; measurements were 345 ft (oa), 330 ft × 54 ft., and troop capacity (in narrow side-deck dormitories, to either side of the upper tank deck space) was for 168.

The contracts for these LSTs were placed under the classification of Transport Ferries. A number of contracts were cancelled when hostilities ended and work ceased on some vessels under construction, these being subsequently completed as merchant ships.

. . .

Some of the ships were transferred to the Ministry of Transport (Army) in 1946 and were named after Army officers. They were placed under the management of the Atlantic Steam Navigation Co. Ltd., London, in 1953 and then passed to British India Steam Navigation Co. Ltd., management in 1961.

LST No.:
3001   Frederick Clover Built: Vickers, Tyne, in 1945.
1966: *Pacific Pioneer* (Philippine American Shipping Corp. Inc., Panama).
9.12.1968: Arrived Hong Kong for breaking up.

3009   Reginald Kerr Built: Harland & Wolff, Belfast, in 1945.
3.1966: Scrapped Singapore.

3021   Charles McLeod Built: Lithgows Ltd., in 1945.
22.7.1968: Arrived Spezia for breaking up.

3024   Maxwell Brander Built: Smiths Dock Co., in 1945.
1968: *Fedredge Isabel* (F. M. V. Holding S.A. (Mollers

Ltd., Hong Kong)).
8.1969: Scrapped Hong Kong.

3028   Snowdon Smith Built: A. Stephen Ltd., in 1945.
14.1.1961: Arrived Spezia for breaking up.

3037   Evan Gibb Built: Fairfield Ltd., in 1945.
11.2.1963: Arrived Spezia for breaking up.

3509   Humphrey Gale Built: Davie Shipbuilding & Repairing Co. Ltd., Lauzon, P.Q., in 1945.
10.1.1961: Arrived Genoa for breaking up.

TRANSPORT FERRIES BUILDING, BUT COMPLETED AS MERCHANT SHIPS

LST No.:
3004 Launched by Vickers, Armstrongs Ltd., Walker, in 1945.
1.1950: Converted and completed at Rio de Janeiro as *Rio Tejo* (4,033 gt) for E. G. Fontes & Cia., Rio de Janeiro.
1955: *Sao Joaquim* (L. Figueiredo Nav. S.A., Rio de Janeiro).
10.1959: Scrapped Porto Alegre, Brazil.

3018 Launched by Hawthorn, Leslie & Co. Ltd., Newcastle, in 1945.
6.1949: Converted and completed at Rio de Janeiro as *Rio Minho* (3,915 gt) for E. G. Fontes & Cia., Rio de Janeiro.

1955: *São Pedro* (L. Figueiredo Nav. S.A., Rio de Janeiro).
10.1959: Scrapped Porto Alegre, Brazil.

3023 Launched by Lithgows Ltd., Port Glasgow, in 1945.
1949: Converted and completed at Rio de Janeiro as *Rio Guadiana* (4,033 gt) for E. G. Fontes & Cia., Rio de Janeiro.
1955: *São Paulo* (L. Figueiredo Nav. S.A., Rio de Janeiro).
1960: *Dom Jose* (Nav. Costa Lima Ltda., Brazil).

On 12 March 1964 the above vessel, under the name of *Guarani*, was reported to be drifting sixty miles north-east of the coast of Surinam, Dutch Guiana, with engine trouble, whilst on a contraband coffee run to the U.S.A. Later, various efforts to tow the ship, made by small tugs of the Alcoa SS Co., and the Surinam vessel *Gran Rio* (1957, 990 gt) all proved abortive, but on 21 March, with the arrival of the Bahamian tug *Ginny* (1944, 683 gt) the *Guarani* was towed to Paramaribo, assisted by Alcoa's tug *Wana*.

On berthing, the *Guarani*'s Paraguayan crew of thirty-three all left without trace while the vessel, although flying the flag of Paraguay, was found to be not registered and carried no identification marks, and no documents or certificates of nationality were found on board. The ship was placed under restraint by the local authorities and the cargo – 50,000 bags of Brazilian coffee – was discharged. Half of it was trans-shipped to New York and most of the remainder to Europe. The balance, water damaged, remained in port custody.

Later, the vessel was allowed to sail and left port in tow of the tug *Ginny*, bound for Georgetown, Guyana, but on 6 April she sank in mysterious circumstances in (approx.) position 6.00N 56.30W.

3032 Launched by C. Connell & Co. Ltd., Glasgow, in 1945.
10.1950: Converted and completed at Rio de Janeiro as *Rio Mondego* (4,033 gt) for E. G. Fontes & Cia., Rio de Janeiro.

The Continental Line Transport Ferry Service was put into operation by Frank Bustard & Sons Ltd. (Atlantic Steam Navigation Co. Ltd.) in view of the growing demand for the movement of road transport by sea. The service began in September 1946 as a six-day round trip, from No. 4 berth, Tilbury Docks, to Hamburg, carrying Government vehicles for the British Forces in Germany and U.N.R.R.A. supplies. This quickly grew to include commercial vehicles and private cars and was extended to Rotterdam and Antwerp.

For this service three ships were chartered from the Ministry of Transport, *LSTs 3512, 3519* and *3534* in their original state and were sent to Harland & Wolff at Tilbury where accommodation for twelve passengers, a merchant crew and fifty lorry drivers was fitted and a new bridge built. The vessels were given the standard M.O.T. 'Empire' nomenclature for ships under their control.

On 20 May 1948 another route was inaugurated from Preston to Larne, Northern Ireland, by the *Empire Cedric* and in January 1949 was joined by the *Empire Gaelic* in a two-ship service, with another ferry, *Empire Doric* in reserve.

By 1957 these services had expanded with a fleet of seven ex-LST(3)-type ships working on six to seven sailings each week on the Irish Sea run and two each week from Tilbury to the Continent. But in that year, two ships of new design were launched at

1955: *Sao Sebastiao* (L. Figueiredo Nav. S.A., Rio de Janeiro).
10.1959: Scrapped Porto Alegre, Brazil.

3039 Launched by Fairfield S.B. & Engineering Co. Ltd., Glasgow, in 1945.
12.1951: Converted and completed at Rio de Janeiro as *Rio Douro* (3,915 gt) for E. G. Fontes & Cia., Rio de Janeiro.
1955: *São Bernardo* (L. Figueiredo Nav. S.A., Rio de Janeiro).
10.1959: Scrapped Port Alegre, Brazil.

3030 Launched by Hall, Russell & Co. Ltd., Aberdeen, in 1945.
1949: Completed for S. Bartz-Johannessen, Bergen, Norway, as a Herring Oil factory, renamed *Clupea*.
1960: (Etab. A. Guelfi and R. Ostrowsky, Mauritania).
3.4.1961: Caught fire in Port Étienne Roads, Mauritania, while serving as a Mother Ship for fishing vessels. Fire extinguished, but:
6.4.1961: Again on fire.
8.4.1961: Sank in position 20.53N 17.03W, with superstructure (above water) still afire.
14.4.1961: Fire extinguished. Total loss.

. . .

Dumbarton for the Atlantic SN Company and the landing ships which had been adapted to peacetime needs were gradually returned to the Ministry of Transport, the last, *Empire Nordic*, in the winter of 1966–1967. Of the seven ships, (listed below) four were Canadian-built.

Empire Baltic ex-*LST 3519* – 1946. Built: Canadian Vickers Ltd., Montreal, in 9.1945.
1961: (Managed by British India SN Co. Ltd.).
10.7.1962: Arrived Spezia for breaking up.

Empire Cedric ex-*LST 3534* – 1946. Built: Yarrows Ltd., Esquimalt, B.C., in 11.1945.
16.9.1960: Arrived Ghent for breaking up.

Empire Celtic ex-*LST 3512* – 1946. Built: Davie SB & Rep. Co. Ltd., Lauzon, P.Q., in 9.1945.
3.1964: Scrapped Spezia.

Empire Doric ex-*LST 3041* – 1948. Built: Harland & Wolff Ltd., Govan, in 6.1945.
13.1.1960: Arrived Port Glasgow for breaking up.

Empire Gaelic ex-*LST 3507* – 1948. Built: Davie SB & Rep. Co. Ltd., Lauzon, P.Q., in 6.1945.
9.1960: Scrapped Burcht, Belgium.

Empire Cymric   ex-*LST 3010* – 1947, ex-*Attacker* – 1954. Built: Harland & Wolff Ltd., Belfast, in 4.1945.
1.10.1963: Arrived Faslane for breaking up.

Empire Nordic   ex-*LST 3026* – 1946, ex-*Charger* – 1955. Built: Blyth DD & SB Co. Ltd., in 6.1945.
1968: Sold to German shipbreakers; resold to Spanish shipbreakers, and
10.10.1968: Arrived Bilbao in tow, from Barrow, for breaking up.

During the Suez crisis of 1956 twelve LST(3)-type ships, cocooned in the River Clyde, were recalled to service and used as military transport ferries. Their bases were at Malta, Aden and Singapore. These ships were given 'Empire' nomenclature and operated for the Ministry of Transport by the Atlantic SN Co. Ltd.

They continued under this arrangement until 1961 when ten of the twelve were transferred to the management of the British India SN Co. Ltd., the exceptions being *Empire Puffin* and *Empire Shearwater*. The ten vessels wore B.I. flags and hull colours, but with buff superstructure.

The twelve ships were:

Empire Curlew   ex-*Hunter*, ex-*LST 3042*. Built: Harland & Wolff Ltd., Govan, in 11.1945.
20.8.1962: Arrived Spezia for breaking up.

Empire Fulmar   ex-*Trumpeter*, ex-*LST 3524*. Built: Davie SB & Rep. Co. Ltd., Lauzon, P.Q., in 11.1945.
1.1969: Scrapped Singapore (where laid up for some time).

Empire Gannet   ex-*Tromso*, ex-*LST 3006*. Built: Harland & Wolff Ltd., Belfast, in 3.1945.
8.1968: Scrapped Singapore.

Empire Grebe   ex-*Fighter*, ex-*LST 3038*. Built: Fairfield SB & Eng. Co. Ltd., in 7.1945.
8.1968: Scrapped Singapore.

Empire Guillemot   ex-*Walcheren*, ex-*LST 3525*. Built: Davie SB & Rep. Co. Ltd., Lauzon, P.Q., in 11.1945.
7.1968: Scrapped Singapore (where laid up for some time).

Empire Gull   ex-*Trouncer*, ex-*LST 3523*. Built: Davie SB & Rep. Co. Ltd., Lauzon, P.Q., in 10.1945.
1968: (Board of Trade Sea Transport Branch).
3.1980: Arrived Santander for breaking up.

Empire Kittiwake   ex-*Slinger*, ex-*LST 3510*. Built: Davie SB & Rep. Co. Ltd., Lauzon, P.Q., in 7.1945.
1.1969: Scrapped Singapore.

Empire Petrel   ex-*Thruster*, ex-*LST 3520*. Built: Canadian Vickers Ltd., Montreal, in 10.1945.
6.1968: Scrapped Singapore (where laid up for some time).

Empire Puffin   ex-*Battler*, ex-*LST 3015*. Built: Barclay, Curle & Co. Ltd., in 1945.
1960: (K. C. Irving, St. John, N.B.).
5.7.1966: Arrived Spezia, in tow, for breaking up.

Empire Shearwater   ex-*LST 3033*. Built: Wm. Pickersgill & Sons Ltd., in 1945.
1958: (European Ferries Ltd. (Townsend Bros. Ferries Ltd.)).
28.11.1962: Arrived Ghent for breaking up.

Empire Skua   ex-*St. Nazaire*, ex-*LST 3517*. Built: Yarrows Ltd., Esquimalt, B.C., in 9.1945.
31.1.1968: Arrived Spezia, in tow, for breaking up.

Empire Tern   ex-*Pursuer*, ex-*LST 3504*. Built: Canadian Vickers Ltd., Montreal, in 5.1945.
9.1968: Scrapped Singapore (where laid up for some time).

Ferries

In 1939 eight ferries were ordered by the Government of Turkey from Swan, Hunter & Wigham Richardson Ltd., and four from Ferguson Bros., Port Glasgow.

They were passenger- and vehicle-carrying ferries with ramps at both ends, for work in the Dardanelles, but could be used by the Turkish Navy as netlayers and, if necessary, quickly converted for minelaying. Dimensions were 187.7 ft (oa), 179.5 ft × 40.2 ft and tonnages were 692 gross, 350 deadweight. Triple-expansion, coal-fired engines were placed aft.

The vessels were constructed in two distinct batches, the first eight launched in 1940 and the latter four in 1941. Some of the vessels were requisitioned by the Royal Navy before hand-over, for use in the North African area of operations.

Delivery of the ships, under the British flag, was contracted to Townsend Bros., who had begun their ship delivery service in 1890 and were later to introduce the car ferry to the English Channel. The delivery voyages of the groups of ferries were astonishing in that after a call at Madeira, they sailed south to round the Cape of Good Hope, up the east coast of Africa and through the Suez Canal to Turkey. Only one was lost, off Lebanon. This was the *Murefte*, which was at Durban in May 1941 and left there on 6 July, bound for Mombasa. The voyages of some of the others to the Mediterranean can be traced by various casualty reports of minor incidents: the *Eceabat* was at Port Said in May 1941; the *Erdek* and *Kilye* both at Istanbul in August 1941; the *Sarkoy* was in collision with the American ship *Lilian Luckenbach* (1919, 6,369 gt) at Port Tewfik on 29 September 1941 and the *Darica* and *Derince* both at Cape Town in June 1942. Strangely, perhaps, the *Silivri* was in the casualty reports while still on the stocks and some three months before being launched when, in May 1941, her hull was damaged during an enemy air raid on Glasgow.

Built by Swan, Hunter & Wigham Richardson Ltd., Newcastle

1662 *Eceabat*
Launched: 17.6.1940.
1942: Turkish Navy (Y.1165).

1664 *Erdek*
Launched: 20.10.1940.
1942: Turkish Navy (Y.1164).
1983: Withdrawn from service.

1666 *Gemlik*
Launched: 1940
6.1941–3.1942: (Royal Navy).
1942: Turkish Navy.

1668 *Kilye*
Launched: 1940.
1942: Turkish Navy (Y.1166).

1670 *Lapseki*
Launched: 10.1940.
6.1941–3.1942: (Royal Navy).
1942: Turkish Navy.
1983: Withdrawn from service.

1672 *Mudanya*
Launched: 11.1940.
1942: Turkish Navy.
1946: (Ministry of National Defence, but for civilian use).
1974: Withdrawn from service; converted to a base for pilotage service.
1984: Laid up at Pendik.

1674 *Murefte*
Launched: 14.11.1940.
19.9.1941: Sunk by Italian submarine (*Topasio*) gunfire, 33.12N 34.35E, off Beirut, Lebanon, on delivery voyage to Turkey.

1676 *Sarkoy*
Launched: 29.11.1940.
6.1941–12.1941: (Royal Navy).
1942: Turkish Navy (Y.1156).

Built by Ferguson Bros. Ltd., Port Glasgow

352   *Cardak*
Launched: 10.4.1941.
Completed: 11.1941.
1942: Turkish Navy.
1946: (Ministry of National Defence – but for civilian use).
1971: Withdrawn from service.

353   *Silivri*
Launched: 8.1941.
1942: Turkish Navy.
1946: (Ministry of National Defence – but for civilian use).
1948: Turkish Navy.

354   *Darica*
Launched: 9.9.1941.
9.1942–11.1943: (Royal Navy).
1943: Turkish Navy.

355   *Derince*
Launched: 8.11.1941.
Completed: 12.1941.
27.12.1941: Aground at Glasgow after trials. Refloated.
14.1.1942: Sailed from Clyde on delivery voyage.
6.1942: At Cape Town, undergoing minor repairs.
1942: Turkish Navy.
1946: (Ministry of National Defence – but for civilian use).
1966: (Canakkale Port Authority).

On 1 November 1966, when the *Derince* was on only her seventh run for the Canakkale Port Authority, she sank after collision during a storm with the Russian mv *Taifun* (1964, 4,727 gt). The *Derince* was on ferry service across the Dardanelles, from Canakkale (Asian side) to Eceabat (European side), laden with passengers and vehicles. In an admission of blame, the Russian authorities immediately offered another ship to compensate for the loss of the ferry, but the offer was rejected.

Four ferries similar to the earlier twelve built for Turkish account were ordered by the Ministry of War Transport. One was released to replace the Turkish loss, with the remaining three completed as 'Empire' ships. They were also equipped with a 25-ton heavy-lift derrick amidships, this situated at the front of the superstructure.

Built by Swan, Hunter & Wigham Richardson Ltd., Newcastle

1752   (Laid down as) *Sarkov*
Launched: 28.7.1942 as *Tuzla* for Turkish Government.
Completed: 9.1942.
3.1943–11.1943: (Royal Navy).
1943: Turkish Navy (Y.1168).

1754   *Empire Dace* 716 gt.
Launched: 11.8.1942.
Completed: 9.1942.
7.1943: Requisitioned by Royal Navy.
1.12.1944: Struck mine at entrance to Missolonghi, north of Gulf of Patras, Greece. Sank. Total loss.

1756   *Empire Roach* 716 gt.
Launched: 25.8.1942.
Completed: 10.1942.

1942: (Operated by Townsend Bros. Ltd.).
1965: (Operated by Ellerman's Westcott & Laurence Line Ltd.).
1968: (Progressive Trading Agency Ltd., Malta).
1970: (Cantieri Navale Giuseppe, Italy). (Vessel at Augusta, Sicily, awaiting conversion to a floating crane), but:
1978: Dismantled; lower part of hull used as a barge at Augusta.

1758   *Empire Chub* 716 gt.
Launched: 10.9.1942.
Completed: 10.1942.
1942: (Operated by Townsend Bros. Ltd.).
1962: *Panther* (Payardi Shipping & Contracting Co., Panama).
9.1968: Converted to a barge in Italy.

Section 3   Water carriers

Built by W. J. Yarwood & Sons (1938) Ltd., Northwich, Cheshire

718   *Empire Billow* 215 gt, 100 ft (oa), 95 ft × 23 ft.
Engines: C2cyl (aft).
Launched: 1943
Completed: 6.1943.
1946: (Admiralty).
10.1963: Scrapped Antwerp.

759   *Empire Barnaby* 222 gt, 106 ft (oa),
100 ft × 23 ft, 251 tdw. Engines: C2cyl (aft) – 7
knots.
Launched: 2.5.1944.
Completed: 7.1944 for the Admiralty.

In January 1967 this vessel, lying in Portsmouth Dockyard, was offered for sale by the Ministry of Transport. Purchased by J. Havens, of London, she later sailed and on 24 June left Brest, France, for Vianna, Portugal, for breaking up. Ten days later she was reported as an overdue vessel, being described as 'painted black, but rusted'. After being adrift with engine trouble for six days, with only two men and no radio installation on board, she was found by a Spanish fishing vessel and towed to Santona, Spain.

Here, the *Empire Barnaby* was detained, as unseaworthy, by the local authorities and the detention continued, later, due to non-payment to the salvors.

760   *Empire Fulham* 222 gt. Details as Yard No. 759.
Launched: 6.1944.
Completed: 10.1944 for the Admiralty.
2.1967: (I. P. Langford Shipping Ltd., Sharpness).
1974: Renamed *Fulham*.

Apart from one dry cargo coaster, *Empire Bridge* (q.v.) and a few small ships for private account, Yarwood's war construction was for dockyard craft. When war ended the company had twelve berths for vessels to 200 ft, and in June 1946 it was acquired by United Molasses Co. Ltd.

The yard ceased building at the end of 1965 after the last ship was delivered. This was the motor tug *St. Elmo* (Yard No. 950), 168 gt, 100.2 ft (oa), 90 ft × 26.9 ft, for the Midmed Towage Co. Ltd., Malta.

SHIPS BUILT UNDER PRIVATE CONTRACT OR LICENCE

667   *Denham* 103 gt, 71 ft × 18.6 ft. Engines: T3cyl.
A tender.
Launched: 1.7.1941.
Completed: 1.1942 for Mersey Docks & Harbour
Board.
18.7.1946: Struck drifting mine in Rock Channel,
Liverpool Bay. Sank. Total loss.

763   *Barnton* 216 gt, 98 ft × 23 ft. Engines: C2cyl. A
lighter.
Launched: 6.1944.
Completed: 1944 for Imperial Chemical Industries
Ltd.
1963: Deleted from shipping registers, as non-
seagoing.

A series of non-propelled cargo lighters were also built:–

–	*Bishops Pointer*	Launched: 1940
–	*Bishops Retriever*	Launched: 1941
–	*Bishops Terrier*	Launched: 1942
766	*Bishops Beagle*	Launched: 1945
767	*Bishops Whippet*	Launched: 1945
–	*Bishops Greyhound*	Launched: 1946
–	*Bishops Foxhound*	Launched: 1946

105 ft × 23.5 ft.
(approx). 185 gt; 260 tdw.
Built for Liverpool Lighterage Co. Ltd., and/or the
associated Bishops Wharf Carrying Co. Ltd.,
London.

Section 4   Floating cranes constructed for the Ministry of War Transport

Crane barges for river service – 615 gt, 125 ft × 62.5 ft.

Fabricated by Fairfield SB & E Co. Ltd., Chepstow and Newport, Mon., some completed by Palmers (Hebburn) Co. Ltd.

Yard No.				Managers during the war:
306/1	*MOWT 1*	Completed:	5.1942	Corporation of Bristol.
		(Newport).		
306/2	*MOWT 2*	Completed:	7.1942.	Mersey Docks & Harbour Board, Liverpool.
306/3	*MOWT 3*	Completed:	10.1942.	Clyde Navigation Trustees, Glasgow.
306/4	*MOWT 4*	Completed:	6.1943.	Port of London Authority.
306/5	*MOWT 5*	Completed:	1.1943.	Great Western Railway, Cardiff.
306/6	*MOWT 6*	Completed:	3.1943.	Mersey Docks & Harbour Board, Liverpool.

. . .

Self-propelled crane barges – 779 gt, 179.8 ft (oa), 173.1 ft × 57.1 ft. Engines: C4cyl (aft). Twin screws

Built by Fleming & Ferguson Ltd., Paisley

Yard No.				Managers during the war:
587	*MOWT 7*	Launched:	28.5.1942.	Mersey Docks & Harbour Board, Liverpool.
		Completed:	8.1942.	
596	*MOWT 8*	Launched:	20.11.1942.	Clyde Navigation Trustees, Glasgow.
		Completed:	2.1943.	
614	*MOWT 9*	Launched:	11.3.1943.	Mersey Docks & Harbour Board, Liverpool.
		Completed:	6.1943.	
615	*MOWT 10*	Launched:	18.5.1943.	Great Western Railway, Cardiff.
		Completed:	9.1943.	

. . .

Crane barges for river service – 613 gt, 125 ft × 62.5 ft.

Fabricated by Palmers (Hebburn) Co. Ltd., completed by J. Russell & Co. Ltd., London

			Managers during the war:
–	*MOWT 11*	Completed: 11.1943.	Southern Railway, London.
–	*MOWT 12*	Completed: 10.1943.	Southern Railway, Southampton.
–	*MOWT 13*	Completed: 1.1944.	Southern Railway, Southampton.
–	*MOWT 14*	Completed: 9.1944.	Port of London Authority.

. . .

Some floating derricks, 289 gt, 74.5 ft × 50 ft were completed by the Barry Graving Dock Co. Ltd., in 1943–1944.

Section 5   Concrete ships

Production of concrete vessels during the war was confined to the building of large numbers of barges by assembly line method and which did not bite into steel stocks or tap the skilled labour of shipyards. However, there were also two cargo ships built of ferro-concrete, the first of which commenced trials in December 1941; the second was built by cement interests and not to Admiralty order.

Built by W. & C. French Ltd., Newport, Mon.

– *Lady Wolmer* 1,883 gt, 277.3 ft (oa), 268.1 ft × 42.3 ft. Engines: Oil.
Launched: 12.1941.
Completed: 4.1942 for Ministry of War Transport (Managers: Walford Lines Ltd.).
1947: (Eastern Asia Navigation Co. Ltd. (Wheelock, Marden & Co. Ltd., Hong Kong)).
20.5.1953: Ashore off Cheju Island, South Korea, 33.32N 126.50E. Total loss (voyage: Kobe/Pusan and India – general).

555 *Lady Kathleen* 1,857 gt, 277 ft (oa), 266.3 ft × 41.9 ft. Engines: Oil.
Launched: 2.4.1943.
Completed: 9.1943 for Concrete Maritime Ltd. (Managers: Wm. Cory & Son Ltd.).
1947: (D/S A/S Phoenix (Paal Wilson & Co. A/S., Norway)).
29.11.1951: Dragged anchor and ashore in Riga Bay, Latvia, during a gale.
1.12.1951: Broke in two. Total loss (voyage: Helsinki/Riga – ballast).

W. & C. French Ltd. also built a number of barges at their Grays, Essex, yard. All were of ferro-concrete, with rolled steel framing. They were 107.5 ft × 25 ft and 192 gt. They were for service on the River Thames and in the port of London; were classed as experimental and subject to annual survey. In 1945 all were in the ownership of F. T. Everard & Sons Ltd., London. They were:

Yard No.			Yard No.		
WCF 2	*St. Anne*	Completed: 8.1943	WCF 5	*St. Bees*	Completed: 3.1944
WCF 3	*St. Asalph*	Completed: 9.1943	WCF 6	*St. Mawes*	Completed: 1944
WCF 4	*St. Austell*	Completed: 1.1944	WCF 7	*St. Michael*	Completed: 1944

Many more concrete, non-propelled barges were mass-produced by assembly line building, being constructed from pre-cast sections made in various sites around the country from concrete placed in moulds and vibrated at high speed to 'shake it down', then moved to the erection yard for completion.

Except for bow and stern shapes, the concrete slabs were of standard shape and size, 7 ft × 3 ft × 2 inches thick. Only a little steel reinforcement was necessary and steel ends projected for the interlocking and knitting process when being assembled. However, a certain amount of reinforcing of the concrete for keelson, floors, frames and hatch coamings was also necessary.

The weight of the barge was 128 tons, made up of 174 pre-cast units and 12¼ tons of reinforcing steel. The deadweight capacity was 200 tons.

Those barges that worked on the canals and narrow rivers had moveable rudders with tillers, but those employed on the reaches of the River Thames were of the familiar swim-ended dumb-barge form with budgett plate – a plate protruding aft, on the centre-line and acting as a fixed rudder.

The Stem-type barges were 84.7 ft long × 22.7 ft deck width and 19.5 ft at bottom; the Swim-type 86 ft × 24 ft. The hatch was 47.7 ft × 16 ft and the sides were fendered with elm timbering.

The first barge was laid down in May 1940; construction time being later worked down to seventy-four hours from launching one barge to launching the next from the same berth. Wates Ltd., Barrow-in-Furness, were major builders of these prefabricated barges; others were produced by Grays Ferrocrete Company, Tarrans and J. Lowe & Sons, of Liverpool.

All the barges were prefixed FB and numbered. Nearly 500 were constructed, of which some 200 could carry liquid cargo in bulk.

Section 6   Ore carriers

Built by Lithgows Ltd., Port Glasgow

All 2,922 gt, 325.8 ft (oa), 315.2 ft × 44.4 ft. Engines: T3cyl (aft). Single deck vessels; no cargo battens fitted.

948 *Empire Stream*
Launched: 2.12.1940.
Completed: 3.1941.
25.9.1941: Sunk by submarine (*U.124*) torpedo in
Atlantic, (approx.) 700 miles west of Cape Finisterre,
Spain, 46.03N 24.40W whilst in convoy HG 73
(Gibraltar/United Kingdom) (voyage:
Huelva/Dundee – iron ore).

949 *Empire Ridge*
Launched: 7.2.1941.
Completed: 4.1941.
19.5.1941: Sunk by submarine (*U.96*) torpedo, ninety
miles west of Bloody Foreland, Donegal, Eire,
55.08N 10.40W (voyage: Melilla/Workington – ore).

950 *Empire Ness*
Launched: 17.3.1941.
Completed: 5.1941.

30.11.1944: Collided with American Liberty ship
William Paca (1942, 7,176 gt) in River Scheldt and
sank near Terneuzen, Holland. Masts and funnel
above water; forward decks blown up due to
explosion of gas bottles in cargo. Salvage not
practicable due to wreck settling rapidly in the mud,
sinking twenty feet in a few days. Total loss (voyage:
Cherbourg/Antwerp – confidential Sea Transport
cargo).

951 *Empire Moat*
Launched: 28.4.1941.
Completed: 7.1941.
20.9.1941: Damaged by submarine (*U.124*) torpedo
approx. 800 miles west of Ushant, France,
48.07N 22.05W, whilst in convoy OG 74 (United
Kingdom/Gibraltar). Abandoned; remained afloat but
salvage not practicable. Presumed to have sunk.

Section 7   Convoy rescue ships

Ships for convoy rescue work were requisitioned mainly from companies engaged in coastal work around Britain's coastline. Many of these were passenger-carrying ships with a speed of 11–12 knots, enabling them to catch up with 10-knot convoys after rescue work.

All eleven ships of the 1939 fleet of the Clyde Shipping Company were requisitioned, seven becoming convoy rescue ships under the Sea Transport Division of the M.O.W.T., and including *Copeland*, *Toward*, *Goodwin* and *Rathlin*. The *Beachy* was the first to be requisitioned and the first to be lost, sunk by enemy bombers some 500 miles west of Ireland on 11 January 1941.

Six ships of the General Steam Navigation Company were taken up as rescue ships and the two G.S.N. ships *Halcyon* and *Philomel*, which had been sold to the Pharoaonic Mail Line, Egypt, in 1934, and renamed *Zamalek* and *Zaafaran* were re-acquired, requisitioned by the M.O.W.T. and placed under G.S.N. management as rescue ships.

In all, twenty-nine ships were taken up. As the war progressed more facilities were added. The ships carried rescue boats and rafts; booms with nets could pick up seamen or drifting rafts; medical facilities included an operating theatre; overall there was warmth and comfort from the heaving sea.

Union-Castle Line's *Walmer Castle*, a feeder motorship in peacetime, was behind convoy OG 74 to Gibraltar on 21 September 1941 when she was bombed and sunk by a solitary German FW 200 plane. At the time the ship was rescuing seamen from the torpedoed ships *Baltallinn* and *Empire Moat*. Another loss was the *Melrose Abbey*, owned by Associated Humber Lines. She was sunk by torpedo on 27 December 1942 while in convoy ONS 154, in the North Atlantic. The London & North Eastern Railway steamer *Stockport*, with distressed seamen from the torpedoed *Empire Trader* and straggling behind convoy ON 166 was herself sunk by U.604 on 23 February 1943 . . .

So it was that these small rescue ships played their part in the rescue of so many seamen, then having to straggle behind the convoy, in great danger, whilst rejoining the formation. The vessels were all mercantile-manned and operated and, not being immune to enemy attack, were armed – generally with AA guns.

Up to June 1945 the rescue ships had covered 2¼ million miles on 796 voyages with convoys and had saved the lives of about 4,200 British and Allied seamen.

Five 'Castle'-class corvettes were completed as Convoy Rescue Ships and given 'Empire' names. After the war, from 1946, they took the role of troopships and/or transports and were based in the Eastern Mediterranean, ferrying troops, etc., between Port Said, Malta, Tobruk, Tripoli and Famagusta.

These ships were 252 ft (oa), 236 ft × 36 ft and their T4cyl engines gave 16½ knots. Gross tonnage was 1,333. All five vessels were managed by City Line Ltd. (Ellerman Lines Ltd.), on behalf of the Ministry of Transport.

Built by Ferguson Bros. Ltd., Port Glasgow

371   *Empire Rest*
Launched: 19.6.1944 as *Rayleigh Castle* for Royal Navy.
Completed: 10.1944 for M.O.W.T.
7.1948: (Laid up at Falmouth).
10.1951: (Lloyds Albert Yard & Motor Boat Packet Services Ltd. (R. A. Beazley), Southampton).
6.6.1952: Arrived Briton Ferry for breaking up.

372   *Empire Comfort*
Launched: 29.9.1944 as *York Castle* for Royal Navy.
Completed: 12.1944 for M.O.W.T.
(*circa*) 1954: (Laid up at Falmouth).
7.1955: Sold to Belgian buyers; towed to Antwerp. Reported to be reconditioned for service in Belgian Congo, but scheme not proceeded with.
12.1955: Scrapped Ghent, Belgium.

Built by Fleming & Ferguson Ltd., Paisley

664   *Empire Lifeguard*
Launched: 8.6.1944 as *Maiden Castle* for Royal Navy.
Completed: 11.1944 for M.O.W.T.
23.7.1947: Holed by underwater explosions of limpet mines fixed to hull in Famagusta; listed and sank in Haifa Harbour soon after disembarking Jewish immigrants brought from detention camps in Cyprus.
8.8.1947: Refloated, and
22.8.1947: Towed to Port Said: drydocked.
9.1947: Caught fire three times whilst under repair; repairs finally completed.
(*circa*) 1954: (Laid up at Falmouth).
22.7.1955: Arrived Antwerp in tow of tug *Marinia* (1955, 392 gt) for breaking up.

9.1955: Scrapping commenced, but
12.11.1955: Moved to Burght for completion of demolition.

665   *Empire Peacemaker*
Launched: 8.9.1944 as *Scarborough Castle* for Royal Navy.
Completed: 1.1945 for M.O.W.T.
(*circa*) 1954: (Laid up at Falmouth).
7.1955: Sold to Belgian buyers; towed to Antwerp. Reported to be reconditioned for service in Belgian Congo, but scheme not proceeded with.
12.1955: Scrapped Ghent, Belgium.

Built by G. Brown & Co. (Marine) Ltd., Greenock

230   *Empire Shelter*
Launched: 5.10.1944 as *Barnard Castle* for Royal Navy.
Completed: 3.1945 for M.O.W.T.

(*circa*) 1954: (Laid up at Falmouth).
22.7.1955: Arrived Antwerp in tow of tug *Marinia* (1955, 392 gt) for breaking up.
9.1955: Scrapped Burght, Belgium.

PART TWELVE

SHIPBUILDERS SOLELY INVOLVED IN THE CONSTRUCTION OF MERCHANT SHIPS UNDER PRIVATE CONTRACT OR LICENCE

John Brown & Co. Ltd., Clydebank, Glasgow

John Brown & Co. Ltd. was a combination of steelworks in Sheffield and J. & G. Thompson's shipbuilding and engineering works on the Clyde. The steelworks was the older, John Brown having started business in the earlier years of the 19th century, in 1854 acquiring Queen's Steelworks which, restyled as Atlas Works, was to lead the industry when the ironclad era began.

James & George Thompson began their small engine and boiler works at Finnieston, Glasgow, in 1846, quickly building up a reputation which induced them to move into the shipbuilding business in 1851 with the small Clyde Bank Yard. But this was merely the beginning and in 1873 they moved to Clydebank where neither housing accommodation for workers nor railway facilities offered. Nevertheless, it was a permanent site, with adjacent land available for expansion, but they were not to know that their infant Clyde yard would one day launch the world's largest liners from its slipways into the River Clyde and where the mouth of its tributary, the River Cart, conveniently opposite, would need to be dredged and so made available to assist in the launching of the huge hulls.

Ten years later their engineering works were also moved from Finnieston to Clydebank and the site area quickly extended to thirty-five acres.

J. & G. Thompson had become closely associated with the Cunard Line over the years and in 1881 completed the 7,390 gt *Servia*, and *Aurania* in 1883. Other Atlantic ships were National Line's *America* of 1883, to be the Blue Riband holder in 1884, and Inman's *City of New York* and *City of Paris* in 1888–1889, which later became *New York* and *Philadelphia* of the American Line.

In 1890 the company became a limited concern; in 1897 it was restyled as the Clydebank Engineering & Shipbuilding Co. Ltd., and in 1899 joined with John Brown to become John Brown & Co. Ltd., now with greater resources to build bigger ships.

In 1905 came two 20,000 ton Cunarders, *Caronia* and *Carmania*; then the Government-financially-assisted *Lusitania* and *Inflexible*, a 20,000-ton displacement battle cruiser in 1908; Cunard's *Aquitania*, 45,000 gt in 1914; the battleship *Barham* of 1915, and 1918 saw completed the largest naval ship, the battle cruiser *Hood*, of 42,000 tons displacement.

In 1930 the yard, already having launched the 42,000 ton *Empress of Britain* on 11 June for Canadian Pacific, laid down Yard No. 534 on 27 December, to be Cunard's 81,000 gt *Queen Mary*. For this, the East (Main) Yard was extended.

But in 1931, in the great depression, work stopped and was not restarted until 1934. On 26 September of that year the huge hull was launched, the River Cart entrance having been considerably dredged for the event. The *Queen Mary* was completed in April 1936. Eight months later, on 4 December 1936, the keel of Yard No. 552 was laid, destined to be the *Queen Elizabeth*, the world's largest passenger liner.

John Brown & Co. Ltd. completed the huge liner in the early months of war and only built four commercial ships to the end of 1944. Their output of warships of many types, however, was enormous.

The yard built the prototype of the last development of the wartime escort, *Loch Fada*, which was really a 'River'-class hull, altered in detail for construction on the pre-fabrication basis. However, the changing pattern of war necessitated ever greater anti-aircraft ability and a number of 'Loch'-class orders were so adapted, these ships becoming the 'Bay'-class. Thirty 'Loch'-class ships were completed and fifty-four orders cancelled; twenty-six ships became the 'Bay'-class. Orders were spread to fourteen yards.

In 1945 the company's yard and works were spread over eighty acres. Five berths for ships 600 ft to 1,000 ft were in the East (Main) yard and three, for vessels 450 ft–600 ft in the West Yard. River frontage was 1,050 yards and there was a 5½ acres tidal basin.

Effective from 7 February 1968 the yard became the Clydebank Division of a new consortium of Clyde shipbuilding yards, Upper Clyde Shipbuilders Ltd. In 1971 Upper Clyde Shipbuilders Ltd. went into liquidation.

MERCHANT SHIPS BUILT UNDER PRIVATE CONTRACT OR LICENCE

552   *Queen Elizabeth* 83,673 gt, 1,031 ft (oa), 987.4 ft × 118.6 ft. Engines: Sixteen steam turbines geared to four shafts.
Launched: 27.9.1938.
Completed: 27.2.1940 for Cunard White Star Ltd., London.
2.3.1940: Left River Clyde, ostensibly for Southampton, but sailed direct to New York, arriving 7 March.
13.11.1940: Left New York for drydocking at Singapore.
2.1941: arrived Sydney for conversion to troopship.
9.4.1941: Left Sydney together with the liner *Queen Mary* with troops for Suez.
4.10.1945: Left Southampton for New York with 15,932 troops and passengers, the largest number carried by the ship on any voyage. In war work carried 811,324 service personnel and steamed a total of 492,635 miles.
16.10.1946: First commercial voyage from Southampton to New York.
23.10.1968: Last voyage Southampton/Cherbourg/New York.
30.10.1968: Last voyage New York/Cherbourg/Southampton, where arrived 4.11.1968.
4.11.1968.
29.11.1968: Left Southampton for Port Everglades, Fla., to be a convention centre.

8.12.1968: Arrived, renamed *Elizabeth* (Elizabeth Corporation (Cunard Steam-Ship Co. Ltd.)).
1969: (Queen Ltd., Port Everglades).
1970: Sold by auction to Seawise Foundations Ltd. (C. Y. Tung, Hong Kong). Renamed *Seawise University*.
16.7.1971: Arrived Hong Kong for conversion to a Floating University but
9.1.1972: On fire, explosions and listing;
10.1.1972: Capsized;
13.1.1972: Fire extinguished.
1974: Broken up, *in situ*, Hong Kong harbour.

566   *Hororata* 12,090 gt, 551.3 ft (oa), 532.2 ft × 70.4 ft. Engines: six steam turbines. Twin screw.
Launched: 9.10.1941.
Completed: 4.1942 for New Zealand Shipping Co. Ltd., London.
1967: (Federal SN Co. Ltd.).
1967: *Nor* (Astroguarda Cia. Nav. S.A. of Panama (Mavroleon Bros. (Ship Management Ltd.)); renamed for delivery voyage to shipbreakers and
6.9.1967: Arrived Kaohsiung for breaking up.

577   (Laid down as) *Port Victor* 528.5 ft (oa), 505.3 ft × 68.3 ft. Engines: Oil. Twin screw. Refrigerated cargo ship.
Laid down: 7.11.1941 for Port Line Ltd.;

requisitioned by the Admiralty and converted to an escort carrier to carry eighteen aircraft; Flight deck: 495 ft.

Launched: 20.5.1943 as H.M.S. *Nairana*.
Completed: 12.12.1943 (Pennant D.05).
1946: *Karel Doorman* (Royal Netherlands Navy).
1948: *Nairana* (Royal Navy).
1949: *Port Victor* (Port Line Ltd.). Converted to a cargo ship (10,409 gt).
1969: (Cunard Steam-Ship Co. Ltd.).
1971: (Port Line Ltd.).
21.7.1971: Arrived Faslane for breaking up.

This vessel was one of the two ships of the 'Port Napier'- (1940 series) to be requisitioned while still under construction and completed as escort carriers. As H.M.S. *Nairana* she hunted U-boats in the Atlantic and escorted convoys to Russia during the 1944–1945 period.

In March 1946 she was transferred to the Royal Dutch Navy where she was used for training flying personnel under the name *Karel Doorman*. Early in 1948 she returned to the Royal Navy and reverted to her former name until June when she was re-acquired by the Port Line and sent to Harland & Wolff, Belfast, for conversion to a cargo liner. After removing 3,000 tons of steel structure and a similar amount of pig iron ballast, some 1,500 tons of new steel was added, to form the normal '3-islands' of an orthodox vessel. Conversion work lasted almost fifteen months and in September 1949 she was named *Port Victor* and sent on trials in Belfast Lough. (See also *Port Vindex*, Yard No. 1783, Swan, Hunter & Wigham Richardson Ltd.)

604   *Norfolk* 11,272 gt, 560.7 ft (oa),
541.3 ft × 70.2 ft. Engines: Oil. Twin screw. Refrigerated cargo ship.
Launched: 13.6.1946.
Completed: 2.1947 for Federal SN Co. Ltd.
1953: *Hauraki* (New Zealand Shipping Co. Ltd., London).
1966: (Federal SN Co. Ltd.).
1973: (P & O SN Co. Ltd.).
22.12.1973: Arrived Kaohsiung for breaking up.

628   *Port Wellington* 10,644 gt, 528.8 ft (oa),
508.5 ft × 68.3 ft. Engines: Oil. Twin screw. Refrigerated cargo ship.
Launched: 4.2.1946.
Completed: 9.1946 for Port Line Ltd.
21.7.1971: Arrived Castellon for breaking up.

Fairfield Shipbuilding & Engineering Co. Ltd., Govan, Glasgow

The roots of the huge Fairfield company are traceable back to the mid-1850s. The outstanding name in its origins is that of John Elder whose early training in the engineering field was given by Robert Napier, at Govan. Elder went on to the firm of engineers, Randolph, Elliott & Company, which in 1852 became Randolph, Elder & Company.

In 1860 Napier's old yard at Govan was acquired and four years later land was bought close to a farm named Fairfield, near to Govan village. By the year 1871 it had become the largest known shipbuilding site.

But in 1869 Elder died and a partnership to continue the business as John Elder & Company was formed by his widow in the following year. This lasted until 1886 when the company was reorganised and renamed the Fairfield Shipbuilding & Engineering Company Ltd., a title which was to become of world-wide significance and was to last for eighty years.

A notable early building success was the *Arizona*, built in 1879 for the Guion Line, which broke both east and west crossing times on the North Atlantic. Many orders for liners were received from the major shipping companies of the age; the *Armadale Castle* in 1903 and *Balmoral Castle* in 1910 were for Union-Castle Line's service to South Africa; Canadian Pacific's *Empress of Britain* was delivered in 1905, *Empress of Ireland* in 1906 and the 16,000 gt *Empress of Russia* and *Empress of Asia* in 1913.

On the naval side, Fairfield's first big order came at the turn of the century with the 17,500 tons (displacement) *Commonwealth*, a 12-inch gun battleship of the 'King Edward VII'-class. And in the Great War the building lists were dominated by naval ships, including the battleship *Valiant*, battle-cruiser *Renown*, the light cruisers *Undaunted* (1914), *Cardiff*, *Carlisle* and *Colombo* in 1917–1919 as well as twenty-four destroyers, including six 'M' and five each of the 'O' and 'S'-classes.

When war ended, Fairfields constructed another four berths, but the anticipated building boom did not last. However, the yard kept busy and in 1921 built Anchor Line's *Tuscania*; then *Athenia* and *Letitia* for Anchor-Donaldson Line in 1923 and 1925 respectively. In 1924 the company completed the 17,000 gt *Aorangi* for the Union SS Company of New Zealand, a quadruple-screw motorship, propelled by four 6-cyl oil engines. She was then the largest and fastest motorship in the world. More Canadian Pacific liners were constructed, the *Montrose* and *Empress of Canada* in 1922 and the 26,000 gt *Empress of Japan* in 1930.

During the depressed years of the early 1930s the yard completed the submarine depot ship *Woolwich* for the Royal Navy in 1934 and went on to build the battleship *Howe*, two aircraft carriers and many lesser ships for the Royal Navy during World War II.

When the war ended there were six building berths for ships to 1,000 ft, a 5½-acre basin with a 270 ft entrance and length of 900 ft, and a 3,000 ft water frontage.

In 1961 the engineering works were merged with David Rowan of Glasgow and restyled as Fairfield-Rowan, but in 1965 Fairfields went into receivership and closed down.

A new company, Fairfield (Glasgow) Ltd., was formed in the following year, but joined the Upper Clyde Shipbuilders group in 1968 as their Govan Division and the Fairfield name ended.

MERCHANT SHIP BUILT UNDER PRIVATE CONTRACT OR LICENCE

728   *Beavercove* 9,824 gt, 497.5 ft (oa), 476 ft × 64 ft. Engines: two turbines to electric motor.
Launched: 16.7.1946.
Completed: 8.1947 for Canadian Pacific SS Ltd. (Canadian Pacific Railway Company).
1952: renamed *Maplecove*.
1956: renamed *Beavercove*.

1963: *Giovanna Costa* (C. Costa fu Andrea, Genoa).
1968: (Costa Armatori SpA).
24.3.1971: Arrived Spezia for breaking up.

Note: Three sisterships, *Beaverdell*, *Beaverglen* and *Beaverlake*, were built by Lithgows Ltd. (Yard Nos. 1001–1003).

Fellows & Co. Ltd., Southtown, Great Yarmouth

MERCHANT SHIPS BUILT UNDER PRIVATE CONTRACT

342   *S. A. Everard* 124 gt, 88.7 ft (oa), 84 ft × 21.6 ft. Engines: Oil. A tug.
Launched: 1939.
Completed: 11.1939 for F. T. Everard & Sons Ltd., London.

345   *Richard Lee Barber* 122 gt, 88.6 ft (oa), 83 ft × 20 ft. Engines: T3cyl. A tug.
Launched: 14.9.1939.
Completed: 2.1940 for Great Yarmouth Port & Haven Commissioners.
4.1966: Scrapped Antwerp.

The company was engaged mainly in the building of landing craft during the 1939–1945 war. In 1947 the yard had three berths to a 120 ft capacity.

Lytham Shipbuilding & Engineering Co. Ltd., Lytham, Lancs.

This small yard on the estuary of the River Ribble built two small steam coasters, for commercial buyers, in the early part of the war, but its main wartime output was a group of fourteen water carriers for the Admiralty, the vessels used for the replenishment of ships in naval dockyards. Their construction stretched over six years, from the first launching (Yard No. 862) in March 1940 to the last (Yard No. 886) in August 1946. The measurements were 121 ft × 25.5 ft and tonnage was 283 gross tons.

The remainder of the yard's war work was in connection with the Mulberry harbours project and the construction of landing craft and naval steam lighters.

The yard, which had been founded in 1892 further up the Ribble, closed in the mid-1950s, one of the last vessels constructed being a motor chain ferry for Windermere, Yard No. 903, with measurements of 95 ft × 30 ft. Launched on 24 June 1954 as *Drake* and completed in July, she was for the Councils of Lancashire and Westmorland.

MERCHANT SHIPS BUILT UNDER PRIVATE CONTRACT OR LICENCE

864 *Maplefield* 492 gt, 148.3 ft (oa), 142.5 ft × 27.2 ft. Engines: T3cyl.
Launched: 28.1.1941.
Completed: 6.1941 for Zillah Shipping & Carrying Co. Ltd. (W. A. Savage & Co. Ltd.).
23.2.1945: In collision with American steamer *Gateway City* (1920, 5,432 gt) four miles east of St. Goven Light, Pembroke (voyage: Penmaenmawr/Holyhead/Swansea – stone). Sank, total loss.

865 *Larchfield* 493 gt. Details as Yard No. 864.
Launched: 11.6.1941.
Completed: 10.1941 for Zillah Shipping & Carrying Co. Ltd. (W. A. Savage & Co. Ltd.).
1950: (Zillah Shipping Co. Ltd. (Coast Lines Ltd.)).
20.2.1957: Arrived Barrow for breaking up.

Henry Robb Ltd., Leith

Henry Robb began his firm on 1 April 1918. His workforce comprised six men. In late 1917 and early 1918 there was much concern regarding the casualties being inflicted by the U-boats and orders for repair work were quickly obtained. Drydocks were rented and within months the workforce neared 1,000 men. But the war had reached its end and after the immediate postwar boom, there began the world slump. However, Robb managed to obtain an order for building, hired a drydock – for the firm had no waterfront – and built their first ship, a dredger. Two waterfront berths were acquired, Ramage & Ferguson's old derelict yard was taken over and the number of berths then numbered eight. Coasters and short sea traders were the main production in the period of the 1930s.

Apart from a few coasters for the General Steam Navigation Company and some tugs for work on the Manchester Ship Canal, the company worked in the construction of naval ships during the years of World War II, particularly of corvettes, frigates and trawlers. The 'Bustler'-class of eight tugs was also built, the first fleet tugs to be fitted with diesel engines. Three of the corvettes were for the New Zealand Navy.

In 1947 the yard had six berths, taking ships to 330 feet in length.

Henry Robb Ltd. acquired the Caledon Shipbuilding & Engineering Co. Ltd., Dundee, in 1968 to become Robb Caledon Shipbuilders Ltd. The yard at Dundee closed down on 17 September 1968; the Leith yard was shut down in 1984.

SHIPS BUILT UNDER PRIVATE CONTRACT OR LICENCE

291   *Underwood* 1,990 gt, 273.5 ft (oa),
263 ft × 45.2 ft. Engines: Oil (aft).
Launched: 15.1.1941.
Completed: 6.1941 for Union SS Company of New Zealand Ltd.
6.1.1944: Sunk by E-boat torpedo in Western Approaches to English Channel, 49.57N 05.28W (approx.) (voyage: Milford Haven/Portsmouth).

Note: The above vessel was originally ordered by Captain A. F. Watchlin, Auckland, and intended to be named *Port Underwood*. Taken over by the Union SS Company of New Zealand, the vessel was requisitioned by the M.O.W.T. on completion.

292   *Oriole* 489 gt, 169 ft (oa), 162.7 ft × 27.2 ft.
Engines: Oil.
Launched: 15.8.1939.
Completed: 10.1939 for General Steam Navigation Co. Ltd., London.
1962: *L'Oriole* (L. Gagne, Canada).
1964: *Cecilienne Marie* (Bouchard Navigation Ltd., Canada).
1967: renamed *Cecilienne*.
1970: *Marine Trader* (Puddister Trading Co. Ltd., Canada).
1983: *Mayan Trader* (Mayan Marble & Stone Ltd., Cayman Islands).
1986: (Inversiones Borman, S.A., Panama).
1988: *Gonaives Trader* (P. A. Simbert, Honduras).

293   *Edina* 489 gt. Details as Yard No. 292.
Launched: 16.10.1939.
Completed: 11.1939 for Leith, Hull & Hamburg S.P. Co. Ltd. (J. Currie & Co., Leith).
1946: (Dundee, Perth & London Shipping Co. Ltd.).
1948: renamed *Gowrie*.
1957: (W. H. McTaggart, Dundee).
1959: *Fordmac* (Fordmac Shipping Co., Cayman Islands).
1961: *Kirk Maid* (N. G. Kirkconnell, Cayman Islands).
7.9.1964: Foundered four miles from Kingston, Jamaica, after leaking and listing (voyage: Dominica/Kingston).

294   *MSC Mallard* 131 gt, 92 ft (oa), 85.4 ft × 23 ft.
Engines: Oil. A Tug.
Launched: 12.12.1939.

Completed: 2.1940 for Manchester Ship Canal Company.
1973: *Twizzle* (Thames Services Marine Ltd., London).
1976: *Aberfoyle* (Londonderry Port & Harbour Commissioners).
1982: (A. H. Clarke, London).
1986: Broken up.

295   *MSC Merlin* Details as Yard No. 294.
Launched: 27.2.1940.
Completed: 4.1940 for Manchester Ship Canal Company.
11.1968: Sold (H. G. Pounds, Portsmouth) for breaking up.

319   *MSC Neptune* Details as Yard No. 294.
Launched: 7.10.1941.
Completed: 1.1942 for Manchester Ship Canal Company.
4.1970: Sold (Shipbreakers (Queenborough) Ltd., Kent); renamed *SQL 2*.
5.1975: At shipbreakers yard at Cairnryan, Scotland.

320   *MSC Nymph* Details as Yard No. 294.
Launched: 17.12.1941.
Completed: 3.1942 for Manchester Ship Canal Company.
3.1970: Sold (Shipbreakers (Queenborough) Ltd., Kent); renamed *SQL 1*.
5.1975: At shipbreakers yard at Cairnryan, Scotland.

332   *Kaimanawa* 2,577 gt, 294.8 ft (oa),
284 ft × 45.2 ft. Engines: T3cyl.
Launched: 11.3.1944.
Completed: 6.1944 for Union SS Company of New Zealand Ltd.
1966: *Rosa Anna* (Madrigal Shipping Co. Inc., Philippines).
15.1.1967: Stranded on Sibulan Island, Philippines. Refloated with extensive bottom damage; towed to Hong Kong; but constructive total loss. Sold, and
7.1967: Scrapped Hong Kong.

333   *Kingfisher* 493 gt. Details as Yard No. 292.
Launched: 15.11.1944.
Completed: 12.1944 for General Steam Navigation Co. Ltd., London.

1966: *Dunure* (Puddister & Bennett Shipping Ltd., St. John's, N.F.).
1974: (new oil engine).
15.12.1983: Scuttled (as useless) off St. John's, N.F.

334   *Stork* 493 gt. Details as Yard No. 292.
Launched: 30.1.1945.
Completed: 4.1945 for General Steam Navigation Co. Ltd., London.
1966: *Nikos Litochoron* (M. Gigilinis & D. Kakassinas (Greece).
1974: (C. Tsintzas & others, Greece).
1982: (Pan Stamoulis, Greece).

351   *Corncrake* 629 gt, 191 ft (oa), 183.6 ft × 33 ft.
Engines: Oil (aft).
Launched: 20.12.1945.
Completed: 5.1946 for General Steam Navigation Co. Ltd., London.
1952: (new oil engine).
1967: *Twillingate* (H. W. C. Gillett Ltd., St. John's, N.F.).
1980: (GVN Inc., Panama).

352   *Redstart* 629 gt. Details as Yard No. 351.
Launched: 5.3.1946.
Completed: 5.1946 for General Steam Navigation Co. Ltd., London.
1967: *Kapta Mathios* (D. Apesakis, Greece).
1969: *Spyros G* (Themis G. Shipping Co. Ltd., Cyprus).
1976: (Spyrthem Shipping Co. Ltd., Cyprus).
7.2.1977: Sprang leak, east of Malta and
8.2.1977: Sank in position 35.46N 20.09E
(voyage: Piraeus/Tripoli (Libya) – cement).

353   *Kanna* 942 gt, 224.5 ft (oa), 214.5 ft × 36.7 ft.
Engines: Oil (aft).
Launched: 23.10.1945.
Completed: 2.1946 for Union SS Company of New Zealand Ltd.
1967: *Luna Marina* (Cia. Nav. La Luna S.A., Panama).

1981: *Seng Giap* (Apollo Agencies (1980) Sdn. Bhd., Malaya).
30.12.1983: Grounded in heavy weather at Tanjong Datu, Borneo, 2.01N 109.39E. Flooded and abandoned (voyage: Sibu/Singapore – general). Constructive total loss.
6.12.1984: Refloated; scrapped locally.

354   *Katui* 942 gt. Details as Yard No. 353.
Launched: 21.11.1945.
Completed: 3.1946 for Union SS Company of New Zealand Ltd.
1967: *Cindee* (Islander Nav. Corp., Panama (Asia–Africa Shipping Co., Hong Kong)).
1973: (Cia. de Nav. Amin S.A., Panama (Unique Shipping & Trading Co., Singapore)).
1974: *Banang* (P. T. Perusahaan Pelayaran Nusantara, Indonesia).
1979: (Nagah Berlian, Indonesia).

355   *Tinto* 1,795 gt, 297 ft (oa), 284.3 ft × 42 ft.
Engines: T3cyl.
Launched: 27.8.1946.
Completed: 1.1947 for Ellerman's Wilson Line Ltd., Hull.
1966: *Kate MG* (M. & G. Shipping Co. Ltd.).
1967: *Bogota* (Western Hydrofoil Ltd., Bahamas).
1967: renamed *Hopi*.
1967: *Bogota* (Victor Stephens, San Domingo).
1968: renamed *Victoria*.
21.5.1972: Broke moorings and grounded in heavy weather at Rio Haina, Dominica. Refloated and
1973: Scrapped Santo Domingo.

356   *Truro* 1,795 gt. Details as Yard No. 355.
Launched: 11.11.1946.
Completed: 3.1947 for Ellerman's Wilson Line Ltd., Hull.
1968: *Gulf Noor* (W. J. Towell & Co., Kuwait).
1972: *Gulf Prosperity* (Five Trust Shipping Co., Panama).
28.5.1972: Arrived Karachi for breaking up.

Scotts' Shipbuilding & Engineering Co. Ltd., Cartsburn Dockyard, Greenock

Considered to be the oldest shipbuilding organisation, Scotts was formed in 1711, in the reign of Queen Anne. John Scott's first site was at Westburn, Greenock and the building of fishing and coastal sailing ships expanded steadily. In the mid-19th century clipper ships were also built and such names as *Lord of the Isles* in 1856 and the last big sailing ship built by Scotts, *Archibald Russell* in 1905 for J. Hardie & Company of Glasgow, are firmly recorded in maritime history. The latter, a 4-masted barque, wore Gustaf Erikson's house flag from 1924, was seized in August 1941 by the Admiralty Marshal when Finland joined the Axis Powers and spent most of the 1939–1945 war laid up at Goole as a store ship for the Ministry of Food. In October 1949 she arrived at Gateshead for breaking up.

But, acknowledging the onset of steam power, the company also built steamships in the early years of the 1800s. In 1819–1821 the three largest British steamships came from Scotts, the 345 ton *Majestic* of 1821 capable of steaming across the Irish Sea at 10 mph on one ton of coal. The first steam frigate, H.M.S. *Greenock* came in 1849, the largest iron warship of the day. Three pioneer steamers *Agamemnon*, *Ajax* and *Achilles*, 2,347 gt, inaugurated the Holt steamship service to China via the Cape of Good Hope in 1865. From Liverpool, they steamed the 8,500 miles to Mauritius without stopping.

A ship which became a legend was the iron-built *Hinemoa*, 542 gt, built in 1876 as a Parliamentary Yacht for the Government of New Zealand. She worked as such until 1922, was laid up for four years, served for another three and was then sold for cruising until 1932 when she was laid up again. On 10 May 1944 she was towed to sea as a target ship, but refused to sink and a charge had to be set to sink her. It was recorded in her papers that Queen Victoria owned the sixty-four shares of the ship.

In 1911 the first super dreadnought battleship *Colossus* was completed, followed in 1913 by the battleship *Ajax*. The first experimental steam submarine *Swordfish* was handed over to the Royal Navy in 1916; she was later converted to a patrol vessel. Three light cruisers were built during the Great War, *Caradoc*, *Dragon* and *Durban*; the latter pair ending up as Mulberry blockships in Normandy in 1944. Fifteen destroyers, nine submarines and a monitor were also completed.

In World War II all building was for Admiralty account and included four cruisers and twenty destroyers. Of these, H.M.S. *Milne* was the ship used in the famous war film 'In Which We Serve', depicting the career of a British destroyer.

When war ended there were eight berths to 800 ft length capacity and a 360 ft drydock.

In June 1965 Scott & Sons (Bowling) Ltd., with no previous connection, was acquired by Scotts, Greenock. In March 1966 the Cartsdyke Shipyard of the Greenock Dockyard Company merged with the adjoining yard of Scotts, the enlarged yard being put under Scotts' control; in 1967 Scotts and Lithgows amalgamated to become Scott, Lithgow Ltd.

SHIPS BUILT UNDER PRIVATE CONTRACT OR LICENCE

638 *Sinkiang* 3,029 gt, 321 ft (oa), 307.2 ft × 46.3 ft. Engines: Oil.
Launched: 22.2.1946.
Completed: 7.1946 for China Navigation Co. Ltd., London.
1966: *Tong Jit* (Asia Selatan Enterprises Ltd., Panama).
1967: *Gamsolo* (Africa Shipping Co., Panama (Kie Hock Shipping Co., Singapore)).
1969: *Kadina* (Kadina Enterprises Co., Panama (Kie Hock Shipping Co., Singapore)).
18.5.1977: Foundered in heavy weather while undergoing repairs in Eastern Anchorage, Singapore.

2.9.1978: Raised, towed in, sold, and 10.1978: Scrapped Singapore.

641 *Shansi* 3,161 gt. Details as Yard No. 638.
Launched: 28.11.1946.
Completed: 2.1947 for China Navigation Co. Ltd., London.
1967: *Kota Rajah* (Pacific International Lines Ltd., Singapore).
1974: *Sang Suria* (Malaysia Shipping Corp., Sdn. Bhd., Malaya).
5.1978: Scrapped Gadani Beach, Karachi.

In 1867 the merchant firm of J. Swire & Sons combined with the Yorkshire merchant R. S. Butterfield to create Butterfield & Swire, to handle textile exports and to hold the agency for Alfred Holt's Ocean SS Co. in China. Five years later the China Navigation Company was formed, for the purpose of breaking the American monopoly of steam navigation on the Yangtse River.

A leading shareholder in the new concern was John Scott of the shipbuilding company which was to build most of the new company's ships for the next eighty years, although the first four vessels ordered were iron paddle steamers from A. & J. Inglis, of Glasgow. Scott's first building for the China Navigation Co. was the *Chefoo* (1,087 gt) in 1876 and up to the start of World War II these builders constructed eighty ships for the company, nineteen of them between the years 1900 and 1905.

By the turn of the century China Navigation's services had expanded from the Chinese rivers and coast to Australia, Java, Siam, French Indo-China, Borneo, the Philippines, Japan and Russia. Replacement and expansion of the fleet continued, further contracts between 1914 and 1925 involving thirty-three vessels, eight built by Scotts and twenty-one by Taikoo Dockyard, Hong Kong, this new shipyard established in 1908 by Swires, with the close co-operation of Scotts.

In the inter-war years trade in China was difficult, mostly due to civil war. Late in the 1920s some political stability was restored, but in 1931 Japan invaded Manchuria and six years later the Sino–Japanese war broke out. Then, in December 1941, came the war in the Pacific.

In 1943 the Allies agreed to reserve future Yangtse river trade for Chinese-flag shipping and after the war, following China Navigation Co.'s withdrawal from much of its Chinese operations, it looked to Australia and Japan for expansion to future trade.

Unique among large British shipping companies in not taking any allocation of wartime standard ships, the company nevertheless added three Wm. Gray-built 'F'-class vessels and four 'S'-class steamers (two by Scotts (as above), one by Caledon and one by Inglis) to its coastal fleet between 1945 and 1947. Attention was then turned to the passenger fleet, with orders for vessels much larger than its pre-war ships. Scotts delivered the 7,000-tonners *Changsha* and *Taiyuan* in 1949 and the *Chungking* and *Changchow*, each of 9,400 tons, in 1950. But the expansion of trade did not materialise and in 1951, when the Communist Government had control of all China and the Taiwan-based Nationalists had imposed a blockade on Chinese ports, the China Navigation Company closed its China coast services. Up to this date Scotts' Shipbuilding & Engineering Co. Ltd. had built a total of eighty-seven ships for the China Navigation Co. Ltd.

Smith's Dock Co. Ltd., Middlesbrough

Smith's Dock Company was a fusion of the family businesses of Smith and Edwards, both of which had histories dating to the 18th century. William Smith acquired his shipbuilding knowledge in William Rowe's yard at St. Peters on the Tyne and in 1810 Smith's father bought the yard and formed a partnership with his two sons. East Indiamen were built for the East India Company by Smiths, two early ships being the *Duke of Roxburgh* (400 tons) and the *George Green* (560 tons), the former recorded as being one of the 'first ships' to arrive at Wellington, in its opening as a port in 1839. By 1851 ships built had reached the 1,600-ton mark with the *Blenheim*, and quite a number were built before the East India Company ceased to exist in 1858 when the Government of India passed to the Crown. T. & W. Smith became a 'limited' company in 1891 – Smith's Dry Dock Co. Ltd. – and eight years later amalgamated with Edwards Brothers, to become Smith's Dock Co. Ltd.

In 1906 the company moved its shipbuilding activities to the River Tees, constructing a yard on the South Bank, near Middlesbrough, South Bank becoming the yard name, operative from 1909.

The Edwards' interest began just prior to the turn of the 18th century when a privateer commander, George Straker, purchased the yard at the High Docks Shipbuilding & Repairing

Company at North Shields. In 1830 the yard was transferred to his son-in-law, James Edwards, but neither he, nor his successor, Harry S. Edwards, remained with the business for long. Nevertheless, the firm expanded and built up a speciality for steam trawlers and between 1893 and 1899, when amalgamation with Smith's Dock Company took place, had built no less than 139 ships.

So Smith's Dock came to be in 1899 and during the Great War turned out 163 vessels, mainly trawlers, and twenty-six gunboats, as well as repair work to some 4,000 ships.

In 1936 Smith's Dock Company completed a whaler, *Southern Pride*, 161 ft long and 30 ft in breadth, 582 gross tons, for the Southern Whaling & Sealing Co. Ltd., London. As war clouds thickened the Admiralty decided that more escort vessels were necessary and a number of the proven-designed 'Southern Pride'-type of ship were ordered from Smith's Dock Company. These became the 'Flower'-class corvettes, of which 221 were built in the United Kingdom and fifty-six in Canada. Nineteen came from Smith's yard. Smith's also built thirteen of the larger escort frigates of the 'River'-class.

When war ceased, the South Bank Yard at Middlesbrough had six berths, and there were four drydocks; the repair works at North Shields had five dry docks to a ship length of 550 ft.

On 5 July 1966 the agreed terms for a merger of Smith's Dock Company and Swan, Hunter & Wigham Richardson Ltd. were announced, the Swan, Hunter name being changed to Associated Shipbuilders Ltd., as the holding company, with a new Swan, Hunter & Wigham Richardson Company being formed. The following month it was stated that Smith's Dock would only undertake servicing and repair work, the building of ships to be by Swan, Hunter & Wigham Richardson on the Tyne. In February 1968 Smith's ended ship repair work at their Graythorp Yard on the Tees.

CARGO SHIPS BUILT UNDER PRIVATE CONTRACT OR LICENCE

1066   *Norman Prince* 1,913 gt, 315 ft (oa), 304 ft × 44.2 ft. Engines: T3cyl.
Launched: 23.12.1939.
Completed: 4.1940 for Prince Line Ltd. (Furness Withy & Co. Ltd.).
29.5.1942: Sunk by submarine (*U.156*) torpedo in Caribbean, 14.40N 62.15W (voyage: Liverpool/St. Lucia – ballast).

1067   *Lancastrian Prince* 1,913 gt. Details as Yard No. 1066.
Launched: 7.3.1940.
Completed: 5.1940 for Prince Line Ltd. (Furness Withy & Co. Ltd.).
12.4.1943: Sunk by submarine (*U.613*) torpedo in North Atlantic, 50.18N 42.48W (Convoy ON 176) (voyage: Liverpool/St. John, N.B.).

1068   *Tudor Prince* 1,948 gt. Details as Yard No. 1066.
Launched: 23.5.1940.
Completed: 8.1940 for Prince Line Ltd. (Furness Withy & Co. Ltd.).
1958: *Croce Italo* (F. Italo Croce SpA., Italy).
1961: *Ornella* (Maritime Enterprise Co., Liberia (S. Scalisi, Italy)).
7.1964: Scrapped Spezia.

1069   *Stuart Prince* 1,948 gt. Details as Yard No. 1066.
Launched: 15.8.1940.
Completed: 10.1940 for Prince Line Ltd. (Furness Withy & Co. Ltd.).
1951: Renamed *Fort Hamilton*.
1958: Renamed *Stuart Prince*.
1959: *Halcyon Med* (Cia. Maritima Med., Costa Rica (D. T. Petroloulos, London)).
24.8.1960: In collision, in fog, with tanker *Esso Switzerland* (1959, 23,363 gt), 120 miles east of Gibraltar. Cut in two; afterpart sank 36.9N 3.36W (approx.). Forepart taken in tow, but:
25.8.1960: Sank in position 36.26N 3.20W (voyage: Arzew/Granton – esparto grass).

1122   *Capitaine Jean Fougere* 3,829 gt, 381 ft (oa), 366 ft × 48.6 ft. Engines: T3cyl and LP turbine.
Launched: 23.11.1946.
Completed: 4.1947 for Union Industrielle & Maritime Soc. Française d'Arm., France.
1960: *Saint Georges* (Soc. Mar. Nationale, France).
1963: *San Giorgio* (Cia. de Nav. Bulk Carriers, Panama (O. Turchi, Italy)).
1963: Renamed *Saint Georges*.
2.3.1970: Sprang leak, abandoned, north-east of Crete, 36.29N 21.54E (voyage: Ravenna/Pazar – ammonia sulphate).

4.3.1970: Towed in, but aground near Cape Akrotiri, four miles south of Korinis, Greece.
10.4.1970: Broke in two during a storm. Afterpart sank, forepart flooded and abandoned. Constructive total loss.

1135 *Southern Strife* 364 gt, 148 ft (oa), 138.6 ft × 26.4 ft. Engines: T3cyl. A whaler.
Launched: 9.7.1945.
Completed: 8.1945 for The South Georgia Co. (C. Salvesen & Co. Ltd.).
1964: *Goltastein* (Atlantic Diesel A/S., Norway).
1966: Converted to a fishing vessel (oil engine fitted).
1968: (Knut Golten, Norway).
1970: Lengthened (166 ft oa., 677 gt).
1978: (New oil engine).

1136 *Southern Truce* 364 gt. Details as Yard No. 1135.
Launched: 9.7.1945.
Completed: 9.1945 for The South Georgia Co. (C. Salvesen & Co. Ltd.).
1963: (B. Berntsen, Norway).
1967: Renamed *Lovisa*; converted to a coaster; lengthened to 172 ft (oa), 463 gt, and fitted with oil engine.
1971: *Stong* (H. Pedersen, Norway).
1973: *Ingmar* (I. Pedersen, Norway).
1977: *Ivo* (A. Valestrand, Norway).
1979: *Famito* (Converted to a standby safety/pollution control vessel (P. R. Famito (K. Misje & Co., Norway)).
1983: *Tamito* (Tamis Ltd., Aberdeen).

1137 *Thorarinn* 361 gt. Details as Yard No. 1135.
Launched: 23.8.1945.
Completed: 9.1945 for Bryde & Dahls Hvalf. A/S. (A/S Thor Dahl, Norway).
1959: *Indus 17* (Cia. Industrial, Chile).
31.3.1983: Scuttled (as useless) off San Vicente, Chile, 36.43S 75.07W.

1138 *Thordr* 361 gt. Details as Yard No. 1135.
Launched: 23.8.1945.
Completed: 9.1945 for Bryde & Dahls Hvalf. A/S. (A/S Thor Dahl, Norway).
1959: *Indus 16* (Cia. Industrial, Chile).

1139 *Southern Wheeler* 427 gt, 158.5 ft (oa), 148.5 ft × 27.6 ft. Engine: T3cyl. A whaler.
Launched: 25.9.1945.
Completed: 11.1945 for South Georgia Co. Ltd. (C. Salvesen & Co. Ltd.).
4.1964: Sold for breaking up at Masnedo, Denmark.

1140 *Southern Wilcox* 427 gt. Details as Yard No. 1139.
Launched: 7.10.1945.
Completed: 12.1945 for South Georgia Co. Ltd. (C. Salvesen & Co. Ltd.).
1961: *Hvalur 7* (Hvalur H/F., Iceland).
9.11.1986: Sunk by sabotage of anti-whaling group at Reykjavik, Iceland.
18.11.1986: Raised; laid up unrepaired.

1141 *Southern Sailor* 434 gt, 154 ft (oa), 148.5 ft × 27.6 ft. Engines: T3cyl. A whaler.
Launched: 14.8.1946.
Completed: 9.1946 for South Georgia Co. Ltd. (C. Salvesen & Co. Ltd.).
1961: *Hvalur 6* (Hvalur H/F., Iceland).
9.11.1986: Sunk by sabotage anti-whaling group at Reykjavik, Iceland.
18.11.1986: Raised; laid up unrepaired.

1142 *Southern Soldier* 434 gt. Details as Yard No. 1141.
Launched: 26.8.1946.
Completed: 10.1946 for South Georgia Co. Ltd. (C. Salvesen & Co. Ltd.).
4.1964: Sold for breaking up at Odense, Denmark.

1157 *Arakaka* 2,814 gt, 351.4 ft (oa), 325 ft × 46.2 ft. Engines: T3cyl
Launched: 15.2.1946.
Completed: 6.1946 for Booker Bros. McConnell & Co. Ltd., Liverpool.
1963: *Aba Prince* (K. S. Potamianos, Greece).
1968: (Soc. Industrielle Commerciale Arm., Somalia).
14.9.1972: Arrived Karachi for breaking up.

The *Kanna*, as *Luna Marina*, at Singapore. (H. Robb Ltd., Yard No. 353.)   *Roy Kittle*

The *Lancastrian Prince*, leaving for trials, 18 May 1940. (Smiths Dock Co. Ltd., Yard No. 1067.)

The *Nottingham*, sunk six days after leaving the Clyde on her maiden voyage. (A. Stephen & Sons Ltd., Yard No. 576.)

Tom Rayner collection

Alexander Stephen & Sons Ltd., Linthouse, Glasgow

Alexander Stephen set up his first shipbuilding yard in 1750 at Burghead, a small fishing port on the Moray Firth on Scotland's north-east coast. It was here that his nephew, William, was apprenticed, later opening his own yard in 1793 at Aberdeen. Over the years shipbuilding was passed from father to son, to yards at Aberdeen, Arbroath and Dundee and it was in 1851 that a move was made from the north-east to a site at Kelvinaugh, on the Clyde, where Alexander Stephen & Sons built 147 ships of wood and iron during the next two decades. Then, in 1869, a 20-acre shipyard site was acquired at Linthouse and here the firm remained to build over 500 ships.

The first launching at Linthouse was Yard No. 148 on 24 November 1870, a 1,500 gt steamer *Glendarroch* for Wm. Ross & Company, Glasgow. In 1878 Clan Line's first two 'Clans' were built, *Clan Alpine* and *Clan Fraser*, just over 2,000 gt, these followed by *Clan Gordon* and *Clan Lamont* in the next year.

Stephens built some notable ships during the 1920–1939 years. The 17,000 gt Anchor Line ships *California* and *Caledonia* were delivered in 1923 and 1925, followed by the smaller *Britannia*, 5,400 gt, in 1926. But no doubt the outstanding building was the *Viceroy of India*, 19,648 gt, completed in 1929 for P & O's London to Bombay run, the first turbo-electric-drive liner built in Britain for British owners. The smaller 14,300 gt *Corfu* and *Carthage* came out in 1931, the *Canton* in 1938, all for the P & O SN Company Ltd.

Stephens built a number of refrigerated cargo liners during the 1939–1945 war, but the yard was used mainly for the construction of naval ships of many types, from sloop to aircraft carrier. In 1947 the yard of Alexander Stephen & Sons Ltd. had six berths for ships to 700 ft, an area of fifty-two acres and a waterfront of 1,500 ft.

In the post-war years the yard built many high standard ships for Elders & Fyffes, British India SN Co. Ltd., Federal SN Company Ltd., and the Union SS Company of New Zealand and in 1964 took over Simons-Lobnitz Ltd., two companies which had amalgamated in 1957. But shipbuilding orders tailed off and in late 1967 the company became the Linthouse Division of the Upper Clyde Shipbuilders Ltd. consortium. One year later the yard launched its last ship when, on 16 April 1968, Yard No. 701 was launched as *Port Caroline* and completed in October 1968 for Port Line Ltd.; the yard was then closed.

SHIPS BUILT UNDER PRIVATE CONTRACT OR LICENCE

570   *Trevethoe* 5,257 gt, 446.7 ft (oa),
432.5 ft × 56.2 ft. Engines: Oil.
Launched: 10.4.1940.
Completed: 6.1940 for Hain SS Co. Ltd., London.
11.3.1941: Sunk by E-boat torpedo in North Sea, north-east of Yarmouth, 52.46N 01.57E (voyage: St. John, N.B./London – wheat).

575   *Gloucester* 8,532 gt, 473 ft (oa),
457.5 ft × 60.3 ft. Engines: Oil. Refrigerated cargo liner.
Launched: 12.3.1941.
Completed: 7.1941 for Federal SN Co. Ltd., London.
1966: *Consulate* (Cia. Nav. Embajada S.A., Panama). Renamed for delivery voyage to Kaohsiung, where ship arrived on

2.10.1966, in tow, from Hong Kong, for breaking up.

576   *Nottingham* 8,532 gt. Details as Yard No. 575.
Launched: 12.8.1941.
Completed: 10.1941 for Federal SN Co. Ltd., London.
1.11.1941: Left Glasgow (on maiden voyage) for New York.
7.11.1941: Sunk by submarine (*U.74*) torpedo 550 miles south-east of Cape Farewell, Greenland, 53.24N 31.51W.

592   *Papanui* 10,006 gt, 495.3 ft (oa),
477 ft × 64.5 ft. Engines: three steam turbines. Refrigerated cargo liner.

Launched: 27.10.1942.
Completed: 6.1943 for New Zealand Shipping Co. Ltd., London.
1965: *Flisvos* (Cia. Nav. Astroguardia S.A., Panama).
5.10.1965: Arrived Kaohsiung for breaking up.

593   *Paparoa* 10,006 gt. Details as Yard No. 592.
Launched: 2.5.1943.
Completed: 1.1944 for New Zealand Shipping Co. Ltd., London.
1967: (Federal SN Co. Ltd., London).
1970: *Margaret* (Renamed for delivery voyage to shipbreakers) (Cia. Nav. Astroguardia S.A., Panama (Mavroleon Bros. Ltd.)).
11.1970: Scrapped Whampoa.

597   *Pipiriki* 10,065 gt. Details as Yard No. 592.
Launched: 28.12.1943.

Completed: 5.1944 for New Zealand Shipping Co. Ltd., London.
1967: (Federal SN Co. Ltd., London).
3.2.1971: Arrived Kaohsiung for breaking up.

602   *Devon* 9,943 gt. Details as Yard No. 592.
Launched: 3.10.1945.
Completed: 2.1946 for Federal SN Co. Ltd., London.
1967: (Overseas Containers Ltd. (Federal SN Co. Ltd., London)).
1971: (Federal SN Co. Ltd., London).
14.7.1971: Arrived Hong Kong for breaking up.

608   *Somerset* 9,943 gt. Details as Yard No. 592.
Launched: 3.1946.
Completed: 9.1946 for Federal SN Co. Ltd., London.
1954: *Aden* (P & O SN Co. Ltd.).
8.10.1967: Arrived Kaohsiung for breaking up.

When war began the New Zealand Shipping Co. Ltd. had twenty ships and the associated Federal SN Co. Ltd. sixteen, a total of thirty-six vessels.

Buildings during the war, to 1946, amounted to nine ships of which seven were constructed by Alex. Stephen & Sons Ltd. Nineteen ships were lost during the war, so that the combined fleets totalled twenty-six ships at the end of 1946. These included two vessels completed during the war by John Brown & Co. Ltd., Clydebank, the *Suffolk*, handed over six days after war broke out and the *Hororata* in April 1942.

The *Paparoa*, ready for her first voyage. (A. Stephen & Sons Ltd., Yard No. 593.)   *Tom Rayner collection*

THE ACQUIRED SHIPS

PART THIRTEEN

SHIPS REQUISITIONED AND PURCHASED

This section is comprised of vessels of all types which were requisitioned, purchased or salved and, given 'Empire' nomenclature, came under the control of the Ministry of War Transport.

Tonnage acquired from the U.S.A., and captured and confiscated enemy tonnage is listed separately.

Empire Adur 1,479 gt. Built: J. F. Duthie & Co., Seattle, in 1920 as *Griffdu*. 220 ft × 40 ft. Engines: T3cyl.
1935: *Noyo* (Union Lumber Company, San Francisco).
1940: *Nang Suang Nawa* (Thai Navigation Co. Ltd., Bangkok).
21.12.1941: (Thailand signed Peace Agreement with Japan).
25.1.1942: (Thailand declared war on Britain and U.S.A.).
1942: Taken by Britain as a prize: renamed *Empire Adur* (M.O.W.T.).
1948: Returned to owners, reverted to former name.
12.11.1955: Left Bangkok for Hong Kong in tow of Philippine tug *Albacore* (1943, 394 gt) for breaking up.

23.11.1955: Last reported north of Paracel Islands, South China Sea, 17.56N 113.45E. No further trace of tug or tow.

During her period as *Empire Adur* the ship suffered constant mechanical problems. Being an old vessel she was never able to steam for long without her furnace burners giving trouble, and crew reports stated that even when in convoy there would be 'frequent loud blasts from down below and flames would shoot from the funnel. Invariably the ship belched volumes of black smoke and threats from the convoy escort to direct her to another port, to let her proceed independently, or even to sink her, were of no avail'.

Not the least of the ship's problems was that the nut holding the steering wheel on would work slack and fall off. It is said that on at least two occasions, in convoy and at night, the Indian helmsman walked out of the wheelhouse onto the deck, still holding the wheel.

The *Empire Bure*, as *Charlton Star*, in Southampton Water in 1950.   *Skyfotos*

Empire Attendant 8,441 gt. Built: Barclay, Curle & Co. Ltd., Glasgow, in 1921 as *Domala*. 450 ft × 58 ft. Engines: Oil.

The motorship *Domala* was the first vessel in the fleet of the British India Steam Navigation Co. Ltd. to be equipped with diesel engines. At the outbreak of war in 1939 she was sailing in the U.K./Calcutta service.

Early in 1940, during a 'quiet' period of the war, the ship was sent to Antwerp to pick up a number of Indian seamen who had been repatriated by the Germans. On 2 March the ship was some thirty miles east of St. Catherine's Point, Isle of Wight, bound for Southampton, when an aircraft was seen overhead. It was thought to be friendly, but was a Heinkel of the German 26 Bomber Group, which flew low over the ship and dropped two sticks of bombs. One penetrated the engine room before exploding. Soon the whole of the vessel's superstructure was ablaze and the order to abandon ship was given.

The German plane machine-gunned survivors attempting to escape in lifeboats and on rafts and 108 of the 291 persons on board were reported missing.

Still on fire, the *Domala* was towed to the Solent, where she was flooded and beached. On 19 March she was refloated and taken to Southampton, then taken over by the M.O.W.T. and converted to a cargo ship, the work involving entire reconstruction. Renamed *Empire Attendant*, she sailed until 15 July 1942, when she was sunk by submarine (*U.582*) torpedo off the west coast of Africa, in position 23.48N 21.51W.

Empire Bell 2,023 gt. Built: Oresundsvarvet, Landskrona, in 1930 as *Belgia* for F. Sternhagen, Gothenburg. 287 ft × 40 ft. Engines: C4cyl.
26.1.1941: Bombed and set on fire by enemy aircraft north-east of Thames Estuary
(voyage: London/Sunderland). Abandoned, drifted ashore completely burnt out. Salvage commenced, and:

14.2.1941: Refloated, towed to Harwich and beached. Patched and pumped out; again refloated, and:
29.4.1941: Anchored in River Stour. Sold to Britain, repaired, and:
1942: *Empire Bell* (M.O.W.T.).
25.9.1942: Sunk by submarine (*U.442*) torpedo south of Iceland, 62.19N 15.27W (voyage: Tyne/Reykjavik – coal).

Empire Blanda 5,693 gt. Built: Lithgows Ltd., Port Glasgow, in 1919 as *Nile*. 424 ft × 56 ft.
Engines: T3cyl.
1933: *Sokol* (Jugoslovensksa Plovidba D.D.).
1939: *Rio Grande* (Cia. Panamena de Vapores, Panama (T. & N. Coumantaros Ltd., Greece).
1940: Requisitioned; renamed *Empire Blanda* (M.O.W.T.).
18.2.1941: Sunk by submarine (*U.69*) torpedo in North Atlantic (position not shown) – a straggler from convoy HX 107S (voyage: Baltimore/Grangemouth – steel scrap).

Empire Bond 2,088 gt. Built: Wm. Gray & Co. Ltd., West Hartlepool, in 1906 as *Ravelston*. 288 ft × 43 ft.
Engines: T3cyl.
4.1940: At Antwerp, under repair. (Owners: Ravelston SS Co., Grangemouth.)
Vessel proceeded to U.K., Repairs completed: requisitioned, and:
1941: *Empire Bond* (M.O.W.T.).
1946: *Prenton* (Rethymnis & Kulukundis, London).
1946: (J. Kattoula, Liverpool).
9.2.1949: Ashore off Mytika, Nikopoli Bay, Greece (voyage: Trieste/Preveza – timber).
11.2.1949: Refloated, and:
13.2.1949: Arrived Preveza. Constructive total loss. Sold, repaired, and
1950: *Agios Dionyssis* (Argo Maritime Transport Co., Greece).
1951: *Sandenis* (D. G. Coucoumbanis, Greece).
1951: *San Denis* (G. Frangistis, Greece).
1959: Scrapped Savona.

Empire Brent 13,876 gt. Built: Fairfield S.B. & Eng. Co. Ltd., Glasgow, in 1925 as *Letitia*. 526 ft × 66 ft.
Engines: six steam turbines

The *Empire Brent*, originally the Donaldson liner *Letitia*, was a near sister-ship to the liner *Athenia*, which was the first British ship to be sunk in the war. Designed for service to Canada from the Clyde, the *Letitia* also cruised and made voyages to India for the associated Anchor Line. In 1935 her owners were retitled Donaldson Atlantic Line when the Anchor Line was sold.

At the outbreak of war the ship was converted to an armed merchant cruiser, but was soon refitted as a troopship. In 1944 she became a Canadian hospital ship and on VJ-Day was outward-bound to the Pacific, after which she was

employed, under her own colours, in repatriating Canadian wives and children.

In 1946 the vessel was sold to the M.O.T., renamed to 'Empire' nomenclature, but remained under Donaldson management. Her repatriation work finished in December 1947; she was overhauled in the Clyde and returned to trooping service to India and the East.

By 1950 she was employed in taking emigrants to Australia and in 1952 was given a name with Antipodean connotations, becoming *Captain Cook*. The ship was scrapped at Inverkeithing in 1960.

Note: With the loss of the liner *Athenia* (1923, 13,581 gt) the war at sea had begun violently. At 9 p.m. on the first day of war, 3 September 1939, she was torpedoed in the North Atlantic by the submarine *U.30* (which had put to sea some days before the declaration of war) some 250 miles north-west of Rathlin Island, off Ireland, in position 56.44N 14.05W. At the time of her loss the liner was taking her 1,418 passengers and crew, mostly women and children, to the safety of Montreal. In all, 112 lives were lost, largely due to accidents with lifeboats.

Empire Bulbul 576 gt. Built: J. I. Thornycroft & Co. Ltd., Southampton, in 1924 as *Jamnagar* for H.H. The Maharajah Jam Sahib of Nawanagar, India.
161 ft × 26 ft. Engines: T3cyl.
1941: (Auxiliary patrol vessel, Royal Indian Navy).
1944: (Hashim Mohomed Ganchi, India).
1944: *Empire Bulbul* (M.O.W.T.).
1947: (Yannoulatos (Far East) Ltd., Hong Kong).
1947: Renamed *Hellenic Bulbul*. To be renamed *Hellenic Bee*, but:
29.8.1948: Ashore near Domanick Island, Bay of Bengal, 21.53N 90.48E. Later sank. Total loss.

Empire Bure 8,178 gt. Built: J. Cockerill S.A., Hoboken, Belgium, in 1921 as *Elisabethville*.
439 ft × 57 ft. Engines: Q8cyl.

As *Elisabethville* this vessel was built for the Belgium–West Africa run of Belge-Maritime du Congo. She remained in this service until the war, although in 1930 her owners amalgamated with Lloyd Royal Belge to become Compagnie Maritime Belge (C.M.B.).

Avoiding capture by the Germans, she was put under British (M.O.W.T.) control for trooping, managed by Lamport & Holt. In 1946 she reverted to her owners and the West Africa service, but in the following year was chartered to, and then sold to, the M.O.T., who renamed her *Empire Bure*, again with the same managers.

The vessel continued trooping until September 1949 and was then laid up in the Holy Loch. Sold in 1950 to the Charlton SS Co. (a Chandris-owned company), she became *Charlton Star*, with the intention of operating a cut-price transatlantic passenger service with dormitory-type accommodation. Instead, she again went trooping, chartered to the British Government for voyages to and from East Africa and Mauritius and later – in 1956 – to Christmas Island.

At the end of 1957 the ship was laid up at Spezia and in the following year was transferred to Greek shipowners A. J.

& D. J. Chandris and placed under the Liberian flag as *Maristrella*. She was sold for breaking up in 1959 and scrapped at Sakai City, Osaka, in 1960.

Empire Chief (tanker) 8,040 gt. Built: Palmers Ltd., Tyne, in 1897 as *Montcalm*. 445 ft × 52 ft.
Engines: T3cyl.

The *Montcalm* was one of the vessels which passed to the ownership of Canadian Pacific Steamships when, in 1903, they acquired the fleet of ships that Elder, Dempster & Co. had been operating as the Beaver Line on the Atlantic.

At the start of World War I the *Montcalm* was requisitioned to serve as a transport and then, in October 1914, was taken over by the Admiralty and fitted out as the dummy battleship H.M.S. *Audacious*. In 1915 it was intended to fill her with cement and, in the event of invasion, scuttle her as a blockship. But the idea was abandoned and she was used as a storeship. Taken by the Shipping Controller in 1916 and converted to an oil tanker, she was transferred to the Anglo-Saxon Petroleum Company, becoming *Crenella*. In November 1917 she was torpedoed off south-west Ireland, but reached port and was repaired. Purchased outright by Anglo-Saxon in 1919, she passed to Runciman & Co. in 1920, but they made no use of her. In 1923 *Crenella* was sold to C. Nielsen & Co., Norway, becoming a whale oil depot ship under the name *Rey Alfonso*. Returning to the British flag in 1927 as *Anglo-Norse*, she worked the South Atlantic whaling grounds for two years and was then acquired by the Falkland Whaling Company (South Georgia Company), who had her rebuilt as a pelagic whaler at Gothenburg, the ship being renamed *Polar Chief*.

Laid up at Tønsberg in September 1939, she escaped before the German invasion of Norway and in 1941 was acquired by the M.O.W.T., becoming *Empire Chief*.

On 16 January 1942 she drifted ashore at Reykjavik, Iceland, in a gale, becoming hard aground with her engine and boiler rooms flooded and her tanks leaking. Refloated on 7 March, temporary repairs were made and at the end of May 1942 the ship was towed to the U.K. for repairs.

In August 1946 the ship reverted to her previous name and owners and in April 1952 was delivered to Dalmuir for breaking up. Three months later the remaining hulk was towed to Troon for final demolition.

Empire Chivalry 6,007 gt. Built: Swan, Hunter & Wigham Richardson Ltd., Newcastle, in 1937 as *Inkosi* for T. & J. Harrison, Liverpool. 415 ft × 56 ft.
Engines: Q4cyl.
15.8.1940: Hired as Ocean Boarding Vessel (R.N.). Fitting out but:
7.9.1940: Bombed by German aircraft and sunk in Royal Albert Dock, London.
4.10.1940: Refloated. Stripped of accommodation and repaired, and:
1941: *Empire Chivalry* (M.O.W.T.).
1946: *Planter* (T. & J. Harrison).
1958: Scrapped Ghent, Belgium.

Note: The air raids on the Port of London during one weekend alone – that of 7–9 September 1940 – caused much devastation in the dock areas and severe damage to a large number of ships.

As well as the *Inkosi* (above) being sunk, her running-sister *Inanda*, lying alongside, met the same fate. Nine other ships were sunk and some twenty others damaged by bombs and fire, with three later found to have unexploded bombs on board.

Vessels sunk or damaged in air raids on London Docks, 7–9 September 1940:

Name:	Built:	Tons:	Remarks:
British flag:			
Inkosi	1937	6,007	
Inanda	1925	5,985	
Baronesa	1918	8,663	Damaged and submerged.
Benevis	1918	5,264	Badly damaged.
Eastwood	1924	1,551	Damaged.
Frumenton	1930	6,675	Unexploded bomb found aboard.
Glenstrae	1922	9,460	Damaged.
Gothland	1932	1,286	Damaged; unexploded bomb found aboard.
Hetton	1924	2,714	Damaged.
Knitsley	1924	2,272	Damaged.
Minnie de Larrinaga	1914	5,046	Fire damaged.
Otaio	1930	10,298	Damaged.
Ryal	1938	367	Damaged.
Sherwood	1924	1,530	Fire damaged.
Tynemouth	1940	3,168	Bomb right through ship; submerged.
Umgeni	1938	8,180	Unexploded bombs in hold; partly flooded.
Umtali	1936	8,162	Damaged. (Again damaged on 11 September.)
William Cash	1929	1,186	Bomb right through ship; submerged.

Name:	Built:	Tons:	Remarks:
Dutch flag:			
Abbekerk	1937	7,906	Damaged and submerged (listing).
Antje	1931	183	Burnt out; submerged.
Moena	1923	9,286	Damaged: Abbekerk (above) leaning on her.
Prins Frederik Hendrik	1936	1,288	Fire damaged.
Prins Maurits	1936	1,287	Fire damaged.
Reiger	1920	168	Burnt out; submerged.
Schie	1922	1,967	Burnt out; submerged.
Thea	1929	273	Burnt out; submerged.
Belgian flag:			
Anna	1928	695	Burnt out; submerged.
President Francqui	1928	4,919	Fire damaged.
Sambre	1917	683	Fire damaged.
Estonian flag:			
Elna	1903	3,195	Damaged; submerged.
Lake Hallwil	1907	3,165	Damaged.

. . .

Empire Claire 5,613 gt. Built: Wm. Hamilton & Co. Ltd., Port Glasgow, in 1919 as *Clan Matheson* for Clan Line Ltd. 410 ft × 51 ft. Engines: T3cyl.
1948: *Harmodius* (British & South American SN Co. (Houston Line Ltd.)).
1951: *Claire T* (Tsavliris Shipping Ltd., London).
1955: *Empire Claire* (M.O.T.). Taken over at Stranraer, Scotland, and partly dismantled, she remained there until loaded with obsolete war materials.
27.7.1955: Taken to sea for the last time, being towed out and a few days later scuttled in the Atlantic.

Empire Clyde 16,584 gt. Built: Wm. Beardmore & Co. Ltd., Dalmuir, in 1920 as *Cameronia* for Anchor Line Ltd. 575 ft × 70 ft. Engines: six steam turbines.
1941: Requisitioned as a troop transport.
22.12.1942: Damaged by submarine (*U.565*) torpedo north-east of Algiers, 37.03N 05.24E. Reached port; repaired.
1945: Laid up.
1947: Returned to trooping duties.
7.1948: Refitted as an emigrant ship for Australian service (1,270 passengers).
1.1953: *Empire Clyde* (M.O.T.). Continued passenger/trooping duties until final return home to Liverpool from a voyage to Christmas Island, Pacific.
22.10.1957: Arrived Newport, Mon., for breaking up.

Empire Corporal (tanker) 6,972 gt. Built: Palmers Ltd., Tyne, in 1922 as *British Corporal* for British Tanker Co. Ltd. 440 ft × 57 ft. Engines: two steam turbines.

4.7.1940: Damaged by E-boat torpedoes in English Channel; anchored at Portland, then towed to Southampton. Repaired, and:
1942: *Empire Corporal* (M.O.W.T.).
14.8.1942: Sunk by submarine (*U.598*) torpedo off Cuba, 21.45N 76.10W (voyage: Curaçao/Key West, Florida).

Empire Crocus 341 gt. Built: Noord Nederland Scheeps., Groningen, in 1936 as *Dr. Colijn* for M. Oosterhuis, Delfzijl, Holland. 133 ft × 23 ft. Engines: Oil.
1940: Requisitioned; renamed *Empire Crocus* (M.O.W.T.).
1947: *Stainton* (H. P. Marshall & Co., Middlesbrough).
1951: *Benwood* (Mountwood Shipping Co., Liverpool).
1955: *Monica* (Rederi A/B Selen, Finland).
1957: *Mona* (N. O. Olausson, Sweden).
1963: *Scantic* (J. L. Hansen, Denmark).
7.12.1964: Foundered after developing leaks in heavy weather in St. George's Channel, 51.10N 7.15W (voyage: Preston/Poole).

Empire Daffodil 394 gt. Built: Van Diepen N.V. Scheeps. Gebr., Waterhuizen, in 1940 as *Caribe II* for S. G. Hallstrom, Amsterdam. 180 ft × 28 ft. Engines: Oil.
1940: Requisitioned; renamed *Empire Daffodil* (M.O.W.T.).
9.7.1940: Damaged by aircraft bombs south-west of Isle of Wight. Taken to Portland, thence Southampton, for repairs.

1946: *Greenfinch* (General Steam Navigation Co. Ltd.).
1966: *Moira* (G. M. Moundreas & Bros., Greece).
1966: *Star of Medina* (Orri Navigation Lines, Saudi Arabia).

Empire Derwent 4,026 gt. Built: Wm. Pickersgill & Sons Ltd., Sunderland, in 1930 as *Stakesby* for Rowland & Marwood SS Co. (Headlam & Son, Whitby). 366 ft × 51 ft. Engines: C4cyl.
25.8.1940: Torpedoed by submarine (*U.124*) twenty-three miles north of Butt of Lewis, Hebrides. Towed in and beached on west coast. Slid off beach in a gale, sank in deep water. Submerged for sixteen months, then raised, towed to port and rebuilt.
1943: *Empire Derwent* (M.O.W.T.).
1946: *Swan Point* (J. D. McLaren & Co., London).
31.7.1949: Stranded in Karnaphuli River, Chittagong. Broke in two. Total loss (voyage: Karachi/Chittagong – general).

Empire Diplomat (tanker) 6,498 gt. Built: J. Brown & Co. Ltd., Clydebank, in 1926 as *British Diplomat* for British Tanker Co. Ltd. 440 ft × 54 ft. Engines: Oil.
1939: (A depot ship at Oran).
3.1940: Returned to U.K. for repairs.
1940: *Empire Diplomat* (M.O.W.T.).
1946: Scrapped Dunston-on-Tyne.

Empire Don 2,553 gt. Built: Ropner & Sons, Stockton, in 1895 as *Barlby*. 290 ft × 43 ft. Engines: T3cyl.
1926: *Noemi* (D. A. Mango, Greece).
1930: *Noemijulia* (Noemijulia SS Co. Ltd. (W. G. Walton)).
1940: (Cia. Maritime Panama Ultramar Ltda, Panama).
1941: *Irish Hazel* (Irish Shipping Ltd., Eire).
17.11.1943: Requisitioned at Newport, Mon., while under repair; renamed *Empire Don* (M.O.W.T.).
1945: Reverted to previous name and owners.
1949: *Uman* (Turk Silepcilik Limitet, Turkey).
6.1.1960: Ashore in fog at Kefken Point, Anatolia (Black Sea); became embedded in sand and flooded. Salvage not possible; Constructive total loss (voyage: Zonguldak/Istanbul – coal).

Empire Estuary 319 gt. Built: Goole Shipbuilding & Repairing Co. Ltd. in 1940 as *Fiddown* for S. Morris Ltd., Goole. 134 ft × 25 ft. Engines: Oil.
29.11.1940: Run down and sunk by H.M.S. *Campbeltown* when entering River Mersey.
7.7.1942: Raised; beached at Tranmere.
10.7.1942: Refloated and repaired; and:
1943: *Empire Estuary* (M.O.W.T.).
1946: *Goldfawn* (E. J. & W. Goldsmith Ltd., London).
1952: *Creekdawn* (Springwell Shipping Co. Ltd.).
1954: *Murell* (J. Tyrell, Eire).
3.1972: Scrapped Eire.
(See also Goole SB & Rep. Co. Ltd. – Ships built for private account.)

Empire Eveleen 502 gt. Built: Ardrossan Dockyard Co. Ltd. in 1920 as *Eveleen* for J. Milligan & Co. Ltd. 160 ft × 25 ft. Engines: T3cyl.
7.11.1942: In collision with steamer *Orchy* (1930, 1,090 gt) off Grey Point, Belfast Lough, while inward-bound with coal cargo. Sank and submerged; settled into mud and sand.
9.11.1943: Refloated, but buckled across deck due to strain of lifting and suction of mud. Beached Ballyholme Bay. Again refloated, taken to Belfast. Repaired, and:
1944: *Empire Eveleen* (M.O.W.T.).
1946: Reverted to original name and owners.
1957: Scrapped Troon.

Empire Explorer 5,985 gt. Built: Swan, Hunter & Wigham Richardson Ltd., Newcastle, in 1925 as *Inanda* for T. & J. Harrison, Liverpool. 407 ft × 52 ft. Engines: Q4cyl.
9.1940: Hired as Ocean Boarding Vessel (R.N.). Fitting out but:
7.9.1940: Bombed and sunk in London Docks. Salved and repaired, and:
1941: *Empire Explorer* (M.O.W.T.).
9.7.1942: Sunk by submarine (*U.575*) torpedo and gunfire off West Indies, 11.40N 60.55W.

Founded in 1853, the British shipowners T. & J. Harrison had, by 1865, a fleet of twenty-five ships – brigs, barques and steamers. In 1887 the last of their sailing vessels was sold.

In 1911 the Aberdeen Direct Line, engaged in the U.K.–Natal trade, was purchased from John T. Rennie Son & Co., and over the following years passenger and cargo vessels on the Harrison–Rennie Line service retained the Rennie style of nomenclature – that of Zulu names commencing with the prefix 'In . . .'. Among the vessels acquired in 1911 was the 1904-built *Inanda*. Disposed of in 1920, another *Inanda* was ordered in 1925, with accommodation for eighty first-class passengers. She remained in company service until 1940, when she was sunk during bombing raids on the Port of London. Taken over by the M.O.W.T. she was raised, stripped of her passenger accommodation and returned to service under 'Empire' nomenclature.

Berthed alongside *Inanda* at the time of her sinking was her running-sister, *Inkosi*, and she met the same fate (see *Empire Chivalry*). A third Harrison vessel, *Dalesman*, also received an 'Empire' name after wartime casualty – becoming *Empire Wily* (q.v.).

Empire Fal 4,880 gt. Built: Irvines SB & DD Co. Ltd., West Hartlepool, in 1914 as *Pengreep* for Chellew Navigation Co., London. 390 ft × 52 ft.
Engines: T3cyl.
6.1941: Seized by Vichy French Forces in Casablanca. Renamed *Ste. Jacqueline*.
11.1942: (Morocco occupied by Allied forces). Vessel seized by British authorities; reported to be damaged and unseaworthy.
1943: Reverted to original name for a short while, then
1943: *Empire Fal* (M.O.W.T.). Repaired.
5.1945: Sailed from Lisbon to Immingham, then:
2.7.1945: Scuttled north-west of Scotland with a cargo of gas bombs (believed carried from Italy) and too dangerous to discharge.

Empire Flaminian 2,763 gt. Built: W. Harkess & Sons Ltd., Middlesbrough, in 1917 as *Flaminian* for Ellerman & Papayanni Lines. 315 ft × 42 ft.
Engines: T3cyl.
1944: *Empire Flaminian* (M.O.W.T.).
1947: Became a Stevedore Training Ship at Marchwood, Southampton, for Royal Engineers Port Unit.
21.7.1950: Arrived Dover, in tow, for scrapping.

Note: Her place as a Stevedore Training Ship was taken by *Empire Stevedore* (q.v.).

Empire Gulf (tanker) 6,401 gt. Built: Short Bros. Ltd., Sunderland, in 1927 as *Laristan* for Common Bros. Ltd. 420 ft × 55 ft. Engines: T3cyl.
15.1.1942: Stranded on Tiree Island, west coast of Scotland. Salved; repaired, and:
1943: *Empire Gulf* (M.O.W.T.).
1946: *Laristan* (Common Bros. Ltd.).
1949: *Cherrywood* (John I. Jacobs & Co. Ltd.).
1953: *Irene M* (Marcou & Sons, London (Costa Rica flag)).
1954: *Semira* (Muzaffer Emin Zorlu, Turkey).
11.1960: Scrapped Kalafatyeri, Turkey.

Empire Hamble 3,260 gt. Built: Submarine Boat Corp., Newark, N.J., in 1920 as *Sulanierco*. 324 ft × 46 ft. Engines: steam turbine.
1931: *Admiral Senn* (Portland California SS Co., Seattle).
1940: *Threpsatri Nawa* (Thai Niyom Panich Co. Ltd., Bangkok).
21.12.1941: (Thailand signed Peace Agreement with Japan).

25.1.1942: (Thailand declared war on Britain and U.S.A.).
1941: Taken by Britain as a prize; renamed *Empire Hamble* (M.O.W.T.).
1947: (Bulk Storage Co. Ltd. – later Basinghall Shipping Co.).
2.1950: Scrapped Bombay.

This vessel was seized from Thailand as a prize (see also *Empire Adur*). Later, due to the war situation in the Pacific, the U.S. Army, anxious to use anything that floated, took over the ship (still as an 'Empire') and operated her from Milne Bay, in New Guinea.

After one particularly hazardous trip, mainly due to her neglected and run-down condition, her crew walked off in protest. A U.S. Army detachment was marched aboard and became the crew: in a count of numbers the even ones went to the engine room and the odd numbers stayed on deck. But as the only ship in the area with a bar on board, she became the 'glamour ship of the East' to American forces.

Nevertheless, by mid-1944 she was only managing six knots and was unable to go astern, and was sent to Sydney for a refit. On 17 October, while in Sydney Harbour, she had another machinery malfunction and was in collision with the American ship *West Cactus* (1919, 5,581 gt), gaining a large hole in No. 2 hold. She sailed to Newcastle, N.S.W., for repairs – the trip of sixty-four miles taking an exciting two full days!

In May 1945 the *Empire Hamble* was involved in the Wewak (New Guinea) landings, when carrying aviation gasoline and torpedoes. Arriving early, she was machine-gunned by the Japanese defenders, so steamed off back to sea, joined the assault craft forming up offshore and steamed in again, with them.

Note: A sistership to *Threpsatri Nawa*, the *Sisunthon Nawa* (1920, 3,286 gt, built in the U.S.A. as *Sugillenco*) was also seized as a prize in 1941 and although operated for the M.O.W.T. (by the Straits SS Co.) was not given an 'Empire' name. Early in 1942 she was reported missing – presumably sunk or captured by the Japanese – although her name appeared in some ship registers even after the end of the war.

Empire Heritage (tanker) 15,702 gt. Built: Armstrong Whitworth & Co. Ltd., Newcastle, in 1930 as *Tafelberg* for Kerguelen Sealing & Whaling Co., Cape Town. 508 ft × 72 ft. Engines: T6cyl.
28.1.1941: Mined in Bristol Channel, 51.21N 03.16W. Beached with after end submerged.
27.3.1941: Refloated; beached on Whitmore Bay Sands, but with flooded fore end and partly flooded stern the vessel could not be held broadside to the beach against the tide, which swung the bows inshore, and during the ebb tide she broke in two amidships. Constructive total loss. Acquired by M.O.W.T., repaired, and:
1943: Renamed *Empire Heritage*.

8.9.1944: Sunk by submarine (*U.482*) torpedo in North Atlantic (convoy HXF 305) in position 55.27N 08.01W (voyage: New York/ Liverpool – oil).

Empire Jonquil 369 gt. Built: Gebr. Bodewes Volharding, Foxhol, Holland, in 1939 as *Venus*. 140 ft × 25 ft. Engines: Oil.
1940: *Begonia* (Dutch flag).
1940: Requisitioned; renamed *Empire Jonquil* (M.O.W.T.).
13.3.1947: Caught fire in North Sea, twenty miles north-east of Outer Dowsing Light Vessel. Abandoned, but engines still 'full ahead', chased for several hours by a trawler. Boarded, taken in tow, still afire, towed in and beached in River Humber. Flooded and fire extinguished. Refloated, taken to Hull docks, but sank. Constructive total loss. Raised, sold, repaired, and:
1948: *Marton* (H. P. Marshall & Co., Middlesbrough).
1952: *Galtee* (Limerick Steamship Co. Ltd.).
1961: *Vittorio Bogazzi* (F. Maggiani & Others, Italy).
1970: *Enrico Effe* (Carlo Figlie, Italy).
1976: Scrapped Italy.

Empire Leech 363 gt. Built: J. Smit, Alblasserdam, Holland, in 1929 as *Escaut* for Wm. Muller & Co., Holland. 145 ft × 25 ft. Engines: Oil.
25.3.1941: Bombed and machine-gunned by German aircraft off North Cornwall. Engine room flooded and ship beached at Cleave Strand, Crackington Haven. Coal cargo caught fire and burned for four weeks. Later refloated by salvage vessel. Rebuilt and repaired, and
1941: *Empire Leech* (M.O.W.T.).
1948: Purchased by original owners; refitted for Paris service, renamed *Seine* – permitting the old name (*Escaut*) to be used for a new building.
16.7.1955: Sank off Dungeness after collision in fog with Russian tanker *Drogobitz* (1954, 3,420 gt) (voyage: Paris/London).

Empire Lethe 369 gt. Built: R. Williamson & Son, Workington, in 1891 as *Black Rock*. 152 ft × 23 ft. Engines: C2cyl.
1913: *Eleth* (Wm. Thomas & Sons, Liverpool).
1941: *Empire Lethe* (M.O.W.T.).
1946: Reverted to previous owners and name.
1.2.1951: Cargo shifted, vessel listed, capsized and sank twelve miles south east of Carlingford, near Dundalk, Ireland (voyage: Birkenhead/Dundalk – coal).

Empire Liddell 1,425 gt. Built: W. Harkess & Sons Ltd., Middlesbrough, in 1920 as *Enugu* for

Government of Nigeria. 235 ft × 36 ft. Engines: T3cyl.
1943: *Empire Liddell* (M.O.W.T.).
1946: *Hoeveld* (Arden Hall SS Co. Ltd., Cape Town).
1951: *Aliwal* (South African National SS Co., Cape Town).
1.1961: Scrapped Durban.

Empire Light (tanker) 6,537 gt. Built: J. Brown & Co. Ltd., Clydebank, in 1925 as *Lumen* for H. E. Moss & Co., Liverpool. 420 ft × 54 ft. Engines: Oil.
9.4.1942: In collision with Dutch steamer *Spar* (1924, 3,616 gt) in River Tyne. Drydocked and repaired, and
1942: *Empire Light* (M.O.W.T.).
7.3.1943: Sunk by submarine (*U.468*) torpedo in North Atlantic, 53.57N 46.14W (voyage: Manchester/New York).

Empire Lizard (tanker) 1,749 gt. Built: Bertram Engine Works Co. Ltd., Toronto, in 1904 as *Haddington*. 256 ft × 43 ft. Engines: T3cyl.
1914: *Maplehill*.
1937: Sold for breaking up, but:
1938: Purchased by Branch Lines Ltd., Montreal; converted to a tanker and renamed *Oakbranch*.
1945: *Empire Lizard* (M.O.W.T.).
1947: *Basingbrook* (Bulk Storage Co. Ltd. – later Basinghall Shipping Co.).
1949: Scrapped Sunderland.

Note: On 2 December 1944 the M.O.W.T. purchased four ageing ships of the five-ship fleet of Branch Lines Ltd. – a subsidiary of Marine Industries Ltd. of Montreal. The other vessels involved were:
Cedarbranch (built 1903) – see *Empire Newt*.
Pinebranch (built 1895) – see *Empire Stickleback*.
Willowbranch (built 1910) – see *Empire Tadpole*.
At the same time the M.O.W.T. also bought a similar vessel, *Riding Mountain Park* (to become *Empire Pike*) from the Canadian Government. These ships had previously traded in the Great Lakes and St. Lawrence areas.

Empire Longford 3,703 gt. Built: Swan, Hunter & Wigham Richardson Ltd., Newcastle, in 1912 as *Dimboola*. 371 ft × 50 ft. Engines: Q4cyl.
1935: *Hong Siang* (Ho Hong SS Co., Singapore).
1951: *Empire Longford* (M.O.W.T.).
1953: Scrapped Dover.

Empire Lotus 3,683 gt. Built: Ropner & Sons, Stockton, in 1920 as *Alness*. 347 ft × 51 ft. Engines: T3cyl.
1933: *Star of Ramleh* (Alexandria Navigation Co., Egypt).
1940: Transferred to Britain, renamed *Empire Lotus* (M.O.W.T.).

The *Stakesby*, as *Empire Derwent*, ready for sea after reconstruction.   *Vic Young*

The *Empire Norse*, in ice off St. John's, N.F., in February 1943, following loss of her rudder. She was later towed to the U.S.A. for repairs.   *Canadian Forces/W.S.P.L.*

The troopship *Empire Parkeston*, arriving at the Hook of Holland.

12.4.1942: Foundered in Atlantic during heavy weather, 44.06N 6.27W (voyage: New York/Belfast).

Empire Medway 10,926 gt. Built: Napier & Miller Ltd., Glasgow, in 1929 as *Eastern Prince*. 496 ft × 65 ft. Engines: Oil.
1953: Scrapped Faslane.

The *Empire Medway*, perhaps better known as Furness, Withy & Co.'s liner *Eastern Prince*, was one of four ships known as the 'Compass' class, designed for the New York–River Plate service.

A twin-screw vessel, her engines developed 10,500 bhp and gave a speed of 17 knots. In addition to her cargo-carrying capacity of almost 9,000 tons, she carried 101 passengers in first-class accommodation.

During the first year of war she made transatlantic voyages, but in November 1940 was requisitioned and converted at Liverpool for trooping duties, making her first sailing in this capacity in June 1941.

Another refit, at Baltimore in 1943, increased her troop capacity to 2,150, and from here she sailed with American troops for Europe and the South of France landings. Towards the end of the war she served as a floating hotel for the British and American representatives at the Yalta Conference. After VE-Day she continued trooping and in 1946 came under M.O.W.T. ownership but without change of name.

In 1950, at the request of her previous owners, she was given an 'Empire' name, thus releasing her 'Prince' title for new tonnage.

Empire Mersey 5,791 gt. Built: R. Duncan & Co. Ltd., Port Glasgow, in 1920 as *Ramon de Larrinaga* for Larrinaga SS Co. Ltd., London. 450 ft × 58 ft. Engines: T3cyl.
8.2.1941: Sprang leak seventy-five miles off New Jersey coast, on voyage from Philadelphia to U.K. with pig iron.
9.2.1941: Beached at Lewes, Delaware.
10.2.1941: Capsized and sank.
26.6.1941: Refloated, towed to Philadelphia, but constructive total loss. Sold and repaired, and:
1942: *Empire Mersey* (M.O.W.T.).
14.10.1942: Sunk by submarine (*U.618*) torpedo in North Atlantic, 54.00N 40.15W (Convoy SC 104).

Empire Newt (tanker) 1,548 gt. Built: Chicago Shipbuilding Company in 1903 as *John Crerar*. 246 ft × 41 ft. Engines: T3cyl.
1918: *Fouras* (Chemins de Fer Francais).
1922: *Glengarnock* (Glen Steamships, Montreal).
1926: *Courtwright* (Canada SS Lines, Montreal).

1940: Purchased by Branch Lines, Montreal, converted to a tanker and renamed *Cedarbranch*.
1945: *Empire Newt* (M.O.W.T.).
7.1946: Scrapped Inverkeithing.
(See also *Empire Lizard*.)

Empire Norse (tanker) 8,120 gt. Built: Palmers Ltd., Tyne, in 1914 as *Maricopa*. 425 ft × 57 ft. Engines: T3cyl.
1929: *Anglo-Norse* (Falkland Shipowners Ltd., London).
19.8.1941: In collision with steamer *Lanark* (1923, 1,904 gt), put into River Tyne with hull damage (voyage: Curaçao/Tyne – oil).
31.8.1941: Caught fire while under repair; beached. Ammunition magazine exploded, vessel scuttled.
3.9.1941: Refloated. Repaired, and
1941: *Empire Norse* (M.O.W.T.).
1946: Reverted to previous owners and name.
1956: *Janina* (Anders Jahre & Co., Norway).
15.1.1957: On fire north-west of Lisbon, 41.33N 9.33W. Abandoned, and:
18.1.1957: Sank (voyage: Odessa/Turku – oil).

Empire Nutfield 1,561 gt. Built: Dublin Dockyard Co. Ltd. in 1919 as *Bermondsey*. 240 ft × 36 ft. Engines: T3cyl.
1928: *Nutfield* (E. T. Lindley, London).
4.12.1942: Sailed from River Tyne, collided with mv *Bornholm* (1930, 3,177 gt). Severely damaged, beached on South Shields Sands. Abandoned.
22.12.1942: Refloated, towed into Tyne, but constructive total loss. Sold, repaired, and:
1943: *Empire Nutfield* (M.O.W.T.).
1.9.1946: Sailed from Barry, South Wales, and:
3.9.1946: Scuttled in Atlantic, 48.03N 8.09W, with a cargo of obsolete chemical warfare ammunition.

Empire Pakeha 8,115 gt. Built: Harland & Wolff Ltd., Belfast, in 1910 as *Pakeha* for Shaw, Savill & Albion Ltd. 477 ft × 63 ft. Engines: Q8cyl.
9.1939: Acquired by Admiralty and converted to a dummy battleship, disguised as H.M.S. *Revenge*; used in Firth of Forth area as a decoy for enemy aircraft.
6.1941: Reconverted to a cargo carrier, but retaining the cruiser stern given her as part of her battleship disguise; renamed *Empire Pakeha* (M.O.W.T.).
1946: Reverted to original owners and name; chartered to Ministry of Food as a meat storage hulk in River Thames.
5.1950: Scrapped Briton Ferry.

Three Shaw Savill ships built at Belfast during 1909–11, the *Pakeha* (above, 10,481 gt when built), *Rangatira* (10,118 gt) and *Waimana* (10,389 gt) – both from Workman, Clark's shipyard – were the first cargo steamers in the New Zealand trade to exceed 10,000 gross tons. A fourth vessel, White Star's *Zealandic* of 10,898 tons, came from Harland & Wolff in 1911. All four were 14-knot ships with large refrigerated and general cargo capacities and had provision for 1,000 emigrant passengers. The *Rangatira* was lost in 1916 when she ran aground on Robben Island, in Table Bay.

In 1926 the Royal Mail group acquired control of the Oceanic SN Co. (White Star Line), which carried with it a large shareholding in Shaw, Savill & Albion. Not long after, the fleet of the Australian Commonwealth Line (five 'Bay'-class passenger ships and two cargo vessels) was acquired by the Oceanic Company. At the time Shaw, Savill – holding shares of the Aberdeen Line – were contemplating the building of new passenger tonnage, but instead chartered that company's latest ships, the 1922-built *Diogenes* and *Sophocles* (renamed *Mataroa* and *Tamaroa*, respectively) in exchange for their own *Waimana* (renamed *Herminius*) and *Zealandic* (renamed *Mamilius*). The *Waimana* became *Empire Waimana* (*q.v.*) in 1942.

The *Mamilius*, at the end of her charter in 1932, became Shaw Savill's *Mamari*. Laid up before the outbreak of war, the Admiralty acquired her in 1939, converting her to represent the aircraft carrier H.M.S. *Hermes*. On 3 June 1941 the *Mamari* (still as the dummy '*Hermes*') was en-route to Chatham Dockyard for reconversion to a refrigerated merchant ship when she ran on to the wreck of the tanker *Ahamo* (1926, 8,621 gt) of Standard Transportation Co. of Hong Kong, which had been mined and sunk on 8 April 1941 off the Norfolk coast, in position 53.22N 00.59E. Salvage attempts were of no avail and the next day the '*Hermes*' was torpedoed by German E-boats, with one torpedo hitting the wreck of the *Ahamo*.

The crew of '*Hermes*' were landed at Grimsby by H.M. Rescue tug *Sabine* and some days later much of '*Hermes*' gear was salved, her 'flight deck', bridge and funnel being above water.

Later, convoys using 'E-boat Alley' used the wreck for target practice, and it was eventually blown up.

Empire Parkeston 5,556 gt. Built: Cammell Laird & Co. Ltd., Birkenhead, in 1930 as *Prince Henry*.
366 ft × 57 ft. Engines: six steam turbines.
1937: *North Star*.
1940: (Auxiliary cruiser, R.C.N.).
1944: H.M.C.S. *Prince Henry* (Landing Ship, Infantry).
1946: *Empire Parkeston* (M.O.W.T.).
1962: Scrapped Spezia.

The *Prince Henry* was built for Canadian National Steamships, a 3-funnelled, twin screw steamer for service on the coast of British Columbia. However, along with her two sisters (*Prince David* and *Prince Robert*) she proved uneconomic on the service and in 1937 she was sold to the Clark SS Co., Quebec, who gave her a refit and the name of *North Star*.

Soon after the outbreak of war she was purchased by the Royal Canadian Navy, converted to an auxiliary cruiser by the Burrard Dry Dock Co., Vancouver, and placed in Pacific service under her original name and at a time when the U.S.A. was still neutral.

On 2 April 1941 the *Prince Henry* intercepted two German merchant ships 200 miles west of Callao, Peru, after they had left that port as part of Germany's fleet of blockade runners to and from Japan with essential war supplies. The two German vessels were *Hermonthis* (1935, 4,833 gt) and *München* (1936, 5,619 gt); both were scuttled by their crews.

Later in the war, after some alteration to the uptakes, the *Prince Henry*'s two forward funnels were trunked into one casing and she was converted to a Landing Ship, taking Canadian troops to the Normandy beaches.

In 1946 the vessel was sold to the M.O.T., refitted at Southampton, given her 'Empire' name and placed on trooping duties, carrying military personnel based in Northern Europe to and from leave across the North Sea between Holland and the U.K.

Empire Pike (tanker) 1,854 gt. Built: Government Shipyard, Sorel, P.Q., in 1905 as *W. S. Fielding*.
240 ft × 43 ft. Engines: T6cyl.
1914: *P.W.D. No. 1* (dredger).
1943: Acquired by Government of Canada, converted to a tanker and renamed *Riding Mountain Park*.
1945: *Empire Pike* (M.O.W.T.).
1947: *Basingford* (Bulk Storage Co. Ltd., London – later Basinghall Shipping Co.).
1949: Scrapped Dunston-on-Tyne.
(See also *Empire Lizard*.)

(Intended to be) *Empire Reserve* (tanker) 5,693 gt. Built: Swan, Hunter & Wigham Richardson Ltd., Newcastle, in 1916 as *Mytilus* for Anglo-Saxon Petroleum Co. Ltd., 414 ft × 54 ft. Engines: T3cyl.
1941: Requisitioned by M.O.W.T.
14.8.1942: Arrived Harwich for use as an oil fuel depot. Intended to be renamed *Empire Reserve*, but name not taken up. Later used only as a storage hulk.
1946: Returned to owners: towed to Plaju, Indonesia; used as a floating oil depot.
11.1950: Scrapped Bombay.

Empire Rother 1,940 gt. Built: Swan, Hunter & Wigham Richardson Ltd., Newcastle, in 1929 as *Imari*. 253 ft × 43 ft. Engines: T3cyl.

1930: *Delaware* (St. Lawrence Steamships Ltd.).
1943: *Empire Rother* (M.O.W.T.).
1949: *Manicouagun* (Quebec North Shore Paper Co., Montreal).

1951: Renamed *Washington Times-Herald*.
1954: Renamed *Manitoulin*.
7.1961: Scrapped Port Dalhousie, Canada.

From 1940 onwards a number of Great Lakes steamers were acquired by the M.O.W.T. from Canadian companies, firstly to ease the pressure on the British coastal trade and, later, to serve in varied European waters. The vessels were of distinctive 'Laker' appearance, with bridges right forward and their engines aft and each was of some 2,000 gross tons.

Companies supplying much of the tonnage included Hall Corporation of Canada; Upper Lakes & St. Lawrence Transportation Company; Keystone Transports Ltd., whose *Trevisa* (1915, 1,813 gt) was sunk on the way across the Atlantic by *U.124* on 16 October 1940, the first loss in the battle for survival of convoy SC 7 (see *Empire Spey*); St. Lawrence Steamships Ltd.; Paterson Steamships and Canada Steamship Lines, a company which had contributed nearly a dozen ships by 1943.

Of these vessels, the *Delaware* (above) was given the name *Empire Rother*. This ship, plus the *Lanark* and *Anticosti* (Canada Steamships) – all managed for the M.O.W.T. by Wm. Cory & Sons – were reconstructed as self-discharging bunkering ships, with grabs. The *Empire Rother* and the *Lanark* served in Icelandic waters for a lengthy spell.

It should be noted that certain other Canadian vessels were also transferred to Britain and were given 'Empire' names (*Empire Lizard*, *Empire Newt*, etc.); these were already classed for 'deep sea' service in the St. Lawrence as well as in the Lakes.

Empire Rowan 9,462 gt. Built: Harland & Wolff Ltd., Glasgow, in 1922 as *Lochgoil* for Royal Mail Lines Ltd. 486 ft × 62 ft. Engines: Oil.
6.10.1939: Damaged by mine five miles from Scarweather Light Vessel, Bristol Channel (voyage: Newport/Vancouver – general). Beached Mumbles, flooded and buckled amidships. Refloated, towed to Swansea. Constructive total loss. Sold and repaired, and:
1940: *Empire Rowan* (M.O.W.T.).
27.3.1943: Sunk by aircraft torpedo in Bay of Collo, north-west of Bone, Algeria, 37.16N 6.54E.
8.1.1951: Wreck exploded under water; cause not established but believed caused by unofficial salvage work by amateur divers.

Empire Severn 6,681 gt. Built: Harland & Wolff Ltd., Glasgow, in 1914 as *Egba* for Elder, Dempster & Co. 406 ft × 54 ft. Engines: T3cyl.
1943: Owners wished to sell vessel for scrapping, due to constant mechanical problems, but:
8.1943: Purchased by M.O.W.T., renamed *Empire Severn*.
10.2.1946: Dragged anchors in Holy Loch, Scotland, and collided with steamer *Leighton* (1921, 7,412 gt); damaged.
19.2.1946: Again broke loose from moorings: again collided with the *Leighton* at the height of the storm. Further damaged. Re-moored three days later. Later loaded at a Continental port, and:
12.10.1946: Scuttled in Atlantic, north-west of Hebrides, 58.18N 9.37E, with a cargo of obsolete ammunition.

The *Leighton* (Lamport & Holt Line) was herself scuttled with a cargo of chemical ammunition in July 1947.

Note: In spite of the urgent need for scrap steel, both in Britain and on the Continent, a number of ships were taken to sea and scuttled with old munitions or poison gas, this being regarded as the only satisfactorily safe means of disposing of such dangerous cargoes.

The *Empire Severn* was one such vessel. As *Egba* she was one of a class of five vessels launched for Elder, Dempster between 1912–1914, their names commencing with the letter 'E'. Her designs had the usual special features required for the West African trade and, put into service just before World War I, she came through unscathed.

Nevertheless, in 1918 she was sent to the White Sea with munitions, but, unable to leave in time, both ship and crew were interned for some months by the Bolshevists. Following a change in the political situation she was released, to return to her owner's service until the summer of 1939, when she was reported sold to Norwegian buyers. But with war only months away, sales to foreign buyers were subject to Government approval. This sale was not approved and, instead, the ship was due to be taken into the Government's Merchant Ship Reserve Fleet. But this was not proceeded with, due to the outbreak of World War II, and the ship continued in her owner's fleet until 1943.

Empire Snowdrop 339 gt. Built: Van Diepen N.V. Scheeps. Gebr., Waterhuizen, Holland, in 1939 as *Caribe I* for S. G. Hallstrom, Amsterdam.
180 ft × 28 ft. Engines: Oil.
1940: Requisitioned; renamed *Empire Snowdrop* (M.O.W.T.).

1946: *De Vilhena* (Malta SS Co. Ltd., Valetta).
2.2.1961: Reported in distress, sinking, off Cape Corse, Corsica (approx.) position 43.00N 8.00E.
3.2.1961: Foundered in heavy seas forty miles north-west of Calvi, Corsica (voyage: La Nouvelle/Italy – maize).

Empire Spey 4,292 gt. Built: Ardrossan Dockyard Co. Ltd. in 1929 as *Blairspey* for Geo. Nisbet & Co., Glasgow. 372 ft × 51 ft. Engines: T3cyl.
18.10.1940: Torpedoed in Atlantic, in position 57.55N 11.10W, in convoy SC 7, by submarine *U.101*. Abandoned.
19.10.1940: Struck by torpedo from *U.100*. Taken in tow, and:
25.10.1940: Beached in Clyde. Refloated, rebuilt at Greenock with a new forepart, and:
1942: *Empire Spey* (M.O.W.T.).
1946: Reverted to previous owners and name.
1961: *Evandros* (Marfuente Cia. Nav., Lebanon).
5.1967: Scrapped Spezia.

Convoy SC 7 sailed from Sydney, N.S., bound for the U.K. on 5 October 1940. It consisted of thirty-five merchant ships with but two escorts – an armed yacht which left for other duties two days later and the sloop (former survey ship) H.M.S. *Scarborough*. Four further escorts joined, the sloops H.M.S. *Fowey* and H.M.S. *Leith* and the corvettes H.M.S. *Bluebell* and H.M.S. *Heartsease*. The first loss was on 16 October, when the 'Laker' *Trevisa* (1915, 1,813 gt) was sunk by *U.124* (see *Empire Rother*) and two days later, when the convoy was north-west of Ireland, it ran into a pack of seven German submarines (U-boat Nos. *38*, *46*, *48*, *99*, *100*, *101* and *123*) and in a four-day battle twenty of the merchant ships were sunk. Fifteen reached port, at Gourock, fourteen on 21 October and, strangely, one – the Canadian 'Laker' *Eaglescliffe Hall* (1928, 1,900 gt) – which had become a straggler and did not rejoin the convoy, the day before.

Empire Stickleback (tanker) 1,984 gt. Built: American Shipbuilding Co., Cleveland, in 1895 as *Malta*. 248 ft × 40 ft. Engines: T3cyl.
1911: Converted to a barge.
1921: Rebuilt as a steamer, renamed *Thunder Bay* (Canada SS Lines Ltd.).
1940: *Plenbranch* (converted to a tanker) (Branch Lines Ltd., Montreal).
1945: *Empire Stickleback* (M.O.W.T.).
1946: Reverted to previous owners and name.
1961: Cut down to deck level, and
24.5.1961: Sunk for use as a wharf at Malignant Cove, Nova Scotia.
(See also *Empire Lizard*.)

Empire Stour 4,696 gt. Built: Bartram & Sons Ltd., Sunderland, in 1930 as *Harpenden* for National SS Co. (J. & C. Harrison). 401 ft × 54 ft. Engines: T3cyl.

11.9.1940: Damaged by submarine (*U.28*) torpedo north-west of Ireland. Remained afloat, but with stern blown off. Towed to River Clyde. Constructive total loss; engines removed.
1941: Repaired and rebuilt; renamed *Empire Stour* (M.O.W.T.).
1946: *Bharatjal* (Bharat Line, Bombay).
1957: *Al-Riyadh* (C. A. Petroutsis, Geneva).
1958: *Spetsai Patriot* (C. A. Petroutsis, Trieste).
1962: Under arrest at Lagos. Sold by Court Order, and
9.1963: Scrapped Split.

Empire Swale 5,452 gt. Built: Deutsche Schiff-und Masch. A.G., Wesermunde, in 1937 as *Takoradian* for United Africa Company, Liverpool. 424 ft × 57 ft. Engines: Oil.
1941: Seized by French authorities at Dakar, renamed *St. Paul* (French flag).
1943: Reverted to Britain (M.O.W.T.) and to original name, then:
1943: Renamed *Empire Swale*.
1946: Reverted to original name and owners.
1949: *Takoradi Palm* (Palm Line Ltd.).
1959: *Irini's Luck* (E. N. Vernicos Shipping Co., Greece).
5.1963: Scrapped Vigo.

The *Takoradian* and her sistership *Gambian* followed very similar careers over a life span of some twenty-six years. Built by the same shipyard for the same owners and their West Africa service the two vessels, by coincidence, were both in Dakar at the end of 1941, when they were seized by the Vichy French authorities and renamed under the French flag. When, later, the Vichy French rejoined the Allies the two vessels were returned, placed under their original names for a short while and were then given 'Empire' nomenclature under the M.O.W.T. After the war the ships reverted to their original names and owners and when Palm Line Ltd. was formed by the United Africa Company in 1949 they took new names with a 'Palm' suffix. In 1959 both vessels were sold to Greek owners and both ships went to shipbreakers four years later, albeit one in Spain and the other in Hong Kong.
(See also *Empire Tweed*.)

Empire Tadpole (tanker) 1,752 gt. Built: Sunderland Shipbuilding Company in 1910 as *Saskatoon*. 250 ft × 43 ft. Engines: Oil.
1927: *Rosemount* (Canada SS Lines).
24.11.1934: Sank alongside Century Coal Dock, Montreal.
25.5.1935: Refloated, but constructive total loss. Sold and dismantled for use as a grain store.
1940: Acquired by Branch Lines Ltd., Montreal; rebuilt and converted to a tanker, renamed *Willowbranch*.
1945: *Empire Tadpole* (M.O.W.T.).

1947: *Basingcreek* (Bulk Storage Co. Ltd., London –
later Basinghall Shipping Co.).
1950: *Coastal Creek* (Coastal Tankers Ltd., Montreal –
later Coastalake Tankers Ltd.).
1964: (Canadian Sealakers Ltd., Edmundston, N.B.).
1968: *Creek Transport* (Hall Corporation of Canada).
1972: *Ile de Montreal* (McNamara Corporation,
Ontario).
1976: (Richelieu Dredging Corporation, Montreal).
1977: (Nittolo Metal Co., Quebec).
1986: Reported broken up.
(See also *Empire Lizard*.)

Empire Taw 1,499 gt. Built: Hawthorns & Co.,
Leith, in 1921 as *London* for Dundee, Perth & London
Shipping Co. Ltd. 250 ft × 35 ft. Engines: T3cyl.
1942: Requisitioned by M.O.W.T. then transferred
to Admiralty; renamed H.M.S. *Holdfast* (auxiliary
cable and pipelaying vessel). Fitted with bow sheave
and cable-laying equipment.
1946: Returned to M.O.W.T., renamed *Empire Taw*.
1952: Scrapped Cork.

In the forward planning for the Allied landings on the
Normandy beaches in June 1944, it was estimated that 14,000
vehicles would be landed on D-Day and that twelve days
later nearly 100,000 vehicles would be ashore.
  The maintenance of a constant fuel supply by conventional
tanker would have been an enormous task, subjecting both
the supply ships, and their necessary numbers, to unacceptable
risks. The solution was an underwater fuel pipeline (PLUTO –
Pipe Line Under The Ocean) across the English Channel.
  It was first tested, on a small scale, in the winter of 1942–
1943, between South Wales and the North Devon coast. The
first tests were made at Westward Ho, but after storms
caused many problems on the open beaches, the tests moved
to Ilfracombe.
  In Wales, the shore end was laid on 27 December 1942
near Swansea, but rough weather prevented coupling it to
the main section on H.M.S. *Holdfast*. Connection was finally
effected on 29 December and H.M.S. *Holdfast* then laid her
25-mile section, dropping the buoyed end 3,000 yards off the
Westward Ho beach. Two days later the Devon section was
laid.
  On 2 February 1943, the Swansea end, which had kinked
in its laying, due to heavy weather, was further damaged by
a U.S. warship dragging its anchor across it in a gale. H.M.S.
Holdfast relaid the section and it was ready for testing by 4
April.
  The full-length PLUTO was laid across the Channel to the
Normandy beach-heads in June 1944.
  (See *Empire Baffin* and *Empire Ridley*.)

Empire Tees 3,101 gt. Built: J. Blumer & Co. Ltd.,
Sunderland, in 1920 as *Daybeam*. 331 ft × 47 ft.
Engines: T3cyl.
1929: *Sebastian* (F. Sainz de Inchaustegui, Spain).
1933: *Azteca* (Marques del Real Socorro, Spain).

1936: *Itxas-Alde* (Name change unconfirmed: deleted
from Register).
1941: *Sebastian* (Comp. Com. de Transportes S.A.,
Spain).
31.10.1943: Vessel seized by Royal Navy and taken
to Gibraltar, owners listed under 'Trading with the
Enemy' Act.
11.1943: (M.O.W.T.).
1944: Renamed *Empire Tees*.
1950: *Tees* (Cia. Mar. Tees, Panama).
1951: *Clonlee* (Shamrock Shipping Co., Belfast).
1954: *Selamet* (Muzaffer Taviloglu, Turkey).
4.4.1968: Arrived Istanbul for breaking up.

Empire Test 8,298 gt. Built: J. Cockerill S.A.,
Hoboken, Belgium, in 1922 as *Thysville*.
442 ft × 57 ft. Engines: Q8cyl.
1947: *Empire Test* (M.O.T.).
1953: Scrapped Faslane.

As *Thysville*, this vessel was a sistership to the *Elisabethville*
(renamed *Empire Bure*, *q.v.*) under the same ownership and
operating in similar West Africa service. Being outside
Belgian waters when that country surrendered in 1940, she
was placed under British control and was employed trooping.
She, too, passed into British ownership in 1947, was given
an 'Empire' name and continued trooping, making her last
run in October 1952 and being scrapped after a life of thirty-
one years.

Empire Thane (tanker) 8,120 gt. Built: Lithgows
Ltd., Port Glasgow, in 1939 as *Desmoulea* for Anglo-
Saxon Petroleum Co. Ltd. 465 ft. × 59 ft.
Engines: Oil.

The *Desmoulea* had an eventful wartime career. On 31 January
1941 she was torpedoed by an enemy destroyer or E-boat in
the Mediterranean, in position 35.31N 02.34E, while on a
voyage from Alexandria to Piraeus. Abandoned, she was
later towed to Suda Bay, Crete, where most of her cargo
was trans-shipped. On 20 April she was towed to Port Said,
then on to Suez. Enemy bombers found her there on 5 August
and she was struck by an aerial torpedo, blasting a 35 ft × 12 ft
hole in her side plating. Considered fit for tow, she left Suez
on 18 August in tow of the motor tanker *Olivia* (1939,
6,250 gt) and arrived at Aden on the 27th. Here she was to
await the cessation of a monsoon before proceeding further,
but was then found to have broken her back, hogged by 4 ft,
buckled down both sides and with very little strength, to
have no power, unable to steer and the engine room full of
water. Nevertheless, she left Aden on 30 December, towed
by the steamer *Malda* (1922, 9,066 gt) and arrived at Bombay
on 12 January 1942.
  By the end of March the expected drydock had not become
available and on 23 April the *Desmoulea* left in tow of the
Dutch tanker *Ondina* – a sistership to the *Olivia* (above) –
arriving on 1 May at Bhavnagar and beaching in a creek. But
her damage was not repairable here and she left the creek,
but grounded, straining her old damage and increasing the
hogging.

On 20 November she departed in tow of the Norwegian steamer *Utsire* (1917, 4,441 gt) but two days later the towline parted and *Desmoulea* went ashore on Goapnath Point. Refloated by a tug four days later, she was towed back to Bombay and used as an oil fuel depot ship.

Drydocked in July 1943, repairs were found possible – providing the previously-ordered materials became available. But two of the vessels carrying consignments from England were sunk on the way out, and thus only some temporary repairs were made. By November 1943 the vessel had become *Empire Thane* under M.O.W.T. control and was then towed to Cochin as a storage hulk.

After the war, in January 1947, she reverted to her original owners and name, and on 21 April commenced a voyage in tow to the U.K., arriving at Falmouth on 16 July, still with a gaping hole in her stern and 5,000 tons of oil fuel on board. In a period of some 6½ years the vessel had been towed more than 12,000 miles, and was finally repaired by her owners. The *Desmoulea* lasted until 1961 and was then scrapped in Hong Kong.

Empire Torridge 4,050 gt. Built: Burntisland Shipbuilding Co. Ltd. in 1923 as *Asiatic*. 350 ft × 50 ft. Engines: T3cyl.
1942: (Hunter Shipping Co., London).
21.1.1942: Ashore North Bay, Tara, Co. Down, N. Ireland (voyage: Liverpool/New York – ballast). Refloated, but regrounded and became tidal. Abandoned.
2.4.1942: Refloated, temporarily repaired for tow to drydock.
9.9.1942: Towed to Belfast, but constructive total loss. Sold; repaired, and:
1943: *Empire Torridge* (M.O.W.T.).
1946: *Huntress* (Fred Hunter (Management) Ltd., London).
1950: *Modesta* (Augusta Paulin, Finland).
2.1962: Scrapped Split.

Empire Tower 4,378 gt. Built: Burntisland Shipbuilding Co. Ltd. in 1935 as *Roxburgh*. 372 ft × 54 ft. Engines: T3cyl.
1937: *Tower Field* (Tower SS Co. (Counties Ship Management, London)).
10.5.1941: Damaged by aircraft bombs off Outer Dowsing Buoy, Thames Estuary (voyage: London/Newcastle – ballast). Repaired.
19.10.1941: Grounded on north bank when entering Workington Channel with cargo of iron ore. Hull fractured, vessel awash, broke in two. Cargo discharged. Refloated, repaired, and:
1942: *Empire Tower* (M.O.W.T.).
5.3.1943: Sunk by submarine (*U.130*) torpedo in Atlantic, north-west of Lisbon, 43.50N 14.46W (Convoy XK 2) (voyage: Huelva/Middlesbrough – ore).

Empire Trader 9,965 gt. Built: Workman, Clark & Co. Ltd., Belfast, in 1908 as *Tainui* for Shaw, Savill & Albion Ltd. 478 ft × 61 ft. Engines: T6cyl.

8.4.1918: Torpedoed by U-boat in approaches to English Channel. Abandoned. Later reboarded and steamed stern-first 130 miles to Falmouth. Beached and later repaired.
1939: Sold to shipbreakers, but sale revoked by Government order, and:
1940: *Empire Trader* (M.O.W.T.).
21.2.1943: Damaged by submarine (*U.92*) torpedo in convoy ON 166 in Atlantic (voyage: Newport, Mon./New York). Escorted towards the Azores by the corvette H.M.C.S. *Dauphin*, but sunk by her on orders from Admiralty, 48.27N 29.47W. The crew were rescued by the convoy ship *Stockport* (1911, 1,683 gt) which, having fallen behind the convoy as a straggler, was then torpedoed and sunk by *U.604* in position 45N 44W, just two days later.

Empire Trent 5,006 gt. Built: Wm. Gray & Co. Ltd., West Hartlepool, in 1927 as *Rockpool* for Sir R. Ropner & Sons. 405 ft × 53 ft. Engines: T3cyl.
1.2.1941: Ran aground in fog on Little Cumbrae Island, Firth of Clyde (voyage: St. John's, N.F./Clyde – pitprops and steel). Became tidal in a gale, with stern gear smashed and extensive bottom damage. Constructive total loss. Raised and repaired, and:
1941: *Empire Trent* (M.O.W.T.).
1946: *General George Brink* (Union SS Co. of South Africa, Cape Town).
1947: *Africana* (Arcturus SS Corp., Panama).
11.1959: Scrapped Osaka.

Empire Tulip 288 gt. Built: Scheeps. Delfzijl v/h Sander, Delfzijl, Holland, in 1939 as *Pallas* for N. Engelsman, Delfzijl. 126 ft × 23 ft. Engines: Oil.
1940: Requisitioned; renamed *Empire Tulip* (M.O.W.T.).
1947: *Goldgnome* (E. J. & W. Goldsmith Ltd., London).
1952: *Insistence* (London & Rochester Trading Co. Ltd.).
1954: New oil engine.
1964: (Another) new oil engine.
3.1970: Sold for breaking up; engine installed in 1964 removed and installed in owner's tug *Draggette* (1947, 50 gt).
12.1970: Scrapped Rochester, Kent.

Empire Tweed 5,452 gt. Built: Deutsche Schiff-und Masch. A.G., Wesermunde, in 1937 as *Gambian* for United Africa Co. Ltd. 424 ft × 57 ft. Engines: Oil.
1941: Seized by Vichy French authorities at Dakar. Renamed *St. Gabriel* (French flag).
1943: Handed back to Britain; reverted to original name, then:
1943: *Empire Tweed* (M.O.W.T.).
1946: Reverted to original owners and name.

1949: *Gambia Palm* (Palm Line Ltd.).
1959: *Irini's Blessing* (E. N. Vernicos Shipping Co., Greece).
7.1963: Scrapped Hong Kong.
(See also *Empire Swale*.)

Empire Tyne 3,724 gt. Built: J. Readhead & Sons Ltd., South Shields, in 1923 as *Steelville*.
347 ft × 49 ft. Engines: T3cyl.
1937: *Francis Dawson* (F. C. Dawson & Co. Ltd.).
8.3.1941: Caught fire at Bedford Basin, Halifax, N.S., while assembling for convoy
(voyage: Portland, Maine/U.K. – grain). Extensively damaged, with midships accommodation burnt out and severe damage to main engine. Constructive total loss; towed to New York: repaired, and:
1941: *Empire Tyne* (M.O.W.T.).
1947: *Inchcrag* (Williamson & Co., Hong Kong).
1952: Scrapped Hong Kong.

Empire Usk 3,229 gt. Built: Tyne Iron Shipbuilding Co. Ltd., Newcastle, in 1918 as *War Combe*.
331 ft × 47 ft. Engines: T3cyl.
1920: *Watsness* (Oakwin SS Co. (Sir W. R. Smith & Sons Ltd.)).
1927: *Marklyn* (Mervyn SS Co., Newport, Mon.).
20.1.1942: Ashore at Crammag Head, Port Logan, Mull of Galloway (voyage: Pepel/Barrow – iron ore). Flooded. Pumped dry and cargo discharge commenced. Reflooded and further damaged during storms. Again pumped out, and:
5.6.1942: Refloated.
17.6.1942: Arrived Glasgow in tow. Repaired, and:
1942: *Empire Usk* (M.O.W.T.).
1946: *Heminge* (Constants (South Wales) Ltd.).
1948: *Bluestone* (Crete Shipping Co., London).
1953: *Grosvenor Mariner* (Grosvenor Shipping Co. (Moller Line (U.K.) Ltd.)).
9.1955: Scrapped Hong Kong.

Empire Viscount (tanker) 8,882 gt. Built: R. Duncan & Co. Ltd., Port Glasgow, in 1929 as *Athelviscount* for United Molasses Co. Ltd. 475 ft × 63 ft.
Engines: Oil.
31.8.1940: Damaged by aircraft bombs at Cammell Laird's shipyard, River Mersey. Repaired.
21.3.1942: Damaged by submarine (*U.202*) torpedo in mid-Atlantic, 38.46N 55.44W. Towed in; repaired, and:
1942: *Empire Viscount* (M.O.W.T.).
1946: Reverted to original name and owners.
10.1957: Scrapped Hendrik Ido Ambacht, Holland.

When, on 21 March 1942, the *Athelviscount* was torpedoed, she was some 600 miles south-east of Newfoundland and almost at the maximum range of the salvage tug sent to assist her. The torpedo struck the tanker 30 ft from her stern, when all the engineers and some of the deck crew were making emergency repairs in the engine room. They were all killed by the blast and those left in the accommodation were injured.

On 26 March, in storm conditions, the tug reached the casualty, now with its bows high in the air and a draught of over 40 ft aft, but some 750 miles from the nearest land and in submarine-infested waters.

In the following days three U-boats were reported on their route to Halifax and four ships were attacked between their position and the coastline. The storm persisted; the towline parted and was reconnected and for four days the two ships drifted further to the eastward. On the fifth day they were just able to regain lost ground. By 4 April the tug and tow were nearing land, but by this time the Admiralty had assumed both vessels had foundered.

Then they were sighted by an aircraft some 100 miles offshore. The tug had been towing for ten days and was almost out of fuel, but managed to reach St. John's with her charge, now drawing more than 41 ft aft.

Due to the days of strain while down by the stern, it was found that *Athelviscount*'s deck and shell plating had fractured and the lower part of the ship was completely severed. Sagging and the lack of trim prevented the ship drydocking, she was moored to a buoy. On 9 April she broke adrift in a gale and stranded at the harbour entrance. Refloated, she finally docked on 23 May for cropping of plating and temporary repairs and on 30 June she left, in tow, bound for New York, for permanent repairs.

Empire Waimana 8,129 gt. Built: Workman, Clark & Co. Ltd., Belfast, in 1911 as *Waimana* for Shaw, Savill & Albion Ltd. 478 ft × 63 ft. Engines: T6cyl.
1926: *Herminius*.
1932: *Waimana* (Shaw, Savill & Albion Ltd.).
1939: Purchased by the Admiralty, converted to a dummy battleship.
1942: *Empire Waimana* (M.O.W.T.).
1946: *Waimana* (Shaw, Savill & Albion Ltd.).

At the outbreak of World War I, the *Waimana*, in New Zealand waters, was requisitioned as a troop transport and on 16 October 1914 sailed from Wellington as part of the convoy carrying the First New Zealand Expeditionary Force. At Albany, W. Australia, they joined with the twenty-eight ships carrying 20,000 troops of the Australian Imperial Force, and on 1 November the convoy, now totalling thirty-eight ships, put to sea. It reached Egypt early in December and there landed the troops who created the ANZAC tradition in the Gallipoli campaign.

In 1915 the *Waimana* became involved in an international incident. She had been defensively armed with a 4.7-inch gun in that year and on the second of two voyages to the River Plate to load meat, she called at Newport News, Virginia, on 26 August to load bunker coal. Two days later she was ready to proceed, but a dispute arose with the neutral United States authorities over her gun. She was detained until 22 September and clearance was not given until the gun had been landed.

In 1926, when three British contenders for the Australian trade – White Star, Blue Funnel and the Aberdeen Line – agreed to run a joint monthly service on the route and thus had a subsequent surplus of tonnage, the *Waimana* was chartered by the Aberdeen Line as *Herminius*, reverting to her owners in 1932. (See also *Empire Pakeha*, *q.v.*) At the outbreak of war in 1939, the *Waimana*, laid up in the Gareloch, was acquired by the Admiralty and converted at Belfast to a dummy battleship, to represent H.M.S. *Resolution*, of the 'Royal Sovereign'-class. She was anchored in the Firth of Forth, but in 1942, due to the growing shortage of insulated tonnage, she was reconverted at Newcastle to commercial trading, acquiring her 'Empire' name. In 1946 the vessel reverted to her original owners and again took her original name.

In February 1951 she towed the disabled Liberty-type cargo ship *San Leonardo* (1944, 7,176 gt), which had lost her propeller and was in danger of going ashore near Cape Northumberland, South Australia, some 300 miles to Melbourne.

On 27 January 1952 the *Waimana* arrived at Milford Haven for breaking up.

Empire Zest (trawler) 316 gt. Built: Gen. Fikkers, Muntendam, Holland, in 1918 as *Amsterdam*.
121 ft × 23 ft. Engines: C2cyl.
1938: *Zeester* (J. L. de Groot, Holland).
1940: Requisitioned; renamed *Empire Zest* (M.O.W.T.).
1957: Transferred to Admiralty.
1962: Reported disposed of.

The *Empire Taw*, formerly the cable and pipelaying vessel HMS *Holdfast*, in July 1949.   *G. A. Osbon*

The *Empire Tyne*, at Halifax, N.S., in May 1943.

PART FOURTEEN

TONNAGE FROM THE UNITED STATES OF AMERICA

Section 1   Purchased Ships

When war broke out in Europe in August 1914 the shipping and shipbuilding industries of the United States were diminished factors in her industrial scene. Her merchant fleet consisted of coasting services and Great Lakes bulk carriers, with but fifteen foreign services worked by a small number of cargo ships, whilst a few liners carried the United States flag across her bordering oceans.

Eastwards, German submarines prowled the Atlantic and within a year of war some 1,200,000 gross tons of British merchant ships had been lost. But these figures paled to insignificance in 1917 when sinkings in the second quarter alone totalled 1,400,000 tons.

Shipyards in Britain were working to full capacity with additional naval work and in 1915 the British Government looked towards the United States to build ships for the British Merchant Marine. British yards on the Clyde and Tyne also built for Scandinavian shipowners, and those and French owners also placed orders with shipyards in the United States.

In 1916 the American loss of prestige in the shipping world over so many decades was acknowledged when, on 7 September, Congress passed an Act creating a United States Shipping Board whose work was to lay in promoting the development of the American Merchant Marine and the control of United States shipping. It was none too soon for such a decision for within a few months the United States declared war on Germany; the date, 6 April 1917.

Normal trading by Britain with the United States had been reduced due to the contingencies of war and Britain had ordered a number of new buildings from them to replace war losses. However, as these were placed prior to 1917 when the United States was a neutral, the orders had to be placed through an agency and not directly by Government. The Cunard Steam Ship Company was the agency through which the transactions were made, although management of the completed ships on behalf of the Shipping Controller was vested in several shipping companies, Furness, Withy & Co., France Fenwick & Co., Lamport & Holt, James Chambers & Co. and others. In March 1917 700,000 tons of shipping was on order for Britain. Many ships were also on order for the French and Scandinavian flags. Britain's reduction in normal Atlantic services encouraged American owners, prior to 1917, to place ships on the Atlantic route and, coupled with overseas orders, output in 1916 from American yards was 174,000 tons.

But the declaration of war by the United States spotlighted the need for ships. In Europe, some 3,000 miles to the East, the war raged on and not only were huge formations of American troops to be transported there but so, too, was their equipment and their stores.

Eleven days after war was declared the United States Shipping Board formed the Emergency Fleet Corporation. It was charged to build a huge fleet of ships, capable of transporting and maintaining the large American Army that was destined for France.

As well as urging the enlarging and improving of existing yards many new shipyards had to be constructed by the Emergency Fleet Corporation and, by the end of 1918, the 1917 take-over figure of sixty-one yards, of which thirty-seven were capable of building steel ships of 3,000 deadweight tons and twenty-four of wooden-hull equivalents, had jumped to 203 yards, with 1,020 shipways, with just a few incomplete. And, in 1918, yards in the United States launched 25 per cent. more merchant tonnage than the rest of the world put together. All these yards were nationally divided to eleven administrative areas, to facilitate speed and efficiency.

In 1917 there were also 431 merchant ships, either partly built or contracted for, in thirty-six of the shipyards for private United States owners, or foreign account, with a deadweight capacity of 2,940,000 tons and on 3 August 1917 all those over 2,500 tons deadweight and built of steel became subject to a requisitioning order. Within this total, 137 ships of some 970,000 tdw were in course of building and of these, seventeen had been launched and were being outfitted. But they were of various sizes and types and standardisation of parts was clearly impossible. Nevertheless, some 300,000 tdw of ships was completed by the end of 1917.

There were no less than ninety-nine different types of requisitioned steel ships, each type varying in design for hull and for main machinery. The E.F.C. was responsible for the design of new ships for the projected fleet and plans were drawn up or revised for ships of 3,500, 5,000, 5,650, 7,500, 8,800, 9,000, 9,400 and 9,600 tdw whilst a plan for a standard wooden-hulled ship was also prepared.

In the last few months before armistice on 11 November 1918, output was steadily rising. In August 1918 forty-one steel ships were completed of 236,000 tdw; in September and October forty-five were completed each month and in November, fifty-two of 303,000 tdw. The 'bridge of ships' frenzy continued until 1921, by which time 1,400 ships had been constructed by the E.F.C.

After hostilities ceased, all merchant ships flying the flag of the United States, with the exception of a few returned to their original owners, were operated under ownership of the U.S.S.B. There were some commandeered ships and some which had worked in the Great Lakes before the war and which had been cut in two and taken through the Welland canal for deep sea work. But American peace-time conditions did not favour the operation of 10½-knot ships; the need was for faster and more up–to-date ships. Some, however, were placed in Government-subsidised company routes, but many were broken up. One large batch of 200 ships which had been built on the Great Lakes was purchased by the Ford Motor Company for scrapping at Detroit and became quite unrecognisable as countless motor cars. Some became barges, particularly Lake-built ships which were purchased by lumber companies, given four masts rigged with long booms, new winches for handling lumber, and worked on the U.S. eastern seaboard. But many were laid up in rivers and backwaters for many years.

At the beginning of World War II the British Ministry of Shipping aimed at time-chartering a block of the laid-up ships, but by the end of February 1940 had purchased some 178,000 tdw, whilst a good deal more tonnage was acquired by neutral nations. Just after the fall of France in 1940 a considerable number were purchased by Great Britain. Many were in poor condition, but owing to the high dollar costs of the United States repair yards, were brought to Britain for repair. Indeed, a few fell victim to the North Atlantic submarine menace even before being given British nomenclature.

About half of the number of ships acquired by Britain became war losses and several more were sunk as blockships in the invasion of Normandy in June 1944. Some were transferred to Allied governments in 1942 from the British flag. Three were transferred to Belgium and put under management of Agence Maritime Internationale S.A. which, as Belgium was under German occupation, was run from their London Office. They took 'Belgian' names. Likewise, six went to Norway with a rename to 'Nor' prefix; two flew the Greek flag and another four the flag of the Netherlands.

The ex-American ships which were transferred to Britain have been listed to three sections: acquisitions of ships that were requisitioned by the U.S.S.B. in 1917; acquisitions of those ordered by the U.S.S.B. and vessels that were under lend/lease conditions, or acquired individually. Many designs were prepared by the Emergency Fleet Corporation and type numbers of accepted designs are shown. E.F.C. design numbers began at 1,001.

Ships building in 1917, requisitioned by the United States Shipping Board

Built by Ames Shipbuilding & Drydock Co., Seattle, Wash.

410 ft × 54 ft. Engines: T3cyl.

6   *Empire Chamois* 5,684 gt. Ordered for Cie. Générale Transatlantique, France.
5.1918: Completed as *Westmount* (U.S.S.B.).
1927: *Pacific Redwood* (Dimon SS Corp. New York).
1932: (U.S.S.B.).
1941: *Empire Chamois* (M.O.W.T.).
1946: *Granview* (Goulandris Bros.).
1949: *Chamois* (Cia. Mar. del Este, Panama).
1958: Scrapped Antwerp.

Note: At the time of her scrapping the above vessel was the last Ames-built ship afloat.

8   *Empire Nightingale* 5,698 gt. Ordered for Cie. Générale Transatlantique, France.
9.1918: Completed as *Westport* (U.S.S.B.).
1941: *Empire Nightingale* (M.O.W.T.).
1946: *Inchmull* (Williamson & Co. Ltd., Hong Kong).
1948: *Jalamatsya* (Scindia SN Co. Ltd.).
1953: *Ricnat* (Richard Nathan Corp., New York), renamed for voyage to shipbreakers.
1953: Scrapped Bo'ness.

9   *Empire Springbuck* 5,591 gt. Ordered as *War Dido* for Shipping Controller, London.
10.1918: Completed as *Westmead* (U.S.S.B.).
1920: (Stand SS Co. New York).
1921: (U.S.S.B.).
1927: *Willanglo* (Williams SS Co. Inc. New York).
1928: (Babcock SS Corpn., New York).
1929: *San Angelo* (Pacific Atlantic SS Co., Portland, Ore.).
1940: *Empire Springbuck* (M.O.S.).
10.9.1941: A straggler in convoy SC 42 (Sydney, N.S./U.K.), was hit by two torpedoes from

submarine *U.81* and sank in position 61.38N 40.40W, off Cape Farewell, Greenland.

10   *Empire Woodcock* 5,572 gt. Ordered for yard account.
11.1918: Completed as *West Cape* (U.S.S.B.).
1927: (McCormick SS Co., San Francisco).
1940: *Empire Woodcock* (M.O.S.).
1942: *Epiros* (Government of Greece).
1948: (Zaunos, Stavrides & Cocolis, Greece).
1951: *San Andrea* (Transworld Lines S.A., Panama).
1.1953: Scrapped Stockton-on-Tees.

11   *Empire Kittiwake* 5,674 gt. Ordered as *War Hector* for Shipping Controller, London.
1.1919: Completed as *Western Ally* (U.S.S.B.).
1929: *Forbes Hauptmann* (McCormick SS Co. San Francisco).
1940: *Empire Kittiwake* (M.O.S.).
1942: *Norfalk* (Norwegian Government).
7.1944: Mined and sank on passage to Normandy (to have been used as an additional blockship).

13   *Empire Gemsbuck* 5,919 gt. Ordered as *War Juno* for Shipping Controller, London.
6.1919: Completed as *Western Glenn* (U.S.S.B.).
1927: *Willwello* (Williams SS Co. Inc., New York).
1928: (American Intercoastal SS Corp., New York).
1929: *San Felipe* (Pacific Atlantic SS Co., Portland, Ore.).
1940: *Empire Gemsbuck* (M.O.S.).
3.11.1941: Sunk by submarine (*U.203*) torpedo, 52.18N 53.05W, NE of Newfoundland whilst in convoy SC 52 (Sydney, N.S./U.K.).

Built by Columbia River Shipbuilding Corporation, Portland, Ore.

Design 1016. 410 ft × 54 ft. DR geared steam turbine.

6 *Empire Turnstone* 5,828 gt. Ordered for Shipping Controller, London.
6.1918: Completed as *Western City* (U.S.S.B.).
1941: *Empire Turnstone* (M.O.W.T.).

23.10.1942: Sunk by submarine (*U.621*) torpedo, 54.40N 28.00W in the Atlantic, a straggler from convoy ONS 136 (U.K./New York) (voyage: Tyne/Port Sulphur).

Built by Bethlehem Shipbuilding Corp., Alameda, Cal.

458 ft (oa), 440 ft × 56 ft. Engines: T3cyl.

165 *Empire Porpoise* 7,592 gt. Ordered as *War Rock* for Shipping Controller, London.
10.1918: Completed as *Invincible* (U.S.S.B.).
1934: (Havemeyers & Elder, New York).
1937: (U.S.M.C.)
1940: (National Bulk Carriers Inc., New York).
1941: *Empire Porpoise* (M.O.W.T.).

1946: *Chrysanthemum* (Marine Enterprises Ltd. (Lyros & Lemos Bros. London)).
1950: *Chryss* (Cia. Maritima Neptuno S.A., Costa Rica).
1952: *Athlit* (Israel America Line Ltd., New York).
10.1954: Scrapped Trieste.

Built by Northwest Steel Co., Portland, Ore.

8,800 tdw, 410 ft × 54 ft. Engines: DR geared steam turbine.

9 *Empire Opossum* 5,760 gt. Ordered for Cie. Générale Transatlantique as *Joffre*.
6.1918: Completed as *Western Ocean* (U.S.S.B.).
1941: *Empire Opossum* (M.O.W.T.).
1949: *Marianne Clunies* (Clunies Shipping Co., Glasgow).

1950: *Ansgaritor* (D. Oltmann & Co., Bremen). Converted to a motor ship.
3.1959: Scrapped Krimpen ad Ysel, Holland.

The following ship was lost before renaming by the Ministry of War Transport:

10 *Western Chief* 5,759 gt. Ordered for Cie Générale Transatlantique as *Marne*.
7.1918: Completed for U.S.S.B.
1937: (U.S.M.C.).
10.1940: (M.O.S.).
14.3.1941: Sunk by Italian submarine (*Emo*) torpedo, 600 miles south of Reykjavik, Iceland, 58.52N 21.13W (voyage: New York/Newport, Mon.).

13 *Empire Cormorant* 5,760 gt. Ordered for Cie Générale Transatlantique as *Aisne*.
8.1918: Completed as *Western Maid* (U.S.S.B.).
1937: (U.S.M.C.).
1941: *Empire Cormorant* (M.O.W.T.).
1.10.1945: Scuttled with chemical ammunition in Bay of Biscay.

Built by Pusey & Jones Co., Gloucester, N.J.

12,500 tdw, 439.6 ft × 60 ft. Engines: Quadruple expansion.

15   *Empire Puma* 7,777 gt. Ordered for Pennsylvania Shipping Co.
3.1920: Completed as *Ethan Allen* (U.S.S.B.).
1933: (Lykes Bros-Ripley SS Co.).
1940: *Empire Puma* (M.O.S.).
1946: *Inchwells* (Williamson & Co. Ltd., Hong Kong).
1951: *Point Clear* (Cia Nav. Bellavista, Panama).
1952: *Giacomo Piaggio* (Soc. Per Azioni 'Stellamaris', Italy).
1954: *Enrichetto* (A. Ravano, Italy).
1958: *Silvana* (Panamanian Oriental SS Co., Panama (Wheelock, Marden & Co., Hong Kong)).

5.1959: Scrapped Hong Kong.

16   *Empire Steelhead* 7,586 gt. Ordered for Pennsylvania Shipping Co.
1920: Completed as *Patrick Henry* (U.S.S.B.).
1933: (Lykes Bros-Ripley SS Co. Inc., New York).
1940: *Empire Steelhead* (M.O.S.).
1942: *Crete* (Government of Greece).
1947: *Vernicos Nicolaos* (D. Vernicos, Greece).
1951: *El Greco* (Cia. Mar. de Petroleo, Panama).
9.1952: Scrapped Savona.

The *Empire Puma*, May 1943. (Pusey & Jones Co., Yard No. 15.)

Built by Skinner & Eddy Corporation, Seattle, Wash.

8,800 tdw, 410 ft × 54 ft. Engines: DR geared steam turbine.

10   *Empire Leopard* 5,676 gt. Ordered for Shipping Controller, London.
12.1917: Completed as *West Haven* (U.S.S.B.).
1918: U.S. Navy.
1920: (U.S.S.B.).
1920: (Atlantic Gulf Pacific SS Co.).
1922: (U.S.S.B.).
1929: *Marian Otis Chandler* (Los Angeles SS Co. Inc.).
1934: *Onomea* (Matson Nav. Co., San Francisco).
1940: *Empire Leopard* (M.O.S.).
2.11.1942: Sunk by submarine (*U.402*) torpedo off Newfoundland, 52.26N 45.22W in convoy SC 107 (Sydney, N.S./Avonmouth).

12   *Black Osprey* 5,802 gt. Building for yard account as *Jas. G. Eddy*. Sold to B. Stolt Nielsen then:
2.1918: Completed as *West Arrow* (U.S.S.B.).
1931: *Black Osprey* (Diamond Lines Inc., New York).
1941: (M.O.S.).
17.2.1941: Sunk by submarine (*U.96*) torpedo 61.30N 18.10W SW of Faroe Islands whilst a straggler from convoy HX 107 (Halifax, New York/U.K.).

Note: 'Empire' name unallocated when sunk.

Built by Texas Steamship Co., Bath, Maine

402 ft × 54 ft. Engines: T3cyl.

1 *Empire Lynx* 6,032 gt. 10.1917: Building for own account, but completed as *Maine* for U.S.S.B.
1920: (Green Star SS Corp., U.S.A.).
1921: (U.S.S.B.).
1922: (C. Barnes, U.S.A.).

1923: (Fairfield SS Corpn. (Seas Shipping Co., New York)).
1940: *Empire Lynx* (M.O.S.).
3.11.1942: Sunk by submarine (*U.132*) torpedo, 55.20N 40.01W, south-east of Greenland.

Built by Todd Drydock & Construction Co., Tacoma, Wash.

7,500 tdw, 380 ft × 53 ft. Engines: T3cyl.

101 *Empire Mallard* 4,957 gt. Ordered as *War Comrade* for Shipping Controller, London.
9.1918: Completed as *Anacortes* (U.S.S.B.).
1920: (French American Line).
1920: (U.S.S.B.).
1941: *Empire Mallard* (M.O.W.T.).
26.9.1941: In collision with *Empire Moon* (1941, 7,424 gt) in fog and in convoy, sank near Point

Amour, Belle Isle Strait (voyage: New York and Sydney, N.S./River Mersey – steel ingots and bars).

Note: The *Empire Moon* was only slightly damaged in the collision.

Three big yards – so-called 'agency yards' – were financed by the United States Government in 1917 where pre-fabricated parts of ships, mass-produced in factories and workshops across the nation and then packed and crated for transport to the yards, could be assembled to ships of standard types. They were at Hog Island, opposite the Philadelphia Navy Yard on the Schuylkill River; at Harriman, Pennsylvania and at Newark Bay, N.J.

At Hog Island the plant of the American International Shipbuilding Corporation was laid out in some 900 acres of marshy ground. Work was begun after the contract of 1917, draining and clearing the ground for road access, ultimately to construct fifty shipways, twenty-eight berths for fitting out the ships, workshops, offices, stores, eighty-two miles of railway tracks and, for a workforce of 30,000, housing and shops. It was hailed as a great industrial marvel.

The ships to be built were planned for simplicity in construction: two decks, five holds, little curvature and no sheer. Measurements were 400 ft length overall, breadth 54 ft, to a gross tonnage of 5,000 and a deadweight capacity of 7,500. Propulsion was by steam turbine, giving 2,500 hp. The design number was 1,022 and known as Type 'A'.

Contracts were let for 110 cargo ships and seventy transports, but before the yard could get into full production the war had ended. The first ship, *Quistconck*, was laid down in June and completed in November 1918, but as the plant began getting into its stride a keel was being laid every 5½ days. All cargo ships ordered were built; four in 1918, sixty-two in 1919 and forty-four in 1920: a total of 110.

But from the order for seventy passenger/cargo ships (Type 'B'), only twelve were built: nine in 1920; three in 1921; with fifty-eight cancelled. These ships were 437 ft in length and 58 ft breadth; gross tonnage was 7,555 and deadweight capacity 8,000 tons. They were driven by turbines of 6,000 hp. Three designs were involved, numbers 1024, 1029 and 1095.

Five of the passenger/cargo carriers formed the American Merchant Lines in 1924 and two more ships joined the fleet in 1931. Later absorbed into the United States Lines, the seven ships became familiar sights on the River Thames in the New York–London service until 1940.

Four were government transports, of which three served as hospital ships, *Samaritan, St. Mihiel* and *Chateau Thierry* in World War II. The twelfth ship, and last keel to be laid down at Hog Island, was commenced on 8 December 1919. On 28 April 1920 she was launched as *Wright* and was moved to Hoboken for completion by Tietjen & Lang as a seaplane carrier (*AV.1*) for the U.S. Navy.

The Hog Island yard closed down in 1921 and in May 1930 was sold to the City of Philadelphia. It became a rail and marine terminal, then an airport.

The total deadweight capacity of all yard building was reckoned to be 921,000 tons.

At Newark Bay, New Jersey, the twenty-eight-shipway plant of the Submarine Boat Corporation was constructed, also on marshy ground.

The contract was set for 150 vessels and Yard No. 1 and the first E.F.C. pre-fabricated ship *Agawam*, was launched in early 1918. In the following year eighty-seven ships were completed, in 1920 came another thirty. But the E.F.C. had, by then, suspended the building of the remaining thirty-two ships, the last keel – for the *Neshobee* – being laid on 11 November 1919 and the ship completed on 11 June 1920. The thirty-two suspended ships were later completed for the account of the Submarine Boat Corporation and with the exception of the first completion, Yard No. 119, named *Italia*, all were named with the prefix 'Su', (see *Empire Hamble*).

All ships were to design 1023: 324 ft in length and 46 ft breadth, with a gross tonnage of 3,545. All were driven by turbines of 1,500 hp except the last, Yard No. 150, *Suphenco*, in which was fitted a six-cylinder oil engine.

The third 'agency yard' involved in the fabricated ship was the Merchant Shipbuilding Corporation, at Harriman, Pa.

A contract was awarded for forty ships to be built at Harriman with another contract for twenty more ships to follow. The chosen site for the yard was considerably drier than those at Hog Island and Newark Bay and twelve shipways were quickly built. By 16 February 1918 Yard No. 1, *Cabegon*, was laid. In 1919 twenty-one ships were completed, fifteen in 1920 and four in 1921, the last, *Arden*, completed on 28 February. Then the yard closed down and was dismantled; the remaining order for twenty ships was cancelled. The ships measured 400 ft × 54 ft, 5,800/6,100 gross tons and had turbines to 3,000 hp.

The Merchant Shipbuilding Corporation also re-opened the yard of J. Roach & Sons at Chester, Pa. which later had become the Delaware River I.S.B. & Engine Works, whose buildings had included steamers for the Ocean SS Company of Savannah and screw vessels and paddle steamers for the New England SS Company of New York, until 1907. Thirty-five ships were constructed between 1918 and 1922 of varying tonnages and propulsion and included nine tankers. The last ships built were the twin screw motorships *Californian* and *Missourian*, 7,900 gt, for the American Hawaiian SS Company. All buildings, however, were only partly pre-fabricated.

These, then, were the main assembly yards for the pre-fabricated ships, totalling ninety shipways, which were financed by the U.S. Government through the Emergency Fleet Corporation. With the armistice in 1918 the E.F.C.'s work was done and it was gradually run down, leaving the United States Shipping Board to administer the vast fleet that had been built in the frenzy of shipbuilding between 1917 and 1921.

Ships built under United States Shipping Board contracts

Design 1013 'Robert Dollar' type – 8,800 tdw, 410 ft × 54 ft. Engines: T3cyl or turbine

Built by J. F. Duthie & Co., Seattle, Wash.

27 *Empire Gannet* 5,672 gt. Ordered as *West Herick*.
1919: Completed as *Dewey* (U.S.S.B.). (Engines T3cyl.).
1928: *Golden Fleece* (Oceanic & Oriental SN Co., San Francisco).
1937: *Louisianan* (American-Hawaiian SS Co., San Francisco).
1941: *Empire Gannet* (M.O.W.T.).
1946: *Arion* (Aurora Shipping Co. (Goulandris Bros.)).
1949: (Cia. Maritima del Este, Panama (Goulandris Bros.)).
1956: *St. Elefterio* (Cia. de Vapores Elefterio Ltd., Costa Rica (Panama flag)).
4.2.1958: Sprung leak in No. 1 hold; diverted to San Juan, P.R., escorted by U.S. destroyers, whose crews attempted to stop the leak.
6.2.1958: Other holds and engine room flooded; rolled over and sank stern first, 21.54N 64.46W (voyage: Nuevitas/U.K. – sugar).

Built by Los Angeles Shipbuilding & Drydock Corporation, San Pedro, Cal.

11 *Empire Crossbill* 5,463 gt.
1919: Completed as *West Amargosa* (U.S.S.B.) (Engines: T3cyl.).
1941: *Empire Crossbill* (M.O.W.T.).
11.9.1941: Sunk by submarine (*U.82*) torpedo, 63.14N 37.12W in convoy SC 42 (voyage: Sydney N.S./Hull).

Built by Northwest Steel Co., Portland, Ore.

19 *Empire Grebe* 5,736 gt.
12.1918: Completed as *West Wauna* (U.S.S.B.). (Engines: DR turbines.)
1941: *Empire Grebe* (M.O.W.T.).
1946: *Inchmark* (Williamson & Co. Ltd., Hong Kong).
29.5.1949: Aground on Schilpad Island Reef, Banda Sea, 7.5S 132.3E. Abandoned. Total loss (voyage: Sydney/Hong Kong – ballast).

33 *Empire Mavis* 5,704 gt.
10.1919: Completed as *West Raritans* (U.S.S.B.). (Engines: DR turbines.)
1941: *Empire Mavis* (M.O.W.T.).
1942: *Jan van Goyen* (Government of Netherlands).
1946: *Stad Maastricht* (Halcyon Lijn N.V., Holland).

1955: *Amaver* (Cia. La Plana, Panama).
1.1959: Scrapped Aviles.

35 *Empire Cougar* 5,758 gt.
10.1919: Completed as *West Saginaw* (U.S.S.B.). (Engines: DR turbines.)
1941: *Empire Cougar* (M.O.W.T.).
1946: *Aurora* (Aurora Shipping Co. (Goulandris Bros)).
1948: *Cougar* (Cia. Maritima del Este, Panama).
1951: *Favola* (Trama Trasporti Marittimi SpA, Genoa).
1959: (Cia. Armatoriale Italiana).
3.1960: Scrapped Spezia.

Built by Skinner & Eddy Corporation, Seattle, Wash.

21   *Empire Cheetah* 5,506 gt.
1918: Completed as *West Lianga* (U.S.S.B.).
(Engines: DR turbines.)
1929: *Helen Whittier* (Los Angeles SS Co. Inc.).
1938: *Kalani* (Matson Nav. Co., San Francisco).
1940: *Empire Cheetah* (M.O.S.).
1942: *Hobbema* (Government of Netherlands).
3.11.1942: Sunk by submarine (*U.132*) torpedo near
Iceland, 55.38N 39.52W, in convoy SC 107
(voyage: Sydney, N.S./Belfast).

24   *Empire Simba* 5,647 gt.
1918: Completed as *West Cohas* (U.S.S.B.).
(Engines: DR turbines.)
1933: (Lykes Bros-Ripley SS Co.).
1940: *Empire Simba* (M.O.S.).
1.3.1941: Damaged by aircraft bomb in Irish Sea,
52.21N 05.23W. Abandoned, leaking. Taken in tow,
docked Liverpool.
12.3.1941: After air raid on Liverpool, parachute mine
found on deck.
14.3.1941: Mine exploded; ship damaged amidships.
Repaired.
9.9.1945: Left Loch Ryan, and:
13.9.1945: scuttled in Atlantic with chemical
ammunition, 55.30N 11.00W.

25   *Empire Wildebeeste* 5,631 gt.
1918: Completed as *West Ekonk* (U.S.S.B.).
(Engines: DR turbines.)
1933: (Lykes Bros-Ripley SS Co.).
1941: *Empire Wildebeeste* (M.O.W.T.).
24.1.1942: Sunk by submarine (*U.106*) torpedo west
of New York, 39.30N 59.54W.

26   *Empire Hartebeeste* 5,676 gt.
1918: Completed as *West Gambo* (U.S.S.B.).
(Engines: DR turbines.)
1933: (Lykes Bros-Ripley SS Co. Inc.).
1941: *Empire Hartebeeste* (M.O.W.T.).
20.9.1942: Sunk by submarine (*U.596*) torpedo
56.20N 38.10W in convoy SC 100 (New
York/U.K.).

28   *West Hobomac* 5,527 gt.
Another Skinner & Eddy-built ship which, although
later flew the British flag, was never under an 'Empire'
name.
1918: Completed as *West Hobomac* (U.S.S.B.).
(Engines: DR turbine.)
1933: (Lykes Bros-Ripley SS Co. Inc.).
1940: *Ile de Batz* (Cie. Générale Transatlantique).
10.1940: Seized by Britain at Falmouth (M.O.S.).
17.3.1942: Sunk by submarine (*U.68*) torpedo off
Gold Coast, 04.04N 08.04W.

Design 1014 'Cascade' type – 7,500 tdw, 380 ft × 53 ft. Engines: T3cyl

Built by Todd Drydock & Construction Corp., Tacoma, Wash.

9   *Empire Antelope* 4,753 gt.
1919: Completed as *Ophis* (U.S.S.B.).
1928: *Bangu* (U.S.S.B.).
1941: *Empire Antelope* (M.O.W.T.).
2.11.1942: Sunk by submarine (*U.402*) torpedo west
of Labrador, 52.26N 45.22W
(voyage: U.S.A./U.K.). (convoy SC 107).

Convoy SC 107 Sydney, N.S./United Kingdom: On 24
October 1942, eleven U-boats formed the 'Veilchen' group,
just east of Newfoundland; five more were placed to the
south; two to the north-east. On 30 October convoy SC 107
was sighted south-west of Cape Race which, with Halifax

and Sydney groups, totalled forty-two ships. Three destroyers and four corvettes were in escort.

For two days the U-boats manoeuvred for attack but were
driven off by the escort ships and Royal Canadian Air Force
planes, but at 02.00 hours on 2 November, *U.402* torpedoed
the *Empire Sunrise*, which was badly damaged and was later
dispatched by *U.84*. Between 04.00 and 06.00 hours the
British ship *Dalcroy* (4,558 gt), the old *Rinos* (4,649 gt) of
1919 wearing the Greek flag of L. A. Embiricos and J. & C.
Harrison's *Hartington* (5,496 gt) were all lost, the latter being
hit by torpedoes from *U.522*, *U.438* and, finally, from *U.521*.

In the first hour of daylight attacks came quickly. The
Canadian frigate *Moosejaw*, which had arrived to reinforce,
was damaged and the *Empire Leopard* and *Empire Antelope*
were both sunk. The 1912-built *Maritima* (5,804 gt) and

another Greek ship, *Mount Pelion* (5,655 gt), were lost. There was a near miss on the 1908-built Greek *Parthenon* (3,189 gt) but she was a victim of an underwater attack by *U.522* later in the day. Some respite came as a mist closed in, but the convoy fell into disarray and the 6,855 gt United States' tanker *Hahira* of the Atlantic Refining Company was spotted by *U.521* just before midday and torpedoed.

Towards midnight on 3 November the attacks were resumed, first on the small Dutch cargo ship *Titus* (1,712 gt). She was abandoned but later re-boarded when it was realised that little damage had occurred. P & O's *Jeypore* (5,318 gt), acting as commodore ship, was hit by a torpedo from *U.89* at about 22.00 hours and within seconds she was ablaze from bridge to forecastle. She was abandoned and sank in twenty minutes.

Just after midnight on 4 November the Dutch-flag *Hobbema* (5,507 gt) and *Empire Lynx* (6,379 gt) were sunk by *U.132* which also hit the British India SN Co.'s *Hatimura* (6,690 gt) which was again torpedoed some three hours later by *U.442* and sunk. The persistent *U.89* sank the Ropner ship *Daleby* (4,640 gt) just before midnight.

On the 5th, Royal Air Force Liberators arrived and, coupled with United States naval reinforcements, dispersed the remainder of the submarines; the operation was broken off on the 6th. The Allies lost fourteen ships totalling 80,000 gross tons with their valuable cargoes. Two submarines were sunk.

10 *Empire Tiger* 4,886 gt.
1919: Completed as *Orcus* (U.S.S.B.).
1923: *Coya* (Grace SS Co. Inc., New York).
1940: *Empire Tiger* (M.O.S.).
Untraced on voyage Halifax/Clyde with cargo of steel.

Last communication on 27.2.1941. Not listed as war loss; considered as foundered in heavy weather.

17 *Empire Elk* 4,748 gt.
1920: Completed as *Rotarian* (U.S.S.B.).
1923: *Condor* (Grace SS Co. Inc., New York).
1940: *Empire Elk* (M.O.S.).
1942: *Norvarg* (Government of Norway).
1946: *Nan Chiang* (Wallem & Co., Shanghai).
1950: *Northern Glow* (Great Northern Shipping Co. Ltd., Hong Kong).
1959: *Hoping Ssu Shi Liu* (Government of China).
1971: Name removed from ship registers.

104 *Empire Wagtail* 4,893 gt.
1919: Completed as *Ossining* (U.S.S.B.).
1932: *Point Lobos* (Gulf Pacific Mail Line Inc., (Swayne & Hoyt Inc., San Francisco)).
1941: *Empire Wagtail* (M.O.W.T.).
28.12.1942: Sunk by submarine (*U.260*) torpedo in mid-Atlantic. 43.17N 27.22W, in convoy ONS 154 (voyage: Cardiff/Halifax – coal).

105 *Empire Gazelle* 4,828 gt.
1919: Completed as *Higho* (U.S.S.B.).
1928: (American West African Line Inc. (Barber SS Lines Inc.)).
1941: *Empire Gazelle* (M.O.W.T.).
1946: *Inchmay* (Williamson & Co. Ltd., Hong Kong).
1954: Scrapped Yawata, Japan.

The following ships were lost before renaming by the Ministry of War Transport:

8 *Berury* 4,924 gt.
1919: Completed for U.S.S.B. as *Olen*.
1928: *Berury* (U.S.S.B.).
1941: (M.O.W.T.).
11.9.1941: Sunk by submarine (*U.207*) torpedo east of Cape Farewell, Greenland, 62.40N 38.50W, in convoy SC 42.

108 *Willimantic* 4,857 gt.
1918: Completed for U.S.S.B.
1942: (M.O.W.T.).
24.6.1942: Sunk by submarine (*U.156*) torpedo north east of St. Thomas, West Indies, 25.55N 51.58W.

110 *Delight* 5,135 gt.
1919: Completed for U.S.S.B.
1928: (J. Griffiths & Sons, Seattle).
1932: *Point Ancha* (Gulf Pacific Mail Line Inc., Swayne & Hoyt Inc., San Francisco).
1941: *Macon* (M.O.S.).
27.7.1941: Sunk by Italian submarine (*Barbarigo*) torpedo, north-west of Canary Islands, 32.48N 26.12W.

Design 1015 – 9,400 tdw, 402 ft × 53 ft. Engines: Geared turbines

Built by Moore Shipbuilding Co., Oakland, Cal.

Eight Moore-built ships were fitted with refrigerating machinery, with a ship capacity of 308,000 cubic feet in eight chambers. Of the eight, five were acquired by Britain and three were transferred to the U.S. Navy in 1921: *Yamhill* (Yard No. 122) which was renamed *Arctic* (AF 7) and scrapped at New Orleans in 1947; *Yaquina* (Yard No. 123) which became *Boreas* (AF 8) until scrapped by Patapsco in 1947 and *Mehanno* (Yard No. 136) renamed *Yukon* (AF 9) and scrapped at Baltimore in 1947.

121   *Empire Raven* 6,100 gt.
11.1918: Completed as *Oskawa* (U.S.S.B.).
1942: *Empire Raven* (M.O.W.T.).
1948: *Southern Raven* (South Georgia Co. Ltd. (Chris Salvesen & Co., Leith)).
11.1952: Scrapped Port Glasgow.

124   *Empire Merganser* 6,220 gt.
1.1919: Completed as *Guimba* (U.S.S.B.).
10.1919: Damaged by mine off mouth of River Elbe; repaired, then:
1921: Laid up until 1941 when reconditioned at Baltimore.
1942: *Empire Merganser* (M.O.W.T.).
1947: *Ketos* (United Whalers Ltd., London).
1949: (Hector Whaling Co. Ltd., London).
2.4.1951: Explosion in engine room; hole blown in side of ship.
3.4.1951: Sank in South Atlantic, 2.25N 30.30W (voyage: Aalborg/Rio de Janeiro – cement).

As *Ketos*, was sometime employed working with the Antarctic whaling fleet, taking stores and returning with whalemeat in her insulated holds.

131   *Empire Whimbrel* 5,983 gt.
6.1919: Completed as *Monasses* (U.S.S.B.).
1941: *Empire Whimbrel* (M.O.W.T.).
11.4.1943: Sunk by submarine (*U.181*) torpedo and gunfire 400 miles SSW of Freetown, 02.31N 15.55W (voyage: Buenos Aires/Freetown (for convoy) – meat).

133   *Empire Avocet* 5,963 gt.
8.1919: Completed as *Cotati* (U.S.S.B.).
1942: *Empire Avocet* (M.O.W.T.).
29.9.1942: Sunk by submarine (*U.125*) torpedo 04.05N 13.23W, 350 miles south of Freetown, homeward bound from River Plate (voyage: (for convoy) Rio Grande do Sul/Freetown – meat).

135   *Empire Starling* 6,060 gt.
10.1919: Completed as *Nockum* (U.S.S.B.).
1941: *Empire Starling* (M.O.W.T.).
21.11.1942: Sunk by submarine (*U.163*) torpedo north east of Barbados, 13.05N 56.20W.

146   *Empire Heron* 6,023 gt.
1920: Completed as *Mosella* (U.S.S.B.).
1940: *Empire Heron* (M.O.S.).
15.10.1941: Sunk by submarine (*U.568*) torpedo in Atlantic 54.05N 27.15W, in convoy SC 48.

147   *Empire Plover* 6,085 gt.
1920: Completed as *Janelew* (U.S.S.B.).
1941: *Empire Plover* (M.O.W.T.).
1946: (to have been named *Granvale*) but:
1948: *Plover* (Cia. Maritima del Este, Panama).
1951: *Marianne* (Soc. de Nav. Magliveras, Panama).
1956: *Nicolas* (Cia. de Nav. Alexander, Panama).
11.1958: Scrapped Vado, Italy.

Built by Groton Iron Works, Groton, Conn.

9 *Empire Tarpon* 6,216 gt.
1920: Completed as *Hopatcong* (U.S.S.B.).
1930: (Jersey American SS Corp., U.S.A.).
3.1931: (Boston I. & M. Co. – at U.S. Marshal's sale). Resold, and:
1931: *Harpoon* (Shepard SS Co., Boston).
1940: *Empire Tarpon* (M.O.S.).

6.10.1942: Engine trouble, in distress 57.20N 15.9W, 500 miles west of Lewis, Hebrides. Took water in holds; Taken in tow, but:
13.10.1942: Abandoned and:
14.10.1942: Sank 57.24N 7.45W, twenty miles SW of South Uist, Hebrides (voyage: Mobile & New York/Milford Haven – general).

Built by Pacific Coast Shipbuilding Co., Bay Point, Cal.

3 *Cockaponset* 5,995 gt.
1919: Completed for U.S.S.B.
1941: (M.O.W.T.).
20.5.1941: Sunk by submarine (*U.111*) torpedo south-east of Cape Farewell, Greenland, 57.28N 41.07W.

Note: 'Empire' name unallocated when sunk.

Built by G. M. Standifer Construction Corp., Vancouver, Wash.

2 *Empire Kingfisher* 6,038 gt.
1919: Completed as *Coaxet* (U.S.S.B.) (Engines: T3cyl.).
1941: *Empire Kingfisher* (M.O.W.T.).
18.1.1942: Struck submerged object four miles off Cape Sable, Nova Scotia. The submerged object (possibly a sunken ship) passed under the *Empire Kingfisher* with a rumbling sound and shock: an explosion was heard. Engines were stopped and the rumbling stopped; engines restarted and sound again heard, followed by jamming of the rudder. Engines again stopped; vessel settled rapidly. Anchored and abandoned, but:
19.1.1942: Sank south of Bantam Rock Buoy before salvage tugs arrived.

3 *Empire Sambar* 6,038 gt.
1919: Completed as *Waban* (U.S.S.B.) (Engines: T3cyl.).
1933: (Lykes Bros-Ripley SS Co.).

1940: *Empire Sambar* (M.O.T.).
6.3.1941: Explosion in engine room while at sea; towed in. Repaired, and:
1941: *Empire Beaver* (M.O.W.T.).
1942: *Norhauk* (Government of Norway).
21.12.1943: Sunk by mine in Thames Estuary, 51.50N 01.33E (voyage: Halifax, N.S./London).

8 *Empire Ptarmigan* 6,103 gt.
1919: Completed as *Abercos* (U.S.S.B.) (Engines: T3cyl).
1941: *Empire Ptarmigan* (M.O.W.T.).
1942: *Norelg* (Government of Norway).
1946: (Wallem & Co., Panama).
1948: *New Asia* (New Continental SS Co., China).
1950: *Norelg* (Wallem & Co., Panama).
1951: (Purple Star Shipping Co., China).
1957: Name deleted from shipping registers due to lack of information.

Built by Virginia Shipbuilding Corp., Alexandria, Va.

6   *Empire Impala* 6,113 gt.
Laid down as *Boshbish* (U.S.S.B.).
1920: Completed as *Clemence C. Morse*
(Engines: T3cyl.) (United States Transportation Co.).
1923: *Oakman* (U.S.S.B.).
1933: (Lykes Bros-Ripley SS Co. Inc.).
1940: *Empire Impala* (M.O.S.).
On 7 March 1943 the Westcott & Laurence Line's *Egyptian* (2,868 gt) and *Empire Impala* were in convoy SC 121 (Sydney N.S./U.K.). Owing to gales there were several stragglers from the convoy. At 02.00 hours the *Egyptian* was torpedoed by *U.230* and sank. The straggling *Empire Impala* came upon survivors, stopped at about 09.00 hours and herself was sunk by torpedoes from *U.591*. She sank in position 58N 15W (approx.).

9   *Empire Moose* 6,103 gt.
1920: Completed as *Colin H. Livingstone*
(Engines: T3cyl.) (United States Transportation Co.).
1923: *Oakwood* (U.S.S.B.).
1933: (Lykes Bros-Ripley SS Co. Inc.).
1940: *Empire Moose* (M.O.S.).
29.8.1940: Sunk by submarine (*U.100*) torpedo, 56.06N 13.33W west of Hebrides. A straggler from convoy OA 204 (Southend/North America).

Design 1016 'Baltimore Drydock' type – 8,800 tdw, 410 ft × 54 ft. Engines: Turbine

Built by Columbia River Shipbuilding Corp., Portland, Ore.

11   *Empire Miniver* 6,055 gt.
12.1918: Completed as *West Cobalt* for U.S.S.B.
1933: (Lykes Bros-Ripley SS Co. Inc.).
1940: *Empire Miniver* (M.O.S.).
18.10.1940: Sunk by submarine (*U.99*) torpedo north-west of Ireland, 250 miles from Rathlin Head.

16   *Empire Moorhen* 5,628 gt.
4.1919: Completed as *West Totant* for U.S.S.B.
1941: *Empire Moorhen* (M.O.W.T.).
9.6.1944: Block ship, Mulberry, Normandy.
1947: Raised, scrapped Troon.

17   *Empire Panther* 5,600 gt.
5.1919: Completed as *West Quechee* for U.S.S.B.
1933: (Lykes Bros-Ripley SS Co. Inc.).
1940: *Empire Panther* (M.O.S.).
1.1.1943: Mined and sank, eight miles off Strumble Head, Pembroke (voyage: New York/Cardiff).

25   *Empire Oryx* 5,756 gt.
Completed as *West Harshaw* for U.S.S.B.
1953: (Lykes Bros.-Ripley SS Co. Inc.).
1940: *Empire Oryx* (M.O.S.).
1941: *Empire Robin* (M.O.W.T.).
1942: *Ferdinand Bol* (Government of Netherlands).
30.7.1942: In collision, in fog with steamer *Norse King* (1920, 5,701 gt), sank 45.21N 59.28W, NE of Cape Breton (voyage: Baltimore and Halifax/Sydney, N.S./Newport – steel and scrap).

The *Empire Oryx* at New York, July 1941. (Columbia River Shipbuilding Corporation, Yard No. 25.)   *U.S.C.G.*

Design 1017 'Downey' type – 7,500 tdw, 387 ft × 52 ft.
Engines: T3cyl.

Built by Downey Shipbuilding Corp., Arlington, N.Y.

10 *Empire Caribou* 4,861 gt.
1919: Completed as *Waterbury* (U.S.S.B.).
1920: *Northern Star* (American Star Line Inc., New York).
1923: *Defacto* (American Sugar Transit Corp., New York).

1940: *Empire Caribou* (M.O.S.).
10.5.1941: Sunk by submarine (*U.556*) torpedo in Atlantic, 59.28N 35.44W after dispersal of convoy OB 318 (voyage: Liverpool/North America).

Design 1019 'Standard Ferris' type – 7,500 tdw, 410 ft × 54 ft.
Engines: T3cyl.

Built by Atlantic Corporation, Portsmouth, N.H.

1 *Empire Dabchick* 6,089 gt.
1919: Completed as *Kisnop* (U.S.S.B.).
1941: *Empire Dabchick* (M.O.W.T.).
3.12.1942: Sunk by submarine (*U.183*) torpedo 43.00N 58.17W about 200 miles SE by S of Sable Island, in convoy ONS 146 (voyage: Liverpool/St John, N.B.).

8 *Empire Dorado* 5,595 gt.
1920: Completed as *Tolosa* (U.S.S.B.).

1940: *Empire Dorado* (M.O.S.).
8.11.1940: Bombed and damaged 55.07N 16.50W, west of Ireland; towed into Clyde; repaired.
20.11.1941: In collision with Greek steamer *Theomitor* (1910, 4,427 gt) WNW of Ireland, 57.58N 20.38W. Taken in tow by H.M. ship. Tow parted. Again taken in tow, but:
22.11.1941: Sank after sixty-five miles of towage (voyage: Halifax, N.S./Manchester – general).

Built by Long Beach Shipbuilding Co., Long Beach, Cal.

137 *Empire Eland* 5,620 gt.
1920: Completed as *West Kedron* (U.S.S.B.).
1940: *Empire Eland* (M.O.S.).

15.9.1941: Sunk by submarine (*U.94*) torpedo in Atlantic approx. 54.00N 28.00W (voyage: Liverpool/Mobile).

Built by Southwestern Shipbuilding Co., San Pedro, Cal.

6   *Empire Bison* 5,612 gt.
1919: Completed as *West Cawthon* (U.S.S.B.).
1920: (Green Star SS Corpn.).
1923: (U.S.S.B.).
1926: (American-South African Line Inc.).
1940: *Empire Bison* (M.O.S.).
1.11.1940: Sunk by submarine (*U.124*) torpedo,
59.30N 17.40W in North Atlantic whilst a straggler
from convoy HX 82 (Halifax/New York/U.K.).

14   *Empire Hawksbill* 5,724 gt.
1920: Completed as *West Nivaria* (U.S.S.B.).
1928: *Golden Coast* (Oceanic & Oriental SS Co., San
Francisco).
1937: *Delawarean* (American Hawaiian SS Co., San
Francisco.).
1940: *Empire Hawksbill* (M.O.S.).
19.7.1942: Sunk by submarine (*U.564*) torpedo
42.29N 25.56W whilst in convoy OS 34, west of
Portugal.

Built by Western Pipe & Steel Co., San Francisco

10   *Empire Guillemot* 5,641 gt.
1919: Completed as *West Caddoa* (U.S.S.B.).
1940: *Empire Guillemot* (M.O.S.).
24.10.1941: Sunk by aircraft torpedo, west of Galita
Island, NW of Bizerta, Tunisia.

The vessel commenced a hazardous voyage when she left
Gourock for Gibraltar on 8 September 1941. The day before

reaching Gibraltar she dropped out of convoy and painted
two big Spanish flags on her sides. Two days later she
changed these for French flags until she reached Cap Bon,
when she became Italian. She steamed along the North
African coast unchallenged and reached Malta safely. On the
return passage she was sunk by Italian aircraft after passing
Cap Bon, Tunisia.

Design 1022 'Standard Fabricated Type A' – 7,500 tdw, 390 ft × 54 ft. Engines: Turbine

Built by American International Shipbuilding Co., Hog Island, Pa.

492   *Empire Falcon* 5,144 gt.
11.1918: Completed as *Quistconck* (U.S.S.B.).
1933: (Lykes Bros.-Ripley SS Co. Inc.).
1941: *Empire Falcon* (M.O.W.T.).
1946: *Barnby* (Rowland & Marwoods SS Co.).
1952: *Mariandrea* (Soc. de Nav. Magliveras S.A.,
Panama).
3.1953: Scrapped Troon.

Quistconck, the first 'Hog Island' ship completed, was
launched by Mrs. Woodrow Wilson on 5 August 1918 and
left Norfolk, Va. on its maiden voyage on 3 January 1919.
The war had ended on 11 November 1918. The name
Quistconck is the name by which Hog Island was known
among the Delaware Indians. 'Quist' means 'Hog' and

'Onck' means 'a place for'. Thus the ship's name was derived
from the name the Indians gave to the swampy, marshy,
island.

494   *Empire Barracuda* 4,926 gt.
1918: Completed as *Sacandaga* (U.S.S.B.).
1918: (Carolina Co. (American Palmetto Line)).
1925: (U.S.S.B.).
1932: *Black Heron* (American Diamond Lines Inc.).
1941: *Empire Barracuda* (M.O.W.T.).
15.12.1941: Sunk by submarine (*U.77*) torpedo, west
of Gibraltar, 35.30N 06.17W in convoy HG 76
(Gibraltar/U.K.).

541 *Empire Ortolan* 4,989 gt.
1919: Completed as *Labette* (U.S.S.B.).
1933: (Lykes Bros.-Ripley SS Co. Inc.)
1941: *Empire Ortolan* (M.O.W.T.).
1946: *Stanland* (Stanhope SS Co. Ltd.).
1949: *Alma* (Alma Shipping Co., S.A. (Faros Shipping Co.)).
5.1953: Scrapped Milford Haven.

1489 *Empire Hawk* 5,032 gt.
1919: Completed as *Coahoma County* (U.S.S.B.).
1931: (American Diamond Lines Inc.).
1932: renamed *Black Tern*.
1941: *Empire Hawk* (M.O.W.T.).
12.12.1942: Sunk by Italian submarine (*Tazzoli*) torpedo in Atlantic, 05.56N 39.50W.

1491 *Empire Shearwater* 4,970 gt.
1919: Completed as *Clearwater* (U.S.S.B.).
1929: (Mississippi Shipping Co. Inc.).
1940: *Empire Shearwater* (M.O.S.).
1946: *St. Jessica* (St. Quentin Shipping Co. Ltd. (South American Saint Line Ltd.)).
1950: *Karsiyaka* (Meserreticoglu (Turkey)).
1.2.1958: Arrived at Istanbul with engine trouble and shaft damage (voyage: Calcutta/Rotterdam – scrap iron, ore and oil cake).
3.9.1958: Discharge of cargo commenced.
12.1958: Vessel sold and scrapped locally.

1507 *Empire Mahseer* 5,107 gt.
1920: Completed as *Liberty Bell* (U.S.S.B.).
1920: (Pioneer SS Corp., New York).
1921: (U.S.S.B.).
1933: (Lykes Bros.-Ripley SS Co. Inc.).
1941: *Empire Mahseer* (M.O.W.T.).
4.3.1943: Sunk by submarine (*U.160*) torpedo, 32.01S 30.48E in Indian Ocean
(voyage: Durban/Bahia & Trinidad).

1521 *Empire Razorbill* 5,117 gt.
1920: Completed as *Conness Peak* (U.S.S.B.).
1920: (Pioneer SS Corp., New York).
1933: (Lykes Bros.-Ripley SS Co. Inc.).
1938: *Erica Reed* (Wisconsin SS Co.).
1939: *Eastern Trader* (American Coast Line Inc.).
1940: *Empire Razorbill* (M.O.S.).
1946: (Williamson & Co. Ltd., Hong Kong).
1947: *M. Xilas* (Xilas Bros. Greece).
4.6.1947: On fire at Kohsichang, Thailand, with rice cargo. Abandoned, beached and burning.
13.7.1947: Sank. Total loss. No salvage facilities available.

1525 *Empire Flamingo* 4,994 gt.
1920: Completed as *Jolee* (U.S.S.B.).
1933: (Lykes Bros.-Ripley SS Co. Inc.).
1941: *Empire Flamingo* (M.O.W.T.).
9.6.1944: Blockship, Mulberry, Normandy.
1948: Forepart salved, to be towed to Newport, Mon., for breaking up, but:
26.10.1948: Sank three miles south of Longships.
1949: Raised, then sunk in deep water 2½ miles south of Gwennap Head.

1540 *Empire Dolphin* 5,037 gt.
1920: Completed as *Vaba* (U.S.S.B.).
1920: (Charbonnier Rajola, U.S.).
1921: (U.S.S.B.).
6.1921: Converted to a tanker by Curtis Bay Copper & Iron Works, Curtis Bay, Md.
1923: (American-Italian SS Co. Inc., New York).
1923: (Tankers Corporation, New York).
1924: (Steamer Vaba Corpn., New York).
1929: *Ruth Kellogg* (Kellogg SS Corp., New York).
1941: *Empire Dolphin* (M.O.W.T.).
2.1947: Scrapped Briton Ferry.

Design 1025 – 9,000 tdw, 400 ft × 54 ft. Engines: Turbine

Built by Merchant Shipbuilding Corp., Harriman, Pa.

39   *Empire Lapwing* 5,358 gt.
1921: Completed as *Ala* (U.S.S.B.).
1931: (American Diamond Lines Inc.).
1935: *Black Condor* (Black Diamond Lines Inc.).

1941: *Empire Lapwing* (M.O.W.T.).
1942: *Belgian Fighter* (Government of Belgium).
9.10.1942: Sunk by submarine (*U.68*) torpedo in
South Atlantic, 35.00S 18.30E, SW of Cape Agulhas.

Design 1027 – 7,500 tdw, 402 ft × 54 ft. Engines: T3cyl.

Built by Oscar Daniels Shipbuilding Co., Tampa, Fla.

6   *Empire Waterhen* 5,948 gt.
1920: Completed as *Manatee* (U.S.S.B.).
1937: (U.S.M.C.).

1941: *Empire Waterhen* (M.O.W.T.).
9.6.1944: Sunk as Blockship, Mulberry, Normandy.
1948: Raised, broken up at Penarth.

Design 1037 – 9,600 tdw, 395.5 ft × 55 ft. Engines: Turbines

Built by Federal Shipbuilding Co., Kearny, N.J.

4   *Empire Kangaroo* 6,219 gt.
1.1919: Completed as *Mercer* (U.S.S.B.).
1941: *Empire Kangaroo* (M.O.W.T.).
1946: *Parthenia* (Donaldson Bros., Glasgow).
1949: *Erminia Mazzella* (P. Mazzella, Naples).
1951: *Pina Onorato* (A. Onorato, Naples).
8.1958: Scrapped Spezia.

8   *Empire Kudu* 6,262 gt.
3.1919: Completed as *Duquesne* (U.S.S.B.).
1933: (Lykes Bros.-Ripley SS Co. Inc.).
1941: *Empire Kudu* (M.O.W.T.).
26.9.1941: Ashore in fog six miles west of Point
Amour, Belle Isle Strait (voyage: Pensacola and
Tampa/Loch Ewe – steel scrap and phosphate).
Abandoned; total loss.

10   *Empire Redshank* 6,615 gt.
4.1919: Completed as *Braddock* (U.S.S.B.).
1941: *Empire Redshank* (M.O.W.T.).

31.1.1942: Damaged by aircraft bomb and gunfire,
63.24N 02.24W, north of Shetland Islands. Repaired.
22.2.1943: Torpedoed by submarine (*U.606*),
47N 34.30W whilst in convoy ON 166 (U.K./North
America).
Abandoned, then sunk by the corvette H.M.C.S.
Trillium.

12   *Empire Thrush* 6,160 gt.
Completed as *Lorain* (U.S.S.B.).
1932: (Cosmopolitan Shipping Co., New York).
1932: (U.S.S.B.).
1942: *Empire Thrush* (M.O.W.T.).
14.4.1942: Sunk by submarine (*U.203*) torpedo
35.08N 75.18W, off Chesapeake Bay.

16   *Empire Reindeer* 6,259 gt.
Completed as *Clairton* (U.S.S.B.).
1941: *Empire Reindeer* (M.O.W.T.).
10.8.1942: Sunk by submarine (*U.660*) torpedo
57.00N 22.30W (convoy SC 94) in mid-Atlantic.

23 *Empire Peacock* 6,098 gt.
Completed as *Bellhaven* (U.S.S.B.).
1941: *Empire Peacock* (M.O.W.T.).
18.5.1942–19.7.1943: At Durban with disabled turbines.
25.8.1946: Scuttled with chemical ammunition in Atlantic, south west of Lands End, 47.55N 08.30W.

24 *Empire Whale* 6,049 gt.
Completed as *Winona County* (U.S.S.B.).
1941: *Empire Whale* (M.O.W.T.).
29.3.1943: Sunk by submarine (*U.662*) torpedo,

south-west of Ireland, 46.44N 16.38W whilst in convoy SL 126 (Sierra Leone/Tyne – ore.)

30 *Empire Magpie* 6,211 gt.
Completed as *Bellemina* (U.S.S.B.).
1941: *Empire Magpie* (M.O.W.T.).
1946: (Williamson & Co., Hong Kong).
1948: *Jui Hsin* (Yui Kong, China).
1950: *Oriental Dragon* (Pacific Union Marine, Panama).
1955: *Atlantic Unity* (Atlantic Bulk Carriers).
4.1959: Scrapped Hirao, Japan.

Design 1042 – 3,350 tdw, 253 ft × 43.5 ft. Engines: T3cyl.

Built by Great Lakes Engineering Works, River Rouge, Ecorse, Michigan

205 *Craycroft* 2,292 gt.
1918: Completed for U.S.S.B.
1927: *Fred W. Green* (J. J. Roen, Charlevoix, Mich.) then (Northwestern Company, Sturgeon Bay, Wis.).

1941: (M.O.W.T.).
31.5.1942: Sunk by submarine (*U.506*) torpedo, 30.20N 62.00W, north east of Bahamas.

Note: 'Empire' name not allocated when sunk.

Design 1043 – 5,350 tdw, 321 ft × 46 ft. Engines: T3cyl.

Built by Hanlon Drydock & Shipbuilding Co., Oakland, Cal.

88 *Empire Mouflon* 3,329 gt.
1921: Completed as *Memnon* (U.S.S.B.).
1925: (Columbia River Packers Association).
1940: *Empire Mouflon* (M.O.S.).
1943: Re-boilered after putting back to various ports on many occasions with constant boiler troubles.

1946: *Preston* (Ropner & Co. Ltd.).
1951: *Avance* (Cia. Mar. Avance S.A., Panama).
1957: *Avlis* (Avlis Sg. Co. S.A. (G. Dracopoulos, Greece)).
6.1962: Scrapped Piraeus.

Design 1046 – 7,400 tdw, 377 ft × 52 ft. Engines: T3cyl.

Built by Bethlehem Shipbuilding Corp., Sparrows Point, Md.

4182   *Empire Albatross* 4,623 gt.
1919: Completed as *Hoxie* (U.S.S.B.).
1941: *Empire Albatross* (M.O.W.T.).
1942: *Belgian Fisherman* (Government of Belgium).
1946: *Belgique* (Government of Belgium).

1947: (Cie. Royale Belgo-Argentine).
1950: *Martha Hendrik Fisser* (Hendrik Fisser A.G., Germany).
1958: Scrapped Hamburg.

Design 1074 'Great Lakes Engineering' type – 5,050 tdw, 253 ft × 43.7 ft. Engines: T3cyl.

Built by Great Lakes Engineering Works, River Rouge, Ecorse, Michigan

230   *Empire Kestrel* 2,674 gt.
1919: Completed as *Lake Ellithorpe* (U.S.S.B.).
1926: (Newtex SS Corp., New York).
1932: Renamed *Texas Trader*.

1940: *Empire Kestrel* (M.O.S.).
16.8.1943: Sunk by German aerial torpedo 37.10N 4.35E, NE of Algiers.

Built by Manitowoc Shipbuilding Corp., Manitowoc, Wisc.

108   *Empire Snipe* 2,689 gt.
Completed as *Lake Gaither* (U.S.S.B.).
1926: (Western Reserve Nav. Co. Inc., Cleveland, Ohio).
1927: (Newtex SS Corp., (New York)).
1932: Renamed *Texas Ranger*.
1940: *Empire Snipe* (M.O.S.).
14.7.1942: Damaged by limpet mine 1½ miles from North Mole Light, Gibraltar (voyage: Lisbon/U.K. –

potash). Flooded, vessel put ashore. Later refloated, and:
14.10.1942: Sailed for U.K. Repaired.
1946: *Staxton* (W. Brown, Atkinson & Co. Ltd.).
1948: *Ileri* (Sirketi Aldikacti, Turkey).
7.1968: Scrapped Halic, Turkey.

Design 1079 'Skinner & Eddy' type – 9,600 tdw, 409 ft × 54 ft. Engines: Turbines

Built by Skinner & Eddy Corp., Seattle, Wash.

42   *Empire Ibex* 7,028 gt.
1918: Completed as *Edgefield* (U.S.S.B.).
1941: *Empire Ibex* (M.O.W.T.).
1.7.1943: In collision with escort aircraft carrier *Empire MacAlpine* in convoy in North Atlantic, 53.30N 36.25W (voyage: Portland (Maine) and

Halifax, N.S./London – general). Shell plating torn open over length of 90 ft. Holds and engine room flooded; bulkheads carried away.
2.7.1943:   Abandoned; sank.

Note: The *Empire MacAlpine* sustained extensive damage to her bows, but continued with the convoy.

Design 1080 'Ames'-type – 8,800 tdw, 410 ft × 54 ft. Engines: T3cyl.

Built by Ames Shipbuilding & Dry Dock Co., Seattle, Wash.

16   *Empire Merlin* 5,680 gt.
1919: Completed as *West Isleta* (U.S.S.B.).
1926: (American South African Line).
1940: *Empire Merlin* (M.O.S.).
25.8.1940: Damaged by submarine (*U.48*) torpedo in North Atlantic 58.30N 10.15W whilst in convoy HX 65A (voyage: U.S.A./U.K. – general). Broke in two; sank.

17   *Empire Eagle* 5,775 gt.
1919: Completed as *West Islip* (U.S.S.B.).
1928: *Golden Rod* (Oceanic & Oriental SN Co., San Francisco).
1935: *Willhilo* (Williams SS Co. Inc., New York).
1937: *Indianan* (American Hawaiian SS Co.).
1940: *Empire Eagle* (M.O.S.).

1942: *Norjerv* (Government of Norway).
8.1944: Sunk as blockship, Mulberry, Normandy.
1949: raised but:
3.6.1949: Broke in two while in tow of tugs *Tradesman* (ex *Empire Julia*) and *Rifleman* (ex *Empire Vera*) bound for Strangford Lough, N. Ireland., for scrapping. Both parts sank.

22   *Empire Ocelot* 5,866 gt.
1919: Completed as *West Jena* (U.S.S.B.).
1925: *Myrtle* (Forest Transport Corp, Portland, Ore.).
1929: *San Marcos* (Pacific Atlantic SS Corp, Portland, Ore.).
1940: *Empire Ocelot* (M.O.S.).
28.9.1940: Torpedoed by submarine (*U.32*) in North Atlantic and sank in position 54.55N 22.06W.

Design 1099 – 4,050 tdw, 251 ft × 43.6 ft. Engines: T3cyl.

Built by Detroit Shipbuilding Co., Wyandotte, Mich.

269   *Empire Tern* 2,606 gt.
11.1919: Completed as *Lake Inglenook* (U.S.S.B.).
1926: (Newtex SS Corp., New York).
1932: Renamed *Texas Banker*.
1940: *Empire Tern* (M.O.S.).

1946: (Williamson & Co., Hong Kong).
1949: Renamed *Inchmull*.
1953: *Sigma Star* (Cia. Sigma, Panama).
10.1953: Scrapped Osaka.

Design 1105 – 9,600 tdw, 401.5 ft × 54.8 ft. Engines: T3cyl.

Built by Skinner & Eddy Corp., Seattle, Wash.

56   *Empire Pelican* 6,463 gt.
1919: Completed as *Stanley* (U.S.S.B.).
1941: *Empire Pelican* (M.O.W.T.).
14.11.1941: Bombed and sunk by Italian aircraft
between Galita Island and Tunisia
(voyage: Gibraltar/Malta – military stores).

57   *Empire Bunting* 6,318 gt.
1919: Completed as *Eelbeck* (U.S.S.B.).
1941: *Empire Bunting* (M.O.W.T.).
9.6.1944: Sunk as a blockship, Mulberry, Normandy.
1947: Raised and scrapped.

58   *Empire Penguin* 6,389 gt.
1919: Completed as *Elkridge* (U.S.S.B.).
1928: *Golden Star* (Oceanic & Oriental SN Co., San
Francisco).
1937: *Tennessean* (American Hawaiian SS Co.).
1940: *Empire Penguin* (M.O.S.).
1942: *Van de Velde* (Government of Netherlands).
1947: *Rijnland* (Royal Holland Lloyd).
1949: Renamed *Rynland*.
1957: *Vaptistis* (Cia. Nav. Maraventure, Panama.
(Lemos & Pateras Ltd.)).
9.1959: Scrapped Lisbon, Portugal.

60   *Empire Dunlin* 6,326 gt.
1919: Completed as *Editor* (U.S.S.B.).
1941: *Empire Dunlin* (M.O.W.T.).
1942: *Norlom* (Government of Norway).
26.4.1942: Aground on Valient Rock, near New

London, Long Island Sound. Leaking; flooded and
abandoned (voyage: New York/U.K. – steel).
11.5.1942: Refloated, towed to New York; repaired.
2.12.1943: Bombed and sunk in Bari Harbour, Italy.

61   *Empire Mermaid* 6,319 gt.
Completed as *Endicott* (U.S.S.B.).
1940: *Empire Mermaid* (M.O.S.).
26.3.1941: Damaged by aircraft bombs 100 miles west
of Hebrides. Flooded, abandoned, and:
28.3.1941: Sank in position 57.33N 12.43W.

63   *Empire Gull* 6,458 gt.
1919: Completed as *Brave Coeur* (U.S.S.B.).
1941: *Empire Gull* (M.O.W.T.).
12.12.1942: Sunk by submarine (*U.177*) torpedo in
Mozambique channel, approx. 26S 35E.

66   *Effna* 6,461 gt.
1919: Completed for U.S.S.B.
1941: (M.O.S.).
1.3.1941: Sunk by submarine (*U.108*) torpedo west
of Faroe Islands, 61.30N 15.45W (voyage: Baltimore
& Halifax, N.S./Newport, Mon.).

Note: 'Empire' name not allocated when sunk.

68   *Empire Buffalo* 6,374 gt.
1919: Completed as *Eglantine* (U.S.S.B.).
1933: (Lykes Bros.-Ripley SS Corp.).
1940: *Empire Buffalo* (M.O.S.).
6.5.1942: Sunk by submarine (*U.125*) torpedo north-
west of Jamaica, 19.14N 82.34W (voyage: Kingston,
Jamaica/New Orleans).

Built by Uchida Shipbuilding & Engineering Co., Yokohama

5   *Empire Jaguar* 5,186 gt. 8,500 tdw,
400 ft × 54.5 ft. Engines: T3cyl.
5.1919: Completed as *Eastern Glade* (U.S.S.B.).
1926: (American South African Line Inc.).

1934: (Postal SS Corpn., New York).
1940: *Empire Jaguar* (M.O.S.).
8.12.1940: Sunk by submarine (*U.103*) torpedo, west of Ireland, 51.34N 17.35W.

Forty-five ships were acquired from Japan for the U.S.A.'s World War One programme, fifteen of which were already under construction or ordered in various yards and the remaining thirty under contracts from the U.S.S.B. with Emergency Fleet Corporation hull numbers 2008–2037. All were given the prefix 'Eastern' to their names on completion.

The *Empire Jaguar* was put under the management of Sir Wm. Reardon Smith & Company, with another eight ex-U.S.S.B. ships. The company was formed in 1905 and became well established as shipowners in the tramp trade. Although based at Cardiff, most of their ships were registered at Bideford, North Devon, near where the founder was born.

By 1926, thirty-six ships were owned, spread over four operating companies. Twenty-five were listed in the fleet as war began and as well as the ex-American ships, Reardon Smith also managed nine British-built 'Empire' ships, three 'Sam' Liberty ships and three Canadian-built 'Fort' standard ships on behalf of the Ministry of War Transport.

Built by Harland & Wolff Ltd., Belfast

349   *Empire Bittern* 8,546 gt. 500 ft × 58 ft.
Engines: Q4cyl. Twin screws.
1902: Completed as *Iowa* for White Diamond SS Co. Ltd. (G. Warren & Co. Ltd.).
1913: *Bohemia* (Hamburg America Line).
1917: *Artemis* (Requisitioned by U.S. Government, (U.S.S.B.)).
1940: *Empire Bittern* (M.O.T.).

23.7.1944: Sunk as an additional blockship, Mulberry, Normandy, after the gales of 19–22 June 1944. (See also Operation 'Overlord'.)

The *Empire Bittern*, known as the 'Five and Ten' ship, at New York, October 1943. (Harland & Wolff Ltd., Belfast, Yard No. 345.)
U.S.C.G.

In 1839 George Warren, of Boston, Massachusetts, founded the White Diamond Line of sailing packets, which became actively engaged in the Boston–Liverpool trade. In 1853 he came to Liverpool and took control of the Line, which came to bear his name. The American Civil War complicated trading conditions and the ships were transferred to the British flag.

The Warren Line specialised in the transportation of cotton and cattle across the Atlantic from America and was a pioneer in the introduction of animal stalls aboard ships; in 1888 it carried over 45,000 head of cattle into the River Mersey.

Between 1892 and 1902 the company had four ships built in Belfast by Harland & Wolff – *Sagamore* (1892), *Sachem* (1893), *Bay State* (1898) and *Iowa* (1902), although in 1898 the White Diamond Steamship Company had been formed to acquire the Warren fleet of steamers, previously run as 'single ship' companies. In 1912 Furness, Withy & Company bought both the White Diamond concern and the Warren trading name.

The *Iowa* was sold to the Hamburg America Line in 1913, becoming *Bohemia* and quickly converted to carry 1,200 persons in steerage class. The ship was interned in the U.S.A. during the war and then seized in April 1917, being transferred to the U.S. Shipping Board and operated by them as *Artemis* until 1919. She was laid up at Galveston and later in the James River, Virginia, and remained there until 1940, when she was offered to the British Government. Refitted, she was taken over by the M.O.W.T. at Newport News in May 1941 as *Empire Bittern*. But she still showed her origins as a cattle carrier and her first cargo, from Savannah, included 400 U.S. Army mules. These were carried in stalls in the 'tween decks and still 'fed' by special pumps which supplied water to the livestock area.

The *Empire Bittern*, a flush-decker of 11,925 tdw, was an unusual vessel and became known as the 'Five and Ten' ship: she had five tall masts and loaded cargo through ten small hatches, with her many ancient steam winches giving constant cargo-handling problems.

Nevertheless, the ship lasted until 1944 and she was at Liverpool, ready to sail for Halifax, N.S., when both her vintage and her length made her a sudden, but ideal, choice to fill a 500-foot gap in the line of blockships off the Normandy beaches.

It may be noted here that in 1922 Furness, Withy amalgamated the Warren Line with their Neptune SN Co. and the Johnson Line, but then decided that the Warren Line should continue, taking over the assets of the Johnson Line. The Neptune SN Co. was put into liquidation.

Built by International Shipbuilding Co., Pascagoula, Miss.

1   *Empire Otter* 4,627 gt. 370 ft × 52 ft.
Engines: T3cyl (aft).
Ordered for Soc. de Nav. Italo-Americana, Italy.
1920: Launched as *Torino*.

The *Empire Otter* was one of a trio of sisters with a unique history. The three ships were ordered from the International Shipbuilding Co. of Pascagoula, Mississippi, by Turin-based shipowners.

Launched in 1920 as Yard Nos. 1–3 (the only vessels from the shipyard) and named *Torino*, *Trento* and *Trieste* respectively, they lay in uncompleted state at Mobile and were never delivered to their Italian owners, whose name had been removed from the List of Shipowners by 1924.

In 1925 all three vessels were listed under the ownership of the Morecraft Transportation Corpn. of New York and seven years later under the Durham Navigation Corpn. Six more years went by, then a ship named *Amsco* 'came on the

scene', owned by American Mineral Spirits Company, of New York. She was the ex-*Torino*, completed and reconstructed in 1938 as a tanker. Transferred to the M.O.T. in 1940, she became *Empire Otter* and sank on 16 February 1941, twenty-five miles south-west of Hartland Point, Bristol Channel, after striking a mine in a British minefield.

Of her sisters, the *Trento* was completed as a motorship in 1941, owned by Norwegian interests, firstly as Thor Dahl's *Philae* and then, in 1948, as *Thorscape*. In 1950 she passed to other Norwegian interests as *Ledaal* and in 1953 to Uruguayan buyers, becoming *Sudelmar*. She was scrapped in Spain in 1974. The third of the trio, *Trieste*, put to sea in 1941 as Gdynia–America Lines *Paderewski*, but sank off Trinidad on 30 December 1942 after being torpedoed and shelled by German submarine *U.214*, whilst on a voyage from Brazil to New York.

Built by Merchant Shipbuilding Corp., Chester, Pa.

445 ft × 59.8 ft. Engines: Oil (twin screw).

385 *Empire Seal* 7,965 gt.
5.1922: Completed as *Californian* for American-Hawaiian SS Co.
1940: *Empire Kite* (M.O.S.).
1940: Renamed *Empire Seal*.
19.2.1942: Sunk by submarine (*U.96*) torpedo, east of Boston, Mass., 43.14N 64.45W.

386 *Empire Swan* 7,965 gt.
6.1922: Completed as *Missourian* for American-Hawaiian SS Co.
1940: *Empire Swan* (M.O.S.).
1942: *Belgian Freighter* (Government of Belgium).
1946: *Capitaine Potie* (Cie. Maritime Belge).
1948: *Genova* (Cia. Genovese di Nav. a Vapore S.A., Genoa (CONGAR)).

1955: *Flaminia* (Cia. Genovese di Armamento, (COGEDAR)) (8,791 gt.)
1963: (Compra Vendita Covena, Genoa).
1964: *King Abdelaziz* (Bakhashab Mohamed Abubakur, Saudi Arabia).
1968: Reported sold to Italian shipbreakers, but:
23.4.1970: Arrived Kaohsiung for breaking up.

Of the (above) two twin-screw motorships built for service between the U.S. north-east coast ports of Boston and New York, via Panama to Pacific ports, it was the *Missourian* that had the long and colourful career. Indeed, when finally scrapped, she had collected seven names and five nationalities. In 1955 she was re-engined and converted to carry 1,000 passengers in berths and more on deck for the pilgrim service to Jeddah, working for some time between 1964 and 1970 under the flag of Saudi Arabia.

Built by Federal Shipbuilding & Drydock Co., Kearny, N.J.

355.5 ft × 52.5 ft. Engines: T3cyl. (aft).

34 *Empire Toucan* 4,421 gt.
1920: Completed as *Freeport Sulphur No. 5* for Freeport Sulphur Transportation Co. Inc., New York.

1940: *Empire Toucan* (M.O.S.).
29.6.1940: Sunk by submarine (*U.47*) torpedo and gunfire, south west of Ireland, 49.20N 13.52W.

Built by New York Shipbuilding Corp., Camden, N.J.

3,400 tdw, 442 ft (oa), 424.8 ft × 54.9 ft. Engines: T6cyl. Twin screws. Two tall, thin funnels.

135 *Empire Woodlark* 7,793 gt.
7.1913: Completed as *Congress* for Pacific Coast SS Co.
1918: *Nanking* (China Mail SS Co., New York).
1923: *Emma Alexander* (Pacific SS Co. Inc., Seattle).
1942: *Empire Woodlark* (M.O.W.T.).
2.11.1946: Scuttled with chemical ammunition, north of Hebrides, 59.00N 7.40W.

The *Congress* was built to carry 500 passengers for the Seattle, San Francisco, Los Angeles and San Diego service, but on 14 September 1916, when off Crescent City, Cal., she caught fire in the after hold, the blaze quickly spreading to the cargo and superstructure. Out of control, the fire burned the ship from stem to stern, all passengers and crew leaving in the lifeboats. Later, when the fire had subsided, the machinery was found undamaged and the ship was sent to Seattle for reconstruction.

In 1918 she became *Nanking*, but in 1922 her owners, China Mail SS Company, were in great financial difficulties and the *Nanking* was seized and auctioned. Her purchasers were the Pacific SS Co., who had acquired the Pacific Coast SS Co. in 1916, and again she was rebuilt and returned to the West Coast run as *Emma Alexander*, this lasting until 1934, when she was laid up at Oakland.

In 1940 the vessel was acquired by the British Government, refitted, and arrived at Liverpool in December 1941. Within a month she was trooping to the Far East.

The *Flaminia*, formerly *Empire Swan*, served in both the Australian emigrant trade and the pilgrim service to Jeddah. (Merchant Shipbuilding Corporation, Yard No. 386.)

The *Empire Gauntlet*, as the Infantry Landing Ship HMS *Sefton*, June 1946. (Consolidated Steel Corporation, Yard No. 356.)
Wright & Logan

The American-built *Empire Pintail*, as *Grand Yaling*. (Federal Shipbuilding & Drydock Co., Yard No. 166.)   *Vic Young*

The following tug was bareboat chartered by the United States War Shipping Administration to Britain, under Lease/Lend arrangements.

Built by Bethlehem Shipbuilding Corp., Elisabeth, N.J.

2136 *Empire Bascobel* 418 gt, 151.5 ft (oa), 142 ft × 27.7 ft. Engines: T3cyl. A tug.
11.1919: Completed as *Bascobel* for U.S.S.B.
1922: (Gulf Coast Transportation Co., New Orleans).
1928: (Tennessee Coal, Iron & Railway Co.).
1936: (U.S.M.C.).
1941: *Empire Bascobel* (M.O.W.T.).
1946: Returned to U.S.M.C.
1948: *Bascobel* (L. & B. Olsson, New York).
1954: (Universal Tank Cleaning Corp., U.S.A.).
1958: (Standard Tank Cleaning Corp., U.S.A.).
18.12.1961: Sank whilst moored alongside a hulk at Mariners Harbor, New York. Raised, but constructive total loss. Sold, and:
12.1953: Scrapped New York.

Note: Some sources suggest that two similar tugs from the same shipbuilders, *Cumco* (ex *Barlow*, 1919, 437 gt, Yard No. 2121) and *Barwick* (1919, 418 gt, Yard No. 2135), also transferred to Britain under Lease/Lend arrangements, were to be given the 'Empire' prefix to their names. There is no official record of such proposed names, but the *Barwick* was taken up by the Royal Navy in 1942, serving under pennant W. 174, and the *Cumco* served the M.O.W.T., also from 1942, on the East Coast of Canada.

Built by Sun Shipbuilding & Drydock Co., Chester, Pa.

184 *Empire Lagan* 11,399 gt. (C3 type.)
468.4 ft × 69.7 ft. Engines: four 7-cyl oil, driving a single screw through electro-magnetic couplings and single-reduction gearing.
4.1940: Completed as *Mormacland* for Moore-McCormack Lines Inc.
3.1941: Rebuilt by Newport News SB & DD Company to an escort carrier, for twenty aircraft.
17.11.1941: To Royal Navy on Lease/Lend arrangements. Renamed H.M.S. *Archer* (D. 78).
13.1.1942: In collision with the *Brazos* (1899, 4,497 gt) and was towed stern-first to Charleston in damaged condition. The *Brazos*, owned by Agwilines Inc., was on voyage San Juan (P.R.) to New York. She sank 32.54N 74.14W (300 miles east of Charleston (SC.). H.M.S. *Archer* was repaired.
11.1943: R.N. stores ship (Clyde and Belfast areas).
3.1945: *Empire Lagan* (M.O.W.T.).
1.1946: *Archer* (U.S.M.C.) Laid up Norfolk, Va.

The post-war activities of the ship began in 1948 when she was sold to Sven Salen, Stockholm, renamed *Anna Salen* and placed under Rederi Pulp AB in 1949, then being given an austerity refit to a passenger ship for emigrants and displaced persons. More lifeboats were added and the superstructure extended from foc's'le to stern (11,672 gt); she worked from Europe to Australia.

In 1955 she moved to the Greek flag of Cia. Nav. Tasmania S.A. and under the name *Tasmania* worked from Greek and French ports to Australia under management of Hellenic Mediterranean Lines.

The China Union Lines of Taipeh bought her in 1961 and she reverted to a cargo ship, *Union Reliance* (7,638 gt). Her end came in 1961 when she was in collision in the Houston Ship Channel on 7 November with the Norwegian motor tanker *Berean* (1961, 9,003 gt) belonging to A. O. Andersen (voyage: Los Angeles/New Orleans – vegetable oil and general). On fire, there was an explosion and she went aground, being refloated on 9 November and towed to Galveston. In March 1962 she was towed to New Orleans and broken up.

Section 2   Landing ships on Lease/Lend

There were thirteen landing ships made available to Britain and bareboat chartered by the Ministry of War Transport, assuming 'Empire' names on their completion. They were fitted out as military transports (Landing Ships, Infantry (Large)) and all were in readiness for the Normandy invasion Armament consisted of one 4 in, and one 12 pdr and twelve 20 mm AA guns.

In 1944–1945 nine were transferred to the Royal Navy and given names of British Derby winning horses (between 1877 and 1924). The *Rocksand*, *Sainfoin*, *Sansovino*, *Sefton* and *Silvio* all went to the Far East, attached to the East Indies fleet; the *Silvio* was mined and damaged in the Rangoon landing on 2 May 1945. When returned to the United States after the war, some retained their 'Empire' nomenclature.

Built by Consolidated Steel Corp., Wilmington, Cal.

Tonnages: 7,177 gross, 11,650 displacement (C1-S-AY1 type). 417.7 ft (oa), 396.3 ft × 60 ft. Engines: Geared turbines.

345   *Empire Battleaxe* Laid down as *Cape Berkeley*.
10.1943: Completed as *Empire Battleaxe* (M.O.W.T.).
1946: *Donovan* (R.N. (F. 161)).
1946: *Empire Battleaxe*.
1947: (U.S.M.C.).
1948: Renamed *Cape Berkeley*.
1948: Sold to China to become *Hai C* but sale cancelled.
1948: *Empire Battleaxe* (U.S.M.C.); Laid up James River, Va.
5.1966: Scrapped Kearny N.J.

346   *Empire Cutlass* Laid down as *Cape Compass*.
11.1943: Completed as *Empire Cutlass* (M.O.W.T.).
21.11.1944: Damaged by mine off Digne Light, Le Havre. Towed to port, flooded. Repaired.
1.1945: *Sansovino* (R.N. (F.162)).
6.1945: Renamed *Empire Cutlass*.
1947: (U.S.M.C.).
1948: Renamed *Cape Compass*.
1948: To be sold to China as *Hai Ou*; sale postponed.
8.1950: *Empire Cutlass* (U.S.M.C.); Laid up James River, Va.
1960: *Hai Ou* (China Merchants SN Co. Ltd., Taiwan).
1970: Scrapped Kaohsiung.

347   *Empire Halberd* Laid down as *Cape Gregory*.
11.1943: Completed as *Empire Halberd* (M.O.W.T.).

6.7.1944: Damaged by mine four miles from Longships Light. Proceeded to port: repaired.
9.1944: *Silvio* (R.N. (F. 160)).
11.1945: *Empire Halberd* (M.O.W.T.).
6.1948: (U.S.M.C.); Laid up James River, Va.
1948: Renamed *Cape Gregory*.
12.1966: Scrapped at Baltimore as *Imperial Halberd*.

348   *Empire Broadsword* Laid down as *Cape Marshall*.
12.1943: Completed as *Empire Broadsword* (M.O.W.T.).
2.7.1944: Mined and sank in English Channel, 49.25N 00.54W, off Normandy beach-head.

349   *Empire Lance* Laid down as *Cape Pine*.
12.1943: Completed as *Empire Lance* (M.O.W.T.).
1945: *Sir Hugo* (R.N.).
1945: *Empire Lance* (M.O.W.T.).
1949: *Cape Pine* (U.S.M.C.).
12.1966: Scrapped at Baltimore as *Imperial Lance*.

350   *Empire Mace* Laid down as *Cape St. Roque*.
12.1943: Completed as *Empire Mace* (M.O.W.T.).
1944: *Galtee More* (R.N. (F. 171)).
1947: *Misr* (Soc. Misr de Nav. Maritime, Egypt).
1959: (Government of Egypt).

351   *Empire Rapier* Laid down as *Cape Turner*.

12.1943: Completed as *Empire Rapier* (M.O.W.T.).
1948: (U.S.M.C.).
1948: *Cape Turner* (U.S.M.C.).
5.1.1966: Scrapped Kearny N.J., under name of *Empire Rapier*.

352 *Empire Anvil* Laid down as *Cape Argos*.
1.1944: Completed as *Empire Anvil* (M.O.W.T.).
11.1944: *Rocksand* (R.N. (F. 184)).
6.1946: *Empire Anvil* (M.O.T.).
1947: (U.S.M.C.).
1948: Renamed *Cape Argos*.
1948: To be sold to China to become *Hai Ya*, but sale postponed.
1948: *Empire Anvil* (U.S.M.C.); Laid up James River, Va.
1960: *Hai Ya* (China Merchants SN Co., Taiwan).
1973: *Fu Ming* (Yangming Marine Transport Corp., Taiwan).
1974: Scrapped Keelung.

353 *Empire Javelin* Laid down as *Cape Lobos*.
1.1944: Completed as *Empire Javelin* (M.O.W.T.).
28.12.1944: Sunk by submarine (*U.772*) torpedo in English Channel, 50.05N 01.00W in convoy TBC 1 (voyage: Southampton/Le Havre – 1,448 servicemen).

The submarine *U.772* spent Christmas of 1944 awaiting victims in the mid-English Channel, particularly those ships employed in the continuing build-up of Allied forces in France. On the morning of 23 December the small Belfast coaster *Slemish* (1909, 1,536 gt) of the Shamrock Shipping Company, moving in coastal convoy WEG 71 was torpedoed and sunk. Two hours later the 5,149 gt *Dumfries* (1935), belonging to B. J. Sutherland & Co., was sunk whilst in coastal convoy MVS 71. On 28 December the *Empire Javelin* embarked American servicemen and sailed from Southampton for Le Havre with the French frigate *L'Escaramouche* as escort. In the afternoon a torpedo from *U.772* hit the transport and she began to sink. Another torpedo followed to sink her. Seven personnel were lost, the remainder being transferred to LSTs. Next day the *U.772* again registered successes with hits on two American Liberty-type ships in convoy TBC 1. First was the *Black Hawk* (1943, 7,191 gt) owned by the U.S.M.C., which was towed in and beached, becoming submerged in Warbarrow Bay, Dorset. The other Liberty ship was the *Arthur Newall*, on her way from France to South Wales, which managed to get to Weymouth Bay and was towed to Portland. She was eventually towed to Bremerhaven in May 1946, loaded with chemical ammunition

and towed to sea and scuttled on 12 October 1946. The *U.772* was sunk by a Wellington bomber of 407 Squadron, Royal Canadian Air Force, on 30 December 1944.

354 *Empire Spearhead* Laid down as *Cape Girardeau*.
1.1944: Completed as *Empire Spearhead* (M.O.W.T.).
1947: (U.S.M.C.).
1948: Renamed *Cape Girardeau*.
5.1948: To be sold to China as *Hai Mei*; sale cancelled.
8.1950: *Empire Spearhead* (U.S.M.C.); Laid up James River, Va.
11.1966: Scrapped Baltimore.

355 *Empire Arquebus* Laid down as *Cape St. Vincent*.
1.1944: Completed as *Empire Arquebus* (M.O.W.T.).
6.1944: *Cicero* (R.N. (F. 170)).
10.1945: *Empire Arquebus* (M.O.W.T.).
11.1946: *Al Sudan* (Soc. Misr de Nav. Maritime, Egypt).
1959: (Government of Egypt).
20.10.1980: Arrived Suez for breaking up but:
7.1984: demolition had not begun.

356 *Empire Gauntlet* Laid down as *Cape Comorin*.
1.1944: Completed as *Empire Gauntlet* (M.O.W.T.).
1944: *Sefton* (R.N. (F. 123)).
9.1946: *Empire Gauntlet* (M.O.W.T.).
1947: *Cape Comorin* (U.S.M.C.).
12.1964: Scrapped Portsmouth, Va.

357 *Empire Crossbow* Laid down as *Cape Washington*.
1.1944: Completed as *Empire Crossbow* (M.O.W.T.).
1944: *Sainfoin* (R.N. (F. 183)).
9.1946: *Empire Crossbow* (M.O.W.T.).
1947: (U.S.M.C.).
1947: Renamed *Cape Washington*.
12.1964: Scrapped Portsmouth, Va.

Note: Yard Nos. 345, 346, 352 and 354 (above): These four vessels were sold to the Government of China in 1948, but the sales were postponed due to the Communist take-over and the vessels were re-possessed by the Maritime Administration. In 1960 the four ships were again authorised for sale, this time to the Nationalist Government of Taiwan. In the event only two were delivered, being allocated to the China Merchants SN Company. The remaining pair (Yard Nos. 345 and 354) were later broken up in the U.S.A.

Section 3   Fast cargo ships on charter

In the autumn of 1941 Britain, already stretched in shipping availability with the movement of 150,000 troops to the Middle East, decided to send a further reinforcement of 40,000 men and sought help from the United States for the loan of troop transports and fast cargo ships. This was readily agreed, the transports to embark 20,000 men in Halifax, N.S., who were already in transit from Britain, and the cargo ships to be placed on the Atlantic run to relieve British cargo ships. These vessels were on loan from October 1941 until February 1942, during which time the war in the Pacific, with Japan, began.

Built by Sun Shipbuilding & Drydock Co., Chester, Pa.

199 *Empire Peregrine* 7,842 gt (C2-SU type). 474 ft (oa), 453.3 ft × 63 ft. Engines: Oil.
10.1941: Completed as *China Mail* for American Mail Line.
1941: *Empire Peregrine* (M.O.W.T.).

1942: *Ocean Mail* (U.S.M.C.).
11.1943: Completed conversion to a transport.
1947: (American Mail Line, Seattle, Wash.).
1959: (U.S. Maritime Administration).
4.1969: Scrapped Tacoma, Wash.

Built by Federal Shipbuilding & Drydock Co., Kearny, N.J.

165 *Empire Condor* 7,773 gt (C3 type). 492 ft (oa), 469 ft × 69.5 ft. Engines: two steam turbines.
7.1940: Completed as *Almeria Lykes* for Lykes Bros. SS Co.
1941: *Empire Condor* (M.O.W.T.).
1942: *Almeria Lykes* (U.S.M.C.).
13.8.1942: Sunk by E-boat torpedo off Cape Bon, Tunisia, 36.40N 11.35E, whilst in convoy WS 21S, Operation 'Pedestal' (voyage: U.K./Malta).

166 *Empire Pintail* 7,773 gt. Details as Yard No. 165.
9.1940: Completed as *Howell Lykes* for Lykes Bros. SS Co.
1941: *Empire Pintail* (M.O.W.T.).
1942: (U.S.M.C.).
12.1943: Completed conversion to transport by Bethlehem Steel Co., Baltimore. Renamed *Howell Lykes*.
2.1946: (Lykes Bros. SS Co.).
1965: *Kings Point* (Sperling SS & Trading Corp., U.S.A.).
1965: *Flying Foam* (American Export Isbrandtsen Lines Inc.).

10.12.1970: Arrived Kaohsiung for breaking up, but resold and renamed *Grand Yaling* (Sea King Corp., New York).
9.1971: Scrapped Kaohsiung.

188 *Empire Fulmar* 7,775 gt. Details as Yard No. 165.
5.1941: Completed as *Hawaiian Shipper* for Matson Nav. Co.
1942: *Empire Fulmar* (M.O.W.T.).
1942: *Hawaiian Shipper* (U.S.M.C.).
2.1943: Completed conversion to a transport for U.S. Navy.
1.1946: (U.S.M.C.).
1948: *America Transport* (Pacific Transport Lines Inc., U.S.A.).
1958: *Washington* (States SS Co., U.S.A.).
1960: Renamed *Michigan*.
1960: (U.S. Maritime Administration).
1969: *Morning Light* (Waterman SS Corp., U.S.A.).
7.1973: Scrapped Kaohsiung.

Built by Bethlehem Steel Co., Quincy, Mass.

1481   *Empire Widgeon* 6,736 gt (C3-E type). 473 ft (oa), 450 ft × 66 ft. Engines: two steam turbines.
8.1940: Completed as *Exemplar* for American Export Lines.
1941: *Empire Widgeon* (M.O.W.T.).
1942: *Exemplar* (U.S.M.C.).

9.1942: Completed conversion to a transport by Bethlehem Steel Co., New York, for U.S. Navy; renamed *Dorothea L. Dix* (AP 67).
4.1946: *Exemplar* (American Export Lines).
11.1968: Scrapped Alicante.

Built by Newport News Shipbuilding & Drydock Co.

373   *Empire Egret* 7,248 gt (C2 type). 459 ft (oa), 439 ft × 63 ft. Engines: two steam turbines.
10.1939: Completed as *Nightingale* for Grace Lines Inc.
1941: *Empire Egret* (M.O.W.T.).
1942: *Nightingale* (U.S.M.C.).

1942: *Santa Isabel* (Grace Lines Inc.).
1.1944: Completed conversion to a transport by Brewer Dockyard Co., New York.
1946: *Guiding Star* (U.S.M.C.).
6.1973: Scrapped Brownsville, Texas.

Built by Bethlehem Steel Co., Sparrows Point, Md.

4342   *Empire Curlew* 7,101 gt (C2-S type). 480 ft (oa), 450 ft × 66 ft. Engines: two steam turbines.
4.1941: Completed as *Robin Doncaster* for Seas Shipping Co. Inc.
1941: *Empire Curlew* (M.O.W.T.).
1942: *Robin Doncaster* (U.S.M.C.).
1.1944: Completed conversion to a transport by Sullivan DD Co., New York, for operation by U.S. Navy.

4.1946: (U.S.M.C.).
1948: (Seas Shipping Co. Inc.).
1957: *Flying Gull* (Isbrandtsen & Co. Inc.).
1962: (American Export Lines Inc.).
6.1968: Scrapped Bilbao.

Built by Bath Iron Works Corp., Bath, Maine

185   *Empire Oriole* 6,551 gt (C2-S-A1 type). 420 ft (oa), 403 ft × 60 ft. Engines: two steam turbines.
10.1941: Completed as *Extavia* for American Export Lines Inc.
1941: *Empire Oriole* (M.O.W.T.).

1942: *Extavia* (U.S.M.C.).
11.1943: Completed conversion to a transport by Todd Shipyards, Brooklyn.
2.1946: (American Export Lines).
7.1968: Scrapped Alicante.

PART FIFTEEN

CAPTURED AND CONFISCATED ENEMY TONNAGE

The seizure of enemy tonnage in Allied ports commenced at the outbreak of war on 3 September 1939 and, as the war progressed, a number of enemy ships were captured on the high seas.

The first vessel captured was the German ship *Hannah Boge* (1938, 2,377 gt), taken in the North Atlantic by the Royal Navy on the first day of war. Placed under Ministry of Transport jurisdiction, she was renamed, a 'Crown' prefix being used for her and she was named *Crown Arun*. In fact, the ship was the only one to carry this prefix – the 'Empire' prefix being immediately adopted for other captured and confiscated tonnage.

Other enemy vessels were scuttled to avoid capture and some German and much Italian shipping was seized or sunk in the Middle East and East African campaigns, and by the time of the Italian surrender, in 1943, only a fraction of the total of pre-war Italian shipping, mostly in poor condition and less than enough to provide for minimum requirements of conquered and Italian territory, fell into Allied hands.

In May 1945, with Germany overrun, all remaining German shipping was seized, only ninety-five dry cargo, twenty general cargo and twenty-one tankers totalling some 200,000 tdw of coastal shipping being left in German hands, this tonnage being considered necessary to assist the German economy, which was dangerously affected by the seriously dislocated internal communications of that time. The position at two particular German ports on 18 May 1945 was that at Flensburg 157 merchant vessels were found in port – only two of them with fuel aboard, while at Brunsbüttel more than twenty merchantmen and some barges were found in port, as well as some naval vessels – an unseaworthy anti-aircraft cruiser, a destroyer, two submarine depot ships, large torpedo boats and E-boats, fifty landing craft and a partly-completed U-boat.

The total number of seized or confiscated ships was 502 and these were allocated to the three great Allied powers – Britain, the United States and Russia. The United States was allocated 167½ ships plus two uncompleted, Russia had 183 ships plus two uncompleted and Britain 136½ ships plus eleven uncompleted. The half-British, half-United States allocation was the *Sierra Cordoba*, this method being adopted to speed the arrangement. The half interest was adjusted later. Under the terms of the agreement, Britain and the United States were to re-distribute their allocations to include other Western Allies whilst Russia was to transfer some of her allocation to Poland.

From the re-distribution, Britain took some ninety ships of about 350,000 gross tons. These were placed under the control of the Ministry of War Transport, given 'Empire' names and managed by various shipping companies on its behalf. Later the vessels were offered for sale after being declared as 'prizes' by the Prize Court. Many ships also took 'Empire' names before being sent to Russia: of these it has not proved possible to trace any subsequent history for a considerable number of them.

The largest class of German 'standard design' ships was known as the Hansa 'A' type, of 3,200 tdw. Constructed between 1943 and 1945 in both German and occupied-territory shipyards, they were just over 1,900 gross tons and had compound engines which gave a speed of 10 knots. In all, nearly forty of the type were confiscated, whilst other vessels taken were of the less-numerous, slightly larger (2,800 gt) Hansa 'B' type. A class of small coastal tankers, each of about 650 gross tons, were also acquired: these, too, were a German standard design. The class, given 'girl' and 'boy' names, was commenced before the war, ostensibly as commercial vessels but in reality as naval vessels for the German Navy (Kriegsmarine) as, in fact, were the majority of the class, most being war-built tonnage.

A number of large passenger liners were also confiscated and brought to the U.K., where they were quickly converted for the transport of troops, and renamed to 'Empire' nomenclature. Among them were the former German East Africa Line's *Ubena* and *Pretoria* (completely rebuilt), the North German Lloyd (Norddeutscher Lloyd) liner *Potsdam* and the Hamburg South America Line's *Monte Rosa* and *Cap Norte*. These ships formed part of a large Sea Transport service for military personnel and dependants and were based at Southampton, whilst from Liverpool and other ports sailed other ex-German liners as troopers, including the former Hamburg South America ship *Antonio Delfino* and also the smaller Polish liner *Kosciusko*.

Section 1   Period 1939–1944

Crown Arun 2,372 gt. Built: Neptun AG., Rostock, in 1938 as *Hannah Boge* for J. M. K. Blumenthal, Hamburg. 302 ft × 45 ft. Engines: C4cyl.
3.9.1939: Captured by Royal Navy in North Atlantic. Renamed *Crown Arun* (M.O.W.T.).
17.9.1940: Sunk by submarine (*U.99*) torpedo off north-west Scotland, 58.02N 14.18W.

On 25 August 1939 a coded radio telegram to almost 2,500 German ships at sea ordered their Masters to open secret orders already on aboard. Subsequent orders directed them to avoid all regular sea routes and to make for home or to seek refuge in friendly or neutral ports. An order dated 3 September 1939 directed Germany-bound ships to use only the route between the Shetland Islands and Norway and, preferably, in bad weather.

The British fleet was already at sea, south of Iceland. Only a few hours after the declaration of war the destroyer H.M.S. *Somali* sighted the *Hannah Boge*, bound from Nova Scotia with a cargo of woodpulp and in the process of disguising herself, but still wearing the German flag. Captured, a prize crew was put aboard and the ship taken to the Pentland Firth, 600 miles away, arriving at Kirkwall on 5 September. Renamed under Ministry jurisdiction, the ship was the only one to be given the 'Crown' prefix, becoming *Crown Arun*. Other captured and confiscated tonnage was given the 'Empire' prefix – including the *Pomona* (renamed *Empire Merchant*) – which was seized in London on the first day of the war.

Empire Ability 7,603 gt. Built: Deutsche Schiff- und Masch., Bremen, in 1931 as *Uhenfels* for Hansa Line,

Bremen. 504 ft × 62 ft.
Engines: T3cyl.
16.10.1939: Sailed from Lourenço Marques disguised as a Dutch ship, in an attempt to break the British blockade and reach Germany.
4.11.1939: Sighted by aircraft from H.M.S. *Ark Royal*, then captured by H.M.S. *Hereward* off Freetown. Taken to U.K., the first German ship to arrive in the River Thames since the outbreak of war, but still wearing 'Dutch' colours. Renamed *Empire Ability* (M.O.W.T.).
23.10.1940: Damaged by aircraft bombs in Garelock, Scotland. Repaired.
27.6.1941: Sunk by submarine (*U.69*) torpedo south-west of Canary Islands, 23.50N 21.10W (voyage: Mauritius and Freetown/Liverpool – sugar and palm kernels).

Empire Activity 5,335 gt. Built: Swan, Hunter & Wigham Richardson Ltd., Newcastle, in 1919 as *Belgian*. 413 ft × 52 ft. Engines: T3cyl.
1934: *Amelia Lauro* (Achille Lauro & Co., Naples).
7.3.1940: Attacked and set on fire by German aircraft in North Sea (voyage: Newcastle/Piombino – coal). Anchored, then abandoned. Later taken in tow for Yarmouth Roads, thence Immingham, with superstructure completely burnt out. Permission granted for temporary repairs, but:

10.6.1940: Seized in prize at Immingham following Italy's declaration of war. Repaired, and renamed *Empire Activity* (M.O.T.).
3.10.1943: Stranded on Peckford Reef, Sir Charles Hamilton Sound, N.F. Holed: filled, slid off reef and sank. Total loss (voyage: Botwood/U.K. – zinc concentrates).

Empire Adventure 5,145 gt. Built: Northumberland Shipbuilding Co. Ltd., Newcastle, in 1921 as *Eastney*. 375 ft × 51 ft. Engines: T3cyl.
1924: *Germaine L. D.* (L. Dreyfus & Co., France).
1932: *Andrea* (Soc. Anon. di Nav. Corrado, Genoa).
6.1940: Taken in prize at Newcastle following Italy's declaration of war. Renamed *Empire Adventure* (M.O.T.).
20.9.1940: Sunk by submarine (*U.138*) torpedo off Islay, Scotland, in convoy OB 216.

Empire Advocate 5,787 gt. Built: J. C. Tecklenborg A.G., Wesermunde, in 1913 as *Solfels*. 437 ft × 56 ft. Engines: T3cyl.
1920: *Bowes Castle* (Lancashire Shipping Co. Ltd.).
1932: *Angelina Lauro* (Achille Lauro & Co., Naples).
23.6.1940: Taken in prize at Liverpool following Italy's declaration of war. Renamed *Empire Advocate* (M.O.T.).
4.1945: Scrapped Bo'ness.

Empire Airman 6,561 gt. Built: Stabilimento Tecnico, Trieste, in 1915 as *Teodo*. 450 ft × 56 ft. Engines: T3cyl.
1924: *Barbana* (Ministry of Marine, Italy).
1926: *Barbana G* (Soc. Anon. di Nav. Garibaldi, Genoa).
9.6.1940: Sailed from Newcastle, but:
10.6.1940: Taken at sea in prize, following Italy's declaration of war; escorted to Methil. Renamed *Empire Airman* (M.O.T.).
21.9.1940: Sunk by submarine (*U.100*) torpedo south-west of Rockall, North Atlantic, 54.00N 18.00W (approx.).

Empire Arun 5,490 gt. Built: Stabilimento Tecnico, Trieste, in 1922 as *Savoia* for Lloyd Triestino. 391 ft × 54 ft. Engines: two steam turbines.
14.2.1941: Taken in prize by Royal Navy at the capture of the port of Kismayu, Italian Somaliland.
1942: *Empire Arun* (M.O.W.T.).
1947: *Granlake* (Goulandris Bros., London).
1949: *Dryad* (Cia. Mar. del Este S.A., Panama (Goulandris Bros. (Hellas) Ltd.)).
1951: *Shiranesan Maru* (Hikari Kisen K.K., Tokyo).
1962: *Tainichi Maru* (a shellfish cannery) (Nichiro Gyogyo K.K., Tokyo).
8.1969: Scrapped Utsumi-Machi, Japan.

Empire Audacity 5,537 gt. Built: Bremer Vulkan Schiff- und Masch., Vegesack, in 1939 as *Hannover* for Norddeutscher Lloyd, Bremen. 435 ft × 56 ft. Engines: Oil.

In 1939 the *Hannover* was still a new ship, having been completed in that year for the banana run from the West Indies. She also carried passengers and was the first freighter with a built-in swimming pool.

When war started she sought refuge at the Dutch island of Curaçao, in the Caribbean. Some six months later, on 5 March 1940, she left port in an attempt to creep home through the British blockade. The night of 7 March found her between the islands of Hispaniola and Puerto Rico and it was here she was found by the cruiser H.M.S. *Dunedin* and the Canadian destroyer *Assiniboine*. The *Hannover* made for the neutral waters of Dominica, was then set on fire and the seacocks opened. But H.M.S. *Dunedin* drew alongside, boarding parties thwarted the scuttling attempts and the ship was towed well back into international waters. Four days later she arrived at Jamaica and in June 1940 was brought to the U.K. under the temporary name of *Sinbad*. Repaired, she was armed for use as an Ocean Boarding Vessel under the name *Empire Audacity*.

By this time the war at sea was going badly for Britain. The nation did not have enough aircraft carriers to give effective convoy protection or to cover the mid-Atlantic 'gap' not covered by shore-based air patrols. The Admiralty decided it needed small carriers – and the quickest way was to take merchantmen and put flight decks on them. And so Britain's first escort carrier was a conversion from the German prize *Hannover*. She was sent to the Northumberland shipyard of Blyth Dry Dock Company, where townsfolk were astonished at the arrival of a 6,000-tonner at a yard which previously had dealt with nothing over 300 feet in length. The official work went ahead and again the townsfolk wondered why, when the nation was short of ships, the entire superstructure and all upperworks were stripped from a perfectly good vessel.

Nevertheless, by June 1941 she had been given a flight deck. Her outfitting was completed at Liverpool: she had no island bridge, no hangar and no lift, but she was able to carry Martlett fighters, which could take off from a 300-ft deck and whose landing speed was less than 70 mph. However, following completion, the Admiralty took a dislike to her merchant ship name and, instead, she became H.M.S. *Audacity*.

H.M.S. *Audacity*'s fighting career was a short one, usually on the Gibraltar run, escorting convoys. On 14 December 1941 she left on a return trip, with thirty-two ships of convoy HG 76. By the 17th they were out of range of air cover from Gibraltar and dependent for cover on *Audacity*'s four aircraft.

It was sometimes the custom for a carrier to leave a convoy at night, for a ship of her type was a prime target among all other ships and a high silhouette could give away the position of a convoy during darkness. On the night of 23 December, as she left the convoy, jittery merchant ships fired 'snowflake', lighting up the sky and revealing the carrier in stark silhouette.

The submarines closed in – they had been given specific orders to sink the carrier – for in fourteen weeks of service she had caused the Germans much trouble, both on the sea and in the air.

A few minutes after being illuminated, the first torpedo, from *U.751*, hit her in the engine room and soon the ship lay helpless. Then she was hit again, by two torpedoes, which blew off her bows. The ship settled deeper in the water, then broke up and sank in position 43.45N 19.54W.

The harassed convoy reached journey's end after thirteen days; it had lost the *Audacity*, one destroyer (H.M.S. *Stanley*), two British merchant ships (*Empire Barracuda* and *Ruckinge*) and the Norwegian vessel *Annavore*, but it had cost Germany four submarines – *U.131*, *U.434*, *U.567* and *U.574*.

Empire Baron 5,894 gt. Built: Cantiere Navali Triestino, Trieste, in 1926 as *Monte Piana* for Nav. Generale Gerolimich & Co., Trieste. 417 ft × 53 ft. Engines: Oil.
12.6.1940: Beached at Aden after an attempt by crew to scuttle, following interception by Royal Navy.
1941: *Empire Baron* (M.O.W.T.). Attempts made to make main machinery and electrical equipment serviceable, but to no avail, and:
23.2.1941: Arrived Vizagapatam, India, in tow of steamer *Nirvana* (1914, 6,044 gt). Vessel repaired; re-entered service.
1947: *Rubystone* (Navigation & Coal Trade Ltd., London).
1951: (Alvion SS Co., Panama).
8.1960: Scrapped Nagasaki.

Empire Brigade 5,154 gt. Built: J. Priestman & Co. Ltd., Sunderland, in 1912 as *Hannington Court*. 400 ft × 54 ft. Engines: T3cyl.
1936: *Elios* (Achille Lauro & Co., Naples).
10.6.1940: Taken in prize at Newcastle. Renamed *Empire Brigade* (M.O.W.T.).
18.10.1940: Sunk by submarine torpedo in North Atlantic, west of Hebrides, 57.12N 10.43W.

On 17 October 1940 the German submarine *U.99* and six other U-boats were converging on convoy SC 7 (Sydney, N.S./U.K.) in the Atlantic. The next night the six started the attack and *U.99*, on the surface, slipped inside the escort screen. At short range she fired a torpedo at one ship – and missed, but hit with a second shot as explosions on the far side of the convoy indicated that other U-boats were finding targets. A sharp alteration of course carried *U.99* right into the convoy, where she headed down the first line, fired at another ship – and missed again.

In the U-boat the conclusion was that the torpedo plotter machine – untested when the submarine sailed – was defective and so her Captain turned to personal judgment of range and distance for subsequent torpedo firings.

Still on the surface, *U.99* dropped back, turned and fired a torpedo at the end ship of the outer column. At the same moment the target started a zig-zag course and the torpedo missed her, but went on to hit a ship in the next column. The vessel broke in two and sank in less than a minute: her radio called for help just once, but only gave her name – *Empire Brigade*. In all, the convoy lost twenty ships in four days of battle between the U-boats and a less-than-adequate escort.

The *U.99* herself sank six ships in some three hours, on a patrol of only nine days before all her torpedoes were expended, these nine days including four days out to the position of the convoy and four days back! (See also *Empire Spey*.)

Empire Citizen 4,683 gt. Built: Reiherstieg Schiffs., Hamburg, in 1922 as *Wahehe* for Woermann Line, Hamburg. 361 ft × 50 ft. Engines: Q4cyl.
9.1939: Took refuge in Vigo, Spain, after sailing from Hamburg prior to outbreak of war.
10.2.1940: Sailed, to return to Germany.
21.2.1940: Intercepted in rough weather south-east of Iceland by H.M.S. *Manchester* and H.M.S. *Kimberley*. Crew ordered not to scuttle ship, or they would be left to their fate.
22.2.1940: Boarded by a prize crew, vessel taken to Kirkwall.
1940: *Empire Citizen* (M.O.T.).
3.2.1941: Sunk by submarine (*U.107*) torpedo in North Atlantic, 58.12N 23.22W, in convoy OB 279 (voyage: Liverpool/U.S.A.).

Empire Clyde 7,515 gt. Built: Ansaldo San Giorgio, Spezia, in 1925 as *Leonardo da Vinci*. 429 ft × 52 ft. Engines: six steam turbines.
1943: *Empire Clyde* (hospital ship).
1948: *Maine* (Admiralty).
1954: Scrapped Hong Kong.

The *Leonardo da Vinci*, ordered before World War I, was not launched until 1921 and was delivered in 1925 to Transatlantica 'Italiana' Societe di Navigazione, of Genoa. Never quite fitting into any of her owner's regular services she went into a three-year lay up in 1926, before making a single voyage to London, in 1929, with art treasures for an exhibition. She then returned to lay up until taken as a transport for Italy's Abyssinian campaign of 1935. Two years later she passed to Lloyd Triestino, when that company was re-formed to take over certain vessels of large Italian fleets.

On 14 February 1941 the *Leonardo da Vinci* fell into the hands of the Royal Navy as a result of the capture of the port of Kismayu, Italian Somaliland. Keeping her Italian name, she was put under the management of the Ellerman group by the M.O.W.T., but was eventually renamed *Empire Clyde* and operated as a military hospital ship. In 1948 she passed to the Admiralty, being renamed *Maine* – the fourth British hospital ship to be so named – this in recognition of the charity of the Americans, who presented the Atlantic Transport liner of that name to Britain during the Boer War.

Note: Five Italian vessels fell into British hands when Kismayu was captured: *Adria* (3,809 gt), *Savoia* (5,490 gt – later *Empire Arun*), *Erminia Mazzella* (5,644 gt), *Manon* (5,597 gt) and *Leonardo da Vinci*. Four other vessels were scuttled in the harbour. At the same time the German ship *Uckermark* (7,021 gt) tried to escape, was intercepted and tried to scuttle herself. This was frustrated but the vessel subsequently sank while in tow. The German steamer *Askari* (590 gt) was driven ashore.

Empire Commerce 3,857 gt. Built: J. L. Thompson & Sons Ltd., Sunderland, in 1928 as *Goodleigh*. 360 ft × 50 ft. Engines: T3cyl.

1937: *Christoph V. Doornum* (Fisser & V. Doornum, Emden).
4.9.1939: Taken in prize by Canadian authorities at Botwood, Newfoundland, while loading concentrates.
1940: *Empire Commerce* (M.O.T.).
9.6.1940: Struck mine off Margate, Kent. Severely damaged, fractured amidships. Beached, but drifted off sandbank. Taken in tow and beached Mucking Sands, River Thames. Discharged, but constructive total loss. Broken up *in situ* (voyage: St. John's, N.F./U.K. – woodpulp).

Empire Confidence 5,023 gt. Built: Bremer Vulkan Schiff- und Masch., Vegesack, in 1935 as *Düsseldorf* for Norddeutscher Lloyd, Bremen. 415 ft × 55 ft. Engines: Oil.
9.1939: Took refuge in Valparaiso, Chile, at outbreak of war.
12.1939: Sailed, in order to proceed to Antofagasta to load fuel, ready for an attempt to break the British blockade and return to Germany; but:
15.12.1939: Captured off Punta Caldera, Chile, by cruiser H.M.S. *Despatch*. Taken into Antofagasta with Chilian permission for repairs and fuel. Then taken, in prize, to Jamaica under temporary name of *Poland* in order to make her appearance 'less German-like'.
1940: *Empire Confidence* (M.O.T.).
1945: *Star of El Nil* (chartered to Alexandria Nav. Co., Egypt).
1950: *Spenser* (Lamport & Holt Ltd.).
1955: Renamed *Roscoe*.
1962: Scrapped Bilbao.

Note: The somewhat unusual temporary name of *Poland* given to a ship captured off Chile, in the South Pacific, is accounted for by the fact that the warship which captured her, H.M.S. *Despatch*, was commanded by Commodore Alan Poland.

The *Empire Confidence* was equipped with German M.A.N.-type engines; there were no spares in Britain and replacement parts had to be copied from existing parts, for she frequently suffered from the bending of her piston rods, a problem which even the Germans had not solved. Nevertheless, some of her exploits will help to exemplify similar wartime service given by hundreds of such vessels while under the jurisdiction of the M.O.W.T.

On 23 October 1942 commenced the Battle of Alamein, the turning point of the war in the deserts of Egypt. Allied forces there formed one claw of a proposed pincer movement on the enemy: the other was an army aboard ships already at sea, taking a force to Morocco and Algeria. The first convoy for French North Africa sailed from the Clyde on 22 October 1942. With it was *Empire Confidence*, carrying landing craft, military vehicles, guns, ammunition and cased petrol. Joining up with troop transports, the ships subsequently anchored in Arzu Bay. A large force was ferried ashore and Oran fell into Allied hands. On 12 November *Empire Confidence* sailed for home, but was back at Oran on 6 January 1943 with another military cargo.

On 7 May the Allies entered Tunis and Bizerta and were planning to invade Sicily. *Empire Confidence* was again fitted out for the task: she left the Clyde in a thirty-ship convoy at the end of June 1943 and by 9 July more convoys were assembling in the Bay of Tripoli. Then, as the invasion of Sicily commenced, the ship took her allotted position off the southern tip of the island and discharged her vital cargo. Following orders, she sailed at exactly 8 p.m. on the 11th, at which time other ships, from precisely-timed convoys, were arriving to take up the vacated places. Then *Empire Confidence* loaded explosives at Algiers, took aboard 400 servicemen and sailed for Salerno. Landings here started on 9 September and the ship then shuttled for six weeks between Tripoli, Alexandria, Augusta and Bari with supplies for the 8th Army.

After her Mediterranean experiences the ship was sent to Baltimore, loading cargo for Karachi and Bombay. She was at Bombay when the *Fort Stikine* blew up, causing widespread destruction to the port and the city. *Empire Confidence*, although damaged, was towed away to safety. But the destruction caused some famine in the area and the ship was sent to Australia for grain. On the way back to India she picked up survivors of the *Helen Moller* (1918, 5,259 gt) which had been sunk by torpedo. *Empire Confidence* arrived back in the U.K., at Hull, on 15 August 1944.

Empire Control 5,612 gt. Built: Reiherstieg Schiffs., Hamburg, in 1913 as *Wotan*. 406 ft × 53 ft. Engines: T3cyl.
1927: *Gianna M* (Comp. Italiana Trasporto Olii Minerali, Genoa).
5.1941: Captured by H.M.S. *Hilary* north of Las Palmas, Canary Islands. Taken to Belfast. Renamed *Empire Control* (M.O.W.T.).
1945: Laid up at Falmouth; intended to become a pelagic herring factory ship, but conversion not carried out. Sold.
1948: *Kleinella* (storage hulk at Gibraltar) (Shell Co. of Gibraltar Ltd. (Anglo-Saxon Petroleum Co. Ltd.)).
12.1953: Scrapped Dunston-on-Tyne.

As *Wotan* this vessel was one of the first ocean-going motor tankers in the world. The first was the Dutch *Vulcanus* (1,179 tons) of 1910, but the Deutsche-Amerikan Petroleum Company introduced a more ambitious programme. They built four vessels in 1913, the twin-screw *Hagen* (5,460 tons), *Loki* (5,456 tons), *Wilhelm A. Reidemann* (9,880 tons) and the *Wotan*, a single-screw vessel, of 5,703 tons. She was propelled by a 2,000 bhp engine – the biggest diesel to be built up to that time.

At the end of World War I the *Wotan* was allocated to the U.S.A. and transferred to the Standard Oil Company. She sailed from London on 22 December 1920, bound for New York, but suffered machinery trouble all the way across. Sent to Baltimore for lay up, the ship remained there until 1927, when she was sold to Italian buyers. Towed back across the Atlantic, her troublesome early diesel engine was replaced with triple-expansion machinery.

Empire Conveyor 5,911 gt. Built: Richardson, Duck & Co. Ltd., Stockton, in 1917 as *Farnworth*. 400 ft × 52 ft. Engines: T3cyl.

The *Empire Clyde*, formerly the Italian liner *Leonardo da Vinci*, as a hospital ship at Malta.

The *Empire Patrol*, on fire off Port Said in September 1945. She carried refugees being repatriated to the Greek Islands.

The *Empire Raja*, as the Japanese-flag *Liverpool Maru*, in the River Thames in 1955.

1926: *Illinois* (Comp. Gen. Transatlantique, France).
1934: *Mount Pentelikon* (Kulukundis Shipping Co., Greece).
1939: *Gloria* (Orion Schiffs., Hamburg).
8.9.1939: Sailed from Buenos Aires in an attempt to break the British blockade and return to Germany.
21.10.1939: Captured south-east of Iceland by H.M.S *Sheffield*. Taken to Leith, and:
1940: *Empire Conveyor* (M.O.T.).
20.6.1940: Sunk by submarine (*U.122*) torpedo fifty miles south-west of Barra Head, Hebrides, 56.16N 8.10W.

Empire Crusader 1,042 gt. Built: Atlas-Werke A.G., Bremen, in 1925 as *Leander* for Neptun Line, Bremen. 224 ft × 33 ft. Engines: T3cyl.
9.11.1939: Captured by H.M. ship off Vigo, Spain; found to have a full cargo of guns. Taken to Falmouth.
1940: *Empire Crusader* (M.O.T.).
8.8.1940: Attacked and set on fire by German aircraft fifteen miles west of St. Catherine's Point, Isle of Wight. Abandoned, capsized and later sank.

Empire Defender 5,649 gt. Built: J. C. Tecklenborg A.G., Wesermunde, in 1910 as *Freienfels*. 435 ft × 55 ft. Engines: Q4cyl.
1914: Seized by Great Britain at Calcutta; transferred to Admiralty.
1920: (Secretary of State for India.).
1925: *Hadiotis* (Rethymnis & Pnevmaticos, Greece).
1929: *Felce* (Achille Lauro & Co., Naples).

The *Felce* was seized at Haifa on 11 June 1940 after Italy declared war on the Allies. She was renamed *Empire Defender* under the M.O.T. Towards the end of 1941 the Admiralty decided to send the vessel on a special mission to Malta with stores and ammunition, unescorted and not in convoy, and without protection in the Mediterranean, the necessity of keeping Malta as a base being of prime importance.

At Glasgow on 20 October 1941 the special cargo was being loaded when her sixty Lascar seamen refused to sail on the ship, following a consecutive two-nights dream by their 'Sarang' that the vessel was 'calash' (finished – sunk) before the next new moon. On sailing day minus one they left the ship and camped in the warehouse alongside, with all their possessions. They had nowhere to go and did not care, setting up their cooking pots and spreading their bedding. The promise of extra wages, more leave, overtime payments and then the threats of the dire consequences of breaking their two-year agreements made no difference – reboard the ship they would not. Other Lascars were not available at short notice and the same number of white ratings were signed on, every man being given ten pounds in cash as inducement to accept the Lascar accommodation, until such time as it could be altered – normally regarded as a six-week job.

Very few persons knew of the ship's destination, even less cared, though the hull had been painted black instead of the usual grey, topsides had become white and funnel buff – all contrary to the wartime regulations. All armament had been removed, as had a minesweeping 'A' frame at the bow. At sea the ship had to appear neutral. Sailing on time, she struck a berthed vessel while swinging, then collided with a new vessel bound upstream. Later, she left a convoy off the Spanish coast and proceeded into the Mediterranean, disguised by painting on her hull the flag of the nation in whose waters she was at the time.

Thus she passed as French, Spanish and Italian through the danger zones until the night before she was due at Malta. Then the prophesy became manifest: at sunset on 14 November she was attacked by an enemy plane, its aerial torpedo struck home and within minutes the vessel was a blazing wreck. Abandoned, her crew had only just cleared the vessel when she blew up and sank, some eighteen miles south of Galita Island.

Empire Defiance 4,667 gt. Built: Reiherstieg Schiffs., Hamburg, in 1909 as *Iserlohn*. 413 ft × 54 ft. Engines: T3cyl.
1921: *Union City* (St. Just SS Co. Ltd.).
1924: *Wasaborg* (J. A. Zachariassen & Co., Finland).
1935: *Erica* (Achille Lauro & Co., Naples).
10.6.1940: Taken in prize at Liverpool. Renamed *Empire Defiance* (M.O.T.).
6.1944: Sunk as a blockship at Gooseberry 5, Ouistreham, Normandy, during Allied invasion of France.
1951: Wreck salved, and:
8.1951: Taken in tow by tugs *Seaman* and *Superman*, bound for shipbreakers. Hull found to be leaking, and:
21.8.1951: Beached off the Mole, Zeebrugge. Refloated and:
15.9.1951: Arrived Antwerp for scrapping.

Empire Endurance 8,570 gt. Built: Deutsche Werft, Hamburg, in 1928 as *Alster*. 513 ft × 64 ft. Engines: T3cyl.

The *Alster* was one of a series of cargo liners built for Norddeutscher Lloyd during 1927–1928. The ten ships of the series, in three classes, came from six different builders and varied from 12,000 tdw coal-burners with triple expansion engines (*Aller*, *Alster* and *Main*) to similar vessels (*Lahn*, *Mosel*, *Neckar* and *Oder*) but with the addition of Bauer-Wach exhaust turbines and to smaller diesel-driven vessels of only 11,000 tdw – the *Havel*, *Saale* and *Trave*. The last-named three vessels were renamed *Coburg*, *Marburg* and *Regensburg* when re-engined and placed on a combined fast service to the Far East, along with the *Potsdam* (see *Empire Fowey*) and her two sisterships.

Only two of the ten ships – *Aller* and *Lahn* – survived the war, the former being interned at Lourenço Marques in 1939 and subsequently becoming the Portuguese *Sofala* and the latter becoming the Argentine-owned *San Martin* and then *Rio Parana*.

On 10 April 1940 the *Alster* was captured off Vestfjord by H.M.S. *Icarus* and became *Empire Endurance*. She served under the M.O.T. for only a year, being sunk by *U.73* on 20 April 1941, in position 53.05N 23.14W, in the North Atlantic, south-west of Rockall.

Empire Energy 6,548 gt. Built: Neptun A.G., Rostock, in 1923 as *Grete*. 462 ft × 57 ft. Engines: T3cyl.
1934: *Gabbiano* (Achille Lauro & Co., Naples).
10.6.1940: Taken in prize at Liverpool; renamed *Empire Energy* (M.O.T.).
5.11.1941: Ashore at Big Brook, eleven miles west of Cape Norman, Belle Isle Strait, N.S. Broadside to beach, resting on a rocky ledge. Total loss (voyage: New York/Belfast – maize).

Empire Engineer 5,358 gt. Built: Canadian Vickers Ltd., Montreal, in 1921 as *Canadian Commander*. 400 ft × 52 ft. Engines: T3cyl.
1932: *Gioacchino Lauro* (Achille Lauro & Co., Naples).
10.6.1940: Seized in prize at Hartlepool; renamed *Empire Engineer* (M.O.T.).
2.2.1941: Sunk by submarine (*U.123*) torpedo in Atlantic (approx.) 54.00N 34.00W (voyage: Halifax/Newport, Mon. – steel).

Empire Fisher (trawler) 268 gt. Built: Reiherstieg Schiffs, Hamburg, in 1922 as *Herlichkeil* for Nordsee Deutsche Hochsee Fischerei Bremen, Cuxhaven. 140 ft × 24 ft. Engines: T3cyl.
13.2.1940: Captured by H.M.S. *Glasgow* in North Sea; taken to Kirkwall. Renamed *Empire Fisher* (M.O.T.).
1947: (Hunter Fishing Company).
2.1948: Sold to BISCO for scrapping, but resold to W. J. Sweeney, Dublin, and:
3.1952: Scrapped Passage West, Cork.

Empire Fusilier 5,404 gt. Built: Cantiere Cerusa, Voltri, Italy, in 1921 as *Mincio* for P. Ravano Fu Marco, Genoa. 394 ft × 52 ft. Engines: T3cyl.
10.6.1940: Taken in prize at Liverpool. Renamed *Empire Fusilier* (M.O.T.).
9.2.1942: Sunk by submarine (*U.85*) torpedo southeast of St. John's, N.F., 44.45N 47.25W.

Empire Garden (tanker) 8,923 gt.
Built: Howaldtswerke, Kiel, in 1919 as *Gedania* for Waried Tankschiff. GmbH, Hamburg. 499 ft × 64 ft. Engines: Q4cyl.
1939: Requisitioned by German Navy.
1941: Converted at St. Nazaire to carry fuel and supplies to German commerce raiders in the Atlantic, and to bring back prisoners taken from sunken ships.
4.6.1941: Captured near Iceland by Ocean Boarding Vessel H.M.S. *Marsdale*, in position 43.38N 28.15W. Renamed *Empire Garden* (M.O.W.T.).
1947: *Southern Garden* (Chr. Salvesen & Co., Leith).
8.1960: Scrapped Inverkeithing.

Empire Governor 8,657 gt. Built: Cantiere San Rocco S.A., Trieste, in 1925 as *Esquilino* for Lloyd Triestino, Trieste. 450 ft × 57 ft. Engines: Oil.

10.6.1940: Taken as a prize at Aden by Royal Navy. Renamed *Empire Governor* (M.O.T.).
1946: Scrapping commenced at Dalmuir, but completed at Troon.

Empire Gunner 4,492 gt. Built: Grangemouth & Greenock Dockyard Co., in 1906 as *Strathearn*. 370 ft × 52 ft. Engines: T3cyl.
1924: *Constantinos* (P. C. Lemos, Greece).
1925: Renamed *Kostantis Lemos*.
1928: *Danaos* (Constantine & Lemos, Greece).
1939: *Moscardin* (Soc. di Nav. Polena, Genoa).
9.6.1940: Sailed from Newcastle, and:
10.6.1940: Captured at sea in prize; taken to Methil. Renamed *Empire Gunner* (M.O.T.).
7.9.1941: Sunk by aircraft bombs in St. George's Channel, 52.08N 5.18W (voyage: Pepel/River Tees – iron ore).

Empire Indus 5,155 gt. Built: Blohm & Voss, Hamburg, in 1923 as *Gera* for Hamburg America Line. 407 ft × 56 ft. Engines: four steam turbines.
4.4.1941: Scuttled at Massowah, Eritrea, just prior to the capture of the port by British forces.
8.9.1942: Refloated; found to have engine damage, bulkheads and bottom distorted and accommodation gutted. Beached in shallow water for temporary repairs. Renamed *Empire Indus* (M.O.W.T.).
2.5.1943: Left in tow of steamer *Mantola* (1921, 9,065 gt) and:
13.5.1943: Arrived Karachi for repairs.
14.4.1944: Badly damaged in *Fort Stikine* explosion at Victoria Dock, Bombay. Forepart and accommodation burnt out, deck plating collapsed, hull distorted.
11.1945: Repairs completed.
1946: (Arden Hall Steamship Co., Cape Town).
1947: Renamed *Bosveld*.
1948: *Pan Ocean* (Pan Ocean Navigation Co., Panama).
6.4.1958: Sprang leak, foundered 160 miles northwest of Alexandria, Egypt, 33.15N 27.55E (voyage: Mormugao/Genoa – iron ore).

Empire Industry 3,721 gt. Built: Vuijk & Son, Capelle, in 1916 as *Leersum*. 361 ft × 48 ft. Engines: T3cyl.
1939: *Henning Oldendorff* (E. Oldendorff, Lübeck).
17.11.1939: Captured in Denmark Strait, off Iceland, by H.M.S. *Colombo*, when trying to reach Germany with iron ore from Huelva. Taken to Kirkwall, thence Liverpool.
1940: *Empire Industry* (M.O.S.).
16.3.1941: Sunk by German battleship *Scharnhorst* south-east of Cape Race, North Atlantic, 43.27N 45.25W.

(Intended to be) *Empire Inventor* 9,515 gt. Built: A.
G. Weser, Bremen, in 1922 as *Werra*. 480 ft × 58 ft.
Engines: T6cyl.
1935: *Calabria* (Lloyd Triestino, Trieste).
10.6.1940: Taken in prize at Calcutta. Intended to be
renamed *Empire Inventor* (M.O.T.), but:
8.12.1940: Sunk (as *Calabria*) by submarine (*U.103*)
torpedo west of Ireland, 52.43N 10.07W.

Empire Kamal 7,862 gt. Built: Bremer Vulkan Schiff-
und Masch., Vegesack, in 1938 as *Hohenfels* for Hansa
Line, Bremen. 488 ft × 61 ft. Engines: Oil.
25.8.1941: Scuttled at Bandar Shapur. Salved by
Royal Navy, and:
1942: *Empire Kamal* (M.O.W.T.).
1944: *Van Ruisdael* (Government of the Netherlands).
1947: *Ridderkerk* (Vereenigde Nederland Scheeps.,
Holland).
9.1962: Scrapped Hong Kong.

Empire Kohinoor 5,225 gt. Built: W. Hamilton & Co.
Ltd., Port Glasgow, in 1919 as *War Celt*.
400 ft × 52 ft. Engines: T3cyl.
1919: *Caboto* (Lloyd Triestino, Trieste).
25.8.1941: Scuttled at Bandar Shapur. Raised and
taken in prize by British. Renamed *Empire Kohinoor*
(M.O.W.T.).
2.7.1943: Damaged by submarine (*U.618*) torpedo
south-west of Freetown, W. Africa, 6.20N 16.30W.
3.7.1943: Torpedoed again by same submarine: sunk.

Note: The Lloyd Triestino also lost another British-built
World War I standard type by scuttling. Built as *War Cobra*
(1917, 5,155 gt) she became *Alberto Treves* in 1919 and *Romolo
Gessi* in 1941. On 4 April 1941 she was scuttled at Massawa.
Later she was raised by the British and cut up for scrap
without being renamed.

Empire Kumari 6,288 gt. Built: A. G. Weser,
Bremen, in 1920 as *Sturmfels* for Hansa Line, Bremen.
431 ft × 56 ft. Engines: T3cyl.
25.8.1941: Scuttled at Bandar Shapur. Salved by
Royal Navy; taken in prize and renamed *Empire
Kumari* (M.O.W.T.).
26.8.1942: Damaged by submarine (*U.375*) torpedo
north of Port Said, 31.58N 34.21E. Towed to Haifa
Bay and beached off harbour breakwater.
Subsequently sank. Total loss.

Note: The Turkish steamer *Gucum Erman* (1910, 4,540 gt)
sank at Haifa on 14 December 1951 after dragging its anchors
and grounding on the wreck of the *Empire Kumari*.

Empire Mariner 4,957 gt. Built: Deutsche Werft,
Hamburg, in 1922 as *Schwarzwald*. 402 ft × 54 ft.
Engines: two steam turbines.
1935: *Rheingold* (H. Vogemann, Hamburg).

10.1939: Sailed from Bahia in an attempt to return to
Germany.
25.10.1939: Captured in North Atlantic by H.M.S.
Delhi. Taken to Kirkwall, then Glasgow.
1940: *Empire Mariner* (M.O.T.).
26.7.1942: Put back to Clyde with machinery
damage. Fitted with new (T3cyl) engine and boilers.
1946: *St. Ina* (South American Saint Line Ltd.).
1948: *Wells City* (Bristol City Line of Steamships
Ltd.).
1951: *Fausta* (East & West Steamship Co., Karachi).
10.1963: Scrapped Karachi.

Empire Merchant 3,457 gt. Built: Deutsche Werft,
Hamburg, in 1938 as *Pomona* for F. Laeisz & Co.,
Hamburg. 399 ft × 53 ft. Engines: Oil.
3.9.1939: Taken in prize in South West India Dock,
London. Renamed *Empire Merchant* (M.O.T.).
16.8.1940: Sunk by submarine (*U.100*) torpedo in
Atlantic, 55.23N 13.24W.

Empire Niger 7,487 gt. Built: J. C. Tecklenborg
A.G., Wesermunde, in 1920 as *Frauenfels* for Hansa
Line, Bremen. 469 ft × 58 ft. Engines: T3cyl.
4.4.1941: Set on fire and scuttled at Massawa. Salved
by Royal Navy; taken in prize, and:
1942: Renamed *Empire Niger*, (M.O.W.T.).
1948: *Belapur* (Oceanic Navigation Co., Calcutta).
1951: (Pang Kwok Sui, Hong Kong).
6.1954: Arrived at Yokohama for scrapping, but
resold, and:
1955: *Snowdon Hill* (Keystone Shipping Co., Hong
Kong).
1957: *Canadian Fir* (Canadian Fir SS Co., Hong
Kong).
1958: *Nan Hai 141* (Government of the People's
Republic of China).
12.1963: Scrapped Hong Kong.

Empire Nile 6,318 gt. Built: A. G. Weser, Bremen,
in 1922 as *Liebenfels* for Hansa Line, Bremen.
432 ft × 56 ft. Engines: T3cyl.
4.4.1941: Set on fire and scuttled at Massowah. Salved
by Royal Navy; taken in prize, and:
1942: *Empire Nile* (M.O.W.T.).
1947: *Alipur* (Oceanic Navigation Co., Calcutta).
1948: *Dah Kiang* (Dah Loh Navigation Co., China).
1951: *El Grande* (Great China SS & Industrial Co.,
Panama).
1951: *Ho Ping I* (Government of the People's Republic
of China).
1967: Renamed *Sheng Li*.
1977: Name removed from shipping registers; vessel
reported scrapped in China.

Note: This vessel was sighted in Shanghai in 1979, with the
new name of *Zhan Dou 75* and with the old name of *Sheng
Li* still clearly showing.

However, some British registers list the *Zhan Dou 75* as the ex-Hansa Line's *Wartenfels*, but it is likely that this vessel (see *Empire Tugela*) carries the unlisted Chinese name of *Zhan Dou 46*, a vessel of this name and obviously an ex-Hansa vessel (although with a new bridge and 'A'-type masts) being sighted at the same time.

Empire Patrol 3,338 gt. Built: Stabilimento Tecnico, Trieste, in 1928 as *Rodi* for Soc. Anon. Adriatica Nav., Trieste. 332 ft × 45 ft. Engines: Oil.
10.6.1940: Taken in prize at Malta, having been intercepted by the British Contraband Control before the Italian declaration of war. Renamed *Empire Patrol* (M.O.W.T.).
29.9.1945: Sailed from Port Said for Castelorizo, Dodecanese Islands, with 496 Greek refugees being repatriated from Abyssinia and East Africa and who had fled from Samos and Kios after the German occupation of those islands. When only thirty-eight miles out of Port Said fire broke out in the passenger quarters. Vessel abandoned with fire out of control and the ship burning from stem to stern.
1.10.1945: Capsized and sank eighteen miles from Port Said after being taken in tow by naval tugs.

Empire Peri (tanker) 4,769 gt. Built: Fratelli Orlando & Co., Leghorn, in 1905 as *Bronte* (Italian Navy water carrier). 381 ft × 47 ft. Engines: T6cyl.
25.8.1941: Captured by Royal Navy at Bandar Shapur. Taken in prize, renamed *Empire Peri* (M.O.W.T.).
1946: In use as a water supply vessel at Bombay.
1947: Scrapped locally.

Empire Planet 4,290 gt. Built: J. Priestman & Co. Ltd., Sunderland, in 1923 as *Barbara Marie*.
365 ft × 52 ft. Engines: T3cyl.
1925: *Portsea* (Sea SS Co. Ltd.).
1933: *Cipro* (Nivose Soc. di Nav., Italy).
1937: *Stella* (Lauro & Montella, Naples).
14.8.1941: Captured by H.M.S. *Circassia* west of Cape Verde Islands. Taken to Bermuda. Renamed *Empire Planet* (M.O.W.T.).
1947: *Inchkeith* (Williamson & Co., Hong Kong).
2.3.1955: Struck uncharted rock after leaving Port Meadows, Andaman Islands, Bay of Bengal. Awash and abandoned. Total loss;
(voyage: Calcutta/Cochin – 5,000 tons of coal, and Port Meadows/Bombay – 700 tons of timber).

Empire Prize (tanker) 3,245 gt. Built: Baltimore Shipbuilding Corporation in 1917 as *Holden Evans*. 306 ft × 47 ft. Engines: T3cyl.
1926: *Olvigore* (European Shipping Co. Ltd.).
1927: Renamed *Oilvigor*.
1930: *Clelia Campanella* (Tito Campanella Fu Pietro, Genoa).

8.4.1941: Scuttled alongside quay at Massowah on capture of port by British forces. Salved by Royal Navy; taken in prize and renamed *Empire Prize* (M.O.W.T.).
1946: *Bankivia* (Anglo-Saxon Petroleum Co. Ltd.).
10.1949: Scrapped Hong Kong.

Empire Progress 5,249 gt. Built: Harland & Wolff Ltd., Glasgow, in 1918 as *War Expert*. 401 ft × 52 ft. Engines: T3cyl.
1919: *Anomia* (Anglo-Saxon Petroleum Co. Ltd.).
1933: *Andrea* (A/S Brovigseil, Norway).
1938: *Mugnone* (converted to dry cargo ship) (M. Querci, Genoa).
10.6.1940: Taken in prize at Newcastle. Renamed *Empire Progress* (M.O.W.T.).
22.5.1941: Bombed and gunned by German aircraft off Needles, Isle of Wight. Repaired.
13.4.1942: Sunk by submarine (*U.402*) torpedo south of Cape Race, North Atlantic, 40.29N 52.35W (voyage: Glasgow/Tampa).

Empire Protector 6,181 gt. Built: Cantiere Officine Savoia, Genoa, in 1921 as *Artena*. 395 ft × 52 ft. Engines: DR turbines.
1928: *Cariddi* (La Mer. di Nav. S.A., Italy).
1932: Renamed *Sebeto*.
1935: *Pamia* (Soc. di Nav. Polena, Genoa).
6.1940: Sailed from Sunderland, but:
10.6.1940: Captured at sea by H.M.S. *Liffey*, taken to Methil. Taken in prize and renamed *Empire Protector* (M.O.W.T.).
30.5.1941: Sunk by submarine (*U.38*) torpedo off West African coast, 6.00N 14.25W (voyage: Cape Town/Freetown).

Empire Raja 6,224 gt. Built: J. C. Tecklenborg A.G., Wesermunde, in 1922 as *Wildenfels* for Hansa Line, Bremen. 431 ft × 56 ft. Engines: T3cyl.
25.8.1941: Scuttled at Bandar Shapur. Salved, taken in prize and renamed *Empire Raja* (M.O.W.T.).
1949: *Lansdowne* (Wheelock, Marden & Co., Hong Kong).
1951: *Liverpool Maru* (Dai-Ichi Kisen K.K., Japan).
11.1960: Scrapped Osaka.

By mid-1941, after the German territorial occupation of Europe had spread into Africa, their High Command was preparing plans for reaching forward to neutral Iran, where control of its oilfields, and the Persian Gulf, would facilitate progress of the German war machine towards India and the East and deny the Allies of much of its fuel supply.
The British Cabinet acted quickly and on 20 August approval was given to disembark troops at the head of the Persian Gulf, using force if necessary; to put the Iranian Navy out of action and to capture the enemy merchant ships which had long been sheltering at Khor Musa, Bandar Shapur. Five days later a landing was made by British and Empire forces,

and success was immediate. By the afternoon of the 25th, Abadan, with its refinery, the naval base at Khorramshahr and the port of Bandar Shapur had been captured, whilst an Army group advancing from Iraq occupied oil fields in the north and dealt with Persian land forces. On 27 August the Iranian Government resigned and in mid-September the Shah abdicated.

A total of seven enemy ships were involved, five German vessels of the Hansa Line and two Italian ships. One German ship, the *Marienfels*, was captured, later becoming the *Empire Rani*. Three others were scuttled by their crews but later raised and repaired – *Sturmfels* (*Empire Kumari*), *Wildenfels* (*Empire Raja*) and *Hohenfels* (*Empire Kamal*). The *Weissenfels*, also scuttled, was raised and scrapped. The Italian vessels captured also became 'Empires' – *Caboto* (*Empire Kohinoor*) and *Bronte* (*Empire Peri*).

A number of other Hansa Line vessels also took 'Empire' nomenclature during the war years, these including ships scuttled in neutral ports in which they had taken refuge: among them were *Frauenfels* and *Liebenfels*, scuttled at Massowah, Eritrea, and later raised to become *Empire Niger* and *Empire Nile*, respectively, and the *Wartenfels*, scuttled at Diego Suarez and later to become *Empire Tugela*.

Empire Rani 7,575 gt. Built: J. C. Tecklenborg A.G., Wesermunde, in 1921 as *Marienfels* for Hansa Line, Bremen. 468 ft × 59 ft. Engines: T3cyl.
25.8.1941: Captured by British forces at Bandar Shapur. Renamed *Empire Rani* (M.O.W.T.).
1950: *Karachi* (San Giorgio del Porto, Italy).
6.1959: Scrapped Osaka.

Empire Resistance 1,631 gt. Built: Fevigs Jernskibsbyg, Fevig, Norway, in 1908 as *Ottar*.
253 ft × 37 ft. Engines: T3cyl.
1935: *Libano* (Servizio Italo–Portoghese Anon. di Nav., Genoa).
6.1940: Taken in prize at Gibraltar. Renamed *Empire Resistance* (M.O.W.T.).
1946: *Resistance* (Resistance Shipping Co., London).
1949: *Beatrice C* (Giacomo Costa, Genoa).
1954: *Acilia* (Raffaele Romano, Naples).
1956: *Cilin* (Apostolo & Ruffini, Genoa).
6.1959: Scrapped Savona.

Empire Sailor 6,086 gt. Built: Stabilimento Tecnico, Trieste, in 1926 as *Cellina* for Soc. Italia di Nav., Genoa. 448 ft × 55 ft. Engines: Oil.
10.6.1940: Taken in prize at Gibraltar. Renamed *Empire Sailor* (M.O.T.).
21.11.1942: Sunk by submarine (*U.518*) torpedo south of Cape Race, 43.53N 55.12W in convoy ON 145 (cargo said to be phosgene and mustard gas).

Empire Salvage (tanker) 10,594 gt. Built: Rotterdam Droogdok Maats N.V., in 1940 as
Papendrecht for Van Ommeren's Scheeps., Rotterdam. 496 ft × 73 ft. Engines: Oil.

5.1940: Seized by Germany at builder's yard. Acquired by German Navy, renamed *Lothringen*; converted for replenishment at sea, used in Atlantic as a supply ship for the battleship *Bismarck*, other raiders and submarines.
15.6.1941: Captured in North Atlantic north-west of Cape Verde Islands by H.M.S. *Dunedin*, in position 19.49N 30.30W. Taken to Bermuda. Renamed *Empire Salvage*; used by Royal Navy as a fleet oiler at Halifax, N.S., and in the Eastern fleet.
1946: Reverted to original Dutch owners and name.
4.1964: Scrapped Onomichi, Japan.

Note: When captured in 1941 the above vessel provided much information relating to the German methods of replenishment at sea. They had evolved rubber hoses for refuelling purposes and it was these, with modifications, that were subsequently used by the Royal Navy.

Empire Scout 2,229 gt. Built: Lübecker Maschinenbau Gesellschaft, Lübeck, in 1936 as *Eilbek* for Knohr & Burchard, Hamburg. 284 ft × 44 ft. Engines: C4cyl.
19.11.1939: Captured south of Iceland while disguised as a Swedish ship, by H.M.S. *Scotstoun*, while attempting to break British blockade and return to Germany – burning her woodpulp cargo as fuel.
1940: *Empire Scout* (M.O.T.).
1946: *Kellwyn* (Dillwyn SS Co.).
1950: *Claus Boge* (J. Blumenthal, Hamburg).
1960: *Antonakis* (Cia. Nav. Viamar, Greece).
8.1968: Scrapped Split.

Empire Seaman 1,927 gt. Built: Schiffs–und Dockbauw. Flender, Lübeck, in 1922 as *Morea* for Deutsche Levant Line, Hamburg. 289 ft × 42 ft. Engines: T3cyl.
9.1939: Took refuge in Vigo, Spain, on outbreak of war.
10.2.1940: Sailed, to return to Germany.
12.2.1940: Sighted 500 miles off Portuguese coast, disguised as a Danish ship, by H.M.S *Hasty*. Scuttling attempts made, but thwarted by a naval boarding party. Vessel taken to U.K., actually joining a Channel convoy and arriving in Falmouth Roads. Renamed *Empire Seaman* (M.O.T.).
4.12.1940: Scuttled as a blockship in a Channel port, south coast of Britain.

Empire Sentinel 638 gt. Built: G. Seebeck A.G., Bremerhaven, in 1898 as *Phaedra* for Neptun Line, Bremen. 171 ft × 27 ft. Engines: T3cyl.
14.1.1940: Captured by Royal Navy in North Sea while on a voyage from Königsberg to Rotterdam. Renamed *Empire Sentinel* (M.O.T.).
1943: Requisitioned by Admiralty, renamed H.M.S. *Rampant* (a Wreck Dispersal ship).

12.1946: Returned to M.O.W.T., then sold.
1947: *Yiaghos* (Wizard Shipping Co., London).
1948: Arrested by Court Order for unpaid debts; reverted to 'Empire' name. Again sold, and:
1948: *Raymond Olivier* (De Malglave Shipping Co.).
1951: (Costa Rican Nav. Co., Honduras (Comp. Italiana Commerciale Maritime, Italy)).
1955: *Mariapaolina* (Costa Rican Nav. Co., (Framar SpA, Italy)).
1.1960: Scrapped Vado.

Empire Soldier 4,536 gt. Built: Lithgows Ltd., Port Glasgow, in 1928 as *Aelybryn*. 385 ft × 52 ft. Engines: T3cyl.
1937: *Konsul Hendrik Fisser* (Fisser & Van Doornum, Emden).
1939: *Empire Soldier* (M.O.T.).
16.9.1942: Sunk in collision in North Atlantic, 47.35N 51.44W (voyage: New York/Hull – grain).

At the start of World War II the *Konsul Hendrik Fisser* was on a voyage from Botwood, N.S., to Antwerp with woodpulp. After a call at Vigo, Spain, she sailed for Germany, flying the Norwegian flag and with Norwegian colours painted on her hull and hatches. On 22 November 1939, north of the Faroe Islands, she was sighted by H.M.S. *Calypso*, but the weather was too rough to launch lifeboats for a boarding party and too rough for the Germans to abandon ship. Under threat from the warship's guns, the freighter made her way into the lee of land, where she was captured next day by trawlers of the Northern Patrol.

Renamed *Empire Soldier* by the M.O.T., she was lost off St. John's, N.F., in 1942 after a collision, in convoy, with the tanker *F. J. Wolfe* (1932, 11,244 gt) – a vessel which was itself damaged, having been torpedoed six days before by the submarine *U.96*.

Empire Statesman 5,306 gt. Built: Soc. per Azioni Ansaldo, Sestri Ponente, Italy, in 1920 as *Ansaldo VIII*. 393 ft × 51 ft. Engines: Oil.
1925: *Ansaldo Ottavo* (Soc. Naz. di Navigazione, Italy).
1928: *Pellice* (Soc. Comm. de Navigazione, Genoa).
9.6.1940: Sailed from River Tyne, and:
10.6.1940: Captured at sea by Royal Navy; taken to Methil. Renamed *Empire Statesman* (M.O.T.).
11.12.1940: Sunk by submarine (*U.94*) torpedo in North Atlantic (voyage: Pepel/Middlesbrough – iron ore).

Empire Success 5,988 gt. Built: Vulkan Werke, Hamburg, in 1921 as *Hagen* for Hamburg America Line. 450 ft × 58 ft. Engines: T3cyl.
8.9.1939: Taken in prize at Durban by South African Navy; renamed *Ixia* (Government of South Africa).
30.9.1940: Damaged by aircraft bombs at Peterhead, Scotland. Repaired and renamed *Empire Success* (M.O.W.T.).

1.1948: Laid up at Liverpool with machinery and collision damage; considered not worthy of repair.
22.8.1948: Scuttled in Bay of Biscay with a cargo of gas bombs.

Empire Tamar 6,640 gt. Built: Workman, Clark & Co. Ltd., Belfast, in 1907 as *Kia Ora*. 463 ft × 56 ft. Engines: T6cyl.
1935: *Verbania* (Achille Lauro & Co., Naples).
10.6.1940: Detained at Port Said by Suez Canal authorities;
7.1940: Taken in prize at Haifa.
1941: *Empire Tamar* (M.O.W.T.).
6.1944: Sunk as a blockship at Gooseberry 5, Oustrieham, Normandy, during Allied invasion of France.

Empire Tana 6,275 gt. Built: Stabilimento Tecnico, Trieste, in 1923 as *Carso* for Lloyd Triestino. 419 ft × 54 ft. Engines: T3cyl.
14.2.1941: Scuttled at Kismayu, Italian Somaliland, when the port captured by British forces. Salved; renamed *Empire Tana* (M.O.W.T.).
9.2.1944: Hull plating and superstructure damaged in multiple collision, in fog, ten miles outside Casablanca, between this vessel and the Dutch steamers *Winsum* (1921, 3,224 gt) and *Jaarstroom* (1922, 2,480 gt), the British vessel *Shirrabank* (1940, 7,274 gt) and the Yugoslav ship *Dunav* (1912, 4,369 gt). The *Empire Tana* considered not worthy of permanent repair, and:
9.6.1944: Sunk as a blockship at Gooseberry 5, Oustrieham, Normandy.
1947: Wreck raised, and:
11.1947: Towed from Arromanches by tug *Zealandia* (ex *Empire Winnie*) for scrapping.
12.11.1947: Broke adrift from tug off Trevose Head, Cornwall; tow later reconnected; vessel towed to Strangford Lough, N. Ireland, for breaking up.

Empire Trooper 14,106 gt. Built: Vulkan Werke, Hamburg, in 1922 as *Cap Norte* for Hamburg Sud America Line. 500 ft × 64 ft. Engines: T6cyl.
1932: *Sierra Salvada* (Charter to Norddeutscher Lloyd).
1934: Reverted to original name and owners.
1940: *Empire Trooper* (M.O.T.).
1955: Scrapped Inverkeithing.

Cap Norte and her sistership *Antonio Delfino* (later renamed *Empire Halladale*, q.v.) were built for their owner's service to South America. They each had accommodation for 200 first-class and 1,400 second-class passengers and carried some 9,000 tons of cargo.

In 1932 the *Cap Norte* and her sister were renamed *Sierra Salvada* and *Sierra Nevada* respectively, for the period of a Norddeutscher Lloyd charter, but two years later reverted to their original names.

On the outbreak of war the *Cap Norte* was homeward bound from Pernambuco. Intending to reach her home waters, she disembarked her passengers at Lisbon and proceeded northward in a wide curve, into the Atlantic. Repainted for disguise, carrying the name *Ancona* and wearing the Swedish flag, she was north-west of the Faroe Islands on 9 October 1939 when she was sighted by H.M.S. *Belfast*. In extremely rough weather, the German captain of *Cap Norte*, to avoid loss of life, did not give the order to scuttle but surrendered his ship instead. Under control of a Royal Navy prize crew the ship headed for Scapa Flow – and a German plan to scuttle the ship when near a British port was thwarted.

The following month the *Cap Norte* was used to block an entrance at Scapa Flow, prior to completion of the boom and after the torpedoing and sinking of the battleship *Royal Oak* in the harbour.

In June 1940 the vessel was taken to the Tyne and converted to a troopship, with very austere outfitting, including hammocks for her passengers. She was renamed *Empire Trooper*, under M.O.T. jurisdiction.

On 25 December 1940 the vessel was hit by shells from the German cruiser *Admiral Hipper* when in convoy in the Atlantic, but the raider was driven off by H.M.S. *Berwick*.

After the war, in 1946, the *Empire Trooper* was refitted to the standard of post-war requirements. In 1950 another refit, this time at Falmouth, reduced her accommodation from 1,521 persons to 924 and recreation and leisure rooms were added.

On 9 April 1955 she arrived at Southampton from Hong Kong on her last trooping voyage, and was sold to shipbreakers. Taken in tow, she broke adrift on 17 May when her towing tugs collided, but she was able to anchor off the South Goodwin Light Vessel, Straits of Dover. The tow later continued, but a week later she grounded on a sandbank near the shipbreaker's yard and was not refloated until four weeks later. At the end of September 1955 she was set afire by acetylene burners at the 'breaker's yard; three levels of deck were affected, with large amounts of valuable timber, decking, panelling and fittings being destroyed. The fire was extinguished and breaking up resumed.

Empire Trophy (tanker) 5,211 gt. Built: Cantiere Navali Riuniti, Palermo, in 1916 as *Giove* (Italian Navy tanker). 399 ft × 51 ft. Engines: T6cyl.
8.4.1941: Scuttled at Massowah, Eritrea, when port captured by British forces.
20.6.1941: Salved; taken in prize; repaired, and:
1942: *Empire Trophy* (M.O.W.T.).
2.9.1944: Arrived Bombay from Persian Gulf, with boiler defects: Laid up.
3.1947: Beached and stripped of usable gear prior to final scrapping, locally.

Empire Tugela 6,181 gt. Built: J. C. Tecklenborg A.G., Wesermunde, in 1921 as *Wartenfels* for Hansa Line, Bremen. 430 ft × 56 ft. Engines: T3cyl.
9.1939: In Red Sea: took refuge in Italian East African port. Later proceeded to Madagascar.
4.5.1942: Captured in drydock at Diego Suarez by Allied forces. Damaged, though most of the explosive scuttling charges set by her crew failed to detonate.

Salved by Royal Navy and renamed *Empire Tugela* (M.O.W.T.).
1947: *Chitpur* (Oceanic Navigation Co., Calcutta).
1948: *Hwah Sung* (Hwah Sung SS Co., Shanghai).
1950: *Navidad* (Wallem & Co., Panama).
1952: (Purple Star Shipping Co., China).
1953: *Hwah Sung* (Hwah Sung SS Co., Shanghai).
1960: Name deleted from ship registers, but:
1983: Reported as *Zhan Dou 75* (Government of People's Republic of China).

Note: A vessel named *Zhan Dou 75*, said to have been built in or about 1921 for the Hansa Line, was listed (but with many details missing) in the 1983 Chinese Ship Register, and in the following year was re-entered in the British Register as the ex-*Wartenfels*. However, from the reports of visual sightings in Shanghai it is likely that the *Zhan Dou 75* is the ex-*Liebenfels* (see *Empire Nile*) and that the *Wartenfels* (above) – a sistership to *Liebenfels* – now carries the (unlisted) name of *Zhan Dou 46*, a vessel bearing this name (and obviously an ex-Hansa ship) also being sighted in Shanghai.

Empire Union 5,952 gt. Built: Stabilimento Tecnico, Trieste, in 1924 as *Salvore*. 406 ft × 54 ft.
Engines: T3cyl.
1937: *Sistiana* (Lloyd Triestino, Trieste).
10.6.1940: Taken in prize in Table Bay by South African Navy; renamed *Myrica* (Government of South Africa).
1941: *Empire Union* (M.O.W.T.).
26.12.1942: Sunk by submarine (*U.356*) torpedo off south-west Ireland, 47.30N 24.30W, in convoy ONS 154.

Empire Unity 6,386 gt. Built: A. G. Weser, Bremen, in 1927 as *Biscaya* for J. T. Essberger, Hamburg. 414 ft × 55 ft. Engines: Oil.
10.1939: Sailed from Las Palmas in an attempt to return to Germany.
19.10.1939: Captured north of Iceland by H.M.S. *Scotstoun*; taken to Leith. Renamed *Empire Unity* (M.O.T.).
4.5.1945: Damaged by torpedoes from submarine (*U.979*) southwest of Iceland, 64.23N 22.37W, on a voyage from Hvalfjordjordur to U.K. Abandoned; reboarded; proceeded to Hvitanes thence Reykjavik for temporary repairs.
20.6.1945: Towed to Methil, then Leith: repaired.
1947: *Stordale* (Storship Transports Ltd., London).
1951: *Mageolia* (T. Pappadrinitriou, Greece).
9.10.1963: Arrived Cerigo, near Piraeus, in tow, for use as a depot ship.
12.4.1966: Arrived in tow at Burriana, Spain, for breaking up.

Empire Volunteer 5,319 gt. Built: Harbour Marine Ltd., Victoria, B.C., in 1921 as *Canadian Traveller*. 400 ft × 52 ft. Engines: T3cyl.

1932: *Procida* (Achille Lauro & Co., Naples).
10.6.1940: Taken in prize at Cardiff. Renamed *Empire Volunteer* (M.O.T.).
15.9.1940: Sunk by submarine (*U.48*) torpedo in North Atlantic, south west of Rockall, 56.43N 15.17W, in convoy SC 3.

Empire Warrior 1,306 gt. Built: Hamburg-Elbe Schiffs., Hamburg, in 1921 as *Bianca*. 245 ft × 36 ft. Engines: T3cyl.
1927: *Elbe* (A. Kirsten, Hamburg.)
1932: Renamed *Bianca*.
20.10.1939: Captured in North Sea by H.M.S. *Transylvania* when on a voyage Rotterdam to Lisbon. Taken to Kirkwall, then Leith.
1940: *Empire Warrior* (M.O.T.).
19.6.1941: Damaged by aircraft bombs off Villa Real, Gulf of Cadiz (voyage: Newcastle/Portugal – coal). Crew rescued by a Portuguese destroyer and attempts made by a trawler to tow the vessel to shallow water, but it broke adrift and sank.

Empire Yukon 7,651 gt. Built: Stabilimento Tecnico, Trieste, in 1921 as *Duchessa D'Aosta* for Lloyd Triestino, Trieste. 451 ft × 57 ft. Engines: T3cyl.

14.1.1942: Found in difficulties off Fernando Po, Guinea, West Africa, after sailing from the port following refuge there. Captured by the Royal Navy; sent to U.K. for discharge, with same name but under British flag.
13.7.1942: Caught fire during discharge at Greenock, all holds extensively damaged; vessel flooded and settled to bottom of the dock.
22.7.1942: Refloated; repaired, and:
1943: *Empire Yukon* (M.O.W.T.).
1946: (Government of Canada).
1947: *Petconnie* (Petrinovic & Co., London).
1951: *Liu O* (C.O.C. Soc. per Azioni, Italy).
11.1952: Scrapped Spezia.

Note: The capture of the *Duchessa D'Aosta* in 1942 was directly due to German propaganda. A German broadcast stated that Allied forces had 'outraged neutrality' by sending a 'cutting out' expedition against Axis ships sheltering in Fernando Po. This the Admiralty denied, but assuming that the story had an ulterior motive, sent a force to investigate. They found the Italian vessel wallowing at sea, hampered by machinery trouble.

Section 2   Period 1945 –

Empire Alde 3,264 gt. Built: Bremer Vulkan Schiffs- und Masch., Vegesack, in 1934 as *Pelikan* for F. Laeisz, Hamburg. 358 ft × 45 ft. Engines: Oil.
1940: Requisitioned by German Navy.
5.1945: Taken in prize at Brunsbüttel.
1946: *Empire Alde* (M.O.W.T.).
1946: *Pelikan* (Elders & Fyffes Ltd.).
1947: Rebuilt; renamed *Pacuare*.
1959: Scrapped Troon.

Empire Annan 2,385 gt. Built: F. Schichau GmbH., Danzig, in 1935 as *Masuren* for Kohlen-Import & Poseidon Co., Königsberg. 281 ft × 44 ft. Engines: C4cyl.
5.1945: Taken in prize at Copenhagen. Renamed *Empire Annan*, (M.O.W.T.).
1947: Allocated to U.S.A. (U.S.M.C.).
1948: (Fanmaur Shipping & Trading Co., New York).
1950: *Thomas N. Epiphaniades* (T. N. Epiphaniades, Greece).
1952: *Helga Boge* (J. Blumenthal, Hamburg).

1960: *Fuhlsbuttel* (Koehn & Bohlmann Reederei, Hamburg).
1964: Scrapped Bremerhaven.

Empire Ardle (Hansa 'B' type) 2,798 gt. Built: Flensburger Schiff-Gesellschaft in 1945 as *Sasbeck* for German account. 344 ft × 51 ft. Engines: C4cyl.
5.1945: Taken in prize, incomplete, at Lübeck.
1946: Completed and renamed *Empire Ardle* (M.O.W.T.).
1947: *Lewis Hamilton* (Rodney SS Co., London).
1950: *Indus* (C. H. Abrahamsen, Stockholm).
1968: (C. Hultstrom, Stockholm).
1968: *Falcon* (Seabird Nav. Inc., Liberia).
1969: *Sea Falcon* (Lilly Nav. Corp., Panama).
1970: (Seabird Nav. Inc., Liberia).
7.1971: Scrapped Aviles.

Empire Ayr 5,064 gt. Built: Oresunds Varvet, Landskrona, in 1943 as *Eberhart Essberger* for J. T. Essberger, Hamburg. 439 ft × 57 ft. Engines: Oil.

5.1945: Taken in prize at Kiel. Renamed *Empire Ayr* (M.O.W.T.).
1946: Allocated to U.S.S.R., renamed *Dimitri Donskoy*.
1974: Scrapped U.S.S.R.

Empire Blackwater 2,917 gt. Built: Flensburger Schiff-Gesellschaft in 1939 as *Pompeji* for German account. 340 ft × 53 ft. Engines: T3cyl.
5.1945: Taken in prize at Kiel. Renamed *Empire Blackwater*, (M.O.W.T.).
1946: Allocated to U.S.A. (U.S.M.C.).
1947: (Seatrade Corp., New York).
1949: *Krusaa* (Basse & Co., Copenhagen).
1960: *Krucia* (Nils Berg, Finland).
1969: *Helvi* (H. Hayrynen O/Y, Finland).
1971: *Eastern Faith* (Nan Sing Nav. Co., Taiwan).
12.1975: Scrapped Kaohsiung.

Empire Calder 2,646 gt. Built: Stettiner Oderwerke A.G., Stettin, in 1923 as *Stettin*. 329 ft × 56 ft. Engines: T3cyl.
1935: *Akka* (Deutsche Levant Line, Hamburg).
5.1945: Taken in prize at Flensburg. Renamed *Empire Calder* (M.O.W.T.).
1947: *Isgo* (Near East Shipping Co., London).
1950: *Erich* (Karl Gross, Bremen).
1960: *Pantera* (Palomba & Salvatori, Italy).
10.1970: Scrapped Italy.

Empire Camel 2,719 gt. Built: Deutsche Werft, Hamburg, in 1929 as *Ceuta* for Oldenburg-Portuguese Line. 283 ft × 46 ft. Engines: C4cyl.
28.3.1943: Sunk by Allied aircraft bombs at Rotterdam. Raised and repaired.
5.1945: Taken in prize at Kiel. Renamed *Empire Camel* (M.O.W.T.).
1946: Allocated to Denmark, renamed *Rinkenaes* (Government of Denmark).
1947: *Oyrnafjell* (Foroya Logting, Faroes).
1956: *Safi* (Oldenburg-Portuguese Line, Hamburg).
1.1960: Scrapped Hamburg.

Empire Carron 5,372 gt. Built: Norderwerft A.G., Hamburg, in 1923 as *Claus Rickmers* for Rickmers Reederei, Hamburg. 402 ft × 53 ft. Engines: T3cyl.
9.1.1945: Damaged by Allied air attack off Lervik, Stord, Norway. Beached, then salved, and:
25.1.1945: Towed to Bergen.
5.1945: Taken in prize at Bergen. Repaired, and:
1947: *Empire Carron* (M.O.T.).
1947: *Andrian* (S. G. Embiricos Ltd., London).
1949: *San Nicolas* (Cia. de Nav. Yavisa, Panama).
12.1964: Scrapped Spezia.

Empire Catcher (Whale catcher) 533 gt. Built: Akers Mek. Verk., Oslo, in 1942 for German account. 159 ft × 29 ft. Engines: T3cyl.

1942: Requisitioned by German Navy on completion by builders, renamed *Flandern*.
1945: Recovered by Norway, renamed *Suderoy VII* (Government of Norway).
1946: Allocated to Britain; renamed *Empire Catcher* (M.O.T.).
1948: *R. K. Fraay* (Union Whaling Co. Ltd., Durban).
1957: *Toshi Maru No. 11* (Taiyo Gyogyo K.K., Japan).
1959: *Daishin Maru No. 2* (Hokuyo Suisan K.K., Japan).
8.1964: Scrapped Onomichi, Japan.

Empire Catcher II (Whale catcher) 533 gt. Built: Akers Mek. Verk., Oslo, in 1942 for German account. 159 ft × 29 ft. Engines: T3cyl.
1942: Requisitioned by German Navy on completion by builders, renamed *Helgoland*.
1945: Recovered by Norway, renamed *Nor IV* (Government of Norway).
1946: Allocated to Britain, renamed *Empire Catcher II* (M.O.T.).
1948: *R. L. Goulding* (Union Whaling Co. Ltd., Durban).
1957: *Toshi Maru No. 8* (Taiyo Gyogyo K.K., Japan).
1959: *Daishin Maru No. 1* (Hokuyo Suisan K.K., Japan).
1963: (Nippon Reizo K.K., Japan).
1967: (Sanwa Sempaku K.K., Japan).
1980: Name removed from ship registers, vessel believed scrapped.

Empire Chelmer 2,299 gt. Built: Burntisland Shipbuilding Co. Ltd., in 1920 as *Sydney Lasry*. 301 ft × 44 ft. Engines: T3cyl.
1935: *Ariege* (Comp. Gen. Transatlantique, France).
1938: *Cap Tafelneh* (Soc. Anon. de Gerance D'Armement, France).
6.1940: Sunk by air attack at Dunkirk. Later salved by Germans; renamed *Carl Arp*.
5.1945: Taken in prize at Hamburg. Renamed *Empire Chelmer*, (M.O.W.T.).
1946: Returned to French owners, name reverted to *Cap Tafelneh*.
1950: *Kandilli* (Mustafa Nuri Andak, Turkey).
1957: *Kahraman Dogan* (Nejat Dogan & Co., Turkey).
1975: Reported scrapped in Turkey in 1972.

Empire Cherwell 2,193 gt. Built: Neptun A.G., Rostock, in 1937 as *Messina* for R. M. Sloman Jr., Hamburg. 303 ft × 44 ft. Engines: C4cyl.
1940: Requisitioned by German Navy.
5.1945: Taken in prize at Travemunde. Renamed *Empire Cherwell* (M.O.W.T.).
1947: Allocated to U.S.S.R., renamed *Polus*.

1961: Name removed from ship registers: no further trace.

Empire Chlorine (liquid chlorine carrier) 307 gt.
Built: D. W. Kremer Sohn, Elmshorn, in 1939 as *Trave* for Lübeck-Wyberger Damps. Gesellschaft, Lübeck. 130 ft × 25 ft. Engines: Oil.
5.1945: Found damaged at Flensburg; taken in prize. Towed to Methil.
10.1945: (M.O.W.T.), but remained laid up until 1952.
1952: Repairs finally completed; converted from dry cargo and fitted with portable tanks for the carriage of corrosive acids. Renamed *Empire Chlorine* (M.O.T.).
1953: Returned to German Government, thence reverted to original name and owners.
1954: *Hybo* (A/S Klorsalg, Norway).
1954: Renamed *Hyborg*.
1954: Renamed *Uniklor*.
1963: (New oil engine).
1978: *Frisnes* (F. Skeie, Norway).

Empire Colne (Hansa 'A' type) 1,923 gt.
Built: Stettiner Vulkan Werft A.G., Stettin, in 1944 as *Peter Rickmers* for Rickmers Reederei, Hamburg. 288 ft × 44 ft. Engines: C4cyl.
5.1945: Taken in prize, incomplete, at builder's yard. Completed at Lubeck and renamed *Empire Colne* (M.O.W.T.).
1947: *Katong* (Straits SS Co. Ltd., Singapore).
1971: *Greengate* (Greenland Ocean Lines, Singapore).
1972: *Ever Glory* (Lam Kok Shipping Co., Singapore).
6.1974: Scrapped China.

Empire Conavon 1,570 gt. Built: Nylands Verk., Oslo, in 1922 as *Minna*. 255 ft × 39 ft. Engines: T3cyl.
1935: *Britt* (H. Jeansson, Stockholm (Kalmar Rederi)).
29.9.1939: Captured in North Sea by German Navy; condemned in prize (voyage: Ulfvik/Aberdeen – woodpulp).
1939–1944: (German Government).
1944: *Leba* (Leth & Co., Hamburg).
5.1945: Taken in prize at Lübeck; renamed *Empire Conavon*, (M.O.W.T.).
1947: *Baltkon* (J. Carlbom & Co. Ltd., Hull).
1959: Scrapped Dunston-on-Tyne.

Empire Concave 1,126 gt. Built: Schiffbau-Ges. Unterweser A.G., Bremen, in 1939 as *Luna* for Neptun Line, Bremen. 235 ft × 35 ft. Engines: Oil.
1940: Requisitioned by German Navy.
5.1945: Taken in prize at Eckernfjord. Renamed *Empire Concave*, (M.O.W.T.).

1946: Allocated to Norway, renamed *Galtnes* (Government of Norway).
1947: *Ila* (Per T. Lykke, Norway).
1952: *Sao Leopoldo* (L. Figueiredo Nav. Ltd., Brazil).
1965: *Mironave* (Casimiro Filho Industria Comercio, Brazil).
1982: (Petrosul, Brazil).

Empire Concern 1,587 gt. Built: Flensburger Schiff-Gesellschaft, in 1927 as *Marquardt Petersen*. 263 ft × 40 ft. Engines: T3cyl.
1935: *Sexta* (Flensburger Damps. Ges. von 1869, Germany).
1938: *Annelis Christophersen* (H. W. Christophersen, Flensburg).
5.1945: Taken in prize at Flensburg. Renamed *Empire Concern* (M.O.W.T.).
1946: Allocated to Norway; renamed *Laksnes* (Government of Norway).
27.11.1946: Grounded at Ronglevaer, near Feje, Norway. Broke in two and sank (voyage: Brevik/Namsos – cement).

Empire Concerto 1,569 gt. Built: Lübecker Maschinenbau-Gesellschaft, in 1922 as *Ingrid Horn*. 273 ft × 38 ft. Engines: T3cyl.
1926: *Margret* (A/S D/S Thorunn, Norway).
1928: *Nelly* (J. Lauritzen, Denmark).
1936: *Corona* (Finska Line, Helsinki).
10.1944: Reported at Holtenau (under Finnish flag).
3.1945: Reported as 'having been unable to escape from a German-controlled port'. Placed under German flag.
5.1945: Taken in prize at Kiel. Renamed *Empire Concerto* (M.O.W.T.).
1946: Returned to Finnish owners and name.
1960: Scrapped Tyko Brok, Finland.

Empire Concession 1,900 gt. Built: Neptun A.G., Rostock, in 1927 as *Ernst Brockelmann* for Erich Ahrens, Rostock. 267 ft × 42 ft. Engines: T3cyl.
5.1945: Taken in prize at Flensburg. Renamed *Empire Concession* (M.O.W.T.).
1947: *Brazen Head* (Blandy Bros. & Co., London).
1950: *Enso* (Baltic Chartering A/B, Finland).
1959: *Hakuni* (E. Fagerstrom O/Y, Finland).
1966: *Isla Del Rey* (Mendez Moreno, Panama).
6.1966: Scrapped Alicante, Spain.

Empire Conclyde 1,409 gt. Built: A. G. Weser, Bremen, in 1924 as *Klio* for Neptun Line, Bremen. 241 ft × 39 ft. Engines: T3cyl.
5.1945: Taken in prize at Rendsburg. Renamed *Empire Conclyde* (M.O.W.T.).
1946: Allocated to U.S.S.R., renamed *Shota Rustavelli*.
No further trace.

Empire Concord (Hansa 'A' type) 1,923 gt.
Built: Deutsche Werft, Hamburg, in 1944 as *Deike
Rickmers* for Rickmers Reederei, Hamburg.
282 ft × 44 ft. Engines: C4cyl.
5.1945: Taken in prize at Kiel. Renamed *Empire
Concord* (M.O.W.T.).
1946: Allocated to U.S.S.R., renamed *Azov*.
3.1973: Scrapped Kure.

(Intended to be) *Empire Concourse* 1,538 gt.
Built: Neptun A.G., Rostock, in 1927 as *Walter L.
M. Russ* for Ernst Russ, Hamburg. 247 ft × 40 ft.
Engines: T3cyl.
5.1945: Taken in prize at Schleswig. To be renamed
Empire Concourse (M.O.W.T.), but:
15.7.1945: Ashore and wrecked on Grassholm Island,
Bristol Channel, still with German name but under
British flag (voyage: Kiel and Methil/Cardiff –
ballast).

Empire Concrete 1,696 gt. Built: Neptun A.G.,
Rostock, in 1927 as *Theresia L. M. Russ* for Ernst
Russ, Hamburg. 258 ft × 42 ft. Engines: T3cyl.
5.1945: Taken in prize at Copenhagen. Renamed
Empire Concrete (M.O.W.T.).
1946: Allocated to Holland, renamed *Velsen*
(Government of Netherlands).
1947: *Cronenburgh* (Wm. H. Muller & Co. N.V.,
Holland).
1955: *Astor* (U. Gennari & Co., Italy (Cia. de Nav.
Cargo Carriers, Panama)).
15.2.1970: Boiler damage on voyage Algiers to Oran.
Repairs uneconomic; sold.
4.1970: Scrapped Spezia.

Empire Condart 310 gt. Built: Lidingo Nya Varv. &
Vaerkstader, Sweden, in 1943 as *Glucksburg* for
German account. 144 ft × 26 ft. Engines: Oil.
1944: Renamed *Stadt Glucksburg*.
5.1945: Taken in prize at Hamburg. Renamed *Empire
Condart* (M.O.W.T.).
1947: *Fredor* (Plym Shipping Co., Plymouth).
1952: (Lengthened to 172 ft, 423 gt).
1957: *Seashell* (Instone Lines Ltd., London).
12.1968: Scrapped Tamise, Belgium.

Empire Condee 215 gt. Built: Van Diepen N.V.
Scheeps. Gebr., Waterhuizen, in 1938 as *Herman
Litmeyer* for Maria Litmeyer, Haren-Ems, Germany.
123 ft × 23 ft. Engines: Oil.
5.1945: Taken in prize at Nyborg, Denmark.
Renamed *Empire Condee* (M.O.W.T.).
1947: *Condee* (Plym Shipping Co., Plymouth).
1950: *Aisne* (Wm. H. Muller & Co. (London) Ltd.).

1960: *Clary* (Channel Shipping Ltd., Jersey).
1976: *Marie Elizabeth* (M. Garzon, Tangier).
20.2.1976: Sustained severe fire damage at Barcelona.
Abandoned; Total loss.

Empire Conderton 1,558 gt. Built: Blyth SB & DD
Co. Ltd., in 1912 as *Thyra Menier*. 240 ft × 36 ft.
Engines: T3cyl.
1918: *Luis Pidal* (F. Lecoeuvre, Belgium).
1925: *Bellini* (Puglisi & Tomasini, Italy).
1928: *Bollan* (August Bolten, Germany).
1936: *Lina Fisser* (Fisser & Van Doornum, Emden).
5.1945: Taken in prize at Kiel. Renamed *Empire
Conderton* (M.O.W.T.).
1947: *Marchmont* (J. P. Hadoulis Ltd., London).
1952: *Irene M* (A. Moschakis Ltd., London).
1955: (Tampa Shipping Ltd., Nova Scotia).
1957: (Marine Industries Ltd., Montreal).
10.1957: Scrapped Sorel, Canada.

Empire Condicote 1,000 gt. Built: Union Giesserei,
Königsberg, in 1923 as *Pickhuben* for H. M.
Gehrckens, Hamburg. 231 ft × 36 ft. Engines: T3cyl.
5.1945: Taken in prize at Lübeck. Renamed *Empire
Condicote*, (M.O.W.T.).
1946: Allocated to Norway, renamed *Grimsnes*
(Government of Norway).
1947: *Tungenes* (Stavanger SS Co., Norway).
6.1961: Scrapped Zalzate, Belgium.

Empire Condor 998 gt. Built: Nordseewerke, Emden,
in 1926 as *Amrum*. 220 ft × 35 ft. Engines: T3cyl.
1931: *Quersee* (W. Schuchmann, Bremerhaven).
5.1945: Taken in prize at Brünsbüttel. Renamed
Empire Condor (M.O.W.T.).
1947: *Mediterranean Trader* (Akritas Nav. Co.,
London).
1949: *Maharashmi* (South East Asia Shipping Co.,
Bombay).
10.6.1951: Ashore on rocks near Bhatkal Fort Light,
India. Abandoned; broke in three; submerged. Total
loss (voyage: Cochin/Bombay – rubber).

Empire Condorrat 998 gt. Built: Stettiner Oderwerke
A.G., in 1921 as *Gunther Russ* for Ernst Russ,
Hamburg. 211 ft × 34 ft. Engines: T3cyl.
5.1945: Taken in prize; renamed *Empire Condorrat*
(M.O.W.T.).
1947: *Kenton* (Whitehaven Shipping Co.).
1950: Purchased by original owners, reverted to
original name.
1957: Scrapped Hamburg.

Empire Condover 1,883 gt. Built: Ostseewerft A.G.,
Stettin, in 1926 as *Siegmund*. 267 ft × 41 ft.
Engines: C4cyl.

1929: *Thielbek* (Knohr & Burchard, Germany).
1939: *Ingrid Traber* (Traber & Co., Hamburg).
5.1945: Taken in prize in a German port; renamed
Empire Condover (M.O.W.T.).
1946: Allocated to Norway, renamed *Fornes*
(Government of Norway).
1948: *I. P. Suhr* (Dansk Kulkompagnie, Denmark).
1.12.1950: Capsized and sank five miles off
Sandhammaren, Sweden (voyage: Gdynia/Aarhus –
coal).
1952: Wreck dispersed with explosives; remains
salved for scrap.

Empire Conexe 921 gt. Built: F. Schichau GmbH,
Elbing, in 1912 as *Badenia* for A. Kirsten, Hamburg.
221 ft × 34 ft. Engines: T6cyl.
1939: Renamed *Titania*.
5.1945: Taken in prize at Rendsburg.
1946: Renamed *Empire Conexe* (M.O.W.T.).
1947: *Ringdove* (General Steam Nav. Co. Ltd.).
1950: Scrapped Bo'ness.

Empire Confal 960 gt. Built: Nuscke & Co., Stettin,
in 1912 as *Borussia* for A. Kirsten, Hamburg.
221 ft × 34 ft. Engines: T6cyl.
1939: Renamed *Timandra*.
5.1945: Taken in prize at Hamburg.
1946: *Empire Confal* (M.O.W.T.).
1947: *Woodwren* (General Steam Nav. Co. Ltd.).
1953: *Artemis* (cut down to deck level, used as a coal
hulk at Gravesend, River Thames).
10.1960: Scrapped Queenborough, Kent.

Empire Confederation 1,199 gt. Built: Nobiskrug
Werft GmbH, Rendsburg, in 1921 as *Elbe* for Bugsier
Reederei, Hamburg. 250 ft × 37 ft. Engines: T3cyl.
5.1945: Taken in prize at Copenhagen. Renamed
Empire Confederation (M.O.W.T.).
1946: Allocated to U.S.S.R., renamed *Jose Dias*.
1966: Scrapped U.S.S.R.

Empire Conference 1,991 gt. Built: Gavle Varv. A.B.,
Gavle, Sweden, in 1943 as *Aletta Noot* for F. Haniel
& Co., Duisburg. 257 ft × 41 ft. Engines: C4cyl.
5.1945: Taken in prize at Flensburg. Renamed *Empire
Conference* (M.O.W.T.).
1946: *Narva* (Glen & Co., Glasgow).
22.12.1957: Foundered in North Sea, 57.28N 3.00E,
150 miles south-west of Lindesnes, Norway, while
going to aid of *Bosworth* (1946, 865 gt) which was
hove-to in a gale with a severe list. The *Narva* was
lost with all hands (voyage: Sweden/Grangemouth –
woodpulp); the *Bosworth* was towed to Aberdeen by
a trawler.

Empire Conforth 854 gt. Built: Howaldtswerke, Kiel,
in 1922 as *Erna*. 195 ft × 33 ft. Engines: T3cyl.

1930: (Ernst Russ, Hamburg).
5.1945: Taken in prize at Kristiansand, Norway.
1946: *Empire Conforth* (M.O.W.T.).
1947: *Troodos* (Cyprus Ship Management Co.,
Cyprus).
1952: *Burica* (Cia. Maritima Punta Burica S.A., Costa
Rica).
1953: *Dimitris* (Comp. Santa Angelica, Costa Rica).
1955: *Cedar* (Metropolitan Agencies Ltd., Panama).
1958: Scrapped Hong Kong.

Empire Congerstone 987 gt. Built: Schiffbau-Ges.
Unterweser A.G., Bremen, in 1920 as *Faust*.
216 ft × 35 ft. Engines: T3cyl.
1926: *Nordmark* (R. Bornhofen, Germany).
1936: Renamed *Angeln*.
1944: *Ermland* (P. Arlt & Co., Germany).
5.1945: Taken in prize at Lübeck. Renamed *Empire
Congerstone* (M.O.W.T.).
1947: *Oakley* (Oakley SS Co., London).
1949: (Goodwin SS Co., London).
1950: (Anthony & Bainbridge Ltd.).
1953: *Lucy* (Nav. de Transportes San José, Costa
Rica).
1960: Scrapped Vado.

Empire Congham 1,499 gt. Built: Helsingors Mask.,
Elsinore, Denmark, in 1899 as *Soderhamn* for H. M.
Gehrckens, Hamburg. 241 ft × 34 ft. Engines: T3cyl.
5.1945: Taken in prize at Kiel. Renamed *Empire
Congham* (M.O.W.T.).
1947: Reverted to original owners and name.
1958: Scrapped Hamburg.

Empire Congleton 1,027 gt. Built: Stettiner
Oderwerke A.G., in 1937 as *Saar* for R. C. Gribel,
Stettin. 209 ft × 32 ft. Engines: C4cyl.
5.1945: Taken in prize at Kolding, Denmark.
Renamed *Empire Congleton* (M.O.W.T.).
1946: Allocated to U.S.S.R., renamed *Donetz*.
No further trace.

Empire Congo 1,059 gt. Built: Nuscke & Co., Stettin,
in 1923 as *Rhenania*. 220 ft × 35 ft. Engines: T3cyl.
1924: *Martha Halm* (E. Halm & Co., Germany).
1926: *Bore VII* (A/B Bore, Finland).
1937: *Gotaalv* (August Bolten, Germany).
1938: *Bernhard Schulte* (Schulte & Bruns, Emden).
3.3.1941: Reported sunk off Lofoten Islands,
Norway. Later salved and repaired.
5.1945: Taken in prize at Flensburg. Renamed *Empire
Congo* (M.O.W.T.).
1947: *Coquetside* (Anthony & Bainbridge Ltd.).
1951: *Deneb* (C. Cosulich, Sicily).
1958: (Nautica SpA, Sardinia).
10.1966: Scrapped Spezia.

Empire Congress 1,442 gt. Built: Deutsche Werft, Hamburg, in 1922 as *Arcadia*. 235 ft × 37 ft. Engines: C4cyl.
1934: *Elbing* (Kohlen-Import und Poseidon Schiffs, Königsberg).
5.1945: Taken in prize in River Elbe. Renamed *Empire Congress* (M.O.W.T.).
1946: Allocated to Norway, renamed *Brunes* (Government of Norway).
1947: *Skuld* (R. Mithassel, Norway).
1948: *Ringas* (Birger Ekerholt, Norway).
1958: *Los Mayas* (C. T. Trapezountios, Liberia).
1959: Renamed *Francisco Morazan*.
29.11.1960: Aground on South Manitou Island, Lake Michigan. Listed and abandoned.
8.12.1960: Salvage commenced but later suspended due to ship being swept by high seas and becoming flooded. Constructive total loss
(voyage: Chicago/Hamburg – general).

Empire Congreve 250 gt. Built: Schulte & Bruns, Emden, in 1939 as *Klaus Wilhelm* for own account. 127 ft × 25 ft. Engines: Oil.
5.1945: Taken in prize in Channel Islands. Renamed *Empire Congreve* (M.O.W.T.).
1946: Allocated to U.S.S.R., renamed *Koida*.
No further trace.

Empire Conifer 1,279 gt. Built: Nordseewerke, Emden, in 1935 as *Adrian* for Ernst Komrowski, Hamburg. 234 ft × 36 ft. Engines: Oil.
5.1945: Taken in prize at Copenhagen. Renamed *Empire Conifer* (M.O.W.T.) Whilst still in Prize Court vessel chartered to Australian Government at nominal sum of 'one penny per year'.
1946: Prize Court awarded the vessel to Australia as its share of German shipping reparations, this being 0.19 per cent of the total available.
12.1946: Delivered at Fremantle (Australian Government, Department of Shipping & Transport).
1947: Refitted and re-equipped at Sydney, renamed *Nyora*, (Australian Shipping Board).
1953: (J. Burke Ltd., Australia).
1963: (Robin & Co., Panama). Resold, and:
1963: *Selat Singkep* (Kie Hock Shipping Co., Singapore).
1964: *Molopo* (Cia. de Nav. Gatun S.A., Panama).
1964: Renamed *Anban*.
1965: *Basongo* (Cia. Nav. Thompson S.A., Panama).
1966: Renamed *Medduno*.
1969: Renamed *Mesawa*.
1976: *Forevergreen* (Uni-Ocean Lines, Singapore).
1977: Renamed *Majullah*. Arrested by Court Order in Malaya. Auctioned at Kuala Lumpur; sold, and:
1978: *Jayawang* (Haw Ben Hock, Singapore).
23.7.1978: Sank near Bangkok (voyage: Bangkok/Philippines – gypsum).

11.1979: Raised, moved to an anchorage nearer Bangkok; Sank again.

Empire Coningsby 1,486 gt. Built: Lübecker Maschinenbau Ges. in 1938 as *Adler* for Argo Line, Bremen. 245 ft × 39 ft. Engines: C4cyl.
1939: Requisitioned by German Navy.
5.1945: Taken in prize at Vordingborg, Denmark. Renamed *Empire Coningsby* (M.O.W.T.).
1946: Allocated to Holland, renamed *Margeca* (Government of Netherlands).
1947: *Wickenburgh* (Wm. H. Muller & Co., Rotterdam).
1963: *Nissos Thassos* (F. C. Georgopulos, Greece).
1970: *Savilco* (Scand–Baltic–Med. Shipping Co., Greece).
1978: (Pythagoras Cia. Nav., Panama).
6.1984: Scrapped Piraeus.

Empire Conington 1,289 gt. Built: F. Krupp A.G., Kiel, in 1920 as *Orlanda*. 238 ft × 37 ft. Engines: T3cyl.
1927: (Argo Line, Bremen).
5.1945: Taken in prize at Hamburg. Renamed *Empire Conington* (M.O.W.T.).
1946: Transferred to Government of Newfoundland, Railways & Steamships Dept.
1949: *Alabe* (Soc. Anon. Mar. et Commerciale, Panama).
1958: Scrapped Sunderland.

Empire Conisborough 1,237 gt. Built: Lübecker Flenderwerke A.G., in 1937 as *Marie Fisser* for Fisser & Van Doornum, Emden. 225 ft × 35 ft. Engines: C4cyl.
5.1945: Taken in prize, in damaged condition, at Emden. Renamed *Empire Conisborough* (M.O.W.T.).
1946: Allocated to U.S.S.R., renamed *Stepan Shaumian*.
No further trace.

Empire Coniston 1,878 gt. Built: A. G. Weser, Bremen, in 1925 as *Sorrento*. 284 ft × 42 ft. Engines: Oil.
1928: *Bessel* (Neptun Line, Bremen).
5.1945: Surrendered to Britain at Vigo, Spain, having put into this neutral port in 1941.
8.1945: Sailed to U.K., renamed *Empire Coniston* (M.O.W.T.).
1946: (Temporarily transferred to Government of Denmark).
1947: Allocated to Denmark; sold; renamed *Birgitte Skou*, (Ove Skou, Denmark).
1959: *N. Martini* (M. Martini, Italy).
1961: Renamed *Nicolo Martini*.

24.4.1972: Grounded in vicinity of Portoscuso, fifty miles from Cagliari, Sardinia (voyage: Carloforte/Genoa – salt). Refloated, but constructive total loss.
12.1972: Sold, and:
10.1973: Scrapped Vado.

Empire Conlea 261 gt. Built: Nobiskrug Werft GmbH, Rendsburg, in 1939 as *Gunther Hartmann* for German account. 129 ft × 23 ft. Engines: Oil.
1945: Taken in prize; renamed *Empire Conlea* (M.O.W.T.).
1950: *Conlea* (Jeppesen, Heaton Ltd., London).
10.2.1956: Forehatch stove in during heavy weather; flooded and sank fifteen miles from Corbiere, Jersey (voyage: Southampton/St. Malo – pitch).

Empire Conleith 1,406 gt. Built: Deutsche Werft, Hamburg, in 1922 as *Ambia*. 234 ft × 37 ft. Engines: C4cyl.
1934: *Gumbinnen* (Kohlen-Import Poseidon Schiffs, Königsberg).
3.3.1941: Reported sunk off Lofoten Islands, Norway. Salved and repaired.
5.1945: Taken in prize at Flensburg. Renamed *Empire Conleith* (M.O.W.T.).
1946: Allocated to Norway, renamed *Dragnes* (Government of Norway).
1947: *Mimona* (K. Andersen & Co., Norway).
1959: *Malay* (T. Halvorsen A/S, Norway).
3.1961: Scrapped Grimstad, Norway.

Empire Conleven 1,642 gt. Built: Furness SB Co. Ltd., Haverton Hill, in 1930 as *Edenhurst*. 245 ft × 39 ft. Engines: T3cyl.
1937: *Ilves* (A/B Dahlberg O/Y, Finland).
1939: *Gluckauf* (Gluckauf Coal Handling Co., Rostock).
1940: Requisitioned by German Navy, renamed *Warnow*.
5.1945: Taken in prize at Flensburg. Renamed *Empire Conleven* (M.O.W.T.).
1946: Allocated to U.S.S.R., renamed *Alexandr Parkohomenko*.
No further trace.

Empire Connah 1,780 gt. Built: Neptun A.G., Rostock, in 1923 as *Charlotte Cords* for August Cords, Rostock. 266 ft × 40 ft. Engines: T3cyl.
5.1945: Taken in prize at Travemunde. Renamed *Empire Connah* (M.O.W.T.).
1946: Allocated to U.S.S.R., renamed *Nicolai Bauman*.
No further trace.

Empire Connaught 999 gt. Built: Stettiner Oderwerke A.G., Stettin, in 1921 as *Johannes C. Russ* for Ernst Russ, Hamburg. 211 ft × 34 ft. Engines: T3cyl.

21.10.1942: Wrecked off Umea, Sweden. Later salved.
5.1945: Taken in prize at Flensburg. Renamed *Empire Connaught* (M.O.W.T.).
1946: Allocated to U.S.S.R., renamed *Nemirovitch Danchenko*.
1971: Scrapped U.S.S.R.

Empire Connell 1,241 gt. Built: Sunderland Shipbuilding Co. in 1908 as *Odland*. 227 ft × 38 ft. Engines: T3cyl.
1922: *Odland 1* (Borre Damps, Norway).
1924: (D/S A/S Martha).
1928: *Brita* (Red. A/B Vasby, Sweden).
9.4.1940: Seized by Germans at Bergen (voyage: Sweden/France – woodpulp).
1940: renamed *Desiderius Siedler* (F. G. Rheingold, Danzig).
5.1945: Taken in prize at Copenhagen, renamed *Empire Connell* (M.O.W.T.).
1947: *Ballyholme Bay* (H. P. Lenaghan & Sons, Belfast).
1951: *Laure Pattison* (Pattison Orient Line Ltd., Hong Kong).
1952: Scrapped Hong Kong.

Empire Connemara 1,428 gt. Built: F. Schichau GmbH., Elbing, in 1924 as *Heinrich Arp* for F. C. Heinrich Arp, Hamburg. 237 ft × 38 ft. Engines: T3cyl.
5.1945: Taken in prize at Hamburg. Renamed *Empire Connemara* (M.O.W.T.).
1946: Allocated to U.S.S.R., renamed *Liza Chaikina*. No further trace.

Empire Conningbeg 1,875 gt. Built: Nobiskrug Werft GmbH, Rendsburg, in 1942. 264 ft × 42 ft. Engines: C4cyl.
1940: Launched as *Justinian* for H. Reksten, Norway. Seized by Germany, completed and renamed *Karl Christian Lohse* (H. P. Vith, Flensburg).
5.1945: Taken in prize at Flensburg. Renamed *Empire Conningbeg* (M.O.W.T.).
1946: Allocated to Norway, renamed *Fuglenes* (Government of Norway).
1947: Reverted to original owners and name.
1954: *Inge R. Christophersen* (H. W. Christophersen, Flensburg).
5.1965: Scrapped Hamburg.

Empire Cononley (ex auxiliary 3-masted schooner) 190 gt. Built: J. Oelkers, Hamburg, in 1922 as *Lucy* (barge). 106 ft × 25 ft.
19..: *Midgard I*.
19..: *Midgard IV*.
19..: *Elisabeth*.

The *Mesawa*, formerly *Empire Conifer*, in Eastern waters.

The *Empire Deben*, as a troopship.   *Vic Young*

The *Empire Fowey* at Southampton.

1935: *Dorothea Weber* (oil engine) (H. J. G. Weber, Hamburg).
5.1945: Taken in prize at Guernsey, Channel Islands. Renamed *Empire Cononley* (M.O.W.T.).
1947: *Coverack* (R. H. Hunt & Son).
1951: (New oil engine).
1953: *River Witham* (Hull Gates Shipping Co., Hull).
1955: Renamed *Rivergate*.
28.7.1959: Grounded off Lowestoft on voyage London to Goole with scrap iron. Refloated and proceeded, but capsized and sank four miles north-west of Inner Dowsing Light Vessel.

Empire Conqueror 1,600 gt. Built: Flensburger Schiff. Gesellschaft in 1926 as *Ilse L. M. Russ* for Ernst Russ, Hamburg. 263 ft × 42 ft. Engines: T3cyl.
5.1945: Taken in prize at Kiel. Renamed *Empire Conqueror* (M.O.W.T.).
1946: Allocated to Norway, renamed *Ekornes* (Government of Norway).
1947: *Elfrida* (Bjorn Tetlie, Norway).
8.12.1959: Leakage in engine room in a gale; took severe list.
9.12.1959: Abandoned, and
10.12.1959: Capsized and sank 100 miles west of Stavanger, Norway (voyage: Archangel/Denmark – timber).

Empire Conquest 1,516 gt. Built: Smit's Machinfabrieken, Kinderdijk, in 1917 as *Tilburg*. 239 ft × 36 ft. Engines: T3cyl.
1922: *Ljusnealf* (Baltische Reederei, Germany).
1938: *Hubert Schroder* (Richard Schroder, Rostock).
5.1945: Taken in prize; renamed *Empire Conquest* (M.O.W.T.).
1947: *Southern Island* (British & Overseas Minerals Ltd., London).
1951: *Verax* (U. Gennari Fu Torquato, Italy).
1960: Renamed *Costance*.
1962: (M. Attanasio (Costance Cia. de Nav., Panama)).
21.4.1966: Aground on rocks in heavy weather at Lampedusa Island, Mediterranean. Flooded and broke up. Total loss.

Empire Consent (Hansa 'A' type) 1,942 gt. Built: Van der Giessen, Krimpen, Holland, in 1944 as *Eichberg* for August Bolten, Hamburg. 283 ft × 44 ft. Engines: C4cyl.
5.1945: Taken in prize at Bremerhaven. Renamed *Empire Consent* (M.O.W.T.).
1949: *Runa* (Glen & Co., Glasgow).
1964: *Karyatis* (Seamasters Shipping Co., Greece).
1968: Scrapped Hong Kong.

Empire Consequence 1,998 gt. Built: Lübecker Maschinenbau Ges., Lübeck, in 1940 as *Friedrich*

Bischoff (German flag). 304 ft × 43 ft. Engines: C4cyl.
13.12.1943: Sunk in Allied air attack at Hamburg. Salved.
5.1945: Taken in prize at Copenhagen. Renamed *Empire Consequence* (M.O.W.T.).
1947: Allocated to U.S.A. (U.S.M.C.).
1950: (Norton Clapp, Seattle).
1951: *Kaisaniemi* (Polttoaine Osuuskunta, Finland).
11.1967: Scrapped Grimstad, Norway.

Empire Consett 1,123 gt. Built: Nordseewerke, Emden, in 1937 as *Thalia* for Neptun Line, Bremen. 235 ft × 35 ft. Engines: Oil.
12.9.1939: At Seville, Spain, on an intended voyage to Huelva.
4.1943: Interned at Cadiz.
5.1945: Surrendered to Britain; taken in prize, and:
8.1945: Engine trouble on voyage to U.K.
25.8.1945: Arrived Falmouth, and:
12.9.1945: Towed to Cardiff; renamed *Empire Consett* (M.O.W.T.).
1946: Allocated to U.S.S.R., renamed *Akademik Karpinsky*.
31.8.1953: Foundered on a voyage Kaliningrad/Amsterdam.

Empire Consistence 1,771 gt. Built: G. Seebeck A.G., Bremerhaven, in 1927 as *Ganter* for Argo Line, Bremen. 277 ft × 42 ft. Engines: T3cyl.
5.1945: Taken in prize at Copenhagen. Renamed *Empire Consistence* (M.O.W.T.).
1951: Bought by Dutch buyers for resale; given temporary names of *Jan Willem*, then *Maria*.
1951: *Dagny* (A. Johansson, Finland).
4.1967: Scrapped Bremen.

Empire Consort 1,175 gt. Built: Stettiner Oderwerke A.G. in 1922 as *Gisela L. M. Russ* for Ernst Russ, Hamburg. 231 ft × 36 ft. Engines: T3cyl.
5.1945: Taken in prize at Flensburg. Renamed *Empire Consort* (M.O.W.T.).
1946: Allocated to Greece, renamed *Volos* (Government of Greece).
1948: *Marios II* (M. A. Karageorgis, Greece).
19.2.1959: Boiler explosion when between Skyros Island and Port Kumi. Abandoned; taken in tow, but sank in position 38.35N 24.21E (voyage: Stratoni/Piraeus – iron ore).

Empire Constable 1,560 gt. Built: Flensburger Schiff. Gesellschaft in 1936 as *Heinrich Schmidt* for H. Schmidt, Flensburg. 263 ft × 41 ft. Engines: T3cyl.
5.1945: Taken in prize at Rendsburg. Renamed *Empire Constable* (M.O.W.T.).
1946: Allocated to U.S.S.R., renamed *Dimitriy Laptev*.
1971: Scrapped U.S.S.R.

Empire Constancy 535 gt. Built: Stettiner Oderwerke
A.G. in 1912 as *Dollart* for Bugsier Line, Hamburg.
166 ft × 28 ft. Engines: C2cyl.
5.1945: Taken in prize at Copenhagen. Renamed
Empire Constancy (M.O.W.T.).
1947: *Polzeath* (S. Hannan & Co., Fowey).
1951: *Meltem* (Azize Arkan v. Ortaklari, Turkey).
1956: *Yener 9* (Erpak Vap. Ithalkat Ihracat, Turkey).
1959: *Yarasli* (Zeki v. Ziya Son. Izzet Kirtil, Turkey).
14.1.1961: Sailed Istanbul for Bagnoli with scrap iron.
25.1.1961: Last reported when passing Cephalonia.
No further trace – presumed lost in Adriatic.

Empire Constellation 1,057 gt. Built: Schiffs–und
Dockbauw. Flender, Lübeck, in 1925 as *Reval*.
222 ft × 35 ft. Engines: T3cyl.
1934: *Memel* (Mathies Reederei, Hamburg).
5.1945: Taken in prize at Flensburg. Renamed *Empire
Constellation* (M.O.W.T.).
1946: Allocated to U.S.S.R., renamed *Ivan Sechenov*.
No further trace.

Empire Constitution 1,598 gt. Built: Flensburger
Schiff. Gesellschaft in 1928 as *Gemma*. 263 ft × 40 ft.
Engines: T3cyl.
1929: *Peter Vith* (H. P. Vith, Flensburg).
5.1945: Taken in prize at Flensburg. Renamed *Empire
Constitution* (M.O.W.T.).
1946: Allocated to Norway, renamed *Grannes*
(Government of Norway).
1946: *Selnes* (Einar Wahlstrom, Norway).
26.11.1950: In collision in fog with *City of Bristol*
(1943, 8,424 gt) off West Barrow Buoy, Thames
Estuary. Holed; beached West Barrow Sands.
Submerged. Total loss (voyage: Oslo/London –
woodpulp).

Empire Constructor 1,201 gt. Built: Nobiskrug Werft
GmbH., Rendsburg, in 1922 as *Pinnau* for Bugsier
Line, Hamburg. 250 ft × 37 ft. Engines: T3cyl.
5.1945: Taken in prize at Lübeck. Renamed *Empire
Constructor* (M.O.W.T.).
1947: *Estkon* (J. Carlbom & Co., Hull).
1959: Scrapped Newport, Mon.

Empire Consumer 1,258 gt. Built: Flensburger Schiff.
Gesellschaft in 1939 as *Haga* for Mathies Reederei,
Hamburg. 283 ft × 38 ft. Engines: C4cyl.
5.1945: Taken in prize at Kiel. Renamed *Empire
Consumer* (M.O.W.T.).
1946: Allocated to Norway, renamed *Hauknes*
(Government of Norway).
1947: *Orm Jarl* (Nordenfjeldske Damps. A/S.,
Norway).

1958: *Travnik* (Atlantska Plovidba, Yugoslavia).
1965: *Komovi* (Prekookeanska Plovidba, Yugoslavia).
1967: *Moschoula* (N. D. Boukouvalas, Greece).
4.1968: Scrapped Split.

Empire Contamar (ex auxiliary 3-masted
schooner) 199 gt. Built: Lübecker Flenderwerke
A.G., in 1935 as *Heimat* (aux. 3-masted schooner) for
H. Rubarth, Hamburg. 129 ft × 23 ft. Auxiliary
engine: Oil.
5.1945: Taken in prize at Kiel. Renamed *Empire
Contamar* (M.O.W.T.).
22.3.1947: Dragged anchor in gale, grounded on
rocks and wrecked St. Austell Bay, Cornwall
(voyage: Maryport/Par – coal).
6.1947: Refloated, but constructive total loss. Sold
and rebuilt (on Clyde) as a motor coaster: renamed
Tyrronall (248 gt) (F. J. Tyrrell, Cardiff).
1950: Again rebuilt.
1961: Further rebuilt (J. Tyrrell, Dublin).
1968: (A. J. Gough, Essex).
6.1974: Sold for breaking up at Santander.

Empire Contay 981 gt. Built: H. C. Stulcken Sohn,
Hamburg, in 1919 as *Malmö* for Bissmark Line,
Hamburg. 219 ft × 33 ft. Engines: T3cyl.
1.6.1942: Mined and sunk south-west of Malmö,
Sweden. Later salved.
5.1945: Taken in prize at Schlei, and:
1946: Renamed *Empire Contay* (M.O.W.T.).
1947: *Reykjanes* (Oddsson & Co. Ltd.).
1949: (Endeavour Shipping Co., Edinburgh).
5.1953: Scrapped Rosyth.

Empire Contees (Hansa 'A' type) 1,923 gt.
Built: Burmeister & Wain, Copenhagen, in 1944 as
Irene Oldendorff for E. Oldendorff, Lübeck.
280 ft × 44 ft. Engines: C4cyl.
14.9.1944: Reported to be in damaged condition at
Copenhagen. Repaired, but:
3.1945: Reported again damaged.
5.1945: Taken in prize at Lübeck. Renamed *Empire
Contees* (M.O.W.T.).
1946: Allocated to U.S.S.R., renamed *Omsk*.
1947: *Opole* (Zegluga Polska S.A., Poland).
1950: *Zetempowiec* (cadet training ship) (Government
of Poland).
1957: *Gryf* (Polish Navy training ship). Subsequently
became an un-named cadet accommodation vessel at
a Polish naval base.

Empire Content 1,453 gt. Built: Deutsche Schiff- und
Masch., Bremen, in 1938 as *Suderau* for Bugsier Line,
Hamburg. 261 ft × 41 gt. Engines: C2cyl.
5.1945: Taken in prize at Bremerhaven. Renamed
Empire Content (M.O.W.T.).

1946: Allocated to Norway, renamed *Svartnes* (Government of Norway).
1947: *Barlind* (F. Olsen & Co., Norway).
1971: *Ikaria* (L. N. Pothas, Greece).
3.1972: Scrapped Aspropyrgos, Greece.

Empire Contest 1,175 gt. Built: Neptun A.G., Rostock, in 1924 as *Alk* for Argo Line, Bremen. 222 ft × 35 ft. Engines: T3cyl.
5.1945: Taken in prize at Brunsbüttel. Renamed *Empire Contest* (M.O.W.T.).
1946: Allocated to U.S.S.R., renamed *Vereshyogin*. No further trace.

Empire Continent 842 gt. Built: Kjobhavens F. & S., Copenhagen, in 1908 as *Laura*. 210 ft × 31 ft. Engines: T3cyl.
1935: *Sylt* (Wendenhof Reederei GmbH, Wismar).
1940: Requisitioned by German Navy.
5.1945: Taken in prize at Trondheim. Renamed *Empire Continent* (M.O.W.T.).
1947: *Master Nicolas* (A. G. Tsavliris Ltd., London).
1952: *Soussana II* (N. T. Papadatos, Greece).
1955: *Georgios Matsas* (L. G. Matsas, Greece).
18.4.1955: Struck rocks, holed, flooded, beached and sank at Muros, Spain.
17.6.1955: Refloated, but constructive total loss. Sold and repaired; renamed *Sur* (Dabaco & Co., Panama).
8.1965: Scrapped Santander.

Empire Contour 965 gt. Built: F. Schichau GmbH., Elbing, in 1922 as *Tertia*. 230 ft × 34 ft. Engines: T3cyl.
1924: *Hornland* (Horn Damps. Rhederei Akt., Germany).
1926: *Taube* (Norddeutscher Lloyd, Germany).
1933: (Argo Line, Bremen).
5.1945: Taken in prize at Flensburg. Renamed *Empire Contour* (M.O.W.T.).
1946: Allocated to Belgium, renamed *Jean Marie* (Vloeberghs Reederij, Belgium).
12.12.1951: Cargo shifted; vessel listed and engine room flooded. Sank in Baltic Sea, 58.40N 20.30E (voyage: Kotka/Ostend – timber).

Empire Contract 965 gt. Built: Norderwerft A.G., Hamburg, in 1925 as *Wiedau* for Bugsier Line, Hamburg. 221 ft × 35 ft. Engines: T3cyl.
5.1945: Taken in prize at Hamburg. Renamed *Empire Contract* (M.O.W.T.).
1945: Allocated to Greece, renamed *Herakleion* (Government of Greece).
1948: *Laconia* (Lakoniki SS Nav. Co. (I. Tsengas & Co., Greece)).
1954: (Hellenic Levant Line, Greece).
1964: (J. Alexatos, Greece).

1965: *Manganese* (Sinai Manganese Co., Egypt).

Empire Contyne (Hansa 'A' type) 1,935 gt. Built: Flensburger Schiff-Gesellschaft in 1944 as *Rodenbek* for Knohr & Burchard, Germany. 280 ft × 44 ft. Engines: C4cyl.
5.1945: Taken in prize at Flensburg. Renamed *Empire Contyne* (M.O.W.T.).
1947: Allocated to U.S.A. (U.S.M.C.).
1948: (Smith-Johnson SS Corpn., New York).
1952: *Aenos* (Cia. Mar. Estrella, Panama (P. D. Marchessini & Co.)).
1963: *Marlin* (Southern Star Shipping Co., Liberia).
17.10.1965: Boiler trouble, lost steering, cargo shifted in heavy weather 130 miles off Cape Fear, N. Carolina. Abandoned, and:
18.10.1965: Sank, 34.38N 75.32W (voyage: Tampa/Port Williams, N.S. – phosphate).

Empire Convention 1,714 gt. Built: Helsingborgs Varv. Akt., Sweden, in 1943 as *Heidberg* for August Bolten, Hamburg. 278 ft × 41 ft. Engines: T3cyl.
5.1945: Taken in prize at Stettin. Renamed *Empire Convention* (M.O.W.T.).
1946: Allocated to U.S.S.R., renamed *Ernst Thaelmann*. No further trace.

Empire Convoy 1,424 gt. Built: Lindenau & Co., Memel, in 1922 as *Cattaro*. 227 ft × 34 ft. Engines: T3cyl.
1930: *Finkenau* (Bugsier Line, Hamburg).
5.1940: Reported damaged by mine in Baltic; later salved and repaired.
1945: Renamed *Levensau*.
5.1945: Taken in prize at Brunsbüttel. Renamed *Empire Convoy* (M.O.W.T.).
1946: Allocated to Holland, renamed *Grebberg* (Government of Netherlands).
1947: *Echo* (Hudig & Veder, Holland).
1952: *Frontier* (African Coasters (Pty.) Ltd., Durban).
27.9.1957: Aground at mouth of Ncera River, twenty-three miles south of East London.
29.9.1957: Broke up; Constructive total loss (voyage: Durban/Port Elizabeth – sugar).

Empire Conway 1,000 gt. Built: Goedhardt Gebr. A.G., Lübeck, in 1925 as *Riga*. 217 ft × 35 ft. Engines: T3cyl.
1934: *Königsberg* (Mathies Reederei, Germany).
1939: Renamed *Stettin*.
5.1945: Taken in prize at Flensburg. Renamed *Empire Conway* (M.O.W.T.).
1946: Allocated to U.S.S.R., renamed *Anakriya*.
1978: Scrapped U.S.S.R.

Empire Conwear 2,487 gt. Built: Lübecker
Flenderwerke A.G., in 1936 as *Nordcoke* for F. Krupp
& Co., Essen. 297 ft × 44 ft. Engines: C4cyl.
1940: Requisitioned by German Navy, renamed
Nordlicht.
5.1945: Taken in prize at Hamburg. Renamed *Empire
Conwear* (M.O.W.T.).
1946: Allocated to U.S.S.R., renamed *Armavir*.
1947: *Kolno* (Zegluga Polska Line, Poland).
6.1971: Scrapped Poland.

Empire Cony 997 gt. Built: Stettiner Oderwerke
A.G., in 1921 as *Wilhelm Russ* for Ernst Russ,
Hamburg. 211 ft × 34 ft. Engines: T3cyl.
5.1945: Taken in prize at Eckernförde, renamed
Empire Cony, (M.O.W.T.).
1947: *Elsie Beth* (Storeship Transport Co., London).
1950: Purchased by original owners, reverted to
original name.
10.1958: Scrapped Hamburg.

Empire Conyngham 1,408 gt. Built: Neptun A.G.,
Rostock, in 1899 as *Marie*. 242 ft × 36 ft.
Engines: T3cyl.
1923: *Norburg* (Ozean Damps. A.G., Germany).
1925: *Gauja* (Government of Latvia).
8.6.1941: Captured in Baltic by German Navy.
Renamed *Friedrich* (Otto Wiggers, Seestadt-Rostock).
5.1945: Taken in prize; renamed *Empire Conyngham*
(M.O.W.T.).
20.6.1949: Scuttled in Atlantic, 47.52N 8.51W with
a cargo of obsolete bombs.

Empire Crouch 4,661 gt. Built: Lithgows Ltd., Port
Glasgow, in 1920; laid down as *War Peshwa* (tanker)
but completed as *Maudie* (whale oil refinery).
385 ft × 52 ft. Engines: T3cyl.
1937: *Angra* (B. Krogius, Finland).
1942: *Mercator* (Finland America Line).
1943: Seized by Germany at Danzig.
16.4.1945: Damaged by aircraft bombs at Hela, Baltic
Sea.
5.1945: Taken in prize at Copenhagen. Renamed
Empire Crouch (M.O.W.T.).
1946: *Mercator* (Chartered to Government of Finland).
1948: Returned to Finnish owners.
1951: (Finska Line, Finland).
1956: *Ruth Nurminen* (J. Nurminen, Finland).
5.1959: Scrapped Yokohama.

Empire Dart 4,186 gt. Built: Kockums Mek. Verk.,
Malmö, in 1925 as *Skaneland*. 377 ft × 54 ft.
Engines: Oil.
1928: *Pernambuco* (Hamburg South America Line).
5.1945: Taken in prize at Kiel: renamed *Empire Dart*
(M.O.W.T.).

1946: Allocated to U.S.S.R., renamed *Krasnodar*.
4.1975: Scrapped Split.

Empire Deben 11,251 gt. Built: Howaldtswerke,
Kiel, in 1922 as *Thuringia*. 474 ft × 61 ft.
Engines: two steam turbines.

The *Thuringia* was built for the Hamburg America Line, one
of the first big class of nine turbine ships with which 'Hapag'
started to rebuild its fleet after World War I. Designed for
the Western Ocean (Atlantic) service, she carried a few first-
class passengers and a large number of emigrants in 'steerage'
quarters.
    She served on the New York and Boston service until
1929, then transferred to the Hamburg South America Line,
being renamed *General San Martin* to please Argentina. From
1940 to 1945 she served the German Navy, first becoming a
barracks ship then, in 1942, a tender. Finally she became a
hospital ship, taking part in the evacuation from the Eastern
Baltic in 1945 when, on eleven voyages, she carried over
29,000 persons back to West Germany.
    Taken in prize at Copenhagen in May 1945, she was
sent to Palmer's shipyard at Hebburn for conversion to
a troopship. Renamed *Empire Deben* under Shaw, Savill
management, she lasted for less than three years before going
to shipbreakers at Newport, Mon., in March 1949.

Empire Dee 7,839 gt. Built: Deutsche Schiff- und
Masch., Bremen, in 1939 as *Neidenfels* for Hansa Line,
Bremen. 489 ft × 61 ft. Engines: Oil.
5.1945: Taken in prize at Eckernförde, Germany,
renamed *Empire Dee* (M.O.W.T.).
1946: Allocated to U.S.S.R., renamed *Admiral
Ushakov*.
10.1975: Scrapped Split.

Empire Doon 17,362 gt. Built: Blohm & Voss,
Hamburg, in 1936 as *Pretoria*. 550 ft × 72 ft.
Engines: eight steam turbines.

The *Pretoria* was built for the German East Africa Line and
their Hamburg–Cape service. Launched on 16 July 1936, she
left Hamburg on her maiden voyage to Cape Town on 19
December 1936, a notable occasion for her passengers to be
Christmas at sea. This they had, but it was marred when the
ship ran aground for thirty-seven hours at East Lepe, in the
Solent. Seven tugs finally refloated her, without damage.
    In 1939 the ship was taken over by the German Navy for
use as a submarine depot ship, and in 1940 she became a
hospital ship. In May 1945 she was taken in prize at Copenhagen, allocated to Britain, then taken to Newcastle and fitted
out as a troopship. Renamed *Empire Doon*, she was managed
by the Orient Line on behalf of the M.O.T.
    But as soon as she came into service she experienced
persistent trouble with her experimental German boilers and
was withdrawn from service, towed home from Port Said
and laid up off Southend. Eventually the ship was re-boilered
and her turbines modified by J. I Thornycroft & Co. at
Southampton, and emerged in January 1950, after 2½ years,
as *Empire Orwell*, with accommodation for 1,500 troops. Her
new name conformed to the M.O.T.'s 'River' style of

nomenclature for troopships and with the Orient Line's tradition of commencing ships names with the letter 'O'.

In December 1957 *Empire Orwell* arrived home from the Far East and was withdrawn, being laid up at Portland. Then, in 1958, she was chartered to the Pan-Islamic SS Co. of Karachi, but later that year was sold to the Ocean Steamship Co. (A. Holt & Co.) Liverpool. Refitted by Barclay, Curle & Co., Glasgow, for the company's pilgrim service between Indonesia and Jeddah, all her troop accommodation was removed and replaced by Indonesian-style accommodation for 2,000 pilgrims. It was intended to rename her *Dardanus* – a well-known 'Blue Funnel' name – but at the suggestion of the pilgrim trade organisers the name *Gunung Djati* was chosen, after an early Moslem Hadji who established Mohammedanism in West Java and became a legendary figure in the Moslem world.

It was envisaged that the ship would stay on the run for twelve years or so, but the political pressure applied in Indonesia's desire to own the pilgrim ship caused her to be sold, in 1962, to that nation's government.

In 1964 she was sold by them to Pelajaran Sang Saka and in the next year passed to Perusahaan Pelarajan Arafat, of Djakarta. Eight years later she was re-engined with diesels at Hong Kong and in 1979 transferred to the Indonesian Navy, becoming the troopship *Kri Tanjung Pandan* (pennant 971). Some two years later she was laid up at Tanjung Priok (the port for Jakarta) as an accommodation vessel and, in 1987, was sold to Taiwan shipbreakers.

Empire Douglas (Hansa 'A' type) 1,925 gt. Built: Van Duivendijks Scheep., Lekkerkerk, in 1943 as *Wilhelmshavn* for Hamburg America Line.
287 ft × 44 ft. Engines: C4cyl.
5.1945: Taken in prize at Kiel. Renamed *Empire Douglas*, (M.O.W.T.).
1946: Allocated to U.S.S.R., renamed *Korsun Shevtshenkovsky*.
3.1972: Scrapped Ghent.

Empire Dove 2,503 gt. Laid down in 1940 by N.V. Scheeps Gebr. Pot., Bolnes, Holland; intended to be *Hermes* for K.N.S.M., Holland. 345 ft × 48 ft. Engines: Oil.
5.1945: Taken in prize (incomplete); and:
6.1949: Completed in Germany. Renamed *Empire Dove* (M.O.T.).
1949: (MacAndrews & Co. Ltd., London).
1953: Renamed *Pozarica*.
1964: *Blue Fin* (Soc. Anon. Letasa, Spain).
27.11.1965: Lost rudder in heavy weather; cargo shifted; taken in tow, but:
28.11.1965: Sank sixty miles west of La Rochelle, Bay of Biscay (voyage: Antwerp/Barcelona).

Empire Dovey 2,883 gt. Built: A. G. Weser, Bremen, in 1929 as *Hercules* for Neptun Line, Bremen.
297 ft × 46 ft. Engines: T3cyl.
5.1945: Taken in prize at Copenhagen. Renamed *Empire Dovey* (M.O.W.T.).

1946: Allocated to U.S.S.R., renamed *Kirovograd*.
9.1968: Scrapped West Germany.

Empire Durant 2,902 gt. Built: Eltringham's Ltd., Willington on Tyne, in 1921 as *Dalewood*.
306 ft × 44 ft. Engines: T3cyl.
1923: *Bernard Blumenfeld* (B. Blumenfeld Akt., Germany).
1938: *Carl Jungst* (F. Krupp & Co., Essen).
5.1945: Taken in prize at Kiel. Renamed *Empire Durant* (M.O.W.T.).
1946: Allocated to U.S.S.R., renamed *Tambov*; became a mother ship for Russian trawler fleets. No trace after 1957.

Empire Eden (Hansa 'A' type) 1,923 gt. Built: Deutsche Werft, Hamburg, in 1944 as *Kattenturm* for Hansa Line, Bremen. 280 ft × 44 ft. Engines: C4cyl.
6.1945: Taken in prize at Brunsbüttel. Renamed *Empire Eden* (M.O.W.T.).
1947: *Lowland* (Currie Line Ltd., Leith).
1959: *Mary Enid* (Poseidon Shipping Co., Bermuda).
1963: *Stelianos* (Delphic Shipping Co., Greece).
1964: *Marynik* (Marynik Cia. Nav., Greece).
1967: *Euripides* (Euripides Shipping Co., Hong Kong, (P. D. Marchessini & Co.)).
7.1969: Scrapped Hong Kong.

Empire Ely 6,112 gt. Built: Lübecker Flenderwerke A.G., in 1944 as *Greifswald* for Norddeutscher Lloyd.
455 ft × 61 ft. Engines: C4cyl.
5.1945: Taken in prize, incomplete, at builder's yard at Lübeck.
1948: Completed; renamed *Empire Ely* (M.O.T.).
1949: Option given to R. Ropner & Sons for purchase, with intended name of *Swiftpool*, but option not taken up.
1954: *Maribella* (Mariblanca Nav. S.A., Liberia).
1955: *Ganges* (F. A. Detjen, Germany).
1959: *Eleni* (Cia. de Nav. Andria, Greece).
5.9.1971: Damaged in collision with Norwegian ferry *Prinsesse Ragnhild* (1966, 7,715 gt) in Kiel Bay (voyage: Rio de Janeiro/Gdynia – general). Arrived in port; repairs uneconomic; sold.
4.1972: Scrapped Santander.

Empire Ettrick 4,622 gt. Built: Deutsche Werft, Hamburg, in 1939 as *Bukarest* for Deutsche Levant Line, Hamburg. 407 ft × 56 ft. Engines: two steam turbines.
5.1945: Taken in prize at Kiel. Renamed *Empire Ettrick* (M.O.W.T.).
1946: Allocated to Norway, renamed *Bremnes* (Government of Norway).
1947: *Clio* (Bergen SS Co., Norway).

1963: *Panorea* (E. T. Kolintzas & Maltakis, Greece).
1974: Scrapped Kaohsiung.

Empire Evenlode 10,254 gt. Built: Scotts SB & Eng.
Co. Ltd., Glasgow, in 1912 as *Talthibius* for A. Holt
& Co., Liverpool. 506 ft × 60 ft. Engines: T6cyl.

The *Talthibius* arrived at Singapore in convoy from Bombay
on 25 January 1942, to discharge military equipment originally
destined for Middle East operations. Unloading, alongside,
proceeded slowly, performed by the ship's crew and volunteer
New Zealand Air Force personnel – the local stevedores
having 'disappeared'.

On 3 February, as the last vehicle was being lifted ashore,
the ship was hit by bombs from Japanese planes and another
salvo burst alongside. Fires broke out, the Asians among the
crew deserted and only the British were left to try to save
the ship.

Later, more bombs burst alongside, damaging the ship
over its entire length. Despite the use of salvage pumps, the
ship slowly filled and on the 7th was moved into the Empire
Dock. But *Talthibius* could not be made seaworthy. Her crew
were fighting fires in sheds alongside, no other assistance was
available, wharfs and godowns were deserted, looting was
rife, air raids frequent and heavy, enemy shells were passing
over the ship and the Japanese Army was advancing rapidly
into the town. The British naval authorities ordered the crew
to abandon ship – now sitting upright on the bottom of the
dock.

Salved by the Japanese, the ship was renamed *Taruyasu
Maru*. After the war she was found submerged off Sado
Island, Japan, having struck an American mine laid on 30
June 1945. Salved again, she was renamed *Empire Evenlode*
under the M.O.W.T. and ordered to return home via the
Cape of Good Hope, after loading scrap metal in Singapore.

Boiler trouble forced her into Mombasa for repairs, into
Durban for overhaul and into Cape Town for new boiler
tubes. The voyage home, which commenced at Hong Kong
on 1 December 1945, ended at Swansea on 8 May 1946. Not
long after, she was put on the sale list, finally being scrapped
at Briton Ferry in 1949.

Empire Exe 2,371 gt. Built: Howaldtswerke, Kiel, in
1921 as *Possehl* for Lübeck Line, Lübeck.
306 ft × 42 ft. Engines: T3cyl.
5.1945: Taken in prize at Lübeck. Renamed *Empire
Exe* (M.O.W.T.).
1947: Allocated to Greece, renamed *Hermoupolis*
(Government of Greece).
1948: (T. J. Lavrangas & Co., Greece) (vessel used as
a depot ship).
1966: *Pilion* (P. Perdikis, Greece).
1967: *Nigma* (Tina Shipping Co., Cyprus).
11.1967: Reported at Aden with boiler damage. Laid
up.
10.1969: Arrived Karachi, in tow, for scrapping.

Empire Farrar (Hansa 'A' type) 1,923 gt.
Built: Stettiner Oderwerke A.G., in 1944 as *Michael*

Ferdinand for H. Ferdinand, Germany. 282 ft × 44 ft.
Engines: C4cyl.
5.1945: Taken in prize at Sønderborg, Denmark.
1946: *Empire Farrar* (M.O.W.T.).
1947: (Stratton Shipping Co. Ltd.).
1949: *Admiral Hardy* (Stanley SS Co., Hong Kong).
1955: (Sig. S. Aarstads Rederi, Norway).
1965: *Dumai Trader* (Scanship Corp., Panama (Sea
Express Line, Norway)).
1967: (Manchester Nav. Ltd., Liberia).
3.1970: Scrapped Kaohsiung.

Empire Forth 2,471 gt. Built: Deutsche Schiff- und
Masch., Bremen, in 1939 as *Mars* for Neptun Line,
Bremen. 333 ft × 48 ft. Engines: Oil.
12.1943: Damaged by air attack at Bremen.
5.1945: Taken in prize at Copenhagen. Renamed
Empire Forth (M.O.W.T.).
1946: Allocated to U.S.S.R., renamed *Equator*.
1949: Renamed *Vityaz* (seagoing training ship).
1982: Reported preserved at Leningrad as a museum
ship.

Empire Fowey 19,047 gt. Built: Blohm & Voss,
Hamburg, in 1936 as *Potsdam*. 605 ft × 74 ft.
Engines: Turbo-electric.

The *Potsdam* was one of a trio of ships ordered by the Hamburg
America Line (Hapag), but while under construction her
owners were forced by the German Nationalist policy of the
mid-1930s to come to an agreement with the North German
Lloyd (Norddeutscher Lloyd) over their future areas of
operation, and the vessel was transferred to the latter company.

Along with her sisters *Scharnhorst* and *Gneisenau*, the
vessels, at 21 knots, became the fastest on the run to the Far
East, the Genoa to Shanghai leg taking little more than three
weeks.

Potsdam commenced another voyage to the East only two
weeks before the start of World War II. But when only a few
days out and still off the coast of Spain, she was recalled,
making her way home via the North Atlantic/North of
Scotland route. Her sisterships became war losses, but *Potsdam*
served in home waters, first as an accommodation ship at
Hamburg, then as a troopship to Norwegian and Baltic ports
and then again as an accommodation ship, this time at Gdynia.
Finally, she took part in the evacuation of German nationals –
refugees – from the Eastern Baltic, back to Germany.

Captured by British forces at Flensburg in May 1945, she
was one of some 150 ships found there when the port was
occupied on 13 May. She was given the name *Empire Jewel*
and, in mid-June, sailed for Kiel, still under her German
captain but without national colours. She arrived on the 19th,
but rumour was that the Germans might block the Kiel Canal
with her and a Royal Navy armed guard contingent was
placed aboard for her canal transit. After arrival at Brunsbüttel
the armed guard left and for three weeks the *Empire Jewel* lay
at anchor, still with her full German crew.

Then, on 20 July, an Army detachment was placed aboard
and she sailed, in a convoy of German ships with a naval
escort, for Methil, on the Firth of Forth.

At the end of July she sailed once more, this time under the British ensign, bound for Belfast and conversion to a troopship by Harland & Wolff. The refit lasted until April 1946, when she emerged for service with a new name – *Empire Fowey*.

However, her turbo-electric machinery and experimental high-pressure boilers were not popular with British engineers, who had little or no experience with this type of installation. In fact, the entire power unit proved so unsatisfactory that in March 1947 the ship was towed to the Clyde, where, in another refit that was to last for three years, she was stripped to a bare hull and geared turbines and new boilers were installed and the troop accommodation completely refitted.

Virtually a new ship, she gave satisfactory trooping service for some ten years. Then, as trooping needs reduced, she was firstly chartered to the Pan-Islamic SS Co. of Pakistan and, in 1960, sold to them, becoming *Safina-E-Hujjaj* and operating mostly in the pilgrim service from East Africa and South East Asia to Jeddah.

By 1976 the vessel was over forty years old and proving too costly to run, burning more than 110 tons of fuel each day. She was sold to Pakistan shipbreakers at Gadani Beach, forty miles from Karachi, where her breaking up commenced in October 1976.

Empire Fraser (Hansa 'A' type) 1,923 gt.
Built: Deutsche Werft, Hamburg, in 1944 as *Weserbrück* for Norddeutscher Lloyd. 282 ft × 44 ft. Engines: C4cyl.
5.1945: Taken in prize, incomplete, at Hamburg.
1946: Completed as *Empire Fraser* (M.O.W.T.).
1947: *Chaksang* (Indo-China SN Co. Ltd.).
7.9.1949: Explosion, due to sabotage, in forward holds while moored in dangerous goods anchorage at Hong Kong, sailing having been delayed due to a typhoon warning. Intensity of subsequent fires prevented cutting of anchor cable to enable beaching of vessel. Typhoon conditions forced salvage and rescue craft to withdraw, with ship settling by the head.
8.9.1949: Sank at moorings, with extensive damage. Total loss (voyage: Hong Kong/N. China – potassium chlorate).
22.3.1950: Refloated, sold locally for scrapping.

Empire Frome (Hansa 'B' type) 2,774 gt. Laid down by Flensburger Schiff-Gesellschaft. 343 ft × 41 ft. Engines: C4cyl.
5.1945: Taken in prize, incomplete, on stocks.
1948: Completed; renamed *Empire Frome* (M.O.T.).
1953: Acquired by Submarine Cables Ltd., London. Converted to a cable ship, and:
1955: renamed *Ocean Layer*.
15.6.1959: Caught fire in crew quarters in Atlantic, position 48.26N 19.03W, during laying of a new lightweight cable between France and Newfoundland. Ship rapidly engulfed in flames and abandoned.
17.6.1959: Taken in tow by German salvage tug *Wotan* (1939, 729 gt) and:

21.6.1959: Arrived Falmouth, still afire and extensively damaged. Constructive total loss. Sold, and:
12.1959: Scrapped Hendrik-Ido-Ambacht.

Empire Gable (Hansa 'A' type) 1,925 gt.
Built: Deutsche Werft, Hamburg, in 1944 as *Benue* for Deutsche Africa Line. 280 ft × 44 ft. Engines: C4cyl.
5.1945: Taken in prize at Cuxhaven. Renamed *Empire Gable* (M.O.W.T.).
1946: Allocated to U.S.S.R., renamed *Sukhumi*.
12.1969: Scrapped Bo'ness.

Empire Gabon (Hansa 'A' type) 1,925 gt.
Built: Flensburger Schiff-Gesellschaft in 1944 as *Licentia* for J. Jost, Flensburg. 280 ft × 44 ft. Engines: C4cyl.
5.1945: Taken in prize at Flensburg. Renamed *Empire Gabon* (M.O.W.T.).
1946: Allocated to U.S.S.R., renamed *Riazan*.
1979: Reported sold to Hamburg buyers, renamed *Rudi* and resold to Spanish shipbreakers at Santander.

Empire Gaffer (Hansa 'A' type) 1,942 gt.
Built: Deutsche Werft, Hamburg, in 1945 as *Betsdorf* for F. Krupp & Co., Essen. 282 ft × 44 ft. Engines: C4cyl.
5.1945: Taken in prize at Kiel. Renamed *Empire Gaffer* (M.O.W.T.).
1947: *Baltrader* (United Baltic Corporation, London).
1952: Renamed *Baltic Fir*.
1956: *Arsterturm* (rebuilt at Bremerhaven) (Hansa Line, Bremen).
1969: *Unigoolnar* (Universal Shipping & Coastal Trading Pte. Ltd., Bombay).
1976: *Sudarsan Shakti* (Sudarsan Liners Ltd., Madras).
1980: Reported in damaged condition; towed from Kuwait to India.
3.1981: Scrapped Bombay.

Empire Gage (Hansa 'A' type) 1,925 gt.
Built: Deutsche Werft, Hamburg, in 1943 as *Santander* for Oldenburg-Portuguese Line. 280 ft × 44 ft. Engines: C4cyl.
5.1945: Taken in prize at Copenhagen. Renamed *Empire Gage* (M.O.W.T.).
8.1945: *Arnhem* (Chartered to Government of Netherlands).
1946: Allocated to U.S.S.R., renamed *Yaroslavl*.
1971: Scrapped U.S.S.R.

Empire Gala (Hansa 'A' type) 1,923 gt. Launched by Nederland Scheeps., Amsterdam, in 1944 as *Weserstrand* for Norddeutscher Lloyd. Completed in Germany in 1945. 282 ft × 44 ft. Engines: C4cyl.

5.1945: Taken in prize at Kiel. Renamed *Empire Gala* (M.O.W.T.).
1946: Allocated to U.S.S.R., renamed *Podolsk*.
9.1.1948: Ashore in heavy weather on Amhurst Rocks, Yangtsze Estuary, sixty miles from Woosung, China. Slowly filled, and:
11.1.1948: Sank in deep water (voyage: Shanghai/Vladivostock – ballast).

Empire Galashiels (Hansa 'A' type) 1,923 gt.
Built: Neptun A.G., Rostock, in 1944 as *Gunther* for Hamburg South America Line. 280 ft × 44 ft.
Engines: C4cyl.
5.1945: Taken in prize at Rostock. Renamed *Empire Galashiels* (M.O.W.T.).
1946: Allocated to U.S.S.R., renamed *Smolensk*.
1976: Scrapped U.S.S.R.

Empire Galaxy 1,849 gt. Built: Neptun A.G., Rostock, in 1927 as *Capri* for R. M. Sloman Jr., Hamburg. 288 ft × 41 ft. Engines: T3cyl.
5.1945: Taken in prize at Kiel. Renamed *Empire Galaxy* (M.O.W.T.).
1946: Allocated to U.S.S.R., renamed *Naderjda Krupskiar* (sometimes shown as *Nadeja Krupskaya*). No trace after 1955.

Empire Galbraith (Hansa 'A' type) 1,923 gt.
Built: Verschure & Co.'s Scheep- en Masch., Amsterdam, in 1944 as *Hendrik Fisser 5* for Fisser & Van Doornum, Emden. 280 ft × 44 ft.
Engines: C4cyl.
5.1945: Taken in prize, in damaged condition, at Kiel. Renamed *Empire Galbraith* (M.O.W.T.).
1946: *Highland* (Currie Line Ltd., Leith).
1959: *Gowrie* (Dundee, Perth & London Shipping Co. Ltd.).
1963: *Hermanos* (G. Vlassis & Co., Greece).
12.1969: Scrapped Vado.

Empire Galena (Hansa 'A' type) 1,925 gt. Built: J. Cockerill S.A., Hoboken, Belgium, in 1943 as *Weserstrom* for Norddeutscher Lloyd. 280 ft × 44 ft. Engines: C4cyl.
5.1945: Taken in prize at Kiel. Renamed *Empire Galena* (M.O.W.T.).
1947: *Albatross* (General Steam Nav. Co. Ltd.).
1958: *Port Capetown* (National Shipping Lines of South Africa).
1959: *Frontier* (African Coasters (Pty.) Ltd., Durban).
1966: *Fortune* (Summit Nav. Co., Hong Kong).
12.1968: Scrapped Hong Kong.

Empire Gallant (Hansa 'A' type) 1,923 gt.
Built: Lübecker Maschinenbau Ges., in 1943 as *Celia*

for A. Kirsten, Hamburg. 280 ft × 44 ft.
Engines: C4cyl.
5.1945: Taken in prize at Flensburg. Renamed *Empire Gallant* (M.O.W.T.).
1947: *Richard Borchard* (Borchard (U.K.) Ltd.).
1960: *Fairwood* (Fairplay Reederi, Richard Borchard GmbH., Hamburg).
1.1963: Scrapped Sarpsborg, Norway.

Empire Galleon (Hansa 'A' type) 1,923 gt. Built: Van Vliet Co., Hardinxveld, Holland, in 1944 as *Elmenhorst* for Bock, Godeffroy & Co., Hamburg. 280 ft × 44 ft. Engines: C4cyl.
5.1945: Taken in prize at Kiel. Renamed *Empire Galleon* (M.O.W.T.).
1946: Allocated to U.S.S.R., renamed *Kazan*.
1973: Scrapped U.S.S.R.

Empire Gallery (Hansa 'A' type) 1,925 gt. Built: P. Smit, Rotterdam, in 1944 as *Weserburg* for Norddeutscher Lloyd. 280 ft × 44 ft. Engines: C4cyl.
5.1945: Taken in prize at Kiel. Renamed *Empire Gallery* (M.O.W.T.).
10.10.1945: Struck mine fifteen miles from Cordouan, France. Engines disabled, towed to Verdon.
7.1.1946: Arrived Penarth in tow. Repaired.
1947: *Kampar* (Straits SS Co. Ltd., Singapore).
1957: *Anglia* (Hellenic Lines Ltd., Greece).
1958: (Universal Cargo Carriers, Panama).
4.1974: Scrapped Gemlik, Turkey.

Empire Gallic (Hansa 'A' type) 1,944 gt. Launched by Deutsche Werft, Hamburg, in 1944. Completed by T. U. K. Smit, Holland, in 1945 as *Hendrik Fisser 7* for Fisser & Van Doornum, Emden. 280 ft × 44 ft. Engines: C4cyl.
5.1945: Taken in prize at Kiel. Renamed *Empire Gallic* (M.O.W.T.).
1946: Allocated to U.S.S.R., renamed *Rjev*.
7.1970: Scrapped Hamburg.

Empire Gallop (Hansa 'A' type) 1,944 gt.
Built: Deutsche Werft, Hamburg, in 1944 as *Fangturm* for Hansa Line, Bremen. 288 ft × 44 ft.
Engines: C4cyl.
5.1945: Taken in prize at Kiel. Renamed *Empire Gallop* (M.O.W.T.).
1947: *Baltonia* (United Baltic Corporation, London).
1953: Renamed *Baltic Oak*.
1957: *Palmyra* (Bock, Godeffroy & Co., Germany).
27.3.1962: In collision with tanker *British Mariner* (1948, 8,576 gt) eighteen miles off Ushant, France. Sank (voyage: Hamburg/Istanbul – general).

(Intended to be) *Empire Galloper* This name was not used and later cancelled. It is likely that such name

was allocated to the following vessel when she came under British control. 7,000 gt. Laid down at Kockums Mek. Verk., Malmö, Sweden, as *Otavi* for German account. Launched in 1940, transferred to Deutsche Werft, Hamburg, for completion. 464 ft × 64 ft. Engines: Oil.
5.1945: Taken in prize, incomplete, at Hamburg. Intended to be given an 'Empire' name, but instead vessel awarded to Belgium. Towed to Antwerp, and:
1946: Completed by Mercantile Marine Engineering & Graving Docks Co. Sold, and:
1946: *El Gaucho* (6,917 gt) (Soc. Anon. Comercial de Exportación y Importación y Financiera, Argentina (Louis Dreyfus & Cie. Ltda.)).
1964: *Rosarino* (Mararte Cia. Nav. S.A. (Dodero Line, Argentina)).
1967: *Plate Lancer* (Mararte Cia. de Nav., Panama (Cie. Mar. et Commerciale, Paris)).
8.4.1969: Damage to main engine while on voyage Bahia Blanca to Rotterdam, with cargo.
15.4.1969: Arrived destination; thence to Hamburg. Repairs found to be uneconomic; sold for breaking up, and:
9.1969: Scrapped Hamburg.

Empire Galveston (Hansa 'A' type) 1,925 gt.
Built: Deutsche Werft, Hamburg, in 1944 as *Weserwald* for Norddeutscher Lloyd. 280 ft × 44 ft. Engines: C4cyl.
5.1945: Taken in prize at Brunsbüttel. Renamed *Empire Galveston* (M.O.W.T.).
1946: Allocated to U.S.S.R., renamed *Volochayevsk*.
1973: Scrapped U.S.S.R.

Empire Galway (Hansa 'A' type) 1,944 gt.
Built: Deutsche Werft, Hamburg, in 1945 as *Schauenburg* for H. Schuldt, Hamburg. 287 ft × 44 ft. Engines: C4cyl.
5.1945: Taken in prize at Flensburg. Renamed *Empire Galway* (M.O.W.T.).
1946: Allocated to Belgium, renamed *Kinshasa* (Government of Belgium – Ministry of Marine).
1950: (Compagnie Maritime Congolaise, Belgium).
1951: *Anne Reed* (D/S A/S Ibis, Norway).
1956: *Pagenturm* (Rebuilt at Hamburg) (Hansa Line, Bremen).
6.1964: Scrapped Spezia.

Empire Game (Hansa 'A' type) 1,925 gt. Built: Van der Giessen, Krimpen, Holland, in 1943 as *Brunhilde* for Hamburg South-America Line. 279 ft × 44 ft. Engines: C4cyl.
5.1945: Taken in prize at Kiel. Renamed *Empire Game* (M.O.W.T.).
1947: *Canford* (Mundus Export & Shipping Co.).
1956: *Fangturm* (rebuilt at Bremerhaven) (Hansa Line, Bremen).

1961: *Panaghia Lourion* (Rio Pardo, Beirut).
1967: *Aghia Thalassini* (Tamara Cia. Nav., Greece).
1970: (Aldebaran Shipping Co., Cyprus).
1974: Scrapped Greece.

Empire Gangway (Hansa 'A' type) 1,942 gt.
Built: Deutsche Werft, Hamburg, in 1944 as *Weserwehr* for Norddeutscher Lloyd. 283 ft × 44 ft. Engines: C4cyl.
5.1945: Taken in prize at Bremerhaven. Renamed *Empire Gangway* (M.O.W.T.).
1946: Allocated to Canada (Government of Canada).
1948: (Clark SS Co., Montreal).
1950: Renamed *Novaport*.
1964: *Fury* (Eagle Ocean Transport Inc., Panama).
1.12.1964: Driven aground on rocks at Wedge Island, 110 miles from Halifax, N.S., in hurricane-force winds and heavy seas. Flooded, tidal and abandoned when breaking up. Driven by mountainous seas over rock ledges and stranded on inshore reef. Total loss (voyage: Quebec/Halifax – ballast).

Empire Gantry (Hansa 'A' type) 1,925 gt. Launched by Werf de Noord, Alblasserdam, Holland, in 1944 as *Imkenturm* for Hansa Line, Bremen. Towed to Flensburg and completed by Flensburger Schiff-Gesellschaft. 288 ft × 44 ft. Engines: C4cyl.
5.1945: Taken in prize at Flensburg. Renamed *Empire Gantry* (M.O.W.T.).
1946: Allocated to U.S.S.R., renamed *Feodosia*.
1947: *Olsztyn* (Gdynia America Lines, Poland).
1951: (Polska Zegluga Morska, Poland).
1.1972: Scrapped Bruges.

Empire Ganymede (Hansa 'A' type) 1,923 gt.
Built: Deutsche Werft, Hamburg, in 1944 as *Adamsturm* for Hansa Line, Bremen. 280 ft × 44 ft. Engines: C4cyl.
5.1945: Taken in prize at Hamburg. Renamed *Empire Ganymede* (M.O.W.T.).
1947: *Baltanglia* (United Baltic Corporation, London).
1952: Renamed *Baltic Pine*.
1954: *Germania* (Hellenic Lines, Greece).
26.4.1955: Collision with ss *Maro* (1919, 7,588 gt) four miles south of Beachy Head, Sussex. Grounded near Beachy Head Lighthouse.
30.11.1955: Refloated, beached Pevensey Bay; back broken; Constructive total loss. Sold, towed to Germany for repair. Renamed *Auriga* (Argo Line, Bremen).
1.1965: Scrapped Bremerhaven.

Empire Garland (Hansa 'A' type) 1,925 gt.
Built: Stettiner Vulkan Werft A.G., in 1944 as *Njong*

for Deutsche-Afrika Line. 288 ft × 44 ft.
Engines: C4cyl.
5.1945: Taken in prize at Flensburg. Renamed *Empire Garland* (M.O.W.T.).
1947: *Sheldrake* (General Steam Nav. Co. Ltd.).
1959: *Salemstar* (Johal Nav. Ltd., Liberia).
1960: *Ambelos* (Johal Nav. Ltd., Greece).
1961: *Marmina* (N. J. Goumas, Greece).
1968: *Filio* (C. Raikos & F. Raikou, Greece).
6.1972: Scrapped Aspropyrgos, Greece.

Empire Garner (Hansa 'A' type) 1,923 gt. Built: N.
V. Werft Gusto, Schiedam, Holland, in 1943 as
Hendrik Fisser 6 for Fisser & Van Doornum, Emden.
280 ft × 44 ft. Engines: C4cyl.
5.1945: Taken in prize at Kiel. Renamed *Empire Garner* (M.O.W.T.).
1946: Allocated to U.S.S.R., renamed *Ribinsk*.
No further trace.

Empire Garrison (Hansa 'A' type) 1,925 gt.
Built: Maats. de Schelde, Flushing, in 1944 as *Kalliope*
for Neptun Line, Bremen. 280 ft × 44 ft.
Engines: C4cyl.
5.1945: Taken in prize at Flensburg. Renamed *Empire Garrison* (M.O.W.T.).
1947: *Bengore Head* (Ulster SS Co., (G. Heyn & Sons)).
1967: *Agios Nectarios* (Canopus Shipping S.A., Greece).
1971: (Aldebaran Shipping Co., Cyprus).
1.1974: Scrapped Spain.

Empire Garry 8,457 gt. Built: Deutsche Schiff- und
Masch., Bremen, in 1928 as *Treuenfels* for Hansa
Line, Bremen. 490 ft × 62 ft. Engines: T3cyl.
6.1945: Taken in prize at Aarhus, Denmark. Taken
to Kiel, where remained for eighteen months.
3.1947: Arrived Leith, renamed *Empire Garry*
(M.O.T.).
1949: *Vergray* (Haddon SS Co.).
1951: *Elath* (Israel-America Line, Israel).
1956: *Shinano Maru* (Nichiro Gyogyo K.K., Japan).
1961: (Converted to a fish factory; re-engined with
oil engine; 9,035 gt).
8.1972: Scrapped Taiwan.

Empire Garston 1,958 gt. Built: Flensburger Schiff-
Gesellschaft in 1930 as *Lipari* for R. M. Sloman,
Hamburg. 301 ft × 43 ft. Engines: T3cyl.
30.12.1942: Interned at Cartagena, Spain.
1945: Surrendered to U.K. in prize. Renamed *Empire Garston* (M.O.W.T.).
1946: Allocated to Holland, renamed *Arnhem*
(Government of Netherlands).
1947: *Orion* (K.N.S.M., Rotterdam).

1960: Scrapped Antwerp.

Empire Gatehouse (Hansa 'A' type) 1,924 gt.
Built: Lübecker Flenderwerke A.G., in 1943 as
Tiefland for Hamburg South-America Line.
280 ft × 44 ft. Engines: C4cyl.
5.1945: Taken in prize at Brunsbüttel. Renamed
Empire Gatehouse (M.O.W.T.).
1947: Allocated to Canada; renamed *Gulfport*
(Gulfport SS Co., Montreal).
1964: *Stefani* (Alma Shipping Co., Liberia).
1966: *Agia Marina* (M. N. Arcadis, Liberia).
1967: *Bright* (Bright Shipping Co., Greece).
1969: *Khalda* (Khalda Shipping Co., Panama).
12.1970: Grounded in Gulf of Suez.
1.1.1971: Refloated.
1974: Under arrest at Massawa. Sold by Court Order,
and:
1977: (A. S. & Y. F. Obeid, Massawa). Vessel
reported to be lying in damaged condition in port.
1984: Reported scrapped in 1982.

Empire Gatwick (Hansa 'A' type) 1,923 gt.
Built: Lübecker Flenderwerke A.G., in 1944 as *Sanga*
for Deutsche Afrika Line. 280 ft × 44 ft.
Engines: C4cyl.
5.1945: Taken in prize at Copenhagen. Renamed
Empire Gatwick (M.O.W.T.).
1947: Allocated to Greece, renamed *Vorios Hellas*
(Government of Greece).
1948: (Hellenic Lines, Greece).
1974: (Papageorgiou Bros., Greece).
4.1974: Scrapped Gemlik, Turkey.

Empire Gavel (Hansa 'A' type) 1,923 gt.
Built: Lübecker Maschinenbau Ges., in 1944 as
Setubal for Oldenburg-Portuguese Line.
280 ft × 44 ft. Engines: C4cyl.
5.1945: Taken in prize at Lübeck. Renamed *Empire Gavel* (M.O.W.T.).
1946: Allocated to Greece, renamed *Rodopi*
(Government of Greece).
1949: (Hellenic Lines, Greece).
4.1974: Scrapped Turkey.

Empire Glencoe 4,854 gt. Launched by Nordseewerke,
Emden, in 1941 as *Atlas* for German account.
416 ft × 57 ft. Engines: Oil.
1941: Sunk during R.A.F. bombing raid on Emden,
before completion. Later raised.
5.1945: Taken in prize, incomplete, at Kiel.
1948: Completed; renamed *Empire Glencoe* (M.O.T.).
1952–1955: To be renamed *Bantry Bay* (H. P.
Lenaghan & Son, Belfast) but transaction for purchase
not completed. Resold by M.O.T., and:
1955: *Regine* (Karl Gross K.G., Bremen).

1956: Renamed *Regine Ohlrogge*.
1959: Renamed *Regine*.
8.1976: Sold to German shipbreakers; resold, and:
9.1976: Scrapped Santander.

Empire Halladale 14,056 gt. Built: Vulkan Werke, Hamburg, in 1921 as *Antonio Delfino* for Hamburg South America Line. 500 ft × 64 ft. Engines: T6cyl.
1932: *Sierra Nevada* (charter to Norddeutscher Lloyd).
1934: (Reverted to original name and owners).
9.1939: At Bahia, Brazil, at outbreak of war; ran Allied blockade and reached Germany.
1940: Requisitioned by German Navy as a barracks ship at Kiel, then, in 1943, at Gdynia.
1944: Became Command Ship for Admiral, Submarines, at Gdynia.
1945: A transport for wounded personnel and refugees from Gdynia to West Germany; made five voyages and carried 20,552 persons.
5.1945: Taken in prize at Copenhagen. Sailed to U.K. and refitted as a troopship by J. Brown & Co., Clydebank.
1946: Renamed *Empire Halladale* (M.O.T.) and:
31.8.1946: Inaugurated a regular service carrying wives and children of British Army personnel based in Germany, when she left Tilbury bound for Cuxhaven. Later the vessel made trooping voyages to the Middle East and Far East.
10.1955: Laid up at Glasgow after making last trooping voyage to Liverpool, and:
2.1956: Scrapped Dalmuir.

Note: This ship was a sistership to *Empire Trooper* (ex *Cap Norte*) which joined the *Empire Halladale* at a later date, sailings from Tilbury then scheduled for every Tuesday and Friday for the 36-hour voyage.
(See also *Empire Trooper*.)

Empire Helford 6,598 gt. Built: Barclay, Curle & Co. Ltd., Glasgow, in 1915 as *Czaritza* for Russian-American Line. 440 ft × 53 ft. Engines: Q8cyl.

During the great trek of emigrants from northern Europe to the New World around the turn of the century, the Germans professed to believe that a cholera epidemic in the greatly-used departure port of Hamburg was started by Russian emigrants and they established 'control stations', ostensibly for severe medical examination and the cleansing of human bodies but, in fact, used to force Russians to use German ships.

Russia needed a liner company under its own national flag. The nation's experience was virtually nil and so it turned to the Danish East Asiatic Company, who formed for them the Russian-American Line, of which it is said that it secured many additional passengers with the advertising slogan 'Travel by our Russian ships and do not be forced to take a bath'.

At first the *Czaritza* ran under the Russian flag between Archangel and New York. After the Revolution she was requisitioned by the British Government, but in 1920 reverted to her original owners, who were now refugees themselves. Renamed *Lituania*, the ship joined the Danish company's emigrant service to New York. Within a few years American restrictions on immigration so curtailed these operations that in 1930 the vessel was sold to the Polish Transatlantic Shipping Company (later Gdynia-America Shipping Lines), becoming *Kosciuszko*.

At the outbreak of World War II she was taken over by the Polish Navy and renamed *Gdynia*, but was soon at Devonport, under the Polish flag and in use as a depot and accommodation ship. Employed on general trooping duties until war's end, but then her crew refused to recognise Russian-controlled Poland and, instead, signed British Articles of maritime employment. The ship's name reverted to *Kosciuszko*.

In 1946 the vessel was renamed *Empire Helford* under the British flag and Lamport & Holt management and continued trooping between Calcutta and Rangoon until the British Army left India. In 1950 she was broken up at Blyth.

Note: A sistership, built as *Czar*, became *Empire Penryn* (*q.v.*).

Empire Helmsdale 2,978 gt. Built: Deutsche Werft, Hamburg, in 1934 as *Sofia*. 353 ft × 50 ft. Engines: Oil.
1938: *Telde* (Oldenburg-Portuguese Line).
1940: Requisitioned by German Navy.
5.1945: Taken in prize at Copenhagen. Renamed *Empire Helmsdale* (M.O.W.T.).
1946: Allocated to U.S.A. (U.S.M.C.).
1948: *Sea Trader* (4,290 gt) (Sea Trade Corporation, New York).
1949: *Risano* (Lloyd Triestino, Italy).
9.1972: Scrapped Trieste.

Empire Humber 9,677 gt. Built: Burmeister & Wain, Copenhagen, in 1939 as *Glengarry*. 475 ft × 66 ft. Engines: Oil.

Launched in November 1939 the *Glengarry*, building for the Glen Line Ltd., London, was not quite completed when seized at her builder's yard by the Germans in April 1940. After successful trials she became *Meerberg* in the October and the next month joined a U-boat flotilla as a target ship. In April 1941 she was chosen for conversion to a raider, given the code name 'Ship No. 5' and was to be fitted with eight 5.9-inch, two 3.1-inch and smaller guns, four torpedo tubes, an aircraft catapult and space for 150 mines.

June 1941 found the ship in Rotterdam, where conversion work was to be carried out at the Wilton Fijenoord shipyard. She was still there two years later, Allied bombing and shortages having delayed delivery of materials, and she was moved to Hamburg for installation of secret equipment. Again, various delays prevented her completion by the stipulated date of October 1943; nevertheless the German Naval Staff persevered in their scheme to convert her into a 'super raider', incorporating into her outfitting all the experiences of earlier raiders, and to get her to sea by 1944. Hopes soon faded and on 10 February 1944 she was renamed

Hansa and commissioned as an artillery cadet training ship. She worked mainly in the Baltic, took part in the evacuation of Revel, Estonia, in September 1944 and then returned to Copenhagen 'to assist in the defence of the port'.

In May 1945 she assisted in the large-scale German evacuation as the Russians swept westward along the Baltic coast, embarking several thousand troops at Hela, near Danzig, for Lübeck Bay. These troops were still aboard her at the time of the German surrender, and the ship was taken in prize at Kiel in May 1945. In mid-June of the same year she passed through the Kiel Canal and joined a convoy of some forty 'prize' vessels bound from Hamburg to Methil, Fife, being the only ship to sail under her 'National colours', the others wearing the flag of surrender.

At Methil the Admiralty considered her a naval prize. Nevertheless, she took the name *Empire Humber* under the M.O.W.T. and was ordered to Rotterdam, via the Clyde and Portsmouth, for conversion to a Combined Operations H.Q. ship, for service in the Pacific. But then followed a long stay in Southampton, during which time Japan surrendered, and the ship was arrested in the name of the Admiralty Marshal. Finding the vessel's mainmast unresponsive, the writ was nailed to the Captain's cabin door. At the same time her managers (Glen Line Ltd.) had ordered the ship to the Gareloch and though the Admiralty representative was adamant that the vessel could not sail, she did.

Nothing more was heard of this infringement of maritime law, the issue evaded being whether the ship, never having served her original owners and having been found, as an ex-warship, in enemy hands was, in truth, a naval prize or not.

By 1946 the ship was again *Glengarry* under her original owners. In 1970 she transferred to her parent company – Ocean SS Co. – becoming *Dardanus*, and in 1971 took the title *Glengarry* again, for her final voyage to shipbreakers at Sakaide, Japan.

Empire Janus (whaler) 575 gt. Built: Kaldnes Mek. Verk., Tønsberg, Norway, in 1944 as *Jan Mayen*. 156 ft × 30 ft. Engines: T3cyl.
1944: Requisitioned by Germany at builder's yard.
5.1945: Taken in prize; renamed *Empire Janus* (M.O.W.T.).
1947: *Southern Main* (Chr. Salvesen & Co., Leith).
1964: Scrapped Odense.

Empire Jewel See *Empire Fowey*.

Empire Ken 9,523 gt. Built: Blohm & Voss, Hamburg, in 1928 as *Ubena* for Deutsche East Africa Line. 469 ft × 60 ft. Engines: four steam turbines.
1939: Requisitioned by German Navy; used as a depot ship for 3rd, 5th and 21st U-Boat flotillas.
1945: Converted to a (German) hospital ship; used in the evacuation of Eastern Baltic territories: in seven voyages carried 27,170 persons to Germany.
5.1945: Taken in prize at Travemunde. Renamed *Empire Ken* (M.O.W.T.).
12.1945: Completed conversion to a troopship on River Clyde. Her trooping service was to last for less

than twelve years, during which time she also helped-out on the Harwich/Hook of Holland run with B.A.O.R. personnel on leave to and from West Germany. Her last trooping voyage was from Cyprus to Southampton.
9.1957: Scrapping commenced at Dalmuir, and:
16.12.1957: Cut-down hulk arrived at Troon for final demolition.

Empire Kennet 2,319 gt. Built: Deutsche Werft, Hamburg, in 1925 as *Las Palmas* for Oldenburg-Portuguese Line. 270 ft × 42 ft. Engines: C4cyl.
5.1945: Taken in prize at Flensburg. Renamed *Empire Kennet* (M.O.W.T.).
1946: Allocated to U.S.S.R., renamed *Brest*. Later converted to a fish factory ship and stationed at Vladivostok.
1955: Name removed from ship registers; vessel later reported broken up in U.S.S.R. in 1971.

Empire Kent 4,769 gt. Built: Nordseewerke, Emden, in 1939 as *Levante* for Deutsche Levante Line. 408 ft × 57 ft. Engines: Oil.
5.1945: Taken in prize at Oslo. Renamed *Empire Kent* (M.O.W.T.).
1947: *Oakmore* (Johnston Warren Lines Ltd.).
4.1967: Scrapped Aviles.

Empire Lark 4,971 gt. Built: Deutsche Werke, Kiel, in 1921 as *Martha Hemsoth*. 408 ft × 54 ft. Engines: two steam turbines.
1926: *Kersten Miles* (Hanseatische Reederei, Hamburg).
27.10.1939: Interned at Las Palmas after arriving with machinery damage on a voyage Argentina to Germany with wheat.
1945: Surrendered to U.K. in prize. Renamed *Empire Lark* (M.O.W.T.).
1946: Selected to be scuttled with obsolete ammunition.
29.1.1947: Left Plymouth in tow, and:
1.2.1947: Arrived at Barry Dock.
3.2.1947: Commenced loading a full cargo of chemical warfare gas bombs and shells. Then experienced long delays on account of severe snow and ice conditions, this curtailing delivery of cargo alongside and causing slow loading due to the nature of the cargo.
18.7.1947: Loading completed, being 7,669 tons of ammunition plus 20 tons of contaminated earth.
27.7.1947: Left in tow of tug *Dexterous*, with a frigate escort, and scuttled in South-West Approaches, 200 miles off Lands End, in position 47.55N 8.25W.

Empire Lea 2,563 gt. Built: Nakskov Skibs Akt. in 1942 as *Karin K. Bornhofen* for R. Bornhofen, Hamburg. 304 ft × 45 ft. Engines: C4cyl.

5.1945: Taken in prize at Copenhagen. Renamed *Empire Lea* (M.O.W.T.).
1946: Allocated to U.S.S.R., renamed *Verkhoyansk*.
1971: Name removed from ship registers: no further trace.

Empire Lune (Hansa 'B' type) 2,837 gt. Launched by Nakskov Skibs Akt. in 1943 as *Millerntor* for Hamburg America Line. Towed to Lübeck and completed in 1945 by Lübecker Flenderwerke A.G. 334 ft × 51 ft. Engines: C4cyl.
5.1945: Taken in prize at Flensburg. Renamed *Empire Lune* (M.O.W.T.).
1947: Allocated to U.S.A., sold and renamed *Alabama Sword* (Sword Line Ltd., New York).
1951: Renamed *Texas Sword*.
1956: *Zephyr* (Cia. de Ultramar S.A., Liberia).
10.11.1962: Grounded off Gladden Spit, British Honduras, 16.32N 87.59W.
17.11.1962: Caught fire while still aground; later extinguished.
27.11.1962: Refloated, but constructive total loss. Sold and repaired, and:
1964: *Carina* (Transcontinental Shipping Corp., Liberia).
1966: *Sapho I* (Astronato Cia. Nav., Liberia).
1967: *Corinthian Glory* (Marvigor Cia. Nav., Liberia).
3.1970: Scrapped Karachi.

Empire Medway 2,391 gt. Built: Moss Vaerft & Dokk, Moss, Norway, in 1938 as *Wandsbek* for Knohr & Burchard, Hamburg. 301 ft × 48 ft.
Engines: T3cyl.
21.7.1941: Sunk by Allied aircraft bombs at Narvik.
29.3.1943: Salved and repaired.
5.1945: Taken in prize; renamed *Empire Medway* (M.O.W.T.).
1946: Allocated to U.S.S.R., renamed *Alexandr Pushkin*.
Vessel not reported since 1955: no further trace.

Empire Mole 4,876 gt. Launched by Deutsche Werft, Hamburg, in 1939 as *Panther* for Laeisz Line. Towed to Copenhagen and completed in 1941 by Burmeister & Wain. 394 ft × 53 ft. Engines: Oil.
1941: Requisitioned by German Navy, converted to an auxiliary cruiser, renamed *Salzburg*.
5.1945: Taken in prize in Kiel Canal. Renamed *Empire Mole* (M.O.W.T.).
1947: *Reventazon* (Elders & Fyffes Ltd.).
1963: *Kimolos* (Jade Co. Inc., Panama).
1972: *Vassilia K* (G. J. Karageorgis Shipping Ltd., Greece).
12.1973: Scrapped Kaohsiung.

Empire Mowddach 3,410 gt. Built: Bremer Vulkan Schiff- und Masch., Vegesack, in 1935 as *Pontos* for F. Laeisz, Hamburg. 366 ft × 45 ft. Engines: Oil.

1940: Requisitioned by German Navy.
5.1945: Taken in prize at Flensburg. Renamed *Empire Mowddach* (M.O.W.T.).
1947: *Nicoya* (Elders & Fyffes Ltd.).
1959: Scrapped Briton Ferry.

Empire Nairn (Hansa 'A' type) 1,923 gt. Launched by Flensburger Schiff-Gesellschaft in 1944 as *Pagenturm* for Hansa Line, Bremen. 287 ft × 44 ft.
Engines: C4cyl.
5.1945: Taken in prize, incomplete, at Flensburg. Completed as *Empire Nairn* (M.O.W.T.).
1947: *Kamuning* (Straits SS Co. Ltd., Singapore).
1956: *Jalatarang* (Scindia SN Co., India).
6.1964: Scrapped Bombay.

Empire Neath 2,150 gt. Built: Neptun A.G., Rostock, in 1935 as *Catania* for R. M. Sloman Jr., Hamburg. 303 ft × 44 ft. Engines: C4cyl.
5.1945: Taken in prize at Aarhus, Denmark. Renamed *Empire Neath* (M.O.W.T.).
1946: Allocated to U.S.S.R., renamed *Meridian*.
1947: Renamed *Equator*.
1949: Converted to a merchant marine training ship.
1982: Moored at Otrada, Bay of Odessa, as a non-seagoing training ship.

Empire Nene 6,113 gt. Laid down by Lübecker Flenderwerke A.G., in 1945 as *Schwarzwald* for Hamburg America Line. 455 ft × 61 ft. Engines: C4cyl.
5.1945: Taken in prize, incomplete and still on stocks, at Lübeck.
8.1947: Completed as *Empire Nene* (M.O.W.T.).
1954: *Mariposa* (Mariblanca Nav. S.A., Liberia).
1956: *Rotenfels* (rebuilt at Bremerhaven) (Hansa Line, Bremen).
1961: (New (oil) engine).
8.1977: Scrapped Karachi.

Empire Nidd 4,742 gt. Laid down by Danziger Werft A.G., in 1939 as *Bielsko* for Polish account. Hull seized by Germany, towed to Helsingborg and completed in 1943 as *Minden* for Norddeutscher Lloyd. 416 ft × 55 ft. Engines: Oil.
5.1945: Taken in prize at Nyborg, Denmark. Renamed *Empire Nidd* (M.O.W.T.).
1946: Allocated to U.S.S.R., renamed *Denis Davydov*.
1947: *General Walter* (Gdynia America Line, Poland).
11.1970: Scrapped Hong Kong.

Empire Ock 6,133 gt. Built: Blohm & Voss, Hamburg, in 1939 as *Dogu*. 385 ft × 53 ft.
Engines: T6cyl.
1940: *Luderitzbucht* (Deutsche Afrika Line, Germany).
1945: Renamed *Duala*.

The *Empire Frome*, as the cable ship *Ocean Layer*, in the River Thames. She was completed from a German 'Hansa B'-type hull.

The *Empire Halladale* in May 1951.   *Tom Rayner collection*

The *Highland*, formerly *Empire Galbraith*, of the German-built 'Hansa A'-type.   *Skyfotos*

5.1945: Taken in prize at Flensburg. Renamed *Empire Ock* (M.O.W.T.).
1946: Allocated to U.S.S.R., renamed *Peotr Weliky*.
1948: *Jagiello* (Gydnia America Line, Poland).
1949: *Petr Velikiy* (U.S.S.R.).
1974: Scrapped Castellon.

In 1939 Blohm & Voss launched three identical passenger-cargo ships for Turkish owners, *Dogu* (above), *Egeman* and *Savas*. At the outbreak of war they were all requisitioned by Germany and upon their completion were allocated to the Deutsche Afrika Line for management, being renamed *Luderitzbucht*, *Swakopmund* and *Dar es Salaam*, respectively.

The *Swakopmund* was bombed and sunk in the Baltic and the *Dar es Salaam*, found bomb-damaged at Kiel at the end of the war, was used as a floating restaurant at Hamburg until 1951 and was then towed to Sheerness, Kent, still minus a large stern section which had been removed after the wartime bomb damage. Later she was broken up at Grays, Essex, without being renamed.

The *Luderitzbucht*, used as an accommodation ship during the war, became *Duala* in 1945 and, soon after, was acquired and given her 'Empire' name.

Empire Orwell 3,132 gt. Built: Armstrong, Whitworth & Co. Ltd., Newcastle, in 1921 as *Vindeggen*. 330 ft × 47 ft. Engines: T3cyl.
1939: *Olga Traber* (W. Traber & Co., Hamburg).
5.1945: Taken in prize at Kiel. Renamed *Empire Orwell* (M.O.W.T.).
1946: Allocated to U.S.S.R., renamed *Poltava*.
No further trace.

Empire Orwell (17,362 gt) See *Empire Doon*.

Empire Ouse 4,833 gt. Built: Burntisland Shipbuilding Co. Ltd., in 1937 as *Ginnheim* for Unterweser Reederei, Bremen. 410 ft × 56 ft. Engines: T3cyl.
5.1945: Taken in prize at Brunsbüttel. Renamed *Empire Ouse* (M.O.W.T.).
1946: Allocated to Holland, renamed *Eindhoven* (Government of Netherlands).
1947: *Parkhaven* (Van Uden Scheeps. Maat., Rotterdam).
1953: *Christopher Oldendorff* (E. Oldendorff, Lübeck).
1963: Scrapped El Ferrol, Spain.

Empire Oykell 2,623 gt. Built: Flensburger Schiff-Gesellschaft in 1939 as *Adele Traber* for W. Traber Pr Co., Hamburg. 284 ft × 46 ft. Engines: T3cyl.
5.1945: Taken in prize in Kiel Canal. Renamed *Empire Oykell* (M.O.W.T.).
1946: Allocated to Norway, renamed *Bruse* (Government of Norway).
1958: *Hoegh Bruse* (Leif Hoegh & Co., Norway).
1959: Renamed *Hoegh Collier*.
1961: *Pomo* (O/Y Propsshipping Ltd., Finland).

1967: *Tomi* (Rauma Chartering Ltd., Finland).
6.1968: Scrapped Spezia.

Empire Patrai See *Empire Towy*.

Empire Penryn 6,515 gt. Built: Barclay, Curle & Co. Ltd., Glasgow, in 1912 as *Czar*. 426 ft × 53 ft. Engines: Q8cyl.
1921: *Estonia* (East Asiatic Company, Denmark).
1930: *Pulaski* (Gdynia America Lines, Poland).
1945: *Empire Penryn* (M.O.W.T.).
1949: Scrapped Blyth.

After the fall of Poland to the Germans in 1939, four Polish passenger ships were placed under British Ministry of Transport control, with Lamport & Holt as managers. The vessels were the sisters *Batory* (1936, 14,287 gt) and *Pilsudski* (1936, 14,294 gt) – their purchase from their Italian builders being partly made by exchanging Polish coal – and the near-sisters *Kosciuszko* and *Pulaski*, all owned by Gdynia America Lines.

The *Pilsudski* left Poland for New York in July 1939; war was declared during her return voyage and she was met in mid-Atlantic by the Royal Navy and ordered into Inverness, where she was converted for trooping. On 26 November 1939, in the North Sea and outward bound for Australia, she detonated two magnetic mines and sank.

The three remaining ships retained their names and their Polish crews throughout the war and were also used as troopships. The *Batory* was returned to Poland in 1945, but the other crews refused repatriation and their ships were placed under the British flag and given 'Empire' names.

The *Pulaski* was built as the *Czar* for the Russian-American Line, backed by the Danish East Asiatic Company, and was intended to break the German monopoly of the Baltic emigrant trade to America. After the Russian Revolution she was requisitioned by the British Government but in 1921 her ownership was established and the vessel was returned to the East Asiatic Company, who renamed her *Estonia* for their Baltic-American Line. In 1930 she went to the Gdynia America Line and was renamed *Pulaski*.

At the fall of France in 1940 she was in port at Konakri and the French authorities there, anxious not to offend the Germans, said she would be detained. But the vessel escaped at night, making her way from the inner harbour under heavy fire from the shore batteries, and joining the Allies. At the end of the war the *Pulaski* was refitted at Calcutta and renamed to *Empire Penryn*. Her near-sister, built as *Czaritza*, became *Empire Helford* (q.v.).

Empire Rhondda 1,096 gt. Built: Schiffswerft A.G., Hamburg, in 1923 as *Pasajes* for Oldenburg-Portuguese Line, Hamburg. 256 ft × 38 ft. Engines: T3cyl.
11.1.1945: Aground in Skagerrak in position 58.05N 8.15E. Salved, taken to Kristiansand for repairs.
5.1945: Taken in prize at Frederikshaven, Denmark. Renamed *Empire Rhondda* (M.O.W.T.).

1946: Allocated to U.S.S.R., renamed *Henri Barbusse*. Vessel not reported since 1955 and name deleted from ship registers in 1968, the existence of the vessel in doubt.

Empire Ribble 4,525 gt. Built: Lithgows Ltd., Port Glasgow, in 1922 as *Dunstaffnage*. 385 ft × 52 ft. Engines: T3cyl.
1939: *Magdalene Vinnen* (F. A. Vinnen & Co., Bremen).
7.1943: Badly damaged in Allied air attack on Hamburg. Towed to Copenhagen for repairs.
5.1945: Taken in prize at Copenhagen, still bearing the scars of the air attack, with her bridge temporarily built up and the vessel painted with black-striped camouflage on a grey hull: at her bows was a long arm which swung out, with a propeller mounted on it, for dealing with acoustic mines. Renamed *Empire Ribble* (M.O.W.T.).
1945: *Oosterbeek* (Charter to Government of Netherlands).
1946: Allocated to Holland, and:
1947: *Winterswijk* (Erhardt & Dekkers, Holland).
1954: *Universal Trader* (Peak SS Co., Hong Kong).
1958: (Great Southern SS Co., Hong Kong).
1959: Scrapped Yokohama.

Empire Roden (Hansa 'B' type) 2,837 gt.
Built: Helsingørs Mask., Elsinore, in 1943 as *Halsnaes* (originally for Danish owners), then renamed *Helgenaes*. 334 ft × 51 ft. Engines: C4cyl.
1943: Requisitioned by Germany, renamed *Krönenfels* (Hansa Line).
5.1945: Taken in prize at Copenhagen. Renamed *Empire Roden*, (M.O.W.T.).
1947: Allocated to U.S.A. (U.S.M.C.), then:
1947: *Florida Sword* (Sword Line Inc., New York).
1956: *Cheyenne* (Gecapo Mar. Nav., Liberia).
1957: *St. Nicholas* (Supreme Nav. Corp., Liberia).
8.8.1958: Stranded on a reef 135 miles off Kingston, Jamaica.
9.1958: Salvage attempts abandoned. Total loss (voyage: Galveston/Colombia – grain).

Empire Roding 2,957 gt. Built: Flensburger Schiff-Gesellschaft in 1937 as *Ernst L. M. Russ* for Ernst Russ, Hamburg. 341 ft × 53 ft. Engines: T3cyl.
5.1945: Taken in prize at Flensburg. Renamed *Empire Roding* (M.O.W.T.).
1946: Allocated to U.S.A. (U.S.M.C.).
1947: *Eastport* (Eastport SS Corp., New York).
1950: *Tsfonit* (Zim Israel Nav. Co., Israel).
1961: *Flamatt* (Agenzia Gen. Nav. Marittima, Italy).
1963: *Florita* (Nana Trading & Shipping Co., Liberia).
1970: *Pamela* (Raffaele Di Maio, Liberia).
8.1972: Scrapped Trieste.

Empire Salerno 877 gt. Built: Earles Shipbuilding Co. Ltd., Hull, in 1920 as *Salerno* for Ellerman Wilson Line. 216 ft × 33 ft. Engines: T3cyl.
15.4.1940: Seized in Sauda Fjord, Norway, by Germans. Renamed *Markirch*: used as a target-towing vessel.
5.1945: Taken in prize at Eckernförde; renamed *Empire Salerno* (M.O.W.T.).
1946: *Salerno* (Ellerman Wilson Line).
1957: *Taxiarchis* (M. A. Karageorgis, Greece).
18.12.1958: Aground on reef between Kos Island (Greece) and Turkish mainland. Hull fractured and leaking (voyage: Izmir/Beirut – tobacco).
23.12.1958: Refloated; proceeded to Kos Island, then towed to Piraeus. Repairs uneconomic: sold, and:
8.1959: Scrapped Perama.

The *Salerno*, owned by the Ellerman Wilson Line, of Hull, was captured by the German invaders of Norway in April 1940 when she was on a voyage from Bergen to Hull. Renamed, she was put into service towing targets for the torpedo school at Eckernförde. Taken by the British following the German collapse, she was sent home, becoming *Empire Salerno*.

As a German vessel the ship was taken in prize, a move which led to a difficult court case. However, in 1946 it was decided that the ship should be returned to her original owners and she recommenced service for them in October 1946 under her original name.

Empire Salmonpool 4,928 gt. Built: Irvines SB & DD Co. Ltd., West Hartlepool, in 1924 as *Salmonpool* for Sir R. Ropner & Sons. 390 ft × 55 ft. Engines: T3cyl.
15.4.1940: (As *Salmonpool*) completed discharge of cargo of coke at Sauda Fjord, Norway, when the country over-run by German forces. An attempt to escape was made, but the vessel was intercepted by German naval units and taken to Trondheim. Renamed *Putzig* and mainly employed in carrying ore from Lulea to German Baltic ports.
5.1945: Taken in prize at Bremerhaven. Renamed *Empire Salmonpool* (M.O.W.T.).
1947: *Irene K* (Kyriakides Shipping Co., London).
1955: Renamed *White Lodge*.
1955: *Puntarenas* (Maritime Transport Overseas S.A., Panama).
1958: Scrapped Aviles, Spain.

Note: Another British vessel, *Salerno*, was also captured by German forces at Sauda Fjord, Norway, on 15 April 1940 (see *Empire Salerno*, above).

Empire Soar 2,740 gt. Built: Blyth SB & DD Co. Ltd. in 1924 as *Tullochmoor*. 320 ft × 43 ft. Engines: T3cyl.
1936: *Brigitte* (Franz L. Nimitz, Stettin).

5.1945: Taken in prize at Hamburg. Renamed *Empire Soar* (M.O.W.T.).
1946: Allocated to Greece, renamed *Preveza* (Government of Greece).
1948: *Danapris* (Synodinos Bros., Greece).
1957: *Armonia* (A. Angelicoussis & Co., Greece).
1959: *Keanyew* (Keanyew Shipping Co., Panama).
1960: Renamed *Charlie* (for sale to shipbreakers) (Southern Commercial Co., Panama).
1.1960: Scrapped Hong Kong.

Empire Spinel 650 gt. Built: Henry Robb Ltd., Leith, in 1937 as *Spinel* for Wm. Robertson, Glasgow. 178 ft × 29 ft. Engines: Oil.
21.5.1940: Sunk by German aircraft bombs at Dunkirk.
4.7.1940: Salved by Germany; repaired.
5.1945: Taken in prize in Channel Islands. Renamed *Empire Spinel* (M.O.W.T.).
1946: Reverted to original name and owner.
4.1970: Scrapped Dalmuir.

Empire Springfjord 2,036 gt. Launched by Trondheims Mek. Verk., Trondheim, in 1940 as *Springfjord* for Springwell Shipping Co. Ltd., London. Seized by Germany while still building; completed as *Rudesheimer* for German account (Hansa Line). 286 ft × 44 ft. Engines: T3cyl.
5.1945: Taken in prize at Tønsberg, and:
1946: *Empire Springfjord* (M.O.T.).
1947: Reverted to original name and owner.
27.6.1954: Bombed by aircraft and set on fire while at anchor at San José, Guatamala, with general cargo, during Guatamalan revolution. Sank. Total loss.

Empire Stevedore 750 gt (approx.). Built as German vessel *KT 3*. 224 ft × 36 ft (approx.).
10.1949: Taken over at Hamburg by the Royal Engineers, and:
1950: Taken to Marchwood, Southampton, for use as a Stevedore Training Ship for their Port Unit. Renamed *Empire Stevedore*. The vessel replaced the former Port Training Ship *Empire Flaminian* (*q.v.*), which was towed to Dover for scrapping in 1950.

Note: 'KT' (Kriegstransporter) vessels were intended to be a class of some fifty-four ships built by the Axis as 'war freighters' for the transport of troops and stores, many of them also equipped for anti-submarine duties. Some of the vessels were built in Italy, these frequently used as blockade runners in the Mediterranean, carrying stores and personnel to the German Afrika Corps in North Africa.
Construction details for these vessels are, generally, shown as 224 ft (oa), 203 ft × 36 ft; 700–800 gross tons, 1,000 tdw, 1,200 tons displacement. Twin-screw, with steam reciprocating machinery and exhaust turbines, 2,400 ihp giving 14½ knots. Fuel, for some of the few vessels of the type listed in postwar ship registers as converted to commercial craft, is shown as coal.
It is doubtful if the entire class of fifty-four vessels was completed and, generally, there is no listing of their builders.

Empire Swallow 209 gt. Built: J. Koster, Groningen, Holland, in 1928 as *Meuse*. 113 ft × 21 ft. Engines: Oil.
1935: *Swallow* (Wm. H. Muller & Co. (London) Ltd.).
12.6.1940: Damaged and abandoned on River Seine, Paris, during German occupation. Salved by Germany, renamed *Schwalbe*.
5.1945: Taken in prize in Channel Islands. Renamed *Empire Swallow* (M.O.W.T.).
1946: Reverted to British owners, again renamed *Swallow*.
1958: *Lies* (H. & T. Schoning, Düsseldorf).
1962: (Lengthened and deepened, 133 ft, 249 gt).
1969: *Mariana J* (M. Harmstorf, Hamburg).
1987: Name deleted from ship registers, existence of vessel in doubt.

Empire Taff 2,296 gt. Built: A. G. Weser, Bremen, in 1927 as *Apollo* for Neptun Line, Bremen. 288 ft × 46 ft. Engines: T3cyl.
5.1945: Taken in prize at Flensburg. Renamed *Empire Taff* (M.O.W.T.).
1947: *Alhama* (John Bruce & Co., Glasgow).
1953: Scrapped Faslane.

Empire Tagalam (tanker) 10,401 gt. Built: F. Schichau, Danzig, in 1936 as *Paul Harneit* for Deutsche Amerikanische Petroleum, Hamburg. 490 ft × 70 ft. Engines: Oil.
5.1945: Taken in prize at Brunsbüttel. Renamed *Empire Tagalam* (M.O.W.T.).
1946: Allocated to U.S.A. (U.S.M.C.).
1947: *Tagalam* (Marine Transport Lines, New York).
1955: *Cassian Sea* (Pioneer Shipping Corp., Liberia).
1960: Scrapped Split.

Empire Taganax (tanker) 10,128 gt. Built: Nakskov Skibs. Akt., Denmark, in 1940 as *Henning Maersk* for A. P. Moller, Copenhagen. 485 ft × 66 ft. Engines: Oil.
1940: Seized by Germany at the builder's yard, renamed *Hydra*.
5.1945: Taken in prize, extensively damaged, at Kiel. Repaired, and:
1946: *Empire Taganax* (M.O.W.T.).
1947: *Busen Star* (St. Helier Shipowners (Falkland Whaling Co., London)).
1961: Scrapped Rotterdam.

(Intended to be) *Empire Tagathel* (tanker) 10,802 gt.
Launched by Burmeister & Wain, Copenhagen, in
1940 as *Theodora* for Comp. Aux. de Navigation,
Paris. 515 ft × 66 ft. Engines: Oil.
1940: Seized by Germany at the builder's yard.
Completed in 1941 and renamed *Heide* (J. T.
Essberger, Hamburg).
5.1945: Taken in prize at Kiel.
30.6.1945: Arrived in River Clyde, to be renamed
Empire Tagathel, but transferred to French
Government, then reverted to original French name
and owners.
1960: *Isly* (S. A. Monegasque D'Armement de Nav.,
Monte Carlo).
1961: *Orval* (C. Audibert, Monte Carlo).
1961: (An oil storage and depot ship at Djibouti) (Soc.
de Travaux Trans. Maritimes, Paris).
2.1965: Scrapped Split.

Empire Tagealand (tanker) 6,492 gt. Built: A. G.
Weser, Bremen, in 1927 as *Mittelmeer* for J. T.
Essberger, Hamburg. 413 ft × 55 ft. Engines: Oil.
1940: Requisitioned by German Navy.
5.1945: Taken in prize at Brunsbüttel. Renamed
Empire Tagealand (M.O.W.T.).
1946: Allocated to U.S.S.R., renamed *Pamir*.
No trace after 1960.

Empire Tageos (tanker) 6,487 gt. Built: A. G. Weser,
Bremen, in 1927 as *Adria* for J. T. Essberger,
Hamburg. 413 ft × 55 ft. Engines: Oil.
1940: Requisitioned by German Navy.
5.1945: Taken in prize at Kiel. Renamed *Empire
Tageos* (M.O.W.T.).
1946: Allocated to U.S.S.R., renamed *Kazbek*.
1947: *Karpaty* (Gdynia America Line, Poland).
1958: Scrapped Spezia.

Empire Taginda (tanker) 2,846 gt. Built: F. Krupp
A.G., Kiel, in 1922 as *Rudolph Albrecht* for Max
Albrecht Kommandit, Hamburg. 377 ft × 46 ft.
Engines: T3cyl.
1940: Requisitioned by German Navy.
5.1945: Taken in prize at Kiel. Renamed *Empire
Taginda* (M.O.W.T.).
1947: *Basingstream* (Salvedor Co. Ltd. (Philip Bauer,
London)).
1949: *Oilstream* (Ship Finance & Management Ltd.,
London).
1952: *Vrissi* (George Nicolaou Ltd., Greece).
11.1960: Scrapped Spezia.

Empire Tagralia (tanker) 5,824 gt. Built: Kockums
Mek. Verk., Malmö, in 1929 as *Max Albrecht* for
Max Albrecht Kommandit, Hamburg. 385 ft × 55 ft.
Engines: Oil.

30.8.1939: Sailed from Houston, Texas, for
Germany. Later put into El Ferrol, Spain. Interned.
5.1945: Surrendered in prize to Britain; brought to
Glasgow for repairs, then renamed *Empire Tagralia*
(M.O.W.T.).
1947: *Repton* (Basra Steam Shipping Co., London).
1952: *Alcantara* (Lloyd Siciliano di Armamento,
Palermo).
9.1960: Scrapped Vado.

Empire Taj (tanker) 3,065 gt. Built: Toledo
Shipbuilding Co., in 1912 as *L. V. Stoddard*.
305 ft × 44 ft. Engines: T3cyl.
1914: *Walter Hardcastle* (Sinclair Navigation Co.,
U.S.A.).
1917: Renamed *W. L. Connelly*.
1937: *Barbara* (Enrico Insom, Italy).
25.8.1941: Taken by Royal Navy in prize at Bandar
Shapur. Towed to Karachi, then renamed *Empire Taj*
(M.O.W.T.).
1948: (Laid up at Abadan, Iran). Sold, and:
10.1949: *Attock* (fuel hulk for Pakistan Navy, at
Karachi).

(Intended to be) *Empire Tarne* 8,800 gt.
Built: Bremer Vulkan Schiff- und Masch., Vegesack,
in 1913 as *Sierra Salvada*. 440 ft × 56 ft.
Engines: T3cyl.
1917: *Avare* (Lloyd Brasileiro, Brazil).
1925: *Peer Gynt* (Soc. Italiana Servizi Marittimi, Italy).
1925: Renamed *Neptunia*.
1927: *Oceana* (Hamburg America Line).
1940: Requisitioned by German Navy; used as
accommodation ship at Gdynia and Stettin.
5.1945: Taken in prize at Flensburg; placed under
British flag (same name).
13.10.1945: Damaged by mine in North Sea, near
Heligoland, 54.00N 7.52E while on voyage Methil
to Hamburg, repatriating German internees. Towed
to Hamburg, drydocked and repaired.
1946: To be renamed *Empire Tarne*, but allocated to
U.S.S.R. and renamed *Sibir* (naval depot ship on
Soviet Pacific coast).
1963: Scrapped Vladivostock.

Empire Tegaden (tanker) 2,579 gt. Launched by
Howaldtswerke, Kiel, in 1940 as *Jeverland*. Towed to
Copenhagen and completed in 1940 by Burmeister &
Wain. 298 ft × 45 ft. Engines: Oil.
1940: Requisitioned by German Navy on completion.
5.1945: Taken in prize at Bergen, Norway. Renamed
Empire Tegaden (M.O.W.T.).
1946: Allocated to U.S.S.R. (as *Jeverland*).
5.8.1946: Reported arrived at Swinemunde, in tow,
from Methil.

Note: Still listed in some 1958 ship registers as named
Jeverland. No further trace.

Empire Tegados (tanker) 692 gt. Built: F. Schichau GmbH., Elbing, in 1938 as *Gabelsflach* for German Navy. 186 ft × 28 ft. Engines: Oil.
5.1945: Taken in prize at Kiel. Renamed *Empire Tegados* (M.O.W.T.).
1946: Allocated to U.S.S.R., renamed *Alexi Tolstoi*. No further trace.

(Intended to be) *Empire Tegaica* (tanker) 650 gt. Built: Gutehoffnungschutte A.G., Walsum, Germany, in 1943 for German Navy. 193 ft × 30 ft. Engines: Oil.
5.1945: Taken in prize at Kiel. Intended to be renamed *Empire Tegaica* (M.O.W.T.), but:
1946: Allocated to U.S.S.R., renamed *Kapitan Plaushevski*.
No further trace.

Empire Tegalta (tanker) 2,299 gt.
Built: Nordseewerke, Emden, in 1944 as *Poseidon* for German account. 287 ft × 43 ft. Engines: Oil.
5.1945: Taken in prize at Kiel. Renamed *Empire Tegalta* (M.O.W.T.).
1946: Allocated to U.S.S.R., renamed *Ararat*. No further trace.

Empire Tegamas (tanker) 708 gt. Built: Schichau GmbH., Danzig, in 1939 as *Oderbank* for German Navy. 176 ft × 28 ft. Engines: Oil.
5.1945: Taken in prize at Trondheim. Renamed *Empire Tegamas* (M.O.W.T.).
1946: Allocated to U.S.S.R., renamed *Khersones*. No further trace.

Empire Tegambia (tanker) 1,156 gt. Built: Lübecker Flenderwerke A.G., in 1936 as *Hermann Andersen* for C. Andersen, Hamburg. 231 ft × 34 ft. Engines: Oil.
5.1945: Taken in prize at Narvik.
1946: Renamed *Empire Tegambia* (M.O.W.T.).
1947: *Pass of Brander* (Bulk Oil SS Co. Ltd.).
1956: Scrapped Dunston-on-Tyne.

Empire Tegaya (tanker) 3,145 gt. Built: Deutsche Werft, Hamburg, in 1921 as *Julius Schindler*.
343 ft × 45 ft. Engines: Oil.
1939: *Thalatta* (Hamburger Tank Reederei, Hamburg)
1940: Requisitioned by German Navy.
5.1945: Taken in prize at Kiel. Renamed *Empire Tegaya* (M.O.W.T.).
1947: *Artist* (Valiant SS Co. Ltd. (Vergottis Ltd., London)).
1949: *Astro* (Fundador Cia. Nav., Panama).
1953: *Franco Lisi* (Nolido Cia. de Nav., Panama).
1960: Scrapped Savona.

Empire Tegenya (tanker) 1,172 gt. Built: Deutsche Werft, Hamburg, in 1930 as *Elsa Essberger*.
235 ft × 37 ft. Engines: Oil.
1938: *Lisa Essberger* (J. T. Essberger, Hamburg).
1940: Requisitioned by German Navy.
5.1945: Taken in prize at Copenhagen. Renamed *Empire Tegenya* (M.O.W.T.).
1947: Returned to German owners, name reverted to *Lisa Essberger*.
1960: *Olstauer* (R. C. Eckelmann, Hamburg).
1964: *Attiki* (C. Diamantis, Greece).
21.9.1967: Fire in engine room in Bay of Eleusis while on voyage to Greece with benzine. Constructive total loss. Repaired by owners, and:
1968: *Peloponnisis* (Greek Tanker Shipping Co. Ltd.).
10.1979: Scrapped Kynossoura, Greece.

Empire Tegidad (tanker) 642 gt. Built: Deutsche Werke, Kiel, in 1934 as *Sylt* for Carl W. Hanssen Tankschiffs, Hamburg. 176 ft × 28 ft. Engines: Oil.
1940: Requisitioned by German Navy.
5.1945: Taken in prize at Trondheim. Renamed *Empire Tegidad* (M.O.W.T.).
1946: Transferred to Allied Control Commission; then returned to Germany, reverted to original name and owners.
1969: *Rovensca* (Cia. de Nav. Lomamar S.A., Panama).
4.1982: Scrapped Trieste.

Empire Tegleone (tanker) 782 gt. Built: Sarpsborg Mek. Verk., Greaker, Norway, in 1942 as *Marsteinen* for German account. 210 ft × 32 ft. Engines: Oil.
1942: Requisitioned by German Navy on completion.
5.1945: Taken in prize at Copenhagen. Renamed *Empire Tegleone* (M.O.W.T.).
1946: Allocated to U.S.S.R., but retained by Britain. Laid up at Queenborough, Kent, for some years. Then sold, and:
1953: *Otto* (Lcth & Co., Hamburg).
1967: *Kali Limenes II* (N. J. Vardinoyannis, Greece).
1980: (Seka S.A., Greece).
1984: (Sekavin Shipping Co., Greece).

Empire Tegoria (tanker) 1,863 gt.
Built: Howaldtswerke, Kiel, in 1916 as *Usedom*.
244 ft × 38 ft. Engines: T6cyl.
1937: *Inga Essberger* (J. T. Essberger, Hamburg).
1940: Requisitioned by German Navy.
5.1945: Taken in prize at Sarpsborg. Renamed *Empire Tegoria* (M.O.W.T.).
1946: Allocated to U.S.S.R., renamed *Beshtau*.
1970: Scrapped U.S.S.R.

Empire Teguda (tanker) 670 gt. Built: Danziger Werft A.G. in 1938 as *Amrum* for German Navy.
177 ft × 28 ft. Engines: Oil.

5.1945: Taken in prize at Kiel. Renamed *Empire Teguda* (M.O.W.T.).
1946: Allocated to U.S.S.R., renamed *Nargin*. No further trace.

Empire Teguto (tanker) 1,338 gt.
Built: Howaldtswerke, Kiel, in 1915 as *Brosen* for German Government account, managed in commercial service by J. T. Essberger, Hamburg. 234 ft × 35 ft. Engines: T3cyl.
5.1945: Surrendered at Pasajes, Spain, to Britain. Renamed *Empire Teguto* (M.O.W.T.).
1946: Allocated to U.S.S.R. (no new name reported).
1950: Reported transferred to Russian Navy.

Empire Tegyika (tanker) 1,623 gt. Built: Stulcken Sohn, Hamburg, in 1935 as *Liselotte Essberger* for J. T. Essberger, Hamburg. 244 ft × 42 ft. Engines: Oil.
1940: Requisitioned by German Navy.
5.1945: Taken in prize at Trondheim. Renamed *Empire Tegyika* (M.O.W.T.).
1947: *Thornol* (Admiralty).
1948: *Caroline M* (Metcalfe Motor Coasters Ltd.).
1958: (New oil engines).
1966: *Kyllini* (C. Diamantis, Greece).
12.1980: Scrapped Salamis Island, Greece.

Empire Teme 3,243 gt. Built: Nordseewerke, Emden, in 1923 as *Ilona Siemers* for G. J. H. Siemers & Co., Hamburg. 332 ft × 46 ft. Engines: T3cyl.
5.1945: Taken in prize at Lübeck. Renamed *Empire Teme* (M.O.W.T.).
1946: Allocated to U.S.S.R., renamed *Aivazovsky*. No further trace.

Empire Tenbrook (tanker) 2,864 gt. Built: Uraga Dockyard, Japan, in 1944 as *Ayakumo Maru*. 307 ft × 45 ft. Engines: steam turbines.
1945: Reported taken in prize.
1947: Acquired by M.O.T., renamed *Empire Tenbrook*.
1950: *Aer Mas* (Government of Indonesia).
1952: Scrapped Hong Kong.

Empire Tenby (tanker) 851 gt. Built in Japan in 1943 as *Leng Maru No. 3*. 193 ft × 33 ft. Engines: Oil.
1945: Reported taken in prize.
1945: Acquired by M.O.W.T., renamed *M.T.S. No. 7*.
1947: *Empire Tenby* (M.O.T.) (converted to dry cargo).
1949: *Leong Bee* (Gwee Au Nua, Singapore).
1952: *Philip Q* (Tan Seck Kay, Singapore).
1954: *Tong Thay* (Kie Hock Shipping Co., Singapore).
1962: Renamed *Hammer* (Panama flag).

1965: renamed *Fajado*.
7.1976: Scrapped Hong Kong.

Empire Teviot 5,337 gt. Built: Flensburger Schiff-Gesellschaft in 1937 as *Mathias Stinnes* for Kohlen-Import und Poseidon Schiffs, Königsberg. 425 ft × 60 ft. Engines: Oil.
5.1945: Taken in prize at Copenhagen. Renamed *Empire Teviot* (M.O.W.T.).
1946: Allocated to U.S.S.R., renamed *Akademik Krilov*.
1975: Scrapped U.S.S.R.

Empire Thames 5,825 gt. Built: Blohm & Voss, Hamburg, in 1920 as *Urundi* for Deutsche East Africa Line. 418 ft × 56 ft. Engines: four steam turbines.
1939: Requisitioned by German Navy.
From 2.1945: Took part in evacuation of German personnel and refugees from the Eastern Baltic and East Prussia. In seven voyages carried 32,716 persons to West Germany.
5.1945: Taken in prize at Copenhagen. Renamed *Empire Thames* (M.O.W.T.).
1945: *Kalamai* (chartered to Government of Greece).
1946: Returned to Britain, renamed *Empire Thames* (M.O.T.).
1947: (Goulandris Bros., London).
1948: *Valparaiso* (Cia. Marit. de Este, Panama).
1949: Renamed *Empire Thames* for voyage to shipbreakers.
3.1949: Scrapped Antwerp.

Empire Tigachi (tanker) 685 gt. Built: Elsflether Werft A.G., in 1942 as *Flemhude* for German Navy. 186 ft × 30 ft. Engines: Oil.
5.1945: Taken in prize, in damaged condition. Renamed *Empire Tigachi* (M.O.W.T.).
3.1.1946: Grounded on a reef at Nidingen, near Gothenburg, Sweden, in heavy seas. Pounded during further gales and severely damaged. Wreck stripped by salvors; later broke in two. Total loss.

(Intended to be) *Empire Tigarth* (tanker) 312 gt. Built: (In Germany?) in 1941 as *Swine* for German Navy. (Approx.) 130 ft × 25 ft. Engines: Oil.
5.1945: Taken in prize at Copenhagen; intended to be renamed *Empire Tigarth*, but:
1946: Allocated to U.S.S.R. (no new name reported). No further trace.

Empire Tigaven (tanker) 972 gt. Built: Deutsche Werft, Hamburg, in 1937 as *Algol* for Trelleborgs Angf. Nya A/B, Sweden. 200 ft × 32 ft. Engines: Oil.
13.12.1939: (As *Algol*) Mined in Swedish waters near a German minefield between Trelleborg and Falsterbo (voyage: Stockholm/Trelleborg – ballast). Sank.

1940: Salved in two parts; sold and rebuilt, and:
1941: Renamed *Soya VII* (O. Wallenius, Stockholm).
1942: Sold to J. T. Essberger, Hamburg, name reverted to *Algol*.
1942: Requisitioned by German Navy.
5.1945: Taken in prize at Arendal, Norway. Renamed *Empire Tigaven* (M.O.W.T.).
1947: *Peter M* (Metcalfe Motor Coasters Ltd.).
1964: *Motol 5* (N. E. Vernicos Ltd., Greece).
1969: (D. & C. Vernicos, Greece).
3.1972: Scrapped Perama.

(Intended to be) *Empire Tigawa* (tanker) 633 gt. Built in Germany in 1940 as *Anna* for German Navy. 189 ft × 30 ft. Engines: Oil.
5.1945: Taken in prize at Kristiansand, Norway. Name of *Empire Tigawa* allocated (M.O.W.T.), but:
27.12.1945: (As *Anna*, under British flag) Stranded at Bolsax, Kattegat. Badly damaged, but refloated and arrived at Kalundborg, Denmark. Constructive total loss.
1946: Towed to Burntisland, Fife. Reported sold to Norway; no further trace.

Empire Tigbart (tanker) 679 gt. Built: Danziger Werft A.G., in 1936 as *Poel* for German Navy. 186 ft × 30 ft. Engines: Oil.
5.1945: Taken in prize at Kiel. Renamed *Empire Tigbart* (M.O.W.T.).
1946: Allocated to U.S.S.R., renamed *Koktebel*. No further trace.

Empire Tigina (tanker) 638 gt. Built: D. W. Kremer Sohn, Elmshorn, in 1940 as *Else* for German Navy. 189 ft × 30 ft. Engines: Oil.
5.1945: Taken in prize at Trondheim. Renamed *Empire Tigina* (M.O.W.T.).
1946: Allocated to U.S.S.R. (no new name reported).
1958: Still listed in some shipping registers.

Empire Tigity (tanker) 465 gt. Built: H. Peters, Beidenfleth, Germany, in 1944 as *Gohren* for German Navy. 144 ft × 26 ft. Engines: Oil.
5.1945: Taken in prize; renamed *Empire Tigity* (M.O.W.T.).
1947: *Anthony M.* (Metcalfe Motor Coasters Ltd.).
1953: (New oil engines).
1970: *Kinder* (Effluent Services Ltd., Macclesfield).
4.1983: Scrapped Garston.

(Intended to be) *Empire Tiglas* (tanker) 510 gt (approx.). Built: (in Germany ?) in 1942 as *Danisch Wohld* (for German Navy ?). Engines: Oil.
5.1945: Taken in prize in Channel Islands. Intended to be renamed *Empire Tiglas* (M.O.W.T.), but:

1946: Allocated to Holland, renamed *Elst* (Government of Netherlands).
1947: Reclassed as a lighter (managed by Van Ommeren N.V., for Dutch Government). No further trace.

Empire Tigness (tanker) 407 gt. Built: Greifenwerft A.G., Stettin, in 1943 as *Georg* for German Navy. 186 ft × 26 ft. Engines: Oil.
5.1945: Taken in prize at Flensburg. Renamed *Empire Tigness* (M.O.W.T.).
1947–1949: Used as a salvage ship for the recovery of 'Pluto' pipeline from the bed of the English Channel.
1949: *Topmast No. 15* (Risdon, Beazley & Co., Southampton).
1953: Sold to Dutch buyers, and:
1959: *Phito* (converted to an inland waterways tank barge).

Empire Tigombo (tanker) 604 gt. Built: Greifenwerft A.G., Stettin, in 1944 as *Howacht* for German Navy. 180 ft × 30 ft. Engines: Oil.
5.1945: Taken in prize at Kiel. Renamed *Empire Tigombo* (M.O.W.T.).
1946: Allocated to U.S.S.R., renamed *Utrish*.
1968: Scrapped U.S.S.R.

Empire Tigonto (tanker) 664 gt. Built: D. W. Kremer Sohn, Elmshorn, in 1940 as *Dora* for German Navy. 192 ft × 30 ft. Engines: Oil.
5.1945: Taken in prize at Flensburg. Renamed *Empire Tigonto* (M.O.W.T.).
1946: Allocated to U.S.S.R. (no new name reported).
1958: Still listed in some ship registers.

Empire Tigoon (tanker) 674 gt. Built: Wilton-Fijenoord N.V., Schiedam, Holland, in 1944 as *Steingrund* for German Navy. 186 ft × 30 ft. Engines: Oil.
5.1945: Taken in prize at Kiel. Renamed *Empire Tigoon* (M.O.W.T.).
1946: Allocated to Greece, renamed *Xanthi* (Government of Greece).
1956: Transferred to Royal Hellenic Navy; renamed *Viviis* (Pennant A.471).

(Intended to be) *Empire Tigosti* (tanker) 638 gt. Built in Germany in 1942 as *Hilde* for German Navy. 189 ft × 30 ft. Engines: Oil.
5.1945: Taken in prize at Kristiansand, Norway. Intended to be renamed *Empire Tigosti* (M.O.W.T.), but:
1946: Allocated to U.S.S.R. (as *Hilde*). No further trace.

The *Caroline M*, formerly *Empire Tegyika*, in 1953.   *Skyfotos*

The *Empire Wansbeck*, arriving at the Hook of Holland in 1958, with British Army-of-the-Rhine personnel.

The *Empire Windrush*, as a troopship, in Southampton Water, May 1953.   *Tom Rayner collection*

Empire Tigouver (tanker) 664 gt. Built: D. W.
Kremer Sohn, Elmshorn, in 1942 as *Grete* for German
Navy. 192 ft × 30 ft. Engines: Oil.
5.1945: Taken in prize; renamed *Empire Tigouver*,
(M.O.W.T.).
1946: Allocated to U.S.S.R., reported renamed *Gret*.
1958: Still listed in some ship registers.

Empire Tintagel 493 gt. Built in Japan in 1941 as *JAP
No. 4000*. 155 ft × 31 ft. Engines: Oil.
1945: Taken in prize (M.O.W.T.), renamed *M.T.S.
No. 12*.
1947: Renamed *Empire Tintagel*.
1951: *Hua Li* (Chan Cheng Kum, Singapore).
1970: (Compass Agencies Pte. Ltd., Singapore).
1974: *Kim Hua Li* (Lawrence Shipping Co., Panama).
28.12.1975: Wrecked in South China Sea,
02.19N 109.01E (voyage: Singapore/Kuching).

Empire Towy (Hansa 'B' type) 2,754 gt. Laid down
by Flensburger Schiff-Gesellschaft in 1943 for German
account. 343 ft × 51 ft. Engines: C4cyl.
5.1945: Taken in prize, incomplete, at builder's yard.
1947: Completed; renamed *Empire Towy* (M.O.T.).
1947: (Fenton SS Co. – purchased from M.O.T.
subject to condemnation of vessel in Prize Court).
1950: renamed *Empire Patrai*.
1953: *Patrai* (Hellenic Lines Ltd., Greece).
1981: (Celika Nav. Co., Cyprus).
1983: (Crystal Breeze Corp. (Roussos Bros.,
Greece)).
1984: Scrapped Perama.

Empire Unitas IV (whaler) 341 gt. Built: Bremer
Vulkan Schiff- und Masch., Vegesack, in 1937 as
Unitas 4 for Jurgens Van Den Bergh Margarine-
Verkaufs Union GmbH, Hamburg. 135 ft × 26 ft.
Engines: T3cyl.
1940: Requisitioned by German Navy.
5.1945: Taken in prize at Flensburg. Renamed *Empire
Unitas IV* (M.O.W.T.).
1955: Scrapped Port Glasgow.

Empire Unitas V (whaler) 341 gt. Built: Bremer
Vulkan Schiff- und Masch., Vegesack, in 1937 as
Unitas 5 for Jurgens Van Den Bergh Margarine-
Verkaufs Union GmbH, Hamburg. 135 ft × 26 ft.
Engines: T3cyl.
1940: Requisitioned by German Navy.
5.1945: Taken in prize at Flensburg. Renamed *Empire
Unitas V* (M.O.W.T.).
1954: Scrapped Port Glasgow.

Empire Unitas 8 (whaler) 341 gt. Built: Bremer
Vulkan Schiff- und Masch., Vegesack, in 1937 as

Unitas 8 for Jurgens Van Den Bergh Margarine-
Verkaufs Union GmbH, Hamburg. 135 ft × 26 ft.
Engines: T3cyl.
1940: Requisitioned by German Navy.
5.1945: Taken in prize at Kiel. Renamed *Empire Unitas
8* (M.O.W.T.).
1956: *Sir Liege* (Union Whaling Co. Ltd., South
Africa).
10.1961: Scrapped Durban.

Empire Unitas X (whaler) 339 gt. Built: F. Schichau
GmbH, Danzig, in 1939 as *Unitas 10* for Jurgens Van
Den Bergh Margarine-Verkaufs Union GmbH,
Hamburg. 135 ft × 26 ft. Engines: T3cyl.
1940: Requisitioned by German Navy.
5.1945: Taken in prize at Emden. Renamed *Empire
Unitas X* (M.O.W.T.).
1956: *C. P. Robinson* (Union Whaling Co. Ltd., South
Africa).
1.1963: Scrapped Durban.

Empire Ure 2,570 gt. Built: Van Duivendijks
Scheep., Lekkerkerk, in 1920 as *Willem Van Driel Sr.*
300 ft × 45 ft. Engines: T3cyl.
1927: *Rheinland* (Kohlen-Import und Poseidon
Schiffs., Königsberg).
1940: Requisitioned by German Navy.
5.1945: Taken in prize at Brunsbüttel. Renamed
Empire Ure (M.O.W.T.).
1947: *Amberstone* (Crete Shipping Co. (Stelp &
Leighton Ltd.)).
1950: *Metamorfosis* (D. A. Psychoyos, Greece).
2.12.1950: Ran aground in a storm near north
breakwater, Ymuiden, Holland. Broke in two, sank.
Total loss (voyage: Ronnskar/Amsterdam – pyrites).

Empire Venture (whale factory) 12,639 gt.
Built: Swan, Hunter & Wigham Richardson Ltd.,
Newcastle, in 1929 as *Vikingen*. 493 ft × 71 ft.
Engines: T6cyl.
1938: *Wikinger* (Hamburger Walfang-Kontor
GmbH., Hamburg).
1939: Requisitioned by German Navy.
5.1945: Taken in prize at Kiel. Renamed *Empire
Venture* (M.O.W.T.).
1946: Allocated to U.S.S.R., renamed *Slava*.
1971: *Fuji Maru* (Japanese flag); Resold, and:
10.1971: Scrapped Kaohsiung.

Empire Victory (whale factory) 21,846 gt.
Built: Deutsche Schiff- und Masch., Bremen, in 1937
as *Unitas* for Unitas Deutsche Walfang GmbH,
Hamburg. 608 ft × 80 ft. Engines: T6cyl.
5.1945: Taken in prize at Flensburg. Renamed *Empire
Victory* (M.O.W.T.).

1950: *Abraham Larsen* (Union Whaling Co. Ltd., South Africa).
1957: *Nisshin Maru No. 2* (27,059 gt, fitted with new (oil) engines) (Taiyo Gyogyo K.K., Japan).
3.1987: Scrapped Kaohsiung.

The *Unitas* was built following the German decision to enter the whaling trade on a large scale. Her deadweight of some 30,000 tons made her the biggest whale oil factory/refinery afloat and in the 1937 to 1939 seasons in the Antarctic she processed large catches made by her attendant catchers, supplying Germany with whale oil and whale meat which was stored for war use. The vessel served the German Navy during the war years.

A post-war problem which had to be overcome before the ship was condemned by the British Prize Court was to determine the percentage of Dutch and British involvement, this due to the fiscal structuring of her German parent company – Jurgens Van Den Bergh Margarine-Verkaufs Union GmbH – which was associated with the British Unilever concern.

In December 1945 the vessel sailed to Methil, Fife, and thence north-about to Southampton, where she was dry-docked by Harland & Wolff in July 1946.

Considerable hull strengthening and bomb damage repairs were carried out, though still leaving her with a large bomb-damage 'blister' and her main deck 'a bit wavy'. She then went to Falmouth, being fitted out by Silley, Cox & Co. Ltd. with equipment including whale oil digesters, meat-meal plant and liver-flake plant for vitamin 'A' production. The ship was operated on behalf of the Ministry of Food by United Whalers Ltd., with nine or ten attendant whale catchers.

Later, in her thirty-year service under the Japanese flag, she continued to serve as a whale factory ship for some ten years. After this she was converted to a fish factory ship.

Empire Viking I (whaler) 250 gt. Built: Smiths Dock Co. Ltd., Middlesbrough, in 1929 as *Vikingen I*. 116 ft × 24 ft. Engines: T3cyl.
1938: *Wiking I* (Hamburger Walfang-Kontor GmbH., Hamburg).
1939: Requisitioned by German Navy.
5.1945: Taken in prize at Kiel. Renamed *Empire Viking I* (M.O.W.T.).
1946: Allocated to U.S.S.R., renamed *Slava VIII*. No further trace.

Empire Viking II (whaler) 250 gt. Built: Smiths Dock Co. Ltd., Middlesbrough, in 1929 as *Vikingen II*. 116 ft × 24 ft. Engines: T3cyl.
1938: *Wiking 2* (Hamburger Walfang-Kontor GmbH., Hamburg).
1939: Requisitioned by German Navy.
5.1945: Taken as a prize at Kiel. Renamed *Empire Viking II* (M.O.W.T.).
1946: Allocated to U.S.S.R., renamed *Slava IX*. No further trace.

Empire Viking III (whaler) 250 gt. Built: Smiths Dock Co. Ltd., Middlesbrough, in 1929 as *Vikingen III*. 116 ft × 24 ft. Engines: T3cyl.
1938: *Wiking 3* (Hamburger Walfang-Kontor GmbH., Hamburg).
1939: Requisitioned by German Navy.
5.1945: Taken in prize at Kiel. Renamed *Empire Viking III* (M.O.W.T.).
1946: Allocated to U.S.S.R., renamed *Slava X*. No further trace.

Empire Viking VI (whaler) 381 gt. Built: Deutsche Schiff- und Masch., Bremen, in 1939 as *Wiking 6* for Hamburger Walfang-Kontor GmbH, Hamburg. 140 ft × 27 ft. Engines: T3cyl.
1940: Requisitioned by German Navy.
5.1945: Taken in prize; renamed *Empire Viking VI* (M.O.W.T.).
1946: Allocated to U.S.S.R., renamed *Slava II*. No further trace.

Empire Viking VIII (whaler) 381 gt. Built: Deutsche Schiff- und Masch., Bremen, in 1939 as *Wiking 8* for Hamburger Walfang-Kontor GmbH, Hamburg. 140 ft × 27 ft. Engines: T3cyl.
1940: Requisitioned by German Navy.
5.1945: Taken in prize; renamed *Empire Viking VIII* (M.O.W.T.).
1946: Allocated to U.S.S.R., renamed *Slava III*. No further trace.

Empire Viking IX (whaler) 370 gt. Built: Deutsche Schiff- und Masch., Bremen, in 1939 as *Wiking 9* for Hamburger Walfang-Kontor GmbH, Hamburg. 134 ft × 26 ft. Engines: T3cyl.
1940: Requisitioned by German Navy.
5.1945: Taken in prize; renamed *Empire Viking IX* (M.O.W.T.).
1946: Allocated to U.S.S.R., renamed *Slava IV*. No further trace.

Empire Viking X (whaler) 370 gt. Built: Deutsche Schiff- und Masch., Bremen, in 1939 as *Wiking 10* for Hamburger Walfang-Kontor GmbH, Hamburg. 134 ft × 26 ft. Engines: T3cyl.
1940: Requisitioned by German Navy.
5.1945: Taken in prize; renamed *Empire Viking X* (M.O.W.T.).
1946: Allocated to U.S.S.R., renamed *Slava V*. No further trace.

Empire Wandle 3.093 gt. Built: Flensburger Schiff-Gesellschaft, in 1935 as *Wilhelm Traber* for W. Traber & Co., Hamburg. 311 ft × 49 ft. Engines: C4cyl.
5.1945: Taken in prize at Brunsbüttel. Renamed *Empire Wandle* (M.O.W.T.).

1947: Allocated to U.S.A. (U.S.M.C.). Sold and renamed *Yankee Dawn* (William C. Atwater & Co. Inc., Fall River, Mass.).
1948: (Fall River Nav. Co., New York).
1950: *Cynthia Olsen* (Oliver J. Olsen & Co., San Francisco).
3.1971: Scrapped U.S.A.

Empire Wansbeck 3,508 gt. Launched by Danziger Werft A.G., in 1939 as *Linz* for Norddeutscher Lloyd. 323 ft × 46 ft. Engines: Oil.

The *Linz* was launched at Danzig in 1939 and completed at Odense in 1943 by Odense Staalskibs Verft. She was one of a class of nine German fruit-carrying ships, the lead ship being the *Saar*, also of Norddeutscher Lloyd, which was commissioned in 1935. Some of the nine vessels became wartime blockade runners and two – including *Linz* – were used as minelayers by the German Navy.

Taken over, in prize, at Kielfjord in May 1945, the *Linz* was converted in Germany to a British troopship with accommodation for 721 persons plus another 283 in cabins and was renamed *Empire Wansbeck* for the M.O.T., under Wilson Line management. She operated on the North Sea (Harwich/Hook of Holland) service for B.A.O.R. (British Army of the Rhine) personnel until 1961. Sold to Greece the following year, she became *Esperos*, a Mediterranean passenger ship owned by Kavounides Bros., of Piraeus.

In March 1980 she left Piraeus, in tow, and was broken up in Spain in the following year.

Empire Waveney 16,754 gt. Built: Blohm & Voss, Hamburg, in 1929 as *Milwaukee* for Hamburg America Line. 547 ft × 72 ft. Engines: Oil.
1940–1945: Used by German Navy as an accommodation and depot ship at Kiel. Bombed by R.A.F. to prevent her intended use by the Nazis as an escape ship for top-rank personnel.
5.1945: Taken in prize at Kiel; used by U.S. Navy as a transport. Allocated to U.S.A., to be taken up by U.S.M.C., but then declined, one main objection believed to be that her electrical wiring was of the single-pole system, by which the hull of the vessel was used as a return circuit.
10.1945: Handed to Britain at New York; renamed *Empire Waveney* (M.O.W.T.); returned to U.K. for repair and overhaul, intended for trooping.

On 8 February 1946 the *Empire Waveney* caught fire while in drydock at Liverpool. The fire was soon under control, with damage confined to cabins on 'D' deck. Then, on 2 March, the vessel again caught fire. At this time she was in the Canada Dock at Liverpool, having left the drydock only the previous day and prior to going on trials at the end of the month. The fire was first discovered on the boat deck, but within minutes the whole of the superstructure was ablaze, with flames to mast height. Soon after the fire spread below decks, the vessel's sides became red-hot and she developed a dangerous list of 30 degrees. Fire-fighting was abandoned due to the possibility of an explosion and danger of the ship capsizing.

Two days later, when the fire had burnt itself out, the ship was gutted and resting on the bottom of the dock.

On 4 May 1946 the ship was refloated – and buried her bows firmly in the dockside as she surged forward – and was then again placed in drydock. Found to be a total loss, the hulk was sold and on 26 January 1947 left the Mersey, in tow, bound for the shipbreaker's yard at Dalmuir, on the Clyde.

On 25 September 1947 the remaining hulk of the ship was towed to Troon for final demolition.

Empire Weaver 2,822 gt. Built: Lübecker Flenderwerke A.G., in 1939 as *Dalbek* for Knohr & Burchard, Hamburg. 326 ft × 48 ft. Engines: C4cyl.
5.1945: Taken in prize at Rendsburg. Renamed *Empire Weaver* (M.O.W.T.).
1946: Allocated to U.S.S.R., renamed *Chernigov*.
6.1969: Scrapped Split.

Empire Welland 17,870 gt. Built: Deutsche Werft, Hamburg, in 1938 as *Patria*. 562 ft × 74 ft. Engines: Oil.

The *Patria* was built at Hamburg as a German 'Strength through Joy' liner, for operating Government-sponsored cruises for certain chosen 'workers' who strongly supported the Nazi regime. Up to the outbreak of war the ship had completed only five voyages.

In 1940 she passed to the German Navy and in May 1945 was the vessel in which Admiral Dönitz and the German High Command surrendered to the Allies at the Baltic port of Flensburg. Taken in prize, the ship was later sent to the Belfast shipyard of Harland & Wolff and there converted to a troopship on behalf of the M.O.W.T. and renamed *Empire Welland*.

The vessel made only two trooping voyages and at the end of December 1945, while lying at Liverpool, a Russian delegation arrived to inspect the ship. The following month a Russian crew was appointed.

On 29 January 1946 the *Empire Welland*, together with forty-nine other former enemy ships, was condemned as a British Prize by the Admiralty Prize Court, thus giving Britain the right to hold her against any Russian claim as part of indemnities. Nevertheless, following an agreement regarding the allocation of ex-enemy ships by the Tripartite Merchant Marine Commission at Potsdam, eleven ex-enemy ships then in the Merseyside docks of Liverpool, Preston and Manchester were awarded to Russia. Included was the *Empire Welland*: she was renamed *Rossia* (*Rossiya*) and later placed in service in the Black Sea. In 1985 the *Rossiya* was renamed *Aniva* and in December of the same year arrived at Kure for breaking up. Nine of the remaining ten ships involved in the transfer were *Empire Conisborough*, *Empire Constable*, *Empire Convention*, *Empire Douglas*, *Empire Dovey*, *Empire Forth*, *Empire Gantry*, *Empire Gable* and *Empire Yare*. The eleventh vessel was the *Caribia* (1933, 12,049 gt) which had retained its original name since being captured at Flensburg and later taken to Liverpool. Allocated to the U.S.A. in July 1945, she was re-allocated to the U.S.S.R. and renamed *Ilitch*, subsequently being based at Vladivostock for Far East service.

Empire Wensum 2,515 gt. Built: Richardson, Duck & Co. Ltd., Stockton, in 1910 as *Rotherhill*.
302 ft × 42 ft. Engines: T3cyl.
1925: *Robert Sauber* (Sauber & Co., Hamburg).
1940: Requisitioned by German Navy.
5.1945: Taken in prize at Flensburg. Renamed *Empire Wensum* (M.O.W.T.).
1947: *Bruce M* (Mooringwell SS Co.).
1956: *Sorengo* (Cia. de Transportes Mar., Panama).
12.1966: Scrapped Spezia.

Empire Wey 2,645 gt. Built: Nakskov Skibs. Akt., Denmark, in 1944 as *Robert Bornhofen* for Robert Bornhofen, Hamburg. 304 ft × 45 ft.
Engines: C4cyl.
1944: Requisitioned by German Navy at builder's yard.
5.1945: Taken in prize at Copenhagen. Renamed *Empire Wey* (M.O.W.T.).
1946: Allocated to U.S.S.R., renamed *Yakutsk*.
1970: Scrapped U.S.S.R.

Empire Wharfe 3,072 gt. Built: Oresunds Varvet, Landskrona, Sweden, in 1938 as *Viator*. 319 ft × 46 ft.
Engines: Oil.

1939: *Angelburg* (H. Schuldt & Co., Hamburg).
1939: Requisitioned by German Navy, used as a target ship for 24th U-Boat flotilla.
1944–1945: Used as a transport to evacuate German forces and refugees from East Prussia to West Germany.
5.1945: Taken in prize at Wilhelmshaven; and:
7.1945: Used as a hospital ship at Flensburg.
1946: *Empire Wharfe* (M.O.W.T.).
31.12.1946: Caught fire in engine room when off Lagos, West Africa, on a voyage from Garston to the Cameroons for a cargo of bananas. Fire spread to holds.
2.1.1947: Arrived Lagos, in tow, beached Badagry Creek. Holds and engine room flooded.
6.1.1947: Refloated; repaired and sold, and:
1947: *Zent* (Intended name of *Jamaica* not used) (Elders & Fyffes Ltd.).
1962: Scrapped Bruges.

In 1939 there were twenty-one ships in the Elders & Fyffes Ltd. fleet. War losses were heavy, nine ships torpedoed, two sunk by mine and one by bombing off the English North East coast in April 1941. Another was caught by the German battleship *Admiral Scheer* on 5 November 1940 and sunk in mid-Atlantic, in position 52.48N 32.15W, whilst the *Matina* left Port Antonio on 12 October 1940 for Garston and was lost without trace.

To offset these severe losses four ships, seized in Prize, were acquired from the Ministry of Transport in 1946–1947, all being former German-owned banana carriers built for the Cameroons trade. Three, renamed *Empire Mole*, *Empire Alde* and *Empire Mowddoch*, were from the Reederei F. Laeisz GmbH and which, in early years, owned many famous sailing ships in their 'Flying P' Line, all names beginning with the letter 'P'. The fourth ship, renamed *Empire Wharfe*, had been owned by H. Schuldt & Company, of Hamburg.

Empire Wily 6,343 gt. Built: Lithgows Ltd., Port Glasgow, in 1940 as *Dalesman* for T. & J. Harrison, Liverpool. 445 ft × 56 ft. Engines: T3cyl.
14.5.1941: Sunk at Suda Bay, Crete. Salved by Germans and renamed *Pluto*. Later sunk again at Trieste.
1946: Refloated; renamed *Empire Wily* (M.O.W.T.).
1946: Reverted to original owners and name.
15.9.1959: Arrived Ghent for scrapping.

As *Dalesman* this vessel commenced her service under war conditions and during the German attack on Crete in May 1941 was engaged in evacuating British troops from the island. She was severely damaged in German bombing attacks and sank in Suda Bay. Later, the ship was salved by the Germans, who repaired her for trooping duties and renamed her *Pluto* for service in the Mediterranean. Later, during an

R.A.F. bombing raid on Trieste harbour the ship was again sunk.

Found in this condition when Allied forces occupied the port in May 1945, she was again raised and completely rebuilt at Trieste. On completion the M.O.W.T. renamed her *Empire Wily*, and in November 1946 the ship reverted to her original owners.

(See also *Empire Chivalry* and *Empire Explorer*.)

Empire Windrush 14,651 gt. Built: Blohm & Voss, Hamburg, in 1930 as *Monte Rosa*. 501 ft × 66 ft.
Engines: Oil.

The *Monte Rosa* was one of a class of five German 'Monte'-class passenger liners dating back to the 1920s and early 1930s. They were all built by Blohm & Voss in Hamburg for Hamburg South America Line's River Plate/Buenos Aires service. Classed as tourist vessels with accommodation for 1,000 'one class' passengers, they were each also fitted to carry an additional 1,500 persons in steerage class, on the lower deck.

The first pair, *Monte Olivia* and *Monte Sarmiento*, delivered in 1924–1925, were followed by the *Monte Cervantes* in 1927. Four years later the class was completed by the addition of the *Monte Pascoal* and the *Monte Rosa*. The *Monte Rosa* was, in fact, to become the sole post-war survivor.

The *Monte Cervantes* saw only two years of service, going ashore and capsizing near Tierra Del Fuego, while cruising in the Straits of Magellan on 23 January 1930. The *Monte Olivia* also capsized, this during an Allied air attack on Kiel on 3 April 1945: her remains were cut up for scrap in 1948. The *Monte Sarmiento* was also damaged by bombs at Kiel, in February 1942, and was later scrapped at Hamburg. Two years later, in February 1944, the *Monte Pascoal* was fire-damaged during an air attack at Wilhelmshaven. On 31 December 1946 she was towed to sea and scuttled in the Skagerrak.

In the early months of the war, in January 1940, the German Navy requisitioned the liner *Monte Rosa*, using her as a barrack ship at Stettin until 1942. Then, for two years, she was on trooping service between Denmark and Norway and in October 1943 was diverted to act as a repair ship to the battleship *Tirpitz*, damaged by British midget submarines the previous month. Again trooping in 1944 she was soon converted to a hospital ship and used in the evacuation of the East Baltic regions, following the Soviet Army's advance into East Prussia. On 16 February 1945 the *Monte Rosa* struck a mine off Hela Spit and was towed to Gdynia. Given temporary repairs and with 5,600 refugees, wounded and sick aboard the ship was towed to Copenhagen without engine power and with her lower compartments full of water. She arrived leaking and slowly sinking, but continued her hospital ship role, being towed to Kiel on 23 June 1945. Allocated to Britain as a prize two months later, she was brought to the Tyne in the November and remained there, moored off Jarrow, for seven months.

In April 1946 the vessel was repainted to British troopship colours, but still bore her German name. Two months later she sailed for the Clyde shipyard of Alex. Stephen & Sons and during the following nine months was converted to a troopship and renamed *Empire Windrush*.

In June 1948 the vessel arrived at Tilbury with 500 Jamaicans seeking work in a new country – the beginning of post-war immigration into the U.K.

In April 1950 the *Empire Windrush* commenced a four-month lay-up at Southampton while alterations were made to her troop and crew accommodation and her main engines were given a major overhaul.

Her final voyage, destination Southampton, commenced from Yokohama early in 1954. She sailed from Port Said on 23 March and five days later caught fire thirty-two miles off Cape Caxine, near Algiers, after an explosion in her engine room. Abandoned, there were only four casualties among her 1,265 passengers – troops, women and children – and the 222 crew, but the ship was gutted.

Several ships responded to the *Empire Windrush*'s S.O.S., including the motor vessels *Mentor* (Dutch) and *Socotra* (British), the Norwegian steamer *Hemsefjell* and the Italian tanker *Taigete*. All the passengers and crew of the stricken ship were picked up and the next day the destroyer H.M.S. *Saintes* took the still-burning hulk in tow, but it sank a day later, stern first, in position 37.00N 02.11E.

Empire Witham (Hansa 'A' type) 1,923 gt. Built: J. Cockerill S.A., Hoboken, Belgium, in 1944 as *Aeolus* for Neptun Line, Bremen. 282 ft × 44 ft. Engines: C4cyl.
5.1945: Taken in prize at Kiel. Renamed *Empire Witham* (M.O.W.T.).
1948: *Choysang* (Indo-China SN Co. Ltd., Hong Kong).
1961: *Milford* (Hemisphere Shipping Co., Hong Kong).
1967: *Salamanca* (Continental Nav. Co., Panama).
5.1969: Scrapped Hong Kong.

Empire Worthtown 805 gt. Built: J. Lewis & Sons Ltd., Aberdeen, in 1939 as *Worthtown* for Williamstown Shipping Co., London. 199 ft × 31 ft. Engines: T3cyl.
27.5.1940: Sunk at Dunkirk by German air attack during evacuation of British and Allied troops.
11.1942: Refloated by Germans: repaired and renamed *Ilse Schulte* (Schulte & Bruns, Emden).
5.1945: Taken in prize at Schlei. Renamed *Empire Worthtown* (M.O.W.T.).
1946: *Glamorganbrook* (Comben Longstaff & Co. Ltd.).
11.10.1946: Sprang leak and abandoned; sank five miles east of Scarborough (voyage: Blyth/Cowes – coal).

Empire Wye 6,446 gt. Launched by Bremer Vulkan Schiff- und Masch., Vegesack, in 1944 as *Esmeralda* for Hamburg South America Line. Completed by Nederland Scheeps., Amsterdam, in 1945.
459 ft × 59 ft. Engines: Oil.
5.1945: Taken in prize in Kiel Canal. Renamed *Empire Wye* (M.O.W.T.).
1947: *Eastern Saga* (Indo-China SN Co. Ltd.).
1968: *Nanfung* (Southen Shipping & Enterprise Co., Hong Kong).
1972: *Nan Fung* (Yick Fung Shipping & Enterprise Co., Hong Kong).
1975: Scrapped China.

Empire Yare 4,701 gt. Built: Reiherstieg Schiffs., Hamburg, in 1922 as *Wadai* for Woermann Line, Hamburg. 362 ft × 50 ft. Engines: Q4cyl.
1939–1945: Used by German Navy as an accommodation ship, a torpedo school ship and a target ship.
5.1945: Taken in prize at Flensburg. Renamed *Empire Yare* (M.O.W.T.).
1946: Allocated to U.S.S.R., renamed *Gogol*. Later converted and used as a fisheries training ship at Petropavlovsk.
1971: Scrapped U.S.S.R.

OPERATION 'OVERLORD'

Bridgehead

In Britain, in 1942, plans were being drawn up for an Allied invasion somewhere along the coasts of Western Europe, coasts that had been continually fortified by the German Wehrmacht since the debacle of Dunkirk in 1940. An invasion to open a door through which Allied forces could enter and sweep in large, mechanised and superbly-trained armies in the liberation of Europe. At the Casablanca summit in January 1943 a decision was taken for the invasion in the summer of 1944; then set for 1 May 1944 at the Washington summit in May 1943. It was code-named 'Overlord'.

The initial assault was to be by five divisions on five code-named beaches, preceded by inland parachute drops. But it was imperative that sufficient forces be landed quickly to maintain the secured bridgeheads.

The Hampshire ports were to be the main assembly areas for the British assault forces. The force for Juno Beach would be from Portsmouth; for Gold Beach from Lymington and the Solent and for Sword Beach from Langston, Shoreham and Newhaven. The U.S. invasion forces would leave from the Dorset ports of Weymouth, Poole and Portland for Omaha Beach and from Torquay, Dartmouth, Brixham and Salcombe for Utah Beach. Follow-up troops would be from Thames ports and Plymouth with more build-up forces from Milford Haven and Swansea.

Along the chosen invasion coast of Normandy were several small ports, but certainly not capable of handling the vast numbers of men and materials that would be arriving. In any case, it was presumed that those ports would have been made inactive.

So there evolved plans for prefabricated ports, able to be towed in pieces to the far shore, assembled in carefully-chosen sites and speedily brought into operation. There were to be two such ports, code-named Mulberry. Mulberry 'A' would be placed off St. Laurent (Omaha Beach) for the American armies and able to transit 5,000 tons of supplies daily, whilst Mulberry 'B' – twelve miles east of 'A' – would be off Arromanches (Gold Beach) in the British sector with a planned throughput of 7,000 tons of supplies daily. The assembly, cross-Channel movement and placing of the prefabricated ports would involve an armada of tugs in the biggest towing feat of all time.

478

The ports plan

The ports were to be based on a system of floating piers and in May 1942 Prime Minister Winston Churchill minuted: 'They must float up and down with the tide; the anchoring problems must be mastered. Let me have the best solution worked out. Don't argue the matter. The difficulties will argue for themselves'.

Numbers of these would form pierheads – 'quays' at which ships discharged – and from the pierhead would be long roadways, floating on pontoons, to the shore. Protection from the turbulent Channel waters would be threefold; with blockships, with concrete caissons sunk in lines and with steel floats, chained together in long lines and anchored outside of each port.

Behind these shelters the ships would also discharge to ferries and small craft in a shuttle service to the beach and there would be shorter piers for Landing Ships (Tank).

At the Quebec Conference in August 1943 the invasion plan had been approved, with the code name of 'Overlord'. There came others. The long piers of the 'Mulberry' harbours were 'Whales', carried on 'Beetles' (pontoons) to the 'Spud' pierheads. The complete blockship operation was 'Corncob' and their placing sites were 'Gooseberry' – numbered 1 to 5. Concrete caissons were 'Phoenixes' and the outside lines of breakwaters were 'Bombardons'. These floating units, each 200 ft in length had a top watertight compartment with the bottom open to water, producing steadiness. They were to break the waves and were built in drydock at Southampton.

Construction

In October 1943 site preparation was started and mass construction of the 'Mulberry' components began in December. There were six months to completion. Work continued day and night and even in air raids, special screened lights were used for it to continue.

The idea for the floating 'Spud' pierhead came from a combined rock-breaker and dumb dipper dredge, *Lucuyan*, just 525 gt and 110 ft long, built in 1923 by Lobnitz & Co., Renfrew, for the Colonial Administration of the Bahamas. She had three legs which could be lowered to the sea bed and locked to hold the vessel stable. By December 1942 Lobnitz had adapted the principal to a pontoon and by the spring it was in experimental stage. The four legs – 'Spuds' – power driven, were thrust down to the sea bed and so lifted the pierhead, or themselves lifted for movement of the pierhead. Construction of the pierheads was at Leith, Conway and Cairnryan, although many steel units were manufactured throughout the country. Then they were towed, overnight, to Southampton where the spud-legs were fitted, after which they were moved to Solent and Selsey anchorages.

Beginning in September 1943 caissons (Phoenixes) were built in a Southampton drydock; some on beaches in the Gosport and Portsmouth areas; in basins on the banks of the Thames, in Tilbury Docks and some at Birkenhead and Hartlepool. Vast amounts of concrete were mixed for their build and they ranged from 1,672 to 6,044 tons in weight. Fifty-seven were built in eight drydocks, eighteen in two wet docks, forty-eight in twelve basins and twenty-three on four slipways. When completed they were towed away to parking areas at Selsey and Dungeness.

The 'Beetles' – the pontoons on which were laid the roadways from the pierheads – were also built of concrete.

The cross-Channel movement

For the cross-Channel tow it was calculated that ninety tugs would be required for the 'Mulberry' ports concept, from a total of 130 needed for the complete 'Overlord' operation.

All equipment built for the 'Mulberry' ports had to be towed from their places of construction to the southern coastal assembly areas for the invasion. For weeks before D-Day every available tug worked at full pressure, towing piers, caissons and pontoons. 'In Operation "Overlord"', a high-ranking planner later said, 'one tug was worth two battleships. It took 200 tugs three months to get down to the South Coast the stuff which made the Mulberry harbours'. Over 500 tows were made, 300 of which were in the month prior to D-Day.

Total British availability was over four hundred tugs, although most were already fully occupied. More tugs were promised from the United States, but many were unsuitable and their crews quite inexperienced for channel towing. On D-Day minus 1 the count was 132 tugs, forty-two from the Ministry of War Transport, thirty from the Admiralty, some of which were rescue tugs withdrawn from the Atlantic convoys; nineteen were U.S. Navy tugs and forty-one were from the U.S. Army. Yet some of these were to be required for other top priority tows and it was decided that the completion date of 'Mulberry' would be put back to D + 27 – over three weeks after D-Day.

By D-Day the tugs had assembled in lines in Areas 20 and 21 of the Solent, off Stokes Bay, Lee-on-the-Solent and Hook shores. On D + 1 (7 June) towing of the caissons ('Phoenixes') began and within a week two-thirds of the planned amount for 'Mulberry A' had been placed. Placing of 'Phoenixes' at 'Mulberry B' began on 10 June and by 18 June most of the breakwaters had been positioned and sunk. Piers, in tow, began arriving at the British 'Mulberry' on 9 June.

Tows were made at an average of 4 knots which, taking in the return leg, storing and bunkering, gave, roughly, a two-day round trip. By the end of July, 295 tows had been made to the invasion coast.

Blockships

In planning the pre-fabricated harbours it was recognised that they would be open to the English Channel, prone to frequent gales, and to give protection for the build-up after the assault, a fleet of blockships was planned. These ships were to be sunk, in line or arc formation, to give shelter to the coasters and myriads of small craft that would be shuttling stores to the beaches and also from the bigger cargo ships outside the protected areas. They were also to be used as stores, repairs and accommodation ships. The whole operation – collection, assembly and placing of the ships was code-named 'Corncob'; the breakwater, 'Gooseberry'.

> *'This project is so vital to the success of Overlord that it might be described as the crux of the whole operation.'*
>
> Extract from a memo from the First Sea Lord.

> *'The blockships fitted for sinking will assemble at Methil and Oban.'*
>
> Extract from Naval Orders for Operation 'Overlord'.

Immediately after the Quebec Conference of August 1943 the Allied merchant fleets were combed for old vessels, damaged vessels and those no longer capable of economic service. The list totalled nearly sixty merchantmen – twenty-two were contributed by the United States (five under the Panama flag), most of the remainder were British with some flying Allied flags. There were also four old warships – two battleships, H.M.S. *Centurion* (for many years a radio-controlled target ship) and the *Courbet* (French) plus two cruisers, H.M.S. *Durban* and the *Sumatra* (Dutch).

Vessels were stripped of their winches, derricks and fittings and the warships of much of their armament, holes were cut in bulkheads to allow free flow of water throughout and the ships wired for scuttling charges. They then sailed to one or other of the assembly ports, to swing forlornly at anchor until required.

The *Durban* and H.N.M.S. *Sumatra* sailed from Portsmouth, west-about, to Oban. There, twenty blockships had already crawled in from the sea, only the numbers painted on their sides disclosing their identity to a chosen few. *Sumatra* stayed to 'mother the chicks' and the *Durban* steamed away, north-about, to Methil and Rosyth, to muster the rest of the force.

> *'The blockships with attendant tugs will proceed to the assault area west-about the United Kingdom.'*
>
> Extract from Naval Orders for Operation 'Overlord'.

And so the last voyage began at Methil. It was D-Day – 10. Forming the convoy, taking up station – and keeping it – was not easy. Speed was 4½ knots, timed to sail through the Pentland Firth on a west-flowing tide, but this was slow and many ships lost steerage way. At greater speed they milled around to waste time and the escorts were despatched to search for and retrieve them. Convoy speed was increased to 5½ knots, but this was the limit. Ship after ship reported mechanical problems but finally they all reached Oban and passed through the boom to the anchorage in Loch Linnhe. Fifty-six blockships were assembled, plus ten tugs and an escort of half-a-dozen corvettes. It was D-Day – 7.

The final convoy conference stressed the routine points and added others: that the ships would sail as an ordinary convoy, that its timing and progress would be re-assessed in the Bristol Channel and that sealed orders would be opened only on command.

And so the ships formed up: twenty-two British and Allied vessels in the lead, sixteen American vessels forming a centre group and the remainder in a third group, astern, each with its attendant tugs. Speed was 5 knots. But in the convoy's two columns, close formation found no favour. Collisions between ships with pierced bulkheads could be fatal and the tendency was to try to widen the margins of safety. They lumbered onward, many with more machinery problems. The *Empire Tamar* and the *Dover Hill* swung across the convoy's course, but recovered their allocated positions. The *Empire Defiance* fell out of line with 'irreparable' machinery damage and was taken in tow by the tug *Empire Winnie*. Miraculously, after seven hours, she was under her own power again. And then the *Innerton* stopped, to be picked up by another tug, *Empire Rupert*.

Off Holyhead two more blockships joined the American contingent as the convoy crawled south. Already nearly-new Liberty ships were there, one with a huge hole in her bow, another with a hogged back. The newcomers were new as well, but different. The *David O. Saylor* and the *Vitruvius*, built of concrete, looked smart enough, even with their straight-line construction, but had failed to take the stresses and strains imposed by the North Atlantic.

In the Bristol Channel time allowed for bad weather had to be wasted, and so the ships were steamed against the ebb tide then, on a reverse course, pushed against the flood.

Lands End was rounded: then came Portland Bill, and anchorage was made in Poole Bay. At last the secret orders were opened: D-Day was the following day – June 6th. At midnight another ship joined the force. It was the *Centurion*, in from the Mediterranean for her last voyage.

The blockship convoy was complete. Division of the fleet was to five groups; two 'Gooseberries' were to be placed in the American sector, three in the British, and on D + 1 they left Poole, steaming some 130 miles across the Channel to where lay a myriad of craft supporting the vast invasion army. And at a five-mile circle of swept waters centred on 'Z buoy' and inevitably known as Piccadilly Circus, the ships separated to reach one of the five lanes cleared through the minefields and leading to Normandy and to their allotted placings, where 'The Planter', as his name implied, would plant them as blockships.

> *'The ships are to be scuttled off the enemy coast in order to form a breakwater giving shelter to the beaches on which the Army has landed.'*
>
> Extract from 'Corncob' special orders.

'Gooseberry 1'

This was at the right of the American flank, off Vierville, protecting Utah Beach and, despite heavy fire from German guns, the first blockship, the Liberty ship *George S. Wasson* was placed, albeit after being hit by a shell and drifting out of position. 'Gooseberry 1' was completed by 13 June.

Ships:	Built:	Tonnage:	Remarks:
George S. Wasson	1943	7,176	Foundered in gales 19/22 June 1944.
Benjamin Contee	1942	7,176	Foundered in gales 19/22 June 1944.
Matt W. Ransom	1943	7,176	Foundered in gales 19/22 June 1944.
David O. Saylor	1943	4,825	C1-S-D1 type (concrete ship).
Vitruvius	1943	4,823	C1-S-D1 type (concrete ship).
West Nohno	1919	5,769	
West Cheswald	1919	5,711	
West Honaker	1920	5,428	
Victory Sword	1906	4,800	

All the above ships were U.S.-flag.

'Gooseberry 2'

The line of blockships which comprised 'Gooseberry 2' was laid off St. Laurent and protected the eastern entrance to 'Mulberry A'. Apart from the 'Bombardons' outside of the port area, the breakwater ran in a line North-west/South-east. A line of 'Phoenixes' to the Middle Entrance gave protection for seven Liberty ships, the main piers and coaster moorings, whilst the old British battleship *Centurion* began the line of blockships at the other side of the Middle Entrance. 'Gooseberry 2' was completed on 10 June.

Ships:	Built:	Tonnage:	Remarks:
H.M.S. *Centurion*	1911	25,000 (displ.)	British: ex-battleship.
James Iredell	1943	7,176	16.7.1944: Abandoned following storms of 19/22 June 1944.
George W. Childs	1943	7,176	16.7.1944: Abandoned following storms of 19/22 June 1944.
Artemas Ward	1942	7,176	16.7.1944: Abandoned following storms of 19/22 June 1944.
James W. Marshall	1942	7,176	16.7.1944: Abandoned following storms of 19/22 June 1944.
Wilscox	1919	5,861	
Galveston	1921	6,173	
Courageous	1918	7,573	
West Grama	1918	5,326	16.7.1944: Sank.

All the above vessels were U.S.-flag.

Potter	1920	6,174	
Baialoide	1914	6,479	1949: Refloated; scrapped Ghent.
Audacious	1913	6,861	
Flight Command	1911	4,341	
Olambala	1901	4,815	12.1941: Seized by U.S. Authorities at Norfolk, Va., as *Antonietta* (ex *Atholl*).

The above five vessels were Panama-flag.

'Gooseberry 3'

This line of blockships was placed off Gold Beach, Arromanches, in the British sector. It stretched from the Northern Entrance to the Eastern Entrance of 'Mulberry B' and was bolstered with 'Phoenix' caissons.

The first ship to be placed was the *Alynbank*, on 9 June, and formerly of Andrew Weir & Co.'s Bank Line, which had been requisitioned in 1939 and fitted out as an anti-aircraft guard ship until late 1941. When being placed she was taken by the current and settled at a 90-degree angle from the intended line of ships.

Ships:	Built:	Tonnage:	Remarks:
Alynbank	1925	5,151	12.1945: Raised, towed to Troon for scrapping.
Elswick Park	1920	4,188	Raised: broken up.
Flowergate	1911	5,156	1946: Raised and beached: later towed to Briton Ferry and broken up.
Ingman	1907	3,619	Raised: broken up.
Innerton	1919	5,276	Raised: broken up.
Saltersgate	1924	3,940	
Vinlake	1913	3,938	Raised: broken up.
Winha	1904	3,391	Raised: broken up.
Parklaan	1911	3,807	(Dutch flag).
Aghios Spyridon	1905	3,338	(Greek flag).
Njegos	1903	4,052	(Yugoslav flag).
Lynghaug	1919	2,809	(Norwegian flag).
Sirehei	1907	3,888	(Norwegian flag).
Modlin	1906	3,569	(Polish flag).
Georgios P	1903	4,052	(Greek flag).

All the above vessels were British flag, except as shown.

'Gooseberry 4'

'Gooseberry 4' provided shelter to Juno Beach at Courseulles, some seven miles east of Arromanches.

Ships:	Built:	Tonnage:	Remarks:
Empire Bunting	1919	6,318	Raised: broken up in 1947.
Empire Flamingo	1920	4,994	
Empire Moorhen	1919	5,628	Raised: broken up.
Empire Waterhen	1920	5,948	1948: Raised: broken up.
Manchester Spinner	1918	4,767	
Bendoran	1910	5,567	Raised: broken up.
Mariposa	1914	3,807	Raised: broken up.
Vera Radcliffe	1925	5,587	
Panos	1920	4,900	(Greek flag).
Belgique	1902	4,606	(Belgian flag).

All the above vessels were British flag, except as shown.

'Gooseberry 5'

Situated off Ouistreham, on the extreme left flank of the British sector. The ships included the battleship *Courbet* and two old cruisers.

Ships:	Built:	Tonnage:	Remarks:
H.M.S. *Durban*	1921	4,850 (displ.)	British 'D'-class cruiser.
H.N.M.S. *Sumatra*	1925	6,670 (displ.)	Dutch cruiser.
F.F.S. *Courbet*	1913	22,189 (displ.)	Free French battleship.
Empire Tana	1923	6,375	1947: Raised: broken up.
Empire Tamar	1907	6,640	
Empire Defiance	1909	4,667	Raised, and: 1951: Scrapped Antwerp.
Dover Hill	1918	5,815	
Becheville	1924	4,228	
Forbin	1922	7,291	

All the above vessels were British flag, except as shown.

The great storm

But fate was to play a hand. On D + 13 (19 June), a strong north-west wind suddenly veered north-east and by mid-day had reached Force 6 and had veered another point by nightfall. This was the worst possible direction from which to blow and reached gale force with waves 10–12 ft high, smashing into the breakwaters and pierheads of the exposed harbours. The 'Bombardon' lines, way out, broke loose and were swept towards shore, but tugs managed to secure them. 'Mulberry A' suffered greatly. Ships dragged anchor; some beached; others drifted, causing damage to pierheads. One pier was destroyed, another turned into a mass of twisted metal. The 'Phoenix' breakwater was rendered almost useless and rogue 'Bombardons' were a great hazard. A number of blockships were wrecked. So serious was the damage to piers and 'Phoenixes' that the port was abandoned. But when the storm eased, the shuttling and supplies from anchored ships to beach began again. Two blockships from 'Gooseberry 1' were lost and several from 'Gooseberry 2' and supplementary ships were later placed to reinforce the line.

Twelve miles eastwards, 'Mulberry B' also suffered, although not as severely as 'Mulberry A', for there was some protection from the Calvados Reef. Some 'Phoenixes', however, were damaged and two blockships wrecked. The fleet of ferrying craft was decimated. However, building and strengthening of the port continued, some equipment being transferred from the abandoned American 'Mulberry'.

The gale blew for three days; it was the worst for forty years. But the shelter of the 'Gooseberries' saved many lives and much equipment. Discharge on the beaches elsewhere was out of the question, but even in the height of the storm some petrol, ammunition and personnel were discharged to beaches behind 'Gooseberries'.

Additional blockships were added after the gales of 19–23 June. Omaha Beach was strengthened with more blockships and twenty-one caissons, but another gale, in early October, wrecked four ships and twelve 'Phoenixes'.

Ships:	Built:	Tonnage:	Remarks:	
Alcoa Leader	1919	5,041	13. 8.1944:	Scuttled as blockship.
Exford	1919	4,969	26. 8.1944:	Scuttled as blockship. 1951: Refloated.
			1.12.1951:	Stranded Vierville whle in tow to Antwerp for scrapping. Broken up *in situ*.
Illinoian	1918	6,473	28. 8.1944:	Scuttled as blockship.
Kentuckian	1910	5,200	12. 8.1944:	Scuttled as blockship.
Kofresi	1920	4,934	14. 8.1944:	Scuttled as blockship.
Lena Luckenbach	1920	5,238	4. 8.1944:	Scuttled as blockship.
Pennsylvanian	1913	5,191	4. 8.1944:	Scuttled as blockship.
Robin Gray	1920	6,896	18. 8.1944:	Scuttled as blockship.
Sahale	1919	5,028	24. 8.1944:	Scuttled as blockship.
West Nilus	1920	5,495	7. 7.1944:	Scuttled as blockship.

All the above ships were U.S.-flag.

Bosworth	1919	6,672		
Empire Bittern	1902	8,546	23. 7.1944:	Scuttled as blockship.
Maycrest	1913	5,923		
Stanwell	1914	5,797		

The above four vessels were British flag.

Persier	1918	5,382	(Belgian flag).
Kelbergen	1914	4,823	(Dutch flag).
Parkhaven	1920	4,803	(Dutch flag).
Norfalk (ex *Empire Kittiwake*)	1919	5,674	(Norwegian flag): 7.1944: Mined and sunk on passage to Normandy.
Norjerv (ex *Empire Eagle*)	1919	5,582	(Norwegian flag): 8.1944: Scuttled as blockship. 1949: Raised, but 6.1949: Sank in tow to U.K. for breaking up.
H.M.S. *Dragon*	1917	4,850 (displ.)	British 'D'-class cruiser. 7.7.1944: Damaged by human torpedo off Normandy whilst with Polish crew. Later joined breakwater off Mulberry.

The 'Mulberry' at Arromanches (A and B designations were withdrawn after the storms of 19–23 June) became the only harbour between Cherbourg and Le Havre, which was liberated on 12 September. Cherbourg and other small ports in Brittany had been liberated by the American armies, but were in a state of destruction and riddled with mines and booby traps, which took time to clear.

The 'Mulberry' therefore, scheduled to cease in mid-October, continued working until 19 November, as did the 'Gooseberries'. Discharging at No. 4 off Courseulles and No. 5 at Ouistreham continued to November, whilst No. 1 at Utah/Omaha beaches, worked until December.

By then Antwerp had been liberated on 4 September, its docks intact, whilst Liberty ships, direct from the United States, had been arriving at Le Havre and discharging there since October.

. . .

In January 1947 the French Mission in the United Kingdom purchased, on behalf of the Ministry of French Colonies, a considerable amount of equipment from the 'Mulberry' harbours, to be used in the construction of a pre-fabricated port off the West African coast.

Among the items available were 'Spud' pierheads, floating roadways, pontoons and floats, much of it unused and available 'from stock'.

. . .

Some experience for the 'Mulberry' project was gained in the construction of two deep water ports on the West Coast of Scotland. When France fell the ports on the South and East coasts were closed to ocean shipping, which was diverted to West Coast ports. These quickly became congested and to help in relieving the problem two ports were built for military purposes; at Gareloch (Military Port No. 1) and at Cairnryan, Loch Ryan (Military Port No. 2). The dredging, construction of the deep water berths and their rails links were all done by units of the Royal Engineers, the Pioneer Corps, and some civilian consultants. Work began at the end of 1940 and the first ship was berthed in July 1942.

Not only were the ports valuable for military operations but they were used as testing grounds for underwater clearance work and training. A number of pierheads for the 'Mulberry' harbour were constructed at Cairnryan. The ports were also used to disembark American troops for the build-up of their forces in Britain in preparation for Operation 'Overlord'.

BIBLIOGRAPHY

F. C. Bowen. *Flag of the Southern Cross* (Shaw, Savill & Albion Ltd.).

J. L. Carvel. *Stephen of Linthouse* (Private publication).

H. T. Lenton and J. J. Colledge. *Warhips of World War II* (Ian Allan Ltd.).

W. A. Meneight. *The United Molasses Company* (Private publication).

M. Moss and J. R. Hume. *Shipbuilders to the World* (Blackstaff Press).

J. Rohwer and G. Hummelchen. *War at Sea* (Ian Allan Ltd.).

J. Rohwer. *Axis Submarine Successes* (Patrick Stephens Ltd.).

Lord Russell of Liverpool. *Knights of the Bushido* (Corgi).

J. D. Scott. *Vickers* (Weidenfeld & Nicolson).

J. D. Taylor. *The Last Passage* (Allen & Unwin Ltd.).

F. Walker. *Song of the Clyde* (W. W. Norton & Company).

Belgian Shiplover. (Journal of the Belgian Nautical Research Association.)

Corporation of Lloyds. (Various shipping publications.)

British Shipping Losses During the Second World War. (H.M.S.O.)

Transactions of the Institute of Naval Architects. (Various editions.)

Janes Fighting Ships. (Various editions.) (Sampson Low Ltd.)

Lloyds Register of Shipping. (Various editions.)

Marine News. (Various editions.) (Journal of the World Ship Society.)

Sea Breezes. (Nautical magazine.) (Various editions.)

Shipbuilding & Shipping Record. (Various editions.)

Shipping World (Nautical magazine.) (Various editions.)

Taikoo Dockyard & Engineering Company. (Private publication.)

INDEX OF SHIPS

INDEX OF SHIPYARD AND COMPANY NOTES